The
NEW
TESTAMENT

The NEW TESTAMENT

A Historical *and* Theological Introduction

DONALD *A.* HAGNER

Baker Academic

a division of Baker Publishing Group
Grand Rapids, Michigan

Published by Baker Academic
a division of Baker Publishing Group
P.O. Box 6287, Grand Rapids, MI 49516-6287
www.bakeracademic.com

Printed in the United States of America

Library of Congress Cataloging-in-Publication Data
Hagner, Donald Alfred.
    The New Testament : a historical and theological introduction / Donald A. Hagner.
        p.   cm.
    Includes bibliographical references and indexes.
    ISBN 978-0-8010-3931-7 (cloth)
    1. Bible. N.T.—Introductions. I. Title.
BS2330.3.H34 2012
225.6′1—dc23   2012025770

12   13   14   15   16   17   18   7   6   5   4   3   2   1

Contents

Illustrations

Preface

The questions of NT introduction are both numerous and complicated. Furthermore, the literature on these questions is voluminous, including not only a long history of the study of the NT but also an ever-increasing flood of contemporary scholarship. No other documents of human history have been subjected to as much study over as long a period as has the Bible as a whole and the NT in particular.

Those unfamiliar with the field may be excused for wondering what more could possibly be said after nearly two thousand years of study of these documents. In fact, progress in the understanding of the NT has been made and continues to be made. This is the result not merely of new discoveries, most famously the Dead Sea Scrolls, but also of the refinement of methods long known, invention of new methods, and in recent decades the application of other academic disciplines to the study of the NT, such as literary criticism, linguistics, sociology, and anthropology.

Occasionally I have been asked why I have written *another* introduction to the NT, and I owe an explanation to you who are reading these lines. What is the purpose and what are the characteristics of the book you hold in your hands?

New introductions to the NT are needed every decade or so in order to reflect the current state of the discussion for new, upcoming students. The present book is meant to be a bread-and-butter introduction to the basic questions of the origins of the NT and the nature of its contents. It is written by a believing Christian primarily for believing Christians—from faith to faith, as Paul would say—for seminary students, for those who would serve God and the church, for disciples who happen to be scholars, not vice versa. In this book, therefore, the material studied—the biblical text—is regarded with a certain reverence as the inspired word of God. But this stance does not prohibit asking the difficult questions with all possible honesty. The book tries to embody the conviction that biblical criticism, sans inimical presuppositions, is consonant with faith and commitment. Holy Scripture, the canon of Old and New Testaments, comes to us as the word of God, but it is given through the words of humans. As such, it demands critical study.

For many or most of the questions that this book explores we do not know the answers. Morna Hooker, Lady Margaret's Professor of Divinity Emerita at the University of Cambridge, suggests, "Perhaps every New Testament scholar should have before him on his desk, as he writes, as a constant reminder of the dangers of dogmatism, the words of R. H. Lightfoot: 'We do not know.'"[1] The truth is that we simply do not know nearly as much we would like to know. "Proof" and "certainty" are words we can rarely use in assessing historical questions.[2] Although we can and do know a lot, it is no good pretending to know more than we *can* know. The great Roman Catholic NT scholar Raymond Brown wisely quipped, "Biblical studies are not helped by being certain about the uncertain."[3]

For a good part of the time, therefore, probable knowledge will have to serve us in the study of the NT. The probabilistic nature of many conclusions in this book should not distress the Christian student. Probable knowledge serves us quite well for most areas of our lives. With the Apostle Paul, here as elsewhere we must be finally content to say, "For now we see in a mirror dimly, but then face to face. Now I know in part; then I shall understand fully, even as I have been fully understood" (1 Cor. 13:12).

The problem with probabilities, of course, is that "arguments from probability are weighed differently by different judges."[4] One person's probability is another person's mere possibility, and vice versa. There is no way around this. One finally has to decide on the basis of one's sense of the force and plausibility of the arguments. Disagreements will remain, but this need not hurt anyone.[5]

This book is written not to provide the sure answers to the questions of introduction, although I am not shy about providing answers that I think are the most persuasive. Although I often indicate alternatives, I have felt no obligation to do so consistently or thoroughly. As much as anything, this book attempts to introduce students to the *status quaestionis* on the subjects

---

1. Hooker, "On Using the Wrong Tool," 581. Hans Dieter Betz calls attention to "what has ever been the surest position of the historical critic, the *ars nesciendi*, 'the art of not knowing'" (*2 Corinthians 8 and 9*, 30).

2. Martin Hengel writes, "*As we know, we cannot solve equations with several unknowns.*" He adds, "We New Testament scholars constantly attempt this" (*The Four Gospels and the One Gospel of Jesus Christ*, 181 and n702, italics in original).

3. Brown, *An Introduction to the New Testament*, 596.

4. Bruce, *The Canon of Scripture*, 41.

5. In another connection, the Apostle Paul notes the appropriateness of humility over against knowledge that puffs up. He writes, "If any one imagines that he knows something, he does not yet know as he ought to know" (1 Cor. 8:2). His point is universally relevant: love should trump our partial knowledge every time. And uncertain, partial knowledge excludes dogmatism.

discussed. I see no need to mention every far-fetched theory and hypothesis, let alone respond to or attempt to counter them. Simplification is essential to a student's introduction. Undoubtedly some will regard my approach in general as reflecting a naive, rosy optimism or an unbelievable chutzpah. If it reflects a naïveté, it is a "second naïveté." I agree with the statement attributed to Justice Oliver Wendell Holmes: "I do not give a fig for the simplicity this side of complexity, but I would give my right arm for the simplicity on the far side of complexity."

If some readers of this book find it a little thin on newer, avant-garde approaches to the NT writings, this is not because I am unaware of them, nor is it because I see no value in them. I regard them as useful and valuable supplements, but supplements nonetheless.[6] One can do only so much in one book, and in an introductory book first things must come first. The present book is already large and pressed by considerations of space. Practically every chapter cries out to be a small (or large!) monograph.

However, it is too easy in this discipline that so quickly spawns new approaches, new theories, and new hypotheses to forget or quickly dismiss scholarship of the past. There can be few subjects that have such a rich history of study as the NT. In this book I argue that some no-longer fashionable views deserve to be considered again, especially the best of them. Some old conclusions are still the best conclusions![7] Although usually there are good reasons for the emergence of consensuses on questions of NT introduction, a consensus should never be allowed to paralyze NT scholarship from its work of examining and reexamining its conclusions.

A distinguishing mark of the present book is its understanding of the NT within the framework of the history of salvation. This refers not to some "special" history or metanarrative above or distinct from ordinary history. Rather, it refers to the grand story of God's work in history, in time and space, to accomplish the redemption of the fallen creation. This orientation accounts for the attention given to the OT in chapter 2 and for the analysis of the main divisions of the book in terms of the kingdom of God (the Gospels as the proclamation of the kingdom; Acts as the earliest preaching of the kingdom; the Epistles as the interpretation of the kingdom; the Apocalypse as the consummation of the kingdom). I have found this a most helpful way to understand the NT and a good way to introduce students to what undergirds the entire NT and what makes it what it is.[8]

This book provides no outlines of the NT books. I have never found other people's outlines very useful. It is far better to do one's own outlines because their real value is in the learning that comes in actually doing them. Nor do

---

6. See Hagner and Young, "The Historical-Critical Method and the Gospel of Matthew."

7. See Gundry, *The Old Is Better*. Gundry presents these essays not to defend traditional interpretations, but because in his opinion they are the interpretations that are the most truthful.

8. Along the same lines, see Ladd, *A Theology of the New Testament*.

I necessarily provide seriatim summaries of the contents of the NT books, although in various ways I do cover much of the content of each book. My focus is more often on the argument of the book. Again, it is far better for students to read the documents for themselves. And thus, like every author of a book such as this, I must beg the reader to keep a copy of the NT open beside this book. Nothing can take the place of the direct encounter with the content of the Bible itself. Unless otherwise noted, Bible quotations in this book are from the RSV,[9] which often follows the Greek text more closely than does the NRSV.

As a service to students wanting to go deeper than this book can take them, I have provided rather full bibliographies, although they are far from exhaustive. I have not included articles and books in languages other than English, despite, for example, the rich resources available in German and French in particular.

An online resource is available providing "questions for review" for students who wish to check up on their comprehension and retention of the important points in each chapter. For professors interested in ideas for exam questions or paper topics, the online resource offers "questions for research and discussion." Thanks go to J. Matthew Barnes for writing this material. These questions are linked under the "resources" heading at www.bakeracademic.com/HagnerNT.

There are many to thank for making the writing of this book possible. First, as always, thanks are due to my dear wife, Beverly, for her unflagging love, support, and encouragement. This book has been written in a variety of academic locations. I especially thank Professor Emerita Morna Hooker and the hospitality of Robinson College, Cambridge, for the privilege of being a bye-fellow for 2009–10. I thank the libraries of Tyndale House, Cambridge, and of the Faculty of Theology at Humboldt University in Berlin. I also thank warmly Professor Bernardo Estrada and the Faculty of Theology at the Pontificia Università della Santa Croce in Rome for their hospitality. Finally, thanks are due to Trinity College, Melbourne, and the Dalton McCaughey Library of the United Faculty of Theology of the University of Melbourne. All the people in these institutions were exceptionally kind and provided excellent, stimulating contexts for researching and writing. I am grateful to the people—too many to name individually—in these places who read chapters of the present book and gave me valuable feedback. I must also render special thanks to my friend Dr. Steve Young, who read and corrected the proofs of the entire manuscript. The shortcomings of this book remain mine.

I thank Thomas Nelson publishers for permission to use material drawn from the introduction to my commentary on Matthew in the Word Biblical Commentary and Baker Books for permission to use material from the

---

9. Unfortunately, the permission to use the RSV stipulates that no changes be made in quoting the translation. As a result, against my wishes, I have had to retain the objectionable masculine language of the RSV. I ask the reader's indulgence.

introduction to my commentary on Hebrews in the Understanding the Bible Commentary Series.

I am also grateful to James Ernest, Jim Kinney, Brian Bolger, and the good folks at Baker Academic for their encouragement and excellent work in the production of this book.

When Charles Bigg sent off his monumental International Critical Commentary on the Epistles of Peter and Jude, he wrote, "I send this laborious volume to the press with a clear sense of its limitations. . . . The shortcomings of the work will be at least as evident to others as to myself."[10] While I would not pretend to possess the stature of a Charles Bigg, these words nevertheless express well my sentiments at this moment.

I wish the reader much joy and excitement in the wonderful adventure of studying the NT—indeed, something of the joy I have experienced in writing this book.

Bibliography

Betz, Hans Dieter. *2 Corinthians 8 and 9: A Commentary on Two Administrative Letters of the Apostle Paul*. Edited by George W. McRae. Hermeneia. Philadelphia: Fortress, 1985.

Bigg, Charles. *A Critical and Exegetical Commentary of the Epistles of St. Peter and St. Jude*. 2nd ed. ICC. Edinburgh: T&T Clark, 1902.

Brown, Raymond E. *An Introduction to the New Testament*. New York: Doubleday, 1997.

Bruce, F. F. *The Canon of Scripture*. Downers Grove, IL: InterVarsity, 1988.

Gundry, Robert H. *The Old Is Better: New Testament Essays in Support of Traditional Interpretations*. WUNT 178. Tübingen: Mohr Siebeck, 2005.

Hagner, Donald A., and Stephen E. Young. "The Historical-Critical Method and the Gospel of Matthew." In *Methods for Matthew,* edited by Mark Allan Powell, 11–43. MBI. Cambridge: Cambridge University Press, 2009.

Hengel, Martin. *The Four Gospels and the One Gospel of Jesus Christ: An Investigation of the Collection and Origin of the Canonical Gospels*. Harrisburg, PA: Trinity Press International, 2000.

Hooker, Morna D. "On Using the Wrong Tool." *Theology* 75 (1972): 570–81.

Ladd, George Eldon. *A Theology of the New Testament*. Revised by Donald A. Hagner. Grand Rapids: Eerdmans, 1993.

10. Bigg, *A Critical and Exegetical Commentary on the Epistles of St. Peter and St. Jude*, v.

Abbreviations

General

//	parallel
ca.	circa
cf.	compare
chap(s).	chapter(s)
col(s).	column(s)
e.g.	for example
esp.	especially
Gk.	Greek
Heb.	Hebrew
ibid.	in the same source
idem	by the same author
lit.	literally
par(s).	parallel(s)
rev.	revised
v(v).	verse(s)
x	times (2x)

Divisions of the Canon

NT	New Testament
OT	Old Testament

Ancient Versions

LXX	Septuagint

Modern Versions

KJV	King James Version
NASB	New American Standard Bible
NIV	New International Version
NJB	New Jerusalem Bible
NRSV	New Revised Standard Version
RSV	Revised Standard Version

Hebrew Bible/Old Testament

Gen.	Genesis
Exod.	Exodus
Lev.	Leviticus
Num.	Numbers
Deut.	Deuteronomy
Josh.	Joshua
Judg.	Judges
Ruth	Ruth
1–2 Sam.	1–2 Samuel
1–2 Kings	1–2 Kings
1–2 Chron.	1–2 Chronicles
Ezra	Ezra
Neh.	Nehemiah
Esther	Esther
Job	Job
Ps./Pss.	Psalms
Prov.	Proverbs
Eccles.	Ecclesiastes
Song	Song of Songs
Isa.	Isaiah
Jer.	Jeremiah
Lam.	Lamentations
Ezek.	Ezekiel
Dan.	Daniel
Hosea	Hosea

Joel	Joel
Amos	Amos
Obad.	Obadiah
Jon.	Jonah
Mic.	Micah
Nah.	Nahum
Hab.	Habakkuk
Zeph.	Zephaniah
Hag.	Haggai
Zech.	Zechariah
Mal.	Malachi

New Testament

Matt.	Matthew
Mark	Mark
Luke	Luke
John	John
Acts	Acts
Rom.	Romans
1–2 Cor.	1–2 Corinthians
Gal.	Galatians
Eph.	Ephesians
Phil.	Philippians
Col.	Colossians
1–2 Thess.	1–2 Thessalonians
1–2 Tim.	1–2 Timothy
Titus	Titus
Philem.	Philemon
Heb.	Hebrews
James	James
1–2 Pet.	1–2 Peter
1–3 John	1–3 John
Jude	Jude
Rev.	Revelation

Apocrypha and Septuagint

1–4 Macc.	1–4 Maccabees
Sir.	Sirach
Wis.	Wisdom of Solomon

Old Testament Pseudepigrapha

2 Bar.	2 Baruch (Syriac Apocalypse)
1 En.	1 Enoch (Ethiopic Apocalypse)
4 Ezra	4 Ezra

L.A.B.	Liber antiquitatum biblicarum (Pseudo-Philo)
Pss. Sol.	Psalms of Solomon
T. Jud.	Testament of Judah

Dead Sea Scrolls

4Q397 (4QMMT^d)	4QHalakhic Letter^d
4Q521	4QMessianic Apocalypse

Targumic Texts

Tg. Onq.	Targum Onqelos

Mishnah and Talmud

b.	Babylonian Talmud
m.	Mishnah
t.	Tosefta
ʾAbot	ʾAbot
Giṭ.	Giṭṭin
Šabb.	Šabbat
Sanh.	Sanhedrin
Soṭah	Soṭah
Sukkah	Sukkah
Yad.	Yadayim

Apostolic Fathers

Barn.	Barnabas
1–2 Clem.	1–2 Clement
Ign. Eph.	Ignatius, To the Ephesians
Ign. Smyrn.	Ignatius, To the Smyrnaeans
Pol. Phil.	Polycarp, To the Philippians

Greek and Latin Works

CLEMENT OF ALEXANDRIA

Strom.	Stromata (Miscellanies)

EPIPHANIUS

Pan.	Panarion (Refutation of All Heresies)

EUSEBIUS

Chron. *Chronicon (Chronicle)*
Hist. eccl. *Historia ecclesias-*
  tica (Ecclesiastical
  History)
Vit. Const. *Vita Constantini (Life*
  of Constantine)

IRENAEUS

Haer. *Adversus haereses*
  (Against Heresies)

JEROME

Vir. ill. *De viris illustribus*
  (On Illustrious Men)

JOSEPHUS

Ag. Ap. *Against Apion*
Ant. *Jewish Antiquities*
J.W. *Jewish War*

JUSTIN

1 Apol. *Apologia i (First*
  Apology)
Dial. *Dialogus cum Try-*
  phone (Dialogue with
  Trypho)

ORIGEN

Comm. Matt. *Commentarium in*
  evangelium Matthaei

PHILO

Contempl. *De vita contemplativa*
  (On the Contempla-
  tive Life)

Hypoth. *Hypothetica*
Leg. *Legum allego-*
  riae (Allegorical
  Interpretation)
Prob. *Quod omnis probus*
  liber sit (That Every
  Good Person Is Free)

PLINY THE YOUNGER

Ep. *Epistulae (Letters)*

SUETONIUS

Claud. *Divus Claudius (Life*
  of Claudius)

TACITUS

Ann. *Annales (Annals)*

TERTULLIAN

Bapt. *De baptismo*
  (Baptism)
Cult. fem. *De cultu feminarum*
  (The Apparel of
  Women)
Marc. *Adversus Marcionem*
  (Against Marcion)

THUCYDIDES

Hist. Pel. *History of the Pelo-*
  ponnesian War

Secondary Sources

AB	Anchor Bible
ABD	*Anchor Bible Dictionary*. Edited by D. N. Freedman. 6 vols. New York: Doubleday, 1992
ABRL	Anchor Bible Reference Library
ABS	Approaches to Biblical Studies
ACCSNT	Ancient Christian Commentary on Scripture: New Testament
ACNT	Augsburg Commentary on the New Testament
AGJU	Arbeiten zur Geschichte des antiken Judentums und des Urchristentums
AJEC	Ancient Judaism and Early Christianity
ALGHJ	Arbeiten zur Literatur und Geschichte des hellenistischen Judentums

AnBib	Analecta biblica
ANF	*Ante-Nicene Fathers*. Edited by A. Roberts and J. Donaldson. 10 vols. 1885–96. Repr., Grand Rapids: Eerdmans, 1986–89
ANRW	*Aufstieg und Niedergang der römischen Welt: Geschichte und Kultur Roms im Spiegel der neueren Forschung*. Edited by H. Temporini and W. Haase. Berlin: de Gruyter, 1972–
ANTC	Abingdon New Testament Commentaries
ASNU	Acta seminarii neotestamentici upsaliensis
AsTJ	*Asbury Theological Journal*
ATJ	*Ashland Theological Journal*
AUS	American University Studies
AUSS	*Andrews University Seminary Series*
AYB	Anchor Yale Bible
BAFCS	The Book of Acts in Its First Century Setting
BBC	Blackwell Bible Commentaries
BBR	*Bulletin for Biblical Research*
BBRNT	Bibliographies for Biblical Research: New Testament Series
BDAG	Danker, F. W., W. Bauer, W. F. Arndt, and F. W. Gingrich. *Greek-English Lexicon of the New Testament and Other Early Christian Literature*. 3rd ed. Chicago: University of Chicago Press, 1999
BECNT	Baker Exegetical Commentary on the New Testament
BETL	Bibliotheca ephemeridum theologicarum lovaniensium
BGBE	Beiträge zur Geschichte der biblischen Exegese
BHGNT	Baylor Handbook on the Greek New Testament
Bib	*Biblica*
BibInt	*Biblical Interpretation*
BibSem	Biblical Seminar
BIS	Biblical Interpretation Series
BJRL	*Bulletin of the John Rylands University Library of Manchester*
BMS	Bibal Monograph Series
BMW	Bible in the Modern World
BNTC	Black's New Testament Commentaries
BP	Bible and Postcolonialism
BRBS	Brill's Readers in Biblical Studies
BRS	Biblical Resource Series
BSac	*Bibliotheca sacra*
BSC	Bible Study Commentary
BT	*The Bible Translator*
BTB	*Biblical Theology Bulletin*
BTCB	Brazos Theological Commentary on the Bible
BTNT	Biblical Theology of the New Testament
BTS	Biblical Tools and Studies
BZ	*Biblische Zeitschrift*
BZNW	Beihefte zur Zeitschrift für die neutestamentliche Wissenschaft
CBC	Cambridge Bible Commentary
CBET	Contributions to Biblical Exegesis and Theology
CBQ	*Catholic Biblical Quarterly*
CBQMS	Catholic Biblical Quarterly Monograph Series
CC	Continental Commentaries
CCL	Classic Commentary Library
CCR	Cambridge Companions to Religion

CCSS	Catholic Commentary on Sacred Scripture
CCT	Chalice Commentaries for Today
CGTC	Cambridge Greek Testament Commentary
ChrCent	*Christian Century*
CJT	*Canadian Journal of Theology*
ConBNT	Coniectanea biblica: New Testament Series
ConC	Concordia Commentary
COQG	Christian Origins and the Question of God
CovQ	*Covenant Quarterly*
CRINT	Compendia rerum Iudaicarum ad Novum Testamentum
CSHJ	Chicago Studies in the History of Judaism
CSR	*Christian Scholar's Review*
CTJ	*Calvin Theological Journal*
Colson	*Philo*. Translated by F. H. Colson and G. H. Whitaker. 11 vols. Loeb Classical Library. Cambridge: Harvard University Press, 1949
CTM	*Concordia Theological Monthly*
CTQ	*Concordia Theological Quarterly*
CurBS	*Currents in Research: Biblical Studies*
CurTM	*Currents in Theology and Mission*
DBC	Daily Bible Commentary
DNTC	Doubleday New Testament Commentary
EBC	Expositor's Bible Commentary
EBib	Études bibliques
EBS	Encountering Biblical Studies
EC	Epworth Commentaries
ECC	Eerdmans Critical Commentary
EGGNT	Exegetical Guide to the Greek New Testament
Ehrman	*The Apostolic Fathers*. Translated by Bart Ehrman. 2 vols. Loeb Classical Library. Cambridge: Harvard University Press, 2003
EpRev	*Epworth Review*
ESEC	Emory Studies in Early Christianity
ESW	Ecumenical Studies in Worship
ETL	*Ephemerides theologicae lovanienses*
EUS	European University Studies
Evans	*Tertullian: Adversus Marcionem*. Edited and translated by Ernest Evans. Oxford: Clarendon, 1972
EvQ	*Evangelical Quarterly*
EvRT	*Evangelical Review of Theology*
ExAud	*Ex auditu*
ExpTim	*Expository Times*
FBBS	Facet Books: Biblical Series
FCBS	Fortress Classics in Biblical Studies
FCNTECW	Feminist Companion to the New Testament and Early Christian Writings
Feldman	*Josephus: Jewish Antiquities, Books 18–20*. Translated by L. H. Feldman. Loeb Classical Library. Cambridge: Harvard University Press, 1998
FM	*Faith and Mission*
FN	*Filología Neotestamentaria*
FRLANT	Forschungen zur Religion und Literatur des Alten und Neuen Testaments

GABR	Guides to Advanced Biblical Research
GBS	Guides to Biblical Scholarship
GNS	Good News Studies
GNTE	Guides to New Testament Exegesis
GP	Gospel Perspectives
GTA	Göttingen theologische Arbeiten
GTJ	*Grace Theological Journal*
HBT	*Horizons in Biblical Theology*
HDR	Harvard Dissertations in Religion
HeyJ	*Heythrop Journal*
HNTC	Harper's New Testament Commentaries
HTB	Histoire du texte biblique
HTKNT	Herders theologischer Kommentar zum Neuen Testament
HTR	*Harvard Theological Review*
HTS	Harvard Theological Studies
HUT	Hermeneutische Untersuchungen zur Theologie
HvTStSup	Supplementum to Hervormde teologiese studies
IBC	Interpretation: A Bible Commentary for Teaching and Preaching
IBRBib	IBR Bibliographies
IBS	*Irish Biblical Studies*
IBT	Interpreting Biblical Texts
ICC	International Critical Commentary
Int	*Interpretation*
IRT	Issues in Religion and Theology
ISFCJ	University of South Florida International Studies in Formative Christianity and Judaism
ITL	International Theological Library
IVPNTC	IVP New Testament Commentary
JBL	*Journal of Biblical Literature*
JETS	*Journal of the Evangelical Theological Society*
JGRChJ	*Journal of Greco-Roman Christianity and Judaism*
Jowett	Thucydides, *History of the Peloponesian War*. Translated by Benjamin Jowett. Amherst, NY: Prometheus Books, 1998
JR	*Journal of Religion*
JSJ	*Journal for the Study of Judaism in the Persian, Hellenistic, and Roman Periods*
JSJSup	Supplements to the Journal for the Study of Judaism
JSNT	*Journal for the Study of the New Testament*
JSNTSup	Journal for the Study of the New Testament: Supplement Series
JSOTSup	Journal for the Study of the Old Testament: Supplement Series
JSPSup	Journal for the Study of the Pseudepigrapha: Supplement Series
JTC	*Journal for Theology and the Church*
JTS	*Journal of Theological Studies*
KPG	Knox Preaching Guides
LAI	Library of Ancient Israel
Lake	*Eusebius: Ecclesiastical History, Books 1–5*. Translated by Kirsopp Lake. Loeb Classical Library. Cambridge: Harvard University Press, 1926
LBC	Layman's Bible Commentary
LCBI	Literary Currents in Biblical Interpretation
LCC	Library of Christian Classics

LEC	Library of Early Christianity
LNTS	Library of New Testament Studies
LPS	Library of Pauline Studies
LSJ	Liddell, H. G., R. Scott, and H. S. Jones. *A Greek-English Lexicon*. 9th ed. with rev. supplement. Oxford: Clarendon, 1996
LTPM	Louvain Theological and Pastoral Monographs
LUÅ	Lunds universitets årsskrift
Martínez	*The Dead Sea Scrolls Translated*. 2nd ed. Edited by Florentino García Martínez. Grand Rapids: Eerdmans, 1997
Mason	*Flavius Josephus: Translation and Commentary*. Edited by Steve Mason. Leiden: Brill, 2006
MBI	Methods in Biblical Interpretation
MBS	Message of Biblical Spirituality
MNTC	Moffatt New Testament Commentary
MNTS	McMaster New Testament Studies
NABPRDS	NABPR Dissertation Series
NABPRSS	NABPR Special Studies
NAC	New American Commentary
NCamBC	New Cambridge Bible Commentary
NCB	New Century Bible
NCBC	New Century Bible Commentary
NCBCNT	New Collegeville Bible Commentary: New Testament
NCC	New Covenant Commentary
NClarB	New Clarendon Bible
Neot	*Neotestamentica*
NIB	*The New Interpreter's Bible*. Edited by Leander E. Keck. 12 vols. Nashville: Abingdon, 1994–2004
NIBC	New International Bible Commentary
NICNT	New International Commentary on the New Testament
NIGTC	New International Greek Testament Commentary
NIVAC	NIV Application Commentary
NovT	*Novum Testamentum*
NovTSup	Novum Testamentum Supplements
NPNF²	*Nicene and Post-Nicene Fathers*, Series 2. Edited by P. Schaff and H. Wace. 14 vols. 1890–1900. Repr., Peabody, MA: Hendrickson, 1994
NSBT	New Studies in Biblical Theology
NTAF	The New Testament and the Apostolic Fathers
NTC	The New Testament in Context
NTComm	New Testament Commentary
NTD	Das Neue Testament Deutsch
NTG	New Testament Guides
NTL	New Testament Library
NTM	New Testament Message
NTMon	New Testament Monographs
NTOA	Novum Testamentum et Orbis Antiquus
NTR	New Testament Readings
NTS	*New Testament Studies*
NTSI	The New Testament and the Scriptures of Israel
NTT	New Testament Theology
NTTS	New Testament Tools and Studies
Numen	*Numen: International Review for the History of Religions*

OBO	Orbis biblicus et orientalis
OBS	Oxford Bible Series
OBT	Overtures to Biblical Theology
Oulton	*Eusebius: Ecclesiastical History, Books 6–10*. Translated by J. E. L. Oulton. Loeb Classical Library. Cambridge: Harvard University Press, 1932
OTM	Oxford Theological Monographs
PBM	Paternoster Biblical Monographs
PBTM	Paternoster Biblical and Theological Monographs
PC	Proclamation Commentaries
PCNT	Paideia Commentaries on the New Testament
PFES	Publications of the Finnish Exegetical Society
PGC	Pelican Gospel Commentaries
PJT	*Pacific Journal of Theology*
PNTC	Pillar New Testament Commentary
PS	Pauline Studies
PSTJ	*Perkins School of Theology Journal*
PTMS	Princeton Theological Monograph Series
PTR	*Princeton Theological Review*
QD	Quaestiones disputatae
RB	*Revue biblique*
RBL	*Review of Biblical Literature*
RBS	Resources for Biblical Study
ResQ	*Restoration Quarterly*
RevExp	*Review and Expositor*
RHC	Romans through History and Cultures
RNBC	Readings: A New Biblical Commentary
RNT	Reading the New Testament
Rolfe	*Suetonius*. Translated by J. C. Rolfe. 2 vols. Loeb Classical Library. Cambridge: Harvard University Press, 1997–98
RTR	*Reformed Theological Review*
SBEC	Studies in the Bible and Early Christianity
SBJT	*Southern Baptist Journal of Theology*
SBL	Studies in Biblical Literature
SBLAB	Society of Biblical Literature Academia Biblica
SBLBMI	Society of Biblical Literature The Bible and Its Modern Interpreters
SBLDS	Society of Biblical Literature Dissertation Series
SBLECL	Society of Biblical Literature Early Christianity and Its Literature
SBLMS	Society of Biblical Literature Monograph Series
SBLRBS	Society of Biblical Literature Resources for Biblical Study
SBLSCS	Society of Biblical Literature Septuagint and Cognate Studies
SBLSP	*Society of Biblical Literature Seminar Papers*
SBLSymS	Society of Biblical Literature Symposium Series
SBT	Studies in Biblical Theology
ScrB	*Scripture Bulletin*
ScrHier	*Scripta hierosolymitana*
ScrMin	Scripta minora
SCSS	Septuagint and Cognate Studies Series
SD	Studies and Documents
SE	*Studia evangelica*
SEÅ	*Svensk exegetisk årsbok*

SecCent	*Second Century*
SFSHJ	South Florida Studies in the History of Judaism
SHBC	Smith & Helwys Bible Commentary
SHCT	Studies in the History of Christian Thought
SJLA	Studies in Judaism in Late Antiquity
SJT	*Scottish Journal of Theology*
SJTOP	Scottish Journal of Theology Occasional Papers
SNTA	Studiorum Novi Testamenti auxilia
SNTG	Sheffield New Testament Guides
SNTI	Studies in New Testament Interpretation
SNTSMS	Society for New Testament Studies Monograph Series
SNTSU	Studien zum Neuen Testament und seiner Umwelt
SNTW	Studies of the New Testament and Its World
SP	Sacra pagina
SPNT	Studies on Personalities of the New Testament
SR	*Studies in Religion*
ST	*Studia theologica*
StBT	*Studia biblica et theologica*
STDJ	Studies on the Texts of the Desert of Judah
StJud	Studies in Judaism
StPatr	*Studia patristica*
SubBi	Subsidia biblica
SUNT	Studien zur Umwelt des Neuen Testaments
SwJT	*Southwestern Journal of Theology*
TBC	Torch Bible Commentaries
TBT	*The Bible Today*
TDNT	*Theological Dictionary of the New Testament*. Edited by G. Kittel and G. Friedrich. Translated by G. W. Bromiley. 10 vols. Grand Rapids: Eerdmans, 1964–1976
TGST	Tesi Gregoriana, Serie teologia
Thackeray	*Josephus: The Life Against Apion*. Translated by H. St. J. Thackeray. Loeb Classical Library 186. Cambridge: Harvard University Press, 1997
THNTC	Two Horizons New Testament Commentary
TI	Theological Inquiries
TJ	*Trinity Journal*
TM	Textus minores
TNTC	Tyndale New Testament Commentaries
TPINTC	Trinity Press International New Testament Commentaries
TS	*Theological Studies*
TSR	*Trinity Seminary Review*
TSt	Texts and Studies
TU	Texte und Untersuchungen
TynBul	*Tyndale Bulletin*
TZ	*Theologische Zeitschrift*
UNDSPR	University of Notre Dame Studies in the Philosophy of Religion
USQR	*Union Seminary Quarterly Review*
VC	*Vigiliae christianae*
VCSup	Supplements to Vigiliae christianae
VE	*Vox evangelica*
WBC	Word Biblical Commentary
WBT	Word Biblical Themes

WeslTJ	*Wesleyan Theological Journal*
WestBC	Westminster Bible Companion
WestPC	Westminster Pelican Commentaries
Whiston	*The Works of Josephus.* Translated by William Whiston. Peabody, MA: Hendrickson, 1987
WTJ	*Westminster Theological Journal*
WUNT	Wissenschaftliche Untersuchungen zum Neuen Testament
WW	*Word and World*
ZECNT	Zondervan Exegetical Commentary: New Testament
ZNW	*Zeitschrift für die neutestamentliche Wissenschaft und die Kunde der älteren Kirche*
ZPE	*Zeitschrift für Papyrologie und Epigraphik*
ZS	Zacchaeus Studies

PART 1

INTRODUCTION
AND BACKGROUND

1

Approaching the New Testament as the Church's Scripture

The Bible is God's gift to the church. Its contents are acknowledged by the church as uniquely inspired by God and revealed to human authors through the inspiration of the Holy Spirit.[1] The NT provides the church not only with the founding story of its incarnate Lord and the salvation accomplished by him but also with a key provision for its ongoing sustenance and guidance. For the church, therefore, Scripture is unique, holy, and possesses irreplaceable, infallible, canonical authority.

The church fully depends on the historical events narrated especially in the Gospels: the ministry, death, and resurrection of Jesus. The Christian faith is more than ethics or philosophy: *it rests squarely on the reality of historical events*. Our salvation, as magnificent and transcendent as it is, was accomplished in datable time and locatable space. The notice in Luke 3:1–2, at the beginning of the story, could hardly be more specific in terms of historical particularity: "In the fifteenth year of the reign of Tiberius Caesar, Pontius Pilate being governor of Judea, and Herod being tetrarch of Galilee, and his

---

1. The classic statement is that of 2 Timothy 3:16: "All scripture is inspired by God," where the word *theopneustos* ("God-breathed") is used. This word may well allude to the work of the "Spirit" (*pneuma*) of God in the production of Scripture. Although the mechanism of inspiration remains mysterious, it is at least clear that Scripture finds its origin in God and thus bears a divine authority. Note also 2 Peter 1:21: "No prophecy ever came by the impulse of man, but men moved by the Holy Spirit spoke from God" (cf. Zech. 7:12; Neh. 9:30). What is spoken of in 2 Timothy 3:16 and 2 Peter 1:21 is, of course, what we call the OT, but the statement may be applied to the NT writings by analogy.

brother Philip tetrarch of the region of Ituraea and Trachonitus, and Lysanias tetrarch of Abilene, in the high-priesthood of Annas and Caiaphas, the word of God came to John the son of Zechariah in the wilderness."

Although Christianity transcends the historical, it is inseparable from the historical. "There cannot therefore be any proclamation of the gospel which is not at the same time a narration of past history."[2] The historical basis of the Christian faith is at once its glory and stumbling block. The glory is in the fact that in the biblical story God enters history, so to speak, for the purpose of rescuing his creation. The eternal intersects the temporal. The stumbling block is that history is fragile: full of uncertainties and subject to human investigation and human doubt. But Christianity nevertheless depends squarely on its contradiction of the famous "ditch" that the eighteenth-century German philosopher G. E. Lessing dug between transcendent truth and the vagaries of history.

The Scriptures as Historical Documents

If the story of salvation is above all a historical story, so too the documents of the NT that record that history are documents that originate in history. The NT did not drop out of heaven directly from God, untouched by human hands. On the contrary, its writings are the products of particular human beings, who lived in specific times and places, and who had their own personalities and their own distinctive viewpoints. Nor were these authors simply empty channels, passively receiving supernatural dictation. As God came to us through the agency of a human being, Jesus, so in an analogous way the word of God comes to us through the agency of human words. This is of the essence of Christianity, and it is of the utmost importance. Thus the record and interpretation of the saving acts of God contained in the NT is itself a collection of historical data, mediated by and through history. Scripture consists of a deed/word or event/interpretation complex where every aspect comes to us through historical means. Indeed, there is a sense in which we may say that God has entrusted the whole process of salvation to history: not merely the acts of redemption themselves, but their record and interpretation in the writing of Scripture, in the formation of the canon, and in the transmission of the text. Theology and history remain inseparably bound together.

This single lapidary fact—the inspired word of God comes to us through the medium of history, through the agency of writers who lived in history and were a part of history—*necessitates the historical and critical study of Scripture*. It is the reason for the writing of the kind of book you have in your hands. In no other way than by historical study can we come to an adequate understanding of the Bible that honors it as God has been pleased to give it to us.

2. Hengel, *Acts and the History of Earliest Christianity*, 44.

Biblical Criticism

Unfortunately, the words "criticism" and "critical" are often misunderstood. As used here, the words do not refer to criticizing Scripture—that is, tearing it down or demeaning it—but rather *to exercising judgment or discernment* concerning every aspect of it.[3] As I use them here, the words indicate nothing other than the good use of reason and the various tools available in understanding and interpreting the Bible.[4] Criticism in this sense is not an option but an absolute necessity if one is going to make any intelligent statement about the Bible or to begin to interpret it responsibly.[5] The question is not whether we should engage in criticism—if we do not, we will be forced to keep silent about the Bible—but whether our critical judgment is good or bad, well founded or without justifiable basis. Studying the Bible critically may be conceived as one way of loving God with all our mind, as we are directed by Jesus, who cites the Shema as the first and greatest commandment (Matt. 22:37, citing Deut. 6:5).

We must engage in historical criticism, in the sense of thoughtful interpretation of the Bible, both because of the way in which God has given Scripture to us and because of its intrinsic nature. To approach the Bible in any other way is to be untrue to its nature. We are called to deal with the Bible that God gave to us, and *as God gave it*, not as we might suppose or wish it to be.

The historical method is indispensable precisely because the Bible is the story of God's acts in history. The salvation-historical narrative that begins in Genesis comes to its climax in the NT account of the appearance of Jesus of Nazareth, the Son of God, at a specific time and place. Since the records and narratives of these salvation-historical acts of God in the Bible are themselves products of history, written by individuals located in specific times and places, it is vitally important to immerse ourselves in the history of that era and that culture. If we are to understand these things, they must be studied historically, using the tools and methods of historical research.[6]

3. Underlying the English words is the Greek word *kritikos*, which occurs in Hebrews 4:12: *kritikos enthymēseōn kai ennoiōn kardias* ("discerning the thoughts and intentions of the heart").

4. "'Historical-critical method' simply represents a necessary collection of the 'tools' for opening up past events" (Hengel, *Acts and the History of Earliest Christianity*, 54).

5. A still-useful introduction and defense of the critical method for the beginner, written from an evangelical perspective, is Ladd, *The New Testament and Criticism*. Ladd, describing the Bible as the word of God in the words of human beings, regarded the historical-critical method as not just useful but also as indispensable. He demonstrated that it was not a contradiction to be both a committed believer *and* a critical scholar. See also Hagner, "The New Testament, History, and the Historical-Critical Method."

6. In recent years there has been a proliferation of new methods for studying the NT. For a description and defense of the continuing indispensability of the historical-critical method, see Hagner and Young, "The Historical-Critical Method and the Gospel of Matthew." Other methods, useful though they may be, must not be allowed to displace the historical-critical method.

For sincere, believing Christians, the word "critical" therefore should be regarded as a good word, and it will be used as such in this book. Only "radical" criticism—that is, a hostile, destructive approach to Scripture—is problematic for faith.

Historical Method and Presuppositions

The main problem with radical, destructive criticism is not the application of critical judgment to Scripture but rather its unjustified presuppositions.

Thus, unfortunately, a feigned neutrality more often than not hides an a priori negative bias. As Colin Hemer notes, "The Enlightenment imposes, not freedom from presupposition, but contrary presuppositions."[7] A naturalistic worldview, which is not subject to proof and can only be presupposed, rules out the possibility of the transcendent or supernatural and thus necessarily closes the mind of the scholar to the truth of the Bible's narratives. Hypotheses built on this presupposition are precarious at best. Many indeed contend that such an attitude is required if one is to practice the historical-critical method with integrity. But Martin Hengel's advice is worth listening to: "The most appropriate attitude for the scholar when dealing with the historical narratives of the New Testament is one which does not disregard *a priori* the testimony and the claim presented in these texts, but is prepared to 'listen' openly to what they have to say. Such an approach takes seriously the content of the texts—however strange they may seem to us—and attempts to understand them in terms of their intrinsic concerns. This also involves accepting, rather than denying, their claim to be kerygmatic historical reports."[8]

It is the bread and butter of the historian to work with causation in history. But historians have no access to the divine causation that is so fundamental to the biblical narratives, a causation outside the closed network of perceivable cause and effect. However, this need not paralyze the historian's critical judgment. Other matters are indeed accessible to the historian, such as the nature and reliability of the evidence, the identity and credibility of the witnesses, and their proximity to the event in question. Purged from unjustifiable presuppositions, the historical-critical method provides wonderful tools to help us understand the Bible.

Keeping an open mind concerning the possibility of the transcendent in history does not entail the suspension of critical judgment. There is no need

7. Hemer, *The Book of Acts in the Setting of Hellenistic History*, 443. It should hardly be surprising that Enlightenment rationalism and its accompanying presuppositions would be so unproductive in the study of the Bible.

8. Hengel, *Acts and the History of Earliest Christianity*, 56. Hengel adds that "the historical method which is appropriate here requires extreme care, guarded intensity, responsibility and reverence towards the truth" (ibid., 57). Hengel's discussion "Historical Methods and the Theological Interpretation of the New Testament" (ibid., 127–36) is filled with wisdom for those who would study the Scriptures.

for a naive credulity and acceptance of anything and everything simply because one's worldview is amenable to the supernatural. A method, however, that excludes the supernatural from the start will not take us far in understanding documents that find their very raison d'être in the activity of God in history.[9] It would be hard to devise a worse match than so-called scientific (= naturalistic) historiography[10] and the Bible, where the method itself cancels out its subject matter a priori.[11] It should be no surprise that this approach has been so unproductive. But as N. T. Wright stresses, "There are more things in heaven and earth than are dreamed of in post-Enlightenment philosophy, as those who have lived and worked in areas of the world less affected by Hume, Lessing and Troeltsch know quite well."[12] The critical method therefore needs to be tempered so that rather than being used against the Bible, it is open to the possibility of the transcendent or miraculous within the historical process and thus is used to provide better understanding of the Bible.[13]

The Spurning of the Historical-Critical Method

Paradoxically, at present it is not only some very conservative scholars who have turned away from the critical method but also more reasonable and even liberal scholars who recognize that the method, as usually practiced, is bankrupt if not dead. Quite remarkably, in recent years the whole enterprise of traditional historical-critical scholarship has come into disrepute. The move away from exclusively historical and theological questions began gently enough with the application of new disciplines to the study of the Bible. Preeminently one thinks of sociology and anthropology, rhetorical and narrative criticism, and especially the new appreciation of the Bible as literature. Although these new approaches are not necessarily antithetical to historical study of Scripture, they

9. "Just as we cannot produce proofs of God with historical methods and from a consideration of history, so it follows that the application of historical-critical methods cannot call for the recognition of an 'atheistic' view of history in which the question of the activity of God becomes illegitimate" (ibid., 52).

10. C. Stephen Evans rightly concludes that the "claim that this approach is more likely to lead to truth because it is 'scientific' seems like an illegitimate attempt to give one party to a dispute an unearned advantage by associating its claims with the deserved and hard-won reputation of the natural sciences" ("The Historical Reliability of John's Gospel," 115).

11. "We are confronted with the paradox of a way of studying the word of God out of which no word of God ever seems to come, with an imposing modern knowledge of the Bible which seems quite incapable of saying anything biblical or thinking biblically" (Casserley, *Toward a Theology of History*, 116). Quoted from L. Morris, *Studies in the Fourth Gospel*, 10.

12. Wright, *Jesus and the Victory of God*, 187.

13. "Historical biblical scholarship that assumes a naturalistic framework is unlikely to be more conducive to truth than other approaches unless metaphysical naturalism is true, and I see little reason to think it is" (Evans, "The Historical Reliability of John's Gospel," 115). See also Stanton, "Presuppositions in New Testament Criticism."

can become so if they are used in a reductionist manner. The same can be said of special-interest hermeneutics such as feminist, liberation, and postcolonial approaches. Unfortunately, however, proponents of these approaches often have been highly critical of the historical approach. But it is especially the so-called new literary criticism that has posed itself as the displacing alternative to historical criticism. In its pure form the literary approach is hostile to history, insisting on understanding the text as a self-contained world and as strictly nonreferential. Here the historicity of events is no longer important, and it gives way to the underlying "message" of the Bible.

It is perhaps not surprising that even some evangelicals have jumped onto the docetic bandwagon of "story but not history."[14] The idea of retaining the Bible's message without having to wrestle with the uncertainties of history is very appealing to them and perhaps reflects a lurking suspicion that the historical basis of Christianity is too fragile to depend upon.

In many circles of the guild these days it is not uncommon to hear the claim that the hegemony of the historical-critical method in the discipline of biblical study has come to an end. The influence of postmodernism is being more and more widely felt, whether it be through the new literary criticism, poststructuralism, or reader-response interpretation.

Postmodernism and Historical Knowledge

For a number of years now there has been an understandable and justifiable reaction under way to the inflated claims of modernism. Postmodernism rightly criticizes modernism's undue confidence in the ability of human reason in itself to arrive at fully objective, exhaustive, and absolute truth. All knowledge is partial and skewed by the perspective of the knower. It would be foolish to deny this. Even the Apostle Paul had to say, "For now we see in a mirror dimly. . . . Now I know in part" (1 Cor. 13:12). But it is equally foolish to go so far as to conclude that no real knowledge is possible and to deny the very idea of universal truth. And although complete objectivity is possible for no one, we should at least strive to be as objective as possible.

Many who are influenced by postmodernism have concluded that it is a serious mistake to think of interpretation as "excavating" the author's meaning in a text. For these scholars, texts serve rather as stimulants to bring out the meanings that interpreters bring to the texts. Meaning thus lies in the reader and not in the text. Attention turns now more often to the reader, the process of reading, and the power of the readers who impose their meanings on texts. The result of such a conclusion is the contention that readers have little chance of hearing anything other than their own thoughts; they can only imagine what

14. For the avoidance of this improper dichotomy, see the excellent discussion in Byrskog, *Story as History—History as Story.*

they see in the text. The inescapable reality of a plurality of interpretations indicates that there is no way to adjudicate between different interpretations. All that we have in the end is the assent of various communities to certain readings of texts that have no objective basis.

Despite the communicable claims of postmodern writers (who presumably believe that what *they* write can be understood more or less correctly!), it is possible to determine the intended meaning of an author in a text, even if that determination is less than perfect and inevitably experiences some interference from the preunderstandings of an interpreter. It is of the greatest importance to insist on the possibility and importance of exegesis.[15] We must indeed fight for the right of texts to be heard, for the autonomy of texts, especially in the case of the biblical texts, the truth of which is all-important to us, and whose teachings we are called to obey. These texts, more perhaps than any others, want to be heard, and it is clear that these authors have something to say. And it is not impossible for us to hear it.

Historical Knowledge and Probability

It may at first be disconcerting to hear the conclusion that all historical knowledge is necessarily only probable rather than certain. The word "prove," although perhaps appropriate in mathematics and science, is out of place when it comes to historical knowledge. Hengel observes, "The demand to 'compellingly prove' something appears all too often in New Testament literature and indicates a lack of historical consciousness"; he continues with a quotation from Adolf Schlatter: "There is no completely accurate historical knowledge for any part of the course of history; we do not even have it for the course of our own life."[16] We function quite well in life with knowledge that usually amounts only to probability and not certainty.

We cannot have perfect knowledge and cannot demonstrate the truth of any particular historical conclusion, but this does not mean that we cannot know or that we cannot have reasonable confidence in our historical conclusions. It is not a matter of either absolute proof or nothing. Certainty is not a requisite to knowledge. Quite the contrary, there are degrees of probability. And in most of the chapters that follow in this book I will speak of probabilities of varying degree rather than of certainties. Many conclusions about the origin of the NT necessarily remain a matter of critical judgment and varying probability rather than of demonstrable truth. This is because of the very nature of historical knowledge.

There is, of course, at the same time a different knowledge that involves another kind of certainty. This is the subjective knowledge that the believer alone

15. See Hagner, "The Place of Exegesis in the Postmodern World."
16. Hengel, "Eye-witness Memory and the Writing of the Gospels," 88n77.

experiences concerning the truth of these matters for his or her existence. Here we know in a unique way, by faith, through the confirmation of the inner witness of the Spirit. This existential certainty should not be thought of as incompatible with the acceptance of probability as the basis of all historical knowledge.

The precarious character of historical knowledge has tempted some believers to the security, or misperceived certainty, of an obscurantist fundamentalism. Repudiation of the critical study of Scripture amounts to a gnostic-like denial of the historical character of the Christian faith. "Fundamentalist polemic against the 'historical-critical method' does not understand historical perception. It can therefore also not perceive the *reality of salvation history*, because in its anxious rationalism, it cannot and will not grasp the true effects of God's action through his Word in history."[17]

The Role of Faith in the Study of Scripture

The NT was written for believers, not for doubters. Believers are the implied readers of the NT texts, and therefore believers are in the best place to make sense of the NT texts.[18] It is to believers that the texts open themselves most readily. This is contrary to the frequently encountered claim that faith is an obstacle to the proper understanding of the NT. Only, however, when faith is characterized by openness rather than an a priori dogmatism is it an aid to the study of Scripture.

The advantage that the believer has in the study of Scripture is openness to the truth of the narratives.[19] A hermeneutic of trust can have the salutary and paradoxical effect of making us better historians and scholars of Scripture than those who do not believe. Options that arise from the material itself may be given fairer consideration; helpful constructions may emerge from a positive approach that would not be seen in a negative orientation. Certainly the approach of the believer will be more fruitful and truthful than a hostile approach of one who is predisposed to deconstruct the Christian faith. Theological presuppositions, of course, inevitably enter into the discussions, as indeed they do for those who consider themselves "neutral."[20] Without ques-

17. Ibid., 94. Hengel adds, "Fundamentalism is a form of 'unbelief' that closes itself to the—God-intended—historical reality" (ibid., 94n100).

18. Markus Bockmuehl makes this point beautifully in *Seeing the Word*.

19. Peter Stuhlmacher calls for a "hermeneutics of consent" that involves "a willingness to open ourselves anew to the claim of tradition, of the present, and of transcendence" (*Historical Criticism and Theological Interpretation of Scripture*, 85). This approach to Scripture employs a "type of interpretation, which not merely critically dissects but also listens," and it involves "exegesis which serves the church" by its openness to "the truth of God encountering us from out of transcendence" (88). See also Snodgrass, "Reading to Hear."

20. For some, "neutrality" means the denial of the church's view of Jesus, or even the possibility that it could be true.

tion presuppositions will remain crucial.[21] "The wise course is to recognize those presuppositions, to make allowance for them, to ensure that they do not exercise an undue influence on our understanding of what we read. It is the unconscious and unsuspected presuppositions that are harmful."[22]

It should be stressed once again that the critical method is indispensable to the study of Scripture. It is the sine qua non of responsible interpretation of God's word. The believer need have no fear of the method itself, but need only be on guard against the employment of improper presuppositions. J. B. Lightfoot gave helpful counsel:

> The timidity, which shrinks from the application of modern science or criticism to the interpretation of Holy Scripture, evinces a very unworthy view of its character. If the Scriptures are indeed true, they must be in accordance with every true principle of whatever kind. It is against the wrong application of such principles, and against the presumption which pushes them too far, that we must protest. It is not much knowledge, but little knowledge, that is the dangerous thing here as elsewhere. From the full light of science or criticism we have nothing to fear: the glimmering light—which rather deserves the name of darkness visible—hides and distorts the truth.[23]

Bibliography

Abraham, W. J. *Divine Revelation an the Limits of Historical Criticism*. New York: Oxford University Press, 1982.

Barton, John. *The Nature of Biblical Criticism*. Louisville: Westminster John Knox, 2007.

Blomberg, Craig L. "Is the New Testament Historically Reliable?" In *Making Sense of the New Testament: Three Crucial Questions*, 17–70. Grand Rapids: Baker Academic, 2004.

Bockmuehl, Markus. *Seeing the Word: Refocusing New Testament Study*. Grand Rapids: Baker Academic, 2006.

Bockmuehl, Markus, and Donald A. Hagner, eds. *The Written Gospel*. Cambridge: Cambridge University Press, 2005.

Brown, Colin, ed. *History, Criticism and Faith: Four Exploratory Studies*. Downers Grove, IL: InterVarsity, 1976.

Brown, R. E. *The Critical Meaning of the Bible: How a Modern Reading of the Bible Challenges Christians, the Church, and the Churches*. Mahwah, NJ: Paulist Press, 1981.

Bruce, F. F. "Primary and Plenary Sense." In *The Canon of Scripture*, 316–34. Downers Grove, IL: InterVarsity, 1988.

Byrskog, Samuel. *Story as History—History as Story: The Gospel Tradition in the Context of Ancient Oral History*. WUNT 123. Tübingen: Mohr Siebeck, 2000.

21. As Evans says, "It is worth reminding ourselves of the elementary fact that judgments of probability are always made relative to a set of background assumptions" (Evans, "The Historical Reliability of John's Gospel," 114).

22. Bruce, "Primary and Plenary Sense," 332.

23. "Greek Testament Lectures, Lent Term 1855" (unpublished lecture notes), cited in James D. G. Dunn, ed., *The Lightfoot Centenary Lectures*, 39–40, 72. See also Treloar, *Lightfoot the Historian*, 307.

Casserley, J. V. L. *Toward a Theology of History*. London: Mowbray, 1965.

Dunn, James D. G. "Criteria for a Wise Reading of a Biblical Text." In *Reading Texts, Seeking Wisdom: Scripture and Theology*, edited by David F. Ford and Graham Stanton, 38–52. London: SCM, 2003.

———, ed. *The Lightfoot Centenary Lectures: To Commemorate the Life and Work of Bishop J. B. Lightfoot (1828–89)*. Durham, UK: Senate of the University of Durham, 1992 (extra issue of *Durham University Journal*).

Evans, C. Stephen. "The Historical Reliability of John's Gospel: From What Perspective Should It Be Assessed?" In *The Gospel of John and Christian Theology*, edited by Richard Bauckham and Carl Mosser, 91–119. Grand Rapids: Eerdmans, 2007.

Fitzmyer, Joseph A. *The Interpretation of Scripture: In Defense of the Historical-Critical Method*. New York: Paulist Press, 2008.

Hagner, Donald A. "The Bible: God's Gift to the Church of the Twenty-First Century." *CurTM* 35 (2008): 19–31.

———. "The New Testament, History, and the Historical-Critical Method." In *New Testament Criticism and Interpretation*, edited by David Alan Black and David S. Dockery, 73–96. Grand Rapids: Zondervan, 1991.

———. "The Place of Exegesis in the Postmodern World." In *History and Exegesis: New Testament Essays in Honor of Dr. E. Earle Ellis for His 80th Birthday*, edited by Sang-Won (Aaron) Son, 292–308. New York: T&T Clark, 2006.

———. "The State of the Bible in the Twenty-First Century." *CurTM* 35 (2008): 6–18.

Hagner, Donald A., and Stephen E. Young. "The Historical-Critical Method and the Gospel of Matthew." In *Methods for Matthew*, edited by Mark Allan Powell, 11–43. MBI. Cambridge: Cambridge University Press, 2009.

Hanson, A. T., ed. *Vindications: Essays on the Historical Basis of Christianity*. London: SCM, 1966.

Hemer, Colin J. *The Book of Acts in the Setting of Hellenistic History*. Edited by Conrad H. Gempf. WUNT 49. Tübingen: Mohr Siebeck, 1989.

Hengel, Martin. *Acts and the History of Earliest Christianity*. Translated by John Bowden. Philadelphia: Fortress, 1980.

———. "Eye-witness Memory and the Writing of the Gospels: Form Criticism, Community Tradition and the Authority of the Authors." In *The Written Gospel*, edited by Markus Bockmuehl and Donald A. Hagner, 70–96. Cambridge: Cambridge University Press, 2005.

Ladd, George Eldon. *The New Testament and Criticism*. Grand Rapids: Eerdmans, 1967.

Morgan, Robert, with John Barton. *Biblical Interpretation*. New York: Oxford University Press, 1988.

Morris, L. *Studies in the Fourth Gospel*. Grand Rapids: Eerdmans, 1969.

Snodgrass, Klyne. "Reading to Hear: A Hermeneutics of Hearing." *HBT* 24 (2002): 1–32.

Stanton, Graham N. "Presuppositions in New Testament Criticism." In *New Testament Interpretation: Essays on Principles and Methods*, edited by I. Howard Marshall, 60–71. Grand Rapids: Eerdmans, 1977.

Stuhlmacher, Peter. *Historical Criticism and Theological Interpretation of Scripture: Towards a Hermeneutics of Consent*. Translated by Roy A. Harrisville. Philadelphia: Fortress, 1977.

Treloar, Geoffrey R. *Lightfoot the Historian: The Nature and Role of History in the Life and Thought of J. B. Lightfoot (1828–1889) as Churchman and Scholar*. WUNT 2/103. Tübingen: Mohr Siebeck, 1998.

Wright, N. T. *Jesus and the Victory of God*. COQG 2. Minneapolis: Fortress, 1996.

2

The Old Testament
as Promise and Preparation

Together with all the people of Israel, the writers of the NT looked to the
Scriptures of Israel as the foundation of their faith and as the expression of
their hopes. The divine inspiration of the *Tanak*—a word created to refer
to the threefold Jewish canon: *Torah* (Law), *Nebiim* (Prophets), *Ketubim*
(Writings)—was taken for granted.[1] The Scriptures recounted the prehistori-
cal stories of the creation and fall, Noah and the flood, Babel, and so forth,
but especially beginning with Abraham they told the story of God entering
into covenant relationship and making covenant promises to Abraham and
his descendants that would remain in the hearts and minds of the people of
Israel through the centuries. From the point of view of the NT writers, who
believed that fulfillment had come in Christ, these Scriptures came to be regarded as a long story of preparation and promise. For them, as we will see,
Christ was the hermeneutical key that unlocked the ultimate meaning of the
Scriptures, and as a consequence they saw the Scriptures as pointing repeatedly
to Christ.[2] *It is virtually impossible to understand the NT without knowledge
of the Scriptures of Israel*. This, therefore, is where we must start.

It is clear that after Eden the world was no longer as God meant it to be
at the beginning, the creation that he had repeatedly pronounced "good."
This reality of a fallen world provides the backdrop for the remainder of the

---

1. The threefold canon was already in place in the first century, except for a few contested
books (see chap. 43 below). It is reflected in, for example, Luke 24:44.
2. See Wright, *Knowing Jesus through the Old Testament*.

story of the Bible. God, however, begins to work to counteract the fall and its effects. With God's promises to Abraham—the Abrahamic covenant—we have the beginning of the history of salvation.[3]

Salvation History: The History of Redemption

The Abrahamic Covenant

Two millennia before Christ, God inaugurated his plan of redemption when he called Abram out of his previous life in Ur and made promises to him and his descendants. This is the beginning of salvation history and what can be designated as the "ascending line of promise," which involves both the building of an expectation and the preparation for its fulfillment.[4]

The first statement of the covenant is found in Genesis 12:1–3, 7, but restatements of its elements occur in 13:14–17; 15:5–6; 17:1–8 (where Abram's name is altered to "Abraham" ["father of a multitude"]); 22:15–18. The covenant promises are renewed to Isaac (26:3–4, 24) and Jacob (28:13–15; 35:9–12 [where Jacob is given the name "Israel"]; cf. 28:3–4; 32:9–12; 48:3–4, 16, 19). Among the various stories of Genesis, the promises of the Abrahamic covenant become a kind of controlling motif. Thus Joseph's final words, at the end of the book, include a reference to the promise that "God will visit you, and bring you up out of this land to the land which he swore to Abraham, to Isaac, and to Jacob" (50:24). And, indeed, the promises of the Abrahamic covenant become of major importance in the thinking of Jews from that time onward.

What specifically are the promises of this covenant? We may list them here as follows (drawn from the Genesis texts listed in the preceding paragraph):

- a great nation
- a blessing
- a great name
- a blessing to others
- in you shall all the families of the earth be blessed[5]

---

3. See Wright, *Salvation Belongs to Our God*. For an older but still helpful review of the OT story of salvation, see Bright, *A History of Israel*.

4. There are, of course, earlier anticipations of the grace of God, who wills to save his creation. Already in the seed of the woman in Genesis 3:15 the church saw a *protevangelium*, an allusion, detected in retrospect, to the redemption to be accomplished through Christ: "I will put enmity between you and the woman, and between your seed and her seed; he shall bruise your head, and you shall bruise his heel."

5. While the meaning of the Hebrew here is ambiguous (the Niphal verb in Gen. 12:3; 18:18 can be translated as a reflexive, "bless themselves," or as a passive, "be blessed"; elsewhere the verb is Hithpael [Gen. 22:18; 26:4], normally a reflexive), the LXX has the unambiguous

Figure 1 **Salvation History (The History of Redemption)**

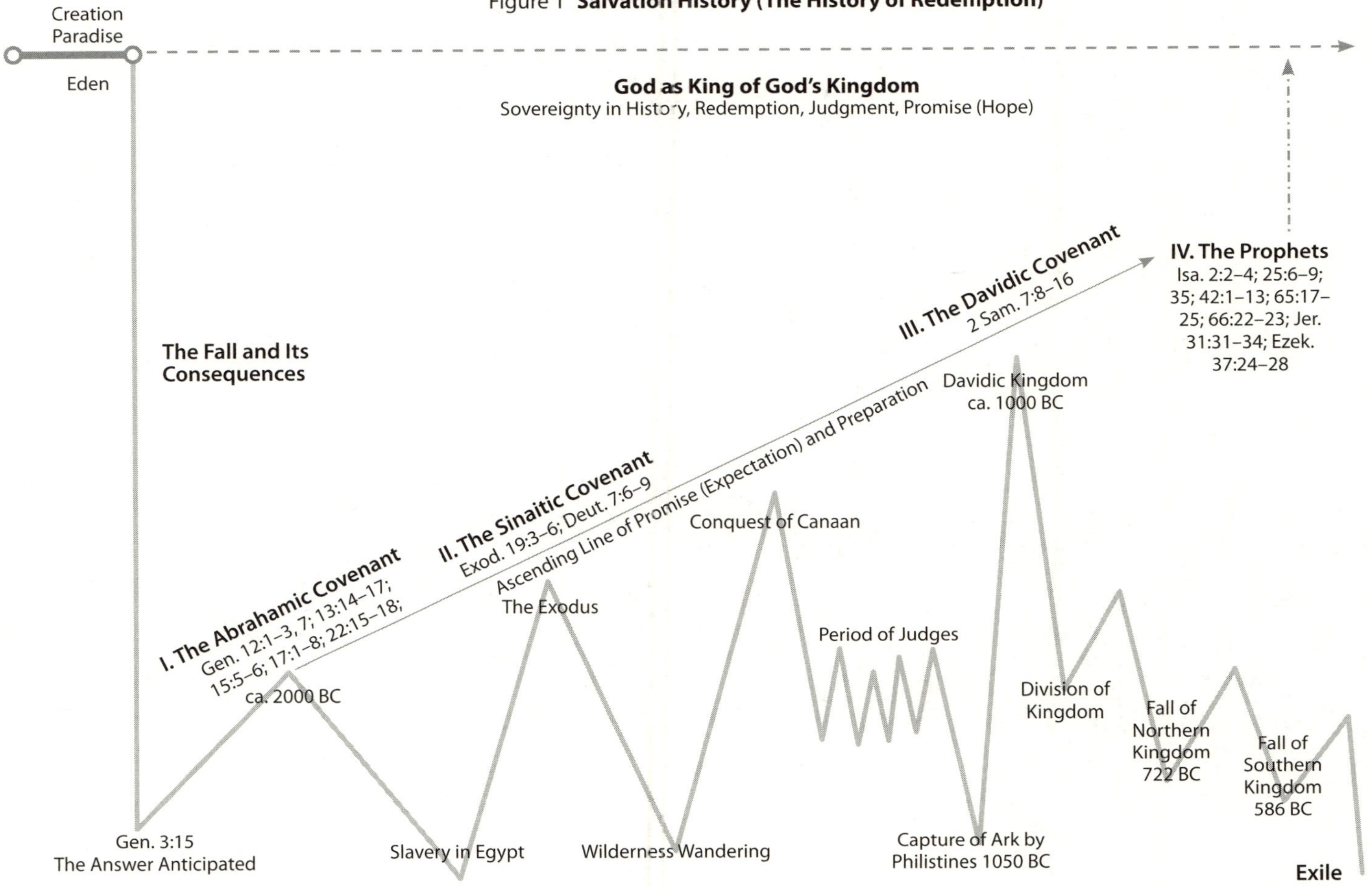

God as King of God's Kingdom

Sovereignty in History, Redemption, Judgment, Promise (Hope)

The Fall and Its Consequences

I. The Abrahamic Covenant
Gen. 12:1–3, 7; 13:14–18;
15:5–6; 17:1–8; 22:15–18;
ca. 2000 BC

II. The Sinaitic Covenant
Exod. 19:3–6; Deut. 7:6–9

Ascending Line of Promise (Expectation) and Preparation

III. The Davidic Covenant
2 Sam. 7:8–16

IV. The Prophets
Isa. 2:2–4; 25:6–9;
35; 42:1–13; 65:17–
25; 66:22–23; Jer.
31:31–34; Ezek.
37:24–28

Creation
Paradise

Eden

Gen. 3:15
The Answer Anticipated

Slavery in Egypt

The Exodus

Wilderness Wandering

Conquest of Canaan

Period of Judges

Capture of Ark by
Philistines 1050 BC

Davidic Kingdom
ca. 1000 BC

Division of
Kingdom

Fall of
Northern
Kingdom
722 BC

Fall of
Southern
Kingdom
586 BC

Exile

- the land to you and your descendants
- descendants as the dust of the earth, the stars in heaven
- the father of a multitude of nations, kings
- an everlasting covenant
- I will be your and their God
- your descendants will possess the gate of their enemies

Already here we have some of the basic components that will characterize the Jewish faith through the centuries: election and covenant (with its promises concerning the future), both depending solely on the grace of God. Also prominent among the covenant promises are those concerning descendants and the land.

The Sinaitic Covenant

The next major covenantal statement in salvation history is found in the complex of events associated with the exodus and the revelation of the law at Sinai. The Sinaitic covenant is not a replacement of the Abrahamic covenant, but in some respects it can be regarded as an extension of it. On the heels of the miraculous deliverance of Israel from Egyptian bondage, God reveals his law—his Torah—on Mount Sinai in Exodus 19:3–6; 20:1–17, and much of the rest of the books of Exodus, Leviticus, and Numbers, together with Deuteronomy, the "second" account of the giving of the law (Deut. 4:13–14, 31, 40). Motifs from the Abrahamic covenant recur throughout this material. Note in Deuteronomy, for example, "Go in and take possession of the land which the LORD swore to your fathers, to Abraham, to Isaac, and to Jacob, to give to them and to their descendants after them" (1:8 [cf. 3:18; 4:1; 6:10, 18, 23]), and "The LORD your God has multiplied you, and behold, you are this day as the stars of heaven for multitude. May the LORD, the God of your fathers, make you a thousand times as many as you are, and bless you, as he has promised you!" (1:10–11 [cf. 7:12–13]). And more generally, "You shall be blessed above all peoples" (7:14).

Election and covenant again emerge with stark clarity: "For you are a people holy to the LORD your God; the LORD your God has chosen you to be a people for his own possession, out of all the peoples that are on the face of the earth" (Deut. 7:6). The Lord's love for Israel is explained as his "keeping the oath which he swore to your fathers" (7:8). "Know therefore that the LORD your God is God, the faithful God who keeps covenant and steadfast love with those who love him and keep his commandments, to a thousand generations" (7:9).

---

eneulogēthēsontai ("they will be blessed"), as do also the NT occurrences (Acts 3:25 [minus the initial en]; Gal. 3:8).

New items also begin to be emphasized: monotheism (Deut. 4:39; 6:4 [the Shema]) and, most dramatically and emphatically, the Torah,[6] the law (4:8; 5:3)—again, two key elements that would continue to characterize the faith of Israel. With the law, of course, comes the instruction for the building of the tabernacle (later the temple) and the accompanying institution of its priesthood and its sacrifices.

In addition to the elements in common with the Abrahamic covenant, we may add the following aspects contained within the Sinaitic material:

- a corpus of commandments
- a temple and sacrifices
- my possession among all peoples
- a kingdom of priests
- a holy nation

The Davidic Covenant

The third covenant of great importance is that made with David, in response to his desire to build "a house" for God—that is, a permanent temple. This too is properly regarded as extending the Abrahamic covenant, but advancing it further. In 2 Samuel 7:4–17 the prophet Nathan is instructed by the Lord to tell David that "the LORD will make you a house," by which is meant a lasting dynasty. Thus, along with other items, such as the promise of "a great name," victory over his enemies, a place (land) where Israel can dwell safely, the astounding promise is made concerning the descendant(s) of David that the Lord "will establish the throne of his kingdom for ever" (7:13).

Of the five promises of the Davidic covenant, the last two take us beyond what has been encountered in the previous covenants:

- I will give you rest from all your enemies
- a great name
- a place (land) for Israel
- the Lord will make you a house (dynasty)
- a kingdom and a throne established forever

New here are the framing of the expectation via the concept of kingship and kingdom and the idea of an eternal kingdom. The expectation of a future Davidic king becomes very important in the Jewish hope for a coming messiah.

---

6. The Hebrew word *tôrâ* can mean several things. Basically, it means "instruction," but it comes also to mean "commandment" and "law," and eventually becomes the regular designation for the Pentateuch.

The content of these three major covenants results in a fixed and recognizable pattern and what could be identified as a relatively unified and general expectation shared widely by the people of Israel in the NT period. These promises dominated the thinking and perspective of the people who were the first to hear the preaching of the Nazarene. And when the NT writers tell the story of salvation accomplished in Jesus, they do so in terms of these covenantal promises.

The Prophets

The expectation outlined thus far is, of course, shared by the prophets. Much of what they say builds on the material outlined above. There is a sense on the part of some, however, that something dramatically *new* must occur if the covenantal promises are to be realized.

A NEW, EVERLASTING COVENANT

Jeremiah 31:31–34 puts forward the idea of "a new covenant," which will succeed where the Sinai covenant did not. These are the elements of this new covenant:

- my law within them, written on their hearts
- I will be their God; they shall be my people
- I will forgive their iniquities and remember their sins no more

Ezekiel 37:24–28 somewhat similarly speaks of "an everlasting covenant," when "my servant David [i.e., a descendant of David] shall be king over them." As in Jeremiah, the observance of the law is assured. We may list the elements of this everlasting covenant as follows:

- they shall dwell in the land
- an everlasting covenant; a covenant of peace
- I will bless them and multiply them
- I will set my sanctuary in the midst of them for evermore
- I will be their God; they shall be my people

In both Jeremiah and Ezekiel we can see continuity with the earlier covenants, but we also encounter some remarkable new promises, and indeed an emphasis on newness.

THE EMERGENCE OF APOCALYPTIC

Several prophets now begin to speak about a future that is no longer realizable within what we might call ordinary history. Here the transition is being made from prophecy to *apocalyptic*—that is, to what can be achieved only by a direct, radical inbreaking of God into the historical process to transform it (see chap. 3 below).[7] Certain sections of Isaiah are remarkable in this respect: 2:2–4; 25:6–9; 35:1–10; 42:9–10; 65:17–25. The following is a list of the things mentioned in these passages:

- all nations shall flow to Zion; out of Zion shall go forth the law
- weapons reshaped into tools; neither shall they learn war any more
- a banquet for all peoples
- death swallowed up forever
- tears wiped away from all faces
- gladness and rejoicing at God's salvation
- desert shall rejoice and blossom; streams in the desert
- sorrow and sighing shall flee away
- everlasting joy shall be upon their heads
- eyes of the blind opened; ears of the deaf unstopped
- the lame shall leap like a hart
- the tongue of the dumb will sing for joy
- the former things have come to pass; new things I now declare
- sing to the Lord a new song
- I create new heavens and a new earth
- no more weeping or cries of distress
- they shall enjoy their inheritance as the blessed of the Lord
- they shall not hurt or destroy in all my holy mountain

Again, the emphasis on newness is obvious in this material. It is as if the prophets said, "We cannot arrive at what God has promised as things currently are." The only way to the amelioration of the ills of Israel, and of the world, is through divine agency, involving a kind of new creation analogous to the original creation, but now unmarred by sin. On God's holy mountain, Zion, God "will destroy . . . the covering that is cast over all peoples, the veil that is spread over all nations" (Isa. 25:7). What God spoke initially to Israel finds its ultimate conclusion in a transformation of the entire created order that will affect all humanity.

THE PROPHETIC REFOCUSING OF THE EXPECTATION

The prophets bring a very important refocusing of Israel's perspective and hopes for the future. Some Jews presumed on their special status as the elect

7. "Increasingly the view of the classical prophets that God's promises to his people would be fulfilled within the context of historical events yielded to the belief that fulfillment would be imposed upon a fallen world in a cataclysmic display of force by the Cosmic Warrior Yahweh" (Paul Hanson, *The Dawn of Apocalyptic*, 405).

people of God, and in so doing they became lax and self-centered. It apparently was easy for some in Israel to think that because they were unlike the other nations, God cared only for them and their future. We may list the prophetic refocusing under four headings.

From physical Jewishness to the remnant concept (e.g., Isa. 10:20–22; 37:31–32; Mic. 5:7–8; Zeph. 2:7; Joel 2:32). Not all Jews will escape future judgment merely because they have Jewish blood in their veins. Only a remnant, those who are faithful, can expect to be saved.

From externalism to internal change (e.g., Isa. 1:12–17; Amos 5:21–24; Mic. 6:6–8). Going through the motions of liturgy and worship avails nothing if integrity and faithfulness are lacking. Conduct in the world must bear some congruence with confession and liturgical service. Genuine internal change will especially reveal itself in appropriate behavior toward the needy.

From ethnocentrism to universalism (e.g., Isa. 42:1, 6; 45:22; 49:6; 60:3; 66:18–21; Zech. 2:11; Mal. 1:11). God's purposes do not begin and end with Israel. Quite the contrary, Isaiah says. Israel's election was ultimately for the sake of the nations. Israel was called to be "as a covenant to the people, a light to the nations" (Isa. 42:6) so that "my salvation may reach to the end of the earth" (49:6). The story of salvation was thus always meant to be bigger than the story of Israel.

From national-political expectation to a transcendent expectation (e.g., Isa. 25:6–9; 35:1–10; 65:17–25). With the emergence of an apocalyptic perspective, as noted above, the goal of God's purposes is broadened to the transformation of the created order: a new heavens and a new earth, a world where the effects of sin are fully removed. The promises and hopes concerning the land are not thereby canceled, but they are relativized or transformed. What God promises to do is no longer simply a matter of establishing a prosperous and secure earthly kingdom for his chosen people in the holy land; rather, it is transcendent and universal in scope.[8]

Although the universal dimensions were already explicit in the Abrahamic covenant, where God promises that in Abraham "all the nations of the world will be blessed," it is in the prophets that we first begin to see the full extent and scope of the promised blessing. What God began with Abraham will ultimately involve a return to the perfection and fulfillment of Eden as it was before the fall, thus affecting the whole of humanity and creation.

The New Testament Understanding of the Old Testament

The earliest Christians immediately regarded their faith as the fulfillment of the cumulative expectation that they knew so well from their Scriptures. It

---

8. For a significant book on the place of the land in the Bible, see Burge, *Jesus and the Land*. See also idem, *Whose Land? Whose Promise?*

is no accident that Matthew refers to Jesus as "the son of David, the son of Abraham" (1:1), evoking both covenants. Nor is it coincidental that Isaiah is by far the most popular prophetic book in the NT. All through the NT writings is the common theme of the fulfillment of the promises of Scripture. This intertextuality, exhibited in the hundreds of quotations and thousands of allusions and echoes of the OT in the NT, is fundamental to the identity and self-understanding of the first Christians. C. H. Dodd argued that the use of the OT to elucidate the kerygma of the early church constitutes no less than "the substructure of New Testament theology."[9]

Without question, then as now, there was disagreement between those who believed in Christ and those who did not about the meaning of specific texts. It is equally clear that the Christians employed a distinctive hermeneutic: a christological hermeneutic of fulfillment based on the conviction that Christ is the hermeneutical key that unlocks the meaning of the Scriptures. In effect, the first Christians started with the answer. They had witnessed the words and deeds of Jesus, and above all they had seen the risen Jesus. This, together with the reality of the experience of the outpouring of the Holy Spirit, assured them that eschatology had begun and that Jesus was the fulfillment of the promises and the hopes of Israel. Salvation history is teleologically oriented, and the telos, the goal, has come in Christ. The central redemptive act of God that reverses the effects of the fall has already occurred in the death and resurrection of Christ.

This conviction enabled them to approach the Scriptures with new eyes and new understanding. What Richard Hays says of Paul applies to virtually all the NT writers: "This means, ultimately, that Scripture becomes—in Paul's reading—a metaphor, a vast trope that signifies and illuminates the gospel of Jesus Christ."[10] The Scriptures, when seen with the eyes of faith, point unmistakably to Christ. Paul alludes to this fact when he writes of non-Christian Jews, "To this day, when they read the old covenant, that same veil remains unlifted, because only through Christ is it taken away. Yes, to this day whenever Moses is read a veil lies over their minds; but when a man turns to the Lord the veil is removed" (2 Cor. 3:14–16). As Hays points out, Paul (and the other writers of the NT too, I would add) enacted "a certain imaginative vision of the relation between Scripture and God's eschatological activity in the present time . . . under the guidance of the Spirit, interpreting Scripture in light of the gospel and the gospel in light of Scripture."[11]

Plenary Sense

The majority of OT quotations in the NT involve finding deeper meanings in texts than the original authors could have realized or intended. We are dealing

9. Dodd, *According to the Scriptures*, 27.
10. Hays, *Echoes of Scripture in the Letters of Paul*, 149.
11. Ibid., 183.

here not with normal exegesis, but rather with a retrospective reunderstanding of texts that is predetermined by the NT authors' conviction that Christ is the goal of the Scriptures. This has been called the *sensus plenior*, the "fuller/deeper sense" of the text—in other words, the ultimate meaning of the text as it can now be determined in light of the fulfillment that has come in Christ.[12] It is a christological exegesis of the Scriptures.

A phenomenon related to *sensus plenior* is found in analogy or typology[13]—that is, in divinely intended patterns of correspondence between what God did or said in the past according to the Scriptures and what is true of the history of Jesus Christ. Because the Bible presents one great story of God redeeming his creation, the correspondences between past and present are regarded not as coincidental but as divinely intended. In these correspondences, which, of course, can be seen only in retrospect, the earlier element (the type) is regarded as prophetic or anticipatory of its later counterpart (the antitype), which in turn can be regarded as its fulfillment. This intertextuality occurs because of the unity of the story of salvation.

This approach to the Scriptures was not the invention of the Christians. It is found already within the OT, where patterns, both of blessing and judgment, are related typologically, former events anticipating later events (e.g., the eschatological restoration of the land reflects the garden of Eden [Ezek. 36:33–35]).[14] Thus, for example, the return from the exile is described in the same language as the exodus deliverance (see, e.g., Jer. 16:14–15; 23:8). The desecration of the temple in 586 BC by the Babylonians, in 187 BC by Antiochus Epiphanes, and in AD 70 by Titus are related in this way. The translators of the Septuagint (the Greek version of the Hebrew Scriptures) saw deeper meaning in Isaiah 7:14 than was understood in Isaiah's day and thus chose to translate the Hebrew word *'almâ*, "young woman," as *parthenos*, "virgin" (cf. Matt. 1:23). A similar approach of finding deeper meaning in texts is found in Jewish literature of the Second Temple period and at Qumran in its pesher ("this is that") interpretation, which is very similar to the NT's use of the OT.

It should be immediately obvious how important and useful this approach to the Scriptures would have been to the earliest Christians. Gerhard von Rad has called attention to the "structural analogy" that exists "between the saving events in the two testaments."[15] The redemption accomplished by Christ is set forth as the analogue to the exodus of Israel from Egypt (cf. Luke 9:31; 1 Cor. 5:7–8; 10:1–5). Most of the quotations of the OT in the NT involve this kind of plenary sense. For example, Matthew 2:15 makes the point that

12. The classic discussion is Brown, *The* Sensus Plenior *of Sacred Scripture*. See also Brown, "The *Sensus Plenior* in the Last Ten Years"; LaSor, "Prophecy, Inspiration, and *Sensus Plenior*."

13. As an antidote for much of the nonsense that passes under the name "typology," nothing is better than the classic work by Lampe and Woollcombe, *Essays on Typology*.

14. On this phenomenon, see von Rad, *Old Testament Theology*, 2:319–429.

15. See von Rad's discussion of typology (ibid., 2:362–74).

the return of Jesus from Egypt with his family is the fulfillment of the statement in Hosea 11:1, "Out of Egypt I called my son." Hosea meant nothing more than the historical fact of the exodus event, referring to Israel as the son of God. But Matthew finds the parallel with the return of Jesus, the Son of God, from Egypt to be a matter of divinely intended correspondence, so that he thinks of the former as an anticipation, or "prophecy," of the latter, and the latter as the "fulfillment" of the former.

Many scholars find this common typological and *sensus plenior* use of the OT in the NT to be arbitrary and indefensible. Although the plenary sense is similar to allegorical interpretation, it is a mistake to think of it as such.[16] The creative aspect is based on the detection of analogical patterns together with the experience of a new revelation in the appearance of Christ. If we make an attempt to understand its underlying rationale, it is not as arbitrary or frivolous as it may at first seem.[17] The *sensus plenior* approach is based on four essential convictions:

1. the sovereignty of God,
2. the inspiration of Scripture,
3. the unity of salvation history, and
4. Christ as the telos.

As we have already noted, the last point here is the determinative principle. Christian interpretation of the OT begins with the telos and then moves to an interpretation of the texts, not vice versa. The telos is by definition Christ, and thus we speak of christological exegesis. This, of course, is the major reason why such interpretation is not compelling for Jews who are not convinced that Jesus is the Messiah.

As for the first point, the sovereignty of God is a basic Jewish conviction. If God is in some sense in control of all that happens, then discernible patterns in history may be thought of as divinely arranged, and movement toward the goal may be assumed. Second, the record of Scripture is verbally inspired by God, so it is no accident how things are expressed. Verbal correspondences therefore are neither accidental nor insignificant.[18] Third, the story of the Bible is one story; it is not two stories, one about Israel and the other about the

16. Allegorical interpretation involves interpreting something in light of something else that is unrelated to it, as, for example, in Philo's interpretation of Moses through the lens of Plato. *Sensus plenior* also involves interpreting something in light of something else, the Christ event, but this is something vitally related to the OT expectation.

17. Granted, it does become stretched in the second-century Apostolic Father Barnabas. But only very seldom does a NT text raise eyebrows (e.g., Matt. 2:23, if "Nazarene" is a play on the word "branch" [*nzr*] in Isa. 11:1).

18. In a well-known text (Gal. 3:16), Paul, in rabbinic fashion, seizes on the singular form of *sperma* ("seed"), even though it is a collective, in order to conclude that the offspring promised to Abraham was Christ.

church, to be kept quite distinct, as classic dispensationalism maintained. As far as the earliest Christians are concerned, there would have been no need to argue for the unity of the great story of the Scriptures and Christ. This was a fundamental, a priori conviction. But, if it is a single story, one may expect interconnectedness and legitimately relate its different parts, the earlier anticipating the later. And it is *Christ as the goal of the story*, from the beginning, that provides the underlying unity and ties the parts together.[19]

One of the most common reservations that scholars have about *sensus plenior* understandably concerns the matter of controls. Do the NT writers find *sensus plenior* everywhere and anywhere, at will? And, on a related point, can later Christian readers employ *sensus plenior* in their interpretation of the OT? I would answer no to the former question and a guarded yes to the latter question.[20]

As a guide to acceptable plenary sense, a few principles in keeping with its nature can be made use of. First, the patterns of correspondence should be parallels involving some perceivable and substantial connections. Second, they should preferably involve patterns of historical sequence. Third, they should involve matters of significance rather than peripheral or trivial details.

The covenantal promises reviewed above, together with the expectations of the prophets, can naturally be interpreted in more than one way. One may say that there are two levels of meaning in the OT texts: one the historical-exegetical meaning intended by the original authors in their original settings, and the other a *sensus plenior* meaning wherein the ultimate significance of the material is understood in light of a perceived fulfillment that enables new meanings for the same texts. The Jews who were not persuaded by the gospel took the former approach; the Christian Jews who did accept the gospel took the latter approach.

Although there were some, like Marcion, who argued that the OT Scriptures had little to do with the Christian faith, the church had no difficulty in seeing its faith as the fulfillment of the Scriptures: the Abrahamic promise that all the nations would be blessed in Abraham was happening through the proclamation of the gospel to the Gentiles; the everlasting kingdom promised to David was now in place through his descendant Jesus; the universal, apocalyptic

---

19. The fact that the LXX translation of the Tetragrammaton (YHWH) is regularly *kyrios* ("Lord"), enabled the earliest Christians to see the Scriptures as referring to the one whom they called "Lord," Jesus. It is interesting, however, that while they often identify Jesus with the LXX's *kyrios*, they do not do so consistently, but only when, for whatever reason, it seems appropriate.

20. On the one hand, if there is an understandable and defensible rationale to *sensus plenior*, as I have argued, then there seems to be no reason why we cannot find more examples of it in the OT than we have in the NT. Some, on the other hand, would limit *sensus plenior* to what we find in the NT. Richard Longenecker, for example, maintains that it is only apostolic authority that legitimates *sensus plenior*. For an informative article, see Longenecker, "Can We Reproduce the Exegesis of the New Testament?" Hays's rejection of this conclusion as less than satisfactory is justified (*Echoes of Scripture in the Letters of Paul*, 180–83).

expectations of the prophets were beginning to be realized in Jesus and the church but would find their consummation in the return of Jesus at the end of the present age.

At the beginning, and for some time afterward, all believers in Jesus were Jews. Never for a moment did any of them think they had left one religion for another. For them, Christianity was the fulfillment of their Scriptures and of their Jewish faith. Their Bible eventually came to be called the "Old Testament," but for them it remained vitally important. Before Christ, no integrating key was available to arrive at the ultimate intention and unity of Scripture. But now in Christ, God has disclosed the true goal of the OT promises (see 2 Cor. 1:20). Now the NT writers are able to understand the OT retrospectively and to conclude "this is that" (see Acts 2:16). This type of interpretation was known in Jewish circles as pesher, and it is found amply in the writings of the Qumran community. The members of that community, however, used pesher interpretation to portray their time as that immediately prior to eschatological fulfillment, whereas the NT writers used it to express the fulfillment that had already begun to occur in Christ.[21]

Richard Hays helpfully detects three substantive "hermeneutical restraints" that control Paul's interpretation of the Scriptures:

1. "God's faithfulness to his promises,"
2. "Scripture must be read as a witness to the gospel of Jesus Christ," and
3. "No reading of Scripture can be legitimate . . . if it fails to shape the readers into a community that embodies the love of God as shown forth in Christ."[22]

These seem to be easily applicable to all of the NT writers.

A New Testament View of the Old Testament

The OT story of God and Israel from the NT point of view is, above all, the preparation of a meaningful context for the central redemptive act of God in Christ for the salvation of the world. As we have seen, the NT writers believe that the OT points consistently to Christ as its telos. Thus the OT does not possess final importance but rather is relativized by the NT. This hardly should be taken to mean that the OT is unimportant. Far from it: the OT is indispensable to the understanding of the NT. There is a sense in which it is a mistake to publish the NT by itself apart from the OT. The two constitute one Bible, and each part needs the other. As the ancients put it, the NT is latent in the OT; the OT is made patent in the NT.

21. See Bruce, *Biblical Exegesis in the Qumran Texts*; idem, *This Is That*.
22. Hays, *Echoes of Scripture in the Letters of Paul*, 191.

What are the key things the NT learns from the OT? We can summarize as follows:

- God in grace and mercy promises salvation (the covenants).
- God is God, with power to deliver and to fulfill covenant promises (the exodus).
- God is holy in an absolute sense (the tabernacle/temple; the priesthood).
- Humankind is sinful and can approach God only through stipulated means (the sacrifices).
- God demands righteousness (the law).
- God purposes to bless all humanity with the benefits of salvation (Abrahamic covenant; the prophets).
- God is faithful, despite how bad things may look in the present, and will surely accomplish his purposes (the prophets).

In addition, and of considerable importance, the OT is a great lesson book concerning the relationship between God and his people. The principles and patterns of obedience and disobedience, and their consequences, remain constant in both Testaments. This is what Paul means when, referring to the wilderness wandering of Israel, he writes, "Now these things happened to them as a warning, but they were written down for our instruction, upon whom the end of the ages has come" (1 Cor. 10.11 [cf. 9.10]). So too Romans 15:4: "For whatever was written in former days was written for our instruction, that by steadfastness and by the encouragement of the scriptures we might have hope."

It should be obvious, then, that of all that could be mentioned as important for the understanding of the NT, including what I will mention in the chapter that follows, nothing supersedes the Scriptures of the OT. Supersession is entirely the wrong language. To be sure, modifications and adjustments are required in light of the new era that has been inaugurated, but the fundamental givenness of the Scriptures is taken for granted throughout the NT. And the OT continues to be Holy Scripture for the Christian. If it is Israel's story, it is also the story of the church. The theological richness caused by the intertextuality of the OT and the NT is one of the major aspects of what makes the NT the exciting collection of writings that it is.

Bibliography

Anderson, Bernhard W. *The Old Testament and Christian Faith: A Theological Discussion.* New York: Harper & Row, 1963.

Baker, D. L. *Two Testaments, One Bible: A Study of the Theological Relationship between the Old and New Testaments.* 3rd ed. Downers Grove, IL: IVP Academic, 2010.

————. "Typology and the Christian Use of the Old Testament." *SJT* 29 (1976): 137–57.

Barr, James. *Old and New in Interpretation: A Study of the Two Testaments*. New York: Harper & Row, 1968.

Beale, G. K., ed. *The Right Doctrine from the Wrong Texts? Essays on the Use of the Old Testament in the New*. Grand Rapids: Baker Academic, 1994.

Beale, G. K., and D. A. Carson, eds. *Commentary on the New Testament Use of the Old Testament*. Grand Rapids: Baker Academic, 2007.

Berding, Kenneth, and Jonathan Lunde, eds. *Three Views on the New Testament Use of the Old Testament*. Grand Rapids: Zondervan, 2007.

Bright, John. *A History of Israel*. 4th ed. Louisville: Westminster John Knox, 2000.

Brown, Raymond E. "The *Sensus Plenior* in the Last Ten Years." *CBQ* 25 (1963): 262–85.

———. *The* Sensus Plenior *of Sacred Scripture*. Baltimore: St. Mary's University, 1955.

Bruce, F. F. *Biblical Exegesis in the Qumran Texts*. Grand Rapids: Eerdmans, 1959.

———. "Primary and Plenary Sense." In *The Canon of Scripture*, 316–34. Downers Grove, IL: InterVarsity, 1988.

———. *This Is That: The New Testament Development of Some Old Testament Themes*. Exeter, UK: Paternoster, 1968.

———. *The Time Is Fulfilled: Five Aspects of the Fulfillment of the Old Testament in the New*. Grand Rapids: Eerdmans, 1978.

Burge, Gary M. *Jesus and the Land: The New Testament Challenge to "Holy Land" Theology*. Grand Rapids: Baker Academic, 2010.

———. *Whose Land? Whose Promise? What Christians Are Not Being Told about Israel and the Palestinians*. Cleveland: Pilgrim Press, 2003.

Carson, D. A., and H. G. M. Williamson. *It Is Written: Scripture Citing Scripture; Essays in Honour of Barnabas Lindars, SSF*. Cambridge: Cambridge University Press, 1988.

Court, John M., ed. *New Testament Writers and the Old Testament: An Introduction*. London: SPCK, 2002.

Dodd, C. H. *According to the Scriptures: The Sub-Structure of New Testament Theology*. London: Nisbet, 1952.

———. *The Old Testament in the New*. Philadelphia: Fortress, 1963.

Ellis, E. Earle. *The Old Testament in Early Christianity: Canon and Interpretation in the Light of Modern Research*. WUNT 54. Tübingen: Mohr Siebeck, 1991.

———. *Paul's Use of the Old Testament*. Reprint, Grand Rapids: Baker Academic, 1981.

Evans, Craig A., and James A. Sanders, eds. *Paul and the Scriptures of Israel*. JSNTSup 83. Sheffield: JSOT Press, 1993.

Foulkes, Francis. *The Acts of God: A Study of the Basis of Typology in the Old Testament*. London: Tyndale, 1955. Reprinted in *The Right Doctrine from the Wrong Texts? Essays on the Use of the Old Testament in the New*, edited by G. K. Beale, 342–71. Grand Rapids: Baker Academic, 1994.

France, R. T. *Jesus and the Old Testament: Application of Old Testament Passages to Himself and His Mission*. Grand Rapids: Baker Academic, 1982.

Goppelt, Leonhard. *Typos: The Typological Interpretation of the Old Testament in the New*. Translated by Donald H. Madvig. Grand Rapids: Eerdmans, 1982.

Hagner, Donald A. "The Use of the Old Testament in the New Testament." In *Interpreting the Word of God: Festschrift in Honor of Steven Barabas*, edited by Samuel J. Schultz and Morris A. Inch, 78–104. Chicago: Moody, 1976.

———. "When the Time Had Fully Come." In *Dreams, Visions, and Oracles: The Layman's Guide to Biblical Prophecy*, edited by Carl Edwin Armerding and W. Ward Gasque, 89–99. Grand Rapids: Baker Academic, 1977.

Hanson, A. T. *The Living Utterances of God: The New Testament Exegesis of the Old*. London: Darton, Longman & Todd, 1983.

Hanson, Paul D. *The Dawn of Apocalyptic*. Philadelphia: Fortress, 1975.

Hay, David M. *Glory at the Right Hand: Psalm 110 in Early Christianity*. SBLMS 18. Nashville: Abingdon, 1973.

Hays, Richard B. *The Conversion of the Imagination: Paul as Interpreter of Israel's Scripture*. Grand Rapids: Eerdmans, 2005.

———. *Echoes of Scripture in the Letters of Paul*. New Haven: Yale University Press, 1989.

Hays, Richard B., Stefan Alkier, and Leroy A. Huizenga, eds. *Reading the Bible Intertextually*. Waco: Baylor University Press, 2009.

Juel, Donald. *Messianic Exegesis: Christological Interpretation of the Old Testament in Early Christianity*. Philadelphia: Fortress, 1988.

Kaiser, Walter C. *The Promise-Plan of God: A Biblical Theology of the Old and New Testaments*. Grand Rapids: Zondervan, 2008.

———. *The Uses of the Old Testament in the New*. Chicago: Moody, 1985.

Lampe, G. W. H., and K. J. Woollcombe. *Essays on Typology*. SBT 22. London: SCM, 1957.

LaSor, William Sanford. "Prophecy, Inspiration, and *Sensus Plenior*." *TynBul* 29 (1978): 49–60.

LaSor, William Sanford, David Allan Hubbard, and Frederic William Bush. *Old Testament Survey: The Message, Form, and Background of the Old Testament*. 2nd ed. Grand Rapids: Eerdmans, 1996.

Lindars, Barnabas. *New Testament Apologetic: The Doctrinal Significance of the Old Testament Quotations*. London: SCM, 1961.

———. "The Place of the Old Testament in the Formation of New Testament Theology." *NTS* 23 (1976–77): 59–66.

Longenecker, Richard N. *Biblical Exegesis in the Apostolic Period*. 2nd ed. Grand Rapids: Eerdmans, 2000.

———. "Can We Reproduce the Exegesis of the New Testament?" *TynBul* 21 (1970): 3–38.

Moo, Douglas J. "The Problem of *Sensus Plenior*." In *Hermeneutics, Authority, and Canon*, edited by D. A. Carson and John D. Woodbridge, 179–211. Grand Rapids: Zondervan, 1986.

Moyise, Steve. *Evoking Scripture: Seeing the Old Testament in the New*. New York: T&T Clark, 2008.

———. *Jesus and Scripture: Studying the New Testament Use of the Old Testament*. Grand Rapids: Baker Academic, 2011.

Porter, Stanley E., and Christopher D. Stanley, eds. *As It Is Written: Studying Paul's Use of Scripture*. SBLSymS 50. Atlanta: Society of Biblical Literature, 2008.

Sparks, Adam. *One of a Kind: The Relationship between Old and New Covenants as the Hermeneutical Key for Christian Theology of Religions*. Eugene, OR: Pickwick, 2010.

Stanley, Christopher D. *Arguing with Scripture: The Rhetoric of Quotations in the Letters of Paul*. New York: T&T Clark International, 2004.

———. *Paul and the Language of Scripture: Citation Technique in the Pauline Epistles and Contemporary Literature*. SNTSMS 74. Cambridge: Cambridge University Press, 1992.

Von Rad, Gerhard. *Old Testament Theology*. Translated by D. M. G. Stalker. 2 vols. London: SCM, 1975.

Wenham, John. *Christ and the Bible*. 3rd ed. Grand Rapids: Baker Academic, 1994.

Wright, Christopher J. H. *Knowing Jesus through the Old Testament*. Downers Grove, IL: InterVarsity, 1995.

———. *Knowing the Holy Spirit through the Old Testament*. Downers Grove, IL: InterVarsity, 2006.

———. *Salvation Belongs to Our God: Celebrating the Bible's Central Story*. Downers Grove, IL: InterVarsity, 2007.

Yarbrough, R. W. *The Salvation Historical Fallacy?: Reassessing the History of New Testament Theology*. Leiden: Deo, 2004.

3

The World of the New Testament

In order to be in a position to understand the NT, it is extremely important to know something of the historical and cultural contexts in which it was written. The more we know of the life setting of these writers and their readers and take it into consideration in our interpretation, the more truthful our exegesis of these texts will be. As we have already noted, God has been pleased to reveal himself through the medium of individuals who were fully and completely a part of their respective societies and cultures. The neglect of this one point has been responsible for much misuse and misinterpretation of the Bible. Above all, we must make the attempt to enter into the mind-set, into the thinking, of these writers, to walk in their shoes, to feel something of their situation, their frustrations and fears, their limitations, their aspirations, their hopes and longings. This means, to begin with, that it is essential to know, among other things, their recent history, developments in their faith, the spread and impact of Hellenism, and the practical effects of Roman rule over Palestine.

The History of Postexilic Israel

The Babylonian Exile

If anything, the history of Israel represents a disheartening series of setbacks that stand in glaring contradiction to the promises that God had made over the centuries. This is depicted in the lower line of figure 1 (p. 15) as the line of Israel's experience. Without question, the lowest point in this dizzying history was the Babylonian exile.

In 586 BC Jerusalem was sacked by Nebuchadnezzar and the Babylonians, and the temple was destroyed (see 2 Kings 24:10–17). The northern kingdom had already fallen to the Assyrians in 722 BC (see 2 Kings 17). It was as if the people of God—his chosen people, the recipients of the covenant promises—had ceased to exist. Moreover, the Solomonic temple, housing the holy of holies and symbolic of the presence of God with Israel, had come to a disastrous end, with its treasures carried off to Babylon. The upper strata of society—the artisans, the wealthy, the educated—were deported to Babylon. Only the poor and destitute were allowed to remain in the land. A sense of hopelessness and despair came over the exiled people. "By the waters of Babylon, there we sat down and wept, when we remembered Zion . . . How shall we sing the LORD's song in a foreign land?" (Ps. 137:1, 4). The book of Lamentations, traditionally ascribed to Jeremiah, eloquently captures the mood.

The impact of the exile on the psyche of the people and its influence in the following centuries, including the era of the NT, can hardly be overemphasized. Since, as we will see, the exile was regarded as the result of Israel's sin, the people now turned away from idolatry and began to pursue righteousness with a new, intense seriousness (see Ezra 9:10–15; Neh. 8–9). Of further importance was the influence of certain ideas in the religions of Mesopotamia, which served together with the experience of Israel as an impetus for a new interest in and growth of ideas about, for example, life after death, dualism, the transcendence of God, angelology, and demonology. These ideas exercise an important influence on the perspective of the NT writers.

Thanks to the conquest of the Babylonians in 539 BC by Cyrus, ruler of the Persians—dubbed God's "anointed" by Isaiah (Isa. 45:1)—after nearly fifty years of exile the people were allowed to return to Palestine (see Ezra 1:2–4). They were even allowed to rebuild their temple, though at the beginning the second temple (ca. 515) was a far cry from the previous Solomonic temple (see Ezra 3:12–13).[1] With the exile and the building of the second temple we reach the period of the beginning of *Judaism* per se.[2]

ALEXANDER THE GREAT, THE PTOLEMIES, AND THE SELEUCIDS

In 332 BC the famous Alexander the Great added Palestine to the long list of nations that he had conquered. As is well known, with the conquests of Alexander came not only foreign rule but also the Greek language and the pervasive influence of Hellenistic culture. The fact that Greek became the lingua franca of the Mediterranean world would have enormous importance even centuries later, accounting not only for the Septuagint (the Greek translations

---

1. Interestingly, a significant number of Jews remained in Babylon, and it became an important Jewish cultural and religious center, where the famous Babylonian Talmud was produced. See "Addendum: The Literary Legacy of the Pharisees" below.

2. Judaism is thus to be distinguished from the earlier, preexilic "religion of Israel."

of the OT, the main translation quoted in the NT) and for the use of Greek for the NT writings but also for facilitating the missionary work of the church in the countries surrounding the Mediterranean.

After the death of Alexander in 323 BC, his conquered territories were split up among his generals, and in turn their descendants: Syria, to the north, came under the rule of the Seleucids; Egypt, to the south, under the Ptolemies. In the ensuing centuries these two Hellenistic kingdoms fought repeatedly for the possession of Palestine; at first the Ptolemies held it, but then, in about 200 BC, it came under the control of the Seleucids, and remained so until the time of the Hasmoneans (see below, under the heading "Independence and the House of Hasmon"). During this period, although obviously taxed by whoever was in power over them, the Jews enjoyed a degree of self-rule, through the high priests and the "elders," and were allowed freedom of worship in the newly rebuilt temple. But the Jews, understandably, still chafed under the rule of foreigners over God's people and the land that God had given them.

ANTIOCHUS IV AND THE MACCABEAN REVOLT

By far the most significant event in this period of the reigns of Alexander's successors was the desecration of the temple by Antiochus IV, the Seleucid king who took the eponym "Epiphanes" (i.e., the "manifestation" of God),[3] along with his attempt to impose Hellenism on Palestine and to rid it of the Jewish faith altogether. The Jews, with rival high priests who had bought their office from Antiochus and who were at one another's throats, were fighting among themselves and seemingly in revolt against Antiochus. He decided that he had had enough of this thorn in his flesh and resolved to destroy Judaism and to impose Greek culture and customs on the Jews. He robbed the temple of its treasures, and in 167 BC he desecrated it by entering the holy of holies and setting an idol upon the altar of sacrifice, the "abomination of desolation" (cf. Dan. 11:31; 12:11; note also reference to the later Roman violation of the temple in AD 70, using the same expression, in Mark 13:14; Matt. 24:15). Antiochus prohibited the practice of the Jewish faith and the observance of the law, including circumcision and the dietary laws, and forced the people to sacrifice to pagan deities. Those who refused to go along with these mandates were put to death. The moving story can be found in the opening chapter of 1 Maccabees.

The story of the Maccabees' response to this persecution was to become one of the great historical symbols of loyalty to the Jewish faith and resistance to assimilation.[4] With unbelievable courage, a certain priest, Mattathias, and

---

3. This quickly was altered to "Epimanes" (i.e., the "madman") by his contemporaries. See Ferguson, *Backgrounds of Early Christianity*, 407.

4. "Maccabee" means "hammer." Other metaphors were used as well: "In his acts he [Judas] was like a lion, and like a lion's whelp roaring for his prey" (1 Macc. 3:4).

his five sons refused to comply with the commands to forsake the practice of their faith (see 1 Macc. 2). They, with others of like mind, formed a guerilla resistance movement that eventually, under the leadership of one of the five sons, Judas Maccabeus, was able to gain an impressive victory over the huge force of the Seleucid armies. In a mere three years the temple was regained, cleansed, and reconsecrated (164 BC).[5] Judas was succeeded by his brothers, Jonathan and Simon. This virtually miraculous deliverance from the powerful Syrian army by the bravery of a greatly outnumbered force of freedom fighters faithful to the Lord remained a fixture in the Jewish mind in the first century, and even down to the present, concerning loyalty and the power of God to deliver.

INDEPENDENCE AND THE HOUSE OF HASMON

Perhaps even more remarkable than the regaining of religious freedom and the reconsecration of the temple is that the Jews were able to regain political sovereignty for a time. By 142 BC the Syrians had been swept out of Palestine, and the land was ruled by Simon, the last of the Maccabee brothers. In 134 John Hyrcanus I, the son of Simon, ruled as high priest, and in 104 his son, Aristobulus, became "king" as well as high priest. From this time the so-called Hasmonean kings (the family name of the Maccabees), although constantly warring among themselves, ruled until the invasion of the Romans in 63. In that year the Roman general Pompey and his army invaded Jerusalem, and he defiled the temple by entering it. Israel and the land of Palestine now came under Roman rule, through puppet kings, for the remainder of its ancient history. In 37 Herod, son of the Idumean Antipater II, became the king of Judea. Herod the Great, as he came to be known (although "the Cruel" would have been a more suitable epithet), advanced Roman Hellenism in Palestine and engaged in grand building projects, including the enlargement and beautification of the Jerusalem temple. After his death (4 BC) the kingdom was divided among three of his sons. The Roman emperor Augustus (30 BC–AD 14), regarded as a kind of "savior," brought an era of peace and stability—the *pax Romana*. This, together with other advantages of the widespread empire, proved very important in the missionary work of the early church.

This interesting period in the history of Israel is full of contradictions. At first glance, it looks like a time of fulfillment. The high priesthood is reestablished, but since the Hasmoneans were not of Zadokite descent many (e.g., the Qumran community) regarded it as illegitimate. There was a succession of kings in Israel, but they were neither of Davidic descent nor of admirable character. The length and breadth of the kingdom had been dramatically increased during this period, but it did not produce the expected promised

---

5. A legend grew up about a miraculous supply of oil for the temple lamps, allowing them to burn for eight days, at the time of the rededication of the temple. This gave rise to the celebration of Hanukkah, which is observed down to the present as a commemoration of loyalty to the Jewish faith in the face of persecution.

blessings. Nevertheless, this period served in a limited and imperfect way as an indication of the presence and power of God as well as a foreshadowing of what might yet come.

The rule of the Romans, like all foreign rule of the Jews in the land, was despised. In no way was it compatible with what God had repeatedly promised to Israel. The might of Rome was undeniable, but so too was that of Antiochus and the Syrians. If God had enabled the Maccabees to win against Antiochus, would he not also come to the aid of Israel in a war against Rome? The result of such thinking was two futile wars against Rome. The first Jewish revolt occurred in AD 66–72, and it resulted not in the mere defilement of the second temple but in its final destruction with the fall of Jerusalem in 70 (in accord with Jesus' prophecy in Mark 13:2 // Matt. 24:2 // Luke 21:6).[6] A half a century later nationalistic fires again ignited against the Romans in the Jewish uprisings of 115–17 and then finally in the second Jewish revolt of 132–35. This constitutes the end of the story of Jews in the land until the establishment of a Jewish state in 1948. Modern Zionism has ancient roots.

Developments in the Jewish Faith

The Dilemma of Israel

From what we have seen so far, it will be no surprise to conclude that the Jewish mind from the exilic period onward was dominated by what may be called "the dilemma of Israel." That dilemma, not altogether new, consisted of the painful, blatant contradiction between the promises of God and the experience of Israel. God had said one thing; Israel had experienced another. In the time of Jesus the Roman rule over Palestine perfectly exemplifies the dilemma. The contrast is depicted in figure 1 (p. 15) in the contrasting lines of promise and Israel's experience. What is the explanation of this contradiction? In the search for the reasons behind this dilemma, again and again it was the sin of Israel that came to the mind of the Jews. It was sin that prevented Israel from experiencing the fulfillment of the promises and brought instead the judgments she had repeatedly experienced. This seemed certainly to be the perceived explanation of the Babylonian exile. God was punishing his people for their unfaithfulness (this is the emphasis especially of Ezra and Nehemiah).

If this was the explanation of the dilemma, what was the answer? What could be done to enable Israel to avoid the disappointments and sufferings of the past and instead to experience at last the fulfillment of the promises? We have evidence from several sources about the emergence of groups with

6. The war came to an end only with the fall of the fortress on Masada on the shore of the Dead Sea in 73 or 74. The story of the heroic Masada martyrs (which can be read in Josephus, *J.W.* 7.389–406) remains forever engraved on Jewish consciousness in the cry, "Never again!"

distinctive perspectives. Especially significant is this statement by Josephus: "The Jews, from the most ancient times, had three philosophies pertaining to their traditions, that of the Essenes, that of the Sadducees, and, thirdly, that of the group called the Pharisees" (*Ant.* 18.11, trans. Feldman). He subsequently speaks of a "fourth philosophy," which probably refers to the Zealots (*Ant.* 18.23).

Answers to Israel's Dilemma

PURSUIT OF RIGHTEOUSNESS

If the reason underlying the dilemma was the sin of Israel, then the first, and most obvious, answer was to pursue righteousness more effectively. This seems clear and logical, and several groups began to emerge in the postexilic era to champion righteousness with great energy: the Hasidim, the Pharisees (and scribes), and the Essenes at Qumran.

The term "*Hasidim*" is a general one that refers to a broad stream of people after the exile who resisted Hellenization and assimilation and promoted a new and serious adherence to the Torah. Their name means "holy ones" or "pious ones." They are, in a sense, the descendants of the reformation brought by Ezra, the protoscribe, the new, vigorous champion of Torah righteousness. They are not properly a sect but rather a kind of general movement of the faithful. Although they receive no specific mention in the NT, they probably are represented by the pious individuals of the Lukan infancy narrative, such as Zechariah and Elizabeth, Simeon, and Anna, not to mention Joseph and Mary.

The Pharisees are the most prominent Jewish sect in the Gospels, and deservedly so, for they were very serious in their quest for righteousness. Their reasoning seemed convincing: the problem that Israel had in successfully obeying the Torah was caused by its lack of specifics. The commandments needed elaboration. It was not enough, for example, to know that one should not work on the Sabbath as the commandment said. The issue was the definition of work. What was work and what was not? So the Pharisees began to elaborate the written law by means of an extensive oral tradition that explained it. In so doing, they were building "a fence around the Torah" (*m. 'Abot* 1.1) in order to ensure its obedience. Much attention was given to issues of ritual purity, a state of holiness of a different order than moral holiness (see below, under the heading "The Basic Elements of the Jewish Faith: Belief and Practice"). This oral law, paralleling the written law, became known as the "tradition of the elders" (as in Mark 7:3, 5; Matt. 15:2–3; cf. Mark 7:8–9).

Not all Pharisees saw everything in the same way, however. Two main schools are well known: that of Shammai and that of Hillel, both teachers active at the beginning of the first century. The Shammaites were far more conservative in all matters. For example, they allowed divorce only on the grounds of sexual immorality, whereas the more liberal Hillelites allowed divorce on practically any grounds. This provides the background of the discussion on divorce that Jesus is drawn into in Matthew 19:3–12. In general, the Talmud tends to favor the views of the Hillelites over those of the Shammaites.

According to Josephus, there were six thousand Pharisees in Israel in the first century, a small proportion (5 percent?) of the population. Their influence obviously was much greater than this number would suggest.

It is a great pity that the word "Pharisee," which ought to be a complimentary term, has become in the English language synonymous with "hypocrite." The word "Pharisee" probably comes from the verb *pāraš*, which means "to separate," in reference to those who were "separatists" by virtue of their serious pursuit of righteousness. This pursuit in itself should make them honorable. According to the Gospel of Matthew, even Jesus could speak in praise of the Pharisees. Insofar as they "sit on Moses' seat," one should "practice and observe whatever they tell you" (Matt. 23:2–3). It is also true that there were hypocrites among the Pharisees[7] (just as there are among Christians). And so in Matthew 23 Jesus, using exceptionally strong language, goes on to warn against their hypocrisy.

It is true that the Pharisees, or at least some of them, fell into a not uncommon trap in the spelling out of details of laws. The forest was lost for the trees. The casuistry of the Pharisees thus sadly and paradoxically often ended up undercutting the very thing that they were after in the first place. This is the complaint of Jesus in Mark 7:8–9: "'You leave the commandment of God, and hold fast the tradition of men.' And he said to them, 'You have a fine way of rejecting the commandment of God, in order to keep your tradition!'" (cf. Matt. 15:3, 6b). Similarly, obsession with trivia sometimes obscured the more important matters of the law: "Woe to you, scribes and Pharisees, hypocrites! For you tithe mint and dill and cumin, and have neglected the weightier matters of the law, justice and mercy and faith" (Matt. 23:23).

Nevertheless, to be a Pharisee was to wear a badge of honor. The Pharisees desired to arrive at a level of righteousness that would finally enable the gap between promise and Israel's experience to be closed. Undoubtedly, to a considerable extent Jesus himself, in his call to righteousness, actually resembled the Pharisees, as has been rightly pointed out by many Jewish scholars. And, of course, one tends to be most harshly critical of those who are closest to the truth.

Although not a sect, the scribes, because of their frequent association with the Pharisees, deserve mention here. "Scribe" (Gk. *grammateus*; Heb. *sōpēr*) refers not to a copyist but rather to a technical legal scholar—that is, an expert in the interpretation of the Mosaic law.[8] Since the interpretation of the law is of the essence of Pharisaism, obviously scribes had a very important role to

---

7. This is noted even in the Babylonian Talmud (*b. Soṭah* 22b).

8. For a classic description of the scribe, see Sirach 39:1–11, where it is said that the scribe "concentrates his mind and his meditation on the law of the Most High. He researches into the wisdom of all the ancients, he occupies his time with the prophecies." These words probably reflect the threefold division of the Hebrew Bible (Law, Prophets, Writings).

play among the Pharisees. Not all scribes, however, were necessarily Pharisees. There were scribes who were Sadducees. Indeed, members of any group could make use of scribes in their attempt to understand the law.

Yet another group that believed the answer to the dilemma of Israel lay in a more successful achievement of righteousness was *the Essenes*, the inhabitants of the monastic community near the northwestern shore of the Dead Sea at Qumran. In their view, what was needed was more focus on the living of the law. The ideal way to get this focus was to leave ordinary society for the monastic life, although there appear to have been gatherings of Essenes even within the villages and towns of Palestine. Josephus puts the number of Essenes at four thousand (*Ant.* 8.20). In the discipline provided by the isolated community there was the possibility of arriving at a high level of righteousness.[9] That goal was also brought closer by the leader of the community, the so-called Teacher of Righteousness, who, somewhat like Jesus, instructed the community in the way of righteousness.

The Qumran community, like the early Christians, believed that they were the people of the promised new covenant spoken of in Jeremiah 31:31. They believed themselves to be on the edge of the eschatological fulfillment promised to Israel. In many ways, of course, they resemble the early Christian community. They too had a specially anointed leader, the Teacher of Righteousness. They practiced ritual washings and had sacramental meals. They believed in the imminent coming of not one but two messiahs: a priestly one of the line of Aaron and a kingly one of the line of David. Despite similarities, however, there was a crucial difference: Christians believed that the Messiah had already come, had been crucified, and had risen from the dead. For them, the new age was not merely imminent; it had arrived and was present in an initial form.

The most dramatic discovery of ancient Jewish literature in the modern period is undoubtedly that of the well-known Dead Sea Scrolls. Between 1947 and 1956 a total of some 930 fragmentary manuscripts were found in eleven caves near Qumran, close to the northwest shore of the Dead Sea, where they had been placed prior to the war of AD 66–72. These manuscripts can be divided into two basic categories: (1) copies of a variety of Scriptures, canonical and noncanonical; and (2) various writings generated by the community. In the first category, all the books of what would become our canonical OT are represented, except for Esther. These biblical manuscripts represent nearly one-fourth of the 930 manuscript fragments found. The books of the Pentateuch are the most common, followed by Psalms and Isaiah. Quite a few manuscripts of what are now known as the Apocrypha and Pseudepigrapha were found, including a number of previously unknown books in the latter category. In the second basic group are a wide variety of manuscripts related

---

9. Josephus speaks glowingly of the Essenes, who, he says, exceeded all others in righteousness (*Ant.* 18.20).

to the community. These include commentaries on biblical books, collections of specific texts, the *Rule of the Community*, the *War Scroll* (an apocalyptic text), and various texts used for worship, such as the hymns, and wisdom texts.[10]

It surely is one of the oddities of history that the Essenes and their community are not mentioned in the NT.[11] This one lesson alone should warn scholars about the danger of the argument from silence, which seems so often to determine conclusions on debated issues within NT scholarship.

VIOLENCE AGAINST ROME

A second answer to the dilemma of Israel, violent acts against the Romans, was offered by *the Zealots* (Gk. *hoi zēlōtai*), freedom fighters known also as the *sicarii*, the "dagger men" (the Latin word *sica* means "dagger"), because they were willing to assassinate those whom they recognized as the enemies of God. They probably are the "fourth philosophy," mentioned by Josephus, who "have a passion for liberty that is almost unconquerable, since they are convinced that God alone is their leader and master" (*Ant.* 18.23, trans. Feldman). Josephus mentions a certain Judas the Galilean, who "set himself up as leader" of the movement (*Ant.* 18.23, trans. Feldman; cf. Acts 5:37). Their argument seems to have been that Israel must force the hand of God by resisting the Romans, as the Maccabees had resisted Antiochus and the Syrians. If they were brave enough to become involved in the great battle that would mark the end of the age, against insuperable odds, God surely would act on their behalf and enable victory, as he had a mere two centuries earlier. This was the way to arrive at the fulfillment of the promises that God had made to Israel. Inspired by such zeal, they felt called to put their lives on the line.[12]

The error of the argument of the Zealots seems confirmed by the two successive revolts (in AD 66–72 and 132–35) under their leadership that ended in defeat. But during the time of the ministry of Jesus, the Zealot mentality is clearly present. Indeed, one or two of the disciples of Jesus, Simon the Zealot (Luke 6:15; Acts 1:13) and possibly Judas Iscariot, seem to have been of the zealotic persuasion.

ACCEPTANCE AND ADAPTATION

A third answer to the dilemma was to take the present reality seriously and simply trim down the expectations. This was the perspective of *the Sadducees*, who rejected the prophets—with what they regarded as their exaggerated apocalyptic expectations—and accepted the canonical authority only of the books of Moses. Of course, they did not thereby dissolve the problem of the dilemma altogether,

10. For details, see the overview in VanderKam, *The Dead Sea Scrolls Today*. Convenient English translations can be found in García Martínez, *The Dead Sea Scrolls Translated* and in Vermes, *The Complete Dead Sea Scrolls in English*.

11. They are, however, mentioned by Philo (*Prob.* 75–87; *Contempl.* 1; *Hypoth.* 11.1–18), as well as Josephus.

12. For a full discussion, see Hengel, *The Zealots*.

but they did lessen the tension to a considerable extent. In the minds of these "realists," the future expectation amounted to little more than idealistic dreaming.

The Sadducees consisted mainly of the aristocracy and the high priesthood. They composed a strong party within the governing Sanhedrin. They are hardly to be thought of as secular in their attitude. The term "Sadducee" probably is derived from the name "Zadok," indicating their claim to be the legitimate descendants of the high priest of the Davidic era. They were in charge of the temple cultus and thus greatly concerned with matters of ritual purity. It seems clear, however, that they also had a vested interest in maintaining the status quo and appeasing the Romans wherever possible. Their openness to compromise in this regard did not endear them to the people, and they are spoken of negatively in the Talmud.

Addendum: The Literary Legacy of the Pharisees

Of the various groups described above, only the Pharisees survived the two Jewish revolts. It is mainly their perspective that is reflected in the literature of post–AD 70 Judaism: the Mishnah, Tosefta, Talmud, targumim, and midrashim. And it is they, therefore, who became the formers of the Judaism that survived through the centuries down to the present.

The Mishnah represents the oral traditions (the oral law) of the Pharisees, collected in about AD 200 by Judah the Patriarch. A difficult question of key importance in NT studies is how much of this material goes back to the NT era. Undoubtedly, much of it does, but often it is difficult to decide what can be safely regarded as reflecting the situation in the first half of the first century.[13] The Tosefta (ca. AD 300) is a large supplement to the Mishnah. The Talmud consists of a commentary on the content of the Mishnah. The commentary ("Gemara") exists in two separate forms, thus producing two Talmuds: the Palestinian (ca. AD 400) and the Babylonian (ca. AD 600). The targumim are free, paraphrastic Aramaic translations of the Hebrew Scriptures (beginning roughly from the first century AD). Midrashim consist of rabbinic exposition and homiletic application of Scripture that probably began to be written down in the second century AD and continued for several centuries.[14]

---

13. See the ambitious work of Instone-Brewer, *Traditions of the Rabbis from the Era of the New Testament*. Two volumes of a projected six are currently available.

14. Most of this literature is available in English translation. Mishnah: Herbert Danby, *The Mishnah* (Oxford: Oxford University Press, 1933); Jacob Neusner, *The Mishnah: A New Translation* (New Haven: Yale University Press, 1987). Tosefta: Jacob Neusner (with Richard S. Sarason for vol. 1), *The Tosefta: Translated from the Hebrew*, 6 vols. (New York: KTAV, 1985 [vol. 1]; Atlanta: Scholars Press, 1990–95 [vols. 2–6]). Babylonian Talmud: I. Epstein, *The Babylonian Talmud*, 18 vols. (London: Soncino, 1935–48). Jerusalem Talmud: Jacob Neusner, *The Talmud of the Land of Israel*, 35 vols. (Chicago: University of Chicago Press, 1982–89). Targumim: Martin McNamara, *Targum Neofiti 1*, 5 vols. (Collegeville, MN: Liturgical Press, 1992–97). Midrashim: Jacob Z. Lauterbach, *Mekilta de Rabbi Ishmael*, 3 vols. (Philadelphia: Jewish Publication Society of America, 1949); Jacob Neusner and Roger Brooks, *Sifra: The Rabbinic Commentary on Leviticus; An American Translation* (Atlanta: Scholars Press, 1986); Jacob

The Rise of Apocalyptic

Although there are earlier anticipations of apocalyptic, it is in the Second Temple period that the apocalyptic perspective begins to emerge with influence, and the classical apocalyptic literature begins to appear. In its own way it too is an answer to the dilemma of Israel, since it grows out of frustration with the present.

Although the word "apocalyptic" comes from the Greek word *apokalyptō*, meaning "reveal" or "unveil," it refers not so much to revelation as such but rather to the revelation specifically of the end of the age. The essence of the apocalyptic perspective is its temporal dualism of two ages: the present age and the age to come. This is accompanied by a metaphysical or cosmological dualism of light and darkness, God and Satan (or evil), engaged in a cosmic struggle. According to the apocalyptic perspective, this age will end, and *the new age will begin only by the direct action of God*. The time of the dawning of the new age can neither be hastened nor delayed. Although the time is set by the hand of God, this did not stop the apocalypticists from attempting to "reveal" the timetable. The present evil age, by divine agency, will move directly into the age of bliss to come. There will be a transformation of the whole of creation, and the judgment of the wicked will occur, as will the resurrection of the righteous dead.

In the Bible well-known books containing apocalyptic are Daniel, Ezekiel, and Zechariah, but other books, such as Deutero-Isaiah (Isa. 40–55), contain apocalyptic passages (see above, p. 19). Famous apocalyptic books from Second Temple Judaism are *2 Baruch*, *4 Ezra* (= 2 Esdras), and *1 Enoch 37–71*.[15] Although there are apocalyptic passages in the Synoptic Gospels and in some of Paul's Letters, the NT contains only one apocalyptic book, Revelation, also known as the Apocalypse.

The Holy Spirit was hardly thought to be inactive in the Second Temple period, yet at the same time there was a conviction that the future would see a dramatic resurgence in the inspiring and empowering activity of the Spirit, especially in connection with the coming of the end of the age (see Joel 2:28–32).[16]

Neusner, *Sifre to Numbers: An American Translation and Explanation* (Atlanta: Scholars Press, 1986); Reuven Hammer, *Sifre: A Tannaitic Commentary on the Book of Deuteronomy* (New Haven: Yale University Press, 1986). For a general introduction, see J. Neusner, *Introduction to Rabbinic Literature* (New York: Doubleday, 1994).

15. For a full collection of apocalyptic texts, see volume 1 of Charlesworth, *The Old Testament Pseudepigrapha*; an earlier translation is available in Charles, *The Apocrypha and Pseudepigrapha of the Old Testament*; see also Charlesworth, *The Pseudepigrapha and Modern Research*. A widely accepted definition of the genre of apocalypse has been developed by John Collins: "revelatory literature with a narrative framework, in which a revelation is mediated by an otherworldly being to a human recipient, disclosing a transcendent reality which is both temporal, insofar as it envisages eschatological salvation, and spatial insofar as it involves another, supernatural world" ("Towards the Morphology of a Genre," 9).

16. This perspective is reflected in the Talmud: "Since the death of the last prophets, Haggai, Zechariah and Malachi, the Holy Spirit [of prophetic inspiration] departed from Israel" (*b. Sanh.* 11a).

The Basic Elements of the Jewish Faith: Belief and Practice

Contemporary scholars stress the variety of first-century Judaism, and rightly so. At the same time, however, all varieties of Judaism share common elements that qualify them to be a form of Judaism. At a minimum, these include the following: monotheism, the election of Israel, covenant, Torah, and temple. For any group to be considered a form of Judaism, there would have to be a basic commitment to these realities. The difficult question of whether Christianity should be thought of as a form of Judaism must be answered in relation to these items. And obviously this bears directly on how, when, and why Christianity and Judaism parted ways already in the first century.[17]

Judaism is more *a religion of praxis* than of doctrine, where what one does matters much more than what one believes. Observance of the Torah is therefore of the greatest importance. One can see this in the opposition that Jesus stirs up when he violates the Sabbath commandment (e.g., Mark 3:2, 6). Torah observance put a premium on circumcision as the sign of the covenant and on Sabbath observance and the dietary laws.

The temple, at the heart of the Jewish religious life, was of great importance. The economy and life of the city revolved around the temple and its cultus. Various daily sacrifices were offered, among which the most important was the *tamid*, the whole burnt offering, offered at sunrise and in the late afternoon. The weekly Sabbath and the monthly new moon were occasions for extra sacrifices in the temple and special observances in Jewish homes. The Sabbath in particular was a joyful celebration and anticipation of the blessings of the eschatological age to come.

The religious year was marked by three main pilgrimage festivals: Passover (also known as Unleavened Bread), which took place around the spring equinox; Pentecost (or Weeks), fifty days, or seven weeks, after Passover; and Booths (or Tabernacles), at the time of the fall equinox. Males technically were required to come to the temple for each festival (see Deut. 16:16; cf. Exod. 23:17), although this was not enforced for those who lived far from the temple; a poor Jew living in the Diaspora would hope to make a pilgrimage perhaps once in a lifetime. But Jews from all over the Diaspora crowded into Jerusalem on these occasions.

Passover celebrated the deliverance of the Jews from Egypt with the sacrifice of the lambs and the Passover meal with its retelling of the story of the exodus, beginning with the child's question, "Why is this night different from all other nights?" Part of the celebration includes eating unleavened bread for the following week. Celebration of the Passover fulfills the command, "This day shall be for you a memorial day, and you shall keep it as a feast to the LORD; throughout your generations you shall observe it as an ordinance for ever" (Exod. 12:14).

17. See chapter 20 below; see also Hagner, "Another Look at 'The Parting of the Ways.'"

Pentecost, seven weeks later (approximately fifty days, hence the name), was the celebration of "the feast of harvest, of the first fruits of your labor, of what you sow in the field" (Exod. 23:16). Originally dedicated to the wheat harvest, Pentecost later became associated with covenant renewal and the giving of the law at Sinai.

The *Festival of Booths* (Sukkoth) was "the feast of ingathering at the end of the year" (Exod. 23:16), an especially joyful harvest festival, now of fruit: grapes and olives. During this festival the Israelites were to live for a week in temporary huts erected to commemorate Israel's wandering in the wilderness (Lev. 23:42–43).

The *Day of Atonement* (Yom Kippur) occurred once a year in the early autumn, just five days before the Festival of Booths. On this day the high priest entered the holy of holies, the inner sanctuary of the temple, with the blood of a bull and of a goat to make atonement for the sins of the people (Lev. 16; 23:26–32). It was a day of repentance and fasting.

The Jews practiced set times of *private prayer* (*tefillah*). The Amidah (the "eighteen benedictions," a set Jewish liturgical prayer) probably was said three times a day—morning, afternoon, and evening (cf. Dan. 5:10; Ps. 55:16–17). And the Shema (Deut. 6:4) was recited both morning and evening, at the beginning and the end of the day, "when you lie down, and when you rise" (Deut. 6:7). The Kaddish was another part of the Jewish prayer liturgy in which God's name was sanctified and the kingdom and age of eschatological blessing were prayed for—a prayer very similar to the Lord's Prayer.

Ritual purity was of great importance in Judaism. To be ritually unclean refers not to any lack of physical cleanness, but instead has to do with a condition that enables relationship with, specifically access or approach to, God. It is a holiness not vis-à-vis other people but rather before God in obedience. This ritual purity or cleanness was meant to be a mark of Israel's calling, separateness, and faithfulness.

The Synagogue

After the catastrophic events of AD 68–72 and the destruction of the second temple, rabbinic Judaism began to consolidate itself in order to survive without nation and temple. The synagogues inside and outside the Holy Land had already become important for Jewish religious life. Now they became still more important.

The institution of the synagogue apparently began in the Diaspora in the exilic period. Jews away from their homeland needed some communal way of expressing and maintaining their Jewish faith and identity. Like the early churches, most of these Jewish assemblies met in private homes long before the construction of buildings dedicated to this purpose. As members of a *religio licita*, a religion recognized by the Romans, Jews were allowed freely to practice their religion. At the heart of the synagogue meetings was the reading and instruction of Torah and the saying of prayers (a synagogue often was called a *proseuchē*, a place of "prayer"). But it also served as a meeting place for the local *beth din*, or "house of judgment," as well as a place of social gathering. The religious service of the synagogue became the model on which the early church service was, to a large extent, based.

The Diaspora

During the exile, and even earlier, Jewish communities began to grow in the major urban centers of the Roman world, including especially, of course, Babylon, but also in cities such as Alexandria, Antioch, and Rome, as well as cities in Asia Minor. Soon the number of Jews living outside Palestine was far greater than in Palestine. Diaspora Judaism undoubtedly was diverse, varying from community to community, but it also shared in the basic beliefs mentioned above as requisite for any manifestation of Judaism: monotheism, the election of Israel, covenant, Torah, and temple (via payment of the temple tax, in particular). Diaspora Judaism in general was understandably more open to the full range of Hellenistic culture, apart from pagan religion, but the degree of assimilation, acculturation, and accommodation varied considerably.[18]

Until recent times it was thought that there was a rather large and important difference between Palestinian and Diaspora ("Hellenistic") Judaism. It is now recognized, however, that Hellenism had a considerable impact even on the Judaism of Palestine.[19] No longer are the two manifestations of Judaism to be thought of as basically different. Hellenism had its influence on both, even if its influence on the Diaspora Jews may have been more conspicuous.

The Hellenistic Culture of the First Century AD

The language and culture of Hellenism are, obviously, enormously important to the NT. All the writings of the NT were written originally in Koine (= "common") Greek, some of a high quality (e.g., Hebrews, Luke-Acts). The letters of the NT often employ various Hellenistic literary and rhetorical devices.[20]

18. For these categories of Hellenization, see Barclay, *Jews in the Mediterranean Diaspora*.

19. The key work here is Hengel, *Judaism and Hellenism*.

20. See Porter (ed.), *Handbook of Classical Rhetoric in the Hellenistic Period, 330 B.C.–A.D. 400*; Aune, *The New Testament in Its Literary Environment*; idem, *The Westminster Dictionary of New Testament and Early Christian Literature and Rhetoric*.

Indeed, it was because Greek was the lingua franca of the Mediterranean world that the NT was written in that language.

The Septuagint

So too the translation of the Bible (i.e., the OT) into Greek, generally referred to as the Septuagint (designated by the symbol "LXX"), owes its existence to the pervasiveness of Greek in the Greco-Roman world. These Greek translations (what we call the LXX is not a single translation, but was translated by different people over a considerable period of time)[21] were extremely important for the writers of the NT, who relied on them rather than the Hebrew Bible the vast majority—perhaps some 90 percent—of the time. The Greek vocabulary of the LXX provided the early church and the writers of the NT with a valuable, ready-made treasury of words that could be used to express its theology and kerygma, thus facilitating the spread of the Christian message in the Hellenistic world.

The legend of the origin of the LXX is contained in the *Letter of Aristeas*, which tells of the Ptolemaic ruler Philadelphus (285–247 BC) requesting of the high priest translators to produce a Greek translation of "the laws of Moses," presumably the Pentateuch, for the famous library at Alexandria. Six elders from each of the twelve tribes were sent to Egypt, making a total of seventy-two. This number becomes abbreviated to seventy, in Latin *septuaginta*, thus giving the translation(s) its name. The fanciful legend goes on to say that after banqueting for seven days they went to the island of Pharos, just off the coast of Egypt, where they finished their work in seventy-two days. Further embroidery of the story has the translators working independently and at the end coming together to find that their translations agreed verbatim.[22] They supposedly translated the whole of the OT, together with twenty-two books of the Apocrypha, although the *Letter of Aristeas* refers only to the law. Before the Christian era, the Jews so highly valued the LXX that they put a curse on any who would revise, add, or omit anything.[23]

The LXX translations vary in quality, from the literal to the paraphrastic. A further complicating factor is that the Hebrew texts that were used are pre-Masoretic and often reflect a different form of the text than we know from

21. Specialists now prefer to use the designation "OG" (Old Greek) to refer to the original layer of the Septuagintal tradition.

22. Irenaeus recounts the story, concluding, "God was glorified and the scriptures were recognized as truly divine: they had all said the same things in the same phrases and the same words from beginning to end, so that even the heathen who were present knew that the scriptures had been translated by the inspiration of God" (Eusebius, *Hist. eccl.* 5.8.14, trans. Lake).

23. By the second century AD, however, the LXX had been used so successfully by Christians (note *parthenos* ["virgin"] in Isa. 7:14), that Jews sternly rejected the LXX and produced new, very literal Greek translations of the Hebrew Bible, three in number: Aquila, Theodotion, and Symmachus.

our OT.[24] The fact that the LXX differs as much as it does from the Masoretic
Hebrew text underlying our English translations means that the serious NT
student *must* become familiar with it.[25] Everett Ferguson does not exagger-
ate when he writes, "The Septuagint was the most important literary event,
perhaps the most important single development of any kind in the Hellenistic
period, for the background of early Christianity."[26]

Hellenization in the Postexilic Period

We have already noted the supreme effort of Antiochus IV to impose Hellenism on the people of Israel by forbidding the practice of Judaism. The heroic
resistance of the Maccabees kept Antiochus from achieving his goal. That did
not mean, however, that the process of Hellenization came to an end. During
the early reign of Antiochus a certain Jason (who took this Greek name in place
of his Hebrew name, "Joshua") bribed his way into the office of high priest. In
2 Maccabees we read that "he at once shifted his countrymen over to the Greek
way of life" (4:10); "he destroyed the lawful ways of living and introduced new
customs contrary to the law" (4:11); "with alacrity he founded a gymnasium
right under the citadel, and he induced the noblest of the young men to wear
the Greek hat" (4:12).[27] The author of 2 Maccabees, not at all in sympathy
with Hellenization, summarizes in these words: "There was such an extreme
of Hellenization and increase in the adoption of foreign ways because of the
surpassing wickedness of Jason, who was ungodly and no true high priest, that
the priests were no longer intent upon their service at the altar" (4:13 NRSV).
This gives an idea of the strength of the Hellenizing process, which continued
with varying degrees of openness and assimilation, even in the Holy Land.

Greco-Roman Philosophy

Greek philosophy serves as a broad background to the intellectual currents
of the NT era. Before the time of Alexander the Great, the *Sophists*, essentially itinerant sages, were the predecessors of the famous Socrates, Plato, and
Aristotle in the fifth and fourth centuries BC. Concurrent with Sophism, but

24. It was previously thought that in many places the LXX translators were incompetent, but
the discovery of the Dead Sea Scrolls revealed Hebrew manuscripts that agreed with the LXX
readings at numerous points and thus, to an extent, vindicated the translators.

25. At a minimum, an English translation is indispensable. Now conveniently available is
Pietersma and Wright, *A New English Translation of the Septuagint* (commonly referred to by
the acronym NETS). On the great importance of the LXX for the study of the NT, see McLay,
The Use of the Septuagint in New Testament Research. For a helpful introduction, see Jobes
and Silva, *Invitation to the Septuagint*.

26. Ferguson, *Backgrounds of Early Christianity*, 436. See also Sundberg, "The Septuagint."

27. A wide-brimmed hat associated with the god Hermes, which was a symbol of appreciation of Greek religion and culture.

influential up to the beginning of the Christian era, was *Skepticism*, the denial of the possibility of absolute knowledge and the doubting of the reliability of sense perception, thus leading to the suspension of judgment. Skepticism led naturally to *Cynicism*, a philosophy promoting the simple life and self-sufficiency. Its famous founder, Diogenes of Sinope (fourth century BC), taught self-denial and living in accord with nature, as well as asceticism, indifference, and boldness of speech. Living as naturally as possible could, however, lead to shameless public conduct, which gave them the name "Cynic" (from the Greek word for "dog"). Probably the most important practical philosophy of the NT period, and in some significant ways similar to Christianity, was *Stoicism*. Stoicism was named for the Stoa (a great colonnaded hall in Athens), where its founder, Zeno (born ca. 335), taught. It was a comprehensive philosophy, including both a pantheistic metaphysics and, more important, a highly influential ethics. In the former, Stoicism taught a doctrine of the *logos*, a rational principle that pervaded all of reality—reality that was fully controlled by a beneficent providence. As for ethics, the goal was to live in harmony with the nature of the universe and of the human being. The key is found in making the right decisions, and therein lie virtue and happiness. One is to live without passions, but rationally, without fear, grief, or anger. Living in agreement with nature means willingly accepting what providence brings. Many scholars have detected Stoic influence in NT ethics. Much admired in the early church were the Stoics Epictetus and Seneca, accepted often as anonymous Christians.

According to Acts 17:18, Paul encountered "Epicurean and Stoic philosophers" in Athens. The founder of *Epicureanism* was the fourth-century BC philosopher Epicurus. He thought of all reality as consisting of uncreated matter, that is, of discrete atoms. But again, far more important than the physical views of Epicureanism is its ethics. The supreme value for Epicureanism is pleasure, by which is meant not excess or self-indulgence, but rather in negative terms the "absence of pain in the body and anxiety in the soul." The goal of philosophy is the wise, moderate, and just life, a life free of vexation and fear, especially fear of death and the gods, a life of quietness, tranquillity, and peace of mind. The followers of Epicurus regularly met in a garden as a fellowship of equals, including without restriction women, slaves, and people of all classes.

Insofar as we think of a religion as a way of thinking and as a way of life, these philosophies have religious dimensions. There is therefore occasionally some overlap between their views and those of the NT, although the amount of direct influence seems small indeed.

Greco-Roman Religions

Again before the time of Alexander, the religions of classical Greece flourished, with their pantheon of deities and the accompanying sacrifices. These continued to have some influence in the Roman period. A variety of *pagan temples* graced every city. Meeting the needs of the populace, *oracles* were consulted through priests or priestesses in local shrines; *healing cults*, such as that of Asclepius, were frequented. Each city had its own patron deity or deities, and there were a variety of *civic cults*. There were also numerous *religious clubs*, groups that met regularly to venerate a particular god. These religious associations also served as occasions for social gatherings where religious meals were enjoyed. Some of these associations existed primarily for arranging and paying for the funerals of its members. To outsiders, the churches of early Christianity would have had the appearance of such religious associations, with various social and cultic dimensions.

The *emperor cult* arose from the widespread belief that rulers, heroes, and other great persons were divinized or transformed into gods at their death. Like the pharaohs of Egypt, ancient kings of the Hellenistic world and heroes, such as Alexander the Great, were deified. Their statues were housed in temples, and cults grew up to render homage to them. Even while still alive, emperors could be recognized as gods. But it was especially after death that their deity became widely accepted. After his death, Julius Caesar was officially acknowledged as a god by the Roman Senate. The same was true of Augustus.

The Christians' confession of Jesus as "Lord" (*Kyrios*) and "Savior" (*Sōtēr*) immediately brought them into tension with the cult of the emperor, since both titles were claimed by emperors. The Christian affirmation of Jesus as Lord inevitably brought their loyalty to the emperor into question (cf. Acts 17:7; John 19:12).

During the NT era, and especially in urban centers and in Asia Minor, many were attracted to the "mysteries," or *mystery religions*, called such because of their secret cults and rites of initiation. Some of these were indigenous to Greece, such as especially the Eleusinian mysteries. Others came from Mesopotamia and Egypt and were, for that reason, exotic. These mystery religions usually were associated with the cycle of nature and seasons of the year and celebrated a myth related to their origin. Among the more important mysteries were those of Dionysius (Bacchus), the god of wine; the Egyptian vegetation god Osiris and his sister/wife, Isis; the fertility goddess Astarte; and the Persian god Mithras.[28] New knowledge of the mysteries in the nineteenth and early twentieth centuries led some scholars of the history-of-religions school to conclude that much of Christianity was borrowed from the mystery religions. The latter had narratives of dying and rising gods, of rites of initiation not unlike baptism, of sacred meals not unlike the Eucharist. Yet the similarities are only of a superficial nature, and there are no real parallels to the Christian

---

28. For descriptions of these mystery religions, see Ferguson, *Backgrounds of Early Christianity*, 251–300; Klauck, *The Religious Context of Early Christianity*, 81–152.

gospel. And the word "mystery" in the NT has the very different sense of something hitherto unknown but now revealed and made plain in Christ.[29]

Gnosticism

One religion of the Roman world, however, has seemed especially attractive to explain the origins of Christianity: Gnosticism. Scholars of the history-of-religions school, led by the premium NT scholar of the early twentieth century, Rudolf Bultmann, argued that the NT gospel was borrowed from the Gnostic myth of the divine redeemer.[30] This was the story of a "divine man" who descends to the world in order to redeem a lost humanity, and then ascends back to heaven. The redemption takes place via *gnōsis*, "knowledge," concerning the heavenly origin of human beings, which enables them to ascend back to the realm of light from which they first came. But the story, as appealed to by Bultmann and others, is drawn from Mandaean literature of the fifth century AD and may, ironically, be dependent on the NT. The problem with all attempts to trace the origins of Christianity to Gnosticism is that there is no evidence of Gnosticism proper—that is, as a religious system—until the second century AD.[31] There were in the NT period certain strains of thought that should be labeled "proto-gnostic," reflecting an incipient gnosticism. But the Gnostic groups known to us from the early church fathers are a second-century phenomenon. The Gnostics held to a cosmic dualism, between matter and spirit, and taught that salvation comes via knowledge.

It was popular in the nineteenth and early twentieth centuries to explain the origins of Christianity as largely due to various influences in Hellenistic culture, especially Gnosticism. As important as the Hellenistic background is to the understanding of Christianity and the NT, very little, if any, of the Christian faith traces back directly to Hellenistic ideas. Most of such ideas come to Christianity through the mediation of Hellenistic Judaism. Thus Martin Hengel concludes "without qualification that Christianity grew *entirely* out of Jewish soil."[32]

Sociological Realities of the First-Century AD Roman World

The disciplines of sociology and anthropology greatly enriched NT studies in the last half of the twentieth century. Again, the more we know of life in the first-century Roman world, the better position we are in to understand the

---

29. A point made by Ferguson, *Backgrounds of Early Christianity*, 299.
30. See Bultmann, *Theology of the New Testament*, 1:166–83.
31. See especially Yamauchi, *Pre-Christian Gnosticism*; see also Wilson, *Gnosis and the New Testament*.
32. Hengel, "Early Christianity as a Jewish-Messianic, Universalistic Movement," 1.

NT. Here I can make only brief reference to these things, but the bibliography contains many resources that can be consulted for further information.

The Roman Rule and Hellenistic Culture

Just as the Jews lamented the Babylonian invasion of Jerusalem and the desecration of the temple in 586 BC, so too they lamented the invasion by the Romans and the desecration of the temple in 63 BC by Pompey. "Arrogantly the sinner broke down the strong walls with a battering ram and you did not interfere. Gentile foreigners went up to your place of sacrifice; they arrogantly trampled (it) with their sandals. . . . The sons and daughters (were) in harsh captivity, their neck in a seal, a spectacle among the gentiles" (*Pss. Sol.* 2:1–2, 6). The explanation was once again the sinfulness of the Jews: "He did (this) to them according to their sins" (*Pss. Sol.* 2:7). Yet again it was hard to reconcile actual events with the power and promises of Israel's God, and so the Jews chafed under Roman rule, even though they were granted extraordinary rights to practice their religion.

The pervasive pressure to Hellenize continued in this period; there was no radical change in the cultural context. The Romans promoted Hellenistic culture. Early Christianity quickly moved from the small villages of an agrarian society to urban centers. There they encountered the gymnasia, with their athletic games, the baths, the theaters, and the large variety of pagan temples that were typical in Roman cities. The polytheism and idolatry against which Jews fought were resisted in the same way by Christians. Slavery was an accepted reality within society. Women generally were regarded as inferior to men. The egalitarianism of the church therefore stood in remarkable contrast to ordinary society. Roman taxation was a burden for most of the population, especially the poor. Poverty was common and separated the poor from the rich. This too was transcended by the church, where rich and poor were equally accepted.

Cultural Norms

Certain codes of conduct were fixed elements of social interaction and were universally operative. One of the most important of these was *honor and shame*, the latter to be avoided, the former to be sought. Honor was given to those who embodied society's or a group's values; shame was experienced by those who flouted them. Honor and shame thus exerted a considerable motivating power for appropriate conduct.[33] This dynamic can also be seen at work in the hortatory material of the NT.

The *patron-client relationship* permeated society, with everyone except the emperor himself beholden to someone else more wealthy and powerful. The

---

33. See Lawrence, *An Ethnography of the Gospel of Matthew*; Neyrey, *Honor and Shame in the Gospel of Matthew*; deSilva, *Despising Shame*.

patron favored the client with various forms of assistance, benefaction, or protection; the client in turn was expected to express gratitude and to behave in certain supportive ways toward the patron. This reciprocity between patron and client was fundamental to the structure and operation of society. The poor especially depended on the generosity of their patron; in turn, they were expected to broadcast that generosity and thus enhance the reputation of the patron. Very naturally, God and the people of God stand in a relationship of patron and client; so too, of course, do Jesus and the church. And within the church horizontally there are patron-client relationships among its members.[34]

Bibliography

General

Aune, David E. *The New Testament in Its Literary Environment*. Philadelphia: Westminster, 1987.

Bell, Albert A., Jr. *Exploring the New Testament World*. Nashville: Thomas Nelson, 1998.

Bruce, F. F. *New Testament History*. Garden City, NY: Doubleday, 1972.

Charlesworth, James H., and Walter P. Weaver, eds. *What Has Archaeology to Do with Faith?* Philadelphia: Trinity Press International, 1992.

Esler, Philip F. *The First Christians in Their Social Worlds: Social-Scientific Approaches to New Testament Interpretation*. London: Routledge, 1994.

Evans, Craig A. *Ancient Texts for New Testament Studies: A Guide to the Background Literature*. Peabody: Hendrickson, 2005.

————. *Noncanonical Writings and New Testament Interpretation*. Peabody, MA: Hendrickson, 1992.

Ferguson, Everett. *Backgrounds of Early Christianity*. 3rd ed. Grand Rapids: Eerdmans, 2003.

Grant, Michael. *Greek and Roman Historians: Information and Misinformation*. New York: Routledge, 1995.

Hengel, Martin. "Early Christianity as a Jewish-Messianic, Universalistic Movement." In *Conflicts and Challenges in Early Christianity*, edited by Donald A. Hagner, 1–41. Harrisburg, PA: Trinity Press International, 1999.

Holman, Susan R., ed. *Wealth and Poverty in Early Church and Society*. Grand Rapids: Baker Academic; Brookline, MA: Holy Cross Orthodox Press, 2008.

Jeffers, James S. *The Greco-Roman World of the New Testament Era: Exploring the Background of Early Christianity*. Downers Grove, IL: InterVarsity, 1999.

Lohse, Eduard. *The New Testament Environment*. Translated by John E. Steely. Nashville: Abingdon, 1976.

Malina, Bruce J. *Windows on the World of Jesus: Time Travel to Ancient Judea*. Louisville: Westminster John Knox, 1993.

Reicke, Bo. *The New Testament Era: The World of the Bible from 500 B.C. to A.D. 100*. Translated by David E. Green. Philadelphia: Fortress, 1968.

Roetzel, Calvin J. *The World That Shaped the New Testament*. Rev. ed. Louisville: Westminster John Knox, 2002.

Stambaugh, John E., and David L. Balch. *The New Testament in Its Social Environment*. Philadelphia: Westminster, 1986.

Stegemann, Ekkehard W., and Wolfgang Stegemann. *The Jesus Movement: A Social History of Its First Century*. Translated by O. C. Dean Jr. Minneapolis: Fortress, 1995.

34. See Chow, *Patronage and Power*.

Judaism in General

Barclay, John M. G. *Jews in the Mediterranean Diaspora: From Alexander to Trajan (323 BC–117 CE)*. Berkeley: University of California Press, 1996.

Boccaccini, Gabriele. *Middle Judaism: Jewish Thought, 300 B.C.E. to 200 C.E.* Minneapolis: Fortress, 1991.

Cohen, Shaye J. D. *From the Maccabees to the Mishnah*. LEC. Philadelphia: Westminster, 1987.

Collins, John J. *Between Athens and Jerusalem: Jewish Identity in the Hellenistic Diaspora*. New York: Crossroad, 1983.

Freyne, Seán. *Galilee, from Alexander the Great to Hadrian, 323 B.C.E. to 135 C.E.: A Study of Second Temple Judaism*. Wilmington, DE: Michael Glazier; Notre Dame, IN: University of Notre Dame Press, 1980.

Grabbe, Lester L. *Judaic Religion in the Second Temple Period: Belief and Practice from the Exile to Yavneh*. New York: Routledge, 2000.

———. *Judaism from Cyrus to Hadrian*. 2 vols. Minneapolis: Fortress, 1991.

Gruen, Erich S. *Diaspora: Jews amidst Greeks and Romans*. Cambridge, MA: Harvard University Press, 2002.

Hanson, K. C., and Douglas E. Oakman. *Palestine in the Time of Jesus: Social Structures and Social Conflicts*. Minneapolis: Fortress, 1998.

Helyer, Larry R. *Exploring Jewish Literature of the Second Temple Period: A Guide for New Testament Students*. Downers Grove, IL: InterVarsity, 2002.

Hengel, Martin. *Judaism and Hellenism: Studies in Their Encounter in Palestine during the Hellenistic Period*. Translated by John Bowden. 2 vols. Philadelphia: Fortress, 1974.

Horbury, William. *Herodian Judaism and New Testament Study*. WUNT 193. Tübingen: Mohr Siebeck, 2006.

Instone-Brewer, David. *Traditions of the Rabbis from the Era of the New Testament*. 2 vols. Grand Rapids: Eerdmans, 2004–11.

Jeremias, Joachim. *Jerusalem in the Time of Jesus: An Investigation into Economic and Social Conditions during the New Testament Period*. Translated by F. H. and C. H. Cave. Philadelphia: Fortress, 1969.

Kraft, Robert A., and George W. E. Nickelsburg, eds. *Early Judaism and Its Modern Interpreters*. SBLBMI 2. Atlanta: Scholars Press, 1986.

McNamara, Martin. *Palestinian Judaism and the New Testament*. Wilmington, DE: Michael Glazier, 1983.

Moore, George Foot. *Judaism in the First Centuries of the Christian Era: The Age of the Tannaim*. 3 vols. Cambridge, MA: Harvard University Press, 1927–30.

Murphy, Frederick J. *Early Judaism: The Exile to the Time of Jesus*. Peabody, MA: Hendrickson, 2002.

Neusner, Jacob. *Judaism in the Beginning of Christianity*. Philadelphia: Fortress, 1984.

Nickelsburg, George W. E. *Jewish Literature between the Bible and the Mishnah*. 2nd ed. Philadelphia: Fortress, 2005.

Safrai, S., and M. Stern, eds. *The Jewish People in the First Century: Historical Geography, Political History, Social, Cultural, and Religious Life and Institutions*. 2 vols. CRINT 1/1. Philadelphia: Fortress, 1974–76.

Sanders, E. P. *Judaism: Practice and Belief 63 BCE–66 CE*. Philadelphia: Trinity Press International, 1992.

Schürer, Emil. *The History of the Jewish People in the Age of Jesus Christ*. Revised and edited by Geza Vermes, Fergus Millar, and Martin Goodman. 4 vols. Edinburgh: T&T Clark, 1986–87.

Smallwood, E. Mary. *The Jews under Roman Rule: From Pompey to Diocletian; A Study in Political Relations*. 2nd ed. SJLA 20. Leiden: Brill, 1981.

Strack, H. L., and Günter Stemberger. *Introduction to the Talmud and Midrash*. Translated and edited by Markus Bockmuehl. Minneapolis: Fortress, 1992.

Trebilco, Paul R. *Jewish Communities in Asia Minor*. SNTSMS 69. Cambridge: Cambridge University Press, 1991.
VanderKam, James C. *An Introduction to Early Judaism*. Grand Rapids: Eerdmans, 2001.

The Pharisees

Finkelstein, Louis. *The Pharisees: The Sociological Background of Their Faith*. 3rd ed. 2 vols. Philadelphia: Jewish Publication Society of America, 1966.
Mason, Steve. "The Problem of the Pharisees in Modern Scholarship." In *Historical and Literary Studies*, vol. 3 of *Approaches to Ancient Judaism*, edited by Jacob Neusner, 103–40. SFSHJ 56. Atlanta: Scholars Press, 1993.
Neusner, Jacob. *From Politics to Piety: The Emergence of Pharisaic Judaism*. Englewood Cliffs, NJ: Prentice-Hall, 1973.
———. *The Rabbinic Traditions about the Pharisees before 70*. 3 vols. Leiden: Brill, 1971.
Neusner, Jacob, and Bruce D. Chilton, eds. *In Quest of the Historical Pharisees*. Waco: Baylor University Press, 2007.
Rivkin, Ellis. *A Hidden Revolution: The Pharisees' Search for the Kingdom Within*. Nashville: Abingdon, 1978.
Saldarini, Anthony J. *Pharisees, Scribes, and Sadducees in Palestinian Society*. Wilmington, DE: Michael Glazier, 1988.
Stemberger, Günter. *Jewish Contemporaries of Jesus: Pharisees, Sadducees, Essenes*. Translated by Allan W. Mahnke. Minneapolis: Fortress, 1995.
Westerholm, Stephen. *Jesus and Scribal Authority*. ConBNT 10. Lund: Gleerup, 1978.

The Zealots

Hengel, M. *The Zealots: Investigations into the Jewish Freedom Movement in the Period from Herod I until 70 A.D.* Translated by D. Smith. Edinburgh: T&T Clark, 1989.

Josephus

Carleton Paget, James. "Some Observations on Josephus and Christianity." *JTS* 52 (2001): 539–624. Reprinted in idem, *Jews, Christians and Jewish Christians in Antiquity*, 185–265. WUNT 251. Tübingen: Mohr Siebeck, 2010.
Feldman, Louis H., and Gohei Hata, eds. *Josephus, the Bible, and History*. Detroit: Wayne State University Press, 1989.
Maier, Paul L., trans. and ed. *Josephus: The Essential Writings; A Condensation of Jewish Antiquities and the Jewish War*. Grand Rapids: Kregel, 1988.
Mason, Steve, ed. *Flavius Josephus: Translation and Commentary*. Leiden: Brill, 2000.
———. *Josephus and the New Testament*. 2nd ed. Peabody, MA: Hendrickson, 2003.
Rajak, Tessa. *Josephus: The Historian and His Society*. 2nd ed. London: Duckworth, 2002.
Sterling, Gregory E. *Historiography and Self-Definition: Josephus, Luke-Acts and Apologetic Historiography*. NovTSup 64. Leiden: Brill, 1992.
Thatcher, Tom. "Literacy, Textual Communities, and Josephus' Jewish War." *JSJ* 29 (1998): 123–42.

The Synagogue

Catto, Stephen K. *Reconstructing the First-Century Synagogue: A Critical Analysis of Current Research*. LNTS 363. London: T&T Clark, 2007.
Fine, Steven, ed. *Sacred Realm: The Emergence of the Synagogue in the Ancient World*. New York: Oxford University Press, 1996.

Olsson, Birger, and Magnus Zetterholm, eds. *The Ancient Synagogue from Its Origins until 200 C.E.: Papers Presented at an International Conference at Lund University, October 14–17, 2001.* ConBNT 39. Stockholm: Almqvist & Wiksell, 2003.

Runesson, Anders. *The Origins of the Synagogue: A Socio-Historical Study.* ConBNT 37. Stockholm: Almqvist & Wiksell, 2001.

Runesson, Anders, Donald Binder, and Birger Olsson. *The Ancient Synagogue from Its Origins to 200 C.E.: A Source Book.* AJEC 72. Leiden: Brill, 2008.

The Dead Sea Scrolls

Charlesworth, James H., ed. *The Bible and the Dead Sea Scrolls: The Second Princeton Symposium on Judaism and Christian Origins.* 3 vols. Waco: Baylor University Press, 2006.

Collins, John J., and Craig A. Evans, eds. *Christian Beginnings and the Dead Sea Scrolls.* Grand Rapids: Baker Academic, 2006.

Cross, Frank Moore. *The Ancient Library of Qumran and Modern Biblical Studies.* Rev. ed. Minneapolis: Augsburg Fortress, 1995.

Fitzmyer, Joseph A. *Responses to 101 Questions on the Dead Sea Scrolls.* New York: Paulist Press, 1992.

Flint, Peter W., and James C. VanderKam, eds. *The Dead Sea Scrolls after Fifty Years: A Comprehensive Assessment.* 2 vols. Leiden: Brill, 1998–99.

García Martínez, Florentino. *The Dead Sea Scrolls Translated: The Qumran Texts in English.* Translated by Wilfred G. E. Watson. Leiden: Brill, 1994.

García Martínez, Florentino, and Julio C. Trebolle Barrera. *The People of the Dead Sea Scrolls: Their Writings, Beliefs, and Practices.* Translated by Wilfred G. E. Watson. Leiden: Brill, 1995.

Schiffman, Lawrence H., and James C. VanderKam, eds. *Encyclopedia of the Dead Sea Scrolls.* 2 vols. New York: Oxford University Press, 2000.

Schuller, Eileen M. *The Dead Sea Scrolls: What Have We Learned?* Louisville: Westminster John Knox, 2006.

VanderKam, James C. *The Dead Sea Scrolls Today.* Grand Rapids: Eerdmans, 2010.

VanderKam, James C., and Peter Flint. *The Meaning of the Dead Sea Scrolls: Their Significance for Understanding the Bible, Judaism, Jesus, and Christianity.* San Francisco: HarperSanFrancisco, 2002.

Vermes, Geza. *The Complete Dead Sea Scrolls in English.* New York: Penguin, 1987.

———. *An Introduction to the Complete Dead Sea Scrolls.* Minneapolis: Fortress, 2000.

Apocalyptic

Aune, David E. "Understanding Jewish and Christian Apocalyptic." *WW* 25 (2005): 233–45.

Charles, R. H. *The Apocrypha and Pseudepigrapha of the Old Testament.* 2 vols. Oxford: Clarendon, 1913.

Charlesworth, James H., ed. *The Old Testament Pseudepigrapha.* 2 vols. Garden City, NY: Doubleday, 1983–85.

———. *The Pseudepigrapha and Modern Research.* Rev. ed. SCSS 7. Chico, CA: Scholars Press, 1981.

Collins, John J. *The Apocalyptic Imagination: An Introduction to Jewish Apocalyptic Literature.* 2nd ed. Grand Rapids: Eerdmans, 1998.

———. "Towards the Morphology of a Genre." *Semeia* 14 (1979): 1–19.

Collins, John J., and James H. Charlesworth, eds. *Mysteries and Revelations: Apocalyptic Studies Since the Uppsala Colloquium.* JSPSup 9. Sheffield: JSOT Press, 1991.

Cook, Stephen L. *The Apocalyptic Literature.* IBT. Nashville: Abingdon, 2003.

Hanson, Paul D. *The Dawn of Apocalyptic.* Philadelphia: Fortress, 1975.

———, ed. *The Origins of Apocalypticism in Judaism and Christianity*. Vol. 1 of *The Encyclopedia of Apocalypticism*. New York: Continuum, 1998.

Hellholm, David, ed. *Apocalypticism in the Mediterranean World and the Near East: Proceedings of the International Colloquium of Apocalypticism, Uppsala, August 12–17, 1979*. Tübingen: Mohr Siebeck, 1983.

Lewis, Scott M. *What Are They Saying about New Testament Apocalyptic?* Mahwah, NJ: Paulist Press, 2003.

Minear, Paul S. *New Testament Apocalyptic*. IBT. Nashville: Abingdon, 1981.

Nicholas, William C., Jr. *I Saw the World End: An Introduction to the Bible's Apocalyptic Literature*. Mahwah, NJ: Paulist Press, 2007.

Rowland, Christopher. *The Open Heaven: A Study of Apocalyptic in Judaism and Early Christianity*. London: SPCK, 1982.

Russell, D. S. *The Method and Message of Jewish Apocalyptic, 200 BC–AD 100*. Philadelphia: Westminster, 1964.

———. *Prophecy and the Apocalyptic Dream: Protest and Promise*. Peabody, MA: Hendrickson, 1994.

VanderKam, James C., and William Adler, eds. *The Jewish Apocalyptic Heritage in Early Christianity*. Minneapolis: Fortress, 1996.

The Greco-Roman World

Bowerstock, G. W. *Hellenism in Late Antiquity*. Ann Arbor: University of Michigan Press, 1990.

Branham, R. Bracht, and Marie-Odile Goulet-Cazé, eds. *The Cynics: The Cynic Movement in Antiquity and Its Legacy*. Berkeley: University of California Press, 1996.

Burkert, Walter. *Ancient Mystery Cults*. Cambridge, MA: Harvard University Press, 1987.

Filorama, Giovanni. *A History of Gnosticism*. Translated by Anthony Alcock. Cambridge, MA: Blackwell, 1990.

Grant, Frederick C. *Roman Hellenism and the New Testament*. New York: Scribner, 1962.

Hedrick, Charles W., and Robert Hodgson Jr., eds. *Nag Hammadi, Gnosticism, and Early Christianity*. Peabody, MA: Hendrickson, 1986.

Jeffers, James S. *The Greco-Roman World of the New Testament Era: Exploring the Background of Early Christianity*. Downers Grove, IL: InterVarsity, 1999.

Jonas, Hans. *The Gnostic Religion: The Message of the Alien God and the Beginnings of Christianity*. New York: Routledge, 1992.

King, Karen L. *What Is Gnosticism?* Cambridge, MA: Harvard University Press, 2003.

Klauck, Hans-Josef. *The Religious Context of Early Christianity: A Guide to Graeco-Roman Religions*. Translated by Brian McNeil. Minneapolis: Fortress, 2003.

Long, A. A. *Hellenistic Philosophy: Stoics, Epicureans, Sceptics*. 2nd ed. Berkeley: University of California Press, 1986.

Long, A. A., and D. N. Sedley. *The Hellenistic Philosophers*. 2 vols. Cambridge: Cambridge University Press, 1987.

MacMullen, Ramsay. *Roman Social Relations, 50 B.C. to A.D. 284*. New Haven: Yale University Press, 1974.

MacRae, George. W. *Studies in the New Testament and Gnosticism*. Edited by Daniel J. Harrington and Stanley B. Marrow. Wilmington, DE: Michael Glazier, 1987.

Pearson, Birger A. *Ancient Gnosticism: Traditions and Literature*. Minneapolis: Fortress, 2007.

Perkins, Pheme. *Gnosticism and the New Testament*. Minneapolis: Fortress, 1993.

Reitzenstein, Richard. *Hellenistic Mystery Religions: Their Basic Ideas and Significance*. Translated by John E. Steely. Pittsburgh: Pickwick, 1978.

Robinson, James M., ed. *The Nag Hammadi Library in English*. 3rd ed. New York: Harper & Row, 1988.

Roetzel, Calvin J. *The World That Shaped the New Testament*. Rev. ed. Louisville: Westminster John Knox, 2002.

Roukema, Riemer. *Gnosis and Faith in Early Christianity: An Introduction to Gnosticism*. Translated by John Bowden. Harrisburg, PA: Trinity Press International, 1999.

Rudolph, Kurt. *Gnosis: The Nature and History of Gnosticism*. Translation edited by Robert McLachlan Wilson. San Francisco: Harper & Row, 1983.

Scheid, John. *An Introduction to Roman Religion*. Translated by Janet Lloyd. Bloomington: Indiana University Press, 2003.

Starr, Chester G. *The Ancient Romans*. New York: Oxford University Press, 1971.

Tripolitis, Antonia. *Religions of the Hellenistic-Roman Age*. Grand Rapids: Eerdmans, 2002.

Wilken, Robert Louis. *The Christians as the Romans Saw Them*. New Haven: Yale University Press, 1984.

Wilson, R. McL. *Gnosis and the New Testament*. Philadelphia: Fortress, 1968.

Yamauchi, Edwin M. *Pre-Christian Gnosticism: A Survey of the Proposed Evidences*. Grand Rapids: Eerdmans, 1973.

The Septuagint

Dines, Jennifer M. *The Septuagint*. Edited by Michael A. Knibb. London: T&T Clark, 2004.

Fernández Marcos, Natalio. *The Septuagint in Context: Introduction to the Greek Versions of the Bible*. Translated by Wilfred G. E. Watson. Leiden: Brill, 2000.

Hengel, Martin, with the assistance of Roland Deines. *The Septuagint as Christian Scripture: Its Prehistory and the Problem of Its Canon*. Translated by Mark E. Biddle. Edinburgh: T&T Clark, 2002.

Jellicoe, Sidney. *The Septuagint and Modern Study*. Oxford: Clarendon, 1968.

Jobes, Karen H., and Moisés Silva. *Invitation to the Septuagint*. Grand Rapids: Baker Academic, 2000.

McLay, R. Timothy. *The Use of the Septuagint in New Testament Research*. Grand Rapids: Eerdmans, 2003.

———. "The Use of the Septuagint in the New Testament." In *The Biblical Canon: Its Origin, Transmission, and Authority*, edited by Lee Martin McDonald, 224–40. Peabody, MA: Hendrickson, 2007.

Müller, Morgens. *The First Bible of the Church: A Plea for the Septuagint*. JSOTSup 206. Sheffield: Sheffield Academic Press, 1996.

Pietersma, Albert, and Benjamin G. Wright, eds. *A New English Translation of the Septuagint: And the Other Greek Translations Traditionally Included under That Title*. New York: Oxford University Press, 2007.

Sundberg, Albert C., Jr. "The Septuagint: The Bible of Hellenistic Judaism." In *The Canon Debate*, edited by Lee Martin McDonald and James A. Sanders, 68–90. Peabody, MA: Hendrickson, 2002.

Other

Aune, David E., ed. *The Blackwell Companion to the New Testament*. Chichester, UK: Wiley-Blackwell, 2010.

———. *The Westminster Dictionary of New Testament and Early Christian Literature and Rhetoric*. Louisville: Westminster John Knox, 2003.

Bultmann, Rudolf. *Theology of the New Testament*. Translated by Kendrick Grobel. Waco: Baylor University Press, 2007.

Chow, John K. *Patronage and Power: A Study of Social Networks in Corinth*. JSNTSup 75. Sheffield: JSOT Press, 1992.

Crown, Alan D., ed. *The Samaritans*. Tübingen: Mohr Siebeck, 1989.

deSilva, David A. *Despising Shame: Honor Discourse and Community Maintenance in the Epistle to the Hebrews*. SBLDS 152. Atlanta: Scholars Press, 1995.

Evans, Craig A. *Ancient Texts for New Testament Studies: A Guide to the Background Literature*. Peabody, MA: Hendrickson, 2005.

Evans, Craig A., and Stanley E. Porter, eds. *Dictionary of New Testament Background*. Downers Grove, IL: InterVarsity, 2000.

Hagner, Donald A. "Another Look at 'The Parting of the Ways.'" In *Earliest Christian History: History, Literature, and Theology. Essays from the Tyndale Fellowship in Honor of Martin Hengel*, edited by Michael F. Bird and Jason Maston, 381–427. WUNT 2/320. Tübingen: Mohr Siebeck, 2012.

Lawrence, Louise Joy. *An Ethnography of the Gospel of Matthew: A Critical Assessment of the Use of the Honour and Shame Model in New Testament Studies*. WUNT 2/165. Tübingen: Mohr Siebeck, 2003.

Millard, Alan. *Reading and Writing in the Time of Jesus*. BibSem 69. Sheffield: Sheffield Academic Press, 2000.

Neyrey, Jerome H. *Honor and Shame in the Gospel of Matthew*. Louisville: Westminster John Knox, 1998.

Orton, David E. *The Understanding Scribe: Matthew and the Apocalyptic Ideal*. JSNTSup 25. Sheffield: Sheffield Academic Press, 1989.

Porter, Stanley E., ed. *Handbook of Classical Rhetoric in the Hellenistic Period, 330 B.C.–A.D. 400*. Leiden: Brill, 1997.

———, ed. *The Language of the New Testament: Classic Essays*. JSNTSup 60. Sheffield: Sheffield Academic Press, 1991.

Porter, Stanley E., and Lee Martin McDonald. *New Testament Introduction*. IBRBib 12. Grand Rapids: Baker Academic, 1995.

Schnabel, Eckhard J. *Early Christian Mission*. 2 vols. Downers Grove, IL: InterVarsity, 2004.

Soulen, Richard N., and R. Kendall Soulen. *Handbook of Biblical Criticism*. 3rd ed. Louisville: Westminster John Knox, 2001.

PART 2

THE GOSPELS

The Proclamation of the Kingdom

4

The Gospels as Historical and Theological Documents

The four Gospels stand at the beginning of the NT because the narrative that they record concerning the ministry, death, and resurrection of Jesus constitutes the very foundation of Christianity. If we were dealing with the books of the NT chronologically, we would discuss the Gospels *after* the Pauline Epistles and perhaps other documents too, because the Gospels were written well into the second half of the first century. The NT tells us that the facts that the Gospels record constitute the turning point and climax of salvation history. This is far from ordinary historical information. It is the story of God at work, fulfilling the promises to Israel and accomplishing the redemption of humanity.

Gospel

The word "gospel" (Gk. *euangelion*) refers at first not to a book but rather to the report of "good news." This was a word well known in the Roman Empire, especially in connection with the imperial cult. It was used to announce the good news of an imperial benefaction, the dawn of a new era (as with Augustus), a victory, the birth or accession of a new emperor, and so forth. There can be little question that "gospel" in the NT stands in deliberate contrast to claims made by the Roman Empire.[1] A more important background for the NT, however, is found in the OT, especially in the verbal forms of the word in Deutero-Isaiah (Isa. 40:9; 52:7; 60:6; 61:1–2; cf. Ps. 96:2–3), where it refers to the coming of salvation.[2]

---

1. What Warren Carter says about Matthew applies equally well to all the Gospels: "The Gospel contests the claims of imperial theology that assert the empire and emperor to represent the gods' sovereignty, will, and blessing on earth" (*Matthew and Empire*, 57).
2. For thorough discussion, see Stanton, *Jesus and Gospel*, 9–62.

In the NT the word first referred to the message proclaimed by Jesus concerning the arrival of the kingdom of God: in Matthew's language, "the gospel of the kingdom [to euangelion tēs basileias]" (Matt. 4:23; 9:35; 24:14), or in Mark's "the gospel of God [to euangelion tou theou]" (Mark 1:14). Very soon in the early church, however, the gospel is equated with Jesus himself, as in the objective genitive of Mark 1:1: "The beginning of the gospel of Jesus Christ [archē tou euangeliou Iēsou Christou]"—that is, the good news about Jesus Christ.

Only later does the word come to designate books as such. In reality there is only one gospel: the "good news" of the coming and work of the Messiah Jesus. For that reason, it is proper to speak, with the early church, of *the gospel of Jesus Christ* "according to" (*kata*) Matthew, according to Mark, according to Luke, and according to John. Indeed, these were the actual titles given to the Gospels already in the second century: "According to Matthew," "According to Mark," and so on.[3] It is true that we have four differing portraits of the life and ministry of Jesus, but it is nonetheless also true that in the four we encounter recognizably one and the same story, one and the same Christ, one gospel.[4] This point has to be made because of the occasional claim that the four Gospels present irreconcilable accounts of Jesus. On the contrary, all four present the same Jesus, and this is especially true of the first three, the Synoptic Gospels. Only the Fourth Gospel, John, presents something of a challenge in this regard, as we will see in chapter 14. But John's portrait of Jesus is hardly irreconcilable with that of the Synoptics.

The four different portraits of Jesus in the NT should be regarded as an enrichment rather than an embarrassment. With the same story told from different perspectives we are able to come to a more adequate understanding of Jesus and his message. The early church realized this and in the second century wisely resisted the temptation to follow Marcion (a mid-second-century gnostic Christian), who accepted only one Gospel as canonical, or Tatian (a late-second-century Syrian Christian), who created one super-Gospel by amalgamating all the material of the four while deleting the duplication that they contain.[5] By the end of the second century the fourfold Gospel was accepted in the early church as a given. The early church certainly did not regard the Gospels, for whatever differences one might care to mention, as incompatible with one another or as presenting irreconcilable portraits of Jesus. Rather, they were perceived as enriching our understanding of Jesus.

It is worth quoting N. B. Stonehouse in this regard:

3. See Hengel, *The Four Gospels and the One Gospel of Jesus Christ*; idem, "The Titles of the Gospels and the Gospel of Mark."

4. See Burridge, *Four Gospels, One Jesus?*

5. Initially this may sound like a good idea, and there have been a number of such amalgamations since Tatian, but the result is the loss of the distinctive and important contribution of each Evangelist, in effect producing an artificial Gospel written by no one.

Conservatives are prone to a traditionalism which is uncritical of the past and is not sufficiently alert to the distinction between what is written and what may have been erroneously inferred from the biblical text. In particular it has seemed to me that Christians who are assured as to the unity of the witness to the Gospels should take greater pains to do justice to the diversity of expression of that witness. . . . [Experience of the unity of the witness to Christ] is far richer and more satisfying if one has been absorbed and captured by each portrait in turn and has conscientiously been concerned with the minutest differentiating details as well as with the total impact of the evangelical witness.[6]

The Genre of the Gospels

As far as literary form goes, beyond those emanating from the Christian church, there are no parallels to the Gospels in the literature of antiquity. Attempts have been made to describe the Gospels by categories such as targum,[7] midrash,[8] and lectionary,[9] but these have not been convincing. The Gospels represent a new and unique literary category, without any exact analogy.

It is clear that the Gospels present themselves as historical narratives in story form.[10] Inasmuch as they center on the life of Jesus, perhaps the closest analogy from antiquity are the lives (*bioi*) or biographies of famous individuals, whether heroes, immortals, or founders of schools of thought.[11] Famous examples are Plutarch's *Lives*, Suetonius's *Lives of the Caesars*, and Diogenes Laertius's *Lives of the Ancient Philosophers*. Perhaps the most interesting parallel, however, is Philostratus's *Life of Apollonius of Tyana*.[12]

But when we liken the Gospels to ancient biographies, the parallels go only so far. The latter are only analogies to the Gospels.[13] The most striking difference is found in what may be called the clear "kerygmatic" or proclamatory

6. Stonehouse, *The Witness of Luke to Christ*, 6.

7. Targums are Aramaic paraphrases of the Hebrew Scriptures designed for reading in the synagogues. There are similarities with the Gospels, and Bruce Chilton concludes that although the Gospels are not targums, "the disciples might have used Targumic methods to transmit the words and deeds of Jesus" ("Targumic Transmission and Dominical Tradition," 39).

8. Midrashim are commentaries on the Hebrew Scriptures. The Gospels have been likened to midrashim by Goulder, *Midrash and Lection in Matthew*; see also Drury, "Midrash and Gospel"; idem, *Tradition and Design in Luke's Gospel*; Miller, *The Gospel of Mark as Midrash on Earlier Jewish and New Testament Literature*. For a balanced treatment of the subject, see France, "Jewish Historiography, Midrash, and the Gospels."

9. See Guilding, *The Fourth Gospel and Jewish Worship*; Goulder, *The Evangelists' Calendar*. For an evaluation of the hypothesis, see Morris, "The Gospels and the Jewish Lectionaries."

10. See Byrskog, *Story as History—History as Story*.

11. See Burridge, *What Are the Gospels?*

12. Plutarch and Suetonius are available in modern editions. Philostratus and Laertius can be found in the Loeb classics series.

13. See Aune, "The Problem of the Genre of the Gospels." Aune's conclusion still stands: "At this point in the history of NT research, it does not appear that a satisfying solution to the

dimension of the Gospels. Whereas ancient biographies were written basically
to provide information, to provide moral or other examples, or perhaps to
entertain, the Gospels intend to witness to and proclaim Jesus as the good news
for which Israel and the world have longed. The basic genre of a Gospel is not
that of a historical novel.[14] The Gospels are interested in providing historical
information about Jesus and to set him forth as an example. They are not,
however, interested in these things for their own sake, but only insofar as they
serve as pointers to the significance of Jesus for the salvation of the world.

These documents are biography-like rather than biographies in the ordinary, modern sense of the word. Thus they have no interest in the childhood
development of Jesus, or his psychological makeup, personal motivation, inner
life, and so on. Certainly there is no criticism of his personality or his calling.
No attempt is made by the Evangelists to provide comprehensive coverage of
what Jesus said and did. Rather, what strikes the reader of the Gospels is their
selectivity. One encounters *representative deeds and teachings* rather than the
whole. Most striking is the sheer amount of space given to the story of the
way in which Jesus' life came to an end. This is obviously the fundamental
point of the story. It was this that inspired Martin Kähler's brilliant observation that the Gospels are passion narratives with extended introductions.[15]
Indeed, it is the remarkable passion narrative that qualifies these documents
to be "Gospels," for it is above all in the death and resurrection of Jesus that
the good news finds its source and content.[16] The biographical elements serve
a single purpose: the presentation of Jesus as the fulfillment of prophecy, as
the one who brings salvation to the world.[17]

History and Theology

The Gospels are, above all, theological documents—documents of faith, written from faith to faith, from commitment in order to encourage commitment.
But this fact should not be taken, as it so often has, to impugn either the importance or the trustworthiness of the history contained in them. To be sure,
for these writers the Jesus of the Gospels was not a person only of the past.
Rather, he was the living, resurrected Lord, present among his people in the
present. Yet the very existence of the church depended on facts accomplished

---

problem of the genre of the gospels can be proposed which could overturn the critical consensus
that the gospels are unique" (ibid., 44).

14. In response to the claims made by Richard Pervo about the book of Acts, see Aune, *The
New Testament in Its Literary Environment*, 81–82.

15. See Kähler, *The So-Called Historical Jesus and the Historic, Biblical Christ*.

16. Thus, the *Gospel of Thomas* is misnamed, since it does not contain the story of Jesus' death
and resurrection, but consists only of 114 sayings of Jesus, with almost no historical narrative.

17. The Gospels "constitute a *subtype* of Greco-Roman biography primarily determined by
content" (Aune, *The New Testament in Its Literary Environment*, 46).

in the past. The one whom the church presently worshiped as Lord had appeared in history, taught, performed deeds, and been crucified and raised from the dead. The subsequent outpouring of the Holy Spirit and the spectacular growth of the church depended on these events. This therefore had to be a history treasured by the early church and valued for its own sake. And, indeed, one of the key roles of the Apostles, as we will see later, was the preservation and transmission of this historical tradition. Justin Martyr in the mid-second century refers to the Gospels as "memoirs of the apostles [*apomnēmoneumata tōn apostolōn*]" (*1 Apol.* 66).

When the canonical Gospels are compared with the apocryphal gospels, one of the most impressive differences is how restrained the former are. There are historical controls at work in the canonical Gospels that were not present in the composition of the apocryphal gospels, which abound in extravagant miracles recorded mainly for effect and to impress the readers. The controlling element in the canonical Gospels is found particularly in the very important continuing availability of eyewitnesses. Eyewitness tradition underlies virtually every stratum of the Gospels.[18] Vincent Taylor wryly called attention to this in a statement that has become famous: "If the Form Critics are right [about their skepticism concerning the reliability of the history recorded in the Gospels], the disciples must have been translated to heaven immediately after the Resurrection."[19]

The Nature of the Historical Reporting in the Gospels

What may we say about the character and quality of the history found in the Gospels? What degree of precision or accuracy may we expect in these accounts? It is important to get our bearings here because conservative interpreters who rightly, in my opinion, regard these documents as divinely inspired nevertheless can be led astray by unnecessary and unjustified expectations.

It is important, first, to realize that the Evangelists are creative writers who exercised considerable freedom in constructing their narratives. They worked with the fund of historical anecdotes available to them from the oral tradition (see chap. 7 below). Although the writers of the Gospels present the story in a chronological framework, apart from a few major fixed points—for example, the birth and baptism narratives, Peter's confession of Christ at Caesarea Philippi, the transfiguration, and the passion narratives—we have no reliable chronology of the ministry of Jesus. Chronology is only one way of organizing a historical narrative. The Evangelists group materials together in whatever way seems compelling to them. Mark, for example, has grouped together the controversy

18. The importance of this fact has hardly been appreciated until the appearance of Richard Bauckham's book *Jesus and the Eyewitnesses*.

19. Taylor, *The Formation of the Gospel Tradition*, 41.

stories that are near the beginning of his narrative (2:1–3:6). Matthew, for another example, groups together representative miracles in chapters 8–9 and sayings of Jesus into five large discourses (chaps. 5–7; 10; 13; 18; 24–25).

The Evangelists furthermore take some freedom in reexpressing the tradition—this in keeping with their own interests and purposes. We can see this clearly in the changes that Matthew and Luke make of their Markan source, and especially in the retelling of the story by the author of the Gospel of John.

A helpful analogy that is sometimes employed is that the Gospels are more like paintings than photographs. A painting, with the interpretive dimension that it affords, often can reveal the truth about a subject more effectively than a photograph.[20] The interpretive dimension provided by the Evangelists enables us to understand the story of Jesus much more effectively than would be possible from a mere transcript of what he said and did.

Because of this freedom in ordering the narrative and in reexpressing it, and because detailed chronology and verbatim repetition were not concerns of the Evangelists, it is both unnecessary and foolish to attempt to harmonize their narratives at the microlevel.

However, the fact that the Gospel writers do not exhibit the kind of concern with exactness and accuracy that we today take to be so important does not mean that their narratives are therefore basically unreliable. That a quotation is not verbatim does not mean that it cannot be truthful. Quite the contrary. Because of the interpretive dimension of the Evangelists' narratives, they can be more truthful.

The statement of the Lukan prologue well describes the character of the tradition and can be applied to all the Gospel writers. There, Luke, referring to his own Gospel, presents the following description of his intent in Luke 1:1–4: "Inasmuch as many have undertaken to compile a narrative of the things which have been accomplished among us, just as they were delivered to us by those who from the beginning were eyewitnesses and ministers of the word, it seemed good to me also, having followed all things closely for some time past, to write an orderly account for you, most excellent Theophilus, that you may know the truth concerning the things of which you have been informed." Luke has gone out of his way to assure his readers that what he writes represents reliable, trustworthy history (for further discussion of the prologue, see chap. 13). Indeed, he writes to strengthen the conviction of his readers in the truth of the gospel concerning which they have been instructed via oral tradition. This strong statement of Luke's purpose to write a trustworthy, truthful narrative based on eyewitness testimony is in no way incompatible with his creative use of his sources and the relative freedom of his reconstruction of the story.

What, then, are we to say of the variations among the Gospels? Most of the time we have the same story told with trivial variations. Such variations should be regarded as within the bounds of an author's license. We need not

20. See Guelich, "The Gospels."

insist on an inconsequential precision. The variations and the chronological discrepancies among the Gospels do not affect their basic reliability and truthfulness. At every point, or nearly every point, we have a historical core that may be relied on to represent historical truth.

To approach these narratives with expectations of a degree of exactness or accuracy that they do not intend to provide is to misuse them and to misunderstand them.[21] Rather, we must accept the Gospels as God gave them to us, and not impose on them external criteria and then force them to agree with those criteria.[22] "Narratives are embodied in natural, phenomenological language, which is not to be judged by over-literal criteria."[23]

Furthermore, all historical narratives must involve interpretation. Even the mere listing of events, which must be selected and ordered, involves a degree of interpretation.[24] In the case of the Gospels, where the writers want not merely to record what happened, but also to tell us something of the meaning of the events, the level of interpretation can be high.[25]

We need not and should not judge ancient historians by the standards of modern historiography. That does not mean, however, that the Gospel writers do not write trustworthy history. The Evangelists compare well with the secular historians of their own day, and their narratives remain basically trustworthy.[26]

Bibliography

Aune, David E. *The New Testament in Its Literary Environment*. Philadelphia: Westminster, 1987.
———. "The Problem of the Genre of the Gospels: A Critique of C. H. Talbert's *What Is a Gospel?*" In *Studies of History and Tradition in the Four Gospels*, edited by R. T. France and David Wenham, 9–60. GP 2. Sheffield: JSOT Press, 1981.

21. See Hemer, "The Meaning of Historicity."
22. This is why it is best to define inspiration inductively, on the basis of the data of Scripture that God has given us, rather than deductively—that is, beginning with the general statements that the Bible is the word of God and God does not speak falsely. The question is not whether it is the word of God, but rather *how God has actually given it*. The Chicago Statement on Biblical Inerrancy (1978) is perceptive when it says: "Since, for instance, non-chronological narration and imprecise citation were conventional and acceptable and violated no expectations in those days, we must not regard these things as faults when we find them in Bible writers. When total precision of a particular kind was not expected nor aimed at, it is no error not to have achieved it. Scripture is inerrant, not in the sense of being absolutely precise by modern standards but in the sense of making good its claims and achieving that measure of focused truth at which its authors aimed."
23. Hemer, "The Meaning of Historicity," 47.
24. We need to remember that in the canonical Gospels we have a very selective account of the ministry of Jesus. The Fourth Evangelist, writing what is in some sense a supplement to the Synoptics, admits how exceedingly selective he has been (John 21:25). As Hemer points out, "Historicity is not necessarily at stake in the phenomena of incomplete or selective narrative" (ibid., 48).
25. See Hagner, "Interpreting the Gospels."
26. See further discussion of this subject in chapters 7, 11, and 13 below.

Bauckham, Richard, ed. *The Gospels for All Christians: Rethinking the Gospel Audiences.* Grand Rapids: Eerdmans, 1998.

———. *Jesus and the Eyewitnesses: The Gospels as Eyewitness Testimony.* Grand Rapids: Eerdmans, 2006.

Blomberg, Craig L. *The Historical Reliability of the Gospels.* 2nd ed. Downers Grove, IL: InterVarsity, 2007.

———. "The Legitimacy and Limits of Harmonization." In *Hermeneutics, Authority, and Canon,* edited by D. A. Carson and John D. Woodbridge, 135–74. Grand Rapids: Academie Books, 1986.

Bockmuehl, Markus, and Donald A. Hagner, eds. *The Written Gospel.* Cambridge: Cambridge University Press, 2005.

Burridge, Richard A. *Four Gospels, One Jesus? A Symbolic Reading.* 2nd ed. Grand Rapids: Eerdmans, 2005.

———. *What Are the Gospels? A Comparison with Graeco-Roman Biography.* 2nd rev. ed. BRS. Grand Rapids: Eerdmans, 2004.

Byrskog, Samuel. *Story as History—History as Story: The Gospel Tradition in the Context of Ancient Oral History.* WUNT 123. Tübingen: Mohr Siebeck, 2000.

Carter, Warren. *Matthew and Empire: Initial Explorations.* Harrisburg, PA: Trinity Press International, 2001.

Chilton, Bruce D. "Targumic Transmission and Dominical Tradition." In *Studies of History and Tradition in the Four Gospels,* edited by R. T. France and David Wenham, 21–45. GP 1. Sheffield: JSOT Press, 1980.

Drury, John. "Midrash and Gospel." *Theology* 77 (1974): 291–96.

———. *Tradition and Design in Luke's Gospel: A Study in Early Christian Historiography.* London: Darton, Longman & Todd, 1976.

Eddy, Paul Rhodes, and Gregory A. Boyd. *The Jesus Legend: A Case for the Historical Reliability of the Synoptic Jesus Tradition.* Grand Rapids: Baker Academic, 2007.

France, R. T. "Jewish Historiography, Midrash, and the Gospels." In *Studies in Midrash and Historiography,* edited by R. T. France and David Wenham, 99–127. GP 3. Sheffield: JSOT Press, 1983.

France, R. T., and David Wenham. *Studies in Midrash and Historiography.* GP 3. Sheffield: JSOT Press, 1983.

———, eds. *Studies of History and Tradition in the Four Gospels.* GP 1. Sheffield: JSOT Press, 1980.

———, eds. *Studies of History and Tradition in the Four Gospels.* GP 2. Sheffield: JSOT Press, 1981.

Goulder, Michael D. *The Evangelists' Calendar: A Lectionary Explanation of the Development of Scripture.* London: SPCK, 1978.

———. *Midrash and Lection in Matthew: The Speaker's Lectures in Biblical Studies, 1969–71.* London: SPCK, 1974.

Grant, Frederick C. *The Gospels: Their Origin and Their Growth.* New York: Harper, 1957.

Guelich, Robert A. "The Gospel Genre." In *The Gospel and the Gospels,* edited by Peter Stuhlmacher, 183–219. Grand Rapids: Eerdmans, 1991.

———. "The Gospels: Portraits of Jesus and His Ministry." *JETS* 24 (1981): 117–25.

Guilding, Aileen. *The Fourth Gospel and Jewish Worship: A Study of the Relation of St. John's Gospel to the Ancient Lectionary System.* Oxford: Clarendon, 1960.

Gundry, Robert H. "Recent Investigations into the Literary Genre 'Gospel.'" In *New Dimensions in New Testament Study,* edited by Richard N. Longenecker and Merrill C. Tenney, 101–13. Grand Rapids: Zondervan, 1974.

Hagner, Donald A. "Interpreting the Gospels: The Landscape and the Quest." *JETS* 24 (1981): 23–37.

Hemer, Colin J. "The Meaning of Historicity." In *The Book of Acts in the Setting of Hellenistic History*, edited by Conrad H. Gempf, 43–49. WUNT 49. Tübingen: Mohr Siebeck, 1989.

Hengel, Martin. *The Four Gospels and the One Gospel of Jesus Christ: An Investigation of the Collection and Origin of the Canonical Gospels*. Harrisburg, PA: Trinity Press International, 2000.

———. "The Titles of the Gospels and the Gospel of Mark." In *Studies in the Gospel of Mark*, translated by John Bowden, 64–84. Reprint, Eugene, OR: Wipf & Stock, 2003.

Kähler, Martin. *The So-Called Historical Jesus and the Historic, Biblical Christ*. Translated and edited by Carl E. Braaten. Minneapolis: Fortress, 1964 [German original, 1896].

Keener, Craig S. "The Character of the Gospels." In *The Historical Jesus of the Gospels*, 71–84. Grand Rapids: Eerdmans, 2009.

Kort, Wesley A. *Story, Text, and Scripture: Literary Interests in Biblical Narrative*. University Park: Pennsylvania State University Press, 1988.

Marsh, Clive, and Steve Moyise. *Jesus and the Gospels*. London: Cassell, 1999.

Miller, Dale. *The Gospel of Mark as Midrash on Earlier Jewish and New Testament Literature*. Lewiston, NY: Mellen, 1990.

Morris, L. "The Gospels and the Jewish Lectionaries." In *Studies in Midrash and Historiography*, edited by R. T. France and David Wenham, 129–56. GP 3. Sheffield: JSOT Press, 1983.

Osborne, Grant R. "History and Theology in the Synoptic Gospels." *TJ* 24 (2003): 5–22.

Porter, Stanley E., ed. *Reading the Gospels Today*. Grand Rapids: Eerdmans, 2004.

Shuler, Philip L. *A Genre for the Gospels: The Biographical Character of Matthew*. Philadelphia: Fortress, 1982.

Stanton, Graham N. *The Gospels and Jesus*. 2nd ed. OBS. Oxford: Oxford University Press, 2002.

———. *Jesus and Gospel*. Cambridge: Cambridge University Press, 2004.

———. *Jesus of Nazareth in New Testament Preaching*. SNTSMS 27. Cambridge: Cambridge University Press, 1974.

Stonehouse, N. B. *The Witness of Luke to Christ*. Grand Rapids: Eerdmans, 1951.

Stuhlmacher, Peter, ed. *The Gospel and the Gospels*. Grand Rapids: Eerdmans, 1991.

Talbert, Charles H. *What Is a Gospel? The Genre of the Canonical Gospels*. Philadelphia: Fortress, 1977.

Taylor, Vincent. *The Formation of the Gospel Tradition*. 2nd ed. London: Macmillan, 1935.

Westcott, B. F. *Introduction to the Study of the Gospels*. 8th ed. London: Macmillan, 1895.

5

The Message of Jesus

All four Gospels, and indeed the entire NT, present Jesus as the one who brings the fulfillment of the promises of the (OT) Scriptures. Despite all the differences between the old covenant and the new covenant that one might tabulate, it remains the case that the Scriptures of the OT and the NT together represent one great story.[1] What exactly was the purpose of Jesus? And how did he express the new reality that he brings?

According to the Synoptic Gospels, Jesus regularly employed the phrase "the kingdom of God" (*hē basileia tou theou*) or, as predominantly in Matthew, the equivalent expression "the kingdom of heaven" (*hē basileia tōn ouranōn*).[2] Although spatial metaphors can be used in referring to it, the kingdom is to be thought of not as a place but rather as the experience of an era in which a new relationship with God, based on the new saving activity of God in Jesus, is made possible. At its heart is the idea of the restoration of the perfect rule or reign (hence "kingdom") of God—that is, the recovery of what was lost through the sin of the garden of Eden. It is a dynamic rather than a static concept. It is the experience of the saving sovereignty of God,[3] not only at the personal level but also the cosmic, and with decidedly eschatological connotations.

1. "The Gospels are simply not understood if one fails to appreciate their fundamental '*salvation-historical*' direction, which presupposes the 'promise history' of the Old Testament, equally narrative in character" (Hengel, "Eye-witness Memory and the Writing of the Gospels," 71).

2. That the two are the same can readily be seen from looking at parallel passages in a synopsis or from Matthew 19:23–24 alone. "Kingdom of heaven" appears to be a circumlocution to avoid too frequent use of "God." In Luke 15:18 one can see the substitution of "heaven" for "God." This does not preclude the possibility that Matthew's "kingdom of heaven" may have a special nuance (see chap. 12, note 19).

3. This is the language of Beasley-Murray, *Jesus and the Kingdom of God*.

Although the reality of which the kingdom speaks is vitally connected to the promises and expectations of the OT Scriptures, surprisingly the phrase "kingdom of God" itself is not found in the OT. Of course, the idea of the rule or reign of God is common there. In principle, God has always remained the ruler of all creation. Yahweh is often identified as "king" (e.g., Pss. 10:16; 29:10; Isa. 6:5; 33:22; 43:15; Jer. 10:7–8; Zeph. 3:15; cf. Ps. 22:28), and there are references to the "kingdom" ruled by Yahweh (1 Chron. 28:5; 29:11; 2 Chron. 13:8; Pss. 103:19; 145:11–13; Dan. 4:3, 34; 6:26; 7:14). But in the fallen world his rule is compromised, even among his covenant people, Israel. In principle, Yahweh presently rules as king, but there is also in the OT the idea of Yahweh's future reign as king (Isa. 24:23; Zech. 14:9), when his enemies will be destroyed and the result will be a universal *shalom* ("peace" in the sense of ultimate well-being in every regard) and universal obedience to his will. The restoration of that rule and the unalloyed experience of it became, as we have seen, increasingly an eschatological hope, standing in very great contrast with present human experience.

The expectation of this new kingdom is also found in the apocalyptic vision of Daniel 7:13–14, where "one like a son of man" comes and is presented to the Ancient of Days. "To him was given dominion and glory and kingdom, that all peoples, nations, and languages should serve him; his dominion is an everlasting dominion, which shall not pass away, and his kingdom one that shall not be destroyed" (Dan. 7:14). Compare Daniel 2:44: "The God of heaven will set up a kingdom which shall never be destroyed." The non-canonical writings of the Second Temple period continue to develop this expectation of the kingdom to come. The apocalyptic book 1 Enoch[4] refers to it in these words: "On that day, I shall cause my Elect One to dwell among them, I shall transform heaven and make it a blessing of light forever. I shall (also) transform the earth and make it a blessing, and cause my Elect One to dwell in her" (45:4–5). The theme of the blessing of the righteous and the judgment of the wicked remains important through to the end of the book. In 2 Baruch, probably late first century AD, chapters 73–74 amount to a midrash on the apocalyptic material of Isaiah (e.g., Isa. 25:6–9; 35:1–10; 65:17–25):

And it will happen that after he has brought down everything which is in the world, and has sat down in eternal peace on the throne of the kingdom, then joy will be revealed and rest will appear. And then health will descend in dew, and illness will vanish, and fear and tribulation and lamentation will pass away

---

4. The date of the Similitudes of 1 Enoch (i.e., chaps. 37–71) presents an infamous problem. A key question is whether this section of 1 Enoch was written after the birth of the church and thus may reflect its theology. James Charlesworth now concludes that the entirety of 1 Enoch, including the Similitudes, is pre-Christian (see The Old Testament Pseudepigrapha and the New Testament, 44).

from among men, and joy will encompass the earth. And nobody will again die untimely, nor will any adversity take place suddenly. Judgment, condemnations, contentions, revenges, blood, passions, zeal, hate and all such things will go into condemnation since they will be uprooted. For these are the things that have filled the earth with evils. . . . And the wild beasts will come from the wood and serve men, and the asps and dragons will come out of their holes to subject themselves to a child. And women will no longer have pain when they bear, nor will they be tormented when they yield the fruits of their womb. . . . For that time is the end of that which is corruptible and the beginning of that which is incorruptible. (2 Bar. 73:1–7; 74:2)

In Jewish apocalyptic of the Second Temple period, as we have already seen, this expectation is articulated in terms of a temporal dualism existing between "this age" and "the age to come." The present age of futility and frustration will give way to a golden age of blessing and fulfillment, the reversal of the effects of Adam's fall. This was the expectation widely shared in Israel, and it is this expectation that Jesus brings to fulfillment, albeit, as we will see, in an unexpected way. Thus, even though the "kingdom of God" language was not current, there would have been little confusion in the minds of those who heard Jesus proclaim the coming of the kingdom concerning what it meant: the fulfillment of the promises so long hoped for by Israel (cf., from Qumran, 4Q521).

Jesus' Proclamation of the Kingdom

The centrality of the kingdom of God in the preaching of Jesus is indisputable. The expression "kingdom of God" occurs fourteen times in Mark, thirty-one times in Luke, and the equivalent "kingdom of heaven" thirty-two times in Matthew (who also has "kingdom of God" 4x). By contrast, in the remainder of the NT the phrase is relatively infrequent (6x in Acts; 2x in John; 12x in the entire Pauline corpus). This shift in vocabulary will be discussed below (see chap. 15). In the Synoptic tradition the expression occurs in some sixty separate logia of Jesus. Virtually all that Jesus says and does is related to the idea of the kingdom. The dawning of the kingdom of God serves well as the integrating key to the Jesus of the Synoptic Gospels, including his words and his deeds:

1. the proclamation of the kingdom as the gift of God's grace (word);
2. the miracles as the embodiment of the message of the kingdom (deed).

In all four Gospels it is John the Baptist who initiates the new work of the Spirit in the announcement of the imminence of the kingdom. All three Synoptics associate John with the prophecy in Malachi 3:1a: "Behold, I send my messenger to prepare the way before me."[5] Mark adds Isaiah 40:3, another passage that alludes to salvation and apocalyptic fulfillment: "The voice of one crying in the wilderness: Prepare the way of the Lord, make his paths straight" (Mark 1:3).[6] Luke continues by quoting apocalyptic words from Isaiah 40:4–5: "Every valley shall be filled, and every mountain and hill shall be brought low, and the crooked shall be made straight, and the rough ways shall be made smooth; and all flesh shall see the salvation of God" (Luke 3:5–6).

John's message is a message of fulfillment: "In those days came John the Baptist, preaching in the wilderness of Judea, 'Repent, for the kingdom of heaven is at hand'" (Matt. 3:1). According to Matthew, Jesus came preaching exactly the same message (4:17). John did this as the one who prepared the way (see Matt. 11:11–15, where Jesus identifies John as the Elijah promised in the book of Malachi as the forerunner of the eschaton [cf. Mal. 3:1; 4:5]);[7] Jesus did this as himself the promised one. John the Baptist becomes a pivotal turning point between promise and fulfillment: "For all the prophets and the law prophesied until John" (Matt. 11:13); "The law and the prophets were until John; since then the good news of the kingdom of God is preached" (Luke 16:16).

Mark sets the tone of his Gospel with this statement: "Now after John was arrested, Jesus came into Galilee, preaching the gospel of God, and saying, 'The time is fulfilled, and the kingdom of God is at hand; repent, and believe in the gospel'" (1:14–15). This message is "the good news of God [*to euangelion tou theou*]"—that is, the announcement of God's grace in the arrival of the promised kingdom.[8] It is this motif of fulfillment that dominates the Gospels, and indeed the entire NT. The message of the dawning of the kingdom is the key to understanding virtually all that Jesus says and does.

Fulfillment dominates the opening chapters, differing though they are, that describe the birth of Jesus in both Matthew and Luke. Both Gospels, but especially Luke, make repeated reference to the Holy Spirit. The very first words

5. Mark, followed by Matthew and Luke, alters the pronoun from "me" to "you," thus addressing the quoted words to Jesus, as the fulfiller of the prophecy. The passage in Malachi continues in an eschatological vein with "and the Lord whom you seek will suddenly come to his temple; the messenger of the covenant in whom you delight, behold, he is coming, says the LORD of hosts. But who can endure the day of his coming, and who can stand when he appears?" (3:1b–2a).

6. For "make his paths straight" the Hebrew text of Isaiah has "make straight in the desert a highway for our God."

7. In the Fourth Gospel, John denies that he is Elijah (John 1:21). This seems to be a denial that he is the final eschatological figure (the name occurs between "the Christ" and "the prophet" [cf. Deut. 18:15]) or perhaps a denial that he is literally Elijah redivivus. The Fourth Gospel, of course, is deliberately subordinating John to Jesus (see John 1:8; 3:28, 30–31), because of the rival sect of John's disciples (John 3:23, 25–26; cf. Acts 19:3).

8. Many manuscripts add *tēs basileias* ("of the kingdom") after "gospel," but the words are lacking in the earliest manuscripts. Note the similarity to the Aramaic paraphrase of Isaiah 40:9; 52:7: "Behold, the kingdom of your God is revealed."

of Matthew refer to Jesus Christ (= Messiah) as "the son of David, the son of Abraham," bringing to the reader's mind the key covenants associated with each figure. In these opening chapters Matthew begins to use his well-known formula to introduce quotations from the OT—for example, "all this took place to fulfill what the Lord had spoken by the prophet" (1:22; cf. 2:15, 17, 23).[9]

The poetic passages in Luke are filled with scriptural allusions meant to underline the fulfillment brought by the coming of Jesus. The prophecy of the birth of John the Baptist (Luke 1:13–17) alludes to his being filled with the Holy Spirit, having the preparatory role of the promised Elijah, with the purpose of making "ready for the Lord a people prepared." The annunciation to Mary (Luke 1:28–35) indicates that her son "will be called the Son of the Most High" and goes on to say, alluding to 2 Samuel 7, "and the Lord God will give to him the throne of his father David, and he will reign over the house of Jacob for ever; and of his kingdom there will be no end." Mary's *Magnificat* (Luke 1:46–55) is a montage of OT allusions, now regarded as coming to realization in the birth of Jesus.[10] Note especially the concluding words: "He has helped his servant Israel, in remembrance of his mercy, as he spoke to the fathers, to Abraham and to his posterity for ever." What begins now to occur in the gospel narrative is a matter of promised covenant faithfulness. Even more specific is the *Benedictus* of Zechariah (Luke 1:68–79). Filled with the Holy Spirit, Zechariah begins with the following words:

> Blessed be the Lord God of Israel,
> for he has visited and redeemed his people,
> and has raised up a horn of salvation for us
> in the house of his servant David,
> as he spoke by the mouth of his holy prophets from of old,
> that we should be saved from our enemies,
> and from the hand of all who hate us;
> to perform the mercy promised to our fathers,
> and to remember his holy covenant,
> the oath which he swore to our father Abraham. (1:68–73)

Then he refers to his son, John, in these words:

> And you, child, will be called the prophet of the Most High;
> for you will go before the Lord to prepare his ways,
> to give knowledge of salvation to his people
> in the forgiveness of their sins,
> through the tender mercy of our God,

9. There are eleven of these in Matthew (see chap. 12 below).

10. For a detailed table showing these allusions, see Plummer, *A Critical and Exegetical Commentary on the Gospel according to St. Luke*, 30–31; and for the *Benedictus* of Zechariah (Luke 1:68–79), ibid., 39.

> when the day shall dawn upon us from on high
> to give light to those who sit in darkness
> and in the shadow of death,
> to guide our feet into the way of peace. (1:76–79)

After the birth of Jesus, Luke refers to the words spoken by Simeon, a man described as "righteous and devout, looking for the consolation of Israel," in the *Nunc Dimittis* (Luke 2:29–32 [cf. 2:34–35]):

> Lord, now lettest thy servant depart in peace,
> according to thy word;
> for mine eyes have seen thy salvation
> which thou hast prepared in the presence of all peoples,
> a light for revelation to the Gentiles,
> and for glory to thy people Israel.

In Luke 2:36–38 the holy prophetess Anna is said to have spoken of Jesus "to all who were looking for the redemption [*lytrōsin*] of Jerusalem."

Luke's emphasis on fulfillment is strong throughout his Gospel. In Luke 4 is the remarkable story of Jesus preaching in the synagogue at Nazareth. The passage that he reads is from Isaiah 61:1–2:

> The Spirit of the Lord is upon me,
> because he has anointed me to preach good news to the poor.
> He has sent me to proclaim release to the captives
> and recovering of sight to the blind,
> to set at liberty those who are oppressed,
> to proclaim the acceptable year of the Lord. (Luke 4:18–19)

This is a messianic passage (note the use of "anointed") that promises eschatological salvation and the coming of "the acceptable year of the Lord," the year when the promises to Israel are at last fulfilled. After reading this passage, Jesus makes this astounding statement: "Today this scripture has been fulfilled in your hearing" (Luke 4:21). The fulfillment motif could not be stronger.

Along the same line, on the return of the Seventy from their missionary work, Jesus, again in shocking terms, says to the disciples, "Blessed are the eyes which see what you see! For I tell you that many prophets and kings desired to see what you see, and did not see it, and to hear what you hear, and did not hear it" (Luke 10:23–24 [cf. Matt. 13:16–17]). Luke's direct statement in 11:20 (cf. Matt. 12:28) is important: "But if it is by the finger of God that I cast out demons, then the kingdom of God has come upon you."[11]

---

11. Here the Greek verb behind "has come" (used also in Matt. 12:28), *phthanō*, is important because it clearly states that the kingdom *has* indeed arrived in the person and ministry of Jesus. This is more explicit than the verb *engizō*, used elsewhere, which can mean "to come near."

Luke 17:20–21 provides an interesting and important confirmation of the fulfillment brought by Jesus: "Being asked by the Pharisees when the kingdom of God was coming, he answered them, 'The kingdom of God is not coming with signs to be observed; nor will they say, "Lo, here it is!" or "There!" for behold, the kingdom of God is in the midst of you.'"[12]

Finally in Luke, we note the closing chapter, where great stress is again put on the fulfillment of Scripture. When he has made himself known to the Emmaus disciples (who "had hoped that he was the one to redeem [*lytrousthai*] Israel" [Luke 24:21]—i.e., hoped until the death of Jesus and the apparent end of the story), Jesus says, "O foolish men, and slow of heart to believe all that the prophets have spoken! Was it not necessary that the Christ should suffer these things and enter into his glory?" Then Luke adds, "And beginning with Moses and all the prophets, he interpreted to them in all the scriptures the things concerning himself" (Luke 24:25–27). And Jesus says similar things to the Eleven in Jerusalem: "These are my words which I spoke to you, while I was still with you, that everything written about me in the law of Moses and the prophets and the psalms must be fulfilled" (Luke 24:44). In this statement is an apparently deliberate allusion to the three divisions of the Hebrew canon: Law, Prophets, and Writings (Psalms being the first of that collection). All of Scripture points to the coming of Jesus.

The ministry of Jesus and his disciples amounts to a kind of invasion of this fallen world, which suffers under the rule of Satan. When Jesus sends out his disciples on their mission, they are told to heal the sick and to say, "The kingdom of God has come near to you" (Luke 10:9 [cf. Matt. 10:7]). On their return they rejoice particularly that the demons were subject to them. Jesus responds, "I saw Satan fall like lightning from heaven" (Luke 10:18). The attack on illness and demons amounts to a head-on confrontation of apocalyptic dimensions.

In short, the Synoptic Gospels are permeated with the theme of the arrival of the kingdom promised in the Scriptures. To miss this is to miss the story of the Gospels altogether. The focus on the hope of Israel is no longer directed to the future but rather to the fulfillment occurring in the present. But since the present is hardly an experience of an unalloyed bliss, and *shalom* is a rare commodity, clearly some explanation is called for.

The Paradoxes of the Kingdom: Fulfillment Short of Consummation

If we are to make any sense of the material just surveyed, we must in some way reconcile it with the world in which we live. It is to be expected that

---

12. Although there is some ambiguity in *entos hymōn*, which could mean "within you," in the larger context of the Gospel it should be taken as meaning "among you." Jesus is speaking to the Pharisees and hardly means to say that the kingdom is "within" them.

non-Christian Jews continue to ask, "But where is this kingdom of which you speak? Don't you read the newspapers?" We are required to grapple with the NT complexity of now and not yet. The Gospel writers were well aware of the problem, to which we now turn by means of discussing several paradoxes.

The Kingdom Is Both Present and Future

Despite the energy behind the proclamation of the presence of the kingdom, the kingdom remains a future reality. Unlike the apocalyptic viewpoint, which expected the present age to end when the new age began, in the NT the new age dawns without bringing the old to an end, resulting in what can be called an "overlap of the ages"[13] (see fig. 2). This means that the old, fallen era continues to exist despite the dawning of the new era. This complexity must be grasped if we are to understand the NT.

Figure 2 **The Overlap of the Ages**

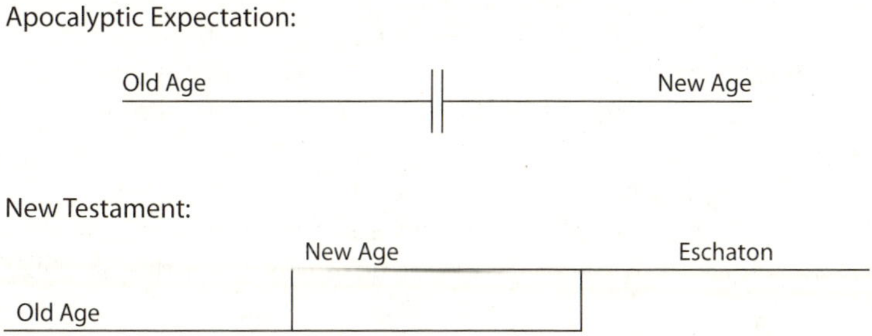

Apocalyptic Expectation:

Old Age | New Age

New Testament:

New Age   Eschaton

Old Age

This idea of an overlap of the ages enables us to assimilate all the material in the NT about present fulfillment along with the material that speaks of the future instead of being forced to choose some to the neglect of the other. Thus, although Jesus continually speaks of the kingdom that he is bringing in his ministry, he also teaches his disciples to pray for the future coming of the kingdom (Matt. 6:10). Each of the Synoptics has an apocalyptic discourse spoken by Jesus concerning events that are to occur in the future (Matt. 24–25; Mark 13; Luke 21). Jesus speaks clearly and often of his return (e.g., Mark 8:38; 13:26; 14:62; Luke 17:24; Matt. 24:30), which will bring the story to a fitting conclusion. This second coming will reveal Jesus in the glory and power that are rightly his, in contrast to his first coming in humility, when according to God's plan he had to suffer and to die. The work of the Messiah is thus divided into two parts separated, as we now know, by a considerable amount of time. The Jewish expectation was of a single work of the Messiah, a final work that Christians believe Jesus will do when he returns. The unique time

13. See especially Cullmann, *Christ and Time.*

frame caused by the overlap of the ages puts the church in the complex situation of being "between the times"—that is, between the first and second comings of the Messiah, a time of fulfillment and a time of waiting. Together with the Jews, Christians await the final work of the Messiah.

The present kingdom thus exists in a veiled form. It is not known or recognized by everyone. There is a sense in which it is "not of this world" (John 18:36). But its reality, perceived by faith, is not doubted by those who have begun to participate in it.[14]

The Kingdom Has Come, but Judgment Is Delayed

This is perhaps the most striking and important of the paradoxes being discussed here because the world that we know seems not to have changed in any radical way. In the day of Jesus it was practically a universal conviction that the new age would bring a division between the wicked and the righteous, with judgment coming to the former and blessing to the latter.

Several parables in Matthew 13 clearly mention this paradox. In this Matthean discourse Jesus refers to the "mysteries of the kingdom." Asking about the parables, the disciples are told by Jesus, "To you it has been given to know the secrets [*mystēria*] of the kingdom of heaven, but to them it has not been given" (Matt. 13:11). These mysteries are facts about the kingdom hitherto unknown but now revealed by Jesus. An important fact is the delay of judgment. It takes faith and receptivity to understand these things which is why those who do not believe do not understand. In the parable of the wheat and the weeds, the servants are told not to gather the weeds "lest in gathering the weeds you root up the wheat along with them. Let both grow together until the harvest; and at harvest time I will tell the reapers, Gather the weeds first and bind them in bundles to be burned, but gather the wheat into my barn" (Matt. 13:29–30). It is not yet the time of harvest—that is, the time of eschatological judgment. "Just as the weeds are gathered and burned with fire, so will it be at the close of the age. The Son of man will send his angels, and they will gather out of his kingdom all causes of sin and all evildoers, and throw them into the furnace of fire. . . . Then the righteous will shine like the sun in the kingdom of their Father. He who has ears, let him hear" (Matt. 13:40–43). A second parable about the delay of judgment is that of the net that caught both good and bad fish. When it was full, the fish were separated. Jesus adds, "So it will be at the close of the age. The angels will come out and separate the evil from the righteous, and throw them into the furnace of fire" (Matt. 13:49–50).[15]

14. See Ladd, "Apocalyptic and New Testament Theology."
15. On the teaching of the parables, see Snodgrass, *Stories with Intent*; Hultgren, *The Parables of Jesus*; Wenham, *The Parables of Jesus*; and the earlier classics Dodd, *The Parables of Jesus*; Jeremias, *The Parables of Jesus*.

The Presence and Power of the Kingdom Are Presently Veiled

Totally unlike the apocalyptic expectation, the kingdom that has come does not overwhelm. On the contrary, it seems to be ineffective. It is visible, indeed, only to those who have a receptive spirit and eyes of faith. It is presently inconspicuous, like a tiny mustard seed that will eventually become a tree (Matt. 13:31–32). And it is like leaven, which when added to loaves of bread cannot be seen but eventually will cause the loaves to rise (Matt. 13:33). It is like a treasure hidden in a field that passersby are unaware of (Matt. 13:44) or a single pearl (Matt. 13:45) that one could put in one's pocket—inconspicuous but, paradoxically, of such a high value as to be worth everything that one has to acquire it.

The Messiah Comes Not as the Expected Triumphant Warrior

The Messiah arrives not sweeping away the Roman occupiers and setting up his throne in Jerusalem, but quite the opposite. He enters the holy city, even as he is acclaimed as the Messiah, riding not a great white steed but instead a lowly donkey (cf. Zech. 9:9). He comes, paradoxically, as a humble servant, and more shocking than that, *as one who suffers and dies as a common criminal on a Roman cross.*

A key turning point in all three Synoptics is Jesus' announcement of the necessity of his death. In all three this comes on the heels of the accompanying key confession of Jesus as the Christ. In retreat with his disciples at Caesarea Philippi, Jesus raises the question about his identity and who the disciples thought he might be. In Matthew's Gospel, Peter excitedly says, "You are the Christ, the Son of the living God" (16:16 [cf. Mark 8:29; Luke 9:20]). After Jesus lauds the confession and installs Peter into office, however, the tonality changes dramatically. "From that time Jesus began to show his disciples that he must go to Jerusalem and suffer many things from the elders and chief priests and scribes, and be killed, and on the third day be raised" (Matt. 16:21). In Peter's view, such talk was out of the question. "And Peter took him and began to rebuke him, saying, 'God forbid, Lord! This shall never happen to you'" (Matt. 16:22). It would have been a shock for Peter to hear himself referred to as "Satan" and to be told that his perspective reflected that of humans and not that of God (Matt. 16:23).

Jesus' prediction of his death assumes a threefold pattern in all of the Synoptics (Mark 8:31; 9:31; 10:33–34, all with parallels in Matthew and Luke). The importance of the death of Jesus in the Gospel narratives can hardly be overemphasized. Rightly did Martin Kähler characterize the Gospels as passion narratives with extended introductions.[16]

It seems as though Jesus conceived of his role as that of the suffering servant in Isaiah 53. In only two places does Jesus directly speak of the meaning of

---

16. Kähler, *The So-Called Historical Jesus and the Historic, Biblical Christ*, 80n11.

his death. In Mark 10:45 (// Matt. 20:28) Jesus says, "For the Son of man also came not to be served but to serve, and to give his life as a ransom [*lytron*] for many." This seems to point back to the prophecy of Isaiah concerning the servant who dies vicariously.[17] The second passage speaks in similar terms. Jesus introduces the cup at the last supper with the words "Drink of it, all of you; for this is my blood of the covenant, which is poured out for many for the forgiveness of sins" (Matt. 26:27–28 [cf. Mark 14:24; Luke 22:20, which has "the new covenant in my blood"]).

The words spoken to Jesus at his baptism (Mark 1:11; Matt. 3:17; cf. Luke 3:22) and again at the transfiguration (Matt. 17:5; cf. Mark 9:3; Luke 9:35), "This is my beloved Son with whom I am well pleased," appear to be a combination of allusions to Psalm 2:7, "He said to me, 'You are my son, today I have begotten you,'" and, in the first of the Servant Songs, Isaiah 42:1, "Behold my servant, whom I uphold, my chosen, in whom my soul delights." This combines the ideas of the triumphant Messiah of Psalm 2 with the servant of Isaiah 42, who gives his life for the transgressions of the people in Isaiah 53.

The idea of a Messiah who dies was something that most Jews could not accept. The Apostle Paul describes it as the great stumbling block for the Jews. Prior to Paul's conversion, it must have been the same for him too. But now it becomes the very cornerstone of his preaching: "For Jews demand signs and Greeks seek wisdom, but we preach Christ crucified, a stumbling block to Jews and folly to Gentiles" (1 Cor. 1:22–23). Paul, along with the other early Christians, was to develop a whole theology of atonement around the death of the Messiah. This apparent oxymoron, a crucified Messiah, turns out to be the very basis of the salvation essential to the kingdom. Christ died *pro nobis*, for us, and without that death humanity and the world remain without hope. Jesus thus comes not only to proclaim the kingdom but also to establish it through his death. The cross is the means of the restoration of God's rule or kingdom and the realization of salvation. And thus "Christ crucified" becomes the heart of the gospel.

Recipients of the Kingdom May Suffer and Even Die

A final paradox to be mentioned here is the astonishing truth that those who receive the kingdom may expect to suffer and even to die. Immediately after the announcement of his own imminent death, Jesus tells the disciples that they may expect something similar: "If any man would come after me, let him deny himself and take up his cross and follow me. For whoever would save his life will lose it; and whoever loses his life for my sake and the gospel's will save it" (Mark 8:34–35; cf. Matt. 16:24–25; Luke 9:23–24). The disciples were dominated by a single thought: the glory of the coming kingdom and their place

---

17. Matthew quotes Isaiah 53:4, applying it to Jesus in 8:17: "This was to fulfill what was spoken by the prophet Isaiah, 'He took our infirmities and bore our diseases.'"

in it. They would sit on either side of Jesus in glory (Mark 10:35–40; Matt. 20:20–23); they are interested in their own greatness (cf. Luke 22:24–30). But in the interim period of the present kingdom they may expect suffering and death.

The ongoing reality of suffering and death, even more the call to suffer and die, must have seemed to be a contradiction of the very idea of the presence of the kingdom. It was not easy to speak of the fulfillment of the Scriptures and the dawn of a new age when the world was not transformed into the promised perfection.[18]

Jesus announces the dawning of the kingdom of God, the fulfillment of the promises. But *that fulfillment is short of consummation*, when everything will come to pass.[19] In the interim, however, the church is to celebrate the fruit of the present reality of the kingdom. Paul will come to speak of the kingdom of God as "righteousness and peace and joy in the Holy Spirit" (Rom. 14:17). And this early fruit of the kingdom is both an anticipation and an assurance of the fullness of the kingdom yet to come.

Universality and Newness of the Kingdom

It has become common in recent years to characterize the message of Jesus as being about the redemption, restoration, or reconstitution of Israel, and the gospel as the announcement of the end of the exile, as though the story of the Bible, both Old and New Testaments, is basically about Israel, with anything else to be put in an appendix. To be sure, the fulfillment of Israel's hopes remains an important part of the biblical story. But that fulfillment is only a part of the larger gospel story, serving as the means to a much greater fulfillment brought by Jesus: the apocalyptic transformation of the world, ultimately a new heaven and a new earth. Israel, rather than being the goal of the story, is the means by which salvation comes to the world. God chose Israel not for its own sake, but in order that Israel might be a light to the nations. It is through Israel that the *shalom* of salvation comes to the world. The language of "restoration," however, implies a return to a glorious past and thus looks backward to a former situation. The language of "restoration" or "reconstitution" cannot adequately depict the radical newness and especially the universalism that the dawning kingdom of God brings. The message of Jesus is for all nations, including Israel, but not just Israel. The new dimension of universality is where the emphasis of the gospel lies.

---

18. The experience of the death of believers at first caused worries in the church at Thessalonica (see 1 Thess. 4:13–18). The return of Christ was expected soon, within that generation. With the lengthening interim period caused by the overlap of the ages, the problem was exacerbated. Later, Paul writes to the Corinthians, "The last enemy to be destroyed is death" (1 Cor. 15:26).

19. On this, see Ladd, *The Presence of the Future*, 105–21.

The Kingdom and Christology

Although Jesus proclaims the kingdom, not himself, in the Gospels, the proc-lamation of the kingdom through his words and deeds is full of christological implications. The vital connection between himself and the kingdom means that a proclamation of the latter inevitably implies a statement about Jesus. Throughout his ministry, down to and including the crucifixion itself, we are confronted with implicit, and sometimes even explicit, christology. Contrary to what some have claimed, christology does not begin with the resurrection narratives. It begins with the appearance of Jesus in the story of the Gospels.[20]

The picture of Jesus that emerges depends not simply on the titles given to Jesus (prophet, Messiah, Son of David, Son of Man, Son of God) or on any specific deeds that could be mentioned (e.g., his forgiving of sins, raising of the dead, healings and exorcisms, nature miracles, authoritative teaching, coming as future judge). Rather, what is decisive for christology is the total picture arrived at through the combination of various individual elements. And although the emphasis is more on function and event than ontology,[21] there is no part of the Synoptic tradition that is not christological.[22]

At a bare minimum, Jesus understood himself to be the Agent (cf. Heb. *šaliaḥ*, the unique Son sent by God as his representative for a special purpose) of that kingdom. But the kingdom material takes us further than that. Jesus speaks not only of the kingdom of the Father (e.g., Matt. 13:43; 26:29) but also of "my" kingdom (Luke 22:30). The kingdom is inseparable from his person and his mission. Where he is, the kingdom is. This intimate associa-tion enabled Origen (*Comm. Matt.* 14.7) to refer to Jesus as the *autobasileia*, the kingdom itself.[23]

Bibliography

Allison, Dale C., Jr. *The End of the Ages Has Come: An Early Interpretation of the Passion and Resurrection of Jesus*. Philadelphia: Fortress, 1985.

Barnett, Paul. *Jesus and the Rise of Early Christianity: A History of New Testament Times*. Downers Grove, IL: InterVarsity, 1999.

Beasley-Murray, George R. *Jesus and the Kingdom of God*. Grand Rapids: Eerdmans, 1986.

Becker, Jürgen. *Jesus of Nazareth*. Translated by James E. Crouch. New York: de Gruyter, 1998.

Betz, Otto. "Jesus' Gospel of the Kingdom." In *The Gospel and the Gospels*, edited by Peter Stuhlmacher, 53–74. Grand Rapids: Eerdmans, 1991.

Bock, Darrell L. *Jesus according to Scripture: Restoring the Portrait from the Gospels*. Grand Rapids: Baker Academic, 2002.

20. On this point see Dunn, *Jesus Remembered*, 882–84.
21. See Cullmann, *The Christology of the New Testament*.
22. Still very much worth reading are two older works, Hoskyns and Davey, *The Riddle of the New Testament*; Denney, *Jesus and the Gospel*.
23. On the self-consciousness of Jesus, see Hagner, "The Self-Understanding of Jesus."

Bockmuehl, Markus, ed. *The Cambridge Companion to Jesus*. CCR. Cambridge: Cambridge University Press, 2001.

Bright, John. *The Kingdom of God: The Biblical Concept and Its Meaning for the Church*. New York: Abingdon, 1953.

Bruce, Alexander B. *The Kingdom of God; or, Christ's Teaching according to the Synoptical Gospels*. 3rd ed. Edinburgh: T&T Clark, 1890.

Burridge, Richard A., and Graham Gould. *Jesus Now and Then*. Grand Rapids: Eerdmans, 2004.

Charlesworth, James H. *The Old Testament Pseudepigrapha and the New Testament: Prolegomena for the Study of Christian Origins*. Rev. ed. Harrisburg, PA: Trinity Press International, 1998.

Chilton, Bruce D. *God in Strength: Jesus' Announcement of the Kingdom*. BibSem 8. Sheffield: JSOT Press, 1987.

———, ed. *The Kingdom of God in the Teaching of Jesus*. Philadelphia: Fortress, 1984.

Cullmann, Oscar. *Christ and Time: The Primitive Christian Conception of Time and History*. Rev. ed. Philadelphia: Westminster, 1962.

———. *The Christology of the New Testament*. Rev. ed. Philadelphia: Westminster, 1963.

Denney, James. *Jesus and the Gospel: Christianity Justified in the Mind of Christ*. London: Hodder & Stoughton, 1908.

Dodd, C. H. *The Parables of Jesus*. Rev. ed. New York: Scribner, 1961.

Dunn, James D. G. *Jesus Remembered*. Christianity in the Making 1. Grand Rapids: Eerdmans, 2003.

Fuellenbach, John. *The Kingdom of God: The Message of Jesus Today*. New York: Orbis, 1995.

Gray, John. *The Biblical Doctrine of the Reign of God*. Edinburgh: T&T Clark, 1979.

Hagner, Donald A. "The Self-Understanding of Jesus." In *Encyclopedia of the Historical Jesus*, edited by Craig A. Evans, 324–33. London: Routledge, 2008.

Hengel, Martin. "Eye-witness Memory and the Writing of the Gospels: Form Criticism, Community Tradition and the Authority of the Authors." In *The Written Gospel*, edited by Markus Bockmuehl and Donald A. Hagner, 70–96. Cambridge: Cambridge University Press, 2005.

Hoskyns, Edwyn, and Noel Davey. *The Riddle of the New Testament*. London: Faber & Faber, 1931.

Hultgren, Arland J. *The Parables of Jesus: A Commentary*. Grand Rapids: Eerdmans, 2000.

Jeremias, Joachim. *New Testament Theology: The Proclamation of Jesus*. Translated by John Bowden. London: SCM, 1971.

———. *The Parables of Jesus*. Translated by S. H. Hooke. New York: Scribner, 1972.

Kähler, Martin. *The So-Called Historical Jesus and the Historic, Biblical Christ*. Translated and edited by Carl E. Braaten. Minneapolis: Fortress, 1964 [German original, 1896].

Kee, Howard Clark. *Jesus in History: An Approach to the Study of the Gospels*. 3rd ed. Fort Worth: Harcourt Brace, 1996.

Ladd, George Eldon. "Apocalyptic and New Testament Theology." In *Reconciliation and Hope: New Testament Essays on Atonement and Eschatology Presented to L. L. Morris on His 60th Birthday*, edited by Robert Banks, 285–96. Grand Rapids: Eerdmans, 1974.

———. *The Gospel of the Kingdom: Scriptural Studies in the Kingdom of God*. Grand Rapids: Eerdmans, 1959.

———. *The Presence of the Future: The Eschatology of Biblical Realism*. Grand Rapids: Eerdmans, 1974. Revision of *Jesus and the Kingdom* (New York: Harper & Row, 1964).

Lundström, Gösta. *The Kingdom of God in the Teaching of Jesus: A History of Interpretation from the Last Decades of the Nineteenth Century to the Present Day*. Translated by Joan Bulman. Richmond, VA: John Knox, 1963.

Manson, T. W. *The Sayings of Jesus: As Recorded in the Gospels according to St. Matthew and St. Luke*. London: SCM, 1949.

Marcus, Joel. *The Mystery of the Kingdom of God*. SBLDS 90. Atlanta: Scholars Press, 1986.

McKnight, Scot. *A New Vision for Israel: The Teachings of the Historical Jesus in National Context*. Grand Rapids: Eerdmans, 1999.

Meadors, Edward P. *Jesus: The Messianic Herald of Salvation*. Peabody, MA: Hendrickson, 1997.

Meyer, Ben F. *The Aims of Jesus*. San Jose, CA: Pickwick, 2002.

Mowinckel, Sigmund. *He that Cometh*. Translated by G. W. Anderson. Oxford: Blackwell, 1956.

Perrin, Norman. *Jesus and the Language of the Kingdom: Symbol and Metaphor in New Testament Interpretation*. Philadelphia: Fortress, 1976.

Plummer, Alfred. *A Critical and Exegetical Commentary on the Gospel according to St. Luke*. 5th ed. ICC. Edinburgh: T&T Clark, 1922.

Reiser, Marius. *Jesus and Judgment: The Eschatological Proclamation in Its Jewish Context*. Translated by Linda M. Maloney. Minneapolis: Fortress, 1997.

Ridderbos, Herman. *The Coming of the Kingdom*. Translated by H. de Jongste. Edited by Raymond O. Zorn. Philadelphia: Presbyterian & Reformed, 1962.

Schnackenburg, Rudolf. *God's Rule and Kingdom*. Translated by John Murray. New York: Herder & Herder, 1963.

Schweitzer, Albert. *The Mystery of the Kingdom of God: The Secret of Jesus' Messiahship and Passion*. Translated by Walter Lowrie. London: Black, 1925.

Snodgrass, Klyne. *Stories with Intent: A Comprehensive Guide to the Parables of Jesus*. Grand Rapids: Eerdmans, 2008.

Stanton, Graham. *The Gospels and Jesus*. 2nd ed. New York: Oxford University Press, 2002.

Stein, Robert H. *Jesus the Messiah: A Survey of the Life of Christ*. Downers Grove, IL: InterVarsity, 1996.

Styler, G. M. "Stages in Christology in the Synoptic Gospels." *NTS* 10 (1963–64): 398–409.

Viviano, Benedict T. *The Kingdom of God in History*. GNS 27. Wilmington, DE: Michael Glazier, 1988.

Weiss, Johannes. *Jesus' Proclamation of the Kingdom of God*. Translated and edited by Richard Hyde Hiers and David Larrimore Holland. Philadelphia: Fortress, 1971.

Wenham, David. *The Parables of Jesus*. Downers Grove, IL: InterVarsity, 1989.

Willis, Wendell, ed. *The Kingdom of God in 20th-Century Interpretation*. Peabody, MA: Hendrickson, 1987.

Wright, N. T. *Jesus and the Victory of God*. COQG 2. Minneapolis: Fortress, 1996.

6

The "Historical" Jesus

It is not surprising that Jesus has been studied intensively from the beginning. For over two millennia the central person of the NT and of the faith of the church has been the subject of endless study and countless books and articles. Only rarely has it been doubted that he was a historical figure who existed in a specific time and place. The canonical Gospels have always been the main source for knowledge about Jesus, and, for the most part, the Gospels were accepted as basically reliable historical reporting. The real Jesus, it was assumed, was the Jesus of the Gospels. But that would all change with the dawn of modernity. Jesus was now to be studied as a specifically historical figure, subjected to historical investigation like any other historical person and, most importantly, altogether apart from, even in opposition to, the faith of the church.

The Initial Quest of the Historical Jesus

Of course, there have always been skeptics who doubted the reliability of the Gospel accounts. But it was the Enlightenment of the eighteenth century, with its confidence in the autonomy of human reason and its eager assault on authority, especially the dogma of the church, that impacted the study of the Gospels and dismantled the idea that what they said about Jesus was historical truth. What determined the new, negative assessment of the truthfulness of the Gospels above all was the emerging naturalistic worldview that prohibited the possibility of supernatural events. Everything now became governed by the "scientific" perspective, including the study of history. So, on the model of science, history too had to be explained on the basis of causation available for the historian's inspection. History was now perceived as a closed continuum of cause and effect that allowed no interference from outside that continuum. There could be no divine causation in the new mechanistic universe that might explain the truly miraculous.[1]

Now, for the first time, given the new rules, it became necessary to distinguish the "real" Jesus, as the historian's Jesus was thought to be, from the Jesus of the Gospels, regarded now as the fictional creation of the church. The new, so-called scientific historiography guaranteed that there would be little congruence between the two.

For the sake of clarity, therefore, it is worth making the following important terminological distinction. "The historical Jesus" refers to the so-called scientific historians' hypothetical product, one that a priori rules out the supernatural or transcendent. "The Jesus of history," by contrast, refers to the way Jesus actually was in history, reflecting an approach that is in principle open to the possibility of the supernatural occurring in history.

Books that gave radical alternatives to the Gospel accounts began to appear. Albert Schweitzer documented this research in a famous book published in 1906, originally titled *Von Reimarus zu Wrede* (From Reimarus to Wrede), the English title of which, *The Quest of the Historical Jesus* (1910),[2] gave its name to the new field of scholarly endeavor that continues a century later with unflagging energy.

As Schweitzer's title indicates, the new "enlightened" study of Jesus began with Hermann Samuel Reimarus (1694–1768),[3] whose reconstruction of the story of Jesus, "On the Intention of Jesus and His Disciples," was published posthumously by Gotthold Lessing in *Fragments from an Unnamed Author* in 1774–78.[4] According to Reimarus, who was not a theologian but rather a professor of Oriental languages, in the last analysis Jesus was no more than another person calling Israel to repentance in preparation for the coming of the kingdom; that is, he was similar to John the Baptist. Such was Jesus' zeal, however, that he had designs of political revolution, aspired to be recognized as the Messiah, but eventually died on the cross in disillusionment. It was his disciples who became the founders of Christianity, when they stole his body, invented the story of the resurrection, and spoke of his imminent return to

---

1. See Fuller, "The Fundamental Presupposition of the Historical Method."

2. The English translation by W. Montgomery, based on the first German edition, has been republished several times. Schweitzer's revised and considerably expanded second German edition is now also available in translation (Schweitzer, *The Quest of the Historical Jesus*).

3. Schweitzer, however, ignores completely the English deists who wrote along similar lines before Reimarus and who heavily influenced him. See Brown, *Jesus in European Protestant Thought, 1778–1860*, 36–55.

4. Known as the Wolfenbüttel Fragments (from the library where they are housed), partly published again, in English translation, nearly two hundred years later, in Talbert, *Reimarus, Fragments*.

set up the kingdom. Some modern accounts of Jesus sound like little more than repeats of Reimarus. Altogether gone from Reimarus's understanding of Jesus is the transcendent, the supernatural, the entering of God into human affairs. Schweitzer believed that much in Reimarus was correct.

The most impressive and influential of the nineteenth-century books on Jesus was that by the twenty-seven-year-old David Friedrich Strauss, *The Life of Jesus Critically Examined* (German original, 1835).[5] William Baird describes this book as "the most revolutionary religious document written since Luther's Ninety-Five Theses."[6] Remarkably, Strauss rejected not only the supernaturalism of the conservatives but also the rationalism of the liberals. He was merciless in his criticism of the latter when they attempted to give rationalistic explanations for the miracle stories of the NT. Not that Strauss in any sense was prepared to accept the historicity of these stories. For him, the bulk of the Gospel narratives, and especially those involving miracles, were "myth," stories not historically true but in various ways symbolic of transcendent truths.

Among the many other works surveyed by Schweitzer, one that should also be mentioned here because of its popularity over a long period of time is by Ernest Renan. His *Vie de Jésus*, which was published in 1863 and went through many editions,[7] rejected the miraculous and portrayed Jesus as a would-be Messiah of a spiritual, rather than earthly, kingdom. Renan's reconstruction of the Gospel stories was highly imaginative and colorful, romantic as well as rationalistic. Jesus is positively put forward as the preacher of morality and spiritual values. Renan's book receives very strong criticism from Schweitzer.

The last figure in Schweitzer's survey, the German scholar William Wrede, reveals the ultimate poverty of the quest for the historical Jesus. Wrede concludes that the Gospels provide us with far more theology than history. The Gospel of Mark, favored by the questers, cannot be relied on for enough history to justify even the liberal lives of Jesus. Wrede's historical skepticism was largely the result of his inability to accept the miraculous dimension of the Gospel narratives. For Wrede, the Apostle Paul, who departed from Jesus' nonmessianic intentions, was the real founder of Christianity.

Schweitzer's own conclusions on Jesus provided a further blow to the liberal lives written in the nineteenth century. He saw that the liberal quest labored to produce a Jesus who was acceptable and appealing to the modern world—a man teaching an exalted ethic, promoting spiritual values, calling people

---

5. The book went through many editions, and Strauss became famous or infamous. He toned down his conclusions to some extent in the third edition of the book (1838) to ease some of the criticism directed at him, but he returned to his radical views in the fourth edition (1839–40). The latter was translated into English by the twenty-three-year-old George Eliot (eventually to become a famous novelist), published in three volumes in 1846, and is presently available as *The Life of Jesus Critically Examined*, edited by Peter C. Hodgson.

6. Baird, *The History of New Testament Research*, 1:246.

7. For an English translation, see Renan, *The Life of Jesus*.

to a higher righteousness. Against that, Schweitzer argues for a thoroughly eschatological Jesus. That is, Jesus gave all his energy to the proclamation of the imminent, apocalyptic kingdom. It was this that led him eventually to martyrdom and to his despair and disillusionment on the cross. If the liberal quest of the historical Jesus ended in a blind alley, as Schweitzer contended, his own reconstruction of Jesus seems to do no better. Neither the thoroughgoing skepticism of Wrede nor the thoroughgoing eschatology of Schweitzer provides an adequate understanding of the Jesus of history.[8]

Schweitzer's impressive book documents the historical study of Jesus through the whole of the nineteenth century. If the quest was productive in some sense, it was often also painful for those engaged in it, as Schweitzer points out. Characteristically, the questers "were eager to picture [Jesus] as an ordinary person, to strip from him the robes of splendour with which he had been apparelled, and clothe him once more with the coarse garments in which he had walked in Galilee."[9] Many lost their academic positions and experienced personal crisis. The sad thing is that the validity of their supposedly scientific portrayals of Jesus was highly questionable. The pictures of Jesus that they produced looked remarkably like themselves. It was as if, looking into the bottom of a well, they saw only their own reflection.[10] Schweitzer himself concludes, "Thus each successive epoch of theology found its own thoughts in Jesus; that was, indeed, the only way in which it could make him live. But it was not only each epoch that found its reflection in Jesus; each individual created Jesus in accordance with his own character."[11] Unfortunately, the same may be said to be true of historical Jesus studies right down to the present.

One German author unfortunately neglected by Schweitzer was Martin Kähler, whose book *The So-Called Historical Jesus and the Historic, Biblical Christ* (1896) took a refreshing change of direction.[12] Kähler rejected the entire enterprise of seeking the historical Jesus, stating forcefully that "*the historical Jesus of modern authors conceals from us the living Christ.*"[13] It is impossible, Kähler argues, to reconstruct the life of Jesus by going beyond the sources available to us in the Gospels. To do so is to put too much trust in the vagaries of historical research. No, Kähler says, the "real" Jesus is none other than the Christ presented in the Gospels and proclaimed by the Apostles. Kähler is in no way against historical research, but he rejects it as *an alternative* to the

8. For a penetrating analysis, see Wright, *Jesus and the Victory of God*, 16–21.

9. Schweitzer, *The Quest of the Historical Jesus*, 6.

10. The famous words of George Tyrrell are often cited: "The Christ that Harnack sees, looking back through nineteen centuries of Catholic darkness, is only the reflection of a Liberal Protestant face, seen at the bottom of a deep well" (*Christianity at the Cross-Roads*, 44).

11. Schweitzer, *The Quest of the Historical Jesus*, 6. He adds, "There is no historical task which so reveals a man's true self as the writing of a Life of Jesus."

12. In this book title "historical" translates *historische* and refers to bare historical fact; "historic" translates *geschichtliche* and refers to existential or interpreted history.

13. Kähler, *The So-Called Historical Jesus and the Historic, Biblical Christ*, 43. Italics in original.

evidence of the Gospels. Historical research itself cannot present us with a better, more accurate picture of Jesus than that of the Gospels.

Several conclusions are to be drawn from the nineteenth-century quest of the historical Jesus as documented by Schweitzer.

1. Beginning with Reimarus, it is clear that the word "historical" has been redefined. No longer does it mean "what happened in history," but rather it refers strictly to what can be established by scientific historiography. For narratives so permeated by the supernatural, the method is inadequate, and the results are bound to be severely distorted. It must be emphasized here, since it holds true down to the present, that the quest of the historical Jesus is a quest for the historian's Jesus, and that the historian's Jesus is a hypothetical construct that depends on presuppositions contrary to the content of the Gospel narratives. It is therefore of necessity a quest for a hypothetical Jesus. This is particularly important to note because often the idea is given that the historian's Jesus is the "real" Jesus. But again it must be emphasized that the so-called historical Jesus is not necessarily the Jesus who existed in history. It is, rather, the hypothetical construction of scholars with a set of presuppositions antithetical to the Gospel narratives.

2. Despite claims of scientific objectivity, the portraits of Jesus produced tended to reflect the values and commitments of the questers. There is no way around it: we tend to see what we want to see, believers and unbelievers alike. Many of the questers, furthermore, were engaged in an attempt to preserve some meaning in Jesus for their world, whether in terms of morality, values, or whatever, and in this way preserve some significance for the church's Jesus.

3. The initial quest of the historical Jesus amounted to a full rejection of the Jesus presented in the Gospels. Growing out of the perspective of the Enlightenment, the quest was determined to discover a Jesus who was fundamentally different from the Jesus worshiped by the church. The authors of the initial quest thus arbitrarily selected bits and pieces of the Gospel narratives, sprinkled in a good dose of imagination, and came up with what was supposed to be the "real" Jesus. That the results were different depending on the cook somehow did not cause any wondering about the correctness or adequacy of the method being employed.

Rudolf Bultmann: Dichotomizing the Jesus of History and the Christ of Faith

Rudolf Bultmann towered over NT scholarship in the first half of the twentieth century. He too was critical of the nineteenth-century quest of the historical

Jesus, which he saw as both impossible and illegitimate. He regarded it as impossible because of the nature of the sources. As documents of faith, the Gospels could not be trusted for reliable historical information. The impact of the resurrection experience (Bultmann denied the reality of the resurrection of Jesus itself) transformed the tradition so that it tells us more about the disciples and the faith of the early church than it does about Jesus. There is no way, according to Bultmann, that one can penetrate behind the barrier of faith in the resurrected Christ to reach the Jesus of history. Many of the sayings of Jesus, Bultmann alleged, were spoken by Christian prophets and then ascribed to Jesus. Particularly debilitating in Bultmann's approach to the question of history in the Gospels was his development of the double criterion of dissimilarity (see below, under the heading "The Birth of the So-Called New Quest in the Mid-Twentieth Century"), whereby an item of the tradition qualifies as reliable history only if it is both unlike what the church believed and unlike anything in contemporaneous Judaism. This cut Jesus off not merely from the faith of his followers but even from his Jewish roots altogether. Ironically, despite this domineering skepticism, Bultmann was able to write his own version of a life of Jesus. In *Jesus and the Word* (German original, 1926) Jesus is presented as a preacher of divine forgiveness who summons his listeners to existential decision.

Bultmann's view of Jesus is captured in his own oft-quoted words: "I do indeed think that we can now know almost nothing concerning the life and personality of Jesus, since the early Christian sources show no interest in either, are moreover fragmentary and often legendary; and other sources about Jesus do not exist."[14]

In Bultmann's view, the quest was illegitimate (evidence is not needed to support faith) and unnecessary because Christian faith depends not on the Jesus of history[15] but rather on the kerygma, the preaching of the early church—that is, the message, not the facts, if you will. It is the message alone that matters, and there is no need for the message to be grounded in historical reality. The message carries its own authority.

Thus, for Bultmann, there is no necessary continuity between the message of Christianity and the person of Jesus. The Christ of faith is what matters, not the Jesus of history. It only matters that there *was* a Jesus (which he refers to as the *Dass*, the "thatness" of Jesus), not what he actually was like, said, or did (the *Was*, i.e., the "what" of Jesus). What matters for Bultmann is the message of the church, the kerygma, which, however, he believes must be "demythologized" in order to become meaningful to the modern world. Thus the language of the first century about sacrifice, atonement, resurrection, and

---

14. Bultmann, *Jesus and the Word*, 14.

15. In Bultmann's *Theology of the New Testament*, where he infamously devotes a mere thirty pages to Jesus, he states that Jesus is not properly a part of NT theology, but only its presupposition.

Jewish apocalyptic and gnostic concepts such as a descending and ascending, dying and rising heavenly redeemer—all are to be understood as a kind of code that really refers to things such as openness to the future, authentic living, and affirmation of life without fear. In this way, using concepts drawn largely from the existential philosophy of his professorial colleague Martin Heidegger, Bultmann believed that he could rescue the Christian faith for his contemporaries.

The Birth of the So-Called New Quest in the Mid-Twentieth Century

It is not uncommon in analyses of the study of the historical Jesus for authors to speak of a "no quest" period between the end of the initial (or "old") quest and the beginning of a renewed effort to get at the historical Jesus that occurred in the mid-twentieth century. But this overlooks the fact that many books on Jesus were written during the half century between Schweitzer and the beginning of the "new quest" of the historical Jesus. There never really was a silent, or "no quest," period.[16]

Nevertheless, something of a turning point in the study of the historical Jesus occurred among the circle of Bultmann's own students, signaled by the famous 1953 essay by Ernst Käsemann, "The Problem of the Historical Jesus." These students (including such notables as Günther Bornkamm and Hans Conzelmann, who were to go on and write their own important Jesus books) were dissatisfied with their teacher's skepticism concerning the historical Jesus. They regarded Bultmann's position as perilously close to docetism (from *dokeō*, "to appear to be"), an ancient heresy that alleged that Jesus appeared to be human but was not. In particular, they were convinced that more continuity was needed between the Jesus of history and the Christ of the kerygma, and that indeed more reliable information could be mined from the Synoptic Gospels than Bultmann had allowed.

Thus a new quest of the historical Jesus was inaugurated. In many important respects, however, there was little new about this new development. Certainly there was no new openness to the possibility of the supernatural occurring in time and space. Basically, what was new was, first, the more careful investigation of elements in the Gospels that could provide some continuity between Jesus and the kerygmatic Christ of the church, and, second, a refinement of criteria by which material in the Gospels could be judged as reliable. The first criterion had been used by Bultmann and is perhaps the most controversial: *double dissimilarity*. For a saying to qualify as historically reliable, it cannot resemble what the church believed about Jesus, and it cannot resemble anything in the Judaism contemporary with Jesus. What is allowed is only that which cannot be explained as having possibly been borrowed from Judaism

16. See Telford, "Major Trends and Interpretive Issues in the Study of Jesus."

or the church. It becomes clear immediately how unreasonable this demand is. It totally isolates Jesus from the world in which he lived. The resultant "critically assured minimum" can amount only to what was eccentric about Jesus, and not what was characteristic of him.[17]

Since the late twentieth century, however, a growing dissatisfaction with the dissimilarity criterion has developed. Gerd Theissen and Dagmar Winter comment, "It is therefore time to replace the criterion of dissimilarity with a new criterion, in the process keeping its legitimate elements and correcting its distortions and one-sidedness."[18] They advocate the "criterion of historical plausibility," giving more positive consideration to contextual plausibility on the Jewish side and to the plausibility of historical effects on the Christian side.

A second criterion is *multiple attestation*. Gospel material that occurs in more than a single strand of the tradition—that is, in Q, in Mark, and in the material unique to Matthew or Luke—has a stronger claim to be accepted as historically reliable than material in one strand. A third criterion is *coherence*. Once one begins to build up a picture through the collection of materials regarded as reliable, other single items that cohere with that picture may also be presumed to have a good claim to reliability. Among further criteria that we may also take notice of is *embarrassment*, where anything that seems out of keeping with the church's view of Jesus has good claim to be original (e.g., when Jesus says he does not know the time of his return [Mark 13:32]).[19] So too the presence of Semitisms or signs of a Palestinian background usually are taken as pointing to historical reliability.[20] At best, the reliability criteria have a limited usefulness.

With the help of criteria such as these, the new questers focused on distinctive aspects of Jesus, such as his table fellowship with sinners, his unique teaching, as well as his unparalleled authority. Building on these materials, they were able to show some of the implicit continuity between history and the kerygma.[21] Bornkamm disagreed with his teacher when he concluded, "Quite clearly what the Gospels report concerning the message, the deeds and the history of Jesus is still distinguished by an authenticity, a freshness, and a distinctiveness not in any way effaced by the Church's Easter faith."[22] This was helpful as far as it could go with the self-imposed restrictions, but the meaning of Jesus was still understood in existential terms. That is, encountering him in the text presents a call to authentic existence, openness to the future, and so forth. Linking

---

17. For the distinction between "unique" and "characteristic," see Hooker, "On Using the Wrong Tool." She points out that the criterion of dissimilarity gives us only the former.

18. Theissen and Winter, *The Quest for the Plausible Jesus*, 67.

19. This was the approach of P. W. Schmiedel (*Encyclopaedia Biblica* [1901], col. 1881), who isolated some nine passages as "the foundation-pillars for a truly scientific life of Jesus." See the response by B. B. Warfield in *Princeton Theological Review* 4 (1906): 121–24.

20. On the criteria, see Porter, *The Criteria for Authenticity in Historical-Jesus Research*; Theissen and Winter, *The Quest for the Plausible Jesus*.

21. Two representative books are Conzelmann, *Jesus*; Bornkamm, *Jesus of Nazareth*.

22. Bornkamm, *Jesus of Nazareth*, 24.

the understanding of Jesus so closely with existential philosophy of the mid-twentieth century assured that this approach would have a limited shelf life.

The So-Called Third Quest

Developments in the study of the historical Jesus, beginning approximately in the 1980s, have been designated as the beginning of a "third quest."[23] This third quest is rather amorphous, and it is difficult sometimes to know which particular quest of the three is the right category for any specific book. According to N. T. Wright, the third quest is characterized by a new attention directed to the historical context of Jesus in all its various aspects, but above all to Second Temple Judaism.

But how new really is the third quest? One could point to a fairer and more nuanced use of the criteria of authenticity. More important is the wider source base employed, together with the concern to place Jesus in broader contexts, openness to new interdisciplinary methods, and a new confidence that a comprehensive account of the historical Jesus is possible. Life of Jesus research, as it is called these days, has become a cottage industry. There seems to be no end to the books, and apparently no end to the public's hunger for such books.[24]

The third quest has made far more progress in understanding the Jewish context of Jesus than in understanding Jesus himself. Again, as in the previous quests, the search is for alternate, naturalistic explanations of Jesus. It is hardly the case that the third quest offers a more strictly historical, and less theological, orientation than previous quests. The ideological commitments of these authors are no less conspicuous than in the earlier quests.[25] Leander Keck, in reviewing the work of John Dominic Crossan and Marcus Borg, key representatives of the latest writing on Jesus, concludes that here, no less than in the original quest, we again encounter modern ideas and values superimposed on the historical Jesus.[26] So although there are some new dimensions to the third quest, in the main there is nothing fundamentally new.[27]

23. Thus N. T. Wright, in Neill and Wright, *The Interpretation of the New Testament, 1861–1986*, 379–403.

24. Especially appealing to the broader public is the idea that "secret" or newly discovered gospels will give us the real Jesus or the real beliefs of the first Christians. See, for example, Sullivan, *Rescuing Jesus from the Christians*. Helpful antidotes to this notion can be found in Bock, *The Missing Gospels*; Craig A. Evans, *Fabricating Jesus*.

25. See Holmén, "A Theologically Disinterested Quest?" He writes: "Within the theological interests of the new research on Jesus, tendencies both to validation and invalidation of traditional Christian convictions are discernible. An antipathy to Church dogma seems no more to guarantee the rigor of the reasoning than does positive sympathy. (The question may be raised whether anyone can ever be truly neutral in this way)" (189–90).

26. Keck, "The Second Coming of the Liberal Jesus?"

27. See Telford, "Major Trends and Interpretive Issues in the Study of Jesus." He argues persuasively that "recent developments are broadly in continuity with the New Quest," and that the new life of Jesus research has decided similarities with even the old quest (ibid., 30).

Given its basic orientation, it is no surprise that even the third quest has for the most part failed to address the question of miracles or else comes to fully negative conclusions. One of the most interesting recent exceptions here is the remarkable conclusion by Wright concerning the historicity of the resurrection. Wright maintains that the empty tomb and the encounters with the risen Jesus belong "in the same sort of category, of historical probability so high as to be virtually certain, as the death of Augustus in AD 14 or the fall of Jerusalem in AD 70."[28] He writes further, "The proposal that Jesus was bodily raised from the dead possesses unrivalled power to explain the historical data at the heart of Christianity."[29] Wright is one of the few questers who does not allow his study to be paralyzed by Enlightenment presuppositions.[30]

The Jesus Seminar

Although the widely publicized Jesus Seminar represents life of Jesus research of a kind, it is so distinctive in its methodology and its conclusions are so skeptical that it is difficult to designate it as part of the third quest. The Jesus Seminar is a group of mainly American scholars, founded by Robert W. Funk in 1985, with the ostensible purpose of examining the materials of the Gospels in order to establish what could be regarded as historically reliable—that is, by the standards of "scientific historiography." In the book that published the results of their study, *The Five Gospels: The Search for the Authentic Words of Jesus*,[31] they concluded that a mere 18 percent of the words of Jesus in the Gospels probably are authentic. In the whole of Mark only one saying of Jesus was regarded as probably authentic: "Render to Caesar the things that are Caesar's and to God the things that are God's" (Mark 12:17). The acts of Jesus (including what he did and what was done to him) fared no better in a subsequent volume, with a meager 16 percent being accorded any historical probability.[32] The conclusions of the second volume are to a considerable extent predetermined by the methodology and negative conclusions of the first volume.[33]

The only "miracles" that are affirmed as authentic seem to be those that are open to being explained psychosomatically. Jesus probably cured Simon's

28. Wright, *The Resurrection of the Son of God*, 710.

29. Ibid., 718.

30. See Wright, *The New Testament and the People of God*, 96–144; *The Resurrection of the Son of God*, 12–31.

31. The fifth gospel referred to in the title is the *Gospel of Thomas*.

32. Funk and the Jesus Seminar, *The Acts of Jesus*.

33. "The representations of social conditions and circumstances in the narrative material should correspond closely to the perception of social reality in the authentic sayings and parables. Any discrepancy between the two automatically raises suspicion about the accuracy of the narrative representation" (ibid., 34–35). There is a suspicious circularity here.

> The rejection as unhistorical of all passages which narrate miracles is sensible if we start by knowing that the miraculous in general never occurs. Now I do not here want to discuss whether the miraculous is possible. I only want to point out that this is a purely philosophical question. Scholars, as scholars, speak on it with no more authority than anyone else. The canon "If miraculous, unhistorical" is one they bring to their study of the texts, not one they have learned from it. If one is speaking of authority, the united authority of all the Biblical critics in the world counts here for nothing. On this they speak simply as men; men obviously influenced by, and perhaps insufficiently critical of, the spirit of the age they grew up in.
>
> C. S. Lewis, "Modern Theology and Biblical Criticism," in *Christian Reflections*,
> edited by Walter Hooper (Grand Rapids: Eerdmans, 1967), 158.

mother-in-law from a fever, a man said to have leprosy (but that was really "some form of dermatitis"), the hemorrhaging woman, and blind Bartimaeus. All these are assigned the color pink (i.e., acceptable for inclusion "in the database for determining who Jesus was"), but "with reservations (or modifications)," and not one is put in red (i.e., included "unequivocally"). Very strangely, not a single exorcism account is accepted as historically probable, although the Jesus Seminar believes that Jesus did practice exorcism.[34] The Jesus Seminar concludes that Jesus was a laconic, itinerant sage, a "social deviant," a healer, and a teacher. What his purpose may have been seems unclear to them. He was put to death by the Romans for something he did in connection with the temple.

The Jesus Seminar seems like little more than a repeat of Reimarus. Granted, its members are more sophisticated and have access to rich contextual materials unknown to Reimarus. But in the end, we come no further than the naturalism of eighteenth-century historicism. The first and the last of the Jesus Seminar's "seven pillars of scholarly wisdom" that support "the edifice of contemporary gospel scholarship" are a good part of the reason.[35] The first of these is "the distinction between the historical Jesus, to be uncovered by historical excavation, and the Christ of faith encapsulated in the first creeds." This methodological pillar assumes the conclusion that the Gospels are untrustworthy sources for the life of Jesus. The last pillar refers to "the reversal that has taken place regarding who bears the burden of proof." They continue: "It was once assumed that scholars had to prove that details in the synoptic gospels were *not* historical. . . . The gospels are now assumed to be narratives in which the memory of Jesus is embellished by the mythic elements that express the church's faith in him. . . . Supposedly historical elements in these narratives must therefore be demonstrated to be so."[36]

34. Does it not indicate a weakness in the voting method when specific conclusions are reached that do not even square with what the Jesus Seminar regards as reality?

35. These are described in Funk, Hoover, and the Jesus Seminar, *The Five Gospels*, 3–5.

36. Ibid., 4–5.

These "pillars" provide the reason for the low percentages of reliability assigned to the Gospels by the Jesus Seminar. Since the Gospels reflect the faith of the authors, it is assumed that they cannot offer any historical knowledge. While for some this might raise the question of the suitability of the method employed in studying the Gospels, books that are avowedly documents of faith, the Jesus Seminar remains untroubled.

This is not the place for a full critique of the Jesus Seminar, but a few points must be made:

1. The members of the Jesus Seminar try hard to convince us that their view, and their view alone, represents what true scholars conclude. They constantly bombard us with the words "scholar," "scholarly," and "scholarship." Their translation of the NT is designated as the "Scholars Version." To the Jesus Seminar, scholarship has become a sacred cow. However the Jesus Seminar represents but a small fraction of critical scholars in the NT guild, to the total neglect of those who happen to disagree with them.[37]

2. Although voting may give the impression of being scientific, everything depends on who the voters are—that is, what the relative percentage is between more conservative and less conservative voters. To the majority of NT scholars, the results of the Jesus Seminar seem skewed. Voting, of course, in itself cannot establish truth or falsehood. At most, what the Jesus Seminar has really accomplished is to see how a small handful of scholars, mainly of a radical persuasion, would vote concerning the material under investigation. Given the makeup of the group, there is nothing really surprising, and certainly nothing normative, about their work.

3. Although it may pose as such, the Jesus Seminar can hardly be considered to represent a neutral scholarship (as if there were any such thing). They are avowedly on a crusade against conservative expressions of Christianity, which they abhor, and therefore they have worked hard to gain wide publicity.

4. Oddly enough, the work of the Jesus Seminar has a fundamentalist feeling to it. In a way similar to the all-or-nothing approach of inerrancy, the Seminar members require the *ipsissima verba*[38] of Jesus, or total narrative accuracy, for something to be designated as historical.

37. A feeble attempt to remedy this by referring to the work of non–Jesus Seminar participants is made in Funk and the Jesus Seminar, *The Acts of Jesus*, but the scholars they have chosen (apart from Raymond Brown) are those who are inclined to agree with many of their conclusions. Also to be noted is that the membership of the Jesus Seminar was much larger at the beginning, but as the bias of the group became clear, many scholars dropped their membership.

38. The verbatim words of Jesus, as from a tape recorder, which in any event we cannot have from the Greek because Jesus taught in Aramaic most, if not all, of the time.

They ignore the possibility that often we may have the *ipsissima vox*[39] of Jesus, or that a narrative could have a historical core even if details are questionable.

5. The Jesus Seminar's Jesus is a naturalistic Jesus, so there is nothing new here that would warrant special attention (despite the claim of "a new venture for gospel scholarship").

6. The picture of Jesus arrived at by the Jesus Seminar is absolutely incapable of explaining the origin of the church. Their conclusion that Jesus did not preach the imminence of the end of the present age goes against not only the third quest but also virtually all the previous quests.

7. Finally, it is historically implausible that only a mere 16 to 18 percent of the Gospel narratives represents true history, and that the remaining material is simply the result of the creative imagination of the Evangelists.

The Endemic Problem of Historical Jesus Studies

Unfortunately, little progress has been made in coming to any common understanding concerning the historical Jesus. The refusal to allow the possibility of the truly supernatural in concrete history takes away the entire interpretive framework that makes possible an adequate understanding of Jesus. As long as historical Jesus studies remain dominated by the scientific historicism and rationalism of the Enlightenment mind-set, they are destined to failure.

This is indicated by the fact that no common understanding of Jesus has emerged; the variety of the results of historical Jesus studies is striking. A partial list of what scholars have concluded shows that Jesus has been described as a radical Jewish cynic, a cynic sage,[40] a charismatic healer, a magician, a marginal Jew, an Essene, a social prophet, a reformer, a zealot, an eschatological preacher, and a noneschatological social critic. "Using the same texts and scholarly apparatus, dozens, perhaps hundreds of different Jesuses can be constructed."[41] Having cut away the essence of the narratives concerning one uniquely sent by God to bring the dawning of a new age and salvation to the world, historical Jesus scholars are forced to use their imagination in constructing new understandings of Jesus. Although they do not quite spin their hypotheses out of thin air, since they draw on the rich contextual materials provided by the contemporaneous sources, their quest must nevertheless

39. The essential voice of Jesus—that is, a fair representation of what he said rather than necessarily a verbatim account.

40. For arguments against this conclusion, see Keener, *The Historical Jesus of the Gospels*, 14–32.

41. Paul Johnson, in his review of Barbara Thiering's book *Jesus the Man* in *The Sunday Telegraph*, September 13, 1992. Telford, from whom I have borrowed the quotation, concludes, "In a nutshell, he has perhaps captured the problem and challenge of Jesus Studies today" ("Major Trends and Interpretive Issues in the Study of Jesus," 46–47).

be said to lack a coherent methodology.[42] Without the interpretive framework provided by the Gospels, which are our only significant sources about
Jesus, the discrete data accepted by these scholars become too fragmentary
and too capable of various construals. It is as if one were confronted with a
large number of discrete dots to be connected together to form a picture but
lacked the numbers that indicate which way the lines are to be drawn. What
happens is that each person connects the dots in his or her own way. The
resultant reconstructions often become little more than brilliant exercises
in subjectivity, and, as in the original quest, the differing portraits of Jesus
noticeably resemble the respective authors. Carl Braaten correctly concludes,
"All three of the quests have failed for the same fundamental reason. They
have fallen into a chasm that separates Jesus from the church. Their approach
to the historical Jesus suspends or brackets out the living reality of the church
as the necessary condition of affirming the essential identity of the earthly
Jesus and the risen Christ."[43]

It is an a priori starting point for most historical Jesus scholars that the
only acceptable approach is to depart from the NT's understanding of Jesus.
Out of a perceived necessity predicated on scientific historicism, Jesus cannot
historically have been what the NT and the church portray him as. Hence,
the real Jesus must be other than the Jesus of the Gospels, and the questers
proceed in their unflinching confidence in judging Gospel material as unreliable. Leander Keck notes that it is one thing to argue that the portrait of
Jesus in the Gospels does not correspond to the historical Jesus, but another
thing to conclude that it is a distortion, since "one can identify a distortion
only when one knows already what was actually the case—precisely what the
quest seeks to learn."[44]

What is positively debilitating in the quest, however, is the shift in the burden of proof that has taken place. Such a negative bias applied to historical
sources would make the historical study of antiquity practically impossible.
Historical knowledge would all but disappear. The shift in the burden of proof
puts a totally unreasonable demand on the historian. "Proof" is not the right
word here in any event, since all that historical knowledge can provide at best
is probable, not certain, knowledge.

Is the Study of the Historical Jesus Necessary?

It is part of orthodox faith that Jesus was fully human. It is a part of NT
christology that the appearance of Jesus in history involved a *kenōsis*, or
"emptying," of some kind (Phil. 2:7). The content of the emptying referred

---

42. So too concludes Telford, "Major Trends and Interpretive Issues in the Study of Jesus," 58.
43. Braaten, "Jesus and the Church," 61.
44. Keck, *Who Is Jesus?*, 19.

to in Philippians 2:7 is not specified, but presumably it was of the divine glory and certain divine prerogatives. We confront here the great mystery of the incarnation. It is worth studying the humanity of Jesus; however, the real story of Jesus is not in the humanity to the exclusion of the transcendent, but rather in the humanity that uniquely manifests deity and uniquely accomplishes the will of God. To limit ourselves to one side (either one) is inevitably to distort. Such is the interconnection attested to by our sources that the humanity cannot be really understood apart from the transcendent, and the transcendent apart from the humanity. We will not make sense of the Jesus of the Gospels if we strictly limit ourselves to the humanity of Jesus and exclude the rest.

That the Jesus of history was to some extent different from the Gospels' portrayal of him can hardly be doubted. It was the resurrection of Jesus, after all, that opened the eyes of the disciples to confirm beyond doubt who this Jesus was (note the experience of the Emmaus disciples [Luke 24:13–35]). After the resurrection of Jesus the disciples understood things with a clarity that they could not have had before the resurrection (see John 12:16). Inevitably, this postresurrection perspective has left its impression on the Gospel narratives. It is the Jesus of their new faith that they present, not some sort of neutral account of something that mattered little to them. The question, of course, is how much this has affected the narratives themselves. It can hardly mean that they created material wholesale to support their new understanding (we could look at the apocryphal gospels to see the sort of thing that the canonical Gospels might have done). Much more likely, it means that sometimes details were added or altered to make the narratives clearer or more applicable to the church. An example, in Peter's confession, is Matthew's alteration of Mark's simple "You are the Christ" to "You are the Christ, the Son of the living God." Another example is the addition of specific details to Jesus' prophecies of his crucifixion. We cannot expect the Jesus of history to correspond exactly to the christology of the church, impacted by, but not created by, the experience of the resurrection.[45] But if we cannot look for a one-to-one correspondence between the Jesus of history and the Jesus of the early church's faith, we can at least establish a degree of continuity between the two. And that continuity is of the greatest importance because without it the Christian faith is in danger of becoming docetic.

How did Jesus think of himself,[46] and how did the disciples think of him during his actual ministry? "God from God, light from light, true God from true God, . . . of one being with the Father," as in the Nicene Creed? The incarnation of the *logos*, as in John 1? Had the disciples any inkling that they were fraternizing with the second person of the Trinity, they would have

---

45. James D. G. Dunn has shown that the christology of the disciples precedes the resurrection experience. See his *Jesus Remembered*.
46. See Hagner, "The Self-Understanding of Jesus."

been paralyzed with fear. How far can we close the gap between the history and the faith?

It must be admitted that we are in no position to write a biography of Jesus. We do not have access to the kind of information that would require. Nor are the Gospels themselves biographies of Jesus in the full sense of the word. They are, rather, kerygmatic portrayals of the story of Jesus. What we can attempt is to lay down some of the simple facts available to us. In my view, a sketch of the historical Jesus would run something like this (and here it is just as important to note what is not said as to note what is said):

> Jesus of Nazareth came proclaiming that the kingdom (i.e., the reign) of God was uniquely dawning in and through his person and ministry, in fulfillment of the expectation of the Scriptures. In this capacity he was conscious of being uniquely the Son of the Father. That kingdom was now beginning in the ministry of Jesus, but it was also still future. In both present and future Jesus knew himself to be the supreme Agent of God's redemptive purposes. He accomplished healings and raisings of the dead as signs of the coming of fulfillment. Although Jesus never spoke of himself as such, he admitted that he was the Messiah (Mark 14:62), accepting the confession and acclaim as Messiah, indeed, Messiah as the unique Son of God. But he redefined the role of the Messiah by going to his death, in obedience to the will of God, conscious that his death was an atoning sacrifice for the sins of the world, on the model of the suffering servant in Isaiah 53. He spoke of and expected his future return to bring God's salvific plan to its consummation, including his role as judge of the wicked and the rewarder of the righteous in glory.

A portrait such as this is not adequate in itself, but it does show sufficient continuity to hold together the Jesus of history and the Christ of faith. The christology of the early church, via the catalyst of the resurrection, drew out the implications in the above material for the understanding of the person of Jesus. The Gospels, reflecting the postresurrection, post-Pentecost interpretation of Jesus, present us with a fully adequate understanding of Jesus. The interpreted Jesus provides the truest understanding of Jesus. Inspired paintings can be more useful and informative than photographs—indeed, more truthful.[47]

There are many like Bultmann who believe that the work of the historian is at best irrelevant to the believer. The need to justify one's position by argument is said to reflect a lack of faith. We cannot, it is sometimes said, make the historian a kind of high priest of the Christian faith, by whose "authoritative" but always changing conclusions we must shape our faith. It is, of course, true that historical scholarship can never prove the truth of Christianity. Nevertheless,

---

47. See Guelich, "The Gospels." Recent Johannine studies are increasingly open to finding information about the historical Jesus even in the Fourth Gospel. See Anderson, Just, and Thatcher, *Glimpses of Jesus through the Johannine Lens*; Anderson, *The Fourth Gospel and the Quest for Jesus*.

Christians must take up the challenge of historical study of Jesus that seems to disprove traditional Christian beliefs. Answers must be given to irresponsible claims and to wild speculations set forth as truth. Perhaps all that historical study can do is to show a sufficient degree of continuity between Jesus and the church. But this is a significant contribution, for it is vitally important that the Gospel story be shown to be rooted in historical fact.[48]

We may ask again, in conclusion, is it not possible to modify the historical method with an openness to the possibility of supernatural causation? We have, after all, entered a post-Newtonian era, where the phenomena of quantum physics have relativized the Newtonian system so that it is not entirely closed. Alongside necessity we now must reckon with contingency. The fact is, we simply do not know enough to be able to exclude the possibility of God's direct intervention in history. Reality, as scientists readily admit, is at bottom filled with the mysterious. The implications, furthermore, of postmodernism for epistemology and the newer understanding of history as necessarily more than brute facts, but as data inescapably interpreted, must now be allowed to affect our thinking and talking about historical reality. We must now take notice of the limitations and the relativity of the historical method as hitherto practiced and to begin to modify the method so as to make it more useful in coming to terms with a universe bigger and more mysterious than Newton's.[49]

As for the historical Jesus, C. F. D. Moule puts his finger on the point that needs to be made:

> The nearer you push the inquiry back to the original Jesus, the more you find that you cannot have him without a transcendental element. What you find is not a rationally intelligible person of past history, but a figure who, although a figure of actual history—datable, placeable—emerges as the fulfilment and crown of a long process of divine education of Israel, and as the one who precipitates decision and brings the Kingship of God to bear on all his circumstances. Here is history which only coheres and makes sense when it is interpreted as "Salvation-history."[50]

A Concluding Remark

The recent flood of books about the historical Jesus, or at least the majority of them, conclude that those who were closest to Jesus—the disciples and the earliest believers in him—either fundamentally misunderstood or misrepresented him in the most culpable manner. They assume that modern scholars, working with a set of presuppositions totally alien to the first century, and with

48. For a helpful treatment of the subject, see Keener, *The Historical Jesus of the Gospels*.
49. See especially the fine work of philosopher C. Stephen Evans, *The Historical Christ and the Jesus of Faith*.
50. Moule, *The Phenomenon of the New Testament*, 80.

ideological commitments no less than those of Christian scholars, know Jesus better! We are asked to believe in the truth of hypothetical reconstructions of Jesus that are totally inadequate to explain the origin of Christianity and the growth of the church, while rejecting the understanding of Jesus that alone can provide such an explanation. The conclusions of the radical historical Jesus scholars require too much of us, but their claims hardly constitute a devastating blow to the church's view of Jesus. Robert Morgan perceptively remarks, "The conflict is thus no longer between faith and reason but between a reasonable faith and a faithless reason."[51]

Bibliography

Akenson, Donald Harmon. *Saint Saul: A Skeleton Key to the Historical Jesus*. New York: Oxford University Press, 2000.

Allison, Dale C., Jr. *Constructing Jesus: Memory, Imagination and History*. Grand Rapids: Baker Academic, 2011.

———. *The Historical Jesus and the Theological Jesus*. Grand Rapids: Eerdmans, 2009.

———. *Jesus of Nazareth: Millenarian Prophet*. Minneapolis: Fortress, 1998.

Anderson, Charles C. *Critical Quests of Jesus*. Grand Rapids: Eerdmans, 1969.

Anderson, Paul N. *The Fourth Gospel and the Quest for Jesus: Modern Foundations Reconsidered*. LNTS. London: T&T Clark, 2006.

Anderson, Paul N., Felix Just, and Tom Thatcher, eds. *Glimpses of Jesus through the Johannine Lens*. Vol. 3 of *John, Jesus, and History*. SBLSymS 44. Atlanta: Society of Biblical Literature, forthcoming.

Aulén, Gustaf. *Jesus in Contemporary Historical Research*. Translated by Ingalill H. Hjelm. Philadelphia: Fortress, 1976.

Baird, William. *The History of New Testament Research*. 2 vols. Minneapolis: Fortress, 1992.

Barnett, Paul. *Finding the Historical Christ*. Grand Rapids: Eerdmans, 2009.

———. *Jesus and the Logic of History*. Grand Rapids: Eerdmans, 1997.

Beilby, James K., and Paul Rhodes Eddy, eds. *The Historical Jesus: Five Views*. Downers Grove, IL: InterVarsity, 2009.

Bock, Darrell L. *Jesus according to Scripture: Restoring the Portrait from the Gospels*. Grand Rapids: Baker Academic, 2002.

———. *The Missing Gospels: Unearthing the Truth behind Alternative Christianities*. Nashville: Thomas Nelson, 2006.

———. *Studying the Historical Jesus: A Guide to Sources and Methods*. Grand Rapids: Baker Academic, 2002.

Bock, Darrell L., and Robert L. Webb. *Key Events in the Life of the Historical Jesus: A Collaborative Exploration of Context and Coherence*. WUNT 247. Tübingen: Mohr Siebeck, 2009.

Bockmuehl, Markus, ed. *The Cambridge Companion to Jesus*. Cambridge: Cambridge University Press, 2001.

Boers, Hendrikus. *Who Was Jesus? The Historical Jesus and the Synoptic Gospels*. San Francisco: Harper & Row, 1989.

Borg, Marcus J. *Jesus, a New Vision: Spirit, Culture, and the Life of Discipleship*. San Francisco: Harper & Row, 1987.

51. Morgan, "The Historical Jesus and the Theology of the New Testament," 199.

Borg, Marcus J., and N. T. Wright. *The Meaning of Jesus: Two Visions*. San Francisco: HarperSanFrancisco, 1998.

Bornkamm, Günther. *Jesus of Nazareth*. Translated by Irene McLuskey and Fraser McLuskey with James M. Robinson. Minneapolis: Fortress, 1995.

Boyd, Gregory A. *Cynic Sage or Son of God? Recovering the Real Jesus in an Age of Revisionist Replies*. Grand Rapids: Baker Academic, 1995.

Braaten, Carl E. "Jesus and the Church: An Essay in Ecclesial Hermeneutics." *Ex Aud* 10 (1994): 59–71.

Braaten, Carl E., and Roy A. Harrisville, trans. and eds. *The Historical Jesus and the Kerygmatic Christ: Essays on the New Quest of the Historical Jesus*. Nashville: Abingdon, 1964.

Brown, Colin. "Historical Jesus, Quest of." In *Dictionary of Jesus and the Gospels*, edited by J. B. Green and S. McKnight, 326–41. Downers Grove, IL: InterVarsity, 1992.

———. *Jesus in European Protestant Thought, 1778–1860*. Reprint, Grand Rapids: Baker Academic, 1988.

Bultmann, Rudolph. *Jesus and the Word*. Translated by Louise Pettibone Smith and Erminie Huntress Lantero. New York: Scribner, 1958 [German original, 1926].

Charlesworth, James H. *The Historical Jesus: An Essential Guide*. Nashville: Abingdon, 2008.

———, ed. *Jesus and the Dead Sea Scrolls*. New York: Doubleday, 1992.

Charlesworth, James H., and Walter P. Weaver, eds. *Jesus Two Thousand Years Later*. Harrisburg, PA: Trinity Press International, 2000.

Chilton, Bruce D., and Craig A. Evans, eds. *Authenticating the Activities of Jesus*. Leiden: Brill, 2002.

———, eds. *Authenticating the Words of Jesus*. Leiden: Brill, 2002.

———, eds. *Studying the Historical Jesus: Evaluations of the State of Current Research*. NTTS 19. Leiden: Brill, 1994.

Conzelmann, Hans. *Jesus: The Classic Article from RGG Expanded and Updated*. Translated by J. Raymond Lord. Edited by John Reumann. Philadelphia: Fortress, 1973.

Crossan, John Dominic. *The Historical Jesus: The Life of a Mediterranean Jewish Peasant*. San Francisco: Harper & Row, 1991.

Crossan, John Dominic, Luke Timothy Johnson, and Werner H. Kelber. *The Jesus Controversy: Perspectives in Conflict*. Harrisburg, PA: Trinity Press International, 1999.

Dawes, Gregory W. *The Historical Jesus Question: The Challenge of History to Religious Authority*. Louisville: Westminster John Knox, 2001.

———, ed. *The Historical Jesus Quest: Landmarks in the Search for the Jesus of History*. Louisville: Westminster John Knox, 2000.

Dodd, C. H. *The Founder of Christianity*. London: Collins, 1971.

Downing, F. Gerald. *Christ and the Cynics: Jesus and Other Radical Preachers in First-Century Tradition*. JSOT Manuals. Sheffield: JSOT Press, 1988.

Dunn, James D. G. *Jesus Remembered*. Christianity in the Making 1. Grand Rapids: Eerdmans, 2003.

———. *A New Perspective on Jesus: What the Quest for the Historical Jesus Missed*. Grand Rapids: Baker Academic, 2005.

Dunn, James D. G., and Scot McKnight, eds. *The Historical Jesus in Recent Research*. Winona Lake, IN: Eisenbrauns, 2005.

Eddy, Paul Rhodes, and Gregory A. Boyd. *The Jesus Legend: A Case for the Historical Reliability of the Synoptic Jesus Tradition*. Grand Rapids: Baker Academic, 2007.

Evans, C. Stephen. *The Historical Christ and the Jesus of Faith: The Incarnational Narrative as History*. Oxford: Clarendon, 1996.

Evans, Craig A., ed. *Encyclopedia of the Historical Jesus*. New York: Routledge, 2008.

———. *Fabricating Jesus: How Modern Scholars Distort the Gospels*. Nottingham, UK: InterVarsity, 2007.

———. "The Historical Jesus and the Christian Faith: A Critical Assessment of a Scholarly Problem." *CSR* 18 (1988): 48–63.

———. "Historical Jesus Studies and the Gospel of Matthew." In *Methods for Matthew*, edited by Mark Allan Powell, 118–53. MBI. Cambridge: Cambridge University Press, 2009.

———. *Jesus*. Grand Rapids: Baker Academic, 1992.

———. *Life of Jesus Research: An Annotated Bibliography*. Rev. ed. NTTS 24. Leiden: Brill, 1996.

Evans, Craig A., and Paul Copan, eds. *Who Was Jesus? A Jewish-Christian Dialogue*. Louisville: Westminster John Knox, 2001.

Freyne, Séan. "Archaeology and the Historical Jesus." In *Galilee and Gospel: Collected Essays*, 160–82. Leiden: Brill, 2002.

———. *Galilee, Jesus, and the Gospels: Literary Approaches and Historical Investigations*. Philadelphia: Fortress, 1988.

Fuller, Daniel P. "The Fundamental Presupposition of the Historical Method." *TZ* 42 (1968): 93–101.

Funk, Robert W., and the Jesus Seminar. *The Acts of Jesus: The Search for the Authentic Deeds of Jesus*. San Francisco: HarperSanFrancisco, 1998.

Funk, Robert W., Roy W. Hoover, and the Jesus Seminar. *The Five Gospels: The Search for the Authentic Words of Jesus*. New York: Macmillan, 1993.

Gaventa, Beverly Roberts, and Richard B. Hays, eds. *Seeking the Identity of Jesus: A Pilgrimage*. Grand Rapids: Eerdmans, 2008.

Gnilka, Joachim. *Jesus of Nazareth: Message and History*. Translated by Siegfried S. Schatzmann. Peabody, MA: Hendrickson, 1997.

Goetz, S. C., and C. L. Blomberg. "The Burden of Proof." *JSNT* 11 (1981): 39–63.

Gowler, David B. *What Are They Saying about the Historical Jesus?* Mahwah, NJ: Paulist Press, 2007.

Gregg, Brian Han. *The Historical Jesus and the Final Judgment Sayings in Q*. WUNT 2/207. Tübingen: Mohr Siebeck, 2006.

Guelich, Robert A. "The Gospels: Portraits of Jesus and His Ministry." *JETS* 24 (1981): 117–25.

Habermas, Gary R. *Ancient Evidence for the Life of Jesus: Historical Records of His Death and Resurrection*. Nashville: Thomas Nelson, 1984.

Hagner, Donald A. "An Analysis of Recent 'Historical Jesus' Studies." In *Religious Diversity in the Graeco-Roman World: A Survey of Recent Scholarship*, edited by Dan Cohn-Sherbok and John M. Court, 81–106. BibSem 79. Sheffield: Sheffield Academic Press, 2001.

———. *The Jewish Reclamation of Jesus: An Analysis and Critique of Modern Jewish Study of Jesus*. Reprint, Eugene, OR: Wipf & Stock, 1997.

———. "The Self-Understanding of Jesus." In *Encyclopedia of the Historical Jesus*, edited by Craig A. Evans, 324–33. London: Routledge, 2008.

Harrington, Daniel J. *Jesus: A Historical Portrait*. Cincinnati: St. Anthony Messenger Press, 2007.

Harvey, A. E. *Jesus and the Constraints of History*. Philadelphia: Westminster, 1982.

Holmén, Tom, ed. *Jesus from Judaism to Christianity: Continuum Approaches to the Historical Jesus*. LNTS 352. London: T&T Clark, 2007.

———. "A Theologically Disinterested Quest? On the Origins of the 'Third Quest' for the Historical Jesus." *ST* 55 (2001): 175–97.

Holmén, Tom, and Stanley E. Porter, eds. *Handbook for the Study of the Historical Jesus*. 4 vols. Leiden: Brill, 2011.

Hooker, Morna D. "Christology and Methodology." *NTS* 17 (1970–71): 480–87.

———. "On Using the Wrong Tool." *Theology* 75 (1972): 570–81.

Jenkins, Philip. *Hidden Gospels: How the Search for Jesus Lost Its Way*. Oxford: Oxford University Press, 2001.

Jeremias, Joachim. *The Problem of the Historical Jesus*. Translated by Norman Perrin. Philadelphia: Fortress, 1964.

Johnson, Luke Timothy. *The Real Jesus: The Misguided Quest for the Historical Jesus and the Truth of the Traditional Gospels*. San Francisco: HarperSanFrancisco, 1997.

Kähler, Martin. *The So-Called Historical Jesus and the Historic, Biblical Christ*. Translated and edited by Carl E. Braaten. Minneapolis: Fortress, 1964 [German original, 1896].

Käsemann, Ernst. "The Problem of the Historical Jesus." In *Essays on New Testament Themes*, translated by W. J. Montague, 15–47. Philadelphia: Fortress, 1982 [German original, 1954].

Keck, Leander E. *A Future for the Historical Jesus: The Place of Jesus in Preaching and Theology*. Philadelphia: Fortress, 1981.

———. "The Second Coming of the Liberal Jesus?" *ChrCent* 111 (1994): 784–87.

———. *Who Is Jesus? History in Perfect Tense*. Minneapolis: Augsburg Fortress, 2000.

Kee, Howard Clark. *What Can We Know about Jesus?* Cambridge: Cambridge University Press, 1990.

Keener, Craig S. *The Historical Jesus of the Gospels*. Grand Rapids: Eerdmans, 2009.

Kissinger, Warren S. *The Lives of Jesus: A History and Bibliography*. New York: Garland, 1985.

Klauck, Hans-Josef. *Apocryphal Gospels: An Introduction*. Translated by Brian McNeil. New York: T&T Clark International, 2003.

Lemcio, Eugene E. *The Past of Jesus in the Gospels*. SNTSMS 68. Cambridge: Cambridge University Press, 1991.

Manson, T. W. "The Quest of the Historical Jesus—Continued." In *Studies in the Gospels and Epistles*, edited by Matthew Black, 3–12. Manchester, UK: Manchester University Press, 1962.

Marshall, I. Howard. *I Believe in the Historical Jesus*. Grand Rapids: Eerdmans, 1977.

Martin, Ralph P. "The New Quest of the Historical Jesus." In *Jesus of Nazareth: Savior and Lord*, edited by Carl F. H. Henry, 31–45. Grand Rapids: Eerdmans, 1966.

McArthur, Harvey K., ed. *In Search of the Historical Jesus*. New York: Scribner, 1969.

McKnight, Scot. *Jesus and His Death: Historiography, the Historical Jesus, and Atonement Theory*. Waco: Baylor University Press, 2005.

Meier, John P. *A Marginal Jew: Rethinking the Historical Jesus*. 4 vols. New York: Doubleday; New Haven: Yale University Press, 1991–2009.

———. "The Present State of the 'Third Quest' for the Historical Jesus: Loss and Gain." *Bib* 80 (1999): 459–87.

Morgan, Robert. "The Historical Jesus and the Theology of the New Testament." In *The Glory of Christ in the New Testament: Studies in Christology in Memory of George Bradford Caird*, edited by L. D. Hurst and N. T. Wright, 187–206. Oxford: Clarendon, 1987.

Moule, C. F. D. *The Phenomenon of the New Testament: An Inquiry into the Implications of Certain Features of the New Testament*. SBT 2/1. London: SCM, 1967.

Neill, Stephen, and N. T. Wright. *The Interpretation of the New Testament, 1861–1986*. 2nd ed. Oxford: Oxford University Press, 1988.

Nodet, Etienne. *The Historical Jesus? Necessity and Limits of an Inquiry*. Translated by J. Edward Crowley. New York: T&T Clark, 2008.

Oakman, Douglas E. *Jesus and the Peasants*. Eugene, OR: Cascade, 2008.

Patterson, Stephen J. *The God of Jesus: The Historical Jesus and the Search for Meaning*. Harrisburg, PA: Trinity Press International, 1998.

Perrin, Nicholas. *Jesus the Temple*. Grand Rapids: Baker Academic, 2010.

Porter, Stanley E. *The Criteria for Authenticity in Historical-Jesus Research: Previous Discussion and New Proposals*. JSNTSup 191. Sheffield: Sheffield Academic Press, 2000.

Powell, Mark Allan. *Jesus as a Figure in History: How Modern Historians View the Man from Galilee*. Louisville: Westminster John Knox, 1998.

Puig i Tàrrech, Armand. *Jesus: An Uncommon Journey; Studies on the Historical Jesus*. WUNT 2/288. Tübingen: Mohr Siebeck, 2010.

Renan, Ernst. *The Life of Jesus*. New York: The Modern Library, 1955.

Richardson, Alan. *History Sacred and Profane*. Philadelphia: Fortress, 1964.

Robinson, James M. *Jesus according to the Earliest Witness*. Minneapolis: Fortress, 2007.

———. *A New Quest of the Historical Jesus and Other Essays*. Philadelphia: Fortress, 1983.

Sanders, E. P. *The Historical Figure of Jesus*. London: Penguin, 1993.

———. *Jesus and Judaism*. Philadelphia: Fortress, 1985.

Schweitzer, Albert. *The Quest of the Historical Jesus*. Translated and edited by John Bowden. Minneapolis: Fortress, 2001.

Stein, Robert H. "The 'Criteria' of Authenticity." In *Studies of History and Tradition in the Four Gospels*, edited by R. T. France and David Wenham, 225–63. GP 1. Sheffield: JSOT Press, 1980.

Strauss, David Friedrich. *The Life of Jesus Critically Examined*. Edited by Peter C. Hodgson. Philadelphia: Fortress, 1972 [German original, 1835].

Sullivan, Clayton. *Rescuing Jesus from the Christians*. Harrisburg, PA: Trinity Press International, 2002.

Talbert, Charles H., ed. *Reimarus, Fragments*. Translated by Ralph S. Fraser. Lives of Jesus Series. London: SCM, 1971.

Tatum, W. Barnes. *In Quest of Jesus*. Rev. ed. Nashville: Abingdon, 1999.

Telford, William R. "Major Trends and Interpretive Issues in the Study of Jesus." In *Studying the Historical Jesus: Evaluations of the State of Current Research*, edited by Bruce Chilton and Craig A. Evans, 33–74. NTTS 19. Leiden: Brill, 1994.

Theissen, Gerd, and Annette Merz. *The Historical Jesus: A Comprehensive Guide*. Translated by John Bowden. Minneapolis: Fortress, 1998.

Theissen, Gerd, and Dagmar Winter. *The Quest for the Plausible Jesus: The Question of Criteria*. Translated by M. Eugene Boring. Louisville: Westminster John Knox, 2002.

Twelftree, Graham. *Jesus the Exorcist: A Contribution to the Study of the Historical Jesus*. Peabody, MA: Hendrickson, 1993.

———. *Jesus the Miracle Worker: A Historical and Theological Study*. Downers Grove, IL: InterVarsity, 1999.

Tyrrell, George. *Christianity at the Cross-Roads*. London: Allen & Unwin, 1963.

Van Voorst, Robert E. *Jesus outside the New Testament: An Introduction to the Ancient Evidence*. Grand Rapids: Eerdmans, 2000.

Wilkins, Michael J., and J. P. Moreland, eds. *Jesus under Fire: Modern Scholarship Reinvents the Historical Jesus*. Grand Rapids: Zondervan, 1995.

Witherington, Ben, III. *The Jesus Quest: The Third Search for the Jew of Nazareth*. Downers Grove, IL: InterVarsity, 1995.

Wright, N. T. *The Challenge of Jesus: Rediscovering Who Jesus Was and Is*. Downers Grove, IL: InterVarsity, 1999.

———. *The Contemporary Quest for Jesus*. Minneapolis: Fortress, 2002.

———. "Five Gospels but No Gospel: Jesus and the Seminar." In *Authenticating the Activities of Jesus*, edited by Bruce Chilton and Craig A. Evans, 83–120. NTTS 28.2. Leiden: Brill, 1999.

———. *Jesus and the Victory of God*. COQG 2. Minneapolis: Fortress, 1992.

———. *The New Testament and the People of God*. COQG 1. Minneapolis: Fortress, 1992.

———. "Quest of the Historical Jesus." *ABD* 3:796–802.

———. *The Resurrection of the Son of God*. COQG 3. Minneapolis: Fortress, 2003.

Zahrnt, Heinz. *The Historical Jesus*. Translated by J. S. Bowden. London: Collins, 1963.

7

The Origin and Reliability
of the Gospel Tradition

In the beginning of the church was the word, but the word of the gospel was oral, a living word (*viva vox*) rather than a written one. Although it is very difficult to know with certainty, the Gospels in our NT probably began to be written some time in the 60s, a generation after the death of Jesus. Although this may seem unduly late, there are good reasons that the Gospels may not have been written sooner than this. First, since the earliest Christians expected Jesus to return in a short time, there must at first have seemed to be no need for written records. Second, and far more important, the words and deeds of Jesus were preserved in a well-formed and stable repository of oral tradition. Indeed, so significant was this body of oral tradition that it continued to be maintained decades after the written Gospels appeared. This oral tradition did not come to an end, as one might have expected, immediately after the writing of the Gospels. Through the second half of the first century up to the opening decades of the second century there was an overlap between oral tradition and the written Gospels.[1]

In recent years there has been much confusion about, and misunderstanding of, oral tradition. The modern world, where memory plays such a small role in life compared to the ancient world, has little respect for oral tradition. Can oral material be passed on accurately for three decades or more? Can

---

1. "The situation of the Church in the years *circa* 60 to *circa* 160 AD is precisely this one, when written and oral tradition are circulating in the Church side by side" (Hanson, *Tradition in the Early Church*, 21).

the Gospels be regarded as trustworthy accounts? Even scholars who often have not studied the subject can perpetuate the popular impression that oral tradition is unreliable. Some like to point to the analogy of the parlor game in which a story is whispered from person to person, and then the last version, some five minutes later, is compared with the original story, usually with enormous and humorous differences. The Jesus Seminar appeals to modern psychological studies: "Short-term memory is able to retain only about seven items at a time. . . . One experiment has shown that most people forget the exact wording of a particular statement after only sixteen syllables intervene between the original statement and the request to recall that wording."[2] There seems to be no realization that these analogies do not at all fit the situation they are intended to describe. Here are four main reasons why this is so:

1. in the ancient world memories were far more practiced and retentive than today;
2. the extraordinary reverence that was given to the material by the disciples of Jesus, whom they regarded as Messiah;
3. the special form of the material that deliberately made it memorable;
4. Jesus undoubtedly often repeated his teaching.

We will look further into these matters below, but for the moment it should be emphasized that the oral tradition underlying the Gospels was quite a different matter from what we think of today as oral transmission and was much more stable than what we ordinarily think of as typically the case.

Memory in the Palestine of the New Testament Period

Memory played a far more important role in NT times than it does in most modern societies today, certainly more than in the modern Western world. Few have studied the role of memory in the Hellenistic and especially the Jewish world of the time of Jesus more thoroughly that the Swedish scholar Birger Gerhardsson. In his landmark book *Memory and Manuscript*[3] he shows how absolutely fundamental memorization was to education in virtually every learning context of the student, whether in the home, the synagogue, or the school. Learning by heart was the central means of learning in these educational contexts, and students therefore developed particularly well-trained memories. Memorization of Scripture was particularly stressed.[4] So too the

2. Funk, Hoover, and the Jesus Seminar, *The Five Gospels*, 28.
3. First published in 1961, it is now available in a reprint together with Gerhardsson's follow-up work, *Tradition and Transmission in Early Christianity*.
4. Gerhardsson refers to a statement in Jerome to the effect that "the Palestinian Jews of his day knew Moses and the Prophets off by heart; even the children demonstrated a remarkable

> "Moses received the Torah from Sinai, and he delivered it to Joshua, and Joshua to the el-
> ders, and the elders to the prophets, and the prophets delivered it to the men of the Great
> Synagogue. They said three things: Be deliberate in judgment; raise up many disciples; and
> make a fence around the Torah" (*m. 'Abot* 1.1).
>
> Among the disciples that Rabban Johanan ben Zakkai praised was Eliezer ben Hyrcanus,
> whom he described as "a plastered cistern which loses not a drop" (*m. 'Abot* 2.8).

tradition of the Pharisees, known also as the oral Torah, was maintained and transmitted by memory.[5] Indeed, there was a prohibition against the writing down of the oral Torah,[6] and yet much of it seems to have been handed down accurately for centuries.

It is, of course, a key and difficult question as to how much of this rabbinic material may be said to be true of the pre–AD 70 period and the time of Jesus. Unfortunately, Gerhardsson's book has been unjustly criticized for relying too heavily on the later materials to make his case.[7] However, Gerhardsson did not claim that the rabbinic materials exactly reflected the situation of the NT era. Rather, he suggests that there is a similarity or analogy between the way rabbinic tradition was handed on and the way the Jesus tradition was handed on. Given the Jewish context of Jesus, it is plausible to think that just as the later rabbis used memorization with their disciples, so too Jesus would have done so with his. Just as the Mishnah, for example, reveals the use of mnemonic patterns and techniques, so too do the Gospels.

Another criticism of Gerhardsson's conclusions is that the differences among the Synoptic Gospels are inconsistent with the idea of memorized material. (At the same time, however, there is a fair amount of material in verbatim agreement that might point to underlying memorization.) Usually it is not noticed that Gerhardsson made room for variations in the handing down of memorized materials. Memorization does not mean that there can be no changes or variations. Indeed, he pointed out this variability not only in halakic material (i.e., legal material, generally handled more conservatively)

---

capacity for memorizing" (*Memory and Manuscript*, 64). Rabbi Eliezer ben Hyrkanus was commended by his teacher as "a well-cemented cistern that never loses a drop" (*Pirqe 'Abot* 2.8).

5. The oral law was regarded as having been transmitted over the generations: "Moses received the Law from Sinai and committed it to Joshua, and Joshua to the elders, and the elders to the Prophets; and the Prophets committed it to the men of the Great Synagogue" (*m. 'Abot* 1.1).

6. See *b. Git.* 60b (cf. *b. Šabb.* 115a). This is a relatively late prohibition, probably unknown to Judah the Patriarch, who, in about AD 200, assembled the oral tradition into the Mishnah. But it reveals a high degree of trust in the reliability of oral tradition.

7. In the foreword to the new edition of Gerhardsson's *Memory and Manuscript* Jacob Neusner indicates how he has changed his mind since he wrote a highly negative review of the book when it first came out.

but also especially in haggadic material (i.e., nonlegal material). It is important to realize that what Gerhardsson's view provides evidence for is not memorization as verbatim repetition but rather as preserving a more general, substantial reliability. In a remarkable and important book showing the importance of eyewitness testimony to the reliability of the Gospel narratives, Richard Bauckham writes:

> In short, memorization was a mechanism of control that preserved the Jesus traditions as faithfully as the early Christian movement required. It was exercised to the extent that stable reproduction was deemed important and in regard to those aspects of the traditions for which stable reproduction was thought appropriate. . . . Factors making for stability and factors making for variability should not be considered in tension with each other. Each balanced the other to produce the combination of fixity and flexibility that was considered appropriate to each of the various types of Jesus tradition.[8]

With this, Gerhardsson would entirely agree.

Testimony in the New Testament and in the Early Church

There is persuasive evidence in early Christianity of the importance of oral tradition and memorization. In Paul's summary of the gospel in 1 Corinthians 15:1–8 he uses the explicit language of oral transmission: "I delivered to you [*paradidōmi*] as of first importance what I also received [*paralambanō*], that Christ died for our sins in accordance with the scriptures, that he was buried, that he was raised on the third day in accordance with the scriptures, and that he appeared to Cephas, then to the twelve" (1 Cor. 15:3–5). He uses similar language in speaking of the tradition of the Last Supper: "For I received [*paralambanō*] from the Lord what I also delivered [*paradidōmi*] to you, that the Lord Jesus on the night when he was betrayed took bread . . ." (1 Cor. 11:23).[9] Paul uses the same word for the reception of oral tradition, *paralambanō* ("to receive"), in Galatians 1:9; 1 Thessalonians 2:13. In 2 Thessalonians 3:6 he refers specifically to "the tradition [*hē paradosis*] that you received [*paralambanō*] from us." These references point to an important and stable handing on of oral tradition. Bauckham rightly concludes, "Thus Paul provides ample evidence of the formal transmission of traditions within the early Christian movement, and good evidence more precisely for *the formal transmission of traditions of the words and deeds of Jesus*."[10]

8. Bauckham, *Jesus and the Eyewitnesses*, 287.
9. When Paul writes "received from the Lord," he does not mean directly from the Lord, in which case it would be more natural to expect the preposition *para* instead of *apo*, but indirectly through oral tradition. The point is that the tradition ultimately goes back to Jesus himself.
10. Bauckham, *Jesus and the Eyewitnesses*, 271. Italics in original.

The word "remember" is used in a few places in the NT where it may refer to oral tradition: John 15:20; Acts 11:16; 2 Peter 3:2; Jude 17; Revelation 3:3. Especially to be noted is Acts 20:35: "remembering [*mnēmoneuein*] the words of the Lord Jesus, how he said, 'It is more blessed to give than to receive.'" Here a saying of Jesus not found in the Gospels (an *agraphon*) is drawn from the living oral tradition introduced with the verb "remember." The use of introductory formulae with this verb occurs after the NT in the Apostolic Fathers. In the two places where *1 Clement* (ca. AD 96) cites words of Jesus, they very probably are drawn from oral tradition, as the parallel structure seems to indicate, rather than from the Gospels. Both passages use an introductory formula that points in the same direction: "most of all remembering [*memnēmenoi*] the words of the Lord Jesus which he spoke, teaching gentleness and patience" (*1 Clem.* 13:1); "remember [*mnēsthēte*] the words of our Lord Jesus" (*1 Clem.* 46:7). Polycarp also introduces words of Jesus with a formula using the verb "remember": "but remembering [*mnēmoneuontes*] what the Lord said when he taught" (Pol. *Phil.* 2:3). Justin Martyr makes a number of references to what he calls "the memoirs [*ta apomnēmoneumata*] of the apostles," "which are called Gospels [*euangelia*]," which he places alongside the writings of the prophets (*1 Apol.* 67.3; 66.3; *Dial.* 101.3; 103.6; 104.1; 105.6; 106.3; 107.1). These references from the Apostolic Fathers and Justin show that memory was of the greatest importance in early Christianity.[11]

Evidence of a living, stable oral tradition is also found in Papias, bishop of Hierapolis in the early second century. Papias says that he preferred the "words of the elders" because "I did not suppose that information from books would help me so much as the word of a living and surviving voice" (Eusebius, *Hist. eccl.* 3.39.4, trans. Lake). Most interesting, and strange to today's world, is the fact that Papias held such a high view of oral tradition that he preferred it over the written sources available to him. He too uses the verb "remember" (*mnēmoneuō*) in referring to the words of the Lord (Eusebius, *Hist. eccl.* 3.39.3).

What is important to note in these second-century references to oral tradition is that oral tradition overlapped the written Gospels and did not come to an immediate end with the appearance of the written documents. It may be that the unknown factor at work in the similarities and differences among the Synoptic Gospels is the continuing presence and influence of the parallel oral tradition.[12] But it is the great similarity between the oral tradition, which our limited evidence reveals, and the written Gospels that provide strong evidence that the words of Jesus were treasured from the beginning and were handed down with the utmost care. This strengthens the conclusion that the Synoptic Gospels are reliable representations of what Jesus said and did.

11. For more detailed discussion, see Young, *Jesus Tradition in the Apostolic Fathers*; Hagner, "The Sayings of Jesus in the Apostolic Fathers and Justin Martyr."
12. See Mournet, *Oral Tradition and Literary Dependency*.

The Role of the Apostles as Custodians of the Jesus Tradition

Jesus chose twelve men to be disciples, to be continuously with him during his ministry, to hear his teaching and to see his deeds, and so to be equipped to be witnesses concerning these things. This was their primary responsibility in extending their master's work of making the kingdom known.

Jesus as Teacher and the Apostles as Learners

All four Gospels frequently present Jesus as a "teacher" (*didaskalos*).[13] It has been estimated that 75 percent of Matthew, 50 percent of Mark, and 66 percent of Luke are composed of teaching content.[14] Jesus even refers to himself as "the teacher" (Mark 14:14; Matt. 26:18; Luke 22:11). Jesus also refers to the teacher/disciple relationship in Luke 6:40 and Matthew 10:24–25 (where it is parallel to the master/servant relationship). "Rabbi," which occurs much less often, and not at all in Luke, also has in mind the teaching activity of Jesus. When in the Fourth Gospel Jesus' disciples address him as "Rabbi," the author defines the word in this way: "which means Teacher" (John 1:38 [cf. 20:16, where the similar word *rabbouni* used by Mary Magdalene to address Jesus, is likewise defined as "Teacher"]). So too Jesus was recognized as a prophet, again with his role of teaching in mind (Mark 6:15; Matt. 21:11, 46; Luke 7:16, 39). The statement of the disillusioned Emmaus disciples should be noted: "Jesus of Nazareth, who was a prophet mighty in deed and word" (Luke 24:19). The teaching activity of Jesus is important and takes up much space in the Gospels. "*Although Jesus is essentially more than the didactic terms can express, his active ministry is from the out-set partly a comprehensive didactic event.*"[15]

But it is not so much the volume of Jesus' teaching that impresses as it is the content and especially the authority of that teaching. This point is frequently noted in the narratives, and it deeply impacted his listeners. "And they were astonished at his teaching, for he taught them as one who had authority, and not as the scribes" (Mark 1:22 [// Matt. 7:29; Luke 4:32]). Jesus is an unparalleled teacher because he comes as the Messiah, the unique teacher of Israel. Matthew 23:8–10 is important here: "But you are not to be called rabbi, for you have one teacher, and you are all brethren. And call no man your father on earth, for you have one Father, who is in heaven. Neither be called masters, for you have one master, the Christ." The word for "master" here, *kathēgētēs*, probably means "tutor," someone who teaches outside the formal structures of education.[16]

13. On this subject, see especially Riesner, "Jesus as Preacher and Teacher." It is regrettable that Riesner's magisterial book *Jesus als Lehrer* (1981) has gone through three editions but never has been translated into English.
14. So Newman, "Some Translational Notes on the Beatitudes."
15. Byrskog, *Jesus the Only Teacher*, 206. Italics in original.
16. So Winter, "The Messiah as Tutor."

It is self-evident that Jesus cared deeply about the preservation of his teaching and would have taken special measures toward that end. This is one of the primary reasons he chose the Twelve: to be those who took into custody the tradition of both his words and the accounts of his deeds. And it is also for this reason that he presented his teaching so often in a form that would facilitate memorization.

The Apostles as Teachers and Servants of the Word

The Apostles were given the commission of maintaining and handing on the tradition about Jesus. They are the custodians of a holy tradition, the teaching and the work of the Messiah. It is important to note that the word "disciple" (*mathētēs*) is derived from the verb *manthanō*, which means "to learn." Thus to be a disciple is preeminently to be a "learner." This fits well the disciples' main function in the early church. Given their conclusion that Jesus was both Lord and Christ, they naturally would have treasured every word of their Master. This was no ordinary material; it was therefore a holy tradition, preserved with the utmost care.

At the end of Matthew, as part of the Great Commission, the risen Jesus tells the eleven disciples to make disciples of all nations and to baptize them, "teaching them to observe all that I have commanded you" (Matt. 28:20). Jesus taught the disciples, and now the disciples are to teach others what they heard from him.[17] The role of the Apostles as guarantors of the Jesus tradition was widely recognized in the early church. When in his prologue Luke indicates the historical reliability of his Gospel and its sequel, the Acts of the Apostles, he refers to his dependence on those who "from the beginning were eyewitnesses and ministers of the word [*hypēretai genomenoi tou logou*]" (Luke 1:2)—that is, the original disciples of Jesus who had been entrusted with the tradition.

Further pointing to the importance of the teaching of the Apostles in the early church is the note in Acts 2:42 that "they devoted themselves to the apostles' teaching and fellowship." Just as Jesus taught in the temple (Luke 19:47), so the Apostles now teach in the temple (Acts 5:25, 42). The Apostles are well aware of their important function as guardians of the tradition, as can be seen from their insistence in Acts 6:4 that they not be distracted from their devotion "to the ministry of the word [*tē diakonia tou logou*]." Indeed, there are repeated references throughout Acts to the importance of teaching in the early church.

While the Twelve remained in Jerusalem, as a kind of collegium,[18] other teachers perpetuated the tradition of the words and deeds of Jesus (e.g., in

---

17. In Matthew 23:8 Jesus admonishes his disciples not to be called "rabbi" (i.e., "teacher") because "you have one teacher." This in no way is a prohibition against teaching; it is meant to be an exhortation to humility, that disciples not desire or use high-sounding titles.

18. Thus Gerhardsson, *Memory and Manuscript*, 279; Riesner, "Jesus as Preacher and Teacher," 200.

Antioch [see Acts 13:1]). It is clear how important teaching was for Paul: in 1 Corinthians 12:28 (cf. Eph. 4:11) he lists teachers as third in the offices of the church, after Apostles and prophets (i.e., prophets within the church). In Paul's Letters we see evidence of the transmission of teaching. For example, in Romans 6:17 Paul thanks God that the Roman Christians were obedient "'to the form of teaching [*typon didachēs*], for the learning of which you were given over,' i.e. by God."[19] So too in Romans 16:17 Paul warns of opposition "to the doctrine which you have been taught [*tēn didachēn hēn hymeis emathēte*]." Even more striking is 1 Corinthians 11:2, where Paul commends his readers because they "maintain the traditions [*tas paradoseis*] even as I have delivered them to you." Paul also alludes to the traditions that he passed on to the Thessalonians (2 Thess. 2:15; 3:6; cf. Phil. 4:9). Gerhardsson's conclusion seems well justified: "In Paul's time there exists a *conscious, deliberate, and programmatic* transmission in the early church."[20]

The Role of the Apostles as Witnesses in Early Christianity

Above all, the Apostles in the book of Acts are designated as "witnesses" (*martyres*). The main criterion for the person replacing Judas among the Twelve was that he be one of those "who have accompanied us during all the time that the Lord Jesus went in and out among us, beginning from the baptism of John until the day when he was taken up from us—one of these men must become with us a witness [*martyra*] to his resurrection" (Acts 1:21–22). From this it can be seen that the Apostles are understood primarily as witnesses to the resurrection, but also to the ministry and teaching of Jesus. It is from the Apostles that the early church receives the truth about Jesus.

Peter, in the house of Cornelius, says specifically, "We are witnesses to all that he [Jesus] did both in the country of the Jews and in Jerusalem" (Acts 10:39). He adds a few lines later that the risen Jesus appeared "not to all the people but to us who were chosen by God as witnesses, who ate and drank with him after he rose from the dead" (Acts 10:41). This motif of the Apostles as witnesses appears frequently in Acts (see Acts 1:8; cf. Luke 24:48). The Apostles themselves clearly are conscious of the important role that they have as witnesses (Acts 2:32; 3:15; 5:32).

In the later documents of the Pauline corpus we encounter evidence of a very self-conscious perpetuation of tradition. Office bearers in the church are called to be effective teachers (in 1 Tim. 3:2 a bishop is to be "an apt teacher"; cf. Titus 1:9; 1 Tim. 5:17). Teaching holds a high priority. Timothy is instructed to "put these instructions before the brethren" (1 Tim. 4:6; cf. 4:11–16). He is exhorted, "Take heed to yourself and to your teaching" (1 Tim. 4:16), and "guard what has been entrusted to you" (1 Tim. 6:20). In this last text (as also

19. This translation is from BDAG 762b.
20. Gerhardsson, *The Reliability of the Gospel Tradition*, 16. Italics in original.

> I can even name the place where the blessed Polycarp sat and taught, where he went out and in. I remember his way of life, what he looked like, the addresses he delivered to the people, how he told of his intercourse with John and with the others who had seen the Lord, how he remembered their words and what he had heard from them about the Lord, about his miracles and about his teaching. As one who had received this from eyewitnesses of the word of life, Polycarp retold everything in accordance with the Scriptures. I listened to this then because of the grace of God which was given me, carefully copying it down, not on paper, but in my heart. And I repeat it constantly in genuine form by the grace of God.
>
> Irenaeus, according to Eusebius, *Hist. eccl.* 5.20 (trans. Gerhardsson, *Memory and Manuscript*, 204)

in 2 Tim. 1:12, 14) the word *parathēkē* is used, meaning "deposit (of truth) to be protected," hence something entrusted to someone to "guard" or "protect" (*phylassō*). In view is an objective chain of transmission: "And what you have heard from me before many witnesses entrust to faithful men who will be able to teach others also" (2 Tim. 2:2). The concern expressed here points to a body of tradition that is regarded as essential to the life of the church and therefore as material requiring the greatest care in preservation and transmission.

The tradition of the Apostles apparently is still intact and highly esteemed toward the end of the second century, long after the Gospels were written. Irenaeus writes that Clement of Rome (at the end of the first century) who "had seen the blessed apostles, and had been conversant with them, might be said to have the preaching of the apostles still echoing [in his ears], and their traditions before his eyes" (*Haer.* 3.3.3, *ANF* 1:416). Irenaeus assures his readers at the end of the second century that the tradition of the Apostles is still available to the church.

The Mnemonic Form of the Sayings of Jesus in the Synoptic Gospels

It is obvious that Jesus cared deeply about the preservation of his teaching, not only from the choosing of the twelve Apostles to be the special custodians of the tradition but also from the very form of his sayings. Most of the time Jesus seems to have used a variety of devices to make his words easy to memorize. The memorable form of Jesus' teachings is clearly evident even from the Greek text of the Gospels, although undoubtedly it was more pronounced in the original Aramaic spoken by Jesus.

In 1925 Oxford professor C. F. Burney published a book in which he compared the reconstructed Aramaic underlying the Greek sayings of Jesus in the Gospels with the poetry of the Hebrew Bible.[21] He was able to demonstrate

21. Burney, *The Poetry of Our Lord*.

that the two main characteristics of Hebrew poetry, parallelism and rhythm, were also clearly evident in the sayings of Jesus. He indicates many examples of synonymous parallelism, where the second line repeats the thought of the first (e.g., "A disciple is not above his teacher, nor a servant above his master" [Matt. 10:24]), and antithetic parallelism, where the second line contrasts the thought of the first (e.g., "Whoever exalts himself will be humbled, and whoever humbles himself will be exalted" [Matt. 23:12]). Burney concludes that "in this and in similar forms of antithesis we may surely believe that we possess our Lord's *ipsissima verba* more nearly than in any sentence otherwise expressed."[22] Burney also found examples of other types of parallelism, such as "step parallelism" (e.g., "He who receives you receives me, and he who receives me receives him who sent me" [Matt. 10:40]).[23] Burney also deals with rhythm, which is seen most easily in cases of synonymous and antithetic parallelism (e.g., "Every good tree | brings forth | good fruits, but the corrupt tree | brings forth | evil fruits" [Matt. 7:17]). Among examples of an antithetic quatrain he gives Matthew 6:14–15: "If you forgive | to men | their trespasses, Your Father | in heaven | will forgive you; But if you forgive not | to men | their trespasses, Neither will your Father | forgive | your trespasses." Among the many examples of rhythm Burney mentions is the two-beat rhythm of Luke 11:9 = Matthew 7:7: "Ásk, and it shall be gíven you; Seék, and you shall fínd; Knóck, and it shall be ópened to you" (another excellent example of this rhythm is Matt. 11:5 = Luke 7:22). Burney finds patterns of two-, three-, and four-beat rhythms in a great number of Gospel passages. In the last chapter of his book, by translating the Greek into Aramaic, Burney establishes that Jesus also made frequent use of rhyme in his teaching.

In more recent times, Joachim Jeremias, building on the work of Burney, made similar observations and drew similar conclusions. He found over a hundred examples of antithetic parallelism in the sayings of Jesus in the Synoptics.[24] Jeremias also discusses alliteration, assonance, and paronomasia in the sayings of Jesus when they are translated back into Aramaic.[25] After his survey of the evidence, Jeremias concludes the following: "The linguistic and stylistic evidence . . . shows so much faithfulness and such respect towards the tradition of the sayings of Jesus that we are justified in drawing up the following principle of method: In the synoptic tradition it is the inauthenticity, and not the authenticity, of the sayings of Jesus that must be demonstrated."[26]

22. Ibid., 84.
23. Ibid., 90–96.
24. Jeremias, *New Testament Theology*, 14–15.
25. Ibid., 27–29. Jeremias gives credit to Matthew Black for pioneering work in this area. See Black, *An Aramaic Approach to the Gospels and Acts*.
26. Jeremias, *New Testament Theology*, 37.

Riesner estimates that 80 percent of the teaching of Jesus is presented in some form of parallelism.[27] Close study of the teaching of Jesus in the Synoptic Gospels shows exactly the various characteristics that one might expect in material meant to be memorized. The sayings of Jesus are presented in memorable form: they are vivid and brief; they are structured and articulated in a way that is helpful to the memory. They make use of a variety of deliberate mnemonic techniques, including such things as alliteration, assonance, parallelism, symmetry, repetition, rhythm, and rhyme.

Conclusion

Contrary to popular thinking, there is no reason to be suspicious about the basic reliability of the oral transmission of the sayings of Jesus over a period three decades and longer. There is every reason, on the contrary, to think that the material was maintained and passed on with care and a remarkably high degree of precision. It was far from ordinary material that was being handed on; it was the teaching of the Messiah and Lord. The tradition of what Jesus said and did is the unique concern of the Gospels. There is no desire to communicate what others among the disciples or early church said and did, except only insofar as it helped to understand Jesus. Provision was made for the transmission of the tradition by the establishment of a special group with special responsibility for its maintenance. The material was presented by Jesus in a way designed to be kept in memory. All of this points to the basic reliability of the Synoptic Gospels. They bring us faithfully back to Jesus.

Gerhardsson's conclusion is apt: "In the Synoptic Gospels we hear not merely the whisper of the voice of Jesus, but are confronted with faithfully preserved words from his mouth and reports which *in the end* go back to those who were with him during his ministry in Galilee and Jerusalem. It is true that the accounts of Jesus' life and, to a certain degree, even a number of his sayings have been reworked by the early church, but the primary goal in all of this has been to understand them better."[28]

Bibliography

Bauckham, Richard. *Jesus and the Eyewitnesses: The Gospels as Eyewitness Testimony*. Grand Rapids: Eerdmans, 2006.
Black, Matthew. *An Aramaic Approach to the Gospels and Acts*. 3rd ed. Oxford: Clarendon, 1967.
Bockmuehl, Markus, and Donald A. Hagner, eds. *The Written Gospel*. Cambridge: Cambridge University Press, 2005.

27. Riesner, "Jesus as Preacher and Teacher," 202.
28. Gerhardsson, *The Reliability of the Gospel Tradition*, 17.

Burney, C. F. *The Poetry of Our Lord: An Examination of the Formal Elements of Hebrew Poetry in the Discourses of Jesus Christ*. Oxford: Clarendon, 1925.

Byrskog, Samuel. *Jesus the Only Teacher: Didactic Authority and Transmission in Ancient Israel, Ancient Judaism and the Matthean Community*. ConBNT 24. Stockholm: Almqvist & Wiksell, 1994.

Dunn, James D. G. "Altering the Default Setting: Re-envisaging the Early Transmission of the Jesus Tradition." *NTS* 49 (2003): 139–75.

———. *Jesus Remembered*. Christianity in the Making 1. Grand Rapids: Eerdmans, 2003.

———. "On History, Memory and Eyewitnesses: In Response to Bengt Holmberg and Samuel Byrskog." *JSNT* 26 (2004): 473–87.

France, R. T. "The Authenticity of the Sayings of Jesus." In *History, Criticism and Faith: Four Exploratory Studies*, edited by Colin Brown, 101–41. Downers Grove, IL: InterVarsity, 1976.

Funk, Robert W., Roy W. Hoover, and the Jesus Seminar. *The Five Gospels: The Search for the Authentic Words of Jesus*. New York: Macmillan, 1993.

Gerhardsson, Birger. *Memory and Manuscript: Oral Tradition and Written Transmission in Rabbinic Judaism and Early Christianity; with, Tradition and Transmission in Early Christianity*. Translated by Eric J. Sharpe. BRS. Grand Rapids: Eerdmans; Livonia, MI: Dove, 1998.

———. *The Reliability of the Gospel Tradition*. Peabody, MA: Hendrickson, 2001.

———. "The Secret of the Transmission of the Unwritten Jesus Tradition." *NTS* 51 (2005): 1–18.

Hagner, Donald A. "The Sayings of Jesus in the Apostolic Fathers and Justin Martyr." In *The Jesus Tradition outside the Gospels*, edited by David Wenham, 233–68. GP 5. Sheffield: JSOT Press, 1985.

Hanson, R. P. C. *Tradition in the Early Church*. Philadelphia: Westminster, 1963.

Hengel, Martin. "Eye-witness Memory and the Writing of the Gospels: Form Criticism, Community Tradition and the Authority of the Authors." In *The Written Gospel*, edited by Markus Bockmuehl and Donald A. Hagner, 70–96. Cambridge: Cambridge University Press, 2005.

Jeremias, Joachim. *New Testament Theology: The Proclamation of Jesus*. Translated by John Bowden. London: SCM, 1971.

Kelber, Werner H., and Samuel Byrskog, eds. *Jesus in Memory: Traditions in Oral and Scribal Perspectives*. Waco: Baylor University Press, 2009.

Knox, Wilfred L. *The Sources of the Synoptic Gospels*. 2 vols. Cambridge: Cambridge University Press, 1953.

Lohr, Charles H. "Oral Techniques in the Gospel of Matthew." *CBQ* 23 (1961): 403–35.

Mournet, Terence C. "The Jesus Tradition as Oral Tradition." In *Jesus in Memory: Traditions in Oral and Scribal Perspectives*, ed. Werner H. Kelber and Samuel Byrskog, 39–62. Waco: Baylor University Press, 2009.

———. *Oral Tradition and Literary Dependency: Variability and Stability in the Synoptic Tradition and Q*. WUNT 2/195. Tübingen: Mohr Siebeck, 2005.

Newman, Barclay M., Jr. "Some Translational Notes on the Beatitudes." *BT* 26 (1975): 106–20.

Riesner, Rainer. "Jesus as Preacher and Teacher." In *Jesus and the Oral Gospel Tradition*, edited by Henry Wansbrough, 185–210. JSNTSup 64. Sheffield: JSOT Press, 1991.

Stuhlmacher, Peter, ed. *The Gospel and the Gospels*. Grand Rapids: Eerdmans, 1991.

Torrey, Charles C. *The Four Gospels: A New Translation*. New York: Harper, 1933.

Wansbrough, Henry, ed. *Jesus and the Oral Gospel Tradition*. JSNTSup 64. Sheffield: JSOT Press, 1991.

Wenham, David, ed. *The Jesus Tradition outside the Gospels*. GP 5. Sheffield: JSOT Press, 1985.

Winter, Bruce W. "The Messiah as Tutor: The Meaning of *kathēgētēs* in Matthew 23:10." *TynBul* 42 (1991): 151–57.

Yarbrough, Robert W. "The Date of Papias: A Reassessment." *JETS* 26 (1983): 181–91.

Young, Stephen E. *Jesus Tradition in the Apostolic Fathers: Their Explicit Appeals to the Words of Jesus in Light of Orality Studies*. WUNT 2/311. Tübingen: Mohr Siebeck, 2011.

8

Form and Redaction Criticism

Two important critical approaches to the Gospels began in the twentieth century: form criticism and redaction criticism. Form criticism (*Formgeschichte*) would be more accurately called "form history." It is the study of the forms of the varying, individual units[1] that compose the Gospel narratives, and in particular the origin and history of these forms in the period of oral tradition prior to the written Gospels—that is, the three or four decades between the resurrection of Jesus and the writing of the Gospels. Redaction criticism is the examination of the process of editing ("to redact" is to edit) that took place in the taking up of the different sources used by the Evangelists. By examining the changes made by the Gospel writers—especially when the source used is available to us—by noting things such as omissions, additions, and alterations, we can deduce the special theological interests of the redactor Evangelist. Before looking further into these two types of Gospel criticism, however, we need to explore the several time frames that enter into the discussion.

The Three Life Settings of the Gospel Tradition

Growing out of form-critical study of the Gospels, three life settings (in German, *Sitze im Leben*) in the history of the tradition began to be employed. This provided a way to think and talk about the process of historical material from event, through interpretation, to recording in the written Gospels.

1. *The life setting of the ministry of Jesus (Sitz im Leben Jesu)*. This time frame comprises the period covered by the Gospels—in other words,

1. Each such unit is known as a "pericope," and often they are approximated by the paragraphs in the RSV translation.

117

the actual time of the life and ministry of Jesus. It provides a means of designating the period in which Jesus spoke and acted. It is the period in which the historical study of Jesus is especially interested.

2. *The life setting of the early church (Sitz im Leben der alten Kirche).* This is the period of oral tradition between the resurrection of Jesus and the writing of the Gospels. The argument of form criticism is that in this period the traditions concerning Jesus received an overlay of faith as a result of the resurrection experience of the disciples. That this happened to some extent can hardly be doubted. The question is to what extent it happened. That is, does the new strength of conviction and new depth of understanding that come to the disciples as a result of the resurrection mean that the tradition now becomes so altered that it is no longer a fair representation of what Jesus said and did? On the one hand, Rudolf Bultmann, a leading form-critical scholar, argued that the resurrection faith provided an impenetrable barrier to accurate information about the Jesus of the first time frame. This means, according to Bultmann, that we cannot get back to the actual Jesus of history. On the other hand, one might well argue that the resurrection, rather than being a barrier, is a lens that makes possible what is ultimately a more accurate understanding of Jesus. Now matters that had to remain implicit in the time of the ministry of Jesus can be made explicit. One sees retrospectively what one could not see in the rush and heat of the moment.

3. *The life setting of the author, the Evangelist (Sitz im Leben des Verfassers).* This is the time frame in which the authors of the Gospels actually write. Clearly, they write with their respective readers and readers' needs in view, and this fact affects the way in which they take up and use the source material available to them. That is, they slightly alter the material, omit, abbreviate, add, emphasize, and in a variety of other ways modify their sources, thus adapting the Jesus tradition to their readers' needs. This frequently happens in the Synoptics and can be clearly seen especially when we can compare the Gospel with its source(s), as when, for instance, Matthew and Luke use Mark. It is obvious, for example, that Matthew 15 considerably reshapes the account of Mark 7 about Jesus and the dietary law in order to make the material more amenable to Jewish Christian readers who continued to observe the law. Similarly, Luke 21 can be seen to recast the eschatological discourse of Mark 13 so as to clarify matters from Luke's post–AD 70 perspective.

The Three Life Settings of the Gospel Tradition

1. Jesus	2. Early Church	3. Evangelist
Jesus' ministry	period of oral tradition (30+ years)	Gospels

That the tradition of Jesus' words and deeds experiences some degree of transformation in the difference between the first and the third time frames seems inevitable. Nevertheless, such a view is not incompatible with the conclusion that the tradition has been handed down in a substantially accurate and trustworthy form. We are not talking about the kind of modifications of the tradition that end up in gross distortion wherein the Jesus of the church bears little relationship to the Jesus of history.

Form Criticism (*Formgeschichte*: "History of Forms")

Form criticism finds its beginning among OT scholars, especially in Hermann Gunkel's work at the start of the twentieth century on the different forms in the book of Genesis. Three major books on form criticism that applied to the NT, two in the same year, came out in Germany early in the twentieth century, inaugurating the discipline. These books focused on the forms of the individual pericopes in the thirty-year period of oral tradition, insofar as it could be determined from our Synoptic Gospels. Form criticism overlaps considerably with tradition criticism (*Traditionsgeschichte*, or "history of traditions"), which also focuses on the preliterary forms of oral tradition and their life settings, and it is therefore often impossible to distinguish the two.

Karl Ludwig Schmidt's 1919 book, *Der Rahmen der Geschichte Jesu*,[2] on the framework of the Gospel narratives, made a strong case that the narrative framework of the Gospels that binds together the discrete pericopes into a continuous story was the creation of the Evangelists. If one were to liken the fund of oral tradition to a basket of pearls, each corresponding to a discrete Synoptic pericope, then what the Evangelists did—Mark in the first instance—was supply the string onto which the pearls were put. The string corresponds to the narrative bits at the beginning and the end of pericopes that enables them to be presented as a coherent story. But this framework is entirely artificial and virtually removes the possibility of arriving at a chronology or specific location for much or most of Jesus' ministry. The one exception allowed is the passion narrative, where a fixed sequence was established early and already transmitted in that connected form in the oral tradition.

In the main, Schmidt's work, though challenged by some, remains convincing. Comparison of the Synoptic Gospels easily shows that the connective material is treated with much more freedom by Matthew and Luke than are the pericopes themselves, which remain much more stable, especially the words of Jesus. The Evangelists exercised the freedom to arrange their narratives in what they believed to be the most convincing manner, and they did not for a

---

2. A translation of the full title is "The Framework of the Story of Jesus: Literary-Critical Investigations of the Oldest Jesus Tradition." But many of Schmidt's insights had already been reached by Menzies, *The Earliest Gospel*, 27–29.

moment think of this as distorting or misrepresenting the story of Jesus. For a chronology of the life and ministry of Jesus we therefore have only a few fixed points, such as Jesus' baptism, Peter's confession that he was the Messiah, and the initial announcement of his sufferings and death, and then the relatively fixed sequence of the passion narrative. The Evangelists did not concern themselves with anything like detailed chronology within these key turning points.

A second book to appear in 1919 was *From Tradition to Gospel*, by Martin Dibelius.[3] He writes at the beginning of his book: "The literary understanding of the synoptics begins with the recognition that they are collections of material. The composers are only to the smallest extent authors. They are principally collectors, vehicles of tradition, editors. Before all else their labour consists in handing down, grouping, and working over the material which has come to them."[4] Turning to the forms themselves, Dibelius finds the major, but not the only, life setting of the materials to be the missionary preaching of the early church. He divides the traditional materials into the following categories: the passion narrative, paradigms, tales, legends, analogies, and exhortations. Paradigms are stories that end with a climactic saying of Jesus applied to matters of faith or conduct, thought by Dibelius and the form critics to be the sole significant purpose of the pericope. Vincent Taylor helpfully renamed this category "pronouncement stories."[5] *Novellen*, or tales, are miracle stories supposed by Dibelius to be told by professional storytellers. Legends, on the contrary, are "narratives of a saintly man in whose works and fate interest is taken."[6]

The third, and generally regarded as the most significant of the three books, is by Bultmann: *The History of the Synoptic Tradition*, first published in 1921.[7] Bultmann used classification categories similar to those of Dibelius, but different language. Dibelius's "paradigms" became "apophthegms" (concise sayings presenting general truth), which Bultmann subdivided into three classes of origin: controversies, schools, and biographical information. He regarded these life settings as ideal scenes, not as historical realities. Dibelius's *Novellen* (tales) Bultmann called *Wundergeschichten* (miracle stories), which he regarded as stories designed to prove the messianic identity of Jesus. Bultmann divides Dibelius's "sayings of Jesus" into five subcategories: logia (or wisdom words), prophetic or apocalyptic words, law words and community rules, I-words, and parables. Finally, Bultmann prefers the term "legends" to Dibelius's "myths." It is worth pointing out, with Vincent Taylor, that several of these categories hardly represent identifiable forms as such.[8]

---

3. The German original was titled *Die Formgeschichte des Evangeliums*.
4. Dibelius, *From Tradition to Gospel*, 3.
5. Taylor, *The Formation of the Gospel Tradition*, 30, 63–87.
6. Dibelius, *From Tradition to Gospel*, 104.
7. The second edition (1963) is much expanded from the 1921 original.
8. Taylor, *The Formation of the Gospel Tradition*, 31–32.

Form Classifications

Martin Dibelius	Rudolf Bultmann	Vincent Taylor
Paradigms	Apophthegms three types: controversy, school, biographical	Pronouncement stories
Novellen (tales) stories of miracles and healings, consisting of three parts	*Wundergeschichten* (miracle stories)	Miracle stories
Sayings of Jesus persuasion, exhortation	Sayings of Jesus five types: logia/wisdom words, prophetic/apocalyptic words, law words/community rules, I-words, parables	Not forms
Mythen (stories about Jesus)	Legends	Not forms

The original task of form criticism was the identification and classification of forms of the pericopes that were passed down via oral tradition together with conjectures about the life settings that gave rise to these forms. The attempt was made to show how the stories took form and shape, using the "laws" (which, however, cannot be demonstrated) of tradition.[9] Specific life settings in the early church, such as preaching, community gatherings, and debates, were suggested as possible situations in which the forms developed. From there, however, the form critics, especially Bultmann, went on to make judgments about the historicity of the pericopes, much of the time arriving at highly negative conclusions. Taylor, not unfairly, refers to Bultmann's work as "a study in the cult of the conceivable" that is "kinder to the possibilities than to the probabilities of things."[10] As the result largely of Bultmann's book, form criticism became known not so much for its study of forms per se but rather as a comprehensive indictment of the historical value of the individual Gospel pericopes.

Here, as everywhere, the valuation of history is governed by the presuppositions of the interpreters.[11] Bultmann's approach to the question is consistent with his approach to the historical Jesus. But Bultmann and those in his train ignore the integrity of oral tradition (explored in the previous chapter) and the ongoing presence of eyewitnesses in the time of the writing

9. For a denial of these so-called laws, see Sanders, *The Tendencies of the Synoptic Tradition*, 272.

10. Taylor, *The Formation of the Gospel Tradition*, 15.

11. See Hooker, "On Using the Wrong Tool," 581.

of the Gospels.[12] Vincent Taylor put a high value on the importance of eye-witness testimony.[13] At the same time, however, he was one of the relatively conservative scholars who saw value in form criticism and tried to rehabilitate it. "If in the hands of Professor Bultmann Form-Criticism has taken a skeptical direction, this is not the necessary trend of the method; on the contrary, when its limitations are recognised, Form-Criticism seems to me to furnish constructive suggestions which in many ways confirm the historical trustworthiness of the Gospel tradition."[14] Even Dibelius protested against Bultmann's skepticism: "It must be said quite emphatically that B's skepticism in all questions of historicity is not necessarily connected with form-critical criteria but with his conception of the nature of the primitive Christian community as well as his emphasis upon the difference between Palestinian and Hellenistic Christianity."[15] T. W. Manson put the matter wonderfully when he said, "A paragraph of Mark is not a penny the better or the worse as historical evidence for being labelled 'Apothegm' or 'Pronouncement Story' or 'Paradigm.'"[16]

Today form criticism per se is quite neglected. The value of identifying forms has been assumed by other subdisciplines of NT study such as rhetorical criticism, as well as literary and genre criticism. The impossibility of doing anything more than conjecture when it comes to the life setting of the preliterary forms of the Gospels is recognized widely. Far more important, however, is that the idea of the Gospel writers as passive compilers of the discrete pericopes of the tradition has given way to the understanding of the Evangelists themselves as active, creative theologians in their own right. Thus in the middle of the twentieth century form criticism began to be superseded by redaction criticism.

Redaction Criticism: Discovering the Theology and Life Setting of the Evangelists

As William Wrede had pointed out already in his influential book *The Messianic Secret* (German original, 1901), the Gospel of Mark is a thoroughly theological document, and the author anything but a neutral chronicler with interest only in passing along the pieces of oral tradition available to him.

12. On this point, see Bauckham, *Jesus and the Eyewitnesses*.

13. Taylor, *The Formation of the Gospel Tradition*, 41.

14. Ibid., vi.

15. This quotation is drawn from Dibelius's 1933 review of *The History of the Synoptic Tradition*, borrowed here from Hengel, "Eye-witness Memory and the Writing of the Gospels," 81–82. Hengel also mentions a 1922 review by Dibelius of the same book, in which he describes Bultmann's book as an example of "unbounded subjectivism" resulting from "a lack of sensitive empathy" (ibid., 82n44).

16. Manson, "The Quest of the Historical Jesus—Continued," 5.

With the growing recognition of the creative role of the Evangelists, attention shifted from preoccupation with discrete pericopes, to the Gospels as whole entities reflecting unique perspectives. It remains the conviction of redaction critics that the Gospels are documents of faith: written from faith (of the authors) to faith (of the readers).

Redaction criticism examines the editorial activity of the Evangelists. It looks in particular for special material added by a writer to what is available in his main source(s). It looks also for omissions and alterations of source material, and also at the order the writers give to their narratives. All these things are potential pointers to the purpose and special interests of the Evangelists, as well as to the identity and situation of their intended readers. Eventually, patterns emerge in these observations, on the basis of which limited but significant conclusions of a more general nature can be drawn (e.g., Matthew reduces the radical Torah critique of Mark; Luke lessens the eschatological imminence of Mark; Matthew is written to Jewish Christians and Luke to Gentile Christians). Of course, redaction criticism is most successful when the source or sources used are available for our examination. Such is presumed to be the case of Matthew and Luke, who very probably made use of Mark's Gospel and also a hypothetical source designated as "Q" (the relationship of Matthew, Luke, and Q will be addressed in the next chapter). Redaction criticism is far more difficult when the source is not available to us, as in the case of Q, to which we have only indirect access, but also in the case of Mark, where we can only guess at what his oral (or written?) sources may have been.

It is, of course, also the case that the Gospels, especially the Synoptics, have much overlapping material in common. The occurrence of so-called double tradition or triple tradition (and rarely quadruple tradition) points to the importance of the core of common material. Identification of this common material has the unintended result of highlighting the unique material in each of the Gospels. As Günther Bornkamm pointed out, "The particular theology and theme of the first three Gospels goes deeper into the substance of them than is generally recognized, and modifies their message not insignificantly, even though over large areas their traditions are the same."[17]

The breakthrough books in redaction criticism started appearing in the 1950s. Here I mention only the pioneering works.[18] Already in 1948 Bornkamm published a short redaction-critical study titled "The Stilling of the Storm in Matthew,"[19] showing how Matthew reinterprets the Markan story to make it

17. In Bornkamm, Barth, and Held, *Tradition and Interpretation in Matthew*, 11, cited in Rohde, *Rediscovering the Teaching of the Evangelists*, 15.

18. For a full review, see Rohde, *Rediscovering the Teaching of the Evangelists*.

19. In Bornkamm, Barth, and Held, *Tradition and Interpretation in Matthew*, 52–57. Included in the same volume is Bornkamm's essay "End-expectation and Church in Matthew," 15–51.

a metaphorical lesson about discipleship. An essay by Heinz Joachim Held, "Matthew as Interpreter of the Miracle Stories," in the same volume provides a further example of redaction criticism at work. It was Hans Conzelmann who did early redaction-critical work on Luke in his *Theology of St. Luke* (German original, 1954).[20] Conzelmann showed that Luke was a theologian who in Luke-Acts presents the tradition in his sources by the use of a salvation-historical line consisting of three time periods—Israel, Jesus, and the church—with Jesus as the center point. This structure had become necessary because of the delay of the *parousia*,[21] a reality that faced Luke more than Mark, whose imminent eschatology Luke abandoned. On the Gospel of Mark itself, Willi Marxsen's *Mark the Evangelist: Studies on the Redaction History of the Gospel* (German original, 1956) was one of the earliest attempts to arrive at its theological perspective. Because we have no direct access to Mark's sources, which probably were oral, the task is especially difficult. Marxsen admits this: "For here we depend on literary-critical analyses for separating tradition from redaction. It is quite clear that *final* certainty can hardly be achieved. But this insight does not exempt us from the attempt."[22] Of course, many more redaction-critical studies were published—particularly in the 1950s and 1960s—as authors became more aware of the active role of the Evangelists in the creation of the Gospels.[23]

It seems undeniable that each of the Evangelists appropriated and adapted the Gospel tradition for his own purposes. "Nowhere in redaction-critical studies does there appear, even merely by way of a suggestion, the view that the Evangelists dealt in an arbitrary way with the shaping of the tradition. On the contrary, it is the explicit opinion of scholars using redaction-critical methods that the Evangelists had fashioned their material to correspond to the needs of their time, and after all, this means the time of the life of the community."[24] So clearly there is a sense in which our Gospels tell us much about the faith and circumstances of the early church, but not necessarily more, as sometimes is claimed, than they do about Jesus himself.

The Problem of Circularity

One of the difficulties of redaction criticism is its obvious circularity. A reading of a Gospel results in the initial construction of a life setting—that is, an idea

20. The more suggestive title of the German original was *Die Mitte der Zeit* ("The Midpoint of Time").

21. This Greek word means "presence" or "arrival," and in the NT it is often used to refer to the second coming of Jesus, his return in glory.

22. Marxsen, *Mark the Evangelist*, 26.

23. For a review and critique of these, see Rohde, *Rediscovering the Teaching of the Evangelists*.

24. Ibid., 257.

of the situation and needs of the readers. Then, however, exegesis of specific passages proceeds confidently on the basis of that assumed life setting. This has resulted in the criticism of the method and of NT commentaries that make use of it. Although this kind of circularity cannot be avoided, it need not vitiate redaction-critical study of the Gospels. As with another famous unavoidable circle—the hermeneutical circle, where one's theological perspective affects the exegesis of texts, and the exegesis of the texts in turn affects one's theological perspective[25]—a conscious awareness of the problem and a continuous moving around the circle can help to avoid being misled. It is furthermore the case that the picture of the life setting of readers is reached by means of an accumulation of evidence, and that then a matter of coherence can give confidence that one is on the right track. So although caution is called for, redaction criticism retains its validity. But the necessarily hypothetical character of its results means that its proposals for the social setting of a particular Gospel remain probabilities at best.

Local or Universal Gospels?

In 1998 Richard Bauckham edited a book in which he argued that, contrary to what has been readily assumed by redaction criticism, the Gospels were written not for specific churches or specific localities but rather for "any and every Christian community in the late-first-century Roman Empire."[26] It seems clear that there are some useful correctives in Bauckham's argument. One wonders, however, whether it is necessary for him to pose his thesis in terms of such a strong either/or. A Gospel author can write for a specific community or communities and also have in mind that his book will be relevant to, and read by, a larger audience at the same time. On the one hand, all the Gospels indeed have a considerable body of basic content marked very little, if at all, by distinctives that can be related to a specific community, content that is universally relevant. On the other hand, each of the Gospels has unique content that in many cases seems explainable only if it is intended for a specific readership.

It is true that some redaction-critical scholars have assumed to know much more than we can know and have painted a picture with far too much definition and specificity. But to correct this does not require that we deny altogether that initially a specific readership may have been in mind. It is difficult not to think that the writer of a Gospel, himself a member of a local church somewhere, would not in the first instance think of his fellow church members and then others like them too as he wrote his Gospel (e.g., Matthew writing for the

25. Or, for another example of circularity, one reads the whole of Scripture in light of the parts, and the parts in light of the whole.
26. Bauckham, *The Gospels for All Christians*, 1.

needs of his community of Jewish Christians and also for Jewish Christians everywhere). Much even of this special material would have a wider application. At the same time, however, there are reasons to connect Mark with churches in Rome, and there are sufficient reasons to connect Matthew with Jewish readers, and Luke, probably the most universal of the Synoptic Gospels, with Gentile readers. It is, of course, absurd to think of an Evangelist writing a Gospel only for a single house church. But the ruling out of that high degree of specificity need not mean that there cannot be at least some reader-specific content in a Gospel.

What we need here is some balance. In the 1998 volume edited by Bauckham, Stephen Barton writes: "This does not mean that the quest for the Gospel *audiences* and their social location(s) is illegitimate. On the contrary, it is an important act of historical and social-scientific imagination. One positive consequence of it is that we are more aware than ever before of (what we might refer to broadly as) the social dimension of the reality of the Gospels."[27] At the same time, however, it remains clear that the Gospel narratives are fundamentally about Jesus rather than "about a hypothetical Christian community that scholars can reconstruct behind the Gospel."[28]

Whither Gospel Studies?

The heyday of form criticism, and to a lesser extent of redaction criticism, is past. But these disciplines still have much to offer in understanding the NT, and they are still worth employing. On the one hand, form criticism keeps us mindful of the importance of the oral-tradition period and of the impact of life settings on the transmission of the accounts of the words and deeds of Jesus. It also enlivens our sensitivity to the forms we encounter in the Gospels, even if their prehistory is hard to determine. Redaction criticism, on the other hand, helps us to appreciate the Evangelists as theologians whose life settings have an impact on the shape that the tradition is given, and it enables us to deal with the Gospels as wholes rather than as mere collections of fragments of oral tradition.

While these approaches to the Gospels will retain their validity, numerous new approaches to the Gospels have come into existence in recent decades. Gospel studies have increasingly moved away from what are now regarded as the outmoded paradigms of historical-critical study. This move is part of a larger shift, like the moving of continental plates, within the whole field of biblical studies. As early as the 1980s one could speak of "a change so radical as to be described . . . as nothing less than a second revolution, analogous to the introduction of the historico-critical method into Biblical studies two

27. Barton, "Can We Identify the Gospel Audiences?" 194. Italics in original.
28. Bauckham, *The Gospels for All Christians*, 2.

centuries ago."[29] The impact of various ancillary disciplines (e.g., linguistics, sociology, psychology, political science, and anthropology) on biblical studies has spawned new methods of studying the biblical texts. This is not the place to deal with these in any detail, but those that impinge the most on the study of the Gospels must at least be mentioned here.

As a way to get an idea of what is happening in Gospel interpretation, we may point to the emergence of three stages of development: interest in the history behind the text (the concern of traditional historical criticism), to the text itself as a literary artifact, and then to the reader in front of the text and to the process of reading itself. Some new trends in Gospel studies that are easily regarded as extensions of the historical-critical approach involve a new attention to matters such as sociology and anthropology, where exploration of the contextual background to the NT can be very rewarding.[30]

If there is a general rubric for the new developments of the second stage, it could be the "new literary criticism." The focus is on the Bible as literature, as a work of art, with a complete lack of interest in historical questions. Linguistics and semiology play a large role. In the Gospels it is the study of narrative, or narrative criticism, that stands at the center. As in a novel, it is the story that matters, in a nonreferential way; that is, it makes no difference whether anything within the text corresponds to historical realities outside the text. The story and the story world are of self-contained importance and worth studying on their own terms. In narrative criticism the focus is on things such as character and plot, narrative flow, the world within the text, the implied author and implied readers in the text (as distinct from the actual author and readers, who are of no concern), and the narrator. Other approaches, such as structuralism (searching for deep structures and universal codes as means of communication) and deconstruction (dismantling a text by showing its inconsistencies and implicit agendas), seem already to have exhausted their potential.

Other text-centered approaches to the Gospels can also be briefly mentioned. Rhetorical criticism (with rhetoric understood as effective communication) focuses on rhetorical structures and textual devices used in the Gospel narratives.[31] This approach is hardly incompatible with, or antithetical to, historical-critical approaches the way some of the other approaches are. So too special-interest methods represent a variety of approaches that can be helpful.[32]

---

29. Soulen, *Handbook of Biblical Criticism*, 5, referring to John Dominic Crossan. The point was already made by D. Robertson in his article on the Bible as literature in the 1976 supplementary volume of *The Interpreter's Dictionary of the Bible*, 547–51.

30. See, for example, Malina, *The Social World of Jesus and the Gospels*; Malina and Rohrbaugh, *Social-Science Commentary on the Synoptic Gospels*.

31. See Wuellner, "Where Is Rhetorical Criticism Taking Us?"

32. As an indication of the diversity of methods and interests, a look at the table of contents of two recent books is revealing. Thus, in Anderson and Moore, *Mark and Method*, the chapter headings, after an introduction, are narrative criticism, reader-response criticism, deconstructive criticism, feminist criticism, social criticism, cultural studies, and postcolonial criticism.

Finally, and very briefly, we note the shift of attention to the third stage, where the focus is in front of the text, on the reader and the construction of meaning by the reader. This moves us away from the meaning of the text in a remarkable manner. In reader-response criticism the reader is in the driver's seat. The text itself has no autonomy as far as meaning goes because meaning is brought *to* the text by the reader, not extracted *from* it. Essentially, readers manufacture meaning for themselves. Reader-response criticism obviously fits hand in glove with the growing postmodernism of our day. In its most potent form it rules out the possibility of any truthful exegesis and the determination of meaning of the text, so that the message of the text becomes no more than the reflection of the reader, the reader's presuppositions and agenda.[33] By its preoccupation with the reader and the process of reading rather than the text itself, this approach can offer little in the way of understanding the Gospels, and one can only hope that this is a temporary phase in biblical studies that will fade away in time.

By no means have I mentioned all the newer approaches to the Gospels, nor in the preceding paragraphs have I been able to do them justice. But it at least should be apparent how much is going on in the field of biblical and Gospel studies. Above all, what characterizes the present situation is a rich methodological pluralism and diversity of viewpoint. Where the diverse methods come together in conclusions that are harmonious, one may be grateful. But more often than not the newer approaches result in disagreement and confusion. Fruitfulness in the end, however, must be judged not by mere activity but by useful results.

Bibliography

Anderson, Janice Capel, and Stephen D. Moore, eds. *Mark and Method: New Approaches in Biblical Studies*. 2nd ed. Minneapolis: Fortress, 2008.

Barton, Stephen C. "Can We Identify the Gospel Audiences?" In *The Gospels for All Christians: Rethinking the Gospel Audiences*, edited by Richard Bauckham, 173–94. Grand Rapids: Eerdmans, 1998.

Bauckham, Richard, ed. *The Gospels for All Christians: Rethinking the Gospel Audiences*. Grand Rapids: Eerdmans, 1998.

———. *Jesus and the Eyewitnesses: The Gospels as Eyewitness Testimony*. Grand Rapids: Eerdmans, 2006.

Bockmuehl, Markus, and Donald A. Hagner, eds. *The Written Gospel*. Cambridge: Cambridge University Press, 2005.

In Powell, *Methods for Matthew*, after an introduction, chapters cover the historical-critical method, literary approaches, feminist criticism, historical Jesus studies, social-scientific studies, and postcolonial criticism.

33. For further discussion of this subject, see Hagner, "The Place of Exegesis in the Postmodern World."

Bornkamm, Günther, Gerhard Barth, and Heinz Joachim Held. *Tradition and Interpretation in Matthew*. Translated by Percy Scott. NTL. Philadelphia: Westminster, 1963.

Bultmann, Rudolf. *The History of the Synoptic Tradition*. Translated by John Marsh. 2nd ed. Peabody, MA: Hendrickson, 1963.

Carson, D. A. "Redaction Criticism: On the Legitimacy and Illegitimacy of a Literary Tool." In *Scripture and Truth*, edited by D. A. Carson and John D. Woodbridge, 119–42. Grand Rapids: Zondervan, 1983.

Conzelmann, Hans. *The Theology of St. Luke*. Translated by Geoffrey Buswell. London: Faber & Faber, 1960.

Dibelius, Martin. *From Tradition to Gospel*. Translated by Bertram Lee Woolf. New York: Scribner, 1965.

Evans, Craig A. "Source, Form and Redaction Criticism: The 'Traditional' Methods of Synoptic Interpretation." In *Approaches to New Testament Study*, edited by Stanley E. Porter and David Tombs, 17–45. JSNTSup 120. Sheffield: JSOT Press, 1995.

Güttgemanns, Erhardt. *Candid Questions concerning Gospel Form Criticism: A Methodological Sketch of the Fundamental Problematics of Form and Redaction Criticism*. Translated by William G. Doty. Pittsburgh: Pickwick, 1979.

Hagner, Donald A. "Interpreting the Gospels: The Landscape and the Quest." *JETS* 24 (1981): 23–37.

———. "The Place of Exegesis in the Postmodern World." In *History and Exegesis: New Testament Essays in Honor of Dr. E. Earle Ellis for His 80th Birthday*, edited by Sang-Won (Aaron) Son, 292–308. New York: T&T Clark, 2006.

Hengel, Martin. "Eye-witness Memory and the Writing of the Gospels: Form Criticism, Community Tradition and the Authority of the Authors." In *The Written Gospel*, edited by Markus Bockmuehl and Donald A. Hagner, 70–96. Cambridge: Cambridge University Press, 2005.

Hooker, Morna D. "In His Own Image?" In *What About the New Testament? Essays in Honour of Christopher Evans*, edited by Morna D. Hooker and Colin Hickling, 28–44. London: SCM, 1975.

———. "On Using the Wrong Tool." *Theology* 75 (1972): 570–81.

Malina, Bruce J. *The Social World of Jesus and the Gospels*. New York: Routledge, 1996.

Malina, Bruce J., and Richard L. Rohrbaugh. *Social-Science Commentary on the Synoptic Gospels*. 2nd ed. Minneapolis: Fortress, 2003.

Manson, T. W. "The Quest of the Historical Jesus—Continued." In *Studies in the Gospels and Epistles*, edited by Matthew Black, 3–12. Manchester, UK: Manchester University Press, 1962.

Marxsen, Willi. *Mark the Evangelist: Studies on the Redaction History of the Gospel*. Translated by James Boyce et al. Nashville: Abingdon, 1969.

McKnight, Edgar V. *What Is Form Criticism?* GBS. Philadelphia: Fortress, 1969.

Menzies, Allan. *The Earliest Gospel: A Historical Study of the Gospel according to Mark*. London: Macmillan, 1901.

Moore, Stephen D. *Literary Criticism and the Gospels: The Theoretical Challenge*. New Haven: Yale University Press, 1989.

Osborne, Grant R. "The Evangelical and Redaction Criticism: Critique and Methodology." *JETS* 22 (1979): 305–22.

Perrin, Norman. *What Is Redaction Criticism?* GBS. Philadelphia: Fortress, 1970.

Porter, Stanley E., ed. *Handbook of Classical Rhetoric in the Hellenistic Period, 330 B.C.– A.D. 400*. Leiden: Brill, 1997.

Powell, Mark Allan, ed. *Methods for Matthew*. MBI. Cambridge: Cambridge University Press, 2009.

———. *What Is Narrative Criticism?* GBS. Minneapolis: Fortress, 1990.

Redlich, E. Basil. *Form Criticism: Its Value and Limitations*. New York: Scribner, 1939.

Rohde, Joachim. *Rediscovering the Teaching of the Evangelists*. Translated by Dorothea M. Barton. Philadelphia: Westminster, 1968.

Sanders, E. P. *The Tendencies of the Synoptic Tradition*. SNTSMS 9. Cambridge: Cambridge University Press, 1969.

Schmidt, Karl Ludwig. *Der Rahmen der Geschichte Jesu: Literarkritische Untersuchungen zur ältesten Jesusüberlieferung*. Berlin: Trowitzsch, 1919.

Silva, Moisés. "Ned B. Stonehouse and Redaction Criticism. I. The Witness of the Synoptic Evangelists to Christ." *WTJ* 40 (1977–1978): 77–88.

———. "Ned B. Stonehouse and Redaction Criticism. II. The Historicity of the Synoptic Tradition." *WTJ* 40 (1977–78): 281–303.

Soulen, Richard N. *Handbook of Biblical Criticism*. 2nd ed. Atlanta: John Knox, 1981.

Stanton, Graham N. "Form Criticism Revisited." In *What About the New Testament? Essays in Honour of Christopher Evans*, edited by Morna D. Hooker and Colin Hickling, 13–27. London: SCM, 1975.

Stein, Robert H. "What Is *Redaktionsgeschichte*?" *JBL* 88 (1969): 45–56.

Taylor, Vincent. *The Formation of the Gospel Tradition*. 2nd ed. London: Macmillan, 1935.

Wrede, William. *The Messianic Secret*. Translated by J. C. G. Greig. Greenwood, SC: Attic Press, 1971.

Wuellner, Wilhelm. "Where Is Rhetorical Criticism Taking Us?" *CBQ* 49 (1987): 448–63.

9

The Synoptic Problem

Since the time of Johann Griesbach (1745–1812), scholars have referred to the first three Gospels of the NT as the Synoptic Gospels. The name refers to the fact that since these Gospels are so similar, have so much material in common, are so often in nearly verbatim agreement, and often present the same order of pericopes, they are easily put in parallel columns and thus "seen together" (*syn-optic*). The fact that there is such a large amount of exact agreement and at the same time significant differences constitutes what is known as the Synoptic Problem, a phenomenon that requires explanation. The problem is to explain the various data that confront us when we look at Matthew, Mark, and Luke (the Gospel of John is very different from the Synoptics and is not part of the problem).

In addition to the intrinsic interest of the problem, the answers to the question of the interrelationship of these three Gospels are important both for their impact on the issue of historicity and for the practice of redaction criticism. Do Matthew and Luke redact Mark, or is Mark a redaction, and reduction, of Matthew and Luke? The answer that one gives has an enormous effect on the interpretation of the Synoptics.

Early in the twentieth century it seemed to many that the Synoptic Problem had essentially been solved in favor of Markan priority, but many continued to question the emerging consensus. The Synoptic Problem, "source criticism" (of the Gospels), is complex and has generated an enormous amount of literature, and the discussion shows no signs of slowing down. It is difficult to deal with it abstractly, as I must here, without delving into specific analyses of the material with synopsis in hand.[1] And indeed, the best way to begin grappling with the Synoptic Problem is to work one's way through a synopsis, pericope by pericope. Again, as in so much, we find ourselves in a realm where there can be no talk of "proof," but only of degrees of probability.

A Look at Some Data

To get an idea of the scope of agreement we have in the Synoptic Gospels, we may indicate the following approximations. Almost all of Mark, some 90 percent, is found in Matthew, while more than 50 percent of Mark is found in Luke. Of Mark's approximately 665 verses (not counting the longer ending of Mark), something like 600 are found in either Matthew or Luke. Thus only about sixty-five verses of Mark are not found in the other two Synoptics; of Mark's eighty-eight pericopes, a mere four or five are missing in the other two Synoptics (Mark 3:7–12; 7:32–37; 8:22–26; 4:26–29; 13:33–36). In triple tradition (i.e., material present in all three Synoptics) passages the wording of Matthew agrees with Luke *against* Mark a mere 6 percent of the time. These data alone suggest that Mark provides the central core of the other two Synoptics. So far as distinctive material goes, Matthew and Luke together have some thirty-six pericopes not found in Mark. The special material of Matthew is designated as "M," that of Luke as "L." Matthew and Luke have a large amount of material in common, known as the double tradition, consisting of more than 230 verses not found in Mark. Just this glance at the data should prepare the student for the complex and interrelated arguments that may be necessary to deal with the Synoptic Problem.

Theories to Explain the Data

Oral Tradition

If, as we saw in chapter 7, oral tradition was a highly effective means of transmission in the ancient world, and if oral tradition is capable of explaining both verbatim agreement and slight differences, why not simply appeal

---

1. The standard Greek-text synopsis is Aland, *Synopsis Quattuor Evangeliorum*; it is available, together with the RSV on facing pages, in Aland, *Synopsis of the Four Gospels*. Also worth noting are Swanson, *The Horizontal Line Synopsis of the Gospels*, which provides the synopsis in lines rather than the customary columns; Orchard, *A Synopsis of the Four Gospels*, which changes the order of the synoptic columns to Matthew, Luke, and then Mark to facilitate seeing the material in a way more amenable to the Griesbach hypothesis. The Eusebian Canons, deriving from the fourth century, divide the four Gospels into small units by content and organize them into ten canons. They still are useful as a provisional synopsis and can be found in Barbara and Kurt Aland et al., eds., *Novum Testamentum Graece*, 27th ed. (Stuttgart: Deutsche Bibelgesellschaft, 1993).

to oral tradition as the source of all three Gospels and the explanation of the Synoptic Problem? This hypothesis is not impossible and cannot be disproven. Moreover, it has the advantage of simplicity, thus heeding the principle of Occam's Razor: the simple explanation is to be preferred to the complex.

At the end of the eighteenth century J. G. Herder (1744–1803) and, somewhat later, J. C. L. Gieseler (1792–1854) argued for the existence of traditions in oral form, rather than literary dependence, that could explain the origin of the Synoptic Gospels.[2] This view was also adopted a hundred years later by B. F. Westcott[3] and nearly another hundred years later by Bo Reicke[4] and John Rist.[5] Rist has argued for the literary independence of Matthew and Mark, suggesting that they derive independently from oral tradition.

Oral tradition is a factor to be reckoned with, and it could well work for some of the pericopes in the Synoptics, but whether it can account for the individual, entire Gospels is very doubtful. And while oral tradition could readily account for the similarities, it seems unlikely that the oral tradition could account for the many and extensive differences among the Synoptics. The fairly clear, observable redaction of Mark by Matthew and Luke here remains unexplained. There is furthermore the issue of the order of the pericopes in the Synoptics. As will be argued below, the Markan order seems to be the foundation of the order in Matthew and Luke. Can oral tradition, which except for the passion account focuses on individual pericopes, account for maintaining the order of lengthy series of pericopes? This grand version of the oral tradition hypothesis as the explanation of the Synoptic Problem has convinced few.

It may seem a little odd, in light of my earlier discussion of the reliability and durability of oral tradition, to dismiss this hypothesis so readily. Perhaps the main reason for doing so is the relative convincing power of the consensus conclusion of literary dependence among the three Synoptic Gospels. I will argue below that oral tradition continues to be an important factor in accounting for aspects of the Synoptic Problem.

An Ur-Gospel or Proto-Gospel

It is possible that a single, primitive (*Ur* in German) gospel underlies our present Gospels. If such a gospel existed, it might have been written in Aramaic rather than Greek. In 1779 (published posthumously in 1784) Gotthold

---

2. See the account of this interesting history in Reicke, *The Roots of the Synoptic Gospels*, 1–23.

3. Westcott, *An Introduction to the Study of the Gospels*, 207–12.

4. Reicke, *The Roots of the Synoptic Gospels*.

5. Rist, *On the Independence of Matthew and Mark*. Oral tradition apparently is the solution also advocated by Eta Linnemann (*Is There a Synoptic Problem?*), who supposes thereby to deny altogether that there is a Synoptic Problem.

Lessing (the same one who published the fragments of Reimarus) set forth just such a hypothesis of an Aramaic Ur-Gospel underlying the canonical (and noncanonical) Gospels. The same proposal was made by Johann Eichhorn in 1796, and the idea of a Greek Ur-Gospel was put forward by Herbert Marsh in 1798. Also subscribing to a form of the Ur-Gospel hypothesis was Friedrich Schleiermacher (1832).[6]

Although it is hardly an impossibility, an oral proto-Gospel is subject to the same criticisms as the appeal to disparate oral traditions. If the Ur-Gospel were in Aramaic, it is almost impossible that independent Greek translations would result in the amount of verbatim agreement that we encounter in the Synoptics. Even if a Greek proto-Gospel is in view, again the redactional changes and differences among the Synoptics are difficult to explain. But perhaps the biggest question about a comprehensive, written proto-Gospel is why it did not survive and why it was replaced by the multiple Gospels that we have.

Literary Interdependence

Since the late eighteenth century, the majority of scholars have been persuaded that the solution to the Synoptic Problem lies in some form of direct dependence among the Synoptics. Only some such solution can explain the data encountered in the Synoptic Gospels. The big question involves who is dependent on whom. Although, as we will see, there remains a strong consensus among scholars about the subject, the question, to an extent, remains an open one.

Theoretically, there are no less than eighteen possible relationships of interdependence among the three Synoptic Gospels (see fig. 3): six of linear descent (e.g., A was used by B, and then B was used by C); three where one Gospel used two of the others (e.g., A and B were used by C); three where two Gospels are dependent on the third (e.g., A was used by B and by C); and six where one Gospel is used by another, and the third Gospel uses the two of them (e.g., A was used by B, and then A and B were used by C).

Figure 3 **Hypothetical Patterns of Literary Dependence**

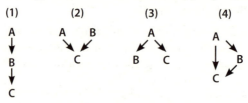

Of all these theoretical possibilities, three have emerged as more probable than the others.

6. For details, see Reicke, *The Roots of the Synoptic Gospels,* 7–9.

1. The Augustinian hypothesis (see fig. 4). This view obviously is based on the canonical order of the Gospels. It was defended by Augustine (354–430)[7] and is the view that the church held until it was challenged in the eighteenth century. Since, as we will see, there was an early tradition that seemed to support the idea that Matthew, regularly the first Gospel in the Gospel codices, was also the earliest of the Synoptics, it may have seemed logical that the order was chronological, and that therefore Mark used Matthew, and then Luke used Mark and Matthew.

Figure 4 **The Augustinian Hypothesis**

Matthew $\rightarrow$ **Mark** $\rightarrow$ **Luke**

2. The Griesbach or Two Gospel hypothesis (see fig. 5). This view also accepts the priority of Matthew, but it puts Mark as the last of the Synoptics. Although anticipated by Henry Owen as early as 1764,[8] this hypothesis is named after Johann Griesbach, who first mooted it in 1783 and then worked it out in detail in 1789.[9] It is also referred to as the Two Gospel hypothesis, which is to be carefully distinguished from the Two Source hypothesis, to be considered next. According to this hypothesis, Mark abbreviated the narratives of Matthew and Luke. As Griesbach put it, Mark omits so much of the other two Gospels because "he sought brevity, as one who wanted to write a book of small compass."[10] But that there was no need for an abridgment of Matthew, such as Mark represents according to the Griesbach hypothesis, is clear from the neglect of Mark in the church once Matthew became available.

Figure 5 **The Two Gospel Hypothesis**

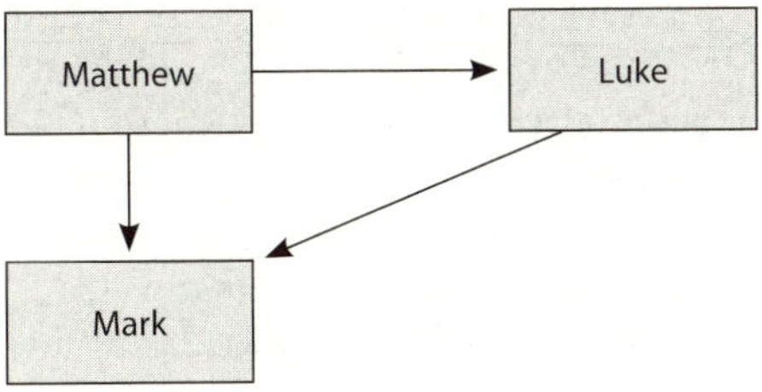

3. The Markan Priority or Two Source hypothesis, sometimes referred to as the Oxford hypothesis (see fig. 6). Supplementary to this hypothesis is the

7. In Augustine's words, "Mark follows him [Matthew] closely and looks as if he were his servant and epitomist [*breviator*]" (*De consensu evangelistarum* 1.2.4).

8. Owen, *Observations on the Four Gospels*.

9. Griesbach's main work, a very brief doctoral dissertation written in Latin, has been translated into English by Bernard Orchard, "A Demonstration That Mark Was Written after Matthew and Luke," in Orchard and Longstaff, *J. J. Griesbach*, 103–35.

10. Ibid., 106.

addition of M to account for the special material in Matthew, and L for the special material of Luke, thus giving us the Four Source hypothesis.

Figure 6 **The Two Source Hypothesis**

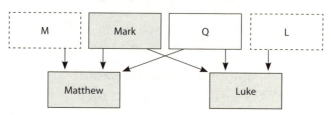

The idea that Mark, not Matthew, is the earliest of the Gospels and was used by Matthew and Luke is relatively recent in the history of the church and the study of the Gospels. This idea, which would become revolutionary for the study of the Gospels, first began to emerge in 1835–38 with the work of Karl Lachmann, Karl Credner, and Christian Weisse, leading from an Ur-Gospel to an Ur-Mark and finally to Mark itself as the earliest Gospel. Some are uncomfortable with the idea that up until this time the church had held the wrong conviction about which Gospel had been written first. But this is not a doctrinal issue, and it is not so unusual for something not examined closely because of a tradition, whose truth was assumed, to yield more truthful results when subjected to close scrutiny.

In the eighteenth century it became increasingly obvious, especially with the emergence of the notion of Markan priority, that the material held in common by Matthew and Luke but not found in Mark required explanation. The majority of scholars saw as unconvincing the possibility that this material could be explained by Luke's use of Matthew or by Matthew's use of Luke. This gave rise to the postulation of a hypothetical sayings source that would receive the designation "Q."[11]

The sayings source came into clearer focus with the work of G. Heinrich Ewald (1803–75) and especially Heinrich Holtzmann (1832–1910), whose name is usually given as the founder of the classic Two Source hypothesis. But above all it was the work of the members of the Synoptic Gospels seminar at the

11. "Q" probably derives from the German word *Quelle*, meaning "source." R. H. Lightfoot (*History and Interpretation in the Gospels*, 27n1), however, relates a story concerning Armitage Robinson, who believed that he might have been the first to use the designation "Q." According to his own account, Robinson was lecturing in Cambridge (in the 1890s) on the Gospel of Mark, which he regularly referred to as "P," considering it to be the reminiscences of Peter. Because "Q" is the next letter in the alphabet, he used it to describe the putative sayings source common to Matthew and Luke. This was several years before the symbol began to be used in Germany at the beginning of the twentieth century. This is challenged by W. F. Howard, "The Origin of the Symbol 'Q.'" For the ongoing discussion, see Neirynck, "The Symbol Q (=Quelle)"; Schmitt, "In Search of the Origin of the *Siglum* Q."

University of Oxford, under the leadership of William Sanday, that established the Two Source hypothesis and served as the real beginning of the current consensus.[12] Two members of the seminar produced particularly important books: John Hawkins, who collected a huge mass of data in his *Horae Synopticae: Contributions to the Study of the Synoptic Problem*, and B. H. Streeter, who set forth the classic statement of the Four Source hypothesis (adding M and L) in his famous *The Four Gospels: A Study of Origins*. Streeter's magisterial book assigned dates and places of origin, perhaps with undue confidence, to the sources and the Gospels.

Figure 7 **The Four Source Hypothesis**

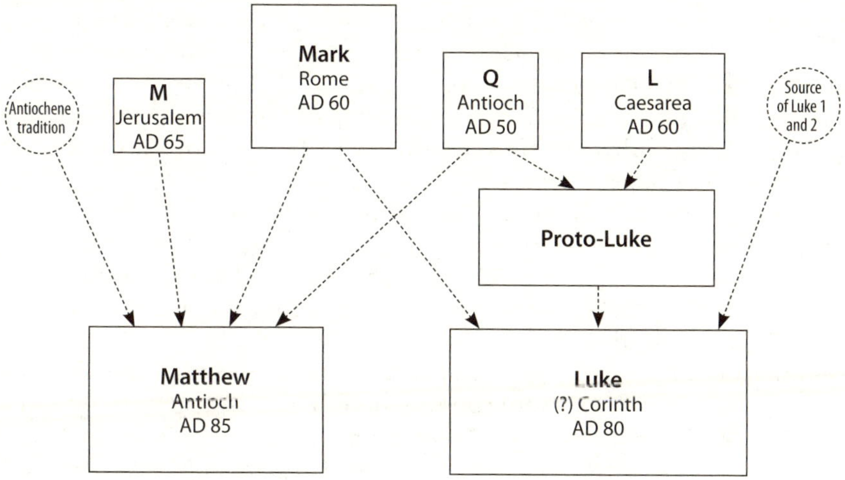

Diagram from B. H. Streeter, *The Four Gospels* (London: Macmillan, 1956), 150.

Was There a Proto-Luke?

B. H. Streeter offers a chapter concerning the hypothesis of a proto-Luke. The hypothesis was prompted by the fact that there are two sections in Luke that are not drawn from Mark, the so-called great (9:51–18:14) and lesser (6:20–8:3) interpolations, to which Streeter added 19:1–27 and 3:1–4:30 as material also not derived from Mark. So little of Mark is there in Luke as a whole (only about a third of the Gospel consists of Markan material) that Streeter no longer considered Mark to be the main source of Luke. Streeter argued that this material was derived from Luke's use of a Gospel-like document, longer than Mark, consisting of Q + L, namely "proto-Luke," which

12. See Sanday, *Studies in the Synoptic Problem*.

was Luke's main source and which he valued above Mark. Streeter argued that proto-Luke was independent of Mark and from about the same date (ca. 66).[13]

Vincent Taylor launched a full-blown defense of the hypothesis, even down to a description of the theology of proto-Luke.[14] He uses the following formula to describe what lies behind our Gospel of Luke: (Q + L) + Mark + Birth Stories = Luke.[15] Taylor presents eight cumulative grounds for the proto-Luke hypothesis.[16] He describes how, in the passion narrative and the eschatological discourse, it appears that the Markan material is inserted into a preexisting narrative. He emphasizes that, on the one hand, the Markan sections give no impression of a continuous whole, nor, on the other hand, does the Markan material by itself seem to present a continuous story. Mark, in short, "is a quarry from which stone is obtained to enlarge an existing building."[17] Luke's preference for his proto-Luke source explains why Luke has taken up only half of Mark. Taylor points out that the proto-Luke hypothesis explains the location in Luke's Gospel of the sixfold date in 3:1–3 (which one expects at the beginning of a book) and also the location of the genealogy in the same chapter. Finally, the hypothesis is consistent with Luke's notice in 1:1–4 about the existence of other accounts.

Among criticisms of the proto-Luke hypothesis, the following can be noted: the presence of phrases in 3:1–4:20 that agree verbatim with Mark; the similarity to Mark in the passion narrative; the sketchy character of the travel narrative of 9:51–18:14; and the fact that the historical framework of Luke seems based on Mark.

If the proto-Luke hypothesis could be demonstrated as true, several consequences would follow: we would possess an early witness to the life, ministry, and death of Jesus independent of, and comparable to, the Gospel of Mark; agreements between proto-Luke and the Gospel of John would have the effect of vindicating the reliability of aspects of the latter; and ideas found in proto-Luke would show that some characteristically Pauline themes are rooted in the Gospel tradition.[18]

Although Streeter's theory was picked up and elaborated by Vincent Taylor and accepted by worthies such as T. W. Manson,[19] G. B. Caird,[20] Joachim Jeremias,[21] and Ralph P. Martin,[22] it has not had a lasting impact, mainly because it rests on what must remain speculation and hence cannot be deter-

---

13. Streeter, *The Four Gospels*, 199–222.
14. Taylor, *Behind the Third Gospel*.
15. Taylor, *The Gospels*, 37.
16. Ibid., 38–40.
17. Ibid., 39.
18. Ibid., 42–43.
19. Manson, *Studies in the Gospels and Epistles*, 54.
20. See Caird, *The Gospel of St. Luke*, 23–27.
21. See Jeremias, *The Eucharistic Words of Jesus*, 97–100.
22. Martin, *New Testament Foundations*, 1:152–56.

mined with any confidence. It still remains a possibility that Luke is in the first instance dependent on Mark. Many introductions to the NT therefore no longer refer to the proto-Luke hypothesis, even in passing. It does, however, remain an intriguing theory worthy of ongoing consideration, and informed students of the Gospels should not neglect it.

Arguments for Markan Priority

The majority opinion among biblical scholars today is that Mark is the earliest of the Gospels. We must now look at the strength of this hypothesis and the reasons that undergird it.

1. Usually thought to be the most significant argument for Markan priority is the matter of the order of the pericopes. It is the Markan order that seems to explain the agreements in order among the three. On examination, the most probable conclusion is that both Matthew and Luke follow the Markan order. Most interesting here is the following observation: although both Matthew and Luke can and do depart from Mark's order, *nowhere do they ever agree together against the Markan order*. Of the pericopes in Matthew and Luke not found in Mark, only once do they occur in the same order. Mark thus appears to be the backbone of the Synoptics, and it is the Markan order that seems to be the fixed order.[23]

2. Although Mark is the shortest of the Synoptic Gospels, *for any single pericope Mark is usually the longest (i.e., wordiest) of the three*. Mark is anything but economical in the wording of his accounts. He regularly includes vivid details that are lacking in the other two Synoptics. These probably depend on eyewitness reports and point to Mark as the earliest of the Synoptics. Matthew and Luke, by comparison, omit redundancies, unnecessary words, and unnecessary details. The expansiveness of Mark does not fit well the view of the Griesbach hypothesis that Mark is an abbreviation of Matthew and Luke.

3. Readily noticeable to those with a knowledge of Greek is *the roughness of Mark's Greek compared to that of Matthew and Luke*. Straight through Mark, Matthew and Luke apparently are at work, continually smoothing out and improving Mark's Greek in a variety of ways. But under the Griesbach hypothesis, one must suppose that the bumbling

23. This argument does not amount to logical proof. As with nearly everything we deal with in the Synoptic Problem, other explanations are possible. Advocates of the Griesbach hypothesis refer to this alleged proof from the order of the Synoptics as the "Lachmann fallacy," wrongly laying it at the feet of Karl Lachmann. For discussion, see Tuckett, "The Argument from Order and the Synoptic Problem."

Mark consistently corrupted the good Greek of his two sources, Matthew and Luke. This seems extremely unlikely.

4. *Matthew and Luke appear to make deliberate changes of Mark for theological or other reasons*. It is extremely difficult to imagine Mark changing Matthew or Luke in these cases. Thus, to illustrate, Matthew appears unhappy with the statement of Jesus in Mark 10:18, "Why do you call me good? No one is good but God alone," and changes it to "Why do you ask me about what is good? One there is who is good" (Matt. 19:17). Matthew changes Mark 6:5, "And he [Jesus] could do no mighty work there," to "And he did not do many mighty works there" (Matt. 13:58). Peter's confession according to Mark is "You are the Christ" (Mark 8:29); in Matthew it is "You are the Christ, the Son of the living God" (Matt. 16:16), while in Luke it is "the Christ of God" (Luke 9:20). There are many more instances of this phenomenon. In general, it may be said that the christology of Matthew and Luke is somewhat higher or more developed.[24]

5. In addition to Mark's vividness of detail, *the presence of Aramaic expressions* in Mark seems to point to its antiquity and priority (see 3:17; 5:41; 7:11, 34; 14:36, none of which finds a parallel in the other Synoptics). These expressions could well go back to the Apostle Peter himself, as we will see in the chapter on Mark.

6. Also in favor of Markan priority is simply the matter of the content of this Gospel: *it is difficult to explain why Mark would have omitted so much of Matthew or Luke*—the birth narratives, the Sermon on the Mount, the Lord's Prayer, and so much more.[25] It is nearly impossible to believe that he omitted material like this, and much easier to conclude that he wrote before the other Synoptics and thus had no access to this material. Furthermore, the actual purpose of such an abbreviated narrative as Mark has never been given an adequate explanation.

7. Perhaps most convincing—and this can be seen only by working through a synopsis of the Gospels page by page—are *the myriad of small differences between Mark and the other two Synoptics that again and again are most satisfactorily explained as redactional changes of Mark made by Matthew or Luke*. That is, again and again the reading in Mark can be seen to give rise to what lies in Matthew or Luke, but not vice versa.[26] To be sure, there are a number of instances where the best explanation

---

24. See Head, *Christology and the Synoptic Problem*.

25. David Dungan (*A History of the Synoptic Problem*, 386) reports that at a 1984 symposium in Jerusalem, Basel professor Bo Reicke said, "It is *inconceivable* that the Gospel authors would omit anything." This is, of course, an exaggeration, but it is not difficult to understand why Reicke would say such a thing.

26. One of the most interesting arguments along this line is that of G. M. Styler, who points to a number of oddities in Matthew's logic or language that can easily (and perhaps only) be

seems to be that Mark has changed Matthew or Luke. But these are relatively few in number, and thus they are anomalies, given the vast number of cases where the redaction is most easily understood as going the other way. Attempts made to explain the differences as the result of Mark's redaction of Matthew or Luke are almost always unconvincing, even if possible.

These arguments, of course, do not amount to proof, but they do have a cumulative effect that has been persuasive to the majority of those who have studied the subject. Although those who disagree with the conclusion just drawn have answers for the various points made above, the arguments for Matthean priority are hardly adequate to overcome the case that has been made.

The Q Hypothesis

Once we grant the probability that Matthew and Luke used Mark as their primary source, the question emerges concerning the material common to Matthew and Luke that is not found in Mark. Where does this material come from? And it is here that the most controversial aspect of the hypothesis of Markan priority enters the picture: the conjectural Q.

For a while, the disillusionment with the positing of a gossamer Q seemed to be growing. There remain a good number of scholars who understandably resist the idea of a source that no one has ever seen,[27] and of course this is a common complaint by advocates of the hypothesis of Matthean priority, where usually it is argued that Luke knew and used Matthew (thus avoiding the need for Q). But in recent years the strength of the Q hypothesis seems again evident. Indeed, there is what amounts to a growing Q industry, with a steady stream of books upholding the Q hypothesis. As part of this renaissance, one thinks of the Jesus Seminar, but others too, especially John Kloppenborg Verbin[28] and James Robinson,[29] who have helped to produce the standard critical edition of Q.[30] What began as a unified Q soon became divided into a version of Q used by Matthew (QMatt) and a version used by Luke (QLuke), and into earlier and later versions of Q (i.e., Q1, Q2, Q3), thereby multiplying theoretical sources at will, but with no solid evidence and no way of verifying the speculations. It seems that one hypothetical source has a way of spawning

---

explained by Matthew's retention of an ill-fitting word drawn from Mark. See Styler, "The Priority of Mark," which remains one of the most persuasive defenses of Markan priority.

27. See, for example, Farrer, "On Dispensing with Q"; Goulder, "Is Q a Juggernaut?"; Goodacre, *The Case against Q*.

28. See Kloppenborg Verbin, *Excavating Q*.

29. See Robinson, *The Sayings Gospel Q*.

30. Robinson, Hoffman, and Kloppenborg, *The Critical Edition of Q*. In this volume, see Robinson, "History of Q Research," xix–lxxi.

others. Perhaps never before has so much been written about something as tenuous as Q necessarily remains.

The Q hypothesis exists solely as an explanation of the rather large amount of material, usually calculated at about 230 verses, that is common to Matthew and Luke but is not found in, and hence not derived from, Mark. This material in Matthew and Luke is not simply similar; *often it is in verbatim agreement that points to a common, though unknown, source.* Unless one posits a hypothetical source such as Q, the only explanation is direct borrowing between the two, whether on Matthew's or Luke's part. But, as I will argue below, such an explanation is unconvincing.

A key fact supporting the existence of Q is that this special material in Matthew and Luke is not simply distributed randomly, here and there, in no order; on the contrary, it is *often, though not always, found in the same order in the two Gospels.*[31] Of the two Gospels, Luke is generally thought to follow Q more closely, and the reconstructed Q is commonly given Lukan verse numberings (e.g., Q 19:26 = Luke 19:26).

Further arguments supporting the existence of Q have been offered. An interesting observation that seems to point to Q concerns doublets—that is, occasions where a story or saying occurs twice in the same Gospel. Thus, for example, the saying of Jesus "For to him who has will more be given" is found in the triple tradition (Matt. 13:12; Mark 4:25; Luke 8:18) *and* in the double tradition or Q (Matt. 25:29; Luke 19:26).[32] In the case of some doublets, the first part of the doublet comes from Mark, while the second is non-Markan—that is, Q material (e.g., Luke 8:16 and Luke 11:33, the first from Mark 4:21, the second paralleled in Matt. 5:15 and hence derived from Q). Another important point often noted is that there is no consistency in whether the Q material in Matthew or in Luke appears to be more "primitive" or original, as one might expect if either were borrowing from the other.

There seem to be good reasons to accept the Q hypothesis, although whether it should be considered a written source or consisting of oral tradition is another question. Oral tradition, as we have seen, is capable of explaining both stability and variability of material. Variations in the wording of Q in Matthew and in Luke are easily explained if Q is conceived as oral tradition(s) rather than a written document. But only a written Q seems able to account for the common order of the material in Matthew and Luke. Since Q material predates the Synoptic Gospels, whether oral or written, it provides us with the earliest layer of tradition about Jesus, and accordingly it lays claim to a high historical reliability. As such, it continues to be of vital importance in the quest of the historical Jesus.

31. See Taylor, "The Original Order of Q."

32. Werner Kümmel (*Introduction to the New Testament*, 66–67) regards the doublets as "decisive evidence" and incontrovertible proof of a document such as Q. For a full list of such doublets, see Hawkins, *Horae Synopticae*, 80–106.

The Question of Whether Luke Might Have Known Matthew or Vice Versa

Those who simply cannot accept the existence of a hypothetical document find their alternative explanation of the double tradition in Luke's use of Matthew (or, for a very few, Matthew's use of Luke). It is true that if Luke made use of Matthew or vice versa, there would be no need for Q, and the economy of Occam's Razor would be satisfied. So too would the advocates of Matthean priority be satisfied, and pleased at the collapse of an important pillar of the Two Source hypothesis.

At the same time, however, the nonexistence of Q is not necessarily the automatic downfall of Markan priority. One significant solution to the Synoptic Problem is *the Farrer hypothesis*, which posits the priority of Mark, but then also the use of Matthew by Luke, thereby avoiding the necessity of Q.[33] In recent years this hypothesis has been championed by Michael Goulder[34] and Mark Goodacre.[35] Their argument is that the non-Markan material in Luke can be explained on the basis of Luke's use of Matthew.[36] And it must be admitted that it can be explained in this way, and that it is attractive not to have to suppose the existence of a hypothetical source. Nevertheless, the question is still whether this explanation is the most probable one.

There are significant reasons why scholars have resisted the Farrer hypothesis. The first is why, if Luke made use of Matthew (or if Matthew made use of Luke[37]), are the two Gospels so different? We may begin with the infancy narratives, which are very different. It begs the question to say that Luke knew Matthew (or vice versa) but chose not to make use of it. Similarly, the post-resurrection narratives of the two Gospels are quite different. Or we may take as an illustration Matthew's Sermon on the Mount. If Luke is dependent on Matthew, he has badly fragmented the Sermon on the Mount and sprinkled it in different places.[38] So too the other major Matthean discourses disappear as such, with their contents distributed here and there. And Matthew's Beatitudes

33. See Farrer, "On Dispensing with Q."

34. See Goulder, *Luke*; idem, "Luke's Knowledge of Matthew"; idem, "Is Q a Juggernaut?"

35. See Goodacre, *Goulder and the Gospels*; idem, *The Case against Q*. See also Goodacre and Perrin, *Questioning Q*; Franklin, *Luke*, 164–375; Gundry, "Matthean Foreign Bodies in Agreements of Luke with Matthew against Mark."

36. For a full defense of this position, see McNicol, Dungan, and Peabody, *Beyond the Q Impasse*.

37. This is a decidedly minority viewpoint because it depends on dating Matthew later than Luke. In recent literature, see Huggins, "Matthean Posteriority"; Hengel, *The Four Gospels and the One Gospel of Jesus Christ*, 169–207. Hengel, however, is not interested in denying the existence of Q.

38. Note Hengel's comment: "[Luke] would not have torn apart discourses which have been worked out so masterfully, but integrated them into his work. One could make a Sermon on the Mount out of the Sermon on the Plain, but not vice versa. . . . In no way may he be made the destroyer of such a grandiose work as that of Matthew, by claiming that he copied out Matthew

and Lord's Prayer are abbreviated. All this could, of course, have been done by Luke. But what would have been his motivation? Moreover, why would he treat the Gospel of Matthew so rudely, when he tends to follow Mark (and possibly Q) rather closely?

Among other problems for arguing that Luke used Matthew is the difficulty of explaining why Luke consistently places Matthew's non-Markan material (Q) in different contexts than it is given in Matthew (the only exceptions are the preaching of John the Baptist and the temptation narrative). Another interesting problem for this view is that in triple tradition passages, material added by Matthew is only in very rare instances picked up by Luke (note Luke's omission of Matt. 16:16–19). It is unlikely that this is due to coincidence. Finally, there seems to be no consistent sense of development from Matthew to Luke in terms of more primitive or developed material.

The Minor Agreements between Matthew and Luke against Mark

The so-called minor agreements are widely thought by advocates of Matthean priority to be the Achilles' heel of the hypothesis of Markan priority, and so they have received considerable attention from both sides. As in the case of the order of pericopes, so too relatively rarely do Matthew and Luke agree in wording against Mark in triple tradition passages. Because, as we have just noted, it is difficult (though not impossible) to think that Luke knew Matthew or that Matthew knew Luke, the majority of scholars have resisted this suggestion as the explanation of the phenomena.

The minor agreements consist of numerous (hundreds, possibly as many as a thousand), generally small, some tiny, agreements between Matthew and Luke that, since they occur in triple tradition passages, are not ordinarily explained by Q. These agreements consist not only in various differences from Mark, involving vocabulary, word order, and so on, but also in common omissions of words or phrases. These have been tabulated in detail.[39] An example of an addition is the presence of *kyrios* ("Lord") in Matthew 8:2 and Luke 5:12, "Lord, if you will," in contrast to the lack of the address in Mark 1:40, "If you will." An example of an omission is the reference to the dazzling white garments of the transfigured Jesus, which Mark describes "as no fuller on earth could bleach them" (Mark 9:3), omitted by both Matthew and Luke.

A key question about the minor agreements is whether (1) differences with Mark are made independently and thus coincidentally happen to agree rather

---

and in so doing—in overweening vanity—destroyed the grandiose architecture of the work along with it impressive theology" (*The Four Gospels and the One Gospel of Jesus Christ*, 176–77).

39. See Neirynck, *The Minor Agreements of Matthew and Luke against Mark*. A comprehensive German discussion, unfortunately, has not been translated: Ennulat, *Die "Minor Agreements."* Ennulat appeals to a hypothetical Deutero-Mark to explain the agreements.

than being the result of dependence of Luke on Matthew or vice versa, or (2) they are the result of direct dependence between the two Synoptics or perhaps dependence on a third source, whether written or oral.

A large number of agreements can be easily explained as the result of independent work by Matthew and Luke. There are several ways in which agreements could simply be coincidental. Thus, for example, Matthew and Luke may easily agree in common omissions from Mark in the attempt that each makes to cut down the redundancies and wordiness in Mark. So too Matthew and Luke may well independently make numerous stylistic improvements and particularly changes to smooth out Mark's awkward grammar. There could also be independent changes where Mark is difficult—for example, the reference to Jesus that says he was angry (Mark 3:5, omitted by both Matthew and Luke); or the apparently incorrect statement that Abiathar was high priest when David entered the temple (Mark 2:26, omitted by Matthew and Luke); or simply an obscure word such as *krabattos*, "pallet," that is, "bed" (Mark 2:4, 9, 11–12, replaced by different words in Matthew and Luke). Hawkins finds more than two hundred instances of agreement that may easily be thought of as coincidental.[40] In his discussion of the problem, Streeter concluded that more than half of the minor agreements were in the category of "irrelevant agreements"—for example, consisting of such minor changes as the substituting of *de* for *kai*, the change from the historical present tense to past tenses, and the specifying of the subject of a sentence.[41]

At the same time, not all the agreements can be explained so easily. Hawkins lists some twenty instances, "and it is reasonable to suspect in others also," where the changes seem due to the influence of a common source.[42] He doubts that this was a proto-Mark, "an early non-Marcan document," or the result of one Evangelist knowing the work of the other. He leans instead to the latter of two possibilities: (1) the influence of copyists or oral tradition, or (2) an early recension of Mark different from the Mark that we know (following a suggestion by William Sanday).[43] Rather than inventing another hypothetical source,[44] however, we do well to put more value on the influence of oral tradition parallel to, and overlapping with, the written Gospels. Robert Stein rightly calls attention to the great significance of oral tradition for explaining similarities between John and the Synoptics, and he argues for a parallel phenomenon in the case of the minor agreements.[45]

40. Hawkins, *Horae Synopticae*, 209.
41. Streeter, *The Four Gospels*, 295–98.
42. Hawkins, *Horae Synopticae*, 210–11.
43. Ibid., 212.
44. Streeter encouraged his readers to "renounce once and for all the chase of the phantom Ur-Marcus" (*The Four Gospels*, 331).
45. Stein, "The Matthew-Luke Agreements against Mark."

Joseph Fitzmyer reduces the list of significant agreements to six: Matthew 26:68, 75; 17:3, 17; 9:7, 20 (and parallels). He rightly points out, "Whatever explanation (or explanations) may account for this phenomenon, it scarcely weighs as evidence that completely counterbalances the other data pointing to a dependence of Luke (and of Matthew) on Mark."[46]

Another factor to keep in mind here is the influence of early textual variants, introduced by copyists who attempted to bring harmony to the Synoptics in parallel passages. This phenomenon, called "assimilation," is readily apparent from a look at the text-critical apparatus of the Nestle-Aland *Novum Testamentum Graece*. As Streeter wrote, "In nearly every case where a minute agreement of Matthew and Luke against Mark is found in B and Aleph it is absent in one or more of the early local texts." His somewhat overstated conclusion was this: "A careful study of the MS. evidence distinctly favours the view that all those minute agreements of Matthew and Luke against Mark, which cannot be attributed to coincidence, were absent from the original text of the Gospels, but have crept in later as a result of 'assimilation' between the texts of the different Gospels."[47] The reality of this kind of cross-transference or assimilation is evident, and it is exactly what one may expect also to occur in the transmission of oral tradition.

The Case for the Priority of Matthew and the Griesbach Hypothesis

The initial piece of evidence for Matthean priority is the testimony of an early second-century Christian, Papias—a piece of evidence that is important, but the interpretation of which is far from clear. It is the fourth-century church historian Eusebius who records what Papias said: "Matthew collected the oracles in the Hebrew language, and each interpreted them as best he could" (*Hist. eccl.* 3.39.16, trans. Lake). Although many take this to be a reference to the Gospel of Matthew, the meaning of "the oracles" (*ta logia*) is highly debatable. Rather than the Gospel of Matthew itself (our Greek Matthew gives no evidence of being a translation), *ta logia* could refer to a collection of the sayings tradition such as Q, or possibly to Matthew's distinctive "formula" quotations of the OT. In addition to the Papias quotation, it is true, as we have already noted, that the church held to the priority of Matthew up until the eighteenth century. With Augustine, the church took for granted that the Gospels were written in the order that they appeared in the Gospel codices: Matthew, Mark, and Luke. Griesbach and his followers built on the priority of Matthew but moved Mark to the place of being the latest Synoptic Gospel.

The new and startling nineteenth-century conclusion that Mark rather than Matthew was the earliest of the Synoptic Gospels began to become the

46. Fitzmyer, "The Priority of Mark and the 'Q' Source in Luke," 15.
47. Streeter, *The Four Gospels*, 181.

dominant viewpoint, displacing the long-held view of Matthean priority. Not all were convinced, however. In 1951 Basil Butler attempted to revive the Griesbach hypothesis, denying the priority of Mark and the existence of Q.[48] Only a few years later, in 1955, Austin Farrer published his now well-known essay, "On Dispensing with Q."[49] But it was especially William Farmer who brought new energy to the Griesbach hypothesis, beginning with his book *The Synoptic Problem* (1964). Throughout the major part of his career Farmer continued his crusade, primarily via a succession of conferences devoted to the question. The result is that today a sizable and vocal minority of scholars subscribe to the Griesbach hypothesis.

The key issue is not so much that Mark is the last of the Synoptics, as Griesbach argued, but rather the dependence of Mark on Matthew—in other words, Matthean priority. Advocates of this hypothesis do have some nineteen centuries of church tradition on their side. It has been shown by these scholars that the possibility of Mark's dependence on Matthew cannot simply be dismissed out of hand. They also have shown that the question of the order of pericopes can be handled by this hypothesis. While Mark clearly is the middle term, or main link, between Matthew and Luke, the issue of the order of pericopes hardly in itself amounts to proof of Markan priority. There is furthermore the issue of the minor agreements. Stein, himself an advocate of the Two Source hypothesis, concludes that "clearly the greatest single argument for the advocacy of the Griesbach hypothesis is the agreements of Matthew and Luke against Mark in the triple tradition. This will always be the single greatest weakness of the two-source hypothesis."[50]

The Griesbach hypothesis serves as a reminder that there are other possible ways of solving the Synoptic Problem, and that Markan priority itself is also a hypothesis that falls short of demonstration. Although Markan priority still seems to most NT scholars the most probable solution, it should never be accepted as a fixed canon of Synoptic criticism. The question deserves to be kept alive as one examines the individual Synoptic pericopes. In the examination of a Synoptic pericope, it is always worth asking: What if Mark were dependent on Matthew?

The Priority of Luke?

Brief mention can be made here of the eccentric idea that the Gospel of Luke is the earliest of the Synoptic Gospels. It has been set forth primarily by Robert Lindsey, who was a missionary in Israel for many years, and has been taken up by several Israeli scholars, including notably David Flusser.[51] Lindsey's unlikely

48. Butler, *The Originality of St. Matthew*.
49. In Nineham, *Studies in the Gospels*, 55–88.
50. Stein, *Studying the Synoptic Gospels*, 146.
51. See Flusser, *Jesus*, 21–22, 221–50.

hypothesis involves the invention of yet another hypothetical document, which he calls the "proto-narrative."[52]

The early dating of Luke, before the other Synoptics, is an uphill climb, to say the least. The dating of the Synoptics, however, is itself extremely difficult, if not impossible. And now, Matthew's use of Luke has surprisingly received support from Martin Hengel.[53]

Concluding Remarks

As will now be clear, the Synoptic Problem is hugely complicated. One reason for this is simply that, having little if any direct evidence, we are forced to work inferentially. Furthermore, various aspects of the problem are interlocked, with a decision concerning one thing often affecting a conclusion on something else. Every argument seems answerable by a counterargument. Scholars on one side continually challenge scholars on the other side by telling them that they must demonstrate this or that to make their position convincing. At the end of the day, there are too many unknowns for anyone to be dogmatic.

But as far as probability goes, the Two Source hypothesis continues to be the most persuasive. It is never to be assumed, however, that this hypothesis has been proven. But with synopsis in hand, proceeding line by line, again and again most readers find that the hypothesis seems vindicated. It is, of course, always worth remembering Occam's Razor, so as to avoid proliferation of documents or sources and to keep a hypothesis as simple as possible. The less ingenious a hypothesis is, the more likely it is to prove true. The scandal of the Two Source hypothesis is its need to posit the existence of the hypothetical Q. It is easy enough to make fun of a hypothetical document that no one has ever seen. Yet Q provides a solution to a problem that seems to most a solution preferable to concluding that Luke knew Matthew or vice versa. Reluctantly we nod to Occam, but we carry on with our convictions about Q. Perhaps the scandal is less if Q consists of oral tradition. Even apart from that conclusion, however, it seems that oral tradition is the wild card capable of explaining the annoying anomalies that one continually encounters in the study of the Synoptic Problem. Terence Mournet is correct in his broad conviction that "any solution to the Synoptic Problem that does not take into serious account the influence of oral tradition in the compositional process must be deemed inadequate."[54]

52. Lindsey, "A Modified Two-Document Theory of Synoptic Dependence and Interdependence" (reprinted in Orton, *The Synoptic Problem and Q*, 7–31). Elsewhere, Lindsey indicates that when translating the NT into modern Hebrew, he noticed that of all the Gospels, Luke was the easiest to back-translate into Hebrew (*A Hebrew Translation of the Gospel of Mark*, 9–65). This led him to the idea of Luke's antiquity.

53. Hengel, *The Four Gospels and the One Gospel of Jesus Christ*, 169–207.

54. Mournet, *Oral Tradition and Literary Dependency*, 149.

A good dose of the Synoptic Problem may well cause the student to think of combining the three or four Gospels into one super-Gospel and be done with the problem altogether. We noted in chapter 4 that this was already a temptation of the early church, beginning with the Syriac *Diatessaron* of Tatian, a melding of the four Gospels accomplished in Syria in about 170.[55] And the temptation has continued down to the present with such attempts as *The Life of Christ in Stereo*.[56] But the church wisely resisted losing the four distinctive Gospels. So too Christians now can and should rejoice in the divinely intended diversity of one Gospel in four differing forms, because the fourfold Gospel enriches us in ways that a single narrative could never do.[57]

Finally, a comment on whether anything significant is at stake theologically in the conclusion that one accepts concerning the Synoptic Problem. Theoretically, Synoptic criticism is a neutral enterprise, a matter of explaining what we have in the NT. At the same time, however, the question of the priority of Mark or of Matthew makes a great difference in the practice of redaction criticism and hence in the determination of the theology of the Evangelists. It has an effect not only on the issue of development in their respective perspectives but also on our understanding of the history of primitive Christianity.

In principle, the positing of Q likewise should be a neutral matter. Without question, the existence of Q has important implications for the quest of the historical Jesus and the origins of Christianity. But when Q is taken in isolation as the expression of a "gospel" very different theologically from that of the Synoptics, as some radical scholars do, the theological consequences can be enormous.[58] Such an approach, even if not intended as such, can be perceived as an attack on the validity of the faith of the NT church. But this minority understanding of Q is hardly a necessity and is held by relatively few advocates of Q, and therefore such an abuse of Q should not be allowed to disqualify it from consideration.[59] (See further the following chapter on Q.)

Bibliography

Synopses

Aland, Kurt. *Synopsis of the Four Gospels: Greek-English Edition of the Synopsis Quattor Evangeliorum*. 10th ed. New York: United Bible Societies, 1987.
———. *Synopsis Quattuor Evangeliorum: Locis Parallelis Evangeliorum Apocryphorum et Patrum Adhibitis Edidit*. 14th ed. Stuttgart: Deutsche Bibelstiftung, 1996.
Barr, Allan. *A Diagram of Synoptic Relationships*. Rev. ed. Edinburgh: T&T Clark, 1995.

55. See Petersen, *Tatian's Diatessaron*.
56. Cheney, *The Life of Christ in Stereo* (published later in several formats).
57. See Burridge, *Four Gospels, One Jesus?*
58. See Kloppenborg, "The Theological Stakes in the Synoptic Problem."
59. What William Farmer is rightly worried about amounts to an abuse of the Two Source hypothesis. See Farmer, *The Gospel of Jesus*.

Orchard, Bernard, ed. *A Synopsis of the Four Gospels: In Greek, Arranged according to the Two-Gospel Hypothesis.* Macon, GA: Mercer University Press; Edinburgh: T&T Clark, 1983.

Swanson, Reuben J. *The Horizontal Line Synopsis of the Gospels.* 2nd ed. Pasadena, CA: William Carey Library, 1984.

Throckmorton, Burton H., Jr., ed. *Gospel Parallels: A Synopsis of the First Three Gospels.* 3rd ed. New York: Nelson, 1967.

Sources Supporting the Two Source Hypothesis

Fitzmyer, Joseph A. "The Priority of Mark and the 'Q' Source in Luke." In *To Advance the Gospel: New Testament Studies*, 3–40. 2nd ed. Grand Rapids: Eerdmans, 1998.

Head, Peter M. *Christology and the Synoptic Problem: An Argument for Markan Priority.* SNTSMS 94. Cambridge: Cambridge University Press, 1997.

Johnson, Sherman E. *The Griesbach Hypothesis and Redaction Criticism.* SBLMS 41. Atlanta: Scholars Press, 1991.

New, David S. *Old Testament Quotations in the Synoptic Gospels, and the Two-Document Hypothesis.* SBLSCS 37. Atlanta: Scholars Press, 1993.

Sanday, William, ed. *Studies in the Synoptic Problem.* Oxford: Clarendon, 1911.

Streeter, B. H. *The Four Gospels: A Study of Origins.* 4th ed. London: Macmillan, 1930.

Styler, G. M. "The Priority of Mark." In *The Birth of the New Testament*, by C. F. D. Moule, 285–316. 3rd ed. BNTC. London: A & C Black, 1982.

Tuckett, C. M. "The Argument from Order and the Synoptic Problem." *TZ* 36 (1980): 338–54.

———. *The Revival of the Griesbach Hypothesis: An Analysis and Appraisal.* Cambridge: Cambridge University Press, 1983.

Westcott, B. F. *An Introduction to the Study of the Gospels.* New York: Macmillan, 1895.

Sources on Q

Catchpole, David R. *The Quest for Q.* Edinburgh: T&T Clark, 1993.

Downing, F. Gerald. "A Paradigm Perplex: Luke, Matthew, and Mark." *NTS* 38 (1992): 15–36.

———. "Towards a Rehabilitation of Q." *NTS* 11 (1964–65): 169–81.

Farrer, Austin. "On Dispensing with Q." In *Studies in the Gospels: Essays in Memory of R. H. Lightfoot*, edited by Dennis E. Nineham, 55–88. Oxford: Blackwell, 1955.

Fleddermann, Harry T. *Mark and Q: A Study of the Overlap Texts.* BETL 122. Leuven: Leuven University Press, 1995.

Foster, Paul. "Is It Possible to Dispense with Q?" *NovT* 45 (2003): 313–26.

Goodacre, Mark S. "The Case Against Q." Website: http://www.markgoodacre.org/Q.

———. *The Case against Q: Studies in Markan Priority and the Synoptic Problem.* Harrisburg, PA: Trinity Press International, 2002.

———. *Goulder and the Gospels: An Examination of a New Paradigm.* JSNTSup 133. Sheffield: Sheffield Academic Press, 1996.

Goodacre, Mark S., and Nicholas Perrin, eds. *Questioning Q: A Multidimensional Critique.* Downers Grove, IL: InterVarsity, 2004.

Goulder, Michael D. "Farrer on Q." *Theology* 83 (1980): 190–95.

———. "Is Q a Juggernaut?" *JBL* 115 (1996): 667–81.

———. "On Putting Q to the Test." *NTS* 24 (1977–78): 218–34.

Head, Peter, and P. J. Williams. "Q Review." *TynBul* 54 (2003): 119–44.

Howard, W. F. "The Origin of the Symbol 'Q.'" *ExpTim* 50 (1938–39): 379–80.

Jacobson, Arland D. *The First Gospel: An Introduction to Q.* Sonoma, CA: Polebridge, 1992.

Kloppenborg, John S. *The Formation of Q: Trajectories in Ancient Wisdom Collections.* Philadelphia: Fortress, 1987.

————. "On Dispensing with Q? Goodacre on the Relation of Luke to Matthew." *NTS* 49 (2003): 210–36.

————. *Q, the Earliest Gospel: An Introduction to the Original Stories and Sayings of Jesus.* Louisville: Westminster John Knox, 2008.

————, ed. *The Shape of Q: Signal Essays on the Sayings Gospel.* Minneapolis: Fortress, 1994.

Kloppenborg Verbin, John S. *Excavating Q: The History and Setting of the Sayings Gospel.* Minneapolis: Fortress, 2000.

Neirynck, Frans. "The Symbol Q (=Quelle)" in *Evangelica: Gospel Studies.* Edited by F. Van Segbroeck. BETL 60. 683–90. Leuven: Leuven University Press, 1982.

Neirynck, F., J. Verheyden, and R. Corstjens, comps. *The Gospel of Matthew and the Sayings Source Q: A Cumulative Bibliography, 1950–1995.* 2 vols. BETL 140. Leuven: Leuven University Press, 1998.

Orton, David E., comp. *The Synoptic Problem and Q: Selected Studies from Novum Testamentum.* BRBS 4. Leiden: Brill, 1999.

Piper, Roland A., ed. *The Gospel behind the Gospels: Current Studies on Q.* NovTSup 75. Leiden: Brill, 1995.

Robinson, James M. *The Sayings Gospel Q: Collected Essays.* BETL 189. Leuven: Leuven University Press, 2005.

Robinson, James M., Paul Hoffman, and John S. Kloppenborg, eds. *The Critical Edition of Q: Synopsis Including the Gospels of Matthew and Luke, Mark and Thomas with English, German, and French Translations of Q and Thomas.* Hermeneia. Minneapolis: Fortress; Leuven: Peeters, 2000.

Schmitt, J. J. "In Search of the Origin of the *Siglum* Q." *ExpTim* 100 (1981): 609–11.

Taylor, Vincent. "The Original Order of Q." In *New Testament Essays: Studies in Memory of Thomas Walter Manson, 1893–1958,* edited by A. J. B. Higgins, 95–118. Manchester, UK: Manchester University Press, 1959.

Tuckett, Christopher M. *Q and the History of Early Christianity: Studies in Q.* Peabody, MA: Hendrickson, 1996.

————, ed. *Synoptic Studies: The Ampleforth Conferences of 1982 and 1983.* JSNTSup 7. Sheffield: JSOT Press, 1984.

Sources on the Minor Agreements

Ennulat, Andreas. *Die "Minor Agreements": Untersuchungen zu einer offenen Frage des synoptischen Problems.* WUNT 2/62. Tübingen: Mohr Siebeck, 1994.

Goulder, Michael D. "Luke's Knowledge of Matthew." In *Minor Agreements: Symposium Göttingen,* edited by Georg Strecker, 143–60. GTA 50. Göttingen: Vandenhoeck & Ruprecht, 1991.

Neirynck, Frans. "The Minor Agreements." In *Evangelica III, 1992–2000: Collected Essays,* 209–339. BETL 150. Leuven: Leuven University Press, 2001.

————, ed. *The Minor Agreements of Matthew and Luke against Mark: With a Cumulative List.* BETL 37. Leuven: Leuven University Press, 1974.

Stein, Robert H. "The Matthew-Luke Agreements against Mark: Insights from John." *CBQ* 54 (1992): 482–502.

Strecker, Georg, ed. *Minor Agreements: Symposium Göttingen 1991.* GTA 50. Göttingen: Vandenhoeck & Ruprecht, 1991.

Sources Supporting the Griesbach or Two Gospel Hypothesis

Butler, Basil C. *The Originality of St. Matthew: A Critique of the Two-Document Hypothesis.* Cambridge: Cambridge University Press, 1951.

Dungan, David L. *A History of the Synoptic Problem: The Canon, the Text, the Composition, and the Interpretation of the Gospels.* New York: Doubleday, 1999.

Farmer, William R. *The Gospel of Jesus: The Pastoral Relevance of the Synoptic Problem.* Louisville: Westminster John Knox, 1994.

———. *The Synoptic Problem: A Critical Analysis.* Dillsboro: Western North Carolina Press, 1976.

McNicol, Allan J., David L. Dungan, and David B. Peabody, eds. *Beyond the Q Impasse: Luke's Use of Matthew; A Demonstration by the Research Team of the International Institute for Gospel Studies.* Valley Forge, PA: Trinity Press International, 1996.

Orchard, Bernard. *Matthew, Luke, and Mark.* Manchester, UK: Koinonia, 1976.

Orchard, Bernard, and Thomas R. W. Longstaff, eds. *J. J. Griesbach: Synoptic and Text-Critical Studies, 1776–1976.* SNTSMS 34. Cambridge: Cambridge University Press, 1978.

Orchard, Bernard, and Harold Riley. *The Order of the Synoptics: Why Three Synoptics?* Macon, GA: Mercer University Press, 1987.

Stoldt, Hans-Herbert. *History and Criticism of the Marcan Hypothesis.* Translated and edited by Donald L. Niewyk. Macon, GA: Mercer University Press; Edinburgh: T&T Clark, 1980.

On Proto-Luke

Brodie, T. L. *Proto-Luke: The Oldest Gospel Account.* Sheffield: Phoenix, 2006.

Caird, G. B. *The Gospel of St. Luke.* Baltimore: Penguin, 1964.

Jeremias, Joachim. *The Eucharistic Words of Jesus.* Translated by Norman Perrin. Philadelphia: Fortress, 1966.

Manson, T. W. *Studies in the Gospels and Epistles.* Edited by Matthew Black. Manchester, UK: Manchester University Press, 1962.

Martin, Ralph P. *New Testament Foundations.* 2 vols. Grand Rapids: Eerdmans, 1975–78.

Taylor, Vincent. *Behind the Third Gospel: A Study of the Proto-Luke Hypothesis.* Oxford: Clarendon, 1926.

Other Sources on the Synoptic Problem

Batovici, Dan. "The Oxford Conference on the Synoptic Problem." *CurBS* 7 (2009): 245–71.

Bellinzoni, Arthur J., Jr., with Joseph B. Tyson and William O. Walker Jr., eds. *The Two-Source Hypothesis: A Critical Appraisal.* Macon, GA: Mercer University Press, 1985.

Black, David Alan, and David R. Beck, eds. *Rethinking the Synoptic Problem.* Grand Rapids: Baker Academic, 2001.

Burkett, Delbert. *Rethinking the Gospel Sources: From Proto-Mark to Mark.* New York: T&T Clark International, 2004.

Burridge, Richard A. *Four Gospels, One Jesus? A Symbolic Reading.* Grand Rapids: Eerdmans, 2005.

Cheney, Johnston M. *The Life of Christ in Stereo: The Four Gospels Combined as One.* Edited by Stanley A. Ellisen. Portland, OR: Western Baptist Seminary Press, 1969.

Farmer, William R., ed. *New Synoptic Studies: The Cambridge Conference and Beyond.* Macon, GA: Mercer University Press, 1983.

Flusser, David. *Jesus.* 2nd ed. Jerusalem: Magnes, 1998.

Franklin, Eric. *Luke: Interpreter of Paul, Critic of Matthew.* JSNTSup 92. Sheffield: JSOT Press, 1994.

Goodacre, Mark S. *The Synoptic Problem: A Way through the Maze.* BibSem 80. London: Sheffield Academic Press, 2001.

Goulder, Michael D. *Luke: A New Paradigm.* 2 vols. JSNTSup 20. Sheffield: JSOT Press, 1989.

Gundry, Robert H. "Matthean Foreign Bodies in Agreements of Luke with Matthew against Mark: Evidence That Luke Used Matthew." In *The Four Gospels, 1992: Festschrift Frans*

Neirynck, edited by Frans van Segbroeck, C. M. Tuckett, G. Van Belle, and J. Verheyden, 2:1467–96. 3 vols. BETL 100. Leuven: Leuven University Press, 1992.

Hawkins, John C. *Horae Synopticae: Contributions to the Study of the Synoptic Problem*. 2nd ed. Oxford: Clarendon, 1909.

Hengel, Martin. *The Four Gospels and the One Gospel of Jesus Christ: An Investigation of the Collection and Origin of the Canonical Gospels*. Harrisburg, PA: Trinity Press International, 2000.

Huggins, R. V. "Matthean Posteriority: A Preliminary Proposal." *NovT* 34 (1992): 1–22.

Klinghardt, Matthias. "The Marcionite Gospel and the Synoptic Problem: A New Suggestion." *NovT* 50 (2008): 1–27.

Kloppenborg, John S. "The Theological Stakes in the Synoptic Problem." In *The Four Gospels, 1992: Festschrift Frans Neirynck*, edited by Frans van Segbroeck, C. M. Tuckett, G. Van Belle, and J. Verheyden, 1:93–120. 3 vols. BETL 100. Leuven: Leuven University Press, 1992.

Kümmel, Werner Georg. *Introduction to the New Testament*. Translated by A. J. Mattill Jr. 14th ed. Nashville: Abingdon, 1966.

Lightfoot, R. H. *History and Interpretation in the Gospels*. London: Hodder & Stoughton, 1935.

Lindsey, Robert. *A Hebrew Translation of the Gospel of Mark*. Jerusalem: Dugith, 1969.

———. "A Modified Two-Document Theory of the Synoptic Dependence and Interdependence." *NovT* 6 (1963): 239–63.

Linnemann, Eta. *Is There a Synoptic Problem? Rethinking the Literary Dependence of the First Three Gospels*. Translated by Robert W. Yarbrough. Grand Rapids: Baker Academic, 1992.

Mournet, Terence C. *Oral Tradition and Literary Dependency: Variability and Stability in the Synoptic Tradition and Q*. WUNT 2/195. Tübingen: Mohr Siebeck, 2005.

Neville, David J. *Arguments from Order in Synoptic Source Criticism: A History and Critique*. Macon, GA: Mercer University Press, 1994.

———. *Mark's Gospel—Prior or Posterior? A Reappraisal of the Phenomenon of Order*. JSNTSup 222. Sheffield: Sheffield Academic Press, 2002.

Owen, Henry. *Observations on the Four Gospels*. London: T. Payne, 1764.

Petersen, William L. *Tatian's Diatessaron: Its Creation, Dissemination, Significance, and History in Scholarship*. VCSup 25. Leiden: Brill, 1994.

Reicke, Bo. *The Roots of the Synoptic Gospels*. Philadelphia: Fortress, 1986.

Rist, John M. *On the Independence of Matthew and Mark*. SNTSMS 32. Cambridge: Cambridge University Press, 1978.

Stein, Robert H. *Studying the Synoptic Gospels: Origin and Interpretation*. 2nd ed. Grand Rapids: Baker Academic, 2001.

Taylor, Vincent. *The Gospels: A Short Introduction*. 5th ed. London: Epworth, 1945.

Westcott, B. F. *An Introduction to the Study of the Gospels*. New York: Macmillan, 1895.

10

Q as an Entity

Because Q remains such an important factor in Synoptic source criticism, we must give some further attention to it.[1]

Defining Q

The quick definition of Q is that material, approximately 230 verses, found in both Matthew and Luke but not in Mark. But is this definition correct, let alone adequate? It is difficult to know much about a hypothetical source unavailable for inspection, as is wittily pointed out by Stewart Petrie in his article "'Q' Is Only What You Make It."[2] It has proved extremely difficult to know exactly what is to be regarded as Q. How close, for example, must the parallel between Matthew and Luke be for it to be considered as Q? Could some of Mark also have been in Q? There are virtually no objective standards by which to answer these questions. The recently published *Critical Edition of Q*,[3] in order "to avoid the endless task of discussing all the verses in Matthew and Luke," began with the reconstruction by John Kloppenborg, including items

1. For a full history of Q research, see Robinson, Hoffmann, and Kloppenborg, *The Critical Edition of Q*, xix–lxxi. See also Piper, "In Quest of Q."
2. Petrie ridicules the efforts at the reconstruction of Q, pointing to the seventeen different reconstructions outlined in James Moffatt's 1918 *Introduction to the Literature of the New Testament*.
3. See Robinson, Hoffmann, and Kloppenborg, *The Critical Edition of Q*. The same texts are conveniently found in Robinson, Hoffmann, and Kloppenborg, *The Sayings Gospel Q in Greek and English*.

Contents of Q according to John Kloppenborg (*Q, the Earliest Gospel*)

(Luke's versification, with overlaps between Mark and Q in italics)

John's preaching (3:7b–9, *16b*–17)

the temptation (*4:1–13*)

Jesus' first speech (6:20b–23, 27–33, 35, 36–*38*, 39–49)

the centurion's serving boy (7:1–2, 6–10)

John's question (7:18–19, 22–23)

Jesus' words about John (7:24–28, 31–35)

two volunteers (9:57–60)

Jesus' mission instructions and thanksgiving (10:2–3, *4–11*, 12–16, 21–22, 23b–24)

instructions on prayer (11:2–4, 9–13)

the Beelzebul accusation and request for a sign (11:*14–18*, 19–20, *21–22*, 23, 24–26, *29–30*, 31–32, 33–35)

woes against the Pharisees and scribes (11:39–44, 46–52)

admonitions on anxiety (12:2–8, *9–12*, 22b–31, 33–34)

the coming Son of Man (12:39–40, 42b–46, 51–53, 54b–56, 58–59)

two parables (13:*18–19*, 20–21)

the two ways (13:24, 26–27, 28–30)

a lament over Jerusalem (13:34–35)

"exalting the humble" (14:11/18:14)

the parable of the great supper and sayings about following Jesus (14:16–24, 26–27; *17:33*)

insipid salt (*14:34–35*)

the parable of the lost sheep (15:4–7)

"God or mammon" (16:13)

sayings on the Torah (16:16, 17, *18*)

sayings on scandals, forgiveness, and faith (17:*1b–2*, 3b–4, *6b*)

the coming of the Son of Man (17:*23–24*, 26–27, 30, 34–35, 37b)

the parable of the entrusted money (19:12–13, 15b–26)

sitting on thrones (22:28–30)

---

that he considered "doubtful" but probable.[4] Initially those "doubtful" but regarded by Kloppenborg as probably not in Q were excluded, but later some were examined for inclusion. The *Critical Edition of Q* is not what could be called minimalist, nor perhaps maximalist either.

4. Robinson, Hoffmann, and Kloppenborg, *The Critical Edition of Q*, lxxx. In this volume numerous debatable passages that might be considered Q are included, but with the verse numbers stricken through so as to indicate the uncertainty.

Given the definition of Q as the material common to Matthew and Luke not found in Mark, we exclude ex hypothesi the possibility that Q contained some further material that we currently know as Mark. But is it necessarily the case that Q had nothing that was in Mark, that Q could not have had any triple tradition material, or could not have had any of the special material (*Sondergut*) M or L? Could not Matthew or Luke, or both, have omitted Q material, which ipso facto drops off our radar screen? We simply do not, and cannot, know exactly what was in Q.

The possibility of the overlapping of Mark and Q has been studied extensively.[5] Christopher Tuckett has called attention to the self-contradictory logic involved in attributing Markan material to Q (and it applies also to the idea that Q could have contained M or L material): overlap material is postulated on the basis of similarity of material, but "relatively *little* verbal agreement between Mark and Matthew/Luke," since a significant amount of agreement would result in the conclusion of straightforward dependence on Mark; "but then the low level of agreement between Mark and Matthew/Luke (= Q) makes it correspondingly harder to plead for any direct literary relationship between Mark and Q, which of necessity has to be based on a relatively *high* level of verbal agreement between Mark and Q (= Matthew/Luke)."[6] One may wonder further why, if Mark knew Q, he did not take up more of it than he has. As Tuckett cautions, "Any attempt to argue for direct dependence between Mark and Q will have to involve a highly sophisticated form of argumentation."[7]

Similar difficulties attend the attempt to answer other questions about the hypothetical Q. Was it a document or several documents, or perhaps oral tradition(s)? Were there several recensions of Q? Was it originally in Aramaic or Greek? Despite the confidence with which some Q specialists answer these questions, it is virtually impossible to do more than to speculate as to what might be the case.

What Kind of Document (or Source) Does Q Represent?

The hypothetical source Q consists almost exclusively of sayings of Jesus, with practically no narrative. For this reason, Q often is referred to as the "Sayings Source" or the "Logia." The only narratives widely believed to have been in Q are the temptation narrative (Luke 4:1–13), the healing of the centurion's

5. For example, Fleddermann, *Mark and Q*. Early on, Streeter studied the question, concluding that Mark knew and quoted Q, adding the qualification that he did so "probably only from memory" ("St. Mark's Knowledge and Use of Q," 165).

6. Tuckett, "Mark and Q," 154. He adds, "A theory of direct dependence of Mark on Q would thus appear to demolish one of the strongest arguments in favour of the very existence of Q in the first place" (ibid.).

7. Ibid.

servant (Luke 7:1–10), and the casting out of a demon (Luke 11:14). Q seems to have no interest in narrative as such, and the narrative it does have is included solely as a means of presenting sayings of Jesus. This is clear from the importance of the words of Jesus in the temptation narrative and also from the fact that the healing of the centurion's servant is a pronouncement story, with emphasis on the saying in Luke 7:9.

Q is thus in essence a collection of sayings of Jesus. It is not at all difficult to believe in the special interest of the early Christians in assembling a collection of the words of Jesus, the words of the one they confessed as Lord. Indeed, such an undertaking has an a priori plausibility. There are parallels to such documents, for example in the so-called *Gospel of Thomas*, which consists exclusively of 114 sayings of Jesus.[8]

It is not uncommon for scholars, especially Q specialists, to refer to Q as a "gospel." But does Q consist of a self-contained kerygma that amounts to a gospel? Everything here, of course, depends on how one defines "gospel." I have already cited with approval Kähler's description of the canonical Gospels as passion narratives with extended introductions. The heart of these Gospels is the cross. As T. W. Manson rightly put it, "For the primitive Church the central thing is the Cross on the Hill rather than the Sermon on the Mount. . . . Christian doctrine and Christian ethics may be the inevitable corollaries of the Christian gospel; but they are corollaries."[9] If the term "gospel" is understood in this way, then neither Q nor *Thomas*[10] should be designated as "gospels," since both lack a passion narrative altogether. Manson concluded that Q "is not the preached Gospel of the primitive Church, but a supplement to the Gospel."[11]

Q by itself *can* be regarded as having a kerygmatic dimension, as we will see below. If one chooses to define the word "gospel" in its basic sense of "good news," it is possible to call Q a kind of "gospel." But this is not the same thing that is meant by the NT word "gospel," which is indistinguishable from the redeeming death of Jesus.

A key question is whether Q presupposes the cross—that is, the passion narrative—or whether it represents a viewpoint in which the cross played no role at all.[12] Some scholars capitalize on the silence of Q about the death of Jesus and conclude that there were very early Christian communities for

8. For sayings collections in the ancient world, see Kloppenborg, *The Formation of Q*, 263–316.

9. Manson, *The Sayings of Jesus*, 9. These words are quoted by Kloppenborg (*Q, the Earliest Gospel*, 73), who refuses to restrict the term "gospel" in this way.

10. Despite the (probably late) colophon stating "Gospel according to Thomas," the document describes itself in the following beginning words: "These are the hidden words which the living Jesus spoke and which Judas, also called Thomas, wrote down."

11. Manson, *The Sayings of Jesus*, 147.

12. Kloppenborg concludes that Q alludes to the death of Jesus at a couple of points, but that this death is the nonsalvific death of a martyred prophet (*Q, the Earliest Gospel*, 76–79).

which the death (and resurrection) of Jesus held no significance. According to Kloppenborg, Q "gives us a glimpse of the earliest Jesus movement in the Galilee, a *different* Gospel with a different view of Jesus' significance."[13] Here the argument from silence is very precarious. It is a priori highly implausible that there was anywhere a Christian community that did not champion the death and resurrection of Jesus, which was the heart of the earliest Christian preaching. Moreover, the idea that Q represents a theological perspective quite different from Mark's has recently been strongly challenged.[14]

The Theology of Q

If we continue to accept the idea of a fairly well-defined Q, especially in written form, but even in oral form, it deserves to be examined on its own terms. Since Q can appear at first glance to be a somewhat random collection of sayings of Jesus, it may seem impossible to find common denominators. There is, however, some coherence in the sayings of Q, and indeed there has been no shortage of treatments of the theology of Q. It is also true that the analysis of Q has sometimes led to very differing results. Not disheartened, some scholars have engaged in the "archaeology of Q," its stratification into various layers—for example, Q1 (sapiential), Q2 (apocalyptic), Q3 ("biographical").[15]

Q contains such a variety of theological emphases that it is difficult, if not impossible, to summarize it under one theme, or even several themes. Among those usually mentioned are wisdom, mission, discipleship, and eschatology. Just this diversity of contents has encouraged some scholars to speak of different redactions of Q. If Q is isolated from the rest of the Gospels and taken by itself, its kerygma would be something like the good news of the presence of the kingdom as "the transformative power in people's lives."[16] Wisdom can enable people to see the kingdom as present here and now. In this way the gospel according to Q is good news to the rural poor. The ethics of the kingdom are meant to protect them at the level of the basics of life.

In addition to ethical instruction on discipleship that could serve as a handbook for church members, we also find in Q the following: eschatological warnings in light of the coming of the Son of Man and imminent judgment (cf. the importance of John the Baptist in Q); prophecy and apocalyptic motifs; emphasis on persecution and suffering; polemic against Israel; and an

13. Ibid., 121. This too was the earlier conclusion of H. E. Tödt, *The Son of Man in the Synoptic Tradition*, 241–45. For a far-fetched expression of the same view, see Mack, *The Lost Gospel*.
14. See the convincing case made by Meadors, *Jesus the Messianic Herald of Salvation*.
15. Note the title of Kloppenborg Verbin's *Excavating Q: The History and Setting of the Sayings Gospel*.
16. Kloppenborg, *Q, the Earliest Gospel*, 71.

assortment of unrelated aphorisms. Perhaps most important in Q is its emphasis on wisdom.[17]

Jesus in an isolated Q becomes little more than a teacher of wisdom, a sage who is particularly sensitive to the presence of the kingdom. It may be true enough to conclude with Kloppenborg that "the center of Q's teachings is not, as it is in Mark, the identity of Jesus as the Son of God, but rather the behavior and attitudes that reflect God's reign."[18] Nevertheless, it is also true that Q has a significant christology that regards him as much more than a teacher of wisdom.[19]

Despite the claims of Kloppenborg and others that Q represents a gospel and a view of Jesus different from that of the canonical Gospels, such a conclusion is hardly a necessary one. Edward Meadors points out that the themes we have seen in Q are also present in Mark, and that there is no incompatibility between Mark and Q.[20] The mistake of those who think otherwise is the assumption that our Q contains everything that the group responsible for the document believed about Jesus and the gospel. But there is no reason to believe that this is the case. The same issue arises with the book of James. Since James contains no reference to the death of Jesus and its atoning significance or to the resurrection, Kloppenborg concludes that it must reflect a Christianity like the kind he detects in Q.[21] But it must be asked of James too, does the document contain reference to everything that his community believed about Jesus and the gospel? Why is this thought necessary? "Why treat Q as a sort of systematic theology, or as an exhaustive statement of someone's christological beliefs?"[22]

For the most part, Q scholars remain oblivious to the question of genre. Q, rather than being a fundamental statement of faith, is much more likely a practical handbook of the sayings of Jesus to be used by Christians as a supplement to what they believe. Rather than itself being the kerygma of a particular community, Q represents a paraenesis (ethical instruction) that presupposes and builds on that kerygma.

Was There a Q Community?

How community-specific is Q? What is its life setting? What is its purpose? These are exceptionally difficult questions to answer. For if a hypothetical document is to be associated with a community, how much more must that

17. See especially Piper, *Wisdom in the Q-Tradition*; Jacobson, *The First Gospel*.
18. Kloppenborg, *Q, the Earliest Gospel*, 97.
19. See Stanton, "On the Christology of Q."
20. Meadors, *Jesus the Messianic Herald of Salvation*.
21. Kloppenborg, *Q, the Earliest Gospel*, 64.
22. Allison, *The Jesus Tradition in Q*, 44.

community itself be hypothetical! Again, however, this challenge does not daunt avid Q scholars.[23] For Kloppenborg, simply put, Q circulated "not among urbanites, but among the rural poor, not in the Gentile cities of the east, but in the towns of Jewish Galilee."[24]

There is little point in reviewing the multitude of conjectures on offer. The difficulty of the task is evident merely from the disparate conclusions that have been drawn.[25] James Dunn calls attention to the "'one document per community' fallacy"[26] and the mistaken assumption that Q by itself can be used to define a community. He rightly argues that "hypotheses that there were distinctively 'Q communities,' in effect isolated from other early Christian communities, depends on deductions which go well beyond what the data of Q itself indicate."[27]

Importance of Q

Q remains an exceptionally important stratum of early Gospel material, even if we cannot know as much about it as we would wish. As such, it remains very important in historical Jesus research.[28] As the earliest stratum (the date is uncertain, but it is commonly thought to be from about AD 50, although some would put it later), it does take us somewhat closer to the events themselves.

It is unnecessary and misleading to take Q as a document that stands entirely on its own legs, presupposing and reflecting a gospel different from that of the Synoptics.

It is almost certainly incorrect to conclude that there was a community that believed only and exclusively what Q contains, and that regarded Jesus as a Cynic sage or prophet and cared nothing of his death and resurrection. On the contrary, Q has value only when taken in conjunction with the framework supplied by the Synoptic Gospels. Q is best understood as a supplement, as teaching (*didachē*) added to kerygma of early church.

Why did Q not survive? On the one hand, possibly because it had been fully taken up into the other Gospels. On the other hand, perhaps Q never existed

23. For an example of remarkable confidence, see Kloppenborg, "Literary Convention, Self-Evidence and the Social History of the Q People."

24. Kloppenborg, *Q, the Earliest Gospel*, 97. His more detailed analysis is linked up with his stratification of Q. See, for example, Kloppenborg Verbin, *Excavating Q*, 166–213.

25. As an illustration, we may point to the *Anchor Bible Dictionary* article "Q (Gospel Source)," by C. M. Tuckett (*ABD* 5:567–72), particularly the section titled "Sitz im Leben."

26. Dunn, *Jesus Remembered*, 150.

27. Ibid., 152.

28. Note James Robinson's statement, "The resultant critical text of Q is (at least) one step removed from Jesus himself" (Robinson, Hoffmann, and Kloppenborg, *The Critical Edition of Q*, lxviii).

as an actual document, but rather consisted of collections of oral tradition.[29] Even if Q was a written document, however, its contents undoubtedly were paralleled in living oral tradition (see chap. 7 above).

Bibliography

See also the bibliography for chapter 9, "The Synoptic Problem."

Allison, Dale C., Jr. *The Jesus Tradition in Q.* Harrisburg, PA: Trinity Press International, 1997.

Dunn, James D. G. *Jesus Remembered.* Christianity in the Making 1. Grand Rapids: Eerdmans, 2003.

———. "Q¹ as Oral Tradition." In *The Written Gospel*, edited by Markus Bockmuehl and Donald A. Hagner, 45–69. Cambridge: Cambridge University Press, 2005.

Fee, Gordon D. "A Text-Critical Look at the Synoptic Problem." In *The Synoptic Problem and Q: Selected Studies from Novum Testamentum*, compiled by David E. Orton, 163–79. BRBS 4. Leiden: Brill, 1999.

Fleddermann, Harry T. *Mark and Q: A Study of the Overlap Texts.* BETL 122. Leuven: Leuven University Press, 1995.

Jacobson, Arland D. *The First Gospel: An Introduction to Q.* Sonoma, CA: Polebridge, 1992.

Kirk, Alan. *The Composition of the Sayings Source: Genre, Synchrony, and Wisdom Redaction in Q.* NovTSup 91. Leiden: Brill, 1998.

Kloppenborg, John S. *The Formation of Q: Trajectories in Ancient Wisdom Collections.* Philadelphia: Fortress, 1987.

———. "Literary Convention, Self-Evidence and the Social History of the Q People." *Semeia* 55 (1992): 77–102.

———. *Q, the Earliest Gospel: An Introduction to the Original Stories and Sayings of Jesus.* Louisville: Westminster John Knox, 2008.

Kloppenborg Verbin, John S. *Excavating Q: The History and Setting of the Sayings Gospel.* Minneapolis: Fortress, 2000.

Mack, Burton L. *The Lost Gospel: The Book of Q and Christian Origins.* San Francisco: HarperSanFrancisco, 1993.

Manson, T. W. *The Sayings of Jesus: As Recorded in the Gospels according to St. Matthew and St. Luke.* Grand Rapids: Eerdmans, 1979.

Meadors, Edward P. *Jesus the Messianic Herald of Salvation.* WUNT 2/72. Tübingen: Mohr Siebeck, 1995.

Orton, David E., comp. *The Synoptic Problem and Q: Selected Studies from Novum Testamentum.* BRBS 4. Leiden: Brill, 1999.

Petrie, Stewart. "'Q' Is Only What You Make It." *NovT* 3 (1959): 28–33. Reprinted in *The Synoptic Problem and Q: Selected Studies from Novum Testamentum*, compiled by David E. Orton, 1–6. BRBS 4. Leiden: Brill, 1999.

Piper, Ronald A., ed. *The Gospel behind the Gospels: Current Studies in Q.* NovTSup 75. Leiden: Brill, 1995.

———. "In Quest of Q: The Direction of Q Studies." In *The Gospel behind the Gospels: Current Studies in Q*, edited by Ronald A. Piper, 1–18. NovTSup 75. Leiden: Brill, 1995.

———. *Wisdom in the Q-Tradition: The Aphoristic Teaching of Jesus.* SNTSMS 61. Cambridge: Cambridge University Press, 1989.

Robinson, James M., Paul Hoffmann, and John S. Kloppenborg, eds. *The Critical Edition of Q: Synopsis Including the Gospels of Matthew and Luke, Mark and Thomas with English,*

29. See Dunn, "Q¹ as Oral Tradition"; Fee, "A Text-Critical Look at the Synoptic Problem."

German, and French Translations of Q and Thomas. Hermeneia. Minneapolis: Fortress; Leuven: Peeters, 2000.

———, eds. *The Sayings Gospel Q in Greek and English: With Parallels from the Gospels of Mark and Thomas.* CBET 30. Leuven: Peeters, 2001.

Stanton, Graham N. "On the Christology of Q." In *Christ and Spirit in the New Testament: Studies in Honour of Charles Francis Digby Moule,* edited by Barnabas Lindars and Stephen S. Smalley, 27–42. Cambridge: Cambridge University Press, 1973.

Streeter, B. H. "St. Mark's Knowledge and Use of Q." In *Studies in the Synoptic Problem,* edited by William Sanday, 165–83. Oxford: Clarendon, 1911.

Tödt, H. E. *The Son of Man in the Synoptic Tradition.* Translated by Dorothea M. Barton. Philadelphia: Westminster, 1965.

Tuckett, Christopher M. "Mark and Q." In *The Synoptic Gospels: Source Criticism and the New Literary Criticism,* edited by Camille Focant, 149–75. BETL 110. Leuven: Leuven University Press, 1993.

———. *Q and the History of Early Christianity.* Peabody, MA: Hendrickson, 1996.

11

The Gospel according to Mark

If the Two Source hypothesis is correct, then Mark is not only the earliest of the Gospels that we know of, but Mark furthermore constitutes the beginning of a new genre: gospel not merely as a message of good news, but gospel also in the sense of a written document, a "Gospel"—indeed, identified by Mark as "the gospel of Jesus Christ, the Son of God" (1:1). And Mark thus serves as a model followed by the Evangelists Matthew and Luke. But where did Mark get his material from, and what explains the basic framework of his Gospel?

Mark's Gospel and the Preaching of the Early Church

Again we turn to the earliest historical information we have about the origin of the Gospels, which is the testimony of Papias, bishop of Hierapolis in the early second century,[1] as recorded in the fourth-century *Ecclesiastical History* of Eusebius (*Hist. eccl.* 3.39.15–16, trans. Lake):

> And the Presbyter used to say this, "Mark became Peter's interpreter [*hermēneutēs*] and wrote accurately [*akribōs*] all that he remembered [*hosa emnēmoneusen*], not, indeed, in order [*ou mentoi taxei*], of the things said or done by the Lord. For he had not heard the Lord, nor had he followed him, but later on, as I said, followed Peter, who used to give teaching as necessity demanded[2] but not making,

---

1. Although it is debated, the *Fragments of Papias* probably are to be dated as early as 110, or perhaps even earlier. See Schoedel, "Papias"; Yarbrough, "The Date of Papias."
2. "As necessity demanded" (*pros tas chreias*) is perhaps better translated "in *chreiai*-form"— that is, in the form of "chreiai," or "useful anecdotes," an elementary type of rhetoric, and

---

Author: *Probably* John Mark, son of Mary of Jerusalem (Acts 12:12), and cousin of Barnabas (Col. 4:10).

Date: *Very tentatively* in about 65, but no later than 75, and possibly much earlier.

Addressees: *Probably* churches of Rome, but not limited to them; a presentation of the gospel especially for Gentile readers in the Roman world.

Purpose: Evangelistic; to give a basic account of the story of Jesus and his proclamation of the kingdom, with a focus on his suffering and death.

Message/Argument: An expansion of the elements of the kerygma, dependent on the preaching of the Apostle Peter; the fundamental statement of the Gospel narratives.

Significance: Mark invents the Gospel genre; serves as the earliest historical narrative of the story of Jesus and hence is vitally important as a historical source, its information based on eyewitness evidence; used by the other Synoptic Gospels and perhaps by John too.

---

as it were, an arrangement of the Lord's oracles [*syntaxin tōn kyriakōn logiōn*] so that Mark did nothing wrong in thus writing down the single points [*enia*] as he remembered them. For to one thing he gave attention, to leave out nothing of what he had heard and to make no false statements [*pseusasthai ti*] in them."

Earlier, Eusebius had written this account (*Hist. eccl.* 2.15.1, trans. Lake):

But a great light of religion shone on the minds of the hearers of Peter, so that they were not satisfied with a single hearing or with the unwritten teaching of the divine proclamation, but with every kind of exhortation besought Mark, whose Gospel is extant, seeing that he was Peter's follower [*akolouthon*], to leave them a written statement [*graphēs hypomnēma*, lit., "remembrance"] of the teaching [*didaskalias*] given them verbally, nor did they cease until they had persuaded him, and so became the cause of the Scripture called the Gospel according to Mark.[3]

Papias is identified by Eusebius as the author of five treatises under the title "Interpretation of the Oracles of the Lord." Part of his fame, however, was that he was "the hearer of John" (thus Irenaeus, according to Eusebius, *Hist. eccl.* 3.39.1). This is the Elder John, not the Apostle John, since, as Eusebius notes, Papias "makes plain that he had in no way been a hearer and eyewitness of the sacred apostles, but teaches that he had received the articles of the faith from those who had known them" (*Hist. eccl.* 3.39.2, trans. Lake). But it seems clear that Papias was a living link with those who knew the Apostles.

---

perhaps referring to "the inadequacy of Mark's account which reflected the undeveloped literary procedures of Peter" (so Schoedel, *Polycarp, Martyrdom of Polycarp, Fragments of Papias*, 106–7).

3. Eusebius indicates that the story is found in Clement of Alexandria, *Hypotyposes*, book 6.

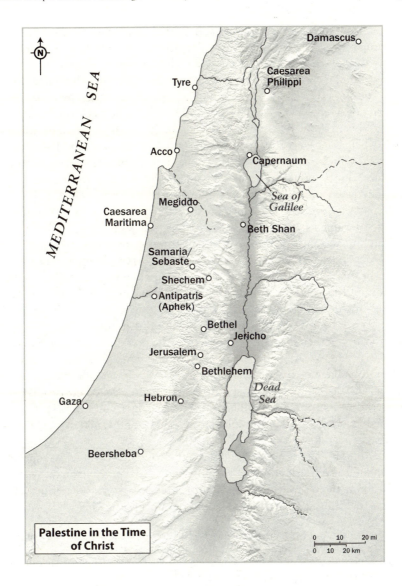

Palestine in the Time of Christ

Assuming that Papias is correct in his information (though this is questioned by many), we may conclude that when Peter preached, Mark was his translator (i.e., the John Mark[4] of Acts 12:12, 25, who was the cousin of Barnabas [Col. 4:10]). Although Peter undoubtedly knew some Greek, he evidently preferred to speak in his native Aramaic, allowing Mark to translate his preaching into Greek. Even Mark's Greek, though better than Peter's, was less than the best,

4. "John" ("Yohanan") would have been his Hebrew name, "Marcus" his Latin name.

however, if we are to judge from what he ended up writing. Traditionally, the preaching referred to was in Rome (for the explicit association of Mark with Peter in Rome, see 1 Pet. 5:13, where "Babylon" refers to Rome).[5]

Many scholars believe that Papias invented this material in order to establish a connection between Mark and the great Apostle and thereby enhance the authority of Mark's Gospel. This possibility cannot be ruled out, but it rests on pure speculation. If Papias is creating ideas ex nihilo, why not attribute this Gospel, or at least the tradition about it, directly to Peter? Patristic testimony, of course, should be subject to the same critical sifting as all ancient literature. But it should never be set aside in deference to mere speculation, especially when good sense can be made of it and when it well explains what needs explanation. And the fact that something is used as a warrant, as in the case of Papias's appeal to Mark's connection with Peter, does not automatically mean that it is unhistorical.[6] Testimony, possibly independent, to Mark's dependence on Peter is found in Justin Martyr, who probably refers to the Gospel of Mark as Peter's "memoirs" (*apomnēmoneumata*) (*Dial.* 106.3), mentioning the name "Boanerges" (which occurs in the NT only in Mark 3:17). Clement of Alexandria's testimony, as conveyed yet again by Eusebius, is this: "When Peter had publicly preached the word at Rome, and by the Spirit had proclaimed the Gospel, those present, who were many, exhorted Mark, as one who had followed him for a long time and remembered what had been spoken, to make a record of what was said [*anagrapsai ta eirēmena*]; and he did this, and distributed the Gospel among those that asked him" (*Hist. eccl.* 6.14.6, trans. Oulton). The connection between Mark and Peter is also noted by Irenaeus (*Haer.* 3.1.1.), though both Clement and Irenaeus may depend on Papias's account.

According to Papias and others, then, the content of Mark's Gospel is to be explained as representative of the preaching of Peter. Consonant with this conclusion is the considerable amount of attention given to Peter in Mark's Gospel (the highest frequency of reference among the Gospels).[7] Another

---

5. Compare the Anti-Marcionite Prologue (probably from the end of the second century, but possibly later) to Mark: "Mark, . . . who is called 'Stump-fingered' because he had short fingers in comparison with the size of the rest of his body. He was Peter's interpreter. After the death of Peter himself he wrote down this same gospel in the regions of Italy."

6. The fully unsympathetic assessment of Papias is unwarranted. For example, here Austin Farrer says far more than he can know: "The whole substance of what he gives us is neither more nor less than an ingenious but false historical hypothesis; and we have confessed that it is hopeless to try to disentangle from it older or more genuine elements" (*A Study in St. Mark*, 20). See Kümmel, *Introduction to the New Testament*, 53. Clifton Black cautiously walks a tightrope between denying and affirming the historical tradition behind Mark, carefully avoiding a slip in either direction (*Mark*). For positive assessments of Papias, see Hengel, *The Four Gospels and the One Gospel of Jesus Christ*, 65–78; Bauckham, *Jesus and the Eyewitnesses*, 202–39.

7. See Feldmeier, "The Portrayal of Peter in the Synoptic Gospels"; see also Bauckham, *Jesus and the Eyewitnesses*, chapter 7, "The Petrine Perspective in the Gospel of Mark," 155–82.

C. H. Dodd's Reconstruction of the Kerygma of the Primitive Church

- The prophecies are fulfilled, and the new age is inaugurated by the coming of Christ.
- He was born of the seed of David.
- He died according to the Scriptures, to deliver us out of the present evil age.
- He was buried.
- He rose on the third day according to the Scriptures.
- He is exalted at the right hand of God, as Son of God and Lord of the quick and the dead.
- He will come again as Judge and Saviour of men.

The Apostolic Preaching and Its Developments, 28

---

pertinent fact is the prominent references to Peter at the beginning and end of the Gospel (1:16; 16:7), which form an inclusio, pointing to the witness of Peter that underlies the whole of the narrative.[8] But even if the connection with Peter were to be ruled out as unconvincing, it remains undeniably the case that Mark's Gospel depends on the preaching of the early church. Mark would have had numerous contexts in which he could have gathered traditions about Jesus.[9] What the earliest Christians remembered and preached about Jesus is what came into the Gospel narrative that we know as Mark.

This understanding of the origin of Mark does not mean that the Evangelist was a passive transmitter of tradition and had little or nothing to do with the way the material is presented. On the contrary, what it underlines is the basic trustworthiness of the narrative, not details such as chronological order, verbatim recording of dialogue, and so on. The Evangelist obviously has considerable freedom to arrange and leave his theological imprint on the material.

The Outline of Mark and the Early Kerygma

It was the British scholar C. H. Dodd's brilliant study of the kerygma of the early church that made possible a new understanding of how Mark might have formed the first written Gospel. By an analysis of the sermons in the book of Acts, Dodd found a common, relatively stable core of the primitive preaching (see sidebar above). Dodd points out that his outline of the kerygma is only schematic, the heart of the kerygma, and that the kerygma included more than is represented here.[10] As an example, we may mention the summaries of

---

8. See Feldmeier, "The Portrayal of Peter in the Synoptic Gospels," 61.
9. So Manson, "The Gospel of Mark," 37.
10. Dodd, *The Apostolic Preaching and Its Developments*, 29.

Jesus' mission—as in Acts 2:22: "Men of Israel, hear these words: Jesus of Nazareth, a man attested to you by God with mighty works and wonders and signs which God did through him in your midst, as you yourselves know . . ." (cf. Acts 3:22, fulfilled in the teaching of Jesus).

Dodd went on from this to argue that the kerygma of the early church to a considerable extent explained the framework of Mark. Dodd referred to three kinds of material taken over by the Evangelist: "(i) Isolated independent *perico-pae*, handed down without any connection. (ii) Larger complexes, which again may be of various kinds: genuinely continuous narratives; *pericopae* strung upon an itinerary; *pericopae* connected by unity of theme. (iii) An outline of the whole ministry, designed, perhaps, as an introduction to the Passion-story, but serving also as a background of reference for separate stories; fragments of this survive in the framework of the Gospel."[11]

It is important here not to overstate Dodd's conclusion. His view does not entail the conclusion that Mark's Gospel presents a detailed and fully reliable chronology.[12] Dodd speaks of two inhibiting factors: "(*a*) the outline was far too meagre to provide a setting for all the detailed narratives at his disposal, while on the other hand it referred to phases of the Ministry not illustrated by the detailed narratives; (*b*) the materials were already partially grouped in ways which cut across a truly chronological order."[13]

Peter's sermon in Acts 10:34–43 is the best example of what Dodd has in mind:

> You know the word which he sent to Israel, preaching good news of peace by Jesus Christ (he is Lord of all), the word which was proclaimed throughout all Judea, beginning from Galilee after the baptism which John preached: how God anointed Jesus of Nazareth with the Holy Spirit and with power; how he went about doing good and healing all that were oppressed by the devil, for God was with him. And we are witnesses to all that he did both in the country of the Jews and in Jerusalem. They put him to death by hanging him on a tree; but God raised him on the third day and made him manifest; not to all the people but to us who were chosen by God as witnesses, who ate and drank with him after he rose from the dead. And he commanded us to preach to the people, and to testify that he is the one ordained by God to be judge of the living and the dead. To him all the prophets bear witness that every one who believes in him receives forgiveness of sins through his name. (Acts 10:36–43 [cf. Paul's sermon in Acts 13:23–33])

This passage is an abbreviated representation of the sort of preaching that Peter and others did everywhere. It is based on an outline of the kerygma. And

---

11. Dodd, "The Framework of the Gospel Narrative," 10. See also Riesenfeld, "On the Composition of Mark."

12. He seems to be misunderstood, for example, by Dennis Nineham, who seems to be working on an "all or nothing" principle ("The Order of Events in St. Mark's Gospel").

13. Dodd, "The Framework of the Gospel Narrative," 10.

it is this schema that presents the most obvious stimulus for the beginning, basic outline of Mark. If Mark was Peter's translator, he would have heard this preaching often. And when he came to writing out the story of Jesus, it very probably was his starting point.

Mark as the Foundation of Matthew and Luke

If Mark is the fundamental source of Matthew and Luke and is taken up by them to the large degree that I have already argued, then it is clear that the content of Mark is of fundamental importance and provides the basic building blocks of the story of Jesus. Mark introduces that story, as we have also seen, as "The beginning of the gospel of Jesus Christ, the Son of God" (1:1). This incomplete sentence functions like a title of the work. In it, Jesus is identified as "Messiah" and probably also as "the Son of God."[14] The good news is bound up with the person of Jesus (note the parallelism between "my sake" and the sake of the gospel in 8:35; 10:29).

The Promise and Fulfillment Perspective

The very next words in Mark, following the title, are "As it is written in Isaiah the prophet." Immediately the reader knows that this is the continuation of an earlier story, indeed, moving toward the climax of that story. The quotation, from Malachi and Isaiah, reads, "Behold, I send my messenger before thy face, who shall prepare thy way; the voice of one crying in the wilderness: Prepare the way of the Lord, make his paths straight" (1:2–3). These words introduce John the Baptist, the one who prepares the way of Jesus the Messiah. Already at this early point we know that this is the astounding announcement of the fulfillment of the promises of Scripture and the hopes of Israel. Thus, "The history of Jesus of Nazareth was already a highly-interpreted history, interpreted through the medium of the Old Testament."[15]

All through Mark this motif of fulfillment is present (e.g., 4:12; 7:6–7; 11:9–10; 12:10–11, 36; 13:26; 14:27, 62), since this was a common element of the preaching of the early church from the beginning.[16] It is something that becomes even more emphatic in the other Gospels. Early Christianity regarded the fulfillment of the Scriptures in Jesus Christ as of supreme importance.

14. The words "the Son of God" are lacking in the first hand of ℵ and also in Θ, but they are found in B and other manuscripts. Because of this division of the significant textual witnesses, these words usually are put in brackets.

15. Hoskyns and Davey, *The Riddle of the New Testament*, 159–60. All NT students should know this classic work. See also Dodd, *According to the Scriptures*.

16. Rikki Watts has shown the importance of the OT for Mark, especially the motif of the new exodus in Isaiah (*Isaiah's New Exodus and Mark*). See too Joel Marcus, *The Way of the Lord*.

The Present Dawning of the Kingdom of God

The essence of the good news of the "gospel" is the announcement of the arrival of the kingdom of God. Thus Mark 1:15: "The time is fulfilled, and the kingdom of God is at hand; repent, and believe in the gospel." This early sentence provides the theme of Mark[17] and of the other Synoptic Gospels. All of Jesus' ministry, including his death, stands under the rubric of the kingdom of God. Everything that Jesus says and does is related to this overarching concept of the presence of the kingdom. His healings are head-on confrontations with the kingdom of darkness. The first healing narrative in Mark concerns a man "with an unclean spirit," which, on seeing Jesus, cries out, "What have you to do with us, Jesus of Nazareth? Have you come to destroy us? I know who you are, the Holy One of God" (1:24). In a summarizing passage about Jesus, Mark records that "he healed many who were sick with various diseases, and cast out many demons; and he would not permit the demons to speak, because they knew him" (1:34). This is no ordinary liberation from human oppression; it is a confrontation with the very powers of hell. The demons, who sense immediately the threat to their dominion, have no doubt concerning the identity of Jesus. The people want Jesus to set up a permanent healing clinic, but Jesus' purpose is the proclamation of the kingdom, and so he continues "preaching in their synagogues and casting out demons" (1:39). This battle with the kingdom of Satan continues to be a strong emphasis in Mark (3:15; 5:1–20; 6:7, 13; 7:25–30; 9:14–29).

The disciples have been given "the secret [*mystērion*][18] of the kingdom of God" (4:11). In parables Jesus indicates the hidden nature of the kingdom: it is presently like secretly growing seed (4:26–29) or an inconspicuous mustard seed (4:30–32). As it has come in the present mysteriously, it will also come in power in the future (9:1; 14:25). Participation in the present dawning kingdom is worth everything (9:47; 10:14–15, 23–25; 12:34).

The Twelve are sent out on a mission to spread the ministry of Jesus by preaching and casting out demons (3:14; 6:7–13).

The Deeds and Words of Jesus

From Mark 1:15 to 8:30 the Evangelist presents a representative sampling of things that Jesus said and did in Galilee. He will present more in the following chapters, but, as we will see, 8:31 is a clear turning point in the narrative. That Mark presents only a sampling should be clear from the summary passages that he includes at certain points in his narrative (e.g., 1:32–34; 3:10; 6:5, 34, 55–56). Mark selects from his memory the most vivid anecdotes that Peter had

---

17. See France, *Divine Government*.

18. Something hitherto unknown but now made clear with the coming of Christ. The Matthean parallel has a plural: "secrets" (13:11).

used in his preaching. He groups some together (e.g., the controversy stories in 2:15–3:6; the parables in 4:1–34), and otherwise he shapes the sequence of the narrative in his own creative way. This is probably what Papias had in mind when he noted that Mark's Gospel was "not in order"—that is, not arranged chronologically.

The deeds of Jesus can be classified in several categories: exorcisms and healings predominate, but there are also "nature" miracles, the stilling of the storm (4:35–41), the feeding of the five thousand (6:35–44), walking on the sea (6:47–52), and the feeding of the four thousand (8:1–10). Sizable selections of Jesus' teaching are provided (2:19–22; 4:1–34; 7:6–23; 8:34–38; 10:2–31, 39–45; 11:22–26; 12:1–44; 13:1–36; 14:17–31). It is seldom realized that as much as one-half of Mark's Gospel is given over to presenting the teaching of Jesus.[19]

The Centrality of the Passion Narrative

At 8:31, at about the midpoint of Mark, the narrative takes a very strange turn. Up to this point, the question implied or explicit has been who Jesus is (e.g., 2:12; 4:41; 7:37). When Jesus finally puts the question to his disciples, Peter, as spokesman for the disciples, answers, "You are the Christ" (8:29). But as soon as Jesus elicits this statement, he surprisingly begins to speak of his death: "And he began to teach them that the Son of man must suffer many things, and be rejected by the elders and the chief priests and the scribes, and be killed, and after three days rise again. And he said this plainly [*parrēsia*]" (8:31–32).[20] Peter's response to the idea of a Messiah who dies shows how ill-prepared he was for such an announcement. His rebuke notwithstanding, this was the will of God (8:33).

We have arrived here at *the central purpose of Jesus*. He has come not to do wonders or to teach, though he did both, but, mysteriously, *to accomplish a redeeming death*. "For the Son of man also came not to be served but to serve, and to give his life as a ransom [*lytron*] for many" (10:45 [cf. 14:24: "This is my blood of the covenant"]). The remainder of Mark's narrative is preparatory for the cross. The prediction of the passion is repeated twice in the next two chapters (9:30–32; 10:32–34). The threefold announcement of the passion is taken up by both Matthew and Luke. After the triumphant entry into Jerusalem (11:1–11), some further teaching in chapter 12, and the great eschatological discourse of chapter 13, chapters 14–15 give the story of the passion in considerable detail. This narrative is undergirded with OT citations to emphasize that what happens is the fulfillment of the will of God (note esp. the use of Pss. 22 and 69 in 15:23–36). This is the heart of the story and the salvific act on which the gospel of the kingdom rests. In the words

19. See France, "Mark and the Teaching of Jesus."
20. There are anticipations of the death of Jesus earlier in Mark. See 1:11 (taking the last clause as an allusion to Isa. 42:1 and connecting it with the suffering servant in Isa. 53); 2:20; 3:6.

of Edwyn Hoskyns and Noel Davey, "This violent and voluntary death is the *opus operatum* which inaugurates the New Order."[21]

As the climax of the story of Jesus and the passion narrative in particular, the resurrection is vitally important. Here, however, apart from the prophecy in each of the three passion predictions that he will arise after three days (8:31; 9:31; 10:34) and the angelic announcement in 16:6, no further attention is given to the resurrection per se. Mark is disappointing in comparison with the other Gospels, but this, as we will see, may well be the result of the original ending having been lost.

Christology

As the story of Jesus, the Gospel of Mark focuses on the key question: "Who is this person?"[22] The question dominates the narrative at least until Peter's statement in 8:29, but also beyond. Who is it who can do these things and speak these words, with such unparalleled power and authority?

Already in the first line of this Gospel the Evangelist gives away the answer: "Jesus Christ, the Son of God." Jesus is the Christ (= the Messiah) and uniquely the Son of God—that is, in a unique relationship with God. One argument for accepting the textually doubtful words "the Son of God" is the inclusio that they form with the words spoken by the centurion near the end of the book: "Truly this man was the Son of God" (15:39). Mark's christology finds its center in this designation. Peter's confession that Jesus is the Christ has been noted above. The Christ, "the anointed one," was unquestionably an exalted, although not necessarily divine, figure. But *this* Messiah, destined to die, is described as David's "Lord" (*kyrios* [12:35–37]). Although Jesus accepts the designation "the Christ" from others, it is only in 14:62 that we have his direct affirmation of the title, when in response to the high priest's question "Are you the Christ, the Son of the Blessed?" Jesus answers, "I am [*egō eimi*]."[23] Mark uses the title "Son" in 1:11 (also in 9:7), and demons recognize Jesus as "the Son of God" in 3:11 and as "Son of the Most High God" in 5:7. Note also the only slightly veiled self-designation of Jesus as the "beloved son" in the parable of the wicked tenants (12:6).

The more deliberately ambiguous expression "Son of Man" is used in a titular sense of a divine agent—that is, the glorious apocalyptic Son of Man, who is to come (in allusion to Dan. 7:13–14), spoken of by Jesus in the third person, but clearly in self-reference (8:38; 13:26; 14:62). Another ambiguous expression in Mark is *kyrios*, which can mean "sir," but also can be a divine

21. Hoskyns and Davey, *The Riddle of the New Testament*, 160.

22. See Hooker, "'Who Can This Be?'"

23. The phrase *egō eimi* is also in the mouth of Jesus as he walks on the sea (6:50). Probably more is meant than the prosaic "It is I." Given its context, it likely is a deliberate allusion to the deity, as in the *egō eimi* in the Greek text of Exodus 3:14.

title referring to a sovereign ruler. Implicitly, the latter is the sense of the word as it is used in 1:3 (the Isaiah quotation implicitly pointing to Jesus) and 12:36–37 (Ps. 110:1 applied to Jesus).

Perhaps equally impressive as the titles is the indirect christology of Mark's Gospel, the things that Jesus says and does that continually raise the question "Who is this man?" Of course, others taught and performed exorcisms and healings, but the power and authority of Jesus exceeded that of others. He forgives the sins of the paralytic (2:1–12), an act regarded as a divine prerogative; he stills the storm (4:35–41; cf. 6:51); he walks on the sea (6:45–52); he raises the dead (6:35–43); he multiplies loaves and fish in two narratives (6:30–44; 8:14–21). Finally, we may mention the one point in the narrative where the disguised glorious identity of Jesus is plainly seen, although only by the inner circle of disciples: his transfiguration (9:2–8), where it is again stressed that Jesus is the unique Son of God, whose authority exceeds even that of the law (Moses) and the prophets (Elijah).

The point to be made here is that Mark, the earliest Gospel, already has a very high christology. This comes to him via the tradition that he received from Peter and others. This view of Jesus is not something later imposed on the tradition; it is part and parcel of the original wellspring from which the Evangelist drank. It is intrinsic to all that Jesus says and does.

Discipleship and Faith

Discipleship is an important theme in Mark.[24] From the start, Jesus calls individuals to follow him (1:16–20; 2:14). There is unmistakable irony in that the disciples—who desired the glory, with its privilege and power, of association with Jesus in his kingdom (10:35–37)—must learn that discipleship means following Jesus in self-denial, suffering, and even death (10:38–39).[25] Immediately after the first announcement of the passion, Jesus defines discipleship as following in his steps: "If any man would come after me, let him deny himself and take up his cross and follow me. For whoever would save his life will lose it; and whoever loses his life for my sake and the gospel's will save it" (8:34–35). Greatness is to be found in the service of others, again in the pattern being set by Jesus (10:42–45).

The initial statement of Jesus about the kingdom in 1:15 includes the command to repent "and believe [*pisteuete*] in the gospel." Faith and believing remain important throughout Mark's Gospel. Disciples of Jesus are described as "those who believe in me" (9:42). Faith is normally requisite for healing, as in 2:5 (where healing is also connected with the forgiveness of sins); 5:36 (in connection with the raising of the dead). In 5:34 and 10:52 the verb *sōzō* is

24. See Best, *Disciples and Discipleship*; Hurtado, "Following Jesus in the Gospel of Mark—and Beyond."

25. See Schweizer, "The Portrayal of the Life of Faith in the Gospel of Mark."

used, in the sense of "your faith has made you well." When the disciples are in mortal danger on the lake, Jesus asks, "Have you no faith?" (4:40). In 9:23 Jesus teaches that "all things are possible to him who believes," and in 11:22–24 Jesus speaks of the power of faith, concluding with the words "Therefore I tell you, whatever you ask in prayer, believe that you have received it, and it will be yours."

The Eschatological Discourse

Occasionally it has been argued that Mark's eschatological discourse (chap. 13) was taken over in toto from a preexisting "apocalypse."[26] There seems little reason, however, to oppose the idea that Mark is reporting the account of Jesus' discourse on the Mount of Olives as he remembered it from Peter's preaching.

It is odd to speak of an eschatological discourse—that is, about the future—in a Gospel that has as its main theme the present realization of the promised hope. We encounter here the "now but not yet" tension that runs throughout the NT. One way to speak about this is to use the word "eschatology" for the present fulfillment described in the NT and the word "consummation" for the future.[27] The consummation cannot happen until evil receives its judgment and the righteous their reward. The purpose of what we now know to be the first coming of the Messiah was the establishment of the kingdom by his death. It will be the return, or second coming, of the Messiah that will finally bring the consummation. The Olivet discourse is concerned with this final sequence of events.

Before the consummation there will be an apparently extended time of various trials and difficulties, described as "but the beginning of the birth-pangs" preceding the consummation (13:8). There will be persecution of the followers of Jesus (13:9–13), but this is still not the end. The difficulty, to put it mildly, of interpreting the remainder of Jesus' eschatological discourse is well known. On the one hand, the section 13:14–23 refers almost certainly to the fall of Jerusalem (as Luke's redaction of the discourse suggests [Luke 21:20–24]). The section that follows (13:24–37), on the other hand, refers to the time of the parousia, the second coming of Jesus. The difficult verse at 13:30 refers most naturally to the fall of Jerusalem, and it occurs here either by dislocation or misunderstanding (i.e., in the expectation that the fall of Jerusalem would necessarily entail the consummation).

Of special importance in the discourse is this incidental notation: "And the gospel must first be preached to all nations" (13:10 [cf. 14:9]). This is evidence that the story of Jesus is not about the restoration of Israel and no more; rather, it is about *the salvation that will now be offered to all the world, Jews*

---

26. For an interesting attempt at reconstruction of the pre-Synoptic discourse, see Wenham, *The Rediscovery of Jesus' Eschatological Discourse.*

27. See, for example, Ladd, *The Presence of the Future,* 105–21.

and Gentiles together. In 7:24–37 Jesus travels to predominantly Gentile areas (see also 5:1–20), while in 8:1–10 he feeds the four thousand, which probably is to be understood as a provision for the Gentiles. The Greek woman in 7:25, whose attitude Jesus admired, was happy if she could but have the crumbs from the table of Israel's blessing. But as we reach the end of Mark's narrative, the Gentiles are enabled to sit at the table with the Jews. They too are to be the recipients of the gospel. When Jesus cleanses the temple, he quotes from Isaiah 56:7: "My house shall be called a house of prayer for all the nations" (11:17). The final confession in Mark's Gospel, that Jesus is the Son of God, comes from a Roman centurion (15:39). Thus the universalism of the story, yet to flower in the period after the resurrection of Jesus, is implicit throughout this Gospel.

These basic building blocks of Markan material bear an interesting relationship to the kerygma of the early church. Mark's Gospel can be thought of as *an expansion of the kerygma*, as we encounter it in the sermons in Acts, and it is not difficult to hear in this material what must have been common elements in the preaching of Peter and others. By virtue of the amount of Mark picked up by Matthew and Luke, the material of these building blocks comes to serve as *the common substructure of the Synoptic Gospels*, as essentially fixed points of the Synoptic tradition. Matthew and Luke will, of course, put their own redactional stamp on the material, and they will add their own material with its distinctive emphases. Nevertheless, their Gospels find their core in the Markan content that they adopt.

There is no need to dismiss this analysis, as some do, because no detailed chronology is offered. It was not the purpose of Mark, nor of Matthew or Luke, to be concerned with chronology.[28] At the same time, however, via Mark we do find common, fixed points in the sequential outline of the Synoptics:

- the appearance of John the Baptist;
- the baptism and temptation of Jesus;
- the Galilean ministry;
- Peter's confession;
- the announcement of the passion;
- the transfiguration;
- the journey to Jerusalem;
- the Jerusalem ministry;
- the cleansing of the temple;

28. "Individuals—and here we may think of Mark himself or an older informant—do remember the general course of events which have taken place within their knowledge, even (or indeed especially) forty years before, although they may find it difficult to say when or where certain incidents took place or certain words were spoken" (Bruce, "The Date and Character of Mark," 72).

- the Passover meal;
- the passion narrative of arrest, trial, condemnation, crucifixion; and
- the resurrection.

This basic Markan story line, but with modifications and especially additions, is found in similar form in Matthew and Luke. Within its framework there is much variation. Nevertheless, these elements remain constant within the Synoptics and even in John to a considerable extent.

Other Characteristics and Distinctives of the Gospel of Mark

The Beginning and the Ending

Mark's Gospel is unusual in both respects.

Mark 1:1 appears to be a title to the book, and 1:2 begins rather awkwardly with the comparative conjunction *kathōs* ("just as"). Unlike Matthew or Luke, Mark lacks a birth narrative or even any mention of the birth of Jesus. One can understand how Matthew and Luke (independently) would have been interested in adding such information to Mark, but it is very difficult to understand how Mark, if it was the latest of the Synoptics (per the Griesbach hypothesis), could have omitted this material without at least a brief note concerning the birth of Jesus.

The abrupt ending of Mark, according to the oldest and best manuscripts, with the statement of the women that "they said nothing to any one, for they were afraid" (16:8), has caused much discussion. It clearly is possible that this Gospel ended with the final two words *ephobounto gar* ("for they were afraid").[29] But this seems improbable to many now, as it did also in the ancient church, with the result that endings were provided to supply the perceived deficiency. Thus there exist a shorter and two longer endings. The vast majority of late manuscripts include one of the longer endings, and it is this that is commonly printed in the NT as 16:9–20.[30]

The ending at 16:8 is capable of explanation in different ways, appeal usually being made to the implied invitation to readers to identify with the ambivalence of the women, their failure, doubt, and fear, or simply to the open-endedness of the story, to be finished by the reader.[31] However, there are good reasons to believe that 16:8 may not have been the original or intended ending. It is not

---

29. It has been shown that a document can end with *gar* ("for"), which as a postpositive must come after the verb. See van der Horst, "Can a Book End with ΓΑΡ?"

30. For full data, see Metzger, *A Textual Commentary on the Greek New Testament*, 102–6. The added endings employ a significant amount of non-Markan vocabulary.

31. See Lincoln, "The Promise and the Failure"; Spencer, "The Denial of the Good News and the Ending of Mark," especially the appendix, 281–83.

difficult to suppose that the last leaf of the manuscript was damaged or lost.[32] (It is intriguing to ponder the possibility that the lost ending of Mark may underlie, as its source, the ending of Matthew's Gospel.) N. Clayton Croy has presented a strong case for the idea of a truncation of both beginning and end of Mark's Gospel owing to the loss of the outside leaf of a codex.[33] Robert Stein presents a convincing case from Mark itself that the ending at 16:8 is very unlikely. His two main arguments are that (1) Mark's pointers to a postresurrection meeting of Jesus with his disciples in Galilee (14:28; 16:7) virtually require a fulfillment to conclude the story; and (2) the emphasis in 16:1–8 is not on the disciples and their failures but rather on Jesus, so that the key verses are 16:6–7, not 16:8.[34] The question must again remain open, but the probability leans in the direction of a lost original ending.

The "Messianic Secret"

One remarkable aspect of Mark's narrative is the repeated instruction to keep silent about the messianic identity of Jesus.[35] This admonition is given to the demons (1:25 ["the Holy One of God"], 34; 3:11 ["the Son of God"]), those who have been healed (1:44; 5:43; 7:36; cf. 8:26), and also to the disciples themselves (8:30 ["the Christ"]; 9:9 [the transfiguration]). This motif is picked up in Matthew and Luke, but it is not as prominent in those Gospels as it is in Mark. The command to secrecy in a Gospel designed to promote Jesus as the promised Messiah produces an unusual paradox, causing Mark to be dubbed a Gospel of "secret epiphanies" (thus Martin Dibelius). The gospel being revealed in the narrative is also kept secret. In a couple of instances those who are healed are, because of their joy, unable to keep the secret. Despite being sternly charged to "say nothing to anyone," the cleansed leper "went out and began to talk freely about it, and to spread the news" (1:44–45).[36] Similarly, after the healing of the deaf mute, the people are charged to tell no one, "but the more he charged them, the more zealously they proclaimed it" (7:36 [no parallel in Matthew or Luke]).

What is the explanation of this phenomenon? An obvious answer is that the reputation of Jesus as a healer, whether messianic or not, drew huge crowds, so that "Jesus could no longer openly enter a town" (1:45). Just as a practical matter, Jesus wanted to avoid the crowds: "He entered a house, and would not have any one know it; yet he could not be hid" (7:24 [cf. 9:30]).

---

32. According to Metzger, this is the probable explanation of the ending at 16:8. It seems "most probable," he writes, that "the Gospel accidentally lost its last leaf before it was multiplied by transcription" (*A Textual Commentary on the Greek New Testament*, 105n7).

33. Croy, *The Mutilation of Mark's Gospel*, following a suggestion by C. F. D. Moule, *The Birth of the New Testament*, 131n1.

34. Stein, "The Ending of Mark."

35. See Aune, "The Problem of the Messianic Secret."

36. Luke relieves the scandal of the disobedience by generalizing the report: "But so much the more the report went abroad concerning him [Jesus]" (5:15).

But more than this has been seen in the call to secrecy. Thus, rather famously, William Wrede came up with the peculiar hypothesis that the secrecy motif was the invention of the early church to cover up the fact that, in Wrede's opinion, Jesus made no claim to be the Messiah.[37] The call to secrecy was a way to explain why there was no (preresurrection) Gospel tradition affirming Jesus as the Messiah. But this conclusion ignores much messianic content, both explicit and implicit, that is in Mark (and arbitrarily rejected by Wrede). One may wonder why, if the early Christians permitted themselves to create tradition at will, they did not simply put messianic content into the mouth of Jesus. That would have taken care of their supposed "embarrassment."

In fact, Wrede's view is too simple and fully misses the significance of the paradox intrinsic to this material. The key to understanding the secrecy motif is in *the paradoxical nature of Jesus' messiahship*. The purpose of the secret is to avoid inflaming messianic expectation among the masses, whose hopes were tied to a militant, triumphant Messiah.[38] Jesus comes, however, not as that kind of Messiah, but as one who has a greater mission, one that can be accomplished only on the cross. The death of the Messiah stands as the central mystery of the Gospel narratives, and it is the mystery that lies behind the so-called messianic secret.

As one begins to move into the passion narrative, the secrecy motif disappears, as no longer relevant,[39] just as after the resurrection the secrecy concerning the transfiguration is no longer binding (9:9). A man on a cross is not likely to incite messianic fervor (cf. 15:31–32).

Just as the gospel of the kingdom involves a present veiling, so too does the messianic identity of Jesus. The kingdom and the Messiah are present, but not in the way expected.

Literary Characteristics

Mark's narrative is well known for its vividness and eyewitness detail. This observation is consonant with the conclusion that the Evangelist depends on the preaching of Peter much of the time. Mark prefers the historical present tense (more than 150x), such as "he says" rather than "he said." Further energy is brought to the narrative by Mark's frequent use (more than 40x) of *euthys* ("immediately") and *palin* ("again") in connecting individual pericopes. The syntax is rapid moving, mostly paratactic, often involving short sentences beginning with *kai* ("and"). Mark's Greek itself, as we have already noted, often is quite rough and anything but polished.

An unusual phenomenon in Mark is intercalation or interpolation: one story is sandwiched inside another, as in the insertion of the story of the healing of the

---

37. See Wrede, *The Messianic Secret*.

38. Note the remark in John 6:15, where, after the feeding of the five thousand, the crowd wants to "take him by force to make him king."

39. See Hengel, *Studies in the Gospel of Mark*, 43.

woman with a hemorrhage (5:25–34) into the middle of the story of the healing of Jairus's daughter (begun in 5:21–24 and continued in 5:35–43). The same phenomenon can be seen in 3:20–35; 6:7–30; 11:12–21; 14:1–11.[40] While these insertions do have the effect of heightening suspense, there may be more going on. James Edwards argues that the insertions "underscore the major motifs" of Mark and provide "the key to the interpretation of the whole."[41] Tom Shepherd finds "dramatized irony" in the intercalations, with christology as a central theme.[42]

The Humanity of Jesus

Alongside his high christology, Mark emphasizes the full humanity of Jesus by indicating that he experienced anger (3:5), was indignant (10:14), felt pity (1:41), marveled (6:6), loved (10:21), and "sighed deeply in his spirit" (8:12). Although all these passages find Synoptic parallels, in every instance this "human" language is studiously avoided by Matthew and Luke (these omissions thus fall in the category of minor agreements against Mark, but they are easily explained). In Mark, Jesus is both the glorious Messiah (though this is for the most part kept secret in the narrative) and the one who is fully human, one who is called indeed to suffer and to die.

The Weakness of the Disciples

Although the disciples clearly are in a favored position by virtue of their relationship to Jesus, they are characterized more by failure than by success.[43] Repeatedly they fail to understand his teaching (7:18; cf. 4:13; 8:21). Not only are they without understanding but also they are described as being hard-hearted (6:52; 8:17; the Matthean parallels omit both references). They lack faith (4:40). They do not understand it when Jesus speaks of his death, and thus they miss the main point of the narrative (8:32–33; 9:32). They fail to grasp the significance of Jesus (9:5–8); they covet positions of power and glory (10:35–45). They forsake Jesus at the end (14:50), and even deny knowing him (14:71). Even the women, who usually do better, are afraid and silent at the end (16:8). Matthew and Luke, however, present a more favorable (though not completely so) picture of the disciples.

Conflict with the Jewish Authorities

Early in the Gospel (2:1–3:6) Mark groups together (topically, not chrono-logically) some confrontation stories where Jesus is opposed by the Jewish

---

40. James Edwards finds four further examples (4:1–20; 14:17–31; 14:53–72; 15:40–16:8) ("Markan Sandwiches").
41. Ibid., 216.
42. Shepherd, "The Narrative Function of Markan Intercalation."
43. See Tannehill, "The Disciples in Mark."

leaders. Already by 3:6 the Pharisees and the Herodians begin to plan "how to destroy him." The issues in this section of Mark concern Jesus' forgiveness of the sins of the paralytic, his table fellowship with "tax collectors and sinners" (2:15, 16), his failure to fast, and his failure to obey the Sabbath.[44] The conflict seems inevitable and increases in succeeding chapters. Jesus portrays the Pharisees as "hypocrites," applying Isaiah 29:13 to them. The effect of their practice is that they "leave the commandment of God, and hold fast the tradition of men" (7:1–13). The Pharisees and Herodians try to "entrap" Jesus in his teaching (12:13–17); the Sadducees do the same and are described by Jesus as those who "know neither the scriptures nor the power of God" (12:18–27). Jesus criticizes the scribes for seeking their own glory (12:38–40). As the passion narrative proper begins, the chief priests and scribes are described as plotting to kill Jesus (14:1). They, together with the elders, arrest Jesus in the garden (14:43) and meet with the whole council (15:1), bringing the narrative to its climax.[45]

The Galilean and Jerusalem Ministries of Jesus

Some Markan scholars have seen the key to the structure of Mark in the geographical division of the narrative into a Galilee section (chaps. 1–9) and a Jerusalem section (chaps. 11–16), separated by the journey to Jerusalem (chap. 10). These scholars have seen here a kind of "theological geography," reflecting the different roles of each respective area—for example, Galilee representing the region of the initial revelation of and response to the kingdom and the place of the apocalyptic appearance of the resurrected Jesus, and Jerusalem representing the rejection and crucifixion of Jesus.[46] But there have been different analyses of the possible symbolism behind Galilee and Jerusalem, with little agreement on conclusions. Werner Kümmel, to offer another explanation, finds Galilee to be "the point of departure for the Gentile mission" and Jerusalem the place of Jewish unbelief. In this way, "Mark demonstrates the theological idea of the transfer of salvation from the unbelieving Jews to the believing Gentiles, and thereby discloses that he is addressing himself to Gentile Christianity, which no longer has any relationship with Jerusalem and the Jews there."[47]

Freedom from the Law of Moses

At one point in Mark's narrative a quite remarkable redactional addition is made. It consists of what appears to be an inserted parenthesis in 7:19: "Thus

44. See Hagner, "Jesus and the Synoptic Sabbath Controversies."
45. On the subject of conflict, see Kingsbury, *Conflict in Mark.*
46. See Marxsen, *Mark the Evangelist,* 54–116.
47. Kümmel, *Introduction to the New Testament,* 88–89.

he declared all foods clean." The awkward syntax of the Greek is caused by the dangling participle *katharizōn*, ("cleansing"), which has no express subject. Possibly it refers to the normal "cleansing" of digestion, but most probably it refers to the point of Jesus' teaching; that is, by saying that what goes into a person's mouth does not defile, he had in effect done away with *kashrut*, the food laws of the Torah. This conclusion would have great significance for Gentiles. And this passage is set in a context that has Gentiles in view: Jesus travels to the region of Tyre and Sidon (7:24), heals the Syrophoenician woman's daughter (7:25–30), and feeds the four thousand, symbolically the Gentiles (8:1–10). This editorial insertion accords with the emphasis on Gentiles (already mentioned above) and strongly supports the conclusion that Mark was written to Gentile readers. The discontinuity between the old and new is stressed in 2:21–22. New cloth and new wine cannot simply be added to the old.

The Splitting of the Temple Curtain at the Moment of Jesus' Death

According to Mark 15:38, when Jesus breathed his last, "the curtain of the temple was torn in two, from top to bottom." The significance of this momentous event is left implicit in the narrative (so too the prophecy of the destruction of the temple [13:2; cf. 14:58; 15:29]). Matthew associates it with the apocalyptic sign of an earthquake (Matt. 27:51). More than a piece of incidental information, this report serves as the symbol of the passing from one era to another, from the sacrificial system of the OT to the finished work accomplished through the sacrifice of Jesus on the cross. As the author of Hebrews puts it, "We have confidence to enter the sanctuary by the blood of Jesus, by the new and living way which he opened for us through the curtain, that is, through his flesh" (Heb. 10:19–20).

The Purpose of Mark

Given that we have no direct access to the oral tradition used by Mark, it is very difficult, if not impossible, to discover Mark's purpose from his redaction of the traditions that serve as his source.[48] For the most part, we must discover Mark's purpose from his Gospel as it stands.[49]

From the very beginning of this Gospel we know that the Evangelist intends to present the story of the "gospel of Jesus Christ, the Son of God." To that

48. Note Clifton Black's justified pessimism along this line: "Markan redaction criticism has emerged as a rather hopeless, if not misbegotten, enterprise" (*The Disciples according to Mark*, 252). See also idem, "The Quest of Mark the Redactor."

49. See the constructive suggestions by Stein, "The Proper Methodology for Ascertaining a Markan Redaction History."

extent, Mark's purpose may be described as evangelistic. If we are correct in concluding that Mark represents the preaching of Peter, then one aspect of his purpose is to make that preaching available to a wide readership. Mark intends to record some of the words and deeds of Jesus, and in particular to show how hostility and opposition to him from his own people began to grow, and how in the end Jesus, now worshiped by Christians as Lord, came to be rejected by the Jewish people and crucified by the Romans like an ordinary criminal. So, as we have seen, the story of the death of Jesus dominates the narrative. Jesus went to the cross willingly, even by design (10:45), not as a criminal, but honorably, as one who was misrepresented and misunderstood, and preeminently as one who gave his life for others.

Another aspect of Mark's purpose may be seen in his emphasis not only on the suffering of Jesus but also on the necessity of suffering in the lives of the disciples. This emphasis makes good sense especially if Mark had in mind a community of believers who were subject to persecution (cf. 4:17; 10:30; 13:9–13). Christians were called to walk in the steps of their Lord.

The repeated motif of the humanity of Jesus and the necessity of his suffering and death has raised in the minds of some scholars the possibility that Mark's picture of Jesus represents a "corrective christology"—that is, a portrait of Jesus that contradicts the idea of Jesus as a Hellenistic "divine man" (*theios anēr*).[50] In this view, Mark writes to counter the triumphalist idea of a Hellenistic wonder worker with the idea of a fully human Christ who suffers and who dies.[51] Robert Gundry has turned this view on its head, arguing that the correction goes the other way: "A theology of glory pervades the Gospel of Mark" and Mark presents "a qualification of suffering by glory."[52] Mark thus writes to emphasize the glory and power of Christ as the context of his suffering and death.

However one looks at it, both the glory and the suffering of Jesus are on display in Mark, and in this Gospel we have the balance of a *theologia gloriae* and a *theologia crucis*. Both must be retained as fundamentally important.

Authorship, Date, Setting

Author

The Gospel of Mark, like all the Gospels, is anonymous. The tradition of the church, however, has always identified this Gospel as "according to Mark." We

---

50. For this hypothesis, see Weeden, "The Heresy That Necessitated Mark's Gospel." Weeden speaks of "a christological dispute raging in Mark's community" (ibid., 91).

51. Ralph P. Martin adds to this the comparison of a Pauline community that emphasized union with a glorious, heavenly Christ to the neglect of an earthly, humble, and suffering Jesus. Mark writes to correct this distortion, as a kind of supplement to Paul's kerygma (*Mark*, 156–62).

52. Gundry, *Mark*, 1024.

began by looking at the testimony of Papias concerning the origin of this Gospel. Papias refers to Mark as one who "had not heard the Lord, nor had he followed him, but later on, as I said, followed Peter." Since, as is often pointed out, the name "Mark" was common in the ancient world, we cannot be absolutely sure that this Mark is the John Mark whom we read of elsewhere in the NT. But in two places we have an association with Peter that would be consistent with this identification. According to Acts 12:12, when Peter was released from his imprisonment, he went "to the house of Mary, the mother of John whose other name was Mark." And in 1 Peter 5:13, Mark is referred to as Peter's "son" and is said to be with Peter in "Babylon" (i.e., Rome). The indirect, incidental way in which this information is offered seems to support the information provided by Papias. In Colossians 4:10 Mark is said to have been "the cousin of Barnabas," which would bear out the other references to Mark in Acts (in 12:25, Mark departs from Jerusalem with Barnabas and Saul; and in 15:36–40 there is the falling out between Barnabas and Paul over Mark).[53] There seems little reason to doubt that all these references have the same Mark in view.

The arguments against the identification of the author of this Gospel as this John Mark are not particularly strong, and they require an inappropriate exactitude of the author. It usually is asserted that as a Jerusalem Jew, John Mark would have known the geography of Palestine better that the author does. However, besides the fact that it is difficult or impossible to know that we have it right and Mark has it wrong, since place names are notoriously tricky, some of the apparent misdirections of the narrative may be the result of the Evangelist's freedom to order his pericopes (with their own geographical tags) at will, which could easily result in confusion. Furthermore, as Martin Hengel points out, it is not always the case that a person knows well the geography even of the region in which he has lived for a long time.[54] Similar arguments that the author does not know Jewish customs demand too high a degree of precision for the author's purposes and do not allow for generalizations. The argument that the author was a Gentile is equally unnecessary. The narrative is exceptionally Jewish, even to the point of being seasoned with Aramaic words.[55] Nothing in it requires a Gentile author.

In short, the evidence, though indirect and certainly short of proof, points in the direction of John Mark as the author. The appeal to some other Mark,

---

53. There are only two other references to Mark in the NT: Philemon 24, where he is one of Paul's "fellow workers," and 2 Timothy 4:11, where Paul writes, "Get Mark and bring him with you; for he is very useful in serving me."

54. Hengel gives an amusing example of a longtime colleague in Tübingen who did not know his local geography (*Studies in the Gospel of Mark*, 148n51).

55. Beyond more than a dozen proper nouns (place or personal names): *abba* (14:36), *ephphatha* (7:34), *korban* (7:11), *pascha* (14:1, 12, 14, 16), *rabbouni* (10:51), *sabbata* (1:21; 2:23–24; 3:2, 4; 16:2), *talitha koum(i)* (5:41), and the Aramaic form of Psalm 22:2 in 15:34. The unusual amount of Aramaic vocabulary indirectly supports the conclusion that the Evangelist depends on the preaching of Peter.

unknown to us, seems the result of unreasonable skepticism and is quite un-necessary and unconvincing by comparison.[56]

Date

If the author of this Gospel really was John Mark, then we have at least that much information about the date of the book, even though we do not know the time of his death (perhaps even before Peter [cf. Eusebius *Hist. eccl.* 2.24: in the eighth year of Nero's reign, thus 62]). An important question is whether this Gospel was written before or after Peter's martyrdom (ca. 64). On the one hand, it is not at all impossible to argue that it was written before Peter's death (thus Clement of Alexandria, *Hypotyposes*, book 6 [see Eusebius, *Hist. eccl.* 6.14.6–7]). There is even some evidence that Mark may have been written as early as 42.[57] On the other hand, other early evidence points to it being written after his death (Anti-Marcionite Prologue to the Gospel of Mark; Irenaeus, *Haer.* 3.1.1).

Although it is not easy to be confident, for *terminus ad quem*, the upper limit, 75 may be suggested, in order for Matthew and Luke to be dependent on Mark (but, of course, this presupposes that we know when those two were written). The *terminus a quo*, the lower limit, is even more difficult, though perhaps it would have to be 42. J. A. T. Robinson presents an interesting, if not persuasive, case for Mark having first put pen to paper to write a kind of proto-Mark as early as 45.[58] It is usually thought, however, whether rightly or wrongly, that the Gospel needs time to develop, and that this prohibits a very early date.[59]

In 1972 José O'Callaghan argued that NT papyri were among the fragments discovered in Cave 7 at Qumran.[60] In 7Q5, he maintained, he had found a tiny piece of Mark 6:52–53. This would provide hard evidence that Mark was written in the mid-60s at the latest. Most scholars, however, have found this conclusion highly unlikely.[61]

Without being able to exclude an earlier (or later) date, we may tentatively opt for a date of about 65, shortly after the death of Peter. This places the initial readers in a time when they would have been subject to persecution, which would make sense of that significant motif in this Gospel.

---

56. The puzzling anecdote in 14:51–52, unique to Mark, has been taken by some to be a reference to the author of the Gospel. This seems unlikely, but even if accepted, it provides no help in identifying the author. The man chooses to flee from following Jesus, even to the point of preferring to run away naked.

57. For an interesting presentation of evidence supporting a date of 42 to 44, see Wenham, *Redating Matthew, Mark and Luke*, 136–82; cf. Hengel, *Studies in the Gospel of Mark*, 5–6.

58. Robinson, *Redating the New Testament*, 116.

59. Robinson points out that guesses about time needed for "development" are too subjective (ibid.).

60. O'Callaghan, "New Testament Papyri in Qumran Cave 7?"

61. See Hemer, "New Testament Fragments at Qumran?"; Förster, "7Q5 = Mark 6:52–53."

Setting

It is equally difficult to establish where and to whom Mark was written.[62] Again, depending on the Papias tradition, we may take the Roman association of this Gospel with some seriousness. Mark is, of course, also associated with Alexandria, as the first to establish churches there (Eusebius, *Hist. eccl.* 2.16). According to Chrysostom (late fourth century), Mark was written in Egypt. Nevertheless, as we have already noted, Clement of Alexandria (ca. 200) accepts the tradition of Mark's Roman origin: "When Peter had publicly preached the word at Rome, and by the Spirit had proclaimed the Gospel, those present, who were many, exhorted Mark . . . to make a record of what was said; and he did this, and distributed the Gospel among those that asked him" (Eusebius, *Hist. eccl.* 6.14.6, trans. Oulton). Several items within this Gospel support the conclusion that Mark wrote with the Roman church in mind. There are a number of Latin words[63] not found in the other Gospels; this Gospel makes modifications with Gentiles in mind (as in 7:19, the revoking of the dietary restrictions; and 10:12, perhaps added for Gentile readers, whose wives had the right to divorce their husbands, unlike Jewish wives [hence omitted by Matthew in 5:32; 19:9]). The bearer of the cross for Jesus on the Via Dolorosa is named in 15:21 as Simon of Cyrene, "the father of Alexander and Rufus" (why mention this Rufus unless he is known to the Roman readers? [cf. Rom. 16:13]). Beyond this, the frequent references to persecution fit well the context of Nero in Rome in the 60s. None of this amounts to demonstration, but it is consistent with a Roman context for Mark's Gospel. There are, of course, other possibilities, such as Galilee[64] or Syria, but the evidence for these options is internal to the book and less convincing than Rome.[65]

The Gospel of Mark has been overshadowed by the Gospel of Matthew for most of church history. But with the revolutionary conclusion that Mark is the earliest of the Gospels, this changed dramatically. Now Mark has come to center stage. And the literature on Mark continues to burgeon. Questions continue to abound, even when our resources for answering them are meager. But Mark has been restored to its rightful place as a treasure of the church. As the distillation of the preaching of the early church and of Peter, the prime Apostle and eyewitness to the story, the Gospel of Mark is in a sense "the

62. For a quite pessimistic account of the possibility of establishing information about the Markan community, see Peterson, *The Origins of Mark*.

63. Werner Kümmel lists these, including explanations where a Latin word explains a Greek word (e.g., 12:42: "two copper coins make a *kodrantēs* [= *quadrans*]"; 15:16: "palace [that is, the *praetorium*]" (*Introduction to the New Testament*, 97–98).

64. "All conjectures about the role of the Galilean communities in the rise of the Gospel of Mark lead to groundless speculations" (Hengel, *Acts and the History of Earliest Christianity*, 76).

65. For a strong defense of Rome as the community addressed, see Incigneri, *The Gospel to the Romans*.

Gospel according to Peter."[66] And this may well be the reason that Mark was regarded so highly at the beginning—indeed, to the point of serving as the main source of the Gospels of Matthew and Luke.

Bibliography

Books and Articles

Anderson, Janice Capel, and Stephen D. Moore, eds. *Mark and Method: New Approaches in Biblical Studies*. 2nd ed. Minneapolis: Fortress, 2008.

Aune, David E. "The Problem of the Messianic Secret." *NovT* 11 (1969): 1–31.

Barta, Karen A. *The Gospel of Mark*. MBS 9. Wilmington, DE: Michael Glazier, 1988.

Barton, Stephen C. *Discipleship and Family Ties in Mark and Matthew*. SNTSMS 80. Cambridge: Cambridge University Press, 1994.

Bauckham, Richard. "The Gospel of Mark: Origins and Eyewitnesses." In *Earliest Christian History: History, Literature, and Theology. Essays from the Tyndale Fellowship in Honor of Martin Hengel*, edited by Michael F. Bird and Jason Maston, 145–69. WUNT 2/320. Tübingen: Mohr Siebeck, 2012.

———. *Jesus and the Eyewitnesses: The Gospels as Eyewitness Testimony*. Grand Rapids: Eerdmans, 2006.

Beck, Robert R. *Nonviolent Story: Narrative Conflict Resolution in the Gospel of Mark*. Maryknoll, NY: Orbis, 2000.

Best, Ernest. *Disciples and Discipleship: Studies in the Gospel according to Mark*. Edinburgh: T&T Clark, 1986.

———. *Following Jesus: Discipleship in the Gospel of Mark*. JSNTSup 4. Sheffield: JSOT Press, 1981.

———. *Mark: The Gospel as Story*. SNTW. Edinburgh: T&T Clark, 1983.

———. *The Temptation and the Passion: The Markan Soteriology*. 2nd ed. SNTSMS 2. Cambridge: Cambridge University Press, 1990.

Bilezikian, Gilbert G. *The Liberated Gospel: A Comparison of the Gospel of Mark and Greek Tragedy*. Grand Rapids: Baker, 1977.

Black, C. Clifton. *The Disciples according to Mark: Markan Redaction in Current Debate*. 2nd ed. Grand Rapids: Eerdmans, 2012.

———. *Mark: Images of an Apostolic Interpreter*. SPNT. Columbia: University of South Carolina Press, 1994.

———. "The Quest of Mark the Redactor: Why Has It Been Pursued, and What Has It Taught Us?" *JSNT* 33 (1988): 19–39.

Black, David A., ed. *Perspectives on the Ending of Mark*. Nashville: Broadman & Holman, 2008.

Blevins, James L. *The Messianic Secret in Markan Research, 1901–1976*. Washington, DC: University Press of America, 1981.

Bolt, Peter. *The Cross from a Distance: Atonement in Mark's Gospel*. NSBT 18. Downers Grove, IL: InterVarsity, 2004.

———. *Jesus' Defeat of Death: Persuading Mark's Early Readers*. SNTSMS 125. Cambridge: Cambridge University Press, 2003.

Broadhead, Edwin K. *Mark*. RNBC. Sheffield: Sheffield Academic Press, 2001.

---

66. Not to be confused with the apocryphal *Gospel of Peter*, a probably late second-century document dependent upon the canonical Gospels and consisting of an abbreviated passion and resurrection narrative. See Elliott, *The Apocryphal New Testament*, 150–58.

————. *Teaching with Authority: Miracles and Christology in the Gospel of Mark*. JSNTSup 74. Sheffield: JSOT Press, 1992.

Bruce, F. F. "The Date and Character of Mark." In *Jesus and the Politics of His Day*, edited by Ernst Bammel and C. F. D. Moule, 69–89. Cambridge: Cambridge University Press, 1984.

Bryan, Christopher. *A Preface to Mark: Notes on the Gospel in Its Literary and Cultural Settings*. Oxford: Oxford University Press, 1993.

Burkett, Delbert. *Rethinking the Gospel Sources: From Proto-Mark to Mark*. New York: T&T Clark International, 2004.

Camery-Hogatt, Jerry. *Irony in Mark's Gospel: Text and Subtext*. SNTSMS 72. Cambridge: Cambridge University Press, 1992.

Collins, Adela Yarbro. *The Beginning of the Gospel: Probings of Mark in Context*. Minneapolis: Fortress, 1992.

Cook, Michael J. *Mark's Treatment of the Jewish Leaders*. NovTSup 51. Leiden: Brill, 1978.

Crossley, James G. *The Date of Mark's Gospel: Insight from the Law in Earliest Christianity*. New York: T&T Clark International, 2004.

Croy, N. Clayton. *The Mutilation of Mark's Gospel*. Nashville: Abingdon, 2003.

Danove, Paul L. *The Rhetoric of the Characterization of God, Jesus, and Jesus' Disciples in the Gospel of Mark*. JSNTSup 290. New York: T&T Clark, 2005.

de Jong, Matthijs J. "Mark 16:8 as a Satisfying Ending to the Gospel." In *Jesus, Paul, and Early Christianity. Studies in Honour of Henk Jan de Jonge*, edited by Rieuwerd Buitenwerf, Harm W. Hollander, and Johannes Tromp, 123–47. NovTSup 130. Leiden: Brill, 2008.

Dodd, C. H. *According to the Scriptures: The Sub-Structure of New Testament Theology*. London: Nisbet, 1952.

————. *The Apostolic Preaching and Its Developments*. London: Hodder & Stoughton, 1936.

————. "The Framework of the Gospel Narrative." In *New Testament Studies*, 1–11. Manchester, UK: Manchester University Press, 1953.

Donahue, John R. *Are You the Christ? The Trial Narrative in the Gospel of Mark*. SBLDS 10. Missoula, MT: Society of Biblical Literature, 1973.

Dowd, Sharyn Echols. *Prayer, Power, and the Problem of Suffering: Mark 11:23–25 in the Context of Markan Theology*. SBLDS 105. Atlanta: Scholars Press, 1988.

Driggers, Ira Brent. *Following God through Mark: Theological Tension in the Second Gospel*. Louisville: Westminster John Knox, 2007.

Edwards, James R. "Markan Sandwiches: The Significance of Interpolations in Markan Narratives." *NovT* 31 (1989): 193–216.

Elliott, J. K., ed. *The Apocryphal New Testament: A Collection of Apocryphal Christian Literature in an English Translation*. Oxford: Clarendon, 1993.

————, ed. *The Language and Style of the Gospel of Mark: An Edition of C. H. Turner's "Notes on Marcan Usage," Together with Other Comparable Studies*. NovTSup 71. Leiden: Brill, 1993.

Farmer, William R. *The Last Twelve Verses of Mark*. SNTSMS 25. Cambridge: Cambridge University Press, 1974.

Farrer, Austin. *A Study in St. Mark*. Westminster, UK: Dacre, 1951.

Feldmeier, Reinhard. "The Portrayal of Peter in the Synoptic Gospels." In *Studies in the Gospel of Mark*, by Martin Hengel, translated by John Bowden, 59–63. Philadelphia: Fortress, 1985.

Förster, Hans. "7Q5 = Mark 6.52–53: A Challenge for Textual Criticism?" *JGRChJ* 2 (2001–5): 27–35.

Fowler, Robert M. *Let the Reader Understand: Reader-Response Criticism and the Gospel of Mark*. Minneapolis: Fortress, 1991.

————. *Loaves and Fishes: The Function of the Feeding Stories in the Gospel of Mark*. SBLDS 54. Chico, CA: Scholars Press, 1981.

France, R. T. *Divine Government: God's Kingship in the Gospel of Mark*. London: SPCK, 1990.

————. "Mark and the Teaching of Jesus." In *Studies of History and Tradition in the Four Gospels*, edited by R. T. France and David Wenham, 103–12. GP 1. Sheffield: JSOT Press, 1980.

Fullmer, Paul M. *Resurrection in Mark's Literary-Historical Perspective*. LNTS 360. London: T&T Clark, 2007.

Gaventa, Beverly Roberts, and Patrick D. Miller, eds. *The Ending of Mark and the Ends of God: Essays in Memory of Donald Harrisville Juel*. Louisville: Westminster John Knox, 2005.

Geddert, Timothy J. *Watchwords: Mark 13 in Markan Eschatology*. JSNTSup 26. Sheffield: JSOT Press, 1989.

Geyer, Douglas W. *Fear, Anomaly, and Uncertainty in the Gospel of Mark*. Lanham, MD: Scarecrow Press, 2001.

Hagner, Donald A. "Jesus and the Synoptic Sabbath Controversies." *BBR* 19 (2009): 215–48. Also published in *Key Events in the Life of the Historical Jesus: A Collaborative Exploration of Context and Coherence*, edited by Darrell L. Bock and Robert L. Webb, 251–92. WUNT 247. Tübingen: Mohr Siebeck, 2009.

Hamerton-Kelly, Robert G. *The Gospel and the Sacred: Poetics of Violence in Mark*. Minneapolis: Fortress, 1994.

Hanson, James S. *The Endangered Promises: Conflict in Mark*. SBLDS 171. Atlanta: SBL, 2000.

Harrington, Daniel J. *What Are They Saying about Mark?* Mahwah, NJ: Paulist Press, 2005.

Hatina, Thomas R. *In Search of a Context: The Function of Scripture in Mark's Narrative*. JSNTSup 232. Sheffield: Sheffield Academic Press, 2002.

Hemer, Colin J. "New Testament Fragments at Qumran?" *TynBul* 23 (1972): 125–28.

Henderson, Suzanne Watts. *Christology and Discipleship in the Gospel of Mark*. SNTSMS 135. Cambridge: Cambridge University Press, 2006.

Hengel, Martin. *Acts and the History of Earliest Christianity*. Translated by John Bowden. Philadelphia: Fortress, 1980.

————. *The Four Gospels and the One Gospel of Jesus Christ: An Investigation of the Collection and Origin of the Canonical Gospels*. Harrisburg, PA: Trinity Press International, 2000.

————. *Studies in the Gospel of Mark*. Translated by John Bowden. Philadelphia: Fortress, 1985.

Hooker, Morna D. *The Message of Mark*. London: Epworth, 1983.

————. *The Son of Man in Mark*. Montreal: McGill University Press, 1967.

————. "'Who Can This Be?' The Christology of Mark's Gospel." In *Contours of Christology in the New Testament*, edited by Richard N. Longenecker, 79–99. Grand Rapids: Eerdmans, 2005.

Horsley, Richard A. *Hearing the Whole Story: The Politics of Plot in Mark's Gospel*. Louisville: Westminster John Knox, 2001.

Hoskyns, Edwyn, and Noel Davey. *The Riddle of the New Testament*. London: Faber & Faber, 1931.

Hurtado, Larry W. "Following Jesus in the Gospel of Mark—and Beyond." In *Patterns of Discipleship in the New Testament*, edited by Richard N. Longenecker, 9–29. Grand Rapids: Eerdmans, 1996.

Incigneri, Brian J. *The Gospel to the Romans: The Setting and Rhetoric of Mark's Gospel*. BIS 65. Leiden: Brill, 2003.

Iverson, Kelly R. *Gentiles in the Gospel of Mark: "Even the Dogs under the Table Eat the Children's Crumbs."* LNTS 339. London: T&T Clark, 2007.

Juel, Donald H. *A Master of Surprise: Mark Interpreted*. Minneapolis: Fortress, 1994.

————. *Messiah and Temple: The Trial of Jesus in the Gospel of Mark*. SBLDS 31. Missoula, MT: Scholars Press, 1977.

Kealy, Sean P. *Mark's Gospel: A History of Its Interpretation, from the Beginning until 1979*. New York: Paulist Press, 1982.

Kee, Howard Clark. *Community of the New Age: Studies in the Gospel of Mark*. Reprint, Macon, GA: Mercer University Press, 1983.

Kelber, Werner H. *The Kingdom in Mark: A New Place and a New Time.* Philadelphia: Fortress, 1974.

———. *Mark's Story of Jesus.* Philadelphia: Fortress, 1974.

———, ed. *The Passion in Mark: Studies on Mark 14–16.* Philadelphia: Fortress, 1976.

Kingsbury, Jack D. *The Christology of Mark's Gospel.* Philadelphia: Fortress, 1983.

———. *Conflict in Mark: Jesus, Authorities, Disciples.* Minneapolis: Fortress, 1989.

Kümmel, Werner Georg. *Introduction to the New Testament.* Translated by A. J. Mattill Jr. 14th ed. Nashville: Abingdon, 1966.

Ladd, George Eldon. *The Presence of the Future: The Eschatology of Biblical Realism.* Grand Rapids: Eerdmans, 1974. Revision of *Jesus and the Kingdom* (New York: Harper & Row, 1964).

Lane, William L. "*Theios Anēr* Christology and the Gospel of Mark." In *New Dimensions in New Testament Study*, edited by Richard N. Longenecker and Merrill C. Tenney, 144–61. Grand Rapids: Zondervan, 1974.

Lincoln, Andrew T. "The Promise and the Failure: Mark 16:7, 8." *JBL* 108 (1989): 283–300.

Malbon, Elizabeth Struthers. *Hearing Mark: A Listener's Guide.* Harrisburg, PA: Trinity Press International, 2002.

———. *In the Company of Jesus: Characters in Mark's Gospel.* Louisville: Westminster John Knox, 2000.

Manson, T. W. "The Gospel of Mark." In *Studies in the Gospels and Epistles*, edited by Matthew Black, 28–45. Manchester, UK: Manchester University Press, 1962.

Marcus, Joel. *The Mystery of the Kingdom of God.* SBLDS 90. Atlanta: Scholars Press, 1986.

———. *The Way of the Lord: Christological Exegesis of the Old Testament in the Gospel of Mark.* Louisville: Westminster John Knox, 1992.

Marshall, Christopher. D. *Faith as a Theme in Mark's Narrative.* SNTSMS 64. Cambridge: Cambridge University Press, 1989.

Martin, Ralph P. *Mark: Evangelist and Theologian.* Grand Rapids: Zondervan, 1973.

———. "The Theology of Mark's Gospel." *SwJT* 21 (1978): 23–36.

Marxsen, Willi. *Mark the Evangelist: Studies on the Redaction History of the Gospel.* Translated by James Boyce et al. Nashville: Abingdon, 1969.

Matera, Frank J. *The Kingship of Jesus: Composition and Theology in Mark 15.* SBLDS 66. Chico, CA: Scholars Press, 1982.

———. *What Are They Saying about Mark?* New York: Paulist Press, 1987.

Metzger, Bruce M. *A Textual Commentary on the Greek New Testament.* 2nd ed. Stuttgart: Deutsche Bibelgesellschaft, 1994.

Miller, Susan. *Women in Mark's Gospel.* JSNTSup 259. New York: T&T Clark, 2004.

Minor, Mitzi L. *The Power of Mark's Story.* St. Louis: Chalice, 2001.

Moloney, Francis J. *Mark: Storyteller, Interpreter, Evangelist.* Peabody, MA: Hendrickson, 2004.

Moule, C. F. D. *The Birth of the New Testament.* 3rd ed. BNTC. London: Black, 1982.

———. "On Defining the Messianic Secret in Mark." In *Jesus und Paulus: Festschrift für Werner Georg Kümmel zum 70. Geburtstag*, edited by E. Earle Ellis and Erich Gräßer, 239–52. Göttingen: Vandenhoeck & Ruprecht, 1975.

Myers, Ched. *Who Will Roll Away the Stone? Discipleship Queries for First World Christians.* Maryknoll, NY: Orbis, 2000.

Neirynck, Frans. *Duality in Mark: Contributions to the Study of the Markan Redaction.* BETL 31. Leuven: University of Leuven Press, 1988.

Neville, David J. *Mark's Gospel: Prior or Posterior? A Reappraisal of the Phenomenon of Order.* JSNTSup 222. Sheffield: Sheffield Academic Press, 2002.

Nineham, Dennis E. "The Order of Events in St. Mark's Gospel—An Examination of Dr. Dodd's Hypothesis." In *Studies in the Gospels: Essays in Memory of R. H. Lightfoot*, 223–39. Oxford: Blackwell, 1955.

O'Callaghan, José. "New Testament Papyri in Qumran Cave 7?" *JBL* 91 (1972): 1–14.

Orton, David E., comp. *The Composition of Mark's Gospel: Selected Studies from Novum Testamentum*. BRBS 3. Leiden: Brill, 1999.

Painter, John. *Mark's Gospel: Worlds in Conflict*. NTR. London: Routledge, 1997.

Peterson, Dwight N. *The Origins of Mark: The Markan Community in Current Debate*. BIS 48. Leiden: Brill, 2000.

Pryke, E. J. *Redactional Style in the Marcan Gospel: A Study of Syntax and Vocabulary as Guides to Redaction in Mark*. SNTSMS 33. Cambridge: Cambridge University Press, 1978.

Räisänen, Heikki. *The "Messianic Secret" in Mark*. Translated by Christopher Tuckett. SNTW. Edinburgh: T&T Clark, 1990.

Rhoads, David. *Reading Mark: Engaging the Gospel*. Minneapolis: Fortress, 2004.

Rhoads, David, Joanna Dewey, and Donald Michie. *Mark as Story: An Introduction to the Narrative of a Gospel*. 2nd ed. Philadelphia: Fortress, 1999.

Riesenfeld, Harald. "On the Composition of Mark." In *The Gospel Tradition: Essays*, 51–74. Philadelphia: Fortress, 1970.

Robbins, Vernon K. *Jesus the Teacher: A Socio-Rhetorical Interpretation of Mark*. Philadelphia: Fortress, 1984.

Robinson, J. A. T. *Redating the New Testament*. Philadelphia: Westminster, 1976.

Robinson, James M. *The Problem of History in Mark and Other Markan Studies*. Philadelphia: Fortress, 1982.

Roskam, H. N. *The Purpose of the Gospel of Mark in Its Historical and Social Context*. NovTSup 114. Leiden: Brill, 2004.

Sabin, Marie Noonan. *Reopening the Word: Reading Mark as Theology in the Context of Early Judaism*. Oxford: Oxford University Press, 2002.

Santos, Narry F. *Slave of All: The Paradox of Authority and Servanthood in the Gospel of Mark*. JSNTSup 237. Sheffield: Sheffield Academic Press, 2000.

Schoedel, William R. "Papias." ANRW II.27.1 (1992): 235–70.

———. *Polycarp, Martyrdom of Polycarp, Fragments of Papias*. Vol. 5 of *The Apostolic Fathers: A New Translation and Commentary*, edited by Robert M. Grant. Camden, NJ: Thomas Nelson, 1967.

Schweizer, Eduard. "The Portrayal of the Life of Faith in the Gospel of Mark." *Int* 32 (1978): 387–99.

Senior, Donald. *The Passion of Jesus in the Gospel of Mark*. Wilmington, DE: Michael Glazier, 1984.

Shepherd, Tom. "The Narrative Function of Markan Intercalation." *NTS* 41 (1995): 522–40.

Shiner, Whitney. *Proclaiming the Gospel: First-Century Performance of Mark*. Harrisburg, PA: Trinity Press International, 2003.

Skeat, T. C. "Irenaeus and the Four-Gospel Canon." *NovT* 34 (1992): 194–99.

Spencer, Aida Besançon. "The Denial of the Good News and the Ending of Mark." *BBR* 17 (2007): 269–83.

Stein, Robert H. "The Ending of Mark." *BBR* 18 (2008): 79–98.

———. "The Proper Methodology for Ascertaining a Markan Redaction History." In *The Composition of Mark's Gospel: Selected Studies from Novum Testamentum*, compiled by David E. Orton, 34–51. BRBS 3. Leiden: Brill, 1999.

Stock, Augustine. *Call to Discipleship: A Literary Study of Mark's Gospel*. GNS 1. Wilmington, DE: Michael Glazier, 1982.

Such, W. A. *The Abomination of Desolation in the Gospel of Mark: Its Historical Reference in Mark 13:14 and Its Impact in the Gospel*. Lanham, MD: University Press of America, 1998.

Tannehill, Robert C. "The Disciples in Mark: The Function of a Narrative Role." In *The Interpretation of Mark*, edited by William R. Telford, 169–95. 2nd ed. SNTI. Edinburgh: T&T Clark, 1995.

Telford, William R. *The Barren Temple and the Withered Tree: A Redaction-Critical Analysis of the Cursing of the Fig-Tree Pericope in Mark's Gospel and Its Relation to the Cleansing of the Temple Tradition*. JSNTSup 1. Sheffield: JSOT Press, 1980.

———, ed. *The Interpretation of Mark*. 2nd ed. Edinburgh: T&T Clark, 1995.

———. *Mark*. NTG. Sheffield: Sheffield Academic Press, 1995.

———. *The Theology of the Gospel of Mark*. NTT. Cambridge: Cambridge University Press, 1999.

———. *Writing on the Gospel of Mark*. GABR 1. Dorchester, UK: Deo, 2009.

Thompson, Mary R. *The Role of Disbelief in Mark: A New Approach to the Second Gospel*. New York: Paulist Press, 1989.

Tolbert, Mary Ann. *Sowing the Gospel: Mark's World in Literary-Historical Perspective*. Minneapolis: Fortress, 1989.

Tuckett, Christopher M., ed. *The Messianic Secret*. IRT 1. Philadelphia: Fortress, 1983.

Upton, Bridget Gilfillan. *Hearing Mark's Endings: Listening to Ancient Popular Texts through Speech Act Theory*. BIS 79. Leiden: Brill, 2006.

van der Horst, P. W. "Can a Book End with ΓΑΡ? A Note on Mark XVI.8." *JTS* 23 (1972): 121–29.

van Iersel, Bas. *Reading Mark*. Translated by W. H. Bisscheroux. Edinburgh: T&T Clark, 1989.

van Oyen, Geert, and Tom Shepherd, eds. *The Trial and Death of Jesus: Essays on the Passion Narrative in Mark*. CBET 45. Leuven: Peeters, 2006.

Via, Dan O., Jr. *The Ethics of Mark's Gospel in the Middle of Time*. Philadelphia: Fortress, 1985.

Vincent, John J., ed. *Mark, Gospel of Action: Personal and Community Responses*. London: SPCK, 2006.

Vines, Michael. *The Problem of Markan Genre: The Gospel of Mark and the Jewish Novel*. SBLAB 3. Atlanta: Society of Biblical Literature, 2002.

Watts, Rikki E. *Isaiah's New Exodus and Mark*. WUNT 2/88. Tübingen: Mohr Siebeck, 1997.

Weeden, Theodore J., Sr. "The Heresy That Necessitated Mark's Gospel." In *The Interpretation of Mark*, edited by William R. Telford, 89–104. 2nd ed. SNTI. Edinburgh: T&T Clark, 1995.

———. *Mark: Traditions in Conflict*. Philadelphia: Fortress, 1971.

Wegener, Mark I. *Cruciformed: The Literary Impact of Mark's Story of Jesus and His Disciples*. Lanham, MD: University Press of America, 1995.

Wenham, David. *The Rediscovery of Jesus' Eschatological Discourse*. GP 4. Sheffield: JSOT Press, 1984.

Wenham, John. *Redating Matthew, Mark and Luke: A Fresh Assault on the Synoptic Problem*. Downers Grove, IL: InterVarsity, 1992.

Wrede, William. *The Messianic Secret*. Translated by J. C. G. Greig. Greenwood, SC: Attic Press, 1971.

Yarbrough, Robert W. "The Date of Papias: A Reassessment." *JETS* 26 (1983): 181–91.

Commentaries

Achtemeier, Paul J. *Mark*. 2nd ed. PC. Philadelphia: Fortress, 1986.

Boring, M. Eugene. *Mark*. NTL. Louisville: Westminster John Knox, 2006.

Collins, Adela Yarbro. *Mark*. Hermeneia. Minneapolis: Fortress, 2007.

Cranfield, C. E. B. *The Gospel according to Saint Mark*. CGTC. Cambridge: Cambridge University Press, 1959.

Culpepper, R. Alan. *Mark*. Macon, GA: Smyth & Helwys, 2007.

Donahue, John R., and Daniel J. Harrington. *The Gospel of Mark*. SP 2. Collegeville, MN: Liturgical Press, 2002.

Dowd, Sharyn Echols. *Reading Mark: A Literary and Theological Commentary on the Second Gospel*. RNT. Macon, GA: Smyth & Helwys, 2000.

Edwards, James R. *The Gospel according to Mark*. PNTC. Grand Rapids: Eerdmans, 2002.

Evans, Craig A. *Mark 8:27–16:20*. WBC 34B. Nashville: Thomas Nelson, 2001.

France, R. T. *The Gospel of Mark: A Commentary on the Greek Text*. NIGTC. Grand Rapids: Eerdmans, 2002.

Guelich, Robert A. *Mark 1–8:26*. WBC 34A. Dallas: Word, 1989.

Gundry, Robert H. *Mark: A Commentary on His Apology for the Cross*. Grand Rapids: Eerdmans, 1993.

Hare, Douglas R. A. *Mark*. WestBC. Louisville: Westminster John Knox, 1996.

Hartman, Lars. *Mark for the Nations: A Text- and Reader-Oriented Commentary*. Eugene, OR: Pickwick, 2010.

Hooker, Morna D. *The Gospel according to St. Mark*. BNTC. Peabody, MA: Hendrikson, 1993.

Juel, Donald H. *The Gospel of Mark*. IBT. Nashville: Abingdon, 1999.

———. *Mark*. ACNT. Minneapolis: Augsburg, 1990.

Lane, William L. *The Gospel according to Mark*. NICNT. Grand Rapids: Eerdmans, 1974.

Marcus, Joel. *Mark 1–8: A New Translation with Introduction and Commentary*. AB 27. New York: Doubleday, 2000.

———. *Mark 9–16: A New Translation with Introduction and Commentary*. AB 27A. New York: Doubleday, 2009.

Moloney, Francis J. *The Gospel of Mark*. Peabody, MA: Hendrickson, 2002.

Nineham, Dennis E. *The Gospel of St. Mark*. PGC. New York: Seabury, 1968.

Swete, H. B. *The Gospel according to St. Mark: The Greek Text with Introduction, Notes and Indices*. 3rd ed. London: Macmillan, 1909.

Taylor, Vincent. *The Gospel according to St. Mark: The Greek Text with Introduction, Notes, and Indexes*. 2nd ed. New York: St. Martin's Press, 1966.

Witherington, Ben, III. *The Gospel of Mark: A Socio-Rhetorical Commentary*. Grand Rapids: Eerdmans, 2001.

12

The Gospel according to Matthew

Matthew stands proudly as the first book of the NT and the first of the four Gospels. Unlike other collections within the NT, such as the Pauline Epistles, the Gospels are not ordered according to length, with the longest coming first. Why is Matthew uniformly the first of the four Gospels in all codices and manuscripts? The reason seems to be the conviction of the early church that it was the earliest of the Gospels, and, most important, that it traced back to the Apostle Matthew himself. It is coincidentally an added advantage that Matthew's fulfillment quotations stress the continuity of the story of Jesus with the promises of the OT Scriptures, and thus this Gospel serves as a bridge from the old to the new.

The Papias Tradition about Matthew

The tantalizing statement of Papias from the first quarter of the second century[1] is at once the earliest, most important, and most bewildering piece of early information that we have concerning the Gospel of Matthew. Papias, whom we have already encountered in the discussion of the Synoptic Problem and Mark's Gospel, is quoted by Eusebius as having said about Matthew, "Matthew collected the oracles in the Hebrew language, and each interpreted them as best he could" (*Hist. eccl.* 3.39.16, trans. Lake). Nearly every element in this

---

1. Schoedel, "Papias," dates the Papias testimony to 110; Yarbrough, "The Date of Papias," puts it even earlier.

Author: Although the disciple Levi-Matthew possibly was the collector and editor of the five Matthean discourses, the Gospel as it stands likely is the work of an unknown disciple or disciples of the Matthean circle—that is, associated with Matthew.

Date: There is a good possibility that Matthew was written a year or two before 70. But it also remains possible that Matthew was written later, in about 80.

Addressees: A Jewish Christian community or communities, or even Jewish Christians generally. If to a specific region, among the most popular of guesses is Antioch of Syria.

Purpose: To write a Gospel modeled on Mark that presents the story of Jesus in a way that both appeals to Jews and helps Jewish Christians to understand and promote their Christian faith to the Jews.

Message/Argument: Jesus is the fulfillment of the OT promises, remained loyal to the Torah as its definitive interpreter, and came initially only to the Jews.

Significance: Combines in a unique way the continuities and discontinuities of Jesus and the faith of Israel, combining old and new (see 13:52).

---

sentence can be understood in more than one way.[2] Since virtually all patristic testimony concerning the origin of Matthew is dependent on this statement of Papias, many scholars believe that Papias is responsible for having misled the entire early church. But the testimony of Papias is worth being taken seriously and examined carefully.

Of key importance to the understanding of the passage is the meaning of "oracles" (*logia*). The early church took it to refer to the Gospel of Matthew itself and thus as establishing the priority of Matthew over the other Gospels. Those who "translated" (or "interpreted" [*hērmēneusen*]) Matthew's oracles became, in this view, the authors of Mark and Luke, for example, who made use of Matthew as their main source. On the one hand, although *logia* strictly means "oracles" and thus most naturally refers to an account of words rather than deeds, the word was also used by Papias in referring to the Gospel of Mark (Eusebius, *Hist. eccl.* 3.39.15). Further to be noted is its use in the title of Papias's own commentary (*Interpretation of the Oracles* [*logia*] *of the Lord*), which probably was not restricted to the words of Jesus. On the other hand, "oracles," as we earlier noted, could refer to words of the OT (so used by the early church fathers [e.g., *1 Clem.* 53:1; 62:3; Clement of Alexandria, *Strom.* 7.18])—that is, to Matthew's distinctive OT quotations in their Hebrew form—or it could refer to words of Jesus in oral tradition, such as perhaps an Aramaic version of Q.[3]

2. For a helpful display of the options, see France, *Matthew*, 56–57.
3. Thus Manson, *The Sayings of Jesus*, 28–30; Black, "The Use of Rhetorical Terminology in Papias on Mark and Matthew."

The interpretation of the word *logia* is naturally dependent on the meaning of the other components of the Papias tradition. Two options are possible for "in the Hebrew language." Most naturally the words mean "written in Hebrew," by which is probably meant Aramaic. Possibly, however, the word translated "language" (*dialektos*, "dialect") is to be taken in a special sense, as documented among ancient technical rhetoricians, to mean "in a Semitic style," referring to the general Jewish "style" or character of Matthew's Gospel.[4] In this view, the verb *hērmēneusen* must be taken in the sense of "explain" rather than "translate." But did the Jewish character of the Gospel of Matthew really need explanation? And would the task of explanation have been so challenging as to account for Papias's words "as each was able"? The combination of the term "dialect" with the verb "interpret" points, on the contrary, to the natural meaning "to translate a language."[5]

If the conclusion is fairly secure that Papias spoke of something in Aramaic that was then translated into Greek, we may return to the discussion of the word *logia*. The major difficulties with the conclusion that it refers to the original Gospel of Matthew are that our Greek Matthew reveals no signs of having been translated from Aramaic (or Hebrew),[6] and that there is abundant evidence that Matthew's Greek is dependent on Mark. The advocates of the priority of Matthew who appeal to the Papias testimony must therefore also argue that the translator had Mark before him and simultaneously redacted Mark's Greek as he translated the putative Aramaic Matthew. Though not impossible, this solution is improbable. It is furthermore difficult, though not impossible, to take the word *logia* as referring to a Gospel. That there was at least one (perhaps more than one) Gospel in Aramaic or Hebrew known to the early church[7] may have added to the confusion caused by Papias's statement, wrongly tempting the early church fathers to think of the Gospel of Matthew.

What of the other two options for the meaning of *logia* mentioned above? We have evidence of the collection of OT prophecies or prooftexts concerning the Messiah or messianic fulfillment (at Qumran, *4QTestimonia*). That Matthew might have collected such texts together in the original Hebrew language seems feasible, especially given the conspicuous use of the OT in this Gospel (see "Matthew's Use of the Old Testament" below). Such a conclusion fits

4. Thus Gundry, *The Use of the Old Testament in St. Matthew's Gospel*, 619–20.

5. Thus rightly France (*Matthew*, 57), who regards it as "most unlikely" that the combination of terms would have been understood in any other way by a Greek reader. See also Schoedel, "Papias," 258.

6. Note, however, the caution of Davies and Allison (*A Critical and Exegetical Commentary on the Gospel according to Matthew*, 1:13), who indicate the difficulty of establishing this point.

7. For example, the *Gospel of the Ebionites*, the *Gospel of the Nazoreans*, the *Gospel of the Hebrews*.

both the point about translation from Hebrew and also the common use of the word *logia* to refer to the OT. The inference that what Papias had in mind was a collection of *testimonia*, however, is only a guess. The collection has not survived, except perhaps indirectly in the quotations of the Gospel itself, and there is no evidence of others having translated or interpreted such OT prooftexts.

More likely is the hypothesis that *logia* refers to sayings of Jesus. The term *logia*, rather than the more normal *logoi*, may be used because of the veneration of the words of Jesus, which were treasured as the supreme authority of the early church. Already by the time of Clement of Rome (ca. 96) they were put alongside words of the OT, even superseding them in authority (see *1 Clem.* 13). The words of Jesus were no less "the oracles" of God than were the OT Scriptures. Matthew, then, may have collected the sayings of Jesus in their original Aramaic, and these were in turn translated by others "as each was able," which could nicely account for some differences among the Synoptic renderings of the sayings.

It is conceivable that this collection was what we call Q or, more precisely, the Aramaic material that underlay Q. However, what Papias may have had in mind is the material contained in the five major discourses of Matthew's Gospel. These discourses are one of the major distinctives of Matthew. Perhaps the Apostle was responsible for the collection of the core material of these discourses, the so-called M material. Such a collection would, in effect, be a proto-Matthew and could explain how the Apostle Matthew's name eventually became attached to this Gospel.[8] This is, of course, speculation, but this solution is most consistent with the testimony of Papias. Papias had reasons for saying what he did, and although our knowledge now is partial, we do well to take it seriously.

Matthew's Sources

In the discussion of the Synoptic Problem (chap. 9) I established the probability of the Two Source hypothesis: Matthew and Luke both made use of Mark and Q. Matthew, as we noted, picks up as much as 90 percent of Mark. In addition to Mark and the Q material, however, Matthew apparently also had access to further oral tradition, which is reflected in the special (i.e., unique) material in his Gospel. Rather than representing a discrete source, this material, usually designated as M, probably was part of a larger stream of tradition, some of it no doubt overlapping with Q—material that we may speculatively also associate in its original Aramaic form with the Apostle Matthew. Less than a third of this Gospel consists of M material.

8. See Allen, *A Critical and Exegetical Commentary on the Gospel according to S. Matthew*, lxxx–lxxxi.

It is sometimes wondered how a Gospel associated with the Apostle Matthew could be so dependent on a Gospel written by one who was not a member of the Twelve. The answer seems to be that the Gospel of Mark, as argued in the preceding chapter, bore the stamp of Peter's authority. The tradition stemming from the prime Apostle would have been highly esteemed.

The Structure of Matthew

Because of the variety of structural elements in Matthew, there has been no consensus on its basic structure.[9] Among these elements are the following.

The Five Discourses

Undoubtedly the most conspicuous structural marker in Matthew's Gospel is the statement (varying only slightly) which ends each of the five major teaching discourses: "And when Jesus finished these sayings [*kai egeneto hote etelesen ho Iēsous tous logous toutous*]" (7:28; cf. 11:1; 13:53; 19:1; 26:1). The Evangelist alternates the teaching discourses with narrative blocks concerning the mighty deeds of Jesus. The discourses in their present form are the construction of the Evangelist and have catechetical interests:

1. The Sermon on the Mount (chaps. 5–7)
2. Mission Directives to the Twelve (chap. 10)
3. Parables of the Kingdom (chap. 13)
4. Discipleship and Discipline (chap. 18)
5. The Olivet Discourse: Eschatology (chaps. 24–25)

Benjamin Bacon suggested that the Evangelist intended the fivefold structure to correspond to the five books of the Pentateuch, with Jesus represented as a new Moses who is the giver of a new law.[10] Although there is an implicit Moses typology in this Gospel,[11] this is not sufficient warrant for Bacon's conclusion. It is also the case that a fivefold structure is found elsewhere in the canonical writings (e.g., the five books of Psalms; the five Scrolls, i.e., the five *Megillot*: the Song of Songs, Ruth, Lamentations, Ecclesiastes, and Esther, often grouped together).

Although these five discourses may be meant to include in each instance a preceding narrative (i.e., chaps. 3–4; 8–9; 11–12; 14–17; 19–22), the fivefold structure hardly seems adequate to be considered the basic plan of this Gospel. The main reason is that certain parts of the book do not fit this structure at

9. The best discussion is Bauer, *The Structure of Matthew's Gospel*.
10. Bacon, *Studies in Matthew*.
11. See Allison, *The New Moses*.

all (e.g., chaps. 11, 23), most significantly, the infancy and passion narratives. The narrative of the death of Jesus is the goal and climax of the story, and any structural analysis must include it as a major element. Thus the fivefold discourse structure, although an important feature of Matthew, must be considered a subsidiary structure rather than the primary one.

Two Major Turning Points

Two pivotal points in Matthew are noted with the repeated clause "from that time Jesus began [*apo tote ērxato ho Iēsous*]" (4:17; 16:21). Jack Kingsbury,[12] followed by David Bauer,[13] has understood the two occurrences of this phrase as indicating the basic structure of this Gospel, which he accordingly describes under the following three headings:

1. the person of Jesus Messiah (1:1–4:16)
2. the proclamation of Jesus Messiah (4:17–16:20)
3. the suffering, death, and resurrection of Jesus Messiah (16:21–28:20)

Because these are such critical junctures in the narrative, they obviously are important to the general shape of the story. But whether they are structural markers in the proper sense of the word is another question. Frans Neirynck, for example, has shown how difficult it is structurally to divide 4:17 from 4:12–16, and 16:21 from the verses that precede it.[14]

A Chiastic Structure

Building on the obvious alternation of narrative with teaching sections, some scholars have detected a symmetrical chiastic structure in Matthew, as in the following example.

```
A  Matt. 1–4: Narrative
   B  Matt. 5–7: Discourse
      C  Matt. 8–9: Narrative
         D  Matt. 10: Discourse
            E Matt. 11–12: Narrative
               F Matt. 13: Discourse
            E' Matt. 14–17: Narrative
         D' Matt. 18: Discourse
      C' Matt. 19–22: Narrative
   B'  Matt. 23–25: Discourse
A'  Matt. 26–28: Narrative
```

12. Kingsbury, *Matthew* (1989).
13. Bauer, *The Structure of Matthew's Gospel*.
14. Neirynck, "ΑΠΟ ΤΟΤΕ ΗΡΞΑΤΟ and the Structure of Matthew."

The chiastic approach can appeal to similar motifs in the content of the infancy and passion narratives and to the similar lengths of *B* and *B'* as well as *D* and *D'*. Although similarity occasionally exists between other corresponding elements, this usually seems arbitrary and uncompelling. No consensus has emerged among those who are inclined to see a chiastic structure as basic to Matthew.[15]

Other Structural Elements

Periodic markers in the flow of Matthew's narrative are provided by the capsule summaries of the ministry of Jesus placed by the Evangelist at 4:23–25; 9:35; 11:1; 14:35–36; 15:29–31; 19:1–2; 21:14. These summaries, however, are not similar enough to be thought of as deliberate macrostructural markers.[16]

Within smaller sections of this Gospel the author displays his literary artistry in the grouping of certain items. As examples, we note his liking of groups of seven—for example, the seven petitions of the Lord's Prayer (6:9–13); the seven parables in chapter 13; the seven woes in chapter 23; and the double sevens of the genealogy (1:1–17). He also favors groups of three—for example, the three divisions of the genealogy (1:1–17); the three kinds of piety (6:1–18); and three polemical parables (21:28–22:14). The Evangelist has other groupings (multiples of three) in instances such as the six antitheses (5:21–48) and the nine benedictions (5:3–11).

The author also apparently has a tendency to double items drawn from his sources, as in the two demoniacs in 8:28–34 (cf. Mark 5:1–20), the two blind men in 20:29–34 (cf. Mark 10:46–52), and the probable doublet of 20:29–34 in 9:27–31. This, like some of the threes in this Gospel, may well result from a concern to have the two or three witnesses required by the law (18:16; cf. 26:60). Many more examples of the author's artistry are apparent if one looks at other literary devices such as repetition, inclusio, leitmotif, and even poetry.[17]

It is virtually impossible to ascertain a unifying overall structure other than of a very general kind. As Floyd Filson pointed out, Matthew has many "broken patterns," patterns that he begins but does not follow through.[18] Also to be remembered in discussions of Matthew's structure is that he is following the outline of Mark, following it very closely indeed from chapter 12 onward. In the final analysis, it may be that the Evangelist really had no grand overall structure in mind other than of the general divisions of the sort that we have noted. Thus a good part of the time this Gospel appears to be a seamless succession of pericopes, alternating presentation of deeds and words of Jesus

---

15. See Fenton, "Inclusio and Chiasmus in Matthew"; Green, "The Structure of St. Matthew's Gospel"; Combrink, "The Structure of the Gospel of Matthew as Narrative."

16. See Gerhardsson, *The Mighty Acts of Jesus according to Matthew*.

17. See Goulder, *Midrash and Lection in Matthew*, 70–94.

18. See Filson, "Broken Patterns in the Gospel of Matthew."

that usually have been collected and arranged topically—seldom is there an interest in chronology—for the sake of the impact on the reader.

Matthew's Use of the Old Testament

Matthew contains well over sixty explicit quotations from the OT (not counting a great number of allusions), more than twice as many as any other Gospel, reflecting Matthew's interest in the gospel as the fulfillment of the OT expectation. Of particular interest are the so-called fulfillment quotations, one of Matthew's most distinctive features. These quotations represent Matthew's own creative interpretation of his narrative. Their reflective character has led to the designation *Reflexionszitate* ("reflection citations").

Ten quotations use an introductory formula, unique to Matthew among the Synoptics, containing the verb "fulfill" (*plēroō*):

    1:22–23 from Isaiah 7:14
    2:15 from Hosea 11:1
    2:17–18 from Jeremiah 31:15
    2:23b from Isaiah 11:1 (?)
    4:14–16 from Isaiah 8:23–9:1
    8:17 from Isaiah 53:4
    12:17–21 from Isaiah 42:1–4
    13:35 from Psalm 78:2
    21:4–5 from Isaiah 62:11; Zechariah 9:9
    27:9–10 from Zechariah 11:12–13 (cf. Jeremiah 32:6–15)

A further quotation uses the synonymous verb *anaplēroō* ("fulfill"):

    13:14–15 from Isaiah 6:9–10

And one further quotation stresses fulfillment, but without the verb "fulfill" ("This is he who was spoken of by the prophet Isaiah when he said . . ."):

    3:3 from Isaiah 40:2 (LXX)

Other quotations, often introduced with the verb *gegraptai* ("it is written"), can also stress fulfillment (e.g., 2:5; 11:10; 26:31; cf. the general statement in 26:54, 56).

The placement of the quotations in the book does not help us to discern the structure of this Gospel: their distribution is not uniform, four occurring in the first two chapters. Their importance is theological, and they undergird the manner in which the events of Matthew's narrative, indeed its totality, are to be understood as the fulfillment of what God had promised in the Scriptures.

The most difficult challenge for modern readers is to understand the hermeneutic that underlies the quotations, which as a rule are not even predictive of future events. We looked earlier at the phenomenon of *sensus plenior* (see chap. 2), which is at work here: the observance of a divinely intended correspondence between God's saving activity at different times in the history of salvation, with the earlier foreshadowing the latter, much in the sense of prophecy and fulfillment. Matthew, together with the whole of the early church, takes as his starting point that Jesus is the one promised by the OT Scriptures. His interpretation involves a christocentric hermeneutic: Christ is the telos, the goal, toward which the whole of the OT pointed.

Matthew's Theology

Since Matthew takes over so much of Mark, we may expect that he shares Mark's theology. At the same time, not only from material unique to Matthew, but also by seeing how Matthew redacts the Markan material, we gain insight into Matthew's particular theological interests.

Fulfillment: The Kingdom of Heaven

The central emphasis of Matthew is found in what is designated (uniquely in the Gospels) as the "gospel of the kingdom" (4:23; 9:35; 24:14; cf. 26:13), the good news that the reign or rule of God has begun to be realized in history through the presence of Jesus Christ. Matthew prefers to refer to "the kingdom of heaven" (*tōn ouranōn*, lit., "of the heavens"), a circumlocution for "the kingdom of God" (which, however, Matthew does use in 12:28; 19:24; 21:31, 43).[19] The importance of the kingdom for the Evangelist is obvious in that he uses the word much more frequently than does any one of the other Gospels, and nearly three times as often as Mark. The message of Jesus, like that of John the Baptist (3:2), is the coming of the kingdom (4:17), and this in turn becomes the message of the disciples (10:7). As in Mark, everything in Matthew relates in some way to this controlling theme. It is true that the kingdom has come presently as a mystery in an unexpected way, as we learn especially from the parables in chapter 13. In particular, the fulfillment brought by Jesus involves a delay in the judgment of the wicked (13:36–42, 47–50).

---

19. Jonathan Pennington argues, however, against the explanation of "kingdom of heaven" as simply a circumlocution. He probably is correct that Matthew's phrase conveys a special nuance: "God's kingdom, which is in heaven and heavenly, is radically different from all earthly kingdoms and will eschatologically replace them (on the earth). It is the coming kingdom which is proclaimed by Jesus and is embodied in himself, the unexpected servant-leader" (*Heaven and Earth in the Gospel of Matthew*, 330).

Nevertheless, the excitement of what has already arrived is not to be missed: "Blessed are your eyes, for they see, and your ears, for they hear. Truly, I say to you, many prophets and righteous men longed to see what you see, and did not see it, and to hear what you hear, and did not hear it" (13:16–17).

Christology

Matthew's doctrine of Jesus as the Christ is fundamentally important to every theological emphasis in his Gospel,[20] for it is the identity of Jesus that determines things such as fulfillment, authoritative exposition of the law, discipleship, ecclesiology, and eschatology. All the main christological titles occur more frequently in Matthew than in the other two Synoptics (except for *kyrios*, which is found most often in Luke). Matthew heightens the christology of Mark, making it more explicit (cf. Matt. 16:16 with Mark 8:29; Matt. 19:17 with Mark 10:18; Matt. 9:3 with Mark 2:7).

The key christological title in Matthew is "Son of God."[21] The importance of this title is seen not only where it is used (e.g., 8:29; 14:33; 16:16; cf. 3:17; 17:5) but also where it is implied, such as in 1:23, "'and his name shall be called Emmanuel' (which means, God with us)"; 14:27, "it is I" (*ego eimi* [cf. Exod. 3:14]); and passages promising the future presence of Jesus with his disciples (18:20; 28:20). Matthew also stresses the sonship of Jesus by having him refer to God as his Father some twenty-three times, fifteen of which are unique to Matthew (eight in original material; seven in redactional alteration). For Matthew, the most exalted confession, which alone expresses the mystery of Jesus' identity, is that he is the Son of God (16:16; also esp. 11:27). This confession in Matthew is made only by believers (except where it is spoken of as blasphemy) and only by revelation (16:7; 11:27; cf. 13:11).

The second major title, "Son of Man," is regularly used by Jesus and thus serves as the public counterpart to the confessional title. In references to the parousia and the eschatological judgment, it tends to coincide with "Son of God." Kingsbury finds no material difference between the titles.[22]

The important title *kyrios* is analogous to "Son of God," being found almost exclusively on the lips of the disciples. The identity of Jesus as the Son of David—that is, the Messiah—linked with the stress on fulfillment is very important to Matthew and his readers. The opening verse of this Gospel identifies Jesus as Messiah, the son of David, and the son of Abraham. The title "Son of David" occurs throughout the narrative (e.g., 12:23; 15:22; 20:30; 21:9); so too Jesus is referred to as the "Christ." The climax of the narrative, short of the passion itself, is Peter's confession that Jesus is the Christ (16:16).

---

20. Warren Carter points out that "the presentation of Jesus as agent of God's sovereignty is part of the Gospel's theological and social challenge to the empire" (*Matthew and Empire*, 57).

21. Thus Kingsbury, *Matthew* (1989).

22. Ibid. So too Meier, *The Vision of Matthew*.

Jesus accepts this designation, and his answer to the high priest's question about whether he is the Christ is a qualified affirmative: he is indeed the Messiah, but not of the sort that was widely expected (26:64). Kingsbury argues that these titles support the title "Son of God."[23] Some have suggested that the key to Matthew's christology is the concept of Jesus as the incarnation of Wisdom (e.g., 11:19, 25–27; 23:34–39) and Torah (e.g., 11:28–30).[24] This analysis is consistent with Matthew's emphasis on a Son of God christology—that is, "God with us."[25]

Righteousness and Discipleship

A term of key importance for the Evangelist is "righteousness" (*dikaiosynē*), which occurs among the Synoptic Gospels only in Matthew (except for Luke 1:75). Especially since the work of Benno Przybylski[26] the view that all seven occurrences of the word refer to the righteousness of ethical demand has become dominant. Although it is clear that several of the seven occurrences of the word in Matthew refer unmistakably to the call to personal righteousness associated with discipleship (e.g., 5:20; 6:1) and other instances are probably so to be interpreted (e.g., 5:10; possibly 6:33), the word in some instances can be understood in a salvation-historical sense—that is, as God's righteousness active in the saving of his people (3:15; 5:6; 21:32; also possibly 6:33).[27]

The cognate word *dikaios* ("just" or "righteous") occurs seventeen times in Matthew, more than all the references in the other three Gospels combined. This righteousness finds its definition and standard in the law, especially as authoritatively interpreted by Jesus. The righteousness to which Jesus calls his disciples, according to Matthew, is a better or higher righteousness (cf. 5:20). In the final analysis, it is a call to do the will of the Father (7:21; 12:50; 21:31).[28]

The Evangelist emphasizes the importance of discipleship. The noun "disciple" (*mathētēs*) occurs much more often in Matthew (73x) than in the other Synoptic Gospels, and the verb *mathēteuō* ("to make disciples") occurs only in Matthew among the four Gospels (13:52; 27:57; 28:19).[29] Disciples are called "sons of God" (5:9, cf. 45), but more frequently by terms meant to emphasize humility, such as "brothers" (esp. 12:49–50; 18:15, 21, 35; 23:8; 25:40; 28:10)

---

23. Kingsbury, *Matthew* (1989).

24. See Suggs, *Wisdom, Christology, and Law in Matthew's Gospel*; Gibbs, "The Son of God as the Torah Incarnate in Matthew;" Hamerton-Kelly, *Pre-Existence, Wisdom, and the Son of Man*; Gench, *Wisdom in the Christology of Matthew*.

25. See Kupp, *Matthew's Emmanuel*.

26. Przybylski, *Righteousness in Matthew and His World of Thought*.

27. See Hagner, "Righteousness in Matthew's Theology."

28. See Hagner, "Holiness and Ecclesiology."

29. See Wilkins, *Discipleship in the Ancient World and in Matthew's Gospel*; Brown, *The Disciples in Narrative Perspective*.

and, most distinctively, "little ones" (*mikroi*) (10:42; 18:6, 10, 14). Discipleship involves following in the steps of the Lord, which entails self-denial and taking up one's cross (10:38–39; 16:24–26), the suffering of persecution (5:10–12; 10:16–25; 24:9–13), and the humility of a servant (20:26–27; 23:11–12) or a child (18:1–4).

Law and Grace

Matthew's Gospel is well known for its emphasis on Jesus' faithfulness to the law, particularly as expressed in 5:17–18: "Think not that I have come to abolish the law and the prophets; I have come not to abolish them but to fulfil them. For truly, I say to you, till heaven and earth pass away, not an iota, not a dot, will pass from the law until all is accomplished." Jesus' teaching about righteousness and the doing of the will of the Father (7:21; 12:50; 21:31) is understood throughout this Gospel as nothing other than the explication of the true meaning of the law. For the sake of his Jewish Christian readers, the Evangelist portrays Jesus as less radical toward the law than does Mark (cf. Mark 7:1–23 with Matt. 15:1–20, where Matthew avoids the conclusion that Jesus "declared all foods clean" and emphasizes only the issue of hand washing). Jesus furthermore is shown to agree in principle with the Pharisees (23:2–3)—that is, to the extent that they truly expound the meaning of the Mosaic law. Even in Matthew, however, Jesus transcends not only the teachings of the Pharisees (9:10–17; 15:1–20) but also the letter of the law, while penetrating to its inner spirit (5:31–42; 12:1–14; 15:11; 19:3–9). Jesus' uniquely authoritative interpretation of the law is possible only because of who he is (the messianic Son of God).[30] Accordingly, the Pharisees are no match for Jesus in their interpretation of the law, and at the same time the author's Jewish Christian church, and not the synagogue, is shown to be in true succession to Moses. The emphasis on the law in Matthew is thus much more probably due to the Jewish Christian orientation of this Gospel than to a direct attempt to counteract a "Pauline" antinomianism, as some have argued.[31]

The law as expounded by Jesus is not a "new" law (note Matthew's omission of Mark's reference to "a new teaching" [Mark 1:27]) but rather the "true" or intended meaning of the Mosaic law. Matthew's stress on the law, however, occurs in the context of the good news of the presence of the kingdom. The announcement of grace is antecedent to the call to live out the righteousness of the law (e.g., the Beatitudes precede the exposition of the law in the Sermon on the Mount). Thus, alongside the stern calls to righteousness (e.g., 5:19–20; 7:21–27; 25:31–46) is also a clear emphasis on grace (e.g., 5:3–12; 9:12–13; 10:7–8; 11:28–30; 18:23–35; 20:1–16; 22:1–10; 26:26–28). The grace of the kingdom and the demands of the law as interpreted by the messianic

30. See Deines, "Not the Law but the Messiah."
31. For example, Barth, "Matthew's Understanding of the Law."

king stand in dynamic tension throughout this Gospel, but it is clear that the former precedes the latter.

Community (Church)

The Greek word *ekklēsia* ("church") occurs among the Gospels only in Matthew (16:18; 18:17 [2x]). Matthew uses this deliberate anachronism to stress that the church was founded by Jesus. In chapter 16, at Peter's confession that Jesus is "the Christ, the Son of the living God," Jesus promises to build his new community (as the underlying Aramaic would have to be translated) upon Peter the rock. The authority bestowed on Peter in 16:19 (singular verbs) is extended to the church in a disciplinary context in 18:18 (plural verbs). Here Matthew's church receives its commission to exercise discipline over believers in the full knowledge that it is being led by the Lord (note 18:19: "If two of you agree on earth about anything they ask, it will be done for them by my Father in heaven"). Matthew has appropriately been called an "ecclesiastical" Gospel for other reasons as well. We have already noted that the Evangelist has collected and shaped the major discourses particularly for the instruction and edification of the church. The disciples and their experiences serve as models for the Evangelist's contemporaries; Peter is a prototype of Christian leadership.

Eschatology

Matthew's special interest in eschatology can be seen simply from the length of the apocalyptic discourse compared with that of Mark 13. Not only is chapter 24 longer than its Markan source (including the warning pericopes in 24:37–51, drawn from Q) but also the author adds an entire chapter of material not found in Mark, centering on the reality of eschatological judgment (the parables of the ten virgins [25:1–13] and the last judgment [25:31–46] are unique to Matthew). Other unique eschatological material in Matthew is found in 13:24–30, 36–43; 20:1–16; 22:1–14. But apocalyptic threads run throughout this Gospel.[32]

The technical word *parousia*, which refers to the eschatological return of Christ, is found only in Matthew (24:3, 27, 37, 39) among the Gospels. Günther Bornkamm has furthermore shown that the Evangelist's eschatology is vitally important to his ecclesiology, christology, and view of the law. As is true throughout the NT, the primary purpose of eschatological teaching for Matthew is not so much to provide information concerning the future as to motivate the church to conduct that is appropriate in light of imminent judgment. Thus in Matthew eschatology is important not only to theology but also to discipleship. The promise of future judgment and deliverance makes perseverance in the present both a possibility and a necessity.

---

32. See Hagner, "Apocalyptic Motifs in the Gospel of Matthew."

The Life Setting of Matthew's Community

The challenge that has always faced students of Matthew is to posit a convincing life setting for the Gospel that can account for its varied perspectives and emphases. Of great importance among these are especially the tension between particularism and universalism within the Gospel and the closely related problem of Israel and the church.

Particularism and Universalism

Matthew is the only Gospel that records Jesus' startling words that restrict his and his disciples' immediate ministry to Israel. When he sends out his disciples he tells them: "Go nowhere among the Gentiles, and enter no town of the Samaritans, but go rather to the lost sheep of the house of Israel" (10:5–6 [cf. 10:23]). Jesus himself responds to the entreaties of a Gentile woman, "I was sent only to the lost sheep of the house of Israel" (15:24). So contradictory is this attitude to that of the Evangelist's day, when the Gentile mission was an undeniable reality, that these passages excellently satisfy the criterion of dissimilarity, and hence most scholars accept their authenticity.

However, seemingly against this particularism, there is an implicit universalism throughout this Gospel: the good news of the gospel is for Gentiles too. Thus, for example, we find Gentile names ("Ruth" and "Rahab") in the genealogy of Christ (1:5); emphasis on Gentile response to the gospel in the magi from the East (2:1–12); the extraordinary faith of the Roman centurion ("Truly, I say to you, not even in Israel have I found such faith" [8:10]); the statements "and in his name will the Gentiles hope" (12:21 [cf. Isa. 42:4]) and "the field is the world" (13:38); the approbation of the Canaanite woman (15:21–28); the parable of the tenants (21:33–43); the parable of the marriage feast (22:1–10); and the Roman soldier's confession of Christ (27:54). What is implicit in these passages becomes explicit in 24:14, where Jesus says, "And this gospel of the kingdom will be preached throughout the whole world, as a testimony to all nations; and then the end will come," and most impressively in the commission in 28:19: "Go therefore and make disciples of all nations [*panta ta ethnē*], baptizing them in the name of the Father and of the Son and of the Holy Spirit."

Israel and the Church

The tension between particularism and universalism is obviously bound up with another polarity in the Gospel, that involving Israel and the church. Matthew contains an apparent polemic against the Jews that is all the more striking because of the favored position of the Jews already noted and because of the generally Jewish tone of this Gospel. Most conspicuous here are the passages referring to a transference of the kingdom from Israel to those who believe (the church) in the gospel. Thus in 8:11–12, just following the compliment given to the Roman centurion for his faith, we read, "I tell you, many will come from east and west and will sit at table with Abraham, Isaac, and Jacob in the kingdom of heaven, while the sons of the kingdom will be thrown into the outer darkness; there men will weep and gnash their teeth." And in 21:41, at the end of the parable of the tenants, the tenants pronounce their own judgment: "He will put those wretches to a miserable death, and let out the vineyard to other tenants who will give him the fruits in their season." This is followed by Jesus' words (21:43): "Therefore I tell you, the kingdom of God will be taken away from you and given to a nation producing the fruits of it." Agreeing with this emphasis is the parable of the marriage feast, where those invited "would not come" (22:3), and thus the invitation is extended to all: "Go therefore to the thoroughfares, and invite to the marriage feast as many as you find" (22:9).

To these passages may be added others that speak of the judgment of unbelieving Israel. Upbraiding the cities of Galilee where his miracles had been done (11:20–24), Jesus concludes, "But I tell you, it shall be more tolerable on the day of judgment for Tyre and Sidon . . . [and the] land of Sodom than for you." In 12:45 he refers to "this evil generation"; in 13:10–15 Matthew alone gives the full quotation of the judgment oracle of Isaiah 6:9–10 concerning the unbelief of Israel (cf. Acts 28:26–27). In the parable of the marriage feast it is noted that "those invited were not worthy" (22:8). In 23:38 Jesus, lamenting over Jerusalem, states, "Behold, your house is forsaken and desolate." And finally we may note the bitter and fateful words of 27:25, unique to Matthew: "And all the people answered, 'His blood be on us and on our children!'" (words that have tragically and unjustifiably been used to promote anti-Semitism).

By contrast, the kingdom is transferred to those who believe, a "nation" (*ethnos*) producing the fruit of the kingdom (righteousness), those who repent, those whose eyes see and whose ears hear what "many prophets and righteous men longed to see . . . and to hear" (13:16–17). In view, of course, is the new community, called with deliberate anachronism the *ekklēsia*, the church.

Also reflecting this tension between the church and Israel are the references to "*their* synagogues" (4:23; 9:35; 10:17; 12:9; 13:54), "*your* synagogues" (23:34), "*their* scribes" (7:29), and "the Jews to this day" (28:15)—most references unique to Matthew and the last comparable to the well-known derogatory reference to "the Jews" in the Fourth Gospel. Throughout the book, moreover, it is the Pharisees who are the main antagonists of Jesus and who are repeatedly shown to be inferior to Jesus in their understanding of Torah. Jesus teaches with a unique authority, "not as their scribes" (7:28–29). Jesus bitterly castigates the Scribes and Pharisees in chapter 23, finally referring to them as "snakes," a "brood of vipers" (cf. John's words in 3:7). Matthew also speaks of the Jewish persecution of the church: "They will deliver you up to the councils and flog you in their synagogues" (10:17 [cf. 23:34]).

Here, then, we have what is probably the major puzzle in the Gospel of Matthew. On the one hand, we have the particularism that limits Jesus' and his disciples' ministry to Israel. Together with this exclusivism—the normal Jewish viewpoint—is the generally Jewish tone of this Gospel, with, among other things, its stress on the abiding validity of the law, the necessity of righteousness, and the fulfillment of messianic prophecy. On the other hand, standing in rather sharp contrast to the preceding, are the universalism of this Gospel, its striking statement concerning the transference of the kingdom to a new community, and the particularly harsh sayings against the Jews.

The Relation of Matthew's Church to Contemporaneous Judaism

A key issue in defining the life setting of Matthew's community is whether by the time of the writing of his Gospel a clear break between the church and synagogue had taken place. Although too much is usually made of it, a relevant issue concerns the decision, which may have been made at Yavneh (Jamnia) in about 85 or 90, to force Jewish Christians out of the synagogue by an addition of a curse against the *minim*, or "heretics," to the liturgy of the synagogue (the *Birkat ha-Minim* in the twelfth of the Eighteen Benedictions, the *Shemoneh Esreh*).[33]

Matthean scholars have tended to work with two false presuppositions about Yavneh: (1) there was no exclusion of Jewish Christians from the synagogue before this date; and (2) after Yavneh the mission to the Jews ceased. However, there is sufficient evidence of an early and continuing hostility between Jews who did not accept the gospel and those who did, including forceful exclusion from the synagogue (cf. Acts 6:12–14; 7:57–8:1; note also Paul's frequent experiences). If any specific date is to be mentioned as a clear turning point for the worse in the relationship between Jews and Christians, it is 70, but even this date does not mark the beginning of hostility between the two groups.[34] Thus the *Birkat ha-Minim*, even on the traditional understanding, amounts only to a formalizing and standardizing of practice, perhaps indeed as the result of mounting hostility, but by no means should it be thought of as an absolute beginning of the hostility or of the practice of exclusion.

33. Possibly Yavneh had no significance for the relationship between Jews and Jewish Christians (thus Kimelman, "*Birkat Ha-Minim* and the Lack of Evidence for an Anti-Christian Prayer in Late Antiquity"). William Horbury concludes that the benediction "was not decisive on its own for the separation of church and synagogue, but it gave solemn liturgical expression to a separation effected in the second half of the first century through the larger group of measures to which it belongs" ("The Benediction of the *Minim* and Early Jewish-Christian Controversy," 61).

34. See the discussion of the parting of the ways in chapter 20 below.

Furthermore, despite the argument by Douglas Hare and Daniel Harrington,[35] there is no need to conclude that Matthew's community had abandoned the mission to the Jews. Even if a mission to the Jews *within* the synagogue must have been abandoned after Jamnia—again on the traditional understanding—the end of the Jewish mission itself is hardly necessitated. Christian Jews would have continued to meet their unbelieving brothers and sisters in the community, where discussions, however tense, undoubtedly continued. It is, in the final analysis, unthinkable both psychologically and theologically that the Jewish Christian community addressed by the Evangelist could have altogether abandoned the mission to members of their own former community.

It seems unlikely, then, that the late 80s or early 90s should be thought of as a watershed providing a radically altered situation that can be used to explain the complex and apparently contradictory data of Matthew's Gospel. The universalism, the sayings about the transference of the kingdom, and the hard sayings against Israel are hardly impossible in the earlier decades. Jesus could have spoken about the future (i.e., the postresurrection period), envisioning a mission to the Gentiles and thus justifying the transference sayings. All this would have been quite meaningful in a context where the Gentile mission was thriving, as would be the sayings against the Jews, which would have reflected the unbelief of the Jews as well as the continuing and probably growing hostility between the church and the synagogue.

The Special Situation of Matthew's Community

Jewish Christians have always found themselves in a kind of existential ambiguity, not least in the first century. To their Jewish family they have always had to answer charges such as disloyalty to the religion of Israel, disloyalty to the Mosaic law (or at least of association with others who fail to observe it), and affiliation with an alien, if not pagan, religion, the large majority of whose adherents are Gentiles.

Matthew's original readers were in an unenviable position, in a kind of "no-man's-land" between the Jews and Gentile Christians, needing to reach back for continuity with the old while at the same time reaching forward to the new work that God was doing in the largely Gentile church—simultaneously answerable, so to speak, to both Jews and Gentile Christians.[36] As James Carleton Paget puts it, "For Christians, Jewish Christians were intolerably Jewish, and for Jews they seemed intolerably Christian."[37]

Finding themselves in this dilemma, Matthew's readers needed an account of the story of Jesus that would enable them to relate both to unbelieving Jews and to Gentile Christians. In particular, the increasing success of the

---

35. Hare and Harrington, "'Make Disciples of All the Gentiles' (Matt. 28:19)."
36. See Hagner, "The Sitz-im-Leben of the Gospel of Matthew."
37. Carleton Paget, "Jewish Christianity," 774.

Gentile mission and the overall failure of the mission to Israel raised questions not only in the readers' minds but also among their Jewish opponents. Thus Matthew's Gospel was written to confirm Jewish believers in the truth of Christianity as the fulfillment of the promises to Israel, which entails the argument that Jesus is the Messiah, that he was loyal to the law, and that he came to the Jews. Through this material the readers could gain confidence in the correctness of their faith as something standing in true succession to the Scriptures and at the same time be in a better position to answer their unbelieving Jewish brothers and sisters in the synagogues.[38]

If this is true, we may well also find here the reason for the preservation of the particularist sayings in Matthew. It was important for the author to be able to stress that Jesus came specifically, indeed exclusively, to the Jews in order to underline God's faithfulness to his covenant people—that is, to stress the continuity of God's salvific promises and the actuality of their fulfillment in the first instance to Israel, as the Scriptures promised. They, unlike the Gentiles, had a place in the ministry of Jesus from the beginning. As Jewish Christians, they were important in the fulfillment of God's plan as a righteous remnant attesting the faithfulness of God to his covenant promises (cf. Rom. 11:1–5). Matthew thus affirms the rightful place of Jewish Christianity as the true Israel. Far from renouncing Judaism, as Kenneth Clark maintains,[39] Matthew finds in Christianity a perfected or fulfilled Judaism, brought to its goal by the long-awaited Christ.

So strongly does Matthew stress the Jewish character of Christian faith that some scholars have argued that Matthew's community should be understood not as a manifestation of Christianity but rather as a sect still within Judaism—that is, a kind of Christian Judaism rather than a Jewish Christianity.[40] This conclusion, however, seriously underestimates the newness of Matthew's Christianity, and especially the shift from a Torah-centered faith to a Christ-centered faith, with all that the latter implies concerning the deity of Christ.[41]

Inevitably and by reason of their unbelieving and hostile brothers and sisters, Jewish Christian congregations must early on have begun to think of themselves as separate from, and even as opposed to, unbelieving Judaism—a righteous remnant against the rabbinic Judaism represented in Matthew's Gospel by the Pharisees. The familiar biblical pattern, denounced so frequently by the prophets, would have been seen in Israel's rejection of God, followed by God's rejection of Israel. And from the latter it is only a step to the sayings about the transference of the kingdom. In the case of these sayings, however,

---

38. See especially Stanton, *A Gospel for a New People*, which convincingly argues for a similar view, buttressing the conclusion with sociological insights.

39. Clark, "The Gentile Bias in Matthew."

40. Thus Saldarini, *Matthew's Christian-Jewish Community*; Sim, *The Gospel of Matthew and Christian Judaism*; Overman, *Matthew's Gospel and Formative Judaism*.

41. See Hagner, "Matthew" (2003); idem, "Matthew" (2004).

our Jewish Christian readers would, of course, have identified themselves as among those nations (*ethnē* ["Gentiles," largely but not exclusively]), *the new people of God*,[42] to whom the kingdom was being transferred.

The Evangelist's community thus shared two worlds, the Jewish and the Christian. Although the members of this community saw their Christianity as the true fulfillment of Judaism, they were quite aware that they had broken with their unbelieving brothers and sisters. This situation explains the basic tensions encountered in Matthew's Gospel. Thus Matthew writes that "new wine is put into fresh wineskins, and so both are preserved" (9:17). Matthew's redactional addition of the last words "and so both are preserved," found neither in Mark or Luke, is congruent with his emphasis on the abiding validity of the law. The new wine of the gospel is preserved together with the new skins—that is, the law as definitively interpreted by Jesus the Messiah. Here we see the Evangelist reaching in both directions to stress the continuity with Moses and the Torah and yet at the same time to affirm the radical newness of the gospel. He writes, in what some think could be an autobiographical allusion, "Therefore every scribe who has been trained for the kingdom of heaven is like a householder who brings out of his treasure what is new and what is old" (13:52).[43]

Genre and Purpose

Matthew, like Mark, is fundamentally a Gospel—good news—a kerygmatic account of the life of Jesus. But Matthew has retold the story of Mark, his main source, with special interests and emphases. With these in mind, is it possible to specify the genre of Matthew more narrowly?

A number of suggestions, not necessarily mutually exclusive, have been put forward. Matthew may be considered as a kind of *midrash*—theological interpretation—on the Gospel of Mark.[44] Some have seen Matthew as a kind of *lectionary*, its composition determined by the lectionary year, so as to provide consecutive liturgical readings in accord with the Jewish festal year.[45] Others have regarded Matthew as a kind of *catechetical handbook* because of its lengthy teaching discourses.[46] In this view, one of Matthew's main purposes is the building up of Christian discipleship through the instruction of its readers.[47] Krister Stendahl went so far as to propose the hypothesis of a

42. See Stanton, *A Gospel for a New People*.
43. See Hagner, "New Things from the Scribe's Treasure Box (Matt. 13:52)."
44. Thus Goulder, *Midrash and Lection in Matthew*. And for the midrashic character of much of Matthew's narrative, Gundry, *Matthew*.
45. See Kilpatrick, *The Origins of the Gospel according to St. Matthew*; Carrington, *The Primitive Christian Calendar*; Goulder, *Midrash and Lection in Matthew*.
46. For example, Minear, *Matthew*.
47. See Wilkins, *Discipleship in the Ancient World and in Matthew's Gospel*.

Matthean school, modeled on the rabbinic schools, that produced a teacher's manual, a Christian equivalent to the Qumran community's *Manual of Discipline*.[48] Another suggestion is that Matthew is a book of *church correctives*, addressing various issues such as division in the community, spiritual malaise, disregard for the law, hypocrisy, and false prophets.[49] Given the burden of this Gospel to demonstrate that Jesus is the Messiah, and especially Matthew's fulfillment quotations, some have described it as basically *missionary propaganda*.[50] Finally, it has been suggested that Matthew basically presents *polemic against the rabbis* concerning the true interpretation of Torah. In this view, Matthew's Gospel draws on the traditions about Jesus and the Pharisees and then uses this material in the struggle with the Pharisaic Judaism of a later time. Matthew is thus a Jewish Christian counterpart of, and response to, the rabbinic activity at Yavneh.[51]

This variety of options indicates the multifaceted character of Matthew. Several of these explanations of this Gospel may be equally true, but this much is clear: Matthew is a "community book," written to meet the immediate needs of a particular readership.[52] The Evangelist intends to help his readers understand their new faith as being in continuity with the faith of their ancestors, as the fulfillment of the Scriptures, and as the beginning of the realization of the hope of Israel. The author wrote, above all, for the church, to interpret the Christ event, but also to instruct and edify the Christians of his own and future generations.

Date and Provenance

Date

Two key questions that pertain to the dating of Matthew are whether the supposed break between the church and synagogue in about 90 had taken place before the Gospel was written, and whether the Gospel reflects a knowledge of the fall of Jerusalem in 70. As already noted, we know very little about the Yavneh decisions, but they are hardly to be conceived of as a watershed in relations between the church and the synagogue. Competition, alienation, and hostility were not unusual before the alleged break. The second question

---

48. Stendahl, *The School of St. Matthew and Its Use of the Old Testament*.

49. For example, Thompson, *Matthew's Advice to a Divided Community*; Schweizer, "Observance of the Law and Charismatic Activity in Matthew."

50. For example, Gärtner, "The Habakkuk Commentary (DSH) and the Gospel of Matthew"; McConnell, *Law and Prophecy in Matthew's Gospel*.

51. Thus Davies, *The Setting of the Sermon on the Mount*, 256–315. See also Hengel, *The Four Gospels and the One Gospel of Jesus Christ*, 169–207.

52. Matthew may well have had a wide readership of Jewish Christians in mind, not necessarily a specific congregation or congregations. See Blomberg, "The Gospels for Specific Communities *and* All Christians."

is not as easy to answer as many have thought. Matthew does refer to the destruction of Jerusalem in 24:2 (cf. 24:15–28), but this can be explained as a record of the prophecy of Jesus, unless the possibility of foretelling the future is ruled out a priori. Nothing in Matthew's redaction of the eschatological discourse of Mark 13 indicates a knowledge of the event.

The reference in 22:7 to the parable of the king who, being angry because those invited to the marriage feast did not come, "sent his troops and destroyed those murderers and burned their city," is too often taken as settling the matter. The reference to "troops" who "burned their city," unnecessary and alien to the context, seems to point to the destruction of Jerusalem. But the language of the parable is hyperbolic and not necessarily to be taken literally. Several scholars have indicated the possibility that the language is a conventional stereotype for punitive expeditions. Robert Gundry shows that the language could be an allusion to Isaiah 5:24–25 (see also Judg. 1:8; 1 Macc. 5:28; *T. Jud.* 5:1–5).[53] Bo Reicke has also indicated the weakness of the usual explanation of 22:7.[54] In short, far too much weight has been put on this text in the confident post-70 dating of Matthew.

Other common objections to an early date of Matthew's Gospel need consideration at this point. First, if it is true that Matthew is dependent on Mark, as I have argued above, and Mark was written in the late 60s, as the consensus holds, must not Matthew be post-70? It should not be assumed, however, that as long as a decade would be needed before Matthew could make use of Mark. There is no reason why more than a year or two at most would be needed, especially if Mark was recognized as Peter's Gospel. Second, it is often alleged that a more "developed" Judaism and a considerably heightened hostility between the church and the synagogue than existed before 70 are needed to account for the content of Matthew. This objection presupposes, on the one hand, more knowledge of pre-70 Judaism than we possess and, on the other hand, that there was only limited hostility between church and synagogue before 70. Third, some have thought Matthew's doctrine too developed to predate 70—for example, in its christology (11:27–30), ecclesiology (16:18–19; 18:15–20), and trinitarian formula (28:19). However, the letters of Paul have similar developed perspectives several years before the destruction of Jerusalem.

Matthew's redaction of the Markan eschatological discourse makes no attempt to disentangle the references to the fall of Jerusalem and the end of the age (chap. 24). Luke very deliberately does so in his redaction of Mark 13, and we might expect Matthew to do the same had it been written after 70. Indeed, the Evangelist aggravates the problem considerably by his insertion of *eutheōs* ("immediately") in 24:29, which leaves the clear impression that

---

53. Gundry, *Matthew.*
54. Reicke, "Synoptic Prophecies on the Destruction of Jerusalem."

he expected the parousia of the Son of Man to occur in close succession to the fall of Jerusalem.[55]

Among further evidence that points to an early date of the Gospel, the following should be mentioned. Unique to Matthew are several redactional additions connected with the temple: the reference to offering and leaving one's "gift" at the altar (5:23–24), the passage on the rightness of paying of the temple tax (17:24–27), and the reference to "swears by the temple" (23:16–22). It is more difficult to believe that these are anachronisms deliberately added by the Evangelist after the temple had been destroyed than that they have relevance because the temple was still standing when this Gospel was written. Similarly, Matthew's redactional addition of the words "Pray that your flight may not be in winter or on a sabbath" (24:20) makes little sense if the destruction of Jerusalem had already occurred.

There is good reason, therefore, to take seriously the possibility of an early (i.e., pre-70) dating for the Gospel, in the late 60s.[56] But there is little room for dogmatism here. We need to remind ourselves how very difficult the dating of the Gospels is and how necessarily speculative our conclusions are.

Provenance

It is equally difficult to know where the Gospel of Matthew was written. The only evidence that we have is indirect: a document written in Greek, mainly to Jewish Christians living probably near Jews and Gentile Christians, perhaps in prosperous communities in an urban context.

Even if we look for a city with a Jewish population where the lingua franca was Greek and where there were also Gentile churches, we have not narrowed the possibilities very much. Dixon Slingerland's hypothesis of a Transjordanian origin (Pella) of Matthew depends altogether on the phrase "across the Jordan" in 4:15; and "beyond the Jordan" in 19:1,[57] which, however, can be explained in other ways. Caesarea Maritima has been favored by Benedict Viviano,[58] and the Phoenician cities of Tyre or Sidon by George Kilpatrick.[59] Other cities such as Alexandria have also been suggested.

One of the most popular options for a long time was a Palestinian origin—such as Jerusalem, Sepphoris, or Tiberias—with support derived from the numerous Jewish characteristics of Matthew's Gospel and especially the idea (from Papias) of an original Aramaic Gospel. With the modern consensus

---

55. See Hagner, "Imminence and Parousia in the Gospel of Matthew"; idem, "Matthew's Eschatology."

56. With, for example, commentators such as Allen, Moule, Reicke, Gundry, Nolland, France, Blomberg, Wilkins, Carson, Gibbs, and Turner. See also Hagner, "Determining the Date of Matthew."

57. Slingerland, "The Transjordanian Origin of St. Matthew's Gospel."

58. Viviano, Matthew and His World.

59. Kilpatrick, The Origins of the Gospel according to St. Matthew.

that Matthew was written originally in Greek, the likelihood of a Palestinian origin diminishes. Diaspora Judaism, moreover, can readily account for the Jewishness of this Gospel.

Of Diaspora cities that might fit what is required, Syrian Antioch has been the clear favorite. Given the population of cosmopolitan Antioch, just the kind of problems that Matthew addressed can easily be imagined as occurring. That is, Jewish Christians would have had to defend their views against the charges of the Jewish community while at the same time relating to the Gentile Christian community. There are, furthermore, some links between the Gospel of Matthew and the *Didache*, which has been related to Syria. And the letters of Ignatius, bishop of Antioch, are the first to indicate a probable knowledge of the Gospel of Matthew.

It may be that Antioch is such an attractive hypothesis simply because we happen to know so much more about it than about most other cities. Antioch, however, can be only a good guess. On this point it is worth quoting a summary of the view held by contributors to an important symposium: "[The Matthean community] was situated in an urban environment, perhaps in Galilee or perhaps more toward the north in Syria but, in any case, not necessarily Antioch."[60]

Authorship

Matthew, like all the canonical Gospels, is an anonymous document. The title *kata Maththaion*, "according to Matthew," was affixed to the Gospel sometime in the second century. From early in the second century the unanimous tradition of the church supports Matthew as the author (e.g., Papias, who received the tradition from the Elder [Apostle?] John, as well as Pantaenus, Irenaeus, Origen, Eusebius, Jerome). The only clues within the text of the Gospel itself are the substitution of the name "Matthew" in 9:9 for "Levi" in the calling of the tax collector to be a disciple (Mark 2:14; cf. Luke 5:27), and the addition of the words "the tax collector" to the name "Matthew" in the listing of the Twelve in 10:3 (cf. Mark 3:18; Luke 6:15). For some reason, the Evangelist wants to show that Levi is the Matthew listed among the Twelve. Is this because he believes that Levi was or should have been one of the Twelve, or is it perhaps because in writing of himself he preferred the name "Matthew" to his own preconversion name, "Levi"?

The real question concerns the reliability of the tradition about the authorship of this Gospel. It is possible, although uncertain, that the whole tradition derives from, and is thus dependent on, the testimony of one man, Papias (as recorded in Eusebius, *Hist. eccl.* 3.39.16). In any event, the tradition appears

60. Kingsbury, "Conclusion," 264.

to have been unchallenged in the early church. It is difficult to believe that this Gospel would have been attributed to Matthew without good reason, since, as far as we can tell from the available data, Matthew was not otherwise a leading figure among the Apostles or in the early church (his name being mentioned only once outside the Gospels, in the list in Acts 1:13). A key objection often set against the traditional ascription of the Gospel to Matthew is the difficulty of believing that one of the Twelve, an eyewitness of the events, could have been so dependent on the account of Mark, a nonparticipant in the narrated events. According to the tradition handed on by Papias (Eusebius, *Hist. eccl.* 3.39.15), however, Mark is essentially the preaching of Peter, and it is not at all inconceivable that Matthew might depend on a Petrine account represented by Mark.

But can Matthew the Apostle have written the Greek document that goes by his name, a document that contains such developed and "late" perspectives? Here it is more difficult to be confident. The tradition about Matthean authorship may be compatible with a conclusion that this Gospel contains traditions stemming from the Apostle (who, as a former tax collector, may well have kept records of Jesus' ministry), perhaps now recognizable particularly in the book's special material—for example, the formula quotations or the material underlying the five discourses. A disciple (or disciples) of Matthew may later have translated and adapted these materials, combined them with the Markan and Q traditions, and reworked the whole to produce the present Gospel of Matthew. Such a hypothesis, speculative though it must be, could account for this Gospel in the form in which we have it.

The argument of a few (e.g., Kenneth Clark, John Meier)[61] that the author was a Gentile rather than a Jew is not convincing. The typical problems that are raised in this connection have better explanations. Thus, for example, the linking of the Sadducees with the Pharisees (e.g., in 16:1, 6, 11–12) is not the result of ignorance concerning the great differences between the two groups, but probably is only an indication of a united front of opposition against Jesus based on the agreement that Jesus was not the Messiah. The mention of two animals in 21:1–9 is not necessarily a misunderstanding of the synonymous parallelism of Zechariah 9:9. The hostility against the Jews in Matthew is not at all unthinkable from the hand of a Jewish Christian; on the contrary, it points to a Jewish author and is exactly what one might expect given the circumstances. Few recent commentators on this Gospel have been inclined to accept the view that the author was a Gentile.

Matthew the Apostle is therefore probably the source of an early form of significant portions of this Gospel, in particular the sayings of Jesus, but perhaps even some of the narrative material. One or more disciples of the Matthean circle may then have put these materials into the form of the Gospel

---

61. Clark, "The Gentile Bias in Matthew"; Meier, *The Vision of Matthew*.

that we have today. The final editing probably was done by an early Hellenistic Jewish Christian, who in transmitting the tradition addressed Jewish fellow believers who, like himself, had come to accept Jesus as the Messiah and now had to articulate that new faith in such a way as to show its continuity with the past as well as to affirm all the newness of the gospel of the kingdom.

Bibliography

Books and Articles

Allison, Dale C., Jr. *The New Moses: A Matthean Typology*. Minneapolis: Fortress, 1993.
———. "The Structure of the Sermon on the Mount." *JBL* 106 (1987): 423–45.
———. *Studies in Matthew: Interpretation Past and Present*. Grand Rapids: Baker Academic, 2005.
Aune, David E., ed. *The Gospel of Matthew in Current Study*. Grand Rapids: Eerdmans, 2001.
Bacon, Benjamin. *Studies in Matthew*. London: Constable, 1930.
Balch, David L., ed. *Social History of the Matthean Community: Cross-Disciplinary Approaches*. Minneapolis: Fortress, 1991.
Banks, Robert. *Jesus and the Law in the Synoptic Tradition*. SNTSMS 28. Cambridge: Cambridge University Press, 1975.
Barth, Gerhard. "Matthew's Understanding of the Law." In *Tradition and Interpretation in Matthew*, by Günther Bornkamm, Gerhard Barth, and Heinz Joachim Held, translated by Percy Scott, 58–164. NTL. Philadelphia: Fortress, 1963.
Barton, Stephen C. *Discipleship and Family Ties in Mark and Matthew*. SNTSMS 80. Cambridge: Cambridge University Press, 1994.
Bauer, David R. *The Structure of Matthew's Gospel: A Study in Literary Design*. JSNTSup 31. Sheffield: Almond, 1988.
Bauer, David R., and Mark Allan Powell, eds. *Treasures New and Old: Contributions to Matthean Studies*. SBLSymS 1. Atlanta: Scholars Press, 1996.
Bauman, Clarence. *The Sermon on the Mount: The Modern Quest for Its Meaning*. Macon, GA: Mercer University Press, 1985.
Beaton, Richard. *Isaiah's Christ in Matthew's Gospel*. SNTSMS 123. Cambridge: Cambridge University Press, 2003.
Betz, Hans Dieter. *Essays on the Sermon on the Mount*. Philadelphia: Fortress, 1985.
Black, Matthew. "The Use of Rhetorical Terminology in Papias on Mark and Matthew." *JSNT* 37 (1989): 31–41.
Blickenstaff, Marianne. *"While the Bridegroom Is with Them": Marriage, Family, Gender, and Violence in the Gospel of Matthew*. JSNTSup 292. London: T&T Clark, 2005.
Blomberg, Craig L. "The Gospels for Specific Communities *and* All Christians." In *The Audience of the Gospels: Further Conversation about the Origin and Function of the Gospels in Early Christianity*, edited by Edward W. Klink III, 111–33. LNTS. London: T&T Clark, 2010.
Bornkamm, Günther, Gerhard Barth, and Heinz Joachim Held. *Tradition and Interpretation in Matthew*. Translated by Percy Scott. NTL. Philadelphia: Westminster, 1963.
Bradley, Marshell Carl. *Matthew: Poet, Historian, Dialectician*. SBL 103. New York: Peter Lang, 2007.
Brooks, Stephenson H. *Matthew's Community: The Evidence of His Special Sayings Material*. JSNTSup 16. Sheffield: JSOT Press, 1987.
Brown, Jeannine K. *The Disciples in Narrative Perspective: The Portrayal and Function of the Matthean Disciples*. SBLAB 9. Atlanta: Society of Biblical Literature, 2002.

Brown, Raymond E. *The Birth of the Messiah: A Commentary on the Infancy Narratives in Matthew and Luke*. Rev. ed. ABRL. New York: Doubleday, 1993.

Bryan, Steven M. *Jesus and Israel's Traditions of Judgement and Restoration*. SNTSMS 117. Cambridge: Cambridge University Press, 2002.

Burnett, Fred W. *The Testament of Jesus-Sophia: A Redaction-Critical Study of the Eschatological Discourse in Matthew*. Washington, DC: University Press of America, 1981.

Byrskog, Samuel. *Jesus the Only Teacher: Didactic Authority and Transmission in Ancient Israel, Ancient Judaism and the Matthean Community*. ConBNT 24. Stockholm: Almqvist & Wiksell, 1994.

Caragounis, Chrys C. *Peter and the Rock*. BZNW 58. Berlin: de Gruyter, 1990.

Carleton Paget, James. "Jewish Christianity." In *The Early Roman Period*. Vol. 3 of *The Cambridge History of Judaism*, edited by William Horbury, W. D. Davies, and John Sturdy, 731–75. Cambridge: Cambridge University Press, 1999.

Carrington, Philip. *The Primitive Christian Calendar: A Study in the Making of the Marcan Gospel*. Cambridge: Cambridge University Press, 1952.

Carson, D. A. "Christological Ambiguities in the Gospel of Matthew." In *Christ the Lord: Studies in Christology Presented to Donald Guthrie*, edited by Harold H. Rowdon, 97–114. Downers Grove, IL: InterVarsity, 1982.

———. "Jewish Leaders in Matthew's Gospel: A Reappraisal." *JETS* 25 (1982): 161–74.

Carter, Warren. *Matthew: Storyteller, Interpreter, Evangelist*. 2nd ed. Peabody, MA: Hendrickson, 2004.

———. *Matthew and Empire: Initial Explorations*. Harrisburg, PA: Trinity Press International, 2001.

———. *What Are They Saying about Matthew's Sermon on the Mount?* Mahwah, NJ: Paulist Press, 1994.

Carter, Warren, and John Paul Heil. *Matthew's Parables: Audience-Oriented Perspectives*. CBQMS 30. Washington, DC: Catholic Biblical Association, 1998.

Chae, Young S. *Jesus as the Eschatological Davidic Shepherd: Studies in the Old Testament, Second Temple Judaism, and in the Gospel of Matthew*. WUNT 2/116. Tübingen: Mohr Siebeck, 2006.

Charette, Blaine. *The Theme of Recompense in Matthew's Gospel*. JSNTSup 79. Sheffield: JSOT Press, 1992.

Clark, Kenneth W. "The Gentile Bias in Matthew." *JBL* 66 (1947): 165–72.

Clarke, Howard. *The Gospel of Matthew and Its Readers: A Historical Introduction to the First Gospel*. Bloomington: Indiana University Press, 2003.

Combrink, H. J. B. "The Structure of the Gospel of Matthew as Narrative." *TynBul* 34 (1983): 61–90.

Cope, O. Lamar. *Matthew, a Scribe Trained for the Kingdom of Heaven*. CBQMS 5. Washington, DC: Catholic Biblical Association, 1976.

Cousland, J. R. C. *The Crowds in the Gospel of Matthew*. NovTSup 102. Leiden: Brill, 2002.

Crosby, Michael. *House of Disciples: Church, Economics, and Justice in Matthew*. Maryknoll, NY: Orbis, 1988.

———. *Spirituality of the Beatitudes: Matthew's Challenge for First World Christians*. Maryknoll, NY: Orbis, 1981.

Davies, W. D. *The Sermon on the Mount*. Cambridge: Cambridge University Press, 1966.

———. *The Setting of the Sermon on the Mount*. Cambridge: Cambridge University Press, 1964.

Davis, James F. *Lex Talionis in Early Judaism and the Exhortation of Jesus in Matthew 5:38–42*. JSNTSup 281. London: T&T Clark, 2005.

Deines, Roland. "Not the Law but the Messiah: Law and Righteousness in the Gospel of Matthew—An Ongoing Debate." In *Built upon the Rock: Studies in the Gospel of Matthew*, edited by D. M. Gurtner and J. Nolland, 53–84. Grand Rapids: Eerdmans, 2008.

Deutsch, Celia. *Hidden Wisdom and the Easy Yoke: Wisdom, Torah and Discipleship in Matthew 11:25–30.* JSNTSup 18. Sheffield: JSOT Press, 1987.

Dodson, Derek S. *Reading Dreams: An Audience-Critical Approach to the Dreams in the Gospel of Matthew.* LNTS 397. New York: T&T Clark, 2009.

Donaldson, Terence L. *Jesus on the Mountain: A Study in Matthean Theology.* JSNTSup 8. Sheffield: JSOT Press, 1985.

Duling, Dennis C. "The Therapeutic Son of David: An Element in Matthew's Christological Apologetic." *NTS* 24 (1977–78): 392–410.

Edwards, Richard A. *Matthew's Story of Jesus.* Philadelphia: Fortress, 1985.

Ellis, Peter R. *Matthew: His Mind and His Message.* Collegeville, MN: Liturgical Press, 1974.

Fenton, J. C. "Inclusio and Chiasmus in Matthew." *SE* 1 [= TU 73] (1959): 174–79.

Filson, Floyd V. "Broken Patterns in the Gospel of Matthew." *JBL* 75 (1956): 227–31.

Foster, Paul. *Community, Law, and Mission in Matthew's Gospel.* WUNT 2/177. Tübingen: Mohr Siebeck, 2004.

France, R. T. *Jesus and the Old Testament: His Application of Old Testament Passages to Himself.* London: Tyndale, 1971.

———. *Matthew: Evangelist and Teacher.* Grand Rapids: Zondervan, 1989.

Gale, Aaron M. *Redefining Ancient Borders: The Jewish Scribal Framework of Matthew's Gospel.* Edinburgh: T&T Clark, 2005.

Garland, David E. *The Intention of Matthew 23.* NovTSup 52. Leiden: Brill, 1979.

Garrow, Alan J. P. *The Gospel of Matthew's Dependence on the Didache.* JSNTSup 254. Sheffield: Sheffield Academic Press, 2003.

Gärtner, Bertil. "The Habakkuk Commentary (DSH) and the Gospel of Matthew." *ST* 8 (1954): 1–24.

Gench, Frances Taylor. *Wisdom in the Christology of Matthew.* Lanham, MD: University Press of America, 1997.

Gerhardsson, Birger. *The Mighty Acts of Jesus according to Matthew.* ScrMin. Lund: Gleerup, 1979.

———. *The Testing of God's Son: An Analysis of Early Christian Midrash.* ConBNT 2. Lund: Gleerup, 1966.

Gibbs, James M. "The Son of God as the Torah Incarnate in Matthew." *SE* 4 [= TU 102] (1968): 38–46.

Gibbs, Jeffrey A. *Jerusalem and Parousia: Jesus' Eschatological Discourse in Matthew's Gospel.* St. Louis: Concordia Academic Press, 2000.

Goodspeed, Edgar J. *Matthew: Apostle and Evangelist.* Philadelphia: Winston, 1959.

Goulder, Michael D. *Midrash and Lection in Matthew: The Speaker's Lectures in Biblical Studies, 1969–71.* London: SPCK, 1974.

Gray, Sherman W. *The Least of My Brothers: Matthew 25:31–46; A History of Interpretation.* SBLDS 114. Atlanta: Scholars Press, 1989.

Green, H. B. "The Structure of St. Matthew's Gospel." *SE* 4 [= TU 102] (1965): 47–59.

Greenman, Jeffrey P., Timothy Larsen, and Stephen R. Spencer, eds. *The Sermon on the Mount through the Centuries: From the Early Church to John Paul II.* Grand Rapids: Brazos Press, 2007.

Gundry, Robert H. *The Use of the Old Testament in St. Matthew's Gospel: With Special Reference to the Messianic Hope.* NovTSup 18. Leiden: Brill, 1967.

Gurtner, Daniel M., and John Nolland, eds. *Built upon the Rock: Studies in the Gospel of Matthew.* Grand Rapids: Eerdmans, 2008.

Hagner, Donald A. "Another Look at 'The Parting of the Ways.'" In *Earliest Christian History: History, Literature, and Theology. Essays from the Tyndale Fellowship in Honor of Martin Hengel*, edited by Michael F. Bird and Jason Maston, 381–427. WUNT 2/320. Tübingen: Mohr Siebeck, 2012.

———. "Apocalyptic Motifs in the Gospel of Matthew: Continuity and Discontinuity." *HBT* 7 (1985): 53–82.

———. "Determining the Date of Matthew." In *Jesus, Matthew's Gospel and Early Christianity: Studies in Memory of Graham N. Stanton*, edited by Daniel M. Gurtner, Joel Willitts, and Richard A. Burridge, 76–92. LNTS 435. London: T&T Clark International, 2012.

———. "Ethics in the Sermon on the Mount." *ST* 51 (1997): 44–59.

———. "Holiness and Ecclesiology: The Church in Matthew." In *Built upon the Rock: Studies in the Gospel of Matthew*, edited by Daniel M. Gurtner and John Nolland, 170–86. Grand Rapids: Eerdmans, 2008.

———. "Imminence and Parousia in the Gospel of Matthew." In *Texts and Contexts: Biblical Texts in Their Textual and Situational Contexts; Essays in Honor of Lars Hartman*, edited by Tord Fornberg and David Hellholm, 77–92. Oslo: Scandinavian University Press, 1995.

———. "Law, Righteousness, and Discipleship in Matthew." *WW* 18 (1998): 364–71.

———. "Matthew: Apostate, Reformer, Revolutionary?" *NTS* 49 (2003): 31–36.

———. "Matthew: Christian Judaism or Jewish Christianity?" In *The Face of New Testament Studies*, edited by Scot McKnight and Grant R. Osborne, 263–82. Grand Rapids: Baker Academic, 2004.

———. "Matthew's Eschatology." In *To Tell the Mystery: Essays on New Testament Eschatology in Honor of Robert H. Gundry*, edited by Thomas E. Schmidt and Moisés Silva, 49–71. JSNTSup 100. Sheffield: JSOT Press, 1994.

———. "New Things from the Scribe's Treasure Box (Matt. 13:52)." *ExpTim* 109 (1998): 329–34.

———. "Righteousness in Matthew's Theology." In *Worship, Theology and Ministry in the Early Church: Essays in Honor of Ralph P. Martin*, edited by Michael J. Wilkins and Terence Paige, 101–20. JSNTSup 87. Sheffield: JSOT Press, 1992.

———. "The Sitz-im-Leben of the Gospel of Matthew." In *Treasures New and Old: Contributions to Matthean Studies*, edited by David R. Bauer and Mark Allan Powell, 27–68. SBLSymS 1. Atlanta: Scholars Press, 1996.

Hagner, Donald A., and Stephen E. Young. "The Historical-Critical Method and the Gospel of Matthew." In *Methods for Matthew*, edited by Mark Allan Powell, 11–43. MBI. Cambridge: Cambridge University Press, 2009.

Ham, Clay Alan. *The Coming King and the Rejected Shepherd: Matthew's Reading of Zechariah's Messianic Hope*. Sheffield: Sheffield Phoenix Press, 2005.

Hamerton-Kelly, Robert G. *Pre-Existence, Wisdom, and the Son of Man: A Study of the Idea of Pre-Existence in the New Testament*. SNTSMS 21. Cambridge: Cambridge University Press, 1973.

Hamm, M. Dennis. *The Beatitudes in Context: What Luke and Matthew Meant*. ZS. Wilmington, DE: Michael Glazier, 1990.

Hare, Douglas R. A. "How Jewish Is the Gospel of Matthew?" *CBQ* 62 (2000): 264–77.

———. *The Theme of Jewish Persecution of Christians in the Gospel according to St. Matthew*. SNTSMS 6. Cambridge: Cambridge University Press, 1967.

Hare, Douglas R. A., and Daniel J. Harrington. "'Make Disciples of All the Gentiles' (Matt. 28:19)." *CBQ* 37 (1975): 359–69.

Heil, John Paul. *The Death and Resurrection of Jesus: A Narrative-Critical Reading of Matthew 26–28*. Minneapolis: Fortress, 1991.

Held, Heinz Joachim. "Matthew as Interpreter of the Miracle Stories." In *Tradition and Interpretation in Matthew*, by Günther Bornkamm, Gerhard Barth, and Heinz Joachim Held, translated by Percy Scott, 165–299. NTL. Philadelphia: Fortress, 1963.

Hendrickx, Herman. *The Infancy Narratives*. London: Geoffrey Chapman, 1984.

Hengel, Martin. *The Four Gospels and the One Gospel of Jesus Christ: An Investigation of the Collection and Origin of the Canonical Gospels*. Harrisburg, PA: Trinity Press International, 2000.

Hill, David. "Son and Servant: An Essay on Matthean Christology." *JSNT* 6 (1980): 2–16.

Horbury, William. "The Benediction of the *Minim* and Early Jewish-Christian Controversy." *JTS* 33 (1982): 19–61. Reprinted in idem, *Jews and Christians in Contact and Controversy*, 67–110. Edinburgh: T&T Clark, 1998.

Horsley, Richard A. *The Liberation of Christmas: The Infancy Narratives in Social Context*. New York: Crossroad, 1989.

Howell, David B. *Matthew's Inclusive Story: A Study in the Narrative Rhetoric of the First Gospel*. JSNTSup 42. Sheffield: JSOT Press, 1990.

Jackson, Glenna S. *"Have Mercy on Me": The Story of the Canaanite Woman in Matthew 15.21–28*. JSNTSup 228. Sheffield: Sheffield Academic Press, 2002.

Jeremias, Joachim. *The Sermon on the Mount*. Translated by Norman Perrin. Philadelphia: Fortress, 1963.

Johnson, Marshall D. *The Purpose of the Biblical Genealogies: With Special Reference to the Setting of the Genealogies of Jesus*. SNTSMS 8. Cambridge: Cambridge University Press, 1969.

Jones, Ivor H. *The Matthean Parables: A Literary and Historical Commentary*. NovTSup 80. Leiden: Brill, 1995.

Kealy, Séan P. *Matthew's Gospel and the History of Biblical Interpretation*. 2 vols. Lewiston, NY: Mellen Biblical Press, 1997.

Kennedy, Joel. *The Recapitulation of Israel: Use of Israel's History in Matthew 1:1–4:11*. WUNT 2/257. Tübingen: Mohr Siebeck, 2008.

Kilpatrick, George D. *The Origins of the Gospel according to St. Matthew*. Oxford: Clarendon, 1946.

Kimelman, Reuven. "*Birkat Ha-Minim* and the Lack of Evidence for an Anti-Christian Jewish Prayer in Late Antiquity." In *Aspects of Judaism in the Greco-Roman Period*. Vol. 2 of *Jewish and Christian Self-Definition*, edited by E. P. Sanders, with A. I. Baumgarten and Alan Mendelson, 226–44, 391–403. Philadelphia: Fortress, 1981.

Kingsbury, Jack D. "Conclusion: Analysis of a Conversation." In *Social History of the Matthean Community: Cross-Disciplinary Approaches*, edited by David L. Balch, 259–69. Minneapolis: Fortress, 1991.

———. *Matthew*. 2nd ed. Philadelphia: Fortress, 1986.

———. *Matthew as Story*. 2nd ed. Philadelphia: Fortress, 1988.

———. *Matthew: Structure, Christology, Kingdom*. 2nd ed. Minneapolis: Fortress, 1989.

———. *The Parables of Jesus in Matthew 13*. 3rd ed. London: SPCK, 1976.

Knowles, Michael. *Jeremiah in Matthew's Gospel: The Rejected Prophet Motif in Matthean Redaction*. JSNTSup 68. Sheffield: JSOT Press, 1993.

Krentz, Edgar. "The Extent of Matthew's Prologue." *JBL* 83 (1964): 409–14.

Kupp, David D. *Matthew's Emmanuel: Divine Presence and God's People in the First Gospel*. SNTSMS 90. Cambridge: Cambridge University Press, 1996.

Kynes, William L. *A Christology of Solidarity: Jesus as the Representative of His People in Matthew*. Lanham, MD: University Press of America, 1991.

LaGrand, James. *The Earliest Christian Mission to "All Nations" in the Light of Matthew's Gospel*. ISFCJ 1. Atlanta: Scholars Press, 1995.

Lambrecht, Jan. *Out of the Treasure: The Parables in the Gospel of Matthew*. LTPM 10. Louvain: Peeters, 1991.

———. *The Sermon on the Mount*. GNS 14. Wilmington, DE: Michael Glazier, 1985.

Lapide, Pinchas. *The Sermon on the Mount: Utopia or Program for Action?* Translated by Arlene Swidler. Maryknoll, NY: Orbis, 1986.

Lawrence, Louise Joy. *An Ethnography of the Gospel of Matthew: A Critical Assessment of the Use of the Honour and Shame Model in New Testament Studies*. WUNT 2/165. Tübingen: Mohr Siebeck, 2003.

Levine, Amy-Jill, ed. *A Feminist Companion to Matthew*. FCNTECW 1. Sheffield: Sheffield Academic Press, 1998.

————. *The Social and Ethnic Dimensions of Matthean Social History*. SBEC 14. Lewiston, NY: Mellen, 1988.

Luomanen, Petri. *Entering the Kingdom of Heaven: A Study on the Structure of Matthew's View of Salvation*. WUNT 2/101. Tübingen: Mohr Siebeck, 1998.

Luz, Ulrich. *Matthew in History: Interpretation, Influence, and Effects*. Minneapolis: Fortress, 1994.

————. *Studies in Matthew*. Grand Rapids: Eerdmans, 2005.

————. *The Theology of the Gospel of Matthew*. Translated by J. Bradford Robinson. Cambridge: Cambridge University Press, 1995.

Malina, Bruce J., and Jerome H. Neyrey. *Calling Jesus Names: The Social Value of Labels in Matthew*. Sonoma, CA: Polebridge, 1988.

Manson, T. W. *The Sayings of Jesus: As Recorded in the Gospels according to St. Matthew and St. Luke*. London: SCM, 1949.

Matthias, Philip. *The Perfect Prayer: Search for the Kingdom through the Lord's Prayer*. Minneapolis: Augsburg, 2005.

McConnell, Richard S. *Law and Prophecy in Matthew's Gospel: The Authority and Use of the Old Testament in the Gospel of St. Matthew*. Basel: Friedrich Reinhart, 1969.

Meier, John P. *Law and History in Matthew's Gospel: A Redactional Study of Matt. 5:17–48*. AnBib 71. Rome: Biblical Institute Press, 1976.

————. *The Vision of Matthew: Christ, Church, and Morality in the First Gospel*. TI. New York: Paulist Press, 1979.

Menninger, Richard E. *Israel and the Church in the Gospel of Matthew*. AUS 7/162. New York: Peter Lang, 1994.

Minear, Paul S. *The Good News according to Matthew: A Training Manual for Prophets*. St. Louis: Chalice, 2000.

————. *Matthew: The Teacher's Gospel*. New York: Pilgrim Press, 1982.

Mohrlang, Roger. *Matthew and Paul: A Comparison of Ethical Perspectives*. SNTSMS 48. Cambridge: Cambridge University Press, 1984.

Moses, A. D. A. *Matthew's Transfiguration Story and Jewish-Christian Controversy*. JSNTSup 122. Sheffield: Sheffield Academic Press, 1996.

Moule, C. F. D. "St. Matthew's Gospel: Some Neglected Features." *SE* 2 [= TU 87] (1964): 90–99.

Murphy, Frederick J. "The Jewishness of Matthew: Another Look." In *Judaism and Christianity in the Beginning*. Vol. 2 of *When Judaism and Christianity Began: Essays in Memory of Anthony J. Saldarini*, edited by Alan J. Avery-Peck, Daniel Harrington, and Jacob Neusner, 377–403. JSJSup 85. Leiden: Brill, 2004.

Neirynck, Frans. "ΑΠΟ ΤΟΤΕ ΗΡΞΑΤΟ and the Structure of Matthew." *ETL* 64 (1988): 21–59.

Newport, Kenneth G. C. *The Sources and Sitz im Leben of Matthew 23*. JSNTSup 117. Sheffield: Sheffield Academic Press, 1995.

Neyrey, Jerome H. *Honor and Shame in the Gospel of Matthew*. Louisville: Westminster John Knox, 1998.

Nolan, Brian M. *The Royal Son of God: The Christology of Matthew 1–2 in the Setting of the Gospel*. OBO 23. Göttingen: Vandenhoeck & Ruprecht, 1979.

Novakovic, Lidija. *Messiah, the Healer of the Sick: A Study of Jesus as the Son of David in the Gospel of Matthew*. WUNT 2/170. Tübingen: Mohr Siebeck, 2003.

O'Collins, Gerald. *The Lord's Prayer*. New York: Paulist Press, 2007.

O'Grady, John F. *The Gospel of Matthew: Question by Question*. Mahwah, NJ: Paulist Press, 2007.

O'Leary, Anne M. *Matthew's Judaization of Mark: Examined in the Context of the Use of Sources in Graeco-Roman Antiquity*. LNTS 323. London: T&T Clark, 2003.

Olmstead, Wesley G. *Matthew's Trilogy of Parables: The Nation, the Nations and the Reader in Matthew 21:28–22:14*. SNTMS 127. Cambridge: Cambridge University Press, 2003.

Orton, David E. *The Understanding Scribe: Matthew and the Apocalyptic Ideal.* JSNTSup 25. Sheffield: Sheffield Academic Press, 1989.

Overman, J. Andrew. *Church and Community in Crisis: The Gospel according to Matthew.* Valley Forge, PA: Trinity Press International, 1996.

———. *Matthew's Gospel and Formative Judaism: The Social World of the Matthean Community.* Minneapolis: Fortress, 1990.

Palachuvattil, Mathew. *"The One Who Does the Will of the Father": Distinguishing Character of Disciples according to Matthew; An Exegetical Theological Study.* TGST 154. Rome: Editrice Pontificio Università Gregoriana, 2007.

Park, Eung Chun. *The Mission Discourse in Matthew's Interpretation.* WUNT 2/121. Tübingen: Mohr Siebeck, 2000.

Pattarumadathil, Henry. *Your Father in Heaven: Discipleship in Matthew as a Process of Becoming Children of God.* AnBib 172. Rome: Editrice Pontificio Istituto Biblico, 2008.

Pennington, Jonathan T. *Heaven and Earth in the Gospel of Matthew.* Grand Rapids: Baker Academic, 2009.

Perlewitz, Miriam. *The Gospel of Matthew.* MBS 8. Wilmington, DE: Michael Glazier, 1989.

Powell, Mark Allan. *Chasing the Eastern Star: Adventures in Reader-Response Criticism.* Louisville: Westminster John Knox, 2001.

———. *God with Us: A Pastoral Theology of Matthew's Gospel.* Minneapolis: Fortress, 1995.

———, ed. *Methods for Matthew.* MBI. Cambridge: Cambridge University Press, 2009.

Pregeant, Russell. *Christology beyond Dogma: Matthew's Christ in Process Hermeneutic.* Philadelphia: Fortress, 1978.

Przybylski, Benno. *Righteousness in Matthew and His World of Thought.* SNTSMS 41. Cambridge: Cambridge University Press, 1980.

Reeves, Keith Howard. *The Resurrection Narrative in Matthew: A Literary-Critical Examination.* Lewiston, NY: Mellen Biblical Press, 1993.

Reicke, Bo. "Synoptic Prophecies on the Destruction of Jerusalem." In *Studies in New Testament and Early Christian Literature: Essays in Honor of Allen P. Wikgren,* edited by David E. Aune, 121–34. NovTSup 33. Leiden: Brill, 1972.

Repschinski, Boris. *The Controversy Stories in the Gospel of Matthew: Their Redaction, Form and Relevance for the Relationship between the Matthean Community and Formative Judaism.* FRLANT 189. Göttingen: Vandenhoeck & Ruprecht, 2000.

Riches, John. *Matthew.* NTG. Sheffield: Sheffield Academic Press, 1996.

Riches, John, and David C. Sim, eds. *The Gospel of Matthew in Its Roman Imperial Context.* JSNTSup 276. London: T&T Clark International, 2005.

Saldarini, Anthony J. "The Gospel of Matthew and Jewish-Christian Conflict." In *Social History of the Matthean Community: Cross-Disciplinary Approaches,* edited by David L. Balch, 37–61. Minneapolis: Fortress, 1991.

———. *Matthew's Christian-Jewish Community.* CSHJ. Chicago: University of Chicago Press, 1994.

Scaer, David P. *Discourses in Matthew: Jesus Teaches the Church.* St. Louis: Concordia, 2004.

Schoedel, William R. "Papias." *ANRW* II.27.1 (1992): 235–70.

Schweizer, Eduard. "Observance of the Law and Charismatic Activity in Matthew." *NTS* 16 (1969–70): 213–30.

Senior, Donald. "Between Two Worlds: Gentile and Jewish Christians in Matthew's Gospel." *CBQ* 61 (1999): 1–23.

———. *The Passion of Jesus in the Gospel of Matthew.* Wilmington, DE: Michael Glazier, 1985.

———. *What Are They Saying about Matthew?* Rev. ed. Mahwah, NJ: Paulist Press, 1995.

Shuler, Philip L. *A Genre for the Gospels: The Biographical Character of Matthew.* Philadelphia: Fortress, 1982.

Sigal, Phillip. *The Halakah of Jesus of Nazareth according to the Gospel of Matthew*. Lanham, MD: University Press of America, 1986.

Sim, David. *Apocalyptic Eschatology in the Gospel of Matthew*. SNTSMS 88. Cambridge: Cambridge University Press, 1996.

———. *The Gospel of Matthew and Christian Judaism: The History and Social Setting of the Matthean Community*. SNTW. Edinburgh: T&T Clark, 1998.

Slingerland, H. Dixon. "The Transjordanian Origin of St. Matthew's Gospel." *JSNT* 3 (1979): 18–28.

Snodgrass, Klyne. "Matthew and the Law." In *Treasures New and Old: Contributions to Matthean Studies*, edited by David R. Bauer and Mark Allan Powell, 99–127. SBLSymS 1. Atlanta: Scholars Press, 1996.

Soarès-Prabhu, George M. *The Formula Quotations in the Infancy Narratives of Matthew: An Enquiry into the Tradition History of Matthew 1–2*. AnBib 63. Rome: Biblical Institute Press, 1976.

Stanton, Graham N. *A Gospel for a New People: Studies in Matthew*. Edinburgh: T&T Clark, 1992.

———, ed. *The Interpretation of Matthew*. SNT 1. 2nd ed. Edinburgh: T&T Clark, 1995.

———. "Matthew." In *It Is Written: Scripture Citing Scripture: Essays in Honour of Barnabas Lindars, SSF*, edited by D. A. Carson and H. G. M. Williamson, 205–19. Cambridge: Cambridge University Press, 1988.

———. "The Origin and Purpose of Matthew's Gospel: Matthean Scholarship from 1945–1980." *ANRW* II.25.3 (1985): 1889–951.

Stendahl, Krister. *The School of St. Matthew and Its Use of the Old Testament*. 2nd ed. Philadelphia: Fortress, 1968.

Stevenson, Kenneth W. *The Lord's Prayer: A Text in Tradition*. Minneapolis: Fortress, 2004.

Stock, Augustine. *The Method and Message of Matthew*. Collegeville, MN: Liturgical Press, 1994.

Suggs, M. Jack. *Wisdom, Christology, and Law in Matthew's Gospel*. Cambridge, MA: Harvard University Press, 1970.

Talbert, Charles H. *Reading the Sermon on the Mount: Character Formation and Decision Making in Matthew 5–7*. Grand Rapids: Baker Academic, 2006.

Thompson, William G. *Matthew's Advice to a Divided Community: Mt. 17,22–18,35*. AnBib 44. Rome: Biblical Institute Press, 1970.

Van Aarde, A. *God-with-Us: The Dominant Perspective in Matthew's Story, and Other Essays*. HvTStSup 5. Pretoria: Periodical Section of the Nederduitsch Hervormde Kerk van Afrika, 1994.

Van de Sandt, Huub, ed. *Matthew and the Didache: Two Documents from the Same Jewish-Christian Milieu?* Assen: Van Gorcum; Minneapolis: Fortress, 2005.

van Tilborg, Sjef. *The Jewish Leaders in Matthew*. Leiden: Brill, 1972.

Vaught, Carl G. *The Sermon on the Mount: A Theological Investigation*. Rev. ed. Waco: Baylor University Press, 2002.

Via, Dan O., Jr. *Self-Deception and Wholeness in Paul and Matthew*. Minneapolis: Fortress, 1990.

Viviano, Benedict. *Matthew and His World: The Gospel of the Open Jewish Christians. Studies in Biblical Theology*. NTOA/SUNT 61. Fribourg: Academic Press; Göttingen: Vandenhoeck & Ruprecht, 2007.

Waetjen, Herman C. *The Origin and Destiny of Humanness: An Interpretation of the Gospel according to Matthew*. Corte Madera, CA: Omega Books, 1976.

Wainwright, Elaine Mary. *Shall We Look for Another? A Feminist Rereading of the Matthean Jesus*. Maryknoll, NY: Orbis, 2000.

Weaver, Dorothy Jean. *Matthew's Missionary Discourse: A Literary-Critical Analysis*. JSNTSup 38. Sheffield: JSOT Press, 1990.

Westerholm, Stephen. *Jesus and Scribal Authority*. ConBNT 10. Lund: Gleerup, 1978.

———. *Understanding Matthew: The Early Christian Worldview of the First Gospel*. Grand Rapids: Baker Academic, 2006.

Wilkins, Michael J. *Discipleship in the Ancient World and in Matthew's Gospel*. 2nd ed. Grand Rapids: Baker Academic, 1995.

Wilson, Alistair I. *When Will These Things Happen? A Study of Jesus as Judge in Matthew 21–25*. PBM. Carlisle, UK: Paternoster, 2004.

Yarbrough, Robert W. "The Date of Papias: A Reassessment." *JETS* 26 (1983): 181–91.

Yieh, John Yueh-Han. *One Teacher: Jesus' Teaching Role in Matthew's Gospel Report*. BZNW 124. Berlin: de Gruyter, 2004.

Commentaries

Albright, W. F., and C. S. Mann. *Matthew: Introduction, Translation, and Notes*. AB 26. Garden City, NY: Doubleday, 1971.

Allen, W. C. *A Critical and Exegetical Commentary on the Gospel according to S. Matthew*. ICC. Edinburgh: T&T Clark, 1912.

Beare, F. W. *The Gospel according to Matthew: A Commentary*. Oxford: Blackwell, 1981.

Betz, Hans Dieter. *The Sermon on the Mount: A Commentary on the Sermon on the Mount, Including the Sermon on the Plain (Matthew 5:3–7:27 and Luke 6:20–49)*. Hermeneia. Minneapolis: Fortress, 1995.

Blomberg, Craig L. *Matthew*. NAC. Nashville: Broadman, 1992.

Boring, M. Eugene. "The Gospel of Matthew: Introduction, Commentary, and Reflections." *NIB* 8:87–506.

Bruner, Frederick Dale. *Matthew: A Commentary*. Rev. ed. 2 vols. Grand Rapids: Eerdmans, 2004.

Carson, D. A. "Matthew." In *Matthew and Mark*, edited by Tremper Longman III and David E. Garland, 23–670. EBC 9. Grand Rapids: Zondervan, 2010.

Carter, Warren. *Matthew and the Margins: A Socio-Political and Religious Reading*. Maryknoll, NY: Orbis, 2000.

Davies, W. D., and D. C. Allison. *A Critical and Exegetical Commentary on the Gospel according to Matthew*. 3 vols. ICC. Edinburgh: T&T Clark, 1988–97.

Fenton, J. C. *The Gospel of St. Matthew*. PGC. Hammondsworth, UK: Penguin, 1963.

Filson, Floyd V. *A Commentary on the Gospel according to St. Matthew*. 2nd ed. BNTC. London: Black, 1971.

France, R. T. *The Gospel according to St. Matthew*. TNTC. Grand Rapids: Eerdmans, 1985.

———. *The Gospel of Matthew*. NICNT. Grand Rapids: Eerdmans, 2007.

Garland, David E. *Reading Matthew: A Literary and Theological Commentary on the First Gospel*. Rev. ed. RNT. Macon, GA: Smyth & Helwys, 1999.

Gibbs, Jeffrey A. *Matthew 1:1–11:1*. ConC. St. Louis: Concordia, 2006.

Guelich, Robert. A. *The Sermon on the Mount: A Foundation for Understanding*. Waco: Word, 1982.

Gundry, Robert H. *Matthew: A Commentary on His Handbook for a Mixed Church under Persecution*. 2nd ed. Grand Rapids: Eerdmans, 1994.

Hagner, Donald A. *Matthew*. 2 vols. WBC 33. Dallas: Word, 1993–95.

Hare, Douglas R. A. *Matthew*. IBC. Louisville: John Knox, 1993.

Harrington, Daniel J. *The Gospel of Matthew*. SP 1. Collegeville, MN: Liturgical Press, 1991.

Hauerwas, Stanley. *Matthew*. BTCB. Grand Rapids: Brazos Press, 2007.

Hendrickx, Herman. *The Sermon on the Mount*. London: Geoffrey Chapman, 1984.

Hill, David. *The Gospel of Matthew*. NCBC. Grand Rapids: Eerdmans, 1972.

Keener, Craig S. *A Commentary on the Gospel of Matthew*. Grand Rapids: Eerdmans, 1999.

Luz, Ulrich. *Matthew: A Commentary*. Translated by James E. Crouch. Edited by Helmut Koester. 3 vols. Hermeneia. Minneapolis: Fortress, 1989–2007.

McNeile, Alan Hugh. *The Gospel according to St. Matthew: The Greek Text with Introduction, Notes, and Indices*. London: Macmillan, 1915.

Meier, John P. *Matthew*. NTM. Collegeville, MN: Liturgical Press, 1980.

Mitch, Curtis, and Edward Sri. *The Gospel of Matthew*. CCSS. Grand Rapids: Baker Academic, 2010.

Montague, George T. *Companion God: A Cross-Cultural Commentary on the Gospel of Matthew*. New York: Paulist Press, 1989.

Morris, Leon. *The Gospel according to Matthew*. PNTC. Grand Rapids: Eerdmans, 1992.

Nolland, John. *The Gospel of Matthew: A Commentary on the Greek Text*. NIGTC. Grand Rapids: Eerdmans, 2005.

Osborne, Grant R. *Matthew*. ZECNT. Grand Rapids: Zondervan, 2010.

Patte, Daniel. *The Gospel according to Matthew: A Structural Commentary on Matthew's Faith*. Philadelphia: Fortress, 1987.

Plummer, Alfred. *An Exegetical Commentary on the Gospel according to St. Matthew*. London: Robert Scott, 1909.

Pregeant, Russell. *Matthew*. CCT. St. Louis: Chalice, 2004.

Ridderbos, Herman. *Matthew*. Translated by Ray Togtman. Grand Rapids: Regency Reference Library, 1987.

Schnackenburg, Rudolf. *The Gospel of Matthew*. Translated by Robert R. Barr. Grand Rapids: Eerdmans, 2002.

Schweizer, Eduard. *The Good News according to Matthew*. Translated by David E. Green. Atlanta: John Knox, 1975.

Senior, Donald. *The Gospel of Matthew*. IBT. Nashville: Abingdon, 1997.

———. *Matthew*. ANTC. Nashville: Abingdon, 1998.

Smith, Robert H. *Matthew*. ACNT. Minneapolis: Augsburg, 1989.

Strecker, Georg. *The Sermon on the Mount: An Exegetical Commentary*. Translated by O. C. Dean Jr. Nashville: Abingdon, 1987.

Turner, David. *Matthew*. BECNT. Grand Rapids: Baker Academic, 2007.

Wilkins, Michael J. *Matthew*. NIVAC. Grand Rapids: Zondervan, 2004.

Witherington, Ben, III. *Matthew*. SHBC. Macon, GA: Smyth & Helwys, 2006.

13

The Gospel according to Luke(-Acts)

One of the oddities of the canonical order of the NT writings is that Luke and Acts, two volumes of a single work (note Acts 1:1: "In the first book, O Theophilus, I have dealt with all that Jesus began to do and teach"), are split apart by the intruding Gospel of John. This happened because of the grouping together of the four Gospels in a single codex in the second century. The unnatural splitting apart of Luke-Acts might have been avoided by making Luke the fourth of the Gospels, but the Gospel of John, as the most developed theological retelling of the story of Jesus, and because of its special character compared to the three Synoptics, was kept as the last of the four. Nevertheless, in analyzing Luke, we must keep Acts in mind, and vice versa.[1] This is true not only for questions such as authorship, date, setting, and purpose, but especially for analyzing Luke's theological perspective.

The Gospel of Luke is unique just by virtue of the fact that it is followed by a second part containing a history of earliest Christianity. This suggests right away that the Evangelist is interested in the story of Jesus and its immediate consequences in the birth of the church.

1. Some caution is due here because there are also various differences between Luke and Acts, among other reasons because of their respective subjects: the stories of Jesus and the church. See Parsons and Pervo, *Rethinking the Unity of Luke and Acts*. Stylometric analysis of the seams and summaries in Luke and Acts leads Patricia Walters, in *The Assumed Authorial Unity of Luke and Acts*, to conclude that the books are by different authors. For defense of the unity of Luke-Acts, see Tannehill, *The Narrative Unity of Luke-Acts*; Marshall, "Acts and the 'Former Treatise.'" See also Verheyden, "The Unity of Luke-Acts."

> **Author**: *Probably* Luke, "the beloved physician" (Col. 4:14) and traveling companion of Paul (cf. the "we" passages [Acts 16:10–17; 20:5–21:18; 27:1–28:16]).
>
> **Date**: *Very tentatively* in the early 70s, possibly a decade earlier or later.
>
> **Addressees**: Theophilus and Gentile Christians throughout the Roman Empire.
>
> **Purpose**: To tell again the story of Jesus, his ministry and death, now as the first stage of the fulfillment of salvation history, but also with various subsidiary theological and apologetic purposes.
>
> **Message/Argument**: In fulfillment of the Scriptures, Jesus announces and brings the kingdom of God through his death, thus making possible a universal salvation.
>
> **Significance**: Presents the story of Jesus from a salvation-historical perspective.

The Lukan Prologue and Address

Although Eusebius provides us with no testimony from Papias concerning the origin of the Gospel of Luke, such as he does for Mark and Matthew, we have a remarkable introduction of the work from the author himself (Luke 1:1–4). Luke alone among the Gospels begins with a prologue, modeled to some extent on the rhetoric of formal Hellenistic prologues,[2] in which he indicates the historical reliability of his account, his purpose in writing, and identifies a specific addressee, the "most excellent Theophilus."

> Inasmuch as many [*polloi*] have undertaken to compile a narrative [*diēgēsis*] of the things which have been accomplished [*peplērophorēmenōn*] among us, just as they were delivered [*paredosan*] to us by those who from the beginning were eyewitnesses [*autoptai*] and ministers [*hypēretai*] of the word, it seemed good to me also, having followed all things closely [*akribōs*] for some time past, to write an orderly [*kathexēs*] account for you, most excellent Theophilus, that you may know the truth [*tēn asphaleian*] concerning the things of which you have been informed [*katēchēthēs*].

Luke writes self-consciously as a historian.[3] He describes his work as a "narrative account."[4] He says that he has followed all things "closely" (i.e.,

2. See especially the standard analysis of the prologue: Alexander, *The Preface to Luke's Gospel*. See also D. Schmidt, "Rhetorical Influences and Genre." It is often pointed out how the elegant Greek of Luke's prologue changes abruptly to a more rugged, paratactic, and Semitic style Greek beginning in 1:5.

3. Brian Rosner shows that Acts "is consciously modelled on the accounts of history found in the Old Testament" ("Acts and Biblical History," 68). He goes on to suggest that Acts may well be thought of as the continuation of the OT story.

4. "The frequency with which the word [*diēgēsis*] occurs in both classical and Hellenistic Greek writers, especially by those who profess to write history or about history and the way it should be written, makes it impossible to miss the intention with which Luke proposes his account of the Christ-event" (Fitzmyer, *The Gospel according to Luke*, 1:173).

"accurately" or "exactly")[5] and has written an "orderly" (i.e., "organized"—not a reference to chronology) account so that Theophilus might know the "reliability" or "certainty" (as *asphaleian* may better be translated)[6] of the things "accomplished among us"[7] that he had been "taught orally" (the Greek word comes into English as "catechized"). Luke indicates that he, like others before him, has made use of apostolic tradition ("eyewitnesses") handed down to the church by "servants" of the word.[8] Although the prologue is styled after the custom of the day, we should not discount the emphasis that Luke wants put upon the reliability of what he writes. Theophilus may safely rely on Luke's account of the story of Jesus. It is furthermore the case that what this prologue affirms stands good for the second volume, the account of the birth of the church.

The Dependence on Mark and the Structure of Luke

Luke, the longest of the four Gospels, depends on Mark for much of its material, but also on the hypothetical source Q, and, third, for the considerable amount of unique material on the special source(s) that we designate "L." Luke picks up a little more than half of Mark (whereas Matthew uses 90 percent of Mark), but given the length of Luke, the Markan material makes up only about one-third of this Gospel. Q makes up about one-fifth of Luke. What is most distinctive is that as much as half of Luke's Gospel consists of L material (whereas less than one-third of Matthew consists of M material). Thus Luke has much more unique material than any of the other Synoptics.

The dependence on Mark means that the outline and core content of Luke remain very much like Mark, as I have earlier described it. The same building blocks of the kerygma are present in Luke, indeed as one might expect, given the kerygmatic sermons of Acts. These common denominators in the Synoptics compose the essence of the gospel.

So too the basic structure of Luke, including its core chronology, follows that of Mark. Joseph Fitzmyer organizes this material into five large blocks of corresponding material:[9]

5. See Moessner, "The Appeal and Power of Poetics (Luke 1:1–4)."

6. This word is placed last in this long Greek sentence for emphasis. Luke wanted "to make known the truth of the Christian message. The surest way to do so was to give historical evidence which was unimpeachable by the standards of his time, 'for this was not done in a corner' (Acts 26:26)" (van Unnik, "Once More St. Luke's Prologue," 19).

7. The participle translated "accomplished" may itself connote fulfillment of the Scriptures.

8. Eusebius comments on the Lukan prologue that Luke "related in his own Gospel the accurate account of the things of which he had himself firmly learnt the truth from his profitable intercourse and life with Paul and his conversation with the other apostles" (*Hist. eccl.* 3.14.15, trans. Lake).

9. Fitzmyer, *The Gospel according to Luke*, 1:67.

1. Mark 1:1–15 = Luke 3:1–4:15
2. Mark 1:21–3:19 = Luke 4:31–6:19
3. Mark 4:1–9:40 = Luke 8:4–9:50
4. Mark 10:13–13:32 = Luke 18:15–21:33
5. Mark 14:1–16:8 = Luke 22:1–24:12

Luke does frequently insert Q and L material into these blocks of material, but these insertions are minor and do not affect the basic Markan order, which is taken over.

But there are notable differences from Mark too. First we may note two substantial blocks of Markan material omitted by Luke: the so-called big omission, Mark 6:45–8:26 (walking on the sea; a miracle summary passage; the discussion of defilement; healing of the Syrophoenician woman's daughter; healing of a deaf mute; feeding of the four thousand; the Pharisees seek a sign; discourse on leaven; healing of a blind man), and the so-called little omission, Mark 9:41–10:12 (teaching of Jesus). It is virtually impossible to explain these omissions beyond simply saying that Luke had limited space and wanted to include his special material.

Corresponding to these omissions are the two substantial blocks of added material known as the big interpolation (9:51–18:14 [or 19:27 or 19:44?]) and the little interpolation (6:20–8:3). The former constitutes the most conspicuous difference between Luke and the other two Synoptic Gospels. This long section, referred to as *Luke's travel narrative*, consists of more than one-third of this Gospel and establishes a turning point in Luke, beginning with the words "When the days drew near for him to be received up, he set his face to go to Jerusalem" (9:51). The travel narrative can be given the title "Journeying toward Jerusalem" (see 13:22; 17:11; 18:31; 19:28). In the transfiguration narrative Moses and Elijah "appeared in glory and spoke of his departure [*exodos*], which he was to accomplish at Jerusalem" (9:31). Jesus goes to Jerusalem to die, as is indicated very clearly in 18:31, introducing the third passion prediction: "Behold, we are going up to Jerusalem, and everything that is written of the Son of man by the prophets will be accomplished." The words in 9:51 thus introduce a lengthy section unparalleled in Mark or Matthew, except for secondary parallels (crossovers of similar material), containing such beloved passages as the parables of the good Samaritan, the lost sheep, the lost coin, the prodigal son, and the Pharisee and the tax collector.[10] Some mark the end of this section with 19:27 because of the reference about going up to Jerusalem in 19:28, but this last section, beginning with 18:15, except for the story

10. For a study of the travel narrative, see especially Moessner, *The Lord of the Banquet*. Moessner explains the disparity between form and content of the narrative by means of the idea that Luke here presents the fulfillment of the new exodus salvation promised in Deuteronomy. See also Evans, "The Central Section of St Luke's Gospel."

of Zacchaeus and the parable of the pounds (19:1–27), seems dependent on Mark (Mark 10:13–52). The little interpolation of 6:20–8:3 consists of Luke's Sermon on the Plain, which has some similarities with Matthew's Sermon on the Mount but at the same time looks independent.

As we saw in chapter 9 on the Synoptic Problem, it was Luke's considerable omissions from Mark that gave rise to the proto-Luke hypothesis advanced initially by B. H. Streeter,[11] who also added 3:1–4:30 as not derived from Mark. According to this hypothesis, Mark was not the primary source of Luke at all. Instead, Luke depended on a source consisting of Q + L material, into which Markan material was subsequently inserted. The hypothesis of a proto-Luke has, however, seemed too speculative to most scholars.

Like Matthew but unlike Mark, Luke has an extended account of the birth of Jesus, including even a story about Jesus when he was twelve years old, dialoguing with the teachers in the temple (2:41–51). And Luke, again like Matthew, has a proper account of the resurrection appearances, including the lengthy story of the Emmaus disciples (24:13–35). These materials are drawn from Luke's special source(s), designated "L," and further mark out the distinctiveness of this Gospel.

The Salvation-Historical Perspective of Luke(-Acts)

Already by virtue of having a second volume, Luke thinks in terms of time frames of salvation history: there is the time of Jesus' ministry and the time of the beginnings of the church. But since Luke places so much importance on the Scriptures of the OT and their fulfillment in Christ, the OT era may also be thought of as a time frame preceding and pointing to the NT era. Luke has a strong sense of salvation history, and he attempts to communicate this perspective through his two volumes.[12]

The Gospel as the Fulfillment of the Promises

The opening chapters of Luke's Gospel are important in setting the tone and direction of the narrative. The so-called infancy narrative of Luke (chaps. 1–2) puts a great emphasis on the fulfillment of the promises of the OT in the birth of Jesus. By means of rhapsodic poetry filled with OT allusions, Luke sets the scene for the story of Jesus. I have already quoted these passages (see above, pp. 72–73), so all that is needed here is a reminder of their content.

First are the words of the angel to Zechariah about the birth of his son, John (the Baptist), in 1:14–17, with its opening emphasis on "joy and gladness," and that "many will rejoice at his birth." He will be "filled with the

---

11. Streeter, *The Four Gospels*, 201–22.
12. See Jervell, "The Future of the Past."

Holy Spirit" (a clear eschatological marker), and he will have a ministry in Israel "in the spirit and power of Elijah," "to make ready for the Lord a people prepared" (thus the messianic forerunner referred to in Mal. 3:1; 4:5–6).

After the annunciation to Mary (1:28–33), with its promise that her son will be "the Son of the Most High," that as Davidic Messiah he will receive the throne of David,[13] and that "of his kingdom there will be no end," Mary responds in the words of the famous *Magnificat* (1:46–55), which is full of eschatological language, ending in the words "He has helped his servant Israel, in remembrance of his mercy, as he spoke to our fathers, to Abraham and to his posterity for ever." In this Son the Abrahamic covenant finds and will find its fulfillment. That is, the reality of the birth of Jesus is itself a present fulfillment that guarantees future and final fulfillment.[14]

The next poetic passage of praise is found in the *Benedictus* of Zechariah (1:68–79), with its opening statement of fulfillment: "Blessed be the Lord God of Israel, for he has visited and redeemed his people, and has raised up a horn of salvation for us in the house of his servant David, as he spoke by the mouth of his holy prophets from of old." The allusion to the Davidic covenant is followed by an allusion to the Abrahamic covenant (1:73).[15] The language is thus couched in terms of national fulfillment for Israel, as indeed has been the case in virtually all the poetic passages thus far. In contrast to this, however, is the *Nunc Dimittis* (2:29–32), where the horizon of fulfillment widens to a universal application. Simeon, "looking for the consolation of Israel," also refers to a salvation "prepared in the presence of all peoples," which he then describes as "a light for revelation to the Gentiles, and for glory to thy people Israel." Here is a deliberate allusion to the eschatological role Isaiah ascribes to Israel as "a light to the nations" (Isa. 42:6; 49:6; cf. 60:3).[16]

Luke, of course, also stresses fulfillment outside the infancy narratives. John the Baptist's appearance is prefaced (3:4–6) with a quotation of Isaiah 40:3–5 (cf. the application of Mal. 3:1 to John in 7:27). Jesus, in the synagogue in Nazareth, reads Isaiah 61:1–2 and says, "Today this scripture has been fulfilled in your hearing" (4:21), a passage regarded by some as programmatic for the whole Gospel of Luke. And particularly striking is the emphasis on

13. See Strauss, *The Davidic Messiah in Luke-Acts.*

14. In 1:49 aorist verbs begin to take the place of the future tense (as also in Zechariah's Benedictus and Simeon's Nunc Dimittis). These aorists appear to be analogous to the Hebrew perfect tense, which speaks of the future, governed as it is by God's sovereign will, in past tenses because of the confidence of future fulfillment.

15. See Dahl, "The Story of Abraham in Luke-Acts."

16. For a defense of the importance of Luke 1–2 for understanding the whole of Luke-Acts, see Minear, "Luke's Use of the Birth Stories." On the fulfillment motif of these chapters, see Farris, *The Hymns of Luke's Infancy Narratives*, 152–54.

the fulfillment of the Scriptures in the last chapter of the book (24:25–27, 32, 44–46). The story of Jesus, including his death, fulfills what stands written in Israel's Scriptures (cf. 18:31; 22:37; Acts 13:29).[17]

So too the story of the church in Acts is presented as a matter of the fulfillment of the Scriptures.[18] What was prophesied in the past is now coming to fulfillment.[19] Even new, Gentile Christians learned the importance of the fulfillment of the Scriptures of Israel.[20]

The Goal of History and the Predetermined Plan of God

The fulfillment of prophecy in itself indicates that the story of Jesus and the church is the outworking of the plan of God. But there are also other indications of this theme in the narrative. In the ancient world the notion of providence and divine control over human history was not unusual. Luke has a similar perspective, but much intensified by the nature of the biblical God and the motif of the fulfillment of Scripture.

Luke plants his narrative squarely in time and space. The story on which the salvation of the world depends is momentous, a pivotal point in human history, and therefore must be located in reference to universal history—the Roman Empire. Thus in Luke 3:1–2 we read, "In the fifteenth year of the reign of Tiberius Caesar, Pontius Pilate being governor of Judea, and Herod being tetrarch of Galilee, and his brother Philip tetrarch of the region of Iturea and Trachonitis, and Lysanias tetrarch of Abilene, in the high-priesthood of Annas and Caiaphas, the word of God came to John the son of Zechariah in the wilderness."

A similar temporal and spatial orientation has already been given in relation to the birth of Jesus: "In those days a decree went out from Caesar Augustus that all the world should be enrolled. This was the first enrollment, when Quirinius was governor of Syria" (2:1–2).[21]

---

17. "In their accounts of the activity and suffering of Jesus of Nazareth, [the Evangelists] were concerned above all to relate the story of God's eschatological revelation of himself, his coming to men, and in so doing to complete the historical narrative of the Old Testament, which they all take up in some way, by describing the fulfilment of the promise" (Hengel, *Acts and the History of Earliest Christianity*, 42).

18. See Kurz, "Promise and Fulfillment in Hellenistic Jewish Narratives and in Luke and Acts"; Bock, "Scripture and the Realisation of God's Promises"; idem, *Proclamation from Prophecy and Pattern*; Litwak, *Echoes of Scripture in Luke-Acts*.

19. See Peterson, "The Motif of Fulfillment and the Purpose of Luke-Acts."

20. See Stenschke, *Luke's Portrait of Gentiles prior to Their Coming to Faith*.

21. The reference to Quirinius presents a notorious difficulty. Historical evidence indicates that Quirinius was governor of Syria AD 6–9, whereas Jesus was born before the death of Herod the Great in 4 BC. After a full survey of the attempts to reconcile Luke's statement with historical sources, Howard Marshall concludes, "No solution is free from difficulty, and the problem can hardly be solved without the discovery of fresh evidence" (*The Gospel of Luke*, 104). With our limited knowledge, it is impossible to be certain that Luke has made an error here, though

In this specific geographical and temporal context God works out his plan of salvation. Luke uses the words "the will [*hē boulē*] of God" (7:30 [used in Acts 20:27 as a summary: lit. "God's plan"]). In reference particularly to the death of Jesus, the cornerstone of this plan, Luke uses the language of predestination: "This Jesus, delivered up according to the definite plan [*tē hōrismenē boulē*] and foreknowledge of God [*prognōsei tou theou*], you crucified and killed by the hands of lawless men" (Acts 2:23 [cf. 10:42; 17:31]); Herod and Pontius Pilate, with the Gentiles and the people of Israel, were gathered against Jesus "to do whatever thy hand [*cheir*] and thy plan [*boulē*] had predestined to take place [*proōrisen genesthai*]" (Acts 4:28). The "will" (*thelēma*) of God is of similar significance (Acts 22:14) and so too the repeated use of *dei* ("it is necessary"), referring to divine necessity—that is, pointing to the outworking of God's will in history.

John Squires has shown how the fulfillment of the plan of God in Luke-Acts is confirmed by signs and wonders in the early church, epiphanies, and fulfilled prophecies. "The interweaving of strands reinforces the function of the central theme of the plan of God as an interpretive key to the events which Luke narrates."[22] The emphasis on the plan of God is most obvious for two particularly difficult and controversial, but absolutely important matters: the death of Jesus (Luke) and the mission to the Gentiles (Acts). Each comes to be fulfilled in its respective volume.

Christ as the Center of Time

In his pioneering redactional-critical study of Luke, Hans Conzelmann focused on Luke's salvation history schema, finding Jesus at the center.[23] He divides all of history between the creation and the parousia into three phases:

1. the period of Israel, of the law and the prophets;
2. the period of Jesus, which gives a foretaste of future salvation;
3. the period between the coming of Jesus and the parousia, which is the period of the church and of the Spirit (this is the last age).[24]

---

that possibility cannot be ruled out. Quirinius may not have been technically "governor" at this time, but that does not affect the reality of an enrollment, prior to the levying of taxes, which was the reason for Joseph and Mary's journey to Bethlehem.

22. Squires, *The Plan of God in Luke-Acts*, 189. See also idem, "The Plan of God in the Acts of the Apostles."

23. The German title of the book, *Die Mitte der Zeit* ("The Midpoint of Time"), is, unfortunately, replaced in the English translation with *The Theology of St. Luke*.

24. Conzelmann, *The Theology of St. Luke*, 150. Many NT scholars have rightly argued that it is equally possible to divide salvation history into two periods, the time of promise and the time of fulfillment, the latter beginning with Jesus and continuing into the church age. The question is how much one emphasizes the continuity and how much the differences between the time of Jesus and the time of the church.

This analysis, although different from the prophecy-fulfillment paradigm mentioned above, is consistent with it. In Luke's view, all Scripture points to Jesus, his coming, his ministry, and especially his death. Thus "the law and the prophets were until John; since then the good news of the kingdom of God is preached" (16:16). The appearance of John the Baptist marks a crucial turning point in salvation history. John is a transitional figure who in one sense belongs to the old period of the law and prophets, as its conclusion, and in another sense belongs to the new period of the kingdom announced by him and Jesus, as its beginning (cf. Matt. 11:11–14).

It is the birth of the church, described by Luke in Acts 2, that constitutes the third time frame—the time of the present era. In his second volume Luke writes an open-ended history of the early church. Jesus brings salvation, enjoyed by the present church, yet it is still not the final salvation promised by the prophets and longed for by Israel. The latter is preceded by the interim period of the church. Although all of Christianity is eschatologically tinged, eschatology proper awaits the future: the return of Christ. Luke's perspective is intrinsically a periodization of history, indeed the outworking of the one great story of salvation history.[25]

Luke as Historian

Much has been written either denying or affirming that Luke is a deliberate and careful historian, intending to write and succeeding at writing an authentic historical account of the life of Jesus and the growth of the early church.[26] Currently many scholars seem uninterested in the historical evaluation of the Gospels and Acts, believing that they are better understood as pure literature and that their value lies in the message rather than the purported history they contain. Acts in particular is regarded by some as not more than a species of romantic fiction.

The foregoing discussion has shown, however, that Luke intends to write history. He may well have other interests too, of course, but these do not necessarily conflict with his desire to tell what happened. History and theology are not irreconcilable enemies, despite what some continue to believe.[27] Nor does Luke's purpose or agenda necessarily cancel out the possibility of the reporting

25. "Oscar Cullmann regarded this work by Conzelmann as a supplement to his *Christ and Time*, a compliment that Conzelmann hardly expected!" (Ellis, *Eschatology in Luke*, 17). Ellis adds that Cullmann would only disagree with Conzelmann's idea that this salvation historical framework was a secondary development.

26. For an excellent and fascinating study, see Gasque, *A History of the Interpretation of the Acts of the Apostles*.

27. On the compatibility of the two, see especially Marshall, *Luke*, 21–52. Morna Hooker rightly points out that "[Luke's] own statement of intent in 1.1–4 scarcely seems to support this antithesis between historical accuracy and theology!" ("In His Own Image?" 37).

of reliable history. C. K. Barrett has written of Luke, "Both the form and the matter of his work place Luke among the historians; . . . he shared, as it were by instinct, and brought to his task, the Hellenistic historian's conception of historiography."[28] Similarly, Martin Hengel writes, "Luke is no less trustworthy than other historians of antiquity. People have done him a great injustice in comparing him too closely with the edifying, largely fictitious, romance-like writings in the style of the later acts of apostles, which freely invent facts as they like and when they need them."[29]

Polybius, for example, has rigorous standards for the writing of history, as can be seen from his strong criticisms of Timaeus's attempt at it.[30] With regard to speeches, this frequently quoted statement by Thucydides indicates the desire to record what was said: "As to the speeches which were made either before or during the war, it was hard for me, and for others who reported them to me, to recollect the exact words. I have therefore put into the mouth of each speaker the sentiments proper to the occasion, expressed as I thought he would be likely to express them, while at the same time I endeavored, as nearly as I could, to give the general purport of what was actually said" (*Hist. Pel.* 1.22, trans. Jowett).

Here, despite the undoubted creative dimension in reconstruction, Thucydides emphasizes his desire to give the essence "*of what was actually said.*" Colin Hemer summarizes the emphases of ancient historiography as including, among others, a rigorous theory of historiography; a stress on eyewitness information; concern for the quality of evidence; a stress on travel to the scene of an event; and a vigorous concept of "truth" in history "as it actually happened."[31]

Despite occasional claims to the contrary, Luke is deeply interested in what happened in history.[32] He makes this point in the prologue to his Gospel (1:1–4), but it is evident also throughout the narrative of Luke-Acts. His stated purpose is to provide Theophilus with a reliable account of the things that had recently happened, to provide him with a confident and truthful knowledge

---

28. Barrett, *Luke the Historian in Recent Study*, 9–10. To illustrate that conception of history, Barrett quotes from Lucian (*On Writing History*), who in turn is dependent on Thucydides: "The one task of the historian is to describe things exactly as they happened." And again, "This is the one essential thing in history, to sacrifice to truth alone." See also Barrett, "The Historicity of Acts"; Bruce, *The Acts of the Apostles*, 27–34.

29. Hengel, *Acts and the History of Earliest Christianity*, 60.

30. See Hemer, "Luke the Historian," 30–31.

31. Hemer, *The Book of Acts in the Setting of Hellenistic History*, 100; see also Marshall, *Luke*, 53–76; Gasque, "The Book of Acts and History."

32. Marshall concludes: "that Luke conceived his task as the writing of history and that we shall fail to do justice to his work if we do not think of him as a historian. . . . Because he was a theologian he had to be a historian. His view of theology led him to write history. . . . The events which faith interprets as divine acts must be real, historical events, or otherwise they cannot be interpreted at all" (*Luke*, 52).

of what Theophilus has heard. In this regard, Luke functions quite like a Hellenistic historian.

A Universal Salvation

The opening chapters of Luke, as we have seen, are dedicated to the statement of the gospel as the fulfillment of Israel's hope, and in that way they underline the faithfulness of God to his promises. This is a point that cannot be missed in Luke-Acts. At the same time, however, from the beginning the Gentiles are also in view.[33] They are implicit in the reference to the Abrahamic covenant alluded to in 1:73, and explicit in the words of Simeon: "Mine eyes have seen thy salvation which thou hast prepared in the presence of all peoples, a light for revelation to the Gentiles, and for glory to thy people Israel" (2:30–32). The fulfillment quotation of Isaiah 40:3–5 is extended by Luke to include the words "and all flesh shall see the salvation of God" (3:6). In 3:8 (// Matt. 3:9) John the Baptist says to the Jews inclined to rest on their lineage that "God is able from these stones to raise up children to Abraham," which in retrospect can be seen to be a reference to perhaps an even greater miracle: the raising up of children to Abraham from the Gentiles. Israel, though remaining special, is not God's sole concern. Jesus reminds the synagogue congregation that in the time of Elisha only Naaman the Syrian, a Gentile, was healed (4:27). In 7:1–10 Jesus heals the Roman centurion's servant and remarks on the faith of the Gentile, "Not even in Israel have I found such faith." The call to evangelize the nations unites the end of Luke's Gospel (24:47) and the beginning of Acts (1:8). "The Gentile mission was not a novel element in the teaching of Jesus, nor did it occur simply as a result of the obduracy of the chosen people; its roots went back far deeper—to the eternal will of God."[34]

All through Luke-Acts the mission to the Gentiles is the plan of God, and in Acts it is fulfilled by divine empowerment, as we see in the narrative of Peter and Cornelius in Acts 10. The Apostle Paul, whose story dominates the last half of Acts, is commissioned specifically to preach the gospel to the Gentiles. The risen Christ says to Ananias, "[Paul] is a chosen instrument of mine to carry my name before the Gentiles and kings and the sons of Israel" (9:15). And in the third account of his conversion in Acts Paul refers to his commission in his defense before Agrippa, citing the words of the Lord: "the Gentiles—to whom I send you to open their eyes, that they may turn from darkness to light and from the power of Satan to God, that they may receive forgiveness of sins and a place among those who are sanctified by faith in me" (26:17–18). And a few lines later the same point is made: "by being the first to rise from the dead, he [Christ] would proclaim light both to the people and to the Gentiles" (26:23).

---

33. See especially Lane, *Luke and the Gentile Mission*.
34. Wilson, *The Gentiles and the Gentile Mission in Luke-Acts*, 244.

Notice that in these last three quoted passages the Jews remain in the picture. The universalism of Luke-Acts is not exclusively Gentile; it continues to include Jews despite their unbelief. That unbelief in the gospel does not mean that the mission to the Jews has come to an end, but only that the emphasis—for the time being at least (cf. Luke 21:24)—has rather dramatically shifted to the Gentiles.[35] Paul and Barnabas say to the crowds at Pisidian Antioch, "For so the Lord has commanded us, saying, 'I have set you to be a light for the Gentiles, that you may bring salvation to the uttermost parts of the earth'" (13:47). It is not difficult to believe that if Luke was a Gentile, as seems very probable, the universality of the gospel message had special meaning to him.[36]

Eschatology in Luke

We may dismiss the claim that eschatology in Luke is vertical (in a Platonic dualism of heaven and earth or time and eternity)[37] rather than horizontal (in the Jewish apocalyptic sense of a future chronological era), in the usual meaning of the word. Luke shares with the other Gospel authors the view that eschatology has begun with the appearance of Jesus, and that this fulfillment is to be followed by the parousia of Jesus, which will bring the consummation of eschatology in the future. The salvation-history perspective that Luke develops, aided by his description of the birth of the church in Acts, was described by Hans Conzelmann, as already noted above. His argument was that Luke developed his perspective as the result of the perceived delay of the parousia, and that therefore the schema Luke presents reflects "early catholicism" (see chap. 33 below).[38]

It cannot be denied that Luke downplays imminent eschatology in his writings (this can be seen at numerous points in Luke's redaction of Mark—e.g., Luke's addition of "for a long while" in 20:9; the understanding of 21:7 [cf. 21:20], edited to refer only to the fall of Jerusalem; 21:25–28, disassociated from the fall of Jerusalem), but although this fits Luke's periodizing of salvation history, it is hardly the cause of it. Nor is the latter the result of the supposed crisis caused by the delay of the parousia.[39] It is also a fact that the delay of the parousia must be balanced with the statements that Luke retains concerning its imminence.[40] Luke apparently attempts to balance these motifs

35. The contention by Jack Sanders (*The Jews in Luke-Acts*) that Luke's polemic against the Jews is anti-Semitic underestimates the positive things said regarding the Jews. For a more adequate perspective, see Brawley, *Luke-Acts and the Jews*.

36. See especially Dupont, *The Salvation of the Gentiles*.

37. Thus Helmut Flender (*St. Luke*), who points to Luke's emphasis on the ascension of Jesus more than his resurrection.

38. Conzelmann, *The Theology of St. Luke*, 207–34.

39. See Aune, "The Significance of the Delay of the Parousia for Early Christianity."

40. See Matill, *Luke and the Last Things*; Hiers, "The Problem of the Delay of the Parousia in Luke-Acts." For an especially clear presentation, see Wilson, "Lukan Eschatology."

derived from his sources, employing the delay motif to quell apocalyptic enthusiasm, and the imminence motif to allay defeatism concerning the delay of the parousia. "Delay, therefore, serves for Luke the opposite function to that identified by Conzelmann. Delay does not oppose but undergirds expectation of an imminent End in Luke's own situation."[41]

Luke's Understanding of the Cross

It has often been pointed out that there is next to nothing in Luke about the meaning of the death of Jesus. This has led some to conclude that Luke has no interest in the atonement. In fact, none of the Synoptics exhibits much interest in spelling out the meaning of the cross. The second half of a key verse in Mark (10:45) that refers to the death of Jesus as having atoning significance is omitted by Luke (22:27), who focuses rather on the service motif of the first part of the verse. The other pertinent passage in Mark, the eucharistic logion of 14:24, is found in the Majority Text of Luke 22:20, but because the verses of 22:17–20 are omitted in the manuscripts containing the Western Text, which routinely have the fullest readings, some doubt its authenticity.[42] If 22:17–20 *is* authentic, then Luke does refer to the significance of the cross: "This cup which is poured out for you is the new covenant in my blood."

In Acts the reference in the basic kerygma to the death of Jesus implies that he "died for our sins" (cf. 1 Cor. 15:3), and it is on the basis of his death that "every one who believes in him receives forgiveness of sins through his name" (10:43). Paul in Acts makes the same appeal: "through this man forgiveness of sins is proclaimed to you" (13:38 [cf. 2:38; 5:31; 26:18]), and "by him every one that believes is freed from everything from which you could not be freed by the law of Moses" (13:39). The Isaiah 53:7–8 passage read by the Ethiopian eunuch (Acts 8:32–33), with its reference to "a sheep led to the slaughter," undoubtedly implies the whole of Isaiah 53, which in its later verses refers to the vicarious death of the servant, a point that Philip no doubt would have been eager to bring out.[43] There are, finally, also the fascinating words in Paul's speech to the Ephesian elders: "the church of God which he obtained with the blood of his own Son [*tou haimatos tou idiou*, lit., "the blood of his own (one)"]" (20:28).

41. Carroll, *Response to the End of History*, 166. Carroll further says, "Luke has presided over a marriage of salvation history and living end-expectation that is without parallel in early Christian literature, particularly in its historical sketch of the status of the promises and hopes of Israel" (ibid., 167). See also Ellis, *Eschatology in Luke*.

42. These verses therefore fall into Westcott and Hort's category of "Western non-interpolations" (see chap. 42 below). They may well have been deliberately omitted in order to avoid the cup-bread-cup sequence in these verses. See Billings, *Do This in Remembrance of Me*.

43. The servant christology of the early chapters of Acts (3:13, 26; 4:27, 30) also probably points to Isaiah 53.

Luke does know and value the atoning significance of the death of Jesus.[44] That he so seldom mentions it specifically is in all probability due to his taking this knowledge for granted. If anything was obvious about the reason for the death of Jesus, this was. While we must not require of Luke that he write about the cross the way Paul did, there is no necessary contradiction of Paul in Luke-Acts. The very idea of salvation, so important to Luke, rests on the reality of the atonement accomplished on the cross.[45]

Other Theological Emphases in the Gospel of Luke

The Holy Spirit

There are some seventy-five references to the Holy Spirit in Luke-Acts, seventeen of them in Luke. It is especially in the early chapters of the Gospel that the references to the Spirit abound. John the Baptist will be filled with the Holy Spirit (1:15); the Holy Spirit will come upon Mary (1:35); Elizabeth was filled with the Holy Spirit (1:41); Zechariah was filled with the Holy Spirit (1:67); the Holy Spirit was upon Simeon (2:25), he receives a revelation from the Holy Spirit (2:26), and is inspired by the Spirit (2:27). In the following chapter John the Baptist prophesies that Jesus will bring the baptism of the Holy Spirit (3:16), and the Holy Spirit comes upon Jesus at his baptism (3:22). This emphasis on the Holy Spirit is closely related to the eschatological aspect of the fulfillment brought by Christ. Indeed, *the Holy Spirit is a prime indicator of eschatological phenomena*. This is abundantly clear in, for example, Jesus' citation of Isaiah 61:1–2 in the synagogue of Nazareth (4:18–19). Luke adds to a Q passage that Jesus "rejoiced in the Holy Spirit" (10:21) and probably has changed "good things" to "the Holy Spirit" in 11:13: "If you then, who are evil, know how to give good gifts to your children, how much more will the heavenly Father give the Holy Spirit to those who ask him!" It is, however, in Acts that the power of the Holy Spirit becomes dominant in the narrative (see chaps. 15 and 16 below).

Salvation

The word "salvation" (*sōtēria* and *sōtērion*) occurs only in Luke's Gospel among the Synoptics (1:69, 71, 77; 2:30; 3:6; 19:9). We have already noted that Luke emphasizes the story of Christ and the church as the culmination of salvation history. "Salvation" is a comprehensive word that refers to

---

44. David Moessner, near the end of his book on the significance of the Lukan travel narrative, writes, "We have brought to light the atoning significance of Jesus's death from the fourfold Deuteronomic-Exodus typology of the travel narrative itself (Luke 9:51–19:44). When, however, the Passion narrative is added, especially the Passion meal, we have seen how consistently the conception of Jesus's atoning death is developed" (*The Lord of the Banquet*, 323).

45. See further Barrett, "Theologia Crucis—in Acts?"; Fuller, "Luke and the Theologia Crucis."

God's gracious act in Jesus that is the antidote to the fallenness of the world. Holding the infant Jesus in his arms, Simeon says, "Mine eyes have seen thy salvation" (2:30). The last line of the Isaiah quotation in 3:4–6 is "and all flesh shall see the salvation of God." Luke alone among the Synoptics refers to Jesus as "Savior" (1:47; 2:11 [cf. Isa. 45:21]). Luke's two-volume story tells of the fulfillment of the saving purpose of God that has begun for Jews and Gentiles alike and ultimately will result in the future "establishing [of] all that God spoke by the mouth of his holy prophets from of old" (Acts 3:21). The word "establishing" (*apokatastasis*) means "restoration" and has in view the realization of the promises of the prophets concerning the transformation of the world into its prefall perfection. Acts continues the emphasis on salvation (4:12; 13:26, 47; 16:17; 28:28); Jesus is the Savior promised to Israel (13:23) and is exalted to God's right hand as such (5:31).[46]

Joy and Praise

The coming of salvation through the appearance and work of Christ is naturally the cause of great rejoicing. Luke stresses this motif far more than do the other Gospels. The jubilation of the first two chapters is unmistakable. The opening words of the first angelic announcement set the tone: "And you will have joy and gladness, and many will rejoice at his birth" (1:14). John the Baptist is joyful even in the womb of his mother (1:44). The beginning of Mary's exultant response includes the words "my spirit rejoices in God my Savior" (1:47). The angel says to the shepherds, "Be not afraid; for behold, I bring you good news of a great joy which will come to all the people" (2:10). The Seventy return from their mission "with joy" (10:17); there is joy in heaven over one sinner who repents (15:7, 10). Jesus too rejoices in the Holy Spirit (10:21), a point not in Matthew but added to Q. Also unique to Luke is the comment made at Jesus' entry into Jerusalem: "As he was now drawing near, at the descent of the Mount of Olives, the whole multitude of the disciples began to rejoice and praise God with a loud voice for all the mighty works that they had seen" (19:37). At the end of Luke's narrative, when the risen Jesus appears to the eleven disciples, "they still disbelieved for joy" (24:41), and the final sentence of this Gospel reports that "they returned to Jerusalem with great joy" (24:52).

Prayer

Luke gives much attention to prayer both in his Gospel and Acts. More than any other Evangelist, Luke records that Jesus prayed, especially at critical junctures of his life. Luke alone records that Jesus was praying at his baptism

---

46. Stressing the importance of the theme in Luke, Marshall writes, "It is our thesis that the idea of salvation supplies the key to the theology of Luke" (*Luke*, 92). The major part of Marshall's book deals with this theme.

(3:21). Luke alone refers to Jesus withdrawing to the wilderness to pray (5:16). When Mark says that Jesus "went up on the mountain" (Mark 3:13), Luke adds "to pray; and all night he continued in prayer to God" (6:12), this prior to the choosing of the Twelve. Luke alone notes that Jesus "was praying alone" just prior to eliciting from the disciples the confession that he is the Christ (9:18); Luke alone indicates that Jesus went up to the Mount of Transfiguration to pray (9:28–29). Luke alone stresses that Jesus, while in the garden of Gethsemane, prayed: "and being in an agony he prayed more earnestly" (22:44, lacking in the best manuscripts). See too the unique reference to Jesus praying in 11:1.

Luke alone has the parable about perseverance in prayer (18:1–8) and the parable about the praying Pharisee and tax collector (18:9–14). Jesus exhorts his disciples to pray (6:28; 22:40).

Luke characterizes the early church as marked by frequent prayer. The abundance of references in Luke's Gospel and in Acts together nearly exceeds all other references to prayer in the NT, and this material can practically serve as a handbook on the importance of prayer.

The Disenfranchised and Downtrodden

No other Gospel gives as much place to women as Luke does. The opening chapters put great emphasis on Mary, Elizabeth, and Anna. Luke is the only Gospel to identify a group of women who were followers of Jesus, some of whom had been healed by him, but also "many others," some of whom were wealthy and provided for Jesus and the Twelve "out of their means" (8:2–3). Luke's unique story of the woman who anointed the feet of Jesus is striking in its affirmation of the woman's deed and her faith (7:36–50). So too the story of Mary and Martha affirms the status of women as disciples (10:38–42). Luke alone has the narrative of the healing of a woman, described as a "daughter of Abraham" (13:10–17), and alone refers to the "daughters of Jerusalem" following him and wailing on the Via Dolorosa (23:27–31). And Luke emphasizes the role of the women as the first witnesses to the empty tomb (24:22–24).

Luke expresses more concern for the poor than the other Gospels do. Luke alone reports Jesus' quotation of Isaiah 61:1–2 in the synagogue at Nazareth: "The Spirit of the Lord is upon me, because he has appointed me to preach good news to the poor . . . to set at liberty those who are oppressed" (4:18 [cf. 7:22]). The beatitude in 6:20, in contrast to Matthew's form, has simply "Blessed are you poor, for yours is the kingdom of God." In Luke alone Jesus teaches, "When you give a feast, invite the poor, the maimed, the lame, the blind, and you will be blessed, because they cannot repay you" (14:13–14). In the parable of the marriage banquet Luke alone extends the invitation to "the poor and maimed and blind and lame" (14:21). Luke follows Mark in recording Jesus' exhortation to the rich young man to sell his possessions and distribute the money to the poor (18:22).

Corresponding to this concern for the poor in Luke is the frequent polemic against the rich. Luke alone has the reference to the rich being sent away empty (1:53) and the four woes corresponding to the Beatitudes, the first three of which are relevant here: "Woe to you that are rich, for you have received your consolation. Woe to you that are full now, for you shall hunger. Woe to you that laugh now, for you shall mourn and weep" (6:24–25). Only in Luke do we find the parable of the rich fool who laid up treasure for himself but was "not rich toward God" (12:13–21), and the parable of the rich man and poor Lazarus, the former being in Hades and the latter in Abraham's bosom (16:19–31).

Luke alone has the story of Zacchaeus, "a chief tax collector" (19:2), who in response to Jesus promises to give half of his goods to the poor (19:8). The crowd was scandalized that Jesus would associate with such a person: "He has gone in to be the guest of a man who is a sinner." Jesus, by contrast, refers to him as "a son of Abraham" to whose house salvation has come. Luke emphasizes that Jesus had table fellowship with the despised, outcasts, and sinners. Luke alone refers to tax collectors coming to John the Baptist for baptism (3:12; cf. 7:29). Following Mark, Luke records the controversy caused not merely by his calling of a tax collector to be one of the Twelve, but by his sitting at the table with tax collectors and sinners in the house of Levi (5:27–30). Like Mark, Luke has the designation of Jesus as "a friend of tax collectors and sinners" (7:34), but only Luke has the note in 15:1–2 that "now the tax collectors and sinners were all drawing near to hear him. And the Pharisees and the scribes murmured, saying, 'This man receives sinners and eats with them.'" And most famously, in 18:9–14 Luke alone has the parable of the Pharisee and the tax collector, in which the latter, asking for mercy as a sinner, returns from the temple "justified" (*dedikaiōmenos*).

Also worth mentioning here is the positive attitude of Luke to the ordinarily despised Samaritans, as reflected in the parable of the good Samaritan (10:29–36), in the single thankful leper who was a Samaritan (17:12–19 [note "this foreigner" in 17:18]), and in the merciful attitude of Jesus in 9:52–55.

Discipleship

In keeping with Luke's polemic against riches, one of the key marks of true discipleship in Luke's Gospel is poverty and generosity to the poor (6:30). This is a fundamental aspect of the Jesus movement according to Luke: "Whoever of you does not renounce all that he has cannot be my disciple" (14:33). The rich fool is told by Jesus, "Take heed, and beware of all covetousness; for a man's life does not consist in the abundance of his possessions" (12:15). Wealth is perceived as a stumbling block to authentic commitment.

The Purposes of Luke-Acts

It is more correct to think of several purposes rather than a single purpose of Luke-Acts. If there is a main purpose of Luke-Acts, however, it has to be the obvious one of telling the story of Jesus and the birth of the church. The prologue of Luke's Gospel (1:1–4) underlines this purpose. This two-volume work is rightly characterized as presenting a history of salvation. In the words of Daniel Marguerat, "Luke recounts a confessional history. . . . Luke does not set out the destiny of a religious movement moving toward Rome from its origin in the Near East, but the expansion of a mission that he intends from the very start to make known as 'a history of salvation.'"[47]

But Luke also has subsidiary purposes in writing. A variety of theological purposes have been suggested. Charles Talbert argues for Luke-Acts as a defense against gnosticism, and in particular against docetism, which explains, among other things, Luke's emphasis on the physicality of Jesus' resurrection body.[48] Hans Conzelmann argues that Luke wrote in order to provide, through his periodizing of salvation history and development of an early catholicism, an antidote to the crisis caused in the early church by the delay of the parousia.[49] It is possible that Luke wrote either for evangelism or edification[50] of Christians, or both. This raises the further question of whether Theophilus and the implied readers should be thought of as Christians or as non-Christians.

A variety of apologetic purposes have also been suggested. F. F. Bruce calls attention to "the outstanding apologetic note throughout the work—the defense of Christianity as a law-abiding movement, constituting no threat to imperial peace and order."[51] In the Gospel Luke presents Jesus as defending the Roman tax (20:20–25) and as being found innocent by Pilate. In Acts Paul is repeatedly vindicated by Roman authorities. The several speeches of Paul before the Roman authorities have an important role to play in this analysis. It has been argued that Luke wrote what amounts to a defense that Paul could use at his trial in Rome.[52] More specifically, some have seen Luke's purpose as that of defending Paul against the attacks of Jewish Christians, by portraying him as loyal to the law of Moses.[53]

Most consonant with the Lukan prologue is the conclusion that Luke wrote his account as "a confirmation of the gospel"—that is, of its reliability and

---

47. Marguerat, *The First Christian Historian*, 25.

48. Talbert, *Luke and the Gnostics*.

49. Conzelmann, *The Theology of St. Luke*.

50. Haenchen, "The Book of Acts as Source Material for the History of Earliest Christianity."

51. Bruce, "The Acts of the Apostles," 2598. See also idem, "Paul's Apologetic and the Purpose of Acts."

52. Thus Mattill, "The Date and Purpose of Luke-Acts"; idem, "The Jesus-Paul Parallels and the Purpose of Luke-Acts."

53. See Jervell, *Luke and the People of God*.

truthfulness.[54] Robert Maddox aptly concludes that Luke "writes to reassure the Christians of his day that their faith in Jesus is no aberration, but the authentic goal towards which God's ancient dealings with Israel were driving. The full stream of God's saving action in history has not passed them by, but has flowed straight into their community-life, in Jesus and the Holy Spirit."[55]

Author, Date, and Addressees of Luke-Acts

Author

From the earliest times, the tradition has unanimously ascribed this Gospel and the book of Acts to Luke, the sometime companion of Paul. We read of this Luke in Colossians 4:14, where he is described as "the beloved physician"; in Philemon 24, where Paul refers to him as among "my fellow workers"; and in 2 Timothy 4:11, as the only one remaining with Paul in Rome.

Late second-century testimony concerning Luke as the author of this Gospel comes from the Muratorian Canon, the colophon of $\mathfrak{P}^{75}$, Irenaeus (*Haer.* 3.1.1; cf. 3.14.1–3), and the Anti-Marcionite Prologue to Luke, which gives this account: "Luke was a Syrian of Antioch, by profession a physician, the disciple of the apostles, and later a follower of Paul until his martyrdom. He served the Lord without distraction, without a wife, and without children. He died at the age of eighty-four in Boetia, full of the Holy Spirit." A few decades later we have this testimony from Eusebius (*Hist. eccl.* 3.4.6, trans. Lake): "Luke, who was by race an Antiochian and a physician by profession, was long a companion of Paul, and had careful conversation with the other apostles, and in two books left us examples of the medicine for souls which he had gained from them—the Gospel . . . and the Acts of the Apostles." If the Gospel and Acts are not by Luke, the question remains why "Luke" rather than, for example, one of the Twelve, was named as the author.

The question of whether Luke-Acts provides any evidence that the author was a physician has generated much discussion. Adolf von Harnack came to a positive conclusion with considerable conviction: "The evidence is of overwhelming force; so that it seems to me that no doubt can exist *that the third gospel and the Acts of the Apostles were composed by a physician.*"[56] Earlier the same conclusion had been reached by William Hobart in a well-known book, *The Medical Language of St. Luke*. Hobart focused on the vocabulary of Luke-Acts, but the weakness of his arguments was shown by Henry Cadbury's refutation.[57]

---

54. Thus van Unnik, "The 'Book of Acts'—the Confirmation of the Gospel"; Maddox, *The Purpose of Luke-Acts*.

55. Maddox, *The Purpose of Luke-Acts*, 187.

56. Harnack, *Luke the Physician*, 198. Italics in original.

57. Cadbury, *The Style and Literary Method of Luke*; see also Foakes-Jackson and Lake, *The Beginnings of Christianity*, 2:349–55.

If Hobart overstated his argument, there are still some intriguing redactional observations that could point to an author who was a physician—for example, Luke's unique proverb, "Physician, heal yourself" (4:23), and Luke's striking omission of Mark's description of the woman with the hemorrhage as one "who had suffered much under many physicians, and had spent all that she had, and was no better but rather grew worse" (Mark 5:26 [omitted in Luke 8:43]).

What is abundantly clear is that the high quality of Luke's Greek fits an educated man. Although some have argued that Luke was a Jew, the theological emphases of Luke-Acts reveal a Gentile orientation, especially, for example, in comparison with Matthew's obvious Jewish cast. Luke does manifest a good knowledge of the synagogue, as well as knowledge of the LXX and Hellenistic Jewish literature. Luke possibly was a proselyte to Judaism before he became a Christian, but more likely he was a Gentile[58] God-fearer who converted, like so many others, to the gospel of grace. Being a God-fearer would have afforded Luke the opportunity to gain the knowledge of the Jewish faith and the Scriptures that he reflects in his narratives (for the categories of proselyte and God-fearer, see chap. 16 below).

The "we" passages in Acts (16:10–17; 20:5–21:18; 27:1–28:16) seem to be travel diary notes, more probably of the author than of his source(s). The author of Acts (and Luke) would thus have been a traveling companion of Paul in his initial journey into Greece, his final journey to Jerusalem, and his journey to Rome. The presence of Luke with Paul in Rome is confirmed by the references in Colossians 4:14; Philemon 24; 2 Timothy 4:11. It thus makes good sense to conclude that Luke refers to himself in the "we" passages.[59]

Date

The issue of the date of Luke-Acts is complicated by the fact that the dating of two volumes is in view. Almost certainly the books were written in close succession. A key factor in the question of the date of Luke-Acts is the ending of the narrative, with Paul living two years under house arrest in Rome (Acts 28:30–31). Does Luke end his narrative at this point because, as he writes, the outcome of Paul's trial was unknown? On the one hand, taken by itself this view has a certain plausibility.[60] On the other hand, if the Gospel of Luke is dependent on Mark, as is commonly argued, and Mark was written probably in the mid- or late 60s, then Luke-Acts would have been written at least several

58. Paul's greetings in Colossians 4:10–17 include a reference to "Luke the beloved physician," but not as a part of the list of those whom Paul describes as "men of the circumcision among my fellow workers for the kingdom of God."

59. For discussion of the "we" passages, see Hemer, *The Book of Acts in the Setting of Hellenistic History*, 312–34. See also Fitzmyer, "The Authorship of Luke-Acts Reconsidered." For a purely literary explanation, see Campbell, *The "We" Passages in the Acts of the Apostles*.

60. Harnack concludes that Luke-Acts was written while Paul was still alive (*The Date of the Acts and of the Synoptic Gospels*, 124).

years after Paul's martyrdom in 64.[61] Luke would therefore have decided not to continue the story beyond Paul's house-prison ministry in Rome, content to leave the narrative open-ended.[62]

If Luke-Acts was not written before Paul's trial, how late might it have been written? Some would put the writing of Luke-Acts late in the first century, a few as late as the mid-second century. Majority opinion puts it sometime in the 80s. There is no reason, however, why Luke-Acts could not have been written in the 70s. Luke's redaction of Mark's eschatological discourse seems to be an attempt to interpret the first part of it as referring to the fall of Jerusalem rather than to yet future events: "But when you see Jerusalem surrounded by armies, then know that its desolation has come near" (Luke 21:20; cf. Mark 13:14). The fall of Jerusalem probably has already happened when Luke writes these words retrospectively (cf. Luke 13:35: "Behold, your house is forsaken").

A further factor for consideration in the dating of Luke-Acts is its perspective or viewpoint. Some think that the author's developed salvation-historical perspective demands a later rather than an earlier date. But a generation after the crucifixion of Jesus seems to afford a sufficient temporal perspective. Elements of "early catholicism" (see chap. 33 below) are fewer and more primitive in Luke-Acts, despite the church consciousness intrinsic to Acts, than one would expect in a late first-century document (contrast, e.g., the Pastoral Epistles).

The question of Luke's understanding of Paul has often been raised, usually with the idea that it is inadequate and points to a late date and non-Lukan authorship. An oft-cited article by Philipp Vielhauer describes differences between the Paul presented in Acts and the Paul of the letters.[63] Although the author of Acts revered Paul, according to Vielhauer, he did not understand Paul's theology, and in the speeches of Paul he failed to present the Pauline view of natural theology, justification, christology, and eschatology. While no doubt there are some differences between Luke's presentation of Paul and the historical Paul, Vielhauer has considerably overstated the case[64] by, among other things, apparently assuming that the sermons are presented in their entirety. Luke's economy in reporting the sermons thus becomes a wedge between Paul and the author

---

61. If the proto-Luke hypothesis is accepted (see p. 137), it is possible to argue that Acts was written *before* our canonical Luke, which only in its final form was dependent on Mark. In that case, Acts can be given an early date (before Paul's trial) while still having the Gospel dependent on Mark.

62. That Luke was aware of Paul's martyrdom may be indicated by the statements in Paul's farewell to the Ephesian elders, that they would not see him again (Acts 20:25, 38). The idea that Luke intended a third volume that, for whatever reason, he never wrote is pure fantasy. Daniel Marguerat suggests that at the end of Acts Luke employs a device of Greco-Roman rhetoric called "narrative suspension," drawing the reader into missionary engagement ("The Enigma of the Silent Closing of Acts [28:16–31]").

63. Vielhauer, "On the 'Paulinism' of Acts." See also Haenchen, *The Acts of the Apostles*, 112–16. For critical evaluation, see Porter, *Paul in Acts*, 187–206.

64. For an examination of the large degree of correspondence between the Paul of Acts and the Paul of the letters, see Bruce, "Is the Paul of Acts the Real Paul?"

of Acts: since Luke did not mention certain things, he therefore must not have understood Paul. This conclusion leads Vielhauer to posit a late date for Acts. Paradoxically, however, the later that one puts the writing of Acts, the more likely it becomes that the Pauline Letters would have been known to the author.

A last point to be mentioned here, consistent with a date of Luke-Acts in the early 70s, is that the apologetic emphases in Acts make the best sense in an atmosphere of persecution,[65] as for example existed during the mid-60s or during the first Jewish revolt (66–74). It was above all such times that made it important to stress that the Christian faith was no threat to the Roman Empire.

Addressees

The specific addressee of the two volumes, Theophilus (Luke 1:3; Acts 1:1), is most probably to be taken as an individual rather than as a cipher for "dear to God" or "lover of God," referring to Christians generally. Nothing, however, is known about him, though probably he was an influential man, possibly from Rome or perhaps Antioch. As with all the Gospels, the determination of a specific life setting is nearly impossible in the case of Luke-Acts. Very tentatively we may suggest that the two-volume work was written in Rome or possibly in Luke's probable home in Antioch. With somewhat more confidence we can conclude that Luke-Acts was written mainly for Gentile Christians.

Bibliography

Books and Articles

Alexander, Loveday. *The Preface to Luke's Gospel: Literary Convention and Social Context in Luke 1:1–4 and Acts 1:1*. SNTSMS 78. Cambridge: Cambridge University Press, 1993.

Aune, David E. "The Significance of the Delay of the Parousia for Early Christianity." In *Current Issues in Biblical and Patristic Interpretation: Studies in Honor of Merrill C. Tenney*, edited by Gerald F. Hawthorne, 87–109. Grand Rapids: Eerdmans, 1975.

Barrett, C. K. "The Historicity of Acts." *JTS* 50 (1999): 515–34.

———. *Luke the Historian in Recent Study*. London: Epworth, 1961.

———. "Theologia Crucis—in Acts?" In *Theologia Crucis, Signum Crucis: Festschrift für Erich Dinkler zum 70. Geburtstag*, edited by Carl Andresen and Günter Klein, 73–84. Tübingen: Mohr Siebeck, 1979.

Bartholomew, Craig G., Joel B. Green, and Anthony C. Thiselton, eds. *Reading Luke: Interpretation, Reflection, Formation*. Grand Rapids: Zondervan, 2005.

Billings, Bradly S. *Do This in Remembrance of Me: The Disputed Words in the Lukan Institution Narrative (Luke 22:19b–20): An Historico-Exegetical, Theological and Sociological Analysis*. LNTS 314. New York: T&T Clark, 2006.

Blomberg, Craig L. "The Law in Luke-Acts." *JSNT* 22 (1984): 53–80.

Bock, Darrell L. *Proclamation from Prophecy and Pattern: Lucan Old Testament Christology*. JSNTSup 12. Sheffield: JSOT Press, 1987.

65. On this theme in Luke-Acts, see Cunningham, *"Through Many Tribulations."*

———. "Scripture and the Realisation of God's Promises." In *Witness to the Gospel: The Theology of Acts*, edited by I. Howard Marshall and David Peterson, 41–62. Grand Rapids: Eerdmans, 1998.

———. *A Theology of Luke and Acts: God's Promised Program, Realized for All Nations*. Grand Rapids: Zondervan, 2012.

Bonz, Marianne Palmer. *The Past as Legacy: Luke-Acts and Ancient Epic*. Minneapolis: Fortress, 2000.

Bovon, François. *Luke the Theologian: Fifty-Five Years of Research (1950–2005)*. Waco: Baylor University Press, 2006.

Brawley, Robert L. *Centering on God: Method and Message in Luke-Acts*. Louisville: Westminster John Knox, 1990.

———. *Luke-Acts and the Jews: Conflict, Apology, and Conciliation*. SBLMS 33. Atlanta: Scholars Press, 1987.

Brown, Schuyler. *Apostasy and Perseverance in the Theology of Luke*. AnBib 36. Rome: Biblical Institute Press, 1969.

Bruce, F. F. "The Acts of the Apostles: Historical Record or Theological Reconstruction?" *ANRW* II.25.3 (1985): 2569–603.

———. "Is the Paul of Acts the Real Paul?" *BJRL* 58 (1975–76): 282–305.

———. "Paul's Apologetic and the Purpose of Acts." *BJRL* 69 (1987): 379–93.

Buckwalter, H. Douglas. *The Character and Purpose of Luke's Christology*. SNTSMS 89. Cambridge: Cambridge University Press, 1996.

Cadbury, Henry J. *The Making of Luke-Acts*. London: Macmillan, 1927.

———. *The Style and Literary Method of Luke*. Cambridge, MA: Harvard University Press, 1920.

Campbell, William Sanger. *The "We" Passages in the Acts of the Apostles: The Narrator as Narrative Character*. SBL 14. Atlanta: Society of Biblical Literature, 2007.

Carroll, John T. *Response to the End of History: Eschatology and Situation in Luke-Acts*. SBLDS 92. Atlanta: Scholars Press, 1986.

Chance, J. Bradley. *Jerusalem, the Temple, and the New Age in Luke-Acts*. Macon, GA: Mercer University Press, 1988.

Coleridge, Mark. *The Birth of the Lukan Narrative: Narrative as Christology in Luke 1–2*. JSNTSup 88. Sheffield: JSOT Press, 1993.

Conzelmann, Hans. *The Theology of St. Luke*. Translated by Geoffrey Buswell. New York: Harper, 1961.

Cunningham, Scott. *"Through Many Tribulations": The Theology of Persecution in Luke-Acts*. JSNTSup 142. Sheffield: Sheffield Academic Press, 1997.

Dahl, Nils A. "The Story of Abraham in Luke-Acts." In *Studies in Luke-Acts: Essays Presented in Honor of Paul Schubert*, edited by Leander E. Keck and J. Louis Martyn, 139–58. Nashville: Abingdon, 1966.

Darr, John A. *On Character Building: The Reader and the Rhetoric of Characterization in Luke-Acts*. Louisville: Westminster John Knox, 1992.

Denova, Rebecca I. *The Things Accomplished among Us: Prophetic Tradition in the Structural Pattern of Luke-Acts*. JSNTSup 141. Sheffield: Sheffield Academic Press, 1997.

Donfried, Karl P. "Attempts at Understanding the Purpose of Luke-Acts: Christology and the Salvation of the Gentiles." In *Christological Perspectives: Essays in Honor of Harvey K. McArthur*, edited by Robert F. Berkey and Sarah A. Edwards, 112–22. New York: Pilgrim Press, 1982.

Dupont, Jacques. *The Salvation of the Gentiles: Essays on the Acts of the Apostles*. Translated by John R. Keating. New York: Paulist Press, 1979.

Ellis, E. Earle. *Eschatology in Luke*. FBBS. Philadelphia: Fortress, 1972.

Esler, Philip Francis. *Community and Gospel in Luke-Acts: The Social and Political Motivations of Lucan Theology*. SNTSMS 57. Cambridge: Cambridge University Press, 1987.

Evans, Christopher F. "The Central Section of St Luke's Gospel." In *Studies in the Gospels: Essays in Memory of R. H. Lightfoot*, edited by Dennis E. Nineham, 55–88. Oxford: Blackwell, 1955.

Evans, Craig A., and James A. Sanders. *Luke and Scripture: The Function of Sacred Tradition in Luke-Acts*. Minneapolis: Fortress, 1993.

Farris, Stephen. *The Hymns of Luke's Infancy Narratives: Their Origin, Meaning and Significance*. JSNTSup 9. Sheffield: JSOT Press, 1985.

Fitzmyer, Joseph A. "The Authorship of Luke-Acts Reconsidered." In *Luke the Theologian: Aspects of His Teaching*, 1–26. New York: Paulist Press, 1989.

Flender, Helmut. *St. Luke: Theologian of Redemptive History*. Translated by Reginald H. Fuller and Ilse Fuller. Philadelphia: Fortress, 1967.

Foakes-Jackson, F. J., and Kirsopp Lake, eds. *The Beginnings of Christianity: The Acts of the Apostles*. 5 vols. Grand Rapids: Baker, 1979.

Franklin, Eric. *Christ the Lord: A Study in the Purpose and Theology of Luke-Acts*. Philadelphia: Westminster, 1975.

Fuller, Reginald H. "Luke and the Theologia Crucis." In *Sin, Salvation, and the Spirit: Commemorating the Fiftieth Year of the Liturgical Press*, edited by Daniel Durken, 214–20. Collegeville, MN: Liturgical Press, 1979.

Garrett, Susan R. *The Demise of the Devil: Magic and the Demonic in Luke's Writings*. Minneapolis: Fortress, 1989.

Gasque, W. Ward. "The Book of Acts and History." In *Unity and Diversity in New Testament Theology*, edited by Robert A. Guelich, 54–72. Grand Rapids: Eerdmans, 1978.

———. *A History of the Interpretation of the Acts of the Apostles*. Peabody, MA: Hendrickson, 1989.

Gill, David W. J., and Conrad Gempf, eds. *The Book of Acts in Its Graeco-Roman Setting*. BAFCS 2. Grand Rapids: Eerdmans, 1994.

Gillman, John. *Possessions and the Life of Faith: A Reading of Luke-Acts*. ZS. Collegeville, MN: Liturgical Press, 1991.

Green, Joel B. *The Theology of the Gospel of Luke*. NTT. Cambridge: Cambridge University Press, 1995.

Green, Joel B., and Michael C. McKeever. *Luke-Acts and New Testament Historiography*. IBRBib 8. Grand Rapids: Baker Academic, 1994.

Haenchen, Ernst. "The Book of Acts as Source Material for the History of Earliest Christianity." In *Studies in Luke-Acts: Essays Presented in Honor of Paul Schubert*, edited by Leander E. Keck and J. Louis Martyn, 258–78. Nashville: Abingdon, 1966.

Harnack, Adolf von. *The Date of the Acts and of the Synoptic Gospels*. Translated by J. R. Wilkinson. London: Williams & Norgate, 1911.

———. *Luke the Physician: The Author of the Third Gospel and the Acts of the Apostles*. Translated by J. R. Wilkinson. New York: G. P. Putnam, 1911.

Hemer, Colin J. *The Book of Acts in the Setting of Hellenistic History*. Edited by Conrad H. Gempf. WUNT 49. Tübingen: Mohr Siebeck, 1989.

———. "First Person Narrative in Acts 27–28." *TynBul* 36 (1985): 80–109.

———. "Luke the Historian." *BJRL* 60 (1977–78): 28–51.

Hengel, Martin. *Acts and the History of Earliest Christianity*. Translated by John Bowden. Philadelphia: Fortress, 1980.

Hiers, Richard H. "The Problem of the Delay of the Parousia in Luke-Acts." *NTS* 20 (1973–74): 145–55.

Hobart, William Kirk. *The Medical Language of St. Luke*. London: Longmans, Green, 1882.

Hooker, Morna D. "'Beginning with Moses and from All the Prophets.'" In *From Jesus to John: Essays on Jesus and New Testament Christology in Honour of Marinus de Jonge*, edited by Martinus C. de Boer, 216–30. JSNTSup 84. Sheffield: JSOT Press, 1993.

———. "In His Own Image?" In *What about the New Testament? Essays in Honour of Christopher Evans*, edited by Morna D. Hooker and Colin Hickling, 28–44. London: SCM, 1975.

Jervell, Jacob. "The Future of the Past: Luke's Vision of Salvation History and Its Bearing on His Writing of History." In *History, Literature, and Society in the Book of Acts*, edited by Ben Witherington III, 104–26. Cambridge: Cambridge University Press, 1996.

———. *Luke and the People of God: A New Look at Luke-Acts*. Minneapolis: Augsburg, 1972.

Johnson, Luke Timothy. *The Literary Function of Possessions in Luke-Acts*. SBLDS 39. Missoula, MT: Scholars Press, 1977.

Juel, Donald. *Luke-Acts: The Promise of History*. Atlanta: John Knox, 1983.

Karris, Robert J. *Luke, Artist and Theologian: Luke's Passion Account as Literature*. TI. New York: Paulist Press, 1985.

Keck, Leander E., and J. Louis Martyn, eds. *Studies in Luke-Acts: Essays Presented in Honor of Paul Schubert*. Nashville: Abingdon, 1966.

Kurz, William S. "Promise and Fulfillment in Hellenistic Jewish Narratives and in Luke and Acts." In *Jesus and the Heritage of Israel: Luke's Narrative Claim upon Israel's Legacy*, edited by David P. Moessner, 147–70. Harrisburg, PA: Trinity Press International, 1999.

———. *Reading Luke-Acts: Dynamics of Biblical Narrative*. Louisville: Westminster John Knox, 1993.

Lane, Thomas J. *Luke and the Gentile Mission: Gospel Anticipates Acts*. EUS 23/571. Frankfurt: Peter Lang, 1996.

Larkin, William J., Jr. "Luke's Use of the Old Testament as a Key to His Soteriology." *JETS* 20 (1977): 325–35.

Litwak, Kenneth Duncan. *Echoes of Scripture in Luke-Acts: Telling the History of God's People Intertextually*. JSNTSup 282. New York: T&T Clark International, 2005.

Maddox, Robert. *The Purpose of Luke-Acts*. Edited by John Riches. SNTW. Edinburgh: T&T Clark, 1982.

Mallen, Peter. *The Reading and Transformation of Isaiah in Luke-Acts*. LNTS 367. London: T&T Clark, 2008.

Marguerat, Daniel. "The Enigma of the Silent Closing of Acts (28:16–31)." In *Jesus and the Heritage of Israel: Luke's Narrative Claim upon Israel's Legacy*, edited by David P. Moessner, 284–304. Harrisburg, PA: Trinity Press International, 1999.

———. *The First Christian Historian: Writing the "Acts of the Apostles."* Translated by Ken McKinney, Gregory J. Laughery, and Richard Bauckham. SNTSMS 121. Cambridge: Cambridge University Press, 2002.

Marshall, I. Howard. "Acts and the 'Former Treatise.'" In *The Book of Acts in Its Ancient Literary Setting*, edited by Bruce W. Winter and Andrew D. Clarke, 163–82. BAFCS 1. Grand Rapids: Eerdmans; Carlisle, UK: Paternoster, 1993.

———. "Luke and His 'Gospel.'" In *The Gospel and the Gospels*, edited by Peter Stuhlmacher, 273–92. Grand Rapids: Eerdmans, 1991.

———. *Luke: Historian and Theologian*. Grand Rapids: Zondervan, 1989.

Marshall, I. Howard, and David Peterson, eds. *Witness to the Gospel: The Theology of Acts*. Grand Rapids: Eerdmans, 1998.

Martin, Ralph P. "Salvation and Discipleship in Luke's Gospel." *Int* 30 (1976): 366–80.

Mattill, A. J., Jr. "The Date and Purpose of Luke-Acts: Rackham Reconsidered." *CBQ* 40 (1978): 335–50.

———. "The Jesus-Paul Parallels and the Purpose of Luke-Acts: H. H. Evans." *NovT* 17 (1975): 15–46.

———. *Luke and the Last Things: A Perspective for the Understanding of Lukan Thought*. Dillsboro: Western North Carolina Press, 1979.

Minear, Paul S. "Luke's Use of the Birth Stories." In *Studies in Luke-Acts: Essays Presented in Honor of Paul Schubert*, edited by Leander E. Keck and J. Louis Martyn, 111–30. Nashville: Abingdon, 1966.

———. *To Heal and to Reveal: The Prophetic Vocation according to Luke*. New York: Seabury, 1976.

Moessner, David P. "The Appeal and Power of Poetics (Luke 1:1–4): Luke's Superior Credentials (παρηκολουθηκότι), Narrative Sequence (καθεξῆς), and Firmness of Understanding
(ἡ ἀσφάλεια) for the Reader." In *Jesus and the Heritage of Israel: Luke's Narrative Claim
upon Israel's Legacy*, edited by David P. Moessner, 84–123. Harrisburg, PA: Trinity Press
International, 1999.

———, ed. *Jesus and the Heritage of Israel: Luke's Narrative Claim upon Israel's Legacy*. Harrisburg, PA: Trinity Press International, 1999.

———. *The Lord of the Banquet: The Literary and Theological Significance of the Lukan Travel
Narrative*. Minneapolis: Fortress, 1989.

Moxnes, Halvor. *The Economy of the Kingdom: Social Conflict and Economic Relations in
Luke's Gospel*. Philadelphia: Fortress, 1988.

Nave, Guy D., Jr. *The Role and Function of Repentance in Luke-Acts*. SBLAB 4. Atlanta:
Scholars Press, 2002.

Navone, J. *Themes of St. Luke*. Rome: Gregorian University Press, 1970.

Neyrey, Jerome H., ed. *The Social World of Luke-Acts: Models for Interpretation*. Peabody,
MA: Hendrickson, 1991.

Orton, David E., comp. *The Composition of Luke's Gospel: Selected Studies from Novum
Testamentum*. BRBS 1. Leiden: Brill, 1999.

O'Toole, Robert F. *The Unity of Luke's Theology: An Analysis of Luke-Acts*. GNS 9. Wilmington, DE: Michael Glazier, 1984.

Parsons, Mikeal C. *Body and Character in Luke and Acts: The Subversion of Physiognomy in
Early Christianity*. Grand Rapids: Baker Academic, 2006.

Parsons, Mikeal C., and Richard I. Pervo. *Rethinking the Unity of Luke and Acts*. Minneapolis:
Fortress, 1993.

Peterson, David. "The Motif of Fulfillment and the Purpose of Luke-Acts." In *The Book of Acts
in Its Ancient Literary Setting*, edited by Bruce W. Winter and Andrew D. Clarke, 83–104.
BAFCS 1. Grand Rapids: Eerdmans; Carlisle, UK: Paternoster, 1993.

Phillips, Thomas E., ed. *Acts and Ethics*. NTMon 9. Sheffield: Sheffield Phoenix Press, 2005.

Pilgrim, Walter E. *Good News to the Poor: Wealth and Poverty in Luke-Acts*. Minneapolis:
Augsburg, 1981.

Porter, Stanley F. *Paul in Acts*. Peabody, MA: Hendrickson, 2001.

Powell, Mark Allan. *What Are They Saying about Luke?* New York: Paulist Press, 1989.

Reumann, J. "Heilsgeschichte in Luke: Some Remarks on Its Background and Comparison with
Paul." *SE* 4 [= TU 102] (1968): 86–115.

Richard, Earl, ed. *New Views on Luke and Acts*. Collegeville, MN: Liturgical Press, 1990.

Rosner, Brian S. "Acts and Biblical History." In *The Book of Acts in Its Ancient Literary Setting*,
edited by Bruce W. Winter and Andrew D. Clarke, 65–82. BAFCS 1. Grand Rapids: Eerdmans;
Carlisle, UK: Paternoster, 1993.

Rowe, C. Kavin. *Early Narrative Christology: The Lord in the Gospel of Luke*. Grand Rapids:
Baker Academic, 2006.

Sanders, Jack T. *The Jews in Luke-Acts*. Philadelphia: Fortress, 1987.

Schmidt, Daryl D. "Rhetorical Influences and Genre: Luke's Preface and the Rhetoric of Hellenistic Historiography." In *Jesus and the Heritage of Israel: Luke's Narrative Claim upon Israel's
Legacy*, edited by David P. Moessner, 27–60. Harrisburg, PA: Trinity Press International, 1999.

Schmidt, Thomas E. *Hostility to Wealth in the Synoptic Gospels*. JSNTSup 15. Sheffield: JSOT
Press, 1987.

Schweizer, Eduard. *Luke: A Challenge to Present Theology*. Atlanta: John Knox, 1982.

Seccombe, David Peter. *Possessions and the Poor in Luke-Acts*. SNTSU 6. Linz: Fuchs, 1982.

Senior, Donald. *The Passion of Jesus in the Gospel of Luke*. Wilmington, DE: Michael Glazier,
1989.

Sheeley, Steven M. *Narrative Asides in Luke-Acts*. JSNTSup 72. Sheffield: JSOT Press, 1992.

Shepherd, William H., Jr. *The Narrative Function of the Holy Spirit as a Character in Luke-Acts.* SBLDS 147. Atlanta: Scholars Press, 1994.

Shillington, V. George. *An Introduction to the Study of Luke-Acts.* London: T&T Clark, 2007.

Squires, John T. *The Plan of God in Luke-Acts.* SNTSMS 76. Cambridge: Cambridge University Press, 1993.

———. "The Plan of God in the Acts of the Apostles." In *Witness to the Gospel: The Theology of Acts,* edited by I. Howard Marshall and David Peterson, 19–39. Grand Rapids: Eerdmans, 1998.

Stenschke, Christoph W. *Luke's Portrait of Gentiles prior to Their Coming to Faith.* WUNT 108. Tübingen: Mohr Siebeck, 1999.

Sterling, Gregory E. *Historiography and Self-Definition: Josephos, Luke-Acts and Apologetic Historiography.* NovTSup 64. Leiden: Brill, 1992.

Stonehouse, N. B. *The Witness of Luke to Christ.* Grand Rapids: Eerdmans, 1951.

Strauss, Mark L. *The Davidic Messiah in Luke-Acts: The Promise and Its Fulfillment in Lukan Christology.* JSNTSup 110. Sheffield: Sheffield Academic Press, 1995.

Streeter, B. H. *The Four Gospels: A Study of Origins.* 4th ed. London: Macmillan, 1930.

Stronstad, Roger. *The Charismatic Theology of St. Luke.* Peabody, MA: Hendrickson, 1984.

Sweetland, Dennis M. *Our Journey with Jesus: Discipleship according to Luke-Acts.* GNS 23. Collegeville, MN: Liturgical Press, 1990.

Talbert, Charles H. *Literary Patterns, Theological Themes, and the Genre of Luke-Acts.* SBLMS 20. Missoula, MT: Society of Biblical Literature, 1974.

———, ed. *Luke-Acts: New Perspectives from the Society of Biblical Literature Seminar.* New York: Crossroad, 1984.

———. *Luke and the Gnostics: An Examination of the Lucan Purpose.* Nashville: Abingdon, 1966.

———, ed. *Perspectives on Luke-Acts.* Edinburgh: T&T Clark, 1978.

———. *Reading Luke-Acts in Its Mediterranean Milieu.* NovTSup 107. Leiden: Brill, 2003.

Tannehill, Robert C. *The Narrative Unity of Luke-Acts: A Literary Interpretation.* 2 vols. Philadelphia: Fortress, 1986–90.

———. *The Shape of Luke's Story: Essays on Luke-Acts.* Eugene, OR: Wipf & Stock, 2005.

Taylor, Vincent. *The Passion Narrative of St. Luke: A Critical and Historical Investigation.* Edited by Owen E. Evans. SNTSMS 19. Cambridge: Cambridge University Press, 1972.

Thompson, Richard P., and Thomas E. Phillips, eds. *Literary Studies in Luke-Acts: Essays in Honor of Joseph B. Tyson.* Macon, GA: Mercer University Press, 1998.

Tiede, David L. *Prophecy and History in Luke-Acts.* Philadelphia: Fortress, 1980.

Tuckett, Christopher M. *Luke.* NTG. Sheffield: Sheffield Academic Press, 1996.

Tyson, Joseph B. *The Death of Jesus in Luke-Acts.* Columbia: University of South Carolina Press, 1986.

———. *Images of Judaism in Luke-Acts.* Columbia: University of South Carolina Press, 1992.

———. *Luke, Judaism, and the Scholars: Critical Approaches to Luke-Acts.* Columbia: University of South Carolina Press, 1999.

———, ed. *Luke-Acts and the Jewish People: Eight Critical Perspectives.* Minneapolis: Augsburg, 1988.

———. *Marcion and Luke-Acts: A Defining Struggle.* Columbia: University of South Carolina Press, 2006.

Van Linden, Philip. *The Gospel of Luke and Acts.* MBS 10. Wilmington, DE: Michael Glazier, 1986.

van Unnik, W. C. "The 'Book of Acts'—the Confirmation of the Gospel." In *The Composition of Luke's Gospel: Selected Studies from Novum Testamentum,* compiled by David E. Orton, 184–217. BRBS 1. Leiden: Brill, 1999.

———. "Once More St. Luke's Prologue." *Neot* 7 (1973): 7–26.

Verheyden, Jozef. "The Unity of Luke-Acts: What Are We Up To?" In *The Unity of Luke-Acts*, edited by Jozef Verheyden, 3–56. BETL 142. Leuven: Leuven University Press, 1999.

Vielhauer, Philipp. "On the 'Paulinism' of Acts." In *Studies in Luke-Acts: Essays Presented in Honor of Paul Schubert*, edited by Leander E. Keck and J. Louis Martyn, 33–50. Nashville: Abingdon, 1966.

Walters, Patricia. *The Assumed Authorial Unity of Luke and Acts: A Reassessment of the Evidence*. SNTSMS 145. Cambridge: Cambridge University Press, 2009.

Wilson, Stephen G. *The Gentiles and the Gentile Mission in Luke-Acts*. SNTSMS 23. Cambridge: Cambridge University Press, 1973.

———. "Lukan Eschatology." *NTS* 16 (1969–70): 330–47.

———. *Luke and the Law*. SNTSMS 50. Cambridge: Cambridge University Press, 1983.

———. *Luke and the Pastoral Epistles*. London: SPCK, 1979.

Winter, Bruce W., and Andrew D. Clarke, eds. *The Book of Acts in Its Ancient Literary Setting*. BAFCS 1. Grand Rapids: Eerdmans; Carlisle, UK: Paternoster, 1993.

Commentaries

Bock, Darrell L. *Luke*. 2 vols. BECNT. Grand Rapids: Baker Academic, 2000.

Bovon, François. *Luke 1: A Commentary on the Gospel of Luke 1:1–9:50*. Translated by Christine M. Thomas. Hermeneia. Minneapolis: Fortress, 2002.

———. *Luke 2: A Commentary on the Gospel of Luke 9:51–19:27*. Translated by Donald S. Deer. Hermeneia. Minneapolis: Fortress, 2012.

———. *Luke 3: A Commentary on the Gospel of Luke 19:28–24:58*. Translated by James E. Crouch. Hermeneia. Minneapolis: Fortress, 2012.

Brown, Raymond E. *The Birth of the Messiah: A Commentary on the Infancy Narratives in the Gospels of Matthew and Luke*. Rev. ed. ABRL. New York: Doubleday, 1993.

Bruce, F. F. *The Acts of the Apostles: The Greek Text with Introduction and Commentary*. 3rd ed. Grand Rapids: Eerdmans, 1990.

Danker, Frederick W. *Luke*. 2nd ed. PC. Philadelphia: Fortress, 1987.

Ellis, E. Earle. *The Gospel of Luke*. NCBC. Reprint, Grand Rapids: Eerdmans, 1981.

Evans, Christopher F. *Saint Luke*. TPINTC. Philadelphia: Trinity Press International, 1990.

Fitzmyer, Joseph A. *The Gospel according to Luke: Introduction, Translation, and Notes*. 2 vols. AB 28, 28A. Garden City, NY: Doubleday, 1981–85.

Green, Joel B. *The Gospel of Luke*. NICNT. Grand Rapids: Eerdmans, 1997.

Haenchen, Ernst. *The Acts of the Apostles: A Commentary*. Translated by Bernard Noble and Gerald Shinn. Philadelphia: Westminster, 1971.

Johnson, Luke Timothy. *The Gospel of Luke*. SP 3. Collegeville, MN: Liturgical Press, 1991.

Just, Arthur, Jr. *Luke*. 2 vols. ConC. St. Louis: Concordia, 2000.

Lieu, Judith. *The Gospel of Luke*. London: Epworth, 1997.

Marshall, I. Howard. *The Gospel of Luke: A Commentary on the Greek Text*. NIGTC. Grand Rapids: Eerdmans, 1978.

Nolland, John. *Luke*. 3 vols. WBC 35A, 35B, 35C. Dallas: Word, 1989–93.

Plummer, Alfred. *A Critical and Exegetical Commentary on the Gospel according to St. Luke*. ICC. 5th ed. Edinburgh: London: T&T Clark, 1906.

Schweizer, Eduard. *The Good News according to Luke*. Translated by David E. Green. Atlanta: John Knox, 1984.

Stein, Robert H. *Luke*. NAC. Nashville: Broadman, 1992.

Talbert, Charles H. *Reading Luke: A Literary and Theological Commentary on the Third Gospel*. New York: Crossroad, 1984.

Tannehill, Robert C. *Luke*. ANTC. Nashville: Abingdon, 1996.

Tiede, David L. *Luke*. ACNT. Minneapolis: Augsburg, 1988.

14

The Gospel according to John

To read the opening lines of the Fourth Gospel is to realize how distinctive this Gospel is compared to the first three in our canon. In a deliberate allusion to the opening words of Genesis, the Fourth Evangelist writes, "In the beginning was the Word [*logos*], and the Word was with God, and the Word was God. He was in the beginning with God; all things were made through him, and without him was not anything made that was made" (1:1–3). The author confronts the reader immediately, and in no uncertain terms, with the divine identity of Jesus. Unlike the Synoptics, here there is no gradual wondering and no growing realization concerning the identity of Jesus: "And the Word became flesh and dwelt among us, full of grace and truth; we have beheld his glory, glory as of the only Son from the Father" (1:14 [cf. 1:18]). Already in chapter 1 Andrew tells his brother Peter, "We have found the Messiah" (1:41), and Nathanael confesses, "Rabbi, you are the Son of God! You are the King of Israel!" (1:49).

John and the Synoptic Gospels

It is not only in the opening paragraphs that John differs greatly from the Synoptics. There is a quite remarkable difference in content, with regard to both the deeds and the words of Jesus, and also in the structure of the book.

Differences

Broad differences between John and the Synoptics will be obvious even to the casual reader. According to John's account the ministry of Jesus lasts between two and three years (three Passover feasts are mentioned), mainly in

Author: Probability tips only very slightly in the direction of identifying the Beloved Disciple with the Apostle John as the author of an initial edition of this Gospel, which was then put into its present form by disciples of the Johannine school in Ephesus. It is possible, however, that the author was John the Elder, to be distinguished from the Apostle.

Date: Almost certainly to be dated at about the end of the first century. But it is possibly somewhat earlier.

Addressees: It is practically impossible to link this Gospel with any specific addressees or community. If it was written in Ephesus, it could be for the Christians of Asia Minor. More probably it was written for the larger Christian church of the Roman world.

Purpose. To retell the Gospel story of Jesus in a new way so as to bring out the true meaning and significance of Jesus, making explicit what lay implicit in the Synoptic Gospels.

Message/Argument: Jesus is the incarnation of God, the unique revealer of God's truth and the one who brings salvation in the form of life to those who believe in him.

Significance: This Gospel is the pinnacle of the accounts of the story of Jesus, bringing out the present meaning of Jesus for the church through its stress on realized eschatology.

Jerusalem and Judea; in the Synoptics his ministry is mainly in Galilee and can easily be contained within a single year. In contrast to the Synoptics, the Fourth Evangelist records not a single demon exorcism and limits himself apparently to seven representative miracles (see discussion of the "signs" below). Unique to John among these are the changing of water into wine at Cana (2:1–12), the healing of a lame man at the pool of Bethzatha (5:1–18) and the man blind from birth (9:1–41), and most notably the raising of Lazarus (11:1–44). John lacks a birth narrative, the story of the wilderness temptation of Jesus and the transfiguration narrative (in a sense, the whole of this Gospel is a revelation of the glory of Jesus). There is no account in John of the Last Supper of Jesus with his disciples—that is, of his giving the cup and the bread (but the meal seems to be in view in 13:2, 21–30; cf. also 6:53). John contains no stories of Jesus eating with tax collectors and sinners, no teaching about loving one's neighbor or enemy (in John the teaching is to love one's fellow disciple), and no teaching about the rich and the poor. In short, John has selected only a small portion of the material available in the tradition (see 20:30; 21:25).

At the same time, John contains notable stories not found in the Synoptics: the calling of the disciples Andrew, Philip, and Nathanael (1:35–51); the meeting with Nicodemus (3:1–21); the conversation with the Samaritan woman (4:1–42); the washing of the disciples' feet (13:1–20); and the resurrection appearance to Thomas (20:24–29). Chapter 21, apparently an appendix to the book (see below), also contains material unique to John.

In the Synoptics Jesus commonly makes use of parables and aphorisms; in John, by contrast, Jesus teaches by means of extensive, repetitive discourses.

In addition to this difference in the form of the teaching, one of the most obvious contrasts in content is the virtually total lack of teaching about the kingdom of God, so prominent in the Synoptics but mentioned in John only in 3:3, 5. John lacks completely an eschatological discourse such as that found in all three Synoptics, preferring to focus instead on realized dimensions of eschatology. In contrast to the Synoptics, much of Jesus' teaching has to do with himself. The Synoptics' proclaimer of the kingdom has, in John, become the proclaimed. This is the first hint that the Gospel of John, far more than the Synoptics, is a deliberately retrospective Gospel, telling the story again with all the advantages of hindsight.

Some differences in order and chronology are also apparent. In contrast to the Synoptics, where Jesus does not begin his ministry until John the Baptist is arrested (cf. Mark 1:14; Matt. 4:12–17), in John there is an overlap, and hence competition, between the ministries of John the Baptist and Jesus (3:22–30; 4:1; cf. 1:9). The Baptist's fate is not mentioned in the Fourth Gospel. No account of the actual baptism of Jesus is presented; it is simply assumed. There is no listing of the twelve Apostles' names. Among further chronological differences is John's placement of the cleansing of the temple at the beginning (2:13–22), rather than at the end, of the ministry of Jesus. Finally, John places the crucifixion of Jesus on the afternoon before the beginning of Passover, "the day of Preparation" (19:14, 31), at about the time of the killing of the sacrificial lambs—this in contrast to the Synoptics, all of which refer to Jesus eating the Passover meal with his disciples.[1]

Common Elements

At the same time, there are common elements between John and the Synoptics. John clearly presents the same basic story about the same Jesus, but with much new material, all expressed in a unique way that gives the Fourth Gospel its own special character.

John the Baptist, as we have seen, is mentioned at the beginning of all four Gospel narratives, although he functions rather differently in John, where he serves primarily as a "witness" to the identity of Jesus as "the Son of God" (1:34). The cleansing of the temple, despite certain differences, is almost certainly the same event transposed by the Fourth Evangelist to the beginning of the ministry of Jesus. Rather less certain is whether the healing of the official's son in 4:46–54 is the same as that of the healing of the centurion's servant/son in Matthew 8:4–13; Luke 7:2–12.[2]

---

1. John's dating of the crucifixion on "the day of Preparation," Nisan 14, agrees with the *baraita* of *b. Sanh*. 43b. This late passage may, however, be dependent on John. This Johannine dating possibly reflects an alternate calendar, such as that used at Qumran, but it may simply be the result of the Evangelist's desire to link the death of Jesus with the sacrifice of the Passover lambs.

2. A recurring problem in the analysis of independent but similar stories is that the similarity itself will often cause a cross-transference of language from one to the other. This happens

The only miracle common to all four Gospels is that of the feeding of the five thousand. The Johannine account, while clearly parallel to the Synoptic account, is also independent.[3] Also apparently parallel but independent is Peter's confession in 6:68–69, where he says, "Lord, to whom shall we go? You have the words of eternal life; and we have believed, and have come to know, that you are the Holy One [*ho hagios*] of God" (cf. Mark 8:29 pars.). Another fairly clear parallel, but also with differences, is in the story of the woman who anoints Jesus with costly ointment at Bethany (identified in John as Mary the sister of Martha).

Apart from similarities in the triumphal entry of Jesus into Jerusalem and the passion narrative itself, the Johannine account of Jesus' last days in Jeru salem is rather different from that of the Synoptics. Again, although the basic story line is similar, the details are often very different.

The Question of Dependence

Even though there are numerous common elements shared by John and the Synoptics, the differences are considerable, and it remains unlikely that we are to explain the similarities as the result of direct dependence. To be sure, there are those who have argued for dependence, and the scholarly pendulum has swung from the conclusion of independence to dependence and then back to independence again.[4]

Up until modern times, it was universally assumed that John knew and made use of the Synoptics. This state of affairs was altered with the important little book by Percival Gardner-Smith, published in 1938,[5] which persuasively argued against the literary dependence of John on the Synoptics. In his view, the many significant differences between John and the Synoptics precluded literary dependence. Instead, he maintained that John was dependent on oral tradition parallel to but different from that underlying the Synoptic Gospels. Many, perhaps even most, Johannine scholars became persuaded with Gardner-Smith that John was independent of the Synoptics. C. H. Dodd, in his famous 1963 book *Historical Tradition in the Fourth Gospel*, took up the argument and traced the influence of an independent oral tradition in John.[6]

---

especially in the period of oral transmission, with the effect that two independent stories may begin to be identified as one and the same.

3. The close study by Percival Gardner-Smith concludes that the Johannine account of the event is "a completely independent account" (*Saint John and the Synoptics*, 29–30).

4. The shifting sands of Johannine scholarship in the middle of the twentieth century were documented in J. A. T. Robinson's informative article "The New Look on the Fourth Gospel." The first of the five major changes documented by Robinson is John's independence from the Synoptics.

5. Gardner-Smith, *Saint John and the Synoptic Gospels*.

6. J. A. T. Robinson also concludes that John relies on "oral tradition with a southern Pal estinian milieu prior to AD 70, parallel to, and independent of, the Synoptic tradition" ("Elijah,

Not all were persuaded, however. Most notably, C. K. Barrett and Frans Neirynck,[7] but others too, continued to argue for some degree of literary dependence of John on the Synoptics. They compose only a minority of Johannine specialists, however, and from the looks of recent volumes,[8] most continue to hold that John depends on its own separate strands of oral tradition.

If the usual dating of John's Gospel to the last decade of the first century is even approximately right, it seems impossible that the author could not have known the other Gospels—at least Mark,[9] but perhaps even Matthew and Luke.[10] Communication among the Christian communities of the Roman world was excellent, and the traveling of teachers between the churches would have been frequent.[11] But even if the author probably was aware of one or more of the Synoptic Gospels, that does not necessarily mean that he used them directly as sources. He could still have preferred to use the oral tradition available to him.[12]

A number of scholars have called attention to the fact that there is a certain "interlocking" of passages wherein the Synoptics help make sense of John, and where John is needed to make sense of the Synoptics.[13] Already John Calvin, in his commentary on John, had noted that "this Gospel is a key to open the door for understanding the rest," although he was thinking of theology rather than source criticism. The evidence of such interlocking of passages points most probably to overlapping of parallel, though separate, strains of tradition, reflecting the underlying historical reality rather than literary dependence.

John and Jesus," 264n2). See also Robinson, *The Priority of John*; Dunn, "John and the Oral Gospel Tradition."

7. See Barrett, *The Gospel according to St. John*, 42–54; idem, "The Place of John and the Synoptics within the Early History of Christian Tradition"; Neirynck, "John and the Synoptics" (1977); idem, "John and the Synoptics" (2001); Brodie, *The Quest for the Origin of John's Gospel*.

8. See especially the three volumes of *John, Jesus, and History*, edited by Paul Anderson, Felix Just, and Tom Thatcher: *Critical Appraisals of Critical Views* (vol. 1); *Aspects of Historicity in the Fourth Gospel* (vol. 2); *Glimpses of Jesus through the Johannine Lens* (vol. 3).

9. See Bauckham, "John for Readers of Mark." John 3:24, for example, presupposes that the readers know that the Baptist had been arrested—something that John does not record. So too 6:67–71 presupposes that the readers already know that Jesus had chosen twelve Apostles; the aside in 4:2 looks like a nod to the Synoptics. See also Bauckham, "The Fourth Gospel as the Testimony of the Beloved Disciple," 132.

10. For example, Andrew Gregory ("The Third Gospel?") points to John's possible knowledge of Luke. See also Bailey, *The Traditions Common to the Gospels of Luke and John*.

11. See the interesting essay by Michael Thompson, "The Holy Internet."

12. Recall from our earlier discussion in chapter 7 the great esteem placed on oral tradition in the early church.

13. Leon Morris discusses this is some detail in *Studies in the Fourth Gospel*, 40–63. "Quite a number of passages in the first three Gospels present very real difficulties taken by themselves, but seem capable of solution when considered in the light of what the Fourth Gospel says" (ibid., 41–42). Morris concludes that there is "a relationship to the tradition in the Synoptics, but not, I think, one of dependence" (ibid., 61). For further discussion of such interlocking connections, see Carson, *The Gospel according to John*, 51–55.

The Question of Historicity

The question of the historical reliability of the Fourth Gospel is caused not just by its contents per se, but especially by the enormous and fundamental difference of its perspective compared to what we have in the other three Gospels.[14] To be sure, John presents what is recognizably the same story: the witness of John the Baptist; the ministry of Jesus in deed and word (but with many differences); the arrest, trial, and crucifixion of Jesus; and finally his resurrection. Although the portrayal can be quite different at times, the subject and the story are the same. Throughout John, however, it is the ultimate significance of Jesus that dominates the narrative—significance drawn out and emphasized by the presentation of theological interpretation as part and parcel of the story.[15] This defining distinctive of the Fourth Gospel is what raises the historical question in such a sharp way. The early church was very aware of these differences and was inclined to consider John as a "spiritual Gospel." In the words of the famous testimony of Clement of Alexandria, "Last of all, John, perceiving that the bodily facts [*ta sōmatika*] had been made plain in the gospel, being urged by his friends, and inspired by the Spirit, composed a spiritual [*pneumatikon*] gospel" (according to Eusebius, *Hist. eccl.* 4.14.7, trans. Lake). Paul Anderson characterizes John's Gospel as the "dialectical reflection of a theologian who also appears to have encountered Jesus of Nazareth and who develops his understanding of the significance of his mission over several decades of Christian history and experience."[16]

Although it seems odd from our perspective, up until the nineteenth century the Gospel of John, regarded as eyewitness testimony of one of the Twelve, was favored *as a historical source* over the Synoptics, or at least over Mark and Luke, neither of them being members of the Twelve. With the coming of nineteenth-century radical criticism, however, this conclusion was reversed. Now the Synoptics and John became increasingly polarized, the former taken as representing "history," and the latter "theology."[17] Although this polarity still haunts Johannine scholarship to some extent, the latest trends see John and the Synoptics as on the same continuum. If John is written from a postresurrection perspective, so too are the Synoptics. If the Synoptics contain accurate

---

14. James Dunn observes that what distinguishes the Fourth Gospel from the Synoptics is "not so much the *content* of the Fourth Evangelist's distinctive christology . . . as the *way* in which he formulates it, as the *degree of development* of the Jesus-tradition" ("Let John Be John," 338).

15. James Dunn comments, "It is the thorough-going portrayal of the Son sent from the Father, conscious of his pre-existence, the descending-ascending Son of Man, making the profoundest claims in his 'I am' assertions, which both *dominates* John's christology *and* distances it most strikingly from the Synoptic tradition" ("Let John Be John," 317).

16. Anderson, *The Riddles of the Fourth Gospel*, 152.

17. As Paul Anderson puts it, over the last two centuries "John has been effectively 'dehistoricized' and Jesus has been likewise 'de-Johannified'" (Anderson, Just, and Thatcher, *Aspects of Historicity in the Fourth Gospel*, 3).

historical information, so too does John. All four Gospels are interpretive; all are theological. The difference between John and the Synoptics here is not absolute, but one of degree. What marks out the Synoptics is the extent to which they restrain letting their privileged postresurrection knowledge influence their narratives, although this surely happens at times. John, on the contrary, seems to be deliberate in drawing out the significance of the story from a later, more explicit, postresurrection perspective.

It is important here to stress that history and theology are not mutually exclusive. History can be the mediator of theology; theology can be expressed in and through history. Against the nineteenth-century polarity spoken of above, nowadays *the Synoptics are regarded as both historical and theological, and John as both theological and historical*, with the respective priorities in that order. In the Synoptics the narratives are mainly historical but not to the exclusion of theology; in John the narratives are mainly theological but not to the exclusion of history. This difference—hardly an absolute one—means that although scholars increasingly look for historical information in the Fourth Gospel,[18] the Synoptic Gospels remain the main sources for our knowledge of the Jesus of history.

Turning from the general to the specific, let us review some of the classic problems. As we have already noted, at least four of the miraculous deeds performed by Jesus according to John are unique, not being found in the Synoptics. Jesus does, of course, heal the lame and the blind in the Synoptics, although the emphasis in John seems to be on the length of time that those healed suffered from their maladies (i.e., the man who had been lame for thirty-eight years, and the man who was blind from birth). The problems revolve instead around the miracles of the changing of the water into wine, and the raising of Lazarus. How, it is often asked, could the Synoptics not refer to these stunning miracles, especially the resurrection of Lazarus? Of course, there is no reason why a miracle that is recorded in only one Gospel should for that reason alone forfeit its claim to historicity. Nor should the striking character of a miracle automatically disqualify it from being historical. All four Gospels have accounts of miraculous multiplication of loaves and fishes; turning the water into wine is no more impressive. In all the Gospels together we receive only a glimpse of the healing ministry of Jesus (see, e.g., Luke 4:40; Matt. 9:35), only representative examples, as also in the Fourth Gospel especially (note 20:30: "Jesus did many other signs in the presence of the disciples, which are not written in this book"; see also 21:25). It does indeed seem striking to *us* that the remarkable narrative of the raising of Lazarus is not found in any of the Synoptics, but given the extensive ministry of Jesus and the necessary selectivity of the Gospels,

18. Unfortunately, it remains the case that many or most critical scholars tend to limit John's historical reliability to things such as accuracy of topological references and time references (e.g., the Passovers).

it perhaps should not surprise us. There are in the Synoptics, of course, other narratives of Jesus raising the dead. Another intriguing explanation has been offered by Richard Bauckham: the omission of the story in the Synoptics is the result of "protective anonymity." After the raising of Lazarus, not only was Jesus' life in danger (11:45–53), but so too was Lazarus's life under threat (12:9–11), and thus the story could not be told in the early Jerusalem church.[19] It may well be that one reason John was written was to record a few further stunning miracles that, for whatever reason, had not become part of the Synoptic tradition but that the Fourth Evangelist wanted to preserve.[20]

More problematic than the deeds of Jesus in John is the teaching of Jesus, both in its form and content. In particular, it is the long, meditative, and repetitive discourses, usually dwelling on the person of Jesus and containing the astounding "I am" sayings,[21] and also Jesus' references to his preexistent glory (17:5, 24) that raise the historical question most sharply. There is practically nothing analogous to this special material in the Synoptic Gospels (but cf. Mark 6:50; 14:62; Luke 20:13; and the "I came" sayings in, e.g., Mark 2:17; 10:45; Matt. 5:17; 10:34–35; Luke 19:10).

Nevertheless, it must be admitted that there is considerable continuity between the Synoptics' view of Jesus and John's. The Synoptics too point to the transcendence of Jesus, his unique sonship, unparalleled authority, and self-understanding.[22] But these emphases are usually more indirect, often left implicit, in the Synoptics. Only rarely do we encounter the direct tone of the famous Johannine-sounding passage in Matthew and Luke: "All things have been delivered to me by my Father; and no one knows the Son except the Father, and no one knows the Father except the Son and any one to whom the Son chooses to reveal him" (Matt. 11:27; cf. Luke 10:22; John 3:35; 10:15). Again, the supposed polarity of a divine Jesus in John and a human Jesus in the Synoptics is incorrect. Jesus is fully human in John; Jesus, as the unique Son of the Father, is the manifestation of God in the Synoptics.[23]

Assessing the Authenticity of the Johannine Sayings of Jesus

One result of nineteenth-century critical study of the Gospels was that the contents of John came to be regarded as simple fiction. However, since C. H.

19. Bauckham, *Jesus and the Eyewitnesses*, 196.
20. Note the conclusion of C. K. Barrett: "He did not hesitate to repress, revise, rewrite or rearrange. On the other hand there is no sufficient evidence for the view that John freely created narrative material for allegorical purposes" (*The Gospel according to St. John*, 141).
21. See Ball, *"I Am" in John's Gospel*.
22. See Hagner, "Jesus' Self-Understanding."
23. As James Dunn rightly indicates, "The recognition that what we have in John is a development of the earlier Christian tradition underscores the importance of these points of continuity"—that is, between John and the earlier Synoptic tradition ("Let John Be John," 338).

Dodd's famous book *Historical Tradition in the Fourth Gospel*, scholars have been more open to the possibility of finding reliable history in John.[24] Dodd repeatedly "found material, closely related to the Synoptic tradition, so deeply embedded in some of the Johannine discourses and dialogues as to be apparently inseparable from the argument of which they form part."[25] Dodd was not alone in this conclusion. A decade earlier, for example, Edwyn Hoskyns had presented a similar argument about the presence of Synoptic sayings in the Johannine discourses.[26] These sayings, he concluded, were

> not so much quoted, or embedded in a discourse; rather, they constitute its theme. It is as though they had been so welded into the author's theology that they had ceased to be detached or even detachable. They lie no longer on the periphery, as though they were just Sayings; rather they have moved into the centre and have taken control, not merely of single discourses, but of the whole presentation of what Jesus was and is.[27]

Dodd's detailed study concluded that "behind the fourth Gospel lies an ancient tradition independent of the other gospels, and meriting serious consideration as a contribution to our knowledge of the historical facts concerning Jesus Christ. For this conclusion I should claim a high degree of probability."[28]

This conclusion does not mean, however, that what we have in John is straightforward history or provides anything like a transcript of what Jesus said.

If we do not doubt that both the Synoptics and John enshrine historical tradition and that both engage in interpretation of the tradition, then we must conclude that John also takes good advantage of his interpretive liberty and puts his own distinctive stamp on the material.[29] When Jesus speaks in the Fourth Gospel, he does so in the idiom of the Evangelist. It is thus difficult

24. See now a similar emphasis in the recent three-volume series *John, Jesus, and History*, edited by Paul Anderson, Felix Just, and Tom Thatcher; and also in Anderson, *The Fourth Gospel and the Quest for Jesus*; idem, *The Riddles of the Fourth Gospel*.

25. Dodd, *Historical Tradition in the Fourth Gospel*, 430. Dodd also thought it proper to add a "warning against a hasty assumption that nothing in the Fourth Gospel which cannot be corroborated from the Synoptics has any claim to be regarded as part of the early tradition of the sayings of Jesus" (ibid., 431).

26. As examples of Synoptic sayings found in John, see 4:44 (Matt. 13:57 pars.); 12:25 (Matt. 16:25 pars.); 13:16 (Matt. 10:24 pars.); 13:20 (Matt. 10:40 par.).

27. Hoskyns, *The Fourth Gospel*, 73–74.

28. Dodd, *Historical Tradition in the Fourth Gospel*, 423. Stephen Smalley similarly remarks, "We can now reckon seriously with the possibility that the Fourth Gospel including John's special material, is grounded in historical tradition when it departs from the synoptics as well as when it overlaps them" (*John*, 29).

29. The occasionally offered explanations of the difference between the Synoptic and Johannine sayings of Jesus—that the latter represents Jesus' teaching in Judea, the former in Galilee, or that the Johannine discourses represent Jesus' private teaching to his disciples—are not borne out in the texts and are therefore inadequate. Indeed, to the contrary, see John 18:19–21.

sometimes to know where Jesus stops speaking and where the Evangelist provides further interpretation (e.g., 3:16–21, 31–36 may be the Evangelist speaking rather than Jesus). In John we have a free representation of things that Jesus said—a representation meant to be not verbatim reporting, but rather a re-presentation that involves deliberate interpretation and elaboration so as to bring out the significance of Jesus for the church.[30] John writes not simply to record history—and the history is very important for him—but also to spell out its significance in ways that are now evident in the postresurrection, post-Pentecost church.

Almost never can we claim we have the *ipsissima verba* of Jesus, the very words themselves, either in the Greek text of the Synoptic Gospels (see the discussion above, ch. 7) or John. Peter Ensor has refined the notion of authenticity by speaking also of *ipsissima dicta*, sayings that "closely represent an original utterance of Jesus," and of *ipsissimae sententiae*, "ideas or notions inherent in" the other categories but "expressed in a different way."[31] On this analysis, the Synoptics generally provide us with *ipsissima dicta*, while John, although containing that type of sayings, mainly contains *ipsissimae sententiae*.

But when the interpretive level becomes as high as it is in John, perhaps it is no longer adequate to argue that what John offers is a loose paraphrase of what Jesus said or to conclude that all the *ipsissimae sententiae* "genuinely reflect the viewpoint of Jesus himself."[32] It is one thing to say, and it is certainly true some of the time, that the Fourth Evangelist "intended to convey the sense or gist of what Jesus said, without feeling bound to reproduce his exact words." So too the Synoptics. But when Ensor adds "aiming to bring out their inner meaning,"[33] that involves something different, for it goes beyond what Jesus *said*. While still wanting to stress continuity with the *ipsissima dicta* of the Synoptic tradition, I see no reason to shy away from the Fourth Evangelist's interpretive liberty, under the inspiration of the Spirit. "When the Spirit of truth comes, he will guide you into all the truth" (16:13).[34] In

---

30. C. K. Barrett comments, "John has liberated his material from particular settings to give it universal applicability." Barrett's own conviction is that "the Jesus of history really did transcend the limitations of space and time" (*Essays on John*, 131).

31. Ensor, "The Johannine Sayings of Jesus and the Question of Authenticity," 23. This is approximately the meaning understood by the more common designation *ipsissima vox*, the "voice" of Jesus—that is, an approximation of what Jesus said. See also Ensor, *Jesus and His "Works."*

32. Ensor, "The Johannine Sayings of Jesus and the Question of Authenticity," 32.

33. Ibid., 31. Ensor quotes J. A. T. Robinson approvingly when he writes that the Fourth Evangelist enables us "to enter at depth into the significance of Jesus's words and works and person" (Robinson, *The Priority of John*, 322).

34. As Clement of Alexandria suggested already toward the end of the second century. There is a sense in which 16:13 can be regarded as an apologia for the Gospel of John:

> I have yet many things to say to you, but you cannot bear them now. When the Spirit of truth comes, he will guide you into all the truth; for he will not speak on his own authority, but whatever he hears he will speak, and he will declare to you the things that are to come. He will glorify me, for he will take what is mine and declare it to you. All

this way, the Fourth Evangelist can bring out the meaning and significance of Jesus for the church as it could now be understood in the waning years of the first century. All the Gospel writers reveal considerable freedom in how they order their narratives and how they reexpress the Jesus tradition (see chap. 4 above). John has taken the furthest step in that liberty by being as explicit as he can in retelling the story. His account reflects what Paul Anderson calls a "dialogical autonomy."[35] John's theological reflection reveals what was inherent or implicit in the historical tradition, and the historicity of that tradition remains of great importance to him.[36] As he draws out the implications and full significance of Jesus in light of the entire Gospel story—in light of the words and deeds of Jesus, together with his resurrection—John does something that Jesus, given the constraints of the moment, could not have done.[37]

It is wrong to conclude, either for the deeds or the discourses, that John engages in creation ex nihilo, or outright fiction.[38] Nor is John distorting or obscuring the facts. On the contrary, there is a sense in which John is not only true but also, because of its explicitness, *the truest of the Gospels.*[39] The Evangelist puts great emphasis on the eyewitness testimony of those who were with Jesus from the beginning (see 15:27; 19:35; 21:24; cf. 1:14).[40] Contrary to the claims of some scholars, despite the obvious differences, there is no fundamental contradiction between the Synoptic Gospels' and John's portraits of Jesus.[41] No Christian reader has trouble moving from one to the other and

that the Father has is mine; therefore I said that he will take what is mine and declare it to you. (16:12–15)

With 14:26 and 15:26 in mind, Herman Ridderbos makes a similar observation: "The operation of the Spirit will be more than merely sharpening the memory of the apostles concerning the exact words of Jesus; it will also be teaching them, expounding all that Jesus had taught" (*Studies in Scripture and Its Authority*, 62).

35. Anderson, *The Riddles of the Fourth Gospel*, 171.

36. As A. C. Headlam rightly points out, "The value of his argument depends upon whether the events he records are true" (*The Fourth Gospel as History*, 14).

37. D. Moody Smith observes, "The most impressive and central divergence of John from the Synoptics is its impressive, christologically elevated portrait of Jesus, which no critical scholar any longer takes to depict the way the historical Jesus presented himself" (*The Fourth Gospel in Four Dimensions*, 177). Smith goes on to say that "when John moves away from the Synoptics, he departs from historical reality" (ibid.). It would be more appropriate and more consistent with the intention of the Fourth Evangelist, in my opinion, to say that where John moves away from the Synoptics, he makes explicit the meaning of historical reality.

38. We find, for example, nothing like the spectacular ad hoc miracles seen in the infancy gospels of the NT Apocrypha. John gives the impression of being much more controlled by historical reality.

39. *Pace* the negativism of Casey, *Is John's Gospel True?*

40. C. K. Barrett notes that for John and the Apostles "the faith of the church rests upon the historical testimony borne by eye-witnesses" and on "the commission given to them by Jesus," which is "dependent on the mission of the Spirit" (*The Gospel according to St. John*, 143). On the subject of eyewitnesses, see especially Bauckham, *Jesus and the Eyewitnesses*.

41. James Dunn comments, "For John's portrayal of Jesus, for all its distinctive development, can still be seen as a continuation of various trends already active in the Synoptics" ("John

back. John offers the same story, the same Lord, and the same salvation, as do the Synoptics,[42] together with the bonus of an authorized, inspired interpretation of the ultimate meaning and significance of it all.

The Question of Authorship

The authorship of the Fourth Gospel remains one of the most difficult puzzles in NT scholarship.[43] The tradition about authorship in the early church is clear and consistent enough from the end of the second century onward. Critical scholarship in the eighteenth and nineteenth centuries, however, raised questions about the reliability of this tradition, and these questions have not gone away. The reasons for this challenge are understandable. Because the content of the Fourth Gospel differs so much from the Synoptics, it is thought impossible that the author could have been an eyewitness of the ministry of Jesus. Added to this is the widespread conviction that a theological perspective as advanced as John's must have taken decades to develop. This concept of a slow, gradual evolution prompted most critical scholars of the nineteenth century to put the writing of John's Gospel in the mid-second century or later, long after the death of the Apostles. The postulation of a late, nonapostolic author who was not an eyewitness seemed a good way to account for the great differences between John and the Synoptics. No attention was paid to how a highly developed christology is found already in Paul's writings, as early as the 50s.[44]

The Beloved Disciple

The mysterious, unnamed Beloved Disciple (lit., "the one whom Jesus loved") is the key to the authorship question, but it is notoriously difficult to

---

and the Synoptics as a Theological Question," 305). Andreas Köstenberger shows how John's transposition of the Synoptic material amounts to "retelling the story of Jesus in another key" ("John's Transposition Theology").

42. Compare this remark, from the late second century, in the Muratorian Canon: "Therefore, while various elements may be taught in the several books of gospels, it makes no difference to the faith of believers, for by the one chief Spirit all things have been declared to all: concerning the nativity, the passion, the resurrection, the life with his disciples and his double advent, first in lowliness and contempt (which has taken place), second in glorious royal power (which is to be)." For the text, see Grant, *Second-Century Christianity*, 118.

43. Indeed, as Felix Just points out, "There is still no consensus on most historical issues surrounding the Fourth Gospel, either in the innumerable details or in the larger picture" (Anderson, Just, and Thatcher, *Aspects of Historicity in the Fourth Gospel*, 388).

44. J. A. T. Robinson is one of the few exceptions. He says that John "bestrides the whole development of New Testament thinking, like a colossus. But so also does Paul; and, like Paul, he will be seen, I believe, to represent its *Alpha* as much as its *Omega*." John's theology, he goes on to say, "had reached its essential, if not its formal, maturity by about the same time as St Paul's, at a date, that is, before any of the Synoptic Gospels were written" ("The New Look on the Fourth Gospel," 102). See also Robinson, *The Priority of John*.

be certain of his identity. He is described in the first reference to him as one who "was lying close to the breast of Jesus" (in 13:23, 25; in the latter verse the Greek vocabulary is totally different). In 19:26–27 "the disciple whom he [Jesus] loved" is described as standing near the cross and is given the care of Jesus' mother[45] (in 19:27 he is described as simply "the disciple"). In the story of 20:1–10 the anonymity of the one "whom Jesus loved" increases by virtue of being strangely referred to several times as "the other disciple" (20:2, 3, 4, 8). In 21:7 "that disciple whom he [Jesus] loved" is the one who recognizes Jesus from the boat. In the strange story of 21:20–23 he is referred to as "the disciple whom Jesus loved, who had lain close to his breast at the supper." Here Peter asks about the fate of "this man," and when Jesus replied that he was to "remain until I come," the rumor started that Jesus had said that "this disciple was not to die," a mistaken deduction that the author corrects in 21:23. The final reference immediately follows in the appended comment, apparently made by a later editor: "This is the disciple who is bearing witness to these things, and who has written these things" (21:24).

There are a few further references to an unnamed disciple or disciples that could have the Beloved Disciple in view.[46] Of the two disciples mentioned in 1:35, only one is eventually named, Andrew (1:40). "Another disciple" is coupled with Peter (18:15) and described twice as "known to the high priest" (18:15–16), but this is not necessarily John. With the reference to the thrusting of the spear into the crucified Jesus and the effluence of blood and water, a typically Johannine note is added: "He who saw it has borne witness—his testimony is true, and he knows that he tells the truth—that you also may believe" (19:35).

Together with these data, two further observations may be useful. First, the name "John" is used in this Gospel only in reference to the Baptist and the father of Simon Peter. John the son of Zebedee, one of the Twelve, is never mentioned by name. It seems strange that such an important disciple should go altogether unmentioned and never appear in the entire Gospel, and this suggests that the references just examined refer to John, especially where there are links with Peter, which is so often the case in the Gospels and Acts. Second, the reference to the one who lay on the breast of Jesus at the supper in 13:1–30 (cf. 21:20) points to one of the Twelve (who are referred to in 6:67, 70, 71; 20:24), if we take the Synoptic information that the meal was a private one with Jesus and the Twelve (Mark 14:17 pars.).

45. The wife of Zebedee and the mother of James and John was Salome, who was a sister of Mary the mother of Jesus, and hence James and John were cousins of Jesus.

46. Alongside a reference to two unnamed disciples, 21:2 mentions "the sons of Zebedee." This is the only time in this Gospel that John is referred to, though he is not mentioned specifically by name. This break in the silence about John is consistent with the conclusion that chapter 21 was not written by the author of the preceding chapters. Richard Bauckham overstates the matter, however, when he says that 21:2 "actually excludes the possibility that he [John] is the Beloved Disciple" (*Jesus and the Eyewitnesses*, 415).

By its nature, the evidence of the Fourth Gospel itself is far from clear. But the conclusion that John the Apostle is the Beloved Disciple is consistent with what we have looked at so far. It fits particularly well with this Gospel's appeal to its basis in eyewitness testimony (19:35; 21:24), and no internal obstacle prohibits this traditional conclusion.[47]

The Patristic Evidence

The evidence from writers of the second century is, at best, ambiguous. Contrary to widespread opinion, there is little clear evidence supporting the identification of the author as John the Apostle, as opposed to a second disciple of Jesus known as John—perhaps to be equated with John the Elder (see below)—until Irenaeus.

The Muratorian Canon, dated to the late second century,[48] contains the following:

> The fourth of the gospels is of John, one of the disciples. To his fellow-disciples and bishops, who were encouraging him, he said, "Fast with me today for three days, and whatever will be revealed to each of us, let us tell to one another." The same night it was revealed to Andrew, one of the apostles, that all should certify what John wrote in his own name. . . . Why, then, is it remarkable that John so constantly brings forth single points even in his epistles, saying of himself, "What we have seen with our eyes and heard with our ears and our hands have handled, these we write to you"? Thus he professes himself not only an eyewitness and hearer but also a writer of all the miracles of our Lord in order.

Here we see an affirmation of both the Gospel and the first of the Johannine Epistles (cf. 1 John 1:1, 4) as written by John, called "one of the disciples" (but contrasted with Andrew, who is designated "one of the apostles").[49]

Justin Martyr, in the mid-second century, may have held that the author of this Gospel was John the Apostle.[50] We have already noted the remark of Clement of Alexandria that "John, last of all . . . divinely moved by the Spirit, composed a spiritual Gospel" (Eusebius, *Hist. eccl.* 6.14.7, trans. Lake). Elsewhere Clement refers to John the Apostle as moving from Patmos to Ephesus (Eusebius, *Hist.*

47. Of course, questions can be raised (e.g., Culpepper, *John, the Son of Zebedee*, 75–76), but none of these overturns the probability that internal evidence of the Gospel points to John the Apostle as the Beloved Disciple.

48. The argument that the Muratorian Canon is to be dated in the fourth century (see Sundberg, "Canon Muratori") has not persuaded most scholars. For defense of the second-century date, see Ferguson, "Canon Muratori."

49. This leads Richard Bauckham to conclude that the John in view is the "Elder" and not the Apostle (*Jesus and the Eyewitnesses*, 429). Bauckham regards the Muratorian Canon as dependent on Papias, whose views on the origin of the Fourth Gospel are not available to us from Eusebius.

50. On the uncertainty, see ibid., 466.

eccl. 3.23.6), probably assuming that he was responsible for the Fourth Gospel as well as the book of Revelation. But again, some uncertainty remains.[51]

No doubt the most influential statement of all, however, is that of Irenaeus, again mediated to us by Eusebius: "Then John, the disciple of the Lord, who had even rested on his breast, himself also gave forth the gospel, while he was living at Ephesus in Asia" (*Hist. eccl.* 5.8.4, trans. Lake = Irenaeus, *Haer.* 3.1.1 [cf. *Hist. eccl.* 3.23.3–4 = Irenaeus, *Haer.* 2.25.5; *Hist. eccl.* 4.14.6 = Irenaeus, *Haer.* 3.3.4]). Irenaeus here clearly identifies John as the Beloved Disciple, but it is still possible that this John is John the Elder.[52]

After surveying the evidence, Richard Bauckham draws the conclusion that "there are only two Christian works of the second century that clearly identify the John who wrote the Gospel with John the son of Zebedee."[53] Both writings are among the NT Apocrypha: *The Acts of John* and *The Epistle of the Apostles.* Elsewhere it is possible that references to John have the Elder in mind.

John the Elder (The Presbyter)

The existence of a second disciple of Jesus with the name "John" obviously adds great uncertainty to our subject.[54] References to John "the disciple of Jesus" automatically become ambiguous, the more so since the Apostles are also called both "disciples" and "presbyters." The most important information about John the Elder comes again from Papias as mediated via Eusebius. Papias (ca. 110) was eager to learn as much as he could from "the presbyters": "If ever anyone came who had followed the presbyters, I inquired into the words of the presbyters, what Andrew or Peter or Philip or Thomas or James or John or Matthew, or any other of the Lord's disciples, had said, and what Aristion and the presbyter John, the Lord's disciples, were saying" (*Hist. eccl.* 3.39.4, trans. Lake).[55] To this quoted material Eusebius adds the following comment: "It is

51. See ibid., 466–67. Bauckham concludes that the use of "apostle" is not necessarily a reference to one of the Twelve.

52. C. K. Barrett concludes, to the contrary, that the "testimony of Irenaeus is simple and complete: John the son of Zebedee (for no other John can be meant) was the beloved disciple; he lived to a great age in Ephesus, and there published the Fourth Gospel" (*The Gospel according to St. John*, 101).

53. Bauckham, *Jesus and the Eyewitnesses*, 463. Compare C. K. Barrett's comment that the second century provides "no plain tale of unquestioned reverence unhesitatingly accorded to a book known from the beginning to have been written by an apostle" (*The Gospel according to St. John*, 125).

54. Richard Bauckham calls attention to the fact that "John" was a very popular name in first-century Palestine, and that fully 5 percent of Palestinian Jewish men bore the name (*Jesus and the Eyewitnesses*, 416). Already in the third century Dionysius makes the same point: "There have been many persons of the same name as John the apostle" (Eusebius, *Hist. eccl.* 7.25.14, trans. Lake).

55. By means of a clever, but perhaps overreaching, argument from this passage, Richard Bauckham suggests that Papias did not equate the Beloved Disciple with John the son of Zebedee (*Jesus and the Eyewitnesses*, 417–20).

here worth noting that he [Papias] twice counts the name of John, and reckons the first John with Peter and James and Matthew and the other apostles, clearly meaning the evangelist, but by changing his statement places the second with the others outside the number of the apostles, putting Aristion before him and clearly calling him a presbyter" (*Hist. eccl.* 3.39.5, trans. Lake).

Eusebius continues by noting the existence of two tombs of John at Ephesus (see also *Hist. eccl.* 7.25.16, quoting Dionysius) and suggests that the Elder John probably was the author of Revelation, of which Eusebius was no fan, "for it is probable that the second [John, i.e., the Elder] (unless anyone prefer the former) saw the revelation which passes under the name of John."

Another pertinent second-century reference comes from Polycrates, who was bishop of Ephesus, in about 190. Eusebius quotes Polycrates's statement about "John, who lay on the Lord's breast, who was a priest, wearing the breastplate, and a martyr, and teacher. He sleeps [i.e., is buried] at Ephesus" (*Hist. eccl.* 5.24.3–4, trans. Lake). This reference to the Beloved Disciple as a high priest (cf. John 18:15; Acts 4:6) eliminates the son of Zebedee here and points to the other John buried in Ephesus, the Elder.[56]

So too we have a third-century reference from Dionysius, whom Eusebius quotes as saying, "There was a certain other [John] among those that were in Asia, since it is said both that there were two tombs at Ephesus, and that each of the two is said to be John's" (*Hist. eccl.* 7.25.16, trans. Oulton). Irenaeus's reference to the Beloved Disciple is ambiguous in the same way as the citation given by Eusebius in *Historia ecclesiastica* 5.8.4 (quoted above).

From the time of Irenaeus onward, however, it appears that the church came to a unified viewpoint in which John the Apostle, one of the Twelve, was the author of the entire Johannine corpus: Gospel, Epistles, Apocalypse. Only in modern times has much attention been given to John the Elder as the possible author of the Gospel (cf. the reference to "the Elder" at the beginning of 2 John and 3 John).

The Beloved Disciple and the Author of the Fourth Gospel

Even if the Beloved Disciple can be identified as the Apostle John, however, that does not automatically establish him as the author of the Gospel. It is possible that he is the basic source of the tradition underlying the Gospel, but that it was actually written by another or others. The third-person pronouns of the relevant passages are easily understood as testimony of the author to the Beloved Disciple, whose eyewitness authority is understood to underlie the narrative.[57] Thus 19:35 looks as though it is written by someone other than the

56. See the argument by Bauckham, ibid., 438–52. He regards it as very significant that the Ephesian church identified John, the Beloved Disciple, not with the son of Zebedee but rather with the John of Acts 4:6 (who is associated with the high-priestly family).

57. George Beasley-Murray writes, "The texts in which the disciple features present him as *the witness* on which the Gospel rests, not its author" (*John*, lxxiii).

Beloved Disciple: "He who saw it has borne witness—his testimony is true, and he knows that he tells the truth—that you also may believe." The same is true of the peculiar statement that occurs almost at the end of the book: "This is the disciple who is bearing witness to these things, and who has written these things; and we know that his testimony is true" (21:24). This at least appears to identify the Beloved Disciple as the author.[58]

As we will see below, however, the entirety of chapter 21 appears to be a supplement, added later, and very possibly written by an individual other than the author of chapters 1–20. This evidence of editorial activity (note also the insertion of 19:35) together with the plural "we" of 21:24 points to the probable existence of a group of disciples associated with the Beloved Disciple—a Johannine school or circle.[59] Much Johannine scholarship has been devoted to reconstructing the history of this community and the stages in the production of the Fourth Gospel, but the conclusions can only be speculative.[60] But this does not cancel out the probable existence of a community originally centered around John the Apostle. John himself would have been the prime source and the interpreter of the traditions about Jesus in the Johannine circle.

There is no insuperable reason that the Apostle cannot also have been the Evangelist if we allow that the book went through a final redaction and was put into its present form by the Beloved Disciple's disciples in Ephesus. It is in this sense only that the Apostle is the author of the Fourth Gospel.

The Continuing Uncertainty and the Ongoing Debate

The result of the uncertainty caused by the nature of both the internal and external data is that there is currently no consensus about the identity of the Beloved Disciple or the author of the Fourth Gospel.

The argument that the Beloved Disciple is understood within the Gospel to be the Apostle John still has much persuasive power. Nevertheless, it must be admitted that this conclusion remains only an inference. For those who resist this inference, it is primarily the content argument that continues to enjoy the most leverage.[61] Once, however, one rejects John the Apostle, it is anyone's guess who

58. True, the words "written these things" (*grapsas tauta*) can be understood as meaning "caused to write" or that the Beloved Disciple's tradition is contained in what has been written. It must be admitted, however, that the natural meaning of this statement is that the Beloved Disciple is the author of this Gospel.

59. See especially Culpepper, *The Johannine School*; Cullmann, *The Johannine Circle*; R. Brown, *The Community of the Beloved Disciple*.

60. "Nowadays we already have too many attempts to reconstruct a 'history of the Johannine community.' They are all doomed to failure, because we know nothing of a real history which even goes back to Palestine, and conjectures about it are idle" (Hengel, *The Johannine Question*, 205n85).

61. But as John Painter rightly points out, "The crucial question is whether eyewitnesses may be significant interpreters rather than straightforward reporters" (*The Quest for the Messiah*, 66).

the Beloved Disciple might be. In the process of examining the numerous other possibilities, Alan Culpepper rightly points out "that *something* could be said in favor of the identification of almost any NT character as the Beloved Disciple. In all cases, the evidence is neither conclusive nor persuasive."[62] Nevertheless, speculation has continued to abound.[63] Some scholars, following Rudolf Bultmann, conclude that the Beloved Disciple refers not to an actual person but rather is to be understood as an ideal, symbolic figure representing the church as the guarantor of the tradition.[64] Many others simply despair at discovering the identity of the Beloved Disciple, cautiously concluding that he was "an eye-witness about whom nothing else is known," "a real person whose identity is lost."[65]

Nevertheless, the traditional conclusion that the Beloved Disciple is the Apostle John, the author of the Fourth Gospel, continues to be held by many scholars.[66] If, for whatever reason, one is doubtful of this conclusion, the presbyter John may be considered an attractive option—a view defended some years ago by Martin Hengel.[67] Richard Bauckham has now effectively shown how amenable the evidence, both internal and external, is to this conclusion.[68] Assuming this conclusion to be correct, it would not be difficult to believe that the early church, deliberately or not, soon understood "John" to be the Apostle rather than the Elder. The advantage of this theory over all alternative suggestions is, of course, that one is still dealing with the same name. Furthermore, as Hengel has noted, the titles of the Gospels go back to the very beginning, and this Gospel was always known as the one "according to John."[69]

62. Culpepper, *John, the Son of Zebedee*, 79. Italics in original.

63. For surveys of the proposals, see ibid., 73–85; also Charlesworth, *The Beloved Disciple*, 127–224. Charlesworth proposes Thomas as the Beloved Disciple. Among other proposals: Matthias, Apollos, the rich young ruler, Judas Iscariot, Andrew, Philip, Nathaniel, Lazarus, John Mark, and Judas the brother of Jesus.

64. See, for example, Lincoln, "The Beloved Disciple as Eyewitness and the Fourth Gospel as Witness." He regards the Beloved Disciple's witness as a literary device.

65. Thus Culpepper himself, *John, the Son of Zebedee*, 84, 141. Among others taking the same view are well-known Johannine scholars such as Oscar Cullmann, D. Moody Smith, Marinus de Jonge, Francis Moloney, and George Beasley-Murray, who writes, "As with the Beloved Disciple, so with the Evangelist: we do not know his name. But our ignorance of his identity entails no detriment to the value of this work" (*John*, lxxiv).

66. Among the scholars who hold that the Beloved Disciple is John the Apostle and, in most cases, also the Evangelist are B. F. Westcott, R. H. Lightfoot, William Sanday, J. H. Bernard, Adolf Schlatter, Leon Morris, F. F. Bruce, Stephen Smalley, J. Ramsey Michaels, D. A. Carson, and Andreas Köstenberger. As an indication of the difficulty of the question, it is interesting that two famous Johannine scholars, Raymond Brown and Rudolf Schnackenburg, who once opted for John the Apostle, in their later writings changed their minds, both independently opting instead for one of the anonymous disciples mentioned in 21:2. For details, see Charlesworth, *The Beloved Disciple*, 217–23.

67. See Hengel, *The Johannine Question*.

68. Bauckham, *Jesus and the Eyewitnesses*, 415–23. Although not all of Bauckham's arguments are equally convincing, the overall strength of his case is impressive.

69. See Hengel, *The Four Gospels and the One Gospel of Jesus Christ*, 48–56.

Adding to the confusion is the fact that the terms "apostle," "disciple," and "elder" are not mutually exclusive. While all Apostles were disciples of Jesus, not all disciples of Jesus were Apostles. At the same time, there are some called "apostle" who were not members of the Twelve (e.g., Paul, Barnabas [Acts 14:14], Andronicus and Junia [Rom. 16:7], Epaphroditus [Phil. 2:25]). And Irenaeus can associate the two terms, as in his reference to his teacher Polycarp as "the blessed and apostolic presbyter [*apostolikos presbyteros*]" (Eusebius, *Hist. eccl.* 5.20.7, trans. Lake).

Many questions remain, of course. Why the anonymity of the Beloved Disciple in the first place? Who would have the audacity to refer to himself as "the disciple whom Jesus loved," and why would he do so? If chapter 13 refers to the Last Supper, would not the Beloved Disciple have to have been one of the Twelve? When did John the son of Zebedee die? Is the elder of 2–3 John to be equated with John the Elder of church tradition? Which John (or yet another?) is the author of the Apocalypse?

Unless new information is forthcoming, we will have to be content with uncertainties. In light of all the evidence, the traditional view that the Apostle John is the Beloved Disciple and the author of the Fourth Gospel, at least in the sense of providing the tradition underlying it, or perhaps a first draft, has a slight edge—but only that—over the other appealing option, John the Elder. This is a subjective call, as all matters of opinion are. But other options are no more compelling—in fact, they are much less so. What should be stressed is that the identity of the author is not crucial to the historical reliability of this Gospel.[70] More important is the reality of eyewitness testimony provided by the Beloved Disciple, whoever he was, as the source and validator of the tradition, endorsed by the disciples associated with him. As they gladly say, "This is the disciple who is bearing witness to these things, and who has written these things; and we know that his testimony is true" (21:24 [cf. 19:35]).

The Enigma of Chapter 21 and the Unity of the Fourth Gospel

A first-time reader of the Gospel of John undoubtedly will think that the book comes to an end with the last sentence of chapter 20 and will be surprised that it is followed by anything at all, let alone a whole chapter introducing new narrative material. In 20:30–31 the Evangelist seems to round off the story, by indicating that his account has been highly selective, and by articulating the purpose of what he has written: "Now Jesus did many other signs in the presence of the disciples, which are not written in this book; but these are written that you may believe that Jesus is the Christ, the Son of God, and that believing you may have life in his name."

---

70. See Dodd, *Historical Tradition in the Fourth Gospel*, 16–17; Robinson, "The New Look on the Fourth Gospel," 106.

At the end of chapter 21, moreover, we read a very similar statement: "But there are also many other things which Jesus did; were every one of them to be written, I suppose that the world itself could not contain the books that would be written" (21:25).[71] This second ending clearly reflects the ending of chapter 20 and indicates that chapter 21 very probably is an added epilogue or appendix to the Gospel proper (cf. the appendix of Sir. 51:1–30).[72] Verse 24, "This is the disciple who is bearing witness to these things, and who has written these things; and we know that his testimony is true," provides virtually indisputable evidence of editorial activity.[73] This epilogue was added very early, as there is no evidence of any manuscript of John's Gospel, including the second-century 𝔓[66], that lacks chapter 21.

What is the purpose of the epilogue of John 21? Three scenes are provided:

1. a miraculous catch of 153 fish[74] involving a (specifically mentioned "third") resurrection appearance (vv. 1–14) and symbolizing the future ministry of the disciples;
2. a moving anecdote about Peter's reinstatement, involving the commission to "feed my sheep" (vv. 15–19);
3. a conversation between Peter and Jesus concerning the fate of the Beloved Disciple (vv. 20–23), who, it seems, has now unexpectedly died (prior to the parousia).

It is possible that the miraculous catch of fish is meant to provide a seventh sign miracle to complete the Gospel.[75]

Not all scholars accept that chapter 21 is another addition to the Gospel from a later hand.[76] The literary style is similar enough to be by the same hand, although this falls short of demonstration. Other literary works in the ancient world provide examples of anticlimactic epilogues and dual endings. Richard

71. Andreas Köstenberger argues that the first-person pronoun of "I suppose" indicates the author of this Gospel and thus its unity, or at least chapter 21 ("'I Suppose' [oimai]"). It is possible, but no more, that the "I suppose" is an editor's way of alluding back to 20:30, indicating that this was the original author's view. It is worth noting that under ultraviolet light, the manuscript of Codex Sinaiticus shows that it originally ended with 21:24.

72. See especially Baum, "The Original Epilogue (John 20:30–31), the Secondary Appendix (21:1–23), and the Editorial Epilogues (21:24–25) of John's Gospel."

73. *Pace* Jackson, "Ancient Self-Referential Conventions and Their Implications for the Authorship and Integrity of the Gospel of John."

74. The symbolism of the 153 fish remains an unsolved mystery. For possible interpretations, see R. Brown, *The Gospel according to John*, 2:1074–76; Beasley-Murray, *John*, 401–4.

75. Unless one counts the walking on the water (6:16–21) as one of the signs—and scholars disagree about this—there are only six sign miracles in chapters 1–20. Richard Bauckham disagrees strongly ("The 153 Fish and the Unity of the Fourth Gospel," 79).

76. Among the minority who do not accept chapter 21 as a later addition are Bauckham, Bruce, Carson, Keener, Köstenberger, Minear, Robinson, and Smalley. See also Porter, "The Ending of John's Gospel."

Bauckham concludes that "there is no reason to doubt [the epilogue] belongs to the original design and form of the Gospel."[77] He defends this conclusion by the observation that there is a correspondence between the 496 syllables of the prologue and the 496 words of the epilogue and by other arguments based on gematria (numerical value of words). Even if there is something to this correspondence, it could be the result of the work of a later author of chapter 21, as Bauckham admits. As for Bauckham's other arguments, it must be said that while practically anything can be alleged as *possible*, it is exceptionally difficult to establish any *probability* in the speculations of gematria. One never knows whether the significance seen in the numbers was intended by the author, or whether it is the result of the ingenuity of the interpreter. There may be something to John Emerton's suggestion that the number 153 corresponds to the Hebrew value of the word "(En-)Eglaim" in Ezekiel 47:10,[78] but there is no way to know whether this is anything more than an interesting coincidence.[79]

It is very unlikely that the original author would have added the new material of chapter 21 in this unusual manner, creating what cannot but seem as an anticlimax. More probably, as C. K. Barrett says, "the supplementary material would have been added by him before 20:30 and the impressive conclusion left undisturbed."[80]

There is one other well-known passage that clearly was added after the Gospel was written: the narrative of the woman caught in adultery (7:53–8:11).[81] This can be said with confidence because although it is an ancient tradition found in many manuscripts, it is lacking in all of the earliest of them ($\mathfrak{P}^{66}$, $\mathfrak{P}^{75}$, ℵ, A, B, C). It also interrupts the narrative flow of 7:52 and 8:12, and thus it is variously placed in the manuscripts that do contain it; even when it occurs after 7:52, it usually is marked by these manuscripts in some way to indicate its doubtful character. In the standard Greek New Testaments it is included in its normal place but within double brackets, indicating its questionable authenticity. Many scholars think that the passage nevertheless may reflect a true story.

77. Bauckham, "The 153 Fish and the Unity of the Fourth Gospel," 79.

78. Which reads, "Fishermen will stand beside the sea; from En-gedi to En-eglaim it will be a place for the spreading of nets; its fish will be of very many kinds, like the fish of the Great Sea." See Emerton, "The Hundred and Fifty-Three Fishes in John xxi.11."

79. Raymond Brown points out that "we know of no speculation or established symbolism related to the number 153 in early thought. . . . Because this symbolism is not immediately evident, it did not prompt the invention of the number; for certainly the writer were he choosing freely, could have come up with a more obviously symbolic number, for example, 144" (*The Gospel according to John*, 2:1075). It remains just possible that a former fisherman might want to count the actual number of fish that were in the net!

80. Barrett, *The Gospel according to St. John*, 577.

81. In a handful of late manuscripts (known as family 13) the passage was also inserted into the Gospel of Luke, after 21:38, in addition to being present in the Fourth Gospel.

The Content and Purpose of the Gospel

John alone among the four Gospels clearly and specifically articulates its purpose: "These [things] are written that you may believe that Jesus is the Christ, the Son of God, and that believing you may have life in his name" (20:31). This Gospel was written to encourage faith in Jesus, whether to initiate faith in unbelievers or to increase and consolidate the faith of those who have already believed.[82] Of course, one would have to say the same thing about the Synoptic Gospels. They too are written to encourage faith in Jesus. John, however, intends to do so by making explicit what the Synoptics have left mostly implicit. This purpose is the underlying explanation of the special character of John, which like no other Gospel brings out the full meaning of Jesus.

John's Gospel divides into six easily recognized main sections.

1. The Prologue (1:1–18)

This opening section is unique and of unique importance, as an introduction to the essential message of this Gospel. It begins with the *logos*, the "Word," identified as God (1:1), as the one through whom everything was created (1:3), and as "the light" (*to phōs*) (1:4; cf. 1:8–9), in whom was "life" (1:4). Already in these references to light and life we have major themes of this Gospel anticipated: "I am the light of the world; he who follows me will not walk in darkness, but will have the light of life [*to phōs tēs zōēs*]" (8:12 [for Jesus as the light, see also 3:19–21; 9:5; 12:35–36, 46]).

The climax of the prologue is reached in 1:14, which is a kind of summary of the book: "And the Word became flesh [*sarx*] and dwelt among us, full of grace and truth; we have beheld his glory [*doxa*], glory as of the only Son from the Father." We must not allow familiarity with this statement to obscure its astounding, radical content. That the *logos*—in Hellenistic thought, the underlying principle of reality that provides coherence and intelligibility to the world—should take on flesh was an absurd idea to the Greeks. To the Jewish mind, the idea of flesh revealing the glory of God—an allusion to the Shekinah glory associated with God's presence in the temple—was scandalous. This Johannine text articulates the very essence of the Christian faith, the incarnation: the great mystery that God has appeared within his own creation, as a fully human man, to rescue the fallen human race. Calling attention to the significance of this assertion, Martin Hengel writes, "In order to interpret this one sentence the

---

82. There is textual uncertainty about the tense of "believe" in the Greek. If it is a present tense (*pisteuēte*), as the earliest manuscripts have it, the idea conveyed would be "keep believing"—that is, the Gospel was written primarily to strengthen the faith of believers. If it is an aorist (*pisteusēte*), the sense would be "begin to believe," thus indicating that the Gospel was written to evangelize unbelievers. But it is doubtful that the tense alone can determine the question. For discussion, see Carson, "The Purpose of the Fourth Gospel"; idem, "Syntactical and Text-Critical Observations on John 20:30–31"; Fee, "On the Text and Meaning of John 20:30–31."

Evangelist could not continue the Synoptic tradition; he had to write a different Gospel that sets out to inculcate in readers the truth of this one sentence."[83]

Equally astounding is the final sentence of the prologue: "No one has ever seen God; the only Son, who is in the bosom of the Father, he has made him known" (1:18). The majority of manuscripts read "the only Son," but the earliest witnesses ($\mathfrak{P}^{66}$, $\mathfrak{P}^{75}$, ℵ, B, C) have *monogenēs theos*, "the one-of-a-kind God." Confronted by this difficult statement, copyists were very tempted to replace *theos* with *huios*, "son," so that it is the unique Son who is

The Seven Signs Manifesting the Glory of Jesus
Chapter 2: changing water into wine
Chapter 4: healing of the nobleman's son
Chapter 5: healing of the lame man
Chapter 6: feeding of the five thousand
[Chapter 6: walking on the water]?
Chapter 9: healing of the blind man
Chapter 11: raising of Lazarus
[Chapter 21: catch of 153 fish]?

in the bosom of the Father. But it may well be, and it is fully in accord with the statement of 1:14, that the Evangelist spoke here of Jesus as God (as is clearly the case in 1:1; 20:28). To see Jesus is, in effect, to see God (cf. 14:9), for Jesus is the "exegesis" of God.[84] This view involves "redefining the basic category of Jewish monotheism itself."[85]

The stunning prologue sets the stage for the entire Gospel that follows, which is intended to be "read through the window of the prologue."[86]

2. The Testimony of John the Baptist and the Calling of the First Disciples (1:19–51)

In contrast to the John the Baptist of the Synoptics, who is merely the forerunner of Jesus, in the Fourth Gospel he is presented as more of a potential competitor of Jesus (see 3:22–30; 4:1–2). John denies that he is *the* eschatological figure, affirming instead, as in the Synoptics, that he is the forerunner (1:23, 27), a witness to the one whom he identifies as not only the "Son of

---

83. Hengel, "The Prologue of the Gospel of John as the Gateway to Christological Truth," 283. A few pages later he writes, "We have the Jesus tradition, which is fundamental to the origin of Christology only in the form of the 'apostolic testimony' in which the 'messianic claim' of Jesus has fused with the first witnesses' experience of Easter and the Spirit. In the Gospel of John the radical concentration on this personal mystery has decisively transformed the Synoptic Jesus tradition" (ibid., 290).

84. In 1:18 "made him known" is a translation of *exēgēsato* (the verb *exēgeomai* means "to relate, expound, explain").

85. Dunn, "Let John Be John," 335. On this, see especially Bauckham, *Jesus and the God of Israel*.

86. Dunn, "Let John Be John," 334. Dunn points out that for John, "the meaning of Christ cannot be expressed except as a christology 'from above'" (ibid.). See also Hengel, "The Prologue of the Gospel of John as the Gateway to Christological Truth."

God" but also as "the Lamb of God, who takes away the sin of the world" (1:29, 36). By the end of the chapter the disciples have already identified Jesus as the Messiah, the King of Israel, and the Son of God.

3. The Public Ministry: Signs and Discourses (2:1–12:50)

The ministry of Jesus begins with the sign miracle performed at the wedding at Cana. The event is highly symbolic and points to the dramatic newness that this Gospel will convey: the stone jars "for the Jewish rites of purification" (2:6) are filled with water that becomes transformed into the incomparable wine of the gospel ("You have kept the good wine until now" [2:10]); the large amount of wine (between 120 and 180 gallons!) itself suggests an anticipation of eschatological fulfillment. The Evangelist notes specifically that this was "the first of his signs" and manifested the glory of Jesus (2:11). The reference to a "second sign" (4:54) leads one to believe that the Evangelist will number all of them. But oddly, no more signs are numbered. Still, one is led now to think about the number of miracles and to discover that there are in this Gospel seven signs, the number of perfection. Jesus did many more, as the Evangelist assures us (2:23; 3:2; 6:2; 11:47; 12:37). The comment toward the end of the narrative that "Jesus did many other signs in the presence of the disciples" (20:30 [cf. 21:25]) indicates that the author has deliberately decided to record seven representative signs, most of which were not part of the Synoptic tradition. These signs (sēmeia) apparently were regarded by the Evangelist as particularly effective in pointing beyond themselves to the identity, the glory, and the meaning of Jesus.

Admittedly, without the Evangelist's enumeration of the signs, there is some uncertainty about the determination of the seven. Six of the signs are clear enough. The key question is whether the walking on the water (6:16–21) is to be regarded as one of the seven. On the one hand, the pericope is short and the readers are left to themselves to draw out its significance (contrast the presentation of the story in Matthew 14:22–33). On the other hand, if the walking on the water is to be counted as one of the signs, the raising of Lazarus seems to be perfect for the seventh and climactic sign. It is just possible, however, that the miraculous catch of chapter 21 was added in the Epilogue to serve as the seventh sign, symbolic perhaps of the fruitfulness of the church's mission.

The lengthy discourses of Jesus comprise the most distinctive aspect of the Fourth Gospel compared to the Synoptics. The so-called public discourses occur in the first major section of the Gospel; the private discourses given by Jesus to his disciples begin in chapter 13. The discourses provide in-depth exposition of the significance of Christ for the church. They move us from the historical past to the present moment. They move us from the theoretical level to the practical—to what the Christ event offers the individual believer

---

The Seven "I Am" Sayings

6:48 "I am the bread of life"; 6:35 "I am the bread of life; he who comes to me shall not
    hunger, and he who believes in me shall never thirst" (cf. 4:14).

9:5 "I am the light of the world"; 8:12 "I am the light of the world; he who follows me will
    not walk in darkness, but will have the light of life."

10:7 "I am the door of the sheep."

10:11 "I am the good shepherd. The good shepherd lays down his life for the sheep."

11:25–26 "I am the resurrection and the life; he who believes in me, though he die, yet
    shall he live, and whoever lives and believes in me shall never die."

14:6 "I am the way, and the truth, and the life; no one comes to the Father, but by me."

15:1 "I am the true vine, and my Father is the vinedresser."

A famous eighth, absolute "I am" saying is different from the preceding inasmuch as it
lacks any predicate nominative: "Before Abraham was, I am" (8:58 [cf. 18:6]).

---

now. If the signs point to Jesus and the new era that he brings, the discourses
indicate the fruit of the new era for those who believe.

The remarkable thing is the extent to which the Evangelist has attempted
to correlate the discourses with the signs. In effect, the signs become teaching
occasions and serve as the example or illustration of the truth of the discourse
material. The correlation is not done systematically or consistently, but in a
few instances, especially for the fourth, fifth (understood as the healing of the
blind man), and sixth (understood as the raising of Lazarus) signs, the design
is unmistakable. Thus after the fourth sign, the feeding of the five thousand
(6:1–14), we encounter the discourse on Jesus as the bread of life (6:25–65).[87]
This discourse finds its immediate stimulus in another miraculous feeding,
the provision of manna to Israel in the wilderness (Exod. 16), described as
"grain from heaven" in Psalm 78:24. Jesus then refers to "the bread which
comes down from heaven" (6:50) and proceeds to identity himself as that
bread (6:51). No longer is the concern with literal food, but rather with a
spiritual provision of eternal life. Here the Evangelist makes use of one of the
"I am" sayings: "I am the bread of life" (6:35). Jesus goes on to say that anyone
who eats this bread, identified now as his flesh, will live forever (6:51). The
following statement, "He who eats my flesh and drinks my blood has eternal
life" (6:54 [cf. 6:55–58]), is unmistakably a eucharistic allusion and a pointer
to the promise of life associated with the Eucharist.

87. As in Mark and Matthew, in John the feeding of the five thousand is followed immediately by the narrative of Jesus walking on the water (6:12–21). This results in some separation
between the sign and the related discourse.

In the case of the fifth sign, understood as the giving of sight to the blind man (9:1–41), it is the discourse material that precedes the miracle that is pertinent. The discourse of 8:12–20 is tied to the sign that follows, since it begins with an "I am" saying that occurs again in 9:5: "I am the light of the world." The same "I am" saying is found in 8:12, followed by these words: "He who follows me will not walk in darkness, but will have the light of life." The intervening material, between the discourse and the sign (8:21–58), is concerned largely with an exchange between Jesus and the Jews who did not believe.

The sixth sign, taken as the resurrection of Lazarus, has no discourse of any length associated with it. There are, however, some connections with material in chapter 10, such as the statement "I give them eternal life, and they shall never perish, and no one shall snatch them out of my hand" (10:28). Most striking, of course, is the "I am" saying in 11:25: "I am the resurrection and the life; he who believes in me, though he die, yet shall he live, and whoever lives and believes in me shall never die."[88]

What is most impressive about the signs and public discourses is their constant emphasis on who Jesus is—the Son of God, the Christ, the Savior of the world, his oneness with the Father—as well as on that which he brings to the world, consistently expressed as "life" or "eternal life." This last phrase is to be understood not so much in quantitative terms as in qualitative terms. It refers to the new state of affairs that comes into existence through the Son, and in that sense it is the equivalent to the Synoptics' theme of the kingdom of God. John retells the story of Jesus in order to draw out its full significance, as it can now be known after the resurrection, the outpouring of the Holy Spirit, and the growth of the church. The discourses draw out the time-transcending significance of Jesus. Who he was, what he did and said, have continuing relevance for the church. John presents, therefore, what can be called a "theological appropriation of the historical." The emphasis moves from the historical to the contemporary. It is as though the Evangelist believed that the story had also to be told in a different way than the Synoptics told it, in a deliberately retrospective way so as to bring out its ultimate meaning, for the benefit of Christians of his and later generations.[89] The Evangelist puts this anachronistic understanding into the discourses by extending, elaborating, and bringing out the implicit meaning of things that Jesus said. He builds

88. It is more difficult to find associated discourse material for the other signs. The first sign, the turning of the water into wine, where the wine symbolizes the newness of the gospel, can be related to the discourse on new life in 3:1–21; the second sign, the healing of the nobleman's son, to the discourse on the water of life (4:7–26); and the third sign, the healing of the lame man, to the discourse on the Son of God as the giver of life (5:17–47). There is little to relate to the added seventh sign of chapter 21.

89. J. Louis Martyn (*History and Theology in the Fourth Gospel*) describes John as having two levels of meaning: the first is the *einmalig* level (the "one-time" original events); the second is the "contemporary" level, wherein the Evangelist finds direct relevance to the specific situation of the readers of his day.

on the tradition that he has access to, but he is able to enrich it through the inspiration of the Spirit and so spell out the truth about Jesus.

4. The Private Teaching to the Apostles: The Farewell Discourse (13:1–17:26)

After the events narrated in chapter 13—the foot-washing, the revealing of the betrayer, the teaching of the "new commandment," and the foretelling of Peter's betrayal—the remaining four chapters of this section consist almost exclusively of words of Jesus. Most notable here are the promise of the Holy Spirit—the *Paraclete* (*paraklētos*, "one who helps")—who functions as the continued presence of Jesus (14:15–31; 15:26; 16:5–15); teaching about Jesus as the true vine (15:1–17); teaching about temporary sorrow and overcoming the world (16:16–24); and finally the so-called high priestly prayer of Jesus (chap. 17).

The gift of the Spirit-Paraclete is of great importance in John. The Spirit, promised as "another Paraclete" (i.e., a Paraclete like Jesus was), will be with (and in) the believer forever (14:16–17). Although when understood in trinitarian terms, the Spirit-Paraclete and Jesus are distinct persons, there is also a sense in which the ministry of the former is a continuation of the latter's ministry (cf. 1 John 2:1, where Jesus is called a *paraklētos*). When Jesus promises, "I will not leave you desolate; I will come to you" (14:18 [cf. 14:28]), he probably means through the Holy Spirit, the second Paraclete. Through the Holy Spirit the absent Jesus is present and actively ministering to the church. The Spirit makes Christ contemporary to us in every age. Jesus thus will "send" the Spirit to his disciples (15:26; 16:7).[90] This is the point of the so-called Johannine Pentecost of 20:22: "he [Jesus] breathed on them, and said to them, 'Receive the Holy Spirit.'" The Spirit in the church carries on the work of Jesus (cf. 7:39).

After the strange interruptive note at the end of chapter 14, "Rise, let us go hence," we encounter the lengthy meditative discourse of chapters 15–16. Using the analogy of a vine and its branches, Jesus speaks of a unique relationship of mutual indwelling (cf. "I in them" [17:23, 26]). Only insofar as the branches abide in the vine can they bear fruit—in this case, the fruit of righteousness, and particularly of love for one another. The disciples must be prepared to endure hatred just as Jesus had done. But the resurrection will turn sorrow into joy. That victory will also be the disciples' victory. They are to have peace, indeed to rejoice, because Jesus has overcome the world.

The discourse material finds its climax in the prayer of Jesus in chapter 17, which provides the occasion for a kind of summary of the work of Jesus and the purpose for which he came. The prayer begins in the third person: "Father, the hour has come; glorify thy Son that the Son may glorify thee, since thou

---

90. These verses caused the addition of the *filioque* clause (i.e., that the Spirit proceeds from the Father "and the Son") to the creed of the Western branch of the early church, causing the rift between the later Roman and Orthodox wings of the church.

hast given him power over all flesh, to give eternal life to all whom thou hast given him. And this is eternal life, that they know thee the only true God, and Jesus Christ whom thou hast sent" (17:1–3). The shift to the first person occurs in the next verse (17:4), but still the prayer summarizes the ministry of Jesus and then provides an allusion to the prologue: "I glorified thee on earth, having accomplished the work which thou gavest me to do; and now, Father, glorify thou me in thy own presence with the glory which I had with thee before the world was made" (17:4–5).[91] The prayer then turns to the Twelve disciples (17:6–19), and then specifically to the church, "for those who believe in me through their word" (17:20–26).

5. Passion Narrative and Resurrection (18:1–20:29)

Along with the basic similarity to the Synoptics' passion and resurrection narratives, John adds some details and provides some new material. Among the most noteworthy additions are the falling of the soldiers to the ground when Jesus identifies himself (18:4–9 [John omits reference to Judas's betraying kiss]); providing the name, "Malchus," of the soldier whose ear was cut off and then restored (18:10; cf. 18:26); the conversation between Pilate and Jesus, with Pilate's famous diversion: "What is truth?" (18:33–38); Pilate's reluctant agreement to put Jesus to death (19:4–15); the gambling of the soldiers for Jesus' seamless tunic (19:23–24); the giving of Mary into the care of the Beloved Disciple (19:26–27); the words from the cross "I thirst" and "It is finished" (19:28–30); that Jesus' legs were not broken, but his side was pierced (19:31–37); the coming of Nicodemus with spices for Jesus' burial (19:39); the condition of the burial clothes in the empty tomb (20:6–7); Mary Magdalene's encounter with the risen Jesus (20:11–17); and finally, the climax of the entire narrative of the Fourth Gospel, the appearance of Jesus to Thomas, his remarkable confession, "My Lord and my God!" (20:28), and the concluding statement by Jesus, "Blessed are those who have not seen and yet believe" (20:29).

6. Epilogue (21:1–25)

We have already noted some of the distinctives of the final chapter of John in the preceding discussion. Clearly of importance is the appearance of the risen Jesus to the seven disciples who went fishing (21:1–3), the third such appearance of the risen Jesus to his disciples (21:14). The restoration of Peter, who had denied Jesus, is brilliantly reported in his repeated affirmations of his love for Jesus. Finally the misunderstanding that the Beloved Disciple would not die is corrected.

---

91. The Fourth Gospel has a much higher frequency of the *doxa-* root ("glory, glorify") than any of the other Gospels.

Characteristics of the Fourth Gospel

In discussing the differences between the Fourth Gospel and the Synoptics, we have already noted some of its special characteristics. The most notable distinctive of John is its discourses, which are lengthy, repetitive, and centered on the person of Jesus and what he offers to the believer.

Literary[92]

Among the special characteristics of the Fourth Gospel we note the following:

- *Repeated use of key terms.* This is to be expected, and it is caused in part by the repetitious character of the lengthy discourses.
- *Key word links.* Important key theological words serve to link various pericopes.
- *Pointless stylistic variations.* At the same time, the Evangelist uses synonyms and can vary the way he expresses himself.
- *Double meanings.* The Evangelist apparently is fond of words that have a dual meaning.[93] Two notable examples: In the statement of John 3:3, 7, that one must be "born anew," the word *anōthen* can also mean "from above." And the verb *hypsoō* can mean both "to lift up" literally and "to exalt"; thus, the lifting up of Jesus on the cross is at the same time his exaltation.
- *Misunderstandings.* Of course, double meanings can lead to misunderstandings, as in John 3. The repeated misunderstandings that occur in the Johannine dialogues usually become vehicles for Jesus' teaching.[94] Familiar examples are the saying about the destruction and raising up of the temple, which was taken literally but was meant by Jesus to refer to the death and resurrection of his body (2:19–21). In the discourse on the bread of life (6:22–59), the eating of Jesus' flesh and drinking of his blood are taken literally but actually are an allusion to the Eucharist.
- *Asides.* The Evangelist often inserts a comment in the form of an aside,[95] as, for example, in 10:6; 12:33.
- *Irony.* This important device pervades the narrative of the Fourth Gospel. Irony effectively conveys the message and truth of the narrative by means of the incongruity of appearance and reality, causing the characters to misunderstand what is happening or to be unaware of the meaning of

---

92. See especially Culpepper, *Anatomy of the Fourth Gospel*.

93. See Wead, "The Johannine Double Meaning."

94. See Culpepper, *Anatomy of the Fourth Gospel*, 152–65, which includes a list of misunderstandings in John; Carson, "Understanding Misunderstandings in the Fourth Gospel."

95. John O'Rourke ("Asides in the Gospel of John") finds more than a hundred examples.

what they themselves say.[96] An excellent example of the author's use of irony is the statement by the Jewish leaders in 11:48, "If we let him go on thus, every one will believe in him, and the Romans will come and destroy both our holy place and our nation," which is exactly what happened when they did *not* let Jesus go (cf. 12:19). Another example is this statement by Caiaphas: "You know nothing at all; you do not understand that it is expedient for you that one man should die for the people, and that the whole nation should not perish" (11:49–50). It was Caiaphas who did not know what he said.

- *Symbolism*. Symbols, so very important in John,[97] are earthly realities that point beyond themselves to a transcendent reality. Just for that reason, they serve a function very close to the purpose of the Gospel itself.[98] Among the many symbols active in the narrative, three core symbols stand out: light, water, and bread,[99] each of which points to the meaning of Jesus. All three symbols are basic to life and thus to the mission of Jesus to bring eternal life.

- *Aporias*. Abrupt transitions in the narrative have been noted, particularly between chapters 4 and 5, and again between chapters 5 and 6. Whereas chapters 4 and 6 take place in Galilee, chapter 5 has Jesus in Jerusalem. This has led some to rearrange the order of the chapters, putting chapters 4 and 6 together, followed by chapter 5, although this results in an awkward transition at the end of chapter 5 and the beginning of chapter 7. No manuscript evidence exists to support this reordering of the content of John's Gospel. The other famous aporia occurs between chapters 20 and 21, a subject examined above. Two factors may be at play here: the probable existence of a later redactor or redactors belonging to the Johannine community, but much more important, what is at work is the freedom of the Evangelist to impose order on the materials as he sees fit and without regard for transitions per se.

Theological

The Gospel of John is fundamentally a theological narrative about the mission of Jesus that focuses intently on the identity and significance of Jesus.

- *Life/salvation*. The offer of life and, more specifically, eternal life, corresponds closely to the Synoptics' offer of the kingdom of God, as its

96. See Culpepper, *Anatomy of the Fourth Gospel*, 165–80; Duke, *Irony in the Fourth Gospel*.
97. See Culpepper, *Anatomy of the Fourth Gospel*, 180–98.
98. Jesus may be regarded as the principal symbol of the Gospel. See Lee, *Symbolic Narratives of the Fourth Gospel*; Schneiders, "History and Symbolism in the Fourth Gospel." See also Léon-Dufour, "Towards a Symbolic Reading of the Fourth Gospel."
99. Thus Culpepper, *Anatomy of the Fourth Gospel*, 189.

virtual equivalent (the noun "life" [*zōē*] occurs 36x in John compared to 16x in the Synoptics altogether). Above all, it is life that Jesus offers those who believe in him (3:15–16, 36; 4:14; 5:24, 40; 6:27, 33, 40, 47; 10:10, 28; 17:2–3; 20:31).

- *Christology*. Jesus is able to offer life because of who he is. "Lord, to whom shall we go? You have the words of eternal life; and we have believed, and have come to know, that you are the Holy One of God" (6:68–69). This title almost certainly is to be understood as a messianic title (cf. the analogous Synoptic passage, Mark 8:29 pars.), but it points to an exalted Anointed One who is nothing less than the incarnation of the *logos* (1:1, 14), who uniquely manifests God (1:18). He is indeed "the Messiah" (1:41; 4:25–26; cf. 11:27; 20:31), the "King of Israel" (1:49; 18:33–37), and "the Savior of the world" (4:42). He is also *kyrios*, "Lord" (4:1; 6:23; 11:2), but most frequently referred to as "the Son of God" (nearly 30x), who is in unique relationship to the Father—a prominent theme in John—and shares the functions of the Father, as giver of life and as judge.[100] And, for the greatest mystery of all, he is somehow the very manifestation of God (1:1, 18; 20:28), the "I AM," Yahweh's self-designation in Exodus 3:14 (4:26; 6:20; 12:58). "You are from below, I am from above; you are of this world, I am not of this world" (8:23). The title "Son of Man" is used of Jesus, but in a less ambiguous way than in the Synoptics. He is a glorious figure, one who descended from, and ascended to, heaven (3:13; cf. 6:62; 1:51; see also 5:27; 6:27). Wisdom motifs surely are at work in John's christology. The titles "Messiah," "Son of God," and "Son of Man" are primarily *"an elaboration of the initial explicit identification of Jesus as the incarnate Wisdom/Logos*—an identification taken over certainly from earlier Christian tradition, but expounded in John's own distinctive fashion."[101] At the same time, however, the full humanity of Jesus, who took on human flesh (1:14), is also a motif of this Gospel not to be forgotten. The Gospel thus is anti-docetic, countering any suggestion that Jesus only "appeared" to be human.[102] A deliberate rejection of docetism is clear in the opening lines of 1 John: "That which was from the beginning, which we have heard, which we have seen with our eyes, which we have looked upon and touched with our hands, concerning the

100. In John's Gospel, to claim to be Son of God amounts to a claim to be God. See 5:18; 10:33, 36; 19:7.

101. So Dunn, "Let John Be John—A Gospel for Its Time," 331. "Wisdom/Logos is *not* a heavenly being over against God, but is *God himself, God in his self-manifestation*, God insofar as he may be known by the mind of man" (ibid).

102. See especially, Thompson, *The Incarnate Word*, which corrects Käsemann's docetic view of the Jesus of the Fourth Gospel as "God striding about the earth."

word of life . . . that which we have seen and heard we proclaim also to you" (1 John 1:1–3 [cf. 2 John 7]).[103]

- *The cross and atonement.* While it has often been noted that John focuses on the theme of revelation, and that the cross plays a less significant role than in the Synoptics, the difference can be overstated. John too knows the significance of the cross as a sacrifice for sin. Already at the beginning of the book the Baptist says, "Behold, the Lamb of God, who takes away the sin of the world" (1:29, cf. 36). The death of Jesus is implied in 3:16–17, "For God so loved the world that he gave his only Son, that whoever believes in him should not perish but have eternal life. . . . God sent the Son into the world . . . that the world might be saved through him." So too the vicarious, sacrificial death of Jesus is indicated when he says, "The bread which I shall give for the life of the world is my flesh" (6:51), in his statement that "the good shepherd lays down his life for the sheep" (10:11 [cf. 10:15, 18]), and in the Evangelist's aside that the high priest unwittingly "prophesied that Jesus should die for the nation" (11:51). The fact that according to the Fourth Gospel Jesus is crucified at the time of the slaying of the Passover lambs points in the same direction, even if the Evangelist does not draw out the parallel.[104] That the meaning of the death of Jesus is understood and assumed in the Fourth Gospel is confirmed by statements in 1 John: "the blood of Jesus his Son cleanses us from all sin" (1 John 1:7) and "he is the expiation [*hilasmos*] for our sins, and not for ours only but also for the sins of the whole world" (1 John 2:2 [cf. 4:10]).[105] A striking distinctive of the Fourth Gospel's perspective on the death of Jesus is that the time of glorification is moved forward from the resurrection, where it occurs in the Synoptics, to the cross itself (see 12:23–24). This is the supreme moment of the glorification of Jesus.[106] The lifting up on the cross is his exaltation. The crucifixion is the goal of the incarnation. The cross thus serves as a key revelation of Jesus.

- *Dualism.* The Gospel of John is full of dualisms. Its main burden, indeed, is dualistic, as reflected already in the prologue: the eternal has entered the temporal; the suprahistorical has entered history; the heavenly has become the earthly; the spiritual has become the material. It is perhaps the vertical dualism of above and below that is most striking in John. Of central importance is the motif of descent and ascent, especially as

103. On John's christology, see Anderson, *The Christology of the Fourth Gospel.*
104. There is significance, however, in the description of the events in 19:31–37, which allude to Numbers 9:12 and Exodus 12:46 (and Exod. 12:10 in the LXX), concerning not breaking any bones of the Passover lamb, and which are said to have occurred in fulfillment of Psalm 34:20, quoted in 19:36. The death of Jesus clearly is in the place of the Passover lamb.
105. See Senior, *The Passion of Jesus in the Gospel of John.*
106. In John, Jesus on the cross does not say, as in Mark and Matthew, "My God, my God, why have you forsaken me," but rather, "It is finished" (19:30).

applied to Jesus: "I came from the Father and have come into the world; again, I am leaving the world and going to the Father" (16:28 [cf. 6:33; 7:33; 13:3]); "No one has ascended into heaven but he who descended from heaven, the Son of man" (3:13 [cf. 6:62]); "For I have come down from heaven, not to do my own will, but the will of him who sent me" (6:38). The sequence of ascent and descent, referring to the ascension and return at the parousia, is also evident: "And when I go and prepare a place for you, I will come again and will take you to myself, that where I am you may be also" (14:3); and, in reference to the Paraclete, "It is to your advantage that I go away . . . ; but if I go, I will send him to you" (16:7). Other dualisms are found throughout John, such as truth/falsehood, life/death, light/darkness, spirit/flesh, good/evil, the believer/the world, and God/Satan. The dualism of belief and unbelief is especially important in this Gospel, prompting Alan Culpepper to say, "The plot of the gospel is propelled by conflict between belief and unbelief as responses to Jesus."[107] Nearly half the NT occurrences of the verb "believe" (*pisteuō*) are in John.

- *Witness.* The vocabulary of "witness" is very important in the Fourth Gospel, with the verb *martyreō* occurring more than thirty times (versus 2x in the Synoptics), and the noun *martyria*, in the sense of "testimony," fourteen times (versus 4x in the Synoptics).[108] This vocabulary is employed to support the truth claims (see 5:14, 32–33; 18:37) of this Gospel. The witness or testimony concerns what has been seen (see 3:11, 32) and heard. Often it is Jesus himself who bears witness to the truth. Also functioning in this role are the Evangelist and members of the Johannine community.[109] The extent of this idea of testimony in this Gospel has given rise to the idea that it is a trial narrative concerning the relationship of God with the world.[110] On trial is God's relationship to the world and, in particular, the identity and role of Jesus as God's Agent.

- *Anti-Judaism.* Although John's Gospel is clearly a very Jewish document, accepting the full authority of the Jewish Scriptures and able to say that "salvation is from the Jews" (4:22), there is at the same time a particularly strong anti-Jewish theme running throughout the book. This motif finds a climax in the exasperation of the bitter and shocking statement "You are of your father the devil, and your will is to do your father's desires" (8:44). This anti-Jewish theme has nothing to do with anti-Semitism or a general prejudice against Jews, although, sadly, it has been used to support the persecution of the Jews. It is, rather, the direct result of

---

107. Culpepper, *Anatomy of the Fourth Gospel*, 97. The final two pericopes of the main discourse section (12:37–50), before Jesus turns to teaching the disciples in private, focus on the importance of belief and unbelief.

108. High occurrence of this vocabulary is also true of the Johannine Epistles (verb 11x; noun 7x).

109. See Painter, *John*.

110. See Lincoln, *Truth on Trial*.

the Jewish rejection of Jesus, and thus it is closely related to the major theme of belief and unbelief, which is of such great importance in John. The importance of this anti-Jewish theme in the Fourth Gospel causes many Johannine scholars to conclude that its main purpose is to react to the Jewish unbelief and hostility (see, e.g., 5:17–18; 6:41–42; 8:37, 40) manifested toward the end of the century in the Evangelist's time, when Jewish Christians were excluded from the synagogues (see 9:22; 12:42; 16:2).[111] From this point of view, John's Gospel is a polemic for the truth of Christ and the gospel against the denials of the Jews.

- *Realized eschatology.* John's retelling of the story of Jesus, as we have seen, intends to draw out the significance of Jesus for the present church. The imminence of Christ's parousia has receded and gives way to an emphasis on the realized dimensions of eschatology—that is, what Christ offers to the believer today. Already, eschatological existence is available to the one who believes: "Truly, truly, I say to you, he who hears my word and believes him who sent me, has eternal life; he does not come into judgment, but has passed from death to life" (5:24). To be noted are the verb tenses of this sentence; John emphasizes the present possession of eternal life (3:36; 5:24). Not only have the blessings of the future entered the present, but so too has judgment (3:19; cf. 12:31). Note the intriguing formula "the hour is coming, and now is" (4:23; 5:25; 16:32). It should not be surprising, then, that in John there is no proper eschatological discourse devoted to the future, analogous to that of the Synoptics. There is, nevertheless, teaching about the future. A future resurrection of the righteous and the wicked is clearly taught in 5:28–29 ("the hour is coming"; note the omission of the second member of the formula, "and now is"), and there are a few other allusions to the future (e.g., 13:36; 14:3, 27; 16:2, 16, 22–26; 17:24; 21:22–23). The Evangelist's emphasis, however, clearly is on the realized dimensions of eschatology and on the richness of what is currently available to the believer.

Use of the Old Testament

John makes frequent use of the OT: there are some fifteen to twenty quotations and many more allusions. Like the Synoptic writers, he regards the story of Jesus as the fulfillment of the OT promises. The texts thus have a clearly christological focus. Jesus accordingly says, "You search the scriptures, because you think that in them you have eternal life; and it is they that bear witness to me" (5:39). Many of the quotations are freely adapted or quite short, so that

---

111. See Martyn, *History and Theology in the Fourth Gospel.* On the subject generally, see Barrett, *The Gospel of John and Judaism.*

sometimes it remains uncertain exactly which texts are being quoted. The OT texts used by the Evangelist often are the same as those used by other NT writers and, likewise, they usually are based on the LXX, although occasionally the Evangelist seems to show a knowledge of Hebrew. The quotations occur in the narrative portions of the Gospel, never in the discourse material. Formula quotations (employing the phrase "it is written" [*estin gegrammenon*]) are found in 2:17; 6:31; 6:45; 10:34; 12:14. Fulfillment quotations (employing the phrase "that it might be fulfilled" [*hina plērōthē*]) are found in 12:38–40; 13:18; 15:25; 19:24; 19:36–37.[112]

The Sources of the Fourth Gospel

John certainly knew the Synoptics, but as we have seen, it is debatable whether he actually made use of any of them. Even less clear is what use, if any, the Evangelist may have made of other sources, whether written or oral. With what is now widely regarded as an unjustifiable confidence, Rudolf Bultmann argued that underlying the first twelve chapters of the Fourth Gospel was a "signs source," and underlying chapters 13–17 was a "revelatory discourse source." He found strong gnostic tendencies in this Gospel that he regarded as derived from gnostic traditions concerning the speeches of a heavenly revealer contained in Mandaean texts much later than John. Most scholars now agree that similarities may have been due to dependence on John's Gospel rather than vice versa. Apart from the posited gnostic influence, Robert Fortna argued for an original signs Gospel,[113] ending with 20:30–31, as the immediate predecessor of the Fourth Gospel. Somewhat more convincingly, C. H. Dodd believed that John's Gospel was dependent on precanonical oral tradition, "whether directly or through the medium of written memoranda."[114] If in fact the Evangelist made use of sources, he has fully integrated them into his Gospel. What makes the question practically unsolvable is that the Johannine idiom is consistent throughout the Gospel.[115]

The Background of the Fourth Gospel

In the first half of the twentieth century, most scholars concluded that the basic background of the Fourth Gospel was to be found in Hellenistic thought. The Gospel's *logos* christology and its dualisms, together with Bultmann's arguments

---

112. For full discussion, see Menken, *Old Testament Quotations in the Fourth Gospel*.

113. Fortna, *The Gospel of Signs*.

114. Dodd, *Historical Tradition in the Fourth Gospel*, 424.

115. For a valuable appraisal of the question, see Carson, "Current Source Criticism of the Fourth Gospel."

concerning the parallel gnostic ideas in the Mandaean and Hermetic literature, seemed to point in this direction. The Jewish aspects of the Fourth Gospel were well known, but its Jewish background was not seen as being able to explain many of its unique characteristics. The discovery of the Dead Sea Scrolls, beginning in 1947, changed everything, for here was first-century evidence of a Judaism on Palestinian soil that was similar to John's, at least in a number of important ways. In particular, the dualism so typical of John, especially the light/darkness and the truth/falsehood motifs, was reflected in the language of the Qumran scrolls.[116] Now this Gospel could be explained as a thoroughly Jewish work, with a Palestinian background. There was no need to appeal to gnostic or other Hellenistic literature to explain John; indeed, it was seen that the Jewish wisdom literature provided more convincing parallels. The work of J. Louis Martyn showed how well the Gospel fit into a late first-century Jewish setting.[117]

The Date of the Fourth Gospel

The highly developed theological understanding of Jesus in the Fourth Gospel has always inclined scholars automatically to a late date. There have been exceptions, of course, notably J. A. T. Robinson, who dates the Gospel to before 70. In the nineteenth century F. C. Baur dated it to about 160, and many others were inclined to a mid-second-century date. It was the dramatic discovery, published in 1935, of an early papyrus fragment of the Fourth Gospel that made such a late dating impossible. This fragment ($\mathfrak{P}^{52}$), discovered in Egypt, has writing on both sides (hence it is from a papyrus codex rather than a scroll), contains only the text of John 18:31–33 and 37–38, and has been dated between 100 and 150. It remains the earliest known extant fragment of the NT.[118] Largely as a result of this discovery, allowing a few decades for the Gospel to establish itself and make its way to Egypt from Ephesus in Asia Minor, the majority of scholars currently date John's Gospel to about the turn of the century.

What is in view here is the dating of John's Gospel as we now have it. If the Gospel was produced in several stages, the bulk of it may well go back to an earlier date. Although Raymond Brown's hypothesis concerning the history

116. This does not mean that John is necessarily dependent on the Qumran documents, but only that it points to a similar thought milieu. See Charlesworth, "The Dead Sea Scrolls and the Gospel according to John." The appreciation of the Jewish background of John has been aided by the influential work of Hengel, *Judaism and Hellenism*, which demolished the firm distinction between Hellenistic and Jewish thought.

117. Martyn, *History and Theology in the Fourth Gospel*. Martyn related the putting of Christians out of the synagogue (*aposynagōgos* [9:22; 12:42; 16:2]) to the liturgical addition to the Eighteen Benedictions, toward the end of the first century. See also Robinson, "The New Look on the Fourth Gospel," 98–100.

118. On display in the John Rylands University of Manchester Library (P. Ryl. Gr. 457), thus sometimes known as the Rylands Fragment.

of the Johannine community and the stages of the production of the Gospel is highly speculative,[119] it does point to the probability of multiple editions of the Gospel. Evidence that we have earlier examined points to an earlier edition of the Gospel, ending with chapter 20, which may to a large extent be the work of the Beloved Disciple himself. To this edition a disciple of the Johannine school may have added chapter 21, and possibly some further redacting, eventually producing our form of the Fourth Gospel. A plausible date, and widely held, for the final form of the Gospel is in the mid-to-late 90s, just at the end of the first century.

The Fourth Gospel in the Church

Evidence for the use of the Gospel of John through most of the second century has been regarded as surprisingly sparse. It has been thought that this was the result of how quickly gnostic Christians seized on this Gospel as promoting their view of a supernatural, docetic Christ, one who only appeared to be human. John is quoted and used extensively by the Valentinian Gnostics in Rome, and in the second-century gnostic *Gospel of Truth* in Egypt. The first commentary on John that we know of was by the gnostic Christian Heracleon (ca. 170). All of this caused C. K. Barrett to conclude, "It was only Irenaeus, who discovered how to use the Gospel in an anti-gnostic sense and thus to turn the Gnostics' weapon against them, who really established its position among the orthodox."[120] Now, however, this standard paradigm of "orthodox Johannophobia" and "gnostic Johannophilia" has been challenged and corrected by Charles Hill.[121] He shows that John was valued by the orthodox church right through the second century, and, on the contrary, that the gnostics had no predilection for the Fourth Gospel, and that the Gospel's roots clearly are not to be found in gnostic soil. As Irenaeus stressed, the Gospel of John is strongly anti-docetic.

Irenaeus was the first to make a case for the apostolic authorship of the Johannine writings. According to him, "John the disciple of the Lord published a gospel in Ephesus" (*Haer.* 3.1.1 = Eusebius, *Hist. eccl.* 5.8.4).[122] Irenaeus makes no reference to John the Elder in this connection. Hill shows that the

---

119. As Raymond Brown himself says, a "perhaps" needs to be added to every sentence (*An Introduction to the New Testament*, 174). He argues for no less than five stages in the history of the community, which need not be reviewed here. As for the production of the Gospel, he locates its first edition, from a disciple of the Beloved Disciple, in the 90s, after some decades of the formation of the community's thought, then a later, redacted edition, our Gospel, in 100–110. See R. Brown, *The Community of the Beloved Disciple*.

120. Barrett, *Essays on John*, 121.

121. See Hill, *The Johannine Corpus in the Early Church*.

122. Another orthodox writer of about the same time who identified the Evangelist as the Apostle John was Theophilus of Antioch. Growing use in orthodox circles was eventually aided

Fourth Gospel was held in high regard from virtually the beginning. It was not long before this Gospel gained the highest respect among the Gospels, accepted now as deriving from the Apostle who was closest to Jesus.

The "Johannine Literature"

In Irenaeus's view, the Apostle John, the Beloved Disciple, the Elder, and the seer were the same person. He thus concluded that John wrote the Gospel and the Epistles (of which he may have known only the first two) in Ephesus and the Apocalypse on the island of Patmos. This conclusion that all these writings stemmed from the same Apostle became the accepted tradition that dominated in the church until the coming of modern criticism. It is thus mainly to Irenaeus that we owe the designation of these five NT books, representing three very different literary genres, as the "Johannine Literature."

Nowadays, as we will see, few would regard the Apocalypse as written by the same author as the Gospel. And there are some, though not many, who would argue that the Epistles are also by another author. One reason that John is unique in the NT is that it is the only Gospel that has an epistle or epistles related to it. What this means is that the one may be of help in the interpretation of the other. Indeed, the specific details afforded by the letters may help to determine the life setting of the Gospel.

Johannine Christianity represents one of the main and most distinctive strains of theology in the NT. At the same time, it bears interesting similarities to other strains, such as the Pauline and that of the book of Hebrews. But its unique richness is not to be denied; it is to be treasured. The Fourth Gospel stands unchallenged as a final, definitive Gospel, presenting to the church the full truth of Jesus as it can now be known through the retelling of history, through the inspired, retrospective interpretation of apostolic tradition.

Bibliography

Books and Articles

Anderson, Paul N. *The Christology of the Fourth Gospel: Its Unity and Disunity in the Light of John 6*. 3rd ed. Eugene, OR: Cascade, 2009.

———. *The Fourth Gospel and the Quest for Jesus: Modern Foundations Reconsidered*. LNTS 321. London: T&T Clark, 2006.

———. *The Riddles of the Fourth Gospel: An Introduction to John*. Minneapolis: Fortress, 2011.

Anderson, Paul N., Felix Just, and Tom Thatcher, eds. *Aspects of Historicity in the Fourth Gospel*. Vol. 2 of *John, Jesus, and History*. SBLSymS 44. Atlanta: Society of Biblical Literature, 2009.

by the Quartodeciman controversy (that Easter was to be celebrated on the same day each year, 14 Nisan [Passover], in keeping with John's dating of the crucifixion).

———, eds. *Critical Appraisals of Critical Views*. Vol. 1 of *John, Jesus, and History*. SBLSymS 44. Atlanta: Society of Biblical Literature, 2007.

———, eds. *Glimpses of Jesus through the Johannine Lens*. Vol. 3 of *John, Jesus, and History*. SBLSym 44. Atlanta: Society of Biblical Literature, forthcoming.

Appold, Mark L. *The Oneness Motif in the Fourth Gospel: Motif Analysis and Exegetical Probe into the Theology of John*. WUNT 2/1. Tübingen: Mohr Siebeck, 1976.

Ashton, John, ed. *The Interpretation of John*. 2nd ed. SNTI. Edinburgh: T&T Clark, 1997.

———. *Studying John: Approaches to the Fourth Gospel*. Oxford: Clarendon, 1994.

———. *Understanding the Fourth Gospel*. Rev. ed. New York: Oxford University Press, 2007.

Bailey, John A. *The Traditions Common to the Gospels of Luke and John*. NovTSup 7. Leiden: Brill, 1963.

Ball, David Mark. *"I Am" in John's Gospel: Literary Function, Background and Theological Implications*. JSNTSup 124. Sheffield: Sheffield Academic Press, 1996.

Barrett, C. K. *Essays on John*. Philadelphia: Westminster, 1982.

———. *The Gospel of John and Judaism*. Translated by D. M. Smith. Philadelphia: Fortress, 1975.

———. "Johannine Christianity." In *Jesus and the Word and Other Essays*, 93–118. Edinburgh: T&T Clark, 1995.

———. "John and the Synoptic Gospels." *ExpTim* 85 (1973–74): 228–33.

———. "The Place of John and the Synoptics within the Early History of Christian Tradition." In *Jesus and the Word and Other Essays*, 119–34. Edinburgh: T&T Clark, 1995.

Bauckham, Richard J. "The Beloved Disciple as Ideal Author." *JSNT* 49 (1993): 21–44.

———. "The Fourth Gospel as the Testimony of the Beloved Disciple." In *The Gospel of John and Christian Theology*, edited by Richard Bauckham and Carl Mosser, 120–39. Grand Rapids: Eerdmans, 2007.

———. *Jesus and the Eyewitnesses: The Gospels as Eyewitness Testimony*. Grand Rapids: Eerdmans, 2006.

———. *Jesus and the God of Israel: God Crucified and Other Studies on the New Testament's Christology of Divine Identity*. Grand Rapids: Eerdmans, 2008.

———. "John for Readers of Mark." In *The Gospels for All Christians: Rethinking the Gospel Audiences*, edited by Richard Bauckham, 147–72. Grand Rapids: Eerdmans, 1998.

———. "Monotheism and Christology in the Gospel of John." In *Contours of Christology in the New Testament*, edited by Richard N. Longenecker, 148–68. Grand Rapids: Eerdmans, 2005.

———. "The 153 Fish and the Unity of the Fourth Gospel." *Neot* 36 (2002): 77–88.

———. *The Testimony of the Beloved Disciple: Narrative, History, and Theology in the Gospel of John*. Grand Rapids: Baker Academic, 2007.

Bauckham, Richard J., and Carl Mosser, eds. *The Gospel of John and Christian Theology*. Grand Rapids: Eerdmans, 2007.

Baum, Armin D. "The Original Epilogue (John 20:30–31), the Secondary Appendix (21:1–23), and the Editorial Epilogues (21:24–25) of John's Gospel: Observations against the Background of Ancient Literary Conventions." In *Earliest Christianity: History, Literature, and Theology. Essays from the Tyndale Fellowship in Honor of Martin Hengel*, edited by Michael F. Bird and Jason Maston, 227–70. WUNT 2/320. Tübingen: Mohr Siebeck, 2012.

Beasley-Murray, George R. *Gospel of Life: Theology in the Fourth Gospel*. Peabody, MA: Hendrickson, 1996.

———. *John*. WBT. Dallas: Word, 1989.

Beirne, Margaret M. *Women and Men in the Fourth Gospel: A Genuine Discipleship of Equals*. JSNTSup 242. Sheffield: Sheffield Academic Press, 2003.

Bieringer, Reimund, Didier Pollefeyt, and Frederique Vandecasteele-Vanneuville, eds. *Anti-Judaism and the Fourth Gospel*. Louisville: Westminster John Knox, 2001.

Blaine, Bradford B., Jr. *Peter in the Gospel of John: The Making of an Authentic Disciple*. SBLAB 27. Atlanta: Society of Biblical Literature, 2007.

Blomberg, Craig L. *The Historical Reliability of John's Gospel*. Downers Grove, IL: InterVarsity, 2002.

Bockmuehl, Markus, and Donald A. Hagner, eds. *The Written Gospel*. Cambridge: Cambridge University Press, 2005.

Boers, Hendrikus. *Neither on This Mountain nor in Jerusalem: A Study of John 4*. SBLMS 35. Atlanta: Scholars Press, 1988.

Boismard, Marie-Émile. *Moses or Jesus: An Essay in Johannine Christology*. Translated by Benedict T. Viviano. Minneapolis: Fortress, 1993.

Borgen, Peder. *Bread from Heaven: An Exegetical Study of the Concept of Manna in the Gospel of John and the Writings of Philo*. NovTSup 10. Leiden: Brill, 1965.

Brant, Jo-Ann A. *Dialogue and Drama: Elements of Greek Tragedy in the Fourth Gospel*. Peabody, MA: Hendrickson, 2004.

Brodie, Thomas L. *The Quest for the Origin of John's Gospel: A Source-Oriented Approach*. New York: Oxford University Press, 1993.

Brooke, George J. "Christ and the Law in John 7–10." In *Law and Religion: Essays on the Place of the Law in Israel and Early Christianity*, edited by Barnabas Lindars, 34–43. London: SPCK, 1988.

Brouwer, Wayne. *The Literary Development of John 13–17: A Chiastic Reading*. SBLDS 182. Atlanta: Scholars Press, 2000.

Brown, Raymond E. *The Community of the Beloved Disciple: The Life, Loves, and Hates of an Individual Church in New Testament Times*. New York: Paulist Press, 1979.

———. *An Introduction to the Gospel of John*. Edited by Francis J. Moloney. New York: Doubleday, 2003.

———. *An Introduction to the New Testament*. New York: Doubleday, 1997.

———. "The Problem of Historicity in John." *CBQ* 24 (1962): 1–14. Reprinted in idem, *New Testament Essays*, 143–67. Milwaukee: Bruce, 1965.

Brown, Tricia Gates. *The Spirit in the Writings of John: Johannine Pneumatology in Social-Scientific Perspective*. JSNTSup 253. Sheffield: Sheffield Academic Press, 2004.

Brunson, Andrew C. *Psalm 118 in the Gospel of John: An Intertextual Study on the New Exodus Pattern in the Theology of John*. WUNT 2/158. Tübingen: Mohr Siebeck, 2003.

Burge, Gary M. *The Anointed Community: The Holy Spirit in the Johannine Tradition*. Grand Rapids: Eerdmans, 1987.

———. *Interpreting the Gospel of John*. Grand Rapids: Baker Academic, 1992.

Burkett, Delbert. *The Son of Man in the Gospel of John*. JSNTSup 56. Sheffield: JSOT Press, 1991.

Byrne, Brendan. *Lazarus: A Contemporary Reading of John 11:1–46*. ZS. Collegeville, MN: Liturgical Press, 1991.

Callahan, Allen Dwight. *A Love Supreme: A History of the Johannine Tradition*. Minneapolis: Fortress, 2005.

Campbell, Joan Cecelia. *Kinship Relations in the Gospel of John*. CBQMS 42. Washington, DC: Catholic Biblical Association of America, 2007.

Carson, D. A. "Current Source Criticism of the Fourth Gospel: Some Methodological Questions." *JBL* 97 (1978): 411–29.

———. "Historical Tradition in the Fourth Gospel: After Dodd, What?" In *Studies of History and Tradition in the Four Gospels*, edited by R. T. France and David Wenham, 83–145. GP 2. Sheffield: JSOT Press, 1981.

———. "John and the Johannine Epistles." In *It Is Written: Scripture Citing Scripture; Essays in Honour of Barnabas Lindars*, edited by D. A. Carson and H. G. M. Williamson, 246–64. Cambridge: Cambridge University Press, 1988.

———. "The Purpose of the Fourth Gospel: John 20:30–31 Reconsidered." *JBL* 108 (1987): 639–51.

———. "Syntactical and Text-Critical Observations on John 20:30–31: One More Round on the Purpose of the Fourth Gospel." *JBL* 124 (2005): 693–714.

———. "Understanding Misunderstandings in the Fourth Gospel." *TynBul* 33 (1982): 59–89.

Carter, Warren. *John: Storyteller, Interpreter, Evangelist*. Peabody, MA: Hendrickson, 2006.

Casey, Maurice. *Is John's Gospel True?* New York: Routledge, 1996.

Cassidy, Richard J. *John's Gospel in New Perspective: Christology and the Realities of Roman Power*. Maryknoll, NY: Orbis, 1992.

Charlesworth, James H. *The Beloved Disciple: Whose Witness Validates the Gospel of John?* Valley Forge, PA: Trinity Press International, 1995.

———. "The Dead Sea Scrolls and the Gospel according to John." In *Exploring the Gospel of John: In Honor of D. Moody Smith*, edited by R. A. Culpepper and C. Clifton Black, 65–97. Louisville: Westminster John Knox, 1996.

———, ed. *John and the Dead Sea Scrolls*. New York: Crossroad, 1991.

Chennattu, Rekha M. *Johannine Discipleship as a Covenant Relationship*. Peabody, MA: Hendrickson, 2006.

Cho, Sukmin. *Jesus as Prophet in the Fourth Gospel*. NTMon 15. Sheffield: Sheffield Phoenix Press, 2006.

Clark-Soles, Jaime. *Scripture Cannot Be Broken: The Social Function of the Use of Scripture in the Fourth Gospel*. Leiden: Brill, 2002.

Collins, Raymond F. *These Things Have Been Written: Studies on the Fourth Gospel*. LTPM 2. Louvain: Peeters, 1990.

Coloe, Mary L. *Dwelling in the Household of God: Johannine Ecclesiology and Spirituality*. Collegeville, MN: Liturgical Press, 2007.

———. *God Dwells with Us: Temple Symbolism in the Fourth Gospel*. Collegeville, MN: Liturgical Press, 2001.

Conway, Colleen M. *Men and Women in the Fourth Gospel: Gender and Johannine Characterization*. SBLDS 167. Atlanta: Society of Biblical Literature, 1999.

———. "The Production of the Johannine Community: A New Historicist Perspective." *JBL* 121 (2002): 479–95.

Cross, F. L., ed. *Studies in the Fourth Gospel*. London: Mowbray, 1957.

Cullmann, Oscar. *The Johannine Circle: Its Place in Judaism, among the Disciples of Jesus and in Early Christianity; A Study in the Origin of the Gospel of John*. Translated by John Bowden. Philadelphia: Westminster, 1976.

Culpepper, R. Alan. *Anatomy of the Fourth Gospel: A Study in Literary Design*. Minneapolis: Fortress, 1983.

———. *The Johannine School: An Evaluation of the Johannine-School Hypothesis Based on an Investigation of the Nature of Ancient Schools*. SBLDS 26. Missoula, MT: Scholars Press, 1975.

———. *John, the Son of Zebedee: The Life of a Legend*. SPNT. Columbia: University of South Carolina Press, 1994.

Culpepper, R. Alan, and C. Clifton Black, eds. *Exploring the Gospel of John: In Honor of D. Moody Smith*. Louisville: Westminster John Knox, 1996.

Davies, W. D. "Reflections on Aspects of the Jewish Background of the Gospel of John." In *Exploring the Gospel of John: In Honor of D. Moody Smith*, edited by R. Alan Culpepper and C. Clifton Black, 43–64. Louisville: Westminster John Knox, 1996.

de Jonge, Marinus. "The Beloved Disciple and the Date of the Gospel of John." In *Text and Interpretation: Studies in the New Testament Presented to Matthew Black*, edited by Ernest Best and R. McL. Wilson, 99–114. Cambridge: Cambridge University Press, 1979.

———, ed. *L'Évangile de Jean: Sources, rédaction, théologie*. BETL 44. Leuven: Leuven University Press, 1977.

Denaux, Adelbert, ed. *John and the Synoptics*. BETL 101. Leuven: University of Leuven Press, 1992.

Dennis, John A. *Jesus' Death and the Gathering of True Israel: The Johannine Appropriation of Restoration Theology in the Light of John 11:47–52*. WUNT 2/217. Tübingen: Mohr Siebeck, 2006.

Diel, Paul, and Jeannine Solotareff. *Symbolism in the Gospel of John*. Translated by Nelly Marans. San Francisco: Harper & Row, 1988.

Dodd, C. H. *Historical Tradition in the Fourth Gospel*. Cambridge: Cambridge University Press, 1963.

———. *The Interpretation of the Fourth Gospel*. Cambridge: Cambridge University Press, 1953.

Dube, Musa W., and Jeffrey L. Staley. *John and Postcolonialism: Travel, Space, and Power*. BP 7. Sheffield: Sheffield Academic Press, 2002.

Duke, Paul D. *Irony in the Fourth Gospel*. Atlanta: John Knox, 1985.

Dumm, Demetrius R. *A Mystical Portrait of Jesus: New Perspectives on John's Gospel*. Collegeville, MN: Liturgical Press, 2001.

Dungan, David L., ed. *The Interrelations of the Gospels: A Symposium Led by M.-É. Boismard, W. R. Farmer, and F. Neirynck*. BETL 95. Leuven: Leuven University Press, 1990.

Dunn, James D. G. "John and the Oral Gospel Tradition." In *Jesus and the Oral Gospel Tradition*, edited by Henry Wansbrough, 351–79. JSNTSup 64. Sheffield: JSOT Press, 1991.

———. "John and the Synoptics as a Theological Question." In *Exploring the Gospel of John: In Honor of D. Moody Smith*, edited by R. Alan Culpepper and C. Clifton Black, 301–13. Louisville: Westminster John Knox, 1996.

———. "Let John Be John—A Gospel for Its Time." In *Das Evangelium und die Evangelien*, edited by Peter Stuhlmacher, 309–39. WUNT 28. Tübingen: Mohr Siebeck, 1983. Reprinted in *The Gospel and the Gospels*, edited by Peter Stuhlmacher, 293–322. Grand Rapids: Eerdmans, 1991.

Ehrman, Bart D. "Jesus and the Adulteress." *NTS* 34 (1988): 24–44.

Ellens, J. H. *The Son of Man in the Gospel of John*. NTM 28. Sheffield: Sheffield Phoenix, 2010.

Ellis, E. Earle. *The World of St. John: The Gospel and the Epistles*. Grand Rapids: Eerdmans, 1984.

Emerton, John. "The Hundred and Fifty-Three Fishes in John xxi.11." *JTS* 9 (1958): 86–89.

Ensor, Peter W. *Jesus and His "Works": The Johannine Sayings in Historical Perspective*. WUNT 2/85. Tübingen: Mohr Siebeck, 1996.

———. "The Johannine Sayings of Jesus and the Question of Authenticity." In *Challenging Perspectives on the Gospel of John*, edited by John Lierman, 14–33. WUNT 2/219. Tübingen: Mohr Siebeck, 2006.

Esler, Philip F., and Ronald A. Piper. *Lazarus, Mary, and Martha: Social-Scientific Approaches to the Gospel of John*. Minneapolis: Fortress, 2006.

Evans, C. Stephen. "The Historical Reliability of John's Gospel: From What Perspective Should It Be Assessed?" In *The Gospel of John and Christian Theology*, edited by Richard Bauckham and Carl Mosser, 91–119. Grand Rapids: Eerdmans, 2007.

Fee, Gordon D. "On the Text and Meaning of John 20:30–31." In *The Four Gospels, 1992: Festschrift Frans Neirynck*, edited by Frans van Segbroeck, C. M. Tuckett, G. Van Belle, and J. Verheyden, 3:2193–205. 3 vols. BETL 100. Leuven: Leuven University Press, 1992.

———. "The Use of the Definite Article with Personal Names in the Gospel of John." *NTS* 17 (1970–71): 168–83.

Ferguson, Everett. "Canon Muratori: Date and Provenance." *StPatr* 17.2 (1982): 677–83.

Forestell, J. Terence. *The Word of the Cross: Salvation as Revelation in the Fourth Gospel*. AnBib 57. Rome: Pontifical Biblical Institute, 1974.

Fortna, Robert T. *The Fourth Gospel and Its Predecessor: From Narrative Source to Present Gospel*. Philadelphia: Fortress, 1988.

———. *The Gospel of Signs: A Reconstruction of the Narrative Source Underlying the Fourth Gospel*. SNTSMS 11. Cambridge: Cambridge University Press, 1970.

Fortna, Robert T., and Tom Thatcher, eds. *Jesus in Johannine Tradition*. Louisville: Westminster John Knox, 2001.

Franck, Eskil. *Revelation Taught: The Paraclete in the Gospel of John*. ConBNT 14. Lund: Gleerup, 1985.

Frey, Jörg, Jan G. van der Watt, and Ruben Zimmerman, eds. *Imagery in the Gospel of John: Terms, Forms, Themes, and Theology of Johannine Figurative Language*. WUNT 200. Tübingen: Mohr Siebeck, 2006.

Fuglseth, Kåre Sigvald. *Johannine Sectarianism in Perspective: A Sociological, Historical, and Comparative Analysis of the Temple and Social Relationships in the Gospel of John, Philo, and Qumran*. NovTSup 119. Leiden: Brill, 2005.

Gardner-Smith, Percival. *Saint John and the Synoptics*. Cambridge: Cambridge University Press, 1938.

Gench, Frances Taylor. *Encounters with Jesus: Studies in the Gospel of John*. Louisville: Westminster John Knox, 2007.

Glasswell, M. E. "The Relationship between John and Mark." *JSNT* 23 (1983): 99–115.

Grant, Robert M. *Second-Century Christianity: A Collection of Fragments*. London: SPCK, 1946.

Gregory, Andrew. "The Third Gospel? The Relationship of John and Luke Reconsidered." In *Challenging Perspectives on the Gospel of John*, edited by John Lierman, 109–34. WUNT 2/219. Tübingen: Mohr Siebeck, 2006.

Gundry, Robert H. *Jesus the Word according to John the Sectarian: A Paleofundamentalist Manifesto for Contemporary Evangelicalism, Especially Its Elites, in North America*. Grand Rapids: Eerdmans, 2001.

Hägerland, Tobias. "John's Gospel: A Two-Level Drama?" *JSNT* 25 (2003): 309–22.

Hagner, Donald A. "Jesus' Self-Understanding." In *Encyclopedia of the Historical Jesus*, edited by Craig A. Evans, 324–33. New York: Routledge, 2008.

Harner, Philip B. *The "I Am" of the Fourth Gospel: A Study in Johannine Usage and Thought*. Philadelphia: Fortress, 1970.

Harrington, Daniel J. *John's Thought and Theology: An Introduction*. GNS 33. Wilmington, DE: Michael Glazier, 1990.

Harris, Murray J. *Jesus as God: The New Testament Use of* Theos *in Reference to Jesus*. Grand Rapids: Baker Academic, 1992.

Harrison, Everett F. "A Study of John 1:14." In *Unity and Diversity in New Testament Theology: Essays in Honor of George E. Ladd*, edited by Robert A. Guelich, 23–36. Grand Rapids: Eerdmans, 1978.

Harstine, Stan. *Moses as a Character in the Fourth Gospel: A Study of Ancient Reading Techniques*. JSNTSup 229. Sheffield: Sheffield Academic Press, 2002.

Harvey, A. E. *Jesus on Trial: A Study in the Fourth Gospel*. London: SPCK, 1976.

Headlam, A. C. *The Fourth Gospel as History*. Oxford: Blackwell, 1948.

Hengel, Martin. *The Four Gospels and the One Gospel of Jesus Christ: An Investigation of the Collection and Origin of the Canonical Gospels*. Harrisburg, PA: Trinity Press International, 2000.

———. *The Johannine Question*. Translated by John Bowden. Philadelphia: Trinity Press International, 1989.

———. *Judaism and Hellenism: Studies in Their Encounter in Palestine during the Hellenistic Period*. Translated by John Bowden. 2 vols. Philadelphia: Fortress, 1974.

———. "The Prologue of the Gospel of John as the Gateway to Christological Truth." In *The Gospel of John and Christian Theology*, edited by Richard Bauckham and Carl Mosser, 265–94. Grand Rapids: Eerdmans, 2007.

Higgins, A. J. B. *The Historicity of the Fourth Gospel*. London: Lutterworth, 1960.

Hill, Charles E. *The Johannine Corpus in the Early Church*. Oxford: Oxford University Press, 2004.

Hooker, Morna D. "The Johannine Prologue and the Messianic Secret." *NTS* 21 (1974–75): 40–58.

Hoskins, Paul M. *Jesus as the Fulfillment of the Temple in the Gospel of John*. PBM. Milton Keynes, UK: Paternoster, 2006.

Howard-Brook, Wes. *Becoming Children of God: John's Gospel and Radical Discipleship*. Maryknoll, NY: Orbis, 1998.

————. *John's Gospel and the Renewal of the Church*. Maryknoll, NY: Orbis, 2000.

Hunter, A. M. *According to John: The New Look at the Fourth Gospel*. London: SPCK, 1968.

Ihenacho, David Asonye. *The Community of Eternal Life: The Study of the Meaning of Life for the Johannine Community*. Lanham, MD: University Press of America, 2001.

Jackson, Howard M. "Ancient Self-Referential Conventions and Their Implications for the Authorship and Integrity of the Gospel of John." *JTS* 50 (1999): 1–34.

Jervell, Jacob. *Jesus in the Gospel of John*. Translated by Harry T. Cleven. Minneapolis: Augsburg, 1984.

Johnston, George. *The Spirit-Paraclete in the Gospel of John*. SNTSMS 12. Cambridge: Cambridge University Press, 1970.

Käsemann, Ernst. *The Testament of Jesus: A Study of the Gospel of John in the Light of Chapter 17*. Translated by Gerhard Krodel. Philadelphia: Fortress, 1968.

Kealy, Sean P. *John's Gospel and the History of Biblical Interpretation*. 2 vols. Lewiston, NY: Mellen, 2002.

Keefer, Kyle. *The Branches of the Gospel of John: The Reception of the Fourth Gospel in the Early Church*. LNTS 332. London: T&T Clark, 2006.

Kellum, L. Scott. *The Unity of the Farewell Discourse: The Literary Integrity of John 13.31–16.33*. JSNTSup 256. London: T&T Clark, 2004.

Kelly, Anthony J., and Francis J. Moloney. *Experiencing God in the Gospel of John*. Mahwah, NJ: Paulist Press, 2003.

Kenney, Garrett C. *Leadership in John: An Analysis of the Situation and Strategy of the Gospel and the Epistles of John*. Lanham, MD: University Press of America, 2000.

Kerr, Alan R. *The Temple of Jesus' Body: The Temple Theme in the Gospel of John*. JSNTSup 220. Sheffield: Sheffield Academic Press, 2002.

Kinlaw, Pamela E. *The Christ Is Jesus: Metamorphosis, Possession, and Johannine Christology*. SBLAB 18. Atlanta: Society of Biblical Literature, 2005.

Koester, Craig R. *Symbolism in the Fourth Gospel: Meaning, Mystery, Community*. 2nd ed. Minneapolis: Fortress, 2003.

————. *The Word of Life: A Theology of John's Gospel*. Grand Rapids: Eerdmans, 2008.

Köstenberger, Andreas J. *Encountering John: The Gospel in Its Historical, Literary, and Theological Perspective*. Grand Rapids: Baker Academic, 1999.

————. "'I Suppose' [*oimai*]: The Conclusion of John's Gospel in Its Literary and Historical Context." In *The New Testament in Its First Century Setting: Essays on Context and Background in Honour of B. W. Winter on His 65th Birthday*, edited by P. J. Williams, Andrew D. Clarke, Peter M. Head, and David Instone-Brewer, 72–88. Grand Rapids: Eerdmans, 2004.

————. "John's Transposition Theology: Retelling the Story of Jesus in a Different Key." In *Earliest Christianity: History, Literature, and Theology; Essays from the Tyndale Fellowship in Honor of Martin Hengel*, edited by Michael F. Bird and Jason Maston, 191–226. WUNT 2/320. Tübingen: Mohr Siebeck, 2012.

————. *The Missions of Jesus and His Disciples according to the Fourth Gospel*. Grand Rapids: Eerdmans, 1998.

————. *Studies on John and Gender: A Decade of Scholarship*. SBL 38. New York: Peter Lang, 2001.

————. *A Theology of John's Gospel and Letters*. BTNT. Grand Rapids: Zondervan, 2009.

Köstenberger, Andreas J., and Scott R. Swain. *Father, Son and Spirit: The Trinity and John's Gospel*. NSBT 24. Downers Grove, IL: InterVarsity, 2008.

Kreitzer, Larry J., and Deborah W. Rooke, eds. *Ciphers in the Sand: Interpretations of the Woman Taken in Adultery (John 7:53–8:11)*. BibSem 74. Sheffield: Sheffield Academic Press, 2000.

Kysar, Robert. *The Fourth Evangelist and His Gospel: An Examination of Contemporary Scholarship*. Minneapolis: Augsburg, 1975.

————. *John, the Maverick Gospel*. 3rd ed. Louisville: Westminster John Knox, 2007.

———. *Voyages with John: Charting the Fourth Gospel*. Waco: Baylor University Press, 2005.

Lee, Dorothy A. *Symbolic Narratives of the Fourth Gospel: The Interplay of Form and Meaning*. JSNTSup 95. Sheffield: JSOT Press, 1994.

Léon-Dufour, Xavier. "Towards a Symbolic Reading of the Fourth Gospel." *NTS* 27 (1980–81): 439–56.

Levine, Amy-Jill, ed. *A Feminist Companion to John*. 2 vols. FCNTECW 4, 5. Sheffield: Sheffield Academic Press, 2001.

Lierman, John, ed. *Challenging Perspectives on the Gospel of John*. WUNT 2/219. Tübingen: Mohr Siebeck, 2006.

Lincoln, Andrew T. "The Beloved Disciple as Eyewitness and the Fourth Gospel as Witness." *JSNT* 85 (2002): 3–26.

———. *Truth on Trial: The Lawsuit Motif in the Fourth Gospel*. Peabody, MA: Hendrickson, 2000.

Lindars, Barnabas. *Essays on John*. Edited by Christopher M. Tuckett. SNTA 17. Leuven: Leuven University Press, 1992.

———. *John*. NTG 4. Sheffield: JSOT Press, 1990. Reprinted in *The Johannine Literature*, by Barnabas Lindars, Ruth B. Edwards, and John M. Court, 29–108. SNTG. Sheffield: Sheffield Academic Press, 2000.

Ling, Timothy J. M. *The Judaean Poor and the Fourth Gospel*. SNTSMS 136. Cambridge: Cambridge University Press, 2006.

Lozada, Francisco, Jr., and Tom Thatcher, eds. *New Currents through John: A Global Perspective*. SBLRBS 54. Atlanta: Society of Biblical Literature, 2007.

Maccini, Robert Gordon. *Her Testimony Is True: Women as Witnesses according to John*. JSNTSup 125. Sheffield: Sheffield Academic Press, 1996.

Malina, Bruce J., and Richard L. Rohrbaugh. *Social-Science Commentary on the Gospel of John*. Minneapolis: Fortress, 2000.

Manning, Gary T., Jr. *Echoes of a Prophet: The Use of Ezekiel in the Gospel of John and in Literature of the Second Temple Period*. JSNTSup 270. London: T&T Clark, 2004.

Martyn, J. Louis. *The Gospel of John in Christian History: Essays for Interpreters*. New York: Paulist Press, 1979.

———. *History and Theology in the Fourth Gospel*. 3rd ed. Louisville: Westminster John Knox, 2000.

McGrath, James F. *John's Apologetic Christology: Legitimation and Development in Johannine Christology*. SNTSMS 111. Cambridge: Cambridge University Press, 2000.

McWhirter, Jocelyn. *The Bridegroom Messiah and the People of God: Marriage in the Fourth Gospel*. SNTSMS 138. Cambridge: Cambridge University Press, 2006.

Meeks, Wayne A. "The Man from Heaven in Johannine Sectarianism." *JBL* 91 (1972): 44–72.

———. *The Prophet-King: Moses Traditions and the Johannine Christology*. NovTSup 14. Leiden: Brill, 1967.

Menken, Maarten J. J. *Old Testament Quotations in the Fourth Gospel: Studies in Textual Form*. CBET 15. Kampen: Kok Pharos, 1996.

Mills, Watson E., comp. *The Gospel of John*. BBRNT 4. Lewiston, NY: Mellen, 1995.

Minear, Paul S. *John: The Martyr's Gospel*. New York: Pilgrim Press, 1984.

———. "The Original Functions of John 21." *JBL* 102 (1983): 85–98.

Moloney, Francis J. *Belief in the Word: Reading the Fourth Gospel, John 1–4*. Minneapolis: Fortress, 1993.

———. "The Fourth Gospel and the Jesus of History." *NTS* 46 (2000): 42–58.

———. *Glory Not Dishonor: Reading John 13–21*. Minneapolis: Augsburg Fortress, 1998.

———. *The Gospel of John: Text and Context*. BIS 72. Leiden: Brill, 2005.

———. *Signs and Shadows: Reading John 5–12*. Minneapolis: Fortress, 1996.

———. *The Theology of the Gospel of John*. NTT. Cambridge: Cambridge University Press, 1995.

————. *What Are They Saying about John?* Rev. ed. Mahwah, NJ: Paulist Press, 2006.

Morris, Leon. *Jesus Is the Christ: Studies in the Theology of John.* Grand Rapids: Eerdmans, 1989.

————. *Studies in the Fourth Gospel.* Grand Rapids: Eerdmans, 1969.

Motyer, Stephen. *Your Father the Devil? A New Approach to John and "the Jews."* PBTM. Carlisle, UK: Paternoster, 1997.

Mussner, Franz. *The Historical Jesus in the Gospel of St. John.* Translated by W. O'Hara. QD 19. Freiburg: Herder; London: Burns & Oates, 1967.

Neirynck, Frans. "John and the Synoptics." In *L'Évangile de Jean: Sources, rédaction, théologie,* edited by Marinus de Jonge, 73–106. BETL 44. Leuven: Leuven University Press, 1977.

————. "John and the Synoptics: 1975–1990." In *Evangelica III, 1992–2000: Collected Essays,* 3–64. BETL 150. Leuven: Leuven University Press, 2001.

Newheart, Michael Willett. *Word and Soul: A Psychological, Literary, and Cultural Reading of the Fourth Gospel.* Collegeville, MN: Liturgical Press, 2001.

Neyrey, Jerome H. *An Ideology of Revolt: John's Christology in Social Science Perspective,* Philadelphia: Fortress, 1988.

North, Wendy E. Sproston. *The Lazarus Story within the Johannine Tradition.* JSNTSup 212. Sheffield: Sheffield Academic Press, 2000.

Nutu, Ela. *Incarnate Word, Inscribed Flesh: John's Prologue and the Postmodern.* BMW 6. Sheffield: Sheffield Phoenix Press, 2007.

O'Day, Gail R. *Revelation in the Fourth Gospel: Narrative Mode and Theological Claim.* Philadelphia: Fortress, 1986.

O'Grady, John F. *According to John: The Witness of the Beloved Disciple.* Mahwah, NJ: Paulist Press, 2000.

Okure, Teresa. *The Johannine Approach to Mission.* WUNT 2/31. Tübingen: Mohr Siebeck, 1988.

Olsson, Birger. *Structure and Meaning of the Fourth Gospel: A Text-Linguistic Analysis of John 2:1–11 and 4:1–42.* ConBNT 6. Lund: Gleerup, 1974.

O'Rourke, John J. "Asides in the Gospel of John." *NovT* 21 (1979): 210–19.

Painter, John. "The Farewell Discourses and the History of Johannine Christianity." *NTS* 27 (1980–81): 525–43.

————. *John: Witness and Theologian.* London: SPCK, 1975.

————. *The Quest for the Messiah: The History, Literature and Theology of the Johannine Community.* 2nd ed. Edinburgh: T&T Clark, 1993.

Painter, John, R. Alan Culpepper, and Fernando F. Segovia, eds. *Word, Theology, and Community in John.* St. Louis: Chalice, 2002.

Pamment, Margaret. "The Fourth Gospel's Beloved Disciple." *ExpTim* 94 (1983): 363–67.

Parker, Pierson. "John the Son of Zebedee and the Fourth Gospel." *JBL* 81 (1962): 35–43.

Parsenios, George L. *Departure and Consolation: The Johannine Farewell Discourses in Light of Greco-Roman Literature.* NovTSup 117. Leiden: Brill, 2005.

Petersen, Norman R. *The Gospel of John and the Sociology of Light: Language and Characterization in the Fourth Gospel.* Valley Forge, PA: Trinity Press International, 1993.

Phillips, Peter M. *The Prologue of the Fourth Gospel: A Sequential Reading.* LNTS 294. London: T&T Clark, 2006.

Pollard, T. E. *Johannine Christology and the Early Church.* SNTSMS 13. Cambridge: Cambridge University Press, 1970.

Porter, Stanley E. "The Ending of John's Gospel." In *From Biblical Criticism to Biblical Faith: Essays in Honor of Lee Martin McDonald,* edited by William H. Brackney and Craig A. Evans, 55–73. Macon, GA: Mercer University Press, 2007.

Porter, Stanley E., and Craig A. Evans, eds. *The Johannine Writings.* BibSem 32. Sheffield: Sheffield Academic Press, 1995.

Pryor, John W. *John, Evangelist of the Covenant People: The Narrative and Themes of the Fourth Gospel.* Downers Grove, IL: InterVarsity, 1992.

Quast, Kevin. *Peter and the Beloved Disciple: Figures for a Community in Crisis.* JSNTSup 32. Sheffield: JSOT Press, 1989.

Reinhartz, Adele, ed. *God the Father in the Gospel of John.* Semeia 85. Atlanta: Scholars Press, 2001.

Rensberger, David. *Johannine Faith and Liberating Community.* Philadelphia: Westminster, 1988.

Richey, Lance Byron. *Roman Imperial Ideology and the Gospel of John.* CBQMS 43. Washington, DC: Catholic Biblical Association of America, 2007.

Ridderbos, Herman. *Studies in Scripture and Its Authority.* Grand Rapids: Eerdmans, 1978.

Ringe, Sharon H. *Wisdom's Friends: Community and Christology in the Fourth Gospel.* Louisville: Westminster John Knox, 1999.

Robinson, J. A. T. "Elijah, John and Jesus: An Essay in Detection." *NTS* 4 (1957–58): 263–81.

———. "The New Look on the Fourth Gospel." In *Twelve New Testament Studies*, 94–106. SBT 34. Naperville, IL: Allenson, 1962.

———. *The Priority of John.* Edited by J. F. Coakley. London: SCM, 1985.

———. "The Relation of the Prologue to the Gospel of John." In *Twelve More New Testament Studies*, 65–76. London: SCM, 1984.

Salier, Willis Hedley. *The Rhetorical Impact of the Sēmeia in the Gospel of John: A Historical and Hermeneutical Perspective.* WUNT 2/186. Tübingen: Mohr Siebeck, 2004.

Sanders, J. N. *The Fourth Gospel in the Early Church, Its Origin and Influence on Christian Theology up to Irenaeus.* Cambridge: Cambridge University Press, 1943.

Schein, Bruce E. *Following the Way: The Setting of John's Gospel.* Minneapolis: Augsburg, 1980.

Schneiders, Sandra M. "History and Symbolism in the Fourth Gospel." In *L'Évangile de Jean: Sources, rédaction, théologie*, edited by Marinus de Jonge, 371–76. BETL 44. Leuven: Leuven University Press, 1977.

———. *Written That You May Believe: Encountering Jesus in the Fourth Gospel.* Rev. ed. New York: Herder & Herder, 2003.

Segovia, Fernando F. *The Farewell of the Word: The Johannine Call to Abide.* Minneapolis: Fortress, 1991.

———, ed. *Literary and Social Readings of the Fourth Gospel.* Vol. 2 of *"What Is John?" Readers and Readings of the Fourth Gospel.* SBLSymS 7. Atlanta: Scholars Press, 1998.

Senior, Donald. *The Passion of Jesus in the Gospel of John.* Collegeville, MN: Liturgical Press, 1991.

Siegman, Edward F. "St. John's Use of Synoptic Material." *CBQ* 30 (1968): 182–98.

Smalley, Stephen S. *John: Evangelist and Interpreter.* Exeter, UK: Paternoster, 1978.

———. "The Sign in John XXI." *NTS* 20 (1973–74): 275–88.

Smith, D. Moody. *The Fourth Gospel in Four Dimensions: Judaism and Jesus, the Gospels and Scripture.* Columbia: University of South Carolina Press, 2008.

———. *Johannine Christianity: Essays on Its Setting, Sources, and Theology.* Columbia: University of South Carolina Press, 1984.

———. *John among the Gospels: The Relationship in Twentieth-Century Research.* 2nd ed. Columbia: University of South Carolina Press, 2001.

———. *The Theology of the Gospel of John.* NTT. Cambridge: Cambridge University Press, 1994.

Staley, Jeffrey Lloyd. *The Print's First Kiss: A Rhetorical Investigation of the Implied Reader in the Fourth Gospel.* SBLDS 82. Atlanta: Scholars Press, 1988.

———. "The Structure of John's Prologue: Its Implications for the Gospel's Narrative Structure." *CBQ* 48 (1986): 241–63.

Stibbe, Mark W. G. "The Elusive Christ: A New Reading of the Fourth Gospel." *JSNT* 44 (1991): 19–38.

———, ed. *The Gospel of John as Literature: An Anthology of Twentieth-Century Perspectives.* NTTS 17. Leiden: Brill, 1993.

————. *John as Storyteller: Narrative Criticism and the Fourth Gospel*. SNTSMS 73. Cambridge: Cambridge University Press, 1992.

Stube, John C. *A Graeco-Roman Rhetorical Reading of the Farewell Discourse*. LNTS 309. London: T&T Clark, 2006.

Sundberg, Albert C., Jr. "Canon Muratori: A Fourth-Century List." *HTR* 66 (1973): 1–41.

Taylor, Michael J. *A Companion to John: Readings in Johannine Theology (John's Gospel and Epistles)*. New York: Alba House, 1977.

Thatcher, Tom. *The Riddles of Jesus in John: A Study in Tradition and Folklore*. SBLMS 53. Atlanta: Society of Biblical Literature, 2000.

————, ed. *What We Have Heard from the Beginning: The Past, Present, and Future of Johannine Studies*. Waco: Baylor University Press, 2007.

————. *Why John Wrote a Gospel: Jesus–Memory–History*. Louisville: Westminster John Knox, 2006.

Thettayil, Benny. *In Spirit and Truth: An Exegetical Study of John 1:19–26 and a Theological Investigation of the Replacement Theme in the Fourth Gospel*. CBET 46. Leuven: Peeters, 2007.

Thompson, Marianne Meye. "Eternal Life in the Gospel of John." *ExAud* 5 (1989): 35–55.

————. *The God of the Gospel of John*. Grand Rapids: Eerdmans, 2001.

————. "The Historical Jesus and the Johannine Christ." In *Exploring the Gospel of John: In Honor of D. Moody Smith*, edited by R. Alan Culpepper and C. Clifton Black, 21–42. Louisville: Westminster John Knox, 1996.

————. *The Incarnate Word: Perspectives on Jesus in the Fourth Gospel*. Peabody, MA: Hendrickson, 1998.

Thompson, Michael B. "The Holy Internet: Communication between Churches in the First Christian Generation." In *The Gospels for All Christians: Rethinking the Gospel Audiences*, edited by Richard Bauckham, 49–70. Grand Rapids: Eerdmans, 1998.

Tovey, Derek. *Narrative Art and Act in the Fourth Gospel*. JSNTSup 151. Sheffield: Sheffield Academic Press, 1997.

Um, Stephen T. *The Theme of Temple Christology in John's Gospel*. LNTS 312. London: T&T Clark, 2006.

van Belle, Gilbert. *Johannine Bibliography 1966–1985: A Cumulative Bibliography on the Fourth Gospel*. BETL 82. Leuven: Leuven University Press, 1988.

————. *The Signs Source in the Fourth Gospel: Historical Survey and Critical Evaluation of the Semeia Hypothesis*. BETL 116. Leuven: Leuven University Press, 1994.

van der Watt, Jan G. *An Introduction to the Johannine Gospel and Letters*. ABS. New York: T&T Clark, 2007.

van Unnik, W. C. "The Purpose of St. John's Gospel." *SE* 1 [= TU 73] (1957): 382–411.

Vellanickal, Matthew. *The Divine Sonship of Christians in the Johannine Writings*. AB 72. Rome: Biblical Institute Press, 977.

Voorwinde, Stephen. *Jesus' Emotions in the Fourth Gospel: Human or Divine?* Harrisburg, PA: Trinity Press International, 2005.

Waetjen, Herman C. *The Gospel of the Beloved Disciple: A Work in Two Editions*. Edinburgh: T&T Clark, 2005.

Wead, David A. "The Johannine Double Meaning." *ResQ* 13 (1970): 106–20.

Webster, Jane S. *Ingesting Jesus: Eating and Drinking in the Gospel of John*. SBLAB 6. Atlanta: Society of Biblical Literature, 2003.

Wenham, David. "The Enigma of the Fourth Gospel: Another Look." *TynBul* 48 (1997): 149–78.

Westermann, Claus. *The Gospel of John in the Light of the Old Testament*. Peabody, MA: Hendrickson, 1996.

Whitacre, Rodney A. *Johannine Polemic: The Role of Tradition and Theology*. SBLDS 67. Chico, CA: Scholars Press, 1982.

Commentaries

Barrett, C. K. *The Gospel according to St. John: An Introduction with Commentary and Notes on the Greek Text*. 2nd ed. Philadelphia: Westminster, 1978.

Beasley-Murray, George R. *John*. 2nd ed. WBC 36. Nashville: Thomas Nelson, 1999.

Bernard, J. H. *The Gospel according to St John*. 2 vols. ICC. Edinburgh: T&T Clark, 1928.

Borchert, Gerald L. *John 1–11*. NAC. Nashville: Broadman & Holman, 1996.

————. *John 12–21*. NAC. Nashville: Broadman & Holman, 2002.

Brodie, Thomas L. *The Gospel according to John: A Literary and Theological Commentary*. Oxford: Oxford University Press, 1993.

Brown, Raymond E. *The Gospel according to John: Introduction, Translation, and Notes*. 2 vols. AB 29, 29A. Garden City, NY: Doubleday, 1966–70.

Bruce, F. F. *The Gospel of John*. Grand Rapids: Eerdmans, 1983.

Bultmann, Rudolf. *The Gospel of John: A Commentary*. Translated by G. R. Beasley-Murray. Edited by R. W. N. Hoare and J. K. Riches. Philadelphia: Westminster, 1971.

Burge, Gary M. *John*. NIVAC. Grand Rapids: Zondervan, 2000.

Burridge, Richard A. *John*. DBC 4. Peabody, MA: Hendrickson, 2007.

Carson, D. A. *The Gospel according to John*. PNTC. Grand Rapids: Eerdmans, 1991.

Culpepper, R. Alan. *The Gospel and Letters of John*. IBT. Nashville: Abingdon, 1998.

Edwards, Mark J. *John*. BBC. Malden, MA: Blackwell, 2004.

Ellis, Peter F. *The Genius of John: A Composition-Critical Commentary on the Fourth Gospel*. Collegeville, MN: Liturgical Press, 1984.

Fenton, J. C. *The Gospel according to St. John in the Revised Standard Version*. Oxford: Clarendon, 1970.

Filson, Floyd V. *The Gospel according to John*. LBC 19. Richmond: John Knox, 1963.

Haenchen, Ernst. *A Commentary on the Gospel of John*. Translated and edited by Robert W. Funk. 2 vols. Hermeneia. Philadelphia: Fortress, 1984.

Hoskyns, Edwyn C. *The Fourth Gospel*. Edited by Francis Noel Davey. London: Faber & Faber, 1954.

Keener, Craig S. *The Gospel of John: A Commentary*. 2 vols. Peabody, MA: Hendrickson; Grand Rapids, Baker Academic, 2010.

Köstenberger, Andreas J. *John*. BECNT. Grand Rapids: Baker Academic, 2004.

Kruse, Colin G. *John*. TNTC. Grand Rapids: Eerdmans, 2003.

Kysar, Robert. *John*. ACNT. Minneapolis: Augsburg, 1986.

Lewis, Scott M. *The Gospel according to John and the Johannine Letters*. NCBCNT 4. Collegeville, MN: Liturgical Press, 2005.

Lightfoot, R. H. *St. John's Gospel: A Commentary*. Edited by C. F. Evans. Oxford: Clarendon, 1956.

Lincoln, Andrew T. *The Gospel according to Saint John*. BNTC. Peabody, MA: Hendrickson, 2005.

Lindars, Barnabas. *The Gospel of John*. NCBC. Grand Rapids: Eerdmans, 1972.

MacRae, George W. *Invitation to John: A Commentary on the Gospel of John, with Complete Text from the Jerusalem Bible*. DNTC. Garden City, NY: Image Books, 1978.

Malina, Bruce J., and Richard L. Rohrbaugh. *Social-Science Commentary on the Gospel of John*. Minneapolis: Fortress, 1998.

Marsh, John. *The Gospel of Saint John*. WestPC. Philadelphia: Westminster, 1978.

McHugh, John F. *A Critical and Exegetical Commentary on John 1–4*. Edited by Graham N. Stanton. ICC. New York: T&T Clark, 2009.

Michaels, J. Ramsey. *The Gospel of John*. NICNT. Grand Rapids: Eerdmans, 2010.

————. *John*. NIBC. Peabody, MA: Hendrickson, 1989.

Moloney, Francis J. *The Gospel of John*. SP 4. Collegeville, MN: Liturgical Press, 1998.

Morris, Leon. *The Gospel according to John*. Rev. ed. NICNT. Grand Rapids: Eerdmans, 1995.

Newbigin, Lesslie. *The Light Has Come: An Exposition of the Fourth Gospel*. Grand Rapids: Eerdmans, 1982.

Neyrey, Jerome H. *The Gospel of John*. NCamBC. Cambridge: Cambridge University Press, 2006.

O'Day, Gail R., and Susan E. Hylen. *John*. WestBC. Louisville: Westminster John Knox, 2006.

Plummer, Alfred. *The Gospel according to St. John*. Reprint, Grand Rapids: Baker Academic, 1981.

Ridderbos, Herman. *The Gospel of John: A Theological Commentary*. Translated by John Vriend. Grand Rapids: Eerdmans, 1997.

Sanders, J. N. *A Commentary on the Gospel according to St. John*. Edited and completed by B. A. Mastin. HNTC. Reprint, Peabody, MA: Hendrickson, 1988.

Schnackenburg, Rudolf. *The Gospel according to St. John*. Translated by Kevin Smyth et al. 3 vols. HTKNT. Reprint, New York: Crossroad, 1990.

Sloyan, Gerard S. *John*. IBC. Atlanta: John Knox, 1988.

Smith, D. Moody. *John*. ANTC. Nashville: Abingdon, 1999.

Stibbe, Mark W. G. *John's Gospel*. NTR. London: Routledge, 1994.

Talbert, Charles H. *Reading John: A Literary and Theological Commentary on the Fourth Gospel and the Johannine Epistles*. Rev. ed. RNT. Macon, GA: Smyth & Helwys, 1999.

Wahlde, Urban C. von. *The Gospel and Letters of John*. 3 vols. Grand Rapids: Eerdmans, 2010.

Westcott, B. F. *The Gospel according to St John: The Authorised Version with Introduction and Notes*. 2 vols. London: John Murray, 1908.

Witherington, Ben, III. *John's Wisdom: A Commentary on the Fourth Gospel*. Louisville: Westminster John Knox, 1995.

PART 3

ACTS

The Earliest Preaching of the Kingdom

15

From the Preaching of Jesus
to the Kerygma of the Early Church

There is no shortage of attempts to pry the preaching of Jesus apart from the kerygma (the preached message) of the early church. Not seldom does one hear it said that Jesus, who came proclaiming the kingdom of God, now himself becomes the message of the early church: the proclaimer becomes the proclaimed, and thereby the message of the proclaimer is transformed into something that Jesus never intended. Luke-Acts is a single work in two parts. It is a single story, as Luke tells us in his opening words of Acts, "In the first book, O Theophilus, I have dealt with all that Jesus began [ērxato] to do and teach" (1:1). The point is that in some sense Luke understands the story of Acts as the continuation of the work of Jesus. Acts is not so much telling an "aftermath" of the story of Jesus, but rather the second part of it. The story of Acts presupposes the story told in the Gospel. This does not mean, however, that there are no differences between what Jesus preached and what the early church preached. What are these differences, and what is their explanation?

Acts as the Continuation of the Gospel Story

The title "The Acts of the Apostles" is misleading. Of the twelve Apostles, apart from a mention of the names of the eleven in 1:13 (to which Matthias, the replacement for Judas Iscariot, is added in 1:26), we hear only of Peter and John in the narrative of Acts (John only in 3:1, 3–4, 11; 4:1), and Peter drops out of the narrative after the puzzling reference in 12:17: "He departed and went to another place [eis heteron topon]." After this Paul, the Apostle extraordinary,

307

Author: *Probably* Luke, "the beloved physician" (Col 4:14) and traveling companion of Paul (cf. the "we" passages [Acts 16:10–17; 20:5–21:18; 27:1–28:16]).

Date: *Very tentatively* in the (early) 70s, possibly a decade earlier or later.

Addressees: Gentile Christians throughout the Roman Empire.

Purpose: To tell the story of the birth and early growth of the church as the second stage of the fulfillment of salvation history, but also with various subsidiary theological and apologetic purposes.

Message/Argument: In fulfillment of the plan of God, a new era of fulfillment has dawned with the outpouring of the Spirit and the proclamation of the gospel to the Gentiles and their positive response.

Significance: Of exceptional importance for the information it provides about the beginnings of the church and the contextual settings for several of Paul's letters.

dominates the story of Acts.[1] And others, not technically Apostles—such as Stephen, Philip, Ananias, Barnabas, and James the brother of Jesus—are important in Acts. Luke has made no attempt whatsoever to be comprehensive in his history of the beginnings of the church. He has been very selective in what he presents, and grateful though we must be for his narrative, it is only a small slice of what happened with this new movement in the middle decades of the first century.

Jesus chose twelve men to be Apostles. We have noted that in the Gospels, especially in Mark, the Apostles often look confused, ineffective, and inadequate. At the end they are particularly disappointing, abandoning their master in fear, with Peter as the prime bad example (Mark 14:66–72; Matt. 26:69–75; Luke 22:56–62).

It is in the narrative of Acts that the Apostles come into their own. They are given a new commission in the closing lines of Luke's Gospel (24:45–49): "Then he opened their minds to understand the scriptures, and said to them, 'Thus it is written, that the Christ should suffer and on the third day rise from the dead, and that repentance and forgiveness of sins should be preached in his name to all nations, beginning from Jerusalem. You are witnesses of these things. And behold I send the promise of my Father upon you; but stay in the city, until you are clothed with power from on high.'" After they have received a blessing from the risen Lord, who ascends into heaven, Luke records that "they returned to Jerusalem with great joy" (24:52). The contrast with the defeated disciples of the passion narrative could not be greater.

In these lines near the end of his Gospel, Luke obviously prepares a bridge to the first chapter of Acts. The reference to the message of "repentance and forgiveness of sins" being "preached [*kērychthēnai*] in his name to all nations, beginning from Jerusalem" together with the promise of being "clothed with

---

1. Martin Hengel rightly notes, "The title 'Acts of the Apostles' has always led the reader of his work astray. It should really be called 'From Jesus to Paul,' with the sub-title 'From Jerusalem to Rome,' and describes very strictly the straight line followed by the gospel from unbelieving Israel to the Gentiles" (*Between Jesus and Paul*, 2).

power from on high" finds its counterpart in the programmatic statement of Acts 1:8: "But you shall receive power when the Holy Spirit has come upon you; and you shall be my witnesses in Jerusalem and in all Judea and Samaria and to the end of the earth."

Above all else, the disciples are called to be *witnesses* (*martyres*) who are to proclaim to all nations repentance and forgiveness of sins in the name of Christ. Both the content and scope of their witness are of great significance. The content of the proclamation causes some surprise. There is no mention of the kingdom (*basileia*) or use of the word "gospel" (*euangelion*). The two occurrences of the word "kingdom" in Acts 1 are interesting. In 1:3 the risen Jesus over a period of some forty days appears to the disciples, "speaking of the kingdom of God." In the second instance the disciples are found asking the ill-considered question, "Lord, will you at this time restore the kingdom to Israel?" (Acts 1:6). Jesus presumably was speaking of the present reality of the kingdom, whereas the disciples, now with a leader who had conquered death, apparently continued to think primarily of a national-political deliverance. Somewhat oddly, there are only two references in the whole of Acts to the "gospel" or "good news": 15:7, "the word of the gospel," and 20:24, "the gospel of the grace of God." It is no surprise, however, that the scope of the proclamation is universal: "to all nations" and "to the end of the earth." The message clearly is one of grace to Israel, "in Jerusalem and in all Judea," but at the same time it applies to all humankind.

The role of the Apostles as witnesses is extremely important in Acts.[2] A witness (*martys*) is someone qualified to give evidence of something as the result of having been present as an observer or participant. The qualifications for a successor to Judas make this clear: "So one of the men who have accompanied us during all the time that the Lord Jesus went in and out among us, beginning from the baptism of John until the day when he was taken up from us—one of these men must become with us a witness to his resurrection" (1:21–22). The Apostles are witnesses to all that Jesus said and did—they will become custodians of this tradition (cf. 5:32; 10:39)—but also and preeminently they are witnesses to his resurrection: "This Jesus God raised up, and of that we all are witnesses" (2:32 [cf. 3:15; 10:41; 13:31]). "And with great power the apostles gave their testimony [*martyrion*] to the resurrection of the Lord Jesus, and great grace [*charis megalē*] was upon them all" (4:33).

The Kerygma in Acts

Acts is the story of the proclamation of the kerygma and the response to it that created house churches throughout the Mediterranean world. It is the

---

2. See especially Clark, "The Role of the Apostles"; Bolt, "Mission and Witness." See also Trites, *The New Testament Concept of Witness*, 128–53.

story of the birth of Christianity as a worldwide faith. What is the message to which the church responds and upon which the church is built?

The Content of the Kerygma

In the discussion of the Gospel of Mark we noted the work of C. H. Dodd on the sermons of the book of Acts (see above, pp. 167–68). From a common pattern in these sermons, Dodd described the earliest preaching as consisting of seven elements:

1. the fulfillment of prophecy,
2. Jesus as the son of David,
3. the death of Jesus,
4. his burial,
5. his resurrection,
6. his exaltation to God's right hand, and
7. his return as judge.[3]

The key elements in the kerygma are the death and the resurrection of Jesus. It is the resurrection above all else to which the Apostles are witnesses.

Paul provides important evidence of the basic kerygma in 1 Corinthians 15, where he speaks of "the gospel" (*euangelion*) he preached, "by which you are saved" (15:1–2). He goes on to describe this gospel in these words (15:3–8):

> For I delivered to you as of first importance what I also received, that Christ died for our sins in accordance with the scriptures, that he was buried, that he was raised on the third day in accordance with the scriptures, and that he appeared to Cephas, then to the twelve. Then he appeared to more than five hundred brethren at one time, most of whom are still alive, although some have fallen asleep. Then he appeared to James, then to all the apostles. Last of all, as to one untimely born, he appeared also to me.

The fulfillment of Scripture in the book of Acts is a theme of great importance. The story that unfolds corresponds to the promises made to Israel.[4]

The Kerygma of Acts and the Good News (Euangelion) of the Synoptic Gospels

The kerygma—the message preached by the Apostles and others—becomes essentially the equivalent of the gospel (*euangelion*). Paul's gospel becomes

---

3. See Dodd, *The Apostolic Preaching and Its Developments*, 28.
4. See Bock, "Scripture and the Realisation of God's Promises."

equivalent to "the preaching [*kērygma*] of Jesus Christ" (Rom. 16:25 [cf. 1 Cor. 1:21; 2:4; 2 Tim. 4:17; Titus 1:3]). The link between the kerygma and the fact of the resurrection is clear: "If Christ has not been raised, then our preaching is in vain and your faith is in vain" (1 Cor. 15:14).

The difference between the good news of the Gospels (the dawning of the kingdom of God) and the kerygma of Acts (the death and resurrection of Jesus) can be regarded only as remarkable and requires explanation. In the Synoptic Gospels the kingdom of God was Jesus' kerygma; in Acts Jesus is the kerygma of the early church. The one who proclaimed the kingdom in the Gospel narratives has now himself become the content of the proclamation. The proclaimer becomes the proclaimed. Another way in which this is often stated is that whereas Jesus announced the coming of the kingdom, what actually came is the church.

It is clear that the ground has shifted somehow. We can describe the changing focus in this way:

The Synoptic Gospels ⟶ the kingdom of God
Acts of the Apostles ⟶ the means by which the kingdom comes
The Epistles ⟶ the fruit of the kingdom

The Synoptic Gospels focus on the announcement of the dawning of the kingdom of God, by which is meant, as we have seen, the coming of the reign or rule of God into history in a dramatically new way that can be described only in terms of the beginning of eschatology. Fulfillment of the promises has come, but leaving us short of the consummation. The world has changed; the world will change. But already in the Gospels there is a foreign body that seems not to fit this theme but clearly is of the greatest significance: the passion narrative. Without the cross there can be no kingdom. Somehow the death of Jesus is vitally important to the announcement of the coming of the new age. His death is the shedding of the blood of *the new covenant*, poured out for the forgiveness of sins (Mark 14:24; Matt. 26:28), foreshadowed in the sacrifices of the old covenant, which it now fulfills.[5]

In the book of Acts the focus shifts from announcement of the dawning reality, which is not denied in any way, to the basis, the grounds, or the agency that makes the new reality a possibility. *What the kingdom depends on has become the good news*—not the kingdom itself, but what makes the kingdom a possibility at all. This is why the kerygma finds its heart in the passion story and its climactic resurrection narrative. Salvation and forgiveness of sins are not only interconnected (as in Luke 1:77); like the kingdom of God and forgiveness of sins (Mark 2:5), they are inseparable. Thus the kerygma of the

---

5. The book of Hebrews makes the argument beautifully. Note Hebrews 9:22: "without the shedding of blood there is no forgiveness of sins."

disciples proclaims "repentance and forgiveness of sins" (Luke 24:47; Acts 2:38; 5:31; 10:43; 13:38; cf. 26:18).[6]

The NT Epistles, to anticipate discussion below, take the announcement of the kingdom and the undergirding kerygma for granted, and they build upon it to focus on the fruit of the kingdom rather than its announcement or the agency by which it comes. The replacement of "kingdom of God" language by the concept of life in the Fourth Gospel similarly involves this shift to the fruit of the kingdom.

The Shift Away from Kingdom-of-God Language

It is quite remarkable that the language about the kingdom of God, used so frequently by Jesus according to the Synoptic Gospels, is allowed to fade so quickly in the early church. One would expect the early church to proclaim above everything else the message of Jesus about the reality of the dawning of the kingdom of God.

However, once we leave the Synoptics "the kingdom of God" is only seldom used. The counterpart in the Fourth Gospel is "life" or "eternal life," with "kingdom" language occurring only in John 3:3, 5 (cf. 18:36). Life in this sense is the result or the fruit of the kingdom announced in the Synoptics. In Acts we find only a relatively few instances where there is reference to the preaching of the kingdom. In Acts 8:12 Philip (one of the seven Jewish Hellenists of chap. 6) is said to have "preached good news about the kingdom of God and the name of Jesus Christ" to the Samaritans. In 19:8 Paul spoke boldly in the synagogue at Ephesus, "arguing and pleading about the kingdom of God." In 20:25 Paul describes his ministry to the Ephesian elders, using the words "among whom I have gone preaching the kingdom." The house prisoner Paul is described as "testifying [*diamartyromenos*] to the kingdom of God and trying to convince them [the Jews] about Jesus both from the law of Moses and from the prophets" (28:23), and then remarkably the last verse of Acts describes Paul as "preaching [to all who came to him] the kingdom of God and teaching about the Lord Jesus Christ quite openly and unhindered" (28:31). Given that Acts is full of accounts of the preaching of the first Christians, this is a surprisingly small number of references to the kingdom. Even more surprising is the fact that the kingdom per se is never mentioned in any of the recorded sermons that Luke offers us. This in itself, together with the association of the "kingdom" language with the person of Jesus (as in 8:3; 28:23, 31), suggests a kind of functional equivalence between the "kingdom of God" language and the kerygma.

6. Richard Bauckham provides a helpful analysis of the kerygma in Acts, arguing that Luke makes use of an oral form of a kerygmatic summary that was "inherently flexible," and that "Luke has taken full advantage of its flexibility in order to suit his narrative contexts and in order to spare his readers the tedium of repetition" ("Kerygmatic Summaries in the Speeches of Acts," 213).

In the remainder of the NT there are not many references to the kingdom of God. More often than not this phrase is used rather vaguely in reference to future eschatology (e.g., 1 Cor. 6:9–10; 15:24, 50; Eph. 4:5; 1 Thess. 2:12; 2 Tim. 4:1, 18; James 2:5; 2 Pet. 1:11; Rev. 11:15). In a few instances the present kingdom seems to be in view. In Colossians 4:11 Paul refers to his "fellow workers for the kingdom of God." The present kingdom is also in view in Hebrews 12:28: "Let us be grateful for receiving a kingdom that cannot be shaken" (so too 2 Thess. 1:5; Rev. 1:6, 9). Colossians 1:13–14 is striking: "He has delivered us from the dominion of darkness and transferred us to the kingdom of his beloved Son, in whom we have redemption, the forgiveness of sins." Perhaps most interesting are two references where the kingdom is described in terms of present experience: 1 Corinthians 4:20, "For the kingdom of God does not consist in talk but in power"; and especially Romans 14:17, "For the kingdom of God is not food and drink but righteousness and peace and joy in the Holy Spirit."

Reasons for the Shift in Terminology

The changes that we have observed in the vocabulary used outside the Synoptic Gospels, especially the decline in the frequency and importance of "kingdom of God" language, occurred for good reasons.

First, talk of a kingdom other than the Roman Empire, with its implication of a king other than Caesar, could easily be misunderstood as treasonous. There is evidence for this possibility in Acts, and, as we have seen, to some extent Acts may have as a purpose the defense of the church as nonthreatening to the Roman Empire. The opponents of Paul and Silas in Philippi say to the magistrates, "These men are Jews and they are disturbing our city. They advocate customs which it is not lawful for us Romans to accept or practice" (16:20–21). In Thessalonica a similar charge is made against Paul and Silas, this time by the Jews: "These men who have turned the world upside down [*tēn oikoumenēn anastatōsantes*] have come here also, and Jason has received them; and they are all acting against the decrees of Caesar, saying that there is another king, Jesus" (17:6–7). When Paul defends himself before Festus, he says, "Neither against the law of the Jews, nor against the temple, nor against Caesar have I offended at all" (25:8). The language of the "kingdom of God" clearly was a liability for the Christians in the Roman Empire. Understandably, it fell into disuse.

A second reason is that the concept of the kingdom had Jewish roots and would not have been easily understood by Gentiles. In an increasingly Gentile church the language of the "kingdom" became less and less meaningful, and hence it was replaced by other language.

Third, when the church began to develop its understanding of what Jesus had brought to them through his death and the outpouring of the Holy Spirit, it became possible to employ new language that focused on the effects—that is, the fruit of the kingdom in the present age. Thus the early

Christians began to appropriate more specific and meaningful terminology to speak of their present experience. We saw this taking place in the definition of the kingdom in Romans 14:17: "righteousness and peace and joy in the Holy Spirit." A variety of terms began to be used that amounted to equivalents to the present experience of the kingdom of God—for example, forgiveness, salvation, reconciliation, justification, regeneration, redemption, and life/eternal life (as in the Gospel of John). These things were largely the fruit of the outpoured Spirit in the lives of the Christians and, at the same time, anticipations of the future consummation that would bring the world to its new perfection.

The Holy Spirit as the Dynamic of the Early Christian Movement

It was the promise of Jesus that the Apostles were to experience a dramatic outpouring of the Holy Spirit that would empower them for the daunting task of spreading the gospel to the ends of the earth (Luke 24:49; Acts 1:5, 8). The Spirit would provide them with the "power" (*dynamis*) that they needed, and the power of the Spirit is displayed through the entirety of the narrative of Acts.

It is on the day of Pentecost that the promise of the Spirit is fulfilled: "They were all filled with the Holy Spirit and began to speak in other tongues, as the Spirit gave them utterance" (2:4). Peter interprets the event as the fulfillment of the prophecy from Joel that in the "last days" God will pour out his Spirit upon all flesh (2:17). In 2:33 the gift of the Spirit is associated with the resurrection and exaltation of Jesus. On the completion of his work, Jesus pours out the Spirit. The gift of the Spirit is not limited to a select group of people, but is offered to all who believe in Jesus. At the end of his sermon Peter says, "Repent, and be baptized every one of you in the name of Jesus Christ for the forgiveness of your sins; and you shall receive the gift of the Holy Spirit. For the promise is to you and to your children and to all that are far off, every one whom the Lord our God calls to him" (2:38–39 [cf. 8:17]).

The power of the Spirit enables the ministry of the disciples. "Luke makes it plain that it is by the power of that same Spirit that all the apostolic acts which he goes on to narrate were performed, so much so that some have suggested as a theologically more appropriate title for his second volume, *The Acts of the Holy Spirit*."[7] Standing before the Jewish authorities to defend his preaching, Peter is "filled with the Holy Spirit" (4:8). There is a second filling of the disciples by the Holy Spirit in 4:31, in a way similar to the Pentecost event, although no longer having the initiatory significance of Pentecost, linked now more directly with proclaiming the gospel: "They were all filled with the Holy Spirit and spoke the word of God with boldness."

7. Bruce, *The Book of the Acts*, 31.

The seven Hellenistic Jewish Christians of Acts 6, chosen to relieve the Twelve from their social work, were "of good repute, full of the Spirit and of wisdom" (6:3). Stephen, who becomes a key figure and the first Christian martyr, is described as "a man full of faith and of the Holy Spirit" (6:5 [cf. 7:55]). Philip, another significant Hellenistic Jewish Christian, is led by the Spirit to the Ethiopian eunuch (8:29; cf. 8:39).

In a summary passage Luke writes, "So the church throughout all Judea and Galilee and Samaria had peace and was built up; and walking in the fear of the Lord and in the comfort [paraklēsis] of the Holy Spirit it was multiplied" (9:31).

At a crucial turning point in the narrative, where the gospel is first brought to the Gentiles, Peter is led by the Spirit (10:19; cf. 11:12). Above all, it is the outpouring of the Holy Spirit upon the Gentiles that is the divine confirmation of the propriety of this new and revolutionary development (10:44–47; 11:15–18; 15:8). So too the very important conclusion of the apostolic council in Jerusalem is directed by the Holy Spirit ("it has seemed good to the Holy Spirit and to us" [15:28]).

Barnabas, though not one of the Twelve, is an important figure in Acts and is described as "a good man, full of the Holy Spirit and of faith" (11:24). Paul was filled with the Holy Spirit just after his conversion (9:17). The Holy Spirit directs Paul and Barnabas in the first of their missionary journeys (13:2, 4). Paul is filled with the Holy Spirit (13:9), led by the Holy Spirit to Europe (16:6–10) and in other instances (19:21; 20:22–23; 21:4, 11).

The Holy Spirit directs in the leadership of the church ("Take heed to yourselves and to all the flock, in which the Holy Spirit has made you overseers, to care for the church of God" [20:28]). And at the end of Acts Paul says that "the Holy Spirit was right" in speaking of the nonresponsiveness of the Jews in Isaiah 6:9–10 (28:25).

In short, in the book of Acts the Holy Spirit equips, empowers, and directs the early church at every stage of its early development. The Spirit is at work not only in special instances through special people, but also generally in all the members of the church.

The Speeches and Sermons in the Book of Acts

Perhaps more revealing than what the key persons of Acts do—and there is no shortage of apostolic miracles in Acts—are the various sermons and speeches that they give. Nearly a quarter of Acts is given over to major speeches.[8] They may be divided into several categories:

8. Marion Soards surveys the speeches and shows how they serve to establish the unity and emphases of Acts, finding among their main themes divine authority, theology, and Christology, the operation of God's plan, the marking of time, and witness (*The Speeches in Acts*, 162–208).

1. evangelistic, subdivided into
   a. to Jews and God-fearers
   b. to pagans
2. deliberative
3. apologetic
4. hortatory[9]

Evangelistic sermons to Jews are delivered by Peter in chapters 2–5, and to the God-fearer Cornelius in chapter 10. Paul speaks to a mixture of Jews and God-fearers at Antioch of Pisidia in chapter 13. Paul evangelizes pagans at Lystra in 14:15–17 and at Athens in 17:22–31.

In the category of *deliberative* speeches are Peter's speech prior to the election of a successor to Judas (1:16–22) and the speeches of Peter and James at the Jerusalem council in chapter 15.

Apologetic (i.e., defense) speeches are given by Stephen in chapter 7; Peter's defense of his having gone to the house of Cornelius (11:4–17); and late in the book the several speeches of Paul defending himself before the Jewish crowd (22:1–21), the Sanhedrin (23:1–6), Felix (24:10–21), Festus (25:8–11), Herod Agrippa II (26:1–29),[10] and finally the Jews of Rome (28:17–20).

The single *hortatory* speech is that given by Paul before the Ephesian elders in 20:18–35.

The content of the evangelistic sermons of Peter in chapter 10 and Paul's in chapter 13 bear remarkable similarity due to their presentation of the basic kerygma of the early church with its emphasis on the death and resurrection of Jesus. Both sermons come to a climax in the offer of the forgiveness of sins (10:43; 13:38). A Pauline touch seems clear in 13:39: "And by him [Jesus] every one that believes is freed from everything from which you could not be freed by the law of Moses" (cf., however, Peter's remark at the Jerusalem council in 15:10). Peter and Paul preached the same gospel (cf. Gal. 2:9).

Paul's preaching to pagans at Lystra and Athens shows how he adapted his message to his non-Jewish listeners. The account of the former (14:15–17) is very abbreviated and therefore contains only natural theology and an anti-idolatry note, but no specifics of the kerygma. It is fair to assume that Paul included the latter in his sermon. The lengthier account of the sermon at the Areopagus also contains motifs of natural theology and more extensive standard Jewish anti-idolatry polemic, together with a climactic statement concerning the resurrection of Jesus (17:31).[11]

9. This follows the categories in Bruce, *The Speeches in the Acts of the Apostles.*
10. See Winter, "Official Proceedings and the Forensic Speeches in Acts 24–26"; Hansen, "The Preaching and Defence of Paul."
11. On this sermon, see Gärtner, *The Areopagus Speech and Natural Revelation*; Stonehouse, *Paul before the Areopagus and Other New Testament Studies*, 1–40; Hemer, "The Speeches of Acts, II."

The deliberative speeches in chapter 15 are of great importance because of the significance of the Jerusalem council. The Apostle of great importance, Peter, is set forth as the protagonist for the Gentiles not being required to be circumcised and is backed up by James, the leader of the Jerusalem church. This Jewish-led stamp of approval is of determinative importance.

Among the apologetic speeches, that of Stephen (7:2–53) is not so much a defense as it is an unrepentant statement of his position. The review of the rebellious history of the Jews is not calculated to appease the members of the Sanhedrin. Paul's defense speeches have the effect of showing that Paul was not regarded as guilty by the Roman authorities.

The hortatory address of chapter 20 is the only Pauline speech addressed to Christians. F. F. Bruce points out that this is the reason why the other speeches, which are directed to non-Christians, differ as much as they do from the Pauline Epistles. By contrast, the speech to the Ephesian elders is filled with parallels to the letters.[12]

There has been much discussion concerning the historicity of these accounts. In Acts Luke gives us only summaries and not transcripts of the sermons and speeches, which must have been much longer than what Luke records (e.g., 20:7 refers to an instance where Paul "prolonged his speech until midnight," to the point of putting some to sleep!). A great amount of discussion has been devoted to the question of how reliable Luke's summaries are. We have already looked at Luke as a historian (see pp. 235–37).

It often has been pointed out that the sermons are all very similar, regardless of the speaker, and that they seem to reflect Luke's own language and theological perspective. As to the latter point, Colin Hemer rightly remarks, "If the speeches recorded are summaries, they are certainly to be regarded as *Lukan summaries* and as such will surely bear the mark of his particular language and interests."[13] As to the similarity of the sermons, Hemer rightly indicates that the observation represents an overstatement. There *are* noticeable differences between the speeches, not only similarities. Some similarities may well be the result of the fact that the early church was united by a common kerygma, as we have already noted. This extends also to its use of common OT apologetic texts, as in the case of Psalm 16:8–11 in Peter's sermon in 2:25–28, and partially in Paul's sermon in 13:35.

In addition to the common elements in the sermons that might be listed, however, they often have distinctive settings and content appropriate to those settings. Perhaps most notable in this regard is Paul's sermon in Athens (17:22–31). There, at the Areopagus, instead of quoting OT texts, as he was wont to do in his synagogue sermons, he quotes pagan literature in 17:28 (Epimenides

12. See Hemer, "The Speeches of Acts, I."; Walton (*Leadership and Lifestyle*) shows the closeness of the Miletus speech to 1 Thessalonians, as well as how few parallels there are to Ephesians and 2 Timothy.

13. Hemer, *The Book of Acts in the Setting of Hellenistic History*, 421. Italics in original.

and Aratus) and makes use of Jewish polemic against idolatry. Paul's speech to the Ephesian elders (20:18–35) is again distinctive, containing typical Pauline biographical references and many allusions to motifs from the Pauline Letters, that fit well the pastoral situation. Finally, we may note Stephen's long (even though apparently truncated) speech (7:2–53). This speech is very different from other speeches—indeed, so different with its review of Israel's history that some have wondered how it fits the particular situation at all.

F. F. Bruce sums up the question of the quality of the history in Acts, when he concludes the following:

> For [Luke's] purpose, despite the clear apologetic and polemic emphases, the record must be recognizably historical. Convenient facts may be stressed, inconvenient facts may be passed over with a brief mention or not mentioned at all; but what is stressed must be factual. The author of Acts has his distinctive theology (a theology recognizably different from Paul's and by no means so deep or rich as his), but his theology is subservient to his main purpose. A writer may be at one and the same time a sound historian and a capable theologian. The author of Acts was both. The quality of his history naturally varied according to the availability and trustworthiness of his sources, but being a good theologian as well as a good historian he did not allow his theology to distort his history.[14]

Concerning the speeches and sermons of Acts we may conclude the following. Luke provides us with reconstructed and interpreted history. His ability to recast his material, select what he wants, abbreviate and emphasize, and at the same time to express his theological and apologetic agendas does not militate against the basic reliability of what he writes.[15] He is very much interested in what happened because this serves as the basis of the message he wants to communicate. He wants to evangelize, but he also wants to vindicate early Christianity in the Roman world and to teach and encourage.

In these speeches and sermons Luke wants to show how what happens fulfills the promises of Scripture. He does this via a christological hermeneutic, wherein Christ is the key to understanding the true meaning of the Scriptures. What happened to Jesus on the cross is regarded as the fulfillment of the plan and purpose of God.

Luke is unwilling in the sermons to indulge in overt theological interpretation and explicit application. There is a clear difference between Acts and the NT Epistles. Acts is ruled by historical narrative. To be sure, that narrative has its own message, its own valuable content. But the genre of Acts restrains the author from offering more than he does.

14. Bruce, "The Acts of the Apostles," 2600. Bruce addressed this subject over a long period of time; see his booklet *The Speeches in the Acts of the Apostles* and his essay "The Speeches in Acts—Thirty Years After." On this subject, see also Gasque, "The Speeches of Acts."

15. The liberal theologian Adolf von Harnack concludes that Acts is "as a whole a genuinely historical work, but even in the majority of its details it is trustworthy" (*The Acts of the Apostles*, 298).

Sources of Acts

Unlike the situation of the Gospel of Luke, where we have the Markan source and indirect evidence of Q, we have no access to sources for Acts that may have been used by Luke. We have no evidence indeed that Luke made use of any sources per se. If he did, they are no longer traceable because of Luke's rewriting. However, given the statement made in the Lukan prologue, which applies also to Acts, we do have reason to think that he would have done historical research by interviewing main characters of the narrative and members of the churches who could supply credible information. An obvious source for the later chapters of Acts is Paul himself, assuming Lukan authorship of the book. The "we" passages possibly are a stylistic device or depend on an unknown written source, but most probably they indicate the author's own diary, or memory, as a source.[16]

Although it is difficult to be optimistic about detecting the sources of Acts,[17] this has not stopped some from speculating about possible Aramaic sources for parts of the book, and especially the earlier chapters. Joseph Fitzmyer builds upon the work of Pierre Benoit, who analyzed three sources for the content of Acts (Palestinian, Antiochene, and Pauline) and assigns every pericope of Acts to one or another of these sources, while insisting at the same time that "Acts is a thoroughly Lucan composition."[18]

The Greek Text of Acts

The Greek text of Acts has a unique history. In addition to the usual array of Greek manuscripts that provide us with the texts of the NT writings (see chap. 42 below), Acts is further witnessed to by a unique textual tradition usually designated as the "Western Text" (primarily the fifth-century uncial D [Codex Bezae], but also in other fragmentary manuscripts, including a few third-century papyri). This Western textual tradition of Acts is, by common estimate, nearly 10 percent longer than the Alexandrian manuscripts of Acts. Although it has been argued by some that the author produced two versions of Acts, more probably the Western Text represents a deliberate, later expansion of an original edition, whether by the author or someone else.[19] For Greek

---

16. Ernst Haenchen concludes this regarding the "we" passages: "If Luke had connected 'we' by literary means with the story of Paul, then this would not have been a story of Paul but a novel about Paul. But Luke, despite his considerable ability as a narrator, is not a novelist but a historian" ("'We' in Acts and the Itinerary," 99).

17. Jaques Dupont comments, "The predominant impression is certainly very negative" (*The Sources of Acts*, 166).

18. Fitzmyer, *The Acts of the Apostles*, 85.

19. For a review of the possibilities, see Metzger, *A Textual Commentary on the Greek New Testament*, 222–36. For a thorough study of the Western Text of Acts, see Read-Heimerdinger,

readers, the interpolations of the Western Text[20] of Acts are available in the text-critical apparatus of the Nestle-Aland Greek New Testament.[21]

Author, Date, Purpose

These are discussed in chapter 13 above.

Bibliography

See also the bibliography for chapter 13, "The Gospel according to Luke(-Acts)."

Books and Articles

Alexander, Loveday C. A. *Acts in Its Ancient Literary Context: A Classicist Looks at the Acts of the Apostles*. LNTS 289. New York: T&T Clark International, 2005.

Anderson, Kevin L. *"But God Raised Him from the Dead": The Theology of Jesus' Resurrection in Luke-Acts*. PBM. Milton Keynes, UK: Paternoster, 2006.

Baban, Octavian D. *On the Road Encounters in Luke-Acts: Hellenistic Mimesis and Luke's Theology of the Way*. PBM. Milton Keynes, UK: Paternoster, 2006.

Barrett, C. K. "The Historicity of Acts." *JTS* 50 (1999): 515–34.

———. "Paul's Address to the Ephesian Elders." In *God's Christ and His People: Studies in Honour of Nils Alstrop Dahl*, edited by Jacob Jervell and Wayne A. Meeks, 107–21. Oslo: Universitetsforlaget, 1977.

Bauckham, Richard. "Kerygmatic Summaries in the Speeches of Acts." In *History, Literature, and Society in the Book of Acts*, edited by Ben Witherington III, 185–217. Cambridge: Cambridge University Press, 1996.

Bock, Darrell L. "Scripture and the Realisation of God's Promises." In *Witness to the Gospel: The Theology of Acts*, edited by I. Howard Marshall and David Peterson, 41–62. Grand Rapids: Eerdmans, 1998.

Bolt, Peter. "Mission and Witness." In *Witness to the Gospel: The Theology of Acts*, edited by I. Howard Marshall and David Peterson, 191–214. Grand Rapids: Eerdmans, 1998.

Borgen, Peder. "From Paul to Luke: Observations toward Clarification of the Theology of Luke-Acts." *CBQ* 31 (1969): 168–82.

Borgman, Paul. *The Way according to Luke: Hearing the Whole Story of Luke-Acts*. Grand Rapids: Eerdmans, 2006.

Bruce, F. F. "The Acts of the Apostles: Historical Record or Theological Reconstruction?" *ANRW* II.25.3 (1985): 2569–603.

———. "Paul's Apologetic and the Purpose of Acts." *BJRL* 69 (1986–87): 379–93.

The Bezan Text of Acts. She concludes that the Bezan text predates the Alexandrian text. See also Parker, *Codex Bezae*; and, earlier, Epp, *The Theological Tendency of Codex Bezae Cantabrigiensis in Acts*.

20. Because the Western Text is generally inclined to include the fullest readings, it is a surprise when it omits material. This phenomenon gave rise to Westcott and Hort's category of "Western non-interpolations," thus calling attention to material omitted by the Western textual tradition. See below chapter 42, "The Transmission of the Text."

21. For an interesting discussion of these interpolations, see Head, "Acts and the Problem of Its Texts."

————. "Paul's Use of the Old Testament in Acts." In *Tradition and Interpretation in the New Testament: Essays in Honor of E. Earle Ellis for His 60th Birthday*, edited by Gerald F. Hawthorne and Otto Betz, 71–79. Grand Rapids: Eerdmans, 1987.

————. "The Speeches in Acts—Thirty Years After." In *Reconciliation and Hope: New Testament Essays on Atonement and Eschatology Presented to L. L. Morris on His 60th Birthday*, edited by Robert Banks, 53–68. Grand Rapids: Eerdmans, 1974.

————. *The Speeches in the Acts of the Apostles*. London: Tyndale, 1942.

Cadbury, Henry J. *The Book of Acts in History*. New York: Harper, 1955.

Clark, Andrew. "The Role of the Apostles." In *Witness to the Gospel: The Theology of Acts*, edited by I. Howard Marshall and David Peterson, 169–90. Grand Rapids: Eerdmans, 1998.

Dibelius, Martin. *The Book of Acts: Form, Style, and Theology*. Edited by K. C. Hanson. FCBS. Minneapolis: Fortress, 2004.

————. *Studies in the Acts of the Apostles*. Edited by Heinrich Greeven. Translated by Mary Ling. New York: Scribner, 1956.

Dodd, C. H. *The Apostolic Preaching and Its Developments*. London: Hodder & Stoughton, 1936.

Dunn, James D. G. *Beginning from Jerusalem*. Christianity in the Making 2. Grand Rapids: Eerdmans, 2009.

Dupont, Jacques. *The Salvation of the Gentiles: Essays on the Acts of the Apostles*. Translated by John R. Keating. New York: Paulist Press, 1979.

————. *The Sources of Acts: The Present Position*. Translated by Kathleen Pond. London: Darton, Longman & Todd, 1964.

Epp, Eldon Jay. *The Theological Tendency of Codex Bezae Cantabrigiensis in Acts*. SNTSMS 3. Cambridge: Cambridge University Press, 1966.

Finger, Reta Halteman. *Of Widows and Meals: Communal Meals in the Book of Acts*. Grand Rapids: Eerdmans, 2007.

Foakes-Jackson, F. J., and Kirsopp Lake, eds. *The Beginnings of Christianity: The Acts of the Apostles*. 5 vols. Reprint, Grand Rapids: Baker, 1979.

Gärtner, Bertil E. *The Areopagus Speech and Natural Revelation*. Translated by Carolyn Hannay King. ASNU 21. Uppsala: Gleerup, 1955.

Gasque, W. Ward. "The Speeches of Acts: Dibelius Reconsidered." In *New Dimensions in New Testament Study*, edited by Richard N. Longenecker and Merrill C. Tenney, 232–50. Grand Rapids: Zondervan, 1974.

Green, Joel B., and Michael C. McKeever. *Luke-Acts and New Testament Historiography*. IBRBib 8. Grand Rapids: Baker Academic, 1994.

Haenchen, Ernst. "'We' in Acts and the Itinerary." Translated by Jack Wilson. *JTC* 1 (1965): 65–99.

Hansen, G. Walter. "The Preaching and Defence of Paul." In *Witness to the Gospel: The Theology of Acts*, edited by I. Howard Marshall and David Peterson, 295–324. Grand Rapids: Eerdmans, 1998.

Harnack, Adolf von. *The Acts of the Apostles*. Translated by J. R. Wilkinson. London: Williams & Norgate, 1909.

Head, Peter. "Acts and the Problem of Its Texts." In *The Book of Acts in Its Ancient Literary Setting*, edited by Bruce W. Winter and Andrew D. Clarke, 415–44. BAFCS 1. Grand Rapids: Eerdmans; Carlisle, UK: Paternoster, 1993.

Hemer, Colin J. *The Book of Acts in the Setting of Hellenistic History*. Edited by Conrad H. Gempf. WUNT 49. Tübingen: Mohr Siebeck, 1989.

————. "First Person Narrative in Acts 27–28." *TynBul* 36 (1985): 79–109.

————. "The Speeches of Acts, I. The Ephesian Elders at Miletus." *TynBul* 40 (1989): 77–85.

————. "The Speeches of Acts, II. The Areopagus Address." *TynBul* 40 (1989): 239–59.

Hengel, Martin. *Acts and the History of Earliest Christianity*. Translated by John Bowden. Philadelphia: Fortress, 1980.

————. *Between Jesus and Paul: Studies in the Earliest History of Christianity.* Translated by John Bowden. Philadelphia: Fortress, 1983.

Jervell, Jacob. *Luke and the People of God: A New Look at Luke-Acts.* Minneapolis: Augsburg, 1972.

————. *The Theology of the Acts of the Apostles.* NTT. Cambridge: Cambridge University Press, 1996.

Kee, Howard Clark. *Good News to the Ends of the Earth: The Theology of Acts.* Philadelphia: Trinity Press International, 1990.

Klauck, Hans-Josef. *Magic and Paganism in Early Christianity: The World of the Acts of the Apostles.* Translated by Brian McNeil. Minneapolis: Fortress, 2003.

Lennartsson, Göran. *Refreshing and Restoration: Two Eschatological Motifs in Acts 3:19–21.* Lund: Lund University Centre for Theology and Religious Studies, 2007.

Lentz, John Clayton, Jr. *Luke's Portrait of Paul.* SNTSMS 77. Cambridge: Cambridge University Press, 1993.

Marguerat, Daniel. *The First Christian Historian: Writing the "Acts of the Apostles."* Translated by Ken McKinney, Gregory J. Laughery, and Richard Bauckham. SNTSMS 121. Cambridge: Cambridge University Press, 2002.

Marshall, I. Howard. *The Acts of the Apostles.* NTG. Sheffield: JSOT Press, 1992.

————. "Luke's View of Paul." *SwJT* 33 (1990): 41–51.

Marshall, I. Howard, and David Peterson, eds. *Witness to the Gospel: The Theology of Acts.* Grand Rapids: Eerdmans, 1998.

Metzger, Bruce M. *A Textual Commentary on the Greek New Testament.* 2nd ed. Stuttgart: Deutsche Bibelgesellschaft, 1994.

Parker, D. C. *Codex Bezae: An Early Christian Manuscript and Its Text.* Cambridge: Cambridge University Press, 1992.

Penner, Todd, and Caroline Vander Stichele, eds. *Contextualizing Acts: Lukan Narrative and Greco-Roman Discourse.* SBLSymS 20. Atlanta: Society of Biblical Literature, 2003.

Pervo, Richard I. *Luke's Story of Paul.* Minneapolis: Fortress, 1990.

————. *Profit with Delight: The Literary Genre of the Acts of the Apostles.* Philadelphia: Fortress, 1987.

Phillips, Thomas E., ed. *Acts and Ethics.* NTMon 9. Sheffield: Sheffield Phoenix Press, 2005.

Porter, Stanley E. *Paul in Acts.* Peabody, MA: Hendrickson, 2001.

————. "The 'We' Passages." In *The Book of Acts in Its Graeco-Roman Setting,* edited by David W. J. Gill and Conrad Gempf, 545–74. BAFCS 2. Grand Rapids: Eerdmans, 1994.

Powell, Mark Allan. *What Are They Saying about Acts?* New York: Paulist Press, 1991.

Read-Heimerdinger, Jenny. *The Bezan Text of Acts: A Contribution of Discourse Analysis to Textual Criticism.* JSNTSup 236. London: Sheffield Academic Press, 2002.

Robinson, Anthony B., and Robert W. Wall. *Called to Be Church: The Book of Acts for a New Day.* Grand Rapids: Eerdmans, 2006.

Scobie, Charles H. H. "The Use of Source Material in the Speeches of Acts III and IV." *NTS* 25 (1978–79): 399–421.

Shiell, William David. *Reading Acts: The Lector and the Early Christian Audience.* BIS 70. Leiden: Brill, 2004.

Shipp, Blake. *Paul the Reluctant Witness: Power and Weakness in Luke's Portrayal.* Eugene, OR: Cascade, 2005.

Soards, Marion L. *The Speeches in Acts: Their Content, Context, and Concerns.* Louisville: Westminster John Knox, 1994.

Spencer, F. Scott. *Journeying through Acts: A Literary-Cultural Reading.* Peabody, MA: Hendrickson, 2004.

Stonehouse, N. B. *Paul before the Areopagus and Other New Testament Studies.* Grand Rapids: Eerdmans, 1957.

Strange, W. A. *The Problem of the Text of Acts*. SNTSMS 71. Cambridge: Cambridge University Press, 1992.

Trites, Allison A. *The New Testament Concept of Witness*. SNTSMS 31. Cambridge: Cambridge University Press, 1977.

Walton, Steve. *Leadership and Lifestyle: The Portrait of Paul in the Miletus Speech and 1 Thessalonians*. SNTSMS 108. Cambridge: Cambridge University Press, 2000.

Wilcox, Max E. *The Semitisms of Acts*. Oxford: Clarendon, 1965.

Winter, Bruce W. "Official Proceedings and the Forensic Speeches in Acts 24–26." In *The Book of Acts in Its Ancient Literary Setting*, edited by Bruce W. Winter and Andrew D. Clarke, 305–36. BAFCS 1. Grand Rapids: Eerdmans; Carlisle, UK: Paternoster, 1993.

Winter, Bruce W., and Andrew D. Clarke, eds. *The Book of Acts in Its Ancient Literary Setting*. BAFCS 1. Grand Rapids: Eerdmans; Carlisle, UK: Paternoster, 1993.

Witherington, Ben, III, ed. *History, Literature, and Society in the Book of Acts*. Cambridge: Cambridge University Press, 1996.

Commentaries

Barrett, C. K. *A Critical and Exegetical Commentary on the Acts of the Apostles*. 2 vols. ICC. Edinburgh: T&T Clark, 1994–98.

Bock, Darrell L. *Acts*. BECNT. Grand Rapids: Baker Academic, 2007.

Bruce, F. F. *The Book of the Acts*. Rev. ed. NICNT. Grand Rapids: Eerdmans, 1988.

———. *The Acts of the Apostles: The Greek Text with Introduction and Commentary*. 3rd rev. ed. Grand Rapids: Eerdmans, 1990.

Conzelmann, Hans. *Acts of the Apostles: A Commentary on the Acts of the Apostles*. Translated by James Limburg, A. Thomas Kraabel, and Donald H. Juel. Edited by Eldon Jay Epp and Christopher R. Matthews. Hermeneia. Philadelphia: Fortress, 1987.

Dunn, James D. G. *The Acts of the Apostles*. Valley Forge, PA: Trinity Press International, 1996.

Fitzmyer, Joseph A. *The Acts of the Apostles: A New Translation with Introduction and Commentary*. AB 31. New York: Doubleday, 1998.

Gaventa, Beverly Roberts. *The Acts of the Apostles*. ANTC. Nashville: Abingdon, 2003.

Haenchen, Ernst. *The Acts of the Apostles: A Commentary*. Translated by Bernard Noble and Gerald Shinn. Philadelphia: Westminster, 1971.

Hamm, Dennis. *The Acts of the Apostles*. NCBCNT. Collegeville, MN: Liturgical Press, 2005.

Johnson, Luke Timothy. *The Acts of the Apostles*. SP 5. Collegeville, MN: Liturgical Press, 1992.

Kee, Howard Clark. *To Every Nation under Heaven: The Acts of the Apostles*. NTC. Harrisburg, PA: Trinity Press International, 1997.

Krodel, Gerhard A. *Acts*. ACNT. Minneapolis: Augsburg, 1986.

Malina, Bruce J., and John J. Pilch. *Social-Science Commentary on the Book of Acts*. Minneapolis: Fortress, 2007.

Marshall, I. Howard. *Acts*. TNTC. Rev. ed. Grand Rapids: Eerdmans, 1980.

Parsons, Mikeal C. *Acts*. Paideia. Grand Rapids: Baker Academic, 2008.

Pelikan, Jaroslav. *Acts*. BTCB. Grand Rapids: Brazos Press, 2005.

Pervo, Richard I. *Acts: A Commentary*. Hermeneia. Minneapolis: Fortress, 2009.

Peterson, David G. *The Acts of the Apostles*. PNTC. Grand Rapids: Eerdmans, 2009.

Talbert, Charles H. *Reading Acts: A Literary and Theological Commentary on the Acts of the Apostles*. Rev. ed. RNT. Macon, GA: Smyth & Helwys, 2005.

Walaskay, Paul W. *Acts*. WestBC. Louisville: Westminster John Knox, 1998.

Willimon, William H. *Acts*. IBC. Atlanta: John Knox, 1988.

Witherington, Ben, III. *The Acts of the Apostles: A Socio-Rhetorical Commentary*. Grand Rapids: Eerdmans, 1998.

16

Acts as a Book of Key Transitions

One of the best ways to comprehend the significance of Acts is to think of it as a book of transitions. Acts covers a period of some three decades, and these decades represent an unparalleled period of change, growth, and development in the history of the church. In the story of Acts we move from a handful of discouraged and bewildered disciples in Jerusalem to churches established around the Mediterranean world, and even so far as the capital of the empire, in Rome. We move, at the same time, from what can initially be conceived of as a sect within Judaism, Jewish believers in Jesus, to a new entity with a distinctly Christian profile, the church. Luke-Acts together spans the whole transition, from the preaching in Galilee of a Jew named Jesus to the largely Gentile church in Rome. Some of the transitions that we will examine here were very gradual. They took place at different speeds, and only rarely is a transition marked with a clear boundary line, as happens to be the case with the first one that we will consider.

From Incarnate Lord to Indwelling Spirit

The Ascension of Jesus

Although the exaltation of Jesus to the right hand of God was a fixture in the faith of the early church, in keeping with its understanding of Psalm 110:1 ("The LORD says to my lord: 'Sit at my right hand, till I make your enemies your footstool'") as applied to Jesus (e.g., Rom. 8:34; Eph. 1:20; Col. 3:1; Heb. 1:3, 13; 8:1; 10:12), an account of the ascension of Jesus is found in the Gospels only in Luke-Acts (cf. John 6:62; 20:17).[1] At the end of Luke's Gospel we read, "While he blessed them, he parted from them, and was carried up into heaven" (24:51), whereas at the beginning of Acts, after Jesus promises the disciples power from on high, Luke writes, "As they were looking on, he was lifted up, and a cloud took him out of their sight" (1:9 [cf. 1:2, 22]). Although they obviously describe the same event, the two accounts do not fit well together. At the end of the Gospel Luke has no interest in mentioning the forty-day period ("many days" according to Acts 13:31) that he refers to at the beginning of Acts, and so apparently he telescopes his narrative so as to include a mention of Jesus' ascension.[2] The ascension proper is simply the final withdrawal of what would have been a series of withdrawals of Jesus during the period of his resurrection appearances.[3] After the ascension of Jesus the resurrection appearances cease (the appearance to Paul in Acts 9:5 is of a special nature; cf. Stephen's vision in 7:56). In the narrative of Acts it is the Holy Spirit who now takes the place of the incarnate Jesus. Thus in 2:33 Jesus is said to be the giver of the Spirit, and in 16:7 the Holy Spirit is referred to as "the Spirit of Jesus."[4]

In the well-known *Paraclete* passages of the Gospel of John, Jesus prepares his disciples for just this transition in the promise of the sending of the Holy Spirit. "And I will pray the Father, and he will give you another Counselor [*paraklētos*], to be with you for ever, even the Spirit of truth, whom the world cannot receive, because it neither sees him nor knows him; you know him, for he dwells with you, and will be in you" (14:16–17 [cf. 14:26: "the Counselor, the Holy Spirit"]). The connection between the departure of Jesus and the coming of the Spirit is made clear in 16:7: "Nevertheless I tell you the truth: it is to your advantage that I go away, for if I do not go away, the Counselor will not come to you; but if I go, I will send him to you." Though not described in John, the ascension is alluded to in 20:17.

Promise and Fulfillment

Above all, the disciples' experience at Pentecost is understood not only as the fulfillment of the promise made by Jesus but also as the fulfillment of OT prophecy and as representing the distinctive mark of an eschatological era. The speech by Peter in Acts 2:14–36 provides the key to the interpretation of this event. Immediately Peter cites Joel 2:28–32 (in the Hebrew text, 3:1–4) in Acts 2:17–21:

1. It is also referred to in the longer ending to the Gospel of Mark supplied in later texts (16:19). There are notable allusions to the ascension in passages such as Philippians 2:9; Ephesians 4:10; 1 Timothy 3:16; 1 Peter 3:22.

2. Unlike modern critical scholars, Luke is oblivious to the discrepancy, of which he surely was aware. Each narrative has its own integrity.

3. See Metzger, "The Ascension of Jesus Christ."

4. The significance of these verses for christology should not be missed. See Turner, "The Spirit of Christ and 'Divine' Christology."

And in the last days it shall be, God declares,
that I will pour out my Spirit upon all flesh,
and your sons and your daughters shall prophesy,
and your young men shall see visions,
and your old men shall dream dreams;
yea, and on my menservants and my maidservants in those days
I will pour out my Spirit; and they shall prophesy.
And I will show wonders in the heaven above
and signs on the earth beneath,
blood, and fire, and vapor of smoke;
the sun shall be turned into darkness
and the moon into blood,
before the day of the Lord comes,
the great and manifest day.
And it shall be that whoever calls on the name of the Lord shall be saved.

"This is what was spoken by the prophet Joel," says Peter (2:16).[5] It is the fulfillment of prophecy, and, astonishingly, prophecy concerning eschatological events. Does Luke regard the entire quoted prophecy as now fulfilled,[6] or does he think of the second half—the wonders in heaven and signs on earth—as still to occur in the near future? The question is difficult to answer, but in keeping with the context of Joel, perhaps the imminence of the day of judgment—not yet here—is what Peter has in mind, and so the signs in the second half of the passage are still future. The beginning of eschatology suggests the imminence of its end, the eschaton proper. No one in the early church at this point had yet to face the idea of *an interim eschatological era*, let alone an extended one, prior to the consummation. But the Evangelist himself is well aware of such a period, and Peter is aware that Jesus must return in order for the end to come in all its fullness. There is the expectation of the return of the just-ascended Christ, probably sooner rather than later, in Acts 3:19–21: "Repent therefore, and turn again, that your sins may be blotted out, that times of refreshing may come from the presence of the Lord, and that he may send the Christ appointed for you, Jesus, whom heaven must receive until the time for establishing all that God spoke by the mouth of his holy prophets from of old."

What is clear from this narrative is that Luke marks out a new time frame, *the age of the church as an eschatological age*, an age of the new, Spirit-endowed community. Peter delivers the first Christian sermon ever preached, an evangelistic sermon addressed mainly to Diaspora Jews who had come

5. Peter could have quoted other prophetic passages concerning the coming of the Spirit as a marker of the eschatological age (e.g., Ezek. 36:27; Isa. 32:15; 44:3). The Spirit was associated with the end time.

6. This is the view of F. F. Bruce, who appeals to the phenomena surrounding the crucifixion of Jesus recorded in Luke 23:44–45 (*The Book of Acts*, 62). There can be no doubt about the hyperbolic nature of the language here.

to Jerusalem for the feast of Pentecost. In this sermon he not only interprets the Pentecost event but also gives the first exposition of the Christian gospel.

A brief reference to the powerful deeds of Jesus leads immediately to the heart of the kerygma: the death of Jesus in accordance with the will and plan of God, and the astounding fact of his resurrection from the dead. Again Peter quotes Scripture, arguing that Psalm 16:8–11 is fulfilled in the resurrection of Jesus (Acts 2:31 is a midrash on the text); then finally he quotes Psalm 110:1, applying it to the ascension of Jesus (2:33–35). The final sentence provides the climax: "Let all the house of Israel therefore know assuredly that God has made him both Lord and Christ, this Jesus whom you crucified" (2:36). This ties in with 2:21, from the Joel quotation, "And it shall be that whoever calls on the name of the Lord shall be saved," thus equating Jesus with Yahweh (cf. Acts 4:12: "And there is salvation in no one else, for there is no other name under heaven given among men by which we must be saved"). With this sermon the Christian mission has begun. The Jewish harvest feast of Pentecost[7] becomes the occasion for the first harvest of the preaching of the gospel in the gaining of three thousand Jewish adherents to the new faith.[8]

The Holy Spirit and the Church

The new time frame of the kingdom of God, the era of the church, is supremely the era of the Holy Spirit. The Spirit is indispensable to the story of Acts—the birth, growth, and life of the church.[9] The new era of the kingdom, dependent on the death, resurrection, and ascension of Jesus, is the era of the outpouring of the Spirit upon all without distinction.

Pentecost was not an ad hoc anointing with the Spirit of a few for their special tasks, as in the empowering of the Spirit in the OT. Rather, here it is initially the endowment of an identity along with an empowerment to realize a new quality of life matching the arrival of this new stage in salvation history. For the believer, the Holy Spirit is the means of incorporation into the church and the personal experience of the powers of the new age. This involves a permanent reality, but with the possibility of subsequent fillings (cf. 4:31). For the narrative of Acts, however, it is especially at key junctures that the leading and enabling of the Spirit are highlighted (see above pp. 314–15).

The Holy Spirit thus replaces the incarnate Jesus. This Jesus, who himself was anointed with the Spirit (Luke 4:18–19, quoting Isa. 61:1–2), now, as he promised, pours out the Holy Spirit upon his people (Acts 2:33; cf. John 1:33). This proves to be a great advantage for the church because the Spirit is not

---

7. For a discussion of the problems concerning the historicity of the Pentecost event, see Marshall, "The Significance of Pentecost."

8. It is important to emphasize that this was not a conversion to a new religion, but rather to a new stage of fulfillment of their Jewish hopes.

9. See Bruce, "The Holy Spirit in the Acts of the Apostles."

limited to being present in one place at a time, as was the incarnate Jesus.[10] This first transition becomes determinative for the entire book of Acts and the Christian mission—indeed, one might say, for the whole of church history.

From Jewish Worship to Christian Worship

Theologically it is not incorrect to say that the church was born on the day of Pentecost. That does not mean, however, that those Jews who believed in Jesus on that day immediately stopped behaving like Jews and became self-consciously "Christians." All the earliest believers in Jesus were Jews, and the new movement at first may be understood as a Jewish sect within Judaism analogous, say, to the Pharisees or the Essenes. Indeed, nowadays it has become fashionable to conclude that one cannot legitimately speak of "Christianity" per se until late in the first century, or even perhaps in the second century. Such a conclusion stresses the Jewish roots of Christianity and the undeniable, extensive continuity between Judaism and Christianity. It builds too on the correct observation that Christianity at first was not perceived as a new religion. Certainly, the early Jewish Christians did not believe that they had changed religions. They had, rather, come into the experience of the fulfillment of their Jewish faith. Christianity for them was *the true Judaism*. There are, however, also strong discontinuities alongside the continuities, and these make it very difficult to keep regarding the new faith for very long as only a sect within Judaism (see chap. 20 below). Eventually, what was implicit from the beginning became more and more explicit, as we will see.

The Exclusively Jewish Church (Acts 1–7)

One of the imponderables in the early part of Acts is that, despite the commission of Acts 1:8, "You shall receive power when the Holy Spirit has come upon you; and you shall be my witnesses in Jerusalem and in all Judea and Samaria and to the end of the earth," the Jewish believers in Jesus seem to have made little if any effort to spread the good news of the gospel outside Jerusalem.[11] At the beginning, their witness is only to the Jerusalem Jews. The first description of the post-Pentecost church says that "they devoted themselves to the apostles' teaching and fellowship, to the breaking of bread and the prayers" (2:42).[12]

10. This probably is the meaning of John 14:12 about the "greater works" that will be done after the ascension. The Spirit-empowered church will do more than Jesus could do.

11. The idea of taking the gospel to non-Jews apparently was too radical to be entertained, as we learn from Acts 10–11. Did they understand the reference to "all nations" (Luke 24:47) and "the end of the earth" (Acts 1:8) to mean only the Jews of the Diaspora?

12. Two items here are distinctively Christian: the apostles' teaching and the breaking of bread, if the latter refers, as seems probable, to the celebration of the Lord's Supper, commemorating the death of Jesus.

In a succession of references we are told that these early believers continued to be loyal to their Jewish practices. The final words of Luke's Gospel refer to the disciples being "continually in the temple blessing God" (24:52). In Acts 2:46–47 we read that they attended the temple together "day by day" and were "praising God." In 3:1 Peter and John are said to be going up to the temple "at the hour of prayer." So too in 5:42 they were "every day in the temple," albeit "teaching and preaching Jesus as the Christ." We also discover that they enjoyed "favor with all the people" (2:47), and that "the people held them in high honor" (5:13). This could not have been true if these Jewish believers in Jesus had stopped obeying the law of Moses. So in these verses we have evidence of their ongoing loyalty to two of the main pillars of Judaism: the temple and, by implication, the law. Peter and John are persecuted for proclaiming the resurrection of Jesus (4:1–22). Again in 5:17–42 they experienced persecution from the authorities, but nonetheless they continued in their evangelistic activities.

It is an interesting question concerning how long the Jewish believers in Jesus continued to participate in the sacrifices of the temple. How long was it before they came to the realization, and were able to act on it, that the sacrificial death of Jesus obviated the sacrificial ritual of the temple, a point made so clearly in the book of Hebrews? We cannot answer this question, of course, but there can be little doubt that the realization was a gradual one, probably earlier than later.

The Hellenistic Jewish Believers in Jesus

In chapter 6 of Acts we are given a glimpse of two groups that made up the early Jerusalem church: the "Hebrews" and the "Hellenists."[13] The latter were Hellenistic Jews and are not to be confused with Gentile believers, who first appear in chapter 10. The difference between these two groups of Jews was both linguistic (the Hellenists speaking mainly Greek while the Hebrews spoke Aramaic) and cultural (the Hellenists being more open to Hellenistic culture while the Hebrews were more conservative and protective of Jewish distinctiveness).[14]

To correct a grievance of the Hellenistic Jewish believers, seven exceptional men were chosen and ordained to the social work of the church. In the providence of God, some of them ended up doing much more than that. Stephen, "a man full of faith and of the Holy Spirit" (6:5), became involved in a debate with other Hellenistic Jews, not believers in Jesus, and appeared to get the best of it: "But they could not withstand the wisdom and the Spirit with which he spoke" (6:10).

13. The Greek word in 6:1 is *hellēnistēs* ("Hellenist"), not *hellēn* ("Greek").
14. Craig Hill (*Hellenists and Hebrews*) attempts to deny significant differences between the two groups. The difference between the two groups perhaps is often exaggerated by scholars, but the existence of clear difference between the two groups seems difficult to deny.

They responded by stirring up opposition to Stephen, spreading the rumor that he spoke "blasphemous words against Moses and God" (6:11). The elders and scribes bring Stephen before the Sanhedrin, where false witnesses (*martyres pseudeis*) report, "This man never ceases to speak words against this holy place and the law; for we have heard him say that this Jesus of Nazareth will destroy this place, and will change the customs which Moses delivered to us" (6:13–14).

As can often be the case with false evidence, there is some truth in what the false witnesses say, probably reflecting things that Stephen had been saying. Stephen's views seemed to threaten two of the fundamental pillars of Judaism: the temple and the law.[15] Regarding the former, although Stephen probably did not say that Jesus would destroy the temple, it may be that he did refer to Jesus' prophecy that the temple was going to be destroyed (e.g., Mark 13.2; Matt. 24:2). The false witnesses in Mark 14:57–58 (cf. Matt. 26:61) seem to represent the same misunderstanding held by the crowd at Jesus' crucifixion (Mark 15:29; Matt. 27:40). But the misunderstanding may have come from the words of Jesus recorded in John 2:19–22, not paralleled in the Synoptics, where John explains that by "temple" Jesus meant his body. As for the law, Stephen undoubtedly had access via oral tradition to some of Jesus' teachings, several of which (e.g., concerning the dietary laws, the Sabbath, and divorce) can be understood as "changing" the law of Moses. So it is not difficult to understand how the accusations against Stephen could have been mounted by witnesses concerned to attack him.

The more important question is whether they reflect a radical perception of irreconcilable differences that eventually would divide Christianity from Judaism. As far as we know from the account in Acts, Stephen was the first to point out key discontinuities that would make it impossible for the new movement to remain as a sect within Judaism. That Stephen began to see the Jerusalem temple as no longer of significance is clearly evident from the content of his defense (Acts 7), where he states that "the Most High does not dwell in houses made with hands" and then supports this statement by quoting Isaiah 66:1–2 (7:48–50). There is no similar polemic against the law in Stephen's defense, perhaps because his speech may have been cut short by the hostile reaction of his listeners. As a Jew, Stephen would have held the law in high regard (cf. "living oracles" [*logia zōnta*] in 7:38), as did all the early Christians, including even Paul.[16] What made them distinctive was not a rejection of the law, but rather their conviction that in the teaching of Jesus they found the true

15. Craig Hill argues to the contrary, "We have no genuine reason to suppose that Stephen was a radical critic of the law or the temple" (ibid., 101). See, however, Kilgallen, "The Function of Stephen's Speech (Acts 7:2–53)." He notes that the speech hints at the destruction of the temple, and that the mention of the law, although only touched on, anticipates the radical conclusion of Acts 15.

16. Stephen anticipates Paul's perspective when he criticizes the Jews for not keeping the law (7:53), although, unlike Paul, he only implies and does not state that they were not able to do so.

interpretation and meaning of the law. At points, however, this made it seem that the law was being changed, if not violated.

The story of Stephen is notable as the first example of the articulation of discontinuities with Judaism that were to become increasingly important.[17] As Martin Hengel puts it, Stephen and the Hellenists are "the real bridge between Jesus and Paul," and it was they who "prepared the way for Paul's preaching of freedom by [their] criticism of the ritual law and the cult."[18] The drawing out of the implications of the new age causes Stephen to become the first Christian martyr.[19] And with this development, the former, positive attitude toward the Jewish believers in Jesus changes dramatically. Thus it is noted in 8:1 that "on that day a great persecution arose against the church in Jerusalem; and they were all scattered throughout the region of Judea and Samaria, except the apostles."[20] The irony is that through this persecution the followers of Jesus begin to fulfill their commission to proclaim the gospel (8:4, 40; 11:19–21).[21]

From Jews to Gentiles

This is a transition of central importance for the story of Christianity, and Luke therefore devotes considerable space to it in Acts. How the barrier of exclusivity came to be broken down and how the Gentiles, who originally were not in the picture (except by anticipation and prophecy), became a part of the family of faith together with the elect, covenant people of God is both interesting and significant.

The Gospel Goes to the Samaritans

As we see in Acts, the first phase in its centrifugal movement from Jerusalem brings the gospel by the hand of Philip, the Hellenistic Jewish Christian, to

17. "The 'Hellenists' put forward the offensive claim that the significance of Jesus as the Messiah of Israel essentially superseded that of Moses in the history of salvation: the gospel of Jesus took the place of the Jewish gospel of exodus and Sinai as God's concluding, incomparable eschatological revelation" (Hengel, *Acts and the History of Earliest Christianity*, 73).

18. Hengel, *Between Jesus and Paul*, 29.

19. Many have pointed out parallels between the "trial" and execution of Jesus and of Stephen. See, for example, Moessner, "'The Christ Must Suffer.'"

20. Possibly only the more liberal Hellenistic Jewish believers had to flee the city, while the more conservative Aramaic-speaking Jewish Christians could have given the impression that they were not interested in criticizing the temple or the law. However, it may well be that the persecution was also directed against the Hebrew Christians, as Craig Hill (*Hellenists and Hebrews*) argues. Were the Twelve able to dissociate themselves from Stephen and the Hellenists, or did they have to go underground? And if the latter, did they feel compelled to remain in Jerusalem to be there for an imminent parousia of Jesus? These are questions without answers.

21. On Stephen, see Scharlemann, *Stephen*; on Stephen's speech, see Kilgallen, *The Stephen Speech*; idem, "The Function of Stephen's Speech (Acts 7:2–53)"; but especially Simon, *St. Stephen and the Hellenists in the Primitive Church*.

the Samaritans (8:5). This development accords with the command of Jesus in 1:8: "You shall be my witnesses in Jerusalem and in all Judea and Samaria and to the end of the earth." That Samaria is singled out for mention, and now the conversion of Samaritans given space in the narrative of Acts, is noteworthy. A significant turn has been reached in the narrative; a significant barrier has been broken down.

There was a general hostility on the part of the Jews toward Samaritans. As a result of their intermarriage with non-Jews, as well as their worship at a rival temple that they had set up on Mount Gerizim, they were regarded, at best, as outside Jewish orthodoxy, and, at worst, as apostates. In John 4:9 the Samaritan woman says, "Jews have no dealings with Samaritans"; in Matthew 10:5 the disciples are to "enter no town of the Samaritans"; James and John are ready to call down fire on a Samaritan village for not receiving Jesus (Luke 9:52–56); Galilean Jews traveling to Jerusalem often crossed the Jordan into Transjordan to avoid going through Samaria; the Jews insult Jesus by calling him "a Samaritan" and demon-possessed (John 8:48). At the same time, the Gospel of Luke can present Samaritans in a very positive light, as in 17:11–19, when of the ten lepers cleansed by Jesus it is only a Samaritan ("this foreigner" [17:18]) who returns to thank Jesus, and in the famous parable of the good Samaritan, who is contrasted favorably with a priest and a Levite (9:29–37).

Philip is thus the first to take the gospel outside the bounds of Judaism to non- or, at best, half-Jews. This momentous development obviously was controversial. Merely the fact that Philip was not one of the Twelve would have raised eyebrows concerning its propriety. It was necessary therefore for the Apostles to investigate the situation and to give it their authoritative approval. "Now when the apostles at Jerusalem heard that Samaria had received the word of God, they sent to them Peter and John" (Acts 8:14). Atypically, the Samaritans had believed in the message and had been baptized, but the Holy Spirit had not yet come upon them.[22] A development this remarkable needed apostolic approval (and here, as in the later admission of the Gentiles, it is Peter, to whom the keys of the kingdom had been given [Matt. 16:19], who provides the final word). When Peter and John laid their hands upon the Samaritans, "they received the Holy Spirit" (8:17). The bestowal of the Spirit is at once evidence of the authenticity of what had happened and also the sign not merely of apostolic approval but of God's approval. Peter and John are not slow in appreciating this new development, and they preach the gospel "to many villages of the Samaritans" on their way back to Jerusalem (8:25).

---

22. This delay is caused by the exceptional nature of the circumstances, and a delayed coming of the Spirit cannot be made normative for Christian experience, as a kind of second work of grace after conversion.

Gentiles: Proselytes, God-Fearers, and Pagans

Before we look at the preaching of the gospel to the Gentiles, it will be useful to note some important distinctions. While the mass of Gentiles in the Roman world were classical pagans, idolatrous and polytheistic, there were many who were attracted to Judaism, to its monotheism and its ethical standards. There were two options for such Gentiles. First, they could become "God-fearers" (technical terms are used, such as *phoboumenoi ton theon*, "fearing God" [Acts 10:2, 22; 13:16, 26], and *sebomenoi*, lit. "worshiping [God]," which the RSV sometimes translates as "devout" [Acts 13:50; 16:14; 17:4, 17; 18:7]; cf. *eusebēs*, "godly" [Acts 10:7, RSV: "devout"]; *theosebēs*, "devout" [John 9:31, RSV: "worshiper of God"]), who believed in the truth of the Jewish faith and its God, and who were willing to live by the moral commandments of the Jewish law. These people often were associated with the synagogue in some (limited) ways, in some instances helping with finances (as in the case of the Roman centurion in Luke 7:5: "he loves our nation, and he built us our synagogue"). God-fearers were thus something like partial converts to Judaism, but in the eyes of the Jews they remained Gentiles. Of course, they were regarded favorably by the Jews, but they were not given full status. It is worth noting here that it was from this group of Gentile God-fearers that Paul was most successful in gaining converts to Christianity. Clearly, Paul's law-free gospel was very appealing to them.[23]

The second option, to become a "proselyte" (*prosēlytos*), did confer full status within Judaism. The demands of becoming a full proselyte were great, however. It meant taking on the whole law of Moses, including circumcision for males (both painful and potentially dangerous), and full observance of the dietary, Sabbath, and purity laws—indeed all the laws—and thus isolation from one's Gentile community. This path was exceptionally demanding, and therefore few had the courage to choose it. There are three references to proselytes in Acts. On the day of Pentecost such Gentile proselytes were among those who had made their way from the Diaspora to the Jewish feast in Jerusalem and who witnessed the outpouring of the Holy Spirit (2:10). One of the seven Hellenists was Nicolaus, described as "a proselyte of Antioch" (6:5). In other words, he was a Gentile who, before he became a believer in Jesus, had converted fully to Judaism. Finally, there is a reference to "many Jews and devout converts [*sebomenōn prosēlytōn*, lit. "proselytes"]" who accepted the message of Paul and Barnabas in the synagogue at Pisidian Antioch (13:43).[24]

---

23. The existence of "God-fearers" as a group has been contested by A. T. Kraabel, who points to the lack of archaeological evidence and regards the idea as a Lukan invention ("The Disappearance of the 'God-fearers'"). For an argument against Kraabel's thesis, see Overman, "The God-Fearers"; Gempf, "Appendix 2."

24. On the subject of proselytes and God-fearers, see Levinskaya, *The Book of Acts in Its Diaspora Setting*.

The Gospel Goes to the Gentiles: Peter's Mission to Cornelius

The centerpiece of the book of Acts is the story of how the gospel was first preached to the Gentiles. The story is told in chapter 10 and then, as an indication of its importance, is repeated in detail in chapter 11, as Peter is forced to defend his actions to the other Apostles in Jerusalem. Luke's narrative spells out in detail how the sovereign guidance of God prepared for this revolutionary development. First, Cornelius, a Roman centurion and God-fearer, receives instructions through an angelic vision to summon Peter (10:1–8). Then Peter learns from the threefold vision of the unclean animals that "what God has cleansed, you must not call common" (10:9–16 [cf. 11:5–10]); as he puzzles over the meaning of this vision, the men from Cornelius arrive and report what Cornelius, "an upright and God-fearing man, who is well spoken of by the whole Jewish nation," had experienced (10:17–23 [cf. 11:11–12]). Then comes the report of Peter's arrival at the house of Cornelius, including his remarkable statement: "You yourselves know how unlawful it is for a Jew to associate with or to visit any one of another nation;[25] but God has shown me that I should not call any man common or unclean" (10:24–29). At this point, Cornelius rehearses once again what had happened to him (10:30–33 = 10:1–8 [cf. 11:13–14]).

Peter's speech begins with an opening sentence about the propriety of proclaiming the gospel to Gentiles: "Truly I perceive that God shows no partiality, but in every nation any one who fears him and does what is right is acceptable to him" (10:34). There follows a brief, no doubt telescoped, statement of the kerygma, ending with the point that "to him all the prophets bear witness that every one who believes in him receives forgiveness of sins through his name" (10:43). At this point, while Peter was still speaking, the Holy Spirit suddenly fell upon Cornelius and his household, as a divine sign of approval of the mission to the Gentiles. "And the believers from among the circumcised who came with Peter were amazed, because the gift of the Holy Spirit had been poured out even on the Gentiles" (10:45). In this exceptional instance baptism follows the reception of the Holy Spirit. Peter notes that baptism here was fully appropriate for "these people who have received the Holy Spirit just as we have" (10:47). Nor is circumcision required of those who have received the Holy Spirit. Cornelius need not become a proselyte in order to become a Christian.

When the report of this event reached the Apostles and their community in Jerusalem, some of them were scandalized. In particular, "the circumcision party"—the ultraconservative Jewish believers who continued to insist

---

25. Peter thus had applied this restriction even to God-fearing Gentiles. The viewpoint is expressed in *Jubilees* 22:16: "Keep yourself separate from the nations, and do not eat with them; for their rites are unclean and all their practices polluted, an abomination and unclean." The contrast between Peter and Philip on the question of the Gentiles is interesting. The more open-minded Philip has no hesitation in proclaiming the gospel to the Ethiopian.

on observance of the law (including circumcision)—criticized Peter, saying, "Why did you go to uncircumcised men and eat with them?" (11:2–3). At this point, Peter recounts the whole story, concluding with these words: "If then God gave the same gift to them as he gave to us when we believed in the Lord Jesus Christ, who was I that I could withstand God?" (11:17). The narrative concludes with these words of the astonished Jewish believers in Jerusalem: "And they glorified God, saying, 'Then to the Gentiles also God has granted repentance unto life'" (11:18).

It is clear that in the full acceptance of the Gentiles into the church we have reached a climactic point in the story of Acts. It is, above all, the authenticating sign of the outpouring of the Holy Spirit that guarantees this development as the will of God. Now the universalism that was implicit from the beginning of salvation history in the Abrahamic covenant, and in the Prophets and other parts of the Scriptures too, comes to its concrete expression in the conversion of Gentiles.[26] *The story of Israel is also the story of the nations*, as is now seen in the outpouring of the Holy Spirit from the ascended Jesus, Israel's Messiah and Lord.

It is no accident that the gospel was first brought to the Gentiles by Peter, the prime Apostle.[27] Had Paul, a latecomer and not one of the Twelve, been the initiator of the Gentile mission, it would have forever remained suspect. Peter, the holder of the keys of the kingdom, is again the one who opens the door, this time to a new group that eventually would come to dominate the membership of the church.

The Crisis of the Jerusalem Council (AD 49)

Chapters 13–14 of Acts record the first missionary journey of Paul and Barnabas, on which they had great success in the conversion especially of Gentiles: God "had opened a door of faith to the Gentiles" (14:27). But not all the believers back in Judea were happy with the easy salvation of the Gentiles. They came to Antioch with this argument: "Unless you are circumcised according to the custom of Moses, you cannot be saved" (15:1). In essence, the argument was that the Gentiles had to become full proselytes to Judaism if they wanted to be Christians. This would seem to assure that Christianity remained a sect

---

26. "Of all the various methods Luke uses to justify the turning to the Gentiles, this appeal to the Old Testament and, by implication, to the eternal will of God, is the most profound and fundamental" (Wilson, *The Gentiles and the Gentile Mission in Luke-Acts*, 244). See also Seccombe, "The New People of God."

27. Technically, of course, Philip brings the gospel first to a Gentile in the person of the Ethiopian eunuch. But this may be thought of as an isolated and unusual instance. In no way does it take away from the showpiece of Peter and Cornelius. Although the chronology is unclear, Luke records (Acts 11:19–20) that some "who were scattered because of the persecution that arose over Stephen" took the gospel only to Jews, but others took the gospel to "Greeks," *hellēnas* (thus 𝔓74, ℵ corrected, A, and the first hand of D, although B, D corrected, E, and the Majority Text have *hellēnistas*, "Hellenists," which makes less sense in contrast to "Jews" in 11:19).

within Judaism. The controversy occasioned the first church council in Jerusalem, where the issue would be debated. In Jerusalem the same argument was presented by "some believers who belonged to the party of the Pharisees" (15:5).

Remarkably, it is Peter rather than Paul who makes the opening argument supporting a law-free gospel for the Gentiles. He begins with these words: "Brethren, you know that in the early days God made choice among you, that by my mouth the Gentiles should hear the word of the gospel and believe" (15:7). Again we see the importance of the fact that it was Peter, not Paul, who was the originator of the Gentile mission. Peter continues with a reference to the authenticating sign of the outpouring of the Holy Spirit upon the house of Cornelius. Then, in a most striking statement, he says, "Now therefore why do you make trial of God by putting a yoke upon the neck of the disciples which neither our fathers nor we have been able to bear? But we believe that we shall be saved through the grace of the Lord Jesus, just as they will" (15:10–11). Here Peter articulates the Pauline gospel to and for Jews.

After Paul and Barnabas give a report of their mission among the Gentiles, it is James (the brother of Jesus), the head of the Jerusalem church, who makes a ruling on the question. He refers to Simeon's (i.e., Peter's) report about "how God first visited the Gentiles, to take out of them a people for his name" (15:14)—the last phrase being language hitherto reserved for Israel. And then he argues that the words of the prophets agree with this development, whereupon he quotes Amos 9:11–12:

> After this I will return,
> and I will rebuild the dwelling of David, which has fallen;
> I will rebuild its ruins,
> and I will set it up,
> that the rest of men may seek the Lord,
> and all the Gentiles who are called by my name,
> says the Lord, who has made these things known from of old. (Acts
>   15:16–18)

The fifth line of the quotation agrees with the LXX against the Hebrew text:

> Hebrew: "that they may possess the remnant of Edom"
> LXX: "that the rest of men may seek the Lord"[28]

Obviously, the LXX fits James's argument better than the Hebrew. It is possible that Greek was the language used at the council, perhaps for the

---

28. The three differences are as follows: (1) in the Hebrew "remnant" is the object; in the LXX "remnant" is the subject; (2) "will possess" or "will inherit" in Hebrew is *yîrĕšû*, while adding one letter gives *yidrĕšû*, "will seek," as in the LXX; (3) "Edom" has the same Hebrew root letters as "Adom" ("men"). This suggests that the translator may have misread the Hebrew text, or perhaps had a different Hebrew text, rather than making arbitrary changes.

sake of Gentile Christian delegates of Antioch who accompanied Paul and Barnabas (cf. 15:2). In that case, the quotation of the LXX would have been natural. However, if the conference was conducted in Aramaic, as seems perhaps more likely, James may have used a Hebrew text different from the later Masoretic Text, one that agreed with what we presently have in the LXX. Be that as it may, the Greek text of Acts as it stands suits James well. If we provide an English midrash on the text, it could run as follows: in the coming of the eschatological age, God will restore Israel in agreement with the Davidic covenant so that the remnant of Israel will seek God with the accompanying result that all the Gentiles, also chosen to be a people for God's name, will turn to the Lord for salvation.

James's conclusion is that what has happened in the success of the Gentile mission is in accord with the promises of Scripture. This is the way Israel fulfills its mission to be a light to the Gentiles (Isa. 42:6), that "salvation may reach to the end of the earth" (Isa. 49:6), and that God becomes the God of all peoples, before whom every knee will bow (Isa. 45:22–23). James also concludes, but without justifying it (at least not in the Acts narrative), that the Gentiles should not be "troubled" with keeping the law, with but a few exceptions, listed in 15:20 (and almost exactly the same in the Letter to the Gentiles of 15:29, but in different order). In what is known as the "apostolic decree," Gentile believers are to be directed to

> abstain from the pollutions of idols,
>> from unchastity,
>> from what is strangled,
>> from blood.[29]

This can seem to be some sort of compromise of the gospel, except that it lacks the crucial circumcision, and it is not related to salvation but rather is imposed to avoid unnecessary offense to Jews, who read the law of Moses "every sabbath in the synagogues" (15:21). It is also difficult to reconcile the decree with the full freedom from the law that is promoted in other parts of the NT. There is no problem with pollutions of idols (yet, see Paul's remark in 1 Cor. 10:25–26), and certainly none with unchastity. Yet the matters of animals strangled and the eating of blood are not the sort of things Paul bothers about.[30] The decree is either to be regarded as local (the letter is addressed

29. Probably in view here is a prohibition against eating blood, as in the Noachic command of Genesis 9:4. Later, however, the word was understood in the ethical sense of shedding blood. Compare the seven Noachic laws (laws that applied to the Gentiles) in b. 'Abodah Zarah 64b: (1) be subject to courts of justice; (2–7) avoid the following six things: blasphemy, idolatry, adultery, bloodshed, robbery, eating flesh cut from living animals.

30. As Martin Hengel notes, "Paul, by contrast, never acknowledged it or practiced [the decree]" (Acts and the History of Earliest Christianity, 117).

to the Gentile brethren of Antioch, Syria, and Cilicia) or as merely having a temporary significance that eventually was lost.[31]

The Transition Complete

The contrast between the opening chapters of Luke and the final chapter of Acts is astonishing. Luke 1–2 is thoroughly Jewish in tonality and outlook. As we have seen, these chapters seem to center on the fulfillment of Israel's expectations and hopes. The Gentiles are barely in the picture at all, only on the periphery despite the occasional anticipation of what is to come. In the middle of the story of Acts the momentous evangelization of the Gentiles begins, and this is followed by the immensely successful mission journeys of Paul and his co-workers, in which largely Gentile churches in Asia Minor and Greece come into existence. The church, which began at Pentecost as an exclusively Jewish community, now rather suddenly becomes increasingly Gentile in makeup. The Gentiles turn out to be far more responsive to the gospel than are the Jews, those to whom the fulfillment is directed in the first instance. Tragically, the Jews for the most part do not accept the salvation offered to them.

This unexpected development is anticipated in the reference to "the times of the Gentiles" in Luke's Gospel (21:24) and also finds expression in the narrative of Acts (13:46; 18:6).

The way in which Luke decides to end his Acts narrative is no accident. He tells of one last encounter between Paul, under house arrest in Rome, and Jews who came to him "in great numbers." Paul expounds the kingdom of God, "trying to convince them about Jesus both from the law of Moses and from the prophets" (28:23). Although "some were convinced by what he said" (28:24), others, by implication the majority, were not. And this motivates Paul to quote the words of Isaiah 6:9–10 concerning the blindness and unresponsiveness of the Jews (28:26–27).[32] But it is the words that he adds to the quotation that contain the sting: "Let it be known to you then that this salvation of God has been sent to the Gentiles; they will listen" (28:28).[33] In this way, Luke describes the direction that his narrative has taken and the outlook of his day. For the time being, the Gentile mission takes priority.[34] This does not exclude an ongoing mission to the Jews or a future turning to God on Israel's part.[35]

---

31. On this passage, see Bauckham, "James and the Gentiles (Acts 15.13–21)."

32. The same passage is quoted by Jesus in Matthew 13:14–15 with Jewish unbelief in view. See Evans, *To See and Not Perceive*.

33. Possibly this ending seemed too sharp or too grim to later copyists who added the sentence, "And when he had said these words, the Jews departed, holding much dispute among themselves" (thus the Textus Receptus, but lacking in all early manuscripts).

34. "The mission to the Gentiles has priority in the history of salvation since it forms the presupposition for the deliverance of Israel at the parousia" (Hengel, *Between Jesus and Paul*, 63).

35. "The anguish of Paul as he speaks his final words to the Roman Jews reflects the anguish of the implied author, who cannot accept this situation as a satisfactory fulfillment of God's

Rather, as Paul indicates in Romans 11:25–26, "a hardening has come upon part of Israel, until the full number of the Gentiles come in, and so all Israel will be saved." For the present era, the church will be composed of many more Gentiles than Jews, but in the future that will change.

From Asia to Europe

With the unqualified admission of Gentiles into its fellowship, the Christian community became a universal faith, inclusive of all humanity. It is also intended to be a worldwide religion geographically, not merely a religion of the Near East or Asia Minor. Thus the forward-looking Acts 1:8 sends the disciples not merely to Judea and Samaria but "to the end of the earth."

Paul's Macedonian call has symbolic significance in this regard even though the gospel had already reached Rome (and elsewhere outside of the Levant). Kept by the Spirit's guidance from going elsewhere in Asia Minor, Paul receives a vision of a Macedonian who cries out, "Come over to Macedonia and help us" (16:9). By means of this divine guidance, Paul's missionary work crosses over into Europe, into Macedonia and Greece. To be sure, all around the Mediterranean, and even in Palestine itself, Christianity had encountered, interacted with, and been influenced by Hellenistic culture. But now, in this turning point, Paul moves into the center of the classical world and Greek culture, preaching even in the Areopagus in Athens (17:22–34).

This underlines the idea of Christianity as a universal faith, for all peoples, for all cultures and contexts. And with Paul's arrival in Rome, even under the circumstance of being a prisoner rather than a free man, Luke has reached a symbolic and climactic ending, indeed, the goal of his narrative. Though Paul was in custody in Jerusalem, "the Lord stood by him and said, 'Take courage, for as you have testified about me at Jerusalem, so you must bear witness also at Rome'" (23:11).

The last stage of the plan of Acts 1:8 has in principle been fulfilled through the work of Paul. Neither Luke nor Paul could have foreseen that in only a few centuries the Roman emperor Constantine would become a Christian, and the empire itself become Christian.

Bibliography

See also the bibliography for chapter 13, "The Gospel according to Luke(-Acts)."

---

promises to Israel" (Tannehill, "The Story of Israel within the Lukan Narrative," 339). See also Wolter, "Israel's Future and the Delay of the Parousia, according to Luke"; Wall, "Israel and the Gentile Mission in Acts and Paul."

Books and Articles

Bauckham, Richard, ed. *The Book of Acts in Its Palestinian Setting.* BAFCS 4. Grand Rapids: Eerdmans, 1995.

———. "James and the Gentiles (Acts 15.13–21)." In *History, Literature, and Society in the Book of Acts,* edited by Ben Witherington III, 154–84. Cambridge: Cambridge University Press, 1996.

Bowman, John. *The Samaritan Problem: Studies in the Relationships of Samaritanism, Judaism, and Early Christianity.* Translated by Alfred M. Johnson. PTMS 4. Pittsburgh: Pickwick, 1975.

Bruce, F. F. "The Holy Spirit in the Acts of the Apostles." *Int* 27 (1973): 166–83.

———. *Peter, Stephen, James, and John: Studies in Early Non-Pauline Christianity.* Grand Rapids: Eerdmans, 1980.

Crown, Alan D., ed. *The Samaritans.* Tübingen: Mohr Siebeck, 1989.

Ehrhardt, Arnold. *The Acts of the Apostles: Ten Lectures.* Manchester, UK: Manchester University Press, 1969.

Evans, Craig A. *To See and Not Perceive: Isaiah 6.9–10 in Early Jewish and Christian Interpretation.* JSNTSup 64. Sheffield: JSOT Press, 1989.

Fitzmyer, Joseph A. "The Ascension of Christ and Pentecost." In *To Advance the Gospel: New Testament Studies,* 265–94. 2nd ed. Grand Rapids: Eerdmans, 1998.

Gempf, Conrad H. "Appendix 2: The God-Fearers." In *The Book of Acts in the Setting of Hellenistic History,* by Colin J. Hemer, edited by Conrad H. Gempf, 444–47. WUNT 49. Tübingen: Mohr Siebeck, 1989.

Gill, David W. J., and Conrad Gempf, eds. *The Book of Acts in Its Graeco-Roman Setting.* BAFCS 2. Grand Rapids: Eerdmans, 1994.

Green, Michael. *Thirty Years That Changed the World: The Book of Acts for Today.* Grand Rapids: Eerdmans, 2004.

Hemer, Colin J. *The Book of Acts in the Setting of Hellenistic History.* Edited by Conrad H. Gempf. WUNT 49. Tübingen: Mohr Siebeck, 1989.

Hengel, Martin. *Acts and the History of Earliest Christianity.* Translated by John Bowden. Philadelphia: Fortress, 1980.

———. *Between Jesus and Paul: Studies in the Earliest History of Christianity.* Translated by John Bowden. Philadelphia: Fortress, 1983.

Hill, Craig C. *Hellenists and Hebrews: Reappraising Division within the Earliest Church.* Minneapolis: Fortress, 1992.

Jervell, Jacob. *The Unknown Paul: Essays on Luke-Acts and Early Christian History.* Minneapolis: Augsburg, 1984.

Kilgallen, John. "The Function of Stephen's Speech (Acts 7:2–53)." *Bib* 70 (1989): 173–93.

———. *The Stephen Speech: A Literary and Redactional Study of Acts 7:2–53.* AnBib 67. Rome: Biblical Institute Press, 1976.

Kraabel, A. T. "The Disappearance of the 'God-fearers.'" *Numen* 28 (1981): 113–26.

Levinskaya, Irina. *The Book of Acts in Its Diaspora Setting.* BAFCS 5. Grand Rapids: Eerdmans, 1996.

MacDonald, John. *The Theology of the Samaritans.* Philadelphia: Westminster, 1964.

Marshall, I. Howard. "The Significance of Pentecost." *SJT* 30 (1977): 347–69.

Marshall, I. Howard, and David Peterson, eds. *Witness to the Gospel: The Theology of Acts.* Grand Rapids: Eerdmans, 1998.

Matthews, Bruce M. *Perfect Martyr: The Stoning of Stephen and the Construction of Christian Identity.* Oxford: Oxford University Press, 2010.

Metzger, Bruce M. "The Ascension of Jesus Christ." In *Historical and Literary Studies: Pagan, Jewish, and Christian,* 77–87. NTTS 8. Leiden: Brill, 1968.

Moessner, David P. "'The Christ Must Suffer': New Light on Jesus—Peter, Stephen, Paul Parallels in Luke-Acts." *NovT* 28 (1986): 220–56.

————, ed. *Jesus and the Heritage of Israel: Luke's Narrative Claim upon Israel's Legacy.* Harrisburg, PA: Trinity Press International, 1999.

Moule, C. F. D. "Once More, Who Were the Hellenists?" *ExpTim* 70 (1958–59): 100–102.

Overman, J. A. "The God-Fearers: Some Neglected Features." *JSNT* 32 (1988): 17–26.

Parsons, Mikeal C. *The Departure of Jesus in Luke-Acts: The Ascension Narratives in Context.* JSNTSup 21. Sheffield: JSOT Press, 1987.

Penner, Todd. *In Praise of Christian Origins: Stephen and the Hellenists in Lukan Apologetic Historiography.* ESEC 10. New York: T&T Clark International, 2003.

Pereira, Francis. *Ephesus, Climax of Universalism in Luke-Acts: A Redaction-Critical Study of Paul's Ephesian Ministry* (Acts 18:23–20:1). Anand: Gujarat Sahitya Prakash, 1983.

Puskas, Charles B. *The Conclusion of Luke-Acts: The Significance of Acts 28:16–31.* Eugene, OR: Pickwick, 2009.

Rapske, Brian M. *The Book of Acts and Paul in Roman Custody.* BAFCS 3. Grand Rapids: Eerdmans, 1994.

Richard, Earl. *Acts 6:1–8:4: The Author's Method of Composition.* SBLDS 41. Missoula, MT: Scholars Press, 1978.

Rowe, C. Kavin. *World Upside Down: Reading Acts in the Graeco-Roman Age.* Oxford: Oxford University Press, 2009.

Samkutty, V. J. *The Samaritan Mission in Acts.* LNTS 328. London: T&T Clark, 2006.

Scharlemann, Martin H. *Stephen: A Singular Saint.* AnBib 34. Rome: Pontifical Biblical Institute, 1968.

Scott, J. Julius, Jr. "The Church's Progress to the Council of Jerusalem according to the Book of Acts." *BBR* 7 (1997): 205–24.

Seccombe, David Peter. "The New People of God." In *Witness to the Gospel: The Theology of Acts,* edited by I. Howard Marshall and David Peterson, 349–72. Grand Rapids: Eerdmans, 1998.

Shelton, James B. *Mighty in Word and Deed: The Role of the Holy Spirit in Luke-Acts.* Peabody, MA: Hendrickson, 1991.

Simon, Marcel. *St. Stephen and the Hellenists in the Primitive Church.* London: Longmans, Green, 1958.

Skinner, Matthew L. *Locating Paul: Places of Custody as Narrative Settings in Acts 21–28.* SBLAB 13. Atlanta: Society of Biblical Literature, 2003.

Spencer, F. Scott. *The Portrait of Philip in Acts: A Study of Roles and Relations.* JSNTSup 67. Sheffield: JSOT Press, 1992.

Tajra, H. W. *The Trial of St. Paul: A Juridical Exegesis of the Second Half of the Acts of the Apostles.* WUNT 2/35. Tübingen: Mohr Siebeck, 1989.

Tannehill, Robert C. "The Story of Israel within the Lukan Narrative." In *Jesus and the Heritage of Israel: Luke's Narrative Claim upon Israel's Legacy,* edited by David P. Moessner, 325–39. Harrisburg, PA: Trinity Press International, 1999.

Thompson, Richard P. *Keeping the Church in Its Place: The Church as Narrative Character in Acts.* New York: T&T Clark, 2006.

Thurston, Bonnie. *Spiritual Life in the Early Church: The Witness of Acts and Ephesians.* Minneapolis: Fortress, 1993.

Tuckett, Christopher M., ed. *Luke's Literary Achievement: Collected Essays.* JSNTSup 116. Sheffield: Sheffield Academic Press, 1995.

Turner, Max. "The Spirit of Christ and 'Divine' Christology." In *Jesus of Nazareth: Lord and Christ; Essays on the Historical Jesus and New Testament Christology,* edited by Joel B. Green and Max Turner, 413–36. Grand Rapids: Eerdmans; Carlisle, UK: Paternoster, 1994.

Wall, Robert. "Israel and the Gentile Mission in Acts and Paul: A Canonical Approach." In *Witness to the Gospel: The Theology of Acts,* edited by I. Howard Marshall and David Peterson, 437–57. Grand Rapids: Eerdmans, 1998.

Wilson, Stephen G. *The Gentiles and the Gentile Mission in Luke-Acts*. SNTSMS 23. Cambridge: Cambridge University Press, 1973.

Wolter, Michael. "Israel's Future and the Delay of the Parousia, according to Luke." In *Jesus and the Heritage of Israel: Luke's Narrative Claim upon Israel's Legacy*, edited by David P. Moessner, 307–24. Harrisburg, PA: Trinity Press International, 1999.

Zehnle, Richard F. *Peter's Pentecost Discourse: Tradition and Lukan Reinterpretation in Peter's Speeches of Acts 2 and 3*. SBLMS 15. Nashville: Abingdon, 1971.

Commentaries

See the bibliography for chapter 15, "From the Preaching of Jesus to the Kerygma of the Early Church."

PART 4

PAUL AND HIS EPISTLES

The Interpretation of the Kingdom

17

Paul, the Man

An enormous amount of literature has been written about Paul over the centuries, and far from subsiding, the writing about Paul continues to increase in our day. On the one hand, of course, this vast literature is a tribute to the crucial importance of Paul to the Christian faith as we know it. On the other hand, it also indicates the challenge of arriving at an adequate understanding of this complex man, and to the continuing fascination for one whose allegiance to the faith of his fathers was absolute and whose encounter with Christ proved so dramatic and revolutionary in its consequences.

It often is pointed out that many find Paul repellent. He is terribly intense and at times can seem distastefully stern. Worse than that, he seems opinionated, dogmatic, and intolerant. He is too assertive of his own authority and far too defensive. Furthermore, he can sound like a misogynist. He clearly is a driven man and would not meet today's criteria for a "psychologically healthy" person. Indeed, he seems very much unlike a twenty-first-century man, at least one whom we might admire. Perhaps not many today would care to be like Paul, though it is interesting that he does call his readers to be like him: "Brothers and sisters, join in imitating me, and observe those who live according to the example you have in us" (Phil. 3:17 NRSV [so too 1 Cor. 4:16; 11:1]). In view, of course, is not the imitation of Paul's personality or personal style, but rather of the absoluteness of his commitment to Christ.[1]

If, however, we make the attempt to understand Paul sympathetically, from within his own frame of reference rather than ours, we may be able not only to appreciate why he exhibits some of the aforementioned characteristics but

---

1. See B. Dodd, *Paul's Paradigmatic "I"*; idem, *The Problem with Paul*.

also to come to a deep appreciation and even admiration of him. The things that strike us negatively about Paul are to be explained largely as the result of the urgency of his mission, the depth of his commitment to Christ, and the severity of the opposition that he encountered. At the same time, Paul exhibits impressive and admirable virtues: love, the desire to nurture and encourage, concern for the welfare of others, self-sacrifice, endurance, and faith. This chapter will approach Paul positively and encourage an appreciation of his greatness.

An important methodological point must be made at the outset. We have two basic sources for information about Paul: his letters and the book of Acts. Of these two, it is the letters, and especially the undisputed letters, that are to be given priority for our historical knowledge of Paul. Acts is clearly secondary in nature, involving the narrative overlay of Luke, with its selectivity, reexpression, and interpretation. While, as we have noted, there is no need for the extreme skepticism of some scholars concerning the historical reliability of Acts (see chaps. 13, 15 above), it is worth being apprized of the problem and in instances where a choice may be required to give preference to the letters.

The Background of Paul

While all agree that Paul is to be understood as the product of both Judaism and Hellenism, there has been much debate concerning which of the two is the primary and which the secondary background. It seems clear that both backgrounds are important, but in determining influence on Paul, eventually one must choose which of the two is the dominant one. At the risk of oversimplifying, we may note that in the late nineteenth and early twentieth centuries, owing to the dominance of the history-of-religions school (*die religionsgeschichtliche Schule*), Paul was explained mainly in Hellenistic terms. More recently, Judaism has perhaps generally been favored as the main background of Paul.[2] We turn first to Paul's Hellenistic background.

Hellenism

Paul the Jew was fully a citizen of the Hellenistic world. Diaspora Jews felt free to imbibe Hellenistic culture more deeply than did their Palestinian counterparts. They used the Greek language, took Greek names, and were more open to, and readily influenced by, their Hellenistic environment. Paul was born and spent at least his early childhood in Tarsus, a city some ten miles from the Mediterranean coast, in eastern Asia Minor (modern Turkey). According to an account in Acts, Paul identifies himself with these words: "I

2. An attempt to overcome the dichotomist approach of Hellenistic versus Jewish is now beginning to emerge. See Engberg-Pedersen, *Paul beyond the Judaism/Hellenism Divide.*

am a Jew, from Tarsus in Cilicia, a citizen of no mean city [lit., "a city not without distinction"]" (Acts 21:39). In addition, Paul was a Roman citizen by birth, as the result of Roman citizenship having been granted to his father or possibly to his grandfather (see Acts 22:27–28, and note the statement made by the tribune). Being a Roman citizen afforded Paul certain privileges, including freedom from certain forms of punishment, such as scourging (see Acts 22:25–26) and execution without due process, as well as the right of final appeal to Caesar (see Acts 25:11–12). Of the three Latin names that Paul the Roman citizen would have had, we know only the third, "Paulus," which could well have been chosen because it was similar in sound to his Jewish name, "Saul."

Had Paul stayed in Tarsus in his formative years, a city known for its university as well as its philosophy, we might conclude that it was there that he acquired the marks of Hellenism. But Paul, as we will see, moved away from there as a very young man, though he was to return in later years (see Acts 9:30; 11:25). As it is, we may safely say only that at Tarsus Paul received his firm grounding in the Greek language, although Aramaic probably was his mother tongue, as we will see. Even the elementary school that he attended may well have been a Jewish Hellenistic one. His knowledge of other Hellenistic philosophy and religions he would have acquired later and by no means only from Tarsus.

In numerous ways Paul reveals that he was a Hellenistic Jew. He wrote his letters in Koine Greek, and there is every reason to believe that the quality of that Greek did not depend on his various secretaries alone. He mainly cites the Septuagint, the Greek translation of the Scriptures, rather than the Hebrew Bible. His letters are written in the customary Greek format and employ typical Hellenistic rhetoric. His style of argument (e.g., diatribe in Rom. 2; 3:1–9; 1 Cor. 9) and his ethical teaching often show a degree of influence from the Cynics and Stoics (e.g., "self-sufficiency" [*autarkeia*] in 2 Cor. 9:8). His metaphors and analogies often are drawn from the Greek games or from the commercial, political, slave trade, and military language of the Hellenistic world. And apparently he was familiar with Greco-Roman writers of the time.[3]

It is undeniable, then, that the framework of Paul's Letters is Greek through and through. But what about the substance of his teaching, the theological content of the epistles? The history-of-religions school tended to explain parallels between Paul's theology and the teachings of the mystery religions as the result of his borrowing from the Greco-Roman cults of his day.[4]

Paul, after all, was born into and moved about in a Hellenistic world, where he would have encountered the exotic sects that had been imported into the Hellenistic culture of Asia Minor. The sacraments of baptism and the Eucharist, it

---

3. See Evans, "Paul and the Pagans."

4. For a contemporary example of this approach, see Maccoby, *The Mythmaker*. The classic refutation of this explanation is found in Machen, *The Origin of Paul's Religion* (first published in 1925).

was claimed, were dependent on similar rites practiced in the mystery religions. The redemption accomplished by Christ's death and resurrection was said to reflect the vegetation deities of the mystery religions or to depend on the gnostic myth of the descending and ascending divine redeemer. Furthermore, it has been claimed, the emperor cult lay behind Paul's christology.

The logical error here, as has often been pointed out, is the fallacy of *post hoc ergo propter hoc* ("after this, therefore on account of this")—that is, the argument that when something comes into existence after something similar to it, causation must be involved. In truth, similar things can exist without there being a connection between them, and in the case of the gnostic redeemer myth, the causation very probably is to be understood as going the other way: the Gnostics of the second century and later borrowed from Christianity.[5]

Judaism

Because of Paul's view of the law and his strong polemic against Jews who do not accept the gospel, Paul has often in the past been thought of as un-Jewish if not anti-Jewish. So glaring is the problem of Paul's theology in comparison to Judaism, indeed, that a few scholars have even tried to argue that Paul was not a Jew, but a Gentile. But there can be no question that Paul was a Jew, and a very devoted one at that—as Morna Hooker once put it, "Jewish down to his fingertips." Paul is very emphatic on this point: "If any other man thinks he has reason for confidence in the flesh, I have more: circumcised on the eighth day, of the people of Israel, of the tribe of Benjamin, a Hebrew born of Hebrews; as to the law a Pharisee, as to zeal a persecutor of the church, as to righteousness under the law blameless" (Phil. 3:4–6 [cf. Rom. 11:1]).[6]

Recent scholarship has taken this statement seriously, and nowadays there is an increasing trend to explain Paul primarily in light of his Jewish background. A better knowledge of Judaism and its diversity, as reflected at Qumran in particular, has enabled recent scholars to explain much in Paul as authentically Jewish that was earlier thought to be essentially Hellenistic. Furthermore, the sharp distinction between Diaspora Judaism and Palestinian Judaism, with the idea that the former was deeply influenced by Hellenism and the latter not at all, has been shown to be false. Such was the pervasive influence of Hellenism that it made its mark even on the Judaism of the Holy Land.[7]

Paul was, in truth, a Hellenistic Jew, with both elements being important, but with the emphasis being on the noun. Before his conversion to Christ, his worldview, his life, his very being, were marked by Judaism rather than Hellenism. Probably at about the time of his bar mitzvah, at the age of thirteen or

---

5. See Yamauchi, *Pre-Christian Gnosticism*.
6. See Hagner, "Paul as a Jewish Believer in Jesus—According to His Letters."
7. See especially Hengel, *Judaism and Hellenism*; see also Newsome, *Greeks, Romans, Jews*.

so, he moved from Tarsus to Jerusalem where he became a *talmid*, a student of the Scriptures, eventually coming to study under one of the greatest scholars of the day: "I am a Jew, born at Tarsus in Cilicia, but brought up in this city at the feet of Gamaliel, educated according to the strict manner of the law of our fathers, being zealous for God as you all are this day" (Acts 22:3); to this we may compare Galatians 1:14: "I advanced in Judaism beyond many of my own age among my people, so extremely zealous was I for the traditions of my fathers." When in Philippians 3:5 Paul refers to himself as a "Hebrew born of Hebrews," he indicates that he spoke Aramaic rather than Greek at home, and his facility in Aramaic is also indicated in Acts 21:40 (cf. Acts 22:2; 2 Cor. 11:22), where he is able to address the crowd in their own tongue ("Hebrew" here is to be understood as referring to Aramaic).

From Paul's Letters we see the ongoing influence of his upbringing and formal training in rabbinic or Pharisaic Judaism. The subjects that he occupies himself with are Jewish subjects: law, covenant, righteousness, christology, salvation, eschatology—granted, all understood anew. He constantly cites the Scriptures (there are nearly a hundred direct citations in the Pauline corpus, together with countless allusions and echoes),[8] and frequently he employs these texts in a midrashic way (i.e., with commentary-like interpretation, as in Gal. 3:15–18; 1 Cor. 9:8–12; 10:1–13), no doubt the sort of practice that he had learned as a *talmid*. It is obvious, as we will see, that for all of the difficulty of understanding his view on the subject, Paul continues to maintain a fundamental loyalty to the law—again, however, in a new way. Furthermore, Paul's method of arguing is often Jewish in format.

Jesus the Jew was the Jewish Messiah. Paul the Jew becomes the definitive interpreter of Jesus, employing Jewish vocabulary, Jewish concepts, and a Jewish framework. The theology of Paul the Apostle to the Gentiles is fundamentally Jewish, and only secondarily Hellenistic.

The Sources of Paul's Christianity: The Damascus Road Experience

If Paul was to some extent the product of the Hellenistic world in which he lived, he was to a far greater extent the product of Pharisaic Judaism. The greatest impact on this remarkable man, however, was an encounter with the risen Christ that took place as Paul was on his way to persecute the Jewish Christians in Damascus. It is hardly possible to overemphasize the significance of this encounter not only in the life of Saul the Pharisee but also for the theology he was to develop, and even for the Christian church of future centuries, which would come to treasure his letters as divinely inspired Scripture alongside what later came to be called "the Old Testament." The story

8. See Hays, *Echoes of Scripture in the Letters of Paul*; Moyise, *Paul and Scripture*; Ellis, *Paul's Use of the Old Testament*.

is so important that it is repeated, with variations, no less than three times in Acts (9:1–9; 22:6–11; 26:12–18). Common to all three accounts are the great light and the words spoken by Jesus to Saul, followed by instructions about what to do. In all three accounts Saul asks the question, "Who are you, Lord?" indicating his intuitive knowledge that he was in the divine presence. Much to his chagrin he was informed, according to all three accounts, that this divine presence was none other than Jesus ("I am Jesus"), and that in persecuting the Christians he was in effect persecuting Jesus the Lord.

From the revelation of the Damascus experience, then, comes above all the revolutionizing knowledge that Jesus is "Lord" (*kyrios*, here a divine title). As part of the Damascus revelation also comes Paul's commission to bring the gospel to the Gentiles. In the third account of the conversion, where it takes the place of the missing Ananias story, the commission is given by Jesus himself: "But rise and stand upon your feet; for I have appeared to you for this purpose, to appoint you to serve and bear witness to the things in which you have seen me and to those in which I will appear to you, delivering you from the people and from the Gentiles—to whom I send you to open their eyes, that they may turn from darkness to light and from the power of Satan to God, that they may receive forgiveness of sins and a place among those who are sanctified by faith in me" (Acts 26:16–18).

Saul's encounter with the risen Jesus on the Damascus Road obviously provides the initial impetus for Paul's christology. It seems probable that Paul's reference to Christ as the "image [*eikōn*] of God" in 2 Corinthians 4:4 ("the light of the gospel of the glory of Christ, who is the likeness of God") and Colossians 1:15 ("he is the image of the invisible God") draws on the Damascus Road experience. Other expressions, such as Christ as the "power of God" (1 Cor. 1:24) and "the Lord of glory" (1 Cor. 2:8), point in the same direction. It is possible to trace even more of Paul's theology back to the Damascus Road experience. If there Paul experienced forgiveness, reconciliation, and renewal, then this could serve as the foundation for his doctrine of salvation and even his eschatology. Thus Paul's very gospel in nuce depends to a considerable extent on the revelation that he experienced at that time.[9]

There have been numerous attempts, especially influenced by Enlightenment thinking, to explain Paul's conversion naturalistically. These appeal to the idea that as he traveled on the road to Damascus, Saul was plagued with guilt, doubt, and frustration—in other words, he was psychologically perfect material for such a conversion experience. This condition was then triggered by a touch of sunstroke to produce in Saul the conviction that he had seen a vision of Jesus. This type of explanation has been totally discredited. There is not the slightest hint that on the road to Damascus Saul was anything other

9. For a full substantiation of the points made in this paragraph, see Kim, *The Origin of Paul's Gospel*.

than a confident man, fully convinced of his own righteousness (cf. Phil. 3:6), certain that he was correct, and that his persecution of Christians was an expression of zeal for God's truth. The words of the proverb in Acts 26:14, "It hurts you to kick against the goads," allude not to a guilty conscience but rather to the difficulty of opposing what is the work of God.

Saul, in short, was not struggling with the problem of righteousness, as was Martin Luther before his discovery of the gospel. Unlike Luther, Saul did not begin with the problem and then find the solution to it. Rather, the reverse is the case. On the Damascus Road Saul was confronted by the solution—the crucified and risen Jesus—without warning or preparation, and from that he was driven to understand the true nature and extent of the human problem. It was this that brought him to comprehend the gravity of sin.

Although Paul had subsequent revelatory experiences (see 2 Cor. 12:1–10; cf. 1 Cor. 2:9–10), none of them came close in significance to the revelation on the Damascus Road. When it came to defending his gospel, Paul was quick to appeal to that experience. Thus he writes, "For I want you to know, brothers and sisters, that the gospel that was proclaimed by me is not of human origin; for I did not receive it from a human source, nor was I taught it, but I received it through a revelation of Jesus Christ" (Gal. 1:11–12 NRSV [followed by a passage alluding to the Damascus Road experience]). It is important to him in the context to show that he was not dependent on the Jerusalem Apostles for the gospel that he preached.

Paul the Christian Theologian

Although his letters contain theology that is brilliant and intellectually challenging, Paul was anything but an armchair theologian sitting in an ivory tower. He was a man not so much of theory as of action. He was first and foremost a preacher of the gospel, particularly among the unevangelized. But once he had evangelized a city and established a community of believers, he did not abandon the new converts. Indeed, it is out of his deep pastoral concern for these churches, and others like them, that he first articulates his theology.

The effect of this is important. What we have of Paul's theological thinking is occasional and pragmatic—that is, directed to deal with problems and issues arising in the specific churches (as particularly, e.g., in Galatians or the Corinthian letters). Very often his theology is shaped by the need to respond to opponents, and thus it is sparked by controversy. All of this, of course, must be kept in mind as we interpret Paul today. It is remarkable, nevertheless, how much emerges from the letters that remains useful for us even today, when the necessary adjustments are made.

Although Paul had no idea that his letters would one day become Scripture alongside the writings of the OT, he does write publicly, with self-conscious authority, occasionally with more than one church in mind. If authentic, Ephesians, probably a circular letter, is an example. Romans, although also dealing with specific or occasional concerns, has in its presentation of the gospel a universality and timelessness that is impressive. It is clearly the most theologically, not to say systematically, coherent of Paul's presentations, and it too seems to have been sent to several other churches.

There is a paradox in Paul the Jewish believer in Jesus. Although he rejects his former Judaism, he regards his *Christianity as the true Judaism*. In no way does he believe that he has abandoned the faith of his fathers. Quite the contrary, Jesus Christ is the fulfillment of the Scriptures, as Paul so eloquently shows again and again.

As with Jesus, so with Paul, we must deal not only with fundamental continuity with the past but also with elements of discontinuity, the latter being caused by the arrival at the turning point of the ages, the beginning of the eschatological era. A current debate asks whether in the case of Paul we should speak of "conversion" or "call." The answer is that both words are appropriate. If one thinks of continuity, and of Paul as faithful to the hope of Israel, then "call" is the right word. That Paul may have thought in terms of a call is evident from his remarks in Romans. The mission to the Gentiles is a part of the larger story of God's grace toward Israel. Paul, like Jesus (Rom. 15:8–9), thus ultimately serves Israel in his service of the Gentiles (cf. Rom. 11:25–32). Paul knows himself called "to be a minister of Christ Jesus to the Gentiles in the priestly service of the gospel of God, so that the offering of the Gentiles may be acceptable, sanctified by the Holy Spirit" (Rom. 15:16). But if one thinks of the dramatic newness brought by Christ and the turnabout in Paul's own life, then "conversion" is the right word. The paradoxes that we encounter here are manifest in the larger paradox of continuity and discontinuity posed by the juxtaposition of the Old and New Testaments itself.

Bibliography

Bassler, Jouette M. *Navigating Paul: An Introduction to Key Theological Concepts*. Louisville: Westminster John Knox, 2007.

Beker, J. Christiaan. *Paul the Apostle: The Triumph of God in Life and Thought*. 2nd ed. Philadelphia: Fortress, 1984.

———. *The Triumph of God: The Essence of Paul's Thought*. Philadelphia: Fortress, 1990.

Betz, Hans Dieter. "Paul." *ABD* 5:186–201.

Bornkamm, Günther. *Paul, Paulus*. Translated by D. M. G. Stalker. New York: Harper & Row, 1971.

Bruce, F. F. *New Testament History*. London: Nelson, 1969.

———. *Paul: Apostle of the Heart Set Free*. Grand Rapids: Eerdmans, 1977.

Davies, W. D. *Jewish and Pauline Studies*. Philadelphia: Fortress, 1984.

———. *Paul and Rabbinic Judaism: Some Rabbinic Elements in Pauline Theology*. 4th ed. Philadelphia: Fortress, 1980.

Dodd, Brian J. *Paul's Paradigmatic "I": Personal Example as Literary Strategy*. JSNTSup 177. Sheffield: Sheffield Academic Press, 1999.

————. *The Problem with Paul*. Downers Grove, IL: InterVarsity, 1996.

Dodd, C. H. *The Meaning of Paul for Today*. New York: Meridian, 1957.

Dunn, James D. G., ed. *The Cambridge Companion to St. Paul*. CCR. Cambridge: Cambridge University Press, 2003.

————. *The Theology of Paul the Apostle*. Grand Rapids: Eerdmans, 1998.

Elliott, Neil, and Mark Reasoner, eds. *Documents and Images for the Study of Paul*. Minneapolis: Fortress, 2010.

Ellis, E. Earle. *Paul's Use of the Old Testament*. Reprint, Grand Rapids: Baker Academic, 1981.

Engberg-Pedersen, Troels. *Paul and the Stoics*. Edinburgh: T&T Clark, 2000.

————, ed. *Paul beyond the Judaism/Hellenism Divide*. Louisville: Westminster John Knox, 2001.

————, ed. *Paul in His Hellenistic Context*. SNTW. Edinburgh: T&T Clark, 1994.

Evans, Craig A. "Paul and the Pagans." In *Paul: Jew, Greek, and Roman*, edited by Stanley E. Porter, 117–39. PS 5. Leiden: Brill, 2008.

Evans, Craig A., and James A. Sanders, eds. *Paul and the Scriptures of Israel*. JSNTSup 83. Sheffield: JSOT Press, 1993.

Given, Mark D., ed. *Paul Unbound: Other Perspectives on the Apostle*. Peabody, MA: Hendrickson, 2010.

Hagner, Donald A. "Paul as a Jewish Believer in Jesus—According to His Letters." In *Jewish Believers in Jesus: The Early Centuries*, edited by Oskar Skarsaune and Reider Hvalvik, 96–120. Peabody, MA: Hendrickson, 2007.

————. "Paul in Modern Jewish Thought." In *Pauline Studies: Essays Presented to Professor F. F. Bruce on His 70th Birthday*, edited by Donald A. Hagner and Murray J. Harris, 143–65. Grand Rapids: Eerdmans, 1980.

Hanson, A. T. *Studies in Paul's Technique and Theology*. London: SPCK, 1974.

Hays, Richard B. *The Conversion of the Imagination: Paul as Interpreter of Israel's Scripture*. Grand Rapids: Eerdmans, 2005.

————. *Echoes of Scripture in the Letters of Paul*. New Haven: Yale University Press, 1989.

Hemer, Colin J. "The Name of Paul." *TynBul* 36 (1986): 179–83.

Hengel, Martin. *Judaism and Hellenism: Studies in Their Encounter in Palestine during the Hellenistic Period*. Translated by John Bowden. 2 vols. Philadelphia: Fortress, 1974.

Hengel, Martin, with Roland Deines. *The Pre-Christian Paul*. Translated by John Bowden. Philadelphia: Trinity Press International, 1991.

Hengel, Martin, and Anna Maria Schwemer. *Paul between Damascus and Antioch: The Unknown Years*. Translated by John Bowden. Louisville: Westminster John Knox, 1997.

Hooker, Morna D. *Paul: A Short Introduction*. Oxford: Oneworld, 2007.

Jewett, Robert. *A Chronology of Paul's Life*. Philadelphia: Fortress, 1979.

Kim, Seyoon. *The Origin of Paul's Gospel*. 2nd ed. Grand Rapids: Eerdmans, 1984.

Maccoby, Hyam. *The Mythmaker: Paul and the Invention of Christianity*. New York: Barnes & Noble, 1986.

Machen, J. Gresham. *The Origin of Paul's Religion*. Reprint, Grand Rapids: Eerdmans, 1973.

Menoud, P.-H. "Revelation and Tradition: The Influence of Paul's Conversion on His Theology." *Int* 7 (1953): 131–41.

Moyise, Steve. *Paul and Scripture: Studying the New Testament Use of the Old Testament*. London: SCM; Grand Rapids: Baker Academic, 2010.

Munck, Johannes. *Paul and the Salvation of Mankind*. Translated by Frank Clarke. Richmond: John Knox, 1959.

Murphy-O'Connor, Jerome. *Paul: A Critical Life*. New York: Oxford University Press, 1996.

————, ed. *Paul and Qumran: Studies in New Testament Exegesis*. Chicago: Priory Press, 1968.

Newsome, James D. *Greeks, Romans, Jews: Currents of Culture and Belief in the New Testament World*. Philadelphia: Trinity Press International, 1992.

Pervo, Richard I. *The Making of Paul: Constructions of the Apostle in Early Christianity.* Minneapolis: Fortress, 2010.

Porter, Stanley E., ed. *Paul and His Opponents.* PS 2. Leiden: Brill, 2005.

———, ed. *Paul and His Theology.* PS 3. Leiden: Brill, 2006.

———, ed. *Paul: Jew, Greek, and Roman.* PS 5. Leiden: Brill, 2008.

———, ed. *Paul's World.* PS 4. Leiden: Brill, 2008.

Porter, Stanley E., and Christopher D. Stanley, eds. *As It Is Written: Studying Paul's Use of Scripture.* SBLSymS 50. Atlanta: Society of Biblical Literature, 2008.

Ridderbos, Herman. *Paul: An Outline of His Theology.* Translated by John Richard de Witt. Grand Rapids: Eerdmans, 1975.

Riesner, Rainer. *Paul's Early Period: Chronology, Mission Strategy, Theology.* Translated by Douglas Stott. Grand Rapids: Eerdmans, 1998.

Roetzel, Calvin J. *Paul: A Jew on the Margins.* Louisville: Westminster John Knox, 2003.

———. *Paul: The Man and the Myth.* SPNT. Columbia: University of South Carolina Press, 1998.

Sanders, E. P. *Paul.* New York: Oxford University Press, 1991.

Schnelle, Udo. *Apostle Paul: His Life and Theology.* Translated by M. Eugene Boring. Grand Rapids: Baker Academic, 2003.

Thiselton, Anthony C. *The Living Paul: An Introduction to the Apostle and His Thought.* Downers Grove, IL: IVP Academic, 2009.

Wallace, Richard, and Wynne Williams. *The Three Worlds of Paul of Tarsus.* London: Routledge, 1994.

Watson, Francis. *Paul and the Hermeneutics of Faith.* London: T&T Clark, 2004.

Whiteley, D. E. H. *The Theology of St. Paul.* Philadelphia: Fortress, 1966.

Yamauchi, Edwin M. *Pre-Christian Gnosticism: A Survey of the Proposed Evidences.* Grand Rapids: Eerdmans, 1973.

18

Jesus and Paul

One of the most important and persistent questions in the study of the NT concerns the continuity, or lack of it, between the teaching of Jesus and that of the early church. For example, one may ask—if a little facetiously—whether Jesus was a Christian. The question, of course, is anachronistic and therefore rather silly. The point behind it, however, is a serious one, for the implication of the question is that what the early church believed about Jesus bears little relationship to what the historical Jesus believed or intended. A more serious form of the question is whether Paul's gospel is in any sense faithful to the teaching of Jesus. Is Paul the great interpreter of Jesus or, as some have supposed, the great betrayer of Jesus' message and purpose?[1] Radical Christian scholarship, followed by modern Jewish scholarship, concludes that Paul was the real creator of Christianity, while Jesus, as a Jewish prophet-like teacher and healer, properly speaking, belongs to Judaism and not to Christianity.

The History of the Debate

Already as early as the eighteenth century, in material published posthumously, Hermann Samuel Reimarus wrote that whereas Jesus was simply a teacher who took up the ethical message of the OT, it was his disciples who created a new religion by means of deception and fraud.[2] F. C. Baur published a book on

1. Larry Hurtado quotes the following aphorism from John Dominic Crossan's book *The Birth of Christianity*: "Start with Paul and you will see Jesus incorrectly"; then Hurtado responds with one of his own: "Fail to take adequate account of Paul and you will describe 'the birth of Christianity' incorrectly" (*Lord Jesus Christ*, 85).

2. The seventh fragment of the famous *Wolfenbuettel Fragments*, published by Lessing in 1778, is devoted to Jesus and his disciples. See above, pp. 84–85.

Paul in 1831 in which he argued that Paul developed his doctrine in complete opposition to that of others in the early church, especially that of Peter.[3] Baur argued that Paul was radically transformed by his faith in the risen Christ, and that he had no need for, or interest in, the Jesus of history. In 1905 William Wrede also published a book on Paul, whom he described as the second founder of Christianity.[4] Wrede found three main differences between Jesus and Paul:

1. the style of their language, Paul writing reflective theology, while Jesus gave simple ethical teaching;
2. the scope of their concern, Jesus worrying about the state of the individual soul, while Paul thought of a universal salvation; and
3. their christology, since Jesus never made himself the object of faith or doctrine, while for Paul, Jesus was the very basis of his theology and was ascribed a deity that Jesus would have vehemently denied.

The history-of-religions school, finding some striking similarities between the mystery religions and Paul's theology, argued that their dying and rising gods greatly influenced Paul, who, they maintained, borrowed freely from them as well as from the gnostic myth of a descending and ascending redeemer.

More recent radical scholarship has continued to follow somewhat the same line of thinking. As we have already had occasion to note, a large number of popular books have appeared in recent times arguing that the "real Jesus" was anything but what the church made him out to be. The public apparently never tires of hearing that the church's view of Jesus is a cooked-up one, and that Jesus has to be "rescued" from the Christians. And modern Jewish scholarship has been more than happy to conclude the same, sensing much in Jesus that is authentically Jewish and hence, by implication, not Christian. Despite the new and growing sensitivity to Paul's own Jewishness, there remains the feeling that Paul and Jesus represent two vastly different worlds.

Paul's Interest in and Knowledge of Jesus

To the question "Was Paul interested in Jesus the Galilean Jew?" one is tempted to respond, "How could he *not* have been?" How could Paul not have been more than mildly curious about the earthly existence, the words and deeds, of the risen one whom he now recognized and proclaimed as Lord? It is a misreading of 2 Corinthians 5:16 that takes the statement to mean that Paul had no interest in the Jesus of history. The verse should not be translated as "If we once knew the fleshly [i.e., human] Christ, now we no longer know him." Rather, the verse means, as the RSV has it, "Even though we once regarded Christ from a human

3. Translated into English in 1873–75. Baur, *Paul, the Apostle of Jesus Christ*.
4. An English translation was published in 1907. Wrede, *Paul*.

point of view, we regard him thus no longer." In other words, the statement is about Paul's earlier misperception of Jesus.

To be sure, Paul constantly focuses on the risen, reigning Lord and on the benefits to Christians of the death and resurrection of Jesus. He writes, after all, not a Gospel, not the story of Jesus, but epistles, the purpose of which are to explore the present meaning of Christ for the church. But although he focuses on the kerygmatic Christ, his view of Jesus is not docetic. He accepts the full humanity of Jesus.

That Paul was not one of the twelve original disciples of Jesus was frequently a problem for him, especially whenever his teaching was challenged. As far as we know, he never saw Jesus or heard him preach. But that he had learned much about the words and deeds of Jesus is clear. Not very long after his conversion, Paul had occasion to stay with Peter in Jerusalem for fifteen days. The translation of the verb *historēsai* in Galatians 1:18 as "to visit" does not bring out its true meaning. More precisely it means "to inquire into or about a thing [or person]" and hence in Galatians 1:18 to "visit a person for the purpose of inquiry."[5] Paul had not come to Jerusalem for a holiday; he was there to obtain information—almost certainly about what Jesus said and did, the meaning of what had happened, but also probably about the birth and mission of the church. Paul, of course, would have had access to the sayings of Jesus and accounts of his deeds through the deposits of oral tradition available in the churches. But he would have been interested in interviewing the prime Apostle, Peter, and acquiring a full and firsthand account of the story.

And indeed, an examination of the Pauline Epistles shows a surprising number of allusions to the earthly Jesus. Putting these together, we could construct a summary such as the following: Jesus was born under the law; was descended from Abraham and David; had brothers; was engaged in ministry to the Jews; was poor, meek, and gentle; had twelve disciples; presented ethical teaching; held a final supper with his disciples at which he instituted the celebration of the Lord's Supper; was crucified and buried.[6] Paul undoubtedly knew the story of Jesus. There are furthermore a few additional instances in which Paul quotes words of Jesus: most probable are 1 Corinthians 7:10–11 (cf. Mark 10:9–12); 9:14 (cf. Luke 10:7). Less probable, because of the availability of other explanations, but still to be considered seriously are 1 Thessalonians 4:15–17 (cf. Matt. 24:30–31) and 1 Corinthians 11:23–25 (cf. Mark 9:31; 10:33; 14:18, 21). Additionally, there is the possibility of "echoes" in other places: especially 1 Thessalonians 5:1–7 (cf. Matt. 24:43);[7] also Romans 14:14 (cf. Mark 7:15); and Romans 12–14 and

5. Thus LSJ, 842a.

6. See Galatians 4:4; 3:16; Romans 1:3; Galatians 1:19; 1 Corinthians 9:5; Romans 15:8; 2 Corinthians 8:9; 10:1; 1 Corinthians 15:5; 7:10; 11:23–26; Galatians 3:1; 1 Corinthians 15:4.

7. On 1 Thessalonians 5:3 (cf. Luke 21:34–36), see Wenham, "Paul's Use of the Jesus Tradition."

1 Thessalonians 4–5, which frequently echo sayings of Jesus. These, together with numerous other echoes, are examined thoroughly by Seyoon Kim.[8]

It is true that one might have expected more specifics, especially more references to specific sayings and deeds of Jesus. But to argue from this relative silence that Paul was uninterested in Jesus and did not know his teachings is to make a huge leap to an exceedingly improbable conclusion. Paul, after all, writes not Gospels but epistles. He presupposes the Gospel tradition in its oral form. His interests, however, are centered not on Jesus the teacher or healer, but rather on Jesus the divine redeemer, who died and was raised for the salvation of the world.

Revelation and Tradition

Paul was the recipient of direct revelations from Christ—preeminently, of course, in his conversion on the Damascus Road, but at other times too (e.g., 2 Cor. 12:1–6; note also the reference to "the abundance of revelations" in 2 Cor. 12:7). The content of these revelations is rarely if ever spelled out. As we noted in the preceding chapter, much of Paul's gospel is contained in seed form in the Damascus Road revelation.[9] It is true at the same time, however, that Paul also depends heavily on tradition inherited from those who were Christians before him.

Paul appeals to tradition for the very heart of his gospel: "For I delivered to you as of first importance what I also received, that Christ died for our sins in accordance with the scriptures, that he was buried, that he was raised on the third day in accordance with the scriptures, and that he appeared to Cephas, then to the twelve" (1 Cor. 15:3–5). As we already noted in our discussion of the origin of the Gospel tradition, the opening clause of this statement employs technical terms referring to the transmission of oral tradition: "deliver" (*paradidōmi*) and "receive" (*paralambanō*). The same two words are used in his account of the Last Supper: "For I received from the Lord what I also delivered to you, that the Lord Jesus on the night when he was betrayed took bread" (1 Cor. 11:23). Although the words "from the Lord" (*apo tou kyriou*) may sound like a matter of special revelation to Paul, received without any mediator, the words "received" and "delivered" point to oral tradition. If direct revelation were in view, we would expect a different preposition, namely, *para tou kyriou*. When Paul says "from the Lord" (*apo tou kyriou*) here, it refers to Jesus as the ultimate source; the tradition itself, however, was mediated by the Apostles. This liturgical tradition of the Eucharist was the common property of the early church.

8. Kim speaks of "over twenty-five instances" of probable reference or allusion and of "over forty possible echoes of a saying of Jesus" ("Jesus, Sayings of," 490). This assertion by Kim is justified: "When in the Pauline letters an echo of a dominical logion is disputed, the burden of proof lies more heavily on those who would deny it, than on those who would accept it" (ibid., 485 [italics removed]).

9. See especially Kim, *The Origin of Paul's Gospel*.

It is not easy to determine exactly what Paul received via revelation and what he received via oral tradition. From his strong statement in Galatians 1:11–12, one might suppose that the answer was clear: "For I would have you know, brethren, that the gospel which was preached by me is not man's gospel. For I did not receive it from man, nor was I taught it, but it came through a revelation of Jesus Christ." Paul insists that his gospel is not dependent on others, not even the Apostles. But it is important to note that Paul writes here in defense of his apostolic authority as well as his gospel. He must, on the one hand, insist on his independence from the Jerusalem Apostles, since his authority does not derive from them; on the other hand, he wants to assert that in its basic content his gospel is no different from theirs. Paul and Peter had been entrusted with the same gospel, with the one difference that Peter was to preach it to the Jews, and Paul to the Gentiles (Gal. 2:7). When the pillars of the church—James, Peter, and John—saw God's grace in Paul, they offered "the right hand of fellowship" to Paul and Barnabas as a sign of unity (Gal. 2:9).

In what sense, then, may we conclude that Paul depends on revelation and in what sense on tradition? It is clear that Paul is dependent on *both* revelation, especially the Damascus revelation, *and* tradition received from those who were Christians before him. Although Paul's encounter with the risen Jesus, his personal authority, and the authority of his gospel are independent of any human mediation, he is dependent on others for the form of the kerygma, the liturgy of the Lord's Supper, and of course for his knowledge of the sayings and deeds of Jesus. It is most probable, for example, that Paul inquired about Jesus when he visited Peter (Gal. 1:18). He needed no one to confirm for him, however, the truth that Jesus was the risen Lord, that salvation had been acquired by the death and resurrection of Jesus, or his own apostolic commission and authority. These he knew directly from his encounter with the risen Jesus. But for other matters maintained by the tradition of those before him, he was happy to be dependent. For although the Damascus Road revelation brought an astounding newness to Paul personally, the gospel that he was now entrusted with had been believed by many before him and was in continuity with that tradition. Paul, independent though he surely was, was no innovator when it came to the substantial matters of the Christian faith.

The Continuity of Paul's Doctrine with That of Earlier Believers in Jesus

It has long been recognized that Paul's Letters are filled with fragments of earlier traditional materials. These occur in a variety of forms—for example, kerygmatic, confessional, liturgical, hymnic, catechetical, and paraenetic (i.e., ethical exhortation).[10] We have already noted the kerygmatic material

10. See especially Hunter, *Paul and His Predecessors*.

of 1 Corinthians 15:3–7 and the liturgical material of 1 Corinthians 11:23–26. Paul, of course, inherits the liturgy of the Lord's Supper and of baptism. But Paul receives much more from those who were Christians before him. In some instances, it is debatable whether we really do have a preliterary form or whether Paul himself composes traditional-sounding material.

In addition to the 1 Corinthians 15 text, an example of a kerygmatic form is 1 Thessalonians 1:9b–10. Confessional forms (*homologia*) can be seen in Romans 10:8–10 and Philippians 2:11. For liturgical forms in Paul, A. M. Hunter refers us to Romans 1:3–5 and 1 Corinthians 8:6 (cf. Eph 4:4–6; 5:14; 1 Tim. 2:5–6). Two famous hymns, probably pre-Pauline, are Philippians 2:6–11 and Colossians 1:12–20 (see also Col. 3:16; and possibly 2 Tim. 2:11–13; Titus 3:4–7). For traditional paraenesis, see Galatians 5:13–6:10; Philippians 4:4–9; and the household codes of Ephesians 4:1–6:20 and Colossians 3:5–4:6. Among other pre-Pauline "formulae," Hunter mentions Romans 4:24–25 and the faith-hope-love triad in 1 Thessalonians 1:3; 5:8; Colossians 1:4–5; Galatians 5:5–6; Romans 5:1–5; and 1 Corinthians 13:13. Finally, there appears to be a pattern of OT texts used in the writers of the NT that probably points to the early tradition. Paul makes use of many of the same OT texts and combinations of texts that may indicate an early collection of testimonies (e.g., the linking of Isa. 28:16; 8:14; Ps. 118:22 occurs in 1 Pet. 2:6–8 and Rom. 9:32–33).

It will be seen that some of these forms understandably overlap. Several of them can be classified as catechetical instruction. What remains clear from these sample passages is that Paul was happy to make frequent use of material that he inherited from the tradition. This is in itself understandable, but it underlines the fact that Paul is not a wholesale innovator, and that he stands within a broad stream of tradition shared by the early church. Paul undoubtedly was creative in his theology, but he was not creative ex nihilo. On the contrary, he carried on the tradition of those who were in Christ before him. Independent of the Jerusalem Apostles though he was, he shared with them a common gospel (see Gal. 2:9; 1 Cor. 15:11).

The Content of Paul's Gospel and the Synoptic Jesus

But, to return to the question of Paul and Jesus, what are we to make of the obvious differences in their teaching and perspective? We look at three key areas that have raised questions.

Justification by Faith

It is fairly easy to argue, especially from Matthew, that Jesus preached a salvation by works. Could anything be clearer than the emphasis at the end of the Sermon on the Mount? "Not every one who says to me, 'Lord, Lord,' shall enter the kingdom of heaven, but he who does the will of my Father who is in heaven. . . . And every one who hears these words of mine and does not do them will be like a foolish man who built his house upon the sand; and the rain fell, and the floods came, and the winds blew and beat against that house, and it fell; and great was the fall of it" (Matt. 7:21, 26–27). At first glance, this looks like an absolute contradiction of Paul's gospel of justification by faith. But that it is not necessarily so should become evident from the fact that Paul himself can make similar statements. Thus in Galatians 5:21, after citing a catalog of sins, he writes, "I warn you, as I warned you before, that those who do such things shall not inherit the kingdom of God." And a few lines later, he writes, "Do not be deceived; God is not mocked, for whatever a man sows, that he will also reap. For he who sows to his own flesh will from the flesh reap corruption; but he who sows to the Spirit will from the Spirit reap eternal life" (Gal. 6:7–8). Similarly, in Romans he writes: "For he [God] will render to every man according to his works: to those who by patience in well-doing seek for glory and honor and immortality, he will give eternal life; but for those who are factious and do not obey the truth, but obey wickedness, there will be wrath and fury. There will be tribulation and distress for every human being who does evil, the Jew first and also the Greek, but glory and honor and peace for every one who does good, the Jew first and also the Greek. For God shows no partiality" (Rom. 2:6–11). "For it is not the hearers of the law who are righteous before God, but the doers of the law who will be justified" (Rom. 2:13).

Clearly, the issue is more complicated than often realized. For Paul, faith and good works belong together; it is not a matter of one or the other. Grace, rather than canceling out practical righteousness, enables it.

However, though often underappreciated, the fact is that grace pervades the Synoptic Gospels. When Jesus announces the dawning of the kingdom in his person and ministry—the very essence of the Synoptics—it is as a gift, not as the reward for any kind of accomplishment that merits the kingdom. That the kingdom is gift rather than reward is clear from the Beatitudes at the beginning of the Sermon on the Mount (Matt. 5:3–11). Jesus calls people to believe in the gospel of the kingdom (Mark 1:15).

The forgiveness of sins is a matter of grace (see Matt. 1:21; 9:2; Mark 2:9; Luke 5:20; 7:48). The parable of the forgiven debt in Matthew 18:23–35 is a parable of the gift of the kingdom. So too are the healings that Jesus performs, depending only on the faith of those who are healed (e.g., Matt. 8:13; 9:28; 11:24). The two key Pauline terms "to believe" and "to be saved" are brought together in the parable of the soils, where the seed that fell along the path is likened to what happens when the devil "takes away the word from their hearts, that they may not believe and be saved [*hina mē pisteusantes sōthōsin*]" (Luke 8:12 [cf. 8:50, where, however, the verb *sōthēsetai* means "shall be well"]).

Two classic parables in Luke's Gospel reveal the connection between salvation and grace. In 15:11–32 the unworthy, prodigal son is gladly accepted back by the waiting, compassionate father. The son "was dead, and is alive," "was lost, and is found" (15:24, 32). The second Lukan parable (18:9–14) likewise is revealing. Of the two men praying in the temple, the Pharisee is actually more righteous than the tax collector, but the latter, who acknowledged his unworthiness and sin, is the one who goes away "*justified* rather than the other." The verb for "justify" here is *dikaioō*, one of Paul's favorite words, meaning "to be reckoned as righteous" (cf. Rom. 3:24, 28; 4:5).

Substitutionary Atonement

Not uncommonly, one hears that Jesus died the death of a martyr but with no sense of the meaning of his own death, even less that he thought of his death as in any sense an atoning sacrifice—something that is crucially important to Paul's soteriology. It has to be admitted that there are few Synoptic texts to help us understand the death of Jesus. But there are two key texts of great importance. The first is Mark 10:45 (// Matt. 20:28): "The Son of man also came not to be served but to serve, and to give his life as a ransom for many." The key word here is *lytron* ("ransom"), which is of the same root as Paul's *apolytrōsis*, meaning "redemption" (Rom. 3:24; 1 Cor. 1:30; Col. 1:14; cf. Eph. 1:7, 14), and the *antilytron* of 1 Timothy 2:6, "who gave himself as a ransom for all" (cf. the cognate verb in Titus 2:14).

The second passage is in the account of the Last Supper where Jesus speaks clearly of his death when he interprets the cup as "my blood of the covenant, which is poured out for many for the forgiveness of sins" (Matt. 26:28; cf. Luke 22:20) and refers to the bread as "my body which is given for you" (Luke 22:19). The sacrificial, atoning aspect of his death is clear in these words. The early church's and Paul's understanding of the significance of the death of Jesus goes back to Jesus himself.

Exalted Christology

Paul's view of Christ as *kyrios* ("Lord"), a divine figure, and perhaps even as *theos* ("God" [see Rom 9:5]), is often said to be an importation of foreign ideas from pagan religions or the emperor cult. The presupposition is that Jesus thought of himself in no such glorified way, but only as a teacher-healer. There is, of course, much in the Synoptic tradition that is consonant with Paul's view, but this material usually is dismissed as the Evangelists' reading of post-Easter theology into the narratives. Although we may well have to allow for the impact of the resurrection experience on the tradition, this hardly justifies wholesale dismissal of the high christology that is endemic to the tradition.

In addition to the direct christology reflected in the titles given to Jesus in the Synoptic tradition, the narratives commonly reflect what can be called an "indirect christology." That is, they consistently raise questions about the unique authority and identity of Jesus. And the implied conclusion, not always expressed, is that Jesus was without parallel, and that he represented a turning point in salvation history. So too the self-consciousness of Jesus reflected in passages such as Matthew 11:25–27; 10:32–33 is consistent with Paul's exalted christology. The restraint of the Synoptics in refusing freely to impose a postresurrection perspective on the tradition, as happens in the Fourth Gospel and to a much greater extent in the apocryphal gospels, is remarkable.

The Newness of Paul

I have been stressing the continuity between Paul and the Christians before him, and ultimately the continuity with Jesus. This does not imply that there is no newness in Paul. Basic to the problem that we have been examining in this chapter is the succession of time frames, particularly from the earthly ministry of Jesus to the time of the church, with the resurrection as the midpoint. With the progress of time, changes are required, and the newness that we encounter in Paul is explained by this development. We may note three factors bearing on the question.

First, and most important: the death and resurrection of Jesus, together with the outpouring of the Spirit, constitutes a new, climactic stage in salvation history. Only with the reaching of this new time frame can the full meaning of the story of Jesus be understood. The accomplishment of these events is responsible for a new perspective that we find not only in Paul but also in all of the early church. Paul speaks of the newness as a "mystery" (*mystērion*, thus $\mathfrak{P}^{46}$, Sinaiticus, Alexandrinus, and other manuscripts; many manuscripts, however, read *martyrion*, which accounts for the RSV's "testimony"), something hidden in ages past but now revealed in the present age of fulfillment (1 Cor. 2:1 [according to $\mathfrak{P}^{46}$, the first hand of Sinaiticus, and Alexandrinus], 7). At the end of Romans he refers to "my gospel and the preaching of Jesus Christ, according to the revelation of the mystery which was kept secret for long ages but is now disclosed and through the prophetic writings is made known to all nations, according to the command of the eternal God, to bring about the obedience of faith" (Rom. 16:25–26).

Paul can now speak in ways that Jesus, under the limitations imposed by that time frame, could not. At the same time, however, there is an essential continuity between the message of Jesus and of Paul. At the heart of both Jesus' and Paul's kerygma is the dawning of the new eschatological reality. Whereas for Jesus it lies in the imminent future, for Paul it is dynamically present, in and through the death and resurrection of Jesus, which serve as the basis of the new reality.

A second concrete factor that impacts Paul's teaching is the mission to the Gentiles. It was his special calling to preach the gospel to the Gentiles. Although it is too much to say, as some have done, that this call is responsible for Paul's law-free gospel, it would be difficult to deny that this calling influenced his theology. What remains remarkable is that Paul puts the Jews in the same needful situation as the pagan Gentiles. All are under sin; all need the remedy provided in the redeeming work of Christ.

Third, in Paul we have the influence of Hellenism as a factor to consider, although, given the pervasiveness of Hellenism even among the Jews, Paul is not unique here. Moreover, the influence appears to be more at the surface level—for example, in Paul's imagery and rhetoric rather than in his theology per se. For despite Paul's background as a Hellenistic Jew, as has been emphasized, his theology remains firmly rooted in the OT and in his Jewish heritage.

Regardless of the newness one may think of in Paul, he is hardly to be regarded as the founder of a new religion. The very suggestion would have been anathema to him. In his perspective, he remained a loyal Jew, faithful to the Scriptures, but having been privileged to see the risen Messiah, who was fulfilling the promises to Israel and accomplishing the salvation that would in time correspond to the prophets' expectation of a renewed creation.

Bibliography

Allison, Dale C., Jr. "The Pauline Epistles and the Synoptic Gospels: The Pattern of the Parallels." *NTS* 28 (1982):1–32.

Barclay, J. M. G. "Jesus and Paul." In *Dictionary of Paul and His Letters*, edited by Gerald F. Hawthorne and Ralph P. Martin, 492–503. Downers Grove, IL: InterVarsity, 1993.

Baur, F. C. *Paul, the Apostle of Jesus Christ: His Life and Work, His Epistles and Doctrine; A Contribution to the Critical History of Primitive Christianity*. Translated by E. Zeller. Edited by A. Menzies. 2 vols. London: Williams & Norgate, 1873–75. Reprint, Grand Rapids: Baker Academic, 2010.

Blomberg, Craig L. "Was Paul the True Founder of Christianity?" In *Making Sense of the New Testament: Three Crucial Questions*, 71–106. Grand Rapids: Baker Academic, 2004.

Bruce, F. F. "Paul and the Historical Jesus." *BJRL* 56 (1973–74): 317–35.

———. *Paul and Jesus*. Grand Rapids: Baker Academic, 1974.

Bultmann, Rudolf. "Jesus and Paul." In *Existence and Faith: Shorter Writings of Rudolf Bultmann*, 183–201. Translated by Schubert M. Ogden. London: Hodder & Stoughton, 1961.

———. "The Significance of the Historical Jesus for the Theology of Paul." In *Faith and Understanding*, edited by Robert W. Funk, translated by Louise Pettibone Smith, 220–46. New York: Harper & Row, 1966.

Dungan, David L. *The Sayings of Jesus in the Churches of Paul*. Philadelphia: Fortress, 1971.

Dunn, James D. G. "Jesus Tradition in Paul." In *Studying the Historical Jesus: Evaluations of the State of the Current Research*, edited by Bruce Chilton and Craig A. Evans, 155–78. NTTS 19. Leiden: Brill, 1994.

Fraser, J. W. *Jesus and Paul: Paul as Interpreter of Jesus from Harnack to Kümmel*. Abingdon, UK: Marcham, 1974.

Furnish, Victor Paul. "The Jesus-Paul Debate: From Baur to Bultmann." *BJRL* 47 (1964–65): 342–81.

Gundry, Robert H. "The Hellenization of Dominical Tradition and Christianization of Jewish Tradition in the Eschatology of 1–2 Thessalonians." *NTS* 33 (1987): 161–78.

Hunter, A. M. *Paul and His Predecessors*. Rev. ed. London: SCM, 1961.

Hurtado, Larry W. *Lord Jesus Christ: Devotion to Jesus in Earliest Christianity*. Grand Rapids: Eerdmans, 2003.

Johnston, George. "'Kingdom of God' Sayings in Paul's Letters." In *From Jesus to Paul: Studies in Honour of Francis Wright Beare*, edited by Peter Richardson and John C. Hurd, 143–56. Waterloo, ON: Wilfrid Laurier University Press, 1984.

Kim, Seyoon. "Jesus, Sayings of." In *Dictionary of Paul and His Letters*, edited by Gerald F. Hawthorne and Ralph P. Martin, 474–92. Downers Grove, IL: InterVarsity, 1993.

———. *The Origin of Paul's Gospel*. 2nd ed. Grand Rapids: Eerdmans, 1984.

Klausner, Joseph. *From Jesus to Paul*. Translated by William Stinespring. New York: Macmillan, 1943.

Longenecker, Bruce W., ed. *Narrative Dynamics in Paul: A Critical Assessment*. Louisville: Westminster John Knox, 2002.

Longenecker, Richard N. *New Wine into Fresh Wineskins: Contextualizing the Early Christian Confessions*. Peabody, MA: Hendrickson, 1999.

Neirynck, Frans. "Paul and the Sayings of Jesus." In *L'Apôtre Paul: Personnalité, style et conception du ministère*, by Albert Vanhoye et al., 265–321. BETL 73. Leuven: Leuven University Press, 1986.

Piper, J. *"Love Your Enemies": Jesus' Love Command in the Synoptic Gospels and the Early Christian Paraenesis; A History of the Tradition and Interpretation of Its Uses*. SNTSMS 38. Cambridge: Cambridge University Press, 1979.

Richardson, Peter, and Peter Gooch. "Logia of Jesus in 1 Corinthians." In *The Jesus Tradition Outside the Gospels*, edited by David Wenham, 39–62. GP 5. Sheffield: JSOT Press, 1985.

Ridderbos, Herman. *Paul and Jesus: Origin and General Character of Paul's Preaching of Christ*. Translated by David H. Freeman. Philadelphia: Presbyterian & Reformed, 1958.

Stanley, David Michael. "Pauline Allusions to the Sayings of Jesus." *CBQ* 23 (1961): 26–39.

Stanton, Graham N. *Jesus of Nazareth in New Testament Preaching*. SNTSMS 27. London: Cambridge University Press, 1974.

Still, Todd D., ed. *Jesus and Paul Reconnected: Fresh Pathways to an Old Debate*. Grand Rapids: Eerdmans, 2006.

Thompson, Michael B. *Clothed with Christ: The Example and Teaching of Jesus in Romans 12:1–15:13*. JSNTSup 37. Sheffield: JSOT Press, 1991.

Walter, N. "Paul and the Early Christian Jesus-Tradition." In *Paul and Jesus: Collected Essays*, edited by A. J. M. Wedderburn, 51–80. JSNTSup 37. Sheffield: JSOT Press, 1989.

Wedderburn, A. J. M., ed. *Paul and Jesus: Collected Essays*. JSNTSup 37. Sheffield: JSOT Press, 1989.

———. "Paul and Jesus: The Problem of Continuity." In *Paul and Jesus: Collected Essays*, edited by A. J. M. Wedderburn, 99–115. JSNTSup 37. Sheffield: JSOT Press, 1989.

———. "Paul and Jesus: Similarity and Continuity." In *Paul and Jesus: Collected Essays*, edited by A. J. M. Wedderburn, 117–43. JSNTSup 37. Sheffield: JSOT Press, 1989.

Wenham, David. *Did St. Paul Get Jesus Right? The Gospel according to Paul*. Oxford: Lion, 2010.

———, ed. *The Jesus Tradition Outside the Gospels*. GP 5. Sheffield: JSOT Press, 1985.

———. *Paul: Follower of Jesus or Founder of Christianity?* Grand Rapids: Eerdmans, 1995.

———. *Paul and Jesus: The True Story*. London: SPCK, 2002.

———. "Paul's Use of the Jesus Tradition: Three Samples." In *The Jesus Tradition outside the Gospels*, edited by David Wenham, 7–37. GP 5. Sheffield: JSOT Press, 1985.

———. *The Rediscovery of Jesus' Eschatological Discourse*. GP 4. Sheffield: JSOT Press, 1984.

Wilson, S. G. "From Jesus to Paul: The Contours and Consequences of a Debate." In *From Jesus to Paul: Studies in Honour of Francis Wright Beare*, edited by Peter Richardson and John C. Hurd, 1–21. Waterloo, ON: Wilfrid Laurier University Press, 1984.

Witherington, Ben, III. *Jesus, Paul, and the End of the World: A Comparative Study in New Testament Eschatology*. Downers Grove, IL: InterVarsity, 1992.

———. *Paul's Narrative Thought World: The Tapestry of Tragedy and Triumph*. Louisville: Westminster John Knox, 1994.

Wrede, William. *Paul*. Translated by Edward Lummis. London: Philip Green, 1907.

Wright, N. T. *What Saint Paul Really Said: Was Paul of Tarsus the Real Founder of Christianity?* Grand Rapids: Eerdmans, 1997.

19

Paul, Judaism, and the Law

Few subjects in Pauline theology have been discussed in recent years as intensively as Paul's understanding of the law. The subject is inherently and notoriously difficult because Paul makes equally strong positive and negative statements about the law of Moses. The challenge is to know how to put these diverse statements together into a coherent view of the subject. The problem has become more difficult than it used to be because of (1) the recent evaluation of first-century Judaism as a religion of grace and not of works righteousness, and (2) the recent emphasis on the continuing Jewishness of Paul's perspective and theology. These developments have caused many scholars to present a "new perspective" on Paul that stands in marked contrast to the traditional "Lutheran" understanding of Paul. The issue is supremely important because it bears on the very center of Paul's theology: his soteriology and the relationship between the new and the old covenants.

The Law in Judaism

The word "Torah" (*tôrâ*) has the broad meaning of "instruction" or "teaching." It thus has several applied meanings: the Scriptures, and more specifically the Pentateuch, but also the commandments of the law per se. In the OT the covenant, founded on God's grace, precedes and takes priority over the law. The call to obey the Torah is the response to the covenant, not its condition; through God's sovereign election Israel already enjoys the unmerited favor of God. Obedience to the law is the human response to the covenant relationship. Thus the account of the giving of the law on Sinai is preceded by a statement

366

of the covenant graciously extended by God to Israel (Exod. 20:1–17; Deut. 5:6–21). The covenant exists for no other reason than God's decree (note Deut. 7:7–8, where it is explained that the Lord loves Israel simply because he loves Israel). And where the law is taught in the OT the covenant is always presupposed as its foundation.

At the same time, however, obedience to the law is a requirement, not merely an option. And since the law is a unity, what is in view is obedience to all the commandments. The people are repeatedly called to be "careful to do all the words of this law which are written in this book" (e.g., Deut. 28:58). They have the choice of experiencing either blessings or curses, "life and good, death and evil," depending on whether they obey or disobey the law (Deut. 30:15–20). There is thus an ambiguity intrinsic to the relationship between the law and the blessings of the covenant. If "getting in" relationship with God is a fact given by God's grace, the line between that and "staying in" the relationship can become almost imperceptibly thin. There are statements that can easily be taken by the unwary to mean that salvation is the result of obedience to the law. The key to a correct understanding, however, was somehow in maintaining a balance between law and covenant.

It is precisely that balance that begins to be lost after the Babylonian exile, which was understood to be caused by the anger of the Lord at the sin of Israel. It was Israel's failure to live in obedience to the law that was responsible for this lowest point in the history of Israel (see, e.g., Ezra 5:12; 9:10–15; Lam. 1:8, 14, 18). The result after the exile was the birth of Judaism through a new turning to the law and a new determined dedication to obey the commandments. This new postexilic stress on the law was inevitable, and with the scribe Ezra we have the beginnings of what we now know as Second Temple Judaism (Ezra 7:10). The reading of "the book of the law of Moses" before all the people in Nehemiah 8 symbolizes this turn in direction. Ezra's prayer in Nehemiah 9 (esp. vv. 26–38) portrays the strong underlying motivation for this new commitment.

The new turning to the law soon finds concrete expression in movements such as the Essenes and the Pharisees, two groups that in their own way focused on the righteousness of the law. And of course Paul, the former Pharisee, stands in this tradition as one who was zealous for the law (see Gal. 1:14; Phil. 3:6).

But the OT prophets already knew that something new was needed; simply more energetic attempts to obey the law could not bring the people of God to the goal of righteousness. They therefore began to speak of a mysterious new future development—a new dynamic, indeed, a new covenant between God and Israel. Thus Jeremiah writes:

> Behold, the days are coming, says the Lord, when I will make a new covenant with the house of Israel and the house of Judah, not like the covenant which I made with their fathers . . . my covenant which they broke. . . . But this is the covenant which I will make with the house of Israel after those days, says the

LORD: I will put my law within them, and I will write it upon their hearts; and I will be their God, and they shall be my people . . . for I will forgive their iniquity, and I will remember their sin no more. (Jer. 31:31–34)

Ezekiel also looks forward to a new time: "A new heart I will give you, and a new spirit I will put within you. . . . And I will put my spirit within you, and cause you to walk in my statutes and be careful to observe my ordinances. . . . And I will deliver you from all your uncleannesses" (Ezek. 36:26–29 [cf. the new era of righteousness anticipated in Isa. 2:2–4; Mic. 4:1–3]). This future era does not involve the giving of a new law; rather, it is the time of a new covenant, a new reality involving both continuity and discontinuity with the past.

The Jewish View of the Law: Blessing or Burden?

The law is the supreme mark of Jewish identity. The law separates Jews out from all other nations. Judaism calls its adherents to a law-centered or nomistic existence—that is, to an ongoing and relentless pursuit of obedience to the law. The challenge of faithfulness to Torah thus governed the daily existence of the Jews. The law was regarded as one, if not the greatest, of God's gifts to Israel. It was thought of as an incomparable blessing, a source of both light and joy (as seen in, e.g., Ps. 119).

At the same time, however, there is evidence in the NT that the law was also burdensome. Peter's remark, as recorded in Acts 15:10, is telling: "Now therefore why do you make trial of God by putting a yoke upon the neck of the disciples which neither our fathers nor we have been able to bear?" According to Matthew, Jesus accused the Pharisees of placing upon the shoulders of their disciples "heavy burdens, hard to bear," an allusion to the demands of their oral law (Matt. 23:4). There are indeed many, many more statements about the law being a blessing than about the law as a burden, but we have just enough of the latter statements to indicate that the law was a problem for some. Paul too had problems with the law. It was not only a blessing but also a curse. "For all who rely on works of the law are under a curse; for it is written, 'Cursed be every one who does not abide by all things written in the book of the law, and do them'" (Gal. 3:10). So too James regards the law as a unity, all of which was to be obeyed, so that "whoever keeps the whole law but fails in one point has become guilty of all of it" (James 2:10). It was in fact impossible to be fully successful in keeping the law, and therein lay its burdensome quality.

The Law in Paul's Life

As an outstanding Pharisee, Saul would have lived as a nomist, a person whose life was centered on the law. For Saul, this would have meant not simply obedience to the written Torah but also obedience to the oral tradition of the Pharisees, which was intended to spell out the meaning of, and thus serve as a fence around, the written Torah. Paul speaks unashamedly of his success in this regard: "as to the law a Pharisee . . . as to righteousness under the law blameless" (Phil. 3:5–6). He speaks of his "former life in Judaism": "I advanced in Judaism beyond many of my own age among my people, so extremely zealous was I for the traditions of my fathers" (Gal. 1:13–14). "Blameless" here does not mean "sinless." Rather it means that by Pharisaic standards Paul was irreproachable.

Remarkably, however, after his encounter with the risen Christ Paul counts all his impressive accomplishments in Judaism as merely rubbish. "For his sake I have suffered the loss of all things, and count them as refuse, in order that I may gain Christ and be found in him, not having a righteousness of my own, based on law, but that which is through faith in Christ, the righteousness from God that depends on faith" (Phil. 3:8–9). The Damascus Road experience caused a complete reversal in Paul's view of the law. Salvation, he now saw, lay not in the possibility of his own righteousness via the law but rather in the death of the risen Messiah. "I do not nullify the grace of God; for if justification were through the law," he writes, "then Christ died to no purpose" (Gal. 2:21). "If it is the adherents of the law who are to be the heirs, faith is null and the promise is void" (Rom. 4:14).

This dramatic reversal forced Paul to reconsider the meaning or purpose of the law. Attempts to obey the law were not the way to righteousness and acceptance by God. How, then, does the law relate to the covenant promises of God? Why was the law given to Israel? Paul poses precisely that question in Galatians 3:19. His response is that the law "was added because of transgressions till the offspring should come to whom the promise [i.e., the promise made to Abraham] had been made." What is meant by the words "because of transgressions" (tōn parabaseōn charin) is not spelled out, but in Romans 5:20 Paul specifies that "law came in, to increase the trespass," and thus, as Paul says earlier, the law brings transgression and wrath (Rom. 4:15).

In contrast to the Jewish thinking of that day, the law is not at all the means to righteousness; it can only multiply sin and provoke God's wrath. Paul makes this unmistakably clear: "If a law had been given which could make alive, then righteousness would indeed be by the law. But the scripture consigned all things to sin, that what was promised to faith in Jesus Christ might be given to those who believe" (Gal. 3:21–22 [cf. Rom. 3:20]). The result, however, was that the law became in effect a curse rather than a blessing.

But this was only a temporary situation, "till the offspring should come to whom the promise had been made" (Gal. 3:19)—that is, until the coming of Christ. The careful explanation is given by Paul in Galatians 3:15–29. In Paul's view, salvation history begins with the promise to Abraham and his "offspring." Reasoning like a rabbi, Paul notes that the word "offspring" (*sperma*, lit., "seed") is singular in form rather than plural, and thus he concludes (ignoring that it is a collective) that it refers to a specific descendant of Abraham, namely Christ. The law, however, came 430 years after the promise to Abraham, and it cannot annul the earlier Abrahamic covenant (Gal. 3:17). The promised inheritance comes not by law but by the earlier promise, Paul says (Gal. 3:18; cf. Rom. 4:13).

The law is not against the promises (Gal. 3:21); it simply had a temporary role to play, and with the coming of Christ, that role had been accomplished. Paul employs two metaphors to describe the function of the law in the interim period between the giving of the law on Sinai and the coming of Christ. First, the law was like a prison; second, the law was like a person in charge of a child (which is the literal meaning of *paidagōgos* in Gal. 3:24), "Before faith came," he writes, "we were confined under the law, kept under restraint until faith should be revealed" (Gal. 3:23). The law brought a kind of temporary imprisonment. Then he adds, "So that the law was our custodian [better: "disciplinarian" or "child guide"] until Christ came" (Gal. 3:24). Most commentators conclude that the "child guide" is to be understood in a negative sense, parallel to the idea of constraint in the preceding verse, rather than positively in the sense of "tutor" or "instructor."

This temporary period of restraint lasted only to the coming of Christ and has now come to an end: "But now that faith has come, we are no longer under a custodian" (Gal. 3:25). It is as though our childhood were past, and therefore we are no longer under "guardians and trustees" (Gal. 4:2). The time has fully come, and we have now moved into full sonship and have become mature heirs (Gal. 4:4–7). We are therefore no longer under the law. Paul is adamant about our freedom from the law: "For freedom Christ has set us free; stand fast therefore, and do not submit again to a yoke of slavery" (Gal. 5:1). To attempt to gain righteousness by the law is to fall away from grace (Gal. 5:4).

In Galatians, then, Paul argues that the law has come to an end, having now served its main purpose, and that Christians have been delivered from being "under" the law (Gal. 3:24–25; 4:4–5). That we are no longer "under the law" (*hypo nomon*) is of categorical importance to Paul. The same emphasis is found in Paul's Letter to the Romans (e.g., Rom. 6:14; 7:4–6; 10:4).

In light of Paul's earlier zeal for the law as a Pharisee, this negation of the law is truly astonishing. He seems to have allowed Jewish believers in Jesus to keep practicing the law, if they were so inclined. Paul himself can be accused of being a model of inconsistency—but deliberately so. According to Acts 16:3, Paul had Timothy, who was only half-Jewish, circumcised, while Paul (along with the Jerusalem Apostles) was content to leave his other co-worker, the Gentile Titus, uncircumcised (see Gal. 2:3). According to Acts 18:18, at Cenchreae, on his way to Jerusalem, Paul cut his hair in connection with a Nazirite vow (see Num. 6:1–21) that would be fulfilled in the temple with, among other things, the giving of sin offerings (Acts 21:26). Paul seems very much a Jew here, and he seems content to have James portray him as one who "live[s] in observance of the law" (Acts 21:24). In fact, Paul lived sometimes in accord with the law and sometimes not. In a most remarkable passage, he says, "To the Jews I became as a Jew, in order to win Jews; to those under the law I became as one under the law—though not being myself under the law—that I might win those under the law. To those outside the law I became as one outside the law—not being without law toward God but under the law of Christ—that I might win those outside the law. . . . I have become all things to all men, that I might by all means save some" (1 Cor. 9:20–22). In a mixed community, where the truth of the gospel was at stake, Paul no doubt would side with the Gentiles. Thus he chides Peter for withdrawing from table fellowship with the Gentiles when the Judaizers arrived in Antioch (Gal. 2:11–16).

The New Perspective on Paul

In the past, the relation of Paul's new faith to Judaism seemed simple enough: Judaism was the polar opposite, the very antithesis to the gospel. It was a matter of righteousness by works versus the gospel of righteousness by faith/grace. The "new perspective on Paul"[1] finds its genesis in the new stress put on Judaism as a religion of grace rather than a religion of works-based righteousness. In an important survey of Second Temple Judaism E. P. Sanders showed that obedience to the law was within the context of the grace of the covenant, and that this Judaism was therefore best characterized as a "covenantal nomism."[2] Judaism, rightly perceived, is a religion of grace as much as Christianity is. The election and covenant on which Judaism rests are God's work for Israel, not Israel's work for God. Both religions, understood correctly, are founded on grace.

Israel is called to obey the law not *in order to* enjoy election and covenant, but rather *because* Israel is elect and in covenant relation with God. In its day-to-day existence, yes, Israel is law-centered or "nomistic." But that is only within the framework of the covenant, and thus Israel's religion is properly to be understood as a "covenantal nomism"—that is, the faithful practice of the law within the covenantal relationship already established by God.

If Judaism is a religion of grace, then much of Paul's teaching must be reunderstood, since he at least appears to argue that Judaism taught, or at least some Jews believed, that salvation depended on the merit of righteousness gained through obedience to the law. Hence the new perspective on Paul. Furthermore, many advocates of the new perspective tend to regard justification by faith as

1. The expression is James Dunn's. See Dunn, *The New Perspective on Paul*. For insightful assessment, see Westerholm, "The 'New Perspective' at Twenty-Five"; see also Hagner, "Paul and Judaism."

2. It was E. P. Sanders's now famous book *Paul and Palestinian Judaism* that gave this subject new prominence. But the point had been made by many before Sanders.

not essential, or at least not central, to Paul's theology, but instead as a pragmatic means of making salvation available to the Gentiles apart from the law.

The key error in the traditional misunderstanding of Paul, according to the new perspective, is that Paul has been read through the lens of Martin Luther and the Reformation. Luther, it is argued, misunderstood Paul because he attributed his own anxiety about salvation to Paul. Luther was unable to achieve the righteousness that he thought was necessary for salvation, and as he studied Paul, he wrongly concluded that Paul too struggled with legalism and eventually argued that salvation could not be obtained by works, but could be received only by faith.[3]

What is fundamental to Paul according to the new perspective is not the universal problem of human sin, but specifically the problem of bringing the Gentiles into the family of faith. Paul had no quarrel with Judaism, except for its exclusiveness, and he had no problem with the law per se. Hence, his polemic against "works of the law" does not concern the commandments in themselves and has nothing to do with the question of righteousness by obedience to the law. It concerns the law only insofar as it represents Jewish badges of identity (circumcision, Sabbath, dietary laws) that separated Jews from the Gentiles and constituted an obstacle to the salvation of the Gentiles. The issue at stake was a matter of race, not grace. Paul's gospel of salvation without works of the law thus has only the salvation of the Gentiles in view. The implication of the new perspective is a double grace-based soteriology: the covenantal nomism of the OT is the way of salvation for Israel, while Paul's law-free gospel is the way of salvation for the Gentiles.

Several things must be said in response to this analysis:

1. The definition of Judaism as a covenantal nomism is correct, but it is an ideal one. The postexilic dedication to the law was so intense that often statements were made that at least gave the impression that salvation had to be earned by obedience to the law.[4] Emphasis on obedience to the law could virtually obscure the reality of covenant grace. While undoubtedly there were some authentic covenantal nomists in the first century, who held matters in proper balance, there were also probably many de facto legalists,[5] who in their very dedication forgot

3. For a convincing answer to this understanding, see Westerholm, *Perspectives Old and New on Paul*.

4. E. P. Sanders (*Paul and the Palestinian Jews*), for example, had to admit that *4 Ezra*, which teaches salvation by works, does not at all fit his analysis. But, as has often been pointed out, there are many places in the literature of the Second Temple that present a legalistic-sounding point of view, wherein salvation is earned by good works.

5. Legalism is the teaching that one earns salvation by one's righteousness deeds. As such, it is to be distinguished from nomism, which is law-centeredness in response to the grace of election (salvation).

or neglected the foundations of grace on which the law rested. These would be the people whom Paul resisted and to whom he proclaimed his law-free gospel. Thus, the traditional view that Paul was attacking legalism—though there should have been none in Judaism—need not be rejected.

2. Paul knows only one gospel, for both Jews and Gentiles, and thus his polemic concerning the law is valid for both groups. Paul's opposition to the law is more fundamental than merely a rejection of its exclusionary aspects. Far from sharing the optimistic view of human nature held by contemporaneous Judaism, Paul believes that both Jews and Gentiles are trapped in sin and need the salvation provided by Christ (see Rom. 3:9, 19–20, 23). The law could not provide the answer, even when kept in proper balance with the covenant. Thus Paul argues that faith in Christ, not obedience to law, is central to salvation (see, e.g., Gal. 3:15–29; Rom. 10:4; 1 Cor. 9:19–23). Paul therefore is unhappy not only with legalism but also with nomism, even of a covenantal variety. Paul regards both Jews and Gentiles as in the same human predicament of captivity to sin, to which there is only one answer: Christ, not the law.

3. It is true that before the Damascus Road experience Paul, as far as we know, had no qualms about his status before God. We have already noted that by the standard of the Pharisees, he thought of himself as blameless. So he seems to have been satisfied enough with his experience as a Pharisee. It was only when he was faced with the indisputable fact that the crucified Nazarene was the risen Messiah that he apparently came to understand the gravity and scope of human sin and the impotence of the law. It cannot be doubted that after his call/conversion Paul argued against the possibility of righteousness through the law in a way that sounds like Luther—or more correctly, we see that Luther had read the post–Damascus Road Paul correctly.

4. While susceptible to different interpretations, in my opinion, certain statements of Paul remain more easily understood as referring to the totality of the law and to the attempt of at least some Jews to establish righteousness by obedience to it, rather than merely to objectionable boundary markers between Jews and Gentiles. Thus in an autobiographical passage, Paul states his goal to "be found in him, not having a righteousness of my own, based on law, but that which is through faith in Christ, the righteousness from God that depends on faith" (Phil. 3:9). And in Romans he writes, "I bear them witness that they [the Jews] have a zeal for God, but it is not enlightened. For, being ignorant of the righteousness that comes from God, and seeking to establish their own, they did not submit to God's righteousness. For Christ is the end of the law, that every one who has faith may be justified" (Rom. 10:2–4).

Paul's Negative and Positive Statements about the Law

One of the reasons for the emergence of the new perspective is the difficulty of reconciling the negative and positive statements about the law. For some, it is difficult to believe that Paul, as a Jew, was critical of the law in any fundamental sense. By restricting Paul's negative statements to the badges of Jewish identity that excluded Gentiles from salvation, it is possible to conclude that Paul otherwise never abandoned his full commitment to the ongoing validity of the law. There can be no question that the badges of Jewish identity would be opposed by Paul, called as he was to evangelize the Gentiles. Some texts fit this hypothesis well, but many more, in my opinion, are difficult to reconcile with it. Paul's view of the law, like his gospel, is global (i.e., universal), and it applied to both Jews and Gentiles.

We do not need here to review all the Pauline passages, negative and positive. We have already noted many of the negative passages.[6] To summarize the main points:

1. The law had a temporary role to play, and that role was not to bring the kind of righteousness that would enable one to stand before God justified, but rather to heighten sin and the awareness of sin.
2. Jews and Gentiles alike are sinful and unable to fulfill the law. Therefore, they are in the same dire situation: without hope apart from the grace of God in Christ.
3. Salvation for both Jews and Gentiles is available only through faith in Christ, not obedience to the law, and for that reason the gospel must be preached to both Jews and Gentiles.

This is a view of the law diametrically opposed to what Paul had earlier believed.

At the same time, alongside his criticism of the law (or at least of the misperception of the law) he continues to esteem it and to say positive things about it. If he says that the law has come to an end, he also says that his gospel does not overthrow the law (Rom. 3:31).

Various solutions have been proposed to reconcile Paul's seemingly contradictory statements about the law. One common suggestion is that Paul opposes the civil and ceremonial (ritual) law, but not the moral law. This view, however, is unconvincing for two reasons. First, the law was accepted as a unity by the Jews, all of it equally binding, so that the distinction itself is artificial. Second, and more important, Paul's statements about no longer being "under the law" are too sweeping and absolute to refer only to the ceremonial law.

---

6. Some of the key texts are Galatians 2:15–16; 3:11–13; Romans 3:19–20, 28; 4:4–6; 5:20–21; 11:5–6.

The "works of the law" against which he militates involve more than simply the ceremonial law or the Jewish badges of identity.[7] This is not to deny that for Paul, as for Jesus, it is the moral law that is of primary interest and that the moral teaching of the law is perpetuated in the church.

Another, perhaps more attractive, way to handle the problem is to take the negative statements as referring to *nomos* understood as the commandments, and the positive statements as referring to the broader meaning of *nomos* as Scripture. In other words, *nomos* as the commandments is done away with, but *nomos* considered as the whole of Scripture is viewed positively, witnessing ultimately to Christ and justification by faith, as well as containing within it the parenthetical *nomos* whose purpose has now been served. This explanation often works well, but not in every instance, and in my view there is a more satisfactory way to deal with the problem.

If we take the negative statements concerning the law as referring to the commandments, it is possible to take the positive statements as referring simply to *the righteousness that is the goal of the law*. Thus, although Christians are no longer "under the law" as commandments, they are still meant to arrive at something approximating the righteousness of the law, so that, *in this sense*, the law in effect is finally upheld. If the moral righteousness that is the heart of the law is mediated to the church through the teaching of Christ and the Apostles and is followed by Christians, then it can be seen that the gospel does not overthrow the law, but rather it produces what the law was after in the first place. The dynamic, however, is totally different. This righteousness is not the result of being "under the law"—language that is anathema to Paul—nor is it derived from tablets of stone, but rather it derives from *the law of the new covenant written on our hearts*, in the life of the Spirit (2 Cor. 3:3).

Paul's Ongoing Commitment to the Importance of Righteousness Apart from the Law

Saul the Pharisee, whether classified as a nomist or a legalist, after his conversion no longer put the law at the center of his life. Having encountered the crucified, risen Christ, Paul could no longer be content with the law, not even as a covenantal nomist. Nor, in Paul's view, could his fellow Jews find salvation in covenantal nomism. In his new understanding of matters the law had only a negative role to play, not a positive one. There was one way of salvation, and that was through Christ, and Christ now took the central place in his life that the law previously held.

7. As Brevard Childs rightly points out, one may see from Philippians 3:2–11 that justification by faith is not a peripheral matter of "defending the inclusion of the Gentiles into the promises of Israel (Stendahl). This passage from Philippians shows that Paul uses the doctrine within a much wider context than in a debate over the inclusion of the Gentiles" (*The New Testament as Canon*, 109).

This does not mean, however, that Paul should be construed as an anti-nomian who now regarded righteousness as unnecessary or merely optional. Paul will make this clear again and again in the very contexts in which he is arguing for freedom from the law (see, e.g., Rom. 3:31). In one of Paul's most remarkable statements he writes, "For I through the law died to the law"; the purpose clause that immediately follows those words must be noted: "that I might live to God" (Gal. 2:19). Here is perhaps the key paradox in the whole question of Paul and the law: we are no longer under the law—we are set free from it—precisely *in order to pursue righteousness more effectively*. This is how Paul puts it: "For you were called to freedom, brethren; only do not use your freedom as an opportunity for the flesh, but through love be servants of one another. For the whole law is fulfilled in one word, 'You shall love your neighbor as yourself'" (Gal. 5:13–14). The goal of the Christian's identification with Christ's death is that "we too might walk in newness of life" (Rom. 6:4; cf. 8:4).

Paul says that Christians, having been set free from slavery to sin, "have become slaves of righteousness" and are to present their members as slaves "to righteousness for sanctification" (Rom. 6:18–19). The metaphor is carried on in Romans 7:6: "But now we are discharged from the law, dead to that which held us captive, so that we serve not under the old written code but in the new life of the Spirit."

For Paul, then, it could hardly be clearer that freedom from the law leads not to sin, but rather, paradoxically, is meant to lead to the practice of righteousness. For Paul, the gospel of Jesus Christ and the practice of righteousness are inseparable: "For God has done what the law, weakened by the flesh, could not do: sending his own Son in the likeness of sinful flesh and for sin, he condemned sin in the flesh, in order that the just requirement of the law might be fulfilled in us, who walk not according to the flesh but according to the Spirit" (Rom. 8:3–4).

Although Paul despairs over the law itself, he never gives up on the righteousness of the law. The difference at the beginning of the present new eschatological era, however, is that the law is interpreted through the teaching of Jesus (thus focusing on the love commandment as supreme). And, most important, one moves out from under bondage to sin and its penalty not by the law, but only by faith in Christ.[8]

Bibliography

Barclay, John M. G. "Paul among Diaspora Jews: Anomaly or Apostate?" *JSNT* 60 (1995): 89–120.

Barclay, John M. G., and Simon J. Gathercole, eds. *Divine and Human Agency in Paul and His Cultural Environment*. LNTS 335. London: T&T Clark, 2006.

Barth, Markus. "St. Paul—A Good Jew." *HBT* 1 (1979): 7–45.

8. See further discussion below in chapter 25, "Galatians."

Bertone, John A. *The Law of the Spirit: Experience of the Spirit and Displacement of the Law in Romans 8:1–16*. SBL 86. New York: Peter Lang, 2005.

Bird, Michael F. *The Saving Righteousness of God: Studies on Paul, Justification and the New Perspective*. PBM. Milton Keynes, UK: Paternoster, 2007.

Bruce, F. F. "The Curse of the Law." In *Paul and Paulinism: Essays in Honour of C. K. Barrett*, edited by Morna D. Hooker and Stephen G. Wilson, 27–36. London: SPCK, 1982.

Carson, D. A., Peter T. O'Brien, and Mark A. Seifrid, eds. *The Complexities of Second Temple Judaism*. Vol. 1 of *Justification and Variegated Nomism*. Grand Rapids: Baker Academic, 2001.

———, eds. *The Paradoxes of Paul*. Vol. 2 of *Justification and Variegated Nomism*. Grand Rapids: Baker Academic, 2004.

Chae, Daniel J.-S. *Paul as Apostle to the Gentiles: His Apostolic Self-Awareness and Its Influence on the Soteriological Argument in Romans*. PBTM. Carlisle, UK: Paternoster, 1997.

Childs, Brevard S. *The New Testament as Canon: An Introduction*. Philadelphia: Fortress, 1985.

Das, A. Andrew. *Paul and the Jews*. Peabody, MA: Hendrickson, 2003.

———. *Paul, the Law, and the Covenant*. Peabody, MA: Hendrickson, 2001.

Davies, W. D. "Paul: From the Jewish Point of View." In *The Early Roman Period*. Vol. 3 of *The Cambridge History of Judaism*, edited by W. D. Davies et al., 678–730. Cambridge: Cambridge University Press, 1999.

———. "Paul and the Law: Reflections on Pitfalls in Interpretation." In *Paul and Paulinism: Essays in Honour of C. K. Barrett*, edited by Morna D. Hooker and Stephen G. Wilson, 4–16. London: SPCK, 1982.

———. *Paul and Rabbinic Judaism: Some Rabbinic Elements in Pauline Theology*. 4th ed. Philadelphia: Fortress, 1980.

Drane, John W. *Paul, Libertine or Legalist? A Study in the Theology of the Major Pauline Epistles*. London: SPCK, 1975.

Dunn, James D. G. *Jesus, Paul and the Law: Studies in Mark and Galatians*. Louisville: Westminster John Knox, 1990.

———. *The New Perspective on Paul*. Rev. ed. Grand Rapids: Eerdmans, 2008.

———, ed. *Paul and the Mosaic Law: The Third Durham-Tübingen Research Symposium on Earliest Christianity and Judaism, Durham, September, 1994*. WUNT 89. Tübingen: Mohr Siebeck, 1996.

Elliott, Mark Adam. *The Survivors of Israel: A Reconsideration of the Theology of Pre-Christian Judaism*. Grand Rapids: Eerdmans, 2000.

Fitzmyer, Joseph A. "Paul and the Law." In *To Advance the Gospel: New Testament Studies*, 186–201. 2nd ed. Grand Rapids: Eerdmans, 1998.

Gager, John G. *Reinventing Paul*. New York: Oxford University Press, 2000.

Garlington, Don B. *"The Obedience of Faith": A Pauline Phrase in Historical Context*. WUNT 2/38. Tübingen: Mohr Siebeck, 1991.

Gaston, Lloyd. *Paul and the Torah*. Vancouver: University of British Columbia Press, 1987.

Gathercole, Simon J. *Where Is Boasting? Early Jewish Soteriology and Paul's Response in Romans 1–5*. Grand Rapids: Eerdmans, 2002.

Gundry, Robert H. "Grace, Works, and Staying Saved in Paul." *Bib* 66 (1985): 1–38.

Hagner, Donald A. "Balancing the Old and the New: The Law of Moses in Matthew and Paul." *Int* 51 (1997): 20–30.

———. "Paul and Judaism: Testing the New Perspective." In *Revisiting Paul's Doctrine of Justification: A Challenge to the New Perspective*, by Peter Stuhlmacher, 75–105. Downers Grove, IL: InterVarsity, 2001.

———. "Paul as a Jewish Believer in Jesus—According to His Letters." In *Jewish Believers in Jesus: The Early Centuries*, edited by Oskar Skarsaune and Reider Hvalvik, 96–120. Peabody, MA: Hendrickson, 2007.

————. "Paul in Modern Jewish Thought." In *Pauline Studies: Essays Presented to Professor F. F. Bruce on His 70th Birthday*, edited by Donald A. Hagner and Murray J. Harris, 143–65. Grand Rapids: Eerdmans, 1980.

————. "Paul's Quarrel with Judaism." In *Anti-Semitism and Early Christianity: Issues of Polemic and Faith*, edited by Craig A. Evans and Donald A. Hagner, 128–50. Minneapolis: Fortress, 1993.

————. "A Positive Theology of Judaism from the New Testament." *SEÅ* 69 (2004): 7–28.

Harrington, Daniel J. *Paul and the Mystery of Israel*. ZS. Collegeville, MN: Liturgical Press, 1992.

Hengel, Martin, with Roland Deines. *The Pre-Christian Paul*. Translated by John Bowden. Philadelphia: Trinity Press International, 1991.

Hübner, Hans. *Law in Paul's Thought: A Contribution to the Development of Pauline Theology*. Translated by James C. G. Greig. Edited by John Riches. SNTW. Edinburgh: T&T Clark, 1984.

Kim, Johann D. *God, Israel, and the Gentiles. Rhetoric and Situation in Romans 9–11*. SBLDS 176. Atlanta: Scholars Press, 2000.

Kim, Seyoon. *Paul and the New Perspective: Second Thoughts on the Origin of Paul's Gospel*. Grand Rapids: Eerdmans, 2002.

Koperski, Veronica. *What Are They Saying about Paul and the Law?* Mahwah, NJ: Paulist Press, 2001.

Kuula, Kari. *Paul's Treatment of the Law and Israel in Romans*. Vol. 2 of *The Law, the Covenant and God's Plan*. PFES 85. Helsinki: Finnish Exegetical Society; Göttingen: Vandenhoeck & Ruprecht, 2003.

Laato, Timo. *Paul and Judaism: An Anthropological Approach*. Translated by T. McElwain. SFSHJ 115. Atlanta: Scholars Press, 1995.

Longenecker, Richard N. *Paul, Apostle of Liberty*. Grand Rapids: Baker, 1964.

Marshall, I. Howard. "Salvation, Grace and Works in the Later Writings in the Pauline Corpus." *NTS* 42 (1996): 339–58.

Martin, Brice L. *Christ and the Law in Paul*. NovTSup 62. Leiden: Brill, 1989.

Moo, Douglas J. "'Law,' 'Works of the Law,' and Legalism in Paul." *WTJ* 45 (1983): 73–100.

Porter, Stanley E. "Was Paul a Good Jew? Fundamental Issues in a Current Debate." In *Christian-Jewish Relations through the Centuries*, edited by Stanley E. Porter and Brook W. R. Pearson, 148–74. JSNTSup 192. Sheffield: Sheffield Academic Press, 2000.

Räisänen, Heikki. *Paul and the Law*. 2nd ed. Philadelphia: Fortress, 1987.

Rapa, Robert Keith. *The Meaning of "Works of the Law" in Galatians and Romans*. SBL 31. New York: Peter Lang, 2001.

Rhyne, C. Thomas. *Faith Establishes the Law*. SBLDS 55. Chico, CA: Scholars Press, 1981.

Sanders, E. P. *Jewish Law from Jesus to the Mishnah: Five Studies*. London: SCM; Philadelphia: Trinity Press International, 1990.

————. *Paul, the Law, and the Jewish People*. Minneapolis: Fortress, 1983.

————. *Paul and Palestinian Judaism*. Philadelphia: Fortress, 1977.

Schoeps, H. J. *Paul: The Theology of the Apostle in the Light of Jewish Religious History*. Translated by Harold Knight. Philadelphia: Westminster, 1961.

Schreiner, Thomas R. *40 Questions about Christians and Biblical Law*. Grand Rapids: Kregel, 2010.

————. "The Abolition and Fulfillment of the Law in Paul." *JSNT* 35 (1989): 47–74.

————. *The Law and Its Fulfillment: A Pauline Theology of Law*. Grand Rapids: Baker Academic, 1993.

————. *Paul, Apostle of God's Glory in Christ: A Pauline Theology*. Downer Grove, IL: InterVarsity, 2001.

————. "'Works of Law' in Paul." *NovT* 33 (1991): 217–44.

Sloan, Robert B. "Paul and the Law: Why the Law Cannot Save." *NovT* 33 (1991): 35–60.

Snodgrass, Klyne. "Spheres of Influence: A Possible Solution to the Problem of Paul and the Law." *JSNT* 32 (1988): 93–113.

Stuhlmacher, Peter. *Revisiting Paul's Doctrine of Justification: A Challenge to the New Perspective*. Downers Grove, IL: InterVarsity, 2001.

Thielman, Frank. *From Plight to Solution: A Jewish Framework for Understanding Paul's View of the Law in Galatians and Romans*. NovTSup 61. Leiden: Brill, 1989.

———. *Paul and the Law: A Contextual Approach*. Downers Grove, IL: InterVarsity, 1994.

Thurén, Lauri. *Derhetorizing Paul: A Dynamic Perspective on Pauline Theology and the Law*. WUNT 124. Tübingen: Mohr Siebeck, 2000.

Tomson, Peter J. *Paul and the Jewish Law: Halakha in the Letters of the Apostle to the Gentiles*. CRINT 3/1. Assen: Van Gorcum; Minneapolis: Fortress, 1990.

Watson, Francis. *Paul, Judaism, and the Gentiles: Beyond the New Perspective*. Rev. ed. Grand Rapids: Eerdmans, 2007.

Westerholm, Stephen. "The 'New Perspective' at Twenty-Five." In *The Paradoxes of Paul*. Vol. 2 of *Justification and Variegated Nomism*, edited by D. A. Carson, Peter T. O'Brien, and Mark A. Seifrid, 1–38. Grand Rapids: Baker Academic, 2004.

———. *Perspectives Old and New on Paul: The "Lutheran" Paul and His Critics*. Grand Rapids: Eerdmans, 2004.

———. "Sinai as Viewed from Damascus: Paul's Reevaluation of the Mosaic Law." In *The Road from Damascus: The Impact of Paul's Conversion on His Life, Thought, and Ministry*, edited by Richard N. Longenecker, 147–65. Grand Rapids: Eerdmans, 1997.

Winger, Michael. *By What Law? The Meaning of Nomos in the Letters of Paul*. SBLDS 128. Atlanta: Scholars Press, 1992.

Wright, N. T. *The Climax of the Covenant: Christ and the Law in Pauline Theology*. Minneapolis: Fortress, 1991.

———. *Paul: In Fresh Perspective*. Minneapolis: Fortress, 2005.

Yinger, Kent L. *The New Perspective on Paul: An Introduction*. Eugene, OR: Wipf & Stock, 2010.

———. *Paul, Judaism, and Judgment according to Deeds*. SNTSMS 105. Cambridge: Cambridge University Press, 1999.

Zetterholm, Magnus. *Approaches to Paul: A Student's Guide to Recent Scholarship*. Minneapolis: Fortress, 2009.

20

Paul's Gospel and
the Parting of the Ways

According to the last chapter of the book of Acts, while the Apostle Paul was under house arrest in Rome awaiting his trial, he called the leaders of the Jews to meet with him. Paul tells them that "it is because of the hope of Israel [*tēs elpidos tou Israēl*] that I am bound with this chain" (Acts 28:20). Paul thus identified the gospel that he preached, for which he was now suffering, as what had been promised to Israel. In no sense does he regard what he preached as alien to his Jewish heritage. When a large crowd of Jews gathered to hear Paul, Luke says that "he expounded the matter to them from morning till evening, testifying to the kingdom of God and trying to convince them about Jesus both from the law of Moses and from the prophets" (Acts 28:23). Although some responded positively, it seems that more did not. Paul then cites the passage from Isaiah about Israel's hard-heartedness (Acts 28:26–27, quoting Isa. 6:9–10)—a text regularly employed by the early church to explain Jewish unbelief in the gospel—adding words that anticipated the parting of the ways between the synagogue and the church that was already beginning to occur: "Let it be known to you then that this salvation of God has been sent to the Gentiles; they will listen" (Acts 28:28).

It was of the highest importance to Paul that his gospel was the fulfillment of what God promised in the Scriptures. The hope of Israel was based on the line of promise and expectation revealed in the Abrahamic, Sinaitic, and Davidic covenants, culminating in the apocalyptic expectation of the Prophets. Saul the Pharisee had based his life on the Scriptures, especially the law of Moses, but as we have noted, his whole life was turned upside down when the risen

Jesus appeared to him on the road to Damascus. There was much new for him to learn, and there were important modifications that he had to make in his previous understanding of God's purposes. At the same time, he has no doubts concerning the continuity of his new understanding with his earlier faith, or that it was the fulfillment of what God had promised to Israel. But now the gospel—the good news—was far different from what he could have imagined as a Pharisee. At its heart was the astounding fact of a crucified Messiah who had risen from the dead.

The Gospel of God Is the Gospel of the Son of God

At the beginning of the Epistle to the Romans Paul identifies himself as "set apart for the gospel of God [*euangelion theou*]" (Rom. 1:1 [the phrase is used again in Rom. 15:16; 1 Thess. 2:2, 8–9; 2 Cor. 11:7]). This gospel is the kerygma that Paul preached. The "good news of God" is what the Scriptures had promised and it concerns "[God's] Son, who was descended from David according to the flesh, and designated Son of God in power according to the Spirit of holiness by his resurrection from the dead, Jesus Christ our Lord" (Rom. 1:3–4). Since the gospel is about the Son, a few lines later Paul describes it as "the gospel of his [God's] Son" (Rom. 1:9). He most commonly refers to it as the "gospel of Christ" (Rom. 15:19; 1 Cor. 9:12; 2 Cor. 2:12; 9:13; Gal. 1:7; Phil. 1:27; 1 Thess. 3:2). He also uses the expression "the gospel of the glory of Christ" (2 Cor. 4:4; cf. 1 Tim. 1:11).

The Gospel of Justification by Faith

In Romans 1:16 Paul further identifies the gospel as "the power of God for salvation to every one who has faith, to the Jew first and also to the Greek." The good news about Jesus Christ brings salvation to all who believe. The determinative word here is "to have faith" (a substantive participle, "to everyone who believes" [*panti tō pisteuonti*]). Paul quotes Habakkuk 2:4 in the verse that follows: "He who through faith [*ek pisteōs*] is righteous shall live" (Rom. 1:17 [cited again in Gal. 3:11]). Admittedly, Paul's Greek is ambiguous.[1] It may also be translated as "The one who is righteous will live by faith" (NRSV). But if we take our cue from the main argument of both Romans and Galatians, it is more likely that Paul means to say that one gains the status of righteousness

---

1. The ambiguity is caused by the uncertainty concerning whether the phrase *ek pisteōs*, "by faith," is to be taken as modifying what precedes or what follows. It fits Paul's argument better to take it as modifying the words that precede—that is, telling how a person becomes righteous rather than merely that a righteous person will live faithfully. Oddly, Paul's version of the verse omits both the pronoun of the Hebrew text ("his faith[fulness]") and the pronoun of the LXX text ("my [*mou*] faith[fulness]").

through believing and in this way has life. Of course, Paul would hardly disagree with the alternative translation, since he also believes that a righteous person will live faithfully. For Paul, salvation is "from faith to faith" (Rom. 1:17, KJV), perhaps meaning from God's faithfulness (see below on Christ's faithfulness, pp. 386–87) to the response of faith in the believer.

Human Sinfulness

As we saw in the preceding chapter, the Christian Paul no longer believed that obeying the law of Moses was the way to righteousness. According to Paul, before the law all stand guilty, both Jew and Gentile. The extensive indictment of humanity in Romans 1:18–3:20 climaxes with this statement: "For no human being will be justified in his sight by works of the law, since through the law comes knowledge of sin." Although Paul, as a Pharisee, no doubt was sensitive to the problem of sin, it was his encounter with Christ and his subsequent need to comprehend the meaning of a crucified Messiah that provided him with this pessimistic view of the law's potentiality. It was when he encountered the solution to the problem that he began for the first time to comprehend the full gravity of the human situation. "I do not nullify the grace of God; for if righteousness were through the law, then Christ died to no purpose" (Gal. 2:21). Again, he writes, "For if a law had been given which could make alive, then righteousness would indeed be by the law. But the scripture consigned all things to sin, that what was promised to faith in Jesus Christ might be given to those who believe" (Gal. 3:21–22). The death of Christ thus delivers us from the law. "Christ redeemed us from the curse of the law, having become a curse for us" (Gal. 3:13).

Today's new perspective on Paul notwithstanding, Paul counterposes "works of the law," in the sense of righteous deeds, to "faith" as the way to righteousness. The problem posed by works of the law is not merely that they are what marked off the Jews from the Gentiles, and Paul's polemic against the works of the law is not merely for the sake of the mission to the Gentiles. The problem addressed by Paul is more basic and of universal scope, and thus common to both Jews and Gentiles: the law—that is, works of the law—cannot produce righteousness. According to Paul, faith, and faith alone, is the way to righteousness, for both Jews and Gentiles.

Making Sense of the Death of Christ: The Justification of Sinners

The good news preached by Paul centers on the saving death of Christ: "We preach Christ crucified, a stumbling block to Jews and folly to Gentiles, but to those who are called, both Jews and Greeks, Christ the power of God and the wisdom of God" (1 Cor. 1:23). It is only through this kerygma concerning the crucified Christ that those who believe can be saved (1 Cor. 1:21). The gospel is therefore "the word of the cross" (1 Cor. 1:18). For Paul, there is not and cannot be any other gospel than the one he preached. And thus he anathematizes any who would bring another, so-claimed but fraudulent, "gospel" (Gal. 1:9).

There is for Paul only one answer to the unavoidable, common plight of fallen humanity. "Since all have sinned and fall short of the glory of God, they are justified by his grace as a gift, through the redemption which is in Christ Jesus" (Rom. 3:23–24). This remarkable pericope, Romans 3:21–26, brings us to the very heart of Paul's soteriology.[2] He describes the death of Christ as "an expiation by his blood, to be received by faith" (3:25). The words "sacrifice of atonement" (NRSV, NIV) translate the single word *hilastērion*, which is drawn from the LXX, where it translates *kappōret*, meaning the lid covering the ark of the covenant (Exod. 25:17–22; 26:34; cf. Heb. 9:5, the only other place where the word is used in the NT).[3] This was the place where the high priest sprinkled blood to make atonement for the sins of the people (Lev. 16:13–16), and thus it comes to be translated "mercy seat," meaning "place of mercy," a metonym for the atoning sacrifice itself.[4] In choosing the word, Paul not only focuses on the death of Christ as an atoning sacrifice but also implies that Christ's sacrifice is the fulfillment of the sacrificial ritual of the OT (cf. his reference to the sacrifice of Christ as "our paschal lamb" in 1 Cor. 5:7). In Romans 3:21–26 Paul succinctly describes the divine solution to sin—the very heart of his gospel. He explains that this gift of God's salvation by means of the blood of Christ is a demonstration "that he [God] himself is righteous [*dikaion*] and that he justifies [*dikaiounta*] him who has faith in Jesus" (Rom. 3:26).[5] He makes his point yet again in Romans 3:28: "For we hold that a man is justified by faith apart from works of law" (cf. Gal. 2:16 [where the verb occurs three times]; 3:11, 24).

The verb *dikaioō* ("to justify") is a key word in the Pauline vocabulary, occurring very frequently in Galatians and Romans. In Greek it has the same root as the common word for "righteousness" (*dikaiosynē*). It means "to regard

2. See Gathercole, "Justified by Faith, Justified by His Blood."

3. The noun *kappōret* is cognate to the verb *kpr*, which means to "cover over" or "make atonement." The root occurs also in "Yom Kippur" ("Day of Atonement"). There are cognates to *hilastērion* in the verb *hilaskomai*, "to have mercy on," "to forgive" (Luke 18:13; Heb. 2:17); *hilasmos*, "atoning sacrifice" (1 John 2:2; 4:10); and *hileōs*, "merciful" (Heb. 8:12; Matt. 16:22).

4. In the middle of the twentieth century there was a famous disagreement between two well-known NT scholars over the meaning of *hilastērion*. Leon Morris (*The Apostolic Preaching of the Cross*, 125–85) defended the idea of "propitiation"—that is, the appeasement of the wrath of God (this is the translation in the KJV). C. H. Dodd ("Atonement"), on the contrary, thought such an idea too pagan and preferred the translation "expiation"—that is, the wiping away or removal of sin. Since Dodd was the chair of the RSV committee, this became the RSV translation. There is no reason, however, why both ideas cannot be implied, and "sacrifice of atonement" is a reasonable alternative.

5. Christ bore the penalty of our sins and died in our place. In defense of the concept of penal substitution, see Marshall's chapter on "The Substitutionary Death of Jesus," in *Aspects of the Atonement*, 34–67.

or declare as righteous"—righteous in the sense of a right relationship with God. To that extent, justification is a forensic idea; it is like the decision of a law court. The startling aspect of justification in Paul's thought is that those who are justified are not actually righteous. If they were actually righteous, there would be no need of the gospel, and the declaration that they were in right relationship with God would amount to a tautology. Being justified, however, they are acquitted from the guilt of sin.

In Romans 4 Paul demonstrates through the examples of Abraham and David that this gospel of justification by faith was already a reality in the OT. Here we encounter, as also in Galatians, the famous Genesis 15:6 text used by Paul: "Abraham believed God, and it was reckoned to him as righteousness" (Rom. 4:3 [cf. Rom. 4:9, 22; cited also in Gal. 3:6]). Paul loves this text because it shows that faith is the way to righteousness. The forensic character of justification is underlined by the repeated use of the verb *logizomai*, meaning "to reckon" or "to count as true," in midrashic treatment of the Genesis text (the word is used an additional ten times in Rom. 4). The illustration of David shows the negative use of the word—that is, where something is *not* reckoned: "Blessed are those whose iniquities are forgiven, and whose sins are covered; blessed is the man against whom the Lord will not reckon his sin" (Rom. 4:7–8, quoting Ps. 32:1–2).

Paul's statements still shock us today: "And to one who does not work but trusts him who justifies the ungodly [*ton asebē*], his faith is reckoned as righteousness" (Rom. 4:5).[6] "While we were still weak, at the right time Christ died for the ungodly" (Rom. 5:6). "But God shows his love for us in that while we were yet sinners Christ died for us" (Rom. 5:8). "While we were enemies we were reconciled to God by the death of his Son" (Rom. 5:10). It is the sacrificial death of Christ that is the source of salvation precisely for sinners: "We are now justified by his blood" (Rom. 5:9). The result of this justification is reconciliation with God and the peace that accompanies it: "Therefore, since we are justified by faith, we have peace with God through our Lord Jesus Christ" (Rom. 5:1). "There is therefore now no condemnation for those who are in Christ Jesus" (Rom. 8:1).

The Righteousness of God

Paul states that in the gospel "the righteousness of God is revealed" (Rom. 1:17). The phrase "righteousness of God" (*dikaiosynē tou theou*) is practically

---

6. This statement stands in tension with some OT texts, such as Exodus 23:7: "I will not acquit the wicked" (LXX: "you will not justify the godless" [*ou dikaioseis ton asebē*]). And among many other passages, note Psalm 1:5–6: "Therefore the wicked will not stand in the judgment, nor sinners in the congregation of the righteous; for the LORD knows the way of the righteous, but the way of the wicked will perish." However, there are also OT passages that express grace toward sinners.

synonymous with the gospel: "But now the righteousness of God has been manifested apart from law, although the law and the prophets bear witness to it, the righteousness of God through faith in Jesus Christ for all who believe" (Rom. 3:21–22). It is clear from just these statements that the righteousness of God refers not so much to God's own (undoubted) moral righteousness as to God's saving activity, to a righteousness of which he is the source—that is, a righteousness that is a gift rather than a demand (Rom. 5:17).[7] Romans 10:3 makes this clear: "For, being ignorant of the righteousness that comes from God, and seeking to establish their own, they did not submit to God's righteousness"; to which Paul adds, "For Christ is the end of the law, that every one who has faith may be justified" (Rom. 10:4).

Frequently in the OT God's righteousness is in synonymous parallelism with salvation provided by God. Thus, for example, in Isaiah 45:8:

> Let the skies rain down righteousness;
> let the earth open, that salvation may sprout forth,
> and let it cause righteousness to spring up also.

Or, in Isaiah 46:13:

> I bring near my deliverance,[8] it is not far off,
> and my salvation will not tarry.

Further examples of this parallelism between righteousness and salvation can be seen in Isaiah 51:5, 6, 8; 56:1.

God's righteousness is thus virtually synonymous with the salvation that he provides. "For our sake he made him to be sin [i.e., a sin offering] who knew no sin, so that in him we might become the righteousness of God" (2 Cor. 5:21).[9] It is obvious that there is a close relationship between the righteousness "of God" and the righteousness that comes "from God." Paul counts his accomplishments as worth nothing, desiring now to "be found in him [Christ], not having a righteousness of my own, based on law, but that which is through faith in Christ, the righteousness from God [*tēn ek theou dikaiosynēn*] that depends on faith" (Phil. 3:9).

Jesus Christ is the righteousness of the Christian. Paul states that God has made Christ "our wisdom, our righteousness and sanctification and

---

7. Martin Luther originally understood the phrase as referring to God's moral perfection, before which he was crushed. When he understood it as God's gracious action of providing the gift of righteousness by faith, he rediscovered the gospel.

8. Unfortunately, the RSV, influenced by the synonymous parallelism, unjustifiably translates *ṣedeq/ṣĕdāqâ* here and in Isaiah 51:5, 6, 8; 56:1 as "deliverance," (the LXX in every instance translates the word using *dikaiosynē*) thus obscuring the connection between righteousness and salvation.

9. See Hooker, "Interchange in Christ."

redemption" (1 Cor. 1:30). Paul may well have had this text from Jeremiah in view: "Behold, the days are coming, says the Lord, when I will raise up for David a righteous Branch, and he shall reign as king and deal wisely, and shall execute justice and righteousness in the land. . . . And this is the name by which he will be called: 'The Lord is our righteousness'" (Jer. 23:5–6 [// 33:15–16]).

Faith in Christ and the Faithfulness of Christ

There is ambiguity in the Greek phrase *pistis Christou* that has caused much discussion among scholars.[10] There is no question that it can be taken as an objective genitive, thus meaning "faith in Christ." But it can also be understood in some places as a subjective genitive, thus meaning "the faithfulness[11] of Christ," in which case the focus is not on the faith of the believer but rather on the faithful obedience of Christ in his atoning death. As an example, it is possible to take it as a subjective genitive in Romans 3:22, producing the following translation: "the righteousness of God through *the faithfulness of* Jesus Christ for all who believe." The saving righteousness of God depends on the faithfulness of Christ. This translation here has the advantage of avoiding the redundancy of the following phrase "for all who believe."

Another example where the subjective genitive is worth considering is Galatians 2:16, where the phrase occurs twice: "Yet who know that a man is not justified by works of the law but through *the faithfulness of* Jesus Christ, even we have believed in Christ Jesus, in order to be justified by *the faithfulness of* Christ, and not by works of the law, because by works of the law shall no one be justified."[12] Other examples are in Galatians 2:20; 3:22; Philippians 3:9. All these passages also refer specifically to the faith of the believer. So again the subjective genitive avoids redundancy, though, admittedly, Paul has no aversion to repeating himself when he is on a point that he regards as of great importance.

The ambiguity here is the result of the fact that faith in Christ and the faithfulness of Christ are two sides of the same coin: the former is made possible only by the latter. This may be the sense of "from faith to faith" in Romans 1:17 (KJV). As Morna Hooker puts it, "Believing faith depends on the faith/faithfulness of Christ: it is the response to Christ's faith and claims it as one's own."[13]

10. The most well-known discussion has been that between Richard Hays and James Dunn, Hays arguing for the subjective genitive, Dunn for the objective genitive. See Hays, *The Faith of Jesus Christ*. The second edition includes republication of key essays by Hays and Dunn. These essays, together with a response from Paul Achtemeier, are available also in Johnson and Hay, *Looking Back, Pressing On*, 33–92.

11. The word *pistis* can mean "faith" or "faithfulness."

12. Morna Hooker writes, "The true antithesis is not between works and faith, but between the works of the *Law* and the saving work of *Christ*" ("ΠΙΣΤΙΣ ΧΡΙΣΤΟΥ," 341).

13. Ibid., 340.

We cannot be certain about this disputed genitive, but the subjective genitive offers much rich insight into the relationship between our faith and Christ's work. In no way should openness to this reading of *pistis Christou* be thought to weaken the important emphasis on *faith in Christ* throughout Paul's writings.[14]

Justification by Faith: The Center of Paul's Theology?

Much of Protestant, and especially Lutheran, theology has strongly affirmed the centrality of justification by faith, not only for Paul's theology but also indeed for the Christian faith itself. This conclusion came under strong criticism in the early twentieth century when Albert Schweitzer argued that justification by faith was not the center of Paul's theology. His oft-quoted statement was that "the doctrine of righteousness by faith is therefore a subsidiary crater, which has formed within the rim of the main crater—the mystical doctrine of redemption through the being-in-Christ."[15]

Critics of the view that justification is the center of Paul's theology often point out that the doctrine is important only in Galatians and Romans and is hardly to be found in the other Pauline Epistles. In response it should be said that it is not necessary for Paul to articulate the center of his theology in every one of his letters. Nothing will qualify as the center if it must be something referred to with equal stress in all of Paul's Letters. Moreover, the center is, by its nature, so basic to everything that it may just for that reason be easily presupposed. The churches knew from Paul's own teaching what the center of his gospel was.

Obviously, the question of the center of Paul's theology depends on what is meant by "center." Most of the proposals for the center, including justification by faith, salvation, redemption, forgiveness of sins, reconciliation, participation in Christ, union with Christ, the inbreaking of a new age, and so on, focus on the fruit of what God has done for us through the coming of Christ. All of these things are true and important, but to decide which one is central is rather like chasing after the wind. A more significant question involves asking what is basic to all of these as their cause. For the answer to that, we must go back to Paul's basic kerygma: the death and resurrection of Christ. It is, above all, *God's grace in the cross* that makes all else possible. And this therefore qualifies to be the center of Paul's theology because all else derives from it. Inasmuch as justification by faith is the clearest articulation of how the grace of the cross is mediated to the believer, how the righteousness of God is received by sinners, it remains an excellent way to express the center. But reconciliation is also an appealing possibility.[16]

Of the greatest importance in Pauline theology is Paul's understanding of the cross and resurrection of Christ as the climactic turning point in salvation

---

14. A result that Dunn thinks is inevitable (see Dunn, "ΕΚ ΠΙΣΤΕΩΣ").

15. Schweitzer, *The Mysticism of Paul the Apostle*, 225.

16. See Martin, *Reconciliation*.

history.[17] For Paul, the cross is the key not only to understanding God's election of Israel and the function of the Mosaic law (e.g., Rom. 9:4–5; Gal. 3:22–29) but also to understanding the whole of human history. The obedient death of Christ, "the last Adam," counteracts the sin of the first Adam (Rom. 5:12–21; 1 Cor. 15:20–22, 45–50) and will bring about the eschatological transformation of the created order. Thus, as Peter Stuhlmacher puts it, "It is precisely the crucified and risen Christ whom Paul proclaims as the one through whom God creates and by whom all God's work is brought to completion; thereby Paul's theology of the cross has a universal scope and covers the history that spans from the first day to the day of eschatological redemption."[18]

The Parting of the Ways

Although many Jews accepted the gospel—the earliest church was composed exclusively of Jews—most did not, for perhaps two main reasons. The first was also the stumbling block that had made Saul a persecutor of the church: the idea that the Messiah had come not to overthrow the Romans and restore the sovereignty to Israel but instead to be crucified and to die as a common criminal. The second was the inclusion of the Gentiles into the people of God without requiring obedience to the law, which seemed to void the uniqueness of Israel.

The parting of the ways between the church and the synagogue was an inevitability. Contrary to some recent arguments,[19] the separation began very early and was a process that continued through the first century, no doubt at different rates of speed in different places. Despite the strong lines of continuity with the old, the degree of newness in the gospel was so great that it was impossible for the church to continue as a sect within Judaism. The old wineskins were unable to contain the new wine of the gospel (see Mark 2:22 pars.). What Jesus suggested by this metaphor (Matt. 9:17) began to be articulated as early as Stephen and the Hellenists (Acts 6:14). That the first-century Jews did not regard the believers in Jesus as a sect within Judaism becomes abundantly clear from the pattern of the Jewish persecution of Jewish Christians in the book of Acts, beginning in earnest in 8:1 (cf. 4:1–3; 5:17–18, 33, 40). Indeed, the whole of the NT and the Christian writers of the second century witness to the early parting of the ways.[20]

17. On the importance of salvation history to Paul, see Yarbrough, "Paul and Salvation History."

18. Stuhlmacher, *Reconciliation, Law, and Righteousness*, 162.

19. See, for example, Becker and Reed, *The Ways that Never Parted*. The contributors to this volume argue that the separation—that is, absolute separation—does not really take place until the fourth century.

20. See Hagner, "Another Look at 'The Parting of the Ways.'"

It is not to be doubted that both Judaism and Christianity were undergoing significant development during the first century. From this, many have claimed that neither one had a stable, ongoing identity through this process, which makes comparisons and contrasts impossible.[21] On the contrary, both Judaism and Christianity were discrete, identifiable entities, each group holding certain fixed core elements or tenets. Christianity represented something radically new in the Jewish tradition. Its gospel, as we have seen, was marked by striking newness—a newness that could not be contained within Judaism. From the beginning, the faith of the Christians was centered in the risen Christ and Lord (Acts 2:36) of the kerygma, whose death was an atoning sacrifice for the sins of the world (1 Cor. 15:3–7).

In the first century, with the fall of Jerusalem and the destruction of the temple in 70, Judaism would make the transition to rabbinic Judaism. As dramatic as this development was, it did not affect the fundamental commitments of all forms of Judaism: monotheism, Torah, the election of Israel, and the temple. Although there are strong continuities between the beliefs of the Christians and the Jews—enough to make it possible for Jewish Christians to claim that their new commitment was the fulfillment of their earlier faith—there was also enough discontinuity to make the two faiths incompatible. Each of the pillars of Judaism was affected in one way or another by the commitments of the Christians. Thus the confession of Jesus as Lord and the devotion to him as a divine figure necessitated a modification, but not a rejection, of monotheism (see below, pp. 398–99). As for Torah, of course Jewish Christians could continue to obey the commandments, but Torah was no longer the center of their lives in the way that it had been previously. Gentile Christians did not abide by the commandments, except insofar as (to a not inconsiderable extent) they were incorporated in the teaching of Jesus and the Apostles. The election of Israel became marginalized by the huge influx of uncircumcised Gentiles into the church (an issue that Paul wrestles with in Rom. 9–11). The sacrificial ritual of the temple became outmoded with the understanding of the death of Jesus as the one sufficient sacrifice for sins (as the book of Hebrews stresses). The destruction of the temple would have confirmed the conviction of the Christians and in any event removed it from their immediate attention, while the rabbis continued their development of regulations concerning the temple long after its destruction.

Another important dividing point, related to the foregoing discussion, needs to be stressed. Although Jews and Christians shared the same Scriptures, they interpreted them in very different ways. Paul read his Bible very differently

21. This exaggerated claim traces back to an influential but misleading book by Walter Bauer, *Orthodoxy and Heresy in Earliest Christianity*. Bauer argued that in the early years the church was characterized by diversity, and that a single orthodoxy emerged only in later centuries. For a more convincing view, see Marshall, "Orthodoxy and Heresy in Earlier Christianity." See also Hultgren, *The Rise of Normative Christianity*; Köstenberger and Kruger, *The Heresy of Orthodoxy*.

after the Damascus Road experience than he did before (see 2 Cor. 3:15–16). The christocentric hermeneutic of the early church (see chap. 2 above) clearly was one of the reasons for the parting of the ways. The Christians now regarded the promises of the Scriptures as in the process of fulfillment, while the Jews continued to look only to the future. The situation was rather like what Martin Buber said in his remark: "To the Christian the Jew is the stubborn fellow who in a redeemed world is still waiting for the Messiah. For the Jew the Christian is a heedless fellow who in an unredeemed world affirms that somehow or other redemption has taken place."[22]

The Jewishness of Christianity is not to be minimized. Jewish Christians in particular recognized their newly found faith as derived from, and the fulfillment of, the faith of Israel. For them, Christianity seemed to involve not so much a parting from their past as a movement toward the goal of their Jewish faith. At the beginning they undoubtedly thought of themselves as within Judaism as its fulfillment, but soon the tensions became such that they recognized that, paradoxically, the fulfillment of Judaism would find its expression outside of unbelieving Judaism.

One can speak of Christianity as a sect of Judaism only for the first transitional year or two of its existence. Gradually, as the radical newness that is intrinsic to the claims of Christianity became evident, the hostility between the Christians and the Jews escalated and the lines hardened. This parting of the ways was not the result of a formal declaration at a particular place and time; rather, it was an unavoidable, painful existential reality that was faced and accepted with differing practical consequences, and with differing rapidity in different places. It goes without saying that the differences can provide no justification for anti-Semitism.

This analysis of the parting of the ways does not entail an anachronistic "essentialism," whereby the Christian doctrinal consolidation of the fourth century is read into the first century. Nor does it entail a triumphalist supersessionism, whereby the church usurps the place of Israel, leaving it no further place in God's plan. The high irony is that, according to Paul, the parting of the ways is, in a strange way, itself the fulfillment of Israel's role in salvation history as the servant to the nations (see Isa. 49:6; 42:6) and at the same time the realization in part of Israel's hope. In the birth of the church Israel has become "a light for revelation to the Gentiles" and at the same time the cause of ultimate "glory to thy people Israel" (Luke 2:32). The salvation of the world is from the Jews.

Bibliography

Aune, David E., ed. *Rereading Paul Together: Protestant and Catholic Perspectives on Justification*. Grand Rapids: Baker Academic, 2006.

22. Cited in Niebuhr, "Martin Buber," 146.

Bauer, Walter. *Orthodoxy and Heresy in Earliest Christianity*. Translated by a team from the Philadelphia Seminar on Christian Origins. Edited by Robert A. Kraft and Gerhard Krodel. Philadelphia: Fortress, 1971.

Becker, Adam H., and Annette Yoshiko Reed, eds. *The Ways that Never Parted: Jews and Christians in Late Antiquity and the Early Middle Ages*. Minneapolis: Fortress, 2007.

Beilby, James K. and Paul Rhodes Eddy, eds. *Justification: Five Views*. Downers Grove, IL: InterVarsity, 2011.

Bird, Michael F. *The Saving Righteousness of God: Studies on Paul, Justification and the New Perspective*. PBM. Milton Keynes, UK: Paternoster, 2007.

Boers, Hendrikus. *The Justification of the Gentiles: Paul's Letters to the Galatians and Romans*. Peabody, MA: Hendrickson, 1994.

Brondos, David A. *Paul on the Cross: Reconstructing the Apostle's Story of Redemption*. Minneapolis: Fortress, 2006.

Carson, D. A., Peter T. O'Brien, and Mark A. Seifrid, eds. *The Complexities of Second Temple Judaism*. Vol. 1 of *Justification and Variegated Nomism*. Grand Rapids: Baker Academic, 2001.

———, eds. *The Paradoxes of Paul*. Vol. 2 of *Justification and Variegated Nomism*. Grand Rapids: Baker Academic, 2004.

Cousar, Charles B. *A Theology of the Cross: The Death of Jesus in the Pauline Letters*. OBT 24. Minneapolis: Fortress, 1990.

Dodd, C. H. "Atonement." In *The Bible and the Greeks*, 82–95. London: Hodder & Stoughton, 1935.

———. "The Mind of Paul." In *New Testament Studies*, 67–128. Manchester, UK: Manchester University Press, 1953.

Donfried, Karl P. "Justification and Last Judgment in Paul." *ZNW* 67 (1976): 90–110.

Dunn, James D. G. "ΕΚ ΠΙΣΤΕΩΣ: A Key to the Meaning of ΠΙΣΤΙΣ ΧΡΙΣΤΟΥ." In *The Word Leaps the Gap: Essays on Scripture and Theology in Honor of Richard B. Hays*, edited by J. Ross Wagner, C. Kavin Rowe, and A. Katherine Grieb, 351–66. Grand Rapids: Eerdmans, 2008.

———, ed. *Jews and Christians: The Parting of the Ways A.D. 70 to 135*. Grand Rapids: Eerdmans, 1999.

———. *The Partings of the Ways between Christianity and Judaism and Their Significance for the Character of Christianity*. Philadelphia: Trinity Press International, 1991.

Finlan, Stephen. *The Background and Content of Paul's Cultic Atonement Metaphors*. SBLAB 19. Atlanta: Society of Biblical Literature, 2004.

Fitzmyer, Joseph A. "The Gospel in the Theology of Paul." In *To Advance the Gospel: New Testament Studies*, 149–61. 2nd ed. Grand Rapids: Eerdmans, 1998.

Gathercole, Simon J. "Justified by Faith, Justified by His Blood: The Evidence of Romans 3:21–4:25." In *The Paradoxes of Paul*. Vol. 2 of *Justification and Variegated Nomism*, edited by D. A. Carson, Peter T. O'Brien, and Mark A. Seifrid, 147–84. Grand Rapids: Baker Academic, 2004.

Hagner, Donald A. "Another Look at 'The Parting of the Ways.'" In *Earliest Christian History: History, Literature, and Theology. Essays from the Tyndale Fellowship in Honor of Martin Hengel*, edited by Michael F. Bird and Jason Maston, 381–427. WUNT 2/320. Tübingen: Mohr Siebeck, 2012.

Hamerton-Kelly, Robert G. *Sacred Violence: Paul's Hermeneutic of the Cross*. Minneapolis: Fortress, 1992.

Hays, Richard B. *The Faith of Jesus Christ: The Narrative Substructure of Galatians 3:1–4:11*. 2nd ed. Grand Rapids: Eerdmans, 2002.

Hengel, Martin. *The Atonement: The Origins of the Doctrine in the New Testament*. Translated by John Bowden. Philadelphia: Fortress, 1981.

Hooker, Morna D. "Interchange in Christ." *JTS* 22 (1971): 349–61.

———. "ΠΙΣΤΙΣ ΧΡΙΣΤΟΥ." *NTS* 35 (1989): 321–42.

Hultgren, Arland J. *Paul's Gospel and Mission: The Outlook from His Letter to the Romans.*
    Philadelphia: Fortress, 1985.

———. "The Pistis Christou Formulation in Paul." *NovT* 22 (1980): 248–63.

———. *The Rise of Normative Christianity.* Minneapolis: Fortress, 1994.

Hunter, A. M. *The Fifth Evangelist.* London: SCM, 1980.

———. *The Gospel according to St. Paul.* London: SCM, 1966.

Husbands, Mark, and Daniel J. Treier, eds. *Justification: What's at Stake in the Current Debates.*
    Downers Grove, IL: InterVarsity, 2004.

Johnson, E. Elizabeth, and David M. Hay, eds. *Looking Back, Pressing On.* Vol. 4 of *Pauline
    Theology.* SBLSymS 4. Atlanta: Scholars Press, 1997.

Johnson, Luke Timothy. "Rom 3:21–26 and the Faith of Jesus." *CBQ* 44 (1982): 77–90.

Johnson, S. Lewis, Jr. "The Gospel that Paul Preached." *BSac* 128 (1971): 327–40.

Käsemann, Ernst. "'The Righteousness of God' in Paul." In *New Testament Questions of Today*,
    168–82. Philadelphia: Fortress, 1969.

Kim, Seyoon. "God Reconciled His Enemy to Himself: The Origin of Paul's Concept of Rec-
    onciliation." In *The Road from Damascus: The Impact of Paul's Conversion on His Life,
    Thought, and Ministry*, edited by Richard N. Longenecker, 102–24. Grand Rapids: Eerdmans,
    1997.

———. *The Origin of Paul's Gospel.* 2nd ed. Grand Rapids: Eerdmans, 1984.

Köstenberger, Andreas J., and Michael J. Kruger. *The Heresy of Orthodoxy: How Contemporary
    Culture's Fascination with Diversity Has Reshaped Our Understanding of Early Christianity.*
    Wheaton, IL: Crossway, 2010.

Ladd, George Eldon. "Righteousness in Romans." *SwJT* 19 (1976): 6–17.

Lambrecht, Jan, and Richard W. Thompson. *Justification by Faith: The Implications of Romans
    3:27–31.* Wilmington, DE: Michael Glazier, 1989.

Lemcio, E. E. "The Unifying Kerygma of the New Testament." *JSNT* 33 (1988): 3–17.

———. "The Unifying Kerygma of the New Testament (II)." *JSNT* 38 (1990): 3–11.

Marshall, I. Howard. *Aspects of the Atonement: Cross and Resurrection in the Reconciling of
    God and Humanity.* Colorado Springs: Paternoster, 2007.

———. "Orthodoxy and Heresy in Earlier Christianity." *Themelios* 2 (1976): 5–14.

Martin, Ralph P. *Reconciliation: A Study of Paul's Theology.* Atlanta: John Knox, 1981.

McGrath, Alister E. *Iustitia Dei: A History of the Christian Doctrine of Justification.* 2 vols.
    Cambridge: Cambridge University Press, 1986.

Morris, Leon. *The Apostolic Preaching of the Cross.* 3rd ed. Grand Rapids: Eerdmans, 2000.

Munck, Johannes. *Paul and the Salvation of Mankind.* Translated by Frank Clarke. Richmond:
    John Knox, 1959.

Niebuhr, Reinhold. "Martin Buber: 1878–1965." *Christianity and Crisis* 25 (1965): 146.

Piper, John. "The Demonstration of the Righteousness of God in Romans 3:25, 26." *JSNT* 7
    (1980): 2–32.

Plevnik, Joseph. "The Center of Paul's Theology." *CBQ* 51 (1989): 46–78.

Reumann, John, with Joseph A. Fitzmyer and Jerome D. Quinn. *Righteousness in the New Tes-
    tament: Justification in the United States Lutheran-Roman Catholic Dialogue.* Philadelphia:
    Fortress; New York: Paulist Press, 1982.

———. *Variety and Unity in New Testament Thought.* OBS. Oxford: Oxford University Press,
    1991.

Schliesser, Benjamin. *Abraham's Faith in Romans 4: Paul's Concept of Faith in Light of the His-
    tory of Reception of Genesis 15:6.* WUNT 2/224. Tübingen: Mohr Siebeck, 2007.

Schreiner, Thomas R. *Paul, Apostle of God's Glory in Christ: A Pauline Theology.* Downers
    Grove, IL: InterVarsity, 2001.

Schweitzer, Albert. *The Mysticism of Paul the Apostle.* Translated by William Montgomery.
    New York: Henry Holt, 1931.

Seifrid, Mark A. *Christ, Our Righteousness: Paul's Theology of Justification*. NSBT. Downers Grove, IL: InterVarsity, 2000.

———. *Justification by Faith: The Origin and Development of a Central Pauline Theme*. NovTSup 68. Leiden: Brill, 1992.

Snodgrass, Klyne. "The Gospel in Romans: A Theology of Revelation." In *Gospel in Paul: Studies on Corinthians, Galatians, and Romans for Richard N. Longenecker*, edited by L. Ann Jervis and Peter Richardson, 288–314. JSNTSup 108. Sheffield: Sheffield Academic Press, 1994.

Soards, Marion L. "The Righteousness of God in the Writings of the Apostle Paul." *BTB* 15 (1985): 104–9.

Stuhlmacher, Peter. "The Apostle Paul's View of Righteousness." In *Reconciliation, Law, and Righteousness: Essays in Biblical Theology*, 68–93. Philadelphia: Fortress, 1986.

———. "The Pauline Gospel." In *The Gospel and the Gospels*, edited by Peter Stuhlmacher, 149–72. Grand Rapids: Eerdmans, 1991.

———. *Reconciliation, Law, and Righteousness: Essays in Biblical Theology*. Philadelphia: Fortress, 1986.

———. *Revisiting Paul's Doctrine of Justification: A Challenge to the New Perspective*. Downers Grove, IL: InterVarsity, 2001.

Turner, H. E. W. *The Pattern of Christian Truth: A Study in Relations between Orthodoxy and Heresy in the Early Christian Church*. London: Mowbray, 1954.

VanLandingham, Chris. *Judgment and Justification in Early Judaism and the Apostle Paul*. Peabody, MA: Hendrickson, 2006.

Wright, N. T. *Justification: God's Plan and Paul's Vision*. Downers Grove, IL: InterVarsity, 2009.

Yarbrough, Robert W. "Paul and Salvation History." In *The Paradoxes of Paul*. Vol. 2 of *Justification and Variegated Nomism*, edited by D. A. Carson, Peter T. O'Brien, and Mark A. Seifrid, 297–342. Grand Rapids: Baker Academic, 2004.

Ziesler, J. A. *The Meaning of Righteousness in Paul: A Linguistic and Theological Inquiry*. SNTSMS 20. Cambridge: Cambridge University Press, 1972.

21

Paul's Christology and Eschatology

It is no exaggeration to say that the whole framework of Paul's theology—his soteriology, his ecclesiology, his conception of life in the present, as well as his eschatology—depends on his understanding of the person of Jesus Christ. Everything is what it is because of who Jesus is. And if Jesus were simply a Jewish prophet-like reformer and healer, and no more, Paul's whole theology would collapse. This is why the encounter on the Damascus Road is of such enormous consequence.

Paul's Christology

Reconceptualizing the Messiah

Saul the Pharisee probably held to the common expectation, dim and unfocused though it may have been, of a coming Messiah, the descendant of David, who would bring foreign domination to an end, restore the fortunes of Israel, and bring about the fulfillment of the prophetic promises. This Messiah would be a gifted, charismatic man, uniquely anointed by God, not a divine figure, but a man who would function as God's agent of salvation. The one who met Paul on that road near Damascus matched this definition of Messiah except in two respects. First, he was a divine figure, whom Paul immediately knew to address as *kyrios* ("Lord"). But unquestionably the second, greatest surprise—something that earlier defied Saul's understanding—was that the Messiah was the man from Nazareth who had been crucified and cursed of God.

Paul now had to confront the reality of what he might well have called the strange work of the Messiah: his death on the cross as an atoning sacrifice.

394

Contrary to Paul's previous expectation, the Messiah had not come in glorious power to overthrow the Romans and set up a new kingdom of Israel, over which he would then reign as king. Along with the rest of the early church, he soon probably made sense of this unfathomable fact of a crucified Messiah by identifying him with the servant in Isaiah 52:13–53:12.[1] Although Isaiah never identifies this servant as the Messiah, what is said in the Isaiah passage corresponds, almost startlingly, to the early church's account and understanding of the death of Jesus, and in remarkable detail. Consider, for example, the following clauses from Isaiah 53:3–12 about the meaning of his death:

> He was despised and rejected by men; a man of sorrows, and acquainted with grief. . . . Surely he has borne our griefs and carried our sorrows; yet we esteemed him stricken, smitten by God, and afflicted. But he was wounded for our transgressions, he was bruised for our iniquities; upon him was the chastisement that made us whole, and with his stripes we are healed. . . . And the Lord has laid on him the iniquity of us all. . . . He was cut off out of the land of the living, stricken for the transgression of my people. . . . Yet it was the will of the LORD to bruise him; he has put him to grief; when he makes himself an offering for sin. . . . By his knowledge shall the righteous one, my servant, make many to be accounted righteous; and he shall bear their iniquities. . . . He poured out his soul to death, and was numbered with the transgressors; yet he bore the sin of many.

Although in his letters Paul does not quote from this passage, he likely alludes to it in, for example, Romans 4:25; 1 Corinthians 15:3b–5 (cf. Rom. 5:6, 8, 15–19; 2 Cor. 5:14–21). Paul reflects a knowledge of Isaiah 53 and uses it in fresh ways to elucidate the meaning of the death of the Messiah.[2] Jesus and the Christians before Paul also probably appealed to Isaiah 53.[3]

The Glory of the Risen Son of God

The crucified Messiah now appeared to Paul as the risen Jesus, in incomparable glory—not simply as a glorified man, but as a divine figure, the unique Son of God, revealed by God to Paul (Gal. 1:15–16).[4] It now became clear to Paul that the man from Nazareth was to be identified as "the Lord of glory." "None of the rulers of this age understood this; for if they had, they would not have crucified the Lord of glory" (1 Cor. 2:8). By contrast, Paul writes,

---

1. See Dodd, *According to the Scriptures*, 92–96.

2. See Hofius, "The Fourth Servant Song in the New Testament Letters," 175–83; Dodd, *According to the Scriptures*, 88–96. See also Bauckham, *Jesus and the God of Israel*, 41–45.

3. Martin Hengel argues tentatively that before Jesus there were "traditions about suffering and atoning eschatological messianic figures" that could have been known to Jesus and the early church and helped them to understand the death of Jesus the Messiah (Hengel, with Bailey, "The Effective History of Isaiah 53 in the Pre-Christian Period," 146).

4. On the significance of the Damascus christophany for Paul's understanding of Christ as the manifestation of God's glory, see Newman, *Paul's Glory-Christology*.

"We all, with unveiled face, beholding the glory of the Lord, are being changed into his likeness from one degree of glory to another; for this comes from the Lord who is the Spirit" (2 Cor. 3:18). According to Paul's analysis, on the one hand, "The god of this world has blinded the minds of the unbelievers, to keep them from seeing the light of the gospel of the glory of Christ, who is the likeness [*eikōn*] of God" (2 Cor. 4:4). On the other hand, "For it is the God who said, 'Let light shine out of darkness,' who has shone in our hearts to give the light of the knowledge of the glory of God in the face of Christ" (2 Cor. 4:6).

Together with Christians before him, Paul believed not only that God had raised Jesus from the dead but also that God exalted him to sit at his right hand (Rom. 8:34; Col. 3:1; cf. Eph. 1:20). Similarly, Paul assigns exalted titles to Jesus: he is not only Messiah (although soon "Christ" is used more as a name than a title) but also the Son of God (e.g., Rom. 1:3–4; 8:3, 32; 2 Cor. 1:19), and Lord (e.g., Rom. 10:9; 1 Cor. 12:3; 2 Cor. 4:5). The identification of Jesus as *kyrios* ("Lord") makes possible the application of certain OT texts to him, since *kyrios* is the regular LXX translation of the Tetragrammaton, "YHWH," the name of God, translated as "LORD" in English Bibles. Thus in Romans 10:13, where Joel 2:32 (LXX) is quoted, Paul understands *kyrios* to be Jesus, so that the statement means that whoever calls on the name of Jesus will be saved. So too when in Philippians 2:10 Paul says that every knee shall bow to Jesus and confess him as Lord, he is quoting from Isaiah 45:23 where it is *kyrios* (i.e., YHWH) who is in view. This same Jesus will function as eschatological Judge at the end of the age (2 Cor. 5:10; 1 Cor. 4:4–5; 1 Thess. 4:6).

Paul furthermore readily associates the name of Jesus with God in the formulaic language of passages such as the familiar opening benediction "Grace to you and peace from God our Father and the Lord Jesus Christ" (e.g., Rom. 1:7; 1 Cor. 1:3; 2 Cor. 1:2; Gal. 1:3; Phil. 1:2). He also uses the simple "The grace of the Lord Jesus be with you" in slightly varying forms (1 Cor. 16:23; Gal. 6:18; 1 Thess. 5:28; Phil. 4:23). He associates the name of Jesus with God in doxological passages (e.g., Rom. 16:27; Phil. 1:11; Eph. 3:21). And quite remarkable is 2 Corinthians 13:14, which anticipates the doctrine of the Trinity: "The grace of the Lord Jesus Christ and the love of God and the fellowship of the Holy Spirit be with you all."

Also notable are the very frequently occurring prepositional phrases "in Christ" and "through Christ." Both incorporation[5] and agency presuppose a high christology.

Two Christological Hymns

It is striking that some of Paul's most significant christological passages are found in the creedal hymns of Philippians 2:6–11 and Colossians 1:15–20.

---

5. On this, see the chapter "The Corporate Christ" in Moule, *The Origin of Christology*, 47–96.

These hymns may well be pre-Pauline;[6] if so, Paul's use of them indicates his full agreement with their affirmations.

Philippians 2:5–11

This hymn may be set out in six couplets:[7]
"Have this mind among yourselves, which is yours in Christ Jesus,

1. "who, though he was in the form of God [*en morphē theou*],
   did not count equality with God [*to einai isa theō*] a thing to be grasped;

2. "but emptied [*ekenōsen*] himself,
   taking the form of a servant [*doulou*],

3. "being born in the likeness [*homoiōmati*] of men;
   And being found in human form [*hōs anthrōpos*]

4. "he humbled [*etapeinōsen*] himself,
   and became obedient unto death, [even death on a cross.]

5. "Therefore God has highly exalted [*hyperypsōsen*] him
   and bestowed on him the name which is above every name,

6. "that at the name of Jesus every knee should bow,
   [in heaven and on earth and under the earth,]
   and every tongue confess [*exomologēsētai*] that Jesus Christ is Lord
   [to the glory of God the Father."]

The hymn takes in the whole scope of the history of Christ and affirms a three-stage christology: (1) preexistence; (2) incarnation; (3) exaltation.

Colossians 1:15–20

This hymn may be set out in two parallel stanzas: (1) verses 15–17; (2) verses 18–20:

6. Although well aware of their poetic form, Gordon Fee doubts that these passages are hymns, preferring to think of them as "exalted Pauline prose" (see "Philippians 2:5–11"; also discussions of both passages in idem, *Pauline Christology*). For a more typical viewpoint, see the chapter "Hymns and Christology" in Hengel, *Between Jesus and Paul*, 78–96; Bauckham, *Jesus and the God of Israel*, 135–39; see also the chapter "Singing Wisdom's Praise" in Witherington, *Jesus the Sage*, 249–94.

7. This form follows the proposal by Martin, *A Hymn of Christ* (earlier title, *Carmen Christi*), 36–38. The English bracketed parts are possibly Paul's additions to the hymn, suggested partly by Ernst Lohmeyer and partly by Joachim Jeremias.

1. "He is the image [*eikōn*] of the invisible God,
   the first-born [*prōtotokos*] of all creation;

   "for in him all thing were created,
   in heaven and on earth,
   visible and invisible,
   whether thrones or dominions or principalities or authorities
   —all things were created through him and for him.

   "He is before all things [*pro pantōn*],
   and in him all things hold together [*synestēken*].

2. "He is the head [*kephalē*] of the body, the church;
   he is the beginning [*archē*], the first-born [*prōtotokos*] from the dead,
   that in everything he might be pre-eminent [*prōteuōn*].

   "For in him all the fulness [*pan to plērōma*] of God was pleased to
   dwell [*katoikēsai*],
   and through him to reconcile to himself all things,
   whether on earth or in heaven,
   making peace by the blood of his cross."

Here, in two parallel stanzas, Christ is shown to be the head of two creations, the original creation and the new creation represented by the church. The work of reconciliation, experienced already in the church, is universal in scope and is accomplished "by the blood of his cross."

Other Key Pauline Texts

Of considerable importance is also 1 Corinthians 8:6:

> Yet for us
>   there is one God, the Father,
>   from whom are all things and for whom we exist,
>
> and one Lord, Jesus Christ,
>   through whom are all things and through whom we exist.

Here, against the background of the confession of the oneness of God in the Shema, Paul adds a second couplet in which he states that as there is "one God, the Father" (*heis theos ho patēr*), so there is one *kyrios*, Jesus Christ. The prepositions of the second line in each couplet are important. Everything is "from" (*ex*) God, and we are "for" (*eis*) God; everything is "through" (*dia*) Christ, and we are "through" (*dia*) Christ.

Also important to consider is Paul's Adam christology, where Christ is the antitype that corresponds to Adam, and whose one act of obedience to God on the cross undoes the effects of Adam's transgression (Rom. 5:12–21; 1 Cor. 15:45 ["the last Adam"], 47 ["the second man"]). It is only by virtue of his divine identity that Christ can become the head of a new stream of redeemed humanity.

We have furthermore in Paul a Wisdom Christology. It is thought by many that the early Christian conception of the divinity of Christ was assisted by the idea of an incarnation of Wisdom. In the OT and in Second Temple literature Wisdom, personified and hypostatized, is said to be present with God at the creation. Thus, according to Proverbs 8, Wisdom speaks the following: "Ages ago I was set up, at the first, before the beginning of the earth. . . . When he established the heavens, I was there. . . . When he marked out the foundations of the earth, then I was beside him, like a master workman" (Prov. 8:23–30 [cf. Col. 1:15, 17]). In Wisdom of Solomon, an OT apocryphal book, Wisdom is spoken of as "the fashioner of all things" (Wis. 7:22). Then Wisdom is spoken of in the following words: "For she is a breath of the power of God, and a pure emanation of the glory of the Almighty. . . . For she is a reflection of eternal light, a spotless mirror of the working of God and an image of his goodness" (Wis. 7:25–26 [cf. Wis. 9; see also Sir. 24]). Paul refers to Christ as "the wisdom of God" (1 Cor. 1:24) and says that God has made Christ "our wisdom, our righteousness and sanctification and redemption" (1 Cor. 1:30).[8]

Just as Wisdom preexisted the creation, so Paul believes in the preexistence of Christ. Like Wisdom, Christ was the agent of creation. Christ "is before all things, and in him all things hold together" (Col. 1:17). In one of the most striking passages Paul refers to Christ as the supernatural (i.e., "spiritual" [*pneumatikos*]) rock that followed Israel in the wilderness, from which they drank (1 Cor. 10:4).[9] The preexistence of the Son is presupposed in passages concerning the sending of the Son (Gal. 4:4; Rom. 8:3; cf. Rom. 10:6–8).

Much debated is whether Paul refers to Christ as God in Romans 9:5, or whether he thinks of Christ as the incarnation of God, as does, for example, the Fourth Evangelist. Although it seems very possible, even probable, that

8. See Dunn, *Christology in the Making*, 176–96; idem, *The Theology of Paul the Apostle*, 272–77; Byrne, "Christ's Pre-existence in Pauline Soteriology"; Witherington, *Jesus the Sage*, 295–33; Gathercole, *The Pre-Existent Son*, 23–31. Gordon Fee argues against a Wisdom Christology in Paul (*Pauline Christology*, 595–630). The exegetical precision that he demands to justify seeing a Wisdom christology in Paul, however, is hardly typical of Paul's (or any of the NT writers') use of the OT.

9. The idea of the rock that followed Israel in the wilderness is drawn from rabbinic tradition (*t. Sukkah* 3.11; *Tg. Onq.* Num. 21:16–20). Compare Wisdom of Solomon 10:17–18; 11:4; *L.A.B.* 10:7.

Christ is referred to as God in Romans 9:5 (cf. Titus 2:13), absolute certainty is impossible because of the ambiguity of the Greek.[10] However, it seems very difficult to deny that the passages we have briefly looked at intend to affirm the preexistence of Christ, despite the possibility of reading them differently.[11] Larry Kreitzer calls attention to the identification of the Messiah with God in 4 *Ezra* and 2 *Baruch* and concludes, "It appears that the two ideas of rigid monotheism and the identification of the Messiah with God are fused in paradox."[12]

A Summary of Paul's Christology

If we put together the various statements that Paul makes about Christ, we come up with the following:

> Jesus Christ is the revelation, the image (*eikōn*), the very expression of God. He preexisted the incarnation, being with God from the beginning. He was the Agent of the initial creation of all and sustains all that exists. He is prior in rank to all that exists (this is the sense of "first-born"). He is the Lord of all. He is God's agent of redemption, which he accomplished through his death on the cross, thereby counteracting the effect of Adam's transgression. He has been exalted to the right hand of God and presently reigns. He will soon return as Judge and as the one who brings to pass the final realization of God's promises.

The similarities between Paul's view of Jesus and the view of Jesus in the Gospel of John (John 1:1–18) and the Epistle to the Hebrews (Heb. 1:1–4) are striking, and they confirm that Paul has not gone off on a tangent of his own but rather is fully in line with two other major strands of NT christology.

How was Paul able to come to this view of Jesus? What is the source of this remarkable christology? The starting point, of course, has to be his

10. It has to be admitted, in my opinion, that the most natural way to take the Greek is the rendering of the RSV footnote: "Christ, who is God over all, blessed for ever." See Metzger, "The Punctuation of Romans 9:5"; Harris, *Jesus as God*, 143–72. Harris concludes appropriately, "Given the high Christology of the Pauline letters, according to which Jesus shares the divine name, exercises divine functions, and is the object of human faith and adoration it should generate no surprise if on occasion Paul should refer to Jesus by the generic title *theos*" (ibid., 171).

11. It is possible to understand these references as only reflections of an Adam christology. James Dunn, for example, does not think that Paul believed in the preexistence of Christ. He explains the passages that seem to speak of Christ's preexistence as reflecting analogies with Wisdom (i.e., the preexistence of Wisdom speaks of Christ) or Adam. Thus Dunn interprets Philippians 2:6–11 as an allusion to Genesis 1:26–27, where God creates Adam in his own image; "taking the form of a slave" refers to the result of Adam's sin; the death suffered alludes to the penalty for Adam's sin. See Dunn, *Christology in the Making*, 114–21. Dunn's conclusion that Paul did not believe in the preexistence of Christ has persuaded very few. Against Dunn, see Hurtado, *Lord Jesus Christ*, 118–26. Dunn responds to some of his critics in the foreword to the second edition of *Christology in the Making*, xi–xxxix.

12. Kreitzer, *Jesus and God in Paul's Eschatology*, 90.

encounter with the risen Jesus, whom he immediately knows is the *kyrios*, the Lord. Undoubtedly, he worked out the full implications of this in the years immediately following his conversion. But he was hardly alone in doing this. The early Judean church had been at work discovering the divine identity of Jesus from the very beginning.

It was once common to trace the development of christology through three evolutionary stages, beginning with the Christianity of Palestinian Judaism, then Hellenistic Judaism, and finally the Hellenistic Gentile church, moving from primitive to more developed.[13] This, however, is an overly precise analysis based on artificial distinctions and indefensible presuppositions, and thus it has lost its power to convince. It alleges far more than it is possible for us to know. Although the christology of Paul and those before him obviously presupposes some early, limited development, it does not require a long, evolutionary process. It seems clear enough that a functional christology contains within itself the seeds of ontological christology. It is the question of the Gospels: Who is it who can say and do these things? So the early church asked: Who is it who has risen from the dead in resurrection glory, is now exalted to God's right hand, ruling over all and will return as Judge? The christology of earliest Christianity was already highly developed, if not articulated, in the first years after the resurrection.

Paul articulates his "high" christology in the 50s, within a couple of decades of the death of Christ. But when we remember that Paul did not invent this christology, we must conclude that it goes back to virtually the beginning of the church. Richard Bauckham concludes that "the highest possible christology—the inclusion of Jesus in the unique divine identity—was central to the faith of the early church even before any of the New Testament writings were written since it occurs in all of them."[14] Similarly, Larry Hurtado writes, "A veritable explosion of devotion to Jesus took place so early, and was so widespread by the time of his Gentile mission, that in the main christological beliefs and devotional practices that he advocated, Paul was not an innovator but a transmitter of tradition."[15] The result of this view of Christ, according to Hurtado, is the rise of "a devotional pattern that is genuinely 'binitarian,'"[16] a christology that involved a mutation in monotheistic devotional practice.[17]

---

13. See, for example, Fuller, *The Foundations of New Testament Christology*. According to this analysis, Palestinian Jewish Christianity viewed Jesus from an eschatological perspective, as the Davidic Messiah, whose work lay primarily in the future (e.g., Acts 3:21). Hellenistic Jewish Christianity then transformed this view into a cosmological perspective with an emphasis on the present work of the exalted Christ. In the third stage, Hellenistic Gentile Christianity began to develop a three-stage christology—preexistence, incarnation, exaltation—thus moving from functional toward ontological christology.

14. Bauckham, *Jesus and the God of Israel*, 19.

15. Hurtado, *Lord Jesus Christ*, 216.

16. Hurtado, *One God, One Lord*, xv. See also the chapter "The Worship of Jesus in Early Christianity" in Bauckham, *Jesus and the God of Israel*, 127–51.

17. See Hurtado, *One God, One Lord*, 93–124.

It is important to insist that although Paul's christology (and John's) necessitates a "modification" of monotheism, it does not amount to a rejection
of it or to the affirmation of two Gods. Christ remains distinct from God
the Father, even subordinate to, and obedient to, the Father. Thus Paul refers
to "the end, when he [Christ] delivers the kingdom to God the Father after
destroying every rule and every authority and power" (1 Cor. 15:24). Paul
adds, "When all things are subjected to him, then the Son himself will also be
subjected to him who put all things under him, that God may be everything
to every one" (1 Cor. 15:28).

None of the NT writers believed that their devotion to Jesus involved a denial
of the oneness of God.[18] Bauckham thus speaks of a "christological monotheism which by no means abandons but maintains precisely the ways Judaism
distinguished God from all other reality and uses these to include Jesus in the
unique divine identity. [Paul] maintains monotheism not by *adding Jesus to*
but by *including Jesus in* his Jewish understanding of the divine uniqueness."[19]

Paul's Eschatology

There is a close relation between Paul's christology and eschatology.[20] Like
all Jewish believers in Jesus, Paul had to reconcile his understanding of Jesus
as the divine Messiah with the fact that Jesus had not brought the messianic
age, or at least not in the way expected. It was of extreme importance to all
Jewish Christians that the Messiah was eventually to act in fulfillment of the
promises made by God in the OT Scriptures. The eschatological parousia,
the second coming of Jesus, therefore was an integral part of their perspective. And it was therefore to future eschatology to which they looked for the
age of bliss of which the prophets spoke. But as with Jesus, so too with Paul,
eschatological fulfillment is a reality of the present as well as an expectation
of the future. The exalted Jesus presently reigns and pours out his blessing
upon the present church.

Present Eschatological Fulfillment

Just as the resurrection of Christ serves as the impetus for Paul's christology,
so too it provides the impetus for his view of the present as an age of inaugurated eschatology. The resurrection is an eschatological event: the beginning of

18. See Hagner, "Jewish Monotheism and Paul's Christology."
19. Bauckham, *Jesus and the God of Israel*, 30. Note now the cautionary remarks in Dunn,
Did the First Christians Worship Jesus? He is concerned to nuance statements about Jesus so as
to protect the monotheistic convictions of the early church.
20. See Kreitzer, *Jesus and God in Paul's Eschatology*.

a new order and a remarkable, vivid sign of a new age.[21] Contrary to popular misunderstanding, the Christian faith is far more a celebration of eschatological reality already accomplished than a celebration of future eschatology—"pie in the sky in the bye and bye." Eschatology is about the present as well as the future. Paul tells the Corinthian Christians that they are those "upon whom the end of the ages [*ta telē tōn aiōnōn*] has come" (1 Cor. 10:11).

The supreme mark of the arrival of a new age is the Holy Spirit in the church. According to Paul, God "has put his seal upon us and given us his Spirit in our hearts as a guarantee" (*arrabōn*, lit., an "earnest" or "down payment") (2 Cor. 1:22; so too in 2 Cor. 5:5; Eph. 1:14). He describes the Holy Spirit as the "first fruits" (*aparchē*) (Rom. 8:23; used in reference to the resurrection of Christ in 1 Cor. 15:20, 23). The ministry of the Holy Spirit in the church represents the first installment of the full blessings of the eschaton. Christians already begin to experience the future fulfillment in the present fruit of the kingdom: righteousness, peace, and joy (Rom. 14:17). "The fruit of the Spirit is love, joy, peace, patience, kindness, goodness, faithfulness, gentleness, self-control" (Gal. 5:22–23). For Paul, the kingdom that has been brought by Christ is more than mere words; it was an experienced reality. "The kingdom of God does not consist in talk but in power" (1 Cor. 4:20).[22]

Fulfillment Short of Consummation: Already/Not Yet

At the same time, however, the present age is highly paradoxical. If there is an "already," there is also a "not yet." The church lives "between the times"—that is, between the time of the first advent and the second advent, the parousia of Christ.[23] Paul is not shy about speaking of the already. "He has delivered us from the dominion of darkness and transferred us to the kingdom of his beloved Son" (Col. 1:13). He speaks to the Corinthians as those "upon whom the end of the ages has come" (1 Cor. 10:11). It was "when the time had fully come" that God sent his Son into the world (Gal. 4:4). "Therefore, if any one is in Christ, he is a new creation; the old has passed away, behold, the new has come" (2 Cor. 5:17 [cf. Gal. 6:15]).

Indeed, so strong was this emphasis on the blessings of the present in Paul's preaching that there was a danger of his listeners espousing an "overrealized" eschatology. The Corinthians apparently were so inclined, and Paul upbraids them for it in 1 Corinthians 4:8. At Thessalonica some argued that the day of

21. As Joseph Plevnik puts it, Christ's resurrection "is the end of the rule of death, the end of dying in all its forms. It is what Jewish apocalyptic more or less hoped would happen in the end of time with an act of God. Paul now asserts that this happened in Christ's resurrection" (*What Are They Saying about Paul and the End Time?*, 36).

22. Apart from a few references, Paul uses "kingdom of God" mainly to refer to the future inheritance of Christians (1 Cor. 6:9–10; 15:50; Gal. 5:21; 1 Thess. 2:12 ["his own kingdom and glory"]; cf. Eph. 5:5).

23. For a full discussion of the subject, see Plevnik, *Paul and the Parousia*.

the Lord had fully arrived (2 Thess. 2:2), and two individuals in a Pauline church argued that the resurrection had already occurred (2 Tim. 2:18; cf. 1 Cor. 15:12).

Paul, however, was a realist, and he never closed his eyes to the continuing reality of evil in the present. In Galatians 1:4 he refers to "the present evil age" (cf. the statement that "the days are evil" in Eph. 5:16; cf. 6:13). The present age is given an evil connotation in Romans 12:2 ("world" translates the word *aiōn* ["age"]), and Paul can even allude to the power of Satan in the present age: "The god [*theos*] of this age has blinded the minds of the unbelievers" (2 Cor. 4:4). But the "rulers of this age" are "doomed to pass away" (1 Cor. 2:6).

Paul thus reveals the same complex perspective of an overlapping of the ages that we noted in the teaching of Jesus (see chap. 5 above). The new has definitely begun, but the old persists.[24] The Messiah has come; the age of the Torah is superseded; the fulfillment of the promises has begun. Yet evil seems to prosper, and death, the last enemy (1 Cor. 15:26), continues to hold sway over those who have entered a new existence. Paul explores both sides of this eschatological tension in considerable detail, and especially the ambiguity of the Christian's existence simultaneously in two ages. There is an analogous overlap of natures in the believer: the new identity in Christ does not yet bring an end to the fallen, Adamic nature and inclination to sin. Martinus de Boer sums up the situation thus: "The eschatological tension between 'already' and 'not yet' means, on the one side that death no less than sin has been defeated by God's invasion of 'this age' in Christ and, on the other side, that sin no less than death remains the mark of 'this age.'"[25]

The Imminence of the End

The early Christians, including Paul, thought that Christ would return in the not-distant future, certainly within their lifetimes. From the oral tradition they knew that Jesus had prophesied the destruction of the temple within that generation, and they naturally concluded that this would happen in conjunction with the end of the present age. Since they had experienced the beginning of eschatological fulfillment, together with the wonders of the new age marked by the power of the Holy Spirit, it is hardly surprising that they supposed that the consummation could not be far off.

In the earlier years of his ministry Paul believed the end of the present age was near. When he writes, for example, to the Thessalonians that they need not worry about those who die before the return of Christ, he says that "we who are alive, who are left until the coming of the Lord, shall not precede those who have fallen asleep" (1 Thess. 4:15). Paul expects that he will still be alive at the parousia.

24. This is explored fully in Vos, *The Pauline Eschatology*; Cullmann, *Christ and Time*. For discussion of the Pauline notion of heaven and the two ages, see Lincoln, *Paradise Now and Not Yet*, 169–95.
25. de Boer, *The Defeat of Death*, 188.

In 1 Corinthians 7:29–31 he writes, "The appointed time has grown very short. . . . For the form of this world is passing away." This expectation accounts for the strange attitude that he takes in that chapter, for example, toward slaves and the unmarried: they are to remain as they are, given the shortness of time until the return of Christ (1 Cor. 7:18–40).

It seems, however, that after a narrow brush with death (see 2 Cor. 1:8–11, possibly with reference to fighting with beasts at Ephesus [1 Cor. 15:32] or possibly a life-threatening illness [2 Cor. 12:7–10]), Paul began to think that he might die before the parousia. In 2 Corinthians 5:1–10, sighing "with anxiety" (cf. Rom. 8:22–23), he discusses the question of the (spiritual) body after death.[26]

Paul may well have thought that his mission to the Gentiles was an essential prerequisite for the ultimate salvation of all Israel and the coming of the end of the age (see Rom. 11:25–26; cf. 15:8–12). In that sense, his missionary work was vital to the whole eschatological schema.

The last element of eschatology, before the establishment of the perfect kingdom of the eschaton, is the final judgment (Rom. 14:10–12 [the judgment seat of God]; 2 Cor. 5:10 [the judgment seat of Christ]). For Paul, and indeed for every Jew, the element of the judgment of the wicked remained important. One aspect of this is the vindication of the righteous. There could be no final resolution without the satisfaction of God's justice.

The Church as the True Israel

For Paul, the church is the eschatological reality of the present. God's purpose all along, from Abraham onward, was to include the Gentiles among those blessed by his grace. Paul concludes in the synagogue of Pisidian Antioch: "It was necessary that the word of God should be spoken first to you. Since you thrust it from you, and judge yourselves unworthy of eternal life, behold we turn to the Gentiles. For so the Lord has commanded us, saying, 'I have set you to be a light for the Gentiles, that you may bring salvation to the uttermost parts of the earth'" (Acts 13:46–47 [cf. 28:25–28]).

The church thus was God's eternal purpose from the beginning. Paul, or at least his disciple, speaks in Ephesians of a plan of universal scope: "a plan for the fulness of time, to unite all things in him, things in heaven and things on earth" (Eph. 1:10). The church is Christ's "body, the fulness of him who fills all in all" (Eph. 1:23). Repeatedly the church is regarded as "the mystery of Christ" (Eph. 3:4)—that is, "how the Gentiles are fellow heirs, members of the same body, and partakers of the promise in Christ Jesus through the gospel" (Eph. 3:6). Paul says this was a "mystery . . . made known to me by revelation" (Eph. 3:3). More exactly, it is "the plan of the mystery hidden

---

26. On the basic unity of Paul's eschatological framework, see Pitts, "Unity and Diversity in Pauline Eschatology."

for ages in God who created all things; that through the church the manifold wisdom of God might now be made known to the principalities and powers in the heavenly places. This was according to the eternal purpose which he has realized in Christ Jesus our Lord" (Eph. 3:9–11). So too in Colossians we read of "the mystery hidden for ages and generations but now made manifest to his saints"—that is, "how great among the Gentiles are the riches of the glory of this mystery, which is Christ in you, the hope of glory" (Col. 1:26–27).

The result of this perspective is that Paul begins to think of the church as the true Israel, though he does not precisely refer to it in those two words. Rather shockingly, Paul writes, "For not all who are descended from Israel belong to Israel, and not all are children of Abraham because they are his descendants. . . . It is not the children of the flesh who are the children of God, but the children of the promise are reckoned as descendants" (Rom. 9:6–8 [cf. 4:16–18]). To the Galatians Paul writes, "And if you are Christ's, then you are Abraham's offspring, heirs according to promise" (Gal. 3:29 [cf. 3:6–9]). Gentile Christians can be described by Paul as "the true circumcision, who worship God in spirit, and glory in Christ Jesus, and put no confidence in the flesh" (Phil. 3:3 [cf. Rom. 2:28–29]).

Terminology hitherto restricted to Israel is now freely applied to the church (Rom. 9:24–26 [most remarkable of all in this respect is 1 Pet. 2:9–10]). Paul may even refer to the church as "the Israel of God" (Gal. 6:16), although the interpretation of this is debatable. Previous distinctions are transcended: "there is neither Jew nor Greek" (Gal. 3:28); "neither circumcision counts for anything, nor uncircumcision" (Gal. 6:15 [1 Cor. 7:19]); "here there cannot be Greek and Jew, circumcised and uncircumcised" (Col. 3:11).

The church represents a new entity in which the Gentiles are united with Jewish believers in one body. Christ is thus "our peace, who has made us both one, and has broken down the dividing wall of hostility, by abolishing in his flesh the law of commandments and ordinances, that he might create in himself one new man in place of the two, so making peace, and might reconcile us both to God in one body through the cross, thereby bringing the hostility to an end" (Eph. 2:14–16).

The Future of Israel

Despite his view of the church as the true Israel, in which the promises are finding their fulfillment, Paul retains the hope of a conversion of "all Israel" (Rom. 11:25–32). It is a fixed point in his universe that "the gifts and the call of God are irrevocable" (Rom. 11:29). God will not abandon his people. Paul refers to the hope of the salvation of Israel as a mystery that has now been made clear. The Jews will be saved, just as will the Gentiles, by faith in Christ, for Paul never envisages anything other than a single way of salvation for all:

the cross of Christ. Thus, at the parousia of Christ, via a special measure of grace, confronted by their Messiah, the Jews will believe in the gospel.[27]

This will serve as the full vindication of God's faithfulness. And it is this toward which the promises to Israel had always pointed. Paul neither speaks of nor looks to an eschatological fulfillment of national-political aspirations. Paul never speaks of the promise of the land.[28] Indeed, it is lacking in the one place where one might well expect a reference to it: Romans 4:13. Here Paul writes about "the promise to Abraham and his descendants, that they should inherit the world [kosmos]," where the expected word is "land" (gē). Paul, however, has universalized the land, so that the promise points to the entire creation.

There is, for Paul and the early church too, ultimately one story of salvation and one people of salvation: the church, including both Jews and Gentiles. The nineteenth-century dispensationalist bifurcation of God's people and promises, in which Israel and the church are kept totally separate, is based on a fully unnecessary assumption about literal OT promises that allegedly still require fulfillment. The limited earthly promises are but foreshadowings of an unlimited reality toward which they point. Nor does Paul ever refer to an earthly millennium for such literal fulfillment of national-political expectations. Rather, his future eschatology concerns a transformation of the created order (see Rom. 8:21–23) that corresponds to the transcendent expectations of the prophets: the full restoration of the created order to its pre-Adamic perfection, when all things are made new. That will be the consummation of the promises to Israel and the salvation of the nations.

Bibliography

Allison, Dale C., Jr. *The End of the Ages Has Come: An Early Interpretation of the Passion and Resurrection of Jesus*. Philadelphia: Fortress, 1987.

Baird, William. "Pauline Eschatology in Hermeneutical Perspective." *NTS* 17 (1970–71): 314–27.

Bauckham, Richard. *Jesus and the God of Israel: God Crucified and Other Studies on the New Testament's Christology of Divine Identity*. Grand Rapids: Eerdmans, 2008.

Beker, J. Christiaan. *Paul's Apocalyptic Gospel: The Coming Triumph of God*. Philadelphia: Fortress, 1982.

Bell, Richard H. *The Irrevocable Call of God: An Inquiry into Paul's Theology of Israel*. WUNT 184. Tübingen: Mohr Siebeck, 2005.

Brueggemann, Walter. *The Land: Place as Gift, Promise, and Challenge in Biblical Faith*. 2nd ed. OBT. Minneapolis: Fortress, 2002.

Burge, Gary M. *Jesus and the Land: The New Testament Challenge to "Holy Land" Theology*. Grand Rapids: Baker Academic, 2010.

Byrne, Brendan T. "Christ's Pre-existence in Pauline Soteriology." *TS* 58 (1997): 308–30.

27. For excellent discussion on this subject, see Bell, *The Irrevocable Call of God*.

28. See especially Davies, *The Gospel and the Land*. Compare Walter Brueggemann's comment: "Land is a central, if not *the central theme* of biblical faith" (*The Land*, 3). For excellent treatment of this theme, see Burge, *Jesus and the Land*.

Capes, David B. *Old Testament Yahweh Texts in Paul's Christology*. WUNT 2/47. Tübingen: Mohr Siebeck, 1992.

Court, John M. "Paul and the Apocalyptic Pattern." In *Paul and Paulinism: Essays in Honour of C. K. Barrett*, edited by Morna D. Hooker and Stephen G. Wilson, 57–66. London: SPCK, 1982.

Cullmann, Oscar. *Christ and Time: The Primitive Christian Conception of Time and History*. Rev. ed. Philadelphia: Westminster, 1962.

Davies, W. D. *The Gospel and the Land: Early Christianity and Jewish Territorial Doctrine*. Berkeley: University of California Press, 1974.

———. "Paul and the People of Israel." In *Jewish and Pauline Studies*, 123–52. Philadelphia: Fortress, 1984.

de Boer, Martinus C. *The Defeat of Death: Apocalyptic Eschatology in 1 Corinthians 15 and Romans 5*. JSNTSup 22. Sheffield: JSOT Press, 1988.

———. "Paul and Jewish Apocalyptic Eschatology." In *Apocalyptic and the New Testament: Essays in Honor of J. Louis Martyn*, edited by Joel Marcus and Marion L. Soards, 169–90. JSNTSup 24. Sheffield: JSOT Press, 1989.

Dodd, C. H. *According to the Scriptures: The Sub-Structure of New Testament Theology*. London: Nisbet, 1952.

Donaldson, Terence L. "Zealot and Convert: The Origin of Paul's Christ-Torah Antithesis." *CBQ* 51 (1989): 655–82.

Dunn, James D. G. *Christology in the Making: An Inquiry into the Origins of the Doctrine of the Incarnation*. 2nd ed. Grand Rapids: Eerdmans, 1996.

———. *Did the First Christians Worship Jesus? The New Testament Evidence*. Louisville: Westminster John Knox, 2010.

———. *The Theology of Paul the Apostle*. Grand Rapids: Eerdmans, 1998.

Fee, Gordon D. *Pauline Christology: An Exegetical-Theological Study*. Peabody, MA: Hendrickson, 2007.

———. "Philippians 2:5–11: Hymn or Exalted Pauline Prose?" In *To What End Exegesis? Essays Textual, Exegetical, and Theological*, 173–94. Grand Rapids: Eerdmans, 2001.

Fuller, Reginald H. *The Foundations of New Testament Christology*. New York: Scribner, 1965.

Gathercole, Simon J. *The Pre-Existent Son: Recovering the Christologies of Matthew, Mark, and Luke*. Grand Rapids: Eerdmans, 2006.

Hagner, Donald A. "Jewish Monotheism and Paul's Christology." In *Perspectives on Christology: Essays in Honor of Paul K. Jewett*, edited by Marguerite Shuster and Richard A. Muller, 19–38. Grand Rapids: Zondervan, 1991.

Harris, Murray J. "2 Corinthians 5:1–10: Watershed in Paul's Eschatology?" *TynBul* 22 (1971): 32–57.

———. *Jesus as God: The New Testament Use of* Theos *as a Christological Term*. Grand Rapids: Baker Academic, 1992.

Hengel, Martin. *Between Jesus and Paul: Studies in the Earliest History of Christianity*. Translated by John Bowden. Philadelphia: Fortress, 1983.

Hengel, Martin, with Daniel P. Bailey. "The Effective History of Isaiah 53 in the Pre-Christian Period." In *The Suffering Servant: Isaiah 53 in Jewish and Christian Sources*, edited by Bernd Janowski and Peter Stuhlmacher, translated by Daniel P. Bailey, 75–146. Grand Rapids: Eerdmans, 2004.

Hofius, Otfried. "The Fourth Servant Song in the New Testament Letters." In *The Suffering Servant: Isaiah 53 in Jewish and Christian Sources*, edited by Bernd Janowski and Peter Stuhlmacher, translated by Daniel P. Bailey, 163–88. Grand Rapids: Eerdmans, 2004.

Hurtado, Larry W. *Lord Jesus Christ: Devotion to Jesus in Earliest Christianity*. Grand Rapids: Eerdmans, 2003.

———. *One God, One Lord: Early Christian Devotion and Ancient Jewish Monotheism*. 2nd ed. New York: T&T Clark, 1998.

Janowski, Bernd, and Peter Stuhlmacher, eds. *The Suffering Servant: Isaiah 53 in Jewish and Christian Sources*. Translated by Daniel P. Bailey. Grand Rapids: Eerdmans, 2004.

Karris, Robert J. *A Symphony of New Testament Hymns: Commentary on Philippians 2:5–11, Colossians 1:15–20, Ephesians 2:14–16, 1 Timothy 3:16, Titus 3:4–7, 1 Peter 3:18–22, and 2 Timothy 2:11–13.* Collegeville, MN: Liturgical Press, 1996.

Keck, Leander E. "Paul and Apocalyptic Theology." *Int* 38 (1984): 229–41.

———. "Toward a Renewal of New Testament Christology." *NTS* 32 (1986): 362–77.

Kennedy, H. A. A. *St. Paul's Conceptions of the Last Things.* London: Hodder & Stoughton, 1904.

Kim, Seyoon. *The Origin of Paul's Gospel.* 2nd ed. Grand Rapids: Eerdmans, 1984.

Kreitzer, Larry J. *Jesus and God in Paul's Eschatology.* JSNTSup 19. Sheffield: JSOT Press, 1987.

Lincoln, Andrew T. *Paradise Now and Not Yet: Studies in the Role of the Heavenly Dimension in Paul's Thought with Special Reference to His Eschatology.* SNTSMS 43. Cambridge: Cambridge University Press, 1981.

Longenecker, Bruce W. *Eschatology and the Covenant: A Comparison of 4 Ezra and Romans 1–11.* JSNTSup 57. Sheffield: JSOT Press, 1991.

Longenecker, Richard N. "The Nature of Paul's Early Eschatology." *NTS* 31 (1985): 85–95.

———. "A Realized Hope, a New Commitment, and a Developed Proclamation: Paul and Jesus." In *The Road from Damascus: The Impact of Paul's Conversion on His Life, Thought, and Ministry*, edited by Richard N. Longenecker, 18–42. Grand Rapids: Eerdmans, 1997.

Luckensmeyer, David. *The Eschatology of First Thessalonians.* NTOA/SUNT 71. Göttingen: Vandenhoeck & Ruprecht, 2009.

Marshall, I. Howard. "A New Understanding of the Present and the Future: Paul and Eschatology." In *The Road from Damascus: The Impact of Paul's Conversion on His Life, Thought, and Ministry*, edited by Richard N. Longenecker, 43–61. Grand Rapids: Eerdmans, 1997.

———. *The Origins of New Testament Christology.* Rev. ed. Downers Grove, IL: InterVarsity, 1990.

Martin, Ralph P. *A Hymn of Christ: Philippians 2:5–11 in Recent Interpretation and in the Setting of Early Christian Worship.* 3rd ed. Downers Grove, IL: InterVarsity, 1997.

Martyn, J. Louis. "Apocalyptic Anomalies in the Letter to the Galatians." *NTS* 31 (1985): 410–24.

Matlock, R. Barry. *Unveiling the Apocalyptic Paul: Paul's Interpreters and the Rhetoric of Criticism.* JSNTSup 127. Sheffield: Sheffield Academic Press, 1996.

Mearns, Christopher L. "Early Eschatological Development in Paul: The Evidence of I and II Thessalonians." *NTS* 27 (1980–81): 137–57.

Metzger, Bruce M. "The Punctuation of Romans 9:5." In *Christ and Spirit in the New Testament: Studies in Honour of Charles Francis Digby Moule*, edited by Barnabas Lindars and Stephen S. Smalley, 95–112. Cambridge: Cambridge University Press, 1973.

Moule, C. F. D. *The Origin of Christology.* Cambridge: Cambridge University Press, 1977.

Newman, Carey C. *Paul's Glory-Christology: Tradition and Rhetoric.* NovTSup 69. Leiden: Brill, 1992.

Pitts, Andrew W. "Unity and Diversity in Pauline Eschatology." In *Paul: Jew, Greek, and Roman*, edited by Stanley E. Porter, 65–91. PS 5. Leiden: Brill, 2008.

Plevnik, Joseph. *Paul and the Parousia: An Exegetical and Theological Investigation.* Peabody, MA: Hendrickson, 1997.

———. *What Are They Saying about Paul and the End Time?* New York: Paulist Press, 2009.

Shires, Henry M. *The Eschatology of Paul in the Light of Modern Scholarship.* Philadelphia: Westminster, 1966.

Thiselton, Anthony C. "Realized Eschatology at Corinth." *NTS* 24 (1977–78): 510–24.

Vos, Geerhardus. *The Pauline Eschatology.* Reprint, Phillipsburg, NJ: Presbyterian & Reformed, 1986.

Witherington, Ben, III. *Jesus, Paul, and the End of the World: A Comparative Study in New Testament Eschatology.* Downers Grove, IL: InterVarsity, 1992.

———. *Jesus the Sage: The Pilgrimage of Wisdom.* Minneapolis: Fortress, 1994.

22

Letters in the Hellenistic World

It is remarkable that a very large portion of the NT consists of actual letters to churches or individuals. This means that much of what Christians regard as uniquely inspired and authoritative Scripture is in the form not of abstract doctrinal essays—indeed, that would be true of none of it—but rather of documents, in this case particular letters, that are historically rooted in specific occasions and circumstances of the first century. The difficulties that this may cause for interpreters who would apply these letters to their own situation twenty centuries later should be readily apparent. When below we consider the individual letters, we will examine their content by locating them in their respective historical contexts, for this is indispensable to their proper interpretation. Here we have in view more generally their form, function, and rhetoric.

Letters in the Hellenistic World

Mainly through the finds of archaeologists we possess a large number of letters from the ancient world. They are of a wide variety, from the most informal "to do" lists to formal letter-treatises; from very personal letters, involving intimate family matters, to impersonal official communications and formal treatises presented as literary letters (e.g., the letters of Cicero or Seneca). The letters of the NT, themselves of various types, are obviously for the most part between these extremes.

In his analysis of ancient letters, Adolf Deissmann made an important distinction between "letter" and "epistle." The former he described as "non-literary," confidential and personal in nature. The latter he calls "an artistic

410

literary form, a species of literature," designed for publicity. His conclusion that Paul's writings were to be categorized not as epistles but rather as letters, has often been challenged, especially since it is clear that Paul usually wrote for his churches and expected his letters to be received as authoritative and to be read publicly. The note at the end of 1 Thessalonians makes this clear: "I solemnly command you by the Lord that this letter be read to all of them" (1 Thess. 5:26); to which we may add this from Colossians: "And when this letter has been read among you, have it read also in the church of the Laodiceans; and see that you read also the letter from Laodicea" (Col. 4:16). This public reading points to the authoritative character of Paul's Letters and plays its role in the eventual canonization of the letters.

Paul's Letters are both personal *and* public documents; they are both occasional, or ad hoc, *and* carefully crafted, often with considerable artistry, from a literary point of view. Some of Paul's Letters are more personal, as, for example, Philemon; others are less personal, as, for example, Romans, Colossians, and, in the Pauline corpus, Ephesians. Paul has created what amounts to a new type of letter. He has taken over and, at the same time, to a certain extent transformed the Hellenistic letter.

The Form of the Hellenistic Letter and the Pauline Letter

This last point can be illustrated by a comparison of the form of Paul's Letters with that of the typical Hellenistic letter. The form of the Hellenistic letter was highly stylized. Ancient handbooks reveal that formal training in letter writing was available in the schools. There, one could obtain information not only on writing different types of letters but also in the formal aspects of the letter. The standard form of the letter consisted in its simplest version of a prescript or opening ("A to B, greetings"—thus, unlike the modern letter form, leaving no doubt from the very beginning concerning the identity of the author); the body of the letter, containing the main concerns of the letter; and the formal closing ("farewell"). Often this form would be expanded to include a wish for health, which followed the prescript, to which was sometimes also appended a prayer or thanksgiving.[1]

Structure of Hellenistic Letter	Structure of Pauline Letter
prescript	prescript
health wish	thanksgiving/blessing
body	body: varied instructions
	ethical exhortation (paraenesis)
closing	closing

1. See O'Brien, *Introductory Thanksgivings in the Letters of Paul.*

Paul takes over this form, which he modifies for his own purposes, and which he uses consistently to articulate his Christian perspective. Each element in turn receives its distinctive Pauline expansion. Thus Paul adds to his name material that affirms his apostolic authority or the authority of his gospel (e.g., Rom. 1:1–6; Gal. 1:1–2; as exceptions, the openings of both letters to the Thessalonians). He adds to the name of the addressees certain things that are true of them as Christians (e.g., 1 Cor. 1:2; 1 Thess. 1:1; 2 Thess. 1:1; as an exception, Gal. 1:2). He consistently alters the traditional "greeting" (*chairein*) to "grace and peace [*charis kai eirēnē*] from God our Father and the Lord Jesus Christ" (Colossians lacks the reference to "the Lord Jesus Christ," while 1 Thessalonians has the simple "Grace to you and peace"). He expands considerably the wish for health into a theologically rich thanksgiving or blessing, often based on OT phraseology, and which often contains implicit, if not explicit, exhortation and anticipates ideas to appear in the body of the letter (e.g., Rom. 1:8–15; 1 Cor. 1:4–9; 2 Cor. 1:3–7; Phil. 1:3–11; as exceptions, Galatians, 1 Timothy, Titus). In the body of the letter—the most varying formal element because it is determined by the actual content—Paul can exercise the greatest freedom. The most remarkable contrast with the Hellenistic letter, however, is that the last main section of the body of a Pauline letter almost consistently is devoted to ethical exhortation ("paraenesis" is the technical word). In this section Paul draws out the implications for conduct from the mainly doctrinal material that precedes. Finally, Paul consistently alters the traditional farewell into a concluding benediction or doxology (e.g., Rom. 16:25–27; 2 Cor. 13:13). Paul, in short, Christianizes the secular Hellenistic letter form. He does not miss an opportunity to enrich his readers with spiritual knowledge and a sense of worship. Indeed, in much of this he may well have had in mind the reading of his letters in a setting of corporate worship.

A few other characteristics often distinguish the Pauline Letters from the typical personal Hellenistic letter. First, Paul's Letters tend to be much longer (Philemon is the exception). The length is the direct result of the character of the letters as public teaching documents (this even for the "personal" letters to Timothy and Titus). Second, a number of the letters are written under more than one name. Thus 1 Corinthians indicates Sosthenes as coauthor. Timothy is coauthor in 2 Corinthians, Philippians, Colossians, and Philemon, while both Silvanus and Timothy are specified in the prescripts of 1 Thessalonians and 2 Thessalonians. Third, except for the Pastoral Epistles (1–2 Timothy, Titus), the addressees are always plural in number, pointing again to the public, corporate, or churchly aspect of the letters.

The Hellenistic Letter Form and Other New Testament Letters

While twenty-two documents of the NT can be classified as letters, some of these are more like tractates written in a quasi-letter form than actual letters. Thus although Hebrews ends like a letter, with greetings and personal notes, it has no customary prescript identifying author and addressees. It is to be classified as a homily partly in the form of a letter. Formally, 1 John has neither the beginning nor the ending of a letter. Other documents, although they have the form of a letter, seem to lack a living context that would qualify them as actual letters. They were created as circular letters (cf. the notion of "general" or "catholic" letters) addressed to a wide, unspecified—except in the most general way—audience (e.g., James, 1–2 Peter, Jude). They may still address quite specific problems and issues confronting the churches, but they lack a rootedness in any specific geographical or ecclesiastical context. These documents likewise reflect the form of the Hellenistic letter, albeit to a more limited extent.

The Function of Letters

Letters in every culture are a substitute for the direct encounter between two parties, whether individuals or groups. The letter therefore is not merely communication but in a real sense represents the absent person. This is the case in the Hellenistic letters, but to a much greater extent in the letters of Paul. One reason for this is the nature of the content of his letters. While trivia sometimes are mentioned in a Pauline letter, no Pauline letter is trivial. There is an urgency in what Paul writes for a variety of reasons. Often this has to do simply with the gravity of the issues and Paul's personal devotion to the churches that he founded, but on many occasions it has to do with a crisis of some kind, imminent or actual, being experienced by various churches. Often the issues deal with salvation and matters of life or death.

To such situations, where Paul cannot personally be present, he writes letters that bear his own apostolic authority. He never writes in a disinterested manner but rather is deeply and personally involved. The letters, in short, represent his apostolic *parousia* or "presence." He would rather be with them and to instruct them personally (see, e.g., Rom. 1:11–13; 1 Cor. 16:5–9; 2 Cor. 1:15; 10:11; 13:10; Gal. 4:18–20; 1 Thess. 2:17–18), and he depends on the letter only as a means of last resort. Paul's travel plans thus assume an importance in the letters. The conveyor of the letter often carries vicariously in his or her person the authority of the Apostle (see 1 Cor. 4:17; 16:10–11; 2 Cor. 8:16–24; Phil. 2:19–29), but it is the letter that stands in the place of the Apostle. By means of the letter, Paul can instruct, answer questions, reprove, encourage, and exhort. Through these letters the apostolic authority of Paul became a reality for communities rooted in the soil of historical particularity,[2] and in a

---

2. The distinction between the "coherent" (the stable core of Paul's theology) and the "contingent" (bearing on specific local particulars) in Paul's Letters is helpful (thus Beker, *Paul the Apostle*).

secondary way, through their canonization, these letters constitute a similar authority for the church of every age.

Greco-Roman Rhetoric and the Letters of Paul

"Rhetoric," as used here, refers not to ornate and flowery language but rather to the persuasive language of effective communication. Rhetoric was a fixed subject in the curriculum of Greco-Roman schools. Students were instructed in the art of rhetoric or effective argumentation by the study of famous orations and their structure. From ancient handbooks on the subject that have survived (e.g., from Quintillian and Cicero), we learn that all persuasive arguments contain at least the following elements:

1. *exordium* = introduction of the subject,
2. *narratio* = description of the facts of the situation,
3. *probatio* (or *argumentatio*) = supporting argument, and
4. *peroratio* (or *conclusio*) = summarizing conclusion.

The third section, containing the argument, sometimes was broken down further into *propositio* = statement of the theses to be demonstrated, *confirmatio* = the logical demonstration itself, and *refutatio* = the refutation of opposing arguments. Three basic types of rhetorical discourse were recognized: forensic (accusation or defense), deliberative (persuasion or dissuasion from future action), and epideictic (praise or blame).

It seems probable that Paul himself had received training in rhetoric. Although in his preaching he largely shunned the tools of oral persuasion advocated in the canons of ancient rhetoric, preferring to rely on the Spirit and the power of God (note his detractors' assessment of him in 2 Cor. 10:10: "His letters are weighty and strong, but his bodily presence is weak, and his speech of no account" [cf. 1 Cor. 1:17–25]), the structure of his letters occasionally bears the marks of the formal rhetoric of the ancient schools. Most remarkable in this regard, perhaps, is Galatians, which Hans Dieter Betz analyzes in his Galatians commentary as a piece of forensic rhetoric, containing, after the epistolary prescript, the following elements: *exordium* (1:6–11), *narratio* (1:12–2:14), *propositio* (2:15–21), *probatio* (3:1–4:31), and *exhortatio* (5:1–6:10). Though recognized by the ancient handbooks, *exhortatio* is not a major structural element of persuasive rhetoric.

Paul's Letters, and other writings of the NT, are increasingly studied from the standpoint of ancient rhetoric. Some are seen as forensic (Romans, 2 Corinthians, Galatians), some deliberative (1 Corinthians, Galatians, Philippians, Philemon), and some epideictic (Romans, 1 Thessalonians). From the overlap we can see that scholars do not agree in every instance. Furthermore, we may have to consider the possibility of mixed genres of rhetoric in the same letter.

Other Aspects of Pauline Rhetoric

Paul employs a large variety of rhetorical devices or techniques in addition to the structure and genre issues that have been discussed. He can use diatribe, a technique favored by the Cynic and Stoic philosophers, whereby discussion is conducted with an imaginary opponent who is allowed to object and cross-examine (Romans provides the best examples). He makes use of different kinds of liturgical elements from the worship of the church, such as hymns, confessions, creedal fragments, prayers, benedictions, and doxologies. He quotes or alludes to the Scriptures to substantiate an argument or otherwise to win over his readers. All of this has to do with persuasive, effective communication and is part of his rhetorical strategy.

The very great importance of paraenesis, or moral exhortation, for Paul is, as we have noted, conspicuous by comparison with the rhetoric of the ancient world. In his paraenesis Paul makes use of much traditional material, including not only the teaching of Jesus, the OT, Jewish material (e.g., the "two ways" tradition), Greco-Roman (e.g., Stoic) ethics, and vice and virtue catalogs, but also mainly the ethical catechesis of the early church, including the "put off . . . put on" pattern and the so-called household codes (instruction to wives, children, slaves, and so on).

The study of rhetoric has shown how intimately form and content are related. The content of the Pauline Letters is unique and categorically different from that of even the literary letters of antiquity. Because Paul desired to communicate effectively, he quite naturally made use of the formal elements of rhetoric that were available to him. The influence of the letter form and the canons of rhetoric on Paul are, however, more indirect than direct. Paul was never a slave to form or convention. He can and does depart from what might be expected at points. For him, the immediate purpose of the communication was everything. It, above all, dictated his rhetorical strategies. Thus the form of certain letters (e.g., 1 Corinthians, Philippians) departs from conventional rhetoric. Paul's language also varies according to his purpose. It can at times be highly polemical, at times encouraging, at times exhorting.

Paul, in short, is his own man. As with his theology, he has taken the things available to him and put his own stamp on them. Thus he displays dependence on the customary letter form and rhetorical conventions but also displays remarkable independence whereby he transforms them for the sake of his own ends. Paul thus became the letter writer par excellence of earliest Christianity.

The Letters of Paul

Paul's Letters constitute a large portion of the canonical NT. They are of the utmost importance because they provide us with the definitive interpretation of the meaning of the kerygma: the death and resurrection of Jesus. Paul draws out that meaning in terms of both its doctrinal and ethical implications. The churches originally addressed by Paul, together with the church of every subsequent age, have found these letters indispensable for an understanding of the Christian faith and have drawn from them nourishment not only for the mind but also for the spirit. To come to grips with the letters of Paul is to begin to understand the mission and work of Jesus and thus to understand Christianity at its very root.

The Pauline Letters in the New Testament

The letters of Paul are placed in the NT immediately after the Acts of the Apostles, which presents an account of the establishing of many of the churches to which Paul writes. As they stand in our NT, Paul's Letters are ordered not chronologically or geographically, but merely by length, from the longest to the shortest,[3] with the exception that letters addressed to individuals come last (the Pastoral Epistles and Philemon, which, however, is addressed also to Apphia, Archippus, and the church in Philemon's house).

Sometimes one hears of reference to the "chief letters" (from the German *Hauptbriefe*) of Paul—Romans, 1–2 Corinthians, Galatians—these being undisputed and the more weighty of Paul's Letters. Another category used in reference to some of Paul's Letters is "prison letters," indicating those that refer to Paul as being incarcerated (though the place is not always certain): Ephesians, Philippians, Colossians, and Philemon (the Pastoral Epistles generally are excluded from this category).

It is remarkable that Romans heads up the Pauline corpus, since it provides such a comprehensive and systematic statement of the gospel as Paul understands it. At the same time, scholars are increasingly sensitive to the fact that in Romans Paul addresses specific problems that he had heard of, though he was not the founder of the church and indeed had never visited it. The only other church that Paul wrote to that he had not founded or visited was that at Colossae (Col. 2:1), and in this letter he also addresses particular problems. The story of the founding of the remaining churches to which he did write is provided in Acts, although, as we will see, it is sometimes a challenge to coordinate Acts and the letters on certain matters. The Corinthian correspondence reflects as many as five original letters, as we eventually will note. The two letters that we do have provide evidence of both Paul's detailed pastoral care and his personal trials with certain opponents. Galatians shows Paul at the peak of aggravation and in the heat of polemic for the sake of the gospel, while Philippians reveals Paul's joy in the midst of adversity. In the Thessalonian letters Paul provides pastoral care and corrective instruction. Paul's deep humanity and compassion come to expression in the request to Philemon.

---

3. A slight exception exists in the case of Galatians, which is a little shorter than Ephesians. This discrepancy, however, may be due to counting lines (*stichoi*) rather than words of a particular manuscript.

In Ephesians and the Pastoral Epistles, if they are by Paul, we find him at the height of his maturity, providing a panoramic view of his theology and showing his deep, practical concern for his successors Timothy and Titus. Or, alternatively, in these letters we have disciples of Paul editing and extending the material of their master for application to the later decades of the first century.

In short, from the letters we can see that Paul was a man of many facets. Common to all those facets is his deep commitment to the gospel of Christ as he understands it. It is that deep commitment that accounts for his emotion and energy in writing to the churches. Above all, it is clear that Paul does not engage in theology for its own sake, not abstractly or theoretically. No, his letters reveal consistently the heart of a pastor with the most pragmatic concerns, burdened constantly with his care for his churches. He puts it vividly himself: "I am under daily pressure because of my anxiety for all the churches" (2 Cor. 11:28 NRSV). It is this that drives Paul to write as he does, instructing, warning, encouraging, exhorting, appealing.

Implied Readers

This single observation points us immediately again to the challenge of the particularity of the letters. Paul has not written timeless treatises or abstract discussions directly relevant or applicable in every era without further thought. Yet, to the extent that we *can* identify ourselves with the original readers, Paul's Letters will have much to offer us. Indeed, literary criticism has taught us to distinguish the original author and readers from the implied author and readers. The implied author and readers are not actual; they are the ideal author and readers implied within the text. The implied readers are those who listen to the author and who respond appropriately. In that sense, the letters may also be understood as addressing readers of the twenty-first century. To the extent that the gospel remains constant and the theological realities described by Paul remain in force, we can find truth in them for ourselves and the generation in which we live.

Bibliography

Aune, David E. "Letters in the Ancient World." In *The New Testament in Its Literary Environment*, 158–82. Philadelphia: Westminster, 1987.

———. *The Westminster Dictionary of New Testament and Early Christian Literature and Rhetoric*. Louisville: Westminster John Knox, 2003.

Beker, J. Christiaan. *Paul the Apostle: The Triumph of God in Life and Thought*. 2nd ed. Philadelphia: Fortress, 1984.

Dormeyer, Detlev. "The Hellenistic Letter-formula and the Pauline Letter-scheme." In *The Pauline Canon*, edited by Stanley E. Porter, 59–93. PS 1. Leiden: Brill, 2004.

Doty, William G. *Letters in Primitive Christianity*. GBS. Philadelphia: Fortress, 1973.

Hansen, G. Walter. "Rhetorical Criticism." In *Dictionary of Paul and His Letters*, edited by Gerald F. Hawthorne and Ralph P. Martin, 822–26. Downers Grove, IL: InterVarsity, 1993.

Klauck, Hans-Josef, with Daniel P. Bailey. *Ancient Letters and the New Testament: A Guide to Context and Exegesis*. Waco: Baylor University Press, 2006.

Meade, David G. *Pseudonymity and Canon: An Investigation into the Relationship of Authorship and Authority in Jewish and Earliest Christian Tradition*. Grand Rapids: Eerdmans, 1987.

Murphy-O'Connor, Jerome. *Paul the Letter-Writer: His World, His Options, His Skills*. GNS 41. Collegeville, MN: Liturgical Press, 1995.

O'Brien, Peter T. *Introductory Thanksgivings in the Letters of Paul*. NovTSup 49. Leiden: Brill, 1977.

———. "Letters, Letter Forms." In *Dictionary of Paul and His Letters*, edited by Gerald F. Hawthorne and Ralph P. Martin, 550–53. Downers Grove, IL: InterVarsity, 1993.

Porter, Stanley E., ed. *The Pauline Canon*. PS 1. Leiden: Brill, 2004.

Porter, Stanley E., and Sean A. Adams, eds. *Paul and the Ancient Letter Form*. PS 6. Leiden: Brill, 2010.

Richards, E. Randolph. *Paul and First-Century Letter Writing: Secretaries, Composition and Collection*. Downers Grove, IL: InterVarsity, 2004.

———. *The Secretary in the Letters of Paul*. WUNT 2/42. Tübingen: Mohr Siebeck, 1991.

Stirewalt, M. Luther, Jr. *Paul the Letter Writer*. Grand Rapids: Eerdmans, 2003.

Stowers, Stanley K. *Letter Writing in Greco-Roman Antiquity*. LEC. Philadelphia: Westminster, 1986.

Trobisch, David. *Paul's Letter Collection: Tracing the Origins*. Minneapolis: Fortress, 1994.

Watson, Duane F. "Rhetorical Criticism of the Pauline Epistles since 1975." *CurBS* 3 (1995): 219–48.

White, John L. *The Form and Function of the Body of the Greek Letter*. SBLDS 2. Missoula, MT: Society of Biblical Literature, 1972.

———. *Light from Ancient Letters*. Philadelphia: Fortress, 1986.

Winter, Bruce W. "Rhetoric." In *Dictionary of Paul and His Letters*, edited by Gerald F. Hawthorne and Ralph P. Martin, 820–23. Downers Grove, IL: InterVarsity, 1993.

23

The Missionary Paul

Without the information provided by the book of Acts, it would be virtually impossible to reconstruct the course of Paul's missionary work. From his letters alone we know little more than that he traveled around, establishing and visiting churches, and that he was persecuted and imprisoned. It is the narrative of Acts that can provide a framework for these bits of information. But it remains a strange fact that Acts mentions no letters of Paul, or even that he was the writer of letters. The task of coordinating the travels and work of Paul with the origin of the specific letters is therefore left to us. Unfortunately, as we have already noted, the book of Acts does not impress most scholars with its historical accuracy. Methodologically, there can be no question that letters of Paul always must take priority over Acts as the primary and most reliable source of historical information about him.

Nevertheless, there is, as I have indicated earlier, too much skepticism about the basic trustworthiness of Acts as a source of historical information. If confidence in Acts is rejected, we will necessarily be limited to speculation and vying conjectures. If we do not want to skate on thinner ice by inventing our own arbitrary chronology for the ministry of Paul, we need to respect what data Acts gives us. When the letters together with Acts *are* taken seriously, as here, a fairly coherent picture emerges. At the same time, it cannot be denied that some challenging problems remain. The following is an attempted integration of the information from the letters of Paul with the narrative of Acts. It should be stressed that the chronology is far from certain and remains only a hypothetical reconstruction, one of several possibilities.

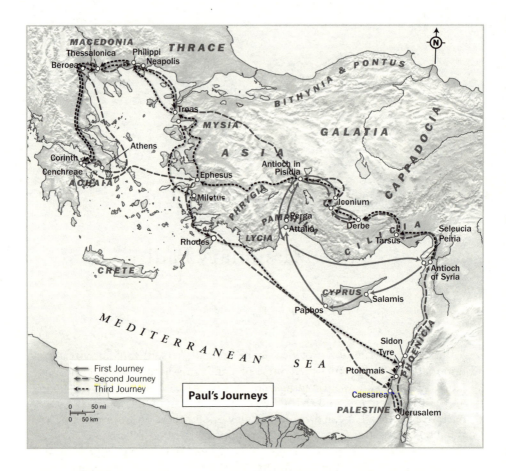

Paul's Journeys

The Years Immediately Following His Conversion

According to Acts, almost immediately after his conversion, generally thought
to be about the year 33, Paul began to proclaim Jesus in the synagogues of
Damascus (9:20). When eventually his life came under threat from Jews there,
Paul escaped by being lowered in a basket over (lit. "through") the city wall at
night, and he came to Jerusalem, where he also preached Christ and again had
to leave because of a further threat to his life. From there he returned to his
home city, Tarsus (9:30). Acts makes no mention of the three years that Paul
spent in Arabia (i.e., Nabataea), according to Galatians 1:17. The common
view now is that he was engaged in evangelism there, although we know next
to nothing about this activity. Acts is silent about Paul for an interim period
that has been estimated as about ten years, at the end of which time Acts
says that Barnabas went to look for Paul in Tarsus in order to bring him to
Antioch as his co-worker (11:25–26). It is difficult to believe that Paul was not

active in evangelization in Tarsus and surrounding areas during this period, especially given his commission on the road to Damascus to preach the gospel, but again we are told nothing about this in Acts or elsewhere in the NT. Acts records that after a year in which they were engaged in teaching the Christians at Antioch (11:26)—the first time the term *Christianoi* is applied to believers in Jesus—Barnabas and Paul made a journey to Judea in order to deliver aid from the church in Antioch (11:29–30). After the fulfillment of their mission, they returned to Antioch, bringing John Mark with them (12:25).

The First Missionary Journey (Acts 13–14)

In about the year 47 the Antiochene church received instructions from the Holy Spirit: "Set apart for me [*aphorisate de moi*] Barnabas and Saul for the work to which I have called them" (13:2). Paul and Barnabas first preached on Cyprus at Salamis, traversed the island, and set sail from Paphos for Perga in Asia Minor (modern Turkey), and from there they moved on to Pisidian Antioch, about a hundred miles into the interior of Asia Minor. At Antioch they encountered Jewish persecution and moved to the east to Iconium, where again they were persecuted and so moved on to Lystra. After an auspicious beginning in Lystra, Jews from Antioch and Iconium came and turned the people against Paul, and they stoned and nearly killed him. From there Paul and Barnabas moved on to Derbe, the last city evangelized on the first journey. They then retraced their steps through the same cities, encouraging the new converts and engaging in further evangelization. Arriving back at the home church in Syrian Antioch within a year or so, they "declared all that God had done with them, and how he had opened a door of faith [*thyran pisteōs*] to the Gentiles" (14:27).

We have one letter from Paul probably addressed to these churches, which are located in the southern part of the Roman province of Galatia. If this is correct, then it would be dated to about 48. The Letter to the **Galatians**, however, is much disputed both as to the location of its actual addressees and its date. These issues will be discussed in the chapter on Galatians (see chap. 25 below).

The Second Missionary Journey (Acts 15:36–18:22)

Luke places this journey after the Jerusalem council, which took place about the year 49 (Acts 15:1–29). The journey was motivated by Paul's pastoral concern for the churches that had been founded on the journey just described. Because of a strong disagreement between Paul and Barnabas over whether to take John Mark (the cousin of Barnabas, who had accompanied them on their first journey as far as the coast of Asia Minor but for some undisclosed reason had returned to Jerusalem), Silas took the place of Barnabas as Paul's companion. Silas (= Silvanus) was a member of the Jerusalem church and is described in 15:32 as a prophet.

The journey began with a visit to the churches of Syria and Cilicia, which Paul had established not on the first journey, but earlier, presumably during his years in Tarsus (see Gal. 1:21). These were on the land route to the churches of Asia Minor, which Paul and Silas in turn visited. Derbe and Lystra are mentioned specifically, and in the latter Paul acquired another member for his team, Timothy. They traveled about in the region of Phrygia and Galatia but were prevented by divine guidance from going into other provinces of Asia Minor. By means of the so-called Macedonian vision (16:9), they were led rather to cross over from Troas to Greece, making the great transition from Asia to Europe. From the seaport of Neapolis in Greece they proceeded along the Egnatian Way, a famous Roman highway, to Philippi, then after some time there they traveled through Amphipolis and Apollonia to Thessalonica. Having experienced imprisonment in Philippi and opposition in Thessalonica, they went on to Beroea, where eventually the Jews of the not-distant Thessalonica also stirred up opposition to Paul. Paul quickly went off alone to Athens, where he preached at the Areopagus (17:16–34) before proceeding to Corinth, where he was rejoined eventually by Silas and Timothy. At Corinth he became acquainted with Aquila and Priscilla, and, since like him they were tentmakers, he stayed with them and worked with them, settling down for a period of a year and a half. Jewish opposition to Paul also arose at Corinth, and Luke, in describing what happened, makes reference to Gallio being proconsul of Achaia at the time. Historically, this places the event rather firmly at 51–52. Accompanied by Priscilla and Aquila, Paul then departed for Syria, traveling by sea, with a stop at Ephesus (where Priscilla and Aquila remained). After discussion with Jews there, he came to Caesarea and then continued on to the home base of Antioch.

Upon the arrival of Timothy in Corinth, with his positive report about the Thessalonian church (to which he had been sent), Paul wrote the letter that we know as **1 Thessalonians**, expressing his relief at the good news of their perseverance (1 Thess. 3:1–10). Perhaps only a few months later, Paul probably wrote **2 Thessalonians** in order to correct some of their misunderstandings concerning the end of the age. But, as we will see, Pauline authorship of this document is doubted by many scholars.

The Third Missionary Journey (Acts 18:23–21:17)

As with the second journey, the third begins with a retracing of earlier steps in Galatia and Phrygia. From there Paul traveled to Ephesus, the important city on the western coast of Asia Minor, where he stayed for more than two years and engaged in daily discussions in the lecture hall of Tyrannus, "so that all the residents of Asia, heard the word of the Lord, both Jews and Greeks" (Acts 19:10). Eventually Paul departed for Macedonia (perhaps going as far as Illyricum at this point [cf. Rom. 15:9]) and Achaia, encouraging the churches in these regions, and eventually staying probably at Corinth for some three months. Although he had planned to sail to Syria, he found it necessary to return by land and did so, passing through Macedonia and sailing from Philippi (Neapolis) to Troas in Asia Minor (Luke says "we sailed" [Acts 20:6], and probably he had joined the party at this point). Paul boarded ship at Assos, a little south of Troas, and then proceeded southward along the coast eventually to Miletus, where he met with elders from the Ephesian church, and then to Patara, where they changed to a ship headed for Tyre. Staying a week with believers in Tyre, the party moved on by ship southward to Ptolemais, and after a day spent with believers there, came to Caesarea, staying for several days in the house of Philip. Finally they arrived in Jerusalem, where they were greeted warmly and met the next day with James and the elders of the Jerusalem church.

Paul's main letters were written during the progress of this "journey," which, as we have seen, included long stays in several locations. During the stay at Ephesus, Paul wrote **1 Corinthians** (see 1 Cor. 16:8, 19) in response to problems and questions conveyed by Stephanus, Fortunatus, and Achaicus (1 Cor. 16:17). Probably **2 Corinthians** was written approximately a year and a half later, from somewhere in Macedonia (see 2 Cor. 7:5; 8:1; 9:2–4). Paul wrote **Romans** during his stay in Corinth (Rom. 16:1–2 implies that Phoebe, from nearby Cenchrae, the port of Corinth, was the bearer of the letter; Gaius, Paul's host, and Erastus of Rom. 16:23 are associated with Corinth; cf. 1 Cor. 1:14; 2 Tim. 4:20). Possibly, Paul wrote the Letter to the Philippians from an Ephesian prison during the time he was in Ephesus (this to be discussed later), but more probably he wrote Philippians from Rome.

The Arrest, Trials, and Roman Imprisonment of Paul

According to the narrative of Acts, Paul had already determined to go to Jerusalem (and Rome too, although not as a prisoner!) during his long stay in Ephesus (19:21). Despite the ominous warnings of the danger that awaited him in Jerusalem (21:4: "through the Spirit they told Paul not to go on to Jerusalem" [cf. 21:10–14]), Paul, "bound in the Spirit" (20:22), will not be turned away from his goal (20:16). The reason Paul desires so earnestly to go to Jerusalem is to bring a gift offering to the Jerusalem saints from the Gentile churches (cf. 1 Cor. 16:1–4; 2 Cor. 8:19; 9:5; Rom. 15:25–26, 31). It is important, however, to realize that Paul's motive is not only the amelioration of poverty but also, ultimately, the symbolic importance of a demonstration of the unity of the Gentile churches with the church of Jerusalem.[1] So important is this latter goal to Paul that he is willing to put his life in danger for it.

1. See Downs, *The Offering of the Gentiles*.

When Paul was seized by the crowds in the temple under the trumped-up charge that he had brought Gentiles into the temple (21:30), a Roman tribune intervened and arrested him. After an address in Aramaic to the people (22:1–21) there follow in rapid order a hearing before the high priest Ananias (23:1–10) and, on a threat to his life, a nighttime transfer to Caesarea. Then comes a trial before Felix, the Roman governor (chap. 24) and, after a two-year interim spent in prison at Caesarea, a trial before his successor, Festus (chap. 25), at which time Paul desperately appealed to Caesar, exercising his right as a Roman citizen. A parenthetical hearing before the Jewish king Agrippa (chap. 26) is held before the required trip to Rome, which was interrupted by a disastrous shipwreck (27:13–44). The forced sheltering on the island of Malta provides Paul with occasion to engage in a ministry of healing (28:7–10). Acts ends with Paul a house prisoner in Rome (28:16, 23, 30) awaiting the outcome of his appeal. Luke ends the narrative here, either because that was as far as the story had come when he wrote or, more likely, because he did not care to carry the story further, having accomplished what he wanted to by recording the arrival of Paul in Rome.

Because we have no data, we are left to speculate what happened next. Basically, there are two choices: either Paul remained in custody for some years and was then put to death, or after a couple of years he was released and carried on further ministry, only again to be arrested for some reason and subsequently put to death. We know only that Paul was put to death by the Romans sometime in the mid-60s. Tradition says that he was beheaded outside the city on the Ostian Way.

While under house imprisonment in Rome, Paul probably wrote **Philippians**, although he could have written this letter from an earlier imprisonment. It is also probable that in Rome he wrote **Colossians** and the closely related **Philemon**, the former in response to reports that he had heard from Epaphras, who had established the Colossian church, the latter on behalf of the slave Onesimus. If **Ephesians** is accepted as a letter of Paul, then it too probably was written from Rome.

According to Philemon 22, Paul was optimistic about being released from his imprisonment. So, if we could be certain that Paul wrote this letter from Rome, we would have some reason to think that he was released from that first Roman imprisonment. If Philippians too was written from Rome, further evidence along the same line is gained from Philippians 1:25; 2:24. Only if we affirm a release from the first imprisonment is it possible to argue for the Pauline authorship of the Pastoral Epistles, or indeed any actual Pauline connection with the letters, since they posit additional travels to the east: Crete, Asia Minor, Macedonia, and Nicopolis.

The Pauline Epistles, the focus of the chapters that follow, are thus to be fitted into the travels and work of the Apostle. They grow out of his career and are the fruit of the commission that he received on the Damascus Road. They are written in different places, at different times, and with different agendas. To understand these letters, one must begin with at least some comprehension of their historical settings. Those settings therefore will be a major feature in the discussion of the content of the specific letters.

Bibliography

Alexander, Loveday C. A. "Chronology of Paul." In *Dictionary of Paul and His Letters*, edited by Gerald F. Hawthorne and Ralph P. Martin, 115–23. Downers Grove, IL: InterVarsity, 1993.

Allen, Roland. *Missionary Methods: St. Paul's or Ours?* 2nd ed. London: World Dominion Press, 1930.

Barnett, Albert E. *Paul Becomes a Literary Influence.* Chicago: University of Chicago Press, 1941.

Barnett, Paul. *Paul: Missionary of Jesus.* Grand Rapids: Eerdmans, 2008.

Barrett, C. K. *Paul: An Introduction to His Thought.* Louisville: Westminster John Knox, 1994.

Bruce, F. F. *Paul: Apostle of the Heart Set Free.* Grand Rapids: Eerdmans, 1977.

Campbell, Thomas H. "Paul's 'Missionary Journeys' as Reflected in His Letters." *JBL* 74 (1955): 80–87.

Childs, Brevard S. *The Church's Guide for Reading Paul: The Canonical Shaping of the Pauline Corpus.* Grand Rapids: Eerdmans, 2008.

Davies, W. D. *Paul and Rabbinic Judaism: Some Rabbinic Elements in Pauline Theology.* 4th ed. Philadelphia: Fortress, 1980.

Donaldson, Terence L. "Israelite, Convert, Apostle to the Gentiles: The Origin of Paul's Gentile Mission." In *The Road from Damascus: The Impact of Paul's Conversion on His Life, Thought, and Ministry*, edited by Richard N. Longenecker, 62–84. Grand Rapids: Eerdmans, 1997.

———. *Paul and the Gentiles: Remapping the Apostle's Convictional World.* Minneapolis: Fortress, 1997.

Downs, David J. *The Offering of the Gentiles: Paul's Collection for Jerusalem in Its Chronological, Cultural, and Cultic Contexts.* WUNT 2/248. Tübingen: Mohr Siebeck, 2008.

Hengel, Martin. *Judaism and Hellenism: Studies in Their Encounter in Palestine during the Hellenistic Period.* Translated by John Bowden. 2 vols. Philadelphia: Fortress, 1974.

Hengel, Martin, with Roland Deines. *The Pre-Christian Paul.* Translated by John Bowden. Philadelphia: Trinity Press International, 1991.

Hengel, Martin, and Anna Maria Schwemer. *Paul between Damascus and Antioch: The Unknown Years.* Translated by John Bowden. Louisville: Westminster John Knox, 1997.

Hock, Ronald F. *The Social Context of Paul's Ministry: Tentmaking and Apostleship.* Philadelphia: Fortress, 1980.

Keck, Leander E. *Paul and His Letters.* Philadelphia: Fortress, 1979.

Kim, Seyoon. *The Origin of Paul's Gospel.* 2nd ed. Grand Rapids: Eerdmans, 1984.

Knox, John. *Chapters in a Life of Paul.* Rev. ed. Macon, GA: Mercer University Press, 1987.

Riesner, Rainer. *Paul's Early Period: Chronology, Mission Strategy, Theology.* Translated by Douglas Stott. Grand Rapids: Eerdmans, 1998.

Sanders, E. P. *Paul and Palestinian Judaism.* Philadelphia: Fortress, 1977.

Schnabel, Eckhard J. *Paul and the Early Church.* Vol. 2 of *Early Christian Mission.* Downers Grove, IL: IVP Academic, 2004.

———. *Paul the Missionary: Realities, Strategies and Methods.* Downers Grove, IL: IVP Academic, 2008.

24

The Authorship Question

Apart from the uncontested letters of Paul, the authorship of the writings of the NT remains one of the most difficult and controversial questions in NT scholarship. Intense study of the content, language, and style of these writings has very often raised doubts concerning the traditional ascriptions of authorship and even the claims of the documents themselves. Although at first this may seem disconcerting, this uncertainty should not be thought of as undermining the authority, inspiration, or canonicity of our NT writings. It would do so only if it could be demonstrated that the actual authors were neither members of the apostolic circle nor associated with the names in the documents—for example, writers of the middle of the second century or later.

The Four Gospels

The writers of all four of our canonical Gospels are anonymous. In each instance, however, there are strong patristic traditions concerning authorship, as we have seen. I have argued that there is good evidence to take the patristic traditions seriously. Furthermore, as Martin Hengel has shown, the titles of the Gospels, "According to Matthew," "According to Mark," and so on, were attached to the Gospel manuscripts from virtually the beginning.[1]

If these were documents looking for names, it remains unclear why anyone would choose "Mark" or "Luke" rather than names of the Twelve. We have

1. See Hengel, "The Titles of the Gospels and the Gospel of Mark." See also idem, *The Four Gospels and the One Gospel of Jesus Christ*.

examined the evidence concerning Mark and Luke, as we have also for Matthew and John. In the case of the latter two, we have seen reason to take the claims of apostolic authorship seriously, even if the final form of these Gospels comes from disciples of the Apostles.

The Pauline Corpus and the Question of Authorship

The letters of Paul in the NT, the so-called Pauline corpus, comprise thirteen documents. That is, thirteen letters begin explicitly with the name of Paul in the prescript. For many centuries the church spoke of fourteen letters of Paul, this including the anonymous Hebrews (which has no prescript), long thought to be by Paul but now almost universally regarded as non-Pauline.[2] For the Pauline Epistles the picture is more complicated than this, however. Some letters, as we already noted, name more than one author/sender. Thus we have to deal also with Sosthenes, Timothy, and Silvanus. Beyond this, we have to consider secretaries, such as Tertius, who is identified by name and rather boldly greets the Romans as "the writer of this letter" (Rom. 16:22), and Silvanus (1 Pet. 5:12), but also other, unnamed secretaries.[3]

Authorship of Paul's Letters

Paul alone: Romans, Galatians, Ephesians, 1 and 2 Timothy, Titus

Paul and Sosthenes: 1 Corinthians

Paul and Timothy: 2 Corinthians, Philippians, Colossians, Philemon

Paul and Silvanus and Timothy: 1 and 2 Thessalonians

It is clear that Paul dictated his letters to professional copyists (the technical word for such a secretary-copyist is "amanuensis"). Frequently at the end of his letters he writes a few lines in his own hand. In no less than four places he makes a specific note of this: "I, Paul, write this greeting with my own hand" (1 Cor. 16:21; Col. 4:4, 18; 2 Thess. 3:17; Philem. 19). At the end of Galatians he even calls attention to his own awkward handwriting: "See with what large letters I am writing to you with my own hand" (Gal. 6:11). There may have been a problem of forged letters, purporting to be by Paul, as this comment in 2 Thessalonians 2:1–2 suggests: "We beg you . . . not to be quickly shaken in mind or alarmed, either by spirit or by word or by letter, as though from us, to the effect that the day of the Lord is already here" (NRSV). Thus at the end of the letter, when he writes, "I, Paul, write this greeting with my own hand," he adds "This is the mark in every letter of mine; it is the way I write" (2 Thess. 3:17). Here we have what amounts

2. That we do not know who wrote Hebrews in no way jeopardizes its canonical authority.
3. See Richards, *The Secretary in the Letters of Paul.*

to an authenticating signature, comparable to our contemporary practice of signing letters.

Only seven of the thirteen letters are widely accepted by scholars as authentic letters of Paul. Most seriously doubted are the Pastoral Epistles (1–2 Timothy and Titus). Considerable doubt also exists, in descending order of degree, for Ephesians, Colossians, and 2 Thessalonians. The reasons for doubt concern not only the observable differences in the style of Greek but also the vocabulary and content, not only because of the presence of material not found in other Pauline Letters but also because of the lack of the usual Pauline language and emphases. In general, most of these doubted letters seem to reflect a situation and perspective rather later than Paul's. Although the stylistic differences might well be accounted for by the use of different secretaries, the differences in content and especially perspective are more problematic. They seem to be too substantial to be attributed merely to secretaries, even secretaries with considerable freedom in putting the dictated material into final form. The argument for pseudonymous Pauline Letters is a cumulative one.

The non-Pauline authorship of these doubted letters is, of course, no more provable than Pauline authorship. As with the question of dates, we are never, or hardly ever, in the realm of what can be proved or demonstrated. At best, here as elsewhere, we deal with historical probabilities. Thus, plenty of room for disagreement should be allowed.[4] The arguments against the Pauline authorship of Colossians and 2 Thessalonians, as we will see, are not very strong. In the case of the Pastoral Epistles and Ephesians, on the contrary, the challenges that have been mounted are of sufficient strength to warrant grouping them, at least tentatively, in a category known as Deutero-Pauline letters.

Deutero-Pauline Letters, Pseudonymity, and the Question of Deception

We have very little to lose in allowing a category of Deutero-Pauline letters. If it happens that some other persons have written these four, or even six, documents in the name of Paul, we are not talking about forgery or deception.[5] The vast majority of scholars assert that these documents contain significant amounts of authentic Pauline material and were put into their present form by immediate disciples or co-workers of Paul. Only if we had here documents

4. Intelligent and worthy arguments have been mounted defending the authenticity of the disputed books. Immediately one thinks of J. A. T. Robinson's remarkable *Redating the New Testament*, in which he dates all the NT books before AD 70. Reasonable defense of the traditional ascriptions can be found in Donald Guthrie's introduction to the NT, as well as other conservative evangelical introductions. Also worth noting is "Did Paul Write Galatians?" which is Harold Hoehner's tongue-in-cheek application of the typical criteria used in arguing for pseudepigraphy to the question of the authorship of Galatians, a letter accepted by all as Pauline.

5. Not even of "the noble lie" variety—that is, a lie "told in the cause of a great truth, and in the service of a great cause." See Harding, "Disputed and Undisputed Letters of Paul," 149.

from well into the second century or later, stemming from people who had no direct connection with Paul, could we justifiably speak of forgery or deception.

The ancient world on the whole did not have the same kind of sensitivity to pseudonymity that is typical in the modern world, with its concern for careful attribution and copyright. It is also important to realize that even by modern standards there is a pseudonymity that can be regarded as morally acceptable, just as there is a blameworthy pseudonymity. In the latter we are dealing with deliberate misrepresentation that amounts to forgery, and in the former with the disciple/co-worker's edition of material that has its roots in the master's actual teaching. Examples of this practice can be seen from Cicero in the first century BC: "If there is anyone to whom you think a letter ought to be sent in my name, please write one and see that it is sent."[6] Sometimes the material as it stands goes back to the master; in other instances it may appropriately extend that teaching in fresh application, something that also honors the master. There is plenty of precedent for this practice. It is widely admitted, even by conservative scholars, that many of the canonical prophetic books of the OT are documents not written by the prophets whose names they bear but instead consist of materials put into their present shape by disciples of the prophets.[7] The authority and canonicity of the material is in no way affected by this fact. The dimension of corporate or shared responsibility for a document is already anticipated in the multiple names associated with Paul in the prescripts noted above. We are not dealing with deception or forgery here.

The fact is that the Pauline corpus, with deutero-letters as well as without them, stands under the banner of the authoritative Paul. From a canonical perspective, the corpus as it stands represents Paul, even if the Deutero-Pauline letters require special awareness and care when they are used to speak of Paul himself. It is not unfair to say that the deutero-letters represent Paul in their own way as much as the authentic letters. But it is indeed Paul whom they represent, and therefore to that extent they involve no deception.[8]

On the one hand, so far as trivial personal details, plans, requests, and so forth in the Pastoral Epistles are concerned—matters incidental to the actual teaching of the letters—if these are artificial, that would hardly impugn the basic integrity of the letter's main content, which represents the Pauline

6. Cicero, *Letters to Atticus* 3.15. Note also: "I am so fearfully upset both in mind and body that I have not been able to write many letters; I have only answered those who have written to me. I should like you to write in my name to Basilus and to anyone else you like, even to Servilius, and say whatever you think fit" (*Letters to Atticus* 11.5).

7. For an exploration not only of the prophets but also of wisdom and apocalyptic as the background for the phenomenon of pseudonymity, see Meade, *Pseudonymity and Canon*, 17–102.

8. Percy Harrison's view is similar: "I do not for a moment believe that [the author of the Pastorals] intended to deceive those for whom he wrote, or that they were in fact deceived by him. He was, in my view, a devout, sincere and earnest Paulinist who set out to express in this familiar form what he and his readers really believed the Apostle would have said had he been still alive" ("Important Hypotheses Reconsidered," 77).

tradition and therefore should be ascribed to Paul. On the other hand, it is entirely possible that these details represent fragments of letters and notes that have been picked up and incorporated into these letters, supplying a framework that employs the familiar Pauline pattern.

The early church rejected pseudonymous writings that were late and had no real connection with the persons under whose names they were written. These they rightly classified as forgeries and as morally culpable. Thus Eusebius records that at the end of the second century Serapion, bishop of Antioch, rejected *The Gospel of Peter* with these words: "For our part, brethren, we receive both Peter and the other apostles as Christ, but the writings which falsely bear their names we reject, as men of experience knowing that such were not handed down to us" (*Hist. eccl.* 6.12.3, trans. Oulton). Another example usually cited in this connection concerns the elder who "out of love for Paul" wrote the *Acts of Paul and Thecla*, which included a letter called "3 Corinthians," and who was deposed from his office for having done so (for a recounting of the story, see Tertullian, *Bapt.* 17). These were the right decisions, because in these instances, unlike the pseudonymous letters of the NT, there was no real connection with the Apostles, and therefore they were forgeries—documents intended to deceive. Only where a close connection exists between the author and the Apostle in question does pseudonymity become innocuous.

The key issue in the minds of many is the matter of deception, since it is rightly maintained that deception is not consonant with the moral integrity of the NT authors and was unacceptable to the early church.[9] Since pseudonymity is someone writing in the name of someone else, it can perhaps be regarded, strictly speaking, or technically, as "deception" from our point of view. But that would be to make a mountain out of a molehill. In the case before us, where there is an ascertainable connection between the Apostle and the author writing in his name, and where the content perpetuates and extends the teaching of the Apostle,[10] the "deception"—if one insists on pressing the issue—is of a very trivial kind and loses its significance. (It might truly have been more deceptive for the author to write in his own name!) Why, it is sometimes asked, would such authors not write in their own name? The answer is that what they were presenting was not fundamentally their own material. Such a technical sense of deception becomes meaningless because in listening to this author we in effect hear the Apostle.[11] The teaching of the document—what really matters—stands as authoritative truth for the church. The proximity of the

9. This appears to be the main concern for scholars such as Donald Guthrie, Earle Ellis, D. A. Carson, and Terry Wilder.

10. David Meade makes the point this way: "In the Pastorals, attribution is primarily an assertion of authoritative tradition, not of literary origins" (*Pseudonymity and Canon*, 139 [italics removed]).

11. Writing about 2 Peter, Richard Bauckham comes to a similar conclusion: "The pseudepigraphal device is therefore not a fraudulent means of claiming apostolic authority but embodies a claim to be a faithful mediator of the apostolic message. Recognising the canonicity of 2 Peter

pseudonymous author to the Apostle is everything. That *these* particular books were received into the canon, under the guidance of the Spirit of God, itself suggests that they are to be differentiated from other, morally reprehensible pseudonymous books or forgeries, texts written for some personal advantage, whether financial or professional.[12]

As Klaus Koch concludes, "Since what is involved is not the conscious use of an inaccurate name, the designation 'pseudonymous' should be used only with reservations."[13] In order to avoid the idea of deceit, Howard Marshall has coined the words "allonymity" and "allepigraphy," in which the prefix *pseudos* ("false") is replaced by *allos* ("other"), which "will refer more positively to the activity of writing in another person's name without intent to deceive."[14] James Dunn comes to a similar conclusion: "The charge of deceit and falsehood leveled against these writings [the canonical pseudepigrapha] becomes inappropriate; what we have rather is a legitimate speaking in and use of the great teacher's name, recognized as such by the churches that first used the letters in question."[15]

It seems advisable, therefore, to defuse the issue of pseudonymity for those who are nervous about it. There is nothing crucial at stake here for those who, like myself, treasure the NT as Scripture. The acceptance of this kind of pseudonymity, based on actual association with and dependence on Paul or other Apostles, should in no way threaten the canonical authority of these documents. As Tertullian says, although admittedly in a different connection, "It is permissible for the works which disciples published to be regarded as belonging to their masters" (*Marc.* 4.5.4, trans. Evans). It was the practice of rabbinic students to hand on materials in the name of their rabbis.[16] The authority of the Apostles extends also to their co-workers, and therefore they could write in the master's name if the occasion required it.[17] The list of Christian Scriptures in the Muratorian Canon includes Wisdom of Solomon—an oddity

---

means recognising the validity of that claim, and it is not clear that this is so alien to the early church's criteria of canonicity as is sometimes alleged" (*Jude, 2 Peter*, 161–62).

12. "In short, since the use of the literary form of pseudepigraphy need not be regarded as necessarily involving fraudulent intent, it cannot be argued that the character of inspiration excludes the possibility of pseudepigraphy among the canonical writings" (Metzger, "Literary Forgeries and Canonical Pseudepigrapha," 20). Werner Kümmel comments, "There still exists in any event no ground for declaring that pseudepigraphic writing is impossible for early Christian epistolary literature, or that it precludes truthfulness" (*Introduction to the New Testament*, 363).

13. Koch, "Pseudonymous Writing," 713.

14. Marshall, *A Critical and Exegetical Commentary on the Pastoral Epistles*, 84.

15. Dunn, "Pseudepigraphy," 984.

16. See Gerhardsson, *Memory and Manuscript*, 131.

17. John Barclay makes the interesting point that "the differences are not large between Paul himself writing this letter [Colossians], Paul writing with the aid of a secretary, Paul authorising an associate to write it, and the letter being composed by a knowledgeable imitator or pupil of Paul." He continues with this observation: "Perhaps with our intense concern to demarcate 'Paul' from 'non-Paul' we are working with an artificial or anachronistic notion of individual uniqueness" (*Colossians and Philemon*, 35).

that we will ignore for the moment. The point to be made here, however, is that Wisdom of Solomon is accepted as Scripture even when the canon compiler, probably toward the end of the second century, recognizes that it was written not by Solomon but rather "by the friends of Solomon in his honor."

Raymond Brown concludes the following about Deutero-Pauline documents in the NT: "Such a situation makes sense if one supposes that Paul was dead and the disciple considered himself an authoritative interpreter of the apostle whose thought he endorsed. Attribution of the letter to Paul in those circumstances would not be using a false name or making a false claim that Paul wrote the letter. It would be treating Paul as the author in the sense of the authority behind a letter that was intended as an extension of his thought—an assumption of the great apostle's mantle to continue his work."[18]

This is a basic principle at work in the formation of the canon. We do not know beyond a shadow of doubt that there are Deutero-Pauline Letters in the Pauline corpus, but if in the weighing of historical probabilities it seems to us that there are, we can admit freely that this too is a way in which God has mediated Scripture to us. What Andrew Lincoln rightly concludes about Ephesians also applies to the Pastoral Epistles and 2 Peter: "There should be no suggestion that to decide that Ephesians is pseudonymous is somehow to detract from the validity or authority of its message as part of the NT canon."[19]

Thus in the discussion of the Pauline Letters below I will separate out the Pastoral Epistles and Ephesians as Deutero-Pauline letters. This is a pragmatic move and rests not on the conviction that the case has been proved beyond a doubt, but rather on how a strong case has been made, that the probabilities point in this direction, and that it therefore may be useful at least to consider these letters separately. There is little to lose and perhaps much to gain insofar as the clarity of the Pauline profile is concerned.

In the Deutero-Pauline letters of Ephesians and the Pastoral Epistles we find a Pauline trajectory that extends the Apostle's teaching to meet the challenges of the later decades of the first century. In Ephesians we encounter a remarkable wide-angle view of Paul's theology; in the Pastoral Epistles we see the clear tendencies of an incipient early catholicism (see chap. 33 below), with preparations for enduring through the lengthening interim period prior to the return of Christ and the consummation of what has already begun.

Other Possibly Pseudonymous Letters in the New Testament

As we proceed, we will see that other letters in the NT possibly are pseudonymous. Indeed, in regard to the seven Catholic Epistles there is hardly a single book for which the question of authenticity does not arise, even if it can be

18. Brown, "Pseudonymity and the Deuteropauline Writings," 586.
19. Lincoln, *Ephesians*, lxxiii.

confidently answered. The letter in the corpus that is almost universally challenged is 2 Peter, which many scholars regard as the last document of the NT to be written, as late as the middle of the second century. Although he would not put it so late, John Calvin regarded the epistle as pseudonymous; Martin Luther and Erasmus also doubted its authenticity. Still, Luther did not relegate it to his appendix to the NT, as he did a few other books. It should be stressed that when we grant that Peter himself did not write the letter, that by no means necessitates a second-century date. Late in the first century is sufficient.

The Johannine Corpus

The authorship of the writings that compose the Johannine corpus (the Gospel of John, 1–3 John, and Revelation) is a very difficult and complicated question that will be dealt with in detail below. John's Gospel and 1 John are, like the other Gospels, Acts, and Hebrews, anonymous. Yet a strong ancient tradition associates them with the Apostle John, and so the question of pseudonymity arises here too.[20] Eastern Orthodoxy affirms John the Apostle as the author of all five documents. All five documents were written in the same sort of simple Semitic Greek; the differences between the documents, it is claimed, are due solely to differences in the genre of the writings. As we will see, questions also arise concerning the identity of John the Elder (2–3 John) and John the seer (Revelation).

Some Concluding Observations

Because our knowledge is so limited, much of the argumentation about authorship presented in chapters that follow necessarily involves possibilities and probabilities. It is very difficult to be fully confident about very much. We are out of the realm of proof and are required instead to depend on cumulative arguments. In this connection, a comment of C. H. Dodd is worth quoting:

> No accumulation of bare possibilities, of course, could amount to more than a possibility in the end and an accumulation of marginal probabilities is not worth much more. But where in one place phenomena pointing to a comparatively modest degree of probability can be shown to be closely related, or significantly analogous, to phenomena in other places where the degree of probability is high, the resultant level of probability is raised; and within such an interlocking structure even mere possibilities may (sometimes) come to wear a different aspect.[21]

What needs to be stressed here, however, is that there is no need to think that the acceptance of pseudonymity in the NT—at least of the kind discussed

---

20. And the question arises very early. The orthodox presbyter and opponent of Montanism, Gaius of Rome (170–80), denied the apostolic authorship of both John's Gospel and Revelation.

21. Dodd, *Historical Tradition in the Fourth Gospel*, 423.

above—in any sense threatens or undermines the authority and canonicity of such writings.

Bibliography

Aland, Kurt. "The Problem of Anonymity and Pseudonymity in Christian Literature of the First Two Centuries." *JTS* 12 (1961): 39–49. Reprinted in *The Authorship and Integrity of the New Testament*, by Kurt Aland, Donald Guthrie, A. Q. Morton, J. A. T. Robinson, G. Bornkamm, A. M. G. Stephenson, and Massey H. Shepherd Jr., 1–13. London: SPCK, 1965.

Aland, Kurt, Donald Guthrie, A. Q. Morton, J. A. T. Robinson, G. Bornkamm, A. M. G. Stephenson, and Massey H. Shepherd Jr. *The Authorship and Integrity of the New Testament*. London: SPCK, 1965.

Barclay, John M. G. *Colossians and Philemon*. NTG. Sheffield: Sheffield Academic Press, 1997.

Bauckham, Richard. *Jude, 2 Peter*. WBC 50. Waco: Word, 1983.

———. "Pseudoapostolic Letters." *JBL* 107 (1988): 469–94.

Brown, Raymond E. "Pseudonymity and the Deuteropauline Writings." In *Introduction to the New Testament*, 585–89. New York: Doubleday, 1997.

Byrskog, Samuel. "Co-Senders, Co-Authors and Paul's Use of the First Person Plural." *ZNW* 87 (1996): 230–50.

Carson, D. A. "Pseudonymity and Pseudepigraphy." In *Dictionary of New Testament Background*, edited by Craig A. Evans and Stanley E. Porter, 857–74. Downers Grove, IL: InterVarsity, 2000.

Clarke, Kent D. "The Problem of Pseudonymity in Biblical Literature and Its Implications for Canon Formation." In *The Canon Debate*, edited by Lee Martin McDonald and James A. Sanders, 440–68. Peabody, MA: Hendrickson, 2002.

DiTommaso, Lorenzo. *A Bibliography of Pseudepigrapha Research, 1850–1999*. JSPSup 39. Sheffield: Sheffield Academic Press, 2001.

Dodd, C. H. *Historical Tradition in the Fourth Gospel*. Cambridge: Cambridge University of Press, 1963.

Donelson, Lewis R. *Pseudepigraphy and Ethical Argument in the Pastoral Epistles*. HUT 22. Tübingen: Mohr Siebeck, 1986.

Dunn, James D. G. "The Problem of Pseudonymity." In *The Living Word*, 65–85. Philadelphia: Fortress, 1987.

———. "Pseudepigraphy." In *Dictionary of the Later New Testament and Its Developments*, edited by Ralph P. Martin and Peter H. Davids, 977–84. Downers Grove, IL: InterVarsity, 1997.

Ellis, E. Earle. "Pseudonymity and Canonicity of New Testament Documents." In *Worship, Theology and Ministry in the Early Church: Essays in Honor of Ralph P. Martin*, edited by Michael J. Wilkins and Terence Paige, 212–24. JSNTSup 87. Sheffield: JSOT Press, 1992.

Gamble, Harry Y. "Pseudonymity and the New Testament Canon." In *Pseudepigraphie und Verfasserfiktion in frühchristlichen Briefen* [*Pseudepigraphy and Author Fiction in Early Christian Letters*], edited by Jörg Frey, Jens Herzer, Martina Janßen, and Clare K. Rothschild, 333–62. WUNT 246. Tübingen: Mohr Siebeck, 2009.

Gerhardsson, Birger. *Memory and Manuscript: Oral Tradition and Written Transmission in Rabbinic Judaism and Early Christianity;* with, *Tradition and Transmission in Early Christianity*. Translated by Eric J. Sharpe. BRS. Grand Rapids: Eerdmans; Livonia, MI: Dove, 1998.

Goodspeed, Edgar J. "Pseudonymity and Pseudepigrapha in Early Christian Literature." In *New Chapters in New Testament Study*, 169–88. New York: Macmillan, 1937.

Guthrie, Donald H. "The Development of the Idea of Canonical Pseudepigrapha in New Testament Criticism." In *The Authorship and Integrity of the New Testament*, by Kurt Aland, Donald Guthrie, A. Q. Morton, J. A. T. Robinson, G. Bornkamm, A. M. G. Stephenson, and Massey H. Shepherd Jr., 14–39. London: SPCK, 1965.

———. "Epistolary Pseudepigraphy." In *New Testament Introduction*, 1011–28. 4th ed. Downers Grove, IL: InterVarsity, 1990.

Harding, Mark. "Disputed and Undisputed Letters of Paul." In *The Pauline Canon*, edited by Stanley E. Porter, 129–68. PS 1. Leiden: Brill, 2004.

Harrison, Percy N. "Important Hypotheses Reconsidered: III. The Authorship of the Pastoral Epistles." *ExpTim* 67 (1955–56): 77–81.

Hengel, Martin. *The Four Gospels and the One Gospel of Jesus Christ: An Investigation of the Collection and Origin of the Canonical Gospels*. Harrisburg, PA: Trinity Press International, 2000.

———. "The Titles of the Gospels and the Gospel of Mark." In *Studies in the Gospel of Mark*, edited by Martin Hengel, translated by John Bowden, 64–84. Reprint, Eugene, OR: Wipf & Stock, 2003.

Hoehner, Harold W. "Did Paul Write Galatians?" In *History and Exegesis: New Testament Essays in Honor of Dr. E. Earle Ellis for His 80th Birthday*, edited by Sang-Won (Aaron) Son, 150–69. New York: T&T Clark, 2006.

Kiley, Mark. *Colossians as Pseudepigraphy*. BibSem 4. Sheffield: JSOT Press, 1986.

Koch, Klaus. "Pseudonymous Writing." In *Interpreter's Dictionary of the Bible: Supplementary Volume*, edited by Keith Crim, 712–14. Nashville: Abingdon, 1976.

Kümmel, Werner Georg. *Introduction to the New Testament*. Translated by A. J. Mattill Jr. 14th ed. Nashville: Abingdon, 1966.

Lea, Thomas D. "Pseudonymity and the New Testament." In *New Testament Criticism and Interpretation*, edited by David Alan Black and David S. Dockery, 533–59. Grand Rapids: Zondervan, 1991.

Lincoln, Andrew T. *Ephesians*. WBC 42. Dallas: Word, 1990.

Marshall, I. Howard. *A Critical and Exegetical Commentary on the Pastoral Epistles*. ICC. Edinburgh: T&T Clark, 1999.

Meade, David G. *Pseudonymity and Canon: An Investigation into the Relationship of Authorship and Authority in Jewish and Earliest Christian Tradition*. Grand Rapids: Eerdmans, 1987.

Metzger, Bruce M. "Literary Forgeries and Canonical Pseudepigrapha." In *New Testament Studies: Philological, Versional, and Patristic*, 1–22. NTTS 10. Leiden: Brill, 1980.

Murphy-O'Connor, Jerome. "Co-Authorship in the Corinthian Correspondence." *RB* 100 (1993): 562–79.

Patzia, Arthur G. "The Deutero-Pauline Hypothesis: An Attempt at Clarification." *EvQ* 52 (1980): 27–42.

Richards, E. Randolph. *Paul and First-Century Letter Writing: Secretaries, Composition and Collection*. Downers Grove, IL: InterVarsity, 2004.

———. *The Secretary in the Letters of Paul*. WUNT 2/42. Tübingen: Mohr Siebeck, 1991.

Rist, Martin. "Pseudepigraphy and the Early Christians." In *Studies in New Testament and Early Christian Literature: Essays in Honor of Allen P. Wikgren*, edited by David E. Aune, 75–91. NovTSup 33. Leiden: Brill, 1972.

Robinson, J. A. T. *Redating the New Testament*. Philadelphia: Westminster, 1976.

Wilder, Terry L. "Pseudonymity and the New Testament." In *Interpreting the New Testament: Essays on Methods and Issues*, edited by David Alan Black and David S. Dockery, 296–335. Nashville: Broadman & Holman, 2001.

———. *Pseudonymity, the New Testament, and Deception: An Inquiry into Intention and Reception*. Lanham, MD: University Press of America, 2004.

25

Galatians

The Letter to the Galatians was composed in the midst of intense theological controversy. For Paul, the crisis that had come upon the Galatian churches threatened the very truth of the gospel, and thus Paul writes with the greatest urgency. Because of the claims of his opponents, he is forced to articulate the gospel in the clearest of terms and at the same time relate it to God's earlier revelation in the law of Moses. The letter that he produced remains one of the most powerful statements of the Christian faith, especially concerning the Christian's freedom from the law; hence, it sometimes has been called the "Magna Carta of the Christian faith." It is, at the same time, a very distinctly Pauline document that states the essential doctrine of justification by faith.

Galatians: The Earliest Letter of Paul?

There are several notable questions in NT studies that have continued to cause disagreement among scholars. One of the most intractable of these concerns the date and addressees of Galatians. The choice to be made is between Galatians as Paul's earliest letter, written in about 48, and addressed to the South Galatian churches established on the first missionary journey (Iconium, Lystra, Derbe),[1] and Galatians as written just prior to Romans, hence in about 55 or

---

1. Among modern commentators accepting the South Galatian hypothesis are Burton, Ridderbos, Guthrie, Bruce, Longenecker, Fung, Morris, Neil, Witherington, George, and Jervis. Among earlier commentators who hold to the South Galatian theory, Burton and Ramsay deserve special mention. It was particularly Ramsay, toward the end of the nineteenth century, who established a sound scholarly basis for the South Galatian theory.

Author: The Apostle Paul. This is one of the four main uncontested Pauline Letters.

Date: Probably before the Jerusalem council, hence 48 or 49, and thus the earliest of Paul's Letters in the canon; but possibly, on the North Galatian hypothesis, in the middle 50s.

Addressees: Probably the churches of South Galatia established on Paul's first missionary journey to Asia Minor, but possibly the churches of North Galatia, agreeing with the later dating of the letter.

Purpose: To set forth a definitive statement of the gospel according to Paul's understanding in order to prevent the Galatians from succumbing to a false gospel of salvation by keeping the commandments.

Message/Argument: Salvation depends on God's grace appropriated by faith, based on the death of Christ, not on the keeping of the Mosaic law, which was in God's plan only a parenthesis between the promise to Abraham and its fulfillment in the coming of Christ.

Significance: Establishes the Christian's freedom from the law of Moses.

56, and addressed to North Galatian churches founded during the second missionary journey (see Acts 16:6; 18:23).[2] There are, to be sure, a few scholars who accept an early date for Galatians but place the addressees in the north (e.g., John Calvin), and vice versa.

Key to the dispute is reconciling the data of Acts with the autobiographical information given by Paul in Galatians 1:18–2:10. A basic question to be answered is whether the narrative of Galatians 2:1–10 is to be equated with the account of the Jerusalem council of Acts 15 (which was held in 49).[3]

Galatians as a Letter from Paul's Middle Years

The North Galatian Hypothesis. That Paul wrote his letter to the cities of North Galatia was universally accepted until it was first challenged in the eighteenth century. This conclusion was, however, not always linked with a late date for the letter. The arguments for a date in the mid-50s, currently the

---

2. Among commentators accepting the North Galatian hypothesis are Hansen, Matera (who hypothesizes that Paul's first missionary journey was *after* the Jerusalem council), Hays, Silva, Williams, and Fee. Among earlier commentators here should be mentioned J. B. Lightfoot. Although J. Louis Martyn accepts North Galatia as the location of the addressees, he dates Galatians to about 50, as the earliest Pauline letter after 1 Thessalonians. Martyn deduces too much from the reference to "Galatians" in 3:1, and his conclusion that there were no Jews in the churches to which Galatians was directed is highly debatable. Frank Matera attempts to avoid the either/or in choosing a viewpoint, but his hypothesis is necessarily an exercise in historical imagination.

3. For a full review of the arguments on both sides, see Longenecker, *Galatians*, lxi–lxxxviii. For an entertaining construction of an imaginary formal debate of the issues, see Hendriksen, *A Commentary on Galatians*, 7–14.

majority opinion, are fairly strong. To begin with, the letter is very similar in content and argument to the Letter to the Romans. This suggests that it may have been written at about the same time as or perhaps just prior to Romans (which probably was written ca. 57), since it is generally regarded as rougher or less polished than the longer letter.

Although the Roman province of Galatia was large and included the southern cities visited by Paul on his first missionary journey, the territory or region technically known as Galatia (1:1) is further to the north. The addressees of the epistle are called *Galatai* ("Galatians") in 3:1, and this term is essentially equivalent to *Keltai* ("Celts"), a people known to have settled more to the north in central Asia Minor early in the third century BC, and who gave the name to that region. Ethnically, the people of South Galatia were not Galatians but rather mainly Phrygians.

According to Acts, Paul's first missionary journey was, after Cyprus and Pisidian Antioch, limited to Iconium, Lystra, and Derbe—all cities of South Galatia.

There is no clear record of Paul evangelizing North Galatia before the Jerusalem council. The first possible time, according to the narrative of Acts, that Paul could have preached the gospel in North Galatia was on the second missionary journey: "they went through the region of Phrygia and Galatia" (16:6). If this reference to "Galatia" means North Galatia and if the mention in Galatians 4:13, when Paul "preached the gospel to you at first," implies that Paul had been to the region twice, then a late date for the letter, in the mid-50s, seems necessary.

But it is not so much these small points by themselves that might seem to favor a late date. Far more important is the conviction of many that Galatians 2:1–10 is an account of the Jerusalem council of Acts 15. In both passages Paul and Barnabas are in Jerusalem confronting the issue of whether circumcision and obedience to the law are to be required of the Gentiles. If this equation is correct, Paul must have written Galatians sometime in the 50s.

Galatians as the First Letter

The South Galatian Hypothesis. Advocates of the South Galatian hypothesis point out that Paul regularly refers to Roman provinces in naming geographical regions (e.g., 1 Cor. 16:5, 15, 19; thus probably also in 16:1). This practice would explain the address "Galatia" (1:1) if Paul writes to Iconium, Lystra, and Derbe. So too the Greek word *proteron*, "first" (Gal. 4:13), could simply refer to a single former visit, the proclamation of the gospel on the first missionary journey. Furthermore, if Galatians and Romans were separated by some nine years, that would provide time for Paul to develop the more nuanced view of the law found in Romans compared with Galatians.

Particularly important is the rich autobiographical account in Galatians 1. In insisting that neither his apostleship nor his gospel depends on the Jerusalem church, Paul documents how little he had been in Jerusalem since the time of his conversion. To stress his independence from the Jerusalem Apostles, Paul stipulates the two times he had visited Jerusalem (1:18; 2:1): the first, three years after his conversion, and the second, fourteen years after his conversion (or, less probably, after the first visit). According to Acts, however, Paul had already visited Jerusalem twice before the visit for the Jerusalem council (9:26; 11:29–30). Thus, if Acts is correct, either Paul in Galatians does not mention all his visits to Jerusalem—but that is exactly what he is required to do for the sake of the argument—or Galatians 2:1–10 must be equated with the famine visit of Acts 11:29–30 and therefore cannot be the visit for the Jerusalem council of Acts 15. Had Paul failed to list in Galatians all his visits to Jerusalem, it would have seriously undermined his argument here and certainly would or could have been seized on by his opponents.[4]

On close examination it is not really so clear that Galatians 2:1–10 is describing the event of Acts 15. There are differences as well as similarities between the two passages. Galatians 2 refers to Titus accompanying Paul and Barnabas; Acts 15 makes no mention of the uncircumcised Titus being present (which would be odd indeed, given the subject being debated). According to Galatians 2:2, Paul went up to Jerusalem in response to a "revelation"; no hint of this is given in Acts 15. But the visit of Acts 11:29–30 is initiated by just such a revelation, through the prophet Agabus. Galatians 2:2 explicitly refers to "a private meeting [*kat' idian*] with the acknowledged leaders" (NRSV); Acts has in view a public meeting with "the apostles and the elders" (15:2) and indeed refers to "all the assembly [*pan to plethos*]" (15:12). The crucial difference between the narratives, however, is that *Galatians makes no mention of the formal decision of the council* or of the letter sent out by the leaders. Had the issue of whether Gentiles needed to be circumcised (and keep the law) been settled so decisively by the Jerusalem leaders, Paul could clearly have mentioned this as his clinching argument in his Letter to the Galatians. His silence on this alone, apart from other difficulties mentioned, is enough to tip the balance, albeit slightly, in favor of the conclusion that Galatians was written before the Jerusalem council.

If this is true, then Galatians 2 must refer to the famine visit of Acts 11:29–30. Granted, the latter passage does not refer to the discussion of the controversy over the circumcision of the Gentiles, which Luke apparently reserves for his account of the Jerusalem council, nor does it mention Titus. It does, as we have noted, concur with the idea of going up to Jerusalem through a revelation. Furthermore, the purpose of the Acts visit was to relieve the hungry, and Galatians 2:10 alludes to the importance of remembering the poor, which, Paul says, "I had been eager to do" (the marginal reading of the NRSV, reflecting the aorist Greek verb).

4. For an argument that Paul was not required to refer to the visit of Acts 11, see Silva, *Interpreting Galatians*, 129–39.

James Dunn correctly sums up the situation as one where the evidence "is actually decisive on neither side."[5] Thus by no means with certainty, but tentatively, we may conclude that Galatians was written before the Jerusalem council, and therefore that it is quite possibly the earliest letter of Paul in the NT,[6] written in about 48 and sent to the churches founded during his first missionary journey.[7] If so, Paul at a very early stage of his career had already hammered out his law-free gospel of justification by faith.[8] This in turn may add strength to the conclusion that justification by faith is of central importance to Paul's theology. Given the great importance of the arguments in Galatians and Romans for Paul's understanding of salvation in Christ, there would furthermore seem to be no insurmountable obstacle in Paul writing so similarly in letters composed some nine years apart. This is consonant with the fact that the similarity between the two letters is more in content rather than actual wording.

The Circumstances at Galatia

Shortly after his first missionary journey (note "so quickly" in 1:6), as I have argued tentatively above, Paul received a report about what was happening in the churches that he had established. From the letter we can reconstruct the circumstances with some confidence.

As had happened in Antioch (2:11–14)—a painful episode that was burned into Paul's memory—certain persons had come from Jerusalem ("from James") with a new message. The Antioch incident concerned table fellowship, and the separation implied that Gentile Christians were not fully members of the people of God. In the Galatian churches the key issue was addressed directly:

5. Dunn, *The Epistle to the Galatians*, 7. Dunn accepts that the letter was written to the South Galatian churches but nevertheless dates the letter to late 50 or early 51. F. F. Bruce, one of the strongest supporters of the South Galatian hypothesis, also admits that the evidence is ambiguous: "The fact that so many competent scholars can be cited in support of either position suggests that the evidence for neither is absolutely conclusive" ("Galatian Problems. 2. North or South Galatians?" 266).

6. The Pauline authorship of Galatians has never been seriously questioned. It, along with Romans and the Corinthian letters, is regarded as one of the *Hauptbriefe* ("chief letters") of the Apostle.

7. See Bruce, "Galatian Problems. 4. The Date of the Epistle"; Hemer, "Acts and Galatians Reconsidered"; idem, "Galatia and the Galatians."

8. As Seyoon Kim has convincingly shown, "Paul's soteriology is strongly stamped by his experience at the Damascus Christophany. The characteristics of his doctrine of justification *sola gratia* and *sola fide* are due to the insights into the questions of the law, human existence and man's relation to God which he developed out of his Damascus experience" (*The Origin of Paul's Gospel*, 329). And as Colin Hemer observes, "Paul's grasp of a matter so central to his message as justification was surely matured even before the earliest feasible dating of Galatians" ("Acts and Galatians Reconsidered," 83).

Gentile Christians needed to be circumcised, and, as always with circumcision, obedience to the entirety of the law was assumed with it. In effect, the Gentile Christians were being told they had to become full proselytes to Judaism in order to belong to the new community of faith. These intruders from Jerusalem probably represented the "brethren" (i.e., Christians) referred to in Acts 15:1, who demanded the circumcision of the Gentile believers (cf. "the circumcision party" in Gal. 2:12; and those "zealous for the law" in Acts 21:20). This in itself, incidentally, would be in agreement with the view that the council of Acts 15 had not yet taken place, for it is difficult to believe that such a demand could be made after the council's decision. Their insistence on circumcision (Gal. 5:2–12; 6:12–13) apparently was being received favorably by some in the church.

We are told little about the troublemakers in Galatians. It is possible, but not at all certain, that they presented themselves as coming from James, in a way similar to the agitators at Antioch (cf. 2:12). This would have added authority to their arguments. Contrary to what some have alleged, it is unlikely that they were Gentile Christians or gnostic Christians (note the libertinism alluded to in 5:13, but Paul probably is only protecting against misunderstanding).[9] Most probably they were Jewish Christians, in which case the name "Judaizers" is, strictly speaking, not appropriate, since only a Gentile could be described as "living like a Jew" (the verb "Judaize" [*ioudaizō*, RSV: "to live like Jews"] occurs in 2:14 in reference to Gentiles).[10] These agitators wanted the Gentiles to Judaize—that is, to accept circumcision and live according to the law, as if they were Jews.

Jewish circumcision was the sign of membership in the covenant, showing that one was a member of the covenant people and thus a participant in election and a recipient of the promises that God made to the patriarchs. It marked a person as a member of the people of God in distinction from all other peoples. It meant in turn, however, that one took on the yoke of the Torah, the responsibility to obey all the commandments of the law. Circumcision was so essential to Judaism that the Jews often are referred to by Paul as simply "the circumcision." So attractive was Judaism in the ancient world that a number of Gentiles were willing to convert and be circumcised, thus becoming full proselytes, although most Gentiles were content to remain "God-fearers," who were required to obey only a handful of commandments.

It is not difficult to imagine the argument of those who came preaching circumcision. "You have made a beginning," they might have said, "but you cannot be full members of the people of God, full-fledged members of Israel, unless you are also willing to go all the way and take upon yourselves the sign

---

9. Against the idea of the agitators being gnostics, see R. Wilson, "Gnostics—in Galatia?"; Jewett, "The Agitators and the Galatian Congregation."

10. Preferable to Paul's "opponents" in Galatians is "the teachers" (Martyn) or "the missionaries" (Dunn; Hays). See their respective commentaries.

of circumcision and obedience to the law given by God at Sinai." To hear this from Jewish Christian brothers, representing the mother church of Jerusalem, must have had a powerful impact on the committed Gentile Christians of Galatia. If, as Acts leads us to believe, some of them had been God-fearers attending the synagogue, they might have heard the argument before, but now it would come home with new force. They now found themselves wanting "to be under law" (4:21).

From other things that Paul says in the letter (1:1, 1–12, 17) we may well imagine further arguments that went along this line: "The gospel that you heard from Paul is not the true, complete gospel. Indeed, Paul had not been one of the original twelve disciples of Jesus, but was a Johnny-come-lately. He was, in fact, dependent on the Jerusalem Apostles for any authority he claimed and any gospel he preached." Again, this could well have sounded persuasive to the Galatian Christians. And apparently they were beginning to yield to the pressure to be circumcised (5:3) and to observe particular aspects of the law (4:10).

Paul too, argued the agitators, was inconsistent on the question, sometimes advocating circumcision (5:11), being eager to please others (1:10) and to avoid persecution. Paul, however, says that those who advocated circumcision did so to escape persecution "for the cross of Christ" (6:12).

It must have sounded to the new Galatian Christians as though they could now simply add circumcision and obedience to the law to their faith in Christ. From Paul's point of view, however, the two were fully irreconcilable. To accept circumcision was automatically to put one's focus on "works of the law" and hence to put oneself outside the realm of grace (5:4).

As proper as it may have sounded, to partake of circumcision was, in effect, to cancel out the true and only gospel. And here we are back to the reason for Paul's aggravation and heated response.

The Argument of Galatians

As we have already noted, Galatians is a highly charged, polemical document. The subject in view is the Mosaic law, and it is hard to imagine a subject of more fundamental importance to the Judaism of the NT period. For this reason, it is worth reviewing Paul's argument in some detail.

Just as Jesus encountered much heated opposition in his understanding of the law, so too Paul had to struggle to define the role of the law in the purpose of God. In particular, the crisis on this issue came about because of the question of whether Gentile Christians had to be circumcised (with the further implication of obedience to the entirety of the law), but Paul's answer has wider implications affecting the whole of humanity, including the Jews.

Paul begins the letter's *praescriptio* (prescript) not merely with an indication of his apostolic office, as he regularly does, but with an immediate and abrupt defense of the divine origin of his apostleship. From the very start, then, we see Paul on the defensive.

Most striking, perhaps shocking, as far as the form of the letter goes, is the oft-noted fact that the epistolary prescript of Galatians lacks even a single word of thanks for the Galatians or a good wish. This traditional section of the Hellenistic letter form is bypassed so that Paul may rush immediately into a statement of his deeply felt concern. The *exordium* (introductory section)[11] of 1:6–10 introduces that concern by characterizing the Galatian crisis as nothing less than a departure from the gospel. Of course, Paul notes, there really is no other gospel. Besides the Pauline gospel, all other gospels are pseudo-gospels. So convinced is he of this that he says that even if an angel were to convey a different gospel than Paul's, it would have to be rejected. With great passion Paul says (1:9) that one who brings another gospel is to be accursed (lit., "anathematized").

When Paul speaks of the gospel, he is talking not about books, but rather about the content of his message. Here "gospel" means "the good news of what God has done in Christ." The point, which will emerge with stark clarity, is that the gospel, the good news, has implications for the place of the law in the Christian life. Paul knows that the intensity of his statement about the single true gospel will not please his opponents, but this is of no concern to him, for he serves not human opinion but Christ.

First Main Section (1:12–2:14)

In the first major section of the letter (the *narratio*, a statement of facts), 1:12–2:14, Paul turns to an autobiographical account that sets the stage for his main argument. He provides an account of his conversion, his contacts with the Jerusalem leaders, with some focus on the second meeting (2:1–10), and finally the confrontation with Peter at Antioch (2:11–14).

His gospel and conversion, like his apostleship, he notes, were a matter of direct revelation of Jesus Christ (1:12), and thus he was in no need of dependence on those who were Apostles before him. He did finally visit Peter, and he also met James the Lord's brother, on his first visit to Jerusalem. The purpose of the visit was not to gain authority or learn the gospel from them but rather to get to know Peter, and we may well surmise that he was also interested in learning what he could about Jesus on that occasion.

The second visit to Jerusalem was more important, again not because of any dependence on Paul's part but because the problem that he is addressing in

---

11. The analysis here follows the categories of Greek rhetoric as outlined in Betz, *Galatians*. Betz regards Galatians as a forensic letter, representing an apologetic speech. See, however, the reservations expressed in Kern, *Rhetoric and Galatians*. Note also Robert Bryant's comment that "Galatians presents a masterful mixture of Greco-Roman communication forms and techniques" (*The Risen Crucified Christ in Galatians*, 232). Most scholars regard Galatians as a species of deliberative rhetoric—that is, an attempt to persuade the Galatians to the proper course of action.

the letter had already been discussed there with the leaders in private. On that occasion Paul outlined the gospel that he was preaching among the Gentiles (2:2)—a law-free gospel—and it was approved by the Jerusalem Apostles. As a concrete demonstration of that fact, Paul notes, the question of circumcising Titus, his Greek assistant, did not even arise. The Jerusalem Apostles were content to let Paul continue his preaching among the Gentiles without requiring circumcision, whereas they would continue to preach to the Jews (2:9).

Paul next recounts a crucial episode that took place at Antioch, where there had been a crisis similar to the one presently confronting the Galatian churches. While Peter was there, emissaries from the Jerusalem church (lit., *apo Iakōbou,* "from James") came and criticized him for eating with Gentiles. Peter, followed by Barnabas, much to the chagrin of Paul, thereupon ceased table fellowship with the Gentiles. Barnabas would have been known to the readers, as he had accompanied Paul on the first missionary journey. The reason is described as fear of "the circumcision party" (2:12), to be understood as either conservative Jewish Christians in Jerusalem or, more probably, Jewish zealots who were putting pressure on the Jewish Christians of Jerusalem. The refusal to eat with the Gentile Christians clearly implied that they were not accepted as full members of the people of God. But this was to question the Pauline gospel at its very heart. If one could have table fellowship only with Gentiles who were full proselytes to Judaism, then the Gentiles were required to observe the law fully. It was for this reason that Paul reacted against Peter with such force. Far from being simply a matter of personal discretion, the very content of the gospel was at stake.

Second Main Section (2:15–4:31)

Paul now moves directly into a statement of his thesis (the *propositio,* a summary of facts) in 2:15–21, followed by a full supporting argument (the *probatio*) in 3:1–4:31. This is the heart of the letter, and at certain points it can be challenging to follow Paul's logic.

Paul begins by admitting the specialness of being Jewish (we "are Jews by birth and not Gentile sinners")—in view would be election, covenant, and law—but then he immediately indicates that Jewish Christians know that no one can achieve righteousness by works of the law and that righteousness is available only by means of faith in Christ.[12] This is repeated emphatically in 2:16 (ending with an allusion to Ps. 143:2). The implication is that as far as the observation of the law is concerned, Jewish Christians may indeed seem to be like Gentile sinners. But this would be to misstate the matter seriously because, as will emerge later in the letter, *righteous conduct is still very much the goal*

---

12. The genitive construction in 2:16, "faith in Jesus Christ" (*pistis Iēsou Christou*), can also be translated "the faithfulness of Jesus Christ." This ambiguous construction is found also in, for example, Galatians 3:22 and Romans 3:22, 26. See Hays, *The Faith of Jesus Christ.*

of every Christian. As Paul puts it vividly in 2:19, he has died to the law, yes, but precisely so that he "might live to God." But, returning to the main point, Paul concludes with the important observation that if righteousness could be gained by keeping the law, "then Christ died to no purpose" (2:21).[13] If it was not to bring humanity out of a hopeless situation, what was the purpose of the death of God's Messiah?

The thesis is now substantiated in a number of different ways:

1. First, Paul asks about the way in which the Galatians initially received the Holy Spirit and continued to enjoy his power in their midst. It was not by works of the law but rather by faith in Christ (3:1–5).

2. He next cites one of his favorite texts (Gen. 15:6): Abraham "believed God, and it was reckoned to him as righteousness" (3:6 [cf. Rom. 4:3]). In this OT text Paul has discovered the very gospel that he preached, his gospel of salvation by faith. But if Abraham was accounted righteous by reason of his faith, so too Gentiles who have faith in Christ may also be declared righteous by faith. Indeed, it was promised to Abraham that "in you shall all the nations [*ethnē*, i.e., Gentiles] be blessed" (3:8, citing Gen. 12:3).[14] To believe in Christ qualifies both Jews and Gentiles to be descendants of Abraham. The operative word is "faith,"[15] not "works."

3. But what of "the works of the law"? To rely on them is only to take on oneself a curse:[16] "Cursed be every one who does not abide by all things written in the book of the law, and do them" (3:10, citing Deut. 27:6).[17] It is for this reason that the gospel was a necessity. Again Paul is able to find his point articulated in the Scriptures: "He who through faith is righteous shall live" (3:11, citing Hab. 2:4 [cited also in Rom. 1:17]).[18] A third citation indicates that the law functioned on a different premise: "Whoever does the works of the law will live by them" (3:12 NRSV, citing Lev. 18:5 [cf. Rom. 10:5]). This explains the curse to which this section refers at its beginning. A final citation in this section returns to the curse motif: "Cursed be everyone who hangs on a tree"

13. On the use of the OT in the first two chapters, see Ciampa, *The Presence and Function of Scripture in Galatians 1 and 2*.

14. See Hansen, *Abraham in Galatians*.

15. In Greek, the verb "to believe" (*pisteuō*) and the noun "faith" (*pistis*) are from the same root.

16. See Morland, *The Rhetoric of Curse in Galatians*; Wisdom, *Blessing for the Nations and the Curse of the Law*.

17. On the difficult passage of 3:1–10, see Longenecker, *The Triumph of Abraham's God*, 134–42; see also Schreiner, "Is Perfect Obedience to the Law Possible?"

18. It is possible to take *ek pisteōs* ("by faith") with *zēsetai* ("will live"), as does the NRSV, "The one who is righteous will live by faith," rather than with *dikaios* ("righteous"), as does the RSV, "He who through faith is righteous shall live." The Greek can fairly be read either way, but keeping Paul's argument in view, both here and in Romans (1:17), the latter rendering is much to be preferred.

(3:13, citing Deut. 21:23). Paul's understanding of the crucifixion is that "Christ redeemed us from the curse of the law, having become a curse for us" (3:13). It was this realization that enabled him to juxtapose the two words "Christ crucified" (1 Cor. 1:23; cf. 2:2 and the reference to "the stumbling block of the cross" in Gal. 5:11).

4. "An example from daily life" is next provided (3:15–18). Given that the Greek word *diathēkē* can mean either "will" or "covenant," Paul draws an analogy between the two. One can no more alter a covenant between God and humanity than one can alter a human will. The covenant between God and Abraham and its promises, therefore, cannot be set aside by the Mosaic law, "which came four hundred and thirty years afterward" (3:17). Referring to Genesis 22:18, Paul also notes that the promise to Abraham included his "offspring" or "seed," which occurs in the singular, allowing Paul to identify that "offspring" specifically as Christ, who was a, or *the*, descendant of Abraham. Christ is the fulfillment of the Abrahamic covenant.

5. The discussion thus far can only raise in a very sharp way the question of the purpose of the law. The first answer is that "it was added because of transgressions till the offspring should come to whom the promise had been made" (3:19). Admittedly, "because of transgressions" (*tōn parabaseōn charin*) is vague, but it appears to mean something like "for the purpose of defining or exposing transgressions" (cf. Rom. 4:15; 5:13) and possibly even "for the purpose of increasing transgressions" (cf. Rom. 5:20). That the law, for Paul, had a temporary function is indicated by the important "until" clause. The law is not opposed [*kata*] to the promises of God (3:21), but it had a limited role to play in God's plan, and a more negative than a positive one. Paul likens the law to a "custodian" (*paidagōgos*, lit., "child guide" [3:24]), whose role, now that Christ has come, is obsolete. In the new situation that exists, among those who have been baptized into Christ, the traditional distinction at the heart of the Galatian controversy—the difference between Jew and Gentile—has been done away with, as have other distinctions such as slave and free, or male and female (3:28). All who belong to Christ will participate in the Abrahamic inheritance.

6. A turning point in the aeons has now been reached, "the time had fully come" (*to plērōma tou chronou*), marked by the coming of God's Son "to redeem those who were under the law" (4:4–5). Those who were infants, hardly distinguishable from slaves before this event, have now been brought to maturity and the status of heirs. How, then, Paul wonders, can the Galatian Christians return to the past and become slaves again of the law (4:1–11)?

7. In a highly personal section (4:12–20) Paul reviews a little of his past history with the Galatians. He hopes that they will not now regard him

as their enemy. He regrets that the letter must substitute for his presence: "I could wish to be present with you now and to change my tone, for I am perplexed about you" (4:20).

8. Paul ends his main argument with a story about Sarah and Hagar, illustrating freedom and slavery (4:21–31). The story is allegorical or symbolic in character. Abraham had a son from each of the two women, from Hagar one born "according to the flesh," and from Sarah one born "through the promise." Paul likens the women to two covenants. Hagar, on the one hand, stands for the Mosaic covenant ("from Mount Sinai"), bears "children for slavery," and "corresponds to the present Jerusalem" (4:25). Sarah, on the other hand, stands for the new covenant (though this is not mentioned), is described as "our mother," and corresponds to "the Jerusalem above" (4:26). The shocking point of the story is that those under the law, the Jews, are in slavery, whereas those who are children of the promise (i.e., those who by sharing the faith of Abraham truly become his descendants), the Christians, are children free from slavery to the law.

Third Main Section (5:1–6:18)

Paul now turns to the application (*exhortatio*) of the preceding argument to the concrete situation of the Galatian churches (5:1–6:10). This is typical of the paraenesis, or moral exhortation, which commonly occurs in the last sections of Paul's Letters.[19] He draws his main conclusion in the opening sentence: "For freedom Christ has set us free. Stand fast, therefore, and do not submit again to a yoke of slavery" (5:1). The word "yoke" (*zygos*) here is the common metaphor for the law. One cannot, in short, be justified by works of the law and by grace at the same time, for the one cancels out the other. "The only thing that counts," Paul writes, "is faith," but to the last remark he adds the very important words "working through love" (5:6). The all-important faith is qualified as active and not passive. It is faith at work (much as James 2:18–26 would have it) and not merely belief.

Once again Paul expresses his frustration at those who have confused the Galatians on the matter of circumcision. If they are so intent on cutting into the flesh, let them "castrate [*apokopsontai*] themselves!" he writes scathingly (5:12 NRSV). Such blistering rhetoric indicates how serious a matter this is to Paul. Nothing less than the gospel itself is at stake.

The freedom from the law that Paul so adamantly defends is not to be misunderstood as a libertinism. This he makes quite clear: "For you were called to freedom, brethren [and sisters]; only do not use your freedom as an opportunity for the flesh, but through love be servants of one another" (5:13).

19. On the paraenesis of Galatians, see Barclay, *Obeying the Truth*.

This emphasis on love is followed up by a vice catalog, listing "works of the flesh" that are to be avoided (5:19–21)—"those who do such things shall not inherit the kingdom of God"—as well as a virtue catalog, listing the "fruit of the Spirit" (5:22–23). "Those who belong to Christ Jesus have crucified the flesh with its passions and desires. If we live by the Spirit, let us also walk by the Spirit" (5:24–25).

There is even paradoxical talk of "the law of Christ" (*ton nomon tou Christou*) in 6:2, but it is clear that Paul does not mean simply that the teaching of Jesus is to be thought of as, or functions as, a new counterpart to the Mosaic law. Here, clearly, Paul shows a deep, ongoing concern for righteousness. When all is said and done, there might appear to be little difference between where Paul comes out and what a good Jew would say. "But let each one test his own work" (6:4). "Do not be deceived; God is not mocked, for whatever a man sows, that he will also reap. For he who sows to his own flesh will from the flesh reap corruption, but he who sows to the Spirit will from the Spirit reap eternal life" (6:7–8). But words such as these must not be understood apart from their larger context. Paul does not urge here a new bondage to the law. He merely wants to protect a misunderstanding of his gospel of grace whereby one might conclude that since we are not under the law, our conduct is no longer important. No, one's personal deeds remain a bottom-line factor that cannot be denied. The gospel, in effect, *upholds the righteousness of the law*. But the gospel does not thereby become law or, indeed, allow us to bring a new slavery to the law in through the back door.

When Paul himself takes up the pen in the epistolary postscript, 6:11–18, he cannot avoid entering into polemics once again. The advocates of circumcision want to impress others: "They desire to have you circumcised that they may glory in your flesh" (6:13), and they want to avoid persecution (probably from zealous Jews, which Paul himself once was). Paul adds emphatically, "I bear on my body the marks of Jesus" (6:17), probably an allusion to his suffering of persecution, indeed stoning, at Lystra (Acts 14:19). Paul makes two remarkable statements in these final verses: first, "even those who receive circumcision do not themselves keep the law" (6:13), confirming his earlier argument that "no man is justified before God by the law" (3:11); second, the revolutionary statement that "neither circumcision counts for anything, nor uncircumcision, but a new creation" (6:15 [cf. 1 Cor. 7:19]). According to Paul, we have entered a new age in which the law is relativized, and righteousness is related to faith and not works of the law.

Justification by Faith and Its Importance in Paul's Theology

Galatians stands in relation to Romans like the rough sketch does to the finished painting of a great master. Many of the key issues that are raised by the argument of Galatians are raised again in Romans, as we will see. But here, at least in a preliminary way, we must look at some of the crucial questions that the letter to the Galatians puts before us.

Without doubt, in Galatians Paul brings definition to his gospel, albeit under the pressure of responding to those who were in error. It is equally true that his gospel in this letter is articulated specifically with the question of Gentile believers in view. Can one say, then, that justification by faith is only a "subsidiary crater" in Paul's theology (using Albert Schweitzer's metapor), and one that was created only in response to the social problem of the rejection of Gentile believers at Galatia, and not a more basic problem than that, as some have contended? If in Galatians we find the doctrine of justification by faith to be essential to the gospel and a fundamental way of expressing the center of Paul's theology, have we unconsciously read Paul through the eyes of Martin Luther and the Protestant Reformation? It is easy to polarize the question unnecessarily, yet it must be asked, for significant matters are at stake.

Is justification by faith little more than a pragmatic ploy to safeguard the full membership of the Gentiles in the people of God by preserving a law-free gospel for Gentiles? Clearly, in Galatians it serves as a stratagem to keep the Gentiles from yielding to circumcision. But the truth of justification by faith is universal, and it is to be applied to Jew as well as to Gentile. Paul's whole premise, indeed, is based on how Gentile believers are justified in the same way that Jewish believers are: by faith and apart from the law (2:15–16). Paul does not contemplate two ways of salvation, but only one and the same, and that way is a law-free gospel based on faith in Christ, valid for both Jews and Gentiles. Any argument, like that of Galatians, that articulates a basic position regarding the Mosaic law and the role it plays in the relation between human beings and God, must have determinative significance for the issue of the salvation not only of the Gentiles but also, obviously, of the Jews.

On the one hand, the importance of justification by faith, apart from the law, for Paul's entire theology should not be underestimated. There is no reason, on the other hand, to insist that this and this alone is to be regarded as the center of Paul's theology. Paul's theology seems far too rich to be reduced to a single center. But that justification by faith is of fundamental, and not just incidental, importance in Paul's theology should not be doubted.

And if the agenda and the argumentation in Galatians are occasional, called forth by a particular problem, this is not the case in Romans. There, especially in the first eleven chapters, Paul desires to lay out the basics of his theology in a clear and persuasive manner with relatively little concern to address particularities of the Roman church. And there we will find the same thesis as outlined here in Galatians, but argued more systematically and in more detail.

The view articulated by Paul here is not opportunistic or ad hoc. We may assume that what he wrote to the Galatians about works of the law and justification by faith was the same message he gave to every church that he founded or to which he ministered. And if it is true that Galatians was Paul's earliest letter, then we can conclude that this was his gospel from the beginning, not something he worked out only later.

Paul's Gospel and the Law

What about the law in Paul's theology? Is Paul's problem with the law merely sociological and not soteriological, a matter of race and not grace, as the "new perspective"[20] on Paul maintains? That is, does Paul reject the law only when or because it is regarded as constituting boundary markers that excluded the Gentiles?

It can hardly be doubted that Paul rejects the law as the demarcation of social identity and, hence, as a limitation of God's grace. The law in this sense is naturally a huge obstacle to the Gentile mission. But Paul's problem with the law runs far deeper.[21] At least two further problems with the law emerge in the Letter to the Galatians.

First, the law seems to hold out a promise that it cannot fulfill: the promise of righteousness. Paul's beginning assumption is that no one can arrive at the goal of righteousness through the law (2:16; 3:10, 21). The effect of the law is quite the opposite: to focus on transgressions (3:19, 22). Works of the law cannot bring a person, Jew or Gentile, into a state of salvation. This conclusion is at the heart of Paul's gospel.

Second, the law had a limited role to play in God's purpose, the role of child guide (3:24), and that role has now been accomplished: "But now that faith has come, we are no longer under a custodian" (3:25). Any attempt to establish an ongoing significance to the law must reckon with the several clauses beginning with "until" in Paul's argument (see 3:23, 24; 4:2). Arguments along the same line eventually will reappear in Romans in refined form.

As the last main part of Galatians shows, however, Paul never gives up on the fundamental importance of righteousness as lived out in the life of the believer. This is a righteousness manifested in the context of freedom from the law (5:1). The statement that those who are "led by the Spirit" are "not under the law" (5:18) is made precisely in a context where there is a great stress on the kind of conduct that must not be found among those who believe in Jesus (see also 5:13). Paul leans on the teaching of Jesus, available to him from the oral tradition, when he writes, "For the whole law is fulfilled in one word, 'You shall love your neighbor as yourself'" (5:14). He can furthermore speak of actions of love as fulfilling "the law of Christ" (6:2), indicating that the teaching of Jesus remains the important standard for measuring righteousness and that toward which believers are required to strive.

---

20. For fuller discussion of the new perspective on Paul, see chapter 19 above.
21. For an insightful study, see Hong, *The Law in Galatians*.

The Legacy of Galatians

This fiery, polemical, and tersely argued letter from Paul remains an extraordinarily important document for Christianity. It has great historical importance because here we can see Paul working out the meaning of the death of God's Messiah and its significance for the gospel. The crucifixion of the Messiah—no doubt an insuperable problem for Saul the Pharisee—now had become the cornerstone of Paul's understanding of salvation. The Messiah was crucified exactly because God meant for him to bear the curse of our inability to obey the law so that we might be redeemed "from the curse of the law" (3:13).

We also discover here how Paul began to work out the relationship between the old and the new. How was the gospel of Jesus Christ to be related to the law of Moses? Because of the death of Christ, that law could no longer be the center of focus. Paul found the answer in the Abrahamic covenant. Indeed, he found in Abraham's faith the confirmation of his law-free gospel, for that faith "was reckoned to him as righteousness" (Gal. 3:6, citing Gen. 15:6). This happened long before the law was given, some 430 years earlier by Paul's calculation. The Mosaic law then becomes, for Paul, *a great parenthesis* in the plan of God, not its center, with the final bracket of that parenthesis occurring with the (first) coming of Christ (3:24). For Paul, the basic line of promise and fulfillment goes directly from Abraham to Christ, with the law becoming but an interim factor. It should be immediately apparent how revolutionary this conclusion was for the Jewish Christian Paul. If there had been any question of whether Christianity was to be construed as a sect of Judaism, that notion was now forever dispelled.

Figure 8 **Abrahamic Covenant
and the New Covenant**

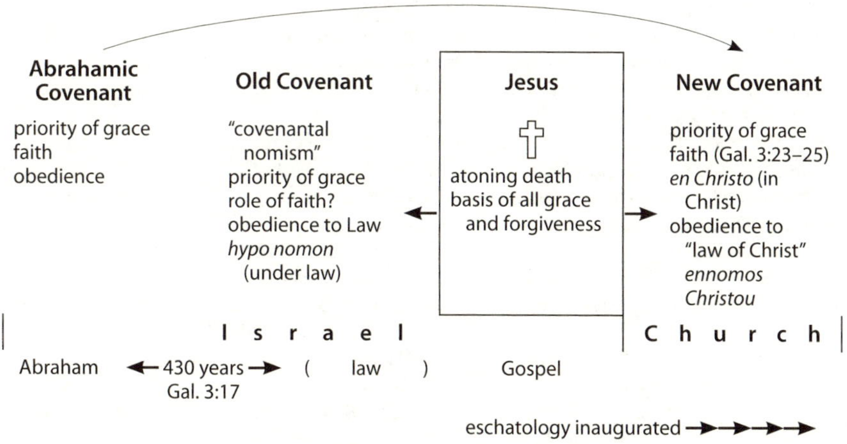

Abrahamic Covenant	Old Covenant	Jesus	New Covenant
priority of grace faith obedience	"covenantal nomism" priority of grace role of faith? obedience to Law *hypo nomon* (under law)	✝ atoning death basis of all grace and forgiveness	priority of grace faith (Gal. 3:23–25) *en Christo* (in Christ) obedience to "law of Christ" *ennomos Christou*

I s r a e l   C h u r c h

Abraham ← 430 years → (law)   Gospel
         Gal. 3:17

eschatology inaugurated →→→→→

Galatians will always retain its timeless character for the Christian church and the understanding of the gospel. It forever stands as the charter of the Christian's liberty from the law with its clarion statement: "For freedom Christ has set us free" (5:1). At the same time, it liberates us finally from the ever-present human propensity to believe that salvation is somehow to be won or lost on the basis of the good works that we perform. If that were the case, grace would be nullified, and Christ would have died for nothing (2:21).

Bibliography

Books and Articles

Asano, Atsuhiro. *Community-Identity Construction in Galatians: Exegetical, Social-Anthropological, and Socio-Historical Studies.* JSNTSup 285. London: T&T Clark, 2005.

Bachmann, Michael. *Anti-Judaism in Galatians? Exegetical Studies on a Polemical Letter and on Paul's Theology.* Translated by Robert L. Brawley. Grand Rapids: Eerdmans, 2008.

Barclay, John M. G. "Mirror-Reading a Polemical Letter: Galatians as a Test Case." *JSNT* 31 (1987): 73–93.

———. *Obeying the Truth: A Study of Paul's Ethics in Galatians.* Edited by John Riches. SNTW. Edinburgh: T&T Clark, 1988.

Barrett, C. K. *Freedom and Obligation: A Study of the Epistle to the Galatians.* Philadelphia: Westminster, 1985.

Barth, Markus. "The Kerygma of Galatians." *Int* 21 (1967): 131–46.

Bassler, Jouette M., ed. *Thessalonians, Philippians, Galatians, Philemon.* Vol. 1 of *Pauline Theology*, 123–79. Minneapolis: Fortress, 1991.

Betz, Hans Dieter. "The Literary Composition and Function of Paul's Letter to the Galatians." *NTS* 21 (1974–75): 353–79.

Boer, Martinus C. de. *Galatians.* NTL. Louisville: Westminster John Knox, 2011.

Bonneau, Normand. "The Logic of Paul's Argument on the Curse of the Law in Galatians 3:10–14." *NovT* 39 (1997): 60–80.

Borgen, Peder. "Paul Preaches Circumcision and Pleases Men." In *Paul and Paulinism: Essays in Honour of C. K. Barrett*, edited by Morna D. Hooker and Stephen G. Wilson, 37–46. London: SPCK, 1982.

Botha, Pieter J. J. "Letter Writing and Oral Communication in Antiquity: Suggested Implications for the Interpretation of Paul's Letter to the Galatians." *Scriptura* 42 (1992): 17–34.

Brinsmead, Bernard Hungerford. *Galatians: Dialogical Response to Opponents.* SBLDS 65. Chico, CA: Scholars Press, 1982.

Bruce, F. F. "'Abraham Had Two Sons': A Study in Pauline Hermeneutics." In *New Testament Studies: Essays in Honor of Ray Summers*, edited by Huber L. Drumwright and Curtis Vaughan, 71–84. Waco: Markham Press Fund, 1975.

———. "The Conference in Jerusalem—Galatians 2:1–10." In *God Who Is Rich in Mercy: Essays Presented to Dr. D. B. Knox*, edited by Peter T. O'Brien and David G. Peterson, 195–212. Homebush West, New South Wales, Australia: Lancer, 1986.

———. "The Curse of the Law." In *Paul and Paulinism: Essays in Honour of C. K. Barrett*, edited by Morna D. Hooker and Stephen G. Wilson, 27–36. London: SPCK, 1982.

———. "Galatian Problems. 1. Autobiographical Data." *BJRL* 51 (1968–69): 292–309.

———. "Galatian Problems. 2. North or South Galatians?" *BJRL* 52 (1969–70): 243–66.

———. "Galatian Problems. 3. The 'Other' Gospel." *BJRL* 53 (1970–71): 253–71.

———. "Galatian Problems. 4. The Date of the Epistle." *BJRL* 54 (1971–72): 250–67.

———. "Galatian Problems. 5. Galatians and Christian Origins." *BJRL* 55 (1972–73): 264–82.

———. "Paul and the Law of Moses." *BJRL* 57 (1974–75): 259–79.

Bryant, Robert A. *The Risen Crucified Christ in Galatians*. SBLDS 185. Atlanta: Society of Biblical Literature, 2001.

Carson, D. A. "Pauline Inconsistency: Reflections on I Corinthians 9:19–23 and Galatians 2:11–14." *Churchman* 100 (1986): 6–45.

Ciampa, Roy E. *The Presence and Function of Scripture in Galatians 1 and 2*. WUNT 2/102. Tübingen: Mohr Siebeck, 1998.

Cosby, Michael R. "Galatians: Red-Hot Rhetoric." In *Rhetorical Argumentation in Biblical Texts: Essays from the Lund 2000 Conference*, edited by Anders Eriksson, Thomas H. Olbricht, and Walter Übelacker, 296–309. Harrisburg, PA: Trinity Press International, 2002.

Cosgrove, Charles H. *The Cross and the Spirit: A Study in the Argument and Theology of Galatians*. Macon, GA: Mercer University Press, 1989.

Cummins, Stephen Anthony. *Paul and the Crucified Christ in Antioch: Maccabean Martyrdom and Galatians 1 and 2*. SNTSMS 114. Cambridge: Cambridge University Press, 2001.

Dahl, Nils A. "Paul's Letter to the Galatians: Epistolary Genre, Content, Structure." In *The Galatians Debate: Contemporary Issues in Rhetorical and Historical Interpretation*, edited by Mark D. Nanos, 117–42. Peabody, MA: Hendrickson, 2002.

Drane, John W. *Paul, Libertine or Legalist? A Study in the Theology of the Major Pauline Epistles*. London: SPCK, 1975.

Dunn, James D. G. "The Incident at Antioch (Gal. 2:11–18)." *JSNT* 18 (1983): 3–57.

———. *Jesus, Paul and the Law: Studies in Mark and Galatians*. Louisville: Westminster John Knox, 1990.

———. "The Relationship between Paul and Jerusalem according to Galatians 1 and 2." *NTS* 28 (1982): 461–78.

———. *The Theology of Paul's Letter to the Galatians*. NTT. Cambridge: Cambridge University Press, 1993.

Elmer, Ian J. *Paul, Jerusalem and the Judaisers: The Galatian Crisis in Its Broadest Historical Context*. WUNT 2/258. Tübingen: Mohr Siebeck, 2009.

Esler, Philip F. *Galatians*. NTR. New York: Routledge, 1998.

Fairweather, Janet. "The Epistle to the Galatians and Classical Rhetoric: Parts 1 and 2." *TynBul* 45 (1994): 1–38.

———. "The Epistle to the Galatians and Classical Rhetoric: Part 3." *TynBul* 45 (1994): 213–43.

Hansen, G. Walter. *Abraham in Galatians: Epistolary and Rhetorical Contexts*. JSNTSup 29. Sheffield: JSOT Press, 1989.

Hardin, Justin K. *Galatians and the Imperial Cult: A Critical Analysis of the First-Century Social Context of Paul's Letter*. WUNT 2/237. Tübingen: Mohr Siebeck, 2008.

Hays, Richard B. "Christology and Ethics in Galatians: The Law of Christ." *CBQ* 49 (1987): 268–90.

———. *The Faith of Jesus Christ: The Narrative Substructure of Galatians 3:1–4:11*. 2nd ed. Grand Rapids: Eerdmans, 2002.

Hemer, Colin J. "Acts and Galatians Reconsidered." *Themelios* 2 (1976–77): 81–88.

———. "Galatia and the Galatians." In *The Book of Acts in the Setting of Hellenistic History*, edited by Conrad H. Gempf, 277–307. WUNT 49. Tübingen: Mohr Siebeck, 1989.

Hietanen, Mika. *Paul's Argumentation in Galatians: A Pragma-Dialectical Analysis*. LNTS 344. London: T&T Clark, 2007.

Holmstrand, Jonas. *Markers and Meaning in Paul: An Analysis of 1 Thessalonians, Philippians and Galatians*. Translated by Martin Naylor. ConBNT 28. Stockholm: Almqvist & Wiksell, 1997.

Hong, In-Gyu. "Does Paul Misrepresent the Jewish Law? Law and Covenant in Gal. 3:1–14." *NovT* 36 (1994): 164–82.

———. *The Law in Galatians*. JSNTSup 81. Sheffield: JSOT Press, 1993.

Hove, Richard W. *Equality in Christ? Galatians 3:28 and the Gender Dispute.* Wheaton, IL: Crossway, 1999.

Howard, George. *Paul: Crisis in Galatia; A Study in Early Christian Theology.* SNTSMS 35. Cambridge: Cambridge University Press, 1989.

Hübner, Hans. *Law in Paul's Thought: A Contribution to the Development of Pauline Theology.* Translated by James C. G. Greig. Edited by John Riches. SNTW. Edinburgh: T&T Clark, 1984.

Jewett, Robert. "The Agitators and the Galatian Congregation." *NTS* 17 (1970–71): 198–212.

Kern, Philip H. *Rhetoric and Galatians: Assessing an Approach to Paul's Epistle.* SNTSMS 101. Cambridge: Cambridge University Press, 1998.

Kilpatrick, G. D. "Peter, Jerusalem, and Galatians 1:13–2:14." *NovT* 25 (1983): 318–26.

Kim, Seyoon. *The Origin of Paul's Gospel.* 2nd ed. WUNT 2/4. Tübingen: Mohr Siebeck, 1984.

Lake, Kirsopp. "The Apostolic Council of Jerusalem." In *Additional Notes to the Commentary.* Vol. 5 of *The Beginnings of Christianity: The Acts of the Apostles*, edited by F. J. Foakes-Jackson and Kirsopp Lake, 195–212. Reprint, Grand Rapids: Baker Academic, 1979.

Longenecker, Bruce W. *The Triumph of Abraham's God: The Transformation of Identity in Galatians.* Edinburgh: T&T Clark, 1998.

Lull, David John. "'The Law Was Our Pedagogue': A Study in Galatians 3:19–25." *JBL* 105 (1986): 481–98.

———. *The Spirit in Galatia: Paul's Interpretation of Pneuma as Divine Power.* SBLDS 49. Chico, CA: Scholars Press, 1980.

Martin, Troy W. "The Covenant of Circumcision (Genesis 17:9–14) and the Situational Antitheses in Galatians 3:28." *JBL* 122 (2003): 111–25.

Martyn, J. Louis. "A Law-Observant Mission to Gentiles: The Background of Galatians." In *Theological Issues in the Letters of Paul*, 7–24. Nashville: Abingdon, 1997.

Matlock, R. Barry. "Detheologizing the *pistis Christou* Debate: Cautionary Remarks from a Lexical Semantic Perspective." *NovT* 42 (2000): 1–23.

———. "Pistis in Galatians 3:26: Neglected Evidence for 'Faith in Christ'?" *NTS* 49 (2003): 433–39.

Morland, Kjell Arne. *The Rhetoric of Curse in Galatians: Paul Confronts Another Gospel.* ESEC 5. Atlanta: Scholars Press, 1995.

Nanos, Mark D., ed. *The Galatians Debate: Contemporary Issues in Rhetorical and Historical Interpretation.* Peabody, MA: Hendrickson, 2002.

———. "Intruding 'Spies' and 'Pseudo-Brethren': The Jewish Intra-Group Politics of Paul's Jerusalem Meeting (Gal. 2:1–10)." In *Paul and His Opponents*, edited by Stanley E. Porter, 59–97. PS 2. Leiden: Brill, 2005.

———. *The Irony of Galatians: Paul's Letter in First-Century Context.* Minneapolis: Fortress, 2002.

Perkins, Pheme. *Abraham's Divided Children: Galatians and the Politics of Faith.* Harrisburg, PA: Trinity Press International, 2001.

Richardson, Peter. "Pauline Inconsistency: I Corinthians 9:19–23—Galatians 2:11–14." *NTS* 26 (1979–80): 347–62.

Ropes, James Hardy. *The Singular Problem of the Epistle to the Galatians.* HTS 14. Cambridge, MA: Harvard University Press, 1929.

Russell, Walter Bo, III. *The Flesh/Spirit Conflict in Galatians.* Lanham, MD: University Press of America, 1997.

Sanders, E. P. *Paul, the Law, and the Jewish People.* Philadelphia: Fortress, 1985.

Scholer, David M. "Galatians 3:28 and the Ministry of Women in the Church." *CovQ* 56 (1998): 2–18.

Schreiner, Thomas R. "Is Perfect Obedience to the Law Possible? A Re-examination of Galatians 3:10." *JETS* 27 (1984): 151–60.

———. "Paul and Perfect Obedience to the Law: An Evaluation of the View of E. P. Sanders." *WTJ* 47 (1985): 245–78.

Scott, James M. *Paul and the Nations: The Old Testament and Jewish Background of Paul's Mission to the Nations with Special Reference to the Destination of Galatians*. WUNT 84. Tübingen: Mohr Siebeck, 1995.

Silva, Moisés. "Betz and Bruce on Galatians," *WTJ* 45 (1983): 371–85.

———. "Faith versus Works of the Law." In *The Paradoxes of Paul*. Vol. 2 of *Justification and Variegated Nomism*, edited by D. A. Carson, Peter T. O'Brien, and Mark A. Seifrid, 217–48. Grand Rapids: Baker Academic, 2004.

———. *Interpreting Galatians: Explorations in Exegetical Method*. 2nd ed. Grand Rapids: Baker Academic, 2001.

Smiles, Vincent M. *The Gospel and the Law in Galatia: Paul's Response to Jewish-Christian Separatism and the Threat of Galatian Apostasy*. Collegeville, MN: Liturgical Press, 1998.

Smit, Joop. "The Letter of Paul to the Galatians: A Deliberative Speech." *NTS* 35 (1989): 1–26.

Stanley, Christopher D. "'Under a Curse': A Fresh Reading of Galatians 3:10–14." *NTS* 36 (1990): 481–511.

Stein, Robert H. "The Relationship of Galatians 2:1–10 and Acts 15:1–35: Two Neglected Arguments." *JETS* 17 (1974): 239–42.

Taylor, Greer M. "The Function of *pistis Christou* in Galatians." *JBL* 85 (1966): 58–76.

Thielman, Frank. *From Plight to Solution: A Jewish Framework for Understanding Paul's View of the Law in Galatians and Romans*. NovTSup 61. Leiden: Brill, 1989.

Tolmie, D. François. *Persuading the Galatians: A Text-Centered Rhetorical Analysis of a Pauline Letter*. WUNT 2/190. Tübingen: Mohr Siebeck, 2005.

Wakefield, Andrew K. *Where to Live: The Hermeneutical Significance of Paul's Citations from Scripture in Galatians 3:1–14*. SBLAB 14. Atlanta: Society of Biblical Literature, 2003.

Westerholm, Stephen. *Perspectives Old and New on Paul: The "Lutheran" Paul and His Critics*. Grand Rapids: Eerdmans, 2004.

White, L. Michael. "Rhetoric and Reality in Galatians: Framing the Social Demands of Friendship." In *Early Christianity and Classical Culture: Comparative Studies in Honor of Abraham J. Malherbe*, edited by John T. Fitzgerald, Thomas H. Olbricht, and L. Michael White, 307–46. NovTSup 110. Leiden: Brill, 2003.

Williams, Sam K. "Justification and the Spirit in Galatians." *JSNT* 29 (1987): 91–100.

Wilson, R. McL. "Gnostics—in Galatia?" *SE* 4 [= TU 102] (1968): 358–67.

Wilson, Todd A. *The Curse of the Law and the Crisis in Galatia: Reassessing the Purpose of Galatians*. WUNT 2/225. Tübingen: Mohr Siebeck, 2007.

Wisdom, Jeffrey R. *Blessing for the Nations and the Curse of the Law: Paul's Citation of Genesis and Deuteronomy in Galatians 3.8–10*. WUNT 2/133. Tübingen: Mohr Siebeck, 2001.

Wright, N. T. *The Climax of the Covenant: Christ and the Law in Pauline Theology*. Edinburgh: T&T Clark, 1991.

———. "Gospel and Theology in Galatians." In *Gospel in Paul: Studies on Corinthians, Galatians, and Romans for Richard N. Longenecker*, edited by L. Ann Jervis and Peter Richardson, 222–39. JSNTSup 108. Sheffield: Sheffield Academic Press, 1994.

Young, Norman H. "Paidagogos: The Social Setting of a Pauline Metaphor." *NovT* 29 (1987): 150–76.

———. "Who's Cursed—And Why? (Galatians 3:10–14)." *JBL* 117 (1998): 79–92.

Commentaries

Betz, Hans Dieter. *Galatians: A Commentary on Paul's Letter to the Churches in Galatia*. Hermeneia. Philadelphia: Fortress, 1979.

Bring, Ragnar. *Commentary on Galatians*. Translated by Eric Wahlstrom. Philadelphia: Muhlenberg, 1961.

Bruce, F. F. *The Epistle to the Galatians: A Commentary on the Greek Text*. NIGTC. Grand Rapids: Eerdmans, 1982.

Burton, Ernest DeWitt. *A Critical and Exegetical Commentary on the Epistle to the Galatians*. ICC. Edinburgh: T&T Clark, 1921.

Cousar, Charles B. *Galatians*. IBC. Atlanta: John Knox, 1982.

Dunn, James D. G. *The Epistle to the Galatians*. BNTC. Peabody, MA: Hendrickson, 1993.

Ebeling, Gerhard. *The Truth of the Gospel: An Exposition of Galatians*. Translated by David Green. Philadelphia: Fortress, 1985.

Edwards, Mark J., ed. *Galatians, Ephesians, Philippians*. ACCSNT 8. Downers Grove, IL: InterVarsity, 1999.

Esler, Philip F. *Galatians*. NTR. London: Routledge, 1998.

Fee, Gordon D. *Galatians*. Pentecostal Commentary. Dorset, UK: Deo, 2007.

Fung, Ronald Y. K. *The Epistle to the Galatians*. NICNT. Grand Rapids: Eerdmans, 1988.

George, Timothy. *Galatians*. NAC. Nashville: Broadman & Holman, 1994.

Guthrie, Donald H. *Galatians*. NCBC. London: Nelson, 1969.

Hansen, G. Walter. *Galatians*. IVPNTC 9. Downers Grove, IL: InterVarsity, 1994.

Hays, Richard B. "The Letter to the Galatians." *NIB* 11:181–348.

Hendriksen, William. *A Commentary on Galatians*. Edinburgh: Banner of Truth Trust, 1968.

Jervis, L. Ann. *Galatians*. NIBC. Peabody, MA: Hendrickson, 1999.

Krentz, Edgar. *Galatians*. ACNT. Minneapolis: Augsburg, 1985.

Lightfoot, J. B. *Saint Paul's Epistle to the Galatians*. London: Macmillan, 1902.

Longenecker, Richard N. *Galatians*. WBC 41. Dallas: Word, 1990.

Luther, Martin. A *Commentary on St. Paul's Epistle to the Galatians*. London: James Clarke, 1953 [German original, 1535].

Martyn, J. Louis. *Galatians*. AB 33A. New York: Doubleday, 1997.

Matera, Frank J. *Galatians*. SP 9. Collegeville, MN: Liturgical Press, 1992.

McKnight, Scot. *Galatians*. NIVAC. Grand Rapids: Zondervan, 1995.

Morris, Leon. *Galatians: Paul's Charter of Christian Freedom*. Downers Grove, IL: InterVarsity, 2004.

Neil, William. *The Letter of Paul to the Galatians*. CBC. Cambridge: Cambridge University Press, 1967.

Ramsay, William M. *Historical Commentary on Galatians*. Edited by Mark Wilson. Reprint, Grand Rapids: Kregel, 1997.

Riches, John. *Galatians through the Centuries*. BBC. Oxford: Blackwell, 2008.

Ridderbos, Herman. *The Epistle of Paul to the Churches of Galatia*. NICNT. Grand Rapids: Eerdmans, 1956.

Schreiner, Thomas R. *Galatians*. ZECNT. Grand Rapids: Zondervan, 2010.

Williams, Sam K. *Galatians*. ANTC. Nashville: Abingdon, 1994.

Witherington, Ben, III. *Grace in Galatia: A Commentary on Paul's Letter to the Galatians*. Grand Rapids: Eerdmans, 1998.

Ziesler, John. *The Epistle to the Galatians*. EC. London: Epworth, 1992.

26

First and Second Thessalonians

Many scholars, as we have already noted, regard 1 Thessalonians as the earliest of Paul's canonical letters. Even if Galatians is to be regarded as earlier, clearly the Thessalonian letters represent a very early Paul, being written close together probably in about 50 or 51. Indeed, recently it has been claimed that 1 Thessalonians was written as early as 43, which clearly would make it Paul's earliest surviving letter.[1] Although many scholars are inclined against the authenticity of 2 Thessalonians, it is nevertheless probable that both letters were written by Paul from Corinth toward the end of his first missionary journey. Both letters are written in the names of Paul, Silvanus, and Timothy and find their origin in the need to encourage the church and to correct misunderstandings of certain things Paul had taught them. Although these letters are best known for eschatological issues, they are of relatively minor importance in the letters.

The story of the founding of the church at Thessalonica, the capital city of Macedonia, is recounted very briefly by Luke in Acts 17:1–9. Paul and Silas (= Silvanus) preached there at least three weeks before Jewish persecution forced them to leave the city. The Thessalonian Jews were so upset by their preaching that they even persecuted Paul and Silas in the next city on their itinerary, Beroea (Acts 17:13). Although some scholars have seen a problem in regarding Luke's account as historically consonant with what can be gained

1. See Donfried, *Paul, Thessalonica, and Early Christianity*, 76. Donfried bases his view on dating the edict of Claudius expelling the Jews from Rome to the year 41 rather than the commonly accepted date, 49. Helmut Koester regards 1 Thessalonians as Paul's invention of a new genre: the Christian letter ("I Thessalonians—Experiment in Christian Writing").

Author: *1 Thessalonians*: universally accepted as by Paul; *2 Thessalonians:* probably by Paul, but very possibly pseudonymous.

Date: *1 Thessalonians*: 50/51, but possibly even earlier; *2 Thessalonians:* probably only a few months after 1 Thessalonians, but if pseudonymous, possibly some years later.

Addressees: Both letters are addressed to the church at Thessalonica in Macedonia.

Purpose: *1 Thessalonians*: thanksgiving for perseverance of their faith, pastoral encouragement, ethical exhortation, instruction concerning those who have died in Christ; *2 Thessalonians:* mainly to correct misunderstanding of eschatological imminence.

Message/Argument: *1 Thessalonians*: teaching; exhortation to holy conduct; *2 Thessalonians*: the revealing of the lawless one, the son of perdition, must happen before the end, but now restrained; exhortation to church members to work.

Significance: *1 Thessalonians*: one of Paul's earliest letters and references to his gospel; teaching about the return of Christ; *2 Thessalonians:* detailed eschatological teaching.

---

from the Thessalonian letters, the differences noted are not very significant (e.g., Paul does not cite the OT in the letters, and the recipients are spoken of as converts from idolatry). That Paul sent Timothy (and Silas) back to Thessalonica is testified both by Acts (18:5) and 1 Thessalonians (3:1–2, 6).

We begin by looking at the letters individually before we turn to the question of their relationship and the issue of the authorship of 2 Thessalonians.

First Thessalonians

The first letter that Paul wrote to the Thessalonian Christians reveals Paul the missionary now acting as pastor and teacher. The warm tone of the letter indicates the closeness that Paul felt to those who came to faith in Christ under his ministry. The pastor here is concerned to teach and correct misunderstandings of what he had taught them while he was among them.[2]

The Content of the Letter

Paul moves from the very brief but formally correct prescript (1:1), modified only by the words "in God the Father and the Lord Jesus Christ," which describe the determining factors in the existence of the church, directly to the thanksgiving (1:2–10), again in good literary form.

The thanksgiving focuses first on the readers' "work of faith and labor of love and steadfastness of hope" (1:3)—that is, on how they were manifesting the basic virtues of the Christian life. Paul expresses gratitude to the readers

---

2. On the role of Paul as pastor to the Thessalonians, see Malherbe, *Paul and the Thessalonians*.

for their reception of the word with joy despite the affliction that they had to endure (1:6). In that respect, they had become imitators of Jesus as well as Paul and his co-workers—probably an allusion to a persecution similar to what Paul and his associates had suffered in Thessalonica (see Acts 17:1–9, 13). The thanksgiving includes the compliment that the report of the faith and faithfulness of the Thessalonian Christians had spread throughout the surrounding region of Macedonia and even to Achaia (1:7–8). Paul's reference to their conversion includes an echo of his gospel that mentions their turning from idols "to serve a living and true God, and to wait for his Son from heaven, whom he raised from the dead, Jesus who delivers us from the wrath to come" (1:9–10).[3]

There is a distinct tone of relief in this thanksgiving, since when Paul had to leave Thessalonica abruptly, he was concerned about their continuing in the faith. The relief comes to expression again in the thanksgiving in 2:13 and in yet a third thanksgiving, in 3:6–10, which is closely related to the thanksgiving proper, but most explicitly in 3:5: "when I could bear it no longer, I sent that I might know your faith, for fear that somehow the tempter had tempted you and that our labor would be in vain." From this it becomes clear that thanksgiving in 1 Thessalonians is itself an important purpose—indeed, one of the main purposes—of the letter, and not merely a formal element as in other letters.

This suggests that the Hellenistic letter form is not strictly followed in this relatively brief letter. Paul is free to adapt that form to his own purposes, and he does so. Thus here, since there is no sustained argument, we lack the usual middle sections of *narratio* (statement of facts) and *probatio* (argument). Two additional main subjects are dealt with briefly before Paul turns in 4:1 to the exhortation section of the letter. The rhetorical genre of the letter has been variously described as deliberative, epideictic, and paraenetic, if it is not sui generis.[4]

First Main Section (2:1–12)

Paul turns first to a defense of his conduct among the Thessalonians.[5] Presumably, this section is a response to charges made against Paul and his companions by his opponents that Timothy may have reported to him.[6] Paul and Timothy supposedly were deceivers who duped others into believing a message that they had invented. Their motives were impure, they were driven by greed, and they got their way by pleasing others. In response, Paul maintains

3. Morna Hooker ("1 Thessalonians 1:9–10") alternatively suggests that 1:9–10 does not represent a summary of the gospel preached by Paul, but rather is in effect an anticipation of the content of the letter that follows. See also Munck, "I Thess. i.9–10 and the Missionary Preaching of Paul."

4. Steve Walton ("What Has Aristotle to Do with Paul?") concludes that the place given to praise and blame points to epideictic.

5. See Weima, "An Apology for the Apologetic Function of 1 Thessalonians 2:1–12."

6. For a discussion of the genre and purpose of 1 Thessalonians 2:1–12, see chapters 1–6 in Donfried and Beutler, *The Thessalonians Debate*. The second part of this book deals with methodology: epistolary analysis versus rhetorical analysis.

that they had been approved and commissioned by God to proclaim the gospel (2:4), they desired neither to please mortals nor did they seek their praise (2:4, 6); and finally that they did not even exercise their right as Apostles to be supported materially but rather worked with their hands to earn their own living (2:7, 9). Their conduct, in short, was "holy and righteous and blameless" (2:10).

The tender side of Paul is apparent when he characterizes his apostolic activity among the Thessalonian Christians as being that of a nurse or father among his children (2:7, 11).[7] And the magnanimity of the man can be seen when he says, "So deeply do we care for you that we are determined to share with you not only the gospel of God but also our own selves, because you have become very dear to us" (2:8 NRSV).

Growing out of the renewed or second thanksgiving in 2:13 is a notorious passage (2:14–16) containing invective against the Jews so scathing that many scholars cannot accept it as authentically Pauline and thus regard it as an interpolation into the letter, even though no extant Greek manuscripts lack these sentences.[8] The passage often is mistakenly taken to be anti-Semitic. Instead, what we have here is a piece of intra-Jewish polemic that partakes of a heated rhetoric familiar in the ancient world. Not unlike an Isaiah, Paul denounces those Jews whom he regards as opposing the purposes of God.[9] The vitriol comes directly out of Paul's personal frustration with the Jewish opposition to his mission, which we read of repeatedly in the book of Acts. We must restrict it to just this limited historical setting and not apply it to modern settings. After the Holocaust, Christians indeed are obligated to stand on guard against any use of the Bible for anti-Semitic purposes. We may be very thankful furthermore that this passage was not the last word of Paul on the Jews (see Rom. 11).

Second Main Section (2:17–3:13)

The next main part of the letter deals with Paul's intention to pay a return visit to the Thessalonian church. He indicates to begin with that he had intended to revisit them earlier but had been hindered from accomplishing that intention (2:18). He assures them of how special they are to him: "We were made orphans by being separated from you" (2:17 NRSV). They are his hope, joy, crown, and glory (2:19). Noting his relief at Timothy's return, Paul reiterates how he longs to see them (3:6; cf. 2:17) and writes that he prays "night and day that we may see you face to face" (3:10). In these remarks we see the letter in its function as the substitute for the personal presence of the Apostle.

7. See Gaventa, "Apostles as Babes and Nurses in 1 Thessalonians 2:7."

8. See especially Pearson, "1 Thessalonians 2:13–16"; see also Schmidt, "1 Thessalonians 2:13–16."

9. For a good explanation of the passage, see Donfried, *Paul, Thessalonica, and Early Christianity*, 195–208. On the hyperbolic character of the passage, see Schlueter, *Filling Up the Measure*.

Finally, he prays for divine enabling to succeed in coming to them, and that they may grow in love and be strengthened in holiness, the last sentences having a little of the tone of a final benediction (3:11–13).

Third Main Section (4:1–5:22)

As usual in Paul's Epistles, the *exhortatio* is substantial. Indeed, it contains a significant teaching section (4:13–5:11) that one might have expected to be found in the earlier parts of the letter. The first part of ethical exhortation (paraenesis) focuses on holiness and love (4:1–12), but a number of other ethical topics come in for mention.[10]

Somewhat abruptly, Paul turns to address a specific matter that was troubling the Thessalonian church. The question had been conveyed to Paul probably by Timothy along with his report. Apparently, Paul's emphasis on the present aspects of eschatology or on the imminence of the return of Christ (the parousia) was such that the death of believers was unexpected and was causing a problem for the church. Would these deceased believers be lost because they were not alive at the return of Christ? It is in answer to that question that Paul presents a bit of his expectation of how the end will be. There is no need to worry about the dead, for "God will bring with him those who have fallen asleep [*koimēthentas*, i.e., died]" (4:14).[11] Moreover, now leaning on "the word of the Lord" (probably from oral tradition),[12] he assures his readers that the dead will be the first to rise. This will happen when Christ returns "with a cry of command, with the archangel's call, and with the sound of the trumpet of God" (4:16). "Then," Paul continues, "we who are alive, who are left, shall be caught up together with them in the clouds to meet the Lord in the air; and so we shall always be with the Lord" (4:17).

In the next subsection, although he notes "you have no need to have anything written to you" on the subject, Paul turns more generally to "the times and the seasons" (5:1–11). Here he indicates that while to the unprepared the coming of the Lord will be "like a thief in the night," this will not be so for the Thessalonian Christians. They are described by contrast as "children of light and children of the day" (5:5 NRSV).[13] The exhortation then comes to the Thessalonians to live as such, putting on "the breastplate of faith and love, and for a helmet the hope of salvation" (5:8 [cf. 1:3]). The end of this subsection, as of the preceding one, concludes with the command to "encourage one another" (5:11 [cf. 4:18]). The close link between eschatology and ethics is evident from this material.

---

10. On this passage, see Weima, "'How You Must Walk to Please God'"; Scott, "Paul and Late-Jewish Eschatology"; Kim, "Paul's Common Paraenesis (1 Thess 4–5; Phil 2–4; Rom 12–13).

11. See Paddison, *Theological Hermeneutics and 1 Thessalonians*.

12. Alternatively, "the salvific message of Jesus' death and resurrection mentioned in 4:14" (thus Pahl, *Discerning the "Word of the Lord,"* 169).

13. See Lövestam, *Spiritual Wakefulness in the New Testament*, 45–58.

The exhortation section concludes with an assortment of admonitions (5:12–22). These appear to be drawn from a reservoir that Paul used in many of his other letters.

Concluding Prayer (5:23–24)

The body of the letter comes to an end with a brief prayer that corresponds to the prayer with which Paul ended the second main section (cf. 3:11–13). It is followed by an appeal for the Thessalonians to pray for Paul and his co-workers (5:25) and then the postscript, or formal closing, of the letter (5:26–28).[14]

The Question of the Unity of First Thessalonians

Because of certain anomalies in form in 1 Thessalonians, some scholars have speculated that it is a combination of what were originally two short, independent letters. The second thanksgiving, in 2:13, it has been argued, reflects what was at the beginning of an independent letter, with its own body and its own conclusion in 3:13 (or 4:1). Hypotheses of this sort, which have minor variations, require of Paul too strict an adherence to the form of the Hellenistic letter. His letters do basically follow that form, but Paul is never a slave to formal conventions. Instead, he freely adapts the form to suit his purposes. Paul, after all, is not writing a formal letter but rather a very practical one that includes deeply felt concerns on several matters. For him to go back and forth on a topic, to repeat, and to digress—all this is only to be expected.[15]

For the same reasons, hypotheses concerning interpolations likewise are unconvincing. The strong reaction to and rejection of 2:14–16 by many, understandable as it is, misconstrues the content, perhaps, but fails also to see how well the passage fits into the context. Other alleged interpolations (e.g., 5:1–11)[16] rest mainly on determined attempts to deconstruct the text of the letter by the discovery of apparent but superficial discrepancies.[17]

Second Thessalonians

Shortly after he wrote 1 Thessalonians, Paul found it necessary to write a second, shorter letter to correct certain misunderstandings that had arisen about the time of the end of the age. It was urgent for Paul to set matters straight if the church was to be what he wanted it to be.

14. See Weima, *Neglected Endings.*
15. See O'Brien, *Introductory Thanksgivings in the Letters of Paul*, 141–66.
16. On the authenticity of this passage, see Plevnik, "I Thess. 5:1–11."
17. See Collins, *Studies on the First Letter to the Thessalonians*, 96–135; Johanson, *To All the Brethren.*

Content of the Letter

The prescript of 2 Thessalonians is identical with that of 1 Thessalonians except for the added words "from God the Father and the Lord Jesus Christ" following "Grace to you and peace" (1:2).

The customary thanksgiving follows (1:3–12). As in the first letter, mention is made of the Thessalonians' faith and love and also of the suffering that they have had to endure (1:3–4). The last part of the thanksgiving includes a fair amount of teaching material focusing on the glorious return of Christ. "When the Lord Jesus is revealed from heaven with his mighty angels in flaming fire," Paul writes, relief will come to those presently afflicted, and there will be "vengeance upon those who do not know God and upon those who do not obey the gospel of our Lord Jesus" (1:7–8). This section ends with reference to Paul's prayers for the Thessalonian Christians that they may be "worthy of his [God's] call," accomplish the "work of faith," and glorify the name of Jesus (1:11–12).

Main Section

The specific purpose of the letter emerges in 2:1–12. Somehow the Christians at Thessalonica apparently had come to the conclusion that "the day of the Lord is already here" (2:2 NRSV). Paul had taught them correctly about this matter, as he gently reminds them (2:5). He points out with some urgency that the day of the Lord will come only after certain things take place: "the rebellion comes first, and the man of lawlessness is revealed, the son of perdition" (2:3). This personage will declare himself to be God (2:4), but at the present moment he is restrained by someone or something not named by Paul. "You know what is restraining him now" (2:6), Paul says simply. But when the time comes that this restrainer is removed, "then the lawless one will be revealed" (2:8). Then, when Jesus returns, he will destroy the lawless one, "the Lord Jesus will slay him with the breath of his mouth and destroy him by his appearing and his coming" (2:8). Paul finally associates the coming of the lawless one with the works of Satan experienced especially by "those who are to perish, because they refused to love the truth and so be saved" (2:10). Those who have not believed the truth will be condemned, he concludes (2:12).[18]

A second thanksgiving is introduced in 2:13, ending with a sentence of exhortation (2:15) and prayer (2:16–17).[19]

Exhortation

The exhortation section begins with a prayer request (3:1–2), and encouragement (3:3–4), and yet another prayer for the Thessalonians (3:5). The exhortation proper (3:6–15) does not present the usual assortment of

---

18. On this passage, see Fee, "Pneuma and Eschatology in 2 Thessalonians 2:1–12."
19. See O'Brien, *Introductory Thanksgivings in the Letters of Paul*, 167–96.

subjects but instead focuses mainly on one particular matter, idleness.[20] Paul refers to his own example of working among them and not exercising his apostolic right to receive his living as a preacher of the word. The Thessalonians are to imitate the example of Paul and his co-workers in this regard (3:7, 9). Indeed, he orders them to work: "Such persons we command and exhort in the Lord Jesus Christ to do their work in quietness and to earn their own living" (3:12).

A benediction (3:16) gives way to the postscript (3:17–18), where Paul takes up the pen and notes that his handwritten postscript marks all of his authentic letters (cf. 2:2). The letter ends with the customary formulaic words "The grace of our Lord Jesus Christ be with all of you."

Did Paul Write Second Thessalonians?

Although only a handful of scholars have doubted the Pauline authorship of 1 Thessalonians, an increasing number have doubted the authenticity of 2 Thessalonians, especially in the late twentieth and early twenty-first centuries.

Against Pauline Authorship

A close comparison of the two letters can give the impression that the second is dependent on and modeled after the first. The shorter 2 Thessalonians has a very similar structure and even very similar wording at points, with the parallels occurring in the same order. As we have noted above, each letter has the oddity of a second thanksgiving section (2:13 in each letter) and a benediction at the end of the body of the letter (1 Thess. 3:11–13; 2 Thess. 2:16). There is at the same time a uniqueness about the vocabulary and literary style of 2 Thessalonians in comparison with the undisputed letters of Paul.

It is also true that the second letter lacks the distinct personal warmth of the first. The tone of the letter is more formal and more distant. Unlike the first letter, furthermore, it gives no personal details concerning Paul and his activities.

There are also some minor theological differences between the letters. On any account, of course, there is the obvious difference between the imminent eschatology of 1 Thessalonians and the delayed eschatology of 2 Thessalonians. The second letter almost certainly is a corrective of a misunderstanding of the first, but was it written by Paul shortly after the first or by a much later corrector in the name of Paul? The letter contains none of the distinctive material familiar to us from the other Pauline Letters.

20. For sociological explanations, see Russell, "The Idle in 2 Thess. 3:6–12"; and Winter, "'If a Man Does Not Wish to Work . . .'" Maarten Menken ("Paradise Regained or Still Lost?") argues, however, that the Thessalonians, believing that the parousia had occurred, apparently thought that paradise had come and thus the curse of Genesis 3:17–19 had been annulled.

Moreover, there appear to be marks in the second letter that may reveal a post-Pauline perspective. For example, some maintain that the emphasis on "truth" (2:10, 12, 13) and on "the gospel" (1:8; 2:14) seems to point to a more developed time than the beginning of Paul's ministry. Further, there is an implicit appeal to apostolic authority in the words "stand firm and hold to the traditions which you were taught by us, whether by word of mouth or by letter" (2:15 [cf. 3:6]). The words "God chose you as the first fruits for salvation" (2:13 NRSV) could possibly point to a somewhat later date. The combination of the theme of eschatological vengeance and judgment in a context of persecution possibly seems to point to a time late in the century, as witnessed by the book of Revelation.

Finally, the defense against pseudonymity in 2:2, 15; 3:17 itself can be taken as a deliberate cover-up of what is actually a pseudonymous document.

It may be that no single argument mentioned here establishes by itself that Paul did not write 2 Thessalonians. It is worth pondering, however, whether the cumulative effect of all the arguments finally makes the conclusion any more than a possible one.

For Pauline Authorship

The single most important fact that must be taken into consideration when examining 2 Thessalonians is its special character as a brief, appendix-like response written for the main purpose of correcting an erroneous understanding of a particular point. What makes 2 Thessalonians unusual is that it assumes 1 Thessalonians, and therefore it should not be finally evaluated independently from that letter.

The shortness of time between the letters, on the traditional view, can account reasonably well for both the similarities and the differences between them. That is, similarities in structure and language appear because of the proximity in time in which they were written, while differences appear because the very purpose of the second letter is to clarify a misunderstanding possibly caused by the first. It remains distinctly possible that the second letter is modeled on the first, but it should furthermore be remembered that some formal similarities can also be purely coincidental. If the second letter was written shortly after the first (say a matter of months), it is understandable that it did not require the same personal warmth, nor did Paul need to include personal details.

It is very difficult to be sure about what is late or not in the literature of the NT because of our comparatively limited knowledge of the full context of earliest Christianity. None of the observations on this score, therefore, can be absolutely compelling. Two other points should be noted here. First, there are almost no marks of the elements of an incipient "early catholicism" that are distinctive to the later letters attributed to Paul.[21] Second, there may be

---

21. For discussion of "early catholicism," see chapter 33 below.

a telltale indication of a relatively early date in the reference to "the man of lawlessness" seating himself "in the temple of God" (2:4). It seems probable from this that the temple had not yet been destroyed, and if so, the letter can have been written no later than the 60s, as the temple was razed in 70.

Without question, 2 Thessalonians contains material not found elsewhere in the Pauline Letters, while at the same time it lacks that which we usually recognize as Pauline. This, however, can be at least partially explained by the special and rather strictly limited purpose of this appendix-like letter.[22]

There are, then, fairly satisfactory answers to the points raised by those arguing for the nonauthenticity of 2 Thessalonians. If we insist furthermore that the burden of proof lies on those who opt for non-Pauline authorship, not on those who accept it, then we must conclude that the case has not quite been established beyond reasonable doubt. Yet this is not a matter on which anyone needs to be dogmatic, and it is possible that one of Paul's associates, such as Silas or Timothy, actually wrote the letter. A conclusion of nonauthenticity would in no way affect the authority of the letter within the NT canon.

The Order of the Letters

A few scholars have challenged the traditional ordering of the Thessalonian letters. That the document we call "First Thessalonians" comes before the one we call "Second Thessalonians" in the NT canon is due solely to the fact that it is the longer of the two.[23] There is no indisputable indication in the letters themselves as to which was written first, and the titles "First Thessalonians" and "Second Thessalonians" are relatively late. So the question is legitimately an open one.

The argument for the priority of 2 Thessalonians rests on the following points. Whereas persecution is spoken of in the past tense in 1 Thessalonians (2:14), it is presented as a vividly present experience in 2 Thessalonians (1:4–5). Awareness of the problem of idleness seems to emerge as a new thing in 2 Thessalonians 3:11, while it is mentioned as something already known in 1 Thessalonians 4:11; 5:14. The note at 2 Thessalonians 3:17 about Paul making a particular mark "in every letter of mine" makes the most sense if this was his first letter. The statement in 1 Thessalonians 5:1 that readers need nothing to be written to them about the last times could be a reference to 2 Thessalonians. Finally, the sections of 1 Thessalonians beginning with "now concerning" may be asking for more information, via return letter, of matters introduced in 2 Thessalonians (cf. 1 Thess. 4:9 and 5:1 with, respectively, 2 Thess. 3:6–15 and 2:1–12). It is very possible, then, that 2 Thessalonians was written first, and even that it

---

22. See Marshall, "Pauline Theology in the Thessalonian Correspondence."
23. The canonical order of the Pauline Epistles depends mainly on length. See chap. 22 above.

was carried to the Thessalonian church by Timothy on the visit referred to in 1 Thessalonians 3:2.

These observations, however, are not sufficient in themselves to have altered the majority opinion on the subject. Each has received its answer. Persecution could well have broken out anew; there may be a new report of idleness; Paul may begin to mark letters with his signature only after he suspected the possibility of a forged letter (cf. 2 Thess. 2:2); the responses ("now concerning . . .") in 1 Thessalonians could well be to a report from the church, and there is no necessity to presuppose knowledge of 2 Thessalonians.

It seems probable that 1 Thessalonians is referred to in 2 Thessalonians 2:15. It is also more likely that the remarks concerning Paul's mission among the Thessalonians (1 Thess. 2–3) would occur in the first letter to the church than in the second. As I have already argued, the very brief 2 Thessalonians is most easily understood as a sequel to 1 Thessalonians and produced not long after it. It is more difficult to believe that 1 Thessalonians is the sequel to 2 Thessalonians. The relation between the teaching concerning eschatology in the two letters, as well as other aspects already mentioned, makes the most sense if we assume the priority of 1 Thessalonians, with 2 Thessalonians as an appendix-like corrective. This will emerge with more clarity in the sections that follow.

The Circumstances of the Thessalonian Church

The church at Thessalonica was a young church that had to face serious opposition in the early months of its existence. From the very start, during Paul and his co-workers' three-week mission, the believers experienced persecution (Acts 17:1–9; 1 Thess. 1:6; 2:2; 3:3–4, 7).[24] Given the zeal of the Jews of the city (cf. Acts 17:13), it is unlikely that the persecution stopped when Paul and his associates departed. On the contrary, it is just the sort of thing that would keep flaring up. Karl Donfried appropriately describes 1 Thessalonians as a "paracletic" letter—that is, one of consolation to those suffering persecution.[25]

Paul had been able to give these new Christians some teaching before he was forced to leave the city, and Timothy may have given further teaching (1 Thess. 3:2). "You learned from us how you ought to live" (1 Thess. 4:1), Paul writes, and there is no need to write anything concerning "the times and the seasons" (1 Thess. 5:1). The last point seems to indicate that Paul had given them some teaching about eschatology (see also 2 Thess. 2:5, 15). Given the specific problem that the death of believers posed for them, it is probable that Paul had taught them concerning the return of Christ in the (relatively) near future. But when some believers died *before* that event, the Thessalonians

24. See especially Still, *Conflict at Thessalonica*.
25. See Donfried, *Paul, Thessalonica, and Early Christianity*, 119–38.

naturally were concerned. That they were surprised at the death of believers may point to an overrealized eschatology (cf. 2 Tim. 2:17–18), perhaps growing out of Paul's stress on the presence of the new age in Christ.

In his response Paul does not play down the imminence of the return of Christ. The parousia continues to receive mention (1 Thess. 1:10; 2:19; 3:13; 5:23) and even its imminence (1 Thess. 5:2). He merely sets their minds at rest concerning the problem of the deceased believers by indicating that Christ will raise them first.

Some months after the first letter was written, Paul apparently received further information about the Thessalonian Christians that caused him to write the second letter. Based on his focus in that letter, we may conclude that he heard of the continued persecution experienced by the church (2 Thess. 1:4–5), the problem of their overrealized eschatology—some arguing "that the day of the Lord has come" (2 Thess. 2:2)—and of a consequent idleness, already noted in the first letter (1 Thess. 4:11; 5:14), now reaching an alarming state (2 Thess. 3:6–13).[26]

Paul encourages them in the face of persecution, and he exhorts them concerning their idleness. In correcting the overrealized eschatology, he presents teaching in which he indicates that certain events must happen before the return of Christ (2 Thess. 2:1–12).[27]

The Eschatology of the Thessalonian Letters

As is the case so often in the Pauline Epistles, teaching grows directly out of the need to address a crisis in the church. What has attracted the most attention in the Thessalonian letters is the teaching on eschatology.[28] These letters have become known precisely for this. Yet, as I have already indicated, both letters, but especially the longer 1 Thessalonians, have larger agendas. First Thessalonians is, above all, the letter of a pastor to his flock; Second Thessalonians is, above all, a letter of comfort and exhortation. The eschatological teaching portions in these letters therefore have only a relative, not absolute, importance. This is not to deny that eschatology is important in these letters or that the second coming of Christ is alluded to more often than usual. Nor is it to deny the apocalyptic character of 2 Thessalonians, with its motif of judgment of the enemies of the truth. But it is especially the interesting nature of the teaching offered in 1 Thessalonians 4:13–18 and 2 Thessalonians 2:1–12, together with understandable

---

26. For the situation of the readers, see Barclay, "Conflict in Thessalonica."

27. For the view that in the two letters we have two stages of a single crisis, see Nicholl, *From Hope to Despair in Thessalonica.*

28. For the similarity between the apocalyptic teaching of the Thessalonian letters and the Jesus traditions of the Synoptic apocalyptic discourse, see Wenham, "Paul and the Synoptic Apocalypse." Against this conclusion, see Tuckett, "Synoptic Tradition in 1 Thessalonians?"

human curiosity about the end times, that have made these passages the focal points.

With these comments in mind, we should not be surprised to note that the eschatological teaching is not given systematically or abstractly; instead, it has, as is consistently so in the NT, an ad hoc character and a vital connection with ethical exhortation (paraenesis). The connection between eschatology and ethics is exceptionally important in the NT, and it is used with good effect in these letters.

But what specifically can be gleaned about the future from the two renowned passages? The passage in 1 Thessalonians assures us that the resurrected dead in Christ will join Christ at his coming (1 Thess. 4:16). In this they will precede living Christians, with whom Paul identifies himself: "we who are alive, who are left"—this leading us to conclude that the early Paul expected the parousia to occur in his own lifetime. The immediately following reference to those alive being "caught up together with them in the clouds to meet the Lord in the air" (1 Thess. 4:17) has given rise to the doctrine of the "rapture" (from the Latin word *rapio*, "to seize, drag away, snatch up"), which has played so large a role in dispensationalist eschatology. It is hard, however, to see any relationship between what this text says and the widely held notion of a "secret rapture" of the saints, according to which, in its classic "pretribulation" form, all Christians will suddenly be removed from the world without any warning whatsoever.[29] On the contrary, the passage in question refers to a gathering up of the saints unto Christ at his parousia, *after* the dead are raised. The particular Greek word used for "meet" (*apantēsis*) is commonly used to refer to honorary processions going outside a city to meet a dignitary in order to accompany that person back into the city (it is used in connection with Paul in Acts 28:15; cf. Matt. 25:6).[30] This suggests that the company of saints may meet the Lord and then come with him to the earth to set up the kingdom (cf. "the coming of our Lord Jesus with all his saints" [1 Thess. 3:13]). However, it is not Paul's purpose to provide much in the way of detail. He intends only to make clear the basic point that the living will not precede the dead in meeting their Lord.

The second passage, 2 Thessalonians 2:1–12, provides substantial teaching on what must precede the coming of the day of the Lord. There is first to be "the rebellion" (*hē apostasia*) and the revelation of a figure called "the man of lawlessness, the son of perdition" (*ho anthrōpos tēs anomias, ho huios tēs apōleias*) (2:3). Although not identified as such by Paul, this lawless one probably is the same as the "beast" in Revelation 13 and the "antichrist" in 1 John 2. This person, "by the activity of Satan" (2:9), "opposes and exalts

---

29. On the rapture question, see Gundry, *The Church and the Tribulation*; Archer et al., *Three Views on the Rapture*; and especially Ladd, *The Blessed Hope*.

30. The differences noted by Michael Cosby ("Hellenistic Formal Receptions and Paul's Use of *apantēsis* in 1 Thessalonians 4:17") do not require the total rejection of this understanding. For a rejoinder, see Gundry, "A Brief Note on 'Hellenistic Formal Receptions and Paul's Use of *apantēsis* in 1 Thessalonians 4:17."

himself against every so-called god or object of worship, so that he takes his seat in the temple of God" (2:4).[31] The most difficult question in this difficult passage is what Paul refers to next: one "who now restrains [*ho katechōn*]"—masculine here, but neuter in 2:6 ("what is restraining")—this evil opponent of God "until he [i.e., the restrainer] is out of the way [*ek mesou genētai*]" (2:7). Paul says that this evil personage, whom Paul had already identified for the readers (2:5–6), "is already at work" (2:7). Although scholars' opinions concerning the identity of the restrainer have ranged the whole gamut from God to Satan, probably we must choose from the following options, all of which involve a person and a process already at work in Paul's day:

1. Paul's own missionary work among the Gentiles;
2. the Roman emperor and state and, by extension, human government; and
3. the Holy Spirit.[32]

On balance, the second option is perhaps the most convincing, especially in that it also explains Paul's decision not to specify the restrainer in the letter, since talk of the end of the Roman Empire would have put Christians under the accusation of treason.

Paul's Gospel

The Letters to the Thessalonians contain a remarkable emphasis on the gospel (*euangelion*) preached by Paul. In 1 Thessalonians 1:5 Paul refers to "our gospel," stating that it "came to you not only in word, but also in power and in the Holy Spirit and with full conviction." It is defined as "the word of the Lord" (1 Thess. 1:8; 2 Thess. 3:1; cf. 1 Thess. 1:6) and identified as "the word of God" (2x in 1 Thess. 2:13). Elements of the Pauline kerygma are echoed in 1 Thessalonians 1:10: "to wait for his Son from heaven, whom he raised from the dead, Jesus who delivers us from the wrath to come."[33] This message is called "the gospel of God" (1 Thess. 2:2, 8, 9). "The gospel" is referred to again in 1 Thessalonians 2:4 and specified as "the gospel of Christ" in 1 Thessalonians 3:2. In 2 Thessalonians 1:8 it is referred to as "the gospel of our Lord Jesus," and in 2 Thessalonians 2:14 as again "our gospel." This foundational message was proclaimed by Paul from his earliest missionary endeavors.[34]

31. The reference to sitting in the temple need not be taken literally; it could refer to a self-exalting claim to deity, perhaps on the model of Caligula setting up his image in the temple in AD 40.

32. For this view, see Powell, "The Identity of the 'Restrainer' in 2 Thessalonians 2:6–7."

33. See Kim, "Jesus the Son of God as the Gospel (1 Thess 1:9–10 and Rom 1:3–4)."

34. See the emphasis in Galatians 1:6–7, where Paul rejects any other gospel than "the gospel of Christ"—that is, the gospel that Paul preached among the Gentiles (Gal. 2:2), "not the gospel of a human" (Gal. 1:11), but a gospel characterized by "truth" (Gal. 2:5, 14).

Bibliography

Books and Articles

Archer, Gleason L., Jr., Paul D. Feinberg, Douglas J. Moo, and Richard R. Reiter. *Three Views on the Rapture: Pre-, Mid- or Post-Tribulation?* Grand Rapids: Zondervan, 1996.

Ascough, Richard S. "The Thessalonian Christian Community as a Professional Voluntary Association." *JBL* 119 (2000): 311–28.

Bailey, John A. "Who Wrote II Thessalonians?" *NTS* 25 (1978–79): 131–45.

Barclay, John M. G. "Conflict in Thessalonica." *CBQ* 55 (1993): 512–30.

Bassler, Jouette M., ed. *Thessalonians, Philippians, Galatians, Philemon.* Vol. 1 of *Pauline Theology*, 37–85. Minneapolis: Fortress, 1991.

Black, David Alan. "The Weak in Thessalonica: A Study in Pauline Lexicography." *JETS* 25 (1982): 307–21.

Bockmuehl, Markus. "1 Thessalonians 2:14–16 and the Church in Jerusalem." *TynBul* 52 (2001): 1–31.

Boers, Hendrikus. "The Form-Critical Study of Paul's Letters: 1 Thessalonians as a Case Study." *NTS* 22 (1975–76): 140–58.

Bridges, Linda McKinnish. "Terms of Endearment: Paul's Words of Comfort in First Thessalonians." *RevExp* 96 (1999): 211–32.

Bruce, F. F. "St. Paul in Macedonia: 2. The Thessalonian Correspondence." *BJRL* 62 (1980): 328–45.

Burke, Trevor J. *Family Matters: A Socio-Historical Study of Kinship Metaphors in 1 Thessalonians.* JSNTSup 247. London: T&T Clark, 2003.

Carroll, John T., Alexandra R. Brown, Claudia J. Setzer, and Jeffrey S. Siker. *The Return of Jesus in Early Christianity.* Peabody, MA: Hendrickson, 2000.

Collins, Raymond F. *Studies on the First Letter to the Thessalonians.* BETL 66. Leuven: Leuven University Press, 1984.

———, ed. *The Thessalonian Correspondence.* BETL 97. Leuven: Leuven University Press, 1990.

Cosby, Michael R. "Hellenistic Formal Receptions and Paul's Use of *apantēsis* in 1 Thessalonians 4:17." *BBR* 4 (1994): 15–33.

Cranfield, C. E. B. "A Study of 1 Thessalonians 2." *IBS* 1 (1979): 215–26.

deSilva, David A. "'Worthy of His Kingdom': Honor Discourse and Social Engineering in 1 Thessalonians." *JSNT* 64 (1996): 49–79.

de Vos, Craig Steven. *Church and Community Conflicts: The Relationship of the Thessalonian, Corinthian, and Philippian Churches with Their Wider Civic Communities.* SBLDS 168. Atlanta: Scholars Press, 1997.

Donfried, Karl P. *Paul, Thessalonica, and Early Christianity.* London: T&T Clark, 2002.

———. "The Theology of 1 Thessalonians." In *The Theology of the Shorter Pauline Letters*, by Karl P. Donfried and I. Howard Marshall, 1–79. NTT. Cambridge: Cambridge University Press, 1993.

———. "The Theology of 2 Thessalonians." In *The Theology of the Shorter Pauline Letters*, by Karl P. Donfried and I. Howard Marshall, 81–113. NTT. Cambridge: Cambridge University Press, 1993.

Donfried, Karl P., and Johannes Beutler, eds. *The Thessalonians Debate: Methodological Discord or Methodological Synthesis?* Grand Rapids: Eerdmans, 2000.

Ellingworth, Paul. "'Which Way Are We Going?' A Verb of Movement, Especially 1 Thessalonians 4:14b." *BT* 25 (1974): 426–31.

Ellis, J. Edward. *Paul and Ancient Views of Sexual Desire: Paul's Sexual Ethics in 1 Thessalonians 4, 1 Corinthians 7 and Romans 1.* LNTS 354. London: T&T Clark, 2007.

Evans, Craig A. "Ascending and Descending with a Shout: Psalm 47:6 and 1 Thessalonians 4:16." In *Paul and the Scriptures of Israel*, edited by Craig A. Evans and James A. Sanders, 238–53. JSNTSup 83. Sheffield: JSOT Press, 1993.

Fee, Gordon D. "Pneuma and Eschatology in 2 Thessalonians 2:1–12: A Proposal about 'Testing the Prophets' and the Purpose of 2 Thessalonians." In *To Tell the Mystery: Essays in Honor of Robert H. Gundry*, edited by Thomas E. Schmidt and Moisés Silva, 196–215. JSNTSup 100. Sheffield: JSOT Press, 1994.

Gaventa, Beverly R. "Apostles as Babes and Nurses in 1 Thessalonians 2:7." In *Faith and History: Essays in Honor of Paul W. Meyer*, edited by John T. Carroll, Charles H. Cosgrove, and E. Elizabeth Johnson, 193–207. Atlanta: Scholars Press, 1990.

Giblin, Charles H. *The Threat to Faith: An Exegetical and Theological Reexamination of 2 Thessalonians*. AnBib 31. Rome: Pontifical Biblical Institute, 1967.

Gillard, Frank D. "The Problem of the Antisemitic Comma between 1 Thessalonians 2:14 and 15." *NTS* 35 (1989): 481–501.

Gillman, John. "Signals of Transformation in 1 Thessalonians 4:13–18." *CBQ* 47 (1985): 263–81.

Goulder, Michael D. "Silas in Thessalonica." *JSNT* 48 (1992): 87–106.

Gundry, Robert H. "A Brief Note on 'Hellenistic Formal Receptions and Paul's Use of *apantēsis* in 1 Thessalonians 4:17.'" *BBR* 6 (1996): 39–41.

———. *The Church and the Tribulation: A Biblical Examination of Posttribulationism*. Grand Rapids: Zondervan, 1973.

———. "The Hellenization of Dominical Tradition and Christianization of Jewish Tradition in the Eschatology of 1–2 Thessalonians." *NTS* 33 (1987): 161–78.

Hester, James D. "The Invention of 1 Thessalonians: A Proposal." In *Rhetoric, Scripture and Theology: Essays from the 1994 Pretoria Conference*, edited by Stanley E. Porter and Thomas H. Olbricht, 251–79. JSNTSup 131. Sheffield: Sheffield Academic Press, 1996.

Hoekema, Anthony A. *The Bible and the Future*. Grand Rapids: Eerdmans, 1979.

Holland, Glenn S. *The Tradition That You Received from Us: 2 Thessalonians in the Pauline Tradition*. HUT 24. Tübingen: Mohr Siebeck, 1988.

Holman, Charles L. *Till Jesus Comes: Origins of Christian Apocalyptic Expectation*. Peabody, MA: Hendrickson, 1996.

Hooker, Morna D. "1 Thessalonians 1:9–10: A Nutshell—but What Kind of Nut?" In *Frühes Christentum*. Vol. 3 of *Geschichte, Tradition, Reflexion: Festschrift für Martin Hengel zum 70. Geburtstag*, edited by Hubert Cancik, Hermann Lichtenberger, and Peter Schäfer, 435–48. Tübingen: Mohr Siebeck, 1996.

Horbury, William. "1 Thessalonians ii.3 as Rebutting the Charge of False Prophecy." *JTS* 33 (1982): 492–508.

Hughes, Frank Witt. *Early Christian Rhetoric and 2 Thessalonians*. JSNTSup 30. Sheffield: JSOT Press, 1989.

Jewett, Robert. *The Thessalonian Correspondence: Pauline Rhetoric and Millenarian Piety*. Philadelphia: Fortress, 1986.

Johanson, Bruce C. *To All the Brethren: A Text-Linguistic and Rhetorical Approach to 1 Thessalonians*. ConBNT 16. Stockholm: Almqvist & Wiksell, 1987.

Kaye, Bruce N. "Eschatology and Ethics in 1 and 2 Thessalonians." *NovT* 17 (1975): 47–57.

Kemmler, Dieter Werner. *Faith and Human Reason: A Study of Paul's Method of Preaching as Illustrated by 1–2 Thessalonians and Acts 17,2–4*. NovTSup 40. Leiden: Brill, 1975.

Kim, Seyoon. "Jesus the Son of God as the Gospel (1 Thess 1:9–10 and Rom 1:3–4)." In *Earliest Christian History: History, Literature, and Theology. Essays from the Tyndale Fellowship in Honor of Martin Hengel*, edited by Michael F. Bird and Jason Maston, 117–141. WUNT 2/230. Tübingen: Mohr Siebeck, 2012.

———. "Paul's Common Paraenesis (1 Thess. 4–5; Phil. 2–4; Rom. 12–13)." *TynBul* 62 (2011): 109–39.

Kloppenborg, John S. "Philadelphia, Theodidaktos and Dioscuri: Rhetorical Engagement in 1 Thessalonians 4:9–2." *NTS* 39 (1993): 265–89.

Koester, Helmut. "I Thessalonians—Experiment in Christian Writing." In *Continuity and Discontinuity in Church History: Essays Presented to George Huntston Williams on the Occasion of His 65th Birthday*, edited by F. Forrester Church and Timothy George, 31–44. SHCT 19. Leiden: Brill, 1979.

Ladd, George Eldon. *The Blessed Hope*. Grand Rapids: Eerdmans, 1956.

Lövestam, Evald. *Spiritual Wakefulness in the New Testament*. Translated by W. F. Salisbury. LUÅ 55/3. Lund: Gleerup, 1963.

Luckensmeyer, David. *The Eschatology of First Thessalonians*. NTOA/SUNT 71. Göttingen: Vandenhoeck & Ruprecht, 2009.

Lyons, George. "Modeling the Holiness Ethos: A Study Based on First Thessalonians." *WTJ* 30 (1995): 187–211.

Malherbe, Abraham J. "Exhortation in First Thessalonians." *NovT* 25 (1983): 238–56.

———. *Paul and the Thessalonians: The Philosophic Tradition of Pastoral Care*. Philadelphia: Fortress, 1987.

Marshall, I. Howard. "Pauline Theology in the Thessalonian Correspondence." In *Paul and Paulinism: Essays in Honour of C. K. Barrett*, edited by Morna D. Hooker and Stephen G. Wilson, 173–83. London: SPCK, 1982.

Mearns, Christopher L. "Early Eschatological Development in Paul: The Evidence of I and II Thessalonians." *NTS* 27 (1980–81): 137–57.

Menken, Maarten J. J. "Paradise Regained or Still Lost? Eschatology and Disorderly Behaviour in 2 Thessalonians." *NTS* 38 (1992): 271–89.

Morris, Leon. *1, 2 Thessalonians*. WBT. Dallas: Word, 1990.

Munck, Johannes. "I Thess. i.9–10 and the Missionary Preaching of Paul: Textual Exegesis and Hermeneutic Reflections." *NTS* 9 (1962–63): 95–110.

Nicholl, Colin R. *From Hope to Despair in Thessalonica: Situating 1 and 2 Thessalonians*. SNTSMS 126. Cambridge: Cambridge University Press, 2004.

O'Brien, Peter T. *Introductory Thanksgivings in the Letters of Paul*. NovTSup 49. Leiden: Brill, 1977.

Okeke, George E. "1 Thessalonians 2:13–16: The Fate of the Unbelieving Jews." *NTS* 27 (1980–81): 127–36.

Otto, Randall E. "The Meeting in the Air (I Thess 4:17)." *HBT* 19 (1997): 192–212.

Paddison, Angus. *Theological Hermeneutics and 1 Thessalonians*. SNTSMS 133. Cambridge: Cambridge University Press, 2005.

Pahl, Michael W. *Discerning the "Word of the Lord": The "Word of the Lord" in 1 Thessalonians 4:15*. LNTS 389. New York: T&T Clark, 2009.

Pearson, Birger A. "1 Thessalonians 2:13–16: A Deutero-Pauline Interpolation." *HTR* 64 (1971): 79–84.

Plevnik, Joseph. "I Thess. 5:1–11: Its Authenticity, Intention and Message." *Bib* 60 (1979): 71–90.

———. *Paul and the Parousia: An Exegetical and Theological Investigation*. Peabody, MA: Hendrickson, 1997.

———. "The Taking Up of the Faithful and the Resurrection of the Dead in 1 Thessalonians 4:13–18." *CBQ* 46 (1984): 274–83.

Polhill, John B. "Hope in the Lord: Introduction to 1–2 Thessalonians." *SBJT* 3 (1999): 22–44.

Porter, Stanley E. "Developments in German and French Thessalonians Research: A Survey and Critique." *CurBS* 7 (1999): 309–34.

Powell, Charles E. "The Identity of the 'Restrainer' in 2 Thessalonians 2:6–7." *BSac* 154 (1997): 320–32.

Poythress, Vern S. "2 Thessalonians 1 Supports Amillennialism." *JETS* 37 (1994): 529–38.

Richard, Earl J. "Contemporary Research on 1 (& 2) Thessalonians." *BTB* 20 (1990): 107–15.

Russell, Ronald. "The Idle in 2 Thess. 3:6–12: An Eschatological or a Social Problem?" *NTS* 34 (1988): 105–19.

Sailors, Timothy B. "Wedding Texual and Rhetorical Criticism to Understanding the Text of 1 Thessalonians 2:7." *JSNT* 80 (2000): 81–98.

Schlueter, Carol J. *Filling up the Measure: Polemical Hyperbole in 1 Thessalonians 2:14–16.* JSNTSup 98. Sheffield: JSOT Press, 1994.

Schmidt, Daryl D. "1 Thessalonians 2:13–16: Linguistic Evidence for an Interpolation." *JBL* 102 (1983): 269–79.

———. "The Authenticity of 2 Thessalonians: Linguistic Arguments." *SBLSP* 22 (1983): 289–93.

Scott, J. Julius, Jr. "Paul and Late-Jewish Eschatology: A Case Study, I Thessalonians 4:13–18 and II Thessalonians 2:1–12." *JETS* 15 (1972): 133–43.

Simpson, John W., Jr. "The Problems Posed by 1 Thessalonians 2:15–16 and a Solution." *HBT* 12 (1990): 42–72.

———. "Shaped by Stories: Narrative in 1 Thessalonians." *AsTJ* 53 (1998): 15–25.

Smith, Abraham. *Comfort One Another: Reconstructing the Rhetoric and Audience of 1 Thessalonians.* Louisville: Westminster John Knox, 1995.

Still, Todd D. *Conflict at Thessalonica: A Pauline Church and Its Neighbours.* JSNTSup 183. Sheffield: Sheffield Academic Press, 1999.

Tellbe, Mikael. *Paul between Synagogue and State: Christians, Jews, and Civic Authorities in 1 Thessalonians, Romans, and Philippians.* ConBNT 34. Stockholm: Almqvist & Wiksell, 2001.

Thurston, Robert W. "The Relationship between the Thessalonian Epistles." *ExpTim* 85 (1973–74): 52–56.

Tuckett, Christopher M. "Synoptic Tradition in 1 Thessalonians?" In *The Thessalonian Correspondence*, edited by Raymond F. Collins, 160–82. BETL 97. Leuven: Leuven University Press, 1990.

Walton, Steve. "What Has Aristotle to Do with Paul? Rhetorical Criticism and 1 Thessalonians." *TynBul* 46 (1995): 229–50.

Ware, James. "The Thessalonians as a Missionary Congregation: 1 Thessalonians 1:5–8." *ZNW* 93 (1992): 126–31.

Weatherly, Jon A. "The Authenticity of 1 Thessalonians 2:13–16: Additional Evidence." *JSNT* 42 (1991): 79–89.

Weima, Jeffrey A. D. "An Apology for the Apologetic Function of 1 Thessalonians 2:1–12." *JSNT* 68 (1997): 73–99.

———. "'But We Became Infants among You': The Case for ΝΗΠΙΟΙ in 1 Thessalonians 2:7." *NTS* 46 (2000): 547–64.

———. "'How You Must Walk to Please God': Holiness and Discipleship in 1 Thessalonians." In *Patterns of Discipleship in the New Testament*, edited by Richard N. Longenecker, 98–119. MNTS. Grand Rapids: Eerdmans, 1996.

———. "Infants, Nursing Mother, and Father: Paul's Portrayal of a Pastor." *CTJ* 37 (2002): 209–29.

———. *Neglected Endings: The Significance of the Pauline Letter Closings.* JSNTSup 101. Sheffield: JSOT Press, 1994.

Weima, Jeffrey A. D., and Stanley E. Porter. *An Annotated Bibliography of 1 and 2 Thessalonians.* NTTS 26. Leiden: Brill, 1998.

Wenham, David. "Paul and the Synoptic Apocalypse." In *Studies of History and Tradition in the Four Gospels*, edited by R. T. France and David Wenham, 345–75. GP 2. Sheffield: JSOT Press, 1981.

Winter, Bruce W. "The Entries and Ethics of Orators and Paul (1 Thess. 2:1–12)." *TynBul* 44 (1993): 55–74.

———. "'If a Man Does Not Wish to Work . . .': A Cultural and Historical Setting for 2 Thessalonians 3:6–16." *TynBul* 40 (1989): 303–15.

Witherington, Ben, III. *Jesus, Paul, and the End of the World: A Comparative Study in New Testament Eschatology*. Downers Grove, IL: InterVarsity, 1992.

Commentaries

Aus, Roger. "2 Thessalonians." In *1–2 Timothy, Titus, 2 Thessalonians*, by Arland J. Hultgren and Roger Aus. ACNT. Minneapolis: Augsburg, 1984.

Beale, G. K. *1–2 Thessalonians*. IVPNTC 13. Downers Grove, IL: InterVarsity, 2003.

Best, Ernest. *1 & 2 Thessalonians*. HNTC. New York: Harper & Row, 1972.

Bridges, Linda McKinnish. *1 & 2 Thessalonians*. SHBC. Macon, GA: Smyth & Helwys, 2008.

Bruce, F. F. *1 & 2 Thessalonians*. WBC 45. Waco: Word, 1982.

Cousar, Charles B. *Reading Galatians, Philippians, and 1 Thessalonians: A Literary and Theological Commentary*. RNT. Macon, GA: Smyth & Helwys, 2001.

Fee, Gordon D. *The First and Second Letters to the Thessalonians*. NICNT. Grand Rapids: Eerdmans, 2009.

Frame, James Everett. *A Critical and Exegetical Commentary on the Epistles of St. Paul to the Thessalonians*. ICC. Edinburgh: T&T Clark, 1912.

Furnish, Victor Paul. *1 Thessalonians, 2 Thessalonians*. ANTC. Nashville: Abingdon, 2004.

Gaventa, Beverly R. *First and Second Thessalonians*. IBC. Louisville: Westminster John Knox, 1998.

Green, Gene L. *The Letters to the Thessalonians*. PNTC. Grand Rapids: Eerdmans, 2002.

Holmes, Michael W. *1 & 2 Thessalonians*. NIVAC. Grand Rapids: Zondervan, 1998.

Juel, Donald H. "1 Thessalonians." In *Galatians, Philippians, Philemon, and 1 Thessalonians*, by Edgar Krentz, John Koenig, and Donald H. Juel. ACNT. Minneapolis: Augsburg, 1985.

Kim, S. *1 and 2 Thessalonians*. WBC. Nashville: Thomas Nelson, forthcoming.

Malherbe, Abraham J. *The Letters to the Thessalonians*. AB 32B. New York: Doubleday, 2000.

Marshall, I. Howard. *1 and 2 Thessalonians*. NCBC. Grand Rapids: Eerdmans, 1983.

Martin, D. Michael. *1, 2 Thessalonians*. NAC. Nashville: Broadman & Holman, 1995.

Menken, Maarten J. J. *2 Thessalonians*. NTR. London: Routledge, 1994.

Moore, A. L. *1 and 2 Thessalonians*. NCBC. London: Nelson, 1969.

Morris, Leon. *The First and Second Epistles to the Thessalonians*. Rev. ed. NICNT. Grand Rapids: Eerdmans, 1991.

Neil, William. *St. Paul's Epistles to the Thessalonians: Introduction and Commentary*. TBC. London: SCM, 1957.

Plummer, Alfred. *A Commentary on St. Paul's First Epistle to the Thessalonians*. London: Robert Scott, 1918.

———. *A Commentary on St. Paul's Second Epistle to the Thessalonians*. London: Robert Scott, 1918.

Richard, Earl J. *First and Second Thessalonians*. SP 11. Collegeville, MN: Liturgical Press, 1995.

Thurston, Bonnie. *Reading Colossians, Ephesians, and 2 Thessalonians: A Literary and Theological Commentary*. RNT. New York: Crossroad, 1995.

Wanamaker, Charles A. *The Epistles to the Thessalonians: A Commentary on the Greek Text*. NIGTC. Grand Rapids: Eerdmans, 1990.

Whiteley, D. E. H. *Thessalonians in the Revised Standard Version: With Introduction and Commentary*. NClarB. Oxford: Oxford University Press, 1969.

Williams, David John. *1 and 2 Thessalonians*. NIBC. Peabody, MA: Hendrickson, 1992.

Witherington, Ben, III. *1 and 2 Thessalonians: A Socio-Rhetorical Commentary*. Grand Rapids: Eerdmans, 2006.

27

First Corinthians

Paul founded the church at Corinth during his second missionary journey, after he had left Athens. Paul emphasizes that he was the founder of the church at Corinth: "For though you have countless guides in Christ, you do not have many fathers. For I became your father in Christ Jesus through the gospel" (1 Cor. 4:15 [cf. 1:14–17; 15:1, 3]). The account in Acts 18 tells how he met Aquila and Priscilla in Corinth (cf. 1 Cor. 16:19), fellow Jewish believers in Jesus who had been driven out of Rome by the edict of Claudius in AD 49[1] and who also happened, like Paul, to be "tentmakers" (i.e., manufacturers of items made of animal skins). After opposition to his preaching, Paul moved from the synagogue[2] to the house next door, the house of Titius Justus (very probably the man whose first name, "Gaius," is used in 1 Cor. 1:14; Rom. 16:23), a wealthy Gentile God-fearer. Also mentioned in Romans 16:23, written from Corinth, is another Corinthian convert, "Erastus, the city treasurer."[3] Many Corinthians believed in the gospel, including even Crispus, the ruler of the synagogue (Acts 18:8; cf. 1 Cor. 1:14). Luke records that Paul remained in Corinth for a year and a half, "teaching the word of God among them" (Acts 18:11).

During the time that Paul stayed in Corinth the Jews eventually brought him before Gallio, the proconsul of Achaea (Acts 18:12–16), an older brother of Seneca, on a charge of persuading people "to worship God contrary to

---

1. Some have favored a date of 41 for the expulsion of the Jews from Rome, but see the persuasive argument in Fitzmyer, *First Corinthians*, 38–40.
2. A Greek inscription on a stone lintel, reading "Synagogue of the Hebrews," has been found at Corinth. See Deissmann, *Light from the Ancient East*, 16.
3. An inscription found at Corinth refers to Erastus, a public official, as having laid a pavement at his own expense. See Harrison, *Paulines and Pastorals*, 100–105.

Author: Universally recognized as one of four main letters of the Apostle Paul.

Date: 54/55, just before Paul's "painful visit" to Corinth.

Addressees: The Christian church at Corinth.

Purpose: To address certain problems that have arisen at Corinth and to answer a number of questions that the church members have raised.

Message/Argument: A wide variety of emphases occur in the book, ranging from discussion of the wisdom of God contrasted with human wisdom, to matters of morality, spiritual gifts, the supremacy of love, and the reality of the resurrection of the body.

Significance: Provides a glimpse into the problems, both practical and doctrinal, faced in a local church and how Paul proceeds to deal with them.

---

the law." Thanks to the discovery of an inscription at Delphi, we know that Gallio was proconsul in 51–52. This provides us with a fixed point in Pauline chronology that enables us to say that Paul was in Corinth very probably from autumn of 50 to early summer of 52.[4] Gallio found no wrongdoing or crime in Paul and thus refused to hear the Jewish complaint, which he referred to as "a matter of questions about words and names and your own law" (Acts 18:15)—that is, an intra-Jewish debate. Undoubtedly it was this decision that made it possible for Paul to remain in Corinth as long as he did. The Jews instead took out their wrath on Sosthenes, described as "the ruler of the synagogue" (probably the successor to Crispus), whom they beat (Acts 18:17) and who himself possibly became a Christian (if we can equate him with the Sosthenes of 1 Cor. 1:1). After this event, Luke says, Paul stayed many days later (to be included in the eighteen months referred to in Acts 18:11) before he sailed for Syria. The final mention of Corinth in Acts tells of Apollos being there (Acts 19:1). For the remainder of Paul's contacts with Corinth we have only the information provided by the Corinthian letters themselves.

The City of Corinth

Corinth was for centuries an important city on the isthmus between central Greece and the Peloponnesus, a north-south crossroad and an east-west corridor because of the two seaports (Cenchreae on the east, Lechaeum on the west) only a few miles apart. Goods were transported across the narrow neck of land from one ship to another. A canal was proposed as early as the sixth century BC and repeatedly afterward, but it came to be built only at the end of the nineteenth century.[5] The ancient Greek Corinth was destroyed by the

---

4. See Hemer, "Observations on Pauline Chronology," 6–9.

5. Murphy-O'Connor, *St. Paul's Corinth*, 88. This monograph is the most helpful text on Corinth.

Romans in 146 BC; Roman Corinth was built anew by Julius Caesar in 44 BC and was made the capital of the Roman province of Achaea (all of Greece south of Macedonia) in 27 BC. Because of its location and its significance, Corinth became well-known in the ancient world. Corinth was one of the most important cities of the Roman world, in Paul's day exceeding even Athens in importance.

Its location made it a place of commerce, wealth, and luxury, which created an upwardly mobile class of nouveau riche. It was known especially for the biennial Isthmian games—athletic games in Greece second only to those of Olympus. It became famous for its valued, especially beautiful "Corinthian bronze."[6] It was diverse in both its population and its religions, which included exotic religions from the East and from Egypt as well as the typical and omnipresent Greek and Roman philosophies and religions, as the ruins of the numerous temples and shrines testify. Corinth put a high value on the Sophistic tradition. It was, furthermore, like other busy cities and seaports, a city where sexual immorality abounded. It was several centuries before Paul, however, that Corinth was most famous for its licentiousness and when the verb "to Corinthianize" became the equivalent of sexual immorality.[7]

The city just described corresponds remarkably with a number of issues raised in the Corinthian letters, to be explored below. The Corinthian church in Paul's day, as we will see, was troubled by divisions (as it was even down to the end of the century, as can be seen from *1 Clement*, written from the church at Rome to the church at Corinth to encourage unity). Jerome Murphy-O'Connor calls attention to the problem of the size of houses: "The difficulty of getting the whole church together regularly in one place goes a long way toward explaining the theological divisions within the Corinthian community (1 Cor. 1–4), but the difficulties of the physical environment also generated other problems when all the believers assembled as a church."[8]

We are, however, not talking about a large community, perhaps as few as fifty or sixty persons. In light of the small numbers, the glory of the first letter written to them by Paul stands out all the more. There were some wealthy and influential church members as well as some from the middle and lower classes (cf. 1:26). It was, furthermore, a church made up not only of some Jewish believers but also mainly of newly converted pagans,[9] and it is perhaps this more than anything else that is responsible for the problems at Corinth, things such as sexual immorality, leanings toward proto-gnostic thinking,

---

6. Ibid., 199–218.

7. Ibid., 56.

8. Ibid., 183.

9. This makes difficult any argument that the basic orientation of the Corinthians goes back to Jewish sources, such as the wisdom speculation of Hellenistic Judaism. See Pearson, *The Pneumatikos-Psychikos Terminology in 1 Corinthians*; Horsley, "Gnosis in Corinth."

ecstatic enthusiasm, attending banquets in idol temples, and an overrealized eschatology.

The Corinthian Correspondence

Paul wrote more letters to Corinth than we have in our NT. These usually are numbered as four or possibly five.[10] After Paul's initial founding of the church in Corinth, he wrote the letters in the following order (note that the fifth one is theoretical, and that the letters in the following list will be used below as references—e.g., "letter A"):

A. The earliest letter that we know of is the one mentioned in 1 Corinthians 5:9: "I wrote to you in my letter not to associate with immoral men" (cf. 5:11, referring probably to the same letter rather than to 1 Corinthians itself). It was written not long after Paul left Corinth, perhaps from Ephesus. Although some have identified this letter with 2 Corinthians 6:14–7:1 (or parts of 1 Corinthians), it almost certainly is no longer extant.[11]

B. **1 Corinthians**, written from Ephesus, in about 54/55.

C. The "sorrowful letter" referred to in 2 Corinthians 2:4; 7:8, written after the "painful visit" made by Paul later in 55. "For I wrote you out of much affliction and anguish of heart and with many tears, not to cause you pain but to let you know the abundant love that I have for you" (2 Cor. 2:4); "For even if I made you sorry with my letter, I do not regret it (though I did regret it), for I see that that letter grieved you, though only for a while. As it is, I rejoice, not because you were grieved, but because you were grieved into repenting; for you felt a godly grief, so that you suffered no loss through us" (2 Cor. 7:8–9 [cf. 7:12]). This letter too is no longer extant, although some have identified it with 2 Corinthians 10–13.

D. **2 Corinthians**, written in 55/56.

E. In theory it is possible that 2 Corinthians 10–13, because of its remarkable change of tone from the immediately preceding chapters, originally was a separate (and last) letter of Paul to Corinth. More likely, however, these chapters were part of 2 Corinthians but were written after Paul had received the most recent report from Corinth.

---

10. If one denies the integrity of one or both of the canonical letters, then the possibility of separate letters can increase at will. Thus, denying the integrity of both letters, Walter Schmithals comes up with a nine-letter hypothesis! See Talbert, *Reading Corinthians*, 6–7.

11. Another well-known reference to a letter of Paul no longer extant is in Colossians 4:16: "And when this letter has been read among you, have it read also in the church of the Laodiceans; and see that you read also the letter from Laodicea."

After the writing of 2 Corinthians Paul once again visited Corinth (ca. 56–57), for a third and apparently last time, as anticipated in 2 Corinthians 12:14; 13:1–2.

The Occasion of First Corinthians

Paul writes 1 Corinthians in response to reports he had received from the church that he had so recently founded. Having already written letter A, he now is forced to write a second letter to address problems reported by the people of Chloe's household (1:11). They have told Paul of quarreling in the church and the emergence of partisans loyal to different key figures: Paul, Apollos, Cephas (= Peter), and even Christ. Just over forty years later, *1 Clement* 47 speaks about factions again evident in the Corinthian church:

> Take up the epistle of that blessed apostle, Paul. What did he write to you at first, at the beginning of his proclamation of the gospel? To be sure he sent you a letter in the Spirit concerning himself and Cephas and Apollos, since you were even then engaged in partisanship. But that partisanship involved you in a relatively minor sin, for you were partisan towards reputable apostles and a man approved by them. But now consider who has corrupted you and diminished the respect you had because of your esteemed love of others. It is shameful, loved ones, exceedingly shameful and unworthy of your conduct in Christ, that the most secure and ancient church of the Corinthians is reported to have created a faction against its presbyters, at the instigation of one or two persons. And this report has reached not only us but even those who stand opposed to us, so that blasphemies have been uttered against the Lord's name because of your foolishness; and you are exposing yourselves to danger. (trans. Ehrman)

The same pattern of conduct criticized by Paul is here criticized in the same church in the mid-90s of the first century, and Clement advises the Corinthians to read again Paul's letter to them.

One of the remarkable things about 1 Corinthians is the extent to which Paul's response to specific problems inspires him to write some of the most glorious passages in his letters.[12] Just after the initial mention of the problem of factions Paul writes a lengthy passage (1:18–2:16) of great beauty and power, contrasting the wisdom of God in the cross with the folly of the world, stressing the impossibility of boasting in the presence of God, his own humility and dependence on the power of the Spirit, and more. Only in 3:3–9 (and 11:18–19) does he return to the problem, with the following conclusion:

> What then is Apollos? What is Paul? Servants through whom you believed, as the Lord assigned to each. I planted, Apollos watered, but God gave the growth. So

---

12. It is perhaps this that causes Raymond Brown to write, "For those studying Paul seriously for the first time, if limitations mean that only one of the thirteen letters can be examined in depth, I Cor may well be the most rewarding" (*An Introduction to the New Testament*, 511).

neither he who plants nor he who waters is anything, but only God who gives the growth. He who plants and he who waters are equal, and each shall receive his wages according to his labor. For we are God's fellow workers; you are God's field, God's building.[13] (3:5–9)

So let no one boast of men. For all things are yours, whether Paul or Apollos or Cephas or the world or life or death or the present or the future, all are yours; and you are Christ's; and Christ is God's. (3:21–23)

Paul briefly addresses one further issue in chapter 4, the apparently over-realized eschatology of the Corinthians, to which he contrasts the sufferings experienced by the Apostles (4:8–13). Then a mention of his sending or having sent Timothy to Corinth (4:17) makes it seem that he might be ready to end his letter. It probably was at this point that he received a new report from Corinth, perhaps delivered by Stephanas, Fortunatus, and Achaicus (16:17), which caused him to take up several new issues.

The beginning of chapter 5 looks very much as if it begins a new section that results from the reception of new information: "It is actually reported that there is immorality among you, and of a kind that is not found even among pagans" (5:1). Similarly, 5:9–10 mentions a misunderstanding of an earlier letter of Paul (letter A).

Apparently, along with the new report from Corinth a list of questions addressed to Paul was delivered to him. Thus at the beginning of chapter 7 we read, "Now concerning the matters about which you wrote" (7:1). The words "now concerning" introduce a formula (*peri de* + genitive) that recurs several times:[14]

- "Now concerning the matters about which you wrote" (7:1)
- "Now concerning the unmarried" (7:25)
- "Now concerning food offered to idols" (8:1)
- "Now concerning spiritual gifts" (12:1)
- "Now concerning the contribution for the saints" (16:1)
- "Now concerning our brother Apollos" (16:12)

These serve as section headings and give 1 Corinthians its unique character among the Pauline Letters. What is really noteworthy, however, is that the sections often deal with a much wider range of content than the questions that were raised. This rich material provides the theological substratum that

13. According to Acts 18:27, Apollos had a significant ministry in Corinth and "greatly helped those who through grace had believed, for he powerfully confuted the Jews in public, showing by the scriptures that the Christ was Jesus."

14. Margaret Mitchell ("Concerning *peri de* in 1 Corinthians") shows, however, that it is hardly a necessity that the formula always introduces a question that had been asked in a communiqué to Paul.

informs the practical instruction given by Paul. This results in the irony that the most significant parts of the letter are those that provide the theological argumentation rather than Paul's answers to specific questions.[15]

An interesting phenomenon occurs in this material whereby Paul apparently quotes slogans of the Corinthians, some of which no doubt had been taught to them by Paul, but which are now being wrongly used:

- "All things are lawful for me" (2x in 6:12)
- "All things are lawful" (2x in 10:23)
- "Food is meant for the stomach and the stomach for food" (6:13)
- "It is well for a man not to touch a woman" (7:1)
- "All of us possess knowledge" (8:1)
- "An idol has no real existence" (8:4)
- "There is no God but one" (8:4)

Paul can agree in principle with these slogans, but he cannot agree with the way in which some of them were being used by the members of the church.

Main Content of First Corinthians

Proceeding consecutively through the letter, we may call attention to various matters that emerge as Paul addresses the key problems in, and the questions of, the Corinthian church.[16]

1 Corinthians 1–4

PROBLEM

Paul tells us next to nothing about what characterized the four parties that he mentions in 1:12. As a pillar of the famous Tübingen hypothesis, F. C. Baur pit Cephas (Peter)[17] and Christ, supposedly arguing for a law-centered gospel, against Paul and Apollos, arguing for a faith-centered gospel.[18] Doubtless there were some differences in the early church on the question of the law,

---

15. John Hurd argues that every part of 1 Corinthians relates to issues that Paul had mentioned in letter A (mentioned in 5:9), and that "every section of this letter relates to the group of disputes which resulted from Paul's attempt to obtain the Corinthians' conformity to the Apostolic Decree" (*The Origin of 1 Corinthians*, 295).

16. For useful discussion, see Hurd, *The Origin of 1 Corinthians*; Horrell, *The Social Ethos of the Corinthian Correspondence*; Eriksson, *Traditions as Rhetorical Proof*; Winter, *After Paul Left Corinth*.

17. See Barrett, "Cephas and Corinth."

18. Michael Goulder (*Paul and the Competing Mission in Corinth*) develops the view of Baur into the unconvincing hypothesis that the two missionizing parties (Paul and the "Petrines")

but not of the dimensions assumed by Baur. Paul himself, however, gives us no hint as to what views may have divided the factions.[19] The problem may have been simply personal loyalties that turned divisive. Although Baur's analysis has long been discredited,[20] the ghost of the Tübingen hypothesis has continued to haunt NT scholarship. What seems significant is not so much what view or views these factions may have held[21] but rather the fact of opposition to Paul himself. "The most serious form of 'division' is that between the majority of the community and Paul himself. They stand over against him on almost every issue. The key issue here is their calling his authority into question."[22]

Although it seems that the Corinthians were all too ready to be influenced by the Sophistic tradition of competitive oratory (note "the debater of this age" in 1:20), on the basis of which they apparently gave their loyalty to one or another orator (e.g., especially Apollos, who was well known for his eloquence [see Acts 18:24]),[23] Paul refuses to depend upon the power of rhetorical persuasion or "eloquent wisdom" (1:17), relying instead upon the "demonstration of the Spirit and of power" (2:4). Yet for those who rightly perceive, Paul's wisdom, "not a wisdom of this age," was "a secret and hidden wisdom of God" (2:6–7), "interpreting spiritual truths to those who possess the Spirit" (2:13).[24]

This language has led some to conclude that Paul had to deal with proto-gnostic ideas at Corinth.[25] Some of the favorite gnostic vocabulary is used often in 1 Corinthians: *gnōsis*, "knowledge" (1:5; 8:1, 7, 10, 11; 12:8; 13:2, 8; 14:6); *sophia*, "wisdom" (1:17, 19, 20, 21, 22, 24, 30; 2:1, 4, 5, 6, 7, 13; 3:19; 12:8);

---

disagreed not just on the place of the law, but on nearly everything discussed in the Corinthian letters and more.

19. L. L. Welborn ("On the Discord in Corinth") finds the key to the factions in political strife rather than in theological differences.

20. "More than one hundred years of research since Baur has made it clear that there is no real trace of 'Judaizers' at Corinth, at least not at the time of 1 Corinthians" (Dahl, "Paul and the Church at Corinth according to 1 Corinthians 1:10–4:21," 314).

21. Margaret Mitchell (*Paul and the Rhetoric of Reconciliation*) concludes that 1 Corinthians as a whole presents deliberative rhetoric that proposes concord in place of the factionalism that has emerged at Corinth. See also Baird, "'One against the Other.'"

22. Fee, *The First Epistle to the Corinthians*, 8. "Thus the letter is basically the apostle vis-à-vis the whole Corinthian congregation" (ibid., 10). See Marshall, *Enmity in Corinth*; Burke and Elliott, *Paul and the Corinthians*.

23. See Winter, *Philo and Paul among the Sophists*, 141–239. See also Litfin, *St. Paul's Theology of Proclamation*; Pogoloff, *Logos and Sophia*.

24. On this passage, see Stuhlmacher, "The Hermeneutical Significance of 1 Corinthians 2:6–16."

25. The tendency to explain 1 Corinthians as responding to full-blown Gnosticism (as argued classically by Schmithals, *Gnosticism in Corinth*) is regarded now as unconvincing because it has become evident that Gnosticism proper is a second-century phenomenon. But that there probably was a kind of incipient gnosticism (i.e., various gnostic tendencies) in the first century seems hard to deny. R. McL. Wilson remarks, "What we have at Corinth, then, is not yet Gnosticism, but a kind of *gnosis*" ("Gnosis at Corinth," 112). See also Barrett, "Christianity at Corinth."

pneumatikos, "spiritual"[26] (2:13, 15; 3:1; 9:11; 10:3, 4; 12:1; 14:1, 37; 15:44, 46). The overrealized eschatology[27] in 4:8–13 expresses a theology of glory consistent with a gnostic perspective, as does also the denial of the resurrection of the body in 15:12–13, 35. The unusual statement "Jesus be cursed!" (12:3) can be explained as a reflection of gnostic dualism[28]—that is, the rejection of the humanity of Jesus in favor of the spiritual Christ. Ecstatic speech (14:1–40) fits the pattern. So too the attitude to practical matters expressing a negative view of materiality, such as being oblivious to food and stomach (6:13) and sexual immorality (6:13–20), and also, paradoxically, the hyper-ascetic denial of marriage relations (7:1–6).

Whether one attributes these phenomena to an incipient gnosticism or to a general Hellenistic dualism does not seem terribly important. More unlikely, however, is the explanation that the Corinthian Christians, who were Gentiles with pagan backgrounds (12:2), could here be under the influence of Jewish wisdom theology[29] or Hellenistic Jewish mysticism.

Response

In dealing with the divisive partisanship exhibiting itself in Corinth, Paul points, in the first instance, to the paradox of the cross as the power of God (1:17, 18) and to "Christ crucified" as "the power of God and the wisdom of God" (1:23, 24). This crucified Christ has been made "our wisdom, our righteousness and sanctification and redemption" (1:30). In the light of the cross of Christ, human wisdom fades to nothing (1:20), and the very possibility of human boasting is excluded (1:29, 31). All through this section Paul quotes or alludes to the OT Scriptures.[30]

And it is for these reasons that Paul did not parade any human wisdom before the Corinthians but instead preached the message of the cross[31] so that their "faith might not rest in the wisdom of men but in the power of God" (2:5). Paul, through the Spirit of God, has been enabled to "understand the gifts bestowed on us by God" (2:12); he has "the mind of Christ" (2:16).

In 3:1–9 Paul reproaches the Corinthians for their fleshly perspective. God alone provides growth; God alone will test the work of his servants, and

26. See Painter, "Paul and the *pneumatikoi* at Corinth."

27. See Thiselton, "Realized Eschatology at Corinth."

28. Anthony Thiselton instead speaks of an "eschatological dualism" (ibid., 516–17). "We have tried to show that at several specific points in the epistle an exegesis in terms of eschatology and spiritual enthusiasm is preferable to one in terms of gnosticism" (ibid., 526).

29. Richard Horsley ("Gnosis in Corinth") finds the source of this perspective in Philo and Wisdom of Solomon. See also Horsley, "Pneumatikos vs. Psychikos." James Davis (*Wisdom and Spirit*) appeals to the connection between Wisdom and Torah.

30. See Williams, *The Wisdom of the Wise*; Heil, *The Rhetorical Role of Scripture in 1 Corinthians*.

31. See Pickett, *The Cross in Corinth*; Lampe, "Theological Wisdom and the 'Word about the Cross.'"

therefore they must be careful in what they do (3:10–17). As the temple of the Spirit, they are holy (3:16–17).[32] Paul once again argues against boasting (note "arrogant people" in 4:19) and human wisdom (3:18–4:7). Worthy commendation comes from God alone, and so Paul is unconcerned about human judgments that may be directed against him (4:1–5).

Paul sets the Corinthians' triumphant, overrealized eschatology against the suffering of the Apostles for the sake of the gospel (4:8–14), and then finally he reasserts his apostolic authority as founder and spiritual father of the church (4:15–16).[33] Paul promises to come to Corinth, but he wonders out loud what his demeanor will need to be (4:21).

1 Corinthians 5

PROBLEM

Paul now turns to a new set of problems (chaps. 5–6) that grow out of a new report that probably he had just received. The first of these involves a grievous example of sexual immorality that exceeds even that of the pagans. Even worse, the Corinthians are arrogant and boastful of their lack of inhibition.

RESPONSE

The man guilty of committing a sexual offense with his father's wife is to be expelled from the fellowship of the church (5:2, 7, 13).[34] Paul's mind turns to the cleansing of the house from leaven in connection with the celebration of Passover, which makes him think automatically of the sacrifice of "Christ, our paschal lamb" (5:7). The last point that he makes is that the separation from sinners (which he had addressed in his earlier letter [letter A] to them) applies only to church members, not to those in the world, "since then you would need to go out of the world" (5:10).[35]

1 Corinthians 6:1–8

PROBLEM

Christians were taking other Christians to secular law courts, where non-Christians adjudicated. Paul emphasizes that if the saints are to judge the world and angels too (6:2–3), they should be entrusted with judging the mundane matters of this life. Paul saw it as scandalous that Christians were bringing their disputes before unbelievers (6:6). He makes his argument using no less than

---

32. See Hogeterp, *Paul and God's Temple*, 295–359.

33. See Burke, "Paul's Role as 'Father' to His Corinthian 'Children' in Socio-Historical Context (1 Cor. 4:14–21")"; Wanamaker, "A Rhetoric of Power."

34. The directive "to deliver this man to Satan for the destruction of the flesh" (5:5) is very obscure, especially if taken as something more than expulsion from the church.

35. See Pascuzzi, *Ethics, Ecclesiology, and Church Discipline*.

eight or nine rhetorical questions. It may well be that the abuses here were on the part of the wealthy of the community against the poor.[36] Bengt Holmberg concludes, "The rich and socially more powerful Christians were the leaders in the Corinthian congregation, and they created most of the problems that the apostle addresses in his Corinthian correspondence."[37]

RESPONSE

Such disputes should be brought before a member of the Christian community. But better than that, Paul encourages them not to bring such cases at all. To have lawsuits at all is a defeat. "Why not rather suffer wrong? Why not rather be defrauded?" (6:7).

1 Corinthians 6:9–20

PROBLEM

The Corinthians continue in immorality, especially sexual immorality, citing the slogan "All things are lawful for me" (6:12). The pagan background of the Corinthian Christians probably explains this problem. There is more than a touch of gnostic dualism in the idea that what one does with one's body in of little significance (6:13).

RESPONSE

They are ignoring their present status. In Christ and in the Spirit they have been "washed . . . sanctified . . . justified" (6:11 [cf. 1:2, 30]). Sexual sins are sins against one's own body and contradict the fact that the "body is a temple of the Holy Spirit." The body is important because it comes "from God" (6:19) and is meant "for the Lord" (6:13). Furthermore, Paul says, alluding to the cross of Christ, "You were bought with a price" (6:20; cf. 7:23) and therefore should "glorify God in your body" (6:20).[38]

1 Corinthians 7:1–24

QUESTION(S)

The initial question in this section concerns the propriety of sexual relations within marriage—again prompted perhaps by gnostic strains of thought—which leads in turn to a discussion of marriage (and divorce) itself, broadening

36. See Horrell, *The Social Ethos of the Corinthian Correspondence*, 111.
37. Holmberg, "The Methods of Historical Reconstruction in the Scholarly 'Recovery' of Corinthian Christianity," 261. "Thus what may look at first like theological and ethical problems and discussions are actually caused more by social factors like stratum-specific behavior patterns operative in the everyday life of these Christians than by differing religious perspectives or theological traditions" (ibid.).
38. See Rosner, "Temple Prostitution in 1 Corinthians 6:12–20."

to other matters in light of Paul's imminent expectation of the end of the present order. Again the Corinthians quote a slogan: "It is well for a man not to touch a woman."[39]

RESPONSE

Sexual relations rightly belong and are vital to the marriage relationship, and they serve as a natural protection against sexual immorality. Depending upon his knowledge of the teaching of Jesus via oral tradition, Paul conveys the charge not to divorce, and he does so, notably, without the so-called Matthean exception (Matt. 6:32; 19:9)—applied both to women and men (who alone, in Judaism, had the right to divorce). Paul himself recommends against a believer divorcing an unbelieving spouse who is willing for the relationship to continue.

1 Corinthians 7:25–40

QUESTION

The implied question apparently concerns whether "the unmarried" (lit., "virgins") should get married or not, and in effect it is an extension of potential changes discussed in 7:17–24.

RESPONSE

The key to understanding Paul's teaching in this section, as in the preceding section (7:17–24), is his conviction that the end of the age was very near: "in view of the present [enestōsan, which can mean "impending"] distress" (7:26); "the appointed time has grown very short" (7:29); "the form [to schēma] of this world is passing away [paragei]" (7:31). This viewpoint is responsible for Paul's acceptance of the status quo for circumcised/uncircumcised, slave/free person, and married/unmarried. Given the shortness of time that remains, changes are unnecessary, and under the circumstances to get married would only increase anxiety (7:32–35).[40]

1 Corinthians 8:1–13

QUESTION

Cannot food that has been offered to idols be eaten by Christians, especially by those who have knowledge that there is only one God and therefore that idols do not exist?

RESPONSE

Reacting to the slogan "There is no God but one" (8:4), Paul writes, in 8:6, one of his most significant christological passages:

39. See Fee, "1 Corinthians 7:1–7 Revisited."
40. See Deming, *Paul on Marriage and Celibacy.*

Yet for us there is one God, the Father,
  from whom are all things and for whom we exist,
and one Lord, Jesus Christ,
  through whom are all things and through whom we exist.[41]

For Paul, eating food offered to idols falls into the category of *adiaphora*, matters of indifference (8:8). He worries only about the conscience of the weaker brother or sister, for whose sake he will deny himself the freedom to eat.[42]

1 Corinthians 9:1–27

QUESTION

Although lacking the usual introductory formula, the question addressed in this chapter concerns Paul's apostolic identity and demeanor. Why does he not receive the material support that he would be entitled to?

RESPONSE

Paul unhesitatingly affirms his apostleship (about which he was never shy!): "Am I not an apostle? Have I not seen Jesus our Lord? . . . If to others I am not an apostle, at least I am to you; for you are the seal of my apostleship in the Lord" (9:1–2). After a forceful defense of his right to material support, that "those who proclaim the gospel should get their living by the gospel" (9:14), he notes his refusal to make use of it, saying, "We endure anything rather than put an obstacle in the way of the gospel of Christ" (9:12), so that "in my preaching I may make the gospel free of charge" (9:18).

This discussion leads Paul to write two remarkable passages. First, he states his willingness to "become all thing to all men," specifically to be like Gentiles when living among the Gentiles and like Jews when among Jews, all "for the sake of the gospel" (9:19–23).[43] Second, making use of athletic metaphors so familiar to the Corinthians, Paul refers to his own agonistic practice of discipleship (9:24–27).

1 Corinthians 10:1–11:1

QUESTION

In this section Paul reverts to the questions discussed in chapter 8 concerning idols and food offered to idols.

---

41. The pronouns are crucial in this quatrain, with the agency of Christ in view ("through," *dia*, used twice). On this passage, see Denaux, "Theology and Christology in 1 Cor 8,4–6."
42. See Dawes, "The Danger of Idolatry"; Cheung, *Idol Food in Corinth*; Newton, *Deity and Diet*.
43. See Barton, "'All Things to All People.'"

RESPONSE

Even though the Israelites had been delivered under Moses' leadership,[44] they lapsed into idol worship. Idols and food offered to idols are nothing, Paul reasserts (10:19; cf. 8:4). In Paul's view, however, demons are real, and he associates them with idols, which therefore are to be avoided (10:20–22). Paul stands by the principle "All things are lawful" (10:23; cf. 6:12). Again he immediately adds the qualification "but not all things are helpful," and further here, "not all things build up." Food that had been offered to idols was not an issue for Paul. What mattered, and was of supreme importance, is not offending the conscience of another for the sake of "my own advantage" (10:33).[45]

1 Corinthians 11:2–34

PROBLEM(S)

Whether asked by the Corinthians or not, Paul turns to address two matters concerning public worship. First, women should be veiled in church. The hierarchical perspective expressed in 11:3, 8–9 is somewhat softened in the teaching of 11:11–12: "Nevertheless, in the Lord woman is not independent of man nor man of woman; for as woman was made from man, so man is now born of woman. And all things are from God."[46] Second, improper conduct at the celebration of the Lord's Supper has been injurious to the fellowship of the church. Some members, probably the wealthy, apparently arrived early, ate their fill, and even became drunk, thus humiliating "those who have nothing" (11:22).

RESPONSE

The actions of these people violated the spirit of the very thing being celebrated, the sacrificial death of Christ. In providing a response, Paul cites the liturgy of the supper (11:23–26), received by him from tradition (11:23). It is unthinkable for him that the selfish behavior of the Corinthians at the celebration of the supper is in any way consistent with the content of this tradition.[47] At the end of this section Paul tantalizingly mentions directions about "other things" that he will give them when he comes (11:34).

---

44. Paul appears to allude to rabbinic tradition in the reference to the rock that followed the Israelites in the wilderness (10:4). He may depend on the association of the rock with Wisdom (as in, e.g., Philo, *Leg.* 2.86) in identifying it as Christ. See Bandstra, "Interpretation in 1 Corinthians 10:1–11"; Collier, "'That We Might Not Crave Evil'"; Enns, "The 'Moveable Well' in 1 Corinthians 10:4."

45. It is important to note that 10:28–29a is a parenthesis, and that the logic of 10:29b ("for") connects with 10:27.

46. See Fitzmyer, "*Kephalē* in 1 Corinthians 11:3."

47. See Das, "1 Corinthians 11:17–34 Revisited."

1 Corinthians 12:1–14:40

PROBLEM

Another specific question is raised by the Corinthians, this time concerning "spiritual gifts" (*tōn pneumatikōn*, possibly to be translated as "spiritual persons"). The issue seems to have been how important particular spiritual gifts were, in particular the gift of speaking in tongues, which occupies most of chapter 14.

RESPONSE

Paul begins with a long section on the diversity of gifts endowed by the same Holy Spirit (12:1–11); then he presents a discourse on the unity of the body of Christ (12:12–31) in which he emphasizes the interdependence of its various parts. He concludes, "Now you are the body of Christ and individually members of it" (12:27). At the end of this section he says, "But earnestly desire the higher gifts" (12:31), but then adds a reference to "a still more excellent way."

This is followed by one of the most glorious passages of the NT—indeed, of all literature—the exalted description of love (chap. 13). The exercise of spiritual gifts without love amounts to nothing. Furthermore, the jealousy, arrogance, and boasting that are reflected in the party spirit at Corinth are simply inconsistent with love (13:4–7).[48]

Finally, in chapter 14 Paul turns directly to the issue of speaking in tongues, a subject indirectly in view in chapters 12–13. Paul's central premise is articulated in 14:12: "So with yourselves; since you are eager for manifestations of the Spirit, strive to excel in building up the church." Speaking in tongues in public worship must therefore always be accompanied by interpretation. "In church I would rather speak five words with my mind, in order to instruct others, than ten thousand words in a tongue" (14:19). "Prophecy"—understood not as foretelling the future but rather as presenting a (spontaneous) message from God to the church—is to be preferred to speaking in tongues.[49] "Let all things be done for edification" (14:26) and "in order," for "God is not a God of confusion but of peace" (14:40, 33).

Because 14:34–35, instruction about women keeping silent in the churches, seems to be an intrusion and is found in the Western textual tradition *after* 14:40, Gordon Fee regards these verses as a marginal gloss later inserted into the text of the letter.[50] But no extant manuscripts of 1 Corinthians lack the verses.[51]

---

48. Omitting the negatives in chapter 13 provides a virtual portrait of the Corinthian church. See Hurd, *The Origin of I Corinthians*, 112.

49. See Sandnes, "Prophecy—A Sign for Believers (1 Cor 14,20–25)."

50. Fee, *The First Epistle to the Corinthians*, 699–708. So too Payne, *Man and Woman, One in Christ*, 263–67.

51. See Niccum, "The Voice of the Manuscripts on the Silence of Women." For a helpful discussion of the meaning of the verses, see Garland, *1 Corinthians*, 664–73.

1 Corinthians 15:1–58

PROBLEM

Some at Corinth apparently denied the resurrection of the dead (15:12).

RESPONSE

Paul presents an important summary of the kerygma that constitutes his gospel (15:1–11), at the heart of which is the death and resurrection of Jesus. He goes on to argue that if there is no resurrection of the dead, then Christ cannot have risen from the dead, and so the faith of Christians is in vain (15:16–17). Paul next engages in a salvation-historical explication of the resurrection of Christ as the answer to Adam's sin and the death that it brought on humankind (15:20–28).[52]

A parenthetical paragraph (15:29–34) interrupts the flow of thought. If the dead are not raised, then why be prepared to die early, as Paul was?[53]

Paul finally turns again to the resurrection and to the nature of the resurrection body (15:35–58). Once again he makes use of the parallel between Adam and Christ (cf. 15:21–22), now referring to the first and the last Adam, the man "of dust" and the man "of heaven" (15:45–50). Believers will bear the image of the latter just as they bear the image of the former, and this will involve a new "spiritual body" (*sōma pneumatikon* [15:44–45]), a body, but not one of flesh and blood (15:50). This leads Paul to the exultant statement in 15:51–57, the jubilant words "death is swallowed up in victory" and the thanksgiving "to God, who gives us the victory through our Lord Jesus Christ."[54]

1 Corinthians 16:1–11

QUESTION AND RESPONSE

How will the contribution to the poor in Jerusalem be accomplished? Paul gives practical instructions about the collecting of money on Sundays. This leads Paul to a brief mention of his evolving plans, subject always to the will of God (16:7). He asks that Timothy be received well (16:10–11; cf. 4:17).

1 Corinthians 16:12

QUESTION AND RESPONSE

If a question underlies this verse, possibly the Corinthians had asked about the plans of Apollos and whether he was coming to Corinth. Paul says that he "strongly urged" Apollos to go to Corinth, but it was not God's will at this point (such is the probable meaning of the absolute use of "will" here).

52. Verse 28 refers probably to a functional subordination rather than an ontological subordination of the Son to the Father.

53. It is difficult to know what is in view in the reference to baptism "on behalf of the dead." For discussion, see Thiselton, *The First Epistle to the Corinthians*, 1242–49.

54. See de Boer, *The Defeat of Death*.

1 Corinthians 16:13–24

This concluding section of the letter contains the usual final exhortations (16:13–18), greetings (especially from Aquila and Prisca), and a final handwritten note from Paul himself.

Major Theological Emphases of First Corinthians

From the letter, it is clear that the Corinthians had, in short, not understood the ramifications of the gospel for the living of daily life in the community of believers. At the end of his initial appeal for unity Paul stresses that he was called "to preach the gospel," which he identifies as "the word of the cross" (1:17–18). This brings him immediately to the articulation of the gospel in these words:"For since, in the wisdom of God, the world did not know God through wisdom, it pleased God through the folly of what we preach [the kerygma] to save those who believe. For Jews demand signs and Greeks seek wisdom, but we preach Christ crucified,[55] a stumbling block to Jews and folly to Gentiles, but to those who are called, both Jews and Greeks, Christ the power of God and the wisdom of God" (1:21–24).

Joseph Fitzmyer regards this passage as expressing the key to Pauline theology in general and as the best summary of "the heart of the Apostle's theological teaching."[56] This "word of the cross" is in view also in other places (15:3–5, 12, 14; so too in "the gospel" [4:15; 9:12–18, 23]). This perspective is basic virtually to all that follows, for the word of the cross turns everything on its head, reversing the world's values. This paradoxical message of weakness that is powerful, of foolishness that is wisdom, of death that leads to life is what is needed for the complete transformation of the worldly perspective and values of the Corinthians. Christ is the power and the wisdom of God; Christ and the message of the cross therefore are the answer to the problems of the Corinthian church.

As we have seen, the combination of time-bound specifics with timeless theological teaching in this letter creates an odd combination. Paul had little interest in abstract theology. For him, theological thinking arises out of and informs the practical life situations of Christians in the world. The result is that, unlike Romans, there is no real organization to the theology in 1 Corinthians, and therefore it is difficult to summarize. Victor Paul Furnish has, however, given us the following helpful sentence:

> Summarized formally, in terms of traditional theological categories, the prevailing Corinthian interpretation of the gospel had departed from Paul's own interpretation of it in four critical respects: christologically, by taking little or

55. As if to emphasize the scandal of the cross to Jews, Paul puts the two words next to each other, "Christ crucified," surely an oxymoron to Jews, as it was to Saul before his conversion.
56. Fitzmyer, *First Corinthians*, 69.

no account of Jesus' death; soteriologically, by misconstruing the meaning of one's freedom in Christ; eschatologically, by failing to appreciate the apostle's dialectical understanding of salvation, as both "already" and "not yet"; and ecclesiologically, by neglecting the corporate dimensions of life in Christ.[57]

Although we have noted these points above, it is worth briefly expanding them as a way to pull the letter together theologically.

1. *Christology*. The high point christologically in the letter is found in 8:6, where Christ is put in parallel with God, the "one Lord" next to the "one God." Christ is also described as "the wisdom of God" (1:24). But Christ is not to be understood apart from the cross. We have already noted the importance of the "word of the cross," which is the heart of the kerygma, "Christ crucified" (1:23; cf. 15:3). Also highly significant is the reference to Christ as the "last Adam" (15:45), which makes him the pivot point of salvation (15:22), analogous to the first Adam, the pivot point of the fall. Christ therefore is described as "our . . . redemption" (1:30), who bought us with a price (6:20; 7:23).

2. *Soteriology*. Salvation by grace—that is, free salvation[58]—becomes a serious distortion if it results in sinful living. The freedom that is rightly the Christian's can easily be misused. The slogan "All things are lawful for me" (6:12; 10:23) must be balanced with the Pauline emphasis that "not all things build up." The Corinthians were not living in accord with what they should have learned from the cross of Christ and the example of Paul. They needed to rediscover the reality of sanctification and the call to holiness. "Although Paul clearly understands that the gospel sets one free and thus gives one *exousia* ('authority, rights,' 6:12; 9:1–2, 19; 10:23), this is not for him the basis of ethical conduct—because as in the case of the Corinthians it can be abused (6:12–20; 8:9)."[59]

3. *Eschatology*. The Corinthians, for whatever reasons, were inclined to an overrealized eschatology (e.g., 4:8). Present fulfillment occupied their triumphalist thoughts to the extent that it obscured the reality of the present overlap of the ages and the actuality of the "not yet" that it necessitates. The church awaits the consummation at the parousia of Christ (15:23), and at the end of the letter Paul utters the Aramaic prayer *marana tha*, "Our Lord, come!" (16:22).

4. *Ecclesiology*. Members of the Corinthian church have not grasped that they had been incorporated into the body of Christ as a unified

57. Furnish, *The Theology of the First Letter to the Corinthians*, 12. For his elaboration of these themes, see ibid., 124–31.

58. On justification by faith in the Corinthian letters, see Fung, "Justification by Faith in 1 & 2 Corinthians."

59. Fee, "Toward a Theology of 1 Corinthians," 53.

communion, of which they were interdependent members. Following the model of Christ and of Paul, they needed to learn to care for others in all that they did, always acting in ways that edified them in their faith. "In their belonging to the resurrected-crucified Christ, believers are formed into a community that lives from the cross and are called to be agents of God's love, both individually and corporately, within the particularities of their own time and place."[60]

Integrity, Date, Author

Integrity

The unity of 1 Corinthians, unlike 2 Corinthians, is accepted by the great majority of NT scholars. Partition theories almost always involve a degree of speculation that far exceeds the probability that Paul's Letters contain tensions.[61] The abrupt shifts in 1 Corinthians that give it its disjointed character usually are explained by how Paul is answering the questions posed to him by the members of the church, probably in the arbitrary order in which he received them. Because, however, as we have seen above, Paul probably received a report from Stephanas, Fortunatus, and Achaicus (16:17) with new information along with the list of questions that caused him to begin a new section of his letter in chapter 5, there is a sense in which the letter may be conceived of as a composite of separate parts. Thus, Martinus de Boer writes, "1 Corinthians, then, is in a qualified sense a composite of two letters, *a composite of Paul's own making.*"[62]

Date

The Gallio inscription, as we have seen, enables us to determine the approximate date of 1 Corinthians with a relative degree of certainty. It was written from Ephesus, probably late in 54, or early in 55, shortly before Paul's "painful visit."

Author

First Corinthians is one of the four *Hauptbriefe* ("chief letters") of Paul (together with Romans, Galatians, and 2 Corinthians), whose authenticity is accepted nearly universally. Paul clearly is the main author of the letter. The

---

60. Furnish, *The Theology of the First Letter to the Corinthians*, 121.

61. For a survey of partition theories, see Hurd, *The Origin of 1 Corinthians*, 43–47. Because of the perceived tensions between 10:1–22 and discussions of the same subject in 8:1–13; 10:23–11:1, some have argued that 10:1–22 was a separate letter. There have also been suggestions that chapter 13 was an independent composition.

62. de Boer, "The Composition of 1 Corinthians," 230–31. On the unity of the letter, see Belleville, "Continuity or Discontinuity." Italics in original.

degree of Sosthenes's involvement (1:1), although difficult to determine, probably was minimal. Since Paul made use of a secretary (cf. 16:21), it is possible that Sosthenes served in that role.

Bibliography

Books and Articles

Adams, Edward, and David G. Horrell, eds. *Christianity at Corinth: The Quest for the Pauline Church*. Louisville: Westminster John Knox, 2004.

Baird, William. "'One against the Other': Intra-Church Conflict in 1 Corinthians." In *The Conversation Continues: Studies in Paul and John in Honor of J. Louis Martyn*, edited by Robert T. Fortna and Beverly R. Gaventa, 116–36. Nashville: Abingdon, 1990.

Bandstra, Andrew J. "Interpretation in 1 Corinthians 10:1–11." *CTJ* 6 (1971): 5–21.

Barclay, John M. G. "Thessalonians and Corinth: Social Contrasts in Pauline Christianity." *JSNT* 47 (1992): 49–74.

Barrett, C. K. "Cephas and Corinth." In *Essays on Paul*, 28–39. Philadelphia: Westminster, 1982.

———. "Christianity at Corinth." In *Essays on Paul*, 1–27. Philadelphia: Westminster, 1982.

———. "Sectarian Diversity at Corinth." In *Paul and the Corinthians: Studies on a Community in Conflict; Essays in Honour of Margaret Thrall*, edited by Trevor J. Burke and J. K. Elliot, 287–302. NovTSup 109. Leiden: Brill, 2003.

Barton, Stephen C. "'All Things to All People': Paul and the Law in the Light of 1 Corinthians 9:19–23." In *Paul and the Mosaic Law: The Third Durham-Tübingen Research Symposium on Earliest Christianity and Judaism, Durham, September, 1994*, edited by James D. G. Dunn, 271–85. WUNT 89. Tübingen: Mohr Siebeck, 1996.

Belleville, Linda L. "Continuity or Discontinuity: A Fresh Look at 1 Corinthians in the Light of First-Century Epistolary Forms and Conventions." *EvQ* 59 (1987): 15–37.

Bieringer, Reimund, ed. *The Corinthian Correspondence*. BETL 125. Leuven: Leuven University Press, 1996.

Borgen, Peder. "'Yes,' 'No,' 'How Far?': The Participation of Jews and Christians in Pagan Cults." In *Paul and His Hellenistic Context*, edited by Troels Engberg-Pedersen, 30–59. SNTW. Edinburgh: T&T Clark, 1994.

Brown, Alexandra R. *The Cross and Human Transformation: Paul's Apocalyptic Word in 1 Corinthians*. Minneapolis: Fortress, 1995.

Brown, Raymond E. *An Introduction to the New Testament*. New York: Doubleday, 1997.

Burke, Trevor J. "Paul's Role as 'Father' to His Corinthian 'Children' in Socio-Historical Context (1 Cor. 4:14–21)." In *Paul and the Corinthians: Studies on a Community in Conflict; Essays in Honour of Margaret Thrall*, edited by Trevor J. Burke and J. K. Elliot, 95–113. NovTSup 109. Leiden: Brill, 2003.

Burke, Trevor J., and J. K. Elliott, eds. *Paul and the Corinthians: Studies on a Community in Conflict; Essays in Honour of Margaret Thrall*. NovTSup 109. Leiden: Brill, 2003.

Carson, D. A. *Showing the Spirit: A Theological Exposition of 1 Corinthians 12–14*. Grand Rapids: Baker Academic, 1987.

Cheung, Alex T. *Idol Food in Corinth: Jewish Background and Pauline Legacy*. JSNTSup 176. Sheffield: Sheffield Academic Press, 1999.

Chow, John K. *Patronage and Power: A Study of Social Networks in Corinth*. JSNTSup 75. Sheffield: JSOT Press, 1992.

Clarke, Andrew D. *Secular and Christian Leadership in Corinth: A Socio-Historical and Exegetical Study of 1 Corinthians 1–6*. AGJU 18. Leiden: Brill, 1993.

Collier, Gary D. "'That We Might Not Crave Evil': The Structure and Argument of 1 Corinthians 10:1–13." *JSNT* 55 (1994): 55–75.

Dahl, Nils A. "A Fragment and Its Context: 2 Corinthians 6:14–7:1." In *Studies in Paul*, 62–69. Minneapolis: Augsburg, 1972.

———. "Paul and the Church at Corinth according to 1 Corinthians 1:10–4:21." In *Christian History and Interpretation: Studies Presented to John Knox*, edited by William R. Farmer, C. F. D. Moule, and Richard R. Niebuhr, 313–35. Cambridge: Cambridge University Press, 1967.

Das, A. Andrew. "1 Corinthians 11:17–34 Revisited." *CTQ* 62 (1998): 187–208.

Davis, James A. *Wisdom and Spirit: An Investigation of 1 Corinthians 1:18–3:20 against the Background of Jewish Sapiential Traditions in the Greco-Roman Period*. Lanham, MD: University Press of America, 1984.

Dawes, Gregory W. "The Danger of Idolatry: First Corinthians 8:7–13." *CBQ* 58 (1996): 82–98.

de Boer, Martinus C. "The Composition of 1 Corinthians." *NTS* 40 (1994): 229–45.

———. *The Defeat of Death: Apocalyptic Eschatology in 1 Corinthians 15 and Romans 5*. JSNTSup 22. Sheffield: JSOT Press, 1988.

Deissmann, Adolf. *Light from the Ancient East: The New Testament Illustrated by Recently Discovered Texts of the Graeco-Roman World*. Translated by Lionel R. M. Strachan. Reprint, Grand Rapids: Baker Academic, 1978.

Deming, Will. *Paul on Marriage and Celibacy: The Hellenistic Background of 1 Corinthians 7*. 2nd ed. Grand Rapids: Eerdmans, 2004.

Denaux, A. "Theology and Christology in 1 Cor 8,4–6: A Contextual-Redactional Reading." In *The Corinthian Correspondence*, edited by Reimund Bieringer, 593–606. BETL 125. Leuven: Leuven University Press, 1996.

Dunn, James D. G. *1 Corinthians*. NTG. Sheffield: Sheffield Academic Press, 1995.

———. "Reconstructions of Corinthian Christianity and the Interpretation of 1 Corinthians." In *Christianity at Corinth: The Quest for the Pauline Church*, edited by Edward Adams and David G. Horrell, 295–310. Louisville: Westminster John Knox, 2004.

Ellis, E. Earle. "*Sōma* in First Corinthians." *Int* 44 (1990): 132–44.

Engels, Donald. *Roman Corinth: An Alternative Model for the Classical City*. Chicago: University of Chicago Press, 1990.

Enns, Peter E. "The 'Moveable Well' in 1 Corinthians 10:4: An Extrabiblical Tradition in an Apostolic Text." *BBR* 6 (1996): 23–38.

Eriksson, Anders. *Traditions as Rhetorical Proof: Pauline Argumentation in 1 Corinthians*. ConBNT 29. Stockholm: Almqvist & Wiksell, 1998.

Fee, Gordon D. "1 Corinthians 7:1–7 Revisited." In *Paul and the Corinthians: Studies on a Community in Conflict; Essays in Honour of Margaret Thrall*, edited by Trevor J. Burke and J. K. Elliott, 197–213. NovTSup 109. Leiden: Brill, 2003.

———. "Toward a Theology of 1 Corinthians." In *1 & 2 Corinthians*. Vol. 2 of *Pauline Theology*, edited by David M. Hay, 37–58. Minneapolis: Fortress, 1993.

Fitzmyer, Joseph A. "*Kephalē* in 1 Corinthians 11:3." *Int* 47 (1993): 32–59.

Fotopoulos, John. *Food Offered to Idols in Roman Corinth: A Social-Rhetorical Reconsideration of 1 Corinthians 8:1–11:1*. WUNT 2/151. Tübingen: Mohr Siebeck, 2003.

Friesen, Steven J., Daniel N. Schowalter, and James C. Walters, eds. *Corinth in Context: Comparative Studies on Religion and Society*. NovTSup 134. Leiden: Brill, 2010.

Fung, Ronald Y. K. "Justification by Faith in 1 & 2 Corinthians." In *Pauline Studies: Essays Presented to F. F. Bruce on His 70th Birthday*, edited by Donald A. Hagner and Murray J. Harris, 246–61. Grand Rapids: Eerdmans, 1980.

Furnish, Victor Paul. *The Theology of the First Letter to the Corinthians*. NTT. Cambridge: Cambridge University Press, 1999.

Garcilazo, Albert V. *The Corinthian Dissenters and the Stoics*. SBL 106. New York: Peter Lang, 2007.

Gardner, Paul Douglas. *The Gifts of God and the Authentication of a Christian: An Exegetical Study of 1 Corinthians 8–11:1*. Lanham, MD: University Press of America, 1994.

Gilchrist, J. M. "Paul and the Corinthians—The Sequence of Letters and Visits." *JSNT* 34 (1988): 47–69.

Gill, David W. J. "Corinth: A Roman Colony in Achaea." *BZ* 37 (1993): 259–64.

Goulder, Michael D. *Paul and the Competing Mission in Corinth*. LPS. Peabody, MA: Hendrickson, 2001.

Grant, Robert M. *Paul in the Roman World: The Conflict at Corinth*. Louisville: Westminster John Knox, 2001.

Harrison, Percy N. *Paulines and Pastorals*. London: Villiers, 1964.

Hay, David M., ed. *1 & 2 Corinthians*. Vol. 2 of *Pauline Theology*, 35–132. Minneapolis: Fortress, 1993.

Hays, Richard B. "The Conversion of the Imagination: Scripture and Eschatology in 1 Corinthians." *NTS* 45 (1999): 391–412.

Heil, John P. *The Rhetorical Role of Scripture in 1 Corinthians*. SBLMS 15. Atlanta: Society of Biblical Literature, 2005.

Hemer, Colin J. "Observations on Pauline Chronology." In *Pauline Studies: Essays Presented to F. F. Bruce on His 70th Birthday*, edited by Donald A. Hagner and Murray J. Harris, 3–18. Grand Rapids: Eerdmans, 1980.

Hogeterp, Albert L. A. *Paul and God's Temple: A Historical Interpretation of Cultic Imagery in the Corinthian Correspondence*. BTS 2. Leuven: Peeters, 2006.

Holmberg, Bengt. "The Methods of Historical Reconstruction in the Scholarly 'Recovery' of Corinthian Christianity." In *Christianity at Corinth: The Quest for the Pauline Church*, edited by Edward Adams and David G. Horrell, 255–71. Louisville: Westminster John Knox, 2004.

Hooker, Morna D. "Authority on Her Head: An Examination of I Corinthians 11:10." *NTS* 10 (1963–64): 410–16.

———. "'Beyond the Things Which Are Written'? An Examination of I Corinthians 4.6." *NTS* 10 (1963–64): 127–32.

Hooker, Morna D., and Stephen G. Wilson, eds. *Paul and Paulinism: Essays in Honour of C. K. Barrett*. London: SPCK, 1982.

Horrell, David G. *The Social Ethos of the Corinthian Correspondence: Interests and Ideology from 1 Corinthians to 1 Clement*. SNTW. Edinburgh: T&T Clark, 1996.

Horsley, Richard A. "Gnosis in Corinth: 1 Corinthians 8:1–6." *NTS* (1980–81): 32–51.

———. "Pneumatikos vs. Psychikos: Distinctions of Spiritual Status among the Corinthians." *HTR* 69 (1976): 269–88.

———. "Wisdom of Word and Words of Wisdom in Corinth." *CBQ* 39 (1977): 224–39.

Hurd, John C. *The Origin of I Corinthians*. New York: Seabury, 1965.

Kuck, David W. *Judgment and Community Conflict: Paul's Use of Apocalyptic Judgment Language in 1 Corinthians 3:5–4:5*. NovTSup 66. Leiden: Brill, 1992.

Lampe, Peter. "Theological Wisdom and the 'Word about the Cross': The Rhetorical Scheme in 1 Corinthians 1–4." *Int* 44 (1990): 117–31.

Liefeld, Walter L. "Women, Submission and Ministry in 1 Corinthians." In *Women, Authority and the Bible*, edited by Alvera Mickelsen, 134–54. Downers Grove, IL: InterVarsity, 1986.

Litfin, A. Duane. *St. Paul's Theology of Proclamation: 1 Corinthians 1–4 and Greco-Roman Rhetoric*. SNTSMS 79. Cambridge: Cambridge University Press, 1994.

Marshall, Peter. *Enmity in Corinth: Social Conventions in Paul's Relations with the Corinthians*. WUNT 2/23. Tübingen: Mohr Siebeck, 1987.

Martin, Dale B. *The Corinthian Body*. New Haven: Yale University Press, 1995.

Martin, Ralph P. *The Spirit and the Congregation: Studies in 1 Corinthians 12–15*. Grand Rapids: Zondervan, 1984.

Meeks, Wayne A. "'And Rose Up to Play': Midrash and Paraenesis in 1 Corinthians 10:1–22." *JSNT* 16 (1982): 64–78.

Meier, John P. "On the Veiling of Hermeneutics (1 Cor. 11:2–16)." *CBQ* 40 (1978): 212–26.

Mihaila, Corin. *The Paul-Apollos Relationship and Paul's Stance toward Greco-Roman Rhetoric: An Exegetical and Socio-Historical Study of 1 Corinthians 1–4.* LNTS 402. Edinburgh: T&T Clark, 2009.

Mitchell, Margaret M. "Concerning *peri de* in 1 Corinthians." *NovT* 31 (1989): 229–56.

———. *Paul and the Rhetoric of Reconciliation: An Exegetical Investigation of the Language and Composition of 1 Corinthians.* HUT 28. Tübingen: Mohr Siebeck, 1991.

———. "Paul's Letters to Corinth: The Interpretive Intertwining of Literary and Historical Reconstruction." In *Urban Religion in Roman Corinth: Interdisciplinary Approaches*, edited by Daniel N. Schowalter and Steven J. Friesen, 307–38. HTS 53. Cambridge, MA: Harvard University Press, 2004.

Murphy-O'Connor, Jerome. "Co-authorship in the Corinthian Correspondence." *RB* 100 (1993): 562–79.

———. *Keys to First Corinthians: Revisiting the Major Issues.* Oxford: Oxford University Press, 2009.

———. *St. Paul's Corinth: Texts and Archaeology.* 3rd ed. Collegeville, MN: Liturgical Press, 2002.

Newton, Derek. *Deity and Diet: The Dilemma of Sacrificial Food at Corinth.* JSNTSup 169. Sheffield: Sheffield Academic Press, 1998.

Niccum, Curt. "The Voice of the Manuscripts on the Silence of Women: The External Evidence for 1 Corinthians 14:34–5." *NTS* 43 (1997): 242–55.

Oropeza, B. J. "Apostasy in the Wilderness: Paul's Message to the Corinthians in a State of Eschatological Liminality." *JSNT* 75 (1999): 69–86.

Paige, Terence. "Stoicism, *Eleutheria*, and Community at Corinth." In *Worship, Theology and Ministry in the Early Church: Essays in Honor of Ralph P. Martin*, edited by Michael J. Wilkins and Terence Paige, 180–93. JSNTSup 87. Sheffield: JSOT Press, 1992.

Painter, John. "Paul and the *pneumatikoi* at Corinth." In *Paul and Paulinism: Essays in Honour of C. K. Barrett*, edited by Morna D. Hooker and Stephen G. Wilson, 237–50. London: SPCK, 1982.

Pascuzzi, Maria. *Ethics, Ecclesiology, and Church Discipline: A Rhetorical Analysis of 1 Corinthians 5.* TGST 32. Rome: Editrice Pontificia Università Gregoriana, 1997.

Payne, Philip B. *Man and Woman, One in Christ: An Exegetical and Theological Study of Paul's Letters.* Grand Rapids: Zondervan, 2009.

Pearson, Birger A. *The Pneumatikos-Psychikos Terminology in 1 Corinthians: A Study in the Theology of the Corinthian Opponents of Paul and Its Relation to Gnosticism.* SBLDS 12. Missoula, MT: Society of Biblical Literature, 1973.

Perriman, A. C. "Paul and the Parousia: 1 Corinthians 15:50–7 and 2 Corinthians 5:1–5." *NTS* 35 (1989): 512–21.

Pickett, Raymond. *The Cross in Corinth: The Social Significance of the Death of Jesus.* JSNTSup 143. Sheffield: Sheffield Academic Press, 1997.

Pogoloff, Stephen M. *Logos and Sophia: The Rhetorical Situation of 1 Corinthians.* SBLDS 134. Atlanta: Scholars Press, 1992.

Rosner, Brian S. *Paul, Scripture, and Ethics: A Study of 1 Corinthians 5–7.* Grand Rapids: Baker Academic, 1999.

———. "Temple Prostitution in 1 Corinthians 6:12–20." *NovT* 60 (1998): 336–51.

Sandnes, Karl O. "Prophecy—A Sign for Believers (1 Cor 14,20–25)." *Bib* 77 (1996): 1–15.

Schmithals, Walter. *Gnosticism in Corinth: An Investigation of the Letters to the Corinthians.* Translated by John E. Steely. Nashville: Abingdon, 1971.

Smit, Joop. "'Do Not Be Idolators': Paul's Rhetoric in First Corinthians 10:1–22." *NovT* 39 (1997): 1–22.

———. "The Function of First Corinthians 10:23–30: A Rhetorical Anticipation." *Bib* 78 (1997): 377–88.

———. "The Rhetorical Disposition of First Corinthians 8:7–9:27." *CBQ* 59 (1997): 476–91.

Stambaugh, John E., and David L. Balch. *The New Testament in Its Social Environment.* Philadelphia: Westminster, 1986.

Stuhlmacher, Peter. "The Hermeneutical Significance of 1 Corinthians 2:6–16." In *Tradition and Interpretation in the New Testament: Essays in Honor of E. Earle Ellis for His 60th Birthday,* edited by Gerald F. Hawthorne and Otto Betz, 328–43. Grand Rapids: Eerdmans, 1987.

Theissen, Gerd. *The Social Setting of Pauline Christianity: Essays on Corinth.* Edited and translated by John H. Schütz. Philadelphia: Fortress, 1982.

Thielman, Frank. "The Coherence of Paul's View of the Law: The Evidence of First Corinthians." *NTS* 38 (1992): 235–53.

Thiselton, Anthony C. "Realized Eschatology at Corinth." *NTS* 24 (1977–78): 510–26.

Tuckett, Christopher M. "The Corinthians Who Say 'There Is No Resurrection of the Dead' (1 Cor 15,12)." In *The Corinthian Correspondence,* edited by Reimund Bieringer, 247–75. BETL 125. Leuven: Leuven University Press, 1996.

van Unnik, W. C. "The Meaning of 1 Corinthians 12:31." *NovT* 35 (1993): 142–59.

Wanamaker, Charles A. "A Rhetoric of Power: Ideology and 1 Corinthians 1–4." In *Paul and the Corinthians: Studies on a Community in Conflict; Essays in Honour of Margaret Thrall,* edited by Trevor J. Burke and J. K. Elliot, 115–37. NovTSup 109. Leiden: Brill, 2003.

Watson, Duane F. "1 Corinthians 10:23–11:1 in the Light of Greco-Roman Rhetoric." *JBL* 108 (1989): 301–18.

Welborn, L. L. "On the Discord in Corinth: 1 Corinthians 1–4 and Ancient Politics." *JBL* 106 (1987): 85–111.

———. *Politics and Rhetoric in the Corinthian Epistles.* Macon, GA: Mercer University Press, 1997.

Williams, H. H. Drake, III. *The Wisdom of the Wise: The Presence and Function of Scripture within 1 Corinthians 1:18–3:23.* AGJU 49. Leiden: Brill, 2001.

Willis, Wendell Lee. *Idol Meat in Corinth: The Pauline Argument in 1 Corinthians 8 and 10.* SBLMS 68. Chico, CA: Scholars Press, 1985.

Wilson, R. McL. "Gnosis at Corinth." In *Paul and Paulinism: Essays in Honour of C. K. Barrett,* edited by Morna D. Hooker and Stephen G. Wilson, 102–14. London: SPCK, 1982.

———. "How Gnostic Were the Corinthians?" *NTS* 19 (1972–73): 65–74.

Winter, Bruce W. *After Paul Left Corinth: The Influence of Secular Ethics and Social Change.* Grand Rapids: Eerdmans, 2001.

———. "Civil Litigation in Secular Corinth and the Church: The Forensic Background to 1 Corinthians 6:1–8." *NTS* 37 (1991): 559–72.

———. *Philo and Paul among the Sophists: Alexandrian and Corinthian Responses to a Julio-Claudian Movement.* 2nd ed. Grand Rapids: Eerdmans, 2002.

———. "Theological and Ethical Responses to Religious Pluralism—1 Corinthians 8–10." *TynBul* 41 (1990): 209–26.

Wire, Antoinette Clark. *The Corinthian Women Prophets: A Reconstruction through Paul's Rhetoric.* Minneapolis: Fortress, 1990.

Wiseman, James. "Corinth and Rome I: 228 B.C.–A.D. 267." *ANRW* II.7.1 (1979): 438–548.

Witherington, Ben, III. "Not So Idle Thoughts about *EIDOLOTHUTON*." *TynBul* 44 (1993): 237–54.

Yeo, Khiok-khing. *Rhetorical Interaction in 1 Corinthians 8 and 10: A Formal Analysis with Preliminary Suggestions for a Chinese, Cross-Cultural Hermeneutic.* BIS 9. Leiden: Brill, 1995.

Commentaries

Barrett, C. K. *The First Epistle to the Corinthians.* HNTC. New York: Harper & Row, 1968.

Blomberg, Craig L. *1 Corinthians.* NIVAC. Grand Rapids: Zondervan, 1994.

Bray, Gerald. *1–2 Corinthians*. ACCSNT 7. Downers Grove, IL: InterVarsity, 1999.

Bruce, F. F. *I and II Corinthians*. NCBC. Grand Rapids: Eerdmans, 1971.

Collins, Raymond F. *First Corinthians*. SP 7. Collegeville, MN: Liturgical Press, 1999.

Conzelmann, Hans. *1 Corinthians: A Commentary on the First Epistle to the Corinthians*. Translated by James W. Leitch. Hermeneia. Philadelphia: Fortress, 1975.

Fee, Gordon D. *The First Epistle to the Corinthians*. NICNT. Grand Rapids: Eerdmans, 1998.

Fitzmyer, Joseph A. *First Corinthians: A New Translation with Introduction and Commentary*. AYB 32. New Haven: Yale University Press, 2008.

Garland, David E. *1 Corinthians*. BECNT. Grand Rapids: Baker Academic, 2003.

Hays, Richard B. *1 Corinthians*. IBC. Louisville: Westminster John Knox, 1997.

Héring, Jean. *The First Epistle of Saint Paul to the Corinthians*. Translated by A. W. Heathcote and P. J. Allcock. London: Epworth, 1962.

Horsley, Richard A. *1 Corinthians*. ANTC. Nashville: Abingdon, 1998.

Keener, Craig S. *1–2 Corinthians*. NCBC. Cambridge: Cambridge University Press, 2005.

Kistemaker, Simon J. *Exposition of the First Epistle to the Corinthians*. NTCom. Grand Rapids: Baker Academic, 1993.

Morris, Leon. *The First Epistle of Paul to the Corinthians*. 2nd ed. TNTC. Grand Rapids: Eerdmans, 1985.

Plummer, Alfred. *A Critical and Exegetical Commentary on the First Epistle of St. Paul to the Corinthians*. ICC. Edinburgh: T&T Clark, 1925.

Snyder, Graydon F. *First Corinthians: A Faith Community Commentary*. Macon, GA: Mercer University Press, 1992.

Talbert, Charles H. *Reading Corinthians: A Literary and Theological Commentary*. RNT. Rev. ed. Macon, GA: Smyth & Helwys, 2002.

Thiselton, Anthony C. *The First Epistle to the Corinthians: A Commentary on the Greek Text*. NIGTC. Grand Rapids: Eerdmans, 2000.

Witherington, Ben, III. *Conflict and Community in Corinth: A Socio-Rhetorical Commentary on 1 and 2 Corinthians*. Grand Rapids: Eerdmans, 1995.

28

Second Corinthians

The fascinating letter that we know as 2 Corinthians is in many ways the most difficult of the Pauline Letters because it is so deeply rooted in specific problems that developed at Corinth, the precise nature of which often remains unclear. Here more than ever in the NT letters we are painfully aware that we are able to hear only one side of the conversation, and so often we must guess about the situation that Paul faces or the underlying situation that he attempts to address. Paul and his apostolic authority clearly are under attack in Corinth, and this has put Paul in a defensive mode. The conflict forces Paul to be more personal than he is elsewhere in his letters, and so he reveals more about himself than usual—information that makes this letter so very valuable in coming to know the Apostle at a deep level.

Author: One of Paul's four main letters, universally accepted as written by the Apostle.

Date: 55 or 56, not long after Paul's "painful visit" to Corinth and the subsequent "painful letter."

Addressees: The Christian church at Corinth.

Purpose: To express relief and thanksgiving for the change of attitude among the Corinthian Christians and their continuing loyalty to him rather than to his opponents.

Message/Argument: A variety of themes, including Paul's affliction, power in weakness, and especially the portrait of ministers of Christ as called to conform to the pattern of the sufferings of Christ.

Significance: Provides a glimpse into Paul's transforming understanding of ministry as strength through weakness and suffering.

Historical Situation and Relation to First Corinthians

As we noted in the preceding chapter, Paul wrote at least four and possibly five (or more) letters to the church at Corinth (see "The Corinthian Correspondence" in the preceding chapter).[1] He wrote 1 Corinthians (letter B) after an initial letter (letter A, mentioned in 1 Cor. 5:9). Following a painful visit to Corinth, Paul had to write a harsh letter (letter C = 2 Cor. 10–13?) "out of much affliction and anguish of heart and with many tears" (2 Cor. 2:3–11; 7:8–12), but that, he says, was written "to let you know the abundant love that I have for you" (2:4). Second Corinthians is thus letter D, very probably the last one that he wrote to Corinth. (If chaps. 10–13 were originally a separate letter, they would compose letter E, and it would possibly be the last letter.)

Although for various reasons Paul's travel plans frequently had to be altered, he did make his way to Asia and Ephesus (see 1 Cor. 16:8–9) and then to Macedonia.[2] It was there at last (see 2 Cor. 2:12–13) that he met Titus, who had delivered the severe letter and now brought with him a positive and encouraging report from the Corinthian church. Paul expresses his relief at the news from Corinth:

> But God, who comforts the downcast, comforted us by the coming of Titus, and not only by his coming but also by the comfort with which he was comforted in you, as he told us of your longing, your mourning, your zeal for me, so that I rejoiced still more. (2 Cor. 7:6–7)

> And besides our own comfort we rejoiced still more at the joy of Titus, because his mind has been set at rest by you all. . . . And his heart goes out all the more to you, as he remembers the obedience of you all, and the fear and trembling with which you received him. I rejoice, because I have perfect confidence in you. (2 Cor. 7:13–16)

It is the report of Titus that explains the basically positive tone of 2 Corinthians 1–9. The Corinthians had taken Paul's rebuke and correction to heart, at least for the time being, if chapters 10–13 reflect the outbreak of new opposition to Paul.

The Occasion of Second Corinthians

Paul has a number of reasons for writing this letter to the Corinthian church. Perhaps most important is his desire to express his joy and relief at the change of heart among the Corinthian Christians and their continuing loyalty to him despite the rough waters that they have had to navigate in their relationship. There is also the need to continue encouraging, edifying, and instructing them in the practice of their faith. In particular, the Corinthians must learn how the

---

1. On the city itself, see "The City of Corinth" in the preceding chapter.
2. For helpful discussion of Paul's itinerary, see Harris, *The Second Epistle to the Corinthians*, 59–64.

cross of Christ transforms the values of the world and presents the attitude and pattern of conduct, including the overturning of the honor/shame paradigm that governs their thinking, that is to be exhibited not just in the Apostles but in all Christians.[3] A second important purpose of the letter is to provide motivation and instructions concerning the offering being collected for the Jerusalem church. And then, finally, there is yet again the urgent need to address problems that seem to have newly emerged in the Corinthian church (chaps. 10–13).[4]

The Theological Context of Paul's Response to the Corinthians

As in 1 Corinthians, the specific problems Paul addresses in 2 Corinthians again draw forth some of the richest theological prose of the NT. Again we see Paul's astounding ability to see everything from the perspective of Christ and the cross. We will see this by exploring the main sections of the letter in sequence.

Paul's Affliction (1:3–11)

At the beginning of the letter Paul blesses God (in the form of a typical Jewish *berakah*) as the "Father of mercies and God of all comfort, who comforts us in all our affliction" (1:3–4). He then states that "we share abundantly in Christ's sufferings" (1:5) and refers several more times to being afflicted and to suffering. At this point, he turns to a specific personal affliction that he had recently experienced in Asia, being "so utterly, unbearably crushed that we despaired of life itself," but also referring to God's deliverance "from so deadly a peril" (1:8–11).

Paul tells us very little about this experience, but it is clear that it was extremely significant for him; indeed, it seems to have constituted a turning

---

> **Chronology of the Corinthian Correspondence**
>
> Paul's initial stay in Corinth (Acts 18:1–18), 50–52
>
> Paul's journey to Caesarea (Acts 18:18–23), 52
>
> Paul's stay in Ephesus (Acts 19:1–41), 52–55
>
> Letter A, corrective letter (1 Cor. 5:9), 53?
>
> Letter B, **1 Corinthians** (from Ephesus), 54/55
>
> Paul's painful visit to Corinth (2 Cor. 2:1; 13:2), 55
>
> Letter C, painful letter (2 Cor. 2:4; 7:8), 55?
>
> Titus delivers the painful letter
>
> Paul stays in Macedonia (Acts 20:1), 55/56
>
> Titus brings good news
>
> Letter D, **2 Corinthians** (from Macedonia), 55/56
>
> [? Letter E (= 2 Cor. 10–13, from Macedonia), 55/56]
>
> Paul stays in Corinth (Acts 20:2–3) 56–57
>
> **Romans**, written from Corinth (Rom. 16:23; cf. 15:26), 57
>
> (Dates are necessarily approximations)

---

3. See Vegge, *2 Corinthians—a Letter about Reconciliation.*
4. See Martin, "The Setting of 2 Corinthians."

point in his life.[5] The "affliction" (*thlipsis*) occurred "in Asia," presumably some time after the writing of 1 Corinthians. Although Paul does not say "in Ephesus," many have associated the affliction with persecution that occurred in Ephesus, a city of Asia, such as either in connection with the riot caused by the silversmith Demetrius, recorded in Acts 19:23–41, or the "fighting with beasts" mentioned in 1 Corinthians 15:32 (cf. 2 Tim. 4:17). The former possibility is improbable because the account in Acts gives no impression that Paul's life was in danger or that he was miraculously delivered. The latter possibility, not referred to in Acts, is very unlikely because the stadium at Ephesus appears to have been open-ended in Paul's time and thus not suitable for combat with beasts.[6] In view, perhaps, is a metaphorical reference to human opposition.

Most probably, Paul's affliction is to be equated with the physical malady referred to as the "thorn . . . in the flesh," the "messenger [*angelos*] of Satan," mentioned in 2 Corinthians 12:7–9, something from which Paul prayed three separate times to be released. It was something that Paul expected to attack him again and from which he expected to be rescued by God again (cf. 1:10). Whatever the illness was, it had a shattering effect on Paul, turning his mind to the real possibility of his own death before the parousia (4:7–18) and hence to the nature of death and the resurrection of the body (5:1–10), while at the same time heightening his sense of dependence on God (1:9).

Paul's Integrity and the Faithfulness of God (1:18–22)

The changes in his plans to visit Corinth do not undercut Paul's integrity or reliability, which he likens to God's faithfulness. God is always for us, "for all the promises of God find their Yes in him" (1:20). God has established the Corinthians in Christ, commissioned the Apostles, and "has put his seal upon us and given us his Spirit in our hearts as a guarantee" (1:22)—all expressed in an incipient trinitarianism.[7]

Paul's Apostolic Ministry (2:14–3:6)

Much discussion has been given to the meaning of the verb *thriambeuō*, "to lead in a triumphal procession," in 2:14 (used also in Col. 2:15). Contrary to what one might expect, this verb plus object points to those being led in the procession as being the captives rather than the victors. The image is derived from the common victory parade in which the victorious general, riding in a chariot, was preceded by some of the spoils of war together with some of those captured, some of whom were to be sacrificed. Paul thus regards himself,

5. For a full discussion, see the excursus in Harris, *The Second Epistle to the Corinthians*, 164–82.
6. Thus George Bean, *Aegean Turkey: An Archaeological Guide* (London: Benn, 1966), cited in Harris, *The Second Epistle to the Corinthians*, 167. But could not temporary barriers have been set up?
7. See Hooker, "From God's Faithfulness to Ours."

and other Christians ("us"), as captives of God. In this way Paul extends the paradoxical theme of power in weakness, suffering, and even death. The fragrance imagery of this passage is also drawn from the victory procession, which included the burning of incense.[8]

Although Paul speaks highly of his ministry, he does not want this to be understood as boasting. The only letter of recommendation that he values is the Corinthian Christians themselves (2:17–3:3). Paul's competence as a minister of the new covenant comes solely from God (3:5).

The Superiority of the New Covenant to the Old Covenant (3:6–18)

In 3:6 Paul refers to himself and his co-workers as "ministers of a new covenant, not in a written code but in the Spirit; for the written code kills, but the Spirit gives life." This leads Paul to a quite remarkable statement in which the old and new covenants are contrasted (3:6–12):

Old Covenant	New Covenant
written code	Spirit
written code kills	Spirit gives life
dispensation of death	dispensation of the Spirit
splendor	greater splendor
dispensation of condemnation	dispensation of righteousness
what has faded away	what is permanent

According to Paul, the Scriptures were not read correctly by the Jews. A veil lies over the eyes of Jewish readers, and that veil is taken away "only through Christ." "But when a man turns to the Lord, the veil is removed" (3:16). Paul adds that the Spirit of the Lord brings "freedom," meaning freedom from the law of Moses. Sanctification, however, is not thereby abandoned, for the Christian is being changed into the likeness of Christ.[9]

Paul's Ministry and the Gospel (4:1–6)

In this brief passage Paul picks up the ideas and terminology of 2:14–17; 3:7–18. In his ministry, he argues, he does not "practice cunning" or "tamper with God's word." His ministry depends on the mercy of God and involves "the open statement of the truth" (4:2)—that is, of "the gospel of the glory

8. On this entire passage, see Hafemann, *Suffering and the Spirit*; see also Aus, *Imagery of Triumph and Rebellion in 2 Corinthians 2:14–17 and Elsewhere in the Epistle*, calling attention to Numbers 16:41–50 as a potential background to the passage.

9. On this passage, see Belleville, *Reflections of Glory*. Scott Hafemann's interpretation of this passage in *Paul, Moses, and the History of Israel* is, however, problematic. See Childs, *The Church's Guide for Reading Paul*, 124–28.

of Christ" (4:4 [cf. 4:6]). "What we preach is not ourselves, but Jesus Christ
as Lord, with ourselves as your servants for Jesus' sake" (4:5).

Treasure in Earthen Vessels (4:7–18)

The glory and "transcendent power" of the gospel, "this treasure," contrasts
dramatically with the perishability of the vessels that transmit it. Yet again
Paul takes up the themes of affliction and mortality: "afflicted in every way"
(4:8); "always carrying in the body the death of Jesus" (4:10); "always being
given up to death for Jesus' sake . . . our mortal flesh" (4:11); "death is at work
in us" (4:12). Confident in the resurrection (4:14), Paul feels impelled to carry
on with his ministry of proclamation and does not lose heart (4:16). Although
his "outer nature is wasting away" (4:16), he is renewed inwardly and looks
for "an eternal weight of glory beyond all comparison" (4:17). "The things
that are seen are transient, but the things that are unseen are eternal" (4:18).[10]

The Expectation of a New, Incorruptible Body (5:1–10)

The reality of mortality turns Paul's thinking to existence after this life. The
present perishable earthly habitation ("tent") of our bodies will be replaced
with "a building from God . . . a house not made with hands . . . our heavenly
dwelling" (5:1–2). In this tent "we groan" (5:2), "we sigh with anxiety" (5:4),
longing for our new dwelling. The present tense of 5:1 ("we have a building"),
together with the statements about not being found naked (5:3) and not un-
clothed but further clothed (5:4), presents the possibility that this new body will
be received at the point of death rather than in a future resurrection, "so that
what is mortal may be swallowed up by life" (5:4). The Holy Spirit has been
given to believers "as a guarantee" (5:5). Paul thus stresses that "we are always
of good courage" (5:6, 8), for to "be away from the body" (i.e., this corruptible
body) is to be "at home with the Lord" (5:8). It remains important to obey
the Lord because all must appear "before the judgment seat of Christ" (5:10).[11]

Controlled by the Love of Christ (5:11–15)

In this memorable passage Paul characterizes his ministry as growing out
of the love of Christ. "For the love of Christ controls us, because we are convinced that one has died for all; therefore all have died. And he died for all,
that those who live might live no longer for themselves but for him who for
their sake died and was raised" (5:14–15). Again we are at the heart of Paul's
gospel: the crucifixion and resurrection of Christ.

10. For an insightful treatment of this section of 2 Corinthians, see Savage, *Power through
Weakness*, 164–86.
11. On this passage, see Harris, "2 Corinthians 5:1–10"; see also Ellis, "The Structure of
Pauline Eschatology (II Corinthians V.1–10)."

The Ministry of Reconciliation: The Gospel according to Paul (5:16–21)

Paul's perspective has changed radically, just as his view of Christ changed.[12] The person who is "in Christ" has become "a new creation": "the old has passed away, behold, the new has come" (5:17). This leads Paul to a glowing statement in 5:18–21 about reconciliation, a theme that some think captures the very center of Paul's theology.[13]

> All this is from God, who through Christ reconciled us to himself and gave us the ministry of reconciliation; that is, in Christ God was reconciling the world to himself, not counting their trespasses against them, and entrusting to us the message of reconciliation. So we are ambassadors for Christ, God making his appeal through us. We beseech you on behalf of Christ, be reconciled to God. For our sake he made him to be sin who knew no sin, so that in him we might become the righteousness of God.

This brief passage on the theme of reconciliation serves well as a summary of the Pauline gospel (cf. Rom. 5:1–11),[14] the message that Paul faithfully preached throughout the Mediterranean world.

The Day of Salvation and the Sufferings of the Apostles (6:1–13)

Paul calls for appropriate conduct from the Corinthians by quoting Isaiah 49:8 and then providing a brief midrash on the passage in the words "Behold, now is the acceptable time; behold, now is the day of salvation" (6:2). Somewhat surprisingly, because they stand in tension with this note of realized eschatology, once again Paul recounts the sufferings of the servants of God (6:4–10).

12. It is possible to take the phrase *kata sarka* ("according to the flesh") adjectivally as modifying the following word, *Christon* ("Christ") resulting in the translation "once we knew Christ according to the flesh; we know him thus no longer." Almost certainly, however, *kata sarka* is adverbial and modifies the verb "knew," in the sense of "know from a human point of view." That is, Paul says that at one time he evaluated Christ according to a (mistaken) human perspective, but now he no longer does so (cf. RSV: "From now on, therefore, we regard no one from a human point of view; even though we once regarded Christ from a human point of view, we regard him thus no longer"). Although Bultmann accepted *kata sarka* as adverbial, he nevertheless insisted that there was no significant difference between the adjectival and adverbial understanding of the phrase: "This decision means nothing for the sense of the total context, for a 'Christ regarded in the manner of the flesh' is just what a 'Christ after the flesh' is" (*Theology of the New Testament*, 1:239). According to Bultmann, Paul had no interest in the historical Jesus, the "Christ after the flesh," but only in the Christ of the kerygma. See *Faith and Understanding*, 1:241.

13. See, for example, Martin, *Reconciliation*.

14. See Belleville, "Gospel and Kerygma in 2 Corinthians." Seyoon Kim ("2 Corinthians 5:11–21 and the Origin of Paul's Concept of 'Reconciliation'") shows how the theme of reconciliation derives from Paul's experience of the risen Christ on the Damascus Road. See also Beale, "The Old Testament Background of Reconciliation in 2 Corinthians 5–7 and Its Bearing on the Literary Problem of 2 Corinthians 6:14–7:1."

Separation from Evil (6:14–7:1)

In a passage that seems unrelated either to what precedes or what follows, Paul cites a collection of OT texts concerning separation from what is unclean and applies it to his readers. He calls himself, together with them, to "make holiness perfect in the fear of God" (7:1). The remainder of chapter 7 concerns the happy report of Titus and Paul's response.

The Offering for Jerusalem (8:1–9:15)

Here a new section of the letter, with a change of subject, begins. With the good example of the Macedonians before them, Paul tells the Corinthians that he is sending Titus to receive their contribution "in the relief of the saints" (8:4), and he exhorts them, "Now as you excel in everything—in faith, in utterance, in knowledge, in all earnestness, and in your love for us—see that you excel in this gracious work also" (8:7). As so often in Paul's argumentation, Jesus is presented as the perfect pattern: "For you know the grace of our Lord Jesus Christ, that though he was rich, yet for your sake he became poor, so that by his poverty you might become rich" (8:9).[15]

Paul tells the Corinthians that along with Titus he is sending two other men, identified only as "brothers" (8:18, 22; 9:3), who were appointed by the churches (of Macedonia) to serve as guarantors of the collection and, perhaps, accompany it all the way to Jerusalem. Why they are unnamed by Paul remains a mystery; possibly, they were already known to the Corinthians, and Paul did not want to detract from the authority of his representative, Titus.

Finally, Paul reminds the Corinthians that "God loves a cheerful giver" (9:7), and that they "will be enriched in every way for great generosity" (9:11). "Under the test of this service, you will glorify God by your obedience in acknowledging the gospel of Christ" (9:13). His final word on the subject is this: "Thanks be to God for his inexpressible gift!" (9:15).

A Sharp Change in Tone: Paul Forced to Defend Himself Again (10:1–18)

If this does not begin a separate letter, then Paul must have received a new, distressing report from Corinth. In contrast to the preceding chapters of 2 Corinthians, where the problems there seem to have been resolved and a positive tone is maintained, now we again encounter Paul wrestling with the difficulties at Corinth. Paul thus speaks of the need of "boldness" on his part (10:2), of a necessary warfare in which he must "destroy arguments and every

---

15. "Although the Corinthians are not called merely to duplicate Christ's self-giving impoverishment (cf. v. 13), their anticipated support of the collection for the saints is implicitly presented as an *imitatio Christi*" (Downs, *The Offering of the Gentiles*, 135). On the centrality of Jesus to Paul's argument in 2 Corinthians, see Stegman, *The Character of Jesus*.

proud obstacle to the knowledge of God, and take every thought captive to obey Christ, being ready to punish every disobedience" (10:5–6).[16]

Competition is once again the problem in the Corinthian church. "Not that we venture to class or compare ourselves with some of those who commend themselves. But when they measure themselves by one another, and compare themselves with one another, they are without understanding" (10:12). Paul allows himself to boast, but "not overextending" himself: "we were the first to come all the way to you with the gospel of Christ" (10:14). His fundamental conviction is that it is God's commendation that matters, not self-boasting (10:15).

False Teaching and False Apostles (11:1–15)

Astonishingly, Paul refers to the readiness of the Corinthian Christians to accept "another Jesus,"[17] "another spirit," "a different gospel," rather than what they had learned from him. They appeared to value "superlative apostles," but Paul feels no inferiority to them and says, "Even if I am unskilled in speaking, I am not in knowledge" (11:5–6). Again Paul defends his practice of accepting financial support from Macedonia and not Corinth (11:7–11). He goes on to describe his competitors as "false apostles, deceitful workmen, disguising themselves as apostles of Christ" (11:13).

Paul Allows Himself Some "Boasting" (11:16–33)

Some of the most intriguing passages in the Pauline corpus occur next as Paul allows himself to boast "as a fool." He will match his competitors at their own game: his Jewish pedigree is as good as any; he is a better servant of Christ. This leads him to a hair-raising catalog of what he has suffered as the apostle to the Gentiles (11:23–27),[18] ending with a poignant reference to "the daily pressure upon me of my anxiety for all the churches" (11:28). "If I must boast, I will boast of the things that show my weakness" (11:30).

Paul's "Visions and Revelations of the Lord" (12:1–10)

Paul briefly recounts (in the third person: "a man") his experience of being "caught up into Paradise," where he "heard things that cannot be told, which man may not utter" (12:3–4). But to this he adds, "And to keep me from being too elated by the abundance of revelations, a thorn was given me in the flesh, a messenger (*angelos*) of Satan, to harass me, to keep me from being too elated" (12:7). When he had prayed three times to be released from this

16. See Lambrecht, "Paul's Appeal and the Obedience to Christ."
17. See Murphy-O'Connor, "Another Jesus (2 Cor. 11:4)."
18. See Hafemann, "The Role of Suffering in the Mission of Paul."

malady, the Lord said to him, "My grace is sufficient for you, for my power is made perfect in weakness" (12:9). Once again asserting one of the main themes in the Corinthian letters, Paul concludes, "I will all the more gladly boast of my weaknesses, that the power of Christ may rest upon me . . . for when I am weak, then I am strong" (12:9–10).[19]

The Signs of a True Apostle (12:11–13)

Once again Paul says, with biting irony, "For I was not at all inferior to these superlative apostles, even though I am nothing" (12:11). Paul had come to Corinth as an authentic Apostle. "The signs of a true apostle were performed among you in all patience, with signs and wonders and mighty works" (12:12). More had taken place at Corinth than we learn from Luke's abbreviated account of the founding of the church in Acts 18.

A Third Visit? (12:14–13:4)

Paul anticipates the necessity of a third visit, but he is filled with fear about what he may encounter (12:20–21). The "second visit" (13:2) must refer to the "painful visit" mentioned earlier in the letter (2:1). In strong contrast to what he has been saying in chapters 1–9, Paul now writes as though the Corinthians had made no progress in the problem areas that he had addressed on that second visit. If he comes to Corinth a third time, Paul warns concerning those who oppose him, "I will not spare them" (13:2 [cf. 13:10]). Paul yet again turns to the model of the cross: Christ "was crucified in weakness, but lives by the power of God. For we are weak in him, but in dealing with you we shall live with him by the power of God" (13:4).

The reference in 12:18 to Titus and "the brother" most probably points to the accomplishment of the recent mission that Paul had sent them on (8:16–24). Perhaps it was they who conveyed the new, discouraging report that becomes the impetus for chapters 10–13.

Final Exhortation and Benediction (13:5–14)

Paul exhorts the Corinthians to "examine yourselves" and "test yourselves" (13:5). He pleads, "Mend your ways, heed my appeal, agree with one another, live in peace, and the God of love and peace will be with you" (13:11). And he closes the letter with a trinitarian benediction: "The grace of the Lord Jesus Christ and the love of God and the fellowship of the Holy Spirit be with you all" (13:14).[20]

19. See Savage, *Power through Weakness*; Black, *Paul, Apostle of Weakness*; Spittler, "The Limits of Ecstasy."

20. See Martin, "The Spirit in 2 Corinthians in Light of the 'Fellowship of the Holy Spirit' in 2 Corinthians 13:14."

Jerome Murphy-O'Connor sums up the contribution of 2 Corinthians to the NT under three points:

1. ministry based on the pattern of Christ and Paul's identification with Christ;
2. weakness and suffering as the characteristic marks of Christ's ministers; and
3. the true evidence of the Holy Spirit is not ecstatic experience but rather an existence marked by the cross.[21]

Paul's Opponents at Corinth

The identity of Paul's opponents is among the most important and most difficult questions in Pauline studies. Despite the amount of information provided in the Corinthian letters, competing hypotheses have proliferated, and little consensus has emerged. The reason is that, as always in the study of letters, we are left to understand the opposition solely on the basis of what Paul says in response to them. Thus, even though almost all the content of 2 Corinthians arises out of response to his opponents, we still puzzle over who they were and what they believed. Paul knows who they were, they knew who they were, and the first readers of the letter knew, but we do not.

Methodological issues have plagued the discussion.[22] Clearly, we must be sensitive to the dangers of "mirror reading," whereby every assertion in the letter is taken to be the refutation of an error held by opponents. Only when the context is polemical or apologetic is one on fairly safe ground in identifying opponents this way. It is furthermore necessary to allow for the possibility of conventional rhetoric that may not entail reference to specific opponents.

One of the debatable questions has to be whether the opponents of Paul were of a single persuasion or whether we have to consider a variety of opponents with different viewpoints. Related is the question of whether the opponents in 2 Corinthians are the same as those in 1 Corinthians. Several scholars have attempted to attribute all the data to a single opposition. Thus, for example, Walter Schmithals finds Gnosticism to be the root of the opposition to Paul throughout the Corinthian letters;[23] John Gunther suggests that the opponents represent a syncretistic, mystic-apocalyptic, ascetic form of

21. Murphy-O'Connor, *The Theology of the Second Letter to the Corinthians*, 140–52.

22. For discussion of method, see Sumney, *Identifying Paul's Opponents*. Applying his method, he comes to the conclusion that the data of 2 Corinthians 1–9 "do not suggest that the opponents are Judaizers, Gnostics, or divine men," but that in the whole of 2 Corinthians Paul opposes "Pneumatics" (ibid., 189–90).

23. See Schmithals, *Gnosticism in Corinth*; idem, *Paul and the Gnostics*.

Palestinian Judaism, "akin to Essenism";[24] Earle Ellis finds the opposition to Paul as coming from pneumatic Hebrews from the Jerusalem church.[25]

Most scholars, however, find variety among the opponents. Murray Harris has summed up the great variety of suggestions on offer for the opponents of 2 Corinthians, helpfully reducing them to four basic categories: Hellenistic Jewish propagandists,[26] pneumatics, gnostics, and Judaizers.[27] Harris himself opts for two groups of opponents: (1) for both 1 Corinthians and 2 Corinthians: proto-gnostics, "in their denial of a future bodily resurrection, their libertinism or asceticism in morals and their pride in *gnosis*";[28] (2) for 2 Corinthians: Palestinian Judaizers who infiltrated the Corinthian church after the writing of 1 Corinthians.[29] If the opponents were Judaizers, however, it seems odd that apparently they did not require circumcision, which, along with the law and justification by faith, is not mentioned in 2 Corinthians 10–13. Did they perhaps only require Gentile adherence to the Jerusalem decree (Acts 15:28–29), and would that have been enough to upset Paul so much?[30] Or was the threat far more serious (2 Cor. 11:4)?

It may be wisest to be content with only a general description of the op-ponents and to say no more than chapters 10–13 say. From these chapters we know that the opponents were Jewish Christians (11:22–23; cf. 10:7) who claimed to be superior to Paul in rhetorical ability (10:10; 11:6) and in their apostleship. Paul sarcastically calls them "superlative apostles" (12:11).[31] Paul insists that he is "not in the least inferior to these superlative apostles" (11:5). They commend themselves (10:12), boasting in letters of recommendation, perhaps from Jerusalem. They criticize Paul's ministry at Corinth (10:14–15) and his refusal to accept the patronage of the Corinthians—that is, financial support (10:7–11; 12:14). They boast in their ministry (11:12). They are fools (11:19) and hypocrites (11:15). They enslave, prey on, take advantage of, and abuse others (11:20). They probably relish boasting in their ecstatic experiences, which is why Paul will foolishly (in his eyes) boast of his own (12:1–10). In sharp contrast to his opponents, Paul will boast only in his weakness (11:23–30). "For we are glad when we are weak" (13:9).

But Paul's unhappiness over the intruders (11:4) is more than just a dislike of their pride, style, demeanor, or even their criticism of him. He obviously

24. See Gunther, *St. Paul's Opponents and Their Background.*

25. See Ellis, "Paul and His Opponents"; idem, "The Circumcision Party and the Early Christian Mission."

26. Thus Georgi, *The Opponents of Paul in Second Corinthians.*

27. Harris, *The Second Epistle to the Corinthians,* 80.

28. Ibid.

29. Ibid., 85–87. This is also the view of C. K. Barrett, "Paul's Opponents in 2 Corinthians"; see also idem, "ΨΕΥΔΑΠΟΣΤΟΛΟΙ (2 Cor. 11:13)."

30. Paul Barnett ("Opposition in Corinth," 6–7) reminds us that Romans, which does address the issues that Judaizers would raise, was written shortly after 2 Corinthians and from Corinth.

31. Probably Paul equates the "superlative apostles" with the "false apostles." See ibid. against distinguishing the two, as does Barrett, "Paul's Opponents in 2 Corinthians."

regards them as exceptionally dangerous. He speaks of them in the strongest language: they are "false apostles, deceitful workmen, disguising themselves as apostles of Christ" (11:13). They come proclaiming "another Jesus than the one we preached," offering "a different spirit" and "a different gospel" (11:4). Little wonder that Paul is as upset with them as he is. One is immediately reminded of the similar situation that he faced in the Galatian churches and of the heated criticism that he directs against the Judaizers (Gal. 1:6–9).

The Integrity of Second Corinthians

Second Corinthians may well be a composite document, but if so, how many are its originally separate parts? As many as six letters have been suggested by Walter Schmithals.[32] The trend, however, seems more and more to favor the integrity or unity of 2 Corinthians as we have it.[33]

Chapters 10–13

The most widely accepted partition in 2 Corinthians is between chapters 1–9 and chapters 10–13. Chapters 10–13 perhaps originally were a separate letter (or part of one), as seems indicated by both the sudden change of tone from the preceding chapters and the shift from the first-person plural to the first-person singular. If these were originally two letters, the possibility exists that chapters 10–13 were written before chapters 1–9 and only later joined to them. It therefore once was popular to identify chapters 10–13 with the painful letter (letter C) mentioned in 2:4, 9; 7:8, 12.[34]

It is much more likely, however, that chapters 10–13 were written after chapters 1–9, so that the visit of Titus mentioned in 12:18 is the one also mentioned in 8:6–24.[35] Another reason why it is difficult to think that chapters 10–13 were the painful letter is that they contain no mention of the key opponent of Paul who was the subject of that letter (see 2:5–6). In spite of some shared elements, these defensive chapters, preparing for the possibility of a visit rather than reacting to one, do not fit well the description of the painful letter, which was written

32. They are 6:14–7:1; 2:14–6:2; 6:3–13 together with 7:2–4; chapters 10–13; chapter 9; 1:1–2:13 together with 7:5–8:24 (Schmithals, "Die Korintherbriefe als Briefsammlung"). For a very similar analysis, see Taylor, "The Composition and Chronology of Second Corinthians."

33. Fredrick Long (*Ancient Rhetoric and Paul's Apology*) defends the integrity of 2 Corinthians by an analysis of the document in terms of ancient forensic discourse. See also Hall, *The Unity of the Corinthian Correspondence*.

34. This view is again defended by Francis Watson ("2 Cor. X–XIII and Paul's Painful Letter to the Corinthians"), who establishes a degree of correspondence between chapters 10–13 and what we know of the painful letter. See also Welborn, "The Identification of 2 Corinthians 10–13 with the 'Letter of Tears.'"

35. See Stephenson, "Partition Theories on II Corinthians."

out of "anguish of heart and with many tears" (2:4). There is furthermore no shred of evidence that these chapters ever actually circulated independently.

The most natural explanation is that when Paul had finished writing chapters 1–9 and perhaps was close to posting the letter to Corinth, he received a disturbing report concerning new developments in the church there.[36] This forced him to add new material of a decidedly different sort. And given what he shares about himself in these concluding chapters, we may almost be grateful that he had to write further.

The Interpolation of 6:14–7:1

Also rather widely accepted is that 6:14–7.1 is a later insertion into Second Corinthians (probably not a separate letter, although some have attempted to equate it with the lost letter mentioned in 1 Cor. 5:9). It sits isolated in its location, like a foreign body, quite unrelated to what precedes and follows—indeed, as an intrusion into the natural succession of 6:13 to 7:2 ("widen your hearts . . . open your hearts to us"). Besides this, the passage is marked by non-Pauline vocabulary (four words are unique, being found in neither the LXX nor the NT), and what Pauline vocabulary there is is not used in a typically Pauline way. The OT quotations are introduced with formulae not used by Paul elsewhere. Then there is also the fact that the passage bears a close affinity to material from Qumran.[37]

However, the passage is not without Pauline content and it is hardly inconceivable that Paul could have written it. It is not lacking in any manuscript of the Pauline Letters we have. And its authenticity therefore has been defended by many.[38]

Chapters 8 and 9 as Separate Letters

As we have already noted, chapter 8 begins addressing a new subject, the offering for the Jerusalem church. This has led some to speculate that it once formed a separate letter, addressed to Corinth, while the somewhat redundant chapter 9, also concerned with the offering, was a separate letter originally addressed to the Christians of Achaia (9:2).[39] Betz works out

---

36. This new report from Corinth need not imply that Titus had fully misunderstood or misrepresented the situation at Corinth in the positive report that brought Paul so much relief. A dramatic shift in the fickle Corinthians is not at all unlikely, especially under the influence of new "apostolic" intruders.

37. See Fitzmyer, "Qumran and the Interpolated Paragraph in 2 Corinthians 6:14–7:1."

38. Notably by commentators such as Thrall and Harris, and others such as Lambrecht, "The Fragment 2 Corinthians 6,14–7,1"; Murphy-O'Connor, "Relating 2 Corinthians 6:14–7:1 to Its Context." See also Webb, *Returning Home*.

39. See especially Betz, *2 Corinthians 8 and 9*. Betz provides an informative history of the partitioning of 2 Corinthians (ibid., 3–36). Stanley Stowers ("*Peri men gar* and the Integrity of 2 Corinthians 8 and 9"), however, makes a strong case against the idea that chapters 8 and 9 are separate letters.

a scenario in which the "reconciliation letter" (= 2 Cor. 1:1–2:13; 7:5–16; 13:11–13), written later than the "second apology" of 10:1–13:10 (and after the "first apology," part of which is found in 2:14–6:13; 7:2–4), "immediately precedes the letters of chaps. 8 and 9."[40] This interpretation of the evidence remains possible, but one may wonder whether this degree of speculation is really necessary.

The Seams at 2:13 and 7:4

Complex partition theories depend on the perceived difficulty in the transition from 2:13 to 2:14[41] and from 7:4 to 7:5.[42] In both cases the second verse rather abruptly introduces a quite different, unrelated subject and involves a change from first-person singular to first-person plural pronouns. Whether shifts such as these can be accepted as occurring within the same letter or whether they necessarily point to the presence of separate letters is a matter of subjective judgment. It is hardly unknown for Paul to shift abruptly to new subjects in letters otherwise normally regarded as single entities.

There should be no objection in principle to the idea of composite documents in the NT. We know that there are (at least) two letters to the Corinthians that we do not possess. Again, there is no objection to the idea that one (or more) of them could have been appended to, or inserted into, 2 Corinthians. The trouble with partition theories, however, is that they can neither be proved nor disproved, and so they necessarily remain in the realm of speculation. Furthermore, the fact that no manuscript evidence exists to support any of the partition theories means that the burden of proof remains on their advocates.

It seems that if ever there was a situation that could explain the disjointed character of a letter, the relations between the Corinthian Christians and Paul would qualify. The fickle Corinthians clearly are unstable, and pretentious intruders aggravate matters considerably, while Paul's deep investment in the church that he founded puts him on an emotional roller coaster—all of this hardly provides a context for the writing of a calm, connected, prose letter-essay.

Addressees, Author, and Date

Addressees

Second Corinthians is addressed not simply "to the church of God which is at Corinth," as is 1 Corinthians, but also to "all the saints who are in the whole of Achaia" (1:1 [cf. 11:10]). This would have included the church of Cenchreae,

40. Betz, *2 Corinthians 8 and 9*, 142.
41. See Murphy-O'Connor, "Paul and Macedonia."
42. Moreover, 2:13 moves very smoothly to 7:5, suggesting that the intervening material may belong to a separate letter.

where Phoebe was a deaconess (Rom. 16:1), as well as other churches of which we know nothing—for example, the believers in Athens (Acts 17:34).

Author

Whereas in 1 Corinthians Paul writes with "our brother Sosthenes" (1 Cor. 1:1), in 2 Corinthians he writes with "Timothy our brother" (2 Cor. 1:1), Paul's trustworthy co-worker who is often mentioned with Paul in this way (in Philippians, Colossians, 1–2 Thessalonians, Philemon). It is unlikely that Timothy played much, if any, of a role in the actual writing of the letter. Rather, it is a matter of Paul wanting to associate Timothy, a key co-worker known to the Corinthians, with the content of the letter and the exhortations to the Corinthians. There is no serious challenge to the Pauline authorship of this letter (or letters).

Date

If 1 Corinthians was written, as I have argued, from Ephesus in 54 or 55, Paul wrote 2 Corinthians from Macedonia (see 2 Cor. 8:1; 9:2), perhaps from Philippi (cf. Phil. 4:15). Because of the need to fit in what happened between the writing of 1 Corinthians and 2 Corinthians, it generally is believed that some eighteen months are needed between the two letters. This being so, we probably are to date 2 Corinthians in 55 or 56.

Bibliography

Books and Articles

Aus, Roger D. *Imagery of Triumph and Rebellion in 2 Corinthians 2:14–17 and Elsewhere in the Epistle: An Example of the Combination of Greco-Roman and Judaic Traditions in the Apostle Paul*. StJud. Lanham, MD: University Press of America, 2005.

Barnett, Paul W. "Opposition in Corinth." *JSNT* 22 (1984): 3–17.

Barrett, C. K. "Paul's Opponents in 2 Corinthians." *NTS* 17 (1970–71): 233–54.

———. "ΨΕΥΔΑΠΟΣΤΟΛΟΙ (2 Cor. 11:13)." In *Essays on Paul*, 87–107. Philadelphia: Westminster, 1982.

Beale, G. K. "The Old Testament Background of Reconciliation in 2 Corinthians 5–7 and Its Bearing on the Literary Problem of 2 Corinthians 6:14–7:1." *NTS* 35 (1989): 550–81.

Belleville, Linda L. "Gospel and Kerygma in 2 Corinthians." In *Gospel in Paul: Studies on Corinthians, Galatians, and Romans for Richard N. Longenecker*, edited by L. Ann Jervis and Peter Richardson, 134–64. JSNTSup 108. Sheffield: Sheffield Academic Press, 1994.

———. "A Letter of Apologetic Self-Commendation: 2 Corinthians 1:8–7:16." *NovT* 31 (1989): 142–63.

———. *Reflections of Glory: Paul's Polemical Use of the Moses-Doxa Tradition in 2 Corinthians 3:1–18*. JSNTSup 52. Sheffield: JSOT Press, 1991.

Betz, Hans Dieter. "2 Corinthians 6:14–7:1: An Anti-Pauline Fragment?" *JBL* 92 (1973): 88–108.

Bieringer, Reimund, ed. *The Corinthian Correspondence*. BETL 125. Leuven: Leuven University Press, 1996.

Bieringer, Reimund, and Jan Lambrecht. *Studies on 2 Corinthians*. BETL 112. Leuven: Leuven University Press, 1994.

Bieringer, Reimund, Emmanuel Nathan, and Dominika Kurek-Chomycz. *2 Corinthians: A Bibliography*. BTS 5. Leuven: Peeters, 2008.

Black, David Alan. *Paul, Apostle of Weakness: Astheneia and Its Cognates in the Pauline Literature*. AUS 7/3. New York: Peter Lang, 1984.

Bornkamm, Günther. "The History of the Origin of the So-called Second Letter to the Corinthians." *NTS* 8 (1961–62): 258–64.

Bultmann, Rudolf. *Faith and Understanding*. Vol. 1. Edited by Robert W. Funk. Translated by Louise Pettibone Smith. London: SCM, 1969.

———. *Theology of the New Testament*. 2 vols. Translated by K. Grobel. Reprint, Waco: Baylor University Press, 2007.

Burke, Trevor J., and J. K. Elliott, eds. *Paul and the Corinthians: Studies on a Community in Conflict; Essays in Honour of Margaret Thrall*. NovTSup 109. Leiden: Brill, 2003.

Byrnes, Michael. *Conformation to the Death of Christ and the Hope of the Resurrection: An Exegetico-Theological Study of 2 Corinthians 4,7–15 and Philippians 3,7–11*. TGST. Rome: Editrice Pontificia Universitá Gregoriana, 2003.

Carson, D. A. *From Triumphalism to Maturity: An Exposition of 2 Corinthians 10–13*. Grand Rapids: Baker Academic, 1984.

Childs, Brevard S. *The Church's Guide for Reading Paul: The Canonical Shaping of the Pauline Corpus*. Grand Rapids: Eerdmans, 2008.

deSilva, David A. *The Credentials of an Apostle: Paul's Gospel in 2 Corinthians 1–7*. BMS 4. North Richland Hills, TX: Bibal Press, 1998.

———. "Measuring Penultimate against Ultimate Reality: An Investigation of the Integrity and Argumentation of 2 Corinthians." *JSNT* 52 (1993): 41–70.

Downs, David J. *The Offering of the Gentiles: Paul's Collection for Jerusalem in Its Chronological, Cultural, and Cultic Contexts*. WUNT 2/248. Tübingen: Mohr Siebeck, 2008.

Ellis, E. Earle. "The Circumcision Party and the Early Christian Mission." In *Prophecy and Hermeneutic in Early Christianity: New Testament Essays*, 116–28. WUNT 18. Tübingen: Mohr Siebeck, 1978.

———. "Paul and His Opponents." In *Prophecy and Hermeneutic in Early Christianity: New Testament Essays*, 80–115. WUNT 18. Tübingen: Mohr Siebeck, 1978.

———. "The Structure of Pauline Eschatology (II Corinthians V.1–10)." In *Paul and His Recent Interpreters*, 35–48. Grand Rapids: Eerdmans, 1961.

Fee, Gordon D. "II Corinthians vi.14—vii.1 and Food Offered to Idols." *NTS* 23 (1976–77): 140–61.

Fitzgerald, John T. *Cracks in an Earthen Vessel: An Examination of the Catalogues of Hardships in the Corinthian Correspondence*. SBLDS 99. Atlanta: Scholars Press, 1988.

Fitzmyer, Joseph A. "Qumran and the Interpolated Paragraph in 2 Corinthians 6:14–7:1." *CBQ* 23 (1961): 271–80.

Georgi, Dieter. *The Opponents of Paul in Second Corinthians*. Philadelphia: Fortress, 1986.

Gnilka, Joachim. "2 Corinthians 6:14–7:1 in Light of the Qumran Texts and the Testaments of the Twelve Patriarchs." In *Paul and Qumran: Studies in New Testament Exegesis*, edited by Jerome Murphy-O'Connor, 48–68. Chicago: Priory Press, 1968.

Gunther, John J. *St. Paul's Opponents and Their Background: A Study of Apocalyptic and Jewish Sectarian Teachings*. NovTSup 35. Leiden: Brill, 1973.

Hafemann, Scott J. *Paul, Moses, and the History of Israel: The Letter/Spirit Contrast and the Argument from Scripture in 2 Corinthians 3*. WUNT 81. Tübingen: Mohr Siebeck, 1995.

———. "The Role of Suffering in the Mission of Paul." In *The Mission of the Early Church to the Jews and Gentiles*, edited by Jostein Ådna and Hans Kvalbein, 165–84. WUNT 127. Tübingen: Mohr Siebeck, 2000.

———. *Suffering and the Spirit: An Exegetical Study of II Corinthians 2:14–3:3 within the Context of the Corinthian Correspondence*. WUNT 2/19. Tübingen: Mohr Siebeck, 1986.

Hall, David R. *The Unity of the Corinthian Correspondence*. JSNTSup 251. New York: T&T Clark International, 2003.

Harris, Murray J. "2 Corinthians 5:1–10: Watershed in Paul's Eschatology?" *TynBul* 22 (1971): 32–57.

Hay, David M., ed. *1 & 2 Corinthians*. Vol. 2 of *Pauline Theology*, 133–208. Minneapolis: Fortress, 1993.

Hooker, Morna D. "From God's Faithfulness to Ours: Another Look at 2 Corinthians 1:17–24." In *Paul and the Corinthians: Studies on a Community in Conflict; Essays in Honour of Margaret Thrall*, edited by Trevor J. Burke and J. K. Elliot, 233–39. NovTSup 109. Leiden: Brill, 2003.

Kim, Seyoon. "2 Corinthians 5:11–21 and the Origin of Paul's Concept of 'Reconciliation.'" *NovT* 39 (1997): 360–84.

Kreitzer, Larry J. *2 Corinthians*. NTG. Sheffield: Sheffield Academic Press, 1996.

Lambrecht, Jan. "The Fragment 2 Corinthians 6,14–7,1: A Plea for Its Authenticity." In *Studies on 2 Corinthians*, by Reimund Bieringer and Jan Lambrecht, 531–49. BETL 112. Leuven: Leuven University Press, 1994.

———. "Paul's Appeal and the Obedience to Christ: The Line of Thought in 2 Corinthians 10,1–6." *Bib* 77 (1996): 398–416.

Lincoln, Andrew T. "Paul the Visionary: The Setting and Significance of the Rapture to Paradise in II Corinthians 12:1–10." *NTS* 25 (1978–79): 204–22.

Long, Fredrick J. *Ancient Rhetoric and Paul's Apology: The Compositional Unity of 2 Corinthians*. SNTSMS 131. Cambridge: Cambridge University Press, 2004.

Martin, Ralph P. "The Opponents of Paul in 2 Corinthians: An Old Issue Revisited." In *Tradition and Interpretation in the New Testament: Essays in Honor of E. Earle Ellis for His 60th Birthday*, edited by Gerald F. Hawthorne and Otto Betz, 279–89. Grand Rapids: Eerdmans, 1987.

———. *Reconciliation: A Study of Paul's Theology*. Reprint, Eugene, OR: Wipf & Stock, 1997.

———. "The Setting of 2 Corinthians." *TynBul* 37 (1986): 3–19.

———. "The Spirit in 2 Corinthians in Light of the 'Fellowship of the Holy Spirit' in 2 Corinthians 13:14." In *Eschatology and the New Testament: Essays in Honor of George Raymond Beasley-Murray*, edited by W. Hulitt Gloer, 113–28. Peabody, MA: Hendrickson, 1988.

Murphy-O'Connor, Jerome. "Another Jesus (2 Cor. 11:4)." *RB* 97 (1990): 238–51.

———. "Paul and Macedonia: The Connection between 2 Corinthians 2:13 and 2:14." *JSNT* 25 (1985): 99–103.

———. "Relating 2 Corinthians 6:14–7:1 to Its Context." *NTS* 33 (1986–1987): 272–75.

———. *The Theology of the Second Letter to the Corinthians*. NTT. Cambridge: Cambridge University Press, 1991.

Savage, Timothy B. *Power through Weakness: Paul's Understanding of the Christian Ministry in 2 Corinthians*. SNTSMS 86. Cambridge: Cambridge University Press, 1996.

Schmithals, Walter. *Gnosticism in Corinth: An Investigation of the Letters to the Corinthians*. Translated by John E. Steely. Nashville: Abingdon, 1971.

———. "Die Korintherbriefe als Briefsammlung." *ZNW* 64 (1973): 263–88.

———. *Paul and the Gnostics*. Translated by John E. Steely. Nashville: Abingdon, 1972.

Spittler, Russell P. "The Limits of Ecstasy: An Exegesis of 2 Corinthians 12:1–10." In *Current Issues in Biblical and Patristic Interpretation: Studies in Honor of Merrill C. Tenney*, edited by Gerald F. Hawthorne, 259–66. Grand Rapids: Eerdmans, 1975.

Stegman, Thomas. *The Character of Jesus: The Linchpin to Paul's Argument in 2 Corinthians*. AnBib 158. Rome: Editrice Pontificio Istituto Biblico, 2005.

Stephenson, A. M. G. "Partition Theories on II Corinthians." *SE* 2 [= TU 87] (1964): 639–46.

Stowers, Stanley K. "*Peri men gar* and the Integrity of 2 Corinthians 8 and 9." *NovT* 32 (1990): 340–48.

Sumney, Jerry L. *Identifying Paul's Opponents: The Question of Method in 2 Corinthians.* JSNTSup 40. Sheffield: JSOT Press, 1990.

Taylor, N. H. "The Composition and Chronology of Second Corinthians." *JSNT* 44 (1991): 67–87.

Thrall, Margaret E. "A Second Thanksgiving Period in II Corinthians." *JSNT* 16 (1982): 101–24.

Vegge, Ivar. *2 Corinthians—a Letter about Reconciliation: A Psychagogical, Epistolographical and Rhetorical Analysis.* WUNT 2/239. Tübingen: Mohr Siebeck, 2008.

Wan, Sze-Kar. *Power in Weakness: Conflict and Rhetoric in Paul's Second Letter to the Corinthians.* NTC. Harrisburg, PA: Trinity Press International, 2000.

Watson, Francis. "2 Cor. X–XIII and Paul's Painful Letter to the Corinthians." *JTS* 35 (1984): 324–46.

Webb, William J. *Returning Home: New Covenant and Second Exodus as the Context for 2 Corinthians 6:14–7:1.* JSNTSup 85. Sheffield: JSOT Press, 1993.

Welborn, L. L. "The Identification of 2 Corinthians 10–13 with the 'Letter of Tears.'" *NovT* 37 (1995): 138–53.

Young, Frances M., and David F. Ford. *Meaning and Truth in 2 Corinthians.* Grand Rapids: Eerdmans, 1988.

Commentaries

Barnett, Paul. *The Second Epistle to the Corinthians.* NICNT. Grand Rapids: Eerdmans, 1997.

Barrett, C. K. *A Commentary on the Second Epistle to the Corinthians.* BNTC. New York: Harper & Row, 1973.

Belleville, Linda L. *2 Corinthians.* IVPNTC. Downers Grove, IL: InterVarsity, 1996.

Betz, Hans Dieter. *2 Corinthians 8 and 9: A Commentary on Two Administrative Letters of the Apostle Paul.* Edited by George W. McRae. Hermeneia. Philadelphia: Fortress, 1985.

Bruce, F. F. *I and II Corinthians.* NCBC. Grand Rapids: Eerdmans, 1971.

Bultmann, Rudolf. *The Second Letter to the Corinthians.* Translated by Roy A. Harrisville. Minneapolis: Augsburg, 1985.

Furnish, Victor Paul. *II Corinthians: Translated with Introduction, Notes, and Commentary.* AB 32A. Garden City, NY: Doubleday, 1984.

Garland, David E. *2 Corinthians.* NAC. Nashville: Broadman & Holman, 1999.

Hafemann, Scott J. *2 Corinthians.* NIVAC. Grand Rapids: Zondervan, 2000.

Harris, Murray J. *The Second Epistle to the Corinthians: A Commentary on the Greek Text.* NIGTC. Grand Rapids: Eerdmans, 2005.

Héring, Jean. *The Second Epistle of Saint Paul to the Corinthians.* Translated by A. W. Heathcote and P. J. Allcock. London: Epworth, 1967.

Hughes, Philip E. *Paul's Second Epistle to the Corinthians.* NICNT. Grand Rapids: Eerdmans, 1962.

Keener, Craig S. *1–2 Corinthians.* NCamBC. Cambridge: Cambridge University Press, 2005.

Kruse, Colin. *2 Corinthians.* TNTC. Grand Rapids: Eerdmans, 1987.

Lambrecht, Jan. *Second Corinthians.* SP 8. Collegeville, MN: Liturgical Press, 1999.

Martin, Ralph P. *2 Corinthians.* WBC 40. Waco: Word, 1986.

Matera, Frank J. *II Corinthians: A Commentary.* NTL. Louisville: Westminster John Knox, 2003.

McCant, Jerry W. *2 Corinthians.* RNBC. Sheffield: Sheffield Academic Press, 1999.

Scott, James M. *2 Corinthians.* NIBC. Peabody, MA: Hendrickson, 1998.

Talbert, Charles H. *Reading Corinthians: A Literary and Theological Commentary.* RNT. Macon, GA: Smyth & Helwys, 2002.

Tasker, R. V. G. *The Second Epistle of Paul to the Corinthians.* TNTC. Grand Rapids: Eerdmans, 1958.

Thrall, Margaret E. *A Critical and Exegetical Commentary on the Second Epistle to the Corinthians.* 2 vols. ICC. London: T&T Clark, 1994–2000.

Witherington, Ben, III. *Conflict and Community in Corinth: A Socio-Rhetorical Commentary on 1 and 2 Corinthians.* Grand Rapids: Eerdmans, 1995.

29

Romans

Romans stands at the head of the Pauline corpus because it is the longest of Paul's Letters. It happens also to be his greatest letter, containing the clearest and most thorough exposition not just of the gospel he preached but of the Christian gospel itself. It is widely acknowledged as one of the foundational documents of the Christian faith, and its impact in the history of the church has been immeasurable.

The Christian Church at Rome

It is appropriate that Paul's greatest letter was written to the empire's capital and greatest city, Rome. Although the church in Rome was to become of great importance, we know nothing about its beginnings. Rome is mentioned in the opening lines of the story of Pentecost, where we read that among those present at this remarkable event were "visitors from Rome, both Jews and proselytes" (Acts 2:10). It seems probable that among those who became believers in Christ that day were some of these Roman pilgrims who had come to Jerusalem to worship the God of Israel. They returned home with a new faith and thus began the Christian church in that city. This is consonant with the testimony of Ambrosiaster (fourth century): "The Romans had embraced the faith of Christ, albeit according to the Jewish rites, although they saw no sign of mighty works nor any of the apostles" (preface, *Ad Romanos*).[1] The

---

1. Irenaeus refers to Peter and Paul preaching at Rome and "laying the foundations of the church" (*Against Heresies* 3.1.1), but this may be understood as simply a reference to their

Author: One of the four main letters of Paul that are uncontested and form the central core of the Pauline corpus.

Date: Probably 57 or 58.

Addressees: In the first instance addressed to the church at Rome, but given its content, probably also circulated to several other churches.

Purpose: Announcement of Paul's intention to visit Rome in the hope of establishing a base for his planned mission to Spain. For the sake of the Romans, who had no direct knowledge of him, Paul outlines his understanding of the gospel in considerable detail.

Message/Argument: The Christian gospel stands in continuity with the OT as its fulfillment. It is of significance to Jews and Gentiles alike because it addresses the human condition and describes the salvation provided for Gentiles and Jews by God's grace in Christ.

Significance: One of the greatest documents of early Christianity, and the most thorough and powerful articulation of the Christian faith.

church in Rome thus probably existed from the very beginning or at least soon thereafter. By the time of Paul it was already well known for its faith (Rom. 1:8).

The church of Rome suffered a great setback in 49 when the emperor Claudius expelled the Jews from Rome—Christian Jews as well as non-Christian Jews. The historian Suetonius describes this expulsion as the result of "disturbances at the instigation of Chrestus" (*Claud.* 25.4, trans. Rolfe).[2] Among those expelled at this time were Aquila and Priscilla, who made their way to Corinth (Acts 18:2), where they would meet Paul and become his co-workers not only in leather products but also in the service of the gospel. By the time Paul writes this epistle they had returned to Rome, where they maintained a church in their house. In the epistle Paul greets them and their house church, referring to them as "my fellow workers in Christ Jesus, who risked their necks for my life, to whom not only I but also all the churches of the Gentiles give thanks" (16:3–4). For some five years, until the Jews were allowed to return in 54, the church at Rome would have been exclusively Gentile. The return of Christian Jews to the church seems to have caused new tensions, apparently explaining Paul's remarks in chapters 11 and 14.

The church at Rome clearly was Jewish at the beginning, but then, perhaps fairly quickly, Gentile believers were added, and it became a mixed church. During the five-year interim period noted above, it became exclusively Gentile. Much discussed, however, is whether the Jewish or the Gentile contingent was

respective ministries in Rome rather than meaning that they were actually the founders of the church.

2. The vowels *i* and *e* often were confused because they were pronounced the same (itacism). Probably the "disturbances" were caused by arguments between Jews who believed that Jesus was the *Christus* and those who did not.

prominent in the house churches (16:3–16 gives evidence of possibly five of these) to which Paul wrote Romans, and which group is addressed in different parts of the letter. On the one hand, at the beginning of the letter Paul clearly implies Gentile readers (1:13; cf. 1:5–6). On the other hand, it seems clear that Jewish readers are occasionally in view. Thus Paul refers to Abraham as "our forefather" (4:1), and he presupposes knowledge of the Mosaic law (chap. 7). Yet Paul affirms the same of Gentile Christians (4:11) and expects knowledge of the law on the part of Gentiles in several of his letters (e.g., 1–2 Corinthians, Galatians), especially, perhaps, those who had been God-fearers before becoming Christians. Sometimes the "weak in faith" referred to in chapter 14 are identified with Jewish Christians. This, however, is by no means a necessary conclusion, and it furthermore seems doubtful because vegetarianism (14.2) was practiced among the pagans but not generally by the Jews. Nevertheless, Jewish readers seem to be addressed in 2:17–24. Furthermore, the exhortation to "welcome one another" (15:7), in the context of the verses that follow, points to a mixed church.

Probably we are to think of the Roman church as consisting of both Gentile and Jewish believers, with the former composing the majority.[3]

A disaster befell the church in 64 when the emperor Nero blamed the Christians for the great fire that destroyed much of the city. The persecution that followed resulted in many martyrs, most notably, of course, of Peter and Paul (1 Clem. 5). The Roman Christians were subject to further persecutions, but with the conversion of Constantine their fortunes changed. "Christianity in Rome, having survived the first attack on its existence, was destined to advance, in spite of subsequent and more severely organized attacks by supreme authority, until at last it was the city and empire that capitulated to the church."[4]

The Destination and Integrity of Romans

Although the title "The Letter of Paul to the Romans" does not derive from Paul himself, it provides us with an early second-century understanding of the destination of the letter. No one doubts that the epistle was written to the church at Rome. There is evidence, however, that Romans may have been sent to more than one church and thus was a kind of circular letter.

A few late Greek manuscripts (G [ninth century], the cursives 1739 and 1908) and other witnesses (Old Latin, some Vulgate manuscripts, Origen, and Ambrosiaster) omit the words "in Rome" in the formal address in 1:7. So too in 1:15 the same words are omitted by G and Origen (Latin translation).

---

3. For the minority view that Romans was written only to Gentiles in the Roman church, see Das, *Solving the Romans Debate.*

4. Bruce, *New Testament History*, 393.

This evidence is so slight that it cannot throw doubt on the authenticity of the words and thus of Rome as the original or main destination of the letter.

The short benediction at 16:20, "The grace of our Lord Jesus Christ be with you," is located at 16:24 in some manuscripts (D, F, G, and Vulgate) and at the end of the chapter after the doxology in other manuscripts (e.g., P, 33, 104, 365). These variations may be due to the different editions of Romans that were in circulation.

But there is other, more significant textual evidence that probably points to the existence of several editions of the book. The doxology in 16:25–27 is found in different places in different manuscripts. The earliest complete manuscript of the Pauline Letters, 𝔓⁴⁶, has the doxology at the end of chapter 15, not chapter 16. A late cursive manuscript, 1506 (dating from 1320), lacks chapter 16 altogether and yet still has the same doxology in two places, at the end of both chapters 14 and 15. One further fact seems highly significant and makes sense of the phenomenon. Chapter 15 ends with the words "The God of peace be with you all. Amen" (15:33). These words are found in all the manuscript evidence that we have, the only exception being the omission of the final "amen" (in 𝔓⁴⁶, A, F, G, a few minuscule manuscripts, and Ambrosiaster). This verse sounds very much like the end of the letter and raises the strong possibility that an original letter contained fifteen chapters, was perhaps sent to more than one church, and chapter 16 was appended to one of the copies of the letter and sent to one particular church. Chapter 16 consists mainly of personal greetings, and some have wondered how Paul could have known so many people (twenty-six names are mentioned) in a city that he had not yet visited. On the one hand, T. W. Manson made the proposal that chapter 16 was added in the copy of the letter sent to Ephesus, where Paul had lived for three years.[5] On the other hand, all roads lead to Rome, and Paul could well be greeting people there whom he had met elsewhere, as, for example, Prisca and Aquila (16:3). Even if chapter 16 was originally a part of the Letter to the Romans, which is far from impossible, the dislocation of the doxology in a few important manuscripts, together with the ostensible ending of chapter 15, makes it likely that copies of the letter, minus chapter 16, were sent to other churches, thereby accounting for the evidence of the twofold omission of the words "in Rome."[6]

Many scholars have doubted the authenticity of the doxology in 16:25–27, not only on the basis of its varying position in the manuscripts, as just noted, but also because of its length, style, vocabulary, and the fact that Paul consistently ends all of his other letters with a benediction rather than a doxology. This formal doxology picks up themes and language from the body of the epistle, with the reference to "the obedience of faith" serving as an inclusion

---

5. Manson, "St. Paul's Letter to the Romans—and Others."
6. See Gamble, *The Textual History of the Letter to the Romans.*

with 1:5. It is, of course, possible that the doxology was composed by a disciple of Paul to conclude one edition of the letter. But it is not at all impossible that Paul himself artfully put the doxology together, making use of key ideas contained in the letter.[7]

The Purpose of Romans

Toward the end of the letter Paul explicitly indicates one reason for writing to the Roman church: "But now, since I no longer have any room for work in these regions, and since I have longed for many years to come to you, I hope to see you in passing as I go to Spain, and to be sped on my journey there by you, once I have enjoyed your company for a little" (15:23–24). With the true heart of a missionary, Paul longed to preach the gospel where it had not yet been preached. He looked to the west and to Spain and thought that Rome would be an ideal base for his future work, no doubt hoping for financial as well as spiritual support from Roman Christians. Paul's intention to go to Rome is mentioned in Acts 19:21: "Now after these events Paul resolved in the Spirit to pass through Macedonia and Achaia and go to Jerusalem, saying, 'After I have been there, I must also see Rome.'" But this simple, pragmatic reason is hardly an adequate explanation for the writing of such a weighty and momentous document as Romans. This book contains the clearest systematic exposition of the Christian gospel in the NT. Almost like a compendium of doctrine, Romans seems as though it could be a final summary of Paul's theology, a kind of "last testament." Still, it has to be clear that Paul does not make an effort to present his theology comprehensively. The focus of the book is on the nature of salvation in Christ; lacking completely, for example, is Paul's ecclesiology, as is also the sort of detail concerning eschatology one might expect if Paul were giving a complete theology. As comprehensive as it is, however, Romans also addresses specific circumstances in the church there.[8] Thus 11:17–24 exhorts the readers not to boast over the unbelieving Jews; chapter 14 addresses the tensions between "the strong" and "the weak" in the church; and 16:17–18 refers to some who were "in opposition to the doctrine which you have been taught." Paul did not have this information about the Roman house churches first hand, but rather was dependent on things he had heard, probably from friends who now lived in Rome. Very perceptively, Werner Kümmel has described Romans as "essentially a debate between the Pauline gospel and Judaism."[9] It is not difficult to believe that one of the sources of tension

7. See Hurtado, "The Doxology at the End of Romans"; Marshall, "Romans 16:25–27—An Apt Conclusion."

8. See Donfried, *The Romans Debate*; Wedderburn, *The Reasons for Romans*; Stuhlmacher, "The Purpose of Romans."

9. Kümmel, *Introduction to the New Testament*, 309.

in the churches of Rome was disagreement between the Christians and the unbelieving Jews that grew to crisis proportions among the Jewish Christians of Rome. This would explain much of the epistle's content.[10] If in Romans Paul deliberately articulates his gospel in relation to Judaism, that would also explain the character and scope of the book as a fundamental exposition of his theology. It would explain the frequent OT quotations in Romans. Martin Luther called Romans "the door and key to Holy Scripture." It furthermore would effectively explain the climactic section of chapters 9–11, its brilliant analogy of the olive tree and the branches (11:17–24), and especially Paul's argument about the election of Israel and his emphasis on God's covenant faithfulness: "the gifts and the call of God are irrevocable" (11:29). Romans would be of enormous help to Jewish Christians in a variety of ways, but it would also help Gentile Christians to remember their indebtedness to the OT Scriptures and the history of God's work with Israel,[11] not to mention the remaining importance of the Jews in God's sight.

Another pragmatic purpose that may explain Romans is Paul's desire to lay his understanding of the gospel before the Roman Christians. It is quite possible that the Romans were aware of the controversy surrounding Paul's law-free gospel, which admittedly was easy to misunderstand, and Paul knew that this needed clarification if he had any hopes of Roman assistance in his projected work in Spain. Along the same lines, Jacob Jervell argued that Romans was essentially written up as a defense of his theology for the church at Jerusalem, which Paul was on his way to visit and where there were suspicions about him.[12]

The Gospel according to Romans 1–8

Already in the prescript Paul refers to "the gospel of God" (1:1), the basic subject of Romans. He describes that gospel as having been "promised beforehand through his prophets in the holy scriptures" (1:2). The gospel of God is nothing other than "the gospel concerning his Son," the descendant of David and at the same time the Son of God, the one risen from the dead, "Jesus Christ our Lord" (1:3–4).[13]

At the end of the introduction to the book Paul introduces the gospel he proclaims as "the power of God for salvation to everyone who has faith, to the

10. John Drane argues that Paul wrote this letter to define his gospel in light of the challenge of the Judaizers: "What we have in this, his *magnum opus*, is therefore a conscious effort to convince himself as well as his opponents that it is possible to articulate a theology which is at once antilegalistic without also being antinomian" ("Why Did Paul Write Romans?" 223–24).

11. Andrew Das is correct about Romans addressing Gentiles in the Roman congregations, but this need not exclude the probability that Paul addresses the Roman Jewish Christians too. Das, *Solving the Romans Debate*.

12. Jervell, "The Letter to Jerusalem."

13. See G. R. Beasley-Murray, "Romans 1:3–4."

Jew first and also the Greek" (1:16). This is the heart of the book's message: salvation is God's work, a demonstration of "the righteousness of God," that is, his covenant loyalty, and most importantly, it is given not as the result of obedience to the law but rather to those who receive it by believing.

In the next verse, Paul says that the gospel is a revelation of "the righteousness of God" (1:17; Paul uses the phrase again in 3:21–22). Here "the righteousness of God" refers not to God's absolute holiness, his righteousness as a general personal attribute, but rather righteousness in the sense of God's covenant loyalty that results in God's saving activity.[14] The gospel is the story of God acting to save the unworthy. It is a demonstration of God's righteousness, that is, his covenant faithfulness, and therefore truly good news.[15]

Paul proceeds to quote the text from Habakkuk 2:4, so important to him (he quotes it again in Gal. 3:11) because it confirmed from the Scriptures the gospel he preached: "He who through faith is righteous shall live."[16] The main body of the Epistle to the Romans could be considered a lengthy midrash on this text.[17]

The content of the book that follows proceeds quite logically from problem to solution, then to the results of the solution, with a section devoted to questions raised by the preceding chapters, and then finally practical exhortations.

The Universal Human Predicament of Sin (1:18–3:20)

The first main part of the book (1:18–3:20) is given over to a universal indictment of humanity, Jews and Gentiles alike, for sinfulness and rebellion against God. Such is the state of human beings that not only is sin an inevitability but they also have nothing in themselves to remedy the situation. In this dire situation they need a salvation that God alone can provide.

Paul begins by referring to the revelation of the wrath of God (1:18), parallel to the revelation of the righteousness of God (1:17). The focus on the wrath of God begins a description and exploration of the plight of humanity to which the only answer is the righteousness of God understood as the salvation he brings. The history of the pagan world with its perversion and corruption is a demonstration of the experience of God's wrath. "Ungodliness and wickedness" (1:18) characterize human history from the beginning. Even with an authentic, if rudimentary, knowledge of God, human beings refused to acknowledge him as God, falling instead into idolatry (1:23, 25) and

14. This phrase, "the righteousness of God," was at first taken by Luther in the sense of God's moral righteousness before which he could not stand. It was his discovery that the phrase in the OT refers repeatedly to God's saving activity that made clear how it could be understood as good news.

15. See Käsemann, "The Righteousness of God in Romans."

16. An alternate translation is possible due to the ambiguity of the Greek: "the one who is righteous will live by faith." See discussion above, p. 445n18.

17. See further, Dockery, "The Use of Habakkuk 2:4 in Romans 1:17."

immorality. God therefore "gave them up" (the formula occurs three times: 1:24, 26, 28) to their evil desires. Having no place for God in their lives, they fell deeper and deeper into sinful acts. This section of Romans comes to a climax in the vice catalog of verses 29–31, concluding with the observation that they know that such conduct puts them under the penalty of death (1:32), yet that does not deter them.

Chapter 2 shifts to a diatribe, a discussion with an imaginary opponent (note now the use of the second person singular verbs), moving from history to the present. "Therefore you have no excuse, O man, whoever you are" (2:1). Paul affirms the theme of chapter 1: "We know that the judgment of God rightly falls upon those who do such things" (2:2), and then applies it to his opponent. "Do you suppose, O man, that when you judge those who do such things and yet do them yourself, you will escape the judgment of God?" (2:3). "By your hard and impenitent heart you are storing up wrath for yourself on the day of wrath when God's righteous judgment will be revealed" (2:5).

Insofar as the opponent is understood to be a Gentile pagan (like the pagans of 1:18–32), Jewish readers of this material would understandably be cheering Paul on. Although the Jews are not totally out of the picture in chapter 2 (cf. 2:9–10, 12b), the focus falls specifically upon the Jews in 2:17–29. Paul concludes that the Jews, despite all their advantages are no better off: "You who boast in the law, do you dishonor God by breaking the law? For, as it is written, 'The name of God is blasphemed among the Gentiles because of you'" (2:23–24, quoting Isa. 52:5). Paul then proceeds to define a true Jew not in terms of externals such as physical circumcision but by internal realities, arguing that "real circumcision is a matter of the heart, spiritual and not literal" (2:29).[18]

Paul asks then whether the Jew has any advantage (3:1), answering first with a positive (3:2) but then with a negative answer: "No, not at all; for I have already charged that all men, both Jews and Greeks are under the power of sin" (3:9). This conclusion is then supported by a chain of OT quotations (3:10–18) drawn mainly from the Psalms. The argument of this section of Romans is summarized in the sweeping conclusion of 3:19b–20: "so that every mouth may be stopped, and the whole world may be held accountable to God. For no human being will be justified in his sight by works of the law, since through the law comes knowledge of sin."[19]

God's Provision of Salvation (3:21–31)

The good news of the gospel is that God has provided the solution to the grim plight of humanity by making it possible for sinners to be justified—declared

18. See Marcus, "The Circumcision and the Uncircumcision in Rome."

19. On "works of the law" see Cranfield, "'The Works of the Law' in the Epistle to the Romans"; Dunn, "Yet Once More—'the Works of the Law'"; Schreiner, "'Works of Law' in Paul"; Moo, "'Law,' 'Works of the Law,' and Legalism in Paul."

righteous—by faith (3:21–31), not works of the law.[20] These eleven verses comprise the most trenchant Pauline articulation of the basis of the salvation brought by Christ.

Although the law and the prophets pointed to this salvation, described as a manifestation of "the righteousness of God" (cf. 1:17), it is also said to be "apart from law" (3:21). Salvation is, rather, "the righteousness of God through faith in Jesus[21] for all who believe" (3:22). All who are justified, that is, declared righteous, "are justified by his grace as a gift" (3:24).

It is usually pointed out that in verses 24–25 Paul uses terminology from three realms: justification (from the law court), redemption (from the slave market), and *hilastērion* (from the temple cultus). It is this last word that is the most important. It is the LXX translation of the Hebrew *kapporeth*, which refers to the lid that covered the ark of the covenant in the holy of holies, the inner sanctuary of the temple. On the annual day of atonement (Yom Kippur) the high priest sprinkled the blood of a sacrificed bull and goat upon the lid to atone for the sins of the people. In English translations of Leviticus 16:13–15 it is usually rendered "mercy seat," that is, place of mercy. *Hilastērion* occurs in the NT in only one other place, Hebrews 9:5, in a description of the furnishings of the temple.[22]

The meaning of the underlying Hebrew root *kpr* has been much debated, affecting the various translations of *hilastērion*. Leon Morris[23] argued for the translation "propitiation" (KJV), that is, the appeasement of the anger of God, while C. H. Dodd[24] opted for "expiation" (RSV), that is, a "wiping away" of sins.

Hilastērion is a metonym for the sacrifice of atonement, and as such could well include both the idea of expiation and propitiation. Recent translations have avoided the choice of one or the other, rightly using the word "sacrifice." Thus the NRSV and NIV translate *hilastērion* with the phrase "a sacrifice of atonement" (cf. NJB: "sacrifice of reconciliation").

Salvation has been accomplished through the atoning death of Christ, whose sacrifice is likened to the atonement accomplished in the holy of holies (3:25). Indeed, the sacrifices of the temple ritual pointed to the one fully efficacious sacrifice, that of Christ, "by his blood." And, Paul stresses, the benefits of this sacrifice are "received by faith" (3:25). Because of the sacrifice of his Son, God's righteous character is not compromised by the gift of justification by

20. For discussion of the "new perspective" on Paul, with its unique understanding of "works of the law," see chapter 19 above.

21. Possibly "through the faithfulness of Jesus." For a discussion of the objective/subjective genitive construction *dia pisteōs Iēsou Christou*, see pp. 386–87.

22. The cognate words, *hilaskomai* (Heb. 2:17; cf. Luke 18:13) and *hilasmos* (1 John 2:2; 4:10) occur in the NT.

23. Morris, *The Apostolic Preaching of the Cross*, 144–213.

24. Dodd, *The Bible and the Greeks*, 82–95.

faith. The price of redemption has been fully paid by Christ the *hilastērion*. Paul makes his point again in the words "We hold that a man is justified by faith apart from works of law" (3:28). Contrary to what one may think, this gospel of salvation by faith does not overthrow the law: "By no means! On the contrary, we uphold the law" (3:31). The law is a subject to which Paul will return later in the Epistle.[25]

Justification by Faith in the OT (4:1–25)

Paul next proceeds to show that the idea of justification by faith was nothing new, but already experienced in the OT, as can be seen preeminently in the example of Abraham. Paul quotes one of his favorite OT texts, Genesis 15:6: "Abraham believed God, and it was reckoned to him as righteousness" (4:3; quoted again in Gal. 3:6). This text has three words that are important for Paul: "believe" (i.e., to have faith), "righteousness," and especially "reckoned" (i.e., to count or declare something as true). Paul uses the verb "reckoned" (*logizomai*) no fewer than ten more times in chapter 4. Genesis 15:6 demonstrates that righteousness is not something gained by doing the works of the law. One believes and is thereby justified, that is, reckoned or counted as righteous. "And to one who does not work but trusts him who justifies the ungodly [*asebē*], his faith is reckoned as righteousness" (4:5). This statement stands in startling disagreement with Exodus 23:7, "I will not acquit the guilty," where the LXX uses the same terminology as Paul does. Paul's emphasis on the grace/gift of salvation could not be stronger.

The nonreckoning of David's sin serves as Paul's obverse example of the grace underlying justification by faith (4:6–8). To be reckoned righteous, of course, necessarily involves the forgiveness of sins. And so Paul quotes Psalm 32:1–2, where he again finds the word "reckon." "Blessed are those whose iniquities are forgiven, and whose sins are covered; blessed is the man against whom the Lord will not reckon his sin" (4:7–8).

Paul understandably makes much of the fact that Abraham was reckoned righteous by faith *before* the account of his circumcision in Genesis 17 (Rom. 4:9–12). This validates his conclusion that justification by faith is available not only to the circumcised (the Jews) but also to the uncircumcised (the Gentiles). According to Paul, Abraham is "the father of us all" (4:16), a point he underscores by a quotation from Genesis 17:5, "I have made you the father of many nations" (4:17).

Paul continues to explore the polarity between law and faith in the second half of chapter 4. The Abrahamic covenant and the promise that Abraham and his descendants would "inherit the world" (4:13; note the universalizing in the change of the word "land" [*gē*] to "world" [*kosmos*]), "did not come

---

25. On the subject of Paul and the Law, see chapter 19 above.

through the law but through the righteousness of faith," to which Paul adds, "If it is the adherents of the law who are to be the heirs, faith is null and the promise is void" (4:13–14). A discussion of Abraham's faith in believing against all odds that God would give him and Sarah a son concludes with the following: "But the words, 'it was reckoned to him,' were written not for his sake alone, but for ours also. It [righteousness] will be reckoned to us who believe in him that raised from the dead Jesus our Lord, who was put to death for our trespasses and raised for our justification" (4:23–25).[26]

The Results of Justification by Faith (5:1–11)

As he begins to canvass the benefits of justification by faith (5:1–11), Paul first emphasizes the fundamental and all-important fact that we have peace with God. Most remarkable is the statement that "While we were still weak [*asthenōn*], at the right time Christ died for the ungodly [*asebōn*]" (5:6), together with the following: "But God shows his love for us in that while we were yet sinners [*hamartōlōn*] Christ died for us" (5:8), and the words of 5:10, "while we were enemies [*echthroi*] we were reconciled to God by the death of his Son." No clearer statement could be made of the grace that underlies the reality of justification by faith.

To the reality of peace with God, Paul adds the hope (in the sense of confident expectation) of the believer, the inner knowledge of the love of God through the gift of the Holy Spirit, the reality of reconciliation, and the promise of future salvation.

Adam and Christ (5:12–21)

Next, in one of the most remarkable of all Pauline passages, Paul steps back to survey the redemptive work of God in Christ within the context of the whole of human history (cf. 1 Cor. 15:21–22, 45–49). In this Adam–Christ typology he compares the two pivotal figures Adam and Christ, showing how all of humanity is affected by their respective acts. Adam's disobedience is counteracted by Christ's act of obedience: "As one man's trespass led to condemnation for all men, so one man's act of righteousness leads to acquittal and life for all men" (5:18).

Underlying this typological parallelism is the notion of corporate solidarity. All human beings are identified with Adam and his act of disobedience. Sin and death entered the world through Adam's sin and passed on to all of humanity, with the result that all have sinned.[27] The doctrine of original sin—the idea that we sinned in Adam—would be unbearable were it not for the fact that no

---

26. See Käsemann, "The Faith of Abraham in Romans 4"; Schliesser, *Abraham's Faith in Rom. 4.*
27. See Cranfield, "On Some Problems in the Interpretation of Romans 5.12"; Danker, "Romans V.12"; Porter, "The Pauline Concept of Original Sin, in Light of Rabbinic Background."

one can claim sinlessness, for "each of us has become our own Adam" (*2 Bar.* 54:19). All are identified with Adam in his disobedience; and all are identified with Christ in his act of obedience. When speaking of the redemptive work of Christ, Paul will only do so in universal terms. To the universal problem of human sin there is one universal solution: the sacrifice of Christ.

Freedom from Sin (Romans 6)

The three final chapters of this section of Romans focus upon the concrete results of justification by faith. Although it is an oversimplification and cannot capture the richness of these chapters, the frequently encountered schema remains convenient: freedom from sin (chap. 6), freedom from the law (chap. 7), and freedom from condemnation and death (chap. 8).

Paul is adamant that sin is to have no place in the life of the Christian. Drawing on the theology of baptism, he refers to the burial of the Christian with Christ in baptism. The result of this is that the Christian has died to sin and has been raised with Christ to "walk in newness of life" (6:4). In a second illustration, Paul refers to our being crucified with Christ (6:6; cf. Gal. 2:20). The result of this death is that we are no longer "enslaved to sin" (6:6), but "freed from sin" (6:7). The challenge, as often suggested by Paul in his ethical exhortation, is to be or become what we are in Christ; the indicative must be accompanied by the imperative. The Christian is dead to sin, through being identified with Christ's death. This is to be counted upon: "So you also must consider yourselves dead to sin and alive to God in Christ Jesus" (6:11). "For sin will have no dominion over you, since you are not under law but under grace" (6:14). The absolute language may seem to imply the possibility of perfection, but that is not a necessary conclusion. What is in view is a degree of sanctification that enables the Christian to live righteously.

Freedom from the Law (Romans 7)

Freedom from the law is a key emphasis of Paul and one that was frequently misunderstood as opening the door to immoral behavior. Often the question was thrown at Paul: "Are we to sin because we are not under law but under grace?" (6:15). The Pauline paradox, however, is that we are free from the law in order to live righteously. The Christian has died to the law, according to Paul, "so that you may belong to another, to him who has been raised from the dead in order that we may bear fruit for God" (7:4). In the new situation that Christ has brought about, "we are discharged from the law, dead to that which held us captive, so that we serve not under the old written code but in the new life of the Spirit" (7:6). Righteous living remains a very important goal for Paul.

One of the more puzzling passages in Romans is 7:7–25. Beginning in 7:7 and continuing to the end of the chapter, Paul uses the first person singular pronoun, "I." Furthermore, from 7:14 to the end of the chapter the verbs are consistently in the present tense. Is the "I" here autobiographical, referring to Paul's own experience, and, if so, is it his experience as a Pharisee or as a Christian? Since 7:7–13 speak of the law of Moses, the "I" must be a Jew or at least a God-fearer. If these verses refer to Paul's own experience, however, they may at the same time mirror the experience of Adam and of Israel.

The content of 7:14–25 seems to have a broader application, referring to the universal truth of the indwelling sin that thwarts any and all who would seek to live a truly moral life. This of course would include the Christian, and perhaps the most natural interpretation of this passage is that it refers to the experience of the Christian. In this present age, even sanctified Christians are unable fully to close the gap between what they are in Adam and their identity in Christ. Perfection is not within their reach, hence the frustration expressed in 7:24. To the question, Who will deliver me? the Christian answer is "Jesus Christ our Lord" (7:25a). But then, in 7:25b comes the surprising summary of the present situation: "So then, I of myself serve the law of God with my mind, but with my flesh I serve the law of sin." Although a number of scholars have argued that 7:25b is misplaced and should come before the victory cry of 7:25a, no manuscripts support this suggestion. The Christian, as Martin Luther put it, is *simul iustus et peccator*, "simultaneously righteous and sinner."[28] It is the righteous, sanctified Christian who feels most the frustration of being unable fully to escape the residue of the Adamic nature and the ongoing failure to arrive at moral perfection.

Freedom from Condemnation and Death (Romans 8)

Romans 8 begins with the triumphant assertion that "There is therefore now no condemnation for those who are in Christ Jesus. For the law of the Spirit of life in Christ Jesus has set me free from the law of sin and death" (Rom. 8:1–2). Despite the pessimism of the last part of chapter 7, Paul concludes that the result of the work of Christ is "that the just requirement of the law might be fulfilled in us, who walk not according to the flesh but according to the Spirit" (8:4). Righteousness is indeed possible; perfection is not. For those in Christ there can be no condemnation.

While earlier chapters have focused on the effects of Christ's redemptive work upon the individual, in chapter 8 Paul for the first time speaks of the effects of Christ's work upon the created order, and this chapter contains the most that Paul has to say about eschatology in Romans. Here he speaks of "the glory that is to be revealed [*apokalyphthēnai*] to us" (8:18). The redemption of humanity has consequences for the created order, and therefore the creation "waits with eager longing for the revealing [*apokalypsin*] of the sons of God" (8:19). According to Paul's apocalyptic perspective, "The creation itself will

---

28. On this passage, see Dunn, "Romans 7:14–25 in the Theology of Paul." On the whole chapter, see Bornkamm, "Sin, Law and Death"; Mitton, "Romans 7 Reconsidered."

be set free from its bondage to decay and obtain the glorious liberty of the children of God" (8:21). And so the whole creation groans together for the time of final redemption (8:22–23).

Considering the scope and grandeur of God's plan leads Paul at the end of chapter 8 to a magnificent rhetorical statement concerning the security of the believer. In the midst of tribulation of whatever kind, he concludes, "we are more than conquerors through him who loved us" (8:37), and in the final moving words of the chapter Paul proclaims that nothing in all creation "will be able to separate us from the love of God in Christ Jesus our Lord" (8:39).

Israel's Unbelief and Salvation (Romans 9–11)

If the exposition of the gospel in the first eight chapters constitutes a self-contained unit of Romans, which seems a reasonable conclusion, then what is the status of chapters 9–11? In the past these chapters commonly were referred to as a kind of appendix or parenthesis, prior to the practical section of the letter beginning in chapter 12, and as such, something that could be dispensed with as not vitally related to the letter. Nowadays, however, these chapters are rightly regarded as an essential part of the first eight. As we have seen, in the first eight chapters Paul has defined his gospel in some detail, but always with attention to its relation to the OT and Judaism. Paul regards his gospel as the fulfillment of Israel's Scriptures and expectation. But the inescapable reality was that only a relatively small remnant of the Jews accepted the gospel. Not only was this a very distressing development emotionally for Paul but also it constituted a theological problem that he was obligated to address (9:1–5). Given the argument Paul has presented in chapters 1 through 8, how can the present unbelief of Israel be explained? Has God's plan failed?[29]

Paul begins with what is the bedrock of Israel's existence: the doctrine of God's election (9:6–29). This brings him down to the idea of the remnant of Israel that experiences salvation (9:27), a subject that he takes up again later (11:1–10).

Before he comes to his resounding affirmation of God's ongoing faithfulness to Israel, however, he turns once again to the theological defense of the gospel and the explanation of where Israel went astray: its reliance on works of the law rather than faith (9:30–10:21). In a statement that sounds almost autobiographical, Paul writes, "For, being ignorant of the righteousness that comes from God, and seeking to establish their own, they did not submit to God's righteousness" (10:3 [cf. Phil. 3:8–9]). There is a supreme irony in that the Gentiles, who did not pursue righteousness, were the ones who obtained it

---

29. On Romans 9–11, see Munck, *Christ and Israel*; G. R. Beasley-Murray, "The Righteousness of God in the History of Israel and the Nations"; Davies, "Paul and the People of Israel"; Corley, "The Jews, the Future and God (Romans 9–11)"; B. W. Longenecker, "Different Answers to Different Issues."

through faith, while Israel pursued the law but did not arrive at righteousness (9:30–31). In 10:4 Paul gives us one of his famous statements: "For Christ is the end of the law, that every one who has faith may be justified." Scholars have debated whether the ambiguous Greek word *telos* is to be understood as "end" (KJV, NASB, RSV, NRSV) or "goal" (cf. NJB: "the Law has found its fulfillment in Christ"; NIV: "culmination"). Either translation fits the argument of Romans, for there is a sense in which both meanings are true, and it is not impossible that Paul has both in mind here.

Paul presents a particularly interesting reinterpretation of Deuteronomy 30:14, "No, the word is very near to you; it is in your mouth and in your heart for you to observe" (NRSV), which he quotes in 10:8. Paul identifies the "word," which in Deuteronomy refers to the commandment, as the gospel, "the word of faith which we preach" (10:8). Picking up the reference to mouth and heart, he explains, "Because, if you confess with your lips that Jesus is Lord and believe in your heart that God raised him from the dead, you will be saved. For one believes with the heart and so is justified, and one confesses with the mouth and so is saved" (10:9–10 NRSV). Paul knows well what he is doing with this text from Deuteronomy. Now that Christ has come, works of the law have given way to faith in the gospel.

The entire discussion comes to a climax in chapter 11. God's faithfulness is established just through the existence of a remnant of Jewish believers in Jesus. The remnant idea is of key importance to Paul. The existence of the remnant in itself is enough to demonstrate that God has not rejected his people (11:1–10). But God will yet extend further grace to Israel. Paul now presents an overarching rationale of salvation history that explains Israel's unbelief from the standpoint of one who believes in the sovereignty of God. This perspective he undoubtedly had worked out in his role as apostle to the Gentiles. God has temporarily "hardened" Israel (11:7), making possible the success of the mission to the Gentiles (11:11).

But Paul sees a different future for Israel and now begins to speak of a brighter time to come, with the salvation of Israel (11:11–32). Israel may have stumbled, but not so as to fall (11:11). And now Paul begins to speak positively of Israel's future, using language such as "their full inclusion" (11:12) and "their acceptance . . . life from the dead" (11:15). The Jews, "if they do not persist in their unbelief,[30] will be grafted in, for God has the power to graft them in again" (11:23). Paul concludes, "how much more will these natural branches be grafted back into their own olive tree" (11:24). The olive tree probably is to be understood as spiritual Israel, with its root being the patriarchs themselves.

---

30. This is an important condition and rules out a *Sonderweg*, or special way of salvation for Israel—that is, apart from Christ. Paul knows of only one source of salvation, for Jews as well as Gentiles, and that is faith in Christ. See Hvalvik, "A 'Sonderweg' for Israel." Günter Wagner rightly concludes, "It should be possible to envisage a self-revelation of Jesus Christ to Israel at the time of the parousia that will awaken a faith response among the Jews who until then resisted the gospel of their Redeemer" ("The Future of Israel," 109).

Then Paul speaks of a "mystery" (in the sense of something hitherto not known but now made clear): "A hardening has come upon part of Israel, until the full number of Gentiles come in, and so all Israel will be saved" (11:25–26). Although the meaning of "and so all Israel will be saved" has been much debated, most interpreters conclude that it refers to a large scale conversion of Jews to faith in the gospel of Christ toward the end of the present age. Paul writes further that "As regards election they are beloved for the sake of their forefathers. For the gifts and the call of God are irrevocable" (11:28–29);[31] "they have now been disobedient in order that by the mercy shown to you they also may receive mercy" (11:31). Then, in a sweeping statement, Paul concludes with these words: "For God has consigned all to disobedience, that he may have mercy upon all" (11:32; cf. 3:23–24; 5:18).

It is worth noting that while Paul had earlier probably thought that Israel would first be saved and then the righteous Gentiles, now he has to adjust his thinking to the Gentiles being saved first and Israel being saved only afterward, at the end of the age.

Paul finally expresses his wonder and amazement at God's plan (11:33–36): "O the depth of the riches and wisdom and knowledge of God! How unsearchable are his judgments and how inscrutable his ways!" (11:33). And he concludes this remarkable passage in the only suitable way, with a doxology: "For from him and through him and to him are all things. To him be glory for ever. Amen" (11:36).

Living the Christian Life (12:1–15:6)

The gospel of Paul as articulated in Romans calls for a particular response in those who are its recipients. So, as is his custom, Paul turns to matters of practice that have their foundation in the doctrine that he has outlined. The rubric for this section of exhortation is found in 12:1: "I appeal to you therefore, brothers and sisters, by the mercies of God, to present your bodies as a living sacrifice, holy and acceptable to God, which is your spiritual worship" (NRSV). The spiritualizing of the language of the temple sacrifices is significant. Discipleship is analogous to giving up one's life to God, with the result that every area of life is lived in accordance with God's will. Chapters 12–13 allude a number of times to the teaching of Jesus, available to Paul from the oral tradition.[32] Chapter 13 includes the summary of the commandments under the love commandment: "'You shall love your neighbor as yourself.' Love does no wrong to a neighbor; therefore love is the fulfilling of the law" (13:9–10; cf. Gal. 5:14; Matt. 22:39–40). This is consonant with the final exhortation of chapter 13, to "put on the Lord Jesus Christ, and make no provision for the flesh, to gratify its desires" (13:14).

31. See especially Bell, *The Irrevocable Call of God.*
32. See Dunn, "Paul's Knowledge of the Jesus Tradition."

Chapter 14 discusses the relationship between "the strong" and "the weak," the latter being those who feel constrained to observe various restrictions concerning such things as foods and observance of days.[33] Paul's response is articulated in a key principle: "Let every one be fully convinced in his own mind" (14:5). The liberty affirmed here is limited by Paul's concern that no one cause another to stumble by his or her conduct (14:21). For Paul the bottom line is "what makes for peace and mutual upbuilding" (14:19). Tying in with the importance of faith throughout the epistle, now applied to the conduct of Christians, is the statement that "whatever does not proceed from faith is sin" (14:23).

In 14:17 Paul makes use of "kingdom of God" language: "For the kingdom of God is not food and drink but righteousness and peace and joy in the Holy Spirit." To this may be compared the final wish in 15:13: "May the God of hope fill you with all joy and peace in believing, so that by the power of the Holy Spirit you may abound in hope." Here the focus is on the fruit of the reign of God in the life of the believer (cf. Gal. 5:22–25).

The Significance of the Gentile Mission and Paul's Plans to Visit Rome (15:7–33)

In chapter 15 yet again we encounter the subject of Jews and Gentiles in salvation history. Paul remarkably refers to Christ as having become "a servant to the circumcised to show God's truthfulness, in order to confirm the promises given to the patriarchs, and in order that the Gentiles might glorify God for his mercy" (15:8–9). In Paul's mind the mission to the Gentiles is thus related to, indeed a vital part of, the story of Israel. The Gentiles have been in the purpose and plan of God all along. Paul collects a number of OT quotations to underscore this point. All these refer to the Gentiles and to their rejoicing at being included in the salvation of God (15:9–12). Paul goes on to speak of himself as, by God's grace, "a minister of Christ Jesus to the Gentiles in the priestly service [*hierourgounta*] of the gospel of God" (15:16).[34] By means of the work of Christ enshrined in the gospel, and through the preaching of Paul, the Apostle to the Gentiles, Israel fulfills its calling to be a servant and "a light to the nations" (Isa. 42:6; 49:6).

Greetings, a Final Warning, and Concluding Doxology (Romans 16)

Among the long list of people in chapter 16, to whom Paul sends greetings, are a number of women who were prominent in the leadership of the church. First Paul mentions Phoebe, a deaconess of the church at Cenchreae, who

---

33. See Watson, "The Two Roman Congregations." Karris ("Romans 14:1–15:3 and the Occasion of Romans") denies that Paul addresses a specific problem in the Roman church.

34. See Robinson, "The Priesthood of Paul in the Gospel of Hope."

brought the letter from Corinth to Rome. Then Prisca, along with her husband Aquila, is mentioned (16:3). Other women about whom we know little or nothing are greeted: Mary (Miriam; 16:6); Tryphaena and Tryphosa, who were probably sisters (16:12); Persis (16:12); the unnamed mother of Rufus (16:13); Julia, the wife of Philologus (and Olympas, probably their daughter; 16:15). Most interesting, however, is the mention in verse 7 of Andronicus and Junias. The latter name in the Greek accusative case used by Paul is *Iounian*, which is the same for both masculine and feminine.[35] Rather than being two men, therefore, Andronicus and Junia (the feminine form of the name, as accepted in NRSV and REB) may be husband and wife. The patristic writers of the early church accepted this understanding up until the Middle Ages. One reason that the issue is of some importance is that if Junia is meant, as seems probable, then this would be an example of a woman being referred to as an apostle: "Greet Andronicus and Junia, my relatives [or compatriots] who were in prison with me; they are prominent among the apostles, and they were in Christ before I was" (NRSV).

It is possible that Paul adds 16:17–20 in his own hand. He warns concerning those who oppose the doctrine they have been taught. Paul is content to assume the orthodoxy of what the Romans had been taught by the others. Paul's imminent eschatology is reflected in the statement of 16:20, "the God of peace will soon crush Satan under your feet."[36]

The final doxology, whether by Paul or not, serves wonderfully as the concluding words of this epistle. It glorifies God for the gospel and the preaching of Jesus Christ, and for making possible the obedience of faith.

Authorship, Date, and Place of Origin

Authorship

The Pauline authorship of Romans, one of Paul's four *Hauptbriefe* ("chief letters"), is one of the few conclusions shared by virtually all NT scholars. Romans is closely related to Galatians, of course, and also contains some content similar to the Corinthian epistles. In the case of Romans, we also know the name of the secretary Paul used when he wrote. With not a shred of shyness, but perhaps because he knew people in the Roman church, he adds his greetings to Paul's: "I Tertius, the writer of this letter, greet you in the Lord" (16:22). As was the custom, Tertius probably took down Paul's dictation by

35. A distinction between the masculine and feminine form of the accusative *Iounian* is made by different accenting of the word. All the early major textual witnesses, however, are without accents and hence the ambiguity remains. An interesting early variant is found in $\mathfrak{P}^{46}$ where *Ioulian*, Julia, is found.

36. On this see Scholer, "'The God of Peace Will Shortly Crush Satan Under Your Feet' (Romans 16:20a)."

shorthand. It may be that the speed of Paul's words and the complexity of the content are responsible for the occasional breaks in syntax, which are not, however, at all unusual in Paul's Letters.

Date

Thanks to the fixed date of 51 for the arrival of Gallio, the new proconsul of Achaia, in Corinth, we have a fair idea of when Paul first came to that city. According to Acts 18:12–17, Paul was brought before Gallio by Jews, hoping for a judgment against him. After three years in Ephesus (Acts 20:31), Paul returned to Corinth for three months (Acts 20:3), probably early in 57. That seems a likely date for the writing of Romans. Probably most important in deciding on the date of the epistle is the indication that the collection for the Jerusalem church was completed and had now only to be delivered, after which Paul planned to go to Rome (Rom. 15:25–29).

Place

Paul probably wrote Romans from Corinth. In Romans 16:23 Paul conveys greetings to the Romans from Gaius, "who is host to me" (one of Paul's converts in Corinth [1 Cor. 1:14]). At the end of Romans (16:1–2) Paul commends Phoebe, "a deaconess of the church at Cenchreae," who probably was the person who delivered the letter. That Paul wrote from Cenchreae is of course a possibility, but no more than a mere guess, with only the proximity to Corinth to recommend it. Macedonia is also a possibility, and appeal has been made to the present tense of the verb in 15:25, "At present, however, I am going [*poreuomai*] to Jerusalem" (15:25), as though indicating that Paul was already on the road. But *poreuomai* can also be taken as a futuristic present, meaning "I am about to go."

The Accomplishment of Romans

It is difficult not to believe that Paul consciously wrote Romans as a kind of definitive statement of his understanding of Christian salvation. Whereas in his other letters we have fragments of that understanding, they are presented not so much for their own sake as to support the practical concerns that Paul addresses in the various churches. Much of the theological substructure is presumed in the letters, probably having been delivered to the churches orally by Paul. In Romans, however, Paul deliberately sets down the basic logic of the work of Christ in a systematic way, relating it to salvation history, indeed universal history, and particularly to the perspectives that had developed within Judaism, many of which he himself has previously held. And so he addresses head-on the issue of how the gospel relates to the law—its promises as well as its demands—and how the response of the Gentiles and the unbelief of Israel are a part of God's larger plan and in no way challenge God's faithfulness. Throughout Romans there is an underlying tone of rejoicing in the grace of God revealed in a salvation so magnificent and comprehensive. The concluding doxology in 16:25–27 could hardly be more appropriate, ending with the words "to the only wise God be glory for evermore through Jesus Christ! Amen."

Romans, in short, is the fullest and clearest exposition in the NT of the meaning of Christ and his work. It is so masterful a document that for many, consciously or unconsciously, it serves as a canon within the canon, as the classic exposition of the essence of the Christian faith. Paul is the church's supreme interpreter of Jesus.

Bibliography

Books and Articles

Aageson, James W. "Scripture and Structure in the Development of the Argument in Romans 9–11." *CBQ* 48 (1986): 265–89.

Abasciano, Brian J. *Paul's Use of the Old Testament in Romans 9:10–18: An Intertextual and Theological Exegesis*. LNTS 301. London: T&T Clark, 2005.

Aune, David E., ed. *Rereading Paul Together: Protestant and Catholic Perspectives on Justification*. Grand Rapids: Baker Academic, 2006.

Beasley-Murray, George R. "The Righteousness of God in the History of Israel and the Nations: Romans 9–11." *RevExp* 73 (1976): 437–50.

Beasley-Murray, Paul. "Romans 1:3–4: An Early Confession of Faith in the Lordship of Jesus." *TynBul* 31 (1980): 147–54.

Bell, Richard H. *The Irrevocable Call of God: An Inquiry into Paul's Theology of Israel*. WUNT 184. Tübingen: Mohr Siebeck, 2005.

———. *No One Seeks for God: An Exegetical and Theological Study of Romans 1:18–3:20*. WUNT 106. Tübingen: Mohr Siebeck, 1998.

———. *Provoked to Jealousy: The Origin and Purpose of the Jealousy Motif in Romans 9–11*. WUNT 2/63. Tübingen: Mohr Siebeck, 1994.

Berkley, Timothy W. *From a Broken Covenant to Circumcision of the Heart: Pauline Intertextual Exegesis in Romans 2:17–29*. SBLDS 175. Atlanta: Society of Biblical Literature, 2000.

Bertone, John A. *"The Law of the Spirit": Experience of the Spirit and Displacement of the Law in Romans 8:1–16*. SBL 86. New York: Peter Lang, 2005.

Boers, Hendrikus. *The Justification of the Gentiles: Paul's Letters to the Galatians and Romans*. Peabody, MA: Hendrickson, 1994.

Borg, Marcus. "A New Context for Romans xiii." *NTS* 19 (1972–73): 205–18.

Bornkamm, Günther. "Sin, Law and Death: An Exegetical Study of Romans 7." In *Early Christian Experience*, 83–94. New York: Harper & Row, 1969.

Botha, Jan. *Subject to Whose Authority? Multiple Readings of Romans 13*. ESEC 4. Atlanta: Scholars Press, 1994.

Bring, Ragnar. "Paul and the Old Testament." *ST* 25 (1971): 21–60.

Brondos, David A. *Paul on the Cross: Reconstructing the Apostle's Story of Redemption*. Minneapolis: Fortress, 2006.

Brown, Raymond E., and John P. Meier. *Antioch and Rome: New Testament Cradles of Catholic Christianity*. New York: Paulist Press, 1983.

Bruce, F. F. *New Testament History*. Garden City, NY: Doubleday, 1972.

Bryan, Christopher. *A Preface to Romans: Notes on the Epistle in Its Literary and Cultural Setting*. New York: Oxford University Press, 2000.

Campbell, Douglas A. *The Rhetoric of Righteousness in Romans 3:21–26*. JSNTSup 65. Sheffield: JSOT Press, 1992.

Campbell, William S., Peter S. Hawkins, and Brenda Schildgen, eds. *Medieval Readings of Romans*. RHC. New York: T&T Clark, 2007.

Corley, Bruce. "The Jews, the Future, and God (Romans 9–11)." *SwJT* 19 (1976–77): 42–56.

Cousar, Charles B. *A Theology of the Cross: The Death of Jesus in the Pauline Letters*. OBT. Minneapolis: Fortress, 1990.

Cranfield, C. E. B. "On Some Problems in the Interpretation of Romans 5.12." *SJT* 22 (1969): 324–41.

———. "'The Works of the Law' in the Epistle to the Romans." *JSNT* 43 (1991): 89–101.

Dabourne, Wendy. *Purpose and Cause in Pauline Exegesis: Romans 1:16–4:25 and a New Approach to the Letters*. SNTSMS 104. Cambridge: Cambridge University Press, 1999.

Danker, Frederick W. "Romans V.12: Sin under Law." *NTS* 14 (1967–68): 424–39.

Das, A. Andrew. *Solving the Romans Debate*. Minneapolis: Fortress, 2007.

Davies, Glenn. *Faith and Obedience in Romans: A Study in Romans 1–4*. JSNTSup 39. Sheffield: JSOT Press, 1990.

Davies, W. D. "Paul and the People of Israel." *NTS* 24 (1977–78): 4–39.

Dinkler, Erich. "The Historical and Eschatological Israel in Romans Chaps. 9–11: A Contribution to the Problem of Predestination and Individual Responsibility." *JR* 36 (1956): 109–27.

Dockery, David S. "The Use of Habakkuk 2:4 in Romans 1:17." *WeslTJ* 22 (1987): 24–36.

Dodd, C. H. *The Bible and the Greeks*. London: Hodder and Stoughton, 1935.

Donfried, Karl P., ed. *The Romans Debate*. Rev. ed. Peabody, MA: Hendrickson, 1991.

Drane, John W. "Why Did Paul Write Romans?" In *Pauline Studies: Essays Presented to F. F. Bruce on His 70th Birthday*, edited by Donald A. Hagner and Murray J. Harris, 208–27. Grand Rapids: Eerdmans, 1980.

Dunn, James D. G. "Paul's Knowledge of the Jesus Tradition: The Evidence of Romans." In *Christus Bezeugen: Für Wolfgang Trilling*, edited by K. Kertelge et al., 193–207. Leipzig: St. Benno, 1990.

———. "Romans 7:14–25 in the Theology of Paul." *TZ* 31 (1975): 257–73.

———. *The Theology of Paul the Apostle*. Grand Rapids: Eerdmans, 1998.

———. "Yet Once More—'The Works of the Law.'" *JSNT* 46 (1992): 99–117.

du Toit, Andrie. *Focusing on Paul: Persuasion and Theological Design in Romans and Galatians*, edited by Cilliers Breytenbach and David S. du Toit. BZNW 151. Berlin: de Gruyter, 2007.

Elliott, Neil. *The Rhetoric of Romans: Argumentative Constraint and Strategy and Paul's Dialogue with Judaism*. JSNTSup 45. Sheffield: JSOT Press, 1990.

Ellis, J. Edward. *Paul and Ancient Views of Sexual Desire: Paul's Sexual Ethics in 1 Thessalonians 4, 1 Corinthians 7, and Romans 1*. LNTS 354. London: T&T Clark, 2007.

Epp, Eldon Jay. *Junia: The First Woman Apostle*. Minneapolis: Fortress, 2005.

Esler, Philip F. *Conflict and Identity in Romans: The Social Setting of Paul's Letter*. Minneapolis: Fortress, 2003.

Fitzmyer, Joseph A. *Spiritual Exercises Based on Paul's Epistle to the Romans*. New York: Paulist Press, 1995.

Gaca, Kathy L., and L. L. Welborn, eds. *Early Patristic Readings of Romans*. RHC. London: T&T Clark, 2005.

Gamble, Harry, Jr. *The Textual History of the Letter to the Romans*. Grand Rapids: Eerdmans, 1977.

Garlington, Don. *Faith, Obedience, and Perseverance: Aspects of Paul's Letter to the Romans*. WUNT 79. Tübingen: Mohr Siebeck, 1994.

Gathercole, Simon J. *Where Is Boasting? Early Jewish Soteriology and Paul's Response in Romans 1–5*. Grand Rapids: Eerdmans, 2002.

Gieniusz, Andrzej. *Romans 8:18–30: "Suffering Does Not Thwart the Future Glory."* ISFCJ 9. Atlanta: Scholars Press, 1999.

Grenholm, Cristina, and Daniel Patte, eds. *Reading Israel in Romans: Legitimacy and Plausibility of Divergent Interpretations*. RHC. Harrisburg, PA: Trinity Press International, 2000.

Grieb, A. Katherine. *The Story of Romans: A Narrative Defense of God's Righteousness*. Louisville: Westminster John Knox, 2002.

Haacker, Klaus. *The Theology of Paul's Letter to the Romans*. NTT. Cambridge: Cambridge University Press, 2003.

Hahne, Harry Alan. *The Corruption and Redemption of Creation: Nature in Romans 8:19–22 and Jewish Apocalyptic Literature*. LNTS 336. London: T&T Clark, 2006.

Hamerton-Kelly, Robert G. *Sacred Violence: Paul's Hermeneutic of the Cross*. Minneapolis: Fortress, 1992.

Harrington, Daniel J. *Paul on the Mystery of Israel*. ZS. Collegeville, MN: Liturgical Press, 1992.

Hay, David M., and E. Elizabeth Johnson, eds. *Romans*. Vol. 3 of *Pauline Theology*. Minneapolis: Fortress, 1995.

Hultgren, Arland J. *Paul's Gospel and Mission: The Outlook from His Letter to the Romans*. Philadelphia: Fortress, 1985.

Hurtado, Larry W. "The Doxology at the End of Romans." In *New Testament Textual Criticism: Its Significance for Exegesis (Essays in Honour of Bruce M. Metzger)*, edited by Eldon J. Epp and Gordon D. Fee, 185–99. Oxford: Clarendon, 1981.

Hvalvik, Reidar. "A 'Sonderweg' for Israel: A Critical Examination of a Current Interpretation of Romans 11:25–27." *JSNT* 38 (1990): 87–107.

Jeffers, James S. *Conflict at Rome: Social Order and Hierarchy in Early Christianity*. Minneapolis: Fortress, 1991.

Jervell, Jacob. "The Letter to Jerusalem." In *The Romans Debate*, edited by Karl P. Donfried, 53–64. Rev. ed. Peabody, MA: Hendrickson, 1991.

———. *The Unknown Paul: Essays on Luke-Acts and Early Christian History*. Minneapolis: Augsburg, 1984.

Karris, Robert J. "Romans 14:1–15:13 and the Occasion of Romans." In *The Romans Debate*, edited by Karl P. Donfried, 65–84. Rev. ed. Peabody, MA: Hendrickson, 1991.

Käsemann, Ernst. "The Faith of Abraham in Romans 4." In *Perspectives on Paul*, 79–101. Philadelphia: Fortress, 1971.

———. "The Righteousness of God in Romans." In *New Testament Questions of Today*, 168–82. Philadelphia: Fortress, 1969.

Kaylor, R. David. *Paul's Covenant Community: Jew and Gentile in Romans*. Atlanta: John Knox, 1988.

Kim, Johann D. *God, Israel, and the Gentiles: Rhetoric and Situation in Romans 9–11*. SBLDS 176. Atlanta: Scholars Press, 2000.

Kümmel, Werner Georg. *Introduction to the New Testament*. Translated by A. J. Mattill Jr. 14th ed. Nashville: Abingdon, 1966.

Kuula, Kari. *Paul's Treatment of the Law and Israel in Romans*. Vol. 2 of *The Law, the Covenant and God's Plan*. PFES 85. Göttingen: Vandenhoeck & Ruprecht, 2003.

Lambrecht, Jan, and Richard W. Thompson. *Justification by Faith: The Implications of Romans 3:27–31*. ZS. Wilmington, DE: Michael Glazier, 1989.

Lampe, Peter. *From Paul to Valentinus: Christians at Rome in the First Two Centuries*. Translated by Michael Steinhauser. Edited by Marshall D. Johnson. Minneapolis: Fortress, 2003.

Landes, Paula Fredriksen. *Augustine on Romans: Propositions from the Epistle to the Romans; Unfinished Commentary on the Epistle to the Romans*. SBLECL 6. Chico, CA: Scholars Press, 1982.

Lincoln, Andrew T. "Abraham Goes to Rome: Paul's Treatment of Abraham in Romans 4." In *Worship, Theology and Ministry in the Early Church: Essays in Honor of Ralph Martin*, edited by Michael J. Wilkins and Terence Paige, 163–79. JSNTSup 87. Sheffield: JSOT Press, 1992.

Longenecker, Bruce W. "Different Answers to Different Issues: Israel, the Gentiles and Salvation History in Romans 9–11." *JSNT* 36 (1989): 95–123.

Longenecker, Richard N. *Introducing Romans: Critical Concerns in Paul's Most Famous Letter*. Grand Rapids: Eerdmans, 2011.

———. "Prolegomena to Paul's Use of Scripture in Romans." *BBR* 7 (1997): 145–68.

Manson, T. W. "St. Paul's Letter to the Romans—and Others." In *Studies in the Gospels and Epistles*, edited by Matthew Black, 225–41. Manchester, UK: Manchester University Press, 1962.

Marcus, Joel. "The Circumcision and the Uncircumcision in Rome." *NTS* 35 (1989): 67–81.

Marshall, I. Howard. "Romans 16:25–27—An Apt Conclusion." In *Romans and the People of God*, edited by Gordon D. Fee, S. K. Soderlund, and N. T. Wright, 170–84. Grand Rapids: Eerdmans, 1999.

McGinn, Sheila E., ed. *Celebrating Romans: Template for Pauline Theology; Essays in Honor of Robert Jewett*. Grand Rapids: Eerdmans, 2004.

McLean, B. Hudson. *The Cursed Christ: Mediterranean Expulsion Rituals and Pauline Soteriology*. JSNTSup 126. Sheffield: Sheffield Academic Press, 1996.

Miller, James C. *The Obedience of Faith, the Eschatological People of God, and the Purpose of Romans*. SBLDS 177. Atlanta: Scholars Press, 2000.

Minear, Paul S. *The Obedience of Faith: The Purposes of Paul in the Epistle to the Romans*. SBT. Naperville, IL: Allenson, 1971.

Mitton, C. L. "Romans 7 Reconsidered." *ExpT* 65 (1953–54): 78–81, 99–103, 132–35.

Moo, Douglas J. *Encountering the Book of Romans: A Theological Survey*. Peabody, MA: Hendrickson, 2002.

———. "'Law,' 'Works of the Law,' and Legalism in Paul." *WTJ* 45 (1985): 90–96.

Morgan, Robert. *Romans*. NTSG. London: Sheffield Academic, 1995.

Morris, Leon. *The Apostolic Preaching of the Cross*. 3rd ed. London: Tyndale, 1965.

Munck, Johannes. *Christ and Israel: An Interpretation of Romans 9–11*. Translated by Ingeborg Nixon. Philadelphia: Fortress, 1967.

———. *Paul and the Salvation of Mankind*. Translated by Frank Clarke. Richmond: John Knox, 1959.

Nanos, Mark D. *The Mystery of Romans. The Jewish Context of Paul's Letters*. Minneapolis: Fortress, 1996.

Odell-Scott, David W., ed. *Reading Romans with Contemporary Philosophers and Theologians*. RHC. New York: T&T Clark, 2007.

Peng, Kuo-Wei. *Hate the Evil, Hold Fast to the Good: Structuring Romans 12:1–15:1*. LNTS 300. London: T&T Clark, 2006.

Porter, Stanley E. "The Pauline Concept of Original Sin, in Light of Rabbinic Background." *TynBul* 41 (1990): 3–30.

Reasoner, Mark. *Romans in Full Circle: A History of Interpretation*. Louisville: Westminster John Knox, 2005.

———. *The Strong and the Weak: Romans 14:1–15:13 in Context*. SNTSMS 103. Cambridge: Cambridge University Press, 1999.

Reumann, John. "The Gospel of the Righteousness of God." *Int* 20 (1966): 432–52.

Richardson, Peter. *Israel in the Apostolic Church*. SNTSMS 10. Cambridge: Cambridge University Press, 1969.

Robinson, D. W. B. "The Priesthood of Paul in the Gospel of Hope." In *Reconcilation and Hope: New Testament Essays on Atonement and Eschatology Presented to L. L. Morris*, edited by R. Banks, 231–45. Grand Rapids: Eerdmans, 1974.

Sabou, Sorin. *Between Horror and Hope: Paul's Metaphorical Language of "Death" in Romans 6:1–11*. PBM. Waynesboro, GA: Paternoster, 2005.

Sanders, E. P. *Paul and Palestinian Judaism*. Philadelphia: Fortress, 1977.

Schliesser, Benjamin. *Abraham's Faith in Romans 4: Paul's Concept of Faith in Light of the History of Reception of Genesis 15:6*. WUNT 2/224. Tübingen: Mohr Siebeck, 2007.

Scholer, David M. "'The God of Peace Will Shortly Crush Satan under Your Feet' (Romans 16:20a): The Function of Apocalyptic Eschatology in Paul." *ExAud* 6 (1990): 53–61.

Schreiner, Thomas R. "'Works of Law' in Paul." *NovT* 33 (1991): 217–44.

Seeley, David. *The Noble Death: Graeco-Roman Martyrology and Paul's Concept of Salvation*. JSNTSup 28. Sheffield: JSOT Press, 1990.

Seifrid, Mark A. *Christ, Our Righteousness: Paul's Theology of Justification*. NSBT. Downers Grove, IL: InterVarsity, 2000.

———. *Justification by Faith: The Origin and Development of a Central Pauline Theme*. NovTSup 68. Leiden: Brill, 1992.

———. "The Subject of Rom 7:14–25." *NovT* 34 (1992): 313–33.

Stendahl, Krister. "The Apostle Paul and the Introspective Conscience of the West." *HTR* 56 (1963): 199–215.

———. *Final Account: Paul's Letter to the Romans*. Minneapolis: Fortress, 1995.

Stowers, Stanley K. *The Diatribe and Paul's Letter to the Romans*. SBLDS 57. Chico, CA: Scholars Press, 1981.

———. *A Rereading of Romans: Justice, Jews, and Gentiles*. New Haven: Yale University Press, 1995.

Stuhlmacher, Peter. "The Purpose of Romans." In *The Romans Debate*, edited by Karl P. Donfried, 231–42. Rev. ed. Peabody, MA: Hendrickson, 1991.

———. *Revisiting Paul's Doctrine of Justification: A Challenge to the New Perspective*. Downers Grove, IL: InterVarsity, 2001.

———. "The Theme of Romans." In *The Romans Debate*, edited by Karl P. Donfried, 333–45. Rev. ed. Peabody, MA: Hendrickson, 1991.

Szypula, Wojciech. *The Holy Spirit in the Eschatological Tension of Christian Life: An Exegetico-Theological Study of 2 Corinthians 5:1–5 and Romans 8:18–27*. TGST 147. Rome: Editrice Pontificia Università Gregoriana, 2007.

Thompson, Michael. *Clothed with Christ: The Example and Teaching of Jesus in Romans 12:1–15:13*. JSNTSup 59. Sheffield: JSOT Press, 1991.

Thorsteinsson, Runar M. *Paul's Interlocutor in Romans 2: Function and Identity in the Context of Ancient Epistolography*. ConBNT 40. Stockholm: Almqvist & Wiksell, 2003.

Tobin, Thomas H. *Paul's Rhetoric in Its Contexts: The Argument of Romans*. Peabody, MA: Hendrickson, 2004.

VanLandingham, Chris. *Judgment and Justification in Early Judaism and the Apostle Paul*. Peabody, MA: Hendrickson, 2006.

Wagner, Günter. "The Future of Israel: Reflections on Romans 9–11." In *Eschatology and the New Testament: Essays in Honor of George Raymond Beasley-Murray*, edited by W. Hulitt Gloer, 77–112. Peabody, MA: Hendrickson, 1988.

Wagner, J. Ross. *Heralds of the Good News: Isaiah and Paul "in Concert" in the Letter to the Romans*. NovTSup 101. Leiden: Brill, 2002.

Watson, Francis. "The Two Roman Congregations: Romans 14:1–15:13." In *The Romans Debate*, edited by Karl P. Donfried, 203–15. Rev. ed. Peabody, MA: Hendrickson, 1991.

Wedderburn, A. J. M. *The Reasons for Romans*. Minneapolis: Fortress, 1991.

Westerholm, Stephen. *Understanding Paul: The Early Christian Worldview of the Letter to the Romans*. 2nd ed. Grand Rapids: Baker Academic, 2004.

Wilk, Florian, and J. Ross Wagner, eds. *Between Gospel and Election: Explorations in the Interpretation of Romans 9–11*. WUNT 257. Tübingen: Mohr Siebeck, 2010.

Ziesler, J. A. *The Meaning of Righteousness in Paul: A Linguistic and Theological Inquiry.* SNTSMS 20. Cambridge: Cambridge University Press, 1972.

Commentaries

Achtemeier, Paul J. *Romans.* IBC. Atlanta: John Knox, 1985.

Barrett, C. K. *A Commentary on the Epistle to the Romans.* HNTC. New York: Harper & Row, 1957.

Barth, Karl. *The Epistle to the Romans.* Translated by Edwyn C. Hoskyns. London: Oxford University Press, 1933.

———. *A Shorter Commentary on Romans.* Translated by Geoffrey Bromiley. Richmond: John Knox, 1959.

Best, Ernest. *The Letter of Paul to the Romans.* CBC. Cambridge: Cambridge University Press, 1967.

Black, Matthew. *Romans.* Greenwood, SC: Attic Press, 1973.

Bruce, F. F. *The Letter of Paul to the Romans.* Rev. ed. TNTC. Grand Rapids: Eerdmans, 1985.

Brunner, Emil. *The Letter to the Romans: A Commentary.* Philadelphia: Westminster, 1959.

Byrne, Brendan. *Romans.* SP 6. Collegeville, MN: Liturgical Press, 1996.

Calvin, John. *Commentary on the Epistle of Paul the Apostle to the Romans.* Translated by Ross Mackenzie. Grand Rapids: Eerdmans, 1961.

Cobb, John B., Jr., and David J. Lull. *Romans.* CCT. St. Louis: Chalice, 2005.

Cranfield, C. E. B. *A Commentary on Romans 12–13.* SJTOP 12. Edinburgh: Oliver & Boyd, 1965.

———. *Romans.* 2 vols. ICC. Edinburgh: T&T Clark, 1975–79.

Denney, James. *St. Paul's Epistle to the Romans.* In vol. 2 of *The Expositor's Greek Testament,* edited by W. Robertson Nicoll, 555–725. London: Hodder & Stoughton, 1917.

Dodd, C. H. *The Epistle of Paul to the Romans.* MNTC. New York: Harper, 1932.

Dunn, James D. G. *Romans 1–8.* WBC 38A. Dallas: Word, 1988.

———. *Romans 9–16.* WBC 38B. Dallas: Word, 1988.

Edwards, James R. *Romans.* NIBC. Peabody, MA: Hendrickson, 1992.

Fitzmyer, Joseph A. *Romans: A New Translation with Introduction and Commentary.* AB 33. New York: Doubleday, 1993.

Godet, Frédéric Louis. *Commentary on Romans.* Translated by A. Cusin. CCL. Grand Rapids: Zondervan, 1956.

Hagner, Donald A., and Everett F. Harrison. "Romans." In *The Expositor's Bible Commentary,* edited by Tremper Longman III and David E. Garland, 11:19–237. Rev. ed. Grand Rapids: Zondervan, 2008.

Harrisville, Roy A. *Romans.* ACNT. Minneapolis: Augsburg, 1980.

Hodge, Charles. *A Commentary on the Epistle to the Romans.* Rev. ed. New York: Armstrong, 1896.

Hunter, A. M. *The Epistle to the Romans.* TBC. London: SCM, 1955.

Jewett, Robert. *Romans: A Commentary.* Hermeneia. Minneapolis: Fortress, 2007.

Johnson, Luke Timothy. *Reading Romans: A Literary and Theological Commentary.* RNT. Macon, GA: Smyth & Helwys, 1999.

Käsemann, Ernst. *Commentary on Romans.* Translated and edited by Geoffrey W. Bromiley. Grand Rapids: Eerdmans, 1980.

Keck, Leander. *Romans.* ANTC. Nashville: Abingdon, 2005.

Leenhardt, Franz J. *The Epistle to the Romans: A Commentary.* Translated by Harold Knight. London: Lutterworth, 1961.

Luther, Martin. *Luther: Lectures on Romans.* LCC 15. Translated and edited by Wilhelm Pauck. Philadelphia: Westminster, 1961.

Manson, T. W. "Romans." In *Peake's Commentary on the Bible*, edited by Matthew Black and H. H. Rowley, 940–53. London: Nelson, 1962.

Matera, Frank J. *Romans*. Paideia. Grand Rapids: Baker Academic, 2011.

Meyer, H. A. W. *Critical and Exegetical Handbook to the Epistle to the Romans*. Translated by John C. Moore and Edwin Johnson. 2 vols. Edinburgh: T&T Clark, 1879.

Moo, Douglas J. *The Epistle to the Romans*. NICNT. Grand Rapids: Eerdmans, 1996.

Morris, Leon. *The Epistle to the Romans*. PNTC. Grand Rapids: Eerdmans, 1988.

Mounce, Robert H. *Romans*. NAC. Nashville: Broadman & Holman, 1995.

Murray, John. *The Epistle to the Romans*. NICNT. Grand Rapids: Eerdmans, 1968.

Nygren, Anders. *Commentary on Romans*. Translated by Carl C. Rasmussen. Philadelphia: Muhlenberg, 1949.

Reumann, John. "Romans." In *Eerdmans Commentary on the Bible*, edited by James D. G. Dunn, 1277–313. Grand Rapids: Eerdmans, 2003.

Robinson, John A. T. *Wrestling with Romans*. Philadelphia: Westminster, 1979.

Sanday, William, and Arthur C. Headlam. *A Critical and Exegetical Commentary on the Epistle to the Romans*. 5th ed. ICC. Edinburgh: T&T Clark, 1925.

Schlatter, Adolf. *Romans: The Righteousness of God*. Translated by Siegfried S. Schatzmann. Peabody, MA: Hendrickson, 1995.

Schreiner, Thomas R. *Romans*. BECNT. Grand Rapids: Baker Academic, 1998.

Stuhlmacher, Peter. *Paul's Letter to the Romans: A Commentary*. Translated by Scott J. Hafemann. Louisville: Westminster John Knox, 1994.

Talbert, Charles H. *Romans*. SHBC. Macon, GA: Smyth & Helwys, 2002.

Taylor, Vincent. *The Epistle to the Romans*. EC. London: Epworth, 1955.

Witherington, Ben, III. *Paul's Letter to the Romans: A Socio-Rhetorical Commentary*. Grand Rapids: Eerdmans, 2003.

Wright, N. T. "The Letter to the Romans." *NIB* 10:393–770.

30

Philippians

Philippians, along with Ephesians, Colossians, and Philemon, belongs to the group of letters commonly known as the Prison Epistles, all of them written ostensibly by an imprisoned Paul. From the joyful tone of this letter, however, one would never have guessed that it was written by a man in prison facing a capital charge. Philippians reveals the positive effects of Christian faith on ordinary, everyday life and in times of suffering and personal trial too. "Even if I am to be poured as a libation upon the sacrificial offering of your faith, I am glad and rejoice with you all. Likewise you also should be glad and rejoice with me" (2:17–18). With the realities of the faith as the foundation of his life, Paul exhorts the Philippian Christians, "Finally, my brothers and sisters, rejoice in the Lord" (3:1 NRSV); "Rejoice in the Lord always; again I will say, Rejoice" (4:4). In Paul's thinking, there is no room for anxiety about anything (4:6). Here he probably depends on the oral tradition of the teaching of Jesus (cf. Matt. 6:25–34; Luke 12:22–31). One is but to pray with thanksgiving, "And the peace of God, which passes all understanding, will keep your hearts and your minds in Christ Jesus" (4:7).

The Church at Philippi

According to the narrative of Acts 16, during the so-called second missionary journey (ca. 49–50), Paul experienced a vision in Troas (northwestern Asia

---

Author: Almost universally accepted as written by Paul.

Date: Probably written from a Roman prison between 60 and 62, perhaps later in the period. If, however, it was written from Caesarea, then sometime in 57–59; if from Ephesus, even earlier, in about 52–55.

Addressees: The church at Philippi.

Purpose: Paul writes for several reasons, among which are to send news concerning his imprisonment, to thank the Philippian Christians for their support, to praise Epaphroditus, and to commend Timothy.

Message/Argument: The letter is dominated by a tone of joy and rejoicing even in the midst of trials, imprisonment, and the possibility of death.

Significance: An unusual Pauline letter because it is not preoccupied with problems in the church, as most of Paul's other letters are. Thus it is an example of a letter of friendship, gratitude, and encouragement.

Minor) consisting of the famous "Macedonian call."[1] In the first of the "we" passages in Acts, Luke records that they sailed westward directly to Samothrace, an island in the Aegean Sea, and from there to Neapolis, the seaport a mere ten miles from Philippi, the latter described by Luke as "the leading city of the district of Macedonia" (Acts 16:12). This description is problematic because Philippi was not such an important city (nearby Amphipolis was more influential). A very slight emendation of the Greek text (reading *prōtēs* for *prōtē*), following the lead of some ancient versions, produces a more probable reading: "a city of the first district of Macedonia."

Philippi had been founded by Greeks in the fourth century BC, taking its name from Philip II of Macedonia, the father of Alexander the Great. In the second century BC it became a Roman city, and eventually in the first century BC, like Corinth, a Roman "colony," as Luke refers to it (Acts 16:12). This was a favored status that brought Roman citizenship to its inhabitants, exemption from taxes, and other legal privileges such as were granted to cities in Italy. Philippi therefore was an exemplary Roman town, with Latin as its official language, strategically located on the Via Egnatia, the main Roman road that ran all the way from Byzantium to the Adriatic.[2] Paul's missionary work in

---

1. Some have suggested that Luke, possibly born in Philippi, may have been the Macedonian man of the vision, but this can only be speculation. See Hemer, *The Book of Acts in the Setting of Hellenistic History*, 346. Just as the first "we" section of Acts ends in Philippi, the second begins in Philippi (Acts 20:6), suggesting that perhaps Luke remained there in the intervening period. It is possible that Luke is to be identified as the "true yokefellow" of Philippians 4:3. See Bruce, *Paul*, 219n28, 221.

2. For an illuminating study of the social composition of the Philippian community, see Oakes, *Philippians*.

Philippi marks a major turning point in his ministry, not only in his entry into Europe but also in his work among predominantly Gentile communities.

There is no evidence, archaeological or otherwise, that Philippi had a Jewish synagogue. Paul, however, discovered a place just outside the town, by the river Gangites, where some women gathered for prayer on the Sabbath. There he met a well-to-do God-fearer (Acts 16:14), Lydia of Thyatira, who believed in Paul's message and was immediately baptized. Paul, Silas, and Luke were invited to stay in her house. Before long, however, Paul and Silas were arrested, beaten, and thrown into jail (cf. the reference to this in 1 Thess. 2:2) for exorcizing a demon (a pythonic spirit) from a slave girl, who had immediately identified them as "servants of the Most High God, who proclaim to you the way of salvation" (Acts 16:17). The trumped-up charge brought against them was that they were Jews who were disturbing the city and advocating "customs which it is not lawful for us Romans to accept or practice" (Acts 16:21). When, after the earthquake and the conversion and baptism of the nameless Philippian jailor, the magistrates discovered that Paul and Silas were Roman citizens and thereby protected against the kind of punishment they had given them without trial, they were obligated to apologize profusely, before requesting them to leave the town.[3]

The next visits of Paul to Philippi apparently were those mentioned in Acts 20:1 and 2 Corinthians 2:13 (in those verses "Macedonia" probably refers to Philippi), and a final visit was made during his journey to Jerusalem with the offering (Acts 20:6), but we are given no information concerning these visits (see also 1 Tim. 1:3).

According to Philippians 2:19–24, Paul intends to send Timothy to Philippi in order to have news, which he hopes will be cheerful, concerning the Philippian church. With Timothy he will also send Epaphroditus, a Philippian Christian described as "my brother and fellow worker and fellow soldier, and your messenger [apostolos] and minister to my need" (2:25). Epaphroditus was distressed that the Philippian church had heard of his serious illness; Paul writes that he had "nearly died for the work of Christ, risking his life to complete your service to me" (2:30 [cf. 4:18]). The only other persons mentioned in the letter are an otherwise unknown Clement and the women Euodia and Syntyche, described by Paul as having "labored side by side with me in the gospel" (4:2–3).[4]

---

3. The accuracy and appropriateness of Luke's technical vocabulary, geographical and official, in this passage has often been remarked on. See Hemer, *The Book of Acts in the Setting of Hellenistic History*, 111–15.

4. These women leaders in the church may well reflect the high status of women generally in Macedonia. "If Macedonia produced perhaps the most competent group of men the world had yet seen, the women were in all respects the men's counterparts; they played a large part in affairs, received envoys and obtained concessions for them from their husbands, built temples, founded cities, engaged mercenaries, commanded armies, held fortresses, and acted on occasion

The Integrity of Philippians

There are several reasons why many scholars have come to the conclusion that Philippians is the combination of several Pauline Letters. Not only does Philippians lack the general coherence of some of the other Pauline Letters but also, most noticeably, it contains some very abrupt transitions and changes of tone. It also contains redundant material at points, while different parts of Philippians address different situations and concerns. In addition to this internal evidence, a statement in Polycarp's *To the Philippians* (early second century) refers to "letters" (plural) that Paul wrote to the Philippians (Pol. *Phil.* 3:2).[5]

The most immediately obvious difficulty concerns the sequence of statements at the beginning of chapter 3. The opening words look very much like the end of a letter: "Finally, my brothers and sisters, rejoice in the Lord" (NRSV). This would fit beautifully with 4:4 (note also the "finally" of 4:8), raising the possibility that the material in between could belong to a separate letter. The transition between 3:1a and 3:2 is terribly abrupt. Suddenly after the call to rejoice and the innocuous statement of 3:1b comes the sudden, vitriolic 3:2: "Look out for the dogs, look out for the evil-workers, look out for those who mutilate the flesh." The situation here is quite parallel to the sudden shift of tone at the beginning of 2 Corinthians 10 that has caused many to think that 2 Corinthians 10–13 was a separate letter (see chap. 28 above).

A further abrupt transition can be seen between 4:9 and 4:10. Whereas 4:9 seems to be winding down to the end of the letter and would be smoothly followed by 4:21–23, suddenly 4:10–20 seems inserted. This passage expresses Paul's gratitude to the Philippians for their gift, but the gift is already alluded to in 1:3–11; 2:25–30. That the thank you of 4:10–20 comes so late in the letter makes it seem that it may originally have been a separate letter or part of a letter earlier sent to Philippi.

These observations, together with the redundancies of material in 4:4–7, 9, 20, 21–23, have led Günther Bornkamm to go so far as to call Philippians "a Pauline letter-collection."[6] Commentators have suggested three separate letters, separated out approximately as follows:

1. 4:10–20 (the original thank-you note, sent soon after the arrival of Epaphroditus)
2. 1:1–3:1 and 4:4–7 (possibly also 4:21–23) (Paul's perspective on his imprisonment)

---

as regents or even co-rulers" (Tarn and Griffith, *Hellenistic Civilization*, 98–99). (I owe this reference to Martin, *Philippians*, 8.)

5. However, see the discussion in Lightfoot, *St. Paul's Epistle to the Philippians*, 140–42, where he shows that the plural *epistolai* can be used of a single document.

6. Bornkamm, "Der Philipperbrief als paulinische Briefsammlung."

3. 3:2–4:3 and 4:8–9 (a sharp attack against Judaizers; no mention of imprisonment in 3:10–11, so perhaps sent before or after)

The conjectural nature of this analysis should be plain to all. We are forced to talk only of possibilities, of which there are many. Paul, moreover, never felt bound to keep to the rules and to write orderly letters.[7] However, rhetorical analysis has shown that Philippians follows the well-established principles of Greco-Roman rhetoric and should therefore be regarded as a unity.[8]

Those commentators who accept the unity of Philippians present a variety of arguments to account for the phenomena observed above. There is furthermore the ongoing challenge to those subscribing to partition theories to account for what looks like the bumbling work of an incompetent editor, not to mention his motivation, in piecing together the putative letters.

It is widely accepted that the Christ hymn in 2:6–11 is an independent piece that preexisted the Letter to the Philippians. However, it is not at all uncommon for Paul to use liturgical and hymnic material in his letters.

The Nature of the Problems at Philippi and the Purpose of the Letter

From the pieces of information that Paul provides, it is difficult to know what problems the Philippian church may have faced. The reason, of course, is that Paul does not write Philippians for the purpose of correcting error. Most "problems" he alludes to only in passing, except for the strife between the two leaders of the community, Euodia and Syntyche (4:2). There is no way to know specifically what lay behind this particular problem. The exhortation in 2:2 may also have this specific situation in view, if it does not refer to other manifestations of strife in the community.[9]

As far as the other issues alluded to by Paul are concerned, these seem not to refer to "opponents" in Philippi.[10] In 1:15–17 the issue is not doctrinal divergence of any kind but rather personal rivalry and conflict, and preaching Christ from the wrong motives. Moreover, those verses refer to Christians who were in the city of Paul's imprisonment, probably, as we will see, Rome. Those who were

7. Loveday Alexander ("Hellenistic Letter-Forms and the Structure of Philippians") concludes that nothing in Philippians is inconsistent with the Hellenistic letter form. See also Garland, "The Composition and Unity of Philippians," arguing that 1:27–4:3 is a literary unit, and that 3:1–21 is a deliberate rhetorical device leading to the climactic appeal concerning Euodia and Syntyche.

8. See Watson, "A Rhetorical Analysis of Philippians and Its Implications for the Unity Question." For another defense of the unity of Philippians, from the standpoint of discourse analysis, see Black, "The Discourse Structure of Philippians." See also the detailed work of Reed, *A Discourse Analysis of Philippians*.

9. See Peterlin, *Paul's Letter to the Philippians in the Light of the Disunity in the Church*.

10. "There is, indeed, *no* evidence that there were *any* 'false teachers' in the Philippian community" (Hooker, "Philippians," 378).

preaching Christ out of selfish ambition did not have a correct understanding of Paul's imprisonment. Paul did not regard his imprisonment as an "affliction," as they apparently did, or indeed as any kind of setback for the gospel. On the contrary, he and others preaching Christ know that he has been put there "for the defense of the gospel" (1:16). And so Paul writes, "I want you to know, beloved, that what has happened to me has actually helped to spread the gospel, so that it has become known throughout the whole imperial guard and to everyone else that my imprisonment is for Christ" (1:12–13 NRSV). Others, as a result, have been emboldened "to speak the word of God without fear" (1:14). Paul's goal here is to set himself forward as a model of Christian suffering to the Philippians. They too must learn to put a positive valuation on suffering (1:28–30).[11] The "opponents" in 1:28 are not identified, but probably they are pagans rather than Christians. They could well be city authorities who saw the church, with its worship of Jesus as Lord, as a clear rival to the emperor cult, which would have been of central importance in a Roman colony such as Philippi. Against the pride of Roman citizenship, so important to the Philippians, Paul deliberately asserts a higher citizenship: "our citizenship [*politeuma*] is in heaven" (3:20 NRSV), where it is not Caesar who is proclaimed as *kyrios*, but Jesus (2:11).

There can be no doubt that the sudden outburst in 3:2–3 refers to Judaizers, those who would impose circumcision and law observance on the Gentiles. It seems very unlikely, however, that this was a present danger confronting the church at Philippi. For if that were the case, Paul would have been much more agitated and certainly would have mounted a direct polemic against this viewpoint, as he does in Galatians. Perhaps it was more of a potential threat that suddenly was brought to Paul's attention for some reason.

It remains difficult to ascertain much more from the letter about problems among the Philippians. Some are tempted to engage in "mirror reading" of certain passages, where behind every exhortation lies a specific problem or shortcoming of the church.[12] For example, does the exhortation in 2:14–16 mean that the Philippian Christians were prone to grumbling and questioning and were not "holding fast the word of life"? Or does 3:12–16 mean that some were claiming to have reached perfection? If so, were they possibly proto-gnostics, as perhaps also the libertinists referred to in 3:18–19? The trouble with an overly aggressive mirror reading of a text is that it becomes no longer possible for the author to make a generalizing exhortation or instruction that has no special meaning for a particular group of readers. Mirror reading almost always leads to overinterpretation.

Paul writes to tell the Philippians of his circumstances in prison (this report, 1:12–26, immediately follows the opening thanksgiving) and to thank the

---

11. For an analysis of Philippians as a letter of consolation relating to Paul's imprisonment and the Philippians' suffering, see Holloway, *Consolation in Philippians*.

12. For caution in this area, see the methodological remarks in Barclay, "Mirror-Reading a Polemical Letter," 84–86.

Philippians for their material support (4:10–20), but also to praise Epaphroditus for his work (2:25–30) and to commend Timothy (2:19–23). That there are several purposes in Philippians does not necessitate that it is composed of several independent letters, since there is no need to require that a letter to be restricted to a single purpose.

Such is the bond of endearment uniting Paul and the Philippian Christians, and such is the warm tone of Philippians, that the letter has been classified as a "hortatory letter of friendship."[13] Already in the opening thanksgiving Paul indicates his thankfulness to the Philippians "for your partnership in the gospel from the first day until now" (1:5), adding "I hold you in my heart," "you are all partakers with me of grace," and "I yearn for you all with the affection of Christ Jesus" (1:7–8). In 4:1 Paul refers to the Philippians as "my brothers and sisters, whom I love and long for, my joy and crown" (NRSV). As a concrete expression of this friendship and fellowship, the Philippians have shared their substance with Paul, as he notes in the tender thank you in 4:10–20.

The Christ Hymn of 2:6–11

No doubt the remarkable christological hymn in chapter 2 is what has captured the widest interest in the letter. I have already set out the stanzas of the hymn above (see "Two Christological Hymns" in chap. 21).

The hymn[14] is doctrinally significant in that it sets forth a three-stage christology: preexistence,[15] incarnation, exaltation. Jesus comes from heaven to earth, accomplishes his work, and then returns to heaven. It thus encapsulates the story of salvation and expresses the heart of the Pauline gospel.[16] Far from being a parenthesis or dispensable accessory in the letter, "the christological statement of 2:6–11 provides the spiritual focus, assurance and incentive for the letter's various instructions."[17] The hymn is closely linked with both the preceding and the subsequent content of the letter. The pattern of Jesus is the pattern of Paul in his imprisonment, and it is meant to be the pattern of the Philippians too. The humility exhibited in Christ is also to be exhibited in the Christian

---

13. Thus Stowers, "Friends and Enemies in the Politics of Heaven," 107–14; see also Stowers, *Letter Writing in Greco-Roman Antiquity*, 58–70; White, "Morality between Two Worlds." On the Philippians' gift, see Peterman, *Paul's Gift from Philippi*.

14. Gordon Fee ("Philippians 2:5–11") argues that the passage should be regarded as exalted Pauline prose and not a hymn. Majority opinion, however, is that the passage is a preformed hymn, not necessarily composed by Paul. The most thorough and authoritative study is Martin, *A Hymn of Christ* (earlier title, *Carmen Christi*).

15. James Dunn, reflecting a minority view, finds no preexistence in the opening lines of the hymn. See Dunn, "Christ, Adam, and Preexistence," and the response by Hurst, "Christ, Adam, and Preexistence Revisited."

16. On the christological hymn, see Hengel, "The Song about Christ in Earliest Worship."

17. Bockmuehl, *A Commentary on the Epistle to the Philippians*, 33.

(2:3). "If the Christians in Philippi fail to live in accordance with this pattern, then they are denying the validity of the events which made them Christian."[18]

Paul's Jewish Credentials and His Status before God (3:3–11)

Paul's sudden warnings about the Judaizers in 3:2 leads to a revealing passage in which he outlines his Jewish credentials. He immediately contrasts the implied Judaizers' claims with the statement, all the more remarkable because it is made to Gentile Christians, that "we are the true circumcision, who worship God in spirit, and glory in Christ Jesus, and put no confidence in the flesh [*ouk en sarki pepoithotes*]" (3:3). Paul goes on to say that if he so desired, he could indeed claim confidence in the flesh, and he gives his Jewish pedigree. Of special interest is the claim "as to righteousness under the law blameless" (3:6), which undoubtedly refers to his dedication and success as a Pharisee, judged by Pharisaic standards. All of this, however, he now counts as worthless because of a new, revolutionary situation described in these words: "that I may gain Christ and be found in him, not having a righteousness of my own, based on law [*emēn dikaiosynēn tēn ek nomou*], but that which is through faith in Christ [*tēn dia pisteōs Christou*], the righteousness from God that depends on faith [*tēn ek theou dikaiosynēn epi tē pistei*]" (3:8–9).

This is an exceptionally important passage in understanding Paul's soteriology. In it he clearly contrasts a righteousness achieved by law (i.e., by doing the works of the law), which was his experience as a Pharisee, with a righteousness received by faith, which is his experience as a Christian. This content is very similar to what Paul says in Galatians and Romans, as traditionally understood, and stands in contrast to the revisionist understanding of the new perspective on Paul (see chap. 19 above). Paul's view of how one becomes righteous has been radically altered. "The fruits of righteousness" now "come through Jesus Christ" (1:11).

Distinctive Emphases

The motif of joy pervades Philippians, even in the midst of everyday realities that seem to prohibit joy. The contradiction here can be explained only by the observation that the joy of the believer derives from a reality that transcends mundane existence. Philippians is an epistle of a joy that "passes all understanding"—words applied to "peace" in 4:7. Philippians uses the verb "rejoice" (*chairō*) more than any letter in the Pauline corpus (9x), as well as the verb "rejoice with" (*synchairō* [2x]) and the noun "joy" (*chara* [5x]).

---

18. Hooker, "Philippians 2:6–11," 154. See also Hellerman, *Reconstructing Honor in Roman Philippi*.

Although Paul expects to be released from his imprisonment, he does not exclude a quite different outcome. He honestly faces the possibility of death. His desire is that Christ be honored in his body, "whether by life or by death" (1:20). He does not provide much detail about what death meant to him, but what he does provide is enlightening: "to die is gain," and therefore most remarkably he says that in the choice between life and death, "My desire is to depart and be with Christ, for that is far better" (1:21–23). For Paul, death is but an entry into a new life with Christ.

The striking passage in 2:12–13 serves as a corrective to any idea that the Pauline gospel proffers a "cheap grace." To encourage obedience (to God), in the pattern of Jesus' obedience, Paul—the absolutely confident advocate of a free salvation by grace, apart from works—writes, "Work out your own salvation with fear and trembling." The verb here (*katergazesthe*) is in the present tense, thus focusing on the ongoing effort, "keep working out"—and with fear and trembling! For Christians, obedience is not optional; it is an extremely serious requirement. But Paul is quick to add that they are not left to their own resources, "for God is at work in you, both to will and to work for his good pleasure."

An emphasis such as this can be demoralizing if it is taken as a call to perfection, and for that reason what Paul says in 3:12–16 is important. "Not that I have already obtained this or am already perfect; but I press on to make it my own, because Christ Jesus has made me his own. Brethren, I do not consider that I have made it my own" (3:12–13a). The great Apostle himself thus confesses his failure, adding, however, "But one thing I do, forgetting what lies behind and straining forward to what lies ahead, I press on toward the goal of the prize of the upward call of God in Christ Jesus" (3:13b–14). Such is the practice that Paul invites his readers to imitate (3:17).

A surprising passage toward the end of the letter, unrelated to its immediate context, gives a call to values and morality that are distinctly Hellenistic rather than specifically Christian. Employing a repetitious structural parallelism, Paul encourages the Philippians to think of things that are true, honorable, just, pure, lovely, and gracious (4:8). As Markus Bockmuehl aptly puts it, "Paul now offers a cross-cultural Christian exhortation *in the language of Philippi*."[19] It is as though the Philippian Christians were not to let the sophisticated Roman-inclined population outdo them in the high standards of Greco-Roman morality.

Paul's Imprisonments and the Provenance of Philippians

Philippians was written from prison (1:7, 12–18), but Paul gives no indication of where the prison is. Traditionally, the Prison Epistles have been considered together—three have close associations, but not Philippians—and held to come

---

19. Bockmuehl, *A Commentary on the Epistle to the Philippians*, 250.

from Paul's Roman imprisonment. But Paul was imprisoned in other places as well (note "far more imprisonments" in 2 Cor. 11:23)[20]—for example, Philippi (Acts 16:24), (possibly) Ephesus,[21] and Caesarea, where Paul was kept for two years, in about 58–60 (Acts 24:27).[22] The complexity of the provenance of the Prison Epistles is daunting.

Affecting the discussion of the provenance of Philippians are facts of geography, where the greater the distance from Philippi, the more difficult it is to fit in the necessary journeys (a minimum of four) that we know from the letter itself had to take place. This alone has caused many to favor Ephesus as the place where Philippians was written. But even if it took a month to travel from Rome to Philippi, compared to a week from Ephesus, the longer distances are hardly an impossibility, either from the west or the east (Caesarea).[23] A further important and complicating issue concerns Paul's expectation of being released (1:19; 2:24).

Caesarea

That Colossians and Philemon were written from an imprisonment in Caesarea is all but impossible, given Paul's expectation of an imminent visit to the Lycus Valley noted in Philemon 22, for Paul at this point had appealed to Caesar and thus was obligated to go to Rome under guard. Since Ephesians, if by Paul, probably was written from the same place as Colossians, this would also rule out Caesarea for the provenance of Ephesians. Philippians, however, possibly was written in Caesarea, where there was a *praetorium* (Acts 23:35) that would satisfy the reference in Philippians 1:13, where those in imperial service could be described as members of "Caesar's household" (Phil. 4:22). The mention in Philippians 1:7 of a defense, if taken as a legal defense already made, corresponds better to the situation of the Caesarean than the Roman imprisonment. On the contrary, Caesarea is even further away from Philippi than Rome is. That Paul has to reckon with the possibility of his death fits the Roman imprisonment better, but given the danger from the Jews in Caesarea, it is not an impossibility for the Caesarean provenance of Philippians.[24]

20. *1 Clement* 5:6 says that Paul had been "seven times in chains," although the number might be taken as symbolic.

21. We have no direct evidence for an Ephesian imprisonment. The Marcionite Prologue to Colossians has the letter written "from Ephesus." Compare *Acts of Paul* 6 and the reference to fighting with beasts at Ephesus in 1 Corinthians 15:32, which, however, probably is metaphorical. The argument for a possible Corinthian imprisonment (see Acts 18:12–17) is equally speculative. For an ambitious hypothesis concerning an Ephesian imprisonment, during which in the spring of 55 Paul is said to have written Colossians and Philemon, see Duncan, *St. Paul's Ephesian Ministry*.

22. On Paul's imprisonments, see Wansink, *Chained in Christ*.

23. On travel times, see Thompson, "The Holy Internet."

24. For a defense of the Caesarean hypothesis, see the introduction in Hawthorne, *Philippians* (2004).

Ephesus

The huge disadvantage of proposing Ephesus as the provenance of Philippians is that we have no solid evidence that Paul was ever actually imprisoned there, even if it may appear likely. Appeal has to be made to Paul's statement about "the affliction we experienced in Asia" (2 Cor. 1:8) or to a literal interpretation of the possibly metaphorical reference to fighting with beasts at Ephesus (1 Cor. 15:32). The major advantage is its relative nearness to Philippi, and it is largely for this reason that it has attracted a considerable number of adherents. As the residence of a provincial governor, like Caesarea, Ephesus can be considered to have had the equivalent of a *praetorium* and members of "Caesar's household"—that is, slaves and freedmen in imperial service.[25] However, if Paul is in Ephesus and contemplating a release and trip to Philippi—all this before the trip to Jerusalem—why, some have asked, is there no reference at all to the collection for Jerusalem that was so important for Paul at this period?

Rome

Rome still remains probably the best guess for the provenance of all the Prison Epistles, including Philippians. The references to the *praetorium* and Caesar's household are most natural here and provide the best explanation for the exuberance of Paul in 1:12, and greetings from Caesar's household in Rome itself would have been especially appreciated by the Christians in the Roman colony of Philippi. The earliest attestation of Philippians is from the Marcionite Prologue (mid-second century), which states that it was written "from Rome in prison by Epaphroditus." The references to the real possibility of Paul's death together with the possibility of a release seem easiest if they stem from the Roman imprisonment.

Frank Thielman, a proponent of an Ephesian provenance for Philippians, fairly concludes after a review of the evidence, "It is difficult to understand the gravity with which the death sentence is pronounced upon a Roman provenance for the letter in the name of distance."[26] Thielman nevertheless rejects Rome, arguing instead that while Philippians is similar to the early letters of Paul, it is quite different from Colossians and Ephesians. It is this agreement in language, style, and content with that of Corinthians and

25. F. F. Bruce, however, notes that whereas the governor of an imperial province would have a *praetorium*, there is no evidence that the governor of a senatorial province, such as the proconsul of Ephesus was, would have one; on this basis he rules out Ephesus ("St. Paul in Macedonia," 263). Frank Thielman counters that it is unnecessary to press the technical use of the term, as Bruce does ("Ephesus and the Literary Setting of Philippians," 222).

26. Thielman, "Ephesus and the Literary Setting of Philippians," 210. Mosés Silva remarks, "It is very difficult to understand why this argument against a Roman origin continues to be taken seriously. The matter should be dropped from consideration" (*Philippians*, 6).

Galatians, which were written from Ephesus, that constitutes the strongest argument for an Ephesian provenance for Philippians.[27] This is a significant and attractive argument, but whether it tips the balance toward Ephesus as "historically probable,"[28] rather than merely enhancing a possibility, is another question.

The amount of discussion of the provenance of Philippians points to the ambiguity of the data and how intractable the question is. Reasonable proposals have been offered for three possibilities, as well as objections and counter-objections. We have here yet again a historical problem that permits no certainty. Opinions therefore are bound to differ, and conclusions may change. But Rome, in my opinion, continues to have a slight edge over the other options.

Authorship and Date

Author

Although Philippians is not reckoned among the four *Hauptbriefe* ("chief letters"), the Pauline authorship of the letter has only rarely been questioned. To be sure, it was the notable F. C. Baur who early in the use of historical criticism questioned Pauline authorship. His conclusion, however, was driven not by the available data but rather by the imposition of a predetermined historical schema on the NT materials, into which he labored to fit Philippians. Early in the age of computer analysis, A. Q. Morton argued that word statistics were inconsistent with Pauline authorship,[29] but the methodology is universally regarded as deeply flawed—to mention one thing alone, because of the brevity of Philippians. Virtually the whole of NT critical scholarship currently accepts Pauline authorship.

Date

The date of Philippians depends directly on the conclusion concerning provenance. If from a Roman imprisonment, which has the slight edge of probability, it is to be dated probably sometime in 60–62, perhaps in the later part of that period. It is clearly possible, however, that Philippians was written earlier. If from an imprisonment in Caesarea, then it was sometime in 57–59. If in Ephesus, it was even earlier, in about 52–55.

27. Ralph Martin argues, however, that "little weight of importance can be attached to the variations in the apostle's vocabulary and style," which can be explained as the result of different subject matter and the more informal and personal character of Philippians (*Philippians* [1976], 37).
28. Thielman, "Ephesus and the Literary Setting of Philippians," 223.
29. See Morton, "The Authorship of the Pauline Corpus."

Bibliography

Books and Articles

Alexander, Loveday. "Hellenistic Letter-Forms and the Structure of Philippians." *JSNT* 37 (1989): 87–110.

Barclay, John M. G. "Mirror-Reading a Polemical Letter: Galatians as a Test Case." *JSNT* 31 (1987): 73–93.

Bassler, Jouette M., ed. *Thessalonians, Philippians, Galatians, Philemon*. Vol. 1 of *Pauline Theology*, 87–121. Minneapolis: Fortress, 1991.

Black, David Alan. "The Discourse Structure of Philippians: A Study in Textlinguistics." *NovT* 37 (1995): 16–49.

Bloomquist, L. Gregory. *The Function of Suffering in Philippians*. JSNTSup 78. Sheffield: JSOT Press, 1993.

Bornkamm, Günther. "Der Philipperbrief als paulinische Briefsammlung." In *Neotestamentica et Patristica*, edited by O. Cullmann, 192–202. Leiden: Brill, 1962.

Bruce, F. F. *Paul: Apostle of the Heart Set Free*. Grand Rapids: Eerdmans, 1977.

———. "St. Paul in Macedonia: 3. The Philippian Correspondence." *BJRL* 63 (1980–81): 260–84.

Carson, D. A. *Basics for Believers: An Exposition of Philippians*. Grand Rapids: Baker Academic, 1996.

deSilva, David A. "No Confidence in the Flesh: The Meaning and Function of Philippians 3:2–21." *TJ* 15 (1994): 27–54.

Duncan, George S. *St. Paul's Ephesian Ministry: A Reconstruction with Special Reference to the Ephesian Origin of the Imprisonment Epistles*. London: Hodder & Stoughton, 1929.

Dunn, James D. G. "Christ, Adam, and Preexistence." In *Where Christology Began: Essays on Philippians 2*, edited by Ralph P. Martin and Brian J. Dodd, 74–83. Louisville: Westminster John Knox, 1998.

Fee, Gordon D. "Philippians 2:5–11: Hymn or Exalted Pauline Prose?" *BBR* 2 (1992): 29–46.

Fitzgerald, John T. "Philippians in the Light of Some Ancient Discussions of Friendship." In *Friendship, Flattery, and Frankness of Speech: Studies on Friendship in the New Testament World*, 141–60. NovTSup 82. Leiden: Brill, 1996.

Garland, David E. "The Composition and Unity of Philippians: Some Neglected Literary Factors." *NovT* 27 (1985): 141–73.

Hansen, G. Walter. "Transformation of Relationships: Partnership, Citizenship, and Friendship in Philippi." In *New Testament Greek and Exegesis: Essays in Honor of Gerald F. Hawthorne*, edited by Amy M. Donaldson and Timothy B. Sailors, 181–204. Grand Rapids: Eerdmans, 2003.

Hawthorne, Gerald F. *Philippians*. WBT. Waco: Word, 1987.

Hellerman, Joseph H. *Reconstructing Honor in Roman Philippi: Carmen Christi as Cursus Pudorum*. SNTSMS 132. Cambridge: Cambridge University Press, 2005.

Hemer, Colin J. *The Book of Acts in the Setting of Hellenistic History*. Edited by Conrad H. Gempf. WUNT 49. Tübingen: Mohr Siebeck, 1989.

Hengel, Martin. "The Song about Christ in Earliest Worship." In *Studies in Early Christology*, 227–91. Edinburgh: T&T Clark, 1995.

Holloway, Paul A. *Consolation in Philippians: Philosophical Sources and Rhetorical Strategy*. SNTSMS 112. Cambridge: Cambridge University Press, 2001.

Hooker, Morna D. "Philippians: Phantom Opponents and the Real Source of Conflict." In *Fair Play: Diversity and Conflicts in Early Christianity; Essays in Honour of Heikke Räisänen*, edited by Ismo Dunderberg, Christopher Tuckett, and Kari Syreeni, 377–95. NovTSup 103. Leiden: Brill, 2002.

———. "Philippians 2:6–11." In *Jesus und Paulus: Festschrift für Werner Georg Kümmel zum 70. Geburtstag*, edited by E. Earle Ellis and Erich Gräßer, 151–64. Göttingen: Vandenhoeck

& Ruprecht, 1975. Reprinted in idem, *From Adam to Christ: Essays on Paul*, 88–100. Cambridge: Cambridge University Press, 1990.

Hurst, L. D. "Christ, Adam, and Preexistence Revisited." In *Where Christology Began: Essays on Philippians 2*, edited by Ralph P. Martin and Brian J. Dodd, 84–95. Louisville: Westminster John Knox, 1998.

Hurtado, Larry W. "Jesus as Lordly Example in Philippians 2:5–11." In *From Jesus to Paul: Studies in Honour of Francis Wright Beare*, edited by Peter Richardson and John C. Hurd, 113–26. Waterloo, ON: Wilfrid Laurier University Press, 1984.

Jewett, Robert. "Conflicting Movements in the Early Church as Reflected in Philippians." *NovT* 12 (1970): 362–90.

———. "The Epistolary Thanksgiving and the Integrity of Philippians." *NovT* 12 (1970): 40–53.

Klijn, A. F. J. "Paul's Opponents in Philippians iii." *NovT* 7 (1964–65): 278–84.

Marshall, I. Howard. "The Theology of Philippians." In *The Theology of the Shorter Pauline Letters*, by Karl P. Donfried and I. Howard Marshall, 115–74. NTT. Cambridge: Cambridge University Press, 1993.

Martin, Ralph P. *A Hymn of Christ: Philippians 2:5–11 in Recent Interpretation and in the Setting of Early Christian Worship*. 3rd ed. Downers Grove, IL: InterVarsity, 1997.

Martin, Ralph P., and Brian J. Dodd, eds. *Where Christology Began: Essays on Philippians 2*. Louisville: Westminster John Knox, 1998.

Mearns, Christopher L. "The Identity of Paul's Opponents at Philippi." *NTS* 33 (1987): 194–204.

Minear, Paul S. "Singing and Suffering in Philippi." In *The Conversation Continues: Studies in Paul and John in Honor of J. Louis Martyn*, edited by Robert T. Fortna and Beverly R. Gaventa, 202–19. Nashville: Abingdon, 1990.

Morton, A. Q. "The Authorship of the Pauline Corpus." In *The New Testament in Historical and Contemporary Perspective: Essays in Memory of G. H. C. MacGregor*, edited by W. Barclay and H. Anderson, 209–35. Oxford: Blackwell, 1965.

Moule, C. F. D. "Further Reflections on Philippians 2:5–11." In *Apostolic History and the Gospel: Biblical and Historical Essays Presented to F. F. Bruce on His 60th Birthday*, edited by W. Ward Gasque and Ralph P. Martin, 264–76. Grand Rapids: Eerdmans, 1970.

Oakes, Peter. *Philippians: From People to Letter*. SNTSMS 110. Cambridge: Cambridge University Press, 2001.

Park, M. Sydney. *Submission within the Godhead and the Church in the Epistle to the Philippians: An Exegetical and Theological Examination of the Concept of Submission in Philippians 2 and 3*. LNTS 361. London: T&T Clark, 2007.

Peterlin, Davorin. *Paul's Letter to the Philippians in the Light of the Disunity in the Church*. NovTSup 79. Leiden: Brill, 1995.

Peterman, Gerald W. *Paul's Gift from Philippi: Conventions of Gift-Exchange and Christian Giving*. SNTSMS 92. Cambridge: Cambridge University Press, 1997.

Pollard, T. E. "The Integrity of Philippians." *NTS* 13 (1966–67): 57–66.

Pretorius, Emil A. C. "Role Models for a Model Church: Typifying Paul's Letter to the Philippians." *Neot* 32 (1998): 547–71.

Rahtjen, B. D. "The Three Letters of Paul to the Philippians." *NTS* 6 (1959–60): 167–73.

Reed, Jeffrey T. *A Discourse Analysis of Philippians: Method and Rhetoric in the Debate over Literary Integrity*. JSNTSup 136. Sheffield: Sheffield Academic Press, 1997.

Reumann, John. "Philippians and the Culture of Friendship." *TSR* 19 (1997): 69–83.

Stowers, Stanley K. "Friends and Enemies in the Politics of Heaven: Reading Theology in Philippians." In *Thessalonians, Philippians, Galatians, Philemon*. Vol. 1 of *Pauline Theology*, edited by Jouette M. Bassler, 105–21. Minneapolis: Fortress, 1991.

———. *Letter Writing in Greco-Roman Antiquity*. LEC. Philadelphia: Westminster, 1986.

Tarn, W. W., and G. T. Griffith. *Hellenistic Civilization*. 3rd ed. London: Arnold, 1952.

Tellbe, Mikael. "The Sociological Factors behind Philippians 3:1–11 and the Conflict at Philippi." *JSNT* 55 (1993): 97–121.

Thielman, Frank. "Ephesus and the Literary Setting of Philippians." In *New Testament Greek and Exegesis: Essays in Honor of Gerald F. Hawthorne*, edited by Amy M. Donaldson and Timothy B. Sailors, 205–23. Grand Rapids: Eerdmans, 2003.

Thompson, Michael B. "The Holy Internet: Communication between Churches in the First Christian Generation." In *The Gospels for All Christians: Rethinking the Gospel Audiences*, edited by Richard Bauckham, 49–70. Grand Rapids: Eerdmans, 1998.

Wansink, Craig S. *Chained in Christ: The Experience and Rhetoric of Paul's Imprisonments.* JSNTSup 130. Sheffield: Sheffield Academic Press, 1996.

Ware, James P. *The Mission of the Church in Paul's Letter to the Philippians in the Context of Ancient Judaism.* NovTSup 120. Reprint, Grand Rapids: Baker Academic, 2011.

Watson, Duane F. "A Rhetorical Analysis of Philippians and Its Implications for the Unity Question." *NovT* 30 (1988): 57–88.

White, L. Michael. "Morality between Two Worlds: A Paradigm of Friendship in Philippians." In *Greeks, Romans, and Christians: Essays in Honor of Abraham J. Malherbe*, edited by David L. Balch, Everett Ferguson, and Wayne A. Meeks, 201–15. Minneapolis: Fortress, 1990.

Williams, Demetrius K. *Enemies of the Cross of Christ: The Terminology of the Cross and Conflict in Philippians.* JSNTSup 223. Sheffield: Sheffield Academic Press, 2002.

Wright, N. T. "*Harpagmos* and the Meaning of Philippians 2:5–11." *JTS* 37 (1986): 321–52.

Commentaries

Barth, Karl. *The Epistle to the Philippians.* Richmond: John Knox, 1962.

Beare, F. W. *A Commentary on the Epistle to the Philippians.* 2nd ed. BNTC. London: Black, 1959.

Bockmuehl, Markus. *A Commentary on the Epistle to the Philippians.* BNTC. London: Black, 1997.

Bruce, F. F. *Philippians.* 2nd ed. NIBC. Peabody, MA: Hendrickson, 1989.

Caird, G. B. *Paul's Letters from Prison: Ephesians, Philippians, Colossians, Philemon.* NClarB. Oxford: Oxford University Press, 1976.

Collange, Jean-François. *The Epistle of St. Paul to the Philippians.* Translated by A. W. Heathcote. London: Epworth, 1979.

Fee, Gordon D. *Paul's Letter to the Philippians.* NICNT. Grand Rapids: Eerdmans, 1995.

Fowl, Stephen E. *Philippians.* THNTC. Grand Rapids: Eerdmans, 2005.

Grayston, Kenneth. *The Letters of Paul to the Philippians and to the Thessalonians.* CBC. Cambridge: Cambridge University Press, 1967.

Hansen, G. Walter. *The Letter to the Philippians.* PNTC. Grand Rapids: Eerdmans, 2009.

Hawthorne, Gerald F. *Philippians.* Revised and expanded by Ralph P. Martin. WBC 43. Nashville: Thomas Nelson, 2004.

Lightfoot, J. B. *St. Paul's Epistle to the Philippians.* London: Macmillan, 1868.

Marshall, I. Howard. *The Epistle to the Philippians.* EC. London: Epworth, 1991.

Martin, Ralph P. *The Epistle of Paul to the Philippians.* 2nd ed. TNTC. Grand Rapids: Eerdmans, 1987.

———. *Philippians.* NCBC. Grand Rapids: Eerdmans, 1976.

Melick, Richard R., Jr. *Philippians, Colossians, Philemon.* NAC. Nashville: Broadman & Holman, 1991.

O'Brien, Peter T. *Philippians: A Commentary on the Greek Text.* NIGTC. Grand Rapids: Eerdmans, 1991.

Osiek, Carolyn. *Philippians, Philemon.* ANTC. Nashville: Abingdon, 2000.

Plummer, Alfred. *A Commentary on St. Paul's Epistle to the Philippians.* London: Macmillan, 1919.

Reumann, John. *Philippians: A New Translation with Introduction and Commentary*. AYB 33B. New Haven: Yale University Press, 2008.

Silva, Moisés. *Philippians*. 2nd ed. BECNT. Grand Rapids: Baker Academic, 2005.

Sumney, Jerry L. *Philippians: A Greek Student's Intermediate Reader*. Peabody, MA: Hendrikson, 2007.

Thielman, Frank. *Philippians*. NIVAC. Grand Rapids: Zondervan, 1995.

Thurston, Bonnie, and Judith Ryan. *Philippians and Philemon*. SP 10. Collegeville, MN: Liturgical Press, 2005.

Vincent, Marvin R. *A Critical and Exegetical Commentary on the Epistles to the Philippians and to Philemon*. 3rd ed. ICC. Edinburgh: T&T Clark, 1922.

Witherington, Ben, III. *Friendship and Finances in Philippi: The Letter of Paul to the Philippians*. Valley Forge, PA: Trinity Press International, 1994.

31

Colossians and Philemon

Colossians and Philemon, two of Paul's Prison Epistles, are almost always linked together because both were sent to the church of Colossae and delivered apparently at the same time by Paul's co-worker Tychicus. Philemon very probably was a member of the church at Colossae (note the name of another member of the church, Archippus in Philem. 2; Col. 4:17). Tychicus furthermore was accompanied by the slave Onesimus (Col. 4:7–9), who is the reason for the writing of the Letter to Philemon. Both letters also mention Epaphras, who first brought the gospel to Colossae (Col. 1:7; 4:12–13; Philem. 23), as well as Mark, Aristarchus, Demas, and Luke (Col. 4:10, 14; Philem. 24). The two letters are therefore closely linked, although not by similar content. Colossians is basically a letter of encouragement; Philemon is a very specific and touching personal request that Paul makes on behalf of the runaway slave Onesimus.

Colossians

Paul did not found the church at Colossae, nor, as far as we know, did he found the nearby churches of Laodicea or Hierapolis (see Col. 2:1; 4:13). All three cities apparently were evangelized initially by Epaphras, Paul's "beloved fellow servant," further described as "a faithful minister of Christ on our behalf" (Col. 1:7). Epaphras is touchingly referred to as Paul's "fellow prisoner in Christ Jesus" in Philemon 23. He therefore was unable to be the bearer of the letters, but both letters convey his greetings (Philem. 23; Col. 4:12). In Colossians 4:12–13 Paul notes specifically that Epaphras, "one of yourselves," was "always remembering you earnestly in his prayers, that you may stand mature

Author: The probability, although not great, is that Paul wrote Colossians. But it is also possible that it was written in Paul's name, perhaps by the same person who wrote Ephesians.

Date: Probably 60–61, from a Roman prison. Possibly, if not by Paul, some years later.

Addressees: To the Christians of Colossae.

Purpose: Written to counter certain Jewish and pagan influences on the Christians of Colossae.

Message/Argument: A proper view of Christ is fundamental to knowledge and ethics, and points to the salvation from the powers announced in the gospel.

Significance: The christological hymn points to the cosmic significance of Christ and the salvation of the Christian. The paraenetic sections and the household code provide for ethical stability in the world.

and fully assured in all the will of God." Paul adds, "For I bear him witness that he has worked hard for you and for those in Laodicea and in Hierapolis."

Colossae, Laodicea, and Hierapolis were located close to one another in the Lycus Valley in Phrygia, approximately 120 miles east of Ephesus (western Asia Minor). Their introduction to the gospel probably is to be understood as included in the statement in Acts 19:10 that "all the residents of Asia [i.e., the Roman province of Asia in today's western Turkey] heard the word of the Lord, both Jews and Greeks"—this during Paul's three-year stay in Ephesus (ca. 53–55).

The Problem of Authorship

Although the prescript refers to Paul and Timothy as the joint authors, Colossians is not among the seven undisputed letters of Paul (Romans, 1–2 Corinthians, Galatians, Philippians, 1 Thessalonians, Philemon). A slight majority of scholars conclude that the letter was not written by Paul, the connections between Colossians and Philemon notwithstanding. We now look at the reasons for this and at possible counterarguments.

Arguments against Pauline Authorship

Vocabulary

This relatively short letter, with a vocabulary of 431 words, contains thirty-four words found in the NT only in Colossians. An additional twenty-eight words, although found elsewhere in the NT, are not in the other Pauline Letters. Colossians has a further twenty-five words in common with Ephesians that are not found in the other letters of the Pauline corpus. While it is true that Colossians has eleven words found only in other Pauline Letters—that is, distinctively Pauline vocabulary—Colossians also lacks many common Pauline words (e.g., sin, revelation, righteousness, freedom, promise, boast, law, believe, salvation, obedience).[1]

The different vocabulary of Colossians proves nothing, however, since a writer's vocabulary can vary greatly depending on the subjects addressed and the purpose of the document. Furthermore, a good amount of Colossians' distinctive vocabulary occurs in a number of preformed traditions, such as the christological hymn in 1:15–20,[2] or in response to the specific issues confronting the Colossians. It often is pointed out that the undisputed Letter to the Philippians also contains a relatively high number of words found nowhere else in the NT.

STYLE

More significant than vocabulary itself is the style (i.e., the syntax) of Colossians in comparison with the undisputed Pauline Letters. The contrast with the style of the undisputed letters is immediately evident: Colossians lacks the array of connective conjunctions that are typical in the acknowledged letters of Paul; five times it employs the phrase *ho estin* ("which is"), which is lacking in the undisputed letters. Most strikingly, however, Colossians exhibits a pleonastic syntax, often with very long, convoluted sentences, frequent participles and relative clauses, the piling up of dependent genitives, redundancies (e.g., adding of synonyms), and a general verbosity—all of this much more easily seen in the Greek than in English translation.[3] This is a distinctive style among the letters of the Pauline corpus, being paralleled only by Ephesians. Eduard Lohse describes the style as "liturgical-hymnic."[4] The great difference between the style of Colossians and that of the undisputed Pauline Letters is undeniable.[5] It therefore is difficult to attribute Colossians directly to the Paul we know from the generally accepted letters.

It is possible to explain the difference as the result of a new situation or as a change in Paul's own style with his advancing age. But this explanation does not seem compelling. More likely, perhaps, is the use of a different secretary—one given unusual freedom—whose own style becomes the vehicle to express

---

1. These statistics are drawn largely from Eduard Lohse (*Colossians and Philemon*, 84–87), who also provides full lists of words.

2. George Cannon points out that since most of the unique words in Colossians, and much of its theology too, are found in the traditional materials taken up by the author, they are of little use in determining the question of authorship (*The Use of Traditional Materials in Colossians*, 177).

3. For a summary of a thorough German analysis (by Walter Bujard) of the stylistic differences, see Kiley, *Colossians as Pseudepigraphy*, 51–59.

4. See Lohse, *Colossians and Philemon*, 90.

5. James Dunn notes that "at point after point in the letter the commentator is confronted with features characteristic of flow of thought and rhetorical technique that are consistently and markedly different from those of the undisputed Paulines" (*The Epistles to the Colossians and to Philemon*, 35).

Paul's thought in new language.[6] In any event, the argument from vocabulary and style, although intriguing, is hardly decisive against Pauline authorship.[7]

THEOLOGY

Colossians presents a more developed or somewhat different theology than the undisputed Pauline Letters at several points. The christological hymn in 1:15–20 is not dissimilar to the hymn in Philippians 2:6–11 and other such Pauline passages (e.g., 1 Cor. 8:6; Rom. 8:31–39), but it goes further in its statement that "in him all the fulness of God was pleased to dwell, and through him to reconcile to himself all things, whether on earth or in heaven, making peace by the blood of his cross" (1:19–20). So too 2:9–10: "For in him the whole fulness of deity dwells bodily . . . who is the head of all rule and authority." The "mystery" of which the author speaks is not the revelation of God's plan or decree, as usual in Paul, but Christ himself: "Christ in you, the hope of glory" (1:27 [cf. 2:2; 4:3, where the gospel is equated with the mystery of Christ]). The cosmic dimensions of this christology are paralleled by the salvation that he has accomplished, now construed not as from sin, law, and death, but rather from the cosmic powers (2:15), over which Christ is not merely head, but creator, "whether thrones or dominions or principalities or authorities" (1:16), and victor (2:15). Realized eschatology takes on new dimensions in Colossians: Christians are already raised with Christ (2:12; 3:1; contrast the future in Rom. 6:5–8); more important than a temporal dualism of ages is a spatial or cosmological dualism of earthly and heavenly things (1:20; 3:2). Totally lacking in Colossians are typical Pauline themes such as justification by faith, imminent eschatology, the parousia, resurrection of the dead, and the final judgment. In the ecclesiology of Colossians the church is conceived of as a universal entity (1:18, 24), in contrast with the church as local assemblies as in the letters of Paul. Aspects of an incipient "early catholicism" (see chap. 33 below) are noticeable in Colossians: the lack of an imminent eschatology, already mentioned, but also reference to "the faith" as the fixed content of what is believed (1:23; 2:7), concern for the preservation of the truth of the gospel, perpetuation of traditional materials, and the household codes (3:18–4:1) as a mark of settling down into the ongoing life and social order of the present age. There is furthermore what looks like later exaltation of the Apostle in the remarks of 1:24–25, where Paul describes himself as "minister" (*diakonos*) of "the church" (universal), "according to the divine office [*oikonomian*] which was given to me for you," and as completing the afflictions of Christ "in my flesh."

6. The key here is the great freedom granted to the secretary, since it is highly unlikely that we can conclude that Paul dictated the letter as it is. Under Paul's direction this secretary becomes the de facto author of the letter. For discussion of the authorship question, see chapter 24 above.

7. So too Lohse (*Colossians and Philemon*, 91), who nevertheless rejects Pauline authorship of Colossians.

By way of response, we may note that nothing here actually contradicts the Pauline theology of the undisputed letters. Rather, what we encounter here are extensions of what is already in Paul. The new dimensions are readily explainable by the situation addressed in Colossians. To conclude that Paul could not have made these adjustments in writing to the Colossians is "seriously to underrate Paul's intelligence and versatility."[8]

The argument against Pauline authorship is cumulative, as it is in every contested instance. Because of the nature of the evidence, there can be no talk of "proof." Again, as in every instance of contested authorship, the question is which way the probability tips, and that is a judgment call. A review of the evidence shows why so many incline to the opinion that Paul did not write Colossians. Inevitably, we must expect judgments to vary. But we must call it the way we see it, even if we have to hold our views with a good measure of tentativeness. The evidence here, unlike what we will see in the case of the Pastoral Epistles and, to a lesser extent, in Ephesians, is not strong enough to overturn the probability of Pauline authorship. Paul probably wrote Colossians, but through the agency of a secretary (perhaps Timothy? [note 1:1]) who was given a very free hand until 4:18, when Paul picks up the pen (no doubt having just read through the finished document) and writes, "I, Paul, write this greeting with my own hand. Remember my fetters. Grace be with you."

Relation to Ephesians

Corresponding to the differences between Colossians and the undisputed Pauline Letters are the similarities between Colossians and Ephesians. Clearly, there is a relationship of dependency between the two letters, but which depends on which? The great majority of scholars conclude that Ephesians is dependent on Colossians. Ephesians is more developed in its perspective and continues further on the trajectory of Colossians, expanding the horizon considerably. As we will see in the next chapter, the arguments against Pauline authorship of Ephesians intensify. If I am correct in my estimation, a disciple of Paul wrote Ephesians, not long after Paul's death, on the model of Colossians and taking up much of its actual wording.

The "Colossian Heresy"

Beyond the authorship of the epistle, the question of what exactly Colossians intends to counteract is the greatest puzzle. A variety of explanations have been offered. Among the ongoing methodological questions is the extent to which we should engage in what is called "mirror reading," whereby positive statements are taken as correctives of defects or errors, even when the latter are not specifically mentioned as such. For example, to what extent, if any, should

8. Bruce, *Paul*, 409.

the christological hymn in 1:15–20 be understood as a corrective of a deficient christology on the part of the Colossians? Another question is whether the errors opposed in the letter reflect a single group or "heresy," or whether a number of the errors are simply independent of any single system of thought.[9]

As we make our way through the letter from beginning to end, we note things such as the following. There is a special emphasis on truth, knowledge, and wisdom: "the word of the truth [*alētheia*], the gospel" (1:5); Paul prays that the Colossians "may be filled with the knowledge [*epignōsis*] of his will in all spiritual wisdom [*sophia*] and understanding . . . increasing in the knowledge [*epignōsis*] of God" (1:9–10); he teaches everyone "in all wisdom [*sophia*]" (1:28); he speaks of "all the riches of assured understanding and the knowledge [*epignōsis*] of God's mystery, of Christ, in whom are hid all the treasures of wisdom [*sophia*] and knowledge [*gnōsis*]" (2:2–3); the new nature of Christians "is being renewed in knowledge [*epignōsis*]" (3:10); the Colossians should "teach and admonish one another in all wisdom [*sophia*]" (3:16).

Paul expresses a concern that they "continue in the faith, stable and steadfast, not shifting from the hope of the gospel which you heard" (1:23); he rejoices "to see your good order and the firmness of your faith in Christ," exhorting them to be "established in the faith, just as you were taught" (2:5, 7).

Only in 2:8 do we first encounter direct information concerning the dangers facing the Colossian church: "philosophy and empty deceit, according to human tradition, according to the elemental spirits [*ta stoicheia*] of the universe" (cf. 2:20). This is followed in 2:16 by a command to resist those who would judge them "in questions of food and drink or with regard to a festival or a new moon or a sabbath."[10] Then in 2:21–22 Paul refers to regulations "according to human precepts and doctrines": do not handle, taste, or touch. Some furthermore were insisting on "self-abasement and worship of angels" and made appeal to "visions," being "puffed up without reason" by a "sensuous mind" (2:18). These regulations, Paul says, "have indeed an appearance of wisdom in promoting rigor of devotion and self-abasement and severity to the body" but, ironically, "are of no value in checking the indulgence of the flesh" (2:23).

What could be the explanation of all of this? Here I select only some of the more popular and more recent proposals, of which there is no shortage.[11] In addition to questions of whether what is in view represents a unified false teaching (a single "philosophy") or whether there are several separate errors in view, broadly speaking, the choice is between a Jewish or Greek background,

---

9. For an excellent discussion of methodological issues, see Barclay, *Colossians and Philemon*, 48–52.

10. See Sumney, "Those Who 'Pass Judgment.'"

11. In 1973 John Gunther could list more than forty different identifications of Paul's opponents at Colossae (*St. Paul's Opponents and Their Background*, 3–4). Even if some of these overlap, it is clear that on the subject of identifying Paul's opponents, Colossians presents the greatest challenge.

or perhaps more probably some combination of the two. A classic explanation, offered by J. B. Lightfoot,[12] was that the false teaching stemmed from a Jewish gnosticism. This would explain the references to sabbaths, lunar cycles, and forbidden foods, on the one hand, and the emphasis on knowledge, dualism, intermediary beings (angels, powers), asceticism, and mystical experience, on the other hand. Others have argued for a Jewish mysticism[13] involving the experience of visions that were enhanced by ascetic practices.[14] Thomas Sappington holds to a combination of Jewish mysticism and gnosticism.[15] James Dunn is of the opinion that ordinary Judaism can readily account for all the problematic factors mentioned by the author.[16] Others have appealed to pagan Hellenism for an explanation—for example, Hellenistic mystery cults, Cynic philosophy,[17] Middle Platonism and pursuit of wisdom,[18] and a syncretistic mixture of Phrygian folk religion (magic), Judaism, and Christianity.[19]

As if to call a halt to these multitudinous speculations, Morna Hooker challenges the idea of there being false teaching in the Colossian church at all.[20] If there had been false teaching that threatened the gospel in any significant way, she argues, Paul would have responded with a much more defined and vigorous counterattack, as he does, for example, in Galatians. What accounts for the matters that Paul does mention is simply the everyday "pressure to conform to the beliefs and practices of their pagan and Jewish neighbors."[21] Most NT scholars, however, are programmed to search for the opposing viewpoint, even though there may not be one. In the case of Colossians, the results have brought us no further than to note that what Paul seems worried about consists of both Jewish and pagan influences.

The Christological Hymn (1:15–20)

A brilliant two-stanza hymn or liturgical piece occurs early in the letter, fixing an important point that is foundational for the instruction and exhortation that follows. Employing parallelism and symmetry, the hymn portrays

---

12. In a famous essay on "The Colossian Heresy," in *St. Paul's Epistles to the Colossians and to Philemon*, 73–113. Lightfoot further identified the heresy as having an Essene character.

13. Most recently, Smith, *Heavenly Perspective*.

14. Such ecstatic experience may explain the reference to "the worship of angels" (2:18), taken as a subjective genitive—that is, the worshiper participated with angels in the worship of God.

15. Sappington, *Revelation and Redemption at Colossae*.

16. Dunn, *The Epistles to the Colossians and to Philemon*, 29–33.

17. T. W. Martin, *By Philosophy and Empty Deceit*.

18. DeMaris, *The Colossian Controversy*.

19. Arnold, *The Colossian Syncretism*.

20. Hooker, "Were There False Teachers in Colossae?" John Barclay does not deny that there was false teaching at Colossae, but he remains pessimistic at finally solving the problem: "We may simply have to accept that [it] is an unsolved, and insoluble, mystery" (*Colossians and Philemon*, 54).

21. Hooker, "Were There False Teachers in Colossae?" 329.

the significance of Christ in the first creation and in the church, which is the new creation. We have already looked at this hymn (see above, pp. 397–98).

The hymn follows the statement, possibly itself a liturgical fragment, "He [the Father] has delivered us from the dominion of darkness and transferred us to the kingdom of his beloved Son, in whom we have redemption, the forgiveness of sins" (1:13–14).

The First Creation (1:15–17)	The New Creation: The Church (1:18–20)
who is the image of the invisible God,	He is the head of the body, the church;[1]
the firstborn of all creation;	who is the beginning, the firstborn from the dead, that in everything he might be preeminent.
for in him all things were created, in heaven and on earth, visible and invisible, whether thrones or dominions or principalities or authorities	For in him all the fullness of God was pleased to dwell, and through him to reconcile to himself
—all things were created through him and for him.	all things, whether on earth or in heaven, making peace by the blood of his cross.[2]
He is before all things, and in him all things hold together.	

[1]Many scholars think that "the church" was added to the original hymn.
[2]Many regard this clause as having been added to the original hymn (cf. "even death on a cross" in Phil. 2:8).

Christ is portrayed in this hymn as the cosmological and redemptive Christ, as the sovereign head of two creations. As the icon of the invisible God, he stands at the apex of creation, not as a created being himself, but as the Agent through whom all that exists was created.[22] The creation was created for him, and he continues to sustain creation ("holds it together"). But he also stands at the apex of the new creation, as the head of the church universal (cf. 2:19), wherein the fallenness of the old creation finds its remedy—this through a reconciliation accomplished by Christ's redemptive death on the cross. The background to this hymn very probably is to be found in the idea of "wisdom" in Hellenistic Judaism (cf. Prov. 8:22–31; Wis. 7:21–8:1; Sir. 24).[23]

Some have concluded that this hymn has as its purpose the correction of false teaching about Christ. That is not impossible, but it may equally be the

22. "The firstborn of all creation" does not mean that Christ was the first creature to be created but instead points to his rank or status over all creation (for this use of the word, see Ps. 89:27, where "firstborn" equals "highest"). It is clear from the following statement in the hymn that Christ belongs on the side of God over against the created order as the Agent of its creation. See Helyer, "Arius Revisited."

23. On the meaning of the hymn, see Hooker, "Where Is Wisdom to Be Found?"; Bauckham, "Where Is Wisdom to Be Found?"

case that the perspective of the hymn is fundamental to the correction of other errors or misapprehensions of the Colossian church.

Ethical Catechesis (3:5–17)

The ethical teaching contained in 3:5–17 probably reflects the primitive form of a baptismal paraenesis that was common in the early church.[24] The pattern of this teaching contained the elements of "putting off" certain behavior and "putting on" new kinds of behavior. A slight variant of the first is in the "put to death" exhortation in 3:5, which is followed by a vice catalog and then again the typical verb *apothesthe* (lit. "put off" [3:8]) and a further list of vices. The heart of this paradigm is expressed in 3:9–10: "Do not lie to one another, seeing that you have put off the old nature [*ton palaion anthrōpon*] with its practices and have put on the new nature [*ton neon*], which is being renewed in knowledge after the image of its creator." The "put on" metaphor is used again in 3:12, 14, together with an extensive virtue catalog. Three further elements of this primitive catechism are found in the imperatives "be subject" (the household code, beginning in 3:18), "being watchful" (4:2), and "stand" (4:12).

The "Household Code" (3:18–4:1)

In Colossians for the first time in the Pauline corpus we encounter a new form of Christian ethical instruction that has been given the name "household code" (or, in German, the word *Haustafel*).[25] The Colossians *Haustafel* provides specific instructions to wives and husbands, children and parents, and slaves and masters. In each case, alongside the command to obey or be subject, a reciprocity and mutual responsibility exist between the two parties. That the instruction to slaves takes up so much space (3:22–25), far more than any other category, suggests that the reason is Onesimus. Paul, who in the accompanying Letter to Philemon requests that Onesimus be accepted as a brother and no longer as a slave, perhaps wants to make clear that he (Paul) knows (and in principle endorses) the responsibilities of a slave to his master. It is also an indication of the significance of the request that Paul makes of Philemon. Standing in remarkable tension with this part of the household code is the statement a few lines earlier that in the new reality of the body of Christ there can be neither slave nor free (3:11).

There has been much discussion concerning the origin of the household code. While some have argued for Stoicism, James Crouch presents a good

---

24. See Carrington, *The Primitive Christian Catechism*, 92–93; Selwyn, *The First Epistle of St. Peter*, 384–439.

25. "The Colossian *Haustafel* is, if not the original, at least the oldest extant *Haustafel* and brings us as near as possible to the beginning of the Christian *Haustafel* tradition" (Crouch, *The Origin and Intention of the Colossian Haustafel*, 32).

case for Hellenistic Judaism. The Christian use of this form of instruction fits well with the interests of early catholicism (see chap. 33 below). As Crouch puts it, the *Haustafel* "was created to serve emerging orthodoxy as a weapon against enthusiastic and heretical threats to the stability of both the church and the social order."[26] The household codes serve as a counterbalance to the implications of radical equality as articulated in, for example, Galatians 3:28, which perhaps some were inclined to take too far for the culture of that day.

Similar household codes are found in Ephesians 5:22–33, the Pastoral Epistles (1 Tim. 2:1–15; 5:1–2; 6:1–2, 17–19; Titus 2:1–3:8), and 1 Peter 2:13–3:7. Speaking of these various household codes, Edward Selwyn concludes, "The NT authors were all writing on the basis of a catechetical pattern well known to their readers, and were developing it, each in his own way."[27]

Theological Emphases

Christology

The view of Christ in Colossians is determinative for the entire epistle. "In the theology of Colossians, christology is central and everything else flows from the belief that Christ is the key to the understanding of reality."[28] The person and work of Christ forge the integrating key to the assertions of the letter.[29] Paul writes to the Colossians in the great desire that they will come "to have all the riches of assured understanding and the knowledge of God's mystery, of Christ, in whom are hid all the treasures of wisdom and knowledge" (2:2–3 [cf. 4:3]). Paul refers to "the riches of the glory of this mystery, which is Christ in you, the hope of glory" (1:27). In the hymn in 1:15–20, as we have seen, Christ is both creator and redeemer. "In him the whole fulness of deity dwells bodily" (2:9 [cf. 1:19]). "Christ is all, and in all" (3:11). Whatever the Christian does "in word or deed" is to be done "in the name of the Lord Jesus" (3:17).

Gospel

The gospel, referred to as the "word of the truth" (1:5 [cf. 1:23]), the "word of God" (1:25), and the "mystery of Christ" (4:3), is of great importance in this epistle. The gospel is "the faith," which the Colossians are to keep "stable and steadfast" (1:23 [cf. 2:7]).

26. Ibid., 151.
27. Selwyn, *The First Epistle of St. Peter*, 435.
28. Lincoln, "The Letter to the Colossians," 569.
29. John Barclay's analysis of the theology of the letter thus relates Christ to each of the following: creation, God, salvation, the powers, the church, the life of the community, the hope of glory, and service in everyday life (*Colossians and Philemon*, 79–92).

Salvation

The good news of the gospel refers to the saving work of Christ. At its heart, this salvation is understood as "redemption, the forgiveness of sins" (1:14). The forgiveness of sins is again in view in 2:13 and 3:13. Christ's redeeming work "has delivered us from the dominion of darkness and transferred us to the kingdom of his [God's] beloved Son" (1:13). Through the blood of Christ's cross "all things" have been reconciled to God (1:20–22). God has made us alive with Christ (2:13). An essentially Pauline emphasis appears in the statement that God has "canceled the bond which stood against us with its legal demands; this he set aside, nailing it to the cross" (2:14). And whatever malevolent powers may be ranged against humans, these have been disarmed in Christ's triumph over them (2:15).

"Now and Not Yet" Eschatology

The stress in Colossians is on the realized dimensions of eschatology, but not to the exclusion of future eschatology. Christians are already delivered from the dominion of darkness and transferred to the kingdom of the Son (1:5). They have already been "raised with Christ" (3:1). At the same time, however, reference is made in 1:5 to "the hope laid up for you in heaven," and in 1:27 to "the hope of glory." The return of Christ is a fixed point: "When Christ who is our life appears, then you also will appear with him in glory" (3:4). That future coming will involve both judgment (3:6) and reward (3:24).

Incorporation into Christ

Again in good Pauline fashion, Colossians indicates that believers are "in Christ" (1:2, 28), and Christ dwells in believers (1:27). The church is the body of Christ (1:24). Believers have died with Christ (2:20; 3:3) and have been "raised with Christ" (3:1). They have been "buried with him in baptism" (2:12) and "made alive together with him" (2:13). Believers furthermore are united with Christ in a spiritual circumcision (2:11). They "have come to fulness of life in him" (2:10), and most dramatically, Paul writes, "Your life is hid with Christ in God" (3:3).

Author, Addressees, Date

Author

The author probably was Paul, but, if so, he employed a secretary to whom he granted an exceptional amount of freedom in framing his thoughts. It is possible, though there can be no way to know with confidence, that the secretary was Timothy. That must remain merely a guess.

Addressees

The town of Colossae was destroyed by an earthquake in 60–61 (Tacitus, *Ann.* 14.27.1). According to Eusebius (*Chron.* 1.21–22, 63–64), all three cities of the Lycus Valley were destroyed. If the letter really was written to the church at Colossae—and there seems little reason to doubt this—then it was written before 60–61. If Colossians was not written by Paul, but later in the first century, one may well wonder why anyone would write a pseudonymous letter to a church that may no longer have existed. Advocates for the pseudonymity of Colossians, however, find the addressees as artificial as the attribution to Paul itself.

Date

Colossians, if by Paul, was written while he was in prison (4:3, 10, 18), but it is not easy to know where that prison was. Traditionally, the prison has been assumed to be in Rome (Acts 28:16, 30). But Paul, as we have already noted (see "Paul's Imprisonments and the Provenance of Philippians" in chap. 30), was also imprisoned in several places. A problem, though hardly insuperable, for the Roman provenance of the letter is the great distance between Rome and the Lycus Valley, and the time it would have taken to travel between them for those mentioned in the letter. Rather more difficult is the reference in Philemon 22, where Paul asks Philemon to prepare a guest room because he plans to visit in the near future. But this is a little difficult to square with Paul's Roman imprisonment unless we posit a release and then later a second Roman imprisonment. Although Paul had hoped to preach the gospel in Spain, he still could have thought of a visit to Colossae. If Colossians and Philemon were written from Rome, the dates probably would be 60–61, perhaps just prior to the disastrous earthquake.

Philemon

The letter known as Philemon is unique among the Pauline Letters because of its brevity (a mere twenty-five verses), its personal nature, and its request. As we have already seen, it probably was sent together with Colossians to the church at Colossae and delivered by Paul's co-worker Tychicus, who actually was accompanied by Onesimus (Col. 4:7–9), the very subject of the Letter to Philemon.

The Situation of Onesimus and Paul's Request

While it is quite clear that Paul wanted very much to have Onesimus with him as an assistant, it is less clear what the situation of Onesimus was. Traditionally,

---

Author: Paul.

Date: Probably delivered with Colossians and to be dated at about the same time (ca. 60–61).

Addressees: To Philemon, Apphia, Achippus, and the church that meets in their house.

Purpose: A personal plea to Philemon to take back the runaway slave Onesimus, but now as a brother in Christ rather than as a slave.

Message/Argument: That the newly converted slave be set free for service to Paul.

Significance: An implicit criticism of slavery and evidence of Paul's generous spirit.

Onesimus has been regarded as a runaway slave. But the fact that he is nowhere in the letter specifically described as a runaway has inevitably caused some to challenge the idea.[30] Perhaps, they argue, Onesimus simply was sent by Philemon to minister to Paul on behalf of the Colossian church, and Paul's request is merely to be able to retain Onesimus as a fellow worker. However, it is quite possible that Onesimus deliberately had sought Paul as an advocate for him for some unknown grievance between him and his master.[31] That Onesimus was in some difficulty with Philemon seems clear enough from verse 11 (cf. v. 18). Since Paul is "sending . . . back" (*anapempō*) Onesimus (v. 12; cf. v. 15), the traditional view that he was a runaway could well be true. Either way, the probability is that Onesimus believed that Paul could be of some assistance to him regarding his master. In the process, however, Onesimus had his life turned around: he became a Christian and thereby was freed from a greater slavery. And thus Paul refers to him as "my child, Onesimus, whose father I have become in my imprisonment" (v. 10).

Onesimus now was in a new relationship to Paul and to Philemon: "a beloved brother, especially to me but how much more to you, both in the flesh and in the Lord" (v. 16). On the basis of this new reality Paul, as an "ambassador" (v. 9), entreats Philemon to receive Onesimus "as you would receive me" (v. 17). Paul could have commanded Philemon; instead, "for love's sake," he appeals to him "for my child Onesimus" (vv. 9–10).

It may seem disappointing that Paul does not directly ask for the manumission of Onesimus. At the same time, however, the request is clearly implied. Paul notes how Onesimus was "useful" to him.[32] So helpful was Onesimus, that sending him back to Philemon was like "sending my very heart" (v. 12).

---

30. Thus John Knox (*Philemon among the Letters of Paul*), who also argues that Archippus, not Philemon, was the owner of Onesimus; see also Winter, "Paul's Letter to Philemon"; Wansink, *Chained in Christ*; Rapske, "The Prisoner Paul in the Eyes of Onesimus."

31. An interesting contemporaneous parallel exists in the letter containing Pliny's appeal to Sabinianus (Pliny, *Ep.* 9.21, 24) on behalf of an unnamed "freedman" who was still obligated to his master. The text is conveniently available in Barclay, *Colossians and Philemon*, 104–5.

32. The name "Onesimus," commonly given to slaves, in Greek means "useful"; verse 11 thus contains a play on words.

Paul continues, "I would have been glad to keep him with me, in order that he might serve me on your behalf during my imprisonment for the gospel" (v. 13). But Paul would not keep Onesimus without Philemon's consent (v. 14). Paul's request is that Philemon would receive Onesimus "no longer as a slave," but rather "as a beloved brother" (v. 16). Paul's request, though indirect, is unmistakable: "Yes, brother, I want some benefit[33] from you in the Lord. Refresh my heart in Christ" (v. 20). It is a little ironic that although Paul did not want to command Philemon "to do what is required" (vv. 8–9), at the end of the letter he nevertheless says, "Confident of your obedience, I write to you, knowing that you will do even more than I say" (v. 21).

The letter is poignant evidence of social relationships in the Pauline churches. Verses 4–7 twice point to Philemon's love not only for Paul but also for the saints. Philemon apparently was an earlier convert of Paul (v. 19), as now Onesimus had become. Paul's concern for Onesimus's situation is impressive, reaching even to Paul's willingness to cover the cost of any losses to Philemon (vv. 18–19). Also touching is the delicate manner in which he approaches Philemon about the issue. Onesimus joins this fellowship, now with all the blessings of full family status.

Slavery in the New Testament

Although the book of Philemon is hardly a clarion call for the emancipation of all Christian slaves, it seems to indicate where Paul's heart is on the subject. When he urges Philemon to receive Onesimus "no longer as a slave but more than a slave, as a beloved brother" (v. 16), he implies that Onesimus is to be freed from being a slave and hence free to return to Paul as his assistant. At the same time, however, it must be admitted that Paul does not—here or anywhere—launch any clear attack against the institution of slavery itself.

Slavery, of course, was a vital part of the fabric of Greco-Roman society. Philemon probably was a wealthy Christian, owning a house large enough to contain church meetings (v. 2), who therefore almost certainly would have had a number of slaves in his household. Paul would have found it nigh unto impossible to attack the institution of slavery head-on. John Barclay attributes the ambiguities of the Epistle to Philemon to the difficult situation of the Christian slave owner, who had the impossible challenge of combining the dynamics of Christian brotherhood with those of the master-slave relationship.[34] Paul's Letter to Philemon leaves his appeal more implicit than explicit. We would have preferred that he took a clear stand, in keeping with his statement in Galatians 3:28 that in Christ the distinction between slave and free is done away with.[35]

---

33. The verb *onaimēn* ("I want to benefit") is a further play on the name "Onesimus."

34. See Barclay, "Paul, Philemon and the Dilemma of Christian Slave-Ownership."

35. It is interesting to wonder how Philemon responded to Paul's letter. Stephen Barton ("Paul and Philemon") has cleverly produced a letter that Philemon might have written to Paul

But it remains regrettably the case that slavery as an institution is accepted and not criticized in the NT. Worse than that, from a modern point of view, slavery is regulated in the household codes, even, as Philemon would have been sure to notice, in the accompanying Letter to the Colossians (3:22–4:1). Although we often have material within the NT that can be used to support social reform, where they are introduced, social agendas are always of secondary importance, subordinate to the direct concerns of the gospel. Nowadays the teachings of the NT about slavery are properly understood as culturally conditioned; that is, they were dictated by social realities of the first century and no longer apply in today's world.

Author, Addressees, Date

Paul, together with Timothy, writes in prison (vv. 1, 9–10, 13), probably in Rome, where he also wrote the Letter to the Colossians (see above). It is perhaps more likely that Onesimus, if a runaway, would have fled to Rome rather than to Ephesus.

The letter is addressed to Philemon "our beloved fellow worker" (v. 1) and to "Apphia our sister and Archippus our fellow soldier, and the church in your house" (v. 2). But although there is a communal aspect to it, and Paul's desire would be known to the congregation, the letter is essentially a personal one to Philemon, as the second-person singular pronouns beginning in verse 4 indicate. Philemon could not but be well aware that the members of the church knew of Paul's request and would have held him accountable.

If Philemon was written at the same time and sent together with Colossians, as argued above, the date would be 60–61.

Philemon is an interesting document not for its theology, as Colossians is, but instead for the window that it provides into social realities of the first century—realities from which the early church could not escape. It reveals much about the truly compassionate heart of Paul, who from other letters can at times seem harsh and imperious. The letter exemplifies the practical application of Christian faith and love,[36] both on the part of Paul and potentially on the part of Philemon.

Unfortunately, we do not know how things turned out. It seems inherently unlikely, however, that Philemon would not have honored Paul's request. A famous hypothesis, put forward by Edgar Goodspeed, argues that Onesimus

and then a second letter from Paul. Philemon's letter protests the suggestion that Onesimus be made a free man; Paul's rejoinder strongly argues not only for Onesimus's freedom but also for human liberty in general. We may wish that Paul had written in this way, but in reality he did not. For an imagined letter from Onesimus to Paul, see Walsh and Keesmaat, *Colossians Remixed*, 202–12. Walsh and Keesmaat's book is a profound application of Colossians to today's world.

36. See Marshall, "The Theology of Philemon," 188.

was actually the author of Ephesians.[37] According to Ignatius (Ign. *Eph*. 1:3; 6:2), a man named "Onesimus" was the bishop of the Ephesian church in the early second century. It is nice to think that this may be the same Onesimus, now a man perhaps in his seventies, but the name was common, and thus it remains only a pleasing possibility. If Onesimus had become a prominent person in the church, it might help to explain the inclusion of the Letter to Philemon in the Pauline corpus and thus in the NT canon. According to later tradition, Philemon and his wife, Apphia, eventually were martyred in Colossae.

Bibliography: Colossians

Books and Articles

Arnold, Clinton E. *The Colossian Syncretism: The Interface between Christianity and Folk Belief at Colossae*. WUNT 2/77. Tübingen: Mohr Siebeck, 1995.

Balch, David L. "Household Codes." In *Greco-Roman Literature and the New Testament: Selected Forms and Genres*, edited by David E. Aune, 25–50. SBLSBS 21. Atlanta: Scholars Press, 1988.

Balchin, John F. "Colossians 1:15–20: An Early Christian Hymn? The Arguments from Style." *VE* 15 (1985): 65–94.

Barbour, R. S. "Salvation and Cosmology: The Setting of the Epistle to the Colossians." *SJT* 20 (1967): 257–71.

Barclay, John M. G. *Colossians and Philemon*. NTG. Sheffield: Sheffield Academic Press, 1997.

Bauckham, Richard. "Where Is Wisdom to Be Found? Colossians 1.15–20 (2)." In *Reading Texts, Seeking Wisdom: Scripture and Theology*, edited by David F. Ford and Graham Stanton, 129–38. London: SCM, 2003.

Beasley-Murray, Paul. "Colossians 1:15–20: An Early Christian Hymn Celebrating the Lordship of Christ." In *Pauline Studies: Essays Presented to F. F. Bruce on His 70th Birthday*, edited by Donald A. Hagner and Murray J. Harris, 169–83. Grand Rapids: Eerdmans, 1980.

Beetham, Christopher A. *Echoes of Scripture in the Letter of Paul to the Colossians*. BIS 96. Leiden: Brill, 2008.

Benoit, Pierre. "The 'plērōma' in the Epistles to the Colossians and the Ephesians." *SEÅ* 49 (1984): 136–58.

Best, Ernest. "Who Used Whom? The Relationship of Ephesians and Colossians." *NTS* 43 (1997): 72–96.

Bevere, Allan R. *Sharing the Inheritance: Identity and the Moral Life in Colossians*. JSNTSup 226. London: Sheffield Academic Press, 2003.

Bradley, James. "The Religious Life-Setting of the Epistle to the Colossians." *StBT* 2 (1972): 17–36.

Bruce, F. F. "Colossian Problems." *BSac* 141 (1984): 3–15, 99–111, 195–208, 291–302.

———. *Paul: Apostle of the Heart Set Free*. Grand Rapids: Eerdmans, 1977.

Cannon, George E. *The Use of Traditional Materials in Colossians*. Macon, GA: Mercer University Press, 1983.

Carrington, Philip. *The Primitive Christian Catechism: A Study in the Epistles*. Cambridge: Cambridge University Press, 1940.

Crouch, James E. *The Origin and Intention of the Colossian Haustafel*. FRLANT 109. Göttingen: Vandenhoeck & Ruprecht, 1972.

37. Goodspeed, *The Meaning of Ephesians*. See further discussion in chapter 32 below.

DeMaris, Richard E. *The Colossian Controversy: Wisdom in Dispute at Colossae.* JSNTSup 96. Sheffield: JSOT Press, 1994.

Duncan, George S. *St. Paul's Ephesian Ministry: A Reconstruction with Special Reference to the Ephesian Origin of the Imprisonment Epistles.* London: Hodder & Stoughton, 1929.

Dunn, James D. G. "The Colossian Philosophy: A Confident Jewish Apologia." *Bib* 76 (1995): 153–81.

Evans, Craig A. "The Colossian Mystics." *Bib* 63 (1982): 188–205.

Francis, Fred O., and Wayne A. Meeks, eds. *Conflict at Colossae: A Problem in the Interpretation of Early Christianity, Illustrated by Selected Modern Studies.* SBLSBS 4. Missoula, MT: Scholars Press, 1973.

Gordley, Matthew E. *The Colossian Hymn in Context: An Exegesis in Light of Jewish and Greco-Roman Hymnic and Epistolary Conventions.* WUNT 2/228. Tübingen: Mohr Siebeck, 2007.

Gunther, John J. *St. Paul's Opponents and Their Background: A Study of Apocalyptic and Jewish Sectarian Teachings.* NovTSup 35. Leiden: Brill, 1973.

Harrington, Daniel J. "Christians and Jews in Colossians." In *Diaspora Jews and Judaism: Essays in Honor of, and in Dialogue with, A. Thomas Kraabel,* edited by J. Andrew Overman and Robert S. MacLennan, 153–61. SFSHJ 41. Atlanta: Scholars Press, 1992.

Hartman, Lars. "Humble and Confident: On the So-Called Philosophers in Colossae." In *Mighty Minorities? Minorities in Early Christianity—Positions and Strategies: Essays in Honour of Jacob Jervell on His 70th Birthday,* edited by David Hellholm, Halvor Moxnes, and Turid Karlsen Seim, 25–39. Oslo: Scandinavian University Press, 1995.

Helyer, Larry R. "Arius Revisited: The Firstborn over All Creation (Col. 1:15)." *JETS* 31 (1988): 59–67.

———. "Cosmic Christology and Col. 1:15–20." *JETS* 37 (1994): 235–46.

Hering, James P. *The Colossian and Ephesian Haustafeln in Theological Context: An Analysis of Their Origins, Relationship, and Message.* AUS 7/260. New York: Peter Lang, 2007.

Hooker, Morna D. "Were There False Teachers in Colossae?" In *Christ and Spirit in the New Testament: Studies in Honour of Charles Francis Digby Moule,* edited by Barnabas Lindars and Stephen S. Smalley, 315–31. Cambridge: Cambridge University Press, 1973.

———. "Where Is Wisdom to Be Found? Colossians 1.15–20 (1)." In *Reading Texts, Seeking Wisdom: Scripture and Theology,* edited by David F. Ford and Graham Stanton, 116–28. London: SCM, 2003.

Karris, Robert J. *A Symphony of New Testament Hymns: Commentary on Philippians 2:5–11, Colossians 1:15–20, Ephesians 2:14–16, 1 Timothy 3:16, Titus 3:4–7, 1 Peter 3:18–22, and 2 Timothy 2:11–13.* Collegeville, MN: Liturgical Press, 1996.

Kiley, Mark. *Colossians as Pseudepigraphy.* BibSem 4. Sheffield: JSOT Press, 1986.

Leppä, Outi. *The Making of Colossians: A Study on the Formation and Purpose of a Deutero-Pauline Letter.* PFES 86. Göttingen: Vandenhoeck & Ruprecht, 2003.

Lincoln, Andrew T. "The Household Code and Wisdom Mode of Colossians." *JSNT* 74 (1999): 93–112.

Lincoln, Andrew T., and A. J. M. Wedderburn. *The Theology of the Later Pauline Letters.* NTT. Cambridge: Cambridge University Press, 1993.

Lohse, Eduard. "Pauline Theology in the Letter to the Colossians." *NTS* 15 (1968–69): 211–20.

Martin, Ralph P. "An Early Christian Hymn (Col 1:15–20)." *EvQ* 36 (1964): 195–205.

———. "Reconciliation and Forgiveness in Colossians." In *Reconciliation and Hope: New Testament Essays on Atonement and Eschatology Presented to L. L. Morris on His 60th Birthday,* edited by Robert Banks, 104–24. Grand Rapids: Eerdmans, 1974.

Martin, Troy W. *By Philosophy and Empty Deceit: Colossians as Response to a Cynic Critique.* JSNTSup 118. Sheffield: Sheffield Academic Press, 1996.

McGuire, Ann. "Equality and Subordination in Christ: Displacing the Powers of the Household Code in Colossians." In *Religion and Economic Ethics*, edited by Joseph F. Gower, 65–85. Lanham, MD: University Press of America, 1990.

Meeks, Wayne A. "'To Walk Worthily of the Lord': Moral Formation in the Pauline School Exemplified by the Letter to Colossians." In *Hermes and Athena: Biblical Exegesis and Philosophical Theology*, edited by Eleonore Stump and Thomas P. Flint, 37–58. UNDSPR 7. Notre Dame, IN: University of Notre Dame Press, 1993.

Murphy-O'Connor, Jerome. "Tradition and Redaction in Col 1:15–20." *RB* 102 (1995): 231–41.

Olbricht, Thomas H. "The Stoicheia and the Rhetoric of Colossians: Then and Now." In *Rhetoric, Scripture and Theology: Essays from the 1994 Pretoria Conference*, edited by Stanley E. Porter and Thomas H. Olbricht, 308–28. JSNTSup 131. Sheffield: Sheffield Academic Press, 1996.

Pizzuto, Vincent A. *A Cosmic Leap of Faith: An Authorial, Structural, and Theological Investigation of the Cosmic Christology in Col. 1:15–20.* CBET 41. Leuven: Peeters, 2006.

Polhill, John B. "The Relationship between Ephesians and Colossians." *RevExp* 70 (1973): 439–50.

Porter, Stanley E., and Kent D. Clarke. "Canonical-Critical Perspective and the Relationship of Colossians and Ephesians." *Bib* 78 (1997): 57–86.

Reicke, Bo. "Caesarea, Rome and the Captivity Letters." In *Apostolic History and the Gospel: Biblical and Historical Essays Presented to F. F. Bruce on His 60th Birthday*, edited by W. Ward Gasque and Ralph P. Martin, 277–86. Grand Rapids: Eerdmans, 1970.

———. "The Historical Setting of Colossians." *RevExp* 70 (1973): 429–38.

Sanders, E. P. "Literary Dependence in Colossians." *JBL* 85 (1966): 28–45.

Sappington, Thomas J. *Revelation and Redemption at Colossae*. JSNTSup 53. Sheffield: JSOT Press, 1991.

Selwyn, Edward G. *The First Epistle of St. Peter: The Greek Text, with Introduction, Notes and Essays*. London: Macmillan, 1946.

Smith, Ian K. *Heavenly Perspective: A Study of the Apostle Paul's Response to a Jewish Mystical Movement at Colossae*. LNTS 326. London: T&T Clark, 2006.

Standhartinger, Angela. "Colossians and the Pauline School." *NTS* 50 (2004): 572–93.

———. "The Origin and Intention of the Household Code in the Letter to the Colossians." *JSNT* 79 (2000): 117–30.

Still, Todd D. "Eschatology in Colossians: How Realized Is It?" *NTS* 50 (2004): 125–38.

Sumney, Jerry L. "Those Who 'Pass Judgment': The Identity of the Opponents in Colossians." *Bib* 74 (1993): 366–88.

Walsh, Brian J., and Sylvia C. Keesmaat. *Colossians Remixed: Subverting the Empire*. Downers Grove, IL: InterVarsity, 2004.

Wilson, Walter T. *The Hope of Glory: Education and Exhortation in the Epistle to the Colossians*. NovTSup 88. Leiden: Brill, 1997.

Wright, N. T. "Poetry and Theology in Colossians 1:15–20." *NTS* 36 (1990): 444–68.

Commentaries

Abbott, T. K. *A Critical and Exegetical Commentary on the Epistles to the Ephesians and to the Colossians*. ICC. Edinburgh: T&T Clark, 1897.

Barth, Markus, and Helmut Blanke. *Colossians: A New Translation with Introduction and Commentary*. Translated by Astrid B. Beck. AB 34B. New York: Doubleday, 1994.

Bruce, F. F. *The Epistles to the Colossians, to Philemon, and to the Ephesians*. NICNT. Grand Rapids: Eerdmans, 1984.

Caird, G. B. *Paul's Letters from Prison: Ephesians, Philippians, Colossians, Philemon*. NClarB. Oxford: Oxford University Press, 1976.

Dunn, James D. G. *The Epistles to the Colossians and to Philemon: A Commentary on the Greek Text*. NIGTC. Grand Rapids: Eerdmans, 1996.

Garland, David E. *Colossians and Philemon*. NIVAC. Grand Rapids: Zondervan, 1998.

Harris, Murray J. *Colossians and Philemon*. EGGNT. Grand Rapids: Eerdmans, 1991.

Hay, David M. *Colossians*. ANTC. Nashville: Abingdon, 2000.

Lightfoot, J. B. *St. Paul's Epistles to the Colossians and to Philemon*. 3rd ed. London: Macmillan, 1879.

Lincoln, Andrew T. "The Letter to the Colossians: Introduction, Commentary, and Reflections." *NIB* 11:551–669.

Lohse, Eduard. *Colossians and Philemon: A Commentary on the Epistles to the Colossians and to Philemon*. Translated by William R. Poehlmann and Robert J. Karris. Edited by Helmut Koester. Hermeneia. Philadelphia: Fortress, 1971.

MacDonald, Margaret Y. *Colossians and Ephesians*. SP 17. Collegeville, MN: Liturgical Press, 2000.

Martin, Ralph P. *Colossians and Philemon*. NCB. Greenwood, SC: Attic Press, 1974.

———. *Ephesians, Colossians, and Philemon*. IBC. Atlanta: John Knox, 1991.

Melick, Richard R., Jr. *Philippians, Colossians, Philemon*. NAC. Nashville: Broadman & Holman, 2000.

Moo, Douglas J. *The Letters to the Colossians and Philemon*. PNTC. Grand Rapids: Eerdmans, 2008.

Moule, C. F. D. *The Epistles of Paul the Apostle to the Colossians and Philemon*. CGTC. Cambridge: Cambridge University Press, 1968.

O'Brien, Peter T. *Colossians, Philemon*. WBC 44. Waco: Word, 1982.

Pokorný, Petr. *Colossians: A Commentary*. Translated by Siegfried S. Schatzmann. Peabody, MA: Hendrickson, 1991.

Schweizer, Eduard. *The Letter to the Colossians: A Commentary*. Translated by Andrew Chester. Minneapolis: Augsburg, 1982.

Sumney, Jerry L. *Colossians: A Commentary*. NTL. Louisville: Westminster John Knox, 2008.

Talbert, Charles H. *Ephesians and Colossians*. PCNT. Grand Rapids: Baker Academic, 2007.

Thompson, Marianne Meye. *Colossians and Philemon*. THNTC. Grand Rapids: Eerdmans, 2005.

Thurston, Bonnie. *Reading Colossians, Ephesians and 2 Thessalonians: A Literary and Theological Commentary*. RNT. Macon, GA: Smyth & Helwys, 1995.

Wall, Robert W. *Colossians and Philemon*. IVPNTC. Downers Grove, IL: InterVarsity, 1993.

Wilson, R. McL. *A Critical and Exegetical Commentary on Colossians and Philemon*. ICC. Edinburgh: T&T Clark, 2005.

Witherington, Ben, III. *The Letters to Philemon, the Colossians, and the Ephesians: A Socio-Rhetorical Commentary on the Captivity Epistles*. Grand Rapids: Eerdmans, 2007.

Wright, N. T. *Colossians and Philemon*. TNTC. Grand Rapids: Eerdmans, 1986.

Bibliography: Philemon

See also the bibliography for Colossians.

Books and Articles

Barclay, John M. G. "Paul, Philemon and the Dilemma of Christian Slave-Ownership." *NTS* 37 (1991): 161–86.

Bartchy, S. Scott. *Mallon Chrēsai: First-Century Slavery and the Interpretation of 1 Corinthians 7:21*. SBLDS 11. Missoula, MT: Scholars Press, 1973.

Barton, Stephen C. "Paul and Philemon: A Correspondence Continued." *Theology* 90 (1987): 97–101.

Burtchaell, James Tunstead. *Philemon's Problem: A Theology of Grace*. Grand Rapids: Eerdmans, 1998.

Callahan, Allen Dwight. "Paul's Epistle to Philemon: Toward an Alternative *Argumentum*." *HTR* 86 (1993): 357–76.

Church, F. Forrester. "Rhetorical Structure and Design in Paul's Letter to Philemon." *HTR* 71 (1978): 17–33.

Frilingos, Chris. "'For My Child, Onesimus': Paul and Domestic Power in Philemon." *JBL* 119 (2000): 91–104.

Goodspeed, Edgar J. *The Meaning of Ephesians*. Chicago: University of Chicago Press, 1933.

Knox, John. *Philemon among the Letters of Paul: A New View of Its Place and Importance*. Chicago: University of Chicago Press, 1935.

Marshall, I. Howard. "The Theology of Philemon." In *The Theology of the Shorter Pauline Letters*, by Karl P. Donfried and I. Howard Marshall, 175–91. NTT. Cambridge: Cambridge University Press, 1993.

Nordling, John G. "Onesimus Fugitivus: A Defense of the Runaway Slave Hypothesis in Philemon." *JSNT* 41 (1991): 97–119.

Petersen, Norman R. *Rediscovering Paul: Philemon and the Sociology of Paul's Narrative World*. Philadelphia: Fortress, 1985.

Rapske, Brian M. "The Prisoner Paul in the Eyes of Onesimus." *NTS* 37 (1991): 187–203.

Sanders, Laura L. "Equality and a Request for the Manumission of Onesimus." *ResQ* 46 (2004): 109–14.

Swartley, Willard M. *Slavery, Sabbath, War, and Women: Case Issues in Biblical Interpretation*. Scottdale, PA: Herald, 1983.

Wansink, Craig S. *Chained in Christ: The Experience and Rhetoric of Paul's Imprisonments*. JSNTSup 130. Sheffield: Sheffield Academic Press, 1996.

Winter, Sara C. "Paul's Letter to Philemon." *NTS* 33 (1987): 1–15.

Commentaries

Barth, Markus, and Helmut Blanke. *The Letter to Philemon: A New Translation with Notes and Commentary*. ECC. Grand Rapids: Eerdmans, 2000.

Fitzmyer, Joseph A. *The Letter to Philemon: A New Translation with Introduction and Commentary*. AB 34C. New York: Doubleday, 2000.

Kreitzer, Larry J. *Philemon*. RNBC. Sheffield: Sheffield Phoenix Press, 2008.

Nordling, John G. *Philemon*. ConC. St. Louis: Concordia, 2004.

PART 5

THE DEUTERO-PAULINE LETTERS

Extending the Teaching of the Apostle

32

Ephesians

The Epistle to the Ephesians is a masterpiece of Pauline theology and the capstone of the Pauline perspective. Ephesians, as much as, or perhaps more than, Romans has a claim to be the most developed statement of Paul's theology. It is a kind of distillation of the basic themes of Paul's theology presented now in the greatest depth and the widest possible scope. From "before the foundation of the world" (1:4) to "the fulness of time" (1:10), it surveys the "mystery of his [God's] will" (1:9), the grand, "eternal purpose" of God (3:11) in and through Christ and the church, "which is his body, the fulness of him who fills all in all" (1:1)—the "mystery hidden for ages in God who created all things" (3:9), and the means of demonstrating "the manifold wisdom of God" in the accomplishing of the cosmic plan of uniting "all things in him, things in heaven and things on earth" (1:10). The cosmic perspective of the Epistle to the Ephesians is continually breathtaking.

It seems natural and obvious to conclude that this glorious letter-treatise was written by Paul—indeed, could only have been written by Paul, unless there was in the early church a greater writer and theologian than Paul himself. Yet there are a number of reasons why a majority of NT scholars have come to doubt, if not outright deny, the Pauline authorship of Ephesians. The title "The Letter of Paul to the Ephesians" is misleading. The book is more of a treatise than a letter; it was not originally addressed to the Ephesians, but was an encyclical; and it perhaps was not written by Paul. But we must begin the discussion with the epistle's relation to Colossians.

Author: Possibly by Paul, but more probably by a disciple of Paul.

Date: If by Paul, early 60s. More probably, however, some twenty years later, perhaps in the 80s.

Addressees: Originally a circular letter to churches in Asia Minor, including Ephesus, the main church of the region.

Purpose: Addresses no specific problems or issues in Ephesus or other churches of Asia Minor. Instead, this is a letter-treatise that generally explores the cosmic significance of the Christian faith.

Message/Argument: The Christian church is nothing less than the purpose that God had from the beginning of salvation history. It is universal, representing God's cosmic purposes, and includes on an equal footing Jews and Gentiles, who are called to respond by living in appropriate ways.

Significance: The letter is the supreme expression of Pauline thought in the New Testament and provides the grandest portrayal of the meaning of Christ and his church.

The Relation of Ephesians to Colossians

No one doubts the very close relationship in language between Ephesians and Colossians. According to Leslie Mitton, more than a quarter (26.5 percent) of the words of Ephesians are the same as in Colossians, or, looked at the other way around, more than a third (34 percent) of the words of Colossians are the same as in Ephesians.[1] Only in one instance, however, do we encounter extensive verbatim agreement (twenty-nine consecutive words): Ephesians 6:21–22 and Colossians 4:7–8. Three instances occur where seven consecutive words are in verbatim agreement: Ephesians 1:1–2 and Colossians 1:1–2; Ephesians 3:2 and Colossians 1:25; Ephesians 3:9 and Colossians 1:26. And in a further two instances five consecutive words are in verbatim agreement: Ephesians 1:7 and Colossians 1:14; Ephesians 4:16 and Colossians 2:19.[2]

Beyond this, Mitton gives nine further examples of near verbatim agreement, where there are only small differences, such as the omission or addition of a phrase or clause, a change of word order, or the use of roughly equivalent language and similar ideas. Many similarities are due to the conflation of phrases and clauses that occur in different parts of either Ephesians or Colossians. Werner Kümmel points out that "only brief portions of Eph (e.g., 2:6–9; 4:5–13; 5:29–33) have no verbal parallels in Col."[3] By modern standards, the extent of dependence would have to be designated as plagiarism.

1. Mitton, *The Epistle to the Ephesians*, 57. In the first of several very useful appendices, Mitton reproduces the entire text of Ephesians together with the parallels from Colossians, the other Pauline Epistles, and 1 Peter (ibid., 279–315).

2. Ibid., 58.

3. Kümmel, *Introduction to the New Testament*, 359. Kümmel says that "of 155 verses in Ephesians, 73 have verbal parallels in Col" (ibid.).

The close similarities in language between the two letters is undeniable. But there has been little agreement on how to explain the similarities. One clear reason for this is that the issue is inevitably linked with the authorship question. Some deny dependence one way or the other, arguing that the two epistles were by the same author, perhaps Paul, and were written close in time to each other, or alternatively by two different authors, perhaps members of the same Pauline "school."[4] Some argue for common dependence on tradition or even on a conjectured third letter.[5] Heinrich Holtzmann offered a complicated theory of mutual dependence and interpolation.[6] And recently John Muddiman argued that Ephesians consists of an expansion of a genuine letter of Paul written to the Laodiceans, edited into its present form by a disciple of Paul.[7]

It seems to most scholars, however, that literary dependence is the most natural explanation of the similarities between the two letters. But which way does the dependence go? There have been advocates on both sides. Despite the fact that plausible arguments can be made either way, and despite the ambiguity of the evidence, relatively few have argued for the dependence of Colossians on Ephesians,[8] while a very large majority of scholars conclude that Ephesians is dependent on Colossians.[9] Generally, the reasons are more than linguistic: the judgment that doctrinally Ephesians is more developed than Colossians,[10] improves Colossians in a variety of ways,[11] follows nearly the same sequence of material through the entire letter, uses Colossians as a model, and modifies Colossians for a more general readership. Ephesians, like Colossians, basks in the glory of Christ and the grandeur and universality of God's purpose. It sets forth the same ethics, including the household code. Eduard Lohse concludes, "In certain passages Ephesians reads like the first commentary on Colossians, though admittedly it does more than explicate the thoughts of Colossians: it also expands them into concepts of its own."[12]

Most seem to agree that the dependence in view is "not that which one would associate with the work of an imitator, hard at work with a copy of Colossians

---

4. Thus Best, "Who Used Whom?," 96.

5. A. van Roon suggests that a common "draft" underlies the two letters (*The Authenticity of Ephesians*, 440). See also Klijn, *An Introduction to the New Testament*, 102.

6. See Mitton, *The Epistle to the Ephesians*, 72–73.

7. Muddiman, *A Commentary on the Epistle to the Ephesians*, 20–41.

8. For example, Coutts, "The Relationship of Ephesians and Colossians"; Synge, *St. Paul's Epistle to the Ephesians*, 70–75. While doubting direct dependence, A. van Roon finds evidence for the priority of Ephesians (*The Authenticity of Ephesians*, 436).

9. This consensus is challenged by Best, "Who Used Whom?," followed by O'Brien, *The Letter to the Ephesians*, 14–21. Best and O'Brien rightly point out that the direction of the dependence has not been proved.

10. See Mitton, *The Epistle to the Ephesians*, 69–70; 82–97. Mitton points out the different meanings of certain words in Colossians and Ephesians (e.g., "mystery," "reconciliation," "head," "fullness" [*pleroma*]).

11. Ibid., 70–71.

12. Lohse, *Colossians and Philemon*, 4.

open in front of him." Rather, as Mitton continues, "His acquaintance with Colossians is not dependent on what he reads in a document, but it is a familiarity which has become part of his own mental equipment."[13] Unquestionably, the author of Ephesians has assimilated the perspective of Colossians and made it his own. At the same time, however, it does seem clear from the places of verbatim agreement, especially at the end of the letters, that the author of Ephesians did have direct access to a copy of Colossians (cf. Eph. 6:21–22 with Col. 4:7–8—not the sort of material that one would commit to memory). "So exact a reproduction could hardly be made from memory alone."[14] It is a good question why, if Paul is the author of Ephesians, he would have been so dependent on Colossians, not to mention the other Pauline Letters, or for that matter, why so dependent on Ephesians if the dependence goes the other way. The nature of the dependence is such that the conclusion of two different authors is the most natural one. Edgar Goodspeed thought that Ephesians reads "like a commentary on the Pauline letters."[15] Of course, one might well expect Paul to be familiar with his own thought! But where there is literary dependence, as seems to be the case with Colossians at least, that argument does not work. If, because of material uncharacteristic of Paul, we may argue against Pauline authorship, we may do the same if Ephesians is "too Pauline"!

Ephesians and the Pauline Corpus: A Circular Letter

Unlike Colossians, which addresses specific problems in a local church, Ephesians expounds its magnificent theology in general terms and lacks specifics that would root it in any particular local church, Ephesus or otherwise. In fact, the words "in Ephesus" in 1:1 are lacking in the earliest and best manuscripts.[16] Although Paul lived in Ephesus for more than two years, the author writes as though he does not know the readers (1:15; 4:21) and they do not know him (3:1–2). Furthermore, no personal greetings occur at the end of Ephesians, which is particularly odd because Paul certainly had many friends there. For these reasons, it seems almost certain that Ephesians was written as an encyclical letter, perhaps to, though not necessarily limited to, the churches of Asia, of which Ephesus was the most prominent. It may well be that the original manuscript of Ephesians had a blank space in 1:1 where different place names could be inserted, and that "in Ephesus" was inserted in the earliest copy. Marcion (according to Tertullian, *Marc.* 5.17) identified

---

13. Mitton, *The Epistle to the Ephesians*, 63.
14. Ibid., 77.
15. Goodspeed, *The Meaning of Ephesians*, 9.
16. They are missing in $\mathfrak{P}^{46}$, the first hand of Sinaiticus and Vaticanus, and in cursive manuscripts 424c and 1739, as well as the text used by Origen, and apparently too in Tertullian and Ephraem. See Metzger, *A Textual Commentary on the Greek New Testament*, 532.

the letter with that to the Laodiceans mentioned in Colossians 4:16, but this is only a possibility at best.

Paul addresses specific issues in Colossians, and it is easy to understand why the letter was written, even if we are uncertain about the errors being opposed. However, Ephesians, as a circular letter-treatise, speaks to no particular problems, and so it is difficult to know why it was written.[17] To answer this question, Edgar Goodspeed came up with an ingenious hypothesis. He proposed that the publication of Acts in the 90s stimulated a new interest in the Apostle Paul that was the cause of the collection of his letters. Ephesians then was written as an introduction to the collection (cf. 3:3–4), thereby transforming the letters written to individual churches "into an encyclical collection, to be appropriated by all."[18] Goodspeed went on to speculate that it may have been Onesimus, who had become bishop of Ephesus (assuming that this was the same Onesimus), who collected the letters and then wrote Ephesians as an introduction to the collection, basing it mainly on Colossians, which of course he would have known well, but also drawing extensively on the letters of the newly compiled collection.[19] Unfortunately, it is impossible to verify this attractive hypothesis. One may object that in no manuscripts of the NT does Ephesians stand at the head of the Pauline Letters, contrary to what we would expect if it were an introduction. Goodspeed's explanation was that Marcion had exchanged the places of Ephesians and Galatians, putting the latter at the head of his Pauline list for doctrinal reasons, and then putting Ephesians (approximately the same length as Galatians) where Galatians had been, and giving the circular letter a name, "To the Laodiceans."[20]

The Authorship Question

After the Pastoral Epistles, Ephesians is the most disputed letter in the Pauline corpus.[21] As we will see, the question of the author of Ephesians is one

---

17. Many therefore think it easier to imagine Colossians being dependent on Ephesians—taking up its thought and applying it to the situation at Colossae—than Ephesians drawing on Colossians to create a universal message.

18. Goodspeed, "Ephesians, the Introduction to the Pauline Collection," 16.

19. Goodspeed writes, "I don't know how this mere conjecture may strike the reader, but it fills my eyes with tears. The emancipated slave lives to build his protector a monument more enduring than bronze! Why, whoever he was, he made Paul a lasting force in Christianity, second only to Jesus himself!" (*The Key to Ephesians*, xv). This book consists almost exclusively of the text of Ephesians and then in successive columns the Colossian parallels, followed by the other Pauline parallels.

20. Goodspeed, *An Introduction to the New Testament*, 224–26.

21. Raymond Brown estimates that approximately 80 percent of NT scholars doubt the Pauline authorship of Ephesians (*An Introduction to the New Testament*, 620). According to Harold Hoehner, that figure is much too high and needs to be adjusted down to about 50 percent (*Ephesians*, 7–20).

of the most difficult in NT scholarship. Good arguments can be mounted both for and against Pauline authorship. Often it is possible to explain the same data quite differently. And when one introduces the idea of a secretary involved in the writing of the letter, the options multiply. Again it needs to be emphasized that we cannot talk about proof or demonstration in a matter such as this. Instead, we can only weigh probabilities against one another, and our conclusion inevitably will be tentative. The issues concern such things as language (i.e., vocabulary and style), theology, and perspective. No single argument is capable of winning the day; one's inclination will depend on the cumulative weight of all the considerations. So difficult is the question that some seasoned scholars, after further consideration, have felt obligated to change their opinions,[22] while others have decided not to decide and thus leave the question open.

From the start, one must admit that Ephesians is a very Pauline document. It is replete with Pauline ideas and Pauline language.[23] C. H. Dodd wrote, "Whether the Epistle is by Paul or not, certainly *its thought is the crown of Paulinism*."[24] F. F. Bruce referred to Ephesians as "the quintessence of Paulinism."[25] But if Paul could write Colossians, why not also the very similar Ephesians? What objections can one have to the Pauline authorship of Ephesians that would not also apply to Colossians?

Yes, the two letters are very similar in content and language. At the same time, however, Ephesians is more developed in its theology and perspective, to the extent that it may be judged to be on a different level than Colossians. And the fact of dependence itself enters into consideration. While it is not difficult to imagine a disciple of Paul making extensive use of Colossians, to think of Paul himself being so dependent on Colossians as he wrote Ephesians, or vice versa for that matter, stretches the imagination to the breaking point. (Galatians and Romans are similar in content and language, but the parallel falls far short.) Of course, scholars who deny the Pauline authorship of Ephesians usually also deny it for Colossians because of the similarity between the two letters. Once one accepts the Pauline authorship of Colossians, however, Pauline authorship of Ephesians hardly remains unthinkable. In the following discussion, rather than separating out the arguments pro and con, I will mention objections and responses on both sides as I proceed.

---

22. See e.g., Lincoln, *Ephesians*, lx.

23. Henry Cadbury asked this interesting question: "Which is more likely—that an imitator of Paul in the first century composed a writing ninety or ninety-five per cent in accordance with Paul's style or that Paul himself wrote a letter diverging five or ten percent from his usual style?" ("The Dilemma of Ephesians," 101). Cadbury nevertheless left the dilemma unresolved, content to suggest that "both sides of the Ephesian debate may take comfort over their fallibility" (ibid.).

24. Dodd, "Ephesians," 1224–25.

25. Bruce, *Paul, Apostle of the Heart Set Free*, 424, borrowing words of A. S. Peake.

Vocabulary

Ephesians contains some ninety-one words not found in the undisputed Pauline Letters; forty of these are found nowhere else in the NT, a number of which, however, are typical in postapostolic literature. But it must be admitted at the same time that the amount of unique vocabulary in Ephesians does not exceed the unique vocabulary of some of the undisputed letters of Paul (e.g., 2 Corinthians, Philippians). Vocabulary naturally varies depending on the purpose and subject of the letter. Nevertheless, it is striking, for example, that Ephesians consistently uses the word *diabolos* ("devil") rather than *satanas* ("Satan"). The former word is used elsewhere in the Pauline corpus only in the Pastoral Epistles; the latter is the common designation in the undisputed Paulines. The unique expression "in the heavenlies" (*en tois epouraniois*)[26] occurs five times in Ephesians but nowhere else in the Pauline Letters (but there we do have the comparable *en tois ouraniois*). There are unique combinations of words, such as "spiritual blessing" (1:3), "the mystery of his will" (1:9), "plan for the fulness of time" (1:10), and "the eternal purpose" (3:11).[27] But as all scholars admit in the end, statistics and data such as these fall short of being proof.

Style

Somewhat more significant is the syntax of Ephesians, which resembles that of Colossians but reaches an even higher level of prolixity. We encounter frequent redundancies (e.g., "the counsel of his will" [1:11], "the working of his great might" [1:19], "pray . . . with all prayer and supplication . . . making supplication" [6:18]), the clustering of synonyms (e.g., "wisdom and insight" [1:9]), and the heavy use of consecutive genitival constructions (e.g., "the measure of the stature of the fulness of Christ" [4:13]). The pleonastic syntax contains a preponderance of prepositions (especially *en* and *kata*), but a conspicuous lack of conjunctions and particles. The first four chapters of Ephesians consist mainly of extremely long and often convoluted sentences (usually broken into separate sentences in English translations), with a heavy use of participles and relative clauses (1:3–14, 15–23; 2:1–7; 3:1–7, 14–19; 4:11–16; see also 5:7–13; 6:14–20). While a heavy, liturgical-hymnic style occasionally is encountered in the undisputed Paulines, nothing there begins to approach the style of Ephesians. By contrast, Paul's prose is crisp and vigorous. Altogether, observations such as these leave the impression of a decidedly un-Pauline style. Mitton calls it "a somewhat artificial eloquence."[28] It is, of

---

26. See Lincoln, "A Re-Examination of 'The Heavenlies' in Ephesians."

27. See Lincoln, *Ephesians*, lxv.

28. Mitton, *The Epistle to the Ephesians*, 11. William Sanday and Arthur Headlam contrast the style of Ephesians with Romans thus: "We cannot speak here of vivacity, hardly of energy. . . . In its place we have a slowly moving, onwards advancing mass, like a glacier working its way inch by inch down the valley" (*A Critical and Exegetical Commentary on the Epistle to the Romans*, lv).

course, at least possible that these stylistic phenomena are due to a secretary used by Paul for both Colossians and Ephesians.

Perspective and Theology

Like the Pastoral Epistles, Ephesians exhibits the tendencies of an incipient early catholicism (see chap. 33 below). The importance of the church in Ephesians can hardly be overemphasized. It is always spoken of as a universal entity, never in local terms (whereas the undisputed Paulines speak almost always only of the local churches). A self-consciousness of the church's importance in the plan of God pervades the epistle. All the designations of the great church of later centuries are here. The church is *one*: "There is one body . . . one faith, one baptism" (4:4–5); *holy*: "that he might present the church to himself in splendor, without spot or wrinkle or any such thing, that she might be holy and without blemish" (5:27); *catholic*: "the church, which is his body, the fulness of him who fills all in all" (1:22–23); and *apostolic*: "the household of God, built upon the foundation of the apostles and prophets, Christ Jesus himself being the cornerstone" (2:19–20 [contrast 1 Cor. 3:11]). This idea of the church itself being built upon the Apostles seems to exalt the importance of the Apostles, almost as figures of the past, in a way that seems a little later than Paul, as does the reference to the unique status of the "holy apostles and prophets" in 3:5. Would Paul really have spoken of himself in such terms?

The church is further described in exalted language as central to the eternal plan of God, already in view "before the foundation of the world" (1:4): "that through the church the manifold wisdom of God might now be made known to the principalities and powers in the heavenly places. This was according to the eternal purpose which he has realized in Christ Jesus our Lord" (3:10–11). This self-consciousness of the church exceeds anything in the undisputed Pauline Letters. The offices of the church, as gifts of God, are stressed: apostles, prophets, evangelists, pastors, and teachers, all having as their purpose "to equip the saints for the work of ministry, for building up the body of Christ" (4:12). But with this we may compare Romans 12:4–8 and 1 Corinthians 12:27–31. Here in Ephesians, however, there is an emphasis on the role of these offices in protecting orthodoxy: "that we may no longer be children, tossed to and fro and carried about with every wind of doctrine by the cunning of men" (4:14). To be sure, Ephesians remains different from the Pastoral Epistles, with their establishment of criteria for the offices and mention of elders and overseers. We have furthermore in Ephesians the formalized catechetical teaching: "put off your old nature" and "put on the new nature" (4:22, 24), "look carefully" (5:15), and "stand" (6:13–14), as well as the household code in 5:21–6:9. These emphases reflect a belief that the church has to find its place in the world and settle down to maintain itself in the ongoing interim period prior to the end of the age.

The emphasis on realized eschatology in Ephesians fits fully with its early catholic tendencies. There is no sense of the imminence of the end and no explicit reference to the parousia of Christ, although the latter is implied in some futuristic passages. What is repeatedly stressed is the present position of Christians, who have been raised with Christ (though there is no mention of dying with Christ) to sit with him "in the heavenly places" (1:3; 2:6). The exaltation and cosmic lordship of Christ are of great importance, not the resurrection. But of course these emphases assume the reality of the resurrection.

A few further items are often mentioned. In contrast to a more balanced view that leaves some ongoing room for the law, Ephesians is not hesitant to state that the law is abolished by the death of Christ (2:15). So too whereas Romans 9–11 continues to affirm a special ongoing importance to Israel, in Ephesians 2:11–21 Israel seems absorbed into the church.

None of this, of course, is fully impossible for Paul, given his genius, his continuing development, and the exigencies of a later situation. Incipient early catholicism, which seems undeniably present in Ephesians, is no sure guarantee that Paul did not write Ephesians. As time passes, even Paul, like other first-generation Christians, can be expected to reveal some of the concerns of incipient early catholicism. And, it should be emphasized, none of this requires a date very late in the first century, let alone the second century.

Still, questions will not go away. It seems strange for Paul to write a general, circular letter when all of his other letters are so thoroughly rooted in particulars (even the Letter to the Romans). Why would Paul write a letter in which he not only copies a previous letter but also seems highly dependent on all of his other letters?[29]

Although none of the arguments against the Pauline authorship of Ephesians provides a knockout punch, together they might provide a narrow victory by points. The cumulative power of the case against Pauline authorship, although hardly overwhelming, is strong and does seem to me to make the affirmation of Pauline authorship more difficult than its denial. To be sure, this conclusion cannot amount to more than a slight probability. "Everything points instead to a later follower of Paul who used Colossians as the basis for his own reinterpretation of the Pauline gospel."[30] It is possible, of course, to argue for a secretary with a distinctive vocabulary and an especially ponderous style. But this is not enough to explain the expansive perspective and theology of Ephesians. For if the necessary degree of freedom and responsibility for content is left to the secretary, then the line between secretary and author virtually vanishes. It is sometimes said that if Ephesians were not written by

29. "Ephesians is almost completely a cento of the known letters of Paul" (Goodspeed, *The Key to Ephesians*, vii). Goodspeed includes a synopsis backing up this statement.

30. Lincoln, *Ephesians*, lxviii.

Paul, then we must accept that there was a theological giant equal to or greater than Paul himself about whom we know nothing. But it is hardly unthinkable that others could be similarly gifted. After all, we do not know the author of the book of Hebrews.

But is there any real obstacle to accepting that Ephesians was written by a disciple of Paul—in Paul's name because of the Pauline content of the letter? Chapter 24 above, "The Authorship Question," contains a discussion of pseudonymity and pseudepigraphy. There I defend the practice of writing in another person's name as a morally acceptable way of a disciple transmitting and adapting the teaching of his master for a new situation. The pseudonymous or "allonymous" (written by "another") document continues to bear the authority of the apostle. It remains canonically authoritative. There seems little to lose if we are open to the "allonymity" of a few documents in our NT. Indeed, we need to be open to it if this is a way in which God has brought our Scriptures to us.[31] It is worth noting that Markus Barth, a commentator on Ephesians who accepts its Pauline authorship,[32] fairly concedes to those who question it: "Inspiration, highest authority, and imperishable value can be ascribed to Ephesians, even when the epistle is 'bereft of its apostolic authorship.'"[33]

Theological Emphases

The Mystery of God's Will

There is a decidedly apocalyptic dimension to Ephesians. The word "mystery" (*mysterion*), which occurs more in Ephesians (6x) than any other NT book, refers to something hitherto unclear but now made plain by revelation.[34] The mystery that Ephesians speaks of involves nothing less than all that exists. This mystery is first articulated early in the book: "For he has made known to us in all wisdom and insight the mystery of his will, according to his purpose which he set forth in Christ as a plan for the fulness of time [*plērōmatos tōn kairōn*], to unite [*anakephalaiōsasthai*, used elsewhere in the NT only in Rom. 13:9, "sum up"] all things in him, things in heaven and things on earth" (1:9–10). The eschatological goal of the transformation of creation is God's plan, and that is to happen "in Christ," or perhaps "through Christ" if we take the dative as instrumental. At the heart of this uniting or summing up

31. Werner Kümmel justifiably writes in his discussion of Ephesians, "There still exists in any event no ground for declaring that pseudepigraphic writing is impossible for early Christian epistolary literature, or that it precludes truthfulness" (*Introduction to the New Testament*, 363).

32. But Barth indicates that "Paul's authorship can only be affirmed with fear and trembling" (*The Broken Wall*, 11).

33. Barth, *Ephesians*, 50, depending on Mitton, *The Epistle to the Ephesians*, 270–77.

34. On this subject, see Caragounis, *The Ephesian* Mysterion.

of all creation is the reconciliation of all things to God (cf. Col. 1:20: "by the blood of his cross"). This refers to a universal salvation that corresponds to the bliss of the garden of Eden. Note too the reference to "the purpose of his will" (1:5) and "according to the purpose of him who accomplishes all things according to the counsel of his will" (1:11).

In chapter 3 the author relates "how the mystery was made known to me by revelation," defining it as "the mystery of Christ, which was not made known to the sons of men in other generations as it has now been revealed to his holy apostles and prophets by the Spirit; that is, how the Gentiles are fellow heirs, members of the same body, and partakers of the promise in Christ Jesus through the gospel" (3:3–6). This passage "already reflects the Gentile apostolate of Paul from the perspective of its role in salvation history."[35]

The Role of the Church

A few lines later, the author refers yet again to "the plan of the mystery hidden for ages in God who created all things," further defining it in these words: "that through the church the manifold wisdom of God might now be made known to the principalities and powers in the heavenly places," adding that "this was according to the eternal purpose which he has realized in Christ Jesus our Lord" (3:9–11). The paradox is that the church, with all its flaws and fallibility has, in God's "eternal purpose," a key cosmological role in the declaration of the highly varied "wisdom of God" to the spiritual entities, "the principalities and powers," of the heavenly sphere. Nothing is left outside God's reconciling power manifested in Christ. If this is in accord with God's "eternal purpose," even "before the foundation of the world," then this is the fulfillment of the covenant promises that God made beginning with Abraham and finding their poetic statement in the apocalyptic portions of the prophets. As promised in the Abrahamic covenant, Gentile believers too are "fellow heirs, members of the same body, and partakers of the promise in Christ Jesus through the gospel" (3:6).

The church is described in Ephesians as Christ's "body, the fulness of him who fills all in all" (1:23); members of the church are members of his body (5:30). The unity of the church is an important concern of Ephesians (4:3–7). The union between husband and wife is likened to that between Christ and the church and is designated "a great mystery" (5:32 KJV). In that context we read that "Christ loved the church and gave himself up for her" (5:25), and so too that "Christ is the head of the church, his body, and is himself its Savior" (5:23). The church is thus the locus of salvation.

Another important metaphor for the church in Ephesians is that of a building or house, and in particular a temple: "the household of God, built upon

---

35. Schnelle, *The History and Theology of the New Testament Writings*, 301.

the foundation of the apostles and prophets, Christ Jesus himself being the cornerstone, in whom the whole structure is joined together and grows into a holy temple in the Lord; in whom you are built into it for a dwelling place of God in the Spirit" (2:19–22).[36]

The Mystery and Glory of the Gospel

The Pauline kerygma is called the proclamation of "the mystery of the gospel" (6:19) and "the word of truth, the gospel of your salvation" (1:13). That gospel is inseparable from Christ and his work. To experience it is to be "in Christ" (1:3–14, and throughout). "Through Jesus Christ" (1:5; cf. 2:18; "through his blood," 1:7; cf. 2:16) becomes interchangeable with "through the gospel" (3:6). The point is made redundantly: "in whom we have boldness and confidence of access through our faith in him" (3:12). The high christological implications of these assertions is plain.

The gospel is none other than the Pauline gospel of salvation by faith, not works. "God, who is rich in mercy, out of the great love with which he loved us, even when we were dead through our trespasses, made us alive together with Christ (by grace you have been saved)" (2:4–5). "For by grace you have been saved through faith; and this is not your own doing, it is the gift of God—not because of works, lest any man should boast" (2:8–9).[37] Or, put alternatively, "In him we have redemption through his blood, the forgiveness of our trespasses, according to the riches of his grace which he lavished upon us" (1:7–8).

Realized Eschatology

Future eschatology has not receded altogether—in "the coming ages" we are to experience the "riches of his grace in kindness" (2:7 [cf. 1:21])—but the emphasis of the epistle clearly is on present realization of salvation. Present salvation and future salvation are held in tension, in good Pauline fashion. Ephesians stresses the noun "fullness" (*plērōma*) and the cognate verb "fulfill" (*plēroō*). These words express the realization of God's purpose and have at times a present and at times a future dimension. Sometimes the words can seem ambiguous, as in 1:10: "a plan [*oikonomian*] for the fulness of time [*tōn kairōn*, lit., "the times"], to unite all things in him, things in heaven and things on earth"—perhaps beginning to be realized now, but fully only in the future. Other uses of the words can also be difficult to understand—for example, the

36. See the excursus "The Church in the Epistle to the Ephesians" in Schnackenburg, *Ephesians*, 293–310.

37. In 2:5, 8 the participle underlying "have been saved" is in the perfect tense, indicating a presently enjoyed reality.

church described as "the fulness of him who fills all in all" (1:23), and Christ's ascension "that he might fill all things" (4:10). Clearly these statements have an eschatological tonality.

Present Christian experience has an eschatological dimension: Paul prays that "according to the riches of his glory he [the Father] may grant you to be strengthened with might through his Spirit in the inner man" (3:16), and that you "may have power to comprehend with all the saints what is the breadth and length and height and depth, and to know the love of Christ which surpasses knowledge, that you may be filled with all the fulness of God" (3:18–19). Comparable is the earlier prayer in 1:17–19, where Paul asks that God will give the readers "a spirit of wisdom and of revelation in the knowledge of him, having the eyes of your hearts enlightened," that they may know "what are the riches of his glorious inheritance in the saints, and what is the immeasurable greatness of his power in us who believe, according to the working of his great might." The power is at work in the present, but the inheritance itself remains future: Christians are "sealed with the promised Holy Spirit, which is the guarantee of our inheritance until we acquire possession of it" (1:13–14), again a very Pauline perspective. Prior to future resurrection, Christians are already "blessed . . . in Christ with every spiritual blessing in the heavenly places" (1:3). God has "raised us up with him, and made us sit with him in the heavenly places in Christ Jesus" (2:6).

Jews and Gentiles in the Church (2:11–22)

One of the most memorable passages in Ephesians describes the unity of Jews and Gentiles in the church. The previous, absolute distinction between Jews and Gentiles, an indisputable fact since the time of the patriarchs, has been overcome in the new entity brought about by the cross: the church, here described under the metaphors of a building, a household, and a temple or dwelling place of God (2:19–22).

The grim plight of the Gentiles before the time of Christ is frankly laid out: "separated from Christ, alienated from the commonwealth of Israel, and strangers to the covenants of promise, having no hope and without God in the world" (2:12). But that situation has dramatically changed: those who were "far off" have now been "brought near" (2:13)—indeed, to the point of experiencing salvation and becoming "fellow citizens with the saints and members of the household of God" (2:19). This remarkable change has become possible by the agency of the death of Christ: "in the blood of Christ" (2:13). The Jews themselves also depend on the cross for this new state of affairs, so that Christ "might reconcile us both to God in one body through the cross, thereby bringing the hostility to an end" (2:16 [cf. 2:15: "in his flesh"]). The new unity of Jews and Gentiles in the church is the result of enjoying a common salvation. Indeed, this passage in itself presents a salvation-historical perspective that moves from the covenants to the eschaton, finding in the church the culmination of God's purpose.

The result is that Christ, described as "our peace," "has made us both one" (2:14), "one new man in place of the two . . . one body" (2:15–16). In the one place in Ephesians where the law of Moses is mentioned, it is identified as the cause of the division and hostility between Jews and Gentiles, since it was the law that marked out Jewish identity over against the Gentiles. The law as a boundary of separation is likened to the physical wall that separated the court of the Gentiles from the inner courts of the temple. That "dividing wall of hostility," the author says, has been "broken down" (*lysas*) by the death of Christ, and, leaving no uncertainty about what he means, he adds "by abolishing [*katargēsas*] in his flesh the law of commandments [*ton nomon tōn entolōn*] and ordinances" (2:15). The commandments per se are no longer of consequence to members of the church, whether Gentile or Jewish.

The new unity of Jews and Gentiles in the church[38] means an end of the traditional hostility and the creation of a new spiritual temple without dividing walls, referred to as "a dwelling place of God in the Spirit" (2:22). This amounts to a new, eschatological temple graced by the presence of God.

Liturgical Aspects of Ephesians

Because of their special style and elevated language, several passages in Ephesians are thought to be, or to be based on, creedal or hymnic traditional materials.[39] The lengthy sentence at the beginning of the epistle, 1:3–14, possibly reflects a hymn; according to some, it was part of an early baptismal liturgy. Other passages that are possibly liturgical are 1:20–23 (especially vv. 20, 22); 2:4–10, possibly a baptismal confession of faith; 2:14–18, thought by many to be based on a hymn because of its parallelisms, participles, and relative clauses; and 2:19–22; 4:4–6; 5:25–27, which seem to represent early creeds. The importance of hymns in the church is indicated explicitly in 5:19: "addressing one another in psalms and hymns and spiritual songs, singing and making melody to the Lord with all your heart." So abundant is the liturgical material in Ephesians that John Kirby has argued that the main content of the letter originally formed a liturgical text related to baptism and used at Pentecost in a covenant renewal service.[40]

---

38. The church has become a third entity, one that transcends the difference between Jew and Gentile. Compare 1 Corinthians 10:32: "Give no offense to Jews or to Greeks or to the church of God."

39. See Best, "The Use of Credal and Liturgical Material in Ephesians"; J. T. Sanders, "Hymnic Elements in Ephesians 1–3."

40. Kirby, *Ephesians*.

Apparently, a line from a hymn, introduced with an introductory formula, is quoted in 5:14: "Awake, O sleeper, and arise from the dead, and Christ shall give you light." The only other explicit quotation introduced with a formula is in 4:8, where Psalm 68:18 is quoted (in a form that agrees with neither the Masoretic Text nor the LXX)[41] and is followed by a midrashic exposition.[42]

Ethical Teaching

The second half of Ephesians is largely devoted to ethical paraenesis. But already in 1:4 the goal of election is expressed as "that we should be holy and blameless before him," and in 1:12 Christians are "destined and appointed to live for the praise of his glory" (1:12). "Good works" (*erga agatha*), language not used positively by Paul, are stressed: "For we are his workmanship, created in Christ Jesus for good works, which God prepared beforehand, that we should walk in them" (2:10); however, this is said in the context of a clear statement about salvation by grace through faith (2:8–9).

A major turning point in the letter is nonetheless reached at 4:1, in the exhortation "to lead a life worthy of the calling to which you have been called." After this initial rubric, the letter stresses the unity of the church in the remarkable creedal passage in 4:4–6: "There is one body and one Spirit, just as you were called to the one hope that belongs to your call, one Lord, one faith, one baptism, one God and Father of us all." Together with the unity of the church are the diverse gifts given by God "to equip the saints for the work of ministry, for building up the body of Christ," with the goal of attaining "the unity of the faith and of the knowledge of the Son of God, to mature manhood, to the measure of the stature of the fulness of Christ" (4:12–13). "Speaking the truth in love, we are to grow up in every way into him who is the head, into Christ" (4:15).

After a brief vice list, the author writes, "You did not so learn [*emathete*] Christ!" (an expression that occurs nowhere else in the Pauline corpus),[43] adding "assuming that you have heard about him and were taught in him, as the truth is in Jesus" (4:20–21). Then comes a long section of ethical catechesis (4:22–5:20), including the pattern of "put off . . . put on" already noted above, together with vice and virtue lists, followed by the directives of the household

41. Psalm 68:18, in both the Masoretic Text (68:19) and the LXX (67:19), says that the Lord "received" rather than "gave" gifts. There are targumic renderings of the verse, however, that apparently follow early traditions that refer to the Lord giving gifts, as in the Ephesians text.

42. Possibly 4:9 refers to Christ's descent into Hades, but more probably "the lower parts of the earth" is an appositional genitive, so that "the lower parts" indicates the earth itself, and hence the passage is a reference to the incarnation.

43. The verb used here, *manthanō*, has as its cognate noun *mathētēs* ("disciple").

code (5:21–6:9). The final exhortation of the epistle employs the metaphor of the armor of God, which Christians are to put on to enable them to stand in the present battle (and also "in the evil day") against principalities, powers, and "the world rulers of this present darkness, against the spiritual hosts of wickedness in the heavenly places" (6:12). That armor consists of truth, righteousness, the gospel of peace, faith, salvation, and the word of God (6:11–17).

Author, Addressees, Date

Author

It remains a fair possibility that Paul himself was the author of Ephesians. In that case, he must have used a secretary—perhaps Timothy or Tychicus or someone like them—to whom he gave an exceptional freedom in putting the letter in its present form. The greater that freedom, however, the more reason we have to speak of an author rather than simply a secretary. If the balance of probability tips somewhat against Pauline authorship, what can be said about other possibilities?

We can at least conclude that the author was a Paulinist—that is, a member of the Pauline circle or school. Several suggestions have been made. One may think of Timothy, whose name, although found at the beginning of Colossians, is lacking at the beginning of Ephesians. Or there is Tychicus, who is mentioned in 6:21, but in a way that perhaps is too glowing for him to have written it himself. We have already noted the hypothesis concerning Onesimus, who, although mentioned in Colossians 4:9, is not mentioned in the close parallel, Ephesians 6:21–22. But the idea of Onesimus as the author is extremely speculative. Appealing to the ideas, vocabulary, imagery, and perspective shared by Ephesians and Luke-Acts, Ralph Martin suggests that Luke, who was present with Paul in prison when he wrote Colossians (Col. 4:14), is the author of Ephesians.[44]

We are forced to admit that if Ephesians was not by Paul, we do not know the gifted author of this remarkable book. He probably was a Hellenistic Jewish Christian and a co-worker or disciple of Paul. It is probable, but not necessary, that the author is someone whose name appears in the Pauline Letters. There are also some interesting similarities between Ephesians and the thought world of Qumran[45] that have led to the bold conjecture that the author was a converted scribe of the Qumran community.[46] That Ephesians was written as an introduction to the Pauline corpus, whether by Onesimus or someone else, remains an unprovable but intriguing hypothesis.

44. See Martin, "An Epistle in Search of a Life-Setting," 301.
45. See the chapter "Ephesians and Qumran" in Dahl, *Studies in Ephesians*, 107–44. Dahl points to things such as dualism; predestination and election; the nature, knowledge, and ethics of the community; the Spirit; and eschatology and hope.
46. Thus Murphy-O'Connor, "Who Wrote Ephesians?"

Addressees

Since Ephesians almost certainly was an encyclical letter, the addressees were Christians generally, probably mainly Gentiles (cf. 2:11–12), and, because of its association with Colossians, perhaps located in the churches of Asia Minor. Some content in Ephesians—for example, the repeated reference to principalities and powers, the realized eschatology, and the ethical paraenesis—suggests that there may have been a threat of incipient gnostic ideas.

Date

If by Paul, Ephesians probably is to be dated from the time of the Roman imprisonment, thus in the early 60s. If, as seems slightly more probable, it was written by a disciple of Paul, since the concerns of an incipient early catholicism are evident already in the second half of the first century, there is really no need to put the document any later than the 70s or, perhaps more likely, the 80s.

Bibliography

Books and Articles

Arnold, Clinton E. *Ephesians: Power and Magic; The Concept of Power in Ephesians in Light of Its Historical Setting*. SNTSMS 63. Cambridge: Cambridge University Press, 1989.

Barth, Markus. *The Broken Wall: A Study of the Epistle to the Ephesians*. Chicago: Judson, 1959.

———. "Conversion and Conversation: Israel and the Church in Paul's Epistle to the Ephesians." *Int* 17 (1963): 3–24.

———. "Traditions in Ephesians." *NTS* 30 (1984): 3–25.

Best, Ernest. *Ephesians*. NTG. Sheffield: JSOT Press, 1993.

———. *Essays on Ephesians*. Edinburgh: T&T Clark, 1997.

———. "Recipients and Title of the Letter to the Ephesians: Why and When the Designation 'Ephesians'?" *ANRW* II.25.4 (1987): 3247–79.

———. "The Use of Credal and Liturgical Material in Ephesians." In *Worship, Theology and Ministry in the Early Church: Essays in Honor of Ralph Martin*, edited by Michael J. Wilkins and Terence Paige, 53–69. JSNTSup 87. Sheffield: JSOT Press, 1992.

———. "Who Used Whom? The Relationship of Ephesians and Colossians." *NTS* 43 (1997): 72–96.

Black, David Alan. "The Peculiarities of Ephesians and the Ephesian Address." *GTJ* 2 (1981): 59–73.

Brown, Raymond E. *An Introduction to the New Testament*. New York: Doubleday, 1997.

Bruce, F. F. *Paul, Apostle of the Heart Set Free*. Grand Rapids: Eerdmans, 2000.

Cadbury, Henry J. "The Dilemma of Ephesians." *NTS* 5 (1958–59): 91–102.

Caragounis, Chrys C. *The Ephesian Mysterion: Meaning and Content*. ConBNT 8. Lund: Gleerup, 1977.

Corley, Bruce. "The Theology of Ephesians." *SwJT* 22 (1979): 24–38.

Coutts, John. "The Relationship of Ephesians and Colossians." *NTS* 4 (1957–58): 201–7.

Cross, Frank L., ed. *Studies in Ephesians*. London: Mowbray, 1956.

Dahl, Nils A. *Studies in Ephesians: Introductory Questions, Text- and Edition-Critical Issues, Interpretation of Texts and Themes*, edited by David Hellholm, Vemund Blomkvist, and Tord Fornberg. WUNT 131. Tübingen: Mohr Siebeck, 2000.

Goodspeed, Edgar J. "Ephesians and the First Edition of Paul." *JBL* 70 (1951): 285–91.

———. "Ephesians, the Introduction to the Pauline Collection." In *New Solutions of New Testament Problems*, 11–20. Chicago: University of Chicago Press, 1927.

———. *An Introduction to the New Testament*. Chicago: University of Chicago Press, 1937.

———. *The Key to Ephesians*. Chicago: University of Chicago Press, 1956.

———. *The Meaning of Ephesians*. Chicago: University of Chicago Press, 1933.

Heil, John Paul. *Ephesians: Empowerment to Walk in Love for the Unity of All in Christ*. SBL 13. Atlanta: Society of Biblical Literature, 2007.

Hering, James P. *The Colossian and Ephesian Haustafeln in Theological Context: An Analysis of Their Origins, Relationship, and Message*. AUS 7/260. New York: Peter Lang, 2007.

Käsemann, Ernst. "Ephesians and Acts." In *Studies in Luke-Acts: Essays Presented in Honor of Paul Schubert*, edited by Leander E. Keck and J. Louis Martyn, 288–97. Nashville: Abingdon, 1966.

Kirby, John C. *Ephesians: Baptism and Pentecost; An Inquiry into the Structure and Purpose of the Epistle to the Ephesians*. London: SPCK, 1968.

Klein, William W. *The Book of Ephesians: An Annotated Bibliography*. New York: Garland, 1996.

Klijn, A. F. J. *An Introduction to the New Testament*. Translated by M. van der Vathorst-Smit. Leiden: Brill, 1967.

Koester, Helmut, ed. *Ephesos, Metropolis of Asia: An Interdisciplinary Approach to Its Archaeology, Religion, and Culture*. HTS 41. Valley Forge, PA: Trinity Press International, 1995.

Kreitzer, Larry J. *Hierapolis in the Heavens: Studies in the Letter to the Ephesians*. LNTS 368. New York: T&T Clark, 2007.

Kümmel, Werner Georg. *Introduction to the New Testament*. Translated by A. J. Mattill Jr. 14th ed. Nashville: Abingdon, 1966.

Larkin, William J. *Ephesians: A Handbook on the Greek Text*. BHGNT. Waco: Baylor University Press, 2009.

Lincoln, Andrew T. "The Church and Israel in Ephesians 2." *CBQ* 49 (1987): 605–24.

———. *Paradise Now and Not Yet: Studies in the Role of the Heavenly Dimension in Paul's Thought with Special Reference to His Eschatology*. SNTSMS 43. Cambridge: Cambridge University Press, 1981.

———. "A Re-Examination of 'The Heavenlies' in Ephesians." *NTS* 19 (1972–73): 468–83.

———. "The Theology of Ephesians." In *The Theology of the Later Pauline Letters*, by Andrew T. Lincoln and A. J. M. Wedderburn, 75–166. NTT. Cambridge: Cambridge University Press, 1993.

———. "The Use of the OT in Ephesians." *JSNT* 14 (1982): 16–57.

Lohse, Eduard. *Colossians and Philemon: A Commentary on the Epistles to the Colossians and to Philemon*. Translated by William R. Poehlmann and Robert J. Karris. Edited by Helmut Koester. Hermeneia. Philadelphia: Fortress, 1971.

Martin, Ralph P. "An Epistle in Search of a Life-Setting." *ExpTim* 79 (1968): 296–302.

McCall, Duke K., ed. "Ephesians." *RevExp* 76 (1979): 463–567.

Metzger, Bruce M. *A Textual Commentary on the Greek New Testament*. 2nd ed. Stuttgart: Deutsche Bibelgesellschaft, 1994.

Mitton, C. Leslie. *The Epistle to the Ephesians: Its Authorship, Origin and Purpose*. Oxford: Clarendon, 1951.

———. "Important Hypotheses Reconsidered: VII. The Authorship of the Epistle to the Ephesians." *ExpTim* 67 (1955–56): 195–98.

Moritz, Thorsten. *A Profound Mystery: The Use of the Old Testament in Ephesians*. NovTSup 85. Leiden: Brill, 1996.

Moule, C. F. D. "E. J. Goodspeed's Theory Regarding the Origin of Ephesians." *ExpTim* 60 (1949): 224–25.

Murphy-O'Connor, Jerome. "Who Wrote Ephesians?" *TBT* 18 (1965): 1201–9.

Neufeld, Thomas Yoder. *"Put on the Armour of God": The Divine Warrior from Isaiah to Ephesians*. JSNTSup 144. Sheffield: Sheffield Academic Press, 1997.

O'Brien, Peter T. "Ephesians 1: An Unusual Introduction to a New Testament Letter." *NTS* 25 (1978–79): 504–16.

Polhill, John B. "The Relationship between Ephesians and Colossians." *RevExp* 70 (1973): 439–50.

Rese, Martin. "Church and Israel in the Deuteropauline Letters." *SJT* 43 (1990): 19–32.

Sampley, J. Paul. *"And the Two Shall Become One Flesh": A Study of Traditions in Ephesians 5:21–33*. SNTSMS 16. Cambridge: Cambridge University Press, 1971.

Sanday, William, and Arthur C. Headlam. *A Critical and Exegetical Commentary on the Epistle to the Romans*. 5th ed. ICC. Edinburgh: T&T Clark, 1925.

Sanders, E. P. "Literary Dependence in Colossians." *JBL* 85 (1966): 28–45.

Sanders, Jack T. "Hymnic Elements in Ephesians 1–3." *ZNW* 56 (1965): 214–32.

Schnelle, Udo. *The History and Theology of the New Testament Writings*. Translated by M. Eugene Boring. Minneapolis: Fortress, 1998.

Tellbe, Mikael. *Christ-Believers in Ephesus: A Textual Analysis of Early Christian Identity Formation in a Local Perspective*. WUNT 242. Tübingen: Mohr Siebeck, 2009.

Trebilco, Paul. *The Early Christians in Ephesus from Paul to Ignatius*. WUNT 166. Tübingen: Mohr Siebeck, 1987.

Turner, Max. "Mission and Meaning in Terms of 'Unity' in Ephesians." In *Mission and Meaning: Essays Presented to Peter Cotterell*, edited by Antony Billington, Tony Lane, and Max Turner, 138–66. Carlisle, UK: Paternoster, 1995.

van Roon, A. *The Authenticity of Ephesians*. NovTSup 39. Leiden: Brill, 1974.

Wall, Robert W. "Wifely Submission in the Context of Ephesians." *CSR* 17 (1988): 272–85.

Wessels, Gabriel F. "The Eschatology of Colossians and Ephesians." *Neot* 21 (1987): 183–202.

Yee, Tet-Lim N. *Jews, Gentiles, and Ethnic Reconciliation: Paul's Jewish Identity and Ephesians*. SNTSMS 130. Cambridge: Cambridge University Press, 2005.

Commentaries

Abbott, T. K. *A Critical and Exegetical Commentary on the Epistles to the Ephesians and to the Colossians*. ICC. Edinburgh: T&T Clark, 1897.

Arnold, Clinton E. *Ephesians*. ZECNT. Grand Rapids: Zondervan, 2010.

Barth, Markus. *Ephesians: Introduction, Translation, and Commentary*. 2 vols. AB 34, 34A. Garden City, NY: Doubleday, 1974.

Best, Ernest. *A Critical and Exegetical Commentary on Ephesians*. ICC. Edinburgh: T&T Clark, 1998.

Bruce, F. F. *The Epistles to the Colossians, to Philemon, and to the Ephesians*. NICNT. Grand Rapids: Eerdmans, 1984.

Caird, G. B. *Paul's Letters from Prison: Ephesians, Philippians, Colossians, Philemon*. NClarB. Oxford: Oxford University Press, 1976.

Dodd, C. H. "Ephesians." In *The Abingdon Bible Commentary*, edited by Frederick Carl Eiselen, Edwin Lewis, and David G. Downey, 1222–37. New York: Abingdon, 1929.

Foulkes, Francis. *The Epistle of Paul to the Ephesians*. 2nd ed. TNTC. Grand Rapids: Eerdmans, 1989.

Hoehner, Harold W. *Ephesians: An Exegetical Commentary*. Grand Rapids: Baker Academic, 2002.

Kreitzer, Larry J. *The Epistle to the Ephesians*. EC. Peterborough, UK: Epworth, 1989.

Liefeld, Walter L. *Ephesians*. IVPNTC. Downers Grove, IL: InterVarsity, 1997.

Lincoln, Andrew T. *Ephesians*. WBC 42. Dallas: Word, 1990.

MacDonald, Margaret Y. *Colossians and Ephesians*. SP 17. Collegeville, MN: Liturgical Press, 2000.

Martin, Ralph P. *Ephesians, Colossians, Philemon*. IBC. Atlanta: John Knox, 1991.

Mitton, C. Leslie. *Ephesians*. NCBC. Grand Rapids: Eerdmans, 1976.

Muddiman, John. *A Commentary on the Epistle to the Ephesians*. BNTC. New York: Continuum, 2001.

O'Brien, Peter T. *The Letter to the Ephesians*. PNTC. Grand Rapids: Eerdmans, 1999.

Patzia, Arthur G. *Ephesians, Colossians, Philemon*. NIBC. Peabody, MA: Hendrickson, 1990.

Perkins, Pheme. *Ephesians*. ANTC. Nashville: Abingdon, 1997.

Schnackenburg, Rudolf. *Ephesians: A Commentary*. Translated by Helen Heron. Edinburgh: T&T Clark, 1991.

Snodgrass, Klyne. *Ephesians*. NIVAC. Grand Rapids: Zondervan, 1996.

Synge, Francis C. *St. Paul's Epistle to the Ephesians: A Theological Commentary*. London: SPCK, 1941.

Talbert, Charles H. *Ephesians and Colossians*. PCNT. Grand Rapids: Baker Academic, 2007.

Theilman, F. *Ephesians*. BECNT. Grand Rapids: Baker Academic, 2011.

Thompson, G. H. P. *The Letters of Paul to the Ephesians, to the Colossians, and to Philemon*. CBC. Cambridge: Cambridge University Press, 1967.

Thurston, Bonnie. *Reading Colossians, Ephesians and 2 Thessalonians: A Literary and Theological Commentary*. RNT. New York: Crossroad, 1995.

Westcott, B. F. *Saint Paul's Epistle to the Ephesians*. New York: Macmillan, 1906.

Witherington, Ben, III. *The Letters to Philemon, the Colossians, and the Ephesians: A Socio-Rhetorical Commentary on the Captivity Epistles*. Grand Rapids: Eerdmans, 2007.

33

The Tendencies of "Early Catholicism"

From its very beginning the Christian church experienced development and change. It could hardly remain static as it actively explored and articulated its theology in continual interaction with varying contexts and issues. As long as the Apostles and their co-workers were still alive, differences between them notwithstanding, development and change could take place with perhaps some sense of security. As the Apostles and the first generation of Christians came to the end of their careers and began to die, however, change undoubtedly was perceived as more of a threat. Thus, in the later decades of the first century the church began to move into a transition that lasted well into the second century and beyond. This period brought a time of consolidation, self-definition, and self-consciousness of the church that has been given the name "early catholicism."

Unfortunately, the expression "early catholicism" carries with it some unwanted baggage. F. C. Baur made it a foundation stone of the (discredited) Tübingen hypothesis, as constituting the "synthesis" in the early church that brought together and reconciled the "thesis" of Petrine Christianity and the "antithesis" of Pauline Christianity. The word "catholicism" worries some Protestants because it might seem to suggest that the NT provides support to the Catholic Church as having such early roots. Some regard the trend as representing an unfortunate departure from the "pure" Pauline gospel.

Martin Hengel suggests doing away with the expression altogether: "The term 'early Catholicism,' so often misused, is inappropriate and does not add anything to our understanding of earliest Christian history. We would do better to avoid it altogether, as it leads us astray into a cliché-ridden approach to earliest Christianity, coupled with distorted judgments. If we want to, we can find 'early-catholic traits' even in Jesus and Paul: the phenomena thus denoted are almost entirely a legacy of Judaism."[1]

Even if we are not persuaded with Hengel to do away with the expression altogether, it does seem more accurate to modify it slightly to something like "incipient early catholicism"—that is, early catholic traits that fall short of a full-blown second-century and later early catholicism that is the precursor of the Catholic Church of later centuries. There is, of course, no such thing as "early catholicism," in the sense of something clearly marked out and with a clear beginning. We are dealing with a transition, a recurring tendency that is gradual and widespread over a considerable period of time. Incipient early catholicism includes the variety of ways by which we move from the church perceiving itself as a band of "aliens and exiles" (1 Pet. 2:11; cf. 1:1) in this world whose "citizenship is in heaven" (Phil. 3:20 NRSV) to, in its most developed form on the trajectory, *una sancta catholica et apostolica ecclesia*, the fully organized custodian of the faith, mediator of salvation, and well settled in the world for the long haul. Incipient early catholicism is the transitional process that brings us from the one to the other. The phrase "early catholicism" is used here in a positive sense, as something that fulfills God's will for the church.

Obviously, it is primarily in the later books of the NT that we can observe the traits of this incipient early catholicism: especially Ephesians, parts of Matthew, Luke-Acts, the Pastoral Epistles, 2 Peter, and Jude. But, as we will see, some of these traits can be found in earlier books too.

The Elements of Incipient Early Catholicism

The essence of incipient early catholicism can best be grasped by looking at some widely recognized tendencies that begin to become evident in the later decades of the first century. These tendencies involve moving from primitive to more developed perspectives. For the sake of clarity, these are strongly stated here, and in contrasting terms. It should be remembered that this involves simplification, and that we are dealing with tendencies over time, with no hard and fast boundaries, relative matters rather than absolutes, and changes occurring at different rates of speed in different places. As will easily be seen, these items are interrelated and mutually supportive. Virtually all of them grow out of the fundamental need to cope with the lengthening period between the first and the second coming of Christ.

1. The fading of an imminent eschatology is widely regarded as fundamental to early catholicism. Understandably, when the parousia of Christ
   recedes into the distant future, thought must be given to maintaining

1. Hengel, *Acts and the History of Earliest Christianity*, 122.

The Tendencies of Incipient Early Catholicism

From	To
imminent eschatology	realized eschatology and salvation-historical perspective
dynamism of Holy Spirit	institutionalism
ad hoc organization	structured ministry/church order
church as proclaimer of the word	church as the means of salvation and dispenser of the sacraments
developing theologies	fixed orthodoxy; custodian of tradition
salvation by faith	moralism
saints	distinction between clergy and laity
prophetic edge	settledness and adaptation to the world
local congregations	a sole, universal church, self-conscious of its unique authority

the church until the time of Christ's return. The emphasis shifts, as one would expect, away from future eschatology and toward realized eschatology. The church must exist in the present and maximize what is available for its life now. The delay in the coming of eschatological consummation in turn emphasizes the significance of the present time, raises a salvation-historical consciousness of the time frame of "the church age," thereby enhancing the importance of the church itself.

2. The dynamism of the Holy Spirit, so vitally significant for the beginning and growth of the church, its decision making, and its direction, now gives way to a formalized institutionalism. Spiritual enthusiasm (e.g., ecstatic experience) soon becomes regarded as more of a danger than an asset.

3. The early lack of organization, when operations were ad hoc, now is replaced with formal church order and a structured authority. Nothing is left to chance. A division of labor takes place, with offices related to personal gifts and qualifications. The ordination of *presbyteroi* ("elders") and *episkopoi* ("bishops"), their increasing authority, and ecclesiastical law begin to emerge.

4. Whereas in the earlier years the church basically was the proclaimer of the word, now the church becomes much more conscious of itself and its importance in God's purposes. It comes to regard itself as the indispensable mediator of salvation to the people and as the sole dispenser of the sacraments, so vitally important for salvation. With this eventually came sacramentalism, with emphasis on the external rite correctly performed by the correct people.

5. In contrast to the relative diversity of theological viewpoint allowed in the earlier years of the church, now the definition of orthodoxy becomes rather narrowly fixed. The church, having received the truth, now becomes the guardian of *the deposit of truth*, identifying itself as the custodian of apostolic tradition. The precise definition of orthodoxy

makes possible the determination of heresy. Heresy, in turn, is forcefully opposed. The *regula fidei*, the "rule of faith," sometimes known
as "the ecclesiastical canon," becomes the standard of orthodoxy and
serves as a guide for the interpretation of Scripture. Faith is objectified
into *fides quae creditur*, "what is believed."

6. A subtle shift takes place wherein the simple Pauline doctrine of justification by faith, not works, gives way to a strong moralism (seeing
   the gospel as new law) that seems to cloud the reality of free grace.
   Early catholicism therefore is seen as a decline from the purity of the
   gospel.

7. In the early church there was an egalitarianism in which all members
   were "saints" responsible for ministry in the church. Incipient early
   catholicism soon begins to develop a distinction between clergy and
   laity, and with it a professional ministry.

8. The church gradually begins to settle into the world as one of its institutions and begins to adapt to the realities of being in the everyday world.
   It tends to lose its prophetic edge, and at least to some extent it begins
   to temper the radical ethic of Jesus.

9. No longer does the church consist merely of local groups of believers,
   with a pilgrim attitude, called to a radical discipleship prior to the return
   of Christ. It now becomes a single, universal church, self-conscious of
   its significance and authority in the world and in the present era.

These developments should hardly be thought of as unfortunate or unde-
sirable in themselves, although of course they may become so. Indeed, it is in
these ways that God leads the church to prepare for and endure through the
lengthening interim period prior to the return of Christ. These were exactly
the things needed, not merely to keep the church on track, but also in order
to counteract two major threats that faced the church in the second century:
Gnosticism and Montanism. It is worth pointing out that in many or most
of the instances mentioned there is no need for the new emphases to exclude
the former realities, as if they were mutually exclusive. Indeed, some of the
marks of incipient early catholicism are already present in early books of the
NT; conversely, some of the characteristics of the early church persist and are
found in the later books.

Incipient Early Catholicism in the Earlier Books of the New Testament

It is easy to spot the tendencies of incipient early catholicism in the books
usually mentioned in this connection (Ephesians, parts of Matthew, Luke-
Acts, the Pastoral Epistles, Jude, and 2 Peter). And it should not be surprising
that early catholicism picks up considerable momentum as the church moves

through the end of the first century and into the second, as can be seen in the Apostolic Fathers[2] and the late second-century apologists Irenaeus and Clement of Alexandria. Although the tendencies of incipient early catholicism are known mainly from the later books of the NT, they are also present to an extent, as we will now see, even in its earlier books.[3]

The earliest church expected the parousia of Christ in the near future; that is, the early Christians had an imminent eschatology. Thus the early Paul expects to be alive at the coming of Christ (1 Thess. 4:15–17; cf. 1 Cor. 7:26–31; 15:51–52). But after his close brush with death (2 Cor. 1:8–11), he began to face the prospect of his death before the parousia (see Phil. 1:20–23). So the expectation of the parousia moved farther into the future, perhaps at first still the relatively near future, but ahead into the unknown, soon with the possibility of a more considerable delay than Paul had ever imagined. In Colossians, although the return of Christ is still expected (3:4), there is no evidence of imminence or urgency. Instead, realized eschatology is emphasized: here it is already true that "he has delivered us from the dominion of darkness and transferred us to the kingdom of his beloved Son" (1:13); already Christians have been raised with Christ (2:12; 3:1). The household code in 3:18–4:1 may also show the influence of the delay of the parousia.[4] James Dunn concludes his discussion of Colossians with this remark: "Here, it could be justly argued, we see the first movement towards early catholicism in Paul himself."[5] Dunn goes on to review the delay of the parousia and the accompanying increased stress on realized eschatology in Ephesians, the Pastoral Epistles, Luke-Acts, John, Hebrews, and 2 Peter.[6]

It is worth underlining that as the emphasis on realized eschatology increases in the later books of the NT, it does not necessarily displace the remaining expectation of the future parousia of Christ and future eschatology.

From practically the beginning, the early church was concerned with the faithful handing on of tradition and with protecting truth and opposing error.

---

2. The letters of Ignatius (ca. 115) are well known for their emphasis on a monarchical bishop and resisting heresy. Likewise, *1 Clement* (ca. 96) speaks of the importance of the office of "bishop" (*1 Clem.* 44), but there the word is still interchangeable with "elder." In Ignatius's *Letter to the Smyrnaeans* (Ign. *Smyrn.* 8.2) is the first use of *hē katholikē ekklēsia* ("the universal church").

3. "The various tendencies which have been lumped together under this designation were not in fact later tendencies but were present, at least in germ, from the beginning" (Marshall, "'Early Catholicism' in the New Testament," 229).

4. Such instructions, however, are not necessarily incompatible with a strong conviction of the imminence of the parousia. See 1 Thessalonians 4:11–12, where, along with the expectation of an imminent parousia, Paul exhorts the Thessalonians "to aspire to live quietly, to mind your own affairs, and to work with your hands, as we charged you; so that you may command the respect of outsiders, and be dependent on nobody."

5. Dunn, "Early Catholicism," 346.

6. At the end of his survey Dunn rightly concludes, "If early catholicism is defined, in part at least, by the fading of the imminent parousia hope, then early catholicism is already well established within the NT" (ibid., 351 [italics removed]).

Orthodoxy is already a concern in earliest Christianity.[7] Paul is adamant about there being only one gospel—the gospel that he preaches (Gal. 1:6–9), interpreted in a specific way (Gal. 2:14; 5:10; cf. 2 Cor. 11:4, 13). That gospel Paul describes as a "treasure" (2 Cor. 4:7). Paul refers to "the word of the truth, the gospel" (Col. 1:5); "the word of God which you heard from us" (1 Thess. 2:13). Paul encourages the Philippians to keep "holding fast the word of life" (Phil. 2:16).

In the earlier letters Paul stresses the necessity of maintaining the traditions. He instructs the Thessalonians to "stand firm and hold to the traditions which you were taught by us" (2 Thess. 2:15). The Philippians are to practice "what you have learned and received and heard and seen in me" (Phil. 4:9). Paul applauds the Corinthians because they "maintain the traditions even as I have delivered them to you" (1 Cor. 11:2). These passages refer not merely to the handing on of tradition; they exalt it and bestow significant authority upon it.

There is even an objectification of the word "faith," as in "the faith of the gospel" (Phil. 1:27) and in the exhortation to "continue in the faith" (Col. 1:23).

If a narrower criterion of orthodoxy is required, we also find in these letters evidence of what can be called a "crystallization of the faith into set forms."[8] Repeatedly we encounter creedal or liturgical fragments, such as Romans 1:3–4; 3:24–26; 10:9; 1 Corinthians 8:6; 11:23–26; 15:3–5; 2 Corinthians 5:18–21. And to these must be added the hymns in Philippians 2:6–11; Colossians 1:15–20.

There is little evidence for the institutionalizing of the church in the early letters. It would hardly seem to be the case, however, that at the beginning there was none. The Jerusalem church had "elders" (*presbyteroi*) who together with the Apostles constituted its leadership (see Acts 11:30; 15:2, 4, 6, 22–23; 16:4; 21:18). Luke tells us furthermore that it was Paul's practice to appoint elders "in every church" (Acts 14:23; cf. James 5:14; 1 Pet. 5:1), and that Paul addressed the elders of the Ephesian church (Acts 20:17). This pattern of leadership, taken over from the synagogue and the Sanhedrin, is exactly what one might expect in the early Christian local churches. That in the main corpus of Pauline Letters (apart from the Pastoral Epistles) the word "elder" does not occur seems to be a mere coincidence.

The office of "bishop" or "overseer" (*episkopos*) also exists early on (Acts 20:28; Phil. 1:1), although at first it is interchangeable with "elder" (so too in *1 Clement*). Although not as defined as they will become, these offices point to "a definite circle whose members may be called *presbyteroi* or *episkopoi* in distinction from others."[9]

The word "deacon" or "minister" (*diakonos*) as an office in the church also occurs in Philippians 1:1 and elsewhere (see Rom. 16:1; Col. 1:7, 23, 25; 4:7),

---

7. See Marshall, "Orthodoxy and Heresy in Earlier Christianity"; Köstenberger and Kruger, *The Heresy of Orthodoxy*.

8. This is the language used by Dunn, "Early Catholicism," 359.

9. Beyer, "ἐπισκέπτομαι, κτλ," 616. Beyer adds in reference to Philippians 1:1 that "it is impossible to argue that [Paul] is simply referring here to an activity . . . and not to an office" (ibid.).

although sometimes the word has the more general sense of "servant." That there was an established leadership in the earliest churches seems evident. Paul exhorts the Thessalonians "to respect those who labor among you and are over [*proïstamenoi*, "leaders"] you in the Lord . . . and to esteem them very highly in love because of their work" (1 Thess. 5:12–13). Similarly, Paul tells the Corinthians to "be subject to" and "give recognition to" those who labor in "the service [*diakonia*] of the saints" (1 Cor. 16:15–18). Among the offices that "God has appointed in the church" is "administrators" (*kybernēseis*), which appears to indicate the governing of the church (1 Cor. 12:28).

We see, then, that the tendencies of incipient early catholicism begin to appear very early, indeed almost from the beginning. It remains true, however, as one would expect, that it is the later books, as a whole, that reflect a more conspicuous pattern of incipient early catholic tendencies.[10]

Early Elements of Christianity in the Later New Testament Books

The impression often is given that the elements of early catholicism are incompatible with the more dynamic realities of earliest Christianity, to the point that the former automatically cancel out some of the latter, but this is greatly exaggerated. Here I merely call attention to some of the ongoing continuities in the books most known for exhibiting early catholicism.

1. While it is true that imminent eschatology recedes in the later books, the expectation of future eschatology often continues unaffected. On eschatology, Ephesians is the weakest, offering only oblique references to, for example, "the hope" and "the riches of his glorious inheritance in the saints" (1:18); the age to come (1:21); "the day of redemption" (4:30); and mention of receiving from the Lord future rewards for doing good (6:8). The Pastoral Epistles have a clear future eschatology. In 1 Timothy 6:14–15 the author speaks of "the appearing of our Lord Jesus Christ," adding "and this will be made manifest at the proper time." There are several references to the day of judgment in 2 Timothy (1:12; 4:8; cf. 4:18), two references to the "appearing" of Christ (4:1, 8), and a denunciation of the overrealized eschatology that claims that the resurrection is already past (2:18). Titus 2:13 is explicit: "awaiting our blessed hope, the appearing of the glory of our great God and Savior Jesus Christ." In 2 Peter there are several references to the "day of judgment" and the coming "day of

---

10. Looking at Galatians and the Corinthian letters, John Drane concludes, "The distinction between the 'early catholic' church and the 'apostolic' church is not so marked as is often supposed. . . . If Paul could hold all these strands together in his own mind, there is no reason to draw a hard and fast line of demarcation between the age of the apostles and what followed it" ("Tradition, Law and Ethics in Pauline Theology," 177).

God" (2:9; 3:7, 12), and to "the day of the Lord," coming "like a thief" (3:10); on the positive side: "according to his promise we wait for new heavens and a new earth in which righteousness dwells" (3:13).

2. The lively role of the Holy Spirit in the Christian and the church is clear in Ephesians. Christians are "sealed" in the Holy Spirit (1:13; 4:30); they are "a dwelling place of God in the Spirit" (2:22); they are called "to maintain the unity of the Spirit in the bond of peace" (4:3). Christians are exhorted to "be filled with the Spirit, . . . making melody to the Lord with all your heart" and giving thanks for everything (5:18–20), and to "pray at all times in the Spirit" (6:18). The Pastoral Epistles mention the role of the Holy Spirit in protecting orthodoxy: "Guard the truth that has been entrusted to you by the Holy Spirit who dwells within us" (2 Tim. 1:14). Titus 3:5–6 refers to "renewal in the Holy Spirit, which he [God] poured out upon us richly through Jesus Christ our Savior." These texts provide evidence that the establishment of church order and offices, so important in these books, is by no means incompatible with the experience of the work of the Spirit. The only reference to the Holy Spirit in 2 Peter is in relation to the inspiration of prophecy by the Holy Spirit (2 Pet. 1:21); Jude 20 exhorts believers to "pray in the Holy Spirit."

3. Another motif that remains evident in these later letters is salvation by faith. Ephesians 2:8–9 says, "For by grace you have been saved through faith; and this is not your own doing, it is the gift of God—not because of works, lest any man should boast." Likewise, we read in 2 Timothy 1:9 that God "saved us and called us with a holy calling, not in virtue of our works but in virtue of his own purpose and the grace which he gave us in Christ Jesus," and in Titus 3:5–7 that God "saved us, not because of deeds done by us in righteousness, but in virtue of his own mercy . . . so that we might be justified by his grace."

The preceding survey is not meant to be a denial that there is a difference between the early and later books of the NT, or that there is much more incipient early catholicism in the latter than in the former. Rather, the purpose has been to soften the polarity, to suggest that much within early catholicism is quite compatible with the life and perspective of the earliest experience of the church.

A Canon within the Canon or the Whole New Testament?

The tendencies of incipient early catholicism need not be rejected as a compromise or departure from the "pure" gospel, as Ernst Käsemann argued when he placed Paul and early catholicism in confrontation.[11] But even Käsemann

---

11. Käsemann, "Paul and Early Catholicism," 237.

had to admit that "from a purely historical viewpoint, Paul himself was a forerunner of early catholicism."[12]

We may well be persuaded that Paul's articulation of the gospel is the clearest and most compelling, and that, in this limited sense, Paul serves as a canon within the canon. But there is a reason for the emphases of the later books of the NT. The tendencies of incipient early catholicism have as their purpose the preservation and protection of the gospel from corruption.[13] Incipient early catholicism is not to be set over against the gospel. Rather than a denial of the gospel, the tendencies of incipient early catholicism exist for the sake of the gospel and the church.

Bibliography

Beker, J. Christian. *Heirs of Paul: Paul's Legacy in the New Testament and in the Church Today*. Minneapolis: Fortress, 1991.

Beyer, Hermann W. "ἐπισκέπτομαι, κτλ." *TDNT* 2:599–622.

Drane, John W. "Eschatology, Ecclesiology and Catholicity in the New Testament." *ExpT* 83 (1971–72): 180–84.

———. "Tradition, Law and Ethics in Pauline Theology." *NovT* 16 (1974): 167–78.

Dunn, James D. G. "Early Catholicism." In *Unity and Diversity in the New Testament: An Inquiry into the Character of Earliest Christianity*, 341–66. 2nd ed. Philadelphia: Trinity Press International, 1990.

Elliott, John H. "A Catholic Gospel: Reflections on 'Early Catholicism' in the New Testament." *CBQ* 31 (1969): 213–23.

Fuller, Reginald H. "Early Catholicism: An Anglican Reaction to a German Debate." In *Die Mitte des Neuen Testaments: Einheit und Vielfalt neutestamentlicher Theologie; Festschrift für Eduard Schweizer zum 70. Geburtstag*, edited by Ulrich Luz and Hans Weder, 34–41. Göttingen: Vandenhoeck & Ruprecht, 1983.

Harrington, Daniel J. "The 'Early Catholic' Writings of the New Testament: The Church Adjusting to World-History." In *The Word and the World: Essays in Honor of Frederick L. Moriarty*, edited by Richard J. Clifford and George W. MacRae, 97–113. Cambridge, MA: Weston College Press, 1973.

Hengel, Martin. *Acts and the History of Earliest Christianity*. Translated by John Bowden. Philadelphia: Fortress, 1980.

Käsemann, Ernst. "Paul and Early Catholicism." In *New Testament Questions of Today*, 236–51. London: SCM, 1969.

Köstenberger, Andreas J., and Michael J. Kruger. *The Heresy of Orthodoxy: How Contemporary Culture's Fascination with Diversity Has Reshaped Our Understanding of Early Christianity*. Wheaton, IL: Crossway, 2010.

Marshall, I. Howard. "'Early Catholicism' in the New Testament." In *New Dimensions in New Testament Study*, edited by Richard N. Longenecker and Merrill C. Tenney, 217–31. Grand Rapids: Zondervan, 1974.

———. "Orthodoxy and Heresy in Earlier Christianity." *Themelios* 2 (1976): 5–14.

Martin, Ralph P. "Early Catholicism." In *Dictionary of the Later New Testament and Its Developments*, edited by Ralph P. Martin and Peter H. Davids, 310–13. Downers Grove, IL: InterVarsity, 1997.

12. Ibid., 238. Käsemann later says, "One can hardly deny that, among other things, he helped prepare the way for early catholicism" (ibid., 249).

13. See Fuller, "Early Catholicism," 38–40.

34

The Pastoral Epistles

The epistles to Timothy and Titus constitute a rather clearly marked out and unique group within the Pauline corpus. These documents (first called "Pastoral Epistles" early in the eighteenth century, and now commonly referred to simply as "the Pastorals") are addressed to two of Paul's key assistants and share similar language, concerns, and directives. Apart from Philemon (which, however, is also written to the church that met in the house of Archippus), these are the only letters of Paul we have where Paul is said to have written to individuals. Of course, it is also true that these letters have a public dimension and assume a wider implied readership.

The Question of Authorship

One of the most difficult problems of the NT is the question of the authorship of the Pastorals, often referred to simply as "the problem of the Pastorals." Only with Johann Schmidt and Friedrich Schleiermacher at the beginning of the nineteenth century was the attack on the Pauline authorship of the letters launched. Endlessly debated since then, this question still yields no definitive answer. At this point, and with the limited information available to us, no one is able to speak of proof. Here, as so often, we are at best in the realm of possibilities and probabilities, not certainties. It appears that good arguments can be put forward on both sides—Pauline or non-Pauline authorship—and judgments are therefore bound to differ.

The arguments against Pauline authorship—the position that I take as having the probabilities on its side—are cumulative; no single argument is

Author: Although quite possibly by Paul (2 Timothy perhaps having the best claim), a slight probability favors a disciple or disciples of Paul, possibly making use of fragments stemming from Paul.

Date: Pauline authorship would put the letters in the early 60s; if written by disciple(s) of Paul, perhaps in the 80s or 90s.

Addressees: Timothy and Titus, two important co-workers of Paul, unless the names are to be understood as ideal figures, representing Christian leaders generally.

Purpose: To provide instruction to church leaders for the effective sustenance of the church during the ongoing interim period between the first coming of Christ and his return.

Message/Argument: Orthodoxy and orthopraxy are to be carefully guarded, maintained by a succession of carefully selected, qualified teacher-leaders.

Significance: Provides a glimpse into the development of the church's self-consciousness and its concern for future survival, as well as advice for the church of every age.

sufficient by itself. That the pseudonymity involved, if these letters are not by Paul himself, is of a harmless kind has been argued above (see chap. 24).

To see the arguments on both sides more clearly, I will proceed by subject, looking first at the argument for pseudonymous authorship and then at the response of those holding the traditional conclusion.

Language and Style

FOR PSEUDONYMITY

It is difficult to deny that the vocabulary and style of the Pastorals are clearly different from the undisputed letters of Paul. It is Percy Harrison who has most diligently set forth the linguistic data that point away from Paul as the author, focusing, in order, on the vocabulary, particles, prepositions, pronouns, grammatical peculiarities, and style.[1] Excluding proper names, there are 848 words in the Pastorals, of which 306 (approximately 36 percent) are not found in any of the other ten letters in the Pauline corpus. Of the 848 words, 175 are unique to the Pastorals in the NT. The vocabulary of the Pastorals is thus highly distinctive. For example, as A. T. Hanson points out,[2] the stress on good conduct employs non-Pauline words such as *eusebeia* ("godliness"), *theosebeia* ("piety"), *semnos* ("honorable" [used once by Paul, in Phil. 4:8]) and *semnotēs* ("seriousness"), and the *sōphrōn* root ("sober-minded" or "disciplined"); the stress on correct doctrine uses *hygiainō* ("to be healthy, sound"). God is referred to as "sovereign," "King of the ages" and "King of kings," as "blessed," as "Savior," and there are repeated references to the "epiphany," in reference not merely to the

1. Harrison, *The Problem of the Pastoral Epistles.*
2. Hanson, *The Pastoral Epistles*, 2–3.

parousia but also to the incarnation. There are the references to the distinctive "a good conscience" and the repeated formula "The saying is sure," not found in Paul. At the same time, however, much of the typical Pauline vocabulary is missing from the Pastorals.[3] Of the 542 words shared, only 50 are exclusively Pauline words; the remaining 492 consist largely of the most common words in the NT, but sometimes they are used in a sense different from Paul's.[4]

But the differences between the Pastorals and Paul also extend to small stylistic matters that are perhaps even more telling than the new vocabulary: the use of connective words, prepositions, and particles so common to Paul's style are lacking in the Pastorals (the Pastorals use less than half of the 214 particles that occur in the other ten letters of the Pauline corpus).[5] Vocabulary may vary according to purpose, but a change of syntactical style seems strange indeed. And, finally, the contrast of style is great: next to the vivid style of Paul, the Pastorals lack any sustained arguments and are "by comparison sober, didactic, static, conscientious, domesticated."[6]

Harrison summarizes: "In vocabulary, grammar, and style, then, the Pastorals show a marked divergence from all other epistles bearing the name of Paul."[7] As we will see, however, this excludes the genuinely Pauline passages in 2 Timothy and Titus containing an abundance of Pauline phrases, which prompted Harrison to formulate his famous "fragment hypothesis."

Against Pseudonymity

A number of things can be said in response to the preceding argument.[8] First, there are clear limitations to what can be established by statistical analysis of vocabulary.[9] Bruce Metzger, not an advocate of the Pauline authorship of the

---

3. For a full chart listing these, see Harrison, *The Problem of the Pastoral Epistles*, 31–32. Harrison makes much of the fact that the words "cross" and "crucifixion" do not occur in the Pastorals.

4. Ibid., 27–28. I deliberately omit mentioning Harrison's faulty argument that the vocabulary of the Pastorals reflects the second century and not the first. In fact, most if not all of the vocabulary is found in both centuries.

5. Again, detailed charts can be found in ibid., 36–37.

6. Ibid., 42.

7. Ibid., 45.

8. Donald Guthrie provides a thorough, critical treatment of Harrison's arguments. See "An Examination of the Linguistic Argument against the Authenticity of the Pastorals," the appendix in Guthrie, *The Pastoral Epistles*, 224–40. See also Guthrie, *The Pastoral Epistles and the Mind of Paul*; idem, *New Testament Introduction*, 607–49.

9. A useful survey that is less than optimistic can be found in Bird, "The Authorship of the Pastoral Epistles—Quantifying Literary Style," although the final sentence seems to contradict what precedes it. See also Kenny, *A Stylometric Study of the New Testament*. Kenny concludes from his study that only Titus comes under suspicion: "I see no reason to reject the hypothesis that twelve of the Pauline Epistles are the work of a single, unusually versatile author" (ibid., 100). Contrast that with the conclusion of Kenneth Grayston and Gustav Herdan, also working with statistical analysis: "Altogether, it may be said that the linguistic evidence is strong enough to justify the conclusion of a very different style in the Pastorals" ("The Authorship of

Pastorals, fairly points this out: "Not only are there different ways of organizing statistics, resulting in diverse evaluations and conclusions but the reliability of the method is far from certain when applied to relatively brief treatises."[10] The argument from vocabulary is not difficult to answer. It should be obvious that new situations and new subjects require new vocabulary.[11] More difficult, however, is not only the lack of so much of Paul's usual vocabulary but also the use of Pauline words with a different meaning. It is stretching the argument to say that this is simply due to differences of context.[12] Donald Guthrie notes a couple of instances of non-Pauline expressions in the Pastorals that are "admittedly unexpected."[13]

On the matter of the style of the prose—that is, the connective particles and prepositions—one may respond that the Pastorals do have many Pauline connectives, although that hardly solves the problem of the long list of Pauline particles *not* used by the Pastorals. It can be noted, however, that the lack of certain of these is the result of the different subject matter of the Pastorals, where, for example, there is no sustained and close argumentation. This too might explain the relatively colorless style of the letters. Even J. N. D. Kelly, a defender of Pauline authorship, notes that the author of the Pastorals "lacks the Apostle's vigour and variety; he writes smooth, often monotonous sentences, instead of piling up parentheses and anacolutha in the struggle to bring his thoughts to birth."[14] The appeal to "advancing age" as an explanation of the different style and vocabulary[15] seems to me like special pleading. After a brief examination of the subject, Howard Marshall concludes, "I am again left with the feeling that this is not the Paul that I know from the genuine letters."[16]

---

the Pastorals in the Light of Statistical Linguistics," 15). David Mealand ("The Extent of the Pauline Corpus") also concludes that the Pastorals reflect a different style from Paul. See also Neumann, *The Authenticity of the Pauline Epistles in the Light of Stylostatistical Analysis*.

10. Metzger, "A Reconsideration of Certain Arguments against the Pauline Authorship of the Pastoral Epistles," 94. Metzger criticizes Harrison for not responding to important criticisms of his arguments in his 1955 *Expository Times* article. In addition to continental works, Harrison fails to note the work of George Yule, *The Statistical Study of Literary Vocabulary* (Cambridge: Cambridge University Press, 1944). Dean Forbes ("Statistical Research on the Bible") also tends to be critical of the claims of most statistical studies.

11. Donald Guthrie surely is right that Harrison's argument from vocabulary has not proved a second-century date for the Pastorals, since that vocabulary is also present in the first century (*The Pastoral Epistles*, 232). Guthrie's appeal, however, to "change of environment" as accounting for a more frequent use of classical words seems unconvincing (ibid., 240).

12. It begs the question to say that an author imitating Paul would have used more of the Pauline vocabulary and would not have assigned new meanings to Pauline words.

13. Guthrie, *The Pastoral Epistles*, 236. He mentions *charin echō* for *eucharisteō* ("I thank"); *di' hēn aitian* for *dio* ("wherefore"); and *despotai* for *kyrioi* ("masters").

14. Kelly, *A Commentary on the Pastoral Epistles*, 21.

15. Guthrie, *The Pastoral Epistles*, 240; idem, *The Pastoral Epistles and the Mind of Paul*, 15, leaning on Ceslas Spicq and E. K. Simpson.

16. Marshall, "Prospects for the Pastoral Epistles," 139. A. T. Hanson speaks of the unusual disconnected style of the Pastorals as like "a meandering brook" and concludes that "it is this

We have nothing like conclusive proof here on either side. There are indeed possible ways to explain the unusual linguistic and stylistic data of the Pastorals and maintain Pauline authorship. The question is whether they constitute a higher degree of probability than the conclusion of non-Pauline authorship.

Church Organization

FOR PSEUDONYMITY

The Pastorals give considerable place to the formalization of church office, quite unlike anything we encounter in the undisputed letters. They assume the fixity of the offices of deacon, elder, and overseer (bishop), who obviously are meant to exercise authority over the congregations. To be sure, in the Pastorals, as in *1 Clement* (ca. 96), the titles "elder" and "bishop" remain interchangeable; nevertheless, clearly the move is under way to an insistence on a difference between the two and the stress on the authority of a single bishop for each community (*episkopos* occurs only in the singular; *presbyteros* only in the plural, except once), as we have it in Ignatius (ca. 115). The criteria for the appointment of persons to these offices are given much attention. The *charisma* associated with the office is granted through the laying on of hands in ordination (1 Tim. 4:14; 2 Tim. 1:6). The total impression is of a church that is fully settled into the world and must take protective measures to ensure its survival into the future.

AGAINST PSEUDONYMITY

The contrast is much overstated. There are clear signs of church organization in the undisputed Pauline Letters (Rom. 16:1; Phil. 1:1; 1 Thess. 5:12; cf. in the disputed letters, Col. 1:7, 25; 4:7; Eph. 6:21) and in the book of Acts (e.g., 14:23). The terms "elder" and "overseer" appear to be interchangeable (compare Acts 20:17 with 20:28), and there is no evidence of a monarchical bishop or of the developed hierarchy that marks the second century. The most that may be fairly said is that Paul addresses the subject of church order directly here in a way that he does not in the undisputed letters. The present situation called for such emphases, whereas the earlier situation had not.

Theology and Ethics

FOR PSEUDONYMITY

Despite the continuities that could be mentioned, there are notable differences between the theology of the Pastorals and that of the undisputed Pauline Letters. The following list gives some indication of the distinctive emphases of the Pastorals versus the Pauline Letters: "epiphany" christology,

---

impression of relative incoherence which, as much as anything else, makes it impossible to believe that the great bulk of the Pastorals is Pauline" (*Studies in the Pastoral Epistles*, 110).

used to refer to both the first and the second coming of Christ (only once in Paul [2 Thess. 2:8]); no reference to Jesus as "Son"; sparse reference to the Holy Spirit; no characteristic use of the Pauline stress on being "in Christ"; "faith" is used to refer to the content of what is believed rather than trust in Christ, and it is not set in opposition to works; the law is spoken of in an uncharacteristic way (1 Tim. 1:8–11);[17] "justification" and "righteousness" are not used to refer to a state of the believer, but only as virtues to be pursued; no mention of the cross or the crucifixion of Jesus; emphasis on "sound" or "healthy doctrine" and the "deposit" of orthodox tradition that is to be carefully guarded. The particular form that the author's protection of orthodoxy takes is quite different from the approach in the undisputed Pauline Letters.

The Pastorals employ an un-Pauline, Hellenistic vocabulary of the Greco-Roman world for ethical conduct (mentioned above)—for example, "godliness," "piety," "seriousness," "disciplined" or "self-controlled," and "good conscience." Why do these words appear only now and not in Paul's earlier, frequent passages of ethical exhortation?

AGAINST PSEUDONYMITY

The differences can be accounted for by factors such as the new situation faced by Paul, that the letters are personal, that Paul's viewpoint has developed, or that a new amanuensis has been used and perhaps given an unusual degree of freedom of expression. Any single one, or a combination, of these factors could explain why these letters differ from the other Pauline Letters. In contrast to the emphasis on difference, attention should be called to the many passages that sound exactly like the Paul of the undisputed letters. Again, it is impossible to rule out this solution. At the same time, the pattern of differences is quite striking, so that the probability of a solution such as this does not seem great. Again the argument concerning theology and ethics is of cumulative force.

Nature of Opposition

FOR PSEUDONYMITY

It is usually assumed, whether correctly or not, that the opposition faced by the author is the same in all three of the Pastoral Epistles. The heresy seems to be from Jewish Christians influenced by Gnosticism (note in 1 Tim. 6:20 the reference to "what is falsely called knowledge [gnōsis]"), exhibiting an overrealized eschatology, a developed asceticism (1 Tim. 4:3), and a preoccupation with "myths and endless genealogies" (1 Tim. 1:4). These

17. Stephen Westerholm ("The Law and the 'Just Man' [1 Tim 1,3–11]"), however, sees no incompatibility between this passage and Paul.

phenomena, even if thought to be proto-gnostic, rather than second-century (Jewish) Gnostic, seem to reflect a time rather later than Paul. Yet there is no evidence of the Judaizing, with its call for circumcision and obedience to the law, that Paul had to fight in his letters. What seems to be more important, however, are the tactics used by the author to combat the heresy. Rather than arguing a position against the heresy as Paul tends to do, he simply employs a harsh condemnation and invective, with very little detail and no attempt to refute the opponents.

Against Pseudonymity

There is abundant evidence in the undisputed Pauline Letters of proto-gnostic elements that he has to oppose. The Pastorals are in this sense not very different from, for example, 1 Corinthians or Colossians. There is no reason to conclude that the author is opposing the full-blown Gnosticism that we know from the second century. The developments and the shift in Paul's concerns can be readily accounted for if these letters were written at the very end of his life, in the mid-60s.

The Picture of Paul

For Pseudonymity

Paul is made to speak of himself in a rather grandiose manner (e.g., 1 Tim. 1:11–12; 2:7; 2 Tim. 1:11–12; 2:8–10; 3:10–11; 4:6–8). This self-exaltation is not typical of the Paul of the undisputed letters. And it is all the stranger when it is articulated to his close co-workers.

Against Pseudonymity

Paul does not hesitate to cite his unique apostolic authority (Gal. 1:1; 2:6–9) and refer to the gospel with which he has been entrusted (Gal. 1:11–16), nor is he reluctant to list his sufferings for Christ (2 Cor. 4:7–12; 6:4–10). He can furthermore exhort the Corinthians to imitate himself (1 Cor. 11:1; Phil. 3:17).

The Personal History of Paul

For Pseudonymity

Since Luke ends his account with Paul's house imprisonment in Rome, with his trial pending, and we have no other sources, the end of Paul's life remains unclear. It therefore is very difficult at best to understand the personal data in the Pastoral Epistles concerning the movements of Paul. According to 1 Timothy 1:3, Paul had been in Ephesus and then traveled to Macedonia. According to Titus 1:5; 3:12, Paul had been in Crete and was planning to go to Nicopolis (Greece) for the winter. In 2 Timothy 1:17 Paul is in Rome, after having been in Troas (2 Tim. 4:13) and Miletus (2 Tim. 4:20). The Pastorals contain no mention of Spain. It is extremely improbable that these data can be made to fit into the career of Paul as known from the letters and Acts. Probably the only viable solution is to conjecture that Paul was released from the Roman imprisonment at the end of Acts, and that he then traveled more, until he was arrested a second time and then martyred. This, however, must remain pure speculation because we have no confirming evidence outside the Pastorals themselves. And if Acts was written late, as majority opinion holds, why does Luke not mention any of this? The release of Paul would have vindicated him in Roman eyes. Unfortunately, it is unclear whether the reference in *1 Clement* 5:7 to Paul having reached the "terminus [*terma*] of the west" refers to Spain or Rome itself, especially since Clement refers to Paul's martyrdom immediately after those words.

AGAINST PSEUDONYMITY

Although difficult, it is not impossible to integrate the Pastorals into the ministry of Paul, even prior to the Roman imprisonment referred to at the end of Acts. The attempt has been made, most notably by J. A. T. Robinson,[18] who places the writing of 1 Timothy between 1 Corinthians and 2 Corinthians; Titus between the writing of Romans and Philippians; and 2 Timothy as the last of Paul's thirteen letters, written in the autumn of 58.[19] Bo Reicke likewise places 1 Timothy between 1 and 2 Corinthians, and Titus immediately after Romans, but he dates 2 Timothy to 60, with Philippians being the last of Paul's Letters, written a year or two later.[20] The fatal flaw in these hypotheses, however, is that they separate the Pastorals from one another and thereby require Paul's style and perspective to change back and forth, in what would be a most strange oscillation. More likely, as argued by most supporters of the authenticity of the Pastorals, we can allow a release from the first imprisonment, followed by a period of further ministry, and then a second imprisonment and martyrdom. Such a conclusion is hardly impossible, but the fact remains that there is not a shred of evidence to support it.

Conclusion on the Authorship Question

Two points should be stressed. First, the arguments against the Pauline authorship of the Pastorals are cumulative. No single argument is totally persuasive, but as the number of arguments against Pauline authorship

18. Robinson, *Redating the New Testament*. Robinson says, "Since there are no controls, we can make Paul do anything, go anywhere" (ibid., 72).

19. Ibid., 84.

20. Reicke, *Re-examining Paul's Letters*, 141.

increase, they grow in strength, and the defense of Pauline authorship becomes an increasingly difficult challenge. Second, the nature of the evidence and arguments falls short of proof or demonstration. We are in a realm of probabilities, where the conclusions of either side cannot be cavalierly dismissed.

In my view, the extensive differences between the Pastoral Epistles and the undisputed Pauline Letters cannot be denied. Most important, the Pastorals breathe a different atmosphere. The landscape and perspective of these letters for the most part seem very unlike Paul's Letters. The Pastorals reflect a conventional, "bourgeois" Christianity—self-conscious, domesticated, institutionalized, finding its place in the world, establishing itself, and settling down in the world for the long haul. Gone are the early days of dynamism and urgency caused by the expectation of the imminent return of Christ. We have here the marks of an incipient early catholicism (see chap. 33 above).

C. F. D. Moule makes the point well:

> Of course we know that writers change their style and their vocabulary, not only with advancing years but with changing situations; and there is no cogent reason for denying Pauline authorship to a letter, merely because its vocabulary and style mark it as different from others which are firmly established as genuine. . . . But the problem of the Pastorals is constituted primarily by much more far-reaching differences than change of phrase or change of emphasis or change of situation. It is constituted by a change of mentality.[21]

Options to Explain the Pastorals

Secretary/Amanuensis

Almost all who accept the Pauline authorship of the Pastorals argue that the differences between them and the other Pauline Letters are due to Paul's use of a different amanuensis. In the use of secretaries in the ancient world there

21. Moule, "The Problem of the Pastoral Epistles," 431–32. Similarly, Howard Marshall says that he gets "the impression of a different way of thinking and expressing theology and ethics in the Pastorals. This is not to say that the theology contradicts that of Paul (which is manifestly not the case) but that the way the author thinks is different. There is a different theological vocabulary and a different manner of argumentation in the PE from Paul. This point weighs with me more strongly than the argument from linguistic style. We have to ask why it could be that when writing to close colleagues Paul would think in a different kind of way" ("Recent Study of the Pastoral Epistles," 12). And Stanley Porter, who supports Pauline authorship of the Pastorals, writes, "Whereas the arguments from chronology, epistolary format, style and content are finally inconclusive, it seems to me that the theological data are the only—or at least the strongest—evidence that raises justifiable doubt regarding Pauline authorship of the Pastorals" ("Pauline Authorship and the Pastoral Epistles" [1995], 113).

was a spectrum ranging from verbatim dictation to complete composition of a letter's contents.[22] Those who appeal to a secretary hypothesis to explain the Pastorals would, given the unity of style in the three letters, think of a single secretary who in these instances had been given great freedom. This can go a long way to account for difference in syntax and style, but it cannot really account for the difference in atmosphere and perspective that mark out these letters. Furthermore, if a secretary were virtually given carte blanche in terms of content and style, how fair is it to call it a letter by Paul and not a pseudonymous document? Another question that remains is why, in contrast to his earlier practice, Paul in these instances gives his secretary such great freedom to compose these letters. It is highly unlikely that the secretary hypothesis, even when combined with other points, such as change of situation and Paul's development, can account for the Pastoral Epistles.

Pseudepigraph

The line becomes thin between a secretary who is given total freedom and an author writing on his own but in the tradition of Paul. Some attempts have been made to identify the secretary used by Paul, such as the suggestion by Joachim Jeremias that it may have been Tychicus.[23] More popular has been the idea that Luke is responsible for the Pastorals. C. F. D. Moule has argued that Luke was their author, but that they were written at Paul's behest while Paul was still alive.[24] Others have opted for Luke, but more as author than as secretary, writing in Paul's name, but after his death. Thus Stephen Wilson accepts Luke as the author, but writing after the death of Paul, so that the Pastorals are pseudepigraphs.[25] Jerome Quinn offered the novel hypothesis that the Pastorals were written by Luke as an epistolary appendix for Luke-Acts, as a kind of third volume.[26] Ralph Martin envisages the combination of "personal memoranda, travel notes, and intimate reflections" as later being written up with the addition of hymns and creedal forms—all put in final form perhaps by Luke.[27]

Pauline Fragments and Personal Notes

It is rather clear to everyone, including those who deny Pauline authorship, that the Pastorals contain materials that go back to Paul in one way or another.

22. See E. R. Richards, *Paul and First-Century Letter Writing*, 64.
23. Jeremias, *Die Briefe an Timotheus und Titus*, 8–9 (cf. Eph. 6:21–22; Col. 4:7–9; Titus 3:12).
24. Moule, "The Problem of the Pastoral Epistles." Moule leans heavily on words, phrases, and significant ideas common to Luke-Acts and the Pastorals.
25. Wilson, *Luke and the Pastoral Epistles*. Facing a crisis caused by false teachers, "Luke wrote three epistles in the name of Paul giving what he imagined Paul's response would have been under the circumstances," 139.
26. Quinn, "The Last Volume of Luke."
27. Martin, *New Testament Foundations*, 2:303, 306.

It is Percy Harrison whose name is associated with the "fragment hypothesis." He isolated Pauline fragments (slightly revised from his 1921 analysis) into three personal notes written by Paul, the third of which he calls "Paul's last letter":[28]

- Titus 3:12–15
- 2 Timothy 4:9–15 + 20–21a, 22b
- 2 Timothy 1:16–18, 3:10, 11; 4:1, 2a, 5b–8, 16–19, 21b–22a; 4:16–18

The complicated analysis of the 2 Timothy material cannot but raise suspicions about its validity. The positing of short, detached papyri letters that were preserved, collected, and inserted into a separate letter in an apparently capricious manner causes C. F. D. Moule to write, "I must confess that it amazes me that such a solution has gained wide currency."[29] Without doubt, the personal notes in the Pastorals (e.g., 1 Tim. 3:14–15; 4:13; Titus 3:12–15; and most famously 2 Tim. 4:9–21) constitute the greatest problem for those who deny their authenticity. Apart from a fragment hypothesis that explains them as really from Paul, with all of its attendant difficulties, one must explain why they were invented and inserted where they are in the letters. The only answer seems to be that they imitate the sort of data well known from the authentic Pauline Letters and present an artificial packaging of the material that is the heart of the letters.[30] Perhaps no one has unflinchingly asserted the deceptive character of the personal information as much as Lewis Donelson.[31] Martin

28. Harrison, *Paulines and Pastorals*, 106–28. For a similar analysis, see Falconer, *The Pastoral Epistles*, 13–17. The latest and most nuanced presentation of the fragment hypothesis comes from James Miller, *The Pastoral Letters as Composite Documents*. According to Miller, the Pastorals are compilations of materials based initially on genuine Pauline fragments, growing over time as a school for pastors gathered traditional materials and edited them into present form. Compare the remarks by Donfried, "Rethinking Scholarly Approaches to 1 Timothy," 156–68. A contrary argument for the cohesive structure of the Pastorals is found in Van Neste, *Cohesion and Structure in the Pastoral Epistles*.

29. Moule, "The Problem of the Pastoral Epistles," 448. A. T. Hanson in his 1966 commentary defended the fragment hypothesis, but in his 1982 commentary he informs us that he has abandoned it because of the great difficulty of explaining the survival of these small fragments. "Paul presumably did not send picture postcards to his friends during his travels!" (*The Pastoral Epistles*, 11).

30. Frances Young, however, turns this argument on its head, asserting that these personal details are "the most compelling evidence for pseudonymity." "Nowhere in the authentic letters," she continues, "do we find Paul worrying about the missing cloaks, but that is just the kind of detail a forger would invent" (*The Theology of the Pastoral Letters*, 139).

31. Donelson, *Pseudepigraphy and Ethical Argument in the Pastoral Epistles*. Donelson regards the deception in the Pastorals as no different from other pseudepigrapha in the ancient world. Pseudepigraphy, he writes, "strikes at the heart of scriptural authority. The vehemence of conservative scholars who resist the whole notion of pseudepigrapha in the canon is well-founded, for to admit it would be to admit that the canon is not what they want it to be" (ibid., 201). But, as I have argued above (chap. 24), not all pseudepigrapha are equally culpable, as, for example, in the instance of a disciple who faithfully perpetuates the tradition of a teacher, extending it to a new situation.

Dibelius and Hans Conzelmann state that "in an age rich in pseudonymous writings one need not postulate any special craftiness nor an ethically questionable character on the part of the creator of such fictitious information."[32] Not surprisingly, this will not be convincing to all.

Paul Himself

It can hardly be denied that the simplest solution is to accept that Paul was the author of the Pastorals. J. A. T. Robinson's view is appealing: the conclusion that the Pastorals are genuinely Pauline documents written to Timothy and Titus is "open to fewer difficulties than any theory that requires the letters to be pseudonymous, whether in whole or part. . . . I am not persuaded that there is anything he *could* not have written."[33] That Paul could change toward the end of his life and write letters with new concerns and a new tonality is hardly to be doubted. All can make reasonably good sense *if* Paul had been released from a first imprisonment in Rome (see Eusebius, *Hist. eccl.* 2.22, trans. Lake, where Paul is said to have been arrested a second time, after further preaching, and that "during this imprisonment he wrote the Second Epistle to Timothy").

If the letters are artificial, why did the author write three letters that often repeat the same or similar material? Why furthermore did he write to individuals rather than to churches? Why to two different individuals? What actual historical situations do the letters presuppose? These are just a few of the questions that remain.

Pauline authorship of the Pastoral Epistles continues to be a valid possibility, and it has been defended by many fine, critical scholars.[34] One the one hand, it is a conclusion that avoids a number of serious problems and enables the explanation of certain phenomena.[35] On the other hand, the question persists concerning whether the cumulative arguments against Pauline authorship have been successfully answered. The bottom line is that despite the presence of Pauline material, these letters are simply too unlike the other letters of Paul to be considered his without qualification. A. T. Hanson observes, "If they are Pauline, they represent a dismal conclusion to Paul's writings; if they are

---

32. Dibelius and Conzelmann, *The Pastoral Epistles*, 127.

33. Robinson, *Redating the New Testament*, 70. Italics in original.

34. A partial list includes Guthrie, Kelly, Robinson, Fee, Knight, Ellis, Johnson, Mounce, Towner, and Witherington.

35. At the invitation of the Society of Biblical Literature's Theology of the Disputed Paulines Group, some years ago I wrote an essay titled "Titus as a Pauline Letter." I was impressed at the case that could be made for Pauline authorship. I quote two sentences from the end of the essay on which my mind has not changed: "The fundamental problem is simply that there are aspects of these documents that are Pauline and other aspects that are unPauline. . . . Allowing fully for the necessary differences between this letter and the undisputed Pauline letters, the possibility that Titus stems from Paul through an amanuensis can by no means be confidently ruled out" (ibid., 558).

post-Pauline, they are an admirable and indispensable illustration of the state of the church at the end of the first century."[36]

Emphases of the Pastoral Epistles

Protecting Orthodoxy and Orthopraxy

The fundamental concern of the Pastoral Epistles is the protection of correct doctrine and the maintenance of appropriate conduct. The two are not separate; indeed, they are vitally interconnected.

In **1 Timothy** we find a series of instructions concerning:

- the charging of certain persons not "to teach a different doctrine" (*heterodidaskalein*) (1:3)
- "the divine order" (*hē oikonomia*) that is in faith (1:4 RSV margin)
- "a pure heart and a good conscience and sincere faith" (1:5)
- "sound doctrine" (*hē hygiainousa didaskalia*) contrasted with immoral behavior (1:10)
- "holding faith and a good conscience" (1:19)
- deacons "must hold the mystery of the faith with a clear conscience" (3:9)
- "how one ought to behave" (3:15)
- "the words of the faith and of the good doctrine [*hē kalē didaskalia*] which you have followed" (4:6)
- "take heed to your teaching" (*didaskalia*) (4:16)
- "teach these things" (6:2)
- opposition to anyone who "teaches otherwise" (*heterodidaskalein*) and affirmation of the "sound words [*hygiainontes logoi*] of our Lord Jesus Christ and the teaching [*didaskalia*] which accords with godliness" (*eusebeia*) (6:3)
- "aim at righteousness, godliness, faith, love, steadfastness, gentleness" (6:11)

So too in **Titus**:

- "knowledge of the truth [*epignōsis alētheias*] which accords with godliness" (*eusebeia*) (1:1)
- a bishop "must hold firm to the sure word as taught [*hē didachē pistou logou*], so that he may be able to give instruction in sound doctrine [*hē didaskalia hē hygiainousa*] and also to confute those who contradict it" (1:9)
- rebuke them "that they may be sound in the faith" (*hina hygiainōsin en tē pistei*) (1:13)

36. Hanson, *Studies in the Pastoral Epistles*, 120.

- "teach what befits sound doctrine" (*hē hygiainousa didaskalia*) (2:1)
- "show yourself in all respects to be a model of good deeds [*typon kalōn ergōn*], and in your teaching show integrity, gravity, and sound speech" (*logos hygiēs*) (2:7–8)
- "in everything adorn the doctrine [*didaskalia*] of God our Savior" (2:10)
- "to live sober [*sōphronōs*], upright [*dikaiōs*], and godly [*eusebōs*] lives in this world" (*en tō nyn aiōni*) (2:12)
- "be careful to apply themselves to good deeds [*kala erga*]; these are excellent and profitable to men" (3:8 [cf. 3:14])

In **2 Timothy**, similarly:

- "follow the pattern of the sound words [*hypotypōsis hygiainontōn logōn*] which you have heard from me" (1:13)
- "rightly handling the word of truth" (*ho logos tēs alētheias*) (2:15)
- "ready for every good work" (*eis pan ergon agathon*) (2:21 NRSV)
- pursue "righteousness, faith, love, and peace" (2:22)
- "these men oppose the truth, men of corrupt mind and counterfeit faith" (*adokimoi peri tēn pistin*) (3:8)
- "continue in what you have learned" (3:14)
- "I have kept the faith" (4:7)

Frances Young cogently remarks that "any attempt to read these letters soon runs up against the fact that they come from a particular social context in which there is an encompassing theological perspective which colours all the material which at first sight appears to be ethical or practical rather than theological in its principle thrust."[37]

"The Deposit"

One of the distinctive ways that the author of the Pastorals encourages the protection of the truth of the faith is by means of the concept of the "deposit" (*parathēkē*) that is to be guarded and handed on. This word is unique to our author in the NT, and in all three instances it occurs with the verb *phylassō* ("to guard"). This idea of guarding or protecting the true ethics or doctrine is of the greatest importance in the Pastorals (see also 1 Tim. 5:21). *Parathēkē* refers to a settled body of truth that is regarded as defining the church and constituting "orthodoxy"—a "deposit" to be protected and carefully handed on.

---

37. Young, *The Theology of the Pastoral Letters*, 2. See also the rich discussion in Towner, *The Goal of Our Instruction*.

- 1 Timothy 6:20: "O Timothy, guard what has been entrusted [*tēn parathēkēn*] to you."
- 2 Timothy 1:12: "I am sure that he is able to guard until that Day what has been entrusted to me [*tēn parathēkēn mou*]."
- 2 Timothy 1:14: "guard the truth that has been entrusted to you [*tēn kalēn parathēkēn*; lit., "the good deposit"]."

The idea of being "entrusted" with a deposit of some kind is found also in 1 Timothy 1:11 ("the gospel") and Titus 1:3 (the "kerygma").

"The Faith"

In most instances in the Pastorals the word "faith" (*pistis*) is used in the objective sense to refer to *what is believed*, rather than to subjective faith or belief. This is true even in some cases where the word lacks the definite article: 1 Timothy 1:2, 18 (first occurrence); 2:7; 3:13; 2 Timothy 1:13; Titus 1:4. More often it occurs in this sense with the article: 1 Timothy 1:19 (second occurrence); 4:1, 6; 5:8; 6:10, 21; 2 Timothy 2:18; 3:8; 4:7; Titus 1:13; 2:2.

One of the most interesting references to "the faith" is where it is described as a "mystery" (*mysterion*), something that has its source in God and is revealed by him. Deacons "must hold the mystery of the faith" (1 Tim. 3:9). In 1 Timothy 3:16 the word "mystery" is used again, this time in the phrase "the mystery of our religion" (*to tēs eusebeias mysterion*), which is then articulated in what may have been the lines of an early Christian hymn:[38]

> He[39] was manifested in the flesh,
> vindicated in the Spirit,
> seen by angels,
> preached among the nations,
> believed on in the world,
> taken up in glory.

These words obviously are a kind of brief credo that summarizes the faith.

"The Truth"

Another way to refer to the doctrine that the church is charged to protect is the word "truth" (*alētheia*). "To come to the knowledge of the truth" is paralleled with salvation in 1 Timothy 2:4. In no less than absolute terms, the

---

38. The symmetry and euphony of these lines can be seen only in the Greek, where each line (except for the opening pronoun) begins with an aorist passive verb, ending in the suffix *-thē*. See Gundry, "The Form, Meaning and Background of the Hymn Quoted in 1 Timothy 3:16."

39. The Greek pronoun at the beginning of the sentence is *hos* ("who"). The majority of later manuscripts read *theos* ("God"), which in its abbreviated form could easily be confused with the pronoun: ΟΣ (= "who"); θ̄Σ̄ (= "God").

truth is what the church believes. This is a constant emphasis in the Pastorals: 1 Timothy 2:7 (second occurrence); 3:15; 4:3; 6:5; 2 Timothy 2:18, 25; 3:7–8; 4:4; Titus 1:1, 14 (cf. "the word of truth" in 2 Tim. 2:15).

"THE TEACHING" OR "DOCTRINE"

The word *didaskalia* occurs far more often in the Pastorals than in the rest of the NT (15x versus 6x in the remainder of the NT). The "teaching" refers to the orthodox doctrine of the church (1 Tim. 4:13, 16). It can also refer to the ethical teaching of the church. In 1 Timothy 6:3 "the teaching which accords with godliness [*eusebeian*]" is paralleled with "the sound words of our Lord Jesus Christ." Titus 2:10, in a passage calling for appropriate Christian behavior, concludes "that in everything they may adorn the doctrine of God our Savior." In 1 Timothy 4:6 the teaching of the church is referred to simply as the "good [*kalē*] doctrine," with which compare "the good confession" (1 Tim. 6:12) and "the good treasure" (2 Tim. 1:14 NRSV [lit. "the good deposit]). Another word for "teaching," *didachē*, occurs in 2 Timothy 4:2 and also in Titus 1:9, where it is said that a bishop "must hold firm to the sure word [*pistou logou*] as taught [*kata tēn didachēn*], so that he may be able to give instruction in sound doctrine and also to confute those who contradict it."

"HEALTHY DOCTRINE"

This language is distinctive to the Pastorals. The idea of "sound doctrine" (*hygiainousa didaskalia*) is an obvious way of referring to orthodox teaching (1 Tim. 1:10; 2 Tim. 4:3; Titus 1:9; 2:1: "teach what befits sound doctrine"). In 1 Timothy 1:10 "sound doctrine" is defined as that which is "in accordance with the glorious gospel of the blessed God" (1:11). With this compare the reference to "sound words" (1 Tim. 6:3; 2 Tim. 1:13) or "sound speech" (Titus 2:8). We also find the exhortation to be "sound in the faith" (Titus 1:13; cf. 2:2).

An important teaching device for the maintenance of proper conduct is the so-called household codes, which provide a guide for church members according to their status or role (see "The 'Household Code' [3:18–4:1]" in chap. 31 above). These do not occur in their fullest form in the Pastorals, but nonetheless they are clearly reflected in passages such as 1 Timothy 2:1–15 (kings and authorities; women); 5:1–16 (older people; widows); 6:1–2 (slaves), 7–19; Titus 2:1–3:8 (older men and women; younger men; slaves; submission to rulers and authorities). The point of the insistence on proper behavior is that proper conduct adorns the doctrine of God ("that in everything they may adorn the doctrine of God our Savior" [Titus 2:10]).

"FAITHFUL IS THE SAYING"

Among the distinctive traits of the Pastorals are the five rich passages introduced with the formula "faithful is the saying" (*pistos ho logos*). In two instances the introductory formula is expanded with the emphatic words "and worthy of full acceptance" (1 Tim. 1:15; 4:9). The sayings represent weighty statements of fundamental significance for the church. The first and the fifth have kerygmatic significance, focusing on the saving death of Jesus. The second brings importance to the office of bishop, which is highly significant to the agenda of the Pastorals, while the third stresses another concern of these letters, "godliness." The fourth also has kerygmatic elements and appears to be based on a hymnic or liturgical fragment.

1. 1 Timothy 1:15: "Christ Jesus came into the world to save sinners."
2. 1 Timothy 3:1: "If any one aspires to the office of bishop, he desires a noble task."[40]
3. 1 Timothy 4:8: "While bodily training is of some value, godliness is of value in every way, as it holds promise for the present life and also for the life to come."[41]
4. 2 Timothy 2:11–13: "If we have died with him, we shall also live with him;
    if we endure, we shall also reign with him;
    if we deny him, he also will deny us;
    if we are faithless, he remains faithful—
    for he cannot deny himself."
5. Titus 3:4–7: "When the goodness and loving kindness of God our Savior appeared, he saved us, not because of deeds done by us in righteousness, but in virtue of his own mercy, by the washing of regeneration and renewal in the Holy Spirit, which he poured out upon us richly through Jesus Christ our Savior, so that we might be justified by his grace and become heirs in hope of eternal life."

These "faithful sayings" represent the doctrine of the church and are emphasized in this way as a sure and trustworthy guide to true belief and conduct.[42]

Preservation and Transmission of Tradition

Since the Pastoral Epistles are supremely concerned with the preservation of the truth of the gospel, they emphasize the great importance of the careful transmission of tradition. There is a deposit to be guarded and handed down from one generation of believers to the next.

40. Some argue that here the (introductory) formula *follows* the saying (as it does for Titus 3:4–7), so that the faithful saying is found in 2:13–15.
41. The majority of commentators conclude that here the (introductory) formula *follows* the saying (as it does for Titus 3:4–7), so it is 4:8, or part of it, that is the faithful saying. However, it remains possible that 4:10 is the faithful saying: "For to this end we toil and strive, because we have our hope set on the living God, who is the Savior of all men, especially of those who believe." This too is a weighty saying, one that speaks of the saving work of God, now with emphasis on faith.
42. See Knight, *The Faithful Sayings in the Pastoral Letters*.

The Pastorals stress the handing on of tradition: "What you have heard from me before many witnesses entrust to faithful men who will be able to teach others also" (2 Tim. 2:2).[43] Timothy is "charged"—that is, he has a commission (1 Tim. 1:3, 5, 18; 5:21; 6:14; 2 Tim. 4:1)—and he is similarly to charge others (2 Tim. 2:14). The continuation of the truth is what matters: "Continue in what you have learned and have firmly believed" (2 Tim. 3:14).

Thus there is abundant evidence of preformed traditions or traditional elements in the Pastorals.[44] Among these are the five "faithful sayings," the creedal fragment in 1 Timothy 3:16, and various hymnic or liturgical fragments. In the last category are passages such as:

For there is one God, and there is one mediator between God and men, the man Christ Jesus, who gave himself as a ransom for all. (1 Tim. 2:5)

. . . the blessed and only Sovereign, the King of kings and Lord of lords, who alone has immortality and dwells in unapproachable light, whom no man has ever seen or can see. To him be honor and eternal dominion. Amen. (1 Tim. 6:15–16)

. . . who saved us and called us with a holy calling, not in virtue of our works but in virtue of his own purpose and the grace which he gave us in Christ Jesus ages ago, and now has manifested through the appearing of our Savior Christ Jesus,[45] who abolished death and brought life and immortality to light through the gospel. (2 Tim. 1:9–10)

For the grace of God has appeared for the salvation of all men, training us to renounce irreligion and worldly passions, and to live sober, upright, and godly lives in this world, awaiting our blessed hope, the appearing of the glory of our great God and Savior Jesus Christ, who gave himself for us to redeem us from all iniquity and to purify for himself a people of his own who are zealous for good deeds (Titus 2:11–14)

The charge to Timothy in 1 Timothy 6:11–16 undoubtedly contains traditional elements. To these passages are to be added the criteria for church officers and the household codes.[46]

Although many of these passages have a Pauline character, the oddity is that they often exhibit a distinctive vocabulary, accounting for approximately

43. Luke Timothy Johnson is correct that this concern for tradition did not begin after Paul's time: "'Tradition' was part of Paul's enterprise from the start and not something invented after his death" (*The First and Second Letters to Timothy*, 59).

44. See Ellis, "Traditions in the Pastoral Letters." Ellis argues that as much as 43 percent of 1 Timothy, 16 percent of 2 Timothy, and 46 percent of Titus consist of preformed traditions (ibid., 418). He refers to the Pastorals as "virtual manuals of traditions" (ibid., 424).

45. For an examination of the Pastorals' epiphany Christology, see Lau, *Manifest in the Flesh*.

46. On the latter, see Verner, *The Household of God*, 83–111.

a third of the non-Pauline words in the Pastorals, as Earle Ellis points out.[47] This assists Ellis in arguing for the Pauline authorship of the letters, which he thinks were addressed to churches in the mid-60s.

Establishing Church Offices

The appointment of qualified individuals for leadership in the church is of very great importance to the agenda of the Pastorals. It is these leaders who have the primary responsibility for the protection of correct teaching and practice and for the maintenance of the traditions that will provide continuity in the church and sustain it in the lengthening interim period between the first and the second coming of Christ. Timothy therefore is instructed, "Do not be hasty in the laying on of hands" (1 Tim. 5:22). Ordination by the laying on of hands is a highly significant practice, performed by the "council of elders" (*presbyterion*), a church group (1 Tim. 4:14) modeled on the similar Jewish council (cf. Luke 22:66; Acts 22:5).

The Criteria for Church Offices

Elder (presbyteros) =	Bishop (episkopos)	Deacon (diakonos)	[Servant (doulos)]
1 Timothy 5:17–22	*1 Timothy 3:2–7*	*1 Timothy 3:8–13*	*2 Timothy 2:24*
rule well	above reproach	serious	not quarrelsome
preaching and teaching	husband of one wife	not double-tongued	kindly to everyone
worthy of double honor	temperate	not addicted to much wine	apt teacher
never admit a charge against an elder except on the evidence of two or three witnesses	sensible	not greedy for gain	forbearing
rebuke elders who persist in sin	dignified	hold faith with clear conscience	correct opponents with gentleness
keep rules without favor	hospitable	be tested first	
	an apt teacher	women must be serious, no slanderers, temperate, faithful in all things	
	no drunkard	husband of one wife	
	not violent, but gentle	manage their children and households well	
	not quarrelsome		
	no lover of money		

47. Ellis, "Traditions in the Pastoral Letters," 418.

Elder (presbyteros) =	Bishop (episkopos)	Deacon (diakonos)	[Servant (doulos)]
1 Timothy 5:17–22	*1 Timothy 3:2–7*	*1 Timothy 3:8–13*	*2 Timothy 2:24*
	manage his household well		
	children submissive and respectful		
	not a recent convert		
	well thought of by outsiders		
Titus 1:5–6	*Titus 1:7–9*		
blameless	blameless		
husband of one wife	not arrogant/quick tempered		
children are believers and not profligate or insubordinate	not drunkard		
	not violent		
	not greedy for gain		
	hospitable		
	lover of goodness		
	master of himself		
	upright		
	holy		
	self-controlled		
	hold firm to the sure word as taught		
	able to give instruction in sound doctrine		
	able to confute those who contradict it		

The lists of criteria for bishops (1 Tim. 3:2–7; Titus 1:7–9) are the longest. There are numerous crossovers in the lists for all three offices (elders: 1 Tim. 5:17–22; Titus 1:5–6; deacons: 1 Tim. 3:8–13), and there appears to be no essential difference between elder and bishop (note the "for" in Titus 1:7, connecting the two lists).[48] The responsibility of teaching is mentioned only for the elders/bishops. "It seems entirely plausible that the 'senior citizen' carried what we

48. For helpful discussion, see Campbell, *The Elders*, 176–204; Meier, "Presbyteros in the Pastoral Epistles."

might call the community memory, and was therefore commissioned to teach the tradition."[49] In the middle of the list of criteria for deacons is a section addressed to "women" (1 Tim. 3:11), probably to be understood not as the wives of the deacons but rather as deaconesses—that is, women engaged in ministry.

The Pastorals present an argument for a structured ministry as the way for the church to survive in the present and into the indefinite future. The structure is important, and therefore care must be taken that the right persons are installed in leadership. It is the job of the elders/bishops, as "God's steward[s]" (Titus 1:7 [cf. "divine training" in 1 Tim. 1:4]), to "care for God's church" (1 Tim. 3:5).

The Self-Consciousness of the Church

One of the most remarkable aspects of the Pastoral Epistles is the self-awareness of the church's importance in the plan of God. The self-definition of the church in 1 Timothy 3:15 is astounding: "the household [*oikos*, lit., "house"] of God, which is the church of the living God, the pillar and bulwark of the truth." A similar self-consciousness is seen in 2 Timothy 2:19: "But God's firm foundation stands, bearing this seal: 'The Lord knows those who are his,' and, 'Let every one who names the name of the Lord depart from iniquity.'" The church is not one organization among others; it is unique, irreplaceable, and central to God's redemptive plan.

In all the emphases of the Pastorals that we have examined we see the unmistakable elements of an incipient early catholicism. Because of the delay of the parousia, the church must reunderstand itself not as a group of believers waiting to be taken away from this world to the next, but rather as the people of God, resident in the world for the foreseeable future, whose unchanging message represents unshakable truth.[50]

Should the Pastoral Letters Be Treated Together?

Some scholars have begun to argue that it is a mistake to deal with the Pastoral Epistles as a unified group. There is a sense, usually felt most keenly by those who allege Pauline authorship of the letters, that it is misleading to do so because it forces the letters "into a restrictive interrelationship that they were never intended to have."[51] It is true that sometimes the grouping of the letters can lead to mischaracterizing the individual letters by reading the characteristics of one letter into the others. It is equally clear that there

---

49. Young, "On ΕΠΙΣΚΟΠΟΣ and ΠΡΕΣΒΥΤΕΡΟΣ," 146.

50. For an examination of the rhetoric of the Pastorals, see Harding, *Tradition and Rhetoric in the Pastoral Epistles*. For the relation of the Pastorals to first-century letter-writing conventions, see Richards, *Difference and Distance in Post-Pauline Christianity*.

51. Towner, *The Letters to Timothy and Titus*, 88. Towner wants to bid "farewell" to the terminology "the Pastoral Epistles." So too Johnson, *The First and Second Letters to Timothy*, 63–64.

is also much to learn from considering each on its own terms.[52] Nevertheless, because the letters display a similar perspective and sufficient commonality and are ostensibly the only letters addressed to Paul's individual co-workers, they warrant consideration as a group. This approach need not close our eyes to the distinctives of the three letters, to which we now turn.

First Timothy

First Timothy is the longest of the Pastorals and the most artificial of the three, having almost no personal notes and no greetings.[53] It consists basically of regulations intended for the church and lacks the closeness between the author and Timothy that one might expect if the author were Paul. With its concerns for orthodoxy and orthopraxy, its emphasis on the preservation and transmission of tradition and its stress on church order, 1 Timothy is perhaps the best example of incipient early catholic interests in the NT. At the same time, there are passages that preserve traditional elements in continuity with the teaching of Paul. For example, the liturgical fragment in 2:3–6: "This is good, and it is acceptable in the sight of God our Savior, who desires all men to be saved and to come to the knowledge of the truth. For there is one God, and there is one mediator [*mesitēs*] between God and men, the man Christ Jesus, who gave himself as a ransom for all, the testimony to which was borne at the proper time." The word "mediator," however, is applied to Christ nowhere else in the Pauline Letters.

One of the most problematic passages in the NT is 1 Timothy 2:11–15, especially verses 11–12: "Let a woman learn in silence with all submissiveness. I permit no woman to teach or to have authority over men; she is to keep silent." The Pauline Letters (e.g., 1 Cor. 11:5) provide evidence that women were active in the church, praying and prophesying (i.e., teaching), and also in positions of leadership,[54] as in the case of Priscilla, who instructed Apollos (Acts 18:26); Euodia and Syntyche, "co-workers" of Paul (Phil. 4:2–3); Phoebe, a deaconess (i.e., minister) in the church of Cenchreae (Rom. 16:1); and Junia, who is called an "apostle" (Rom. 16:7). Despite this evidence, many feel compelled by this controversial passage (along with 1 Cor. 14:34–35) to deny women key leadership roles in the church.[55] Those who are unhappy with this conclusion have two possible courses to take: they can reunderstand the passages in question,[56]

---

52. Luke Timothy Johnson makes the interesting point that if one compares point by point Titus with Galatians, 1 Timothy with 1 Corinthians, and 2 Timothy with Philippians, "the letters look less alien" (*The First and Second Letters to Timothy*, 64).

53. For the interesting results of a 2006 symposium on 1 Timothy, see Donfried, *1 Timothy Reconsidered*.

54. See Belleville, *Women Leaders and the Church*.

55. See especially Köstenberger and Schreiner, *Women in the Church*.

56. It is possible to argue, as does Craig Keener (*Paul, Women and Wives*), that the silence imposed in our passage refers to unorthodox teaching, and that the authority refers only to a

or they can reject the teaching as conditioned by first-century culture,[57] as in the case of the NT teaching about slavery (cf. 6:1–2), and as inconsistent with the practice of the early church and the stress on equality in the NT (e.g., Gal. 3:28),[58] but most of all as making little sense in contemporary society and ultimately damaging to the witness of the church.[59]

Another notable point stressed in 1 Timothy, one that remains as obviously valid today, or more so, as in the first century, is the observation in 6:10: "For the love of money is the root of all evils; it is through this craving that some have wandered away from the faith and pierced their hearts with many pangs."

Second Timothy

Second Timothy is the most personal letter of the Pastorals and the one that sounds the most like an authentic letter of Paul. The personal details referring to Paul's imprisonment in Rome (1:16–17; especially 4:6–8, 18) seem very much like authentic Pauline fragments, and which therefore form the heart of the "fragment hypothesis." Second Timothy also contains the smallest amount of the kind of content that we have been noticing in the Pastorals.[60] Thus, for example, there are no instructions concerning church order, no lists of criteria for church offices.[61] However, 1:13–14 does reflect some of the essential concerns of the Pastorals: "Follow the pattern of the sound words which you have heard from me, in the faith and love which are in Christ Jesus; guard the truth that has been entrusted to you by the Holy Spirit who dwells within us." So too the exhortation in 3:14, "But as for you, continue in what you have learned and have firmly believed, knowing from whom you learned it," and the reference to "sound teaching" (4:3). Also to be noted is the "faithful saying" in 2:11–13.

Although the idea of an imminent end has weakened, eschatology has not receded altogether: "in the last days there will come times of stress" (3:1), words that are followed by a vice list, at the end of which is the exhortation "Avoid such people" (3:5). The author thus regards the present as "the last days." Future eschatology, however, remains a fixed point (4:8).

---

domineering expression of authority. See also Gritz, *Paul, Women Teachers, and the Mother Goddess at Ephesus*; Payne, *Man and Woman, One in Christ*.

57. See Bruce, "Women in the Church." The typical argument that these verses reflect a "creation ordinance" and therefore cannot be regarded as culturally conditioned ignores the fact that the pertinent Genesis material is capable of more than one interpretation.

58. Is there a retreat in the Pastorals caused by newly liberated women going too far too fast for that culture?

59. I find it ludicrous that while women in the modern world can be prime ministers, presidents, governors, legislators, mayors, military officers, and CEOs, they are denied positions of leadership, to which they believe they are called by God, only in the church.

60. See Murphy-O'Connor, "Second Timothy Contrasted with 1 Timothy and Titus."

61. But 2:24–25, applied generally to "the Lord's servant [*doulos*]," comes close to the heart of the Pastorals.

The mention of the "sacred writings" leads the author to this famous description: "All scripture is inspired by God and profitable for teaching, for reproof, for correction, and for training in righteousness, that the man of God may be complete, equipped for every good work" (3:16–17). Here what we call the "Old Testament" is described as "inspired"—literally, "God-breathed" (*theopneustos*)—and effective in accomplishing the sorts of things needed by the readers. This text can be applied to inspiration of the NT only by analogy.

Titus

Titus resembles 1 Timothy much more than it does 2 Timothy. The agenda of the book is indicated in the opening sentence: "to further the faith of God's elect and their knowledge of the truth which accords with godliness" (1:1). We find here all the concerns typical of the Pastorals—for example, the appointing of church officers (1:5–9), the insistence on "sound doctrine" (2:1; cf. 2:8), and household codes (2:1–10; 3:1–2). Christians are called "to live sober, upright, and godly lives in this world" (2:12).

In 2:13 the author speaks of "our blessed hope, the appearing of the glory of our great God and Savior Jesus Christ."[62] Nowhere does Paul unambiguously refer to Jesus as God.[63]

Authorship, Recipients, and Date

If Paul did not write the Pastoral Epistles, the actual author remains unknown to us.[64] It might have been Luke, but there are other possibilities, including even Timothy himself.[65] A reasonable argument can be put forward that 2 Timothy was written by Paul.[66] But probably the most we can say is that these letters were written by someone who was a close and trustworthy associate of Paul. Perhaps we may conclude with a slight modification of what Origen said concerning the Epistle to the Hebrews: "But who wrote these epistles, in truth only God knows" (see Eusebius, *Hist. eccl.* 6.25.13–14, trans. Oulton).

If the letters are pseudonymous or "allonymous," it is probable, though not absolutely necessary, that the addressees were not actually Timothy and Titus.

---

62. For thorough treatment of this text, see Harris, "Titus 2:13 and the Deity of Christ."

63. Romans 9:5 may come close, however. See Harris, *Jesus as God*.

64. For recent discussion of Pauline authorship of the Pastorals, see Donfried, "Rethinking Scholarly Approaches to 1 Timothy."

65. "If the Pastorals were written after Paul's death but within Timothy's lifetime, then most probably they were written by Timothy himself" (Bauckham, "Pseudo-Apostolic Letters," 494).

66. See Prior, *Paul the Letter-Writer and the Second Letter to Timothy*. For the conclusion that the author of 2 Timothy was different from the author of the other two Pastorals, see Aageson, *Paul, the Pastoral Epistles, and the Early Church*, 87–89.

The letters may, in their name, speak generally to implied readers—those in leadership in the early church.

Again, it is impossible to specify a specific date for the letters, other than to say that there is no need to assign them to the second century. The nature of the opposition, the ecclesiology, and the concerns of these letters point not to the second century (contrast, e.g., Ignatius's letters) but rather to a time in the last third of the first century, not long after Paul's death. We can only guess as to the order of the writing of the letters, except that 2 Timothy was probably the last to be written.

It should be obvious from the foregoing discussion that the Pastorals have much to offer to the church of the twenty first century. The call to remain faithful to the tradition of the church, its doctrine and ethics, in the face of various contemporary challenges could hardly be more timely. The church, if it is to survive this lengthening interim period until the return of Christ, needs to regain a sense of its identity as "the household of God, . . . the church of the living God, the pillar and bulwark of the truth" (1 Tim. 3:15).

Bibliography

Books and Articles

Aageson, James W. *Paul, the Pastoral Epistles, and the Early Church*. Peabody, MA: Hendrickson, 2008.

Bauckham, Richard. "Pseudo-Apostolic Letters." *JBL* 107 (1988): 469–94.

Beattie, Gillian. *Women and Marriage in Paul and His Early Interpreters*. JSNTSup 296. London: T&T Clark, 2005.

Beck, James R., ed. *Two Views on Women in Ministry*. Rev. ed. Grand Rapids: Zondervan, 2005.

Beker, J. Christiaan. *Heirs of Paul: Paul's Legacy in the New Testament and in the Church Today*. Minneapolis: Fortress, 1991.

Belleville, Linda L. *Women Leaders and the Church: Three Crucial Questions*. Grand Rapids: Baker Academic, 2000.

Bilezikian, Gilbert. *Beyond Sex Roles: What the Bible Says about a Woman's Place in Church and Family*. 3rd ed. Grand Rapids: Baker Academic, 2006.

Bird, Anthony E. "The Authorship of the Pastoral Epistles—Quantifying Literary Style." *RTR* 56 (1997): 118–37.

Brown, Raymond E. "*Episkopē* and *Episkopos*: The New Testament Evidence." *TS* 41 (1980): 322–38.

Bruce, F. F. "Women in the Church: A Biblical Survey." In *A Mind for What Matters: Collected Essays of F. F. Bruce*, 259–66. Grand Rapids: Eerdmans, 1990.

Campbell, R. Alastair. *The Elders: Seniority within Earliest Christianity*. SNTW. Edinburgh: T&T Clark, 1994.

———. "Identifying the Faithful Sayings in the Pastoral Epistles." *JSNT* 54 (1994): 73–86.

Davies, Margaret. *The Pastoral Epistles*. NTG. Sheffield: Sheffield Academic Press, 1996.

Donelson, Lewis R. *Pseudepigraphy and Ethical Argument in the Pastoral Epistles*. HUT 22. Tübingen: Mohr Siebeck, 1986.

Donfried, Karl P., ed., *1 Timothy Reconsidered*. Leuven: Peeters, 2008.

———. "Rethinking Scholarly Approaches to 1 Timothy." In *1 Timothy Reconsidered*, edited by Karl P. Donfried, 153–68. Monographic Series of "Benedictina": Biblical-Ecumenical Section 18. Leuven: Peeters, 2008.

Ellis, E. Earle. "The Authorship of the Pastorals: A Résumé and Assessment of Recent Trends." In *Paul and His Recent Interpreters*, 49–57. Grand Rapids: Eerdmans, 1961.

———. "The Pastorals and Paul." *ExpTim* 104 (1992): 45–47.

———. "Traditions in the Pastoral Letters." In *The Making of the New Testament Documents*, 406–25. BIS 39. Leiden: Brill, 1999.

Fiore, Benjamin. *The Function of Personal Example in the Socratic and Pastoral Epistles*. AnBib 105. Rome: Biblical Institute Press, 1986.

Forbes, A. Dean. "Statistical Research on the Bible." *ABD* 6:185–206.

Grayston, Kenneth, and Gustav Herdan. "The Authorship of the Pastorals in the Light of Statistical Linguistics." *NTS* 6 (1959–60): 1–15.

Gritz, Sharon Hodgin. *Paul, Women Teachers, and the Mother Goddess at Ephesus: A Study of 1 Timothy 2:9–15 in Light of the Religious and Cultural Milieu of the First Century*. Lanham, MD: University Press of America, 1991.

Gundry, Robert H. "The Form, Meaning and Background of the Hymn Quoted in 1 Timothy 3:16." In *Apostolic History and the Gospel: Biblical and Historical Essays Presented to F. F. Bruce on His 60th Birthday*, edited by W. Ward Gasque and Ralph P. Martin, 203–22. Grand Rapids: Eerdmans, 1970.

Guthrie, Donald H. *New Testament Introduction*. 4th rev. ed. Downers Grove, IL: InterVarsity, 1990.

———. *The Pastoral Epistles and the Mind of Paul*. London: Tyndale, 1956.

Hagner, Donald A. "Titus as a Pauline Letter." *SBLSP* 37 (1998): 546–58.

Hanson, A. T. *Studies in the Pastoral Epistles*. London: SPCK, 1968.

Harding, Mark. *Tradition and Rhetoric in the Pastoral Epistles*. SBL 3. New York: Peter Lang, 1998.

———. *What Are They Saying about the Pastoral Epistles?* New York: Paulist Press, 2001.

Harris, Murray J. *Jesus as God: The New Testament Use of* Theos *in Reference to Jesus*. Grand Rapids: Baker Academic, 1992.

———. "Titus 2:13 and the Deity of Christ." In *Pauline Studies: Essays Presented to F. F. Bruce on His 70th Birthday*, edited by Donald A. Hagner and Murray J. Harris, 262–77. Grand Rapids: Eerdmans, 1980.

Harrison, Percy N. "Important Hypotheses Reconsidered: III. The Authorship of the Pastoral Epistles." *ExpTim* 67 (1955–56): 77–81.

———. *Paulines and Pastorals*. London: Villiers, 1964.

———. *The Problem of the Pastoral Epistles*. London: Oxford University Press, 1921.

Holmes, J. M. *Text in a Whirlwind: A Critique of Four Exegetical Devices at 1 Timothy 2.9–15*. JSNTSup 196. Sheffield: Sheffield Academic Press, 2000.

Karris, Robert J. "The Background and Significance of the Polemic of the Pastoral Epistles." *JBL* 92 (1973): 549–64.

Keener, Craig S. *Paul, Women and Wives: Marriage and Women's Ministry in the Letters of Paul*. Peabody, MA: Hendrickson; Grand Rapids: Baker Academic, 1992.

Kenny, Anthony. *A Stylometric Study of the New Testament*. Oxford: Clarendon, 1986.

Kidd, Reggie M. *Wealth and Beneficence in the Pastoral Epistles: A "Bourgeois" Form of Early Christianity?* SBLDS 122. Atlanta: Scholars Press, 1990.

Knight, George W., III. *The Faithful Sayings in the Pastoral Letters*. Kampen: J. H. Kok, 1968.

Köstenberger, Andreas J., and Thomas R. Schreiner, eds. *Women in the Church: An Analysis and Application of 1 Timothy 2:9–15*. 2nd ed. Grand Rapids: Baker Academic, 2005.

Köstenberger, Andreas J., and Terry L. Wilder, eds. *Entrusted with the Gospel: Paul's Theology in the Pastoral Epistles*. Nashville: Broadman & Holman, 2010.

Kroeger, Richard Clark, and Catherine Clark Kroeger. *I Suffer Not a Woman: Rethinking 1 Timothy 2:11–15 in Light of Ancient Evidence*. Grand Rapids: Baker Academic, 1992.

Lau, Andrew Y. *Manifest in the Flesh: The Epiphany Christology of the Pastoral Letters*. WUNT 2/86. Tübingen: Mohr Siebeck, 1996.

MacDonald, Margaret Y. *The Pauline Churches: A Socio-Historical Study of Institutionalization in the Pauline and Deutero-Pauline Writings*. SNTSMS 60. Cambridge: Cambridge University Press, 1988.

Malina, Bruce J. *Timothy: Paul's Closest Associate*. Collegeville, MN: Liturgical Press, 2008.

Marshall, I. Howard. "Prospects for the Pastoral Epistles." In *Doing Theology for the People of God: Studies in Honour of J. I. Packer*, edited by Donald Lewis and Alister McGrath, 137–55. Leicester: Apollos, 1996.

———. "Recent Study of the Pastoral Epistles." *Themelios* 23 (1997): 3–29.

———. "Salvation, Grace and Works in the Later Writings in the Pauline Corpus." *NTS* 42 (1996): 339–58.

———. "'Sometimes Only Orthodox': Is There More to the Pastoral Epistles?" *EpRev* 20 (1993): 12–24.

Martin, Ralph P. *New Testament Foundations*. 2 vols. Grand Rapids: Eerdmans, 1975–78.

Mealand, David L. "The Extent of the Pauline Corpus: A Multivariate Approach." *JSNT* 59 (1995): 61–92.

———. "Positional Stylometry Reassessed: Testing a Seven-Epistle Theory of Pauline Authorship." *NTS* 35 (1989): 266–86.

Meier, John P. "Presbyteros in the Pastoral Epistles." *CBQ* 35 (1973): 323–45.

Metzger, Bruce M. "A Reconsideration of Certain Arguments against the Pauline Authorship of the Pastoral Epistles." *ExpTim* 70 (1958–59): 91–94.

Mickelsen, Alvera, ed. *Women, Authority and the Bible*. Downers Grove, IL: InterVarsity, 1986.

Miller, James D. *The Pastoral Letters as Composite Documents*. SNTSMS 93. Cambridge: Cambridge University Press, 1997.

Moule, C. F. D. "The Problem of the Pastoral Epistles: A Reappraisal." *BJRL* 47 (1964–65): 430–52.

Murphy-O'Connor, Jerome. *Paul the Letter-Writer: His World, His Options, His Skills*. GNS 41. Collegeville, MN: Liturgical Press, 1995.

———. "Second Timothy Contrasted with 1 Timothy and Titus." *RB* 98 (1991): 403–10.

Neumann, Kenneth J. *The Authenticity of the Pauline Epistles in the Light of Stylostatistical Analysis*. SBLDS 120. Atlanta: Scholars Press, 1990.

Payne, Philip B. *Man and Woman, One in Christ: An Exegetical and Theological Study of Paul's Letters*. Grand Rapids: Zondervan, 2009.

Porter, Stanley E. "Pauline Authorship and the Pastoral Epistles: A Response to R. W. Wall's Response." *BBR* 6 (1996): 133–38.

———. "Pauline Authorship and the Pastoral Epistles: Implications for Canon." *BBR* 5 (1995): 105–23.

Prior, Michael. *Paul the Letter-Writer and the Second Letter to Timothy*. JSNTSup 23. Sheffield: JSOT Press, 1989.

Quinn, Jerome D. "The Last Volume of Luke: The Relation of Luke-Acts to the Pastoral Epistles." In *Perspectives on Luke-Acts*, edited by Charles H. Talbert, 62–75. Edinburgh: T&T Clark, 1978.

Reicke, Bo. *Re-examining Paul's Letters: The History of the Pauline Correspondence*. Edited by David Moessner and Ingalisa Reicke. Harrisburg, PA: Trinity Press International, 2001.

Richards, E. Randolph. *Paul and First-Century Letter Writing: Secretaries, Composition and Collection*. Downers Grove, IL: InterVarsity, 2004.

———. *The Secretary in the Letters of Paul*. WUNT 2/42. Tübingen: Mohr Siebeck, 1991.

Richards, William A. *Difference and Distance in Post-Pauline Christianity: An Epistolary Analysis of the Pastorals*. SBL 44. New York: Peter Lang, 2002.

Robinson, J. A. T. *Redating the New Testament*. Philadelphia: Westminster, 1976.

Simpson, E. K. *The Authenticity and Authorship of the Pastoral Epistles: An Address Delivered at the Third Conference of the Theological Students' Prayer Union, Swanwick, April 1939.* London: James Clarke, 1939.

Towner, Philip H. "Gnosis and Realized Eschatology in Ephesus (of the Pastoral Epistles) and the Corinthian Enthusiasm." *JSNT* 31 (1987): 95–124.

———. *The Goal of Our Instruction: The Structure of Theology and Ethics in the Pastoral Epistles.* JSNTSup 34. Sheffield: JSOT Press, 1989.

———. "Pauline Theology or Pauline Tradition in the Pastoral Epistles: The Question of Method." *TynBul* 46 (1995): 287–314.

Van Neste, Ray. *Cohesion and Structure in the Pastoral Epistles.* JSNTSup 280. London: T&T Clark International, 2004.

Verner, David C. *The Household of God: The Social World of the Pastoral Epistles.* SBLDS 71. Chico, CA: Scholars Press, 1983.

Wall, Robert W. "The Function of the Pastoral Letters within the Pauline Canon of the New Testament: A Canonical Approach." In *The Pauline Canon,* edited by Stanley E. Porter, 27–44. PS 1. Leiden: Brill, 2004.

———. "Pauline Authorship and the Pastoral Epistles: A Response to S. E. Porter." *BBR* 5 (1995): 125–28.

Westerholm, Stephen. "The Law and the 'Just Man' (1 Tim 1,3–11)." *ST* 36 (1982): 79–95.

Wilson, Stephen G. *Luke and the Pastoral Epistles.* London: SPCK, 1979.

Witherington, Ben, III. *Women in the Earliest Churches.* SNTSMS 59. Cambridge: Cambridge University Press, 1988.

Young, Frances M. "On ΕΠΙΣΚΟΠΟΣ and ΠΡΕΣΒΥΤΕΡΟΣ." *JTS* 45 (1994): 142–48.

———. *The Theology of the Pastoral Letters.* NTT. Cambridge: Cambridge University Press, 1994.

Commentaries

Barrett, C. K. *The Pastoral Epistles.* NClarB. Oxford: Clarendon, 1963.

Collins, Raymond F. *1 & 2 Timothy and Titus: A Commentary.* NTL. Louisville: Westminster John Knox, 2002.

Dibelius, Martin, and Hans Conzelmann. *The Pastoral Epistles.* Translated by Philip Buttolph and Adela Yarbro. Edited by Helmut Koester. Hermeneia. Philadelphia: Fortress, 1972.

Dunn, James D. G. "The First and Second Letters to Timothy and the Letter to Titus." *NIB* 11:773–880.

Easton, Burton Scott. *The Pastoral Epistles: Introduction, Translation, Commentary and Word Studies.* London: SCM, 1948.

Falconer, Robert. *The Pastoral Epistles: Introduction, Translation and Notes.* Oxford: Clarendon, 1937.

Fee, Gordon D. *1 and 2 Timothy, Titus.* NIBC. Peabody, MA: Hendrickson, 1988.

Fiore, Benjamin. *The Pastoral Epistles: First Timothy, Second Timothy, Titus.* SP 12. Collegeville, MN: Liturgical Press, 2007.

Guthrie, Donald H. *The Pastoral Epistles.* Rev. ed. TNTC. Grand Rapids: Eerdmans, 1990.

Hanson, A. T. *The Pastoral Epistles.* NCBC. Grand Rapids: Eerdmans, 1982.

———. *The Pastoral Letters: Commentary on the First and Second Letters to Timothy and the Letter to Titus.* CBC. Cambridge: Cambridge University Press, 1966.

Houlden, James L. *The Pastoral Epistles: I and II Timothy, Titus.* TPINTC. Philadelphia: Trinity Press International, 1989.

Hultgren, Arland J. *1 & 2 Timothy, Titus.* ACNT. Minneapolis: Augsburg, 1984.

Jeremias, Joachim. *Die Briefe an Timotheus und Titus.* NTD 9. Göttingen: Vandenhoeck & Ruprecht, 1953.

Johnson, Luke Timothy. *The First and Second Letters to Timothy: A New Translation with Introduction and Commentary*. AB 35A. New York: Doubleday, 2001.

Karris, Robert J. *The Pastoral Epistles*. NTM 17. Wilmington, DE: Michael Glazier, 1979.

Kelly, J. N. D. *A Commentary on the Pastoral Epistles*. BNTC. New York: Harper & Row, 1963.

Knight, George W., III. *The Pastoral Epistles: A Commentary on the Greek Text*. NIGTC. Grand Rapids: Eerdmans, 1992.

Marshall, I. Howard. *A Critical and Exegetical Commentary on the Pastoral Epistles*. ICC. Edinburgh: T&T Clark, 1999.

Mounce, William D. *Pastoral Epistles*. WBC 46. Nashville: Thomas Nelson, 2000.

Quinn, Jerome D. *The Letter to Titus: A New Translation with Notes and Commentary and an Introduction to Titus, I and II Timothy, the Pastoral Epistles*. AB 35. New York: Doubleday, 1990.

Quinn, Jerome D., and William C. Wacker. *The First and Second Letters to Timothy: A New Translation with Notes and Commentary*. ECC. Grand Rapids: Eerdmans, 2000.

Simpson, E. K. *The Pastoral Epistles*. London: Tyndale, 1954.

Towner, Philip H. *The Letters to Timothy and Titus*. NICNT. Grand Rapids: Eerdmans, 2006.

Witherington, Ben, III. *A Socio-Rhetorical Commentary on Titus, 1–2 Timothy, and 1–3 John*. Vol. 1 of *Letters and Homilies for Hellenized Christians*. Downers Grove, IL: IVP Academic, 2006.

PART 6

HEBREWS AND THE CATHOLIC EPISTLES

Non-Pauline Christianity

35

The Book of Hebrews

As distinctive among the writings of the NT as Hebrews is, we know very little about its origin, its author, and its first readers. The traditional and ancient designation of the book as "The Epistle of Paul the Apostle to the Hebrews," found, for example, at the head of the book in the KJV, is not a part of the original document but rather is a later ecclesiastical opinion that first comes to expression in the Eastern church (Alexandria) late in the second century and in the Western church two centuries after that. Moreover, this ascription appears to have been inferred from the document itself, much in the manner of modern scholarship, rather than derived from any independent tradition about its origin. It has been challenged on all three points: it is almost unanimously agreed that Paul did not write Hebrews; the document is more a sermon-treatise than an epistle; and some have challenged whether it was written to Hebrews—that is, to Jewish Christians.

The Addressees

Unlike most of the NT letters, Hebrews does not begin with an identification of the author and the addressees. Nor, indeed, does it begin like a letter at all, despite its typical epistolary ending. Nowhere in this document, furthermore, are the original readers referred to as "Hebrews" or "Jews." The title "To the Hebrews" is first attested at the end of the second century (by Clement of Alexandria and Tertullian). Although it is also found in the oldest manuscript

---

Author: We can only guess at the author of this anonymous book. The author appears to have been a member of the circle of workers associated with Paul or one of the other Apostles.

Date: With no reference in the book to the fall of Jerusalem, it probably is to be dated before 70, and since no martyrdoms have yet been experienced by members of the community, before the persecution by Nero—therefore probably in the early 60s.

Addressees: Probably written to the Jewish Christian community of Rome.

Purpose: To present reasons why the readers should not revert to their (pre-Christian) Jewish faith.

Message/Argument: Jesus Christ is the supreme, definitive, and final revelation of God, whose atoning sacrifice is the fulfillment of the promises of Scripture and of universal import.

Significance: An extremely rich exposition of the meaning of Christ and his sacrifice through midrashic interpretation of the Scriptures. The one sacrifice of Christ replaces the repeated sacrifices of the temple ritual.

---

of the Pauline Epistles ($\mathfrak{P}^{46}$) from about the same time, this may reflect only the emerging opinion in the Eastern church that it was Pauline.[1]

Jewish or Gentile Christians?

Nevertheless, the early church very probably was correct in understanding the first readers to have been Jewish Christians. The vast majority of modern scholars agree with this conclusion because of the content of the book. The OT is of enormous importance for Hebrews: it is quoted often and expounded in midrashic fashion (see below, pp. 658–59), and the argument of the book to a large extent depends on this use of the OT. More specifically, the stress on the Levitical liturgy and priesthood, the sanctuary of the wilderness tabernacle, and the Mosaic covenant, all of which in such a detailed manner are contrasted with the fulfillment brought by Christ, points to the high probability of Jewish readers.

The same is true of the book's interest in christology and the fulfillment of OT promises, as well as the way in which the experiences of Israel are used by the author as warnings for the community. Certain passages seem particularly appropriate for Jewish readers. For example, the opening words, "In many and various ways God spoke of old to our fathers by the prophets" (1:1), refer most naturally to physical fathers, the forebears of the readers. Again, this is

---

1. In $\mathfrak{P}^{46}$, the earliest complete manuscript of the Pauline Epistles, dating from about 200, Hebrews appears as the second writing—that is, between Romans and 1 Corinthians. For the heading "To the Hebrews" in Clement of Alexandria, see Eusebius, *Hist. Eccl.* 6.14.4; for Tertullian, see *On Modesty*, 20. See too Anderson, "Hebrews among the Letters of Paul."

a compelling conclusion from 2:16: "For surely it is not with angels that he is concerned but with the descendants of Abraham." In this passage the incarnation is explained as due to Christ's identification with humankind (and not angels), yet this is expressed through the allusion to Isaiah 41:8–9, where it is specifically Israel that is in view. This obviously would have had special relevance to Jewish readers. And it is particularly Jewish readers, more than any others, who, because of the intrinsic excellence of Judaism, would have been tempted to return to their earlier religious faith—something that our author warns against repeatedly in the book. They, more than any others, would have been forced to grapple with the relation between the old covenant and the new covenant.

That the first readers of the book were Jewish Christians remained the unanimous conviction of scholars until the end of the nineteenth century. Since that time, some scholars have argued that the first readers were Gentiles, not Jews.[2] Since the superscription "To the Hebrews" is traditional rather than original, the determination of whether the readers were Jews or Gentiles can be made only from the book itself. These scholars argue that nothing about the content of the book necessitates Jewish readers. Although this assertion is quite true in itself, the question remains as to which hypothesis is more successful in accounting for the content of the book as a whole.

The following objections have been raised to the identification of the readers as Jewish. The potential apostasy described in 3:12, "Take care, brethren, lest there be in any of you an evil, unbelieving heart, leading you to fall away from the living God," seems difficult if it is a return to Judaism that is contemplated. If Gentiles return to their paganism, they can indeed be understood as turning away from the living God. And yet, given our understanding of the author's larger argument, to turn away from the fulfillment brought in Christ is indeed so grievous that, even for Jewish readers, it would be to "fall away from the living God." From our author's perspective, the old covenant is passé; to return to it would not have been thought by him to be a return to a valid faith.

Similarly, although some are of the opinion that the reference to "dead works" in 6:1 and 9:14 is a more appropriate description of paganism than Judaism, our author's perspective may well make such a description of Judaism possible. Further, the references to gnostic-related views in 13:4, 9 need not imply a Gentile readership; Diaspora Judaism in particular was subject to such gnostic influence (cf. Col. 2:16, 21–22). Neither the elegant Greek of the book nor the regular citation of the OT from the LXX necessarily points to Gentile readers. Again, the fact that it is not Judaism and the temple but rather the Levitical ritual and the wilderness tabernacle that are the focus of the author's appeal to the past and to what is recorded in Scripture is the result of the author's desire to stress the motif of promise and fulfillment. Thus the new that has come in Christ succeeds not simply the present manifestation

2. For example, von Soden, Zahn, Moffatt, Windisch, Scott, Käsemann, Vos.

of Judaism but also its ideal statement in the Torah (Genesis through Deuteronomy). If the originally intended readers were Jewish, we very probably should conceive of them as Hellenistic or Greek-speaking Jews whose Judaism was of a nonconformist variety (i.e., other than typical rabbinic Judaism, though not necessarily uninfluenced by it).

It must be admitted, however, that just as nothing in the book necessitates that the original readers be Jewish, despite strong probability in favor of such a view, so nothing in the book excludes the possibility of a Gentile readership. Some scholars, indeed, argue for a mixed readership of both Jews and Gentiles. By virtue of its contents, the book possesses a universal applicability.

Related to the Qumran Essenes?

If, as I have argued, the most natural explanation of the book, taking into account its total contents, is that the original readers were Jewish Christians, can anything more specific be said about them? Some have maintained that the readers were converts, perhaps former priests,[3] from the Essene community at Qumran,[4] known to us through the discovery of the Dead Sea Scrolls. However, on closer analysis, the similarities can be shown to be more superficial than substantial.[5] Furthermore, the stress on the Levitical priesthood and ritual in Hebrews need not indicate that the readers were former priests (cf. Acts 6:7). The author's argumentation is not so technical as to be beyond Jews who had converted to Christianity. Similarly, the author's criticism of the readers when he says that they ought to have been teachers (5:12) does not necessarily indicate professionals in contrast to laity. It could well mean that they as Jewish Christians, with their intimate understanding of the OT, ought to have been in a superior position to teach others (especially Gentiles) about the full significance of Christianity.

The History of the Community

Although the hypothesis that the readers were Jewish Christians remains at best only highly probable, some things about the readers are certain. First, it is plain that the recipients of the book formed a specific community with a specific history. We learn that although they had been Christians for some time, they remained immature in their understanding of the Christian faith

---

3. Acts 6:7 tells us that "a great many of the priests were obedient to the faith." This identification of the addressees is argued extensively by Spicq, *L'Epître aux Hébreux*, 1:226–31.

4. Among those who see Qumranic influence in Hebrews are Braun, Kosmala, Bowman, Yadin, Flusser, Buchanan, and Hughes.

5. See Bruce, "'To the Hebrews' or 'To the Essenes'?"

(5:11–6:3). The reason for this seems to have been their fear of persecution and their reluctance to separate from Judaism rather than mental dullness on their part. This failure is all the more striking given their earlier history, in which they demonstrated their love of their fellow Christians through service to them (6:9–10). In a time of persecution, during which they themselves suffered considerably, they nevertheless identified with those whose sufferings were worse and thereby suffered all the more, including loss of personal property (10:32–39). But despite this honorable past, there seems to be evidence that they were weakening in their commitment, perhaps in the face of the threat of new persecution. Although apparently they had not previously suffered martyrdom, perhaps this now loomed as a threatening possibility (10:35–36; 12:4).

We may further say of the readers that the author did not simply know them but was somehow related to them, perhaps as a former leader of the community (13:18–19, 22–24; cf. 13:7, 17).

It is less certain, but nevertheless a good possibility, that the community of Jewish believers was, or at least once had been, part of a larger Christian community, perhaps the Jewish wing of a larger congregation (note the reference to "all your leaders" in 13:24). They may have met together as a house church, but new pressures appear to have discouraged them from meeting this way (cf. 10:25). Indeed, perhaps the imminence of persecution caused them to separate themselves from the main body of Christians.

Location of the Readers

Rome

Can we say with any certainty where this group of Jewish Christians lived? Jewish converts to Christianity lived throughout the Mediterranean world as well as in Palestine. The only geographical clue in the epistle is in 13:24, and it is an ambiguous one. The words "Those who come from Italy send you greetings" probably mean that Italian compatriots, away from home and with our author, send greetings back to their brothers and sisters in the homeland. This is more natural than to conclude that Christians in Rome (in which case we would not expect the preposition "from") send their greetings elsewhere. Furthermore, our earliest knowledge of Hebrews—and a very early one at that—comes from Clement of Rome in 96 (*1 Clement*). *First Clement* quotes from Hebrews extensively[6] but unfortunately gives us no hint of its author, whose identity Clement probably knew if the letter was addressed to Jewish Christians in Rome. Also to be noted is that the Roman church, like the first readers of Hebrews, had suffered persecutions and was known for its generos-

---

6. See Hagner, *The Use of the Old and New Testaments in Clement of Rome*, 179–95.

ity (cf. 6:10–20; 10:32–39). Timothy, mentioned in 13:23, was also known to the Roman church (cf. Rom. 16:21).

Palestine

Some scholars maintain, however, that the letter was sent to Jewish Christians in Palestine. Would not Jewish Christians there be under the greatest pressure to return to their former faith? They had suffered persecution from their unbelieving brethren, and some had even died (cf. 12:4, where the readers are said not to have shed their blood). The imminent crisis that they seem to face in Hebrews could be the destruction of Jerusalem by the Romans. Against this view, however, is the strongly Hellenistic character of the book, which does not fit very well with, for example, a Jerusalem readership. It is further to be noted that the Jerusalem church was poverty-stricken and therefore hardly capable of the generosity for which the author compliments the readers (6:10; 10:34; 13:16).

Alexandria

Because of apparent signs of an Alexandrian perspective—for example, the dualism between heavenly archetypes and earthly copies, the use of the OT, similarities with the Alexandrian Jewish scholar Philo—some scholars propose Alexandria as the destination of the epistle. This evidence, however, is possibly more pertinent to the author's background than to the readers. It would also be strange that the Alexandrian church would not remember the name of the author, for it is in Alexandria late in the second century that Hebrews was first attributed to Paul. But there it was also believed that the letter originally had been sent to Jewish Christians in Palestine, not to Alexandria.

The Lycus Valley

T. W. Manson suggested that Hebrews was directed to Jewish Christians who faced the same problems as those addressed by Paul in his Letter to the Colossians, and thus that Hebrews also had been sent to the churches of the Lycus Valley.[7] Both Colossians and Hebrews refer to scruples about certain foods (Col. 2:16; Heb. 13:9; cf. Col. 2:20–23; Heb. 9:10) and also to the veneration of angels (Col. 2:18; Heb. 1:4–14). Yet there is no reason to believe that these manifestations of an early form of Jewish gnosticism would have been limited to the Lycus Valley.

Other Suggestions

A number of other places, such as Ephesus, Syria, Asia, Galatia, Corinth, and Cyprus, have also been suggested as the location of the readers, but these

7. Manson, "The Problem of the Epistle to the Hebrews."

involve an even higher degree of speculation than those just mentioned. When all the data have been considered, Rome still remains the most attractive hypothesis concerning the destination of the letter. But a hypothesis it remains.

Date

If, then, it is tentatively accepted that the original readers of Hebrews were Jewish Christians forming a part of the larger Christian church in Rome, what may be said concerning the date of its composition? Because of the use of Hebrews by Clement of Rome, we can be certain that it was written earlier than 95. The most important factor in determining the approximate date of the epistle is the identification of the persecution referred to in 10:32–34. According to this passage, sometime in "the former days" the readers had suffered abuse, public insult, and the loss of possessions. There are three conspicuous Roman persecutions to consider: that under the emperor Domitian in the 80s and 90s of the first century, that under Nero beginning in 64, and that under Claudius in 49. The persecutions under Nero and Domitian, on the one hand, involved considerable loss of life, whereas our readers seem clearly not to have suffered a persecution that involved martyrdom (12:4). The persecution under Claudius, on the other hand, fits well the description given in 10:32–34. Claudius expelled the Jews from Rome, and this included Jewish Christians (among whom were Priscilla and Aquila [see Acts 18:2]). Indeed, according to the Roman historian Suetonius (*Claud.* 25.4), as we have previously noted, the expulsion was due to riots having to do with one named *Chrestus* (probably a misspelling of *Christus* ["Christ"]). These riots likely had to do with the recent conversion of Jews to faith in Christ and with the consequent turmoil caused within the Jewish community. The difficulties of this time would have afforded the readers ample opportunity to demonstrate the love and service for which the author compliments them.

A second important issue involved in dating Hebrews is whether it was written before or after the fall of Jerusalem and the destruction of the temple in 70. The sacrificial ritual and the work of the Levitical priesthood are described in the present tense throughout the book. Yet it must be remembered that what is described in this way is not the ritual of the second temple but rather the one described in the OT. Hence the description is set forth in ideal terms. It is furthermore the case that Christian writers after 70 can still describe the temple ritual using present tenses (e.g., Clement of Rome and Justin Martyr). Despite these observations, however, the present tense could be an indicator that Hebrews was written before 70. It is highly remarkable—indeed, unbelievable—that had our author written after the destruction of the temple he could have failed to mention it, since this historical event could have been seen as the divine authentication of the author's central argument that the Levitical ritual was outmoded and hence without remaining significance (cf. 8:13: "And what is becoming obsolete and growing old is ready to vanish away"). Indeed, it would have provided the perfect capstone to his attempt to persuade his readers not to return to Judaism. It is, therefore, especially the silence about the events of 70 that leads us to the probability of an earlier date for the writing of the book. And if Nero's persecution had not yet taken place, as seems to be the case, then we are drawn to a date somewhere in the early 60s. This date seems compatible with the statement in 2:3 that the readers heard the gospel from those who had heard Jesus, assuming this statement to be literal and not simply a general statement about the integrity of the tradition. When and by whom in particular this message first came to the readers remain beyond our reach, however, as does knowledge about the founding of the church at Rome.

Author

A secure place in the NT canon came early for Hebrews with the attribution of the book to Paul in the Eastern church by the end of the second century. Clement of Alexandria (ca. 200), following his teacher Pantaenus, held to Pauline authorship of Hebrews, but because of the different character of its Greek he postulated that Paul had written the letter in Hebrew (Aramaic), and that Luke translated it into Greek. Several decades later Origen, although denying Pauline authorship (even of a Hebrew original), affirmed the content of the book to be essentially Pauline. After Origen, Pauline authorship of Hebrews remained unchallenged in the East, where by the middle of the third century it was placed immediately after Romans in the midst of the Pauline corpus in $\mathfrak{P}^{46}$, the earliest papyrus copy of that corpus to survive into the modern era.

Pauline authorship of Hebrews was disputed in the Western church until the late fourth and early fifth centuries. Only with Jerome and Augustine was Pauline authorship accepted, but more so because of the strong tradition confirming it in the Eastern church, as well as canonical considerations, than because of any genuine conviction on their part. This conclusion remained established in the West until the Reformation period, when Erasmus, Luther, and Calvin again challenged it.

It is difficult to accept Paul as the author of Hebrews for four significant reasons. First, unlike all the undisputed Pauline Letters, this writing is anonymous. There are, furthermore, no personal allusions in the letter that would lead us to the conclusion that Paul was the author. Nowhere does the personal experience of the author intrude into the content of the letter, contrary to the frequent practice of Paul. Second, the author aligns himself with those who have only a secondhand knowledge of the Lord (2:3), whereas Paul vigorously defends his firsthand experience of Christ (e.g., 1 Cor. 9:1; Gal. 1:12). Paul will admit no inferiority to the Twelve Apostles, the more so because exactly this charge was repeatedly leveled at him. Third, as was already noticed in the early church, the style of the Greek in this book—the most elegant in the NT—is unlike that of any of the epistles in the Pauline corpus. It is, of course, possible to attribute this to the use of a different secretary, although this seems unlikely. Fourth, and most important, there are considerable theological differences between Hebrews and the Pauline Epistles. Most prominent among these is the major significance of the high priesthood of Christ for the author of Hebrews, a concept which is absent altogether from Paul's writings. In addition, several emphases common in Paul's Letters are not found in Hebrews: union with Christ ("in Christ"), justification by faith, the work of the Holy Spirit, the opposition of faith and works, and the tension between flesh and spirit are lacking; the resurrection of Christ (mentioned only in 13:20) has given way to repeated emphasis on his exaltation to God's right hand; and Paul's common emphasis on the redemptive character of Christ's work is subordinated to an emphasis on Christ's cleansing and sanctifying of his people.[8]

The Reformers were not inclined to accept the Pauline authorship of Hebrews. In his commentary on Hebrews, John Calvin concluded, "I can adduce no reason to show that Paul was its author." In the prologue to Hebrews in his translation of the NT, William Tyndale wrote, "It is easy to see that he [the author of Hebrews] was a faithful servant of Christ's and of the same doctrine that Timothy was of, yea and Paul himself was, and that he was an apostle or in the apostles' time or near thereunto" (*Preface to Hebrews*). Nothing in Hebrews is contradictory of Paul; indeed, they share many things in common. This circumstance led Origen to conclude that although the book itself was not by Paul, much of its contents were of a Pauline character.[9] This, together with the mention of Timothy (13:23), suggests that the author was associated with the Pauline circle.

Since, therefore, the ancient tradition that Paul was the author of Hebrews cannot be relied on, we are left to speculate concerning the author's identity from the content of the book. An increasingly popular proposal, apparently first made by Martin Luther, is that the author was Apollos, the Jewish convert from Alexandria, described in Acts 18:24 as "an eloquent man, well versed in the scriptures." It is also said of Apollos that "he powerfully confuted the Jews in public, showing by the scriptures that the Christ was Jesus" (Acts 18:28). Both his background and his abilities thus accord well with what we know of the author of Hebrews. Further, it is clear that Apollos knew Paul and indeed had been instructed by him indirectly through Priscilla and Aquila. He would also have been acquainted with Timothy. The only drawback to the suggestion of Apollos as the author of Hebrews is the lack of ancient testimony supporting

---

8. On the attribution of Hebrews to Paul, see Rothschild, *Hebrews as Pseudepigraphon*.

9. "Not without reason have the men of old time handed it down as Paul's" (quoted in Eusebius, *Hist. eccl.* 6.25.13, trans. Oulton).

it. Because our knowledge is so limited, Apollos can only be a guess. But it is a very good guess, perhaps the best that can be offered.

Another person proposed is Barnabas, who does have the support of the early church father Tertullian (*On Modesty*, 20), ca. 200. Barnabas (see Acts 4:36) was a Levite and therefore would have been interested in, and knowledge-able about, the Levitical system. He was from Cyprus, where he would have been influenced by Hellenistic culture and Greek of a high caliber. Another striking point, if of minor importance, is the translation of Barnabas's name (Acts 4:36) as "Son of encouragement" and the corresponding self-descrip-tion of Hebrews as a "word of exhortation" (Heb. 13:22); the Greek word (*paraklēsis*) is the same in both texts, and the expression in Hebrews can well be translated as "word of encouragement."

The suggestion that Barnabas was the author of Hebrews is thus tenable, but it is still worth wondering whether Tertullian's view depended on an inference from the contents of the letter, as did Luther's, rather than on any authentic tradition to that effect. But that does not mean that it is not a good guess.

Several other guesses, all of them speculative, have been put forward at one time or another for the author of Hebrews. These may be mentioned briefly with the main claim made in their support: Luke (similarities in style and in the content of Acts, especially Stephen's speech); Silvanus (similarities in style between 1 Peter and Hebrews); Philip (commending Paulinism to Jewish Chris-tians of Jerusalem); Clement of Rome (nearly identical wording in places); Epaphras (similar anti-gnostic concerns in Colossians); Priscilla (anonymity of the letter and her tutelage of Apollos);[10] and even Mary the mother of Jesus (a "feminine" touch plus affinity with Luke 1–2).

This multitude of candidates itself reflects the difficulty of discovering the identity of the author. It was Origen in the third century who, after surveying a list of possible authors, uttered these famous words: "But who wrote the epistle, in truth God knows" (quoted in Eusebius, *Hist. eccl.* 6.25.14, trans. Oulton). The author, whoever he or she was, had an exceptional knowledge of the OT, interpreted the OT midrashically in terms of Christ, probably was acquainted with the Platonic idealism popular in Alexandria, enjoyed the best training in the use of the Greek language, and shared the universal perspective of the early Hellenistic Christians. This person probably was a member of the Pauline circle and very probably was a converted Jew. The author's burden for the situation and plight of the readers is evident throughout the letter. He or she writes as one of them, as one who apparently has had previous contact with them in the form of some kind of ministry. More than this is difficult to say. If Origen was unable to establish the author's identity in the third

---

10. The Greek participle *diēgoumenon* in the author's self-reference in Hebrews 11:32 is masculine, but presumably Priscilla would have been clever enough not to reveal herself by a telltale feminine participle.

century, it is unlikely that we will succeed where he failed. Origen's comment via Eusebius is worth quoting in full:

> That the character of the diction of the epistle entitled To the Hebrews has not the apostle's rudeness in speech, who confessed himself rude in speech, that is, in style, but that the epistle is better Greek in the framing of its diction, will be admitted by everyone who is able to discern differences of style. But again on the other hand, that the thoughts of the epistle are admirable, and not inferior to the acknowledged writings of the apostle, to this also everyone will consent as true who has given attention to reading the apostle. . . . But as for myself, if I were to state my own opinion I should say that the thoughts are the apostle's, but that the style and composition belong to one who called to mind the apostle's teachings and, as it were, made short notes of what his master said. If any church, therefore, holds this epistle as Paul's, let it be commended for this also. For not without reason have the men of old time handed it down as Paul's. But who wrote the epistle, in truth God knows. (Eusebius, *Hist. eccl.* 6.25.11–14, trans. Oulton)

Purpose

Discernment of the author's purpose in this letter depends, of course, to a very large degree on the identification of the addressees. There can be no question but that it is a major, probably *the* major, purpose of the book to warn the readers of a danger and to exhort them to faithfulness (thus the frequent applications [e.g., 2:1–3; 3:6, 12–14; 4:1, 11–13; 6:1–12; 10:26–31, 35–39; 12:3–17; 13:9]). If the argument presented above is correct, then it is the author's concern to warn Jewish Christian readers against apostatizing to their former Judaism. Possibly the readers were in danger of retreating into a proto-gnosticism, with its angel worship (cf. 1:5–14; 2:5–9), its "diverse and strange teachings" (13:9), and its concern with foods (cf. 9:10).[11] The author himself refers to his writing as "my word of exhortation" (13:22).

If the readers are to be motivated to remain faithful, they must come to an understanding of the true significance of Christianity. Accordingly, the author sets forth the incomparable superiority, together with the utter finality and definitive nature, of God's work in Jesus Christ. Christianity rightly understood is thus absolute in character and universal in scope. It is indeed nothing less than the fruition of God's intended purposes from the beginning and therefore the fulfillment of what "in many and various ways God spoke of old to our fathers by the prophets" (1:1). The inescapable conclusion is that a turning away from Christianity to any other way, regardless of how excellent in itself, is altogether ruled out. The answer to any such tendency is to be found in an

---

11. T. W. Manson ("The Problem of the Epistle to the Hebrews") went so far as to identify the addressees as members of the church at Colossae, who were subject to the heretical, gnostic teachings countered by Paul in his Letter to the Colossians (see Col. 2).

understanding of the true significance of Jesus Christ and his work.[12] It is this, therefore, that accounts for the high christology of the book together with its full explanation of Christ's priestly work. Christianity by its nature is far more than a new Jewish sect; it is of absolute, universal, and permanent significance.

All other motifs in Hebrews are subordinate to this central purpose of the author. Although there is evidence in the book that the author intends to combat heretical teachings of what probably was a form of Jewish gnosticism, this is decidedly a secondary concern.

Form and Structure

The literary genre of Hebrews is an exhortatory sermon ("word of exhortation," 13:22; cf. the same expression in Acts 13:15). It begins not with the usual identification of author and readers followed by a salutation and thanksgiving, but rather with an impressive christological prologue that in many respects resembles the prologue to the Gospel of John. Nevertheless, it is plain, as we have seen, that Hebrews is directed to a specific community. Moreover, the book does end like an epistle, including some items of personal information about the author's circumstances and those of a mutual friend, Timothy, as well as greetings and benedictions.

What we have in the book of Hebrews, then, is a sermon-treatise that the author sent to a particular community as a letter. The distinctive alternation of exhortation and argumentative discourse is striking and is a fundamental characteristic of the book:

Discourse	Mixed	Exhortation/Application
1:1–14		2:1–4
2:5–3:6		3:7–19
	4:1–16	
5:1–10		5:11–6:12
6:13–10:18		10:19–39
11:1–40		12:1–17
12:18–24		12:25–13:6
	13:7–21	

Although the central purpose of Hebrews is clear, it is precisely its alternating mixture of discourse and exhortation that sometimes makes the structure of the book and the sequence of the argument difficult to discern. In addition to the frequent insertion of exhortations, sections of the discourse often are

12. See Webster, "One Who Is Son."

bridged by no more than a common word, the same argument can be restated often with only slight variations, and summarizing sections can obscure the flow of the argument.

Accordingly, the structure of the book has generated considerable discussion.[13] Albert Vanhoye has devoted great time and energy to the literary analysis of Hebrews in a series of publications, mainly in French,[14] yet not all have been convinced by his arguments.[15] In very general terms it may be said that the argument of the book proceeds from christology (1:1–3:6), to the high priesthood of Jesus (4:14–5:10; 7:1–8:6), to the superiority of the new covenant[16] and Christ's sacrificial work (8:7–10:18). But interspersed throughout are warnings and exhortations. George Guthrie rightly observes that "the expositional material serves the hortatory purpose of the whole work."[17] Since Hebrews is a work that intends to persuade, its rhetoric has been the focus of much study. The author makes use of many rhetorical devices familiar to us from the ancient world.[18]

A major turning point of the book comes in 10:19. To be sure, exhortation and application are mixed in with the argument before this point, but the heart of the epistle's main doctrinal argument is concluded with 10:18. The last part of the letter focuses on faith (10:19–11:40) but includes various applications, sprinkled, as in the first part, with repeated warnings.[19]

It is agreed on by all that the literary style of the author involves an impressive artistry. Often, on close examination, a concentric symmetry can be discerned and also an abundance of small and large chiastic structures.[20] For example, 2:1–4 is symmetrically shaped; the sequence of Christ-angels-Christ in 1:5–8 is repeated in 1:13–2:4; and 3:1 is found again in nearly symmetrical form in 4:14.

Unity of the Book

Some scholars have regarded chapter 13 as not originally belonging with the first twelve chapters but added only later to give the treatise the appearance of

13. See Guthrie, *The Structure of Hebrews*.

14. For a convenient summary, see Black, "The Problem of the Literary Structure of Hebrews."

15. See especially Swetnam, "Form and Content in Hebrews 1–6"; idem, "Form and Content in Hebrews 7–13."

16. On this subject, see Lehne, *The New Covenant in Hebrews*.

17. Guthrie, *The Structure of Hebrews*, 143. Barnabas Lindars observes, "The author is dealing with an extremely urgent practical situation which demands his utmost skill in the art of persuasion" ("The Rhetorical Structure of Hebrews," 384).

18. See the excellent discussion in deSilva, *Perseverance in Gratitude*, 35–58. In an earlier work deSilva (*Despising Shame*) focused on the importance of the honor/shame paradigm for the author's rhetoric. For the author's style, in particular the use of rhetorical devices, see Trotter, *Interpreting the Epistle to the Hebrews*, 163–84.

19. Because of the intensely practical concern of the author, Barnabas Lindars argues that the climax of the book is 10:19–12:29 ("The Rhetorical Structure of Hebrews," 384).

20. See the exhaustive study of this in Heil, *Hebrews*.

a letter. Admittedly, it is not a part of the argument of the book and consists mainly of an assortment of unconnected ethical injunctions, an elaborate doxology, and personal information, including salutations and a benediction. Nevertheless, much of the content of chapter 13 is closely related to the emphases of chapters 1–12, and the way in which pentateuchal material (i.e., material from Genesis through Deuteronomy) is midrashically elaborated and applied in 13:10–15 is quite similar to the use of the OT throughout the book. There is no compelling reason to deny that chapter 13 belongs with the preceding twelve chapters.[21]

The Midrashic Use of the Old Testament

About thirty citations and more than seventy allusions to the OT have been counted in Hebrews. The author regularly follows the Greek (LXX) rather than the Hebrew (Masoretic) text that has come down to us. It is primarily this that accounts for differences between the citations as found in Hebrews and in our English translations of the OT (which are based on the Masoretic Text).[22]

The author employs a christological hermeneutic (discussed in chap. 2 above). That is, Christ is seen to be the key to the real meaning of the OT as it can now be understood in this era of fulfillment. This involves a recontextualizing of the OT texts. From this point of view, all of the OT points directly or indirectly to Christ, who is by definition the telos (goal) of God's saving purposes.[23] The dawning of the eschatological age in Christ[24] and the experience of fulfillment through his death and resurrection provide the writers of the NT, including the anonymous author of Hebrews, with a dramatically new point of orientation from which the OT can be read with new understanding.

A remarkable feature of Hebrews is its prominent use of the OT and the midrashic treatment of the texts—that is, practical exposition of the quotation, employing specific words taken from the quotation. The argument of the book is largely carried on through the midrashic treatment of OT material.[25] Chapter 1, after the opening sentence, consists of an argument concerning the superiority of the Son to the angels based on seven OT quotations that are presented with virtually no comment. In 2:6–8 a quotation from Psalm 8:4–6 is presented followed by a midrashic commentary. Probably most im-

21. For a brilliant demonstration that chapter 13 belongs with the preceding twelve chapters, see Filson, "*Yesterday.*"

22. See Thomas, "The Old Testament Citations in Hebrews"; France, "The Writer of Hebrews as a Biblical Expositor"; Guthrie, "Hebrews' Use of the Old Testament."

23. In Hebrews "perfection" is a teleological idea that refers to the reaching of a goal. See Peterson, *Hebrews and Perfection.*

24. On the importance of eschatology for the author, see Mackie, *Eschatology and Exhortation in the Epistle to the Hebrews.*

25. See Caird, "The Exegetical Method of the Epistle to the Hebrews."

pressive in this regard is the author's artistic construction of 3:12–4:11, which is based on the quotation (with several refrains) of Psalm 95:7–11 together with a midrashic application of the passage to the situation of the readers.[26] The next major section of the book may be said to depend on the citation of Psalm 2:7 and Psalm 110:4 in 5:5–6. The connection of these two passages is one of the author's greatest contributions to the understanding of the priestly work of Christ.[27]

The argument about the priesthood of Melchizedek, interrupted by a lengthy discussion (5:11–6:12), resumes in 7:1, where (in addition to the use of Gen. 14) Psalm 110:4 is cited again twice.[28] The argument of chapter 7 consists of a skillful elaboration of OT texts. Chapter 8 depends on the lengthy quotation from Jeremiah 31:31–34. In chapter 9 we again encounter a midrash-like presentation of material drawn from the Pentateuch, but with little explicit quotation. Chapter 10 combines a quotation of Psalm 40:6–8 with a brief midrashic commentary, followed by the requoting of Jeremiah 31:33–34, and an exhortation that concludes with the citation of Habakkuk 2:3–4. Chapter 11, of course, depends heavily on the OT in its description of the heroes of faith. In chapter 12 we again encounter in the midst of exhortation the quotation and midrashic treatment of OT material (Prov. 3:11–12; Hag. 2:6). In short, OT material is pervasive in Hebrews, indeed, one may say, indispensable to the author.

Thus practically the entire argument of the book rests on OT passages. Indeed, the author seems to have structured his argument around key quotations. His favorite practice is to quote an appropriate passage and then comment on the passage in the manner of Jewish midrash, applying its truth to the readers in a most practical way. This procedure is reminiscent of the commentaries on Scripture produced by the Qumran community (cf. the commentaries on Habakkuk, Micah, Nahum, and Psalm 37 found among the Dead Sea Scrolls).

In the view of the early church and the author of Hebrews, a christocentric interpretation of the OT entails the determination of the ultimate intention of the divine inspirer of Scripture and the recognition of the underlying unity of God's work in history. Only from a perspective such as this can the fundamental importance of the OT and the interpretive procedure of the author be appreciated. In his approach to the OT he is similar to other NT writers, for with them he shares the excitement of the joy and fulfillment of the gospel.[29]

26. See Enns, "Creation and Re-Creation."

27. See Hagner, "The Son of God as Unique High Priest."

28. The prominence of Psalm 110 in the author's argument led George Buchanan to refer to Hebrews as "a homiletical midrash based on Psalm 110" (*To the Hebrews*, xix.). Although this is an overstatement, it is not without truth. On the parallels between Hebrews' view of Melchizedek and those at Qumran, see Mason, *"You Are a Priest Forever."*

29. For helpful comparison with postbiblical Jewish exegesis, see Docherty, *The Use of the Old Testament in Hebrews.*

Theological Emphases

In its broader outlines, the perspective of the author is in accord with other writers of the NT. His high christology[30] and his use of dualistic language to speak of the world above and the world below, resembles the Gospel of John. His similarities with Paul have often been noted. I mention only the high view of Christ, the substitutionary atonement accomplished by Christ, and the contrasting of old and new covenants.

Certain theological emphases of the book, however, may stem from the Hellenistic Jewish circle represented by Stephen and the seven men chosen to relieve the Twelve from their social work. Stephen (Acts 7) was, to our knowledge, the first in the early church to begin to articulate the true, and hence universal, significance of Christianity and the implications of this for the Jerusalem temple and Judaism itself. The stress in Hebrews on these matters is very similar. There is, of course, a clear sense in which the OT is upheld in Hebrews. The OT is repeatedly appealed to and cited as the very oracles of God, who continues to speak through these ancient writings. Yet the authority of these writings is not self-contained but rather is recognized only in the sense that they point to what has occurred in and through Christ. For the old order, pointing to what yet lay in the future, was intrinsically incomplete. It was valid as preparation, but as one of its own authors admitted, something new was needed (Jer. 31:31–34). And thus our author, with a courage resembling Stephen's, points out the invalidity of the old now that the new has come. Like all NT writers, he works within the tension existing between the continuing authority of the OT, as a witness to the truth of Christianity, and the obvious sense in which the old must give away to the new. Indeed, for him the old no longer finds meaning in itself but only in that to which it points, God's definitive revelation in his Son. The new is what the old had promised. Since what Jeremiah had prophesied has now come, the old takes on not less meaning but more meaning; always, however, the old finds meaning not in itself, but as if it were a series of arrows pointing to God's definitive revelation in his Son (see 1:1–2).

The very strong emphasis on the discontinuity between the old and the new that we encounter in Hebrews raises difficult problems with regard to the Christian perception of Judaism. For our author, Judaism is outmoded. It has performed its necessary task in preparation for the universal work that God had always intended to do through Israel, from the promise that in Abraham all the nations of the earth would be blessed to Isaiah's repeated stress on the calling of Israel to be a light to the nations. Israel is a blessing and light to the Gentiles through the Christian church. From our author's perspective, Judaism finds its fulfillment in Christianity.

30. See Bauckham, "The Divinity of Jesus Christ in the Epistle to the Hebrews."

It is crucial, however, to note that neither the author nor his readers believed that they had become disloyal to their Jewish heritage or had stopped being Jews in becoming Christians. On the contrary, their Christian faith was the flowering of Israel's hope. Thus there is a strong continuity between Judaism and Christianity. But with the coming of the Messiah, the Son of God and "great high priest" (4:14), Judaism had reached its goal. And thus we also confront the strong motifs of discontinuity in Hebrews. That discontinuity cannot be denied even if anti-Judaism is not the most appropriate way to describe it.[31] Salvation is no longer to be found in the sacrifices of the temple but in what they pointed forward to: *the all-sufficient, once-for-all sacrifice of Christ*. The Jewish Christian readers, therefore, must not contemplate returning to their earlier Judaism.

Hellenistic Philosophy and Hebrews

The language and theology of Hebrews are those of a Christian who was a Hellenistic Jew. But how much was he influenced by his Hellenism? In particular, to what degree, if at all, does he owe his unique perspective about heavenly archetypes and earthly copies to the Alexandrian Jew Philo (ca. 20 BC to AD 50)? Philo's view of reality was derived from the dualistic idealism of Plato, in which for every object perceived with the senses there is a corresponding perfect, changeless archetypal "idea" or "form" that can be known only through the intellect. There is an obvious similarity between this perspective and that of our author when he speaks of earthly copies of heavenly realities (e.g., 8:1, 5; 9:11, 23, 24; 10:1; 11:1, 3). The language of 8:5 may indeed seem Platonic in tone, yet it must be noted that this view of the earthly sanctuary predates Plato, being found within the Pentateuch (Exod. 25:9, 40; 26:30; 27:8; cf. 1 Chron. 28:19; Wis. 9:8). But more important is that the dualism in Hebrews is not oriented toward the metaphysical questions of the philosophers. The author's basic framework is *a temporal or eschatological one* in which Christ and his work bring a fulfillment that corresponds with God's perfect and eternal purpose. The heavenly realm has been entered by Christ (something impossible in the Platonic scheme), and there he has accomplished what the earthly prototypes pointed toward. The earthly copies and the heavenly realities correspond as promise and fulfillment. The promise is the shadow or copy; the fulfillment is the good things that have come. Christ on the cross, and thus in the historical process, accomplished what the earthly prototypes pointed toward. Because of its glorious nature and its definitive character, the fulfillment brought by Christ in history is expressed in the exalted language of the spiritual realm, the language of eternal reality. But this is far removed from the perspective of Plato and Philo.[32]

---

31. See Kim, *Polemic in the Book of Hebrews*.

32. See Williamson, "Platonism and Hebrews;" idem, *Philo and the Epistle to the Hebrews*. The most useful book on the background of Hebrews remains Hurst, *The Epistle to the Hebrews*.

The Legacy of Hebrews

The unknown author of Hebrews almost certainly was a Hellenistic Jew. His elegant style and vocabulary are clearly Hellenistic, but his orientation is much more that of a Jewish Christian with an overarching paradigm of promise and fulfillment. As a Hellenistic Jew, he is open to the radical consequences for the old now that the new has come. The theology of Hebrews is, at the same time, in basic accord with other NT writings. Thus, in agreement with Paul and others, Hebrews stresses the definitive, eschatological character and the universal significance of Christ.

Hebrews, like every book of the NT, must be understood in its own historical context, even if that must be, to some degree, a product of inference. Yet there is also a sense in which the message of Hebrews transcends its own historical situation. This message has a universal applicability and an ongoing relevance to every generation of Christians, whatever their cultural context. For the main themes of this book—the incomparable superiority and finality of Christ, the fulfillment of the old covenant, the universal significance of the Christian faith—must always be central wherever authentic Christianity is to be found. But more than that, this book, with its rich theological content, is at the same time wonderfully practical. From its pages Christians of every era, Jewish and Gentile alike, can learn of the pilgrimage of faith and of the great personal resources available to them through the once-for-all, finished work of Christ.[33]

Bibliography

Books and Articles

Allen, David L. *Lukan Authorship of Hebrews.* NAC Studies in Bible and Theology. Nashville: B&H Publishing Group, 2010.

Allen, David M. *Deuteronomy and Exhortation in Hebrews: A Study in Narrative Representation.* WUNT 2/238. Tübingen: Mohr Siebeck, 2008.

———. "More Than Just Numbers: Deuteronomic Influence in Hebrews 3:7–4:11." *TynBul* 58 (2007): 129–49.

Anderson, Charles P. "The Epistle to the Hebrews and the Pauline Letter Collection." *HTR* 59 (1966): 429–38.

———. "Hebrews among the Letters of Paul." *SR* 5 (1975–76): 258–66.

Barrett, C. K. "The Eschatology of the Epistle to the Hebrews." In *The Background of the New Testament and Its Eschatology: Edited by W. D. Davies and W. Daube in Honour of Charles Harold Dodd,* 363–93. Cambridge: Cambridge University Press, 1956.

Bateman, Herbert W., IV. *Early Jewish Hermeneutics and Hebrews 1:5–13: The Impact of Early Jewish Exegesis on the Interpretation of a Significant New Testament Passage.* AUS 7/193. New York: Peter Lang, 1997.

———, ed. *Four Views on the Warning Passages in Hebrews.* Grand Rapids: Kregel, 2007.

———. "Psalm 45:6–7 and Its Christological Contributions to Hebrews." *TJ* 22 (2001): 3–21.

33. See Lane, *Hebrews.*

Bauckham, Richard. "The Divinity of Jesus Christ in the Epistle to the Hebrews." In *The Epistle to the Hebrews and Christian Theology*, edited by Richard Bauckham, Daniel R. Driver, Trevor A. Hart, and Nathan MacDonald, 15–36. Grand Rapids: Eerdmans, 2009.

Bauckham, Richard, Daniel R. Driver, Trevor A. Hart, and Nathan MacDonald, eds. *A Cloud of Witnesses: The Theology of Hebrews in its Ancient Contexts*. LNTS 387. London: T&T Clark, 2008.

———, eds. *The Epistle to the Hebrews and Christian Theology*. Grand Rapids: Eerdmans, 2009.

Baugh, Steven M. "The Cloud of Witnesses in Hebrews 11." *WTJ* 68 (2006): 113–32.

Betz, Otto. "Firmness in Faith: Hebrews 11:1 and Isaiah 28:16." In *Jesus, der Herr der Kirche: Aufsätze zur biblischen Theologie II*, 425–46. WUNT 52. Tübingen: Mohr Siebeck, 1990.

Black, David Alan. "Hebrews 1:1–4: A Study in Discourse Analysis." *WTJ* 49 (1987): 175–94.

———. "On the Pauline Authorship of Hebrews." *FM* 16 (1999): 32–51, 78–86.

———. "The Problem of the Literary Structure of Hebrews: An Evaluation and Proposal." *GTJ* 7 (1986): 163–77.

Bligh, John. *Chiastic Analysis of the Epistle to the Hebrews*. Oxford: Athenaeum, 1966.

———. "The Structure of Hebrews." *HeyJ* 5 (1964): 170.

Brown, Raymond E., and John P. Meier. *Antioch and Rome: New Testament Cradles of Catholic Christianity*. New York: Paulist Press, 1983.

Bruce, F. F. "The Kerygma of Hebrews." *Int* 23 (1969): 3–19.

———. "'To the Hebrews': A Document of Roman Christianity?" *ANRW* II.25.4 (1987): 3496–521.

———. "'To the Hebrews' or 'To the Essenes'?" *NTS* 9 (1962–63): 217–32.

Bulley, Alan D. "Death and Rhetoric in the Hebrews 'Hymn to Faith.'" *SR* 25 (1996): 409–23.

Burns, Lanier. "Hermeneutical Issues and Principles in Hebrews as Exemplified in the Second Chapter." *JETS* 39 (1996): 587–607.

Caird, G. B. "The Exegetical Method of the Epistle to the Hebrews." *CJT* 5 (1959): 44–51.

Carlston, Charles E. "Eschatology and Repentance in the Epistle to the Hebrews." *JBL* 78 (1959): 296–302.

Cockerill, Gareth Lee. "The Better Resurrection (Heb. 11:35): A Key to the Structure and Rhetorical Purpose of Hebrews 11." *TynBul* 51 (2000): 214–34.

———. "Hebrews 1:6: Source and Significance." *BBR* 9 (1999): 51–64.

———. "Structure and Interpretation in Hebrews 8:1–10:18: A Symphony in Three Movements." *BBR* 11 (2001): 179–201.

Cody, Aelred. *Heavenly Sanctuary and Liturgy in the Epistle to the Hebrews: The Achievement of Salvation in the Epistle's Perspective*. St. Meinrad, IN: Grail, 1960.

Collins, Raymond F. *Letters That Paul Did Not Write: The Epistle to the Hebrews and the Pauline Pseudepigrapha*. Wilmington, DE: Michael Glazier, 1988.

Cosby, Michael R. *The Rhetorical Composition and Function of Hebrews 11 in Light of Example Lists in Antiquity*. Macon, GA: Mercer University Press, 1988.

Croy, N. Clayton. *Endurance in Suffering: Hebrews 12:1–13 in Its Rhetorical, Religious, and Philosophical Context*. SNTSMS 98. Cambridge: Cambridge University Press, 1998.

Dahl, Nils A. "'A New and Living Way': The Approach to God according to Hebrews 10:19–25." *Int* 5 (1951): 401–12.

Dahms, John V. "The First Readers of Hebrews." *JETS* 20 (1977): 365–75.

D'Angelo, Mary Rose. *Moses in the Letter to the Hebrews*. SBLDS 42. Missoula, MT: Scholars Press, 1979.

Demarest, Bruce. *A History of the Interpretation of Hebrews 7:1–10 from the Reformation to the Present*. BGBE 19. Tübingen: Mohr Siebeck, 1976.

deSilva, David A. *Bearing Christ's Reproach: The Challenge of Hebrews in an Honor Culture*. North Richland Hills, TX: Bibal Press, 1999.

———. *Despising Shame: Honor Discourse and Community Maintenance in the Epistle to the Hebrews*. SBLDS 152. Atlanta: Scholars Press, 1995.

———. "Entering God's Rest: Eschatology and the Socio-Rhetorical Strategy of Hebrews." *TJ* 21 (2000): 25–43.

Dey, Lala Kalyan Kumar. *The Intermediary World and Patterns of Perfection in Philo and Hebrews*. SBLDS 25. Missoula, MT: Scholars Press, 1975.

Docherty, Susan E. *The Use of the Old Testament in Hebrews: A Case Study in Early Jewish Bible Interpretation*. WUNT 2/260. Tübingen: Mohr Siebeck, 2009.

Dolfe, Karl-Gustav E. "Hebrews 2,16 under the Magnifying Glass." *ZNW* 84 (1993): 289–94.

Donelson, Lewis R. *From Hebrews to Revelation: A Theological Introduction*. Louisville: Westminster John Knox, 2000.

Dumbrell, William J. "The Spirits of Just Men Made Perfect." *EvQ* 48 (1976): 154–59.

Dunnill, John. *Covenant and Sacrifice in the Letter to the Hebrews*. SNTSMS 75. Cambridge: Cambridge University Press, 1992.

Ebert, Daniel J., IV. "The Chiastic Structure of the Prologue to Hebrews." *TJ* 13 (1992): 163–79.

Eisenbaum, Pamela Michelle. *The Jewish Heroes of Christian History: Hebrews 11 in Its Literary Context*. SBLDS 156. Atlanta: Scholars Press, 1997.

Emmrich, Martin. "Hebrews 6:4–6—Again! (A Pneumatological Inquiry)." *WTJ* 65 (2003): 83–95.

———. *Pneumatological Concepts in the Epistle to the Hebrews: Amtcharisma, Prophet, and Guide of the Eschatological Exodus*. Lanham, MD: University Press of America, 2003.

Enns, Peter E. "Creation and Re-Creation: Psalm 95 and Its Interpretation in Hebrews 3:1–4:13." *WTJ* 55 (1993): 255–80.

Filson, Floyd V. *"Yesterday": A Study of Hebrews in Light of Chapter 13*. SBT 4. Naperville, IL: Allenson, 1967.

France, R. T. "The Writer of Hebrews as a Biblical Expositor." *TynBul* 47 (1996): 245–76.

Gelardini, Gabriella, ed. *Hebrews: Contemporary Methods, New Insights*. BIS 75. Leiden: Brill, 2005.

Gheorghita, Radu. *The Role of the Septuagint in Hebrews: An Investigation of Its Influence with Special Consideration to the Use of Habakkuk 2:3–4 in Hebrews 10:37–38*. WUNT 2/160. Tübingen: Mohr Siebeck, 2003.

Gleason, Randall C. "Angels and the Eschatology of Heb 1–2." *NTS* 49 (2003): 90–107.

———. "The Eschatology of the Warning in Hebrews 10:26–31." *TynBul* 53 (2002): 97–120.

———. "The Old Testament Background of Rest in Hebrews 3:7–4:11." *BSac* 157 (2000): 281–303.

———. "The Old Testament Background of the Warning in Hebrews 6:4–8." *BSac* 155 (1998): 62–91.

Gooding, David. *An Unshakeable Kingdom: The Letter to the Hebrews for Today*. Grand Rapids: Eerdmans, 1989.

Gray, Patrick. *Godly Fear: The Epistle to the Hebrews and Greco-Roman Critiques of Superstition*. SBLAB 16. Atlanta: Society of Biblical Literature, 2003.

Guthrie, George H. "Hebrews in Its First-Century Contexts: Recent Research." In *The Face of New Testament Studies*, edited by Scot McKnight and Grant R. Osborne, 414–43. Grand Rapids: Baker Academic, 2004.

———. "Hebrews' Use of the Old Testament: Recent Trends in Research." *CurBS* 1 (2003): 271–94.

———. *The Structure of Hebrews: A Text-Linguistic Analysis*. Grand Rapids: Baker Academic, 1998.

Hagner, Donald A. *Encountering the Book of Hebrews: An Exposition*. EBS. Grand Rapids: Baker Academic, 2002.

———. "Hebrews: A Book for Today." In *Christology, Hermeneutics, and Hebrews. Profiles from the History of Interpretation*, edited by Jon C. Laansma and Daniel J. Treier, 213–24. LNTS 423. New York: T&T Clark, 2012.

———. "Interpreting the Epistle to the Hebrews." In *The Literature and Meaning of Scripture*, edited by Morris A. Inch and C. Hassell Bullock, 217–42. Grand Rapids: Baker Academic, 1981.

———. "The Son of God as Unique High Priest: The Christology of the Epistle to the Hebrews." In *Contours of Christology in the New Testament*, edited by Richard N. Longenecker, 247–67. Grand Rapids: Eerdmans, 2005.

———. *The Use of the Old and New Testaments in Clement of Rome*. NovTSup 34. Leiden: Brill, 1973.

Hahn, Scott W. "A Broken Covenant and the Curse of Death: A Study of Hebrews 9:15–22." *CBQ* 66 (2004): 416–36.

Hamm, Dennis. "Faith in the Epistle to the Hebrews: The Jesus Factor." *CBQ* 52 (1990): 270–91.

Harrington, Daniel J. *What Are They Saying about the Letter to the Hebrews?* Mahwah, NJ: Paulist Press, 2005.

Hay, David M. *Glory at the Right Hand: Psalm 110 in Early Christianity*. SBLMS 18. Nashville: Abingdon, 1973.

Heil, John Paul. *Hebrews: Chiastic Structures and Audience Response*. CBQMS 46. Washington, DC: Catholic Biblical Association of America, 2010.

Horbury, William. "The Aaronic Priesthood in the Epistle to the Hebrews." In *Messianism among Jews and Christians: Twelve Biblical and Historical Studies*, 227–54. New York: T&T Clark, 2003.

Horton, Fred L., Jr. *The Melchizedek Tradition: A Critical Examination of the Sources to the Fifth Century A.D. and in the Epistle to the Hebrews*. SNTSMS 30. Cambridge: Cambridge University Press, 1976.

Hughes, Graham. *Hebrews and Hermeneutics: The Epistle to the Hebrews as a New Testament Example of Biblical Interpretation*. SNTSMS 36. Cambridge: Cambridge University Press, 1979.

Hurst, L. D. "Apollos, Hebrews, and Corinth: Bishop Montefiore's Theory Examined." *SJT* 38 (1985): 505–13.

———. "The Christology of Hebrews 1 and 2." In *The Glory of Christ in the New Testament: Studies in Christology in Memory of George Bradford Caird*, edited by L. D. Hurst and N. T. Wright, 151–64. Oxford: Clarendon, 1987.

———. *The Epistle to the Hebrews: Its Background and Thought*. SNTSMS 65. Cambridge: Cambridge University Press, 1990.

Isaacs, Marie E. *Sacred Space: An Approach to the Theology of the Epistle to the Hebrews*. JSNTSup 73. Sheffield: JSOT Press, 1992.

Johnson, Richard W. *Going outside the Camp: The Soteriological Function of the Levitical Critique in the Epistle to the Hebrews*. JSNTSup 209. Sheffield: Sheffield Academic Press, 2001.

Johnsson, William G. "The Pilgrimage Motif in the Book of Hebrews." *JBL* 97 (1978): 239–51.

Joslin, Barry C. "Can Hebrews Be Structured? An Assessment of Eight Approaches." *CurBS* 6 (2007): 99–129.

Käsemann, Ernst. *The Wandering People of God: An Investigation of the Letter to the Hebrews*. Translated by Roy A. Harrisville and Irving L. Sandberg. 2nd ed. Minneapolis: Augsburg, 1984.

Kim, Lloyd. *Polemic in the Book of Hebrews: Anti-Judaism, Anti-Semitism, Supersessionism?* PTMS 64. Eugene, OR: Wipf & Stock, 2006.

Kistemaker, Simon J. *The Psalm Citations in the Epistle to the Hebrews*. Amsterdam: G. van Soest, 1961.

Kobelski, Paul J. *Melchizedek and Melchireša*. CBQMS 10. Washington, DC: Catholic Biblical Association, 1981.

Koester, Craig R. *The Dwelling of God: Tabernacle in the Old Testament, Intertestamental Jewish Literature, and the New Testament*. CBQMS 22. Washington, DC: Catholic Biblical Association, 1989.

Koester, Helmut. "'Outside the Camp': Hebrews 13:9–14." *HTR* 55 (1963): 299–315.

Köstenberger, Andreas J. "Jesus, the Mediator of a 'Better Covenant': Comparatives in the Book of Hebrews." *FM* 21 (2004): 30–49.

Kurianal, James. *Jesus Our High Priest: Ps 110,4 as the Substructure of Heb 5,1–7,28*. EUS 23/693. New York: Peter Lang, 2000.

Laansma, Jon. *"I Will Give You Rest": The Rest Motif in the New Testament with Special Reference to Matthew 11 and Hebrews 3–4*. WUNT 98. Tübingen: Mohr Siebeck, 1997.

Lane, William. *Hebrews: A Call to Commitment*. Peabody, MA: Hendrickson, 1998.

Lehne, Susanne. *The New Covenant in Hebrews*. JSNTSup 44. Sheffield: JSOT Press, 1990.

Leithart, Peter J. "Womb of the World: Baptism and Priesthood of the New Covenant in Hebrews 10:19–22." *JSNT* 78 (2000): 49–65.

Leschert, Dale F. *Hermeneutical Foundations of Hebrews: A Study in the Validity of the Epistle's Interpretation of Some Core Citations from the Psalms*. NABPRDS 10. Lewiston, NY: Mellen, 1994.

Lincoln, Andrew T. *Hebrews: A Guide*. New York: T&T Clark, 2006.

———. "Sabbath, Rest, and Eschatology in the New Testament." In *From Sabbath to Lord's Day: A Biblical, Historical, and Theological Investigation*, edited by D. A. Carson, 197–220. Grand Rapids: Zondervan, 1982.

Lindars, Barnabas. "The Rhetorical Structure of Hebrews." *NTS* 35 (1989): 382–406.

———. *The Theology of the Letter to the Hebrews*. NTT. Cambridge: Cambridge University Press, 1991.

Loader, William R. G. "Christ at the Right Hand—Ps. cx.1 in the New Testament." *NTS* 24 (1977–78): 199–217.

Mackie, Scott D. *Eschatology and Exhortation in the Epistle to the Hebrews*. WUNT 2/223. Tübingen: Mohr Siebeck, 2007.

MacRae, George W. "Heavenly Temple and Eschatology in the Letter to the Hebrews." *Semeia* 12 (1978): 179–99.

Manson, T. W. "The Problem of the Epistle to the Hebrews." In *Studies in the Gospels and Epistles*, 242–58. Philadelphia: Westminster, 1962.

Manson, William. *The Epistle to the Hebrews*. London: Hodder & Stoughton, 1951.

Marshall, I. Howard. "Soteriology in Hebrews." In *The Epistle to the Hebrews and Christian Theology*, edited by Richard Bauckham, Daniel R. Driver, Trevor A. Hart, and Nathan MacDonald, 253–77. Grand Rapids: Eerdmans, 2009.

Mason, Eric F. *"You Are a Priest Forever": Second Temple Jewish Messianism and the Priestly Christology of the Epistle to the Hebrews*. STDJ 74. Leiden: Brill, 2008.

Mason, Eric F., and Kevin B. McCruden. *Reading the Epistle to the Hebrews: A Resource for Students*. Leiden: Brill, 2011.

Mathewson, Dave. "Reading Heb 6:4–6 in Light of the Old Testament." *WTJ* 61 (1999): 209–25.

McCown, Wayne G. "Holiness in Hebrews." *WeslTJ* 16 (1981): 58–78.

McKnight, Scot. "The Warning Passages of Hebrews: A Formal Analysis and Theological Conclusions." *TJ* 13 (1992): 21–59.

Meier, John P. "Structure and Theology in Heb 1,1–14." *Bib* 66 (1985): 168–89.

———. "Symmetry and Theology in the Old Testament Citations of Hebrews 1:5–14." *Bib* 66 (1985): 504–33.

Mitchell, Alan C. "Holding On to Confidence: Παρρησία in Hebrews." In *Friendship, Flattery, and Frankness of Speech: Studies on Friendship in the New Testament World*, edited by John T. Fitzgerald, 203–26. NovTSup 82. Leiden: Brill, 1996.

———. "The Use of πρεπειν and Rhetorical Propriety in Hebrews 2:10." *CBQ* 54 (1992): 681–701.

Motyer, Stephen. "The Psalm Quotations of Hebrews 1: A Hermeneutic-Free Zone?" *TynBul* 50 (1999): 3–22.

Muddiman, John. "Wresting with Hebrews: τετραχηλισμένα at Hebrews 4.13." In *Understanding, Studying and Reading: New Testament Essays in Honour of John Ashton*, edited by Christopher Rowland and Crispin H. T. Fletcher-Louis, 165–73. JSNTSup 153. Sheffield: Sheffield Academic Press, 1998.

Nairne, Alexander. *The Epistle of Priesthood: Studies in the Epistle to the Hebrews*. Edinburgh: T&T Clark, 1915.

Neyrey, Jerome H. "'Without Beginning of Days or End of Life' (Hebrews 7:3): Topos for a True Deity." *CBQ* 53 (1991): 439–55.

Oberholtzer, Thomas K. "The Warning Passages in Hebrews, Part 1: The Eschatological Salvation in Hebrews 1:5–2:5." *BSac* 145 (1988): 83–97.

———. "The Warning Passages in Hebrews, Part 2: The Kingdom Rest in Hebrews 3:1–4:13." *BSac* 145 (1988): 185–96.

———. "The Warning Passages in Hebrews, Part 3: The Thorn-Infested Ground in Hebrews 6:4–12." *BSac* 145 (1988): 319–28.

———. "The Warning Passages in Hebrews, Part 4: The Danger of Willful Sin in Hebrews 10:26–39." *BSac* 145 (1988): 410–19.

———. "The Warning Passages in Hebrews, Part 5: The Failure to Heed His Speaking in Hebrews 12:25–29." *BSac* 146 (1989): 67–75.

Olbricht, Thomas H. "Hebrews as Amplification." In *Rhetoric and the New Testament: Essays from the 1992 Heidelberg Conference*, edited by Stanley E. Porter and Thomas H. Olbricht, 375–87. JSNTSup 90. Sheffield: JSOT Press, 1993.

Owen, Huw P. "The 'Stages of Ascent' in Heb. 5.11–6.3." *NTS* 3 (1956–57): 243–53.

Peterson, David G. *Hebrews and Perfection: An Examination of the Concept of Perfection in the "Epistle to the Hebrews."* SNTSMS 47. Cambridge: Cambridge University Press, 1982.

———. "The Situation of the 'Hebrews' (5:11–6:12)." *RTR* 35 (1976): 14–21.

Proctor, John. "Judgement or Vindication? Deuteronomy 32 in Hebrews 10:30." *TynBul* 55 (2004): 65–80.

Rhee, Victor. *Faith in Hebrews: Analysis within the Context of Christology, Eschatology and Ethics*. SBL 19. New York: Peter Lang, 2001.

Rice, George E. "Hebrews 6:19: Analysis of Some Assumptions concerning *Katapetasma*." *AUSS* 25 (1987): 65–71.

Rothschild, Clare K. *Hebrews as Pseudepigraphon: The History and Significance of the Pauline Attribution of Hebrews*. WUNT 235. Tübingen: Mohr Siebeck, 2009.

Salevao, Iutisone. *Legitimation in the Letter to the Hebrews: The Construction and Maintenance of a Symbolic Universe*. JSNTSup 219. Sheffield: Sheffield Academic Press, 2002.

Schaefer, James R. "The Relationship between Priestly and Servant Messianism in the Epistle to the Hebrews." *CBQ* 30 (1968): 359–85.

Schenck, Kenneth. *Cosmology and Eschatology in Hebrews: The Settings of the Sacrifice*. SNTSMS 143. Cambridge: Cambridge University Press, 2007.

———. *Understanding the Book of Hebrews: The Story behind the Sermon*. Louisville: Westminster John Knox, 2003.

Scholer, John M. *Proleptic Priests: Priesthood in the Epistle to the Hebrews*. JSNTSup 49. Sheffield: JSOT Press, 1991.

Scott, J. Julius, Jr. "*Archēgos* in the Salvation History of the Epistle to the Hebrews." *JETS* 29 (1986): 47–54.

Silva, Moisés. "Perfection and Eschatology in Hebrews." *WTJ* 39 (1977): 60–71.

Smillie, Gene R. "Contrast or Continuity in Hebrews 1.1–2?" *NTS* 51 (2005): 543–60.

———. "Ο ΛΟΓΟΣ ΤΟΥ ΘΕΟΥ in Hebrews 4:12–13." *NovT* 46 (2004): 338–59.

———. "'The One Who Is Speaking' in Hebrews 12:25." *TynBul* 55 (2004): 275–94.

———. "'The Other ΛΟΓΟΣ at the End of Heb. 4:13." *NovT* 47 (2005): 19–25.

Son, Kiwoong. *Zion Symbolism in Hebrews: Hebrews 12:18–24 as a Hermeneutical Key to the Epistle*. PBM. Waynesboro, GA: Paternoster, 2006.

Sowers, Sidney G. *The Hermeneutics of Philo and Hebrews: The Epistle to the Hebrews as a New Testament Example of Biblical Interpretation*. SNTSMS 36. Cambridge: Cambridge University Press, 1979.

Stanley, Steve. "Hebrews 9:6–10: The 'Parable' of the Tabernacle." *NovT* 37 (1995): 385–99.

———. "The Structure of Hebrews from Three Perspectives." *TynBul* 45 (1994): 245–71.

Swetnam, James. "Form and Content in Hebrews 1–6." *Bib* 53 (1972): 368–85.

———. "Form and Content in Hebrews 7–13." *Bib* 55 (1974): 333–48.

———. *Jesus and Isaac: A Study of the Epistle to the Hebrews in the Light of the Aqedah.* AnBib 94. Rome: Biblical Institute Press, 1981.

———. "A Merciful and Trustworthy High Priest: Interpreting Hebrews 2:17." *PJT* 21 (1999): 6–25.

———. "On the Literary Genre of the 'Epistle' to the Hebrews." *NovT* 11 (1969): 261–69.

———. "Sacrifice and Revelation in the Epistle to the Hebrews: Observations and Surmises on Hebrews 9:26." *CBQ* 30 (1968): 227–34.

Tasker, R. V. G. *The Gospel in the Epistle to the Hebrews.* London: Tyndale, 1950.

Thomas, Kenneth J. "The Old Testament Citations in Hebrews." *NTS* 11 (1964–65): 303–25.

Thompson, James W. *The Beginnings of Christian Philosophy: The Epistle to the Hebrews.* CBQMS 13. Washington, DC: Catholic Biblical Association, 1982.

Trompf, Garry W. "The Conception of God in Hebrews 4:12–13." *ST* 25 (1971): 123–32.

Trotter, Andrew H., Jr. *Interpreting the Epistle to the Hebrews.* GNTE. Grand Rapids: Baker Academic, 1997.

Übelacker, Walter G. "Paraenesis or Paraclesis—Hebrews as a Test Case." In *Early Christian Paraenesis in Context*, edited by James Starr and Troels Engberg-Pedersen, 319–52. BZNW 125. Berlin: de Gruyter, 2004.

Vanhoye, Albert. *Old Testament Priests and the New Priest according to the New Testament.* Petersham, MA: St. Bede's Publications, 1986.

———. *Structure and Message of the Epistle to the Hebrews.* SubBi 12. Rome: Editrice Pontificio Istituto Biblico, 1989.

Verbrugge, Verlyn D. "Towards a New Interpretation of Hebrews 6:4–6." *CTJ* 15 (1980): 61–73.

Vos, Geerhardus. "The Priesthood of Christ in the Epistle to the Hebrews." *PTR* 5 (1907): 423–47, 579–604.

———. *The Teaching of the Epistle to the Hebrews.* Grand Rapids: Eerdmans, 1956.

Webster, John. "One Who Is Son: Theological Reflections on the Exordium to the Epistle to the Hebrews." In *The Epistle to the Hebrews and Christian Theology*, edited by Richard Bauckham, Daniel R. Driver, Trevor A. Hart, and Nathan MacDonald, 69–94. Grand Rapids: Eerdmans, 2009.

Wedderburn, A. J. M. "The 'Letter' to the Hebrews and Its Thirteenth Chapter." *NTS* 50 (2004): 390–405.

Weeks, Noel K. "Admonition and Error in Hebrews." *WTJ* 39 (1976): 72–80.

Westfall, Cynthia Long. *A Discourse Analysis of the Letter to the Hebrews: The Relationship between Form and Meaning.* LNTS. New York: T&T Clark, 2005.

Williamson, Ronald. *Philo and the Epistle to the Hebrews.* ALGHJ 4. Leiden: Brill, 1970.

———. "Platonism and Hebrews." *SJT* 16 (1963): 415–24.

Wray, Judith Hoch. *Rest as a Theological Metaphor in the Epistle to the Hebrews and the Gospel of Truth: Early Christian Homiletics of Rest.* SBLDS 166. Atlanta: Scholars Press, 1998.

Yadin, Yigael. "The Dead Sea Scrolls and the Epistle to the Hebrews." *ScrHier* 4 (1958): 36–55.

Young, Norman H. "'Bearing His Reproach' (Heb 13.9–14)." *NTS* 48 (2002): 243–61.

———. "'The Day of Dedication or the Day of Atonement?'" The Old Testament Background to Hebrews 6:19–20 Revisited." *AUSS* 40 (2002): 61–68.

———. "The Gospel according to Hebrews 9." *NTS* 27 (1980–81): 198–210.

———. "ΤΟΥΤ᾽ ΕΣΤΙΝ ΤΗΣ ΣΑΡΚΟΣ ΑΥΤΟΥ (Heb. X.20): Apposition, Dependent or Explicative?" *NTS* 20 (1973–74): 100–114.

———. "'Where Jesus Has Gone as a Forerunner on Our Behalf' (Hebrews 6:20)." *AUSS* 39 (2001): 165–73.

Commentaries

Attridge, Harold. W. *The Epistle to the Hebrews*. Hermeneia. Philadelphia: Fortress, 1989.
Bruce, F. F. *The Epistle to the Hebrews*. Rev. ed. NICNT. Grand Rapids: Eerdmans, 1990.
Buchanan, George W. *To the Hebrews: Translation, Comment, and Conclusions*. AB 36. Garden City, NY: Doubleday, 1972.
Cockerill, Gareth Lee. *The Epistle to the Hebrews*. NICNT. Grand Rapids: Eerdmans, 2012.
Davies, J. H. *A Letter to Hebrews*. CBC. Cambridge: Cambridge University Press, 1967.
Delitzsch, Franz. *Commentary on the Epistle to the Hebrews*. Translated by Thomas L. Kingsbury. 2 vols. Minneapolis: Klock & Klock, 1978.
deSilva, David A. *Perseverance in Gratitude: A Socio-Rhetorical Commentary on the Epistle "to the Hebrews."* Grand Rapids: Eerdmans, 2000.
Ellingworth, Paul. *The Epistle to Hebrews: A Commentary on the Greek Text*. NIGTC. Grand Rapids: Eerdmans, 1993.
France, R. T. "Hebrews." In *The Expositor's Bible Commentary*, edited by Tremper Longman III and David E. Garland, 13:17–195. Rev. ed. Grand Rapids: Zondervan, 2005.
Gench, Frances Taylor. *Hebrews and James*. WestBC. Louisville: Westminster John Knox, 1996.
Gordon, Robert P. *Hebrews*. RNBC. Sheffield: Sheffield Academic Press, 2000.
Guthrie, Donald H. *The Letter to the Hebrews*. TNTC. 2nd ed. Grand Rapids: Eerdmans, 1990.
Guthrie, George H. *Hebrews*. NIVAC. Grand Rapids: Zondervan, 1998.
Hagner, Donald A. *Hebrews*. NIBC. Peabody, MA: Hendrickson; Grand Rapids: Baker Academic, 2011.
Harrington, Daniel J. *The Letter to the Hebrews*. NCBCNT 11. Collegeville, MN: Liturgical Press, 2005.
Héring, Jean. *The Epistle to the Hebrews*. Translated by A. W. Heathcote and P. J. Allcock. London: Epworth, 1970.
Hughes, Philip E. *A Commentary on the Epistle to the Hebrews*. Grand Rapids: Eerdmans, 2002.
Isaacs, Marie E. *Reading Hebrews and James: A Literary and Theological Commentary*. RNT. Macon, GA: Smyth & Helwys, 2002.
Jewett, Robert. *Letter to Pilgrims: A Commentary on the Epistle to the Hebrews*. New York: Pilgrim Press, 1981.
Johnson, Luke Timothy. *Hebrews*. NTL. Louisville: Westminster John Knox, 2006.
Kistemaker, Simon J. *Exposition of the Epistle to the Hebrews*. NTComm. Grand Rapids: Baker Academic, 1984.
Koester, Craig R. *Hebrews: A New Translation with Introduction and Commentary*. AB 36. New York: Doubleday, 2001.
Lane, William L. *Hebrews 1–8*. WBC 47A. Dallas: Word, 1991.
———. *Hebrews 9–13*. WBC 47B. Dallas: Word, 1991.
Long, Thomas G. *Hebrews*. IBC. Louisville: Westminster John Knox, 1997.
McKnight, Edgar V., and Christopher Church. *Hebrews-James*. SHBC. Macon, GA: Smyth & Helwys, 2004.
Mitchell, Alan C. *Hebrews*. SP 13. Collegeville, MN: Liturgical Press, 2007.
Moffatt, James. *A Critical and Exegetical Commentary on the Epistle to the Hebrews*. Edinburgh: T&T Clark, 1924.
Montefiore, Hugh. *A Commentary on the Epistle to the Hebrews*. HNTC. New York: Harper & Row, 1964.
Morris, Leon. *Hebrews*. BSC. Grand Rapids: Zondervan, 1983.
O'Brien, Peter T. *The Letter to the Hebrews*. PNTC. Grand Rapids: Eerdmans, 2010.
Pfitzner, Victor C. *Hebrews*. ANTC. Nashville: Abingdon, 1997.
Robinson, Theodore H. *The Epistle to the Hebrews*. MNTC. London: Hodder & Stoughton, 1933.
Smith, Robert H. *Hebrews*. ACNT. Minneapolis: Augsburg, 1984.

Spicq, Ceslas. *L'Epître aux Hébreux*. 3rd ed. 2 vols. EBib. Paris: Gabalda, 1952.
Stedman, Ray C. *Hebrews*. IVPNTC. Downers Grove, IL: InterVarsity, 1992.
Westcott, B. F. *The Epistle to the Hebrews: The Greek Text with Notes and Essays*. London: Macmillan, 1892.
Wilson, R. McL. *Hebrews*. NCBC. Grand Rapids: Eerdmans, 1987.
Witherington, Ben, III. *Letters and Homilies for Jewish Christians: A Socio-Rhetorical Commentary on Hebrews, James, and Jude*. Downers Grove, IL: IVP Academic, 2007.

36

James

James has been acknowledged as perhaps the most puzzling book of the NT and for a variety of reasons. Its fragmented form and content are unusual, its organization is unclear, its authorship and therefore date and provenance are uncertain, its addressees a question mark, its purpose vague, its Christian doctrine practically nil, and hence its reception in the early church was notably slow. Very little indeed is known concerning this document, and the challenge is to make what we can from its content alone.

The Traditional View of Its Authorship

The opening words of this book identify the author as "James, a servant of God and of the Lord Jesus Christ." The name "James" (Gk. *Iakōbus*) was very common in first-century Palestine. From the NT alone we know of at least five different Jameses, and there are possibly two others. Only three are of much significance in the NT. Among the twelve disciples of Jesus, two bear the name: James the son of Zebedee, and James the son of Alphaeus. The third is James the brother or half-brother of Jesus.[1] We know next to nothing about James the son of Alphaeus, but there is a slim possibility that he could be the author of the book. The other two are far more prominent. James the son of Zebedee is never mentioned apart from his younger brother John. As far as we know, he was the first of the Twelve to suffer martyrdom (Acts 12:1–2), probably in 44, but not later. If he is the author of the book, then it was written very early.

---

1. Of two other Jameses, James the son of Mary (not the mother of Jesus, but the "other Mary" present at the tomb of Jesus) and James the father of Judas (not Iscariot), we know nothing.

Author: Very possibly by James, the brother of Jesus. But it is equally possible that the prescript is pseudonymous (or "allonymous"), so that the real author is unknown to us. A third possibility is that the material of the epistle traces back to James but was put into its present shape by a later redactor.

Date: Extremely difficult to decide. If authored by the brother of Jesus, then written sometime before 62, the date of James's martyrdom. If authored by someone else, perhaps sometime between 70 and 90, though perhaps earlier.

Addressees: Possibly Jewish Christians, but possibly both Jewish and Gentile Christians. It is impossible to place the addressees in any specific locale.

Purpose: To promote righteous living.

Message/Argument: Sermonic paraenesis based largely on the teaching of Jesus, presented in the mode of Jewish wisdom literature.

Significance: Particularly important for the correction of any distortion of Paul's law-free gospel to the effect that righteous living is not required of Christians.

It is James the brother of Jesus who from earliest times has been regarded as the author of the book of James. His name is found in the mention of Jesus' family in Mark 6:3 (// Matt. 13:55; cf. Jude 1). Although we have no evidence that he followed Jesus during his ministry (cf. John 7:5), the tradition contains a reference to a special resurrection appearance of Jesus to him (1 Cor. 15:7). Note too the presence of the brothers of Jesus at prayer in "the upper room" (Acts 1:13). Subsequently, James became a "pillar" of the church in Jerusalem (Gal. 2:9) and its functional leader, presiding over the Jerusalem council and the Christian community there (Acts 15:13–21; cf. Gal. 1:19; 2:12; see also Acts 12:17; 21:18). James "the Just," as he came to be called, enjoyed a reputation for his exceptional righteousness. Eusebius records that "James was indeed a remarkable man and famous among all for righteousness" (*Hist. eccl.* 2.23.19, trans. Lake). A late tradition from Hegesippus notes that James was so often on his knees in prayer that they became like the knees of a camel (Eusebius, *Hist. eccl.* 2.23.6). Reportedly, he was martyred by the scribes and Pharisees by being thrown off the pinnacle of the temple (ironically, on the charge of "breaking the law") in about 62 (Josephus, *Ant.* 20.200).[2]

Objections to the traditional conclusion that James the brother of Jesus was the author of the book of James are the following:

1. The author does not identify himself as "the brother of Jesus" or an "apostle" (cf. Gal. 1:19) or as a leader in any other way, when to do so could have only enhanced the letter's authority. Given the commonness

---

2. For a full study of James in history and tradition, see Painter, *Just James*.

of the name "James," why would he not have done so? Nor, beyond the perfunctory 1:1; 2:1, does he refer to Jesus, contrary to what we might well expect him to do.

2. The Greek of James is of a very high quality, second in the NT only to that of the book of Hebrews.[3] This Greek fits well that of a Hellenistic Jew living in the Diaspora. Is it conceivable that a Galilean Jew who grew up in a carpenter's shop could write Greek of this quality?

3. The author regularly uses the LXX in his allusions to the OT, this again reflecting more of a Hellenistic than Palestinian context.

4. There are occasional marks of Cynic-Stoic ethics, Greek diatribe, and Hellenistic rhetoric in the book that seem strange coming from a Galilean Jew.

5. The book does not emphasize the agenda that James is known for according to other NT passages. That is, in particular, the author does not place the kind of emphasis on the law, including its ritual aspects, that one finds in, for example, Acts 21:20, 24.[4] Instead, he can refer to "the perfect law, the law of liberty" (1:25). Moreover, in 2:14–26 he seems either to misunderstand or to misrepresent the Pauline view of salvation by faith.

6. There is a notable lack of Christian doctrine in James. Not even the basic elements of the kerygma, such as the death and resurrection of Jesus, are mentioned. Could James, who agreed with Paul on the essentials of the Christian gospel (cf. Gal. 2:2, 9; Acts 15:19), have avoided all allusion to the kerygma as the basis for his ethical exhortation?

7. The early church apparently was unsure that the document was written by the brother of Jesus. Eusebius is thus obligated to put James among the *antilegomena*, the books disputed in the early church (*Hist. eccl.* 3.25.3). "It is to be observed that its authenticity is denied, since few of the ancients quote it, as is also the case with the Epistle called Jude's, which is itself one of the seven called Catholic" (*Hist. eccl.* 2.23.24, trans. Lake). Eusebius adds, "Nevertheless we know that these letters have been used publicly with the rest in most churches" (*Hist. eccl.* 2.23.24–25, trans. Lake).

Origen is the first to mention the epistle. It is not mentioned in the Muratorian Canon, a list of NT writings that goes back to the second half of the second century (see chap. 43 below).

3. Joseph Mayor writes, "On the whole, I should be inclined to rate the Greek of this Epistle as approaching more nearly to the standard of classical purity than that of any other book of the NT with the exception perhaps of the Epistle to the Hebrews" (*The Epistle of St. James*, ccxliv). He adds, however, that this Greek is not "such as could be mistaken for that of a classical writer" (ibid., ccxlv).

4. The reference to the Judaizers in Galatians 2:12 as certain men who "came from James," even if true, does not necessarily mean that they correctly represented the viewpoint of James.

The question to be asked here is whether these various observations amount to a cumulative case that tips the probability away from the traditional conclusion concerning the authorship of James. Before attempting an answer, we should note that responses can be made to each of the seven objections just described:

1. It is perhaps a little strange, but seemingly true, that only the real author would have been content to refer to himself as simply "James." A pseudonymous author could hardly have kept from specifying "an apostle" or "head of the Jerusalem church" or "brother of Jesus."
2. The excellent Greek of James should not be judged an impossibility for the brother of Jesus. A survey of the literary and archaeological data points to what is often a quite high level of Greek in Palestine, so that "the possibility can no longer be precluded that a Palestinian Jewish Christian of the first century AD wrote an epistle in good Greek."[5] There is furthermore, if preferred, the possibility of the use of a secretary to explain the quality of the letter's Greek (cf. 1 Pet. 5:12). There are also some striking vocabulary parallels in the book of James to James's speech and the apostolic letter as recorded in Acts 15:13–29.
3. For anyone writing in Greek, whether in Palestine or not, it would be natural to make use of the LXX.
4. The presence of Hellenistic thought forms in James or elsewhere in the NT, given the pervasive influence of Hellenism even in Palestine,[6] is hardly impossible.
5. James is not fundamentally at odds with Paul on the issue of the law, especially relating to the Gentiles. What he argues against in 2:14–26 is, instead, a perversion of the Pauline teaching. This need not point to a late date, since Paul himself had to defend against a similar misunderstanding already in his own lifetime (see "James and Paul" below).
6. The lack of kerygmatic content in James is due simply to the special genre and purpose of the material presented. In no way need it be assumed that James did not share the basic doctrine of the early church.
7. It should be little surprise, given its unusual content in comparison with other NT letters and its uncertain authenticity, that James was slow to be accepted in the early church. However, James does seem to have been known and used by 1 Clement in 96.[7]

5. Sevenster, Do You Know Greek?, 191. First-century Palestine was a strongly bilingual environment. "To suggest that a Jewish boy growing up in Galilee would not know Greek would be rather like suggesting that a Welsh boy brought up in Cardiff would not know English" (Argyle, "Greek among the Jews of Palestine in New Testament Times," 88).

6. As demonstrated by Hengel, Judaism and Hellenism.

7. See Hagner, The Use of the Old and New Testaments in Clement of Rome, 248–56, where the probability, "although not very considerable," is affirmed.

It will be evident from this discussion that the decision about the author-ship of James is a very difficult one. As an interesting alternative possibility, Ralph Martin and a few others have proposed a two-stage production of our book of James. In this attractive view, authentic tradition deriving from the brother of Jesus was put into its present form by a disciple-editor in Syrian Antioch who is responsible for the more Hellenistic traits of the document in our canon.[8] Unfortunately, its plausibility notwithstanding, there is not enough evidence to advance this speculation from possibility to probability.

This review of the evidence, though brief, indicates that it is impossible to rule out James the brother of Jesus as the author of the book. There is a satisfying congruence between the tradition about James being an exception-ally righteous man and the emphases of the epistle. There is no compelling reason why the author cannot have been James the brother of Jesus.[9] At the same time, however, we cannot completely exclude the alternate possibility that the book is pseudonymous. Already in the time of Jerome it was regarded as such. Jerome writes that the book of James was claimed by some to have been published by someone else under his name (*Vir. ill.* 2). Least likely of all, but again not impossible, the letter could have been written by another, little known or unknown, person named "James."

The Genre of James

Although James begins with the classic opening of a Hellenistic letter, it ends quite abruptly, and not like an actual letter.[10] It is thus more of a "literary let-ter"—that is, the use of the letter form as a means of a general publication. It most resembles a Jewish paraenetic tract or synagogue sermon, or perhaps frag-ments of different sermons. The content of James employs various rhetorical devices (such as rhetorical questions, appeals, exhortations) and vivid imagery and metaphors (a great variety, from the wind-tossed sea and scorching sun [1:6, 11] to the disappearing mist [4:14]) that are characteristic homiletical aids. If James is an actual letter, it may be classified as a "paraenetic encyclical."[11]

The organization of James has defied analysis.[12] There is no apparent pat-tern or coherent outline, and little logic to the sequence of materials. In this regard, it resembles much of the Jewish wisdom literature. The Epistle of James

8. See Martin, *James*, lxxvi–lxxvii. Syria is chosen because of the literary connections be-tween the book of James and the Gospel of Matthew, the *Didache*, and the letters of Ignatius.

9. The thoroughly Palestinian background of the epistle is demonstrated in Davids, "Pales-tinian Traditions in the Epistle of James."

10. But on this, see Francis, "The Form and Function of the Opening and Closing Paragraphs of James and I John."

11. Thus Bauckham, *James*, 13.

12. But see Taylor, *A Text-Linguistic Investigation into the Discourse Structure of James*; Cargal, *Restoring the Diaspora*.

can be classified as a kind of ad hoc Christian appropriation of wisdom. It contains an exceptionally large number of imperative verbs. The beginning of the book calls its readers to wisdom: "If any of you lack wisdom, ask God, who gives to all generously and ungrudgingly, and it will be given to you" (1:5 NRSV). And a little further on: "Who is wise and understanding among you? Show by your good life that your works are done with gentleness born of wisdom" (3:13 NRSV). James regularly employs the devices of wisdom literature: maxims, proverbs, memorable images—all devoted to the promoting of an intensely practical righteousness. "The wisdom from above is first pure, then peaceable, gentle, open to reason, full of mercy and good fruits, without uncertainty or insincerity" (3:17).

So Jewish are both the form and content of James that some have suggested that originally it was a purely Jewish document that was co-opted by a Christian writer and applied to Christian readers. This is possible, but hardly a necessary conclusion. Such a hypothesis becomes difficult when one considers the material woven into the whole of the letter that goes back to Jesus' teaching (see "James and Jesus Tradition" below). There is no reason why a Jewish Christian could not compile this wisdom document de novo. Notoriously, James, as a wisdom document, lacks gospel or kerygma, and it lacks christology. Indeed, the only explicit references to Christ are in 1:1, which is formulaic, and in 2:1. Both, however, refer to Jesus as *kyrios*. As is also the case in wisdom literature, the substructure of theology that undergirds the moral exhortation is assumed, not stated.

Themes of Jewish Wisdom

Many of the themes of Jewish wisdom are found in James. At times too the social concerns in James make him sound very much like the NT equivalent of the OT prophet Amos. Dominant, of course, is the general paraenesis (moral exhortation) itself. Among specific themes we may note the following examples:

- a theology of suffering (1:2–4, 12–15; cf. 5:10); trials and testings are to be received positively as opportunities to demonstrate steadfastness;
- emphasis on doing the law (1:25; 2:8–12; 4:11–12); "Be doers of the word, and not hearers only, deceiving yourselves" (1:22);
- the challenge of bridling the tongue (1:26; 3:3–12);[13]
- polemic against the rich (2:1–7; 5:1–6);
- concern for the afflicted: visit orphans and widows (1:27);
- prohibition of taking oaths (5:12);

13. On the importance of controlling speech in James, see Baker, *Personal Speech-Ethics in the Epistle of James*.

- keep oneself unstained from the world; "Do you not know that friendship with the world is enmity with God?" (4:4);[14]
- the brevity of life; "What is your life? For you are a mist that appears for a little time and then vanishes" (4:14);
- apocalyptic eschatology (5:7–11).[15]

James and the Jesus Tradition

Paradoxically, James has only a modicum of explicitly Christian content, while at the same time it contains many allusions to the sayings of Jesus. From this point of view, James is a most Christian book indeed. In a study of the Synoptic tradition in James, Peter Davids finds twenty "close allusions," not to mention a further twenty-eight instances of possible influence.[16] These appear to come mainly from the oral tradition underlying Q and Matthew (half of the twenty close allusions are designated as Q material by Davids). Q has long been recognized as giving an important place to wisdom. Since the ethical teaching of Jesus draws so heavily on the OT, so here too, via Jesus, is OT influence in James.

Some of the more striking examples are the following:

James 1:5: "If any of you lacks wisdom, let him ask God, who gives to all men generously and without reproaching, and it will be given him."

Matthew 7:7–8: "Ask, and it will be given you; seek, and you will find; knock, and it will be opened to you. For every one who asks receives, and he who seeks finds, and to him who knocks it will be opened."

James 1:22: "Be doers of the word, and not hearers only, deceiving yourselves."

Matthew 7:24: "Every one then who hears these words of mine and does them will be like a wise man who built his house upon the rock."

James 2:5: "Has not God chosen those who are poor in the world to be rich in faith and heirs of the kingdom which he has promised to those who love him?"

Luke 6:20: "Blessed are you poor, for yours is the kingdom of God."

Luke 7:22: "The poor have good news preached to them."

14. See Lockett, *Purity and Worldview in the Epistle of James*.

15. On eschatology as a key to understanding James, see Penner, *The Epistle of James and Eschatology*.

16. See Davids, "James and Jesus," 66–67; idem, *The Epistle of James*, 47–48. For other lists of correspondences between James and the Synoptic tradition, see Mayor, *The Epistle of St. James*, lxxxv–lxxxviii; Davies, *The Setting of the Sermon on the Mount*, 402–3; Hartin, *James and the "Q" Sayings of Jesus*, 141–42.

James 2:8: "If you really fulfill the royal law, according to the scripture, 'You shall love your neighbor as yourself,' you do well."

Matthew 22:39–40: "And a second is like it, You shall love your neighbor as yourself. On these two commandments depend all the law and the prophets."

James 2:13: "For judgment is without mercy to one who has shown no mercy; yet mercy triumphs over judgment."

Matthew 5:7: "Blessed are the merciful, for they shall obtain mercy."

James 3:12: "Can a fig tree, my brethren, yield olives, or a grapevine figs?"

Matthew 7:16: "Are grapes gathered from thorns, or figs from thistles?"

James 4:10: "Humble yourselves before the Lord and he will exalt you."

Matthew 23:12: "Whoever exalts himself will be humbled, and whoever humbles himself will be exalted."

James 4:11–12: "Do not speak evil against one another. . . . But who are you that you judge your neighbor?"

Matthew 7:1: "Judge not, that you be not judged."

James 4:13–14: "Come now, you who say, 'Today or tomorrow we will go into such and such a town and spend a year there and trade and get gain'; whereas you do not know about tomorrow."

Matthew 6:34: "Therefore do not be anxious about tomorrow, for tomorrow will be anxious for itself. Let the day's own trouble be sufficient for the day."

James 5:1: "Come now, you rich, weep and howl for the miseries that are coming upon you."

Luke 6:24–25: "But woe to you that are rich, for you have received your consolation. Woe to you that are full now, for you shall hunger."

James 5:12: "But above all, my brethren, do not swear, either by heaven or by earth or with any other oath, but let your yes be yes and your no be no, that you may not fall under condemnation."

Matthew 5:34–37: "But I say to you, Do not swear at all, either by heaven, for it is the throne of God, or by the earth, for it is his footstool. . . . Let what you say be simply 'Yes' or 'No'; anything more than this comes from evil."

This is only a small sample of the parallel Synoptic material distributed throughout James. Davids rightly concludes that "there existed an early paraenetic collection of the sayings of Jesus (oral or written)," and that "James knew a version of that block of tradition."[17] That block of tradition apparently consisted mainly of Sermon on the Mount/Sermon on the Plain material.

Christian Theology?

It is rightly said that James articulates no christology, but that is different from saying that he has none. James assumes his and his readers' christology. In two places James refers explicitly to Jesus as *kyrios* (1:1; 2:1). In the second of these, the reference to "our Lord Jesus Christ" is extended with the phrase "the Lord of glory [*tēs doxēs*]" (or perhaps "our glorious Lord"). James must be considered to hold a "high" christology.

But are there further instances of Christian theology in James? If we can assume that the epistle was originally written for Christians, then language that might otherwise be ambiguous can be taken in a Christian sense. It is not at all difficult to take the following verse as a reference to new birth through the gospel and the eschatological new creation: "Of his own will he brought us forth by the word of truth that we should be a kind of first fruits of his creatures" (1:18). Similarly, these words have Christian significance: "Receive with meekness the implanted word, which is able to save your souls" (1:21).[18]

The statement that the readers "hold the faith of our Lord Jesus Christ" (2:1) can be understood either as a subjective genitive (the faith or faithfulness that Jesus exhibited) or as an objective genitive (faith in Jesus). The "kingdom" mentioned in 2:5 is undoubtedly the kingdom proclaimed by Jesus. "The honorable name which was invoked over you" (2:7) is almost certainly the name of Jesus. Possibly the spirit that God "has made to dwell in us" (4:5) refers to the Holy Spirit, and possibly "the Lord" (4:10, 15; 5:11) refers to Jesus. Almost certainly "the Lord" refers to Jesus in 5:7–8: "Be patient, therefore, brethren, until the coming of the Lord . . . for the coming of the Lord is at hand"; as also in 5:14–15: anointing a sick person "in the name of the Lord . . . and the Lord will raise him up."

James and Paul

Undoubtedly the most famous or infamous passage in James, despite all the other wonderful material in the letter, is the discussion of faith and works in

17. Davids, "James and Jesus," 67.

18. On the possible Stoic influence in the reference to the "implanted word" (*emphytos logosn*), see Jackson-McCabe, *Logos and Law in the Letter of James.*

2:14–26, widely understood to be a blatant contradiction of Paul's teaching of salvation by faith alone.

This passage in James seems to presuppose a knowledge of either Galatians or Romans or both, unless, as is more probable, the author had only heard reports of Paul's view. It cannot be doubted that he is responding to Paul. The appeal to Genesis 15:6, a text famously used by Paul, and to the example of Abraham, demonstrates this knowledge. The problem is that James seems to have misunderstood Paul badly. He seems to argue against a perversion of Pauline teaching that turned Paul into an antinomian.

It is, of course, easy to portray Paul and James as diametrically opposed. Note, for example, these two contradictory verses:

Romans 3:28: "For we hold that a man is justified by faith apart from works of law."
James 2:24: "You see that a man is justified by works and not by faith alone."

Although we should always resist the tendency to downplay differences between NT writers and to harmonize too quickly, without listening to the distinct contrasting voices, in this case we must resist polarizing James and Paul. There is a contradiction here, but ultimately it is superficial rather than essential, more terminological than substantial. And unfortunately, it has resulted in a distortion of both Paul and James.

Paul would not have disagreed with James about the vital importance of a righteous life, and he would have readily agreed that faith without works is dead. But in Paul's mind, authentic faith includes appropriate response. Righteousness, for Paul, is not merely an option that a Christian may decide to choose or not to choose. For Paul, to have faith is to respond to the call to righteousness. Anyone who reads Paul must know immediately that this is true. Nevertheless, there were some who pushed Paul's statements to mean that salvation by grace canceled the necessity of righteous living. And thus they mocked Paul with the contemptuous remark "Since we are not under law but under grace, let us sin" (this is the statement underlying the question in Rom. 6:15; cf. 6:1; 3:8; 3:31).

No one was more upset about this misunderstanding than Paul himself. He responds several times with the strong *mē genoito*—"God forbid!" or, more accurately, "May it never be!" (Rom. 3:31; 6:2, 15). The importance of practical righteousness for Paul could hardly be clearer, and this is the case in the very books, Galatians and Romans, where he argues so strongly for salvation apart from the works of the law. For example, after a long list of "the works of the flesh," he writes, "I warn you, as I warned you before, that those who do such things shall not inherit the kingdom of God" (Gal. 5:21). And a little further on: "Do not be deceived; God is not mocked, for whatever a man sows, that he will also reap. For he who sows to his own flesh will from the flesh reap corruption; but he who sows to the Spirit will from the Spirit reap eternal life" (Gal. 6:7–8). Similarly, Romans 2:6–8: "For he will render to every man according to his works: to those who by patience in well-doing seek for glory and honor and immortality, he will give eternal life; but for those who are factious and do not obey the truth, but obey wickedness, there will be wrath and fury." Very simply, sin leads to death, and obedience leads to righteousness (Rom. 6:16). For Paul, the Christian's call to righteousness is a given. "How can we who died to sin still live in it?" (Rom. 6:2). "If you live according to the flesh you will die, but if by the Spirit you put to death the deeds of the body you will live" (Rom. 8:13). The Christian is to "walk in newness of life" (Rom. 6:4), by the Spirit, "in order that the just requirement of the law might be fulfilled in us" (Rom. 8:4).

And yet despite this unrelenting insistence on its necessity, righteousness will never be described by Paul as the cause of our salvation. That remains a matter of grace. The broken parallelism of 6:23 is evidence of this: "For the wages of sin is death, but the free gift of God is eternal life in Christ Jesus our Lord." As Martin Luther liked to put it, righteous deeds, rather than preceding salvation as its cause, follow salvation as its result.

So it is not fair to say that Paul and James are contradictory in any significant way. To be sure, Paul would not articulate the importance of righteousness using the language of James. He would never have spoken of being "justified by works" (as James does in 2:21, 24), nor would he be fond of the way James uses Genesis 15:6 and the example of Abraham. Paul can, however, at times sound exactly like James: "For it is not the hearers of the law who are righteous before God, but the doers of the law who will be justified" (Rom. 2:13). At bottom, although they express themselves differently, both Paul and James have a nonnegotiable commitment to the importance and necessity of practical righteousness.

James, however, should not be misunderstood as proclaiming a salvation by works. Although the word "works" (*erga*) often has negative connotations for Paul, James uses the word basically to mean "obedience." For him being "justified by works" is a way of referring to the indispensability of righteousness in the believer. James does not deny the priority and fundamental importance of faith. What James insists on is that faith be "completed by works" (James 2:22) and thus shown to be living rather than dead. James seems to understand "faith" not as Paul does (i.e., as itself involving the response of righteousness) but rather as mere intellectual assent to a proposition (in which sense even the demons "believe" [2:19]). James's purpose is not to articulate a soteriology but instead, by means of the teachings of wisdom, to drive home the importance of righteous living. It is probably for this reason that the word "grace" (*charis*) occurs only in James 4:6. It would be a mistake to assume that James viewed salvation as based on anything other than the work of Christ. Brevard Childs rightly concludes, "In no sense does James derive salvation from a syncretism of human and divine co-operation. God is the source of every benefit."[19]

From the preceding discussion, we may conclude that what James says about these things, and the problem thereby caused, are the result of the kind of book that he produced: not a book of doctrine, but rather a book of wisdom that presupposes doctrine—that is, a book of paraenesis or moral exhortation.

Addressees, Author, and Date

Addressees

All of the NT epistles we have looked at thus far take their names from the addressees (e.g., Romans, Corinthians, Galatians). The seven Catholic Epistles, or General Epistles, however, are called such either because we do not know the addressees or because they are addressed to a broad, varied audience rather than a specific one. The result is that these epistles get their names from their putative authors (James, Peter, John, Jude).

James is addressed to "the twelve tribes in the Dispersion," but exactly what is meant by this remains unclear. The "Dispersion" (*diaspora*) normally would refer to Jews outside the Holy Land, unless a "spiritual" dispersion and exile is in view. Are these dispersed persons exclusively Jewish Christians, or can Gentile Christians be included in the designation? On the one hand, the reference to the "twelve tribes" seems to point specifically to Jewish believers in Jesus, as would also the appropriateness of the wisdom genre for such a readership.[20] On the other hand, it is possible that the Christian community in general is understood as the manifestation of a new Israel (note that Gentile Christians are addressed as "exiles of the Dispersion" in 1 Pet. 1:1). The "twelve tribes" takes on a symbolic nuance pointing to the fulfillment of the promises to Israel in the new entity of the church (cf. Matt. 19:28; Rev. 21:12–14). James is thus an encyclical letter and applicable to a wide readership quite independent of the specific circumstances of any intended readers.

Author

As we have seen, it is very difficult to know who actually wrote this epistle. It may well have been James the brother of Jesus (cf. Gal. 1:19), as tradition has maintained. Despite questions that can be raised, nothing prohibits this conclusion. At the same time, however, possibly the book is pseudonymous

---

19. Childs, *The New Testament as Canon*, 439.

20. Dale Allison finds reasons to include non-Christian Jews among the addressees. "James reflects a first-century Christian group still battling for its place within the Jewish community, a Christian group that wishes to remain faithful members of the synagogue" ("The Fiction of James and Its *Sitz im Leben*," 570).

or by some other James. If so, little can be said of the author, other than that he was a Hellenistically influenced Jew, and perhaps that he was a teacher, if we may judge from the comment in 3:1–2.

Date

Perhaps no other NT book has been assigned such a wide variety of dates as James, ranging from early in the 40s to as late as the mid-second century.[21] This fact reflects the indeterminate character of James as a circular letter, sent to no specific community and therefore rooted in no specifics that might help in dating the document. It is simply very difficult to know the date of the epistle.

Arguing against a late date is the lack of the marks of incipient early catholicism. The contrast with the Pastoral Epistles is notable. The call to be patient in waiting for the parousia in 5:7–8 need not point to a very late date, although it does make one hesitant to put the book as early as the 40s or 50s, which seems prohibited also by the interaction with teaching related to Paul. As mentioned above, the use of Synoptic tradition in oral rather than written form probably speaks also for a first-century date, as does the probable use of James in *1 Clement*.

If the book was actually written by James the brother of Jesus, then it cannot be later than 62, the traditional date of his martyrdom. If our James is someone else, then the question remains rather open, although a somewhat later date, say between 70 and 90, might be a good guess, without ruling out the possibility of an earlier date.

The Book of James in the Church

Although he often is cast as someone who intensely disliked the book of James, Martin Luther said a few positive things about it. "I praise it and hold it a good book, because it sets up no doctrine of men and lays great stress upon God's law. . . . I cannot put him among the chief books, though I would not thereby prevent anyone from putting him where he pleases and estimating him as he pleases; for there are many good sayings in him."[22] Although it is true that Luther thought that James contradicted his beloved Paul,[23] Luther's real complaint was that James did not contain the gospel and therefore was inferior. "In a word, St. John's Gospel and his first epistle, St. Paul's epistles, especially Romans, Galatians, and Ephesians, and St. Peter's first epistle are

21. David Nienhuis (*Not by Paul Alone*) dates James in the mid-second century on the basis of his hypothesis concerning its role in the formation of the corpus of the seven Catholic Epistles.
22. Luther, *Word and Sacrament I*, 362.
23. In a humorous mood, Luther once said, "I will place my doctor's hat upon anyone who can reconcile the two [James and Paul], and let that person scold me as a fool" (*Table Talk*, no. 3292a).

the books that show you Christ and teach you all that it is necessary and salvatory for you to know, even if you were never to see or hear any other book or doctrine. St. James' epistle is really an epistle of straw, compared to the others, for it has nothing of the nature of the gospel about it."[24] For Luther, James simply was not of the same order of significance as other NT books.

One sometimes gets the impression from some people that all twenty-seven books of the NT, since they are inspired, canonical books, must be of equal importance and value. As a canonical book, James must be heard in the church, and it has much to offer. However, it does not express the gospel, and for that reason it is not the equal of other books. This conclusion does not depend on some predetermined canon within the canon, as some fear, or the favoring of one author over another. It is just a simple fact about the content of books James is a worthy book and, *pace* Luther, does not contradict the real Paul. Nevertheless, it does not contain, but rather presupposes, the gospel.

Bibliography

Books and Articles

Adamson, James B. *James: The Man and His Message*. Grand Rapids: Eerdmans, 1989.

Allison, Dale C., Jr. "The Fiction of James and Its *Sitz im Leben*." *RB* 108 (2001): 529–70.

Argyle, A. W. "Greek among the Jews of Palestine in New Testament Times." *NTS* 20 (1973–74): 87–89.

Baker, William R. "Christology in the Epistle of James." *EvQ* 74 (2002): 47–57.

———. *Personal Speech-Ethics in the Epistle of James*. WUNT 2/68. Tübingen: Mohr Siebeck, 1995.

Bauckham, Richard. "James and Jesus." In *The Brother of Jesus: James the Just and His Mission*, edited by Bruce D. Chilton and Jacob Neusner, 100–137. Louisville: Westminster John Knox, 2001.

———. "James and the Gentiles (Acts 15.13–21)." In *History, Literature, and Society in the Book of Acts*, edited by Ben Witherington III, 154–84. Cambridge: Cambridge University Press, 1996.

———. "James and the Jerusalem Church." In *The Book of Acts in Its Palestinian Setting*, edited by Richard Bauckham, 415–80. BAFCS 4. Grand Rapids: Eerdmans, 1995.

———. *James: The Wisdom of James, Disciple of Jesus the Sage*. New York: Routledge, 1999.

Boyle, Marjorie O'Rourke. "The Stoic Paradox of James 2:10." *NTS* 31 (1985): 611–17.

Cargal, Timothy B. *Restoring the Diaspora: Discursive Structure and Purpose in the Epistle of James*. SBLDS 144. Atlanta: Scholars Press, 1993.

Carpenter, Craig B. "James 4:5 Reconsidered." *NTS* 46 (2001): 189–205.

Chester, Andrew. "The Theology of James." In *The Theology of the Letters of James, Peter, and Jude*, by Andrew Chester and Ralph P. Martin, 1–62. NTT. Cambridge: Cambridge University Press, 1994.

Cheung, Luke Leuk. *The Genre, Composition and Hermeneutics of the Epistle of James*. PBTM. Carlisle, UK: Paternoster, 2003.

Childs, Brevard S. *The New Testament as Canon: An Introduction*. Philadelphia: Fortress, 1985.

Chilton, Bruce D., and Craig A. Evans, eds. *James the Just and Christian Origins*. NovTSup 98. Leiden: Brill, 1999.

24. Luther, *Word and Sacrament I*, 395–96.

Chilton, Bruce D., and Jacob Neusner, eds. *The Brother of Jesus: James the Just and His Mission*. Louisville: Westminster John Knox, 2001.

Cranfield, C. E. B. "The Message of James." *SJT* 18 (1965): 182–93, 338–45.

Davids, Peter H. "The Epistle of James in Modern Discussion." *ANRW* II.25.5 (1988): 3621–45.

———. "James and Jesus." In *The Jesus Tradition Outside the Gospels*, edited by David Wenham, 63–84. GP 5. Sheffield: JSOT Press, 1985.

———. "James's Message: The Literary Record." In *The Brother of Jesus: James the Just and His Mission*, edited by Bruce D. Chilton and Jacob Neusner, 66–87. Louisville: Westminster John Knox, 2001.

———. "Palestinian Traditions in the Epistle of James." In *James the Just and Christian Origins*, edited by Bruce D. Chilton and Craig A. Evans, 33–57. NovTSup 98. Leiden: Brill, 1999.

———. "Theological Perspectives on the Epistle of James." *JETS* 23 (1980): 97–103.

Davies, W. D. *The Setting of the Sermon on the Mount*. Cambridge: Cambridge University Press, 1964.

Edgar, David Hutchinson. *Has God Not Chosen the Poor? The Social Setting of the Epistle of James*. JSNTSup 206. Sheffield: Sheffield Academic Press, 2001.

Eisenman, Robert. *James the Brother of Jesus: The Key to Unlocking the Secrets of Early Christianity and the Dead Sea Scrolls*. New York: Viking, 1997.

Elliott, John H. "The Epistle of James in Rhetorical and Social Scientific Perspective: Holiness-Wholeness Patterns of Replication." *BTB* 23 (1993): 71–81.

Francis, Fred O. "The Form and Function of the Opening and Closing Paragraphs of James and I John." *ZNW* 61 (1970): 110–26.

Gowan, Donald E. "Wisdom and Endurance in James." *HBT* 15 (1993): 145–53.

Hagner, Donald A. *The Use of the Old and New Testaments in Clement of Rome*. NovTSup 34. Leiden: Brill, 1973.

Hartin, Patrick J. *James and the "Q" Sayings of Jesus*. JSNTSup 47. Sheffield: JSOT Press, 1991.

———. *A Spirituality of Perfection: Faith in Action in the Letter of James*. Collegeville, MN: Liturgical Press, 1999.

Hengel, Martin. *Judaism and Hellenism: Studies in Their Encounter in Palestine during the Hellenistic Period*. Translated by John Bowden. 2 vols. Philadelphia: Fortress, 1974.

Jackson-McCabe, Matt A. "A Letter to the Twelve Tribes of the Diaspora: Wisdom and 'Apocalyptic' Eschatology in the Letter of James." *SBLSP* 35 (1996): 504–17.

———. *Logos and Law in the Letter of James: The Law of Nature, the Law of Moses, and the Law of Freedom*. NovTSup 100. Leiden: Brill, 2001.

———. "The Messiah Jesus in the Mythic World of James." *JBL* 122 (2003): 701–30.

Jacobs, Irving. "The Midrashic Background for James II, 21–23." *NTS* 22 (1975–76): 457–64.

Jeremias, Joachim. "Paul and James." *ExpTim* 66 (1954–55): 368–71.

Johnson, Luke Timothy. *Brother of Jesus, Friend of God: Studies in the Letter of James*. Grand Rapids: Eerdmans, 2004.

Kloppenborg, John S. "The Reception of the Jesus Tradition in James." In *The Catholic Epistles and the Tradition*, edited by Jacques Schlosser, 93–141. BETL 176. Leuven: Leuven University Press, 2004.

Laato, Timo. "Justification according to James: A Comparison with Paul." Translated by Mark A. Seifrid. *TJ* 18 (1997): 43–84.

Lockett, Darian R. *Purity and Worldview in the Epistle of James*. LNTS 366. New York: T&T Clark, 2008.

Luther, Martin. *Word and Sacrament I*. Vol. 35 of *Luther's Works*. Edited by E. Theodore Bachmann. Philadelphia: Muhlenberg, 1960.

Marcus, Joel. "The Evil Inclination in the Epistle of James." *CBQ* 44 (1982): 606–21.

Maynard-Reid, Pedrito U. *Poverty and Wealth in James*. Maryknoll, NY: Orbis, 1987.

McCartney, Dan G. "The Wisdom of James the Just." *SBJT* 4 (2002): 52–64.

McKnight, Scot. "James 2:18a: The Unidentifiable Interlocutor." *WTJ* 52 (1990): 355–64.

Niebuhr, Karl-Wilhelm. "James in the Minds of the Recipients." In *The Catholic Epistles and Apostolic Tradition: A New Perspective on James to Jude*, edited by Karl-Wilhelm Niebuhr and Robert W. Wall, 43–54. Waco: Baylor University Press, 2009.

Nienhuis, David R. "The Letter of James as a Canon-Conscious Pseudepigraph." In *The Catholic Epistles and Apostolic Tradition: A New Perspective on James to Jude*, edited by Karl-Wilhelm Niebuhr and Robert W. Wall, 183–200. Waco: Baylor University Press, 2009.

———. *Not by Paul Alone: The Formation of the Catholic Epistle Collection and the Christian Canon*. Waco: Baylor University Press, 2007.

Painter, John. "James as the First Catholic Epistle." In *The Catholic Epistles and Apostolic Tradition: A New Perspective on James to Jude*, edited by Karl-Wilhelm Niebuhr and Robert W. Wall, 161–81. Waco: Baylor University Press, 2009.

———. *Just James: The Brother of Jesus in History and Tradition*. SPNT. Columbia: University of South Carolina Press, 1997.

Penner, Todd C. *The Epistle of James and Eschatology: Re-reading an Ancient Christian Letter*. JSNTSup 121. Sheffield: Sheffield Academic Press, 1996.

Popkes, Wiard. "The Mission of James in His Time." In *The Brother of Jesus: James the Just and His Mission*, edited by Bruce D. Chilton and Jacob Neusner, 88–99. Louisville: Westminster John Knox, 2001.

Porter, Stanley E. "Is *dipsychos* (James 1,8; 4,8) a 'Christian' Word?" *Bib* 71 (1990): 469–98.

Rendall, Gerald H. *The Epistle of St. James and Judaic Christianity*. Cambridge: Cambridge University Press, 1927.

Schnabel, Eckhard J. *Law and Wisdom from Ben Sira to Paul: A Tradition Historical Enquiry into the Relation of Law, Wisdom, and Ethics*. WUNT 2/16. Tübingen: Mohr Siebeck, 1985.

Sevenster, Jan N. *Do You Know Greek? How Much Greek Could the First Jewish Christians Have Known?* Translated by J. de Bruin. NovTSup 19. Leiden: Brill, 1968.

Taylor, Mark Edward. *A Text-Linguistic Investigation into the Discourse Structure of James*. LNTS 311. New York: T&T Clark, 2006.

Verseput, Donald J. "James 1:17 and the Jewish Morning Prayers." *NovT* 39 (1997): 177–91.

———. "Reworking the Puzzle of Faith and Deeds in James 2:24–26." *NTS* 43 (1997): 97–115.

———. "Wisdom, 4Q185, and the Epistle of James." *JBL* 117 (1998): 691–707.

Wachob, Wesley Hiram. *The Voice of Jesus in the Social Rhetoric of James*. SNTSMS 106. Cambridge: Cambridge University Press, 2000.

Wall, Robert W. "James as Apocalyptic Paraenesis." *ResQ* 32 (1990): 11–22.

———. "The Priority of James." In *The Catholic Epistles and Apostolic Tradition: A New Perspective on James to Jude*, edited by Karl-Wilhelm Niebuhr and Robert W. Wall, 153–60. Waco: Baylor University Press, 2009.

Watson, Duane F. "James 2 in the Light of Greco-Roman Schemes of Argumentation." *NTS* 39 (1993): 94–121.

———. "The Rhetoric of James 3:1–12 and a Classical Pattern of Argumentation." *NovT* 35 (1993): 48–64.

Webb, Robert L., and John S. Kloppenborg, eds. *Reading James with New Eyes: Methodological Reassessments of the Letter of James*. LNTS 342. New York: T&T Clark, 2007.

Wilkinson, John. "Healing in the Epistle of James." *SJT* 24 (1971): 326–45.

Commentaries

Adamson, James B. *The Epistle of James*. NICNT. Grand Rapids: Eerdmans, 1976.

Davids, Peter H. *The Epistle of James: A Commentary on the Greek Text*. NIGTC. Grand Rapids: Eerdmans, 1982.

———. *James*. NIBC. Peabody, MA: Hendrickson, 1989.

Dibelius, Martin. *James: A Commentary on the Epistle of James*. Revised by Heinrich Greeven. Translated by Michael A. Williams. Edited by Helmut Koester. Hermeneia. Philadelphia: Fortress, 1975.

Hartin, Patrick J. *James*. SP 14. Collegeville, MN: Liturgical Press, 2003.

Hort, F. J. A. *The Epistle of James: The Greek Text with Introduction, Commentary as Far as Chapter IV Verse 7, and Additional Notes*. London: Macmillan, 1909.

Johnson, Luke Timothy. *The Letter of James: A New Translation with Introduction and Commentary*. AB 37A. New York: Doubleday, 1995.

Laws, Sophie. *A Commentary on the Epistle of James*. HNTC. San Francisco: Harper & Row, 1980.

Martin, Ralph P. *James*. WBC 48. Waco: Word, 1988.

Mayor, Joseph B. *The Epistle of St. James: The Greek Text with Introduction, Notes and Comments*. Reprint, Grand Rapids: Baker Academic, 1978.

McCartney, Dan G. *James*. BECNT. Grand Rapids: Baker Academic, 2009.

Mitton, C. Leslie. *The Epistle of James*. Grand Rapids: Eerdmans, 1966.

Moo, Douglas J. *The Letter of James*. TNTC. Grand Rapids: Eerdmans, 1985.

———. *The Letter of James*. PNTC. Grand Rapids: Eerdmans, 2000.

Painter, John, and David A. deSilva. *James and Jude*. Paideia. Grand Rapids: Baker Academic, 2012.

Reicke, Bo. *The Epistles of James, Peter, and Jude: Introduction, Translation, and Notes*. AB 37. Garden City, NY: Doubleday, 1964.

Ropes, James H. *A Critical and Exegetical Commentary on the Epistle of St. James*. ICC. Edinburgh: T&T Clark, 1916.

Scaer, David P. *James, the Apostle of Faith: A Primary Christological Epistle for the Persecuted Church*. St. Louis: Concordia, 1983.

Sidebottom, E. M. *James, Jude, 2 Peter*. NCBC. Grand Rapids: Eerdmans, 1982.

Sleeper, C. Freeman. *James*. ANTC. Nashville: Abingdon, 1998.

Tasker, R. V. G. *The General Epistle of James*. TNTC. Grand Rapids: Eerdmans, 1957.

Wall, Robert W. *Community of the Wise: The Letter of James*. NTC. Valley Forge, PA: Trinity Press International, 1997.

37

First Peter

No document among the Catholic Epistles provides quite as varied and rich a theological feast as does 1 Peter. Although 1 Peter apparently speaks to some specific circumstances, as a circular letter written to several Christian communities in Asia Minor it lacks the kind of rootedness and particularity that would enable us to understand it as fully as we would like. Like the other Catholic letters, 1 Peter remains enigmatic in many ways.

The Authorship Question

The question of who wrote 1 Peter is not easy to decide. The author identifies himself as "Peter, an apostle of Jesus Christ" (1:1), and the authenticity of the letter was never questioned in the early church, where it was widely known.[1] Eusebius (*Hist. eccl.* 3.25.3) places 1 Peter among the "undisputed" books (the only Catholic Epistle in that category), but inexplicably it is lacking in the list known as the Muratorian Canon (ca. 180). With the dawn of the historical-critical method, however, questions about its authorship began to be raised.

Doubts about whether the Apostle Peter wrote 1 Peter began with the observation that the polished Greek, the rhetoric, and the extensive vocabulary of the document seem to be beyond the capability of the former Galilean

---

1. Already before the end of the first century, the letter is clearly alluded to in *1 Clement* (ca. 96). See Hagner, *The Use of the Old and New Testaments in Clement of Rome*, 239–48. Among the possible allusions, three instances are regarded as especially probable.

Author: Very possibly Peter, through Silvanus, but if not, possibly by a disciple or associate of the Apostle.

Date: If by Peter, then probably early 60s. If by an associate of Peter, not later than the 80s.

Addressees: A circular letter addressed to the "exiles of the Dispersion," by which is meant Gentile Christians living in eastern Asia Minor.

Purpose: To edify Christian readers by stressing their new identity in Christ and their membership in a new family of faith, and by addressing the challenge of persecution.

Message/Argument: Perhaps an adaptation of an original baptismal homily, employing liturgical elements to explore a variety of appropriate themes such as rebirth and new life.

Significance: A fundamental statement of the Christian faith ultimately from the prime Apostle, Peter, analogous in content and scope to Paul's gospel.

---

fisherman. Peter and John are described as "uneducated [*agrammatoi*, lit., "unlettered"], common men" (Acts 4:13). But rather than meaning that they were unable to read or write, probably this refers to their lack of formal training in the law (Torah)—that is, their lack of a proper rabbinic education of the sort, for example, that Paul had. As we noted in the discussion of James in the preceding chapter, it is by no means impossible that a Galilean Jew such as Peter could have acquired an excellent facility in Greek and indeed made regular use of the LXX in the letter.[2] Against this conclusion is the fact that Peter apparently preferred to make use of Mark as his interpreter when he preached in Rome (see chap. 11 above). If the excellence of Peter's Greek is regarded as improbable, however, appeal may be made to the statement in 5:12: "By Silvanus, a faithful brother as I regard him, I have written briefly to you." Silvanus (whose name is the Latinized equivalent of "Silas") was one of the leading men in the Jerusalem church (Acts 15:22, 32). Like Paul, Silas was a Roman citizen (Acts 16:37–38). He accompanied Paul on the second missionary journey (Acts 15:40) and is mentioned as a coauthor, along with Paul and Timothy, of the Thessalonian letters (see also 2 Cor. 1:19). The effectiveness of the appeal to Silvanus is weakened, however, by the observation that the formula "I have written through [*dia*, "by"]" probably refers to the one who delivers the letter rather than the one who writes it.[3] But still this does not make it impossible that in the present case Silvanus served also as secretary. If the quality of the language in the letter is due to Silvanus, then it follows that he would have been granted considerable freedom in its composition, and

2. Karen Jobes has studied "linguistic interference" (i.e., influence of one language upon another), using a method of syntax criticism developed by Raymond Martin, and concludes that "the Greek of 1 Peter indicates an author whose first language was not Greek" (*1 Peter*, 337). See the excursus "The Syntax of 1 Peter: How Good Is the Greek?" in ibid., 325–38.

3. See Richards, "Silvanus Was Not Peter's Secretary."

the line between a secretary and a disciple writing in the name of his master becomes exceedingly thin.

The appeal to Silvanus's role in the production of 1 Peter can help to answer a further objection to Petrine authorship that has been raised: the letter is quite Pauline in much of its content. Paul's familiar "in Christ" formula, for example, is found in 3:16; 5:10, 14. Some have suggested that were it not for the opening identification of the author, one might easily have taken 1 Peter as a Pauline Letter. These echoes of Paul's theology would be explainable through Silvanus's close association with Paul over many years.[4] This objection may well accept too quickly the supposition that Peter's theology necessarily diverged in fundamental ways from Paul's, as the old Tübingen hypothesis maintained. But the possibility that Peter and Paul shared a common apostolic tradition and much of the same theology should not be dismissed.

Another objection to the authenticity of 1 Peter is that one might well expect an abundance of references to Jesus and his ministry in a letter written by one of the chief eyewitnesses of that ministry. Although perhaps not as much as to be expected, there do seem to be some possible allusions to the ministry of Jesus. The statement that the readers love Christ "without having seen him" (1:8) implies that the writer did see Jesus. He describes himself as "a witness of the sufferings of Christ" (cf. 2:4), and it is possible that the reference to being "a partaker in the glory that is to be" alludes to the transfiguration (5:1). References to the resurrection of Christ (1:3; 3:21) could find their background in Peter's own experience of the resurrected Christ, and Peter's restoration after denying Christ could be alluded to in 5:10. Most impressive of all are the numerous allusions to sayings of Jesus (see "First Peter's Use of Traditional Materials," below). That there are not more allusions to the ministry of Jesus is due to the genre of the document. According to early tradition, Peter's reminiscences about Jesus are extensively preserved in the Gospel of Mark.

Some have thought that 1 Peter reflects a church order that is too developed for the time of Peter. Thus, for example, 5:2 uses the participle "exercising the oversight" (RSV margin: *episkopountes* is lacking in some early manuscripts), which could point to the office of "bishop." But the subject of the participle is "elders" (*presbyteroi*), which points, as in the Pastoral Epistles, to the early period when "elder" and "bishop" were interchangeable. The author's reference to himself as "a fellow elder" in 5:1 is sometimes thought to be contradictory of the apostolic office and authority indicated in 1:1. But it is extremely unlikely that a pseudonymous writer would have used the word "elder" here instead of repeating "apostle" from 1:1.

---

4. Edward Selwyn explores in detail the similarities between the Thessalonian epistles and 1 Peter, suggesting that they are due to the influence of Silvanus (*The First Epistle of St. Peter*, 369–84).

First Peter exhibits little of the influence of the incipient early catholic perspective. Quite against the later perspective, 1 Peter preserves an imminent eschatology: "The end of all things is at hand [*pantōn de to telos ēngiken*]" (4:7 [cf. 4:17]), unless this is to be understood as a kind of theological rather than chronological imminence. Some have maintained, however, that the sense of Christian identity in 1 Peter, where the church seems to take the place of Israel (cf. the OT language applied to Gentile Christians in 2:9), also reflects a time later than Peter.

Finally, the suffering and persecution mentioned in 4:14–16, explicitly "for the name of Christ" and "as a Christian," are thought by some to point to a time in the late first century (Domitian) or early second century (Trajan) rather than to the time of Peter (the persecution by Nero is less of a possibility). But the suffering mentioned in 1 Peter apparently involved no martyrdoms and need not point to an empire-wide, systematic persecution, but only to sporadic and local outbreaks of persecution. Since the loyalties of Christians inevitably clashed with the claims of the emperor and social mores of the Greco-Roman world, hostility against them would not have been unexpected or unusual.[5] The references to persecution thus provide no real assistance in dating the letter or identifying the author.

Once again we face a situation where important objections are raised against the authenticity of a NT document, but where at the same time the objections can be answered to some extent. Unlike the situation of the Pauline Epistles, where we have several uncontested documents to use for comparison, in the present case we have no body of genuine Petrine material to help us.[6] (The document known as 2 Peter almost certainly is not by Peter, as we will see in the next chapter.) Again we are in the realm of probabilities where dogmatic or overconfident assertions are unwarranted. The probabilities in this case do not tip one way or the other. We can exclude neither the possibility that Peter, using Silvanus as his secretary, wrote the letter nor the possibility that it is pseudonymous.[7]

To opt for a pseudonymous author does not automatically necessitate a late date (e.g., late in the first century), nor does it preclude any connection with Peter. The attribution of the document to Peter could be explained by the author being a part of a circle or school of Peter,[8] a follower of Peter who

5. For an analysis of the hostility toward the Christian readers as a matter of "social prejudice," see Holloway, *Coping with Prejudice*.

6. Some have detected a similarity to 1 Peter in the vocabulary of Peter's sermons in Acts, but one can hardly build much on this given that Luke's reports are not verbatim. The similarities can be explained as a common, shared Christian tradition.

7. As J. N. D. Kelly points out, "Critical scholarship is not equipped to produce a finally convincing settlement" (*A Commentary on the Epistles of Peter and of Jude*, 30). Paul Achtemeier notes, "Evidence to solve definitively the question of the authorship of 1 Peter remains unavailable" (*1 Peter*, 42).

8. For an argument for the existence of such a school, see Soards, "1 Peter, 2 Peter, and Jude as Evidence for a Petrine School." See also Elliott, "Peter, Silvanus and Mark in 1 Peter and Acts"; idem, *A Home for the Homeless*, 270–82.

sets down some of the teachings of his master. Alternatively, the document could be explained as more general traditions of the church at Rome set forth in the name of the prime apostle.[9]

The Form and Integrity of First Peter

There is little doubt among scholars that 1 Peter is a real letter, with formulaic address and final greetings, sent to a number of communities in Asia Minor. For all of its theological similarities with the Pauline Epistles, however, there are also notable differences in form. First Peter contains no sustained argument but instead consists basically of a series of alternating indicatives and participial imperatives, of assertions and admonitions. In place of a connected, lengthy exposition we encounter pithy theological statements of key ideas that remain largely undeveloped. The organization and structure of 1 Peter has continued to challenge scholars.[10]

The integrity of 1 Peter has not gone unchallenged. A clear break at 4:11, with what seems to be an ending doxology and "Amen," leads to a new section beginning in 4:12, where the reference to suffering, "the fiery ordeal," seems heightened, possibly pointing to a new stage of development (cf. 1:6). What appears to be a second ending occurs in 5:11. This has led to the speculation that 1 Peter represents two letters or perhaps the combination of a sermon (1:3–4:11) and a letter (1:1–2 plus 4:12–5:11).[11] C. F. D. Moule suggested that two letters were sent, one for those facing the threat of persecution (not official, but at the personal level) and the other for those presently experiencing it.[12] It seems to be a good possibility that we have two conjoined documents here, but such a conclusion is not a necessary one, nor can it be definitely established.

A Baptismal Homily or Liturgy?

The baptismal connections of 1 Peter have long been noted. The references to rebirth provide evidence of the interest in baptism. Already in 1:3, in the first statement of the letter, we read, "By his great mercy we have been born anew [*anagennēsas*] to a living hope through the resurrection of Jesus Christ from the dead." Similarly in 1:23: "You have been born anew [*anagegennēmenoi*],

9. This is the view of Horrell ("The Product of a Petrine Circle?"), who finds the evidence for a Petrine school too insubstantial.

10. Troy Martin (*Metaphor and Compostion in 1 Peter*) finds the body-middle of the letter as organized under three "metaphor clusters": "the elect household of God" (1:14–2:10); "aliens in this world" (2:11–3:12); and "sufferers in the Diaspora" (3:13–5:11).

11. See Beare, *The First Epistle of Peter*, 25–28.

12. Moule, "The Nature and Purpose of I Peter," 7–11.

not of perishable seed but of imperishable, through the living and abiding word of God."

There is, furthermore, the catechetical exhortation to "put away all malice and all guile and insincerity and envy and all slander," followed by words appropriate to a person being baptized: "Like newborn babes, long for the pure spiritual milk, that by it you may grow up to salvation; for you have tasted the kindness of the Lord" (2:1–3). And then, most strikingly: "Baptism, which corresponds to this, now saves you, not as a removal of dirt from the body but as an appeal to God for a clear conscience, through the resurrection of Jesus Christ" (3:21).

So too have the liturgical, hymnic, and creedal aspects of much of the material in 1 Peter often been observed. This material has caused many to think that 1 Peter is largely a baptismal sermon. F. L. Cross came up with the most developed hypothesis, in which he suggested that the frequent reference to suffering (the verb is *paschō*) in 1 Peter is to be connected with the Pascha, or Easter Vigil, and the baptism and Eucharist that took place then.[13] According to Cross, 1:3–4:11 presents the words of the actual baptismal liturgy spoken by the celebrant. The analysis is ingenious, but probably overly contrived. There can be little doubt, however, that 1 Peter has a homiletical character and a special interest in baptism.

First Peter's Use of Traditional Materials

Traditional materials abound in 1 Peter. The author is not an innovator, unless in the sense of one who very skillfully employs tradition to convey his own message.

1. The number of possible allusions to the sayings of Jesus in 1 Peter is impressive. These appear to consist of various layers of traditions underlying each of the four Gospels. Especially noteworthy are parallels to material in Luke 6; 12; 22 (e.g., 1:4 is similar to Luke 12:33; 1:13 to Luke 12:35; 2:18–23 to Luke 6:27–36; 2:19–20 to Luke 6:32–35; 3:9 to Luke 6:27–28; 5:8–9 to Luke 22:31–32; 5:3–5 to Luke 22:25–30). Parallels to Matthean tradition also occur (e.g., 1:17 is similar to Matt. 6:9; 2:12 to Matt. 5:16; 2:13–17 to Matt. 17:24–27; 3:14 to Matt. 5:10; 4:13–14 to Matt. 5:10–11). Johannine traditions are also evident (e.g., 1:8 is similar to John 20:29; the "rebirth" passages in 1 Peter recall John 3:3, 7). Almost all of these allusions are from contexts where Peter is involved

13. Cross, *I Peter, a Paschal Liturgy*. Cross finds other details supporting his hypothesis: the girding of the loins (taken literally) before baptism (1:13), even locating the baptism itself between 1:21 and 1:22, and an allusion to the baptismal Eucharist in 2:3. For a critique of Cross, see Moule, "The Nature and Purpose of I Peter."

in some way. According to Robert Gundry, this unique phenomenon can be explained only by Petrine authorship and the authenticity of the Gospel traditions.[14] In his commentary, Edward Selwyn surmised that the allusions were largely drawn from Q.

2. There are numerous parallels with other NT writings, especially the Pauline Epistles. For just a sampling from Romans, compare 1:17 and Romans 13:1–7; 2:5 and Romans 12:1; 2:6–8 and Romans 9:32–33; 2:10 and Romans 9:25; 2:24 and Romans 6:11; 4:10–11 and Romans 12:6–7. There are many other Pauline parallels. From Ephesians, compare 1:20 and Ephesians 1:4; 2:2–6 and Ephesians 2:18–22. Compare also 2:16 and Galatians 5:13. There are also a number of parallels to James—for example, 1:6–7 and James 1:2–3; 4:8 and James 5:20; 5:5–9 and James 4:6–10.

3. First Peter makes frequent use of the OT. There are some eight explicit quotations, but also many more allusions. Most notable among the quotations are the three "stone" logia in 2:6–8, all of which refer to Christ and are of great importance in earliest Christianity. The first of these concerns the "cornerstone chosen and precious" laid in Zion (Isa. 28:16); the second is about the stone rejected by the builders becoming the head of the corner (Ps. 118:22); the third refers to a stone that causes people to stumble (Isa. 8:14–15). Also of very great interest is the use of Isaiah 53 in 2:22–25. As important as Isaiah 53 must have been in the early church, it is, surprisingly, not quoted in the NT very often. First Peter provides the most extensive application of the passage to Christ. Another feature of 1 Peter's use of the OT is that not only is Psalm 34:12–16 quoted in 3:10–12, applied directly to the Christian readers, but also the psalm is alluded to throughout the book.[15] There are, furthermore, allusions to the Passover (1:19) as well as references to Abraham and Sarah (3:6) and to Noah (3:20). The quantity of quotation and allusion to the OT has prompted one scholar to refer to 1 Peter as essentially a "homiletical midrash."[16] Rather than being the results of literary dependence, it is "more likely" that "the many reflections of both NT and OT in 1 Peter show the author to be anchored in common early Christian tradition."[17]

4. Catechetical tradition is also found in 1 Peter. The ethical exhortation of the epistle employs paraenetic materials common to Romans,

14. Gundry, "'Verba Christi' in I Peter." This conclusion is challenged by Best, "I Peter and the Gospel Tradition," and Gundry's rejoinder is found in "Further Verba on Verba Christi in First Peter."

15. See Jobes, "Got Milk?"

16. That is, a running sermonic interpretation of OT texts. Thus Schutter, *Hermeneutic and Composition in 1 Peter.*

17. Achtemeier, *1 Peter,* 21.

Colossians, and James.[18] We see evidence of the "put off . . . put on" paradigm (see 2:1, 11–12; 5:5), perhaps, as we have noted, in relation to a baptismal liturgy. Included here too are the household codes regulating behavior (2:13–3:7).

5. The author includes hymnic (or creedal) fragments here and there in the letter. Possibly to be identified as such are 1:3–5; 1:18–21; 2:22–25; 3:18, 22; 4:6; 5:5b–9.[19] These passages embody some of the especially rich theology that is so characteristic of 1 Peter.

The author of 1 Peter has creatively and brilliantly woven these various traditional materials, often seamlessly, into the tapestry of the letter.

The Emergence of Christian Identity

One of the remarkable passages in 1 Peter is in 2:9–10: "But you are a chosen race, a royal priesthood,[20] a holy nation, God's own people, that you may declare the wonderful deeds of him who called you out of darkness into his marvelous light. Once you were no people but now you are God's people; once you had not received mercy but now you have received mercy." Language that in the history of salvation has been carefully restricted to Israel (cf. Exod. 19:5–6; Isa. 43:20–21) is now freely applied to Gentile Christians. What appears to be a confusion of categories is an astounding theological assertion. The church is understood to possess fully the status and privileges of Israel.

An important issue is whether a passage such as this should be understood as saying that the church has taken the place of Israel as the new people of God. It is clear that we must reckon with the concept of a new Israel here. But is this a matter of shared status or of displacement? What is clear in this passage is that the prerogatives of Israel belong now to the church. Whether Israel, the previous owner of the language, is thereby excluded or not is a question that 1 Peter does not choose to address. But the author, like Paul, sees the unbelief of Israel as something mysteriously within the plan of God: "They stumble because they disobey the word, as they were destined to do" (2:8).

The teaching of this passage apparently intends to encourage the readers who had experienced a loss of identity through conversion to Christianity, and who therefore felt like "aliens and exiles" (2:11; cf. 1:1, 17) in a hostile world responsible for their suffering. Their real home now was their spiritual home, and their new identity was their identity as the people of God. Providing an

18. See Selwyn, *The First Epistle of St. Peter*, 384–439.

19. On the first four of these passages, see Pearson, *The Christological and Rhetorical Properties of 1 Peter*. She emphasizes the suffering/exaltation pattern of christology in 2:21–25, based on Isaiah 53.

20. On this, see Elliott, *The Elect and the Holy*.

alternative analysis, John Elliott explains the "aliens and exiles" in exclusively sociological terms as displaced persons without a true home.[21] Ralph Martin gets to the heart of the epistle in these words: "By a common participation in the messianic blessing realized in Christ and the new age and through a shared study of ancient scriptures, both first generation Christians (represented by Peter the apostle at the fountainhead) and any subsequent generation of responsive believers stand together as on the same ground."[22]

Theological Themes

1. Hope is presented as the antidote to suffering. The initial readers of 1 Peter were experiencing suffering (1:6; 2:21; 3:9, 14, 17; 4:12–19; 5:9–10), and a central purpose of the letter is to encourage them in their trying circumstances.[23] The word "hope" (*elpis*) in the NT does not refer to wishful thinking. It has the connotation of "confident expectation" because of the knowledge that the future, like the present, is fully in God's hands. At the beginning of the book we find a reference to "a living hope" that is the result of the new birth (1:3), and then in 1:13 the readers are exhorted to "set your hope fully upon the grace that is coming to you at the revelation of Jesus Christ." Hope is linked with confidence and faith in 1:21. The readers are instructed: "Always be prepared to make a defense to any one who calls you to account for the hope that is in you, yet do it with gentleness and reverence" (3:15).

2. Christology and atonement play a large role. Christ is, first of all, a model of righteous suffering for the readers. "Christ also suffered for you, leaving you an example, that you should follow in his steps" (2:21 [cf. 1:11, 19; 3:18; 4:1]). Among the remarkable christological passages are the following:

   • 1:18–21: Christians are "ransomed" from their past condition "not with perishable things such as silver or gold, but with the precious blood of Christ, like that of a lamb without blemish or spot." Christ was "destined before the foundation of the world but was made manifest at the end of the times for your sake."
   • 2:4–8: Three "stone" logia, with midrashic interpretation, describing Christ as "that living stone rejected by men but in God's sight chosen and precious," and as the cause of stumbling (cf. Rom. 9:33).

---

21. See Elliott, *A Home for the Homeless*. For a critique, see Chin, "A Heavenly Home for the Homeless."

22. R. P. Martin, "The Theology of Jude, 1 Peter, and 2 Peter," 89.

23. For a discussion of suffering in 1 Peter (esp. 4:12–19) as "messianic woes" preceding the eschaton, see Dubis, *Messianic Woes in First Peter*.

- 2:21–25: A paraphrase of the suffering servant in Isaiah 53 describes the suffering of Christ (cf. 1:11) and concludes with a reference to Christ as "the Shepherd and Guardian [*episkopos*, "Bishop"] of your souls."
- 3:18–22: "For Christ also died for sins once for all, the righteous for the unrighteous, that he might bring us to God, being put to death in the flesh but made alive in the spirit." This statement is followed by the difficult reference to Christ in Hades (see "Christ Preaching in Hades?" below).

3. The resurrection and return of Christ are very important. The resurrection of Christ is brought to the front in the statement of the opening blessing of God: "By his great mercy we have been born anew to a living hope through the resurrection of Jesus Christ from the dead" (1:3). In 1:21 it is again mentioned: "Through him you have confidence in God, who raised him from the dead and gave him glory." Christ was "put to death in the flesh" but "made alive in the spirit" (3:18).[24] Christ's resurrection and ascension are spoken of together in 3:21–22: "through the resurrection of Jesus Christ, who has gone into heaven and is at the right hand of God, with angels, authorities, and powers subject to him." The return of Christ is in view in the reference to "the revelation of Jesus Christ" (1:7, 13 [cf. 1:5; 4:13]) and perhaps too in the mention of "the subsequent glory" (1:11). The reality of eschatological fulfillment is a fixed point in the author's mind. Thus he refers to "the day of visitation" (2:12), "the end of all things" (4:7), and the beginning of judgment (4:17). The epistle ends with the comforting promise that expresses its central theme of hope: "And after you have suffered a little while, the God of all grace, who has called you to his eternal glory in Christ, will himself restore, establish and strengthen you" (5:10).

4. The church as a community or family is emphasized. We have already noted the establishing of the new identity of the readers in 2:4–10. They now constitute "a spiritual house" (2:5). Once "no people," they are now "God's people" (2:10), indeed, "the household [*oikos*] of God" (4:17 [an idea familiar from the Pastorals]). Fellow Christians are referred to as brothers/sisters (cf. 5:9), and the readers are repeatedly exhorted concerning the importance of love of the brothers/sisters (1:22; 2:17; 3:8; cf. "love for one another" in 4:8).

5. There is strong emphasis on holiness and the call to the church to live righteously in the world. "As obedient children, do not be conformed to the passions of your former ignorance, but as he who called you is holy,

24. "In this way the paraenesis finds its anchoring in the kerygma, and the inherited material of varied origin is tuned to the one basic tone that sounds through the epistle from beginning to end. Christ has suffered, and the Christians are called upon to follow in his steps" (Lohse, "Paraenesis and Kerygma in 1 Peter," 59).

be holy yourselves in all your conduct; since it is written, 'You shall be holy, for I am holy'" (1:14–16). The readers are to avoid their previous patterns of conduct, to "put away all malice and all guile and insincerity and envy and all slander" (2:1). As "aliens and exiles" in this world, they are to "abstain from the passions of the flesh that wage war against your soul" (2:11 [cf. 4:3]). "Good deeds" assume great importance, as God "judges each one impartially according to his deeds" (1:17 [cf. 2:12]). Paraenesis, or ethical exhortation, assumes a remarkably large role in this letter.[25]

6. The ethical catechesis sprinkled throughout the letter is strengthened and given structure by means of the use of traditional household codes, which do not appear in immediate succession. The readers are to "be subject for the Lord's sake to every human institution" (2:13–17); servants (*oiketai*) are to be submissive to their masters (2:18), and wives to their husbands (3:1–7); the younger are to be subject to the elder (5:5). Elders themselves are exhorted to "tend the flock of God that is your charge" (5:2).

Christ Preaching in Hades?

Two of the most obscure and problematic passages in the NT are 3:18–22 and 4:6. They often have been taken together to refer to Christ preaching to the dead in Hades. Indeed, the ancient Apostles' Creed confesses, "He descended into Hell." But nowadays this interpretation of the passages is held by very few.

The basic options for understanding the first passage, where Christ in the spirit "went and preached to the spirits in prison" (3:19) are the following:

1. Between his death and resurrection Christ preached the gospel to the spirits of the disobedient who perished in the days of Noah,[26] perhaps giving them a second chance of salvation; or, alternatively, Christ preached to the OT saints.
2. The preexistent Christ preached through Noah to his contemporaries, but they did not respond and hence are in prison.
3. After his resurrection Christ proclaimed triumph over the imprisoned "spirits" (there is no mention of "the dead")—that is, fallen supernatural powers (including those of Gen. 6:1–4).

The last view has become dominant because it fits the immediate context in 1 Peter far better than do the others (cf. 3:22).[27] Christ descended (or it could

25. See Thurén, *Argument and Theology in 1 Peter*.
26. The background provided by *1 Enoch* 6–11; 64–69; 106–8 is of great importance in understanding this passage.
27. See Dalton, *Christ's Proclamation to the Spirits*.

be ascended, since no direction is indicated) to the supernatural realm to proclaim victory over the evil principalities and powers.

The equally difficult second passage, with its reference to preaching the gospel to the dead (4:6), has lately been understood as not referring to the same thing as the first passage. Interpreted on its own terms, it simply refers to the preaching (not by Christ, who is not mentioned) of the gospel and the conversion of saints now dead.[28] Here the passive verb is "evangelized" (*euēngelisthē*), not "preached" (*ekēryxen*) as in 3:19. The possibility remains open, however, that the dead generally are in view, not just those already converted.[29]

Author, Addressees, Date

Author

The author possibly is Peter. If the letter is not by Peter, why is it written in his name? Given the amount of Pauline-sounding theology in the letter, an ordinary pseudonymous writer might have written in Paul's name. If the letter is not by Peter, the most natural conclusion is that the author had some association with him either as his disciple or as a member of a Petrine circle or school.

Addressees

As already noted, 1 Peter is a kind of limited circular letter, addressed to "the exiles of the Dispersion in Pontus, Galatia, Cappadocia, Asia, and Bithynia" (1:1)—that is, mainly eastern Asia Minor. These cities probably are listed in the order of the route traveled by the messenger (Silvanus?). Whereas "exiles of the Dispersion" might well give the impression that the letter is written to Jewish Christians, actually it is meant mainly for Gentile Christians (cf. 1:14, 18) living in a hostile world. They are no longer regarded as Gentiles (note the statement in 4:3–4); they are no longer a people without an identity (2:10). But why is it that Peter writes to Gentile Christians?

Peter had an evident concern not just for Jewish Christians but for the whole church, Gentiles and Jews together. And, like Paul, he was concerned to hold together the Jewish and Gentile believers in Jesus. It was Peter who became "the focal point of unity for the whole Church . . . in fact and effect the bridge-man who did more than any other to hold together the diversity of first-century Christianity."[30]

---

28. So Dalton, ibid. The problem of the death of Christians prior to the parousia of Christ may lie behind the statement in 4:6 (cf. 1 Thess. 4:13–18).

29. For this view, see Horrell, "Who Are 'The Dead' and When was the Gospel Preached to Them?" Horrell is content to leave the passage as an enigma.

30. Dunn, *Unity and Diversity in the New Testament*, 385 (italics removed).

Date

It is very difficult to date 1 Peter because we cannot be sure of the actual author, and therefore we must depend solely on the contents of the letter. If it was written by Peter (using Silvanus as secretary), then we must date the epistle to about 63–64, just prior to his martyrdom. If it is not by Peter, but rather by one of his disciple/associates, it still need not be dated very late, probably not later than the 80s. First Peter does not bear many of the typical marks of incipient early catholicism. As we have already noted, the references to persecution are too vague to be identified confidently with any of the major imperial persecutions. Almost certainly the letter is written from Rome, here called "Babylon" (5:13). This reference itself may have something to contribute to the dating of the letter, since the use of the cryptogram "Babylon" for Rome seems not to be attested until after AD 70. This hardly means, however, that it could not have been used earlier, but it may just possibly be another pointer to a time after the death of Peter.

Bibliography

Books and Articles

Achtemeier, Paul J. "The Christology of 1 Peter: Some Reflections." In *Who Do You Say That I Am? Essays on Christology*, edited by Mark Alan Powell and David R. Bauer, 140–54. Louisville: Westminster John Knox, 1999.

———. "Newborn Babes and Living Stones: Literal and Figurative in 1 Peter." In *To Touch the Text: Biblical and Related Studies in Honor of Joseph A. Fitzmyer*, edited by Maurya P. Horgan and Paul J. Kobelski, 207–36. New York: Crossroad, 1989.

———. "Suffering Servant and Suffering Christ in 1 Peter." In *The Future of Christology: Essays in Honor of Leander E. Keck*, edited by Abraham J. Malherbe and Wayne A. Meeks, 176–88. Minneapolis: Fortress, 1993.

Balch, David L. "Early Christian Criticism of Patriarchal Authority: 1 Peter 2:11–3:12." *USQR* 39 (1984): 161–73.

———. *Let Wives Be Submissive: The Domestic Code in 1 Peter*. SBLDS 26. Atlanta: Scholars Press, 1981.

Bandstra, Andrew J. "'Making Proclamation to the Spirits in Prison': Another Look at 1 Peter 3:19." *CTJ* 38 (2003): 120–24.

Bechtler, Steven Richard. *Following in His Steps: Suffering, Community, and Christology in 1 Peter*. SBLDS 162. Atlanta: Scholars Press, 1998.

Best, Ernest. "I Peter and the Gospel Tradition." *NTS* 16 (1969–70): 95–113.

———. "I Peter II 4–10—A Reconsideration." *NovT* 11 (1969): 270–93.

Blevins, James L. "Introduction to 1 Peter." *RevExp* 79 (1982): 401–25.

Bockmuehl, Markus. "Peter's Death in Rome? Back to Front and Upside Down," *SJT* 60 (2007): 1–23.

———. *Simon Peter in Scripture and Memory: The New Testament Apostle in the Early Church*. Grand Rapids: Baker Academic, 2012.

Brooks, Oscar S. "I Peter 3:21—The Clue to the Literary Structure of the Epistle." *NovT* 16 (1974): 290–305.

Brown, Raymond E., Karl P. Donfried, and John Reumann, eds. *Peter in the New Testament: A Collaborative Assessment by Protestant and Roman Catholic Scholars*. Minneapolis: Augsburg, 1973.

Campbell, Barth L. *Honor, Shame, and the Rhetoric of 1 Peter*. SBLDS 160. Atlanta: Scholars Press, 1998.

Casurella, Anthony. *Bibliography of Literature on First Peter*. NTTS 23. Leiden: Brill, 1996.

Chin, Moses. "A Heavenly Home for the Homeless: Aliens and Strangers in 1 Peter." *TynBul* 42 (1991): 96–112.

Coutts, John. "Ephesians 1.3–14 and 1 Peter 1.3–12." *NTS* 3 (1956–57): 115–27.

Cross, F. L. *I Peter, a Paschal Liturgy*. London: Mowbray, 1954.

Cullmann, Oscar. *Peter: Disciple, Apostle, Martyr; A Historical and Theological Study*. Translated by Floyd V. Filson. London: SCM, 1953.

Dalton, William J. *Christ's Proclamation to the Spirits: A Study of 1 Peter 3:18–4:6*. AnBib 23. 2nd ed. Rome: Editrice Pontificio Istituto Biblico, 1989.

———. "The Interpretation of 1 Peter 3:19 and 4:6: Light from 2 Peter." *Bib* 60 (1979): 547–55.

Danker, Frederick W. "I Peter 1:24–2:17—A Consolatory Pericope." *ZNW* 58 (1967): 93–102.

deSilva, David. "1 Peter: Strategies for Counseling Individuals on the Way to a New Heritage." *ATJ* 32 (2000): 33–52.

Doering, Lutz. "First Peter as Early Christian Diaspora Letter." In *The Catholic Epistles and Apostolic Tradition: A New Perspective on James to Jude*, edited by Karl-Wilhelm Niebuhr and Robert W. Wall, 215–36. Waco: Baylor University Press, 2009.

Downing, F. Gerald. "Pliny's Prosecutions of Christians: Revelation and 1 Peter." *JSNT* 34 (1988): 105–23.

Dryden, J. de Waal. *Theology and Ethics in 1 Peter: Paraenetic Strategies for Christian Character Formation*. WUNT 2/209. Tübingen: Mohr Siebeck, 2006.

Dubis, Mark. *Messianic Woes in First Peter: Suffering and Eschatology in 1 Peter 4:12–19*. SBL 33. New York: Peter Lang, 2002.

———. "Research on 1 Peter: A Survey of Scholarly Literature since 1985." *CurBS* 4 (2006): 199–239.

Dunn, James D. G. *Unity and Diversity in the New Testament: An Inquiry into the Character of Earliest Christianity*. 2nd ed. Philadelphia: Trinity Press International, 1990.

Elliott, John H. *Conflict, Community, and Honor: 1 Peter in Social-Scientific Perspective*. Eugene, OR: Cascade, 2007.

———. "Elders as Leaders in 1 Peter and the Early Church." *CurTM* 28 (2001): 549–59.

———. *The Elect and the Holy: An Exegetical Examination of I Peter 2:4–10 and the Phrase basileion hierateuma*. NovTSup 12. Leiden: Brill, 1966.

———. *A Home for the Homeless: A Sociological Exegesis of 1 Peter, Its Situation and Strategy*. Philadelphia: Fortress, 1981.

———. "Peter, Silvanus and Mark in 1 Peter and Acts: Sociological-Exegetical Perspectives on a Petrine Group in Rome." In *Wort in der Zeit: Neutestamentliche Studien; Festgabe für Karl Heinrich Rengstorf zum 75. Geburtstag*, edited by Wilfrid Haubeck and Michael Bachmann, 250–67. Leiden: Brill, 1980.

Feldmeier, Reinhard. "The 'Nation' of Strangers: Social Contempt and Its Theological Interpretations in Ancient Judaism and Early Christianity." In *Ethnicity and the Bible*, edited by Mark G. Brett, 240–70. BIS 19. Leiden: Brill, 1996.

———. "Salvation and Anthropology in First Peter." In *The Catholic Epistles and Apostolic Tradition: A New Perspective on James to Jude*, edited by Karl-Wilhelm Niebuhr and Robert W. Wall, 203–13. Waco: Baylor University Press, 2009.

Foakes-Jackson, F. J. *Peter, Prince of the Apostles: A Study in the History and Tradition of Christianity*. London: Hodder & Stoughton, 1927.

Furnish, Victor P. "Elect Sojourners in Christ: An Approach to the Theology of 1 Peter." *PSTJ* 28 (1975): 1–11.

Green, Gene L. "The Use of the Old Testament for Christian Ethics in 1 Peter." *TynBul* 41 (1993): 276–89.

Gundry, Robert H. "Further Verba on Verba Christi in First Peter." *Bib* 55 (1974): 211–32.

———. "'Verba Christi' in I Peter: Their Implications concerning the Authorship of I Peter and the Authenticity of the Gospel Tradition." *NTS* 13 (1966–67): 336–50.

Hagner, Donald A. *The Use of the Old and New Testaments in Clement of Rome.* NovTSup 34. Leiden: Brill, 1973.

Hanson, A. T. "Salvation Proclaimed. I. 1 Peter 3.18–22." *ExpTim* 93 (1981–1982): 100–105.

Harner, Philip B. *What Are They Saying about the Catholic Epistles?* Mahwah, NJ: Paulist Press, 2004.

Helyer, Larry R. *The Life and Witness of Peter.* Downers Grove, IL: IVP Academic, 2012.

Hemer, Colin J. "The Address of 1 Peter." *ExpTim* 89 (1977–78): 239–43.

Hengel, Martin. *Saint Peter: The Underestimated Apostle.* Translated by Thomas Trapp. Grand Rapids: Eerdmans, 2010.

Hill, David. "On Suffering and Baptism in 1 Peter." *NovT* 18 (1976): 181–89.

———. "'To Offer Spiritual Sacrifices . . .' (1 Peter 2:5): Liturgical Formulations and Christian Paraenesis in 1 Peter." *JSNT* 16 (1982): 45–63.

Hillyer, Norman. "First Peter and the Feast of Tabernacles." *TynBul* 21 (1970): 39–70.

Holloway, Paul A. *Coping with Prejudice: 1 Peter in Social-Psychological Perspective.* WUNT 244. Tübingen: Mohr Siebeck, 2009.

Horrell, David G. *1 Peter.* NTG. London: T&T Clark, 2008.

———. "The Label Χριστιανός: 1 Peter 4:16 and the Formation of Christian Identity." *JBL* 126 (2007): 361–81.

———. "The Product of a Petrine Circle? A Reassessment of the Origin and Character of 1 Peter." *JSNT* 86 (2002): 29–60.

———. "Who Are 'The Dead' and When Was the Gospel Preached to Them? The Interpretation of 1 Peter 4:6." *NTS* 49 (2003): 70–89.

Jobes, Karen H. "Got Milk? Septuagint Psalm 33 and the Interpretation of 1 Peter 2:1–3." *WTJ* 64 (2002): 1–14.

Lapham, Fred. *Peter: The Myth, the Man and the Writings; A Study of Early Petrine Text and Traditions.* JSNTSup 239. Sheffield: Sheffield Academic Press, 2000.

Lohse, Eduard. "Paraenesis and Kerygma in 1 Peter." In *Perspectives on First Peter*, edited by Charles H. Talbert, 37–59. NABPRSS 9. Macon, GA: Mercer University Press, 1986.

Martin, Ralph P. "The Composition of I Peter in Recent Study." *VE* 1 (1962): 29–42.

———. "The Theology of Jude, 1 Peter, and 2 Peter." In *The Theology of the Letters of James, Peter, and Jude*, by Andrew Chester and Ralph P. Martin, 63–163. NTT. Cambridge: Cambridge University Press, 1994.

Martin, Troy W. *Metaphor and Composition in 1 Peter.* SBLDS 131. Atlanta: Scholars Press, 1992.

———. "The Present Indicative in the Eschatological Statements of 1 Peter 1:6, 8." *JBL* 111 (1992): 307–14.

———. "The TestAbr and the Background of 1 Peter 3,6." *ZNW* 90 (1999): 139–46.

Mbuvi, Andrew Mutua. *Temple, Exile, and Identity in 1 Peter.* LNTS 345. New York: T&T Clark, 2007.

Michaels, J. Ramsey. "Eschatology in I Peter III.17." *NTS* 13 (1966–67): 394–401.

Mitton, C. Leslie. "The Relationship between 1 Peter and Ephesians." *JTS* 1 (1950): 67–73.

Moule, C. F. D. "The Nature and Purpose of I Peter." *NTS* 3 (1956–57): 1–11.

Moyise, Steve. "Isaiah in 1 Peter." In *Isaiah in the New Testament*, edited by Steve Moyise and Maarten J. J. Menken, 175–88. NTSI. New York: T&T Clark, 2005.

Osborne, Thomas P. "Guide Lines for Christian Suffering: A Source-Critical and Theological Study of 1 Peter 2:21–25." *Bib* 64 (1983): 381–408.

Parker, David C. "The Eschatology of 1 Peter." *BTB* 24 (1994): 27–32.

Pearson, Sharon Clark. *The Christological and Rhetorical Properties of 1 Peter*. SBEC 45. Lewiston, NY: Mellen, 2001.

Perkins, Pheme. *Peter: Apostle for the Whole Church*. SPNT. Columbia: University of South Carolina Press, 1994.

Piper, John. "Hope as the Motivation of Love: I Peter 3:9–12." *NTS* 26 (1978–79): 212–31.

Reicke, Bo. *The Disobedient Spirits and Christian Baptism: A Study of 1 Pet. III:19 and Its Context*. ASNU 13. Copenhagen: Munksgaard, 1946.

Richards, E. Randolph. "Silvanus Was Not Peter's Secretary: Theological Bias in Interpreting διὰ Σιλουανοῦ . . . ἔγραψα." *JETS* 43 (2000): 417–32.

Scharlemann, Martin H. "'He Descended into Hell': An Interpretation of 1 Peter 3:18–20." *CTM* 15 (1989): 311–22.

Schutter, William L. *Hermeneutic and Composition in 1 Peter*. WUNT 2/30. Tübingen: Mohr Siebeck, 1989.

Seland, Torrey. "The 'Common Priesthood' of Philo and 1 Peter: A Philonic Reading of 1 Peter 2:5, 9." *JSNT* 57 (1995): 87–119.

———. *Strangers in the Light: Philonic Perspectives on Christian Identity in 1 Peter*. BIS 76. Leiden: Brill, 2005.

———. "πάροικος καὶ παρεπίδημος: Proselyte Characterizations in 1 Peter?" *BBR* 11 (2001): 239–68.

Sleeper, C. Freeman. "Political Responsibility according to I Peter." *NovT* 10 (1968): 270–86.

Snodgrass, Klyne. "I Peter II.1–10: Its Formation and Literary Affinities." *NTS* 24 (1977–78): 97–106.

Snyder, Scot. "Participles and Imperatives in 1 Peter: A Re-examination in the Light of Recent Scholarly Trends." *FN* 8 (1995): 187–98.

Soards, Marion L. "1 Peter, 2 Peter, and Jude as Evidence for a Petrine School (with Addenda by V. Oliver Ward)." *ANRW* II.25.5 (1988): 3827–49.

Spencer, Aída Besançon. "Peter's Pedagogical Method in 1 Peter 3:6." *BBR* 10 (2000): 107–19.

Stewart-Sykes, Alistair. "The Function of 'Peter' in I Peter." *ScrB* 27 (1997): 8–21.

Talbert, Charles H., ed. *Perspectives on First Peter*. NABPRSS 9. Macon, GA: Mercer University Press, 1986.

Thompson, James W. "'Be Submissive to Your Masters': A Study of 1 Peter 2:18–25." *ResQ* 9 (1966): 66–78.

Thurén, Lauri. *Argument and Theology in 1 Peter: The Origins of Christian Paraenesis*. SBLDS 114. Atlanta: Scholars Press, 1995.

———. *The Rhetorical Strategy of 1 Peter: With Special Regard to Ambiguous Expressions*. Åbo: Åbo Academy Press, 1990.

van Unnik, W. C. "The Teaching of Good Works in I Peter." *NTS* 1 (1954–55): 92–110.

Volf, Miroslav. "Soft Difference: Theological Reflections on the Relation between Church and Culture in 1 Peter." *ExAud* 10 (1994): 15–30.

Warden, Duane. "The Prophets of 1 Peter 1:10–12." *ResQ* 31 (1989): 1–12.

Webb, Robert L., and Betsy Bauman-Martin, eds. *Reading First Peter with New Eyes: Methodological Reassessments of the Letter of First Peter*. LNTS 364. New York: T&T Clark, 2007.

Westfall, Cynthia Long. "The Relationship between the Resurrection, the Proclamation to the Spirits in Prison and Baptismal Regeneration: 1 Peter 3:19–22." In *Resurrection*, edited by Stanley E. Porter, Michael A. Hayes, and David Tombs, 106–35. JSNTSup 186. London: Sheffield Academic Press, 1999.

Woan, Sue. "The Psalms in 1 Peter." In *The Psalms in the New Testament*, edited by Steve Moyise and Maarten J. J. Menken, 213–29. NTSI. New York: T&T Clark, 2004.

Commentaries

Achtemeier, Paul J. *1 Peter: A Commentary on First Peter*. Edited by Eldon Jay Epp. Hermeneia. Minneapolis: Fortress, 1996.

Beare, F. W. *The First Epistle of Peter: The Greek Text with Introduction and Notes*. 3rd ed. Oxford: Blackwell, 1970.

Best, Ernest. *1 Peter*. NCBC. Grand Rapids: Eerdmans, 1982.

Bigg, Charles. *A Critical and Exegetical Commentary on the Epistles of St. Peter and St. Jude*. ICC. Edinburgh: T&T Clark, 1956.

Boring, M. Eugene. *1 Peter*. ANTC. Nashville: Abingdon, 1999.

Craddock, Fred B. *First and Second Peter and Jude*. WestBC. Louisville: Westminster John Knox, 1995.

Cranfield, C. E. B. *I & II Peter and Jude: Introduction and Commentary*. TBC. London: SCM, 1960.

———. *The First Epistle of Peter*. London: SCM, 1950.

Davids, Peter H. *The First Epistle of Peter*. NICNT. Grand Rapids: Eerdmans, 1990.

Donelson, Lewis R. *I & II Peter and Jude*. NTL. Louisville: Westminster John Knox, 2010.

Elliott, John H. *1 Peter: A New Translation with Introduction and Commentary*. AB 37B. New York: Doubleday, 2000.

Feldmeier, Reinhard. *The First Letter of Peter: A Commentary on the Greek Text*. Translated by Peter H. Davids. Waco: Baylor University Press, 2008.

Goppelt, Leonhard. *A Commentary on I Peter*. Translated and augmented by John E. Alsup. Edited by Ferdinand Hahn. Grand Rapids: Eerdmans, 1993.

Green, Joel B. *1 Peter*. THNTC. Grand Rapids: Eerdmans, 2007.

Grudem, Wayne. *The First Epistle of Peter*. TNTC. Grand Rapids: Eerdmans, 1988.

Hillyer, Norman. *1 and 2 Peter, Jude*. NIBC. Peabody, MA: Hendrickson, 1992.

Horrell, David G. *The Epistles of Peter and Jude*. EC. London: Epworth, 1998.

Hort, F. J. A. *The First Epistle of St Peter I.1–II.17: The Greek Text, with Introductory Lecture, Commentary, and Additional Notes*. London: Macmillan, 1898.

Jobes, Karen H. *1 Peter*. BECNT. Grand Rapids: Baker Academic, 2005.

Kelly, J. N. D. *A Commentary on the Epistles of Peter and Jude*. BNTC. London: Black, 1969.

Leaney, A. R. C. *The Letters of Peter and Jude: A Commentary on the First Letter of Peter, a Letter of Jude and the Second Letter of Peter*. CBC. Cambridge: Cambridge University Press, 1967.

Marshall, I. Howard. *1 Peter*. IVPNTC. Downers Grove, IL: InterVarsity, 1991.

McKnight, Scot. *1 Peter*. NIVAC. Grand Rapids: Zondervan, 1996.

Michaels, J. Ramsey. *1 Peter*. WBC 49. Waco: Word, 1988.

Perkins, Pheme. *First and Second Peter, James, and Jude*. IBC. Louisville: John Knox, 1995.

Reicke, Bo. *The Epistles of James, Peter, and Jude: Introduction, Translation, and Notes*. 2nd ed. AB 37. Garden City, NY: Doubleday, 1964.

Richard, Earl Jeffrey. *Reading 1 Peter, Jude, and 2 Peter: A Literary and Theological Commentary*. RNT. Macon, GA: Smyth & Helwys, 2000.

Schreiner, Thomas R. *1, 2 Peter, Jude*. NAC. Nashville: Broadman & Holman, 2003.

Selwyn, Edward G. *The First Epistle of St. Peter: The Greek Text, with Introduction, Notes and Essays*. London: Macmillan, 1946.

Senior, Donald. *1 Peter*. SP 15. Collegeville, MN: Liturgical Press, 2003.

Stibbs, Alan M. *The First Epistle General of Peter: A Commentary*. TNTC. Grand Rapids: Eerdmans, 1979.

38

Jude and Second Peter

Jude and 2 Peter are among the most neglected books of the NT canon. They are short and often rather difficult to understand. As is the case with most of the other Catholic Epistles, we know next to nothing about the origin or life setting of these books. They are nonetheless interesting early Christian documents that have their own unique contribution to make to the church.

The Relation between Jude and Second Peter

The two books share much common material—so much, in fact, that very probably we have to conclude literary dependence one way or the other. As many as nineteen of Jude's total twenty-five verses find full or partial parallels in 2 Peter.[1] Similarities pointing to literary dependence are found mainly between Jude 4–13, 16–18; and 2 Peter 2:1–18; 3:1–3. For a few examples: both refer to "denying the Master [*despotēn arnoumenoi*]" (2 Pet. 2:1; Jude 4); both give OT examples, and both refer to Balaam (Jude 11; 2 Pet. 2:15); both mention "the nether gloom of darkness that has been reserved" (Jude 13; 2 Pet. 2:17); both exhort the readers to "remember . . . the predictions of the apostles/holy prophets" (Jude 17; 2 Pet. 3:2); and both refer to "scoffers" who will come in the last days (Jude 18; 2 Pet. 3:3). We may quickly put aside other possible explanations of the similarities, such as common dependence on an unknown

1. Thus M. Green, *2 Peter Reconsidered*, 10.

third source[2] and common authorship.[3] But if we have here an instance of literary dependence, who depends on whom?

A number of factors point to the priority of Jude and to 2 Peter's dependence on Jude:

1. Jude is much shorter. It is easier to think that 2 Peter is an expansion of Jude than that Jude is an abbreviation of 2 Peter. Why would Jude have omitted so much of 2 Peter? And, indeed, since most of it is already in 2 Peter, why would Jude have been written at all?

2. Jude 4–18 consists of a detailed and carefully structured midrashic treatment of OT texts and *1 Enoch* that can hardly have been produced from the parallels in 2 Peter 2; at the same time, it is not difficult to imagine that the material in 2 Peter 2 can be the result of a mining and alteration of Jude. Redaction-critical analysis points most often to the probable use of Jude by 2 Peter.[4]

3. It is more likely that 2 Peter reorders (and supplements) the references to OT examples in Jude 5–7 so as to have them in chronological order.
   Jude 5–7: exodus/wilderness, fallen angels, Sodom and Gomorrah
   2 Peter 2:4–8: fallen angels, flood (Noah), Sodom and Gomorrah, Lot

4. Second Peter omits Jude's references to apocryphal or pseudepigraphal writings, thereby suggesting a considerably later date for 2 Peter, at a time when canon issues were developing. Thus the material drawn from *Assumption of Moses* or from *Testament of Moses* in Jude 9 is omitted in the parallel 2 Peter 2:10–11,[5] and the reference to Enoch and the citation of *1 Enoch* in Jude 14–15 are lacking in 2 Peter altogether.

5. The "scoffers [who] will come in the last days" (2 Pet. 3:3) scoff, according to Jude, at nothing specific but are said simply to follow "their own ungodly passions" (Jude 4), whereas in 2 Peter they are said to scoff specifically at the delay of the parousia: "Where is the promise of his coming?" This concern is a fundamental point of early catholicism and may point to a time of two or three decades after the death of Peter.

6. The Greek of 2 Peter is inferior to the more refined Hellenistic Greek of Jude, and is most probably a corruption of it.[6]

2. Thus Reicke, *The Epistles of James, Peter, and Jude*; M. Green, *2 Peter and Jude*. The existence of this hypothetical source is, of course, a matter of pure speculation.

3. Robinson, *Redating the New Testament*, 192–95. This conclusion, however, encounters obstacles in the different styles and viewpoints of Jude and 2 Peter.

4. Thus Bauckham, *Jude, 2 Peter*, 142–43.

5. The result of this is that the 2 Peter passage is left quite unclear in meaning. See Gilmour, *The Significance of Parallels between 2 Peter and Other Early Christian Literature*, 84–85.

6. It has also been pointed out that the tone of Jude is rather more direct and harsh than that of 2 Peter, suggesting that the author of the latter modifies it for his readers.

At the end of an exhaustive discussion of the question, Joseph Mayor makes the following remark: "In Jude we have the first thought, in 2 Peter the second thought; . . . we can generally see a reason why 2 Peter should have altered Jude, but very rarely a reason why what we read in 2 Peter should have been altered to what we find in Jude. Second Peter is more reflective, Jude more spontaneous."[7]

Although none of these arguments is conclusive in itself, together they do make it probable that 2 Peter is the later of the two documents and dependent on Jude. The majority opinion by far is that Jude is the earlier document, and that 2 Peter has made use of Jude.[8] If accepted, this conclusion may have some implications for the question of authorship. It may be a little unlikely that the Apostle Peter, if taken as the author of 2 Peter, would be dependent on the writing of a nonapostle, even if the latter was, or claimed to be, the brother of Jesus.

The Epistle of Jude

Jude is a letter written apparently to address a specific situation in the early church, whether in one locality or several. But it is as much a treatise or sermon as it is a letter, and therefore it has been appropriately described as an "epistolary sermon."[9]

The author, however, does not provide enough information for us to know the particulars that caused him to write. Although it has been called "the most neglected book of the New Testament,"[10] it is hardly lacking in either interest or value.

Intruders

The author indicates that he writes under an urgent necessity. Some "false brethren" had "secretly" (cf. Gal. 2:4) infiltrated the church and were perverting "the grace of our God into licentiousness" and denying "our only Master and Lord, Jesus Christ" (v. 4). Among other things, "these men" (v. 8 [cf. the parallel "these" in vv. 10, 12, 14, 16, 19]) "defile the flesh" and "reject authority" (v. 8). They "revile whatever they do not understand" (v. 10) and "boldly carouse together" (v. 12); they are selfish, fruitless, and shameful (vv. 12–13). They are described as "grumblers, malcontents, following their own passions, loud-mouthed boasters, flattering people to gain advantage" (v. 16). They are "scoffers, following their own ungodly passions" (v. 18). They "set up divisions" and are "worldly people, devoid of the Spirit" (v. 19).

7. Mayor, *The Epistle of St. Jude and the Second Epistle of St. Peter*, xxv.
8. This too is the conclusion of the most recent thorough discussion: Wasserman, *The Epistle of Jude*, 73–98. See also Fornberg, *An Early Church in a Pluralistic Society*, 33–59.
9. Thus Bauckham, *Jude, 2 Peter*, 3.
10. See Rowston, "The Most Neglected Book in the New Testament."

> **Author**: No certainty possible, but probably Judas, the brother of Jesus and James.
>
> **Date**: Very difficult to know, but perhaps in about 70, but probably not later than 80.
>
> **Addressees**: Although specific Jewish Christian or mixed congregations appear to be in view, it is impossible to know where they were located.
>
> **Purpose**: To warn with urgency against the influence of ungodly persons who have come into the church, mainly with respect to conduct, but also doctrine.
>
> **Message/Argument**: A letter-sermon based to a considerable extent on analogies of the past applied to the present, indicating the dangers confronting the readers.
>
> **Significance**: Provides a good example of the defensive posture of the early church concerning proper Christian conduct and how Scripture was used to support the argument.

Who are these people? Are these merely general descriptions of unacceptable conduct of different people—that is, an example of stock ancient rhetoric (*vituperatio*) used against opponents—or do they profile one or more particular groups? On the one hand, it is possible that they were Pauline antinomians who were distorting the Pauline gospel. But if that were the case, one might expect some appeal to the law. It is perhaps more probable, on the other hand, that the libertinism of these intruders could represent a kind of incipient gnosticism beginning to infect the church. But again, nothing beyond the ungodly behavior, and perhaps the reference to their "dreamings" (v. 8), assures us that we are on the right track. The author simply does not provide us with enough information to identify the intruders.

The body of Jude's letter begins with the appeal to "contend for the faith which was once for all delivered to the saints" (v. 3) and leads one to expect that the danger confronting the readers is one of false doctrine. Yet the remainder of the letter is concerned with the problem of ungodly conduct. The intruders concerning whom the author cautions his readers do not live as Christians are called to live. The heart of the "epistolary sermon" of Jude is this warning against sinful conduct. The "common salvation" (v. 3) that the author originally intended to address[11] has given way to ethical issues. Doctrine, whether christology or soteriology, is simply assumed by the author and is given no place in the epistle. There can hardly be any doubt, however, that for the author, as for all the early church, truth in doctrine and in conduct were inseparable.

Genre

We noted above that Jude has been described as a sermon in the form of a letter. To a large extent the sermon accomplishes its goal by means of negative

---

11. It is possible, though not necessary, that verse 3a refers to a different letter than our present Jude. In that case, the author was sidetracked from his original intention perhaps by a report concerning the intruders.

examples drawn from both the OT Scriptures and noncanonical writings (vv. 5–16).[12] The sermon is essentially a grave warning. Only at the end of the sermon do we encounter positive exhortation (vv. 20–23), followed by the marvelous doxology in verses 24–25.

The author gathers together passages that exhibit the sequence of unbelief, disobedience, and judgment. In this paradigm unbelief refers not so much to doctrinal heresy as to the cause of disobedience. By means of midrashic treatment (contemporary application) of these passages, he draws parallels with the situation of the intruders and, potentially, the readers. The destruction that came upon those of the past or has been prophesied for the future will come upon those guilty of a similar unrighteousness in the present. "These" are the ones to whom the text applies.[13]

The first example, the exodus from Egypt, is especially apt because it refers to those who were "saved" being then "destroyed" in the wilderness because of their disobedience (v. 5). Next come the examples of the fallen angels (v. 6 [cf. Gen. 6:1–3; 1 En. 6–19]) and the familiar story of Sodom and Gomorrah (v. 7). Not so familiar, however, is the episode referred to in verse 9, which alludes to a story in the pseudepigraphal writing *Assumption of Moses*.[14] Only fragments of this book have survived, none containing the story about the dispute over Moses' body. Further biblical examples refer to Cain, Balaam, and Korah's rebellion (v. 11).

Jude 14–15 is famous for being one of the very few citations of noncanonical books in the NT. The author regards the passage, *1 Enoch* 1:9, as inspired prophecy going back to Enoch in the seventh generation from Adam. Although very close in wording, the quotation is not verbatim. In the reference to the Lord coming "to execute judgment on all, and to convict all the ungodly of all their deeds of ungodliness which they have committed in such an ungodly way" (v. 15), the author has found a statement that exactly supports his argument.

The counteracting, positive charge to the readers comes only in the brief passage in verses 20–21: "But you, beloved, build yourselves up on your most holy faith; pray in the Holy Spirit; keep yourselves in the love of God; wait for the mercy of our Lord Jesus Christ unto eternal life." After a call to "convince some, who doubt," to "save some, by snatching them out of the fire," and "on some have mercy with fear" (vv. 22–23), the author concludes his admonitory sermon with his grand doxology and its note of comfort (vv. 24–25): God is able to keep the Christian from falling.

---

12. For a study of Jude's use of literary-rhetorical conventions, see Charles, *Literary Strategy in the Epistle of Jude*; Watson, *Invention, Arrangement, and Style*.

13. Richard Bauckham has called attention to the similarity between this hermeneutic and the pesher interpretation ("this is that") employed in the Qumran writings (*Jude and the Relatives of Jesus in the Early Church*, 179–234).

14. Alternatively, it may be derived from the lost ending of *Testament of Moses*. For full discussion, see ibid., 235–80.

Theological Emphases: Incipient Early Catholicism?

Given its intense, pragmatic concern with the avoidance of ungodly living, there is still a fair amount of theological content in Jude. Much is assumed of the readers, often with a single word made to carry an understood theological content. Already in the opening words we find reference to the calling and the security of the Christian: "called, beloved in God the Father and kept for Jesus Christ" (v. 1). "Mercy, peace, and love" (v. 2) are words closely associated with the gospel and "our common salvation" (v. 3).

Some of the emphases in Jude indicate concerns usually associated with incipient early catholicism. Thus already in verse 3 we encounter the exhortation "to contend for the faith which was once for all delivered to the saints." Here "the faith" refers to the objective body of truth believed by Christians, not the subjective belief that appropriates the gifts of God. Its once-for-all character points to a well-established tradition that has been "handed down" (the participle is *paradotheisē*) to the church represented by the author and initial readers. Unlike the Pastoral Epistles, here we find no exhortation to guard and pass on that tradition, since that is not the particular concern of the author of Jude. But that it refers to the same well-defined reality can hardly be doubted. It is also in view in the reference to "your most holy faith [*hagiōtatē hymōn pistei*]" (v. 20). Although Jude does not mention church offices per se, it does exalt the apostolic office as the unique guarantor of the tradition, thus providing another early catholic tone. The Apostles are looked back on corporately, with awe: "You must remember, beloved, the predictions of the apostles of our Lord Jesus Christ" (v. 17).

That we do not have early catholicism proper in Jude is fully evident in that the epistle contains no hint of the delay of the parousia or the weakening of eschatological expectation, a primary pillar of early catholicism.[15] On the contrary, Jude if anything seems to hold the expectation of an imminent coming of the Lord and the accompanying judgment (note the words "in the last time" in v. 18, and especially in v. 21 the exhortation to "wait" [*prosdechomenoi*] for "the mercy of Jesus," presumably at the parousia). And, as already mentioned, there are no references to church offices or other instances of the settling down of the church in the world. Furthermore, the Holy Spirit is mentioned twice (vv. 19–20), with no sense that the work of the Spirit has ceased. At most, therefore, we may say that although a few of the important emphases of an incipient early catholicism are evident in Jude, we have no evidence of a full-blown early catholicism, and certainly nothing that would necessitate a particularly late date for the epistle.

Although the author assumes rather than articulates it, he has an obviously high christology. He refers to Jesus Christ as "our only Master [*despotēs*] and Lord [*kyrios*]" (v. 4) and repeatedly as "Lord" (vv. 17, 21, 25). Given his

---

15. See the discussion of early catholicism in chapter 33 above.

purpose, Jude's christology centers on Christ as coming eschatological Judge. He inserts the reference to "Lord" in the quotation in verse 14 probably because he understands Jesus as the one who comes to judge.[16] This clearly is the point of verse 21: "wait for the mercy of our Lord Jesus Christ unto eternal life." As throughout the NT, Jesus is the divine Agent who functions in the role of God and is thus uniquely related to the being of God. The mystery is articulated in verse 25: "to the only God, our Savior through Jesus Christ our Lord."

Canon Difficulties

Jude, like several other Catholic Epistles, had a slow and difficult time in being accepted into the evolving canon of the early church. However, it does appear in the Muratorian Canon and was commented on by Clement of Alexandria in about 200.

Eusebius classifies the book as among the "disputed" books (*antilegomena*), along with James, 2 Peter, and 2–3 John (*Hist. eccl.* 3.25.3). Elsewhere Eusebius notes that the authenticity of Jude was *denied*, although he also mentions that "these letters [James and Jude] have been used publicly with the rest in most churches" (*Hist. eccl.* 2.23.25, trans. Lake). In the fourth-century manuscript Vaticanus the ancient "chapter" divisions are not present for 2 Peter, suggesting that it was not yet regarded as canonical.[17]

Jude is not included in the fourth-century Syrian translation known as the Peshitta, and it was not accepted in the Syrian church until as late as the Philoxenian version of the sixth century. Martin Luther relegated Jude to the inferior books of the NT, placing it at the end of his NT.

It seems that perhaps the main reason for the hesitation concerning Jude in the early church was that it quoted (in vv. 14–15), and thus apparently sanctioned, the noncanonical book *1 Enoch*. However, the earliest church employed a rather larger "OT canon" than did the church of later centuries (which eventually felt compelled to tailor its OT canon to agree with the established Jewish canon).[18]

Text, Author, Date, Addressees

Text

Jude is infamous for its text-critical problems, the number of which, for whatever reason, is out of all proportion to the epistle's brevity. Joseph Mayor concludes that "the text is in a less satisfactory condition than that of any

---

16. See Bauckham, *Jude and the Relatives of Jesus in the Early Church*, 288–302.
17. Thus Metzger and Ehrman, *The Text of the New Testament*, 69. See chapter 42 below.
18. See chapter 43 below.

other portion of the New Testament."[19] Among the more notable textual difficulties are those in verses 1–5, 12, 18–19, and especially 22–23.[20]

Author and Date

The author identifies himself as "Jude, a servant of Jesus Christ and brother of James" (v. 1). Because "Jude" and "James" were very common names, when they are written here without further specification, they must refer to well-known persons in the early church. The James who immediately comes to mind is James the brother of Jesus (see Gal. 1:19) and the head of the Jerusalem church. "Jude" is simply an alternate, English form of "Judas" (as in the Greek text of v. 1). James and Judas are listed as among the brothers of Jesus in the Gospel narratives (Mark 6:3; Matt. 13:55; cf. Eusebius, *Hist. eccl.* 3.19.1). The Judas referred to in the list of Apostles in Luke 6:6 and Acts 1:13 (lit., "Judas of James") is the son, not brother, of James and thus cannot be the author of Jude (*pace* John Calvin). The Jewishness of the book's perspective, its midrashic interpretation of Palestinian Jewish literature, and its concern with ethical paraenesis are fully consistent with what we might expect from Judas, the brother of Jesus and James. The rather high quality of the epistle's Greek is surprising but probably not out of the range of what Judas perhaps could have achieved toward the end of his life. Thus, although the possibility of pseudepigraphy need not be ruled out—one may wonder, however, at the choice of the otherwise obscure "Jude" for a pseudonym—there seems to be no compelling reason to deny the traditional conclusion concerning its authorship by Judas the brother of Jesus.

As pointed out above, there is no need to date Jude very late. The incipient early catholic traits probably rule out an early date as well. A date of about 70, but probably not later than 80, seems a good guess.

Addressees

No assistance concerning the location of the addressees is provided in the opening sentence. But since the epistle has quite specific concerns, it must have been written to congregations of a certain area. Probably these were Jewish Christians, though the existence of Gentiles in the church(es) cannot be excluded. If we speculate—and that is all that can be done—Jude could have been addressed to almost anywhere. Alexandria in Egypt is often mentioned, but there are many other possibilities. The only place that seems an unlikely suggestion from the start is Syrian Antioch (in Syria, as noted above, Jude was accepted only very late).

19. Mayor, *The Epistle of St. Jude and the Second Epistle of St. Peter*, clxxxi.
20. The definitive study of the text of Jude is Wasserman, *The Epistle of Jude*. See also Landon, *A Text-Critical Study of the Epistle of Jude*.

Second Peter

As was explained above, we can be fairly certain that 2 Peter is dependent on Jude. Second Peter, more than twice as long as Jude, contains much the same material and probably is rightly understood to be a creative expansion and application of the basic content of Jude to a new situation. It is thought by many to be the latest book in the NT canon.

The Authorship Question

According to the opening words of the letter, 2 Peter was written by "Simeon Peter, a servant and apostle of Jesus Christ." But for several reasons many scholars have doubted this statement as being literally true.

ARGUMENTS AGAINST PETRINE AUTHORSHIP

Several strong arguments oppose the authenticity of 2 Peter.

1. The language of 2 Peter is very different from that of 1 Peter, both in vocabulary and literary style. The vocabulary of 2 Peter is highly distinctive, with the highest proportion of *hapax legomena* (i.e., words occurring only once in the NT) of any NT book: out of a vocabulary of 401 words, 57 are unique in the NT, and 32 of those are lacking in the whole of the Greek Bible. Only a very few of 2 Peter's rare words are shared with Jude. The style of 2 Peter's language is artificial and highly contrived. The author's "grandiose language" gives the impression of "aiming at ambitious literary effect."[21] It seems very unlikely that Peter would have written this kind of Greek.

   The contrast with the Greek vocabulary and style of 1 Peter is striking. The majority of words shared by 2 Peter and 1 Peter are common words. Richard Bauckham notes that of the thirty-eight words occurring elsewhere in the NT only once or twice—that is, 2 Peter's distinctive vocabulary—a mere two occur in 1 Peter. "None of the really characteristic terminology of either epistle reappears in the other."[22] The two letters also differ greatly in substance and tone. So too 2 Peter addresses the problem of the delay of the parousia, while this problem is absent from 1 Peter.

2. Second Peter's dependence on Jude. It seems rather unlikely that an Apostle—indeed, the prime Apostle, Peter—would so depend on and

---

21. Thus Bauckham, *Jude, 2 Peter*, 137. For a thorough discussion of the epistle's language, see ibid., 135–38. Nigel Turner concludes that the Greek of 2 Peter is "too sophisticated to substantiate any claim that it belongs to the vernacular Koine" ("The Literary Character of New Testament Greek," 107).

22. Bauckham, *Jude, 2 Peter*, 144.

Author: Almost certainly not by Peter. Very probably written by a disciple of Peter or a member of the Petrine circle.

Date: Probably to be put in the 80s or possibly the 90s. But there is little reason to put it confidently in the second century.

Addressees: Probably an unknown community or communities, if the letter is not addressing general problems faced by many churches.

Purpose: A warning against false teaching and improper conduct.

Message/Argument: Presented somewhat in the form of a testament of Peter—that is, providing some final admonitions and instructions from the prime Apostle.

Significance: Stress on the truth of Christianity, the reality of future judgment, and the certainty of the future parousia of Christ.

take up so much of a letter written by a nonapostle, and one so little known, even if purportedly a brother of James and hence of Jesus.

3. Evidence of a time later than the Apostle Peter (martyred ca. 64). Second Peter reveals clear marks of an incipient early catholicism (see "Incipient Early Catholicism" below) that seem to point, at the earliest, to the later decades of the first century. Perhaps most striking among these marks is the reference to the letters of Paul: "So also our beloved brother Paul wrote to you according to the wisdom given him, speaking of this as he does in all his letters. There are some things in them hard to understand,[23] which the ignorant and unstable twist to their own destruction, as they do the other scriptures" (3:15–16). Two issues emerge from this statement: the collection of Paul's Letters and the implication that they are regarded as "scriptures." Both point to a time later than Peter himself. The letters of Paul were collected probably no earlier than 85 or 90 (see discussion in chapter 43 below), and it is doubtful that they would have been regarded as "scriptures" (*graphai*) to be put alongside the OT Scriptures much before that, even if they were earlier accepted as bearing apostolic authority. Second Peter's omission of the quotation from *1 Enoch* suggests a consciousness of OT canonical issues, also suggesting a somewhat later date. Similarly, the reference to "your apostles" (3:2) and the statement "ever since the fathers fell asleep" (3:4) seem to refer to a time no earlier than late in the first century.

4. The presence of what sounds like a late, gnostic concept of apotheosis. It is difficult to imagine Peter writing in 1:4 that Christians may escape the corruption of the present world "and become partakers of the divine

23. This does not mean that the author presents Peter as unable to understand Paul's Letters (*pace* Guthrie, *New Testament Introduction*, 814, 827). The point seems to be that others, not Peter, misunderstood Paul, as the following clause indicates.

nature [*theias koinōnoi physeōs*]."[24] Other Hellenistic concepts also seem strange coming from Peter: "moral excellence" (*aretē*) (1:3, 5) and "eyewitnesses" (*epoptai*) (1:16). There are also pointers to incipient gnostic tendencies among the false teachers, which are more likely after the time of Peter than earlier.

5. The use of personal allusions look specially contrived to support the claim that Peter is the author, a typical device of pseudonymous writers. The double name of the salutation, "Simeon Peter," seems unnecessary. But more symptomatic verisimilitude is seen in the following: the deliberate allusion to the first letter (i.e., 1 Peter, almost certainly known to the author) in 3:1: "This is now the second letter that I have written to you, beloved, and in both of them I have aroused your sincere mind by way of reminder"; and the allusion to the transfiguration in 1:16–18: "But we were eyewitnesses of his majesty. For when he received honor and glory from God the Father and the voice was borne to him by the Majestic Glory, 'This is my beloved Son, with whom I am well pleased,' we heard this voice borne from heaven, for we were with him on the holy mountain." This seems to be a labored and artificial attempt to show that the author was Peter. A further instance that looks suspicious is the statement in 1:14, "I know that the putting off of my body will be soon, as our Lord Jesus Christ showed me," which looks very much as though it may be an allusion to John 21:18–19.

6. The difficulty that 2 Peter had in being admitted into the canon. As will be examined more fully below, there was considerable doubt in the early church concerning whether this letter rightly belonged in the canon.

RESPONSES TO THE CHALLENGE

Defenders of the authenticity of 2 Peter have attempted to answer the objections just surveyed.[25] The question is whether the answers are sufficient to overcome the cumulative argument against authenticity.

1. The issue of differing language, both vocabulary and style, can be readily answered by appealing to the use of a different amanuensis for 2 Peter (cf. 1 Peter 5:12, although Silvanus may have been only the bearer of the letter). Ever since the time of Jerome the hypothesis of different secretaries has been used to explain the differences in Greek vocabulary

24. For a thorough study on this, see Starr, *Sharers in the Divine Nature*. Starr does not see the passage as referring to gnostic ideas of apotheosis. Rather, he finds abundant source material in Jewish literature and interprets the passage as referring to the Christian's sharing of the moral excellence of Christ now, and in the future the sharing of his immortality.

25. Two of the most thorough defenses of the authenticity of 2 Peter are M. Green, *2 Peter Reconsidered* (see also idem, *2 Peter and Jude*, 13–39); Guthrie, *New Testament Introduction*, 820–42.

and style. In this case, however, the secretary has been given such free rein that the line between secretary and pseudonymous author again all but disappears. Although it is important, this argument against authenticity is probably the least significant of all.

2. We cannot be certain that Jude is prior to 2 Peter; perhaps it is Jude who is dependent on 2 Peter. But even if the majority opinion that 2 Peter depends on Jude is correct, that does not mean that the Apostle Peter cannot have seen valuable material coming from Jude, the brother of James, and thus made use of it. Because something is unlikely hardly makes it impossible.

3. The reference in 3:16 to "all" Paul's Letters does not necessarily mean a collection of the complete Pauline corpus, whether of ten or thirteen letters. It may refer only to several letters known to Peter. The Greek word *graphai* can mean "writings" and need not mean "holy scriptures." It is not impossible, however, that Peter could have thought of Paul's Letters as inspired Scriptures. The "fathers" who have died (3:4) could be OT patriarchs rather than the first generation of Christians; "your apostles" (3:2) possibly refers to no more than those who had worked among the readers.

4. There is no reason to think that Peter cannot have been influenced to some extent by Hellenistic ideas, which had permeated first-century Palestine. This is also true to an extent concerning the ideas and vocabulary of incipient gnosticism.[26]

5. If the traditional authorship is accepted, then the personal allusions make perfect sense. They need not be taken as the literary devices of a pseudepigraphist. The judgment that these references display artificiality is a decidedly subjective one.

6. The slowness of acceptance for 2 Peter simply points to the care with which the early church considered the formation of the canon. In the end, the authenticity of the letter was accepted by the church.

Two other considerations often raised in support of the authenticity of 2 Peter are: first, the similarities that can be pointed out between it and the narratives about Peter's words in the Gospels and Acts, as well as a variety of similarities with 1 Peter; and, second, the great differences between 2 Peter and the universally acknowledged body of pseudonymous Petrine literature (e.g., the apocryphal *Acts of Peter*, *Apocalypse of Peter*, and *Kerygma of Peter*).

---

26. The typical response to gnostic or incipient gnostic ideas on the part of those defending authenticity is to say (rightly) that there is no evidence in the NT of the developed Gnosticism of the second century and then to conclude (wrongly) that the document in question is therefore not pseudonymous. The later decades of the first century provide considerable evidence of the growing influence of incipient gnostic thought before the rise of the full-blown Gnosticism.

Conclusion

As we have seen often in earlier discussions of cases of disputed authorship, no knockout blow can be delivered by either side; instead, we are dealing with a series of arguments that build to a cumulative case of probability. Petrine authorship of 2 Peter cannot be absolutely excluded. It must be admitted that answers can be given to the arguments against Petrine authorship. Nevertheless, the defense of the authenticity of 2 Peter remains very much an uphill argument, and it depends mainly on possibilities rather than probabilities. John Calvin, following the lead of Jerome, concluded, "I do not here recognize the language of Peter." He says further that "it must have proceeded from Peter; not that he himself wrote it, but that some one of his disciples set forth in writing, by his command, those things which the necessity of the times required."[27]

After extensive study, that masterful commentator on the epistle, Joseph Mayor, wrote:

> When I began to pay special attention to [2 Peter] . . . my own feeling was that the traditional view must be accepted, unless it could be disproved by positive evidence on the other side; and I was not satisfied that such positive evidence had yet been adduced in proof of its spuriousness. Further consideration, however, of the language, matter, and the tone of the two Petrine epistles has gradually forced me to the conclusion already arrived at by Calvin and Grotius, as well as by many modern commentators, that the second epistle is not written by the author of the first epistle—a conclusion which in my view is equivalent to saying that it is not by the Apostle St. Peter.[28]

Genre and Purpose

As the opening salutation indicates, 2 Peter is a letter, although the specific readers are identified only very generally. There is no evidence of a personal relationship between the author and the readers, and there are no greetings at the end of the letter. Second Peter also bears the marks of a "testament," a document written as a kind of farewell address before the imminent death of the author (cf. 1:14), containing final counsel for the future. The testament was a popular Jewish and Christian form of pseudepigraphy in the ancient world. It may be that this document was intended to be a "Testament of Peter," containing a variety of last warnings and exhortations, so "that after my departure you may be able at any time to recall these things" (1:15).

Second Peter, like Jude, addresses a situation of danger for the church. Despite the similarities, however, it is a mistake to assume that the situation

27. See the introduction to Calvin's commentary on 2 Peter.
28. Mayor, *The Epistle of St. Jude and the Second Epistle of St. Peter*, vii.

was exactly the same. In both cases we have little idea where the addressees lived. Like Jude, 2 Peter earnestly warns against immoral conduct. The opening of the letter points in this direction, from the mention of "righteousness" in 1:1 to the call to "escape from the corruption that is in the world" (1:4) and the list of virtues in 1:5–7. "Whoever lacks these things is blind and shortsighted and has forgotten that he was cleansed from his old sins" (1:9).

At the same time, the author explicitly writes to warn against false teachers:

> But false prophets also arose among the people, just as there will be false teachers [*pseudodidaskaloi*] among you, who will secretly bring in destructive heresies [*haireseis apōleias*], even denying the Master who bought them, bringing upon themselves swift destruction. (2:1)

> Because of them the way of truth will be reviled. And in their greed, they will exploit you with false words. (2:2–3)

But not only are these teachers purveyors of false teaching; they also are guilty of a gross immorality ("their licentiousness" [2:2]; "those who indulge in the lust of defiling passion" [2:10]), which they also promote among those who listen to them. "They count it pleasure to revel in the daytime. . . . They have eyes full of adultery, insatiable for sin. . . . Forsaking the right way they have gone astray" (2:13–15). They "entice" others, promising them a "freedom" that ends in corruption (2:19). The author warns that "it would have been better for them never to have known the way of righteousness than after knowing it to turn back from the holy commandment delivered to them" (2:21).

These false teachers "despise authority" (2:10) and have no regard for the authority or tradition of the Apostles (cf. 3:2), or even of Christ himself (2:1). They deny the coming eschatological judgment and are oblivious to the threat that it poses to them.

Can these false teachers be identified with any groups that we are familiar with from elsewhere in the NT? Although it would be a mistake to identify them as Gnostics as we know them from the second century, they do seem to exhibit some of the traits of a proto-gnostic perspective. Does the reference to "cleverly devised myths" (*sesophismenoi mythoi*) in 1:16 refer to their doctrines? Does our author's repeated use of "knowledge" point to the heretical teachers' emphasis on *gnōsis* (1:5–6; 3:18) and *epignōsis* (emphatic, 1:2–3, 8; 2:20; verbal form twice in 2:21)? The point of these references would then be that Christians possess the true knowledge compared with the false knowledge of those emphasizing *gnōsis*. The opening statement of the letter seems aimed at outdoing gnostic claims: "His divine power has granted to us all things that pertain to life and godliness, through the knowledge of him who called us to his own glory and excellence, by which he has granted to us his precious and very great promises, that through these you may escape from the corruption that is in the world because of passion, and become partakers of the divine nature" (1:3–4 [cf. 2:20]). The last part of this statement more than hints at a dualistic perspective associated with gnostic thinking. The immorality and licentiousness of the false teachers are readily explainable from that strain of gnostic thinking that paid no regard to the body and its activities. The insistent ethical paraenesis of 2 Peter fits this analysis, as does the teachers' denial of eschatology and eschatological judgment.

Some have pointed to another area of Hellenistic influence among the false teachers in 2 Peter: Epicureanism. Thus Jerome Neyrey notes that the Epicureans rejected divine providence as well as judgment or reward after death,[29] the very thing that 2 Peter is so determined to affirm.

A conclusion that 2 Peter exhibits evidence of an incipient gnosticism on the part of the false teachers by no means necessitates a second-century date for the epistle, since traits of an incipient gnosticism already make their appearance by the middle of the first century, increasing as the century wore on. What is opposed in 2 Peter is not Gnosticism proper.

The immediate purpose of the epistle is given in the penultimate statement of the letter: "You therefore, beloved, knowing this beforehand, beware lest you be carried away with the error of lawless men and lose your own stability" (3:17 [cf. 1:10–11]).

Incipient Early Catholicism

It is exactly the sort of threat just outlined that the various emphases of early catholicism are designed to address. Although it is hardly to be thought of as an example of classic early catholicism, 2 Peter exhibits some of the tendencies of an incipient form of early catholicism that point to the later decades of the first century.[30]

Although it is the false teachers who challenge the reality of the promised parousia (3:3–4), the delay of the parousia is something against which the author has to defend. He and his readers surely retain their future eschatological expectation (cf. 3:11–13), expressed so beautifully in the words of 1:19: "You will do well to pay attention to this as to a lamp shining in a dark place, until the day dawns and the morning star [an allusion to Num. 24:17; cf. Rev. 22:16]

---

29. Neyrey, 2 Peter, Jude, 122–28.
30. Ernst Käsemann's "An Apologia for Primitive Christian Eschatology," an anaylsis of early catholic elements in 2 Peter, is insightful, but it presses the evidence to an unjustifiably radical conclusion, forcing the book into the mid-second century.

rises in your hearts." At the same time, however, it is necessary for the author and the readers to work through the problem of the delay. "The fathers" have died (3:4); that is, the first generation of Christian believers has passed from the scene without the return of Christ. Thus the author exhorts his readers: "But do not ignore this one fact, beloved, that with the Lord one day is as a thousand years, and a thousand years as one day. The Lord is not slow about his promise as some count slowness, but is forbearing toward you, not wishing that any should perish, but that all should reach repentance" (3:8–9). This suggests a later date for the epistle. Second Peter may also be said to have its share of realized eschatology.

In the polemic against the heresy of the false teachers 2 Peter puts a premium on orthodoxy and knowledge of the truth. The "faith" (1:1) refers to something fixed, a body of truth including both doctrine and ethical paraenesis, of which the Apostles in particular are regarded as the revered custodians ("through your apostles" [3:2]; cf. "the holy commandment delivered to them" [2:21]). The readers are "established in the truth that [they] have" (1:12). Christian teaching is "the way of truth" (2:2) and "the way of righteousness" (2:21). Second Peter's shying away from the citation of noncanonical writings also points to an increased sensitivity to the authority of the developing canon.

Second Peter is marked by a strong moralism, from the Hellenistic catalog of virtues in 1:5–7 (the words "virtue" [aretē], "self-control" [enkrateia], and "godliness" [eusebeia] are important in Hellenistic ethical admonition) to the ethical exhortation that occurs throughout the epistle. The stress is on the importance of righteousness and obedience to the holy commandment that goes back to Jesus (2:21; 3:2). Despite the allusion to Paul's Letters in 3:15–16, there is no articulation of salvation by faith in 2 Peter, although the twice-repeated word "granted" (dōreomai) in 1:3–4 points to the grace (see also 3:18) that underlies salvation (cf. 3:15).

The reference to Paul as "our beloved brother" and to "the wisdom given him" (3:15) seems a little forced and is perhaps an attempt to smooth over differences between the two Apostles, not that we need think that they were polarized against each other. What also seems to be an example of late first-century catholic interests in the authority of the church and its Scriptures is the reference to the collection of Paul's Letters and the esteem of them as Scripture.

Some of the emphases that we associate with early catholicism, however, even in an incipient manifestation as in the Pastoral Epistles, do not appear in 2 Peter. While there is a noticeable absence of reference to the Holy Spirit (1:21 refers to the work of the Spirit in connection with the OT Scriptures), we do not find in 2 Peter the corresponding emphasis on church order or offices. And, perhaps surprisingly, the household codes for regulating behavior make no appearance in 2 Peter. Similarly, there is little evidence of a self-consciousness of the church such as we find in the Pastorals.

Theological Emphases

The heart of 2 Peter is its emphasis on the reality of eschatological judgment as the motivation for living righteously. This emphasis is made repeatedly and by means of a series of illustrations (see esp. 2:4–16; 3:6). Thus Jewish apocalyptic looms large in 2 Peter (see 3:3–13, sometimes referred to as a "little apocalypse"). "The day of the Lord will come like a thief," and the heavens and earth will be destroyed (3:10; cf. 3:7). "The coming of the day of God" (synonymous with "the day of the Lord") will mean the dissolving of the heavens and in due time the coming of "new heavens and a new earth in which righteousness dwells" (3:12–13 [cf. Isa. 65:17; 66:22; Rev. 21:1]). Immediately after these words the author characteristically brings the application: "Therefore, beloved, since you wait for these, be zealous to be found by him without spot or blemish, and at peace" (3:14).

The reality of the eventual, if seemingly delayed, parousia of Christ (3:4) becomes an important point for the author. He confirms its reality by an allusion to Psalm 90:4 (3:8): a thousand years is as nothing before the Lord. The story of the transfiguration of Christ is an account of a parousia (1:16, where the Greek word *parousia* is used) that had already happened and thus serves as an anticipation and guarantee of the eschatological parousia. "We have the prophetic word made more sure" (1:19).

The high christology of 2 Peter is also remarkable. In one of the small handful of cases in the NT where Jesus perhaps is referred to as God,[31] 1:1 refers to Jesus as "our God and Savior," where the two nouns are governed by a single definite article, meaning that they refer to the same person. In 1:11 there is a reference to "the eternal kingdom of our Lord and Savior Jesus Christ." Christ is called "Lord and Savior" also in 2:20; 3:2, 18. Also to be noted is the application of *despotēs* ("master" or "sovereign") to Christ (2:1). The transfiguration story refers not only to the "majesty" of Christ but also to the "honor and glory" that he received from God, who referred to him as "my beloved Son, with whom I am well pleased" (1:16–17).

Finally, we may note 1:20–21: "First of all you must understand this, that no prophecy of scripture is a matter of one's own interpretation, because no prophecy ever came by the impulse of man, but men moved by the Holy Spirit spoke from God." Here we have both an allusion to a tradition of hermeneutical consensus and also a doctrine of inspiration. The interpretation of prophecy is not a matter of private opinion; rather, it belongs in the domain of the community of faith. The reason is that prophecy comes from God and is not

31. See Harris, *Jesus as God*.

of human origin. What differentiates prophecy (and, by extension, Scripture) from ordinary discourse is its divine origin. It is human beings who speak, but they do so "from God [*apo theou*]," as a source, being "moved [*pheromenoi*, lit., "being carried"] by the Holy Spirit."

Author, Addressees, Date

Author

It may be that this document was intended to be a "Testament of Peter," enshrining Petrine traditions, written by someone associated with Peter in some way, perhaps as a disciple in a Petrine school in Rome.[32] The author probably was an educated Hellenistic Jewish Christian.

Addressees

Since it is concerned with specific problems faced by the readers, 2 Peter was written probably to a specific church or, more likely, to a group of churches in a particular region. It is difficult to guess where in the Mediterranean world these churches might have been located. The original readers could have been either Jews or Gentiles or, more likely, a combination of the two.

Date

The discussion of authorship and early catholicism earlier in this chapter indicated a number of reasons that make it difficult to date the epistle in the lifetime of Peter. The evidence of gnosticism and early catholicism is all of an incipient kind, quite obviously short of the full manifestation of these phenomena in the second century. We may tentatively suggest a date between 80 and 90, or possibly sometime in the last decade of the century.

Entry into the Canon

No other book of the NT was accepted into the NT canon with more hesitance than 2 Peter, and no canonical book is so poorly attested in the early church. A papyrus manuscript, $\mathfrak{P}^{72}$, from the first half of the second century contains 2 Peter. There is no convincing evidence, however, that the earliest fathers before Clement of Alexandria, at the end of the second century, knew 2 Peter, and it is lacking in the Muratorian Canon (which, however, also lacks 1 Peter and is fragmentary). For probably the earliest sure record of a knowledge of the epistle we have Origen's remark: "Peter . . . has

---

32. See Soards, "1 Peter, 2 Peter, and Jude as Evidence for a Petrine School."

left one acknowledged [*homologoumenēn*] epistle, and, it may be, a second also; for it is doubted [*amphiballetai*]" (according to Eusebius, *Hist. eccl.* 6.25.8, trans. Oulton). Eusebius gives his own assessment in these words: "Of Peter, one epistle, that which is called his first, is admitted, and the ancient presbyters used this in their own writings as unquestioned, but the so-called second epistle we have not received as canonical, but nevertheless it has appeared useful to many, and has been studied with other Scriptures" (*Hist. eccl.* 3.3.1, trans. Lake). Eusebius places 2 Peter, along with James, Jude, and 2–3 John, among "the disputed books [*tōn antilegomenōn*] which are nevertheless known to most" (*Hist. eccl.* 3.25.3, trans. Lake). Jerome, as we have already noted, had questions about 2 Peter, centering on the style of the Greek compared to 1 Peter.

In the sixteenth century Erasmus, Calvin, and Luther had their doubts about the authenticity of 2 Peter. Calvin appreciated the content of the book and wrote that "to repudiate it is what I dread, though I do not here recognize the language of Peter."[33] Nevertheless, 2 Peter well deserves its place in the NT canon as inspired Scripture, and our NT would be the poorer without it.

Bibliography

Books and Articles

Adams, Edward. "Where Is the Promise of His Coming? The Complaint of the Scoffers in 2 Peter 3:4." *NTS* 51 (2005): 106–22.

Allen, Joel S. "A New Possibility for the Three-Clause Format of Jude 22–23." *NTS* 44 (1998): 133–43.

Bauckham, Richard. "James, 1 Peter, Jude, and 2 Peter." In *Vision for the Church: Studies in Early Christian Ecclesiology in Honour of J. P. M. Sweet*, edited by Markus Bockmuehl and Michael B. Thompson, 153–66. Edinburgh: T&T Clark, 1997.

———. *Jude and the Relatives of Jesus in the Early Church*. Edinburgh: T&T Clark, 1990.

———. "The Letter of Jude: An Account of Research." *ANRW* II.25.5 (1988): 3791–826.

———. "2 Peter: An Account of Research." *ANRW* II.25.5 (1988): 3713–52.

Boobyer, G. H. "The Indebtedness of 2 Peter to 1 Peter." In *New Testament Essays: Studies in Memory of Thomas Walter Manson, 1893–1958*, edited by A. J. B. Higgins, 34–53. Manchester, UK: Manchester University Press, 1959.

Callan, Terrance. "The Christology of the Second Letter of Peter." *Bib* 82 (2001): 253–63.

———. "The Soteriology of the Second Letter of Peter." *Bib* 82 (2001): 549–59.

———. "Use of the Letter of Jude by the Second Letter of Peter." *Bib* 85 (2004): 42–64.

Cavallin, Hans C. C. "The False Teachers of 2 Peter as Pseudo-Prophets." *NovT* 21 (1979): 263–70.

Charles, J. Daryl. "The Angels under Reserve in 2 Peter and Jude." *BBR* 15 (2005): 39–48.

———. "Jude's Use of Pseudepigraphical Source-Material as Part of a Literary Strategy." *NTS* 37 (1991): 130–45.

———. "The Language and Logic of Virtue in 2 Peter 1:5–7." *BBR* 8 (1998): 55–73.

———. "Literary Artifice in the Epistle of Jude." *ZNW* 82 (1991): 106–24.

33. Calvin, in the introduction to his commentary on 2 Peter.

———. *Literary Strategy in the Epistle of Jude*. Scranton, PA: University of Scranton Press, 1993.

———. "'Those' and 'These': The Use of the Old Testament in the Epistle of Jude." *JSNT* 38 (1990): 109–24.

———. *Virtue amidst Vice: The Catalogue of Virtues in 2 Peter 1*. JSNTSup 150. Sheffield: Sheffield Academic Press, 1997.

Countryman, L. William. "Asceticism or Household Morality: 1 and 2 Peter and Jude." In *Asceticism and the New Testament*, edited by Leif E. Vaage and Vincent L. Wimbush, 371–82. New York: Routledge, 1999.

Danker, Frederick W. "2 Peter 1: A Solemn Decree." *CBQ* 40 (1978): 64–82.

Desjardins, Michel. "The Portrayal of the Dissidents in 2 Peter and Jude: Does It Tell Us More about the 'Godly' than the 'Ungodly'?" *JSNT* 30 (1987): 89–102.

Duke, Thomas H. "An Exegetical Analysis of 2 Peter 3:9." *FM* 16 (1999): 6–13.

Dunnett, Walter M. "The Hermeneutics of Jude and 2 Peter: The Use of Ancient Jewish Traditions." *JETS* 31 (1988): 287–92.

Ellis, E. Earle. "Prophecy and Hermeneutic in Jude." *Prophecy and Hermeneutic in Early Christianity: New Testament Essays*, 220–36. WUNT 18. Tübingen: Mohr Siebeck, 1978.

Fornberg, Tord. *An Early Church in a Pluralistic Society: A Study of 2 Peter*. Translated by Jean Gray. ConBNT 9. Lund: Gleerup, 1977.

Fossum, Jarl. "Kyrios Jesus as the Angel of the Lord in Jude 5–7." *NTS* 33 (1987): 226–43.

Frey, Jörg. "The Epistle of Jude between Judaism and Hellenism." In *The Catholic Epistles and Apostolic Tradition: A New Perspective on James to Jude*, edited by Karl-Wilhelm Niebuhr and Robert W. Wall, 309–29. Waco: Baylor University Press, 2009.

Gerdmar, Anders. *Rethinking the Judaism-Hellenism Dichotomy: A Historiographical Study of Second Peter and Jude*. ConBNT 36. Stockholm: Almqvist & Wiksell, 2001.

Gilmour, Michael J. "Reflections on the Authorship of 2 Peter." *EvQ* 73 (2001): 291–309.

———. "2 Peter in Recent Research: A Bibliography." *JETS* 42 (1999): 673–78.

———. *The Significance of Parallels between 2 Peter and Other Early Christian Literature*. SBLAB 10. Atlanta: Society of Biblical Literature, 2002.

Green, Michael. *2 Peter Reconsidered*. London: Tyndale, 1961.

Guthrie, Donald H. *New Testament Introduction*. 4th rev. ed. Downers Grove, IL: InterVarsity, 1990.

Hafemann, Scott J. "Salvation in Jude 5 and the Argument of 2 Peter 1:3–11." In *The Catholic Epistles and Apostolic Tradition: A New Perspective on James to Jude*, edited by Karl-Wilhelm Niebuhr and Robert W. Wall, 331–42. Waco: Baylor University Press, 2009.

Harris, Murray J. *Jesus as God: The New Testament Use of* Theos *in Reference to Jesus*. Grand Rapids: Baker Academic, 1992.

Heide, Gale Z. "What Is New about the New Heaven and the New Earth? A Theology of Creation from Revelation 21 and 2 Peter 3." *JETS* 40 (1997): 37–56.

Joubert, Stephan J. "Language, Ideology, and the Social Context of the Letter of Jude." *Neot* 24 (1990): 335–49.

———. "Persuasion in the Letter of Jude." *JSNT* 58 (1995): 75–87.

Käsemann, Ernst. "An Apologia for Primitive Christian Eschatology." In *Essays on New Testament Themes*, translated by W. J. Montague, 169–95. Philadelphia: Fortress, 1982 [German original, 1954].

Knight, Jonathan. *2 Peter and Jude*. NTG. Sheffield: Sheffield Academic Press, 1995.

Kruger, Michael J. "The Authenticity of 2 Peter." *JETS* 42 (1999): 647–71.

Landon, Charles. *A Text-Critical Study of the Epistle of Jude*. JSNTSup 135. Sheffield: Sheffield Academic Press, 1996.

Lapham, Fred. *Peter: The Myth, the Man and the Writings; A Study of Early Petrine Text and Traditions*. JSNTSup 239. Sheffield: Sheffield Academic Press, 2000.

Lyle, Kenneth R., Jr. *Ethical Admonition in the Epistle of Jude*. SBL 4. New York: Peter Lang, 1998.

Martin, Ralph P. "The Theology of Jude, 1 Peter, and 2 Peter." In *The Theology of the Letters of James, Peter, and Jude*, by Andrew Chester and Ralph P. Martin, 63–163. NTT. Cambridge: Cambridge University Press, 1994.

Metzger, Bruce M., and Bart D. Ehrman. *The Text of the New Testament: Its Transmission, Corruption, and Restoration*. 4th ed. New York: Oxford University Press, 2005.

Miller, Robert J. "Is There Independent Attestation for the Transfiguration in 2 Peter?" *NTS* 42 (1996): 620–25.

Neyrey, Jerome H. "The Apologetic Use of the Transfiguration in 2 Peter 1:16–21." *CBQ* 42 (1980): 504–19.

———. "The Form and Background of the Polemic in 2 Peter." *JBL* 99 (1980): 407–31.

Osburn, Carroll D. "The Christological Use of I Enoch i.9 in Jude 14, 15." *NTS* 23 (1976–77): 334–41.

———. "Discourse Analysis and Jewish Apocalyptic in the Epistle of Jude." In *Linguistics and New Testament Interpretation: Essays on Discourse Analysis*, edited by David Alan Black, Katharine Barnwell, and Stephen Levinsohn, 287–319. Nashville: Broadman, 1992.

———. "1 Enoch 80:2–8 (67:5–7) and Jude 12–13." *CBQ* 47 (1985): 296–303.

———. "The Text of Jude 5." *Bib* 62 (1981): 107–15.

Perkins, Pheme. "Christ in Jude and 2 Peter." In *Who Do You Say That I Am? Essays on Christology*, edited by Mark Alan Powell and David R. Bauer, 155–65. Louisville: Westminster John Knox, 1999.

Reese, Ruth Anne. *Writing Jude: The Reader, the Text, and the Author in Constructs of Power and Desire*. BIS 51. Leiden: Brill, 2000.

Robinson, J. A. T. *Redating the New Testament*. Philadelphia: Westminster, 1976.

Rowston, Douglas J. "The Most Neglected Book in the New Testament." *NTS* 21 (1974–75): 554–63.

Soards, Marion L. "1 Peter, 2 Peter, and Jude as Evidence for a Petrine School (with Addenda by V. Oliver Ward)." *ANRW* II.25.5 (1988): 3827–49.

Starr, James M. *Sharers in the Divine Nature: 2 Peter 1:4 in Its Hellenistic Context*. ConBNT 33. Stockholm: Almqvist & Wiksell, 2000.

Talbert, Charles H. "II Peter and the Delay of the Parousia." *VC* 20 (1966): 137–45.

Taylor, Vincent. "The Message of the Epistles—2 Peter and Jude." *ExpTim* 45 (1933–34): 437–41.

Thurén, Lauri. "Hey Jude! Asking for the Original Situation and Message of a Catholic Epistle." *NTS* 43 (1997): 451–65.

———. "The Relationship between 2 Peter and Jude—A Classical Problem Resolved?" In *The Catholic Epistles and the Tradition*, edited by Jacques Schlosser, 451–60. BETL 176. Leuven: Leuven University Press, 2004.

———. "Style Never Goes Out of Fashion: 2 Peter Re-evaluated." In *Rhetoric, Scripture and Theology: Essays from the 1994 Pretoria Conference*, edited by Stanley E. Porter and Thomas H. Olbricht, 329–47. JSNTSup 131. Sheffield: Sheffield Academic Press, 1996.

Turner, Nigel. "The Literary Character of New Testament Greek." *NTS* 20 (1973–74): 107–14.

Wall, Robert W. "The Canonical Function of 2 Peter." *BibInt* 9 (2001): 64–81.

Wasserman, Tommy. *The Epistle of Jude: Its Text and Transmission*. ConBNT 43. Stockholm: Almqvist & Wiksell, 2006.

Watson, Duane F. *Invention, Arrangement, and Style: Rhetorical Criticism of Jude and 2 Peter*. SBLDS 104. Atlanta: Scholars Press, 1988.

Webb, Robert L. "The Eschatology of the Epistle of Jude and Its Rhetorical and Social Functions." *BBR* 6 (1996): 139–51.

Webb, Robert L., and Peter H. Davids, eds. *Reading Jude with New Eyes: Methodological Reassessments of the Letter of Jude*. LNTS 383. New York: T&T Clark, 2008.

Wenham, David. "Being 'Found' on the Last Day: New Light on 2 Peter 3:10 and 2 Corinthians 5:3." *NTS* 33 (1987): 477–79.

Wolters, Al. "'Partners of the Deity': A Covenantal Reading of 2 Peter 1:4." *CTJ* 25 (1990): 28–44.

———. "Postscript to 'Partners of the Deity.'" *CTJ* 26 (1991): 418–20.

Wolthuis, Thomas R. "Jude and Jewish Traditions." *CTJ* 22 (1987): 21–45.

———. "Jude and the Rhetorician: A Dialogue on the Rhetorical Nature of the Epistle of Jude." *CTJ* 24 (1989): 126–34.

Commentaries

Bauckham, Richard. *Jude, 2 Peter*. WBC 50. Waco: Word, 1983.

Bigg, Charles. *A Critical and Exegetical Commentary on the Epistles of St. Peter and St. Jude*. ICC. Edinburgh: T&T Clark, 1956.

Craddock, Fred B. *First and Second Peter and Jude*. WestBC. Louisville: Westminster John Knox, 1995.

Cranfield, C. E. B. *I & II Peter and Jude: Introduction and Commentary*. TBC. London: SCM, 1960.

Davids, Peter H. *The Letters of 2 Peter and Jude*. PNTC. Grand Rapids: Eerdmans, 2006.

Donelson, Lewis R. *I & II Peter and Jude*. NTL. Louisville: Westminster John Knox, 2010.

Elliott, John H. *I and II Peter, Jude*. ACNT. Minneapolis: Augsburg, 1982.

Green, Gene L. *Jude and 2 Peter*. BECNT. Grand Rapids: Baker Academic, 2008.

Green, Michael. *2 Peter and Jude: An Introduction and Commentary*. Rev. ed. TNTC. Grand Rapids: Eerdmans, 1987.

Harrington, Daniel J. *Jude and 2 Peter*. SP 15. Collegeville, MN: Liturgical Press, 2003.

Hillyer, Norman. *1 and 2 Peter, Jude*. NIBC. Peabody, MA: Hendrickson, 1992.

Horrell, David G. *The Epistles of Peter and Jude*. EC. London: Epworth, 1998.

Kelly, J. N. D. *A Commentary on the Epistles of Peter and Jude*. BNTC. London: Black, 1969.

Kraftchick, Steven J. *Jude, 2 Peter*. ANTC. Nashville: Abingdon, 2002.

Leaney, A. R. C. *The Letters of Peter and Jude: A Commentary on the First Letter of Peter, a Letter of Jude and the Second Letter of Peter*. CBC. Cambridge: Cambridge University Press, 1967.

Mayor, Joseph B. *The Epistle of St. Jude and the Second Epistle of St. Peter: Greek Text with Introductions, Notes, and Comments*. London: Macmillan, 1907.

Moo, Douglas J. *2 Peter, Jude*. NIVAC. Grand Rapids: Zondervan, 1996.

Neyrey, Jerome H. *2 Peter, Jude: A New Translation with Introduction and Commentary*. AB 37C. New York: Doubleday, 1993.

Painter, John, and David A. deSilva. *James and Jude*. Paideia. Grand Rapids: Baker Academic, 2012.

Perkins, Pheme. *First and Second Peter, James, and Jude*. IBC. Louisville: John Knox, 1995.

Reese, Ruth Anne. *2 Peter and Jude*. THNTC. Grand Rapids: Eerdmans, 2007.

Reicke, Bo. *The Epistles of James, Peter, and Jude: Introduction, Translation, and Notes*. 2nd ed. AB 37. Garden City, NY: Doubleday, 1964.

Richard, Earl Jeffrey. *Reading 1 Peter, Jude, and 2 Peter: A Literary and Theological Commentary*. RNT. Macon, GA: Smyth & Helwys, 2000.

Schreiner, Thomas R. *1, 2 Peter, Jude*. NAC. Nashville: Broadman & Holman, 2003.

Senior, Donald. *1 and 2 Peter*. NTM. Wilmington, DE: Michael Glazier, 1980.

Sidebottom, E. M. *James, Jude and 2 Peter*. NCB. London: Thomas Nelson, 1967.

39

The Johannine Epistles

Only the first of the three Johannine Epistles is familiar in the church. The second and third letters are very short, at least by NT standards (thirteen verses and fifteen verses, respectively), and deal with specific matters that seem vague at best. Perhaps just for these reasons 2 John and 3 John were especially slow to be accepted into the canon. The Johannine Epistles constitute a group within the NT not so much because of any intrinsic connection between them (although 2 John and 3 John are linked through the author who is mysteriously designated as "the Elder," and 1 John and 2 John have some common language), but because of tradition going back to the second century that linked them together with the Gospel of John and the book of Revelation (the Apocalypse) as all written by the same author, thought to be the Apostle John. Like the Gospel of John itself, 1 John is anonymous, while the identity of the "Elder" of 2 John and 3 John remains uncertain. Whether the John of Revelation 1:1 (cf. 1:4, 9; 22:8) is to be related to either remains very doubtful.

The Relationship between the Gospel of John and the Johannine Epistles

Aside from the testimony of church tradition, is there internal evidence of any relationship among these writings? An affirmative answer has to be given at least for the Fourth Gospel and 1 John. The language and theology of the two documents is the same. The description of the theology of the Fourth Gospel given earlier in this book (see chap. 14) is relevant also for 1 John and should be consulted here. The similarity between John's Gospel and the (First) Epistle

---

Author: A slight probability favors the conclusion that all three letters, and the Fourth Gospel too, are by the Apostle John, also known as "the Elder." The writings are linked through the close relationship between the Fourth Gospel and 1 John, on the one hand, and between 1 John and 2 John, on the other hand. Authorship of the letters by a member of the Johannine circle remains a possibility.

Date: Since 1 John seems to presuppose the Gospel of John, it would have been written a little later, hence at the end of the first century or the beginning of the second. Probably, 2 John and 3 John were written about the same time.

Addressees: 1 John is written apparently to several churches, unknown to us; 2 John to one church, addressed as "the elect lady"; 3 John to one person, Gaius.

Purpose: 1 John is written to deal with the serious problem of "antichrists," probably proto-gnostics, who deny the incarnation. It also gives much further general teaching, similar to that of the Gospel of John. Second John also addresses a specific problem of the same sort dealt with in 1 John. Third John affirms Gaius and rebukes Diotrephes.

Message/Argument: 1 John is a sermon or tract, stressing orthodoxy and right conduct; 2 John and 3 John are proper letters, with 2 John resembling 1 John. Third John is quite distinctive, with a very specific purpose.

Significance: These letters are important for illustrating an extension of the thought and perspective of the Fourth Gospel, in practical application.

---

of John was pointed out as early as the third century by Dionysius (bishop of Alexandria), as cited by Eusebius (*Hist. eccl.* 7.25.20, trans. Oulton):

> [The author of the two documents] is consistent with himself and does not depart from what he has proposed, but proceeds throughout under the same heads and expressions, certain of which we shall mention concisely. But the attentive reader will find frequently in one and the other "the life," "the light," "turning from darkness"; continually "the truth," "the grace," "the joy," "the flesh and blood of the Lord," "the judgment," "the forgiveness of sins," "the love of God toward us," the "commandment" that we should "love one another," that we should "keep all the commandments"; the "conviction" of "the world," of "the devil," of "the antichrist"; the promise of the Holy Spirit; the adoption of the sons of God; the "faith" that is demanded of us throughout; "the Father" and "the Son"; these are to be found everywhere. In a word, it is obvious that those who observe their character throughout will see at a glance that the Gospel and Epistle have one and the same complexion.

The first four verses of 1 John allude to the opening of the Fourth Gospel and provide strong evidence of the connection between the two. The relationship is unmistakable in the statement "the life was made manifest, and we saw it, and testify to it, and proclaim to you the eternal life which was with the

Father and was made manifest to us" (1 John 1:2). A. E. Brooke comments, "To quote all [the similarities] that exist would involve printing practically the whole of the Epistle and a large part of the Gospel."[1] Some therefore have argued for a direct relationship between the Fourth Gospel and 1 John, that the latter was written as a cover letter introducing the former[2] or possibly as a corrective to a perceived misunderstanding of the Fourth Gospel.

Although the case is less impressive for the second and third epistles, probably due to their brevity, there are some striking similarities here too, both with the Fourth Gospel and with 1 John. Thus in 2 John we find "know the truth," "the truth which abides in us and will be with us forever," "in truth and love," and "following in the truth" (vv. 1–4). There is also reference to "a new commandment . . . the one we have had from the beginning, that we love one another. And this is love, that we follow his commandments; this is the commandment, as you have heard from the beginning, that you follow love" (vv. 5–6). So too, "Any one who goes ahead and does not abide in the doctrine of Christ does not have God; he who abides in the doctrine has both the Father and the Son" (v. 9). Style, content, and vocabulary here are typical of John's Gospel and 1 John. Add to this the anti-docetic emphasis in verse 7, about "the coming of Jesus Christ in the flesh," and it seems difficult to dissociate 2 John from either John's Gospel or 1 John. The third epistle, the most distinctive of the three because of the specific problem that it addresses, contains less material in common with the other Johannine writings: some in the church testified to the "truth" of Gaius's life, "as indeed you do follow the truth" (v. 3); and the author adds, "No greater joy can I have than this, to hear that my children follow the truth" (v. 4); "He who does good is of God; he who does evil has not seen God" (v. 11). Finally, we may note the Johannine-sounding witness statement: "I testify to him [Demetrius] too, and you know my testimony [*martyria*] is true" (v. 12).

The data just briefly surveyed have convinced most scholars that these epistles are by the same author as the Fourth Gospel, but one eminent Johannine scholar dissents. C. H. Dodd finds too many differences between the Fourth Gospel and these letters to maintain common authorship. Working mainly with 1 John, he points to differences in the style and language,[3] the absence of OT quotations in the epistles, and the Hellenistic aspects of the epistles (e.g., the purely abstract "God is love" in 1 John 4:8, 16; the use of rhetorical questions), compared to the more Jewish Fourth Gospel. He also finds a rather more primitive theology in 1 John: it maintains an imminent

---

1. Brooke, *A Critical and Exegetical Commentary on the Johannine Epistles*, ix. Brooke quotes a statement by Schulze via Holtzmann: "In the whole of the first Epistle there is hardly a single thought that is not found in the Gospel" (ibid.). For a helpful tabulation of linguistic data, see ibid., i–xix, 229–42.

2. Thus Lightfoot, *Biblical Essays*, 194–98.

3. For detailed information, see Dodd, "The First Epistle of John and the Fourth Gospel."

eschatology (2:18, 28; 3:2) and does not put the same emphasis on the Holy
Spirit as does the Fourth Gospel; it also explicitly stresses the death of Christ
as an atonement: "And he is the expiation [*hilasmos*] for our sins, and not for
ours only but also for the sins of the whole world" (2:2 [cf. 4:10]). All of this
points to different authors, in Dodd's opinion.[4]

Although Dodd has made an interesting case for different authorship of the
Fourth Gospel and 1 John (and 2–3 John too), his arguments have persuaded
few.[5] The dissimilarities are more of degree than absolute. The language and
style remain quite similar; the lack of OT quotations may be due to the brevity of the letters; certain rhetorical devices can be explained by the difference
in genre between gospel and letter; the Fourth Gospel contains a future eschatology alongside its realized eschatology, and it alludes to Christ's death
as a sacrifice for sin. The Evangelist's statement in John 3:16–17, "God so
loved the world that he gave [*edōken*] his only Son, that whoever believes in
him should not perish but have eternal life . . . that the world might be saved
through him" (cf. reference to the Lamb who "takes away the sin of the world"
[1:29; cf. 1:36]), is not different from 1 John's atonement theology, and it is
the concrete historical truth that lies behind and informs 1 John's abstract
statement "God is love." In short, the similarities between the Fourth Gospel
and 1 John are more substantial than the dissimilarities, and Dodd's account
of the latter cannot overturn the probability of a common author.[6]

Authorship of the Epistles

As we have already had occasion to note, early church tradition is of little help
to us on this question because the viewpoint of Irenaeus seems immediately to
have become dominant, namely that the Apostle John was the author of the
entire Johannine corpus, Gospel, Epistles, and Apocalypse. There did remain
in some minds, however, a lingering suspicion concerning 2 John and 3 John,
and for some, the Apocalypse too. The fact that the author of 2 John and
3 John identified himself as "the Elder," while no such identification is made
in 1 John, separated the former from the latter, giving rise to some skepticism.
Origen says that John, "who leaned back on Jesus' breast," wrote the Gospel
and the Apocalypse and "has left also an epistle of a very few lines, and it may
be, a second and third: for not all say that these are genuine. Only, the two
of them together are not a hundred lines long" (according to Eusebius, *Hist.*

---

4. Dodd, *The Johannine Epistles*, xlvii–lvi.
5. Some weighty names are in agreement with Dodd, however: Bultmann, Barrett, Klein,
McNeile, Moffatt, Brown, and Schnackenburg, this last scholar having earlier argued for a single
author of John's Gospel and 1 John.
6. Dodd himself admits, "In such matters strict proof is seldom attainable" (*The Johannine
Epistles*, lvi).

eccl. 6.25.9–10, trans. Oulton). Dionysius called attention to the problem: "Nay, not even in the second or third extant epistles of John, although they are short, is John set forth by name; but he has written 'the Elder,' without giving his name" (according to Eusebius, *Hist. eccl.* 7.25.11, trans. Oulton).

While 1 John is fully anonymous, 2 John and 3 John may be said to be partially anonymous. That is, we know they were written by "the Elder" (or "the presbyter"), but exactly who this Elder was remains unclear. It is not even certain how we should understand the word "elder" here, since the word can refer to the advanced age of a person or to a position of authority in the church distinct from the question of age. Papias, we may remember, seems to have thought of "elders" as the successors to the Apostles, as representing the second generation of transmitters of tradition (according to Eusebius, *Hist. eccl.* 3.39.4).

Because of the relation that exists between 1 John and 2 John, and then between 2 John and 3 John, it is probable that all three letters derive from the same author. Given the reference in the early church to an "Elder" named "John" (see discussion in chap. 14 above), it seems natural to identify this particular John as the author of 2 John and 3 John, although this still can be only a conjecture. The unknowns are too numerous and the evidence too tenuous for any confidence, but it seems that a slight probability favors all three letters, together with the Fourth Gospel, as having been written by the Apostle John. Nothing seems definitively to prohibit this conclusion. Other possibilities remain, however, such as that 2 John and 3 John are by the Elder, and the Fourth Gospel and 1 John are by the Apostle, or perhaps only John's Gospel is by the Apostle. Or indeed the possibility can hardly be excluded that all three Johannine Epistles and John's Gospel are by the Elder. In Dodd's tentative view, the author of the letters was "a disciple of the Evangelist and a student of his work."[7] He conjectures that the author was one of the presbyters of the province of Asia sometime between 96 and 110.

If all of these documents are not by the same hand, they are at least from the same milieu, such as a single community or school, of which we saw evidence in the discussion of John's Gospel (chap. 14 above).[8] "The fact that they share language, style, terminology and patterns of theological thought and outlook points to a tradition which was encapsulated within a defined group."[9] It is

7. Ibid., lvi. J. A. T. Robinson holds that the Fourth Gospel and all three Johannine Epistles come from the same hand and are addressed to the same community ("The Destination and Purpose of the Johannine Epistles," 126).

8. A. E. Brooke comments, "We are always on safer ground when we speak of the 'Ephesian Canonical Writings' than when we assign them definitely to St. John, Apostle or Elder. But there are no adequate reasons for setting aside the traditional view which attributes the Epistle and Gospel to the same authorship" (*A Critical and Exegetical Commentary on the Johannine Epistles*, xviii).

9. Lieu, *The Theology of the Johannine Epistles*, 98–99.

perhaps the authority of this group, which initially had the Apostle John as its founder and head, that finally stands behind the testimony of these documents.

Order and Date of the Epistles

Uncertainties about the Johannine Epistles are not limited to the question of authorship. It is impossible to determine with any confidence the order in which they were written and whether they were written before or after John's Gospel, let alone assign even approximate dates to them.

It is possible, or even probable, that the three letters were written over a very short time span and possibly were sent together to their (unknown) destination(s), so that the order in which they were written becomes unimportant. More significant is whether they (or at least 1 John) were written before or after the Fourth Gospel. The Johannine Epistles concern practical matters in a way that John's Gospel does not, and so they have been likened to the Pastoral Epistles in relation to the undisputed Pauline Epistles. "In each case there is a concretizing of insights, an appeal to tradition, a defensiveness against dangers from within, and a certain cautious retrenchment—the marks of the second generation of a community now more concerned with survival and preservation than with the conversion of Jews and Gentiles."[10] This makes it likely that these epistles were written after John's Gospel. The readers of these epistles are assumed to be familiar with John's Gospel. This statement by B. F. Westcott remains convincing: "It can only be said with confidence that the Epistle [1 John] presupposes in those for whom it was composed a familiar acquaintance with the characteristic truths which are preserved for us in the Gospel."[11] Indeed, 1 John is regarded by some as a corrective, orthodox commentary on the Fourth Gospel.[12]

In the early history of the formation of the canon, John's Gospel and 1 John usually are linked and receive early and consistent recognition. Not so with 2 John and 3 John. Where they are mentioned at all, their authority often is debated. In his account of the state of the canon in the early fourth century, Eusebius lists among the "disputed books" (*antilegomena*) "the so-called second and third Epistles of John which may be the work of the Evangelist or of some other with the same name" (*Hist. eccl.* 3.25.3, trans. Lake). An example of this uncertainty is their omission from the Syriac translation of the NT until at least the fifth century. By contrast, 1 John, like the Fourth Gospel, finds a place in Eusebius's category of "recognized books" (*homolegoumenoi*) (*Hist. eccl.* 3.25.2). Already in the early second century Polycarp shows that he probably knew 1 John 4:2–3 (and/or 2 John 7): "Everyone who does not

---

10. Brown, *The Epistles of John*, 35.
11. Westcott, *The Epistles of St. John*, xxxi (cited by Brown, *The Epistles of John*, 35).
12. Thus, for example, Brown, *The Epistles of John*, 90–92.

confess that Jesus Christ has come in the flesh is an Antichrist; and whoever does not confess the witness of the cross is of the devil" (Pol. *Phil.* 7:1). And Eusebius informs us that Papias "used quotations [*martyriais*] from the first Epistle of John" (*Hist. eccl.* 3.39.17, trans. Lake). This suggests a date for 1 John, and probably 2 John and 3 John as well, at the end of the first century or the beginning of the second.

First John

Although we commonly speak of the three Johannine Epistles, only the second two are really letters. First John, by contrast, resembles the book of Hebrews in that it is more of a sermon or tract, in this case devoted to the practical application of the content of the Fourth Gospel, but also directed to specific readers and addressing a specific problem. In contrast to 2 John and 3 John, it lacks the formulaic letter opening that identifies the author, and it lacks the closing greetings usually found in letters.

On the one hand, the lack of an address to any specific readers at the beginning of 1 John suggests that it may have been a circular document, meant for readers in several communities. On the other hand, there seems to be a close relationship with the readers, unless the terms of endearment ("my children," "brothers") are no more than rhetorical devices. Clearly, 1 John is a document dominated by pastoral concerns. It stresses not only understanding but also conduct.

Theological and Ethical Motifs

Life

The opening of the letter recalls the prologue of the Fourth Gospel:[13] "that which was from the beginning [*ho ēn ap' archēs*]." So too the themes of the first three verses, especially "the word of life" and "eternal life," allude to the Gospel. Indeed, what these first three verses say about life is virtually what the Gospel prologue says about Jesus. It is "life" (*zōē*) that has been "manifested" (*ephanerōthē*) and "seen" (1:1–2). The shared witness of the community, reflected in the repeated plural "we," concerns "the word [*logos*] of life." The community proclaims "the eternal life which was with the Father [*pros ton patera*] and was made manifest to us" (1:2). It is as though the author wants to say that Jesus *is* life, in accord with the statement "In him was life" in John 1:4. This corresponds to the inclusio at the end of the letter, where the author writes, "And this is the testimony, that God gave us eternal life, and

---

13. Dionysius made this observation in the third century: "There is indeed a mutual agreement between the Gospel and the Epistle, and they begin alike" (according to Eusebius, *Hist. eccl.* 7.25.18, trans. Oulton).

this life is in his Son. He who has the Son has life; he who has not the Son of God has not life" (5:11–12 [cf. 2:25]). The author continues by expressing his purpose for writing: "I write this to you who believe in the name of the Son of God, that you may know that you have eternal life" (5:13 [cf. John 20:31]). The penultimate sentence states the implied equivalence quite clearly, when he says that we are "in his [God's] Son Jesus Christ. This is the true God and eternal life" (5:20).

WITNESS AND TRUTH

As in the Fourth Gospel, witness and truth are important concepts in 1 John. The idea of witness or testimony is linked with seeing. What the author and the community proclaim is that "which we have seen with our eyes, which we have looked upon . . . and we saw it, and testify to it . . . that which we have seen" (1:1–3). "And we have seen and testify that the Father has sent his Son as the Savior of the world" (4:14). Testimony is also linked with the Spirit in the remarkable passage in 5:6–12. "And the Spirit is the witness, because the Spirit is the truth" (5:7).[14] This is equated with the testimony of God. "If we receive the testimony of men, the testimony of God is greater; for this is the testimony of God that he has borne witness to his Son" (5:9). "And this is the testimony, that God gave us eternal life, and this life is in his Son" (5:11). Witness and truth also become allied concepts. The person who does not receive God's testimony "has made him a liar" (5:10). Truthfulness is contrasted to falsehood (2:21; 4:6; cf. 1:6; 2:4). In keeping with these emphases is the stress on knowing and being sure. The phrase "by this we know," or an equivalent, occurs repeatedly (2:5; 3:16, 19, 24; 4:2, 6, 13; 5:2). The truth is what has been heard from the beginning (2:7, 24; 3:11).

SIN AND CHRISTIAN IDENTITY

The author counterposes walking in light with walking in darkness, and these are paralleled with the concept of living according to the truth or not doing so (1:6–8; cf. 2:9–11), or in other terms, keeping or disobeying Christ's commandments (2:3–6). The author will not allow the reality of sin to be brushed away: "If we say we have no sin, we deceive ourselves" (1:8; cf. 1:10). However, so contradictory is sin to the identity of a Christian that he can also say, "No one who abides in him sins; no one who sins has either seen him or known him," and "No one born of God commits sin; for God's nature [*sperma*, lit., "seed"] abides in him, and he cannot sin because he is born of God" (3:6, 9 [cf. 5:18]). This is a remarkable tension[15] that has caused com-

---

14. The verse numbering in the Greek text differs slightly, where this sentence is a part of 5:6.

15. Raymond Brown says, "No other NT author contradicts himself so sharply within such a short span of writing." He goes on to say, however, "We should never assume that ancient authors were stupid or illogical and could not see difficulties, especially within the same brief piece of writing" (*The Epistles of John*, 413).

mentators a considerable headache.[16] One of the most common solutions is to take the present tenses as progressive presents: the Christian does not keep on sinning—that is, does not continually or habitually sin. As true as this may be, it does not explain the statement in 3:9 that the Christian "cannot sin" (*ou dynatai hamartanein*, lit., "is not able to sin"). What we have here is a tension, not unlike that in Paul, between our present identity in Christ and the ongoing fact that we live our lives in an overlap of the ages, short of the consummation. This tension is evident just a few verses earlier, where the author affirms our present identity as "children of God" (3:1) but goes on to say, "Beloved, we are God's children now; it does not yet appear what we shall be, but we know that when he appears we shall be like him, for we shall see him as he is. And every one who thus hopes in him purifies himself as he is pure" (3:2–3 [cf. 2:8]). The Christian is already perfect in Christ, ideally or positionally, but not yet perfect in present experience.[17] Just for that reason the author can also write, "If we confess our sins, he is faithful and just, and will forgive our sins and cleanse us from all unrighteousness" (1:9). The ultimate purpose of this teaching is to prompt Christians to live in a way that is consistent with their identity in Christ, to express their real identity by pressing on in righteousness. "My little children, I am writing this to you so that you may not sin; but if any one does sin, we have an advocate with the Father, Jesus Christ the righteous" (2:1). The Son is "the Savior of the world" (4:14).

LOVE AS THE SUPREME MARK OF THE CHRISTIAN

The verb "to love" (*agapaō*) occurs almost as many times (31x) in the three brief Johannine Letters as it does in the entire Pauline corpus. The noun "love" (*agapē*) also occurs frequently (21x). The person who loves brother or sister "abides in the light" (2:10). "For this is the message which you have heard from the beginning, that we should love one another" (3:11 [cf. 4:21]).

Here 1 John provides one of the most memorable passages in the NT: "Beloved, let us love one another, because love is from God, and everyone who loves is born of God and knows God. Whoever does not love does not know God, for God is love" (4:7–8 NRSV). But the climactic passage on the subject comes in 4:9–12: "In this the love of God was made manifest among us, that God sent his only Son into the world, so that we might live through him. In this is love, not that we loved God but that he loved us and sent his Son to be the expiation [*hilasmos*] for our sins. Beloved, if God so loved us, we also ought to love one another. No man has ever seen God; if we love one another, God abides in us and his love is perfected in us." Christians are to love others because God loves them: "We love, because he first loved us" (4:19).

---

16. Raymond Brown (ibid.) groups the various attempts to solve the problem into no less than seven general approaches. For a full list, see Stott, *The Letters of John*, 130–36.

17. This brings to mind Martin Luther's statement that the Christian is *simul iustus et peccator* ("at once righteous and a sinner").

For the author, the love commandment is linked with "righteousness" (a word that occurs only 3x in 1 John). "Doing righteousness" is paralleled to loving one's brother and sister (3:10–11). Love for others is neither abstract nor narrow in scope; it sums up the Christian ethic. And so he exhorts his readers, "Let us not love in word or speech but in deed and truth" (3:18).

Abiding in God

The verb "to abide" (*menō*) is also of great importance in the Johannine literature (40x in John; 27x in 1–3 John). Closely related is the idea of "being in" (*einai en*), which also occurs frequently in the Johannine Gospel and Epistles.[18] The idea of abiding in love is correlated with abiding in God. "So we know and believe the love God has for us. God is love, and he who abides in love abides in God, and God abides in him" (4:16). "To abide in someone" is to have an intimate personal relationship, involving a deep, steady communion with that person. To abide in God involves a communion that results in a right kind of living, particularly in a way that demonstrates love to others in the family of faith. God loved us; so should we love others. "For this is the love of God, that we keep his commandments. And his commandments are not burdensome" (5:3).

The Life Setting and Purpose of the Epistle

First John is not an abstract theological treatise dwelling on the themes just examined, attempting to deepen the spiritual life of the readers. A specific problem seems to have called forth the document. Some people have left the Johannine community (2:19), and not over a minor issue. They are castigated in harsh language as "antichrists," liars who denied that Jesus is the Christ (2:18, 22). "This is the antichrist, he who denies the Father and the Son" (2:22). The author very specifically indicates this lie as the reason, or at least one of the main reasons, he writes. "I write this to you about those who would deceive you" (2:26). They are further described as "false prophets" (4:1) who follow "the spirit of antichrist" (4:3) rather than the Spirit of God, and who confess that "Jesus Christ has come in the flesh" (4:2). They are "of the world," whereas "we are of God" (4:5–6). The reality of antichrists and false prophets points to the nearness of eschatological fulfillment.

The concern over the denial that Jesus Christ has come in the flesh indicates that those who had left the community apparently were gnostic dualists whose arguments continued to have influence. A major, if not *the* major, concern of the author is to counter this incipient gnosticism. Jesus Christ came in flesh (4:2; cf. 2 John 7); he "came by water and blood"—that is, by baptism and the cross (5:6). Some have seen a connection between the

18. See Malatesta, *Interiority and Covenant*.

gnostic beliefs of those who left the community and the early gnostic Cerinthus, who lived in Asia Minor. According to Irenaeus, the Gospel of John was written to counteract the teaching of Cerinthus, who was a precursor of the Gnostics; he perhaps also is the target of the correctives offered in 1 John.[19] In J. A. T. Robinson's view, the Johannine Epistles were written to a Hellenistic Jewish Christian community as "necessary correctives to deductions drawn from the teaching of the fourth Gospel by a gnosticizing movement within Greek-speaking Diaspora Judaism."[20] Much in 1 John can be explained on this basis.

If we engage in mirror reading of 1 John, the strong emphasis on love in the epistle may point to a lack of love among the readers. Similarly, the argument against worldliness (2:15–17) may point to the sinful inclinations of those addressed.

The "Johannine Comma" (Inserted Words of First John 5:7–8)

A brief trinitarian statement is found in a handful of late manuscripts of the Textus Receptus, and thus made its way into the KJV: "For there are three that bear record in heaven, the Father, the Word, and the Holy Ghost: and these three are one. And there are three that bear witness in earth" (5:7–8). Only in early fourth-century Latin manuscripts do the words begin to appear, composed apparently to provide ammunition in the church's fourth-century christological controversies. It is something like a thousand years later before they are found in a Greek manuscript of the NT. Erasmus, who in the sixteenth century produced the first printed Greek NT, did not at first include the words, since he knew of no Greek manuscript that contained them. But to those who complained about their omission he rashly promised to include them if a single Greek manuscript could be found that contained them. It was not long before such a manuscript appeared (Codex Montfortianus, assigned the number 61 and now housed in Trinity College in Dublin)—apparently manufactured on demand in Oxford by a Franciscan monk in 1520, as eventually emerged—and

19. A tradition that goes back to Polycarp tells the story of John the Apostle immediately departing from a bath house when he heard that Cerinthus was present (see Eusebius, *Hist. eccl.* 3.28.6; 4.14.6).

20. Robinson, "The Destination and Purpose of the Johannine Epistles," 138. This was a view held much earlier by Robert Law (see *The Tests of Life* [originally published in 1909]). Robinson observes, "Even if Gnosticism was eventually to lead to 'an acute Hellenizing' of Christianity, we must question the assumption that it was a growth which in NT times flourished in Gentile rather than Jewish circles within the Church. All the pointers are in fact the other way" (ibid., 137). He mentions as NT examples of this gnostic tendency in Diaspora Judaism, the Colossian heresy and passages opposing a false knowledge (*gnōsis*) and Jewish myths in 1 Timothy and Titus. The Wisdom mysticism of Judaism became the source of gnostic tendencies and easily led to a metaphysical dualism.

Erasmus somewhat reluctantly included the words in the third edition (1522) of his Greek Testament.[21]

Second John

As we have noted, the author of 2 John and 3 John identifies himself as "the Elder." It is probable, though hardly certain, that we should identify him with John the Elder, spoken of in the early tradition of the church. The similarity between 2 John and 1 John makes it very likely that the latter was written by the same author, perhaps at about the same time. This person could well be the author of the Fourth Gospel too, and if so, he may be the Beloved Disciple—the Apostle-Elder John, as I have tentatively argued. If this is asserting too much on evidence that is too tenuous, we may at the least speak of a Johannine school or circle as being responsible for these letters and accounting for their commonality.

Second John is addressed to "the elect lady and her children" (v. 1), while at the end of the letter the author sends greetings from "the children of your elect sister" (v. 13). It is not impossible that these are individual women in the church, although why they would be referred to so secretively seems strange.[22] It seems more likely that "the elect lady" (*kyria*) is a way of referring to local churches (the Greek word *ekklēsia* being a feminine noun), a metaphor for the church (so too in v. 5), whose members are accordingly referred to as "children." The "children" mentioned in verse 4 seem not to be the actual children of the elect lady (note the repeated metaphorical reference to "children" in 1 John 2:1, 12, 13, 18, 28; 3:2, 7, 10, 18; 4:4; 5:2). Despite its seemingly personal form, the letter is not a private letter at all, but rather a pastoral letter to a local church, probably somewhere in Asia Minor, perhaps not far from Ephesus.

The relation of 2 John to the content of 1 John is immediately evident. The theme of truth dominates the opening four verses. The author speaks of "knowing the truth" and of "the truth which abides in us and will be with us for ever" (vv. 1–2); he links "truth and love" (v. 3) and uses the expression "walking in the truth" (v. 4 NRSV). Verses 5–7 contain strong parallels to 1 John, especially in the commandment "from the beginning" to love one another (vv. 5–6; cf. 1 John 2:7–8) and in the reference to deceivers and antichrists, defined as those "who will not acknowledge the coming of Jesus Christ in the flesh" (v. 7; cf. 1 John 2:18–19; 4:1–2). This marks out the boundaries of orthodoxy, and the readers are exhorted to "abide in the doctrine [*didachē*] of Christ"; the one who does so "has both the Father and the Son," while the one who does not "does not have God" (v. 9). Those who do not share this

---

21. See Metzger and Ehrman, *The Text of the New Testament*, 146. See chapter 42 below.
22. It has been suggested, implausibly it seems to me, that the Greek represents personal names rather than nouns, thus *Kyria* and *Adelpha*.

didachē ("teaching") are not to be welcomed but rather are to be shunned as those who do wickedness (vv. 10–11).

Both 2 John and 3 John end with a statement that the author has more to say but prefers to do so face-to-face rather than with papyrus and ink (2 John 12; 3 John 13–14).

Third John

Of all the letters of the NT, the very short 3 John is the closest in form (address, expression of good wishes to the addressee, closing greetings) and in length to a typical Hellenistic letter. It would fit easily onto a single sheet of papyrus. Although 3 John is quite short, it is at the same time the most specific of the three Johannine Letters.

Third John is addressed to "the beloved Gaius," a man whom we know only from this letter, but who probably was a leader in one of the Johannine congregations in Asia Minor. The author is convinced that all is well with Gaius's soul (v. 2) because he has heard about "the truth" of Gaius's life, that he "follows the truth" (v. 4). Service to the brothers and sisters and especially hospitality[23] to strangers are lifted up as examples of love shown by Gaius (vv. 5–6).

By contrast to Gaius, the author criticizes Diotrephes for putting himself first, for not acknowledging the author's authority, and for speaking against him with evil words (vv. 9–10). No details are given concerning how or why this was so; no doubt it was known to the readers. It is difficult to say more than that the authority of the Elder was under challenge. Then, in direct contrast to the laudable conduct of Gaius, the author notes Diotrephes's refusal to show hospitality, indeed his casting out of the church of those who would show hospitality. No issue of doctrine is raised in connection with Diotrephes, or in any other connection. It seems that his desire for a closed community was intended to be protective, perhaps against the doctrinal deviation of a gnostic/docetic kind. Diotrephes seems to have been guilty not of heterodoxy but rather of a conduct that did not manifest the supreme virtue of love. Perhaps the statement of verse 11 is directed against him: "Do not imitate evil but imitate good. He who does good is of God; he who does evil has not seen God."

The few words of praise for Demetrius in verse 12 do not provide the reason for the praise, but they do provide opportunity for a Johannine-type statement: "I testify to him too, and you know my testimony is true."

Third John is marked by typical Hellenistic rhetoric, earning the goodwill of the reader and employing praise and blame for the purpose of motivating change in behavior.[24] The final benediction confers peace on Gaius and offers

23. On the importance of this theme in 3 John, see Malherbe, "Hospitality and Inhospitality in the Church."

24. See Watson, "A Rhetorical Analysis of 3 John."

greetings to "the friends," each by name (*kat' onoma*), suggesting that the author had an especially close relationship with this congregation. If so, this would have aggravated the conduct of Diotrephes.

The three Johannine Epistles belong together and are also in some clear and definite way related to the Fourth Gospel. The same language and motifs are found in all four documents. Even apart from the uncertainties that remain concerning authorship, and even if they are not written by the same person, they constitute a collection of documents that at least reflects the influence of a Johannine circle or school. As we will see in the following chapters, it is unlikely that the Apocalypse, despite some points of contact, is to be included in this corpus.

Bibliography

See also the bibliography for chapter 14, "The Gospel according to John."

Books and Articles

Bogart, John. *Orthodox and Heretical Perfectionism in the Johannine Community as Evident in the First Epistle of John.* SBLDS 33. Missoula, MT: Scholars Press, 1977.
Briggs, Robert C. "Contemporary Study of the Johannine Epistles." *RevExp* 67 (1970): 411–22.
Brown, Raymond E. *The Community of the Beloved Disciple: The Life, Loves, and Hates of an Individual Church in New Testament Times.* New York: Paulist Press, 1979.
Bruce, F. F. "Johannine Studies since Westcott's Day." In *The Epistles of John: The Greek Text with Notes,* by B. F. Westcott, lix–lxxvi. Grand Rapids: Eerdmans, 1966.
Dodd, C. H. "The First Epistle of John and the Fourth Gospel." *BJRL* 21 (1937): 129–56.
Donelson, Lewis R. *From Hebrews to Revelation: A Theological Introduction.* Louisville: Westminster John Knox, 2001.
Donfried, Karl P. "Ecclesiastical Authority in 2–3 John." In *L'Évangile de Jean: Sources, rédaction, théologie,* edited by Marinus de Jonge, 325–33. BETL 44. Gembloux: Duculot; Leuven: Leuven University Press, 1977.
Edwards, Ruth B. *The Johannine Epistles.* NTG. Sheffield: Sheffield Academic Press, 1996.
Francis, Fred O. "The Form and Function of the Opening and Closing Paragraphs of James and I John." *ZNW* 61 (1970): 110–26.
Funk, Robert W. "The Form and Structure of II and III John." *JBL* 86 (1967): 424–30.
Griffith, Terry. *Keep Yourselves from Idols: A New Look at 1 John.* JSNTSup 233. Sheffield: Sheffield Academic Press, 2002.
Harner, Philip B. *What Are They Saying about the Catholic Epistles?* Mahwah, NJ: Paulist Press, 2004.
Hill, Charles E. *The Johannine Corpus in the Early Church.* Oxford: Oxford University Press, 2004.
Howard, Wilbert F. "The Common Authorship of the Johannine Gospel and Epistles." *JTS* 48 (1947): 12–25.
Kenney, Garrett C. *The Relation of Christology to Ethics in the First Epistle of John.* Lanham, MD: University Press of America, 2001.
Law, Robert. *The Tests of Life: A Study of the First Epistle of St. John.* 3rd ed. Grand Rapids: Baker, 1979.
Lieu, Judith M. "'Authority to Become Children of God': A Study of 1 John." *NovT* 23 (1981): 210–28.

———. *The Second and Third Epistles of John: History and Background.* SNTW. Edinburgh: T&T Clark, 1986.

———. *The Theology of the Johannine Epistles.* NTT. Cambridge: Cambridge University Press, 1991.

Lightfoot, J. B. *Biblical Essays.* New York: Macmillan, 1893.

Longacre, Robert E. "Towards an Exegesis of 1 John Based on the Discourse Analysis of the Greek Text." In *Linguistics and New Testament Interpretation: Essays on Discourse Analysis,* edited by David Alan Black, Katharine Barnwell, and Stephen Levinsohn, 271–86. Nashville: Broadman, 1992.

Malatesta, Edward. *Interiority and Covenant: A Study of* εἶναι ἐν *and* μένειν ἐν *in the First Letter of John.* AnBib 69. Rome: Biblical Institute Press, 1978.

Malherbe, Abraham J. "Hospitality and Inhospitality in the Church." In *Social Aspects of Early Christianity,* 92–112. Philadelphia: Fortress, 1983.

Metzger, Bruce M., and Bart D. Ehrman. *The Text of the New Testament: Its Transmission, Corruption, and Restoration.* 4th ed. New York: Oxford University Press, 2005.

O'Neill, J. C. *The Puzzle of 1 John: A New Examination of Origins.* London: SPCK, 1966.

Painter, John. "The 'Opponents' in 1 John." *NTS* 32 (1986): 48–71.

Piper, Otto A. "1 John and the Didache of the Primitive Church." *JBL* 66 (1947): 437–51.

Poythress, Vern S. "Testing for Johannine Authorship by Examining the Use of Conjunctions." *WTJ* 46 (1984): 350–69.

Robinson, J. A. T. "The Destination and Purpose of the Johannine Epistles." In *Twelve New Testament Studies,* 126–38. SBT 34. London: SCM, 1962.

Salom, A. P. "Some Aspects of the Grammatical Style of 1 John." *JBL* 74 (1955): 96–102.

Scholer, David M. "1 John 4:7–21." *RevExp* 87 (1990): 309–14.

Segovia, Fernando F. *Love Relationships in the Johannine Tradition: Agapē/Agapan in 1 John and the Fourth Gospel.* SBLDS 58. Chico, CA: Scholars Press, 1982.

Smith, D. Moody. *Johannine Christianity: Essays on Its Setting, Sources, and Theology.* Columbia: University of South Carolina Press, 1989.

Songer, Harold S. "The Life Situation of the Johannine Epistles." *RevExp* 67 (1970): 399–409.

Stagg, Frank. "Orthodoxy and Orthopraxy in the Johannine Epistles." *RevExp* 67 (1970): 423–32.

Vorster, W. S. "Heterodoxy in 1 John." *Neot* 9 (1975): 87–97.

Wahlde, Urban C. von. *The Johannine Commandments: 1 John and the Struggle for the Johannine Tradition.* New York: Paulist Press, 1990.

Watson, Duane F. "Amplification Techniques in 1 John: The Interaction of Rhetorical Style and Invention." *JSNT* 51 (1993): 99–123.

———. "A Rhetorical Analysis of 2 John according to Greco-Roman Convention." *NTS* 35 (1989): 104–30.

———. "A Rhetorical Analysis of 3 John: A Study in Epistolary Rhetoric." *CBQ* 51 (1989): 479–501.

Whitacre, Rodney A. *Johannine Polemic: The Role of Tradition and Theology.* SBLDS 67. Chico, CA: Scholars Press, 1982.

Wilson, W. G. "An Examination of the Linguistic Evidence Adduced against the Unity of Authorship of the First Epistle of John and the Fourth Gospel." *JTS* 49 (1948): 147–56.

Wohl, D. Bruce. *Johannine Christianity in Conflict: Authority, Rank, and Succession in the First Farewell Discourse.* SBLDS 60. Chico, CA: Scholars Press, 1981.

Commentaries

Akin, Daniel L. *1, 2, 3 John.* NAC. Nashville: Broadman & Holman, 2001.

Black, C. Clifton. "The First, Second, and Third Letters of John." *NIB* 12:363–469.

Brooke, A. E. *A Critical and Exegetical Commentary on the Johannine Epistles.* ICC. Edinburgh: T&T Clark, 1912.

Brown, Raymond E. *The Epistles of John: Translated, with Introduction, Notes, and Commentary*. AB 30. New York: Doubleday, 1982.

Bruce, F. F. *The Epistles of John: Introduction, Exposition, and Notes*. Grand Rapids: Eerdmans, 1979.

Bultmann, Rudolf. *The Johannine Epistles: A Commentary on the Johannine Epistles*. Translated R. Philip O'Hara with Lane C. McGaughy and Robert W. Funk. Edited by Robert W. Funk. Hermeneia. Philadelphia: Fortress, 1973.

Burge, Gary M. *The Letters of John: From Biblical Text to Contemporary Life*. NIVAC. Grand Rapids: Zondervan, 1996.

Culpepper, R. Alan. *1 John, 2 John, 3 John*. KPG. Atlanta: John Knox, 1985.

———. *The Gospel and Letters of John*. IBT. Nashville: Abingdon, 1998.

Dodd, C. H. *The Johannine Epistles*. MNTC. London: Hodder & Stoughton, 1946.

Grayston, Kenneth. *The Johannine Epistles*. NCBC. Grand Rapids: Eerdmans, 1984.

Houlden, James L. *A Commentary on the Johannine Epistles*. HNTC. New York: Harper & Row, 1973.

Kruse, Colin G. *The Letters of John*. PNTC. Grand Rapids: Eerdmans, 2000.

Kysar, Robert. *1, 2, 3 John*. ACNT. Minneapolis: Augsburg, 1986.

Lewis, Scott M. *The Gospel according to John and the Johannine Letters*. NCBCNT 4. Collegeville, MN: Liturgical Press, 2005.

Lieu, Judith M. *I, II, & III John: A Commentary*. NTL. Louisville: Westminster John Knox, 2008.

Loader, William. *The Johannine Epistles*. EC. London: Epworth, 1992.

Marshall, I. Howard. *The Epistles of John*. NICNT. Grand Rapids: Eerdmans, 1978.

Painter, John. *1, 2, and 3 John*. PNTC. Grand Rapids: Eerdmans, 2000.

———. *1, 2, and 3 John*. SP 18. Collegeville, MN: Liturgical Press, 2002.

Perkins, Pheme. *The Johannine Epistles*. NTM. Wilmington, DE: Michael Glazier, 1979.

Rensberger, David. *1 John, 2 John, 3 John*. ANTC. Nashville: Abingdon, 1997.

Schnackenburg, Rudolf. *The Johannine Epistles*. Translated by Reginald and Ilse Fuller. New York: Crossroad, 1992.

Sloyan, Gerard S. *Walking in the Truth: Perseverers and Deserters; The First, Second, and Third Letters of John*. NTC. Harrisburg, PA: Trinity Press International, 1995.

Smalley, Stephen S. *1, 2, 3 John*. WBC 51. Waco: Word, 1984.

Smith, D. Moody. *First, Second, and Third John*. IBC. Louisville: John Knox, 1991.

Stott, John R. W. *The Letters of John: An Introduction and Commentary*. Rev. ed. TNTC. Grand Rapids: Eerdmans, 1988.

Strecker, Georg. *The Johannine Letters: A Commentary on 1, 2, and 3 John*. Translated by Linda M. Mahoney. Edited by Harold Attridge. Hermeneia. Minneapolis: Fortress, 1996.

Talbert, Charles H. *Reading John: A Literary and Theological Commentary on the Fourth Gospel and the Johannine Epistles*. RNT. Rev. ed. Macon, GA: Smyth & Helwys, 1999.

Thompson, Marianne Meye. *1–3 John*. IVPNTC. Downers Grove, IL: InterVarsity, 1992.

Wahlde, Urban C. von. *The Gospel and Letters of John*. 3 vols. Grand Rapids: Eerdmans, 2010.

Westcott, B. F. *The Epistles of St. John: The Greek Text with Notes*. 3rd ed. Grand Rapids: Eerdmans, 1966.

Williams, Ronald R. *The Letters of John and James: Commentary on the Three Letters of John and the Letter of James*. CBC. Cambridge: Cambridge University Press, 1965.

Witherington, Ben, III. *A Socio-Rhetorical Commentary on Titus, 1–2 Timothy, and 1–3 John*. Vol. 1 of *Letters and Homilies for Hellenized Christians*. Downers Grove, IL: IVP Academic, 2006.

Yarbrough, Robert W. *1–3 John*. BECNT. Grand Rapids: Baker Academic, 2008.

PART 7

THE APOCALYPSE

The Consummation of the Kingdom

40

The Message of the Apocalypse

No book of the NT has been as much abused and misunderstood as the book of Revelation, otherwise known as the Apocalypse (from its Greek name, *apokalypsis*). Its cryptic language and symbols have fascinated readers from the beginning, often mesmerizing them and luring them to crash on the rocks of allegory and speculative interpretation. Dionysius, bishop of Alexandria in the third century, who did not particularly care for the book, nevertheless respected it and noted its appeal: "I hold that the interpretation of each several passage is in some way hidden and more wonderful. For even although I do not understand it, yet I suspect that some deeper meaning underlies the words" (according to Eusebius, *Hist. eccl.* 7.25.4, trans. Oulton). This is a very typical response to the content of the book. The book cries out to be "decoded" in order to arrive at its secret message, its "deeper" meaning. But how can something so encrypted rightly be called a "revelation"—that is, an unveiling? What really does the book of Revelation reveal?

The Misuse of the Apocalypse

Revelation is the final book of the NT, located at the end of the NT canon precisely because it looks forward to the future. The purpose of Revelation, however, is wrongly taken by many as providing detailed prophecy of what is to come—a virtual blueprint of the end times—available through a decoding of the text. We will see that several basic approaches to understanding what the book says about the future have emerged. Here I want to argue that the purpose of the book is not to convey information per se about the future. Although this book *is* about the future, it presents not a detailed prediction of future events but a more basic and significant message concerning the sovereignty of God and the consummation of God's plan of salvation. The end of the last book of the NT deliberately corresponds to the opening book of the Bible; like bookends, Genesis and Revelation enclose the library containing the story of salvation history. The Apocalypse shows that eschatology corresponds to protology, as fulfillment does to promise.

But no more than Genesis provides details about precisely how God created the world does Revelation provide details about how all things will come to an end. It is not the purpose of the book to provide information or chronology for its own sake. Only in the most general sense is information or chronology the concern of the author. The Apocalypse was not written to satisfy human curiosity about end-time matters. Indeed, if anything, the whole of the NT is reluctant to disclose details about the end. In the eschatological discourse itself Jesus comments, "But of that day or that hour no one knows, not even the angels in heaven, nor the Son, but only the Father" (Mark 13:32; cf. Matt. 24:36). And when the disciples ask the risen Lord about the time of the end, Jesus responds, "It is not for you to know times or seasons which the Father has fixed by his own authority" (Acts 1:7). But even a direct statement like this has not deterred the efforts of many to determine a detailed end-time chronology, even among those who would say that they accept the inspiration and authority of Acts 1:7.

The Apocalypse is regularly subjected to this type of predetermined approach, and it is especially in times of crisis that it flourishes. The number of books written to interpret the Apocalypse increases dramatically in times of war and crisis, from generation to generation. Times of tribulation are likely to be thought of as those spoken of in Revelation. The key enemy of any such period of suffering is likely to be identified as the antichrist. The end of all things is thus said to be imminent. Again and again, of course, the predictions have proved wrong.[1] What the authors of popular eschatology books fail to say is that their interpretations are little more than speculations, for that is all that they can be. Nobody can know the time of the end or lay out a chronological blueprint of the future. This is not for us to know, and more than that, the very nature of the Apocalypse is such that it does not provide the material that we would need.

Most notable in the United States, of course, is the dispensational eschatology that has captured the imagination of so many conservative and fundamentalist churches.[2] With a sublime, yet totally unwarranted, confidence,

1. It is rather astonishing that the repeated miscalculations about the coming of the end never seem to dishearten those who have repeatedly been wrong. On this phenomenon, see Festinger, Riecken, and Schachter, *When Prophecy Fails*; Stone, *Expecting Armageddon*.

2. It is unfathomable that a system of interpretation that began in the mid-nineteenth century could come to possess virtually canonical authority in so many churches that desire to take the

these Christians await an at-any-moment, "secret rapture" that will take them out of this world so that they will escape the tribulations described in the Apocalypse.[3] For the preachers of this message (e.g., Hal Lindsey), escaping these tribulations becomes virtually the gospel itself: one need not be "left behind" to endure the final period of suffering. Dispensational eschatology comes as a neatly wrapped package: pretribulation rapture followed by the tribulation, a literal millennium, yet another rebellion against God, followed finally by the eschaton.[4]

The author of Revelation no doubt would have been amazed at the conclusions drawn by these interpreters. Their failure is largely due to a neglect of the genre of apocalyptic and a misunderstanding of the basic purpose of the Apocalypse. Although it sounds shocking, I do not think that Raymond Brown overstates the matter when he says, "*The author of Rev did not know how or when the world will end, and neither does anyone else.*"[5]

The Message of the Book

If the point of Revelation is not primarily to supply information to those curious about the future, what is its message? Revelation is basically a message of comfort and hope for the church of John's day, and in effect, also for the church present and future. It is addressed in the first instance to a church undergoing persecution, a church struggling against supernatural evil in what seems to be an apparently hopeless battle. Revelation unveils reality in contrast to appearances; it provides a true understanding of the present and therefore also of the future. Things are not the way they seem to present perception. On the contrary, it is God who is triumphant, and with him his people, who are victorious over the powers of evil. The Apocalypse therefore provides assurance to its readers and also hope (i.e., confident expectation) for the future. Although addressed to the particular circumstances of John's day, it has a timeless message for the church of every age in its existence prior to the parousia of Christ.

At the very heart of Revelation are the hymnic and doxological passages that pervade the book (e.g., 1:4–8, 12–19; 4:1–11; 5:9–14; 11:15–18; 15:2–4; 19:1–8).

Bible seriously. This no doubt happened because of its articulation in the notes of the Scofield Bible in 1909, which forever linked dispensational eschatology with the fundamentalist cause and the King James Bible.

3. Popularized now in no less than sixteen novels of the "Left Behind" series by Tim LaHaye and Jerry Jenkins.

4. For this reason, the eschatological expectations spelled out in many conservative statements of faith became much too detailed. Many of these were drawn up during the fundamentalist-modernist controversies of the early twentieth century, when the choice appeared to be between the eschatological package of dispensationalism or unbelief in eschatology altogether.

5. Brown, *An Introduction to the New Testament*, 810 (note Brown's emphatic italics).

R. H. Charles, one of the twentieth century's greatest commentators on the Apocalypse, put it this way: "Though our author has for his theme the inevitable conflict and antagonisms of good and evil, of God and the powers of darkness, yet his book is emphatically a Book of Songs."[6] The huge difference between this perception of the book and that of popular-eschatology buffs is an indication of how off-target the latter are. Charles is worth quoting further: "A faith immeasurable, an optimism inexpugnable, a joy inextinguishable press for utterance and *take form in anthems of praise and gladness and thanksgiving,* as the Seer follows in vision the varying fortunes of the world struggle, till at last he sees evil fully and finally destroyed, righteousness established for evermore, and all the faithful—even the weakest of God's servants amongst them—enjoying everlasting blessedness in the eternal City of God, bearing His name on their foreheads, and growing more and more into His likeness."[7]

Revelation is a book that celebrates the proleptic victory of Christ and his church. It is the paradoxical victory song of the persecuted church. It points to the truth that cannot yet be seen by human eyes, the truth of the way things really are, not the way they may seem. The pervasive hymnic aspects of the book may point to the liturgical genesis of the material, or at least its use in the worship of the church, which reflects the worship in heaven (note the liturgical formulae in 4:8; 5:14; 7:12; 19:1–6). The liturgy of heaven is meant to inform and inspire the liturgy of those on the earth.

The Goal of Salvation History

Revelation reaches from the present to the end of this age. Christians are meant to know beyond any doubt that the end is secure because it is fully in God's hands. As the book proceeds to its climax in the final four chapters, it increasingly employs various eschatological images from the OT and Second Temple Jewish literature to point to the arrival of the goal of salvation history. In chapter 19 we read of "the marriage supper of the Lamb" (19:9; cf. 19:7), in chapter 20 of the resurrection of the dead, and in chapters 19–20 of the judgment of God's enemies.

But it is particularly in chapters 21–22 that we encounter statements concerning the realization of apocalyptic expectations and the fulfillment of salvation history (cf. earlier, 7:16–17). The opening words of chapter 21 allude to Isaiah 65:17; 66:22: "Then I saw a new heaven and a new earth; for the first heaven and the first earth had passed away" (21:1). And in 21:5, "He who sat upon the throne said, 'Behold, I make all things new'" (cf. Isa. 43:19). The new, perfect creation is the answer to the old, fallen creation. Thus in 21:3–4 we find the fulfillment of the hope expressed in various places in Isaiah: "Behold,

---

6. Charles, *A Critical and Exegetical Commentary on the Revelation of St. John,* 1:xiv.
7. Ibid., 1:xiv–xv (italics added).

the dwelling of God is with men. He will dwell with them, and they shall be his people, and God himself will be with them; he will wipe away every tear from their eyes, and death shall be no more, neither shall there be mourning nor crying nor pain any more, for the former things have passed away" (21:3–4 [cf. Isa. 25:8; 35:10; 51:11; see also Ezek. 37:27]). As 21:6 emphasizes, "It is done [*gegonan*]! I am the Alpha and the Omega, the beginning and the end [*to telos*]." The goal has been reached. The enemies of God and their evil fruit have been vanquished. The story has gone from beginning to end, covering all of time, as the inclusio of 1:8, 17; and 22:13 emphasizes.

Chapter 21 continues with references to the fulfillment of OT expectations: "To the thirsty I will give from the fountain of the water of life without payment" (21:6 [cf. Isa. 55:1; 49:10]). In 21:24–26 we see allusions to Isaiah 60:3, 5, 11. "By its light [i.e., of the glory of God] shall the nations walk" (21:24) fulfills the promise of Isaiah 25:7 that on God's holy mountain, Zion, God "will destroy . . . the covering that is cast over all peoples, the veil that is spread over all nations."

Chapter 22 refers to "the river of the water of life" that flows "from the throne of God and of the Lamb" (22:1 [cf. Ezek. 47:1–9; Zech. 14:8; see also Joel 3:18]) and also to "the tree of life with its twelve kinds of fruit, yielding its fruit each month; and the leaves of the tree were for the healing of the nations" (22:2 [cf. Ezek. 47:12: "Their fruit will be for food, and their leaves for healing"]). "The tree of life" (22:2, 14, 19) clearly is an allusion to Genesis 2:9. What Adam and Eve grasped for in their disobedience at the beginning of the story God now offers freely at the conclusion of the story. God has set right what went so tragically wrong at the beginning.

This section of Revelation ends with a final, resounding statement in 22:3–5, a grand theological inclusio in which the promises of God from the beginning come to their corresponding fulfillment: "There shall no more be anything accursed, but the throne of God and of the Lamb shall be in it [i.e., the new Jerusalem], and his servants shall worship him; they shall see his face, and his name shall be on their foreheads. And night shall be no more; they need no light of lamp or sun, for the Lord God will be their light, and they shall reign for ever and ever." The goal of a long, protracted salvation history has been reached. This, of course, is the language of realized eschatology: the future is fully secure and is just around the corner. The last book of the Bible could end in no more suitable way.

Interpreting the Apocalypse

One of the reasons for the all-too-common misunderstanding and misuse of Revelation is the failure to appreciate its special literary genre. Many interpreters with the best of intentions approach the book as though it were written in straightforward prose and end up with flatly literal interpretations. But apocalyptic is a special and unique genre, familiar to those living in the first century. It draws on a common stock of apocalyptic images and language, and it makes heavy use of symbolism. It may be said to resemble parables in that it speaks obliquely rather than directly, through pictorial images rather than prose statements. And, as with parables, the details of the images often have no self-contained importance, but instead are present merely to contribute to the total impression and the main ideas—that is, to support the main message. Apocalyptic can be likened to the political cartoon in today's newspapers. Here strange images, exaggerated features, and distorted perspectives are not meant to be taken literally; rather, they serve a greater purpose: to make the impact and to communicate the point that the cartoonist intended. Apocalyptic language functions in a similar way.

The rich symbolism of Revelation makes it a difficult book. That the symbols of the book are not stable, but constantly shifting, constitutes a considerable challenge for the interpreter. People, places, things, and numbers can bear a symbolic significance that is to be determined only from the context, if at all.[8] Frequently the meaning is far from clear.

As far as a general approach to the interpretation of the book is concerned, four basic perspectives have emerged in the history of the study of the book. Many commentators have found truth in more than one of these, combining aspects from more than one of the approaches.

Preterist

This approach sees the book as addressed exclusively to the past, to the time of the original readers at the end of the first century. In this view, Revelation, like other apocalypses of the era known to us (e.g., *Apocalypse of Enoch, 4 Ezra, Baruch*, and *Assumption of Moses*), directly addresses the suffering and persecution of its readers by its promise of an imminent reversal of fortunes. Thus Revelation is not seen to be offering prophecies concerning the future, certainly not the distant future. Rather, it concerns the judgment of the present enemies of God, possibly, on an early dating of the book, apostate Israel and thus a prophecy of the destruction of Jerusalem, or more commonly, the Roman Empire, emperors, and the cult of emperor worship are thought to be in view. Their demise, it is promised, will come in the near future. But despite the various similarities between Revelation and other apocalypses of its time, the differences are of enormous consequence. There is nothing in them like Revelation's songs of joy concerning the accomplishment of salvation history.

8. For example, the number 666 probably refers to Nero (the name "Nero" written in Hebrew letters equals 666; some manuscripts have 616, which is the number of the Latin letters that spell "Nero"). The numerical equivalent of "Jesus" is 888, which excels a perfect 777 by the same extent that 666 falls short. Numerology is an ever-inviting and ever-uncertain enterprise.

Historicist

According to this analysis, the sequence of events spoken of in Revelation amounts to a history of the church from the beginning to the time of the interpreter. The various sections of the book are seen to correspond to ages or epochs of world history, or, alternatively, to eras of church history. This view, which became popular in the Reformation period, identified the beast and the false prophet with the papacy and the Catholic Church. In the historicist approach the seals, trumpets, and bowls are taken as corresponding to particular persons or movements in history, even down to the recent past, with the beast identified as a Stalin or a Hitler. This approach calls attention again to the presence of symbols in Revelation and to the difficulty of interpreting them.

Idealist

This approach goes in a different direction altogether, denying any specific reference to historical realities whatsoever. Here Revelation is a purely symbolic, ideal portrayal of the ongoing struggle between good and evil, together with the assurance of the eventual victory of the former. Like a grand parable or series of parables, Revelation provides a timeless message, referring to history only in the sense of assuring the church of its ultimate victory, but without providing any details or correspondences with historical events past, present, or future. This approach has the advantage of making Revelation generally relevant to readers of every era. But it tears the book away from its historical context and ignores the clear historical connections with the first-century churches of Asia Minor that are addressed.

Futurist

Understandably, the most popular approach to Revelation, because it is in some ways the most natural, has been the futurist. Emphasis here is on how the book defines itself as a "prophecy" (1:3), a revelation of "what must soon take place" (1:1). Jesus tells John, "Write what you see, what is and what is to take place hereafter" (1:19). The inclusio at the end of the book makes the same points: the purpose of the revealing angel was to show "what must soon take place" (22:6); the book is a "prophecy" (22:10, 18–19). In a fundamental sense the book is about the future, and thus it seems that any approach to the interpretation of the book must at least to some degree be futurist. At issue, then, is not whether the book speaks of the future, but rather how much detail is provided about how and when the future will unfold.

Undoubtedly, the most complex and detailed eschatological blueprint drawn from Revelation in particular, but from other parts of Scripture too, is that of dispensationalism, an interpretive approach that emerged only in the nineteenth century. Dispensationalists quote texts abundantly from all over the Bible, usually with little regard for their context or intended meaning, treating the Bible like a vast collection of self-standing prooftexts.[9] And when one is dealing with apocalyptic texts laden with symbolism, the literalistic and simplistic approach of dispensationalism becomes all the more indefensible.

There is no single place in Scripture where the dispensationalist system is set forth. What dispensationalist interpretation reveals more than anything else is the ingenuity of the interpreter. Once the basic rules have been set—for example, the airtight separation of Israel and the church, a literalistic OT hermeneutic, the existence of seven dispensations (eras in which God deals with humanity differently)—then it becomes a simple matter of bringing "similar" verses together from all over the Bible, taking them as referring to the same thing, or discovering some distinction that enables the separating of verses that look like they might otherwise belong together. In a disturbingly facile way all is made to fit the predetermined system. But the implausibility of the resultant reading of the texts, which ends up with a "secret" rapture, two parousias, two resurrections, two final judgments, two final rebellions, separated by an earthly millennium of imperfect semi-bliss, somehow does not dawn on its adherents. It must be asked, however, whether the apocalyptic texts of the Bible, including those of Revelation, really have as their purpose the conveying of this kind of specific and detailed information. Or is this a stunning example of the overinterpretation and misuse of Revelation?

Given the nature of Revelation and its inherent difficulties, the most satisfactory way to proceed is by using a mix of interpretive methods, which should not be thought of as mutually exclusive. Brevard Childs draws an appropriate conclusion: "The issues of symbolism, literary genre, and fluctuating tradition pose a complexity which does not allow for a simple method of 'decoding' the text."[10]

Millennialism (Chiliasm)

From the earliest time, the particular teaching in Revelation 20:1–6 concerning the millennium, the centerpiece in futurist interpretation, caused controversy in the church. Millennialism, or chiliasm (to use the corresponding Greek root), has remained a dividing point in the church ever since. The issue is whether the reference (in the NT only here) to the thousand-year reign of Christ on earth,

---

9. Indeed, there is commonly a disdain for "interpreting" texts, with the express preference for "letting the texts speak for themselves" and "taking the verses as they stand," as though that did not involve interpretation. Such counsel not only begs the question, of course, but also amounts to a carte blanche approval of arbitrary interpretation—for interpretation there will be, unless one simply repeats the texts and says no more.

10. Childs, *The New Testament as Canon*, 304.

prior to the end of all things, is to be taken literally or symbolically.[11] There is no satisfying answer to the question of why God would imprison Satan for a thousand years only to let him loose on the world to do his evil work again, or what the purpose of a literal earthly reign of Christ that falls short of the perfection of the eschaton might be. Nor are there passages anywhere else in the Bible that contain these ideas. A literal millennium, therefore, did not make sense to many Christians. Unfortunately, it was also a fact that some millennialists crassly looked forward to the millennium as a time of unbridled hedonism.

Already in the fourth century opposition to the literal understanding of the millennium was growing in parts of the church. Origen understood it spiritually, and Tyconius, the author of one of the earliest commentaries on the Apocalypse (ca. 380), interpreted the thousand years symbolically as a reference to the church age—that is, the time of the reign of Christ between his first and second coming. This viewpoint, which came to be known as amillennialism, persuaded the influential Augustine, who earlier had accepted a literal millennium. In the Reformation period, Martin Luther and John Calvin, neither of whom thought much of the Apocalypse (it is the only book of the NT on which Calvin did not write a commentary, and Luther placed it in an appendix to the NT), assumed the amillennialist perspective. Neither of the classic Reformation statements of faith, the Augsburg Confession and the Second Helvetic Confession, gave any place to chiliasm.

In the eighteenth century a viewpoint known as postmillennialism began to emerge. The prefix "post" refers to the conclusion that the return of Christ will take place only *after* the millennium has been experienced.[12] The millennium is thus not the supernatural work of Christ produced on his return, but rather is the work of the church and its transforming impact on the world, leading to the return of Christ. Postmillennialists combined the liberal dream of a perfect society, brought about by the progress of science, technology, and human equality, with the theology of Christ's present reign and the spread of the gospel to produce the idea of an age of near perfection realized in history. It was above all the horrors of the early twentieth century, with its demonstration of the extent of human evil, that demolished the optimistic notion that the kingdom could be realized on earth through human effort, even if aided by God.

11. Vern Poythress ("Genre and Hermeneutics in Rev 20:1–6") has shown how premillennialists neglect the visionary and symbolic levels of the text, reducing all to the referential, historical level.

12. This contrasting view of when Christ would return made it necessary to change the name of classic millennialism to "premillennialism." In this view, Christ returns at the end of seven years of tribulation in order to set up the thousand-year period. Classic dispensationalism teaches a pretribulation rapture of the church, though some premillennialists teach a midtribulation rapture, and others a posttribulation rapture. Nondispensationalist premillennialists who believe that the church will go through the tribulation are known as historic premillennialists. On the rapture question, see "The Eschatology of the Thessalonian Letters" in chapter 26 above. See also Ladd, *The Blessed Hope*; Gundry, *The Church and the Tribulation*.

Chiliasts of every generation have found it hard to resist the temptation to predict the imminent approach of the millennium in their time. By arbitrarily identifying catastrophes of their time with events described in Revelation, they thought they could predict its arrival in their own day. This pattern has been repeated again and again, down to present-day televangelists, showing the futility of the exercise.

At the heart of dispensationalist eschatology is the conviction that the promises of an earthly kingdom made to Israel in the OT must be taken literally. Since these promises have not yet been literally fulfilled, and God's faithfulness is on the line, they require a future fulfillment; according to this view, the millennium is the time of that earthly fulfillment. The difficulty with this idea is that a mere thousand years cannot literally fulfill the promise of a Davidic kingdom that will last forever ("And your house and your kingdom shall be made sure for ever before me; your throne shall be established for ever" [2 Sam. 7:16; cf. 7:13]), nor does it constitute the time when death is no more and every tear is wiped away. The promises to Israel require fulfillment not in an interim period, but in eternity, in the new earth to be created by God. Daniel 7:18 speaks not of an interim period, but of a final reign of the saints: "The saints of the Most High shall receive the kingdom, and possess the kingdom for ever, for ever and ever." It cannot be said that dispensationalists are consistent in their intention to take the texts literally.

Dispensationalism unfortunately ignores the possibility that the promises to Israel could point beyond themselves to a greater reality than a national-political one, a transcendent reality that rounds out the whole of salvation history by bringing us again to the perfection of Eden.

Being Content with Basic Truths

With an amazing but unwarranted confidence, dispensationalism imposes a complicated system on the data of Revelation (and other biblical texts). Highly questionable interpretations abound; meanings are forced on texts; gaps have to be imagined where there are none, while those that do exist must be ignored; the harmonizing of disparate texts is the order of the day. The coherence that emerges does so only by means of a random association of texts and a creative cleverness.

In principle, of course, there is nothing wrong with speculating about the possible meaning of the prophecies of Revelation and other books of the Bible. But when we deal with eschatology we must allow a diversity of views. Because the meaning of many of these texts is far from clear, there should therefore be no room for dogmatism or for the dismissal of other views as heretical. Problems begin when one treats speculation as dogmatic truth and when that speculation becomes kerygma, such as when the good news seems to be reduced to the escape from the tribulation.

If it was the purpose of Revelation to reveal a detailed blueprint of the future, it has not succeeded. The end is so mysterious and beyond what we know that it can be referred to only in figures, symbols, and images, such as Revelation does. The third-century bishop Dionysius reported, "Some indeed of those before our time rejected and altogether impugned the book, examining it chapter by chapter and declaring it to be unintelligible and illogical, and its title false. For they say that it is not John's, no, nor yet an apocalypse (unveiling), since it is veiled by its heavy, thick curtain of unintelligibility" (according to Eusebius, *Hist. eccl.* 7.25.1, trans. Oulton). Although exaggerated, there is some truth in this reaction. That does not mean, however, that nothing about the future is clear in Revelation or the NT.

The NT does provide us with good news concerning the future, even if its burden is the good news of salvation already accomplished in the cross of Christ, and the focus of the NT is more on the dimensions of realized eschatology available now in the church. There are, nevertheless, both in Revelation and in the NT, quite clear, fixed points in the expectation of the future: the return of Christ, the victory of Christians in their suffering, the resurrection of the dead, the future judgment and the end of evil, the guaranteed coming of the eschaton with its unalloyed, promised blessings—all of this, in contrast to Jewish apocalyptic books, dependent on the reality of the cross, the "Lamb that was slain" (13:8; cf. 5:6–14). These are the things that the Apocalypse sings about! The basic truths are the important things; details of how and when are irrelevant, and our ignorance of them is unimportant.

Does an Apocalyptic Book Belong in the New Testament?

Because the NT is a book much more of present fulfillment than of future promise, it may well be asked, as it has been throughout the history of the church, whether an apocalyptic book really belongs in the NT. If the Apocalypse of John were fully analogous to, and parallel with, other Jewish apocalyptic books, I think that the answer would have to be no. But the unique aspects of the book that we have observed make it a very special apocalyptic book. Its celebratory, liturgical character, championing what God has accomplished in the slain Lamb, differentiates it from typical apocalypses. The stress in the final chapters on the arrival of the culmination of salvation history, with the transformation of the whole of creation, make it an ideal concluding book of the NT canon.

It is true that as far as the end itself is concerned, Revelation takes us no further than other NT books. What it does vividly, however, is emphasize the theme of judgment—which Jesus took trouble to emphasize was something delayed, despite the dawning of the kingdom—and press it to the point of certain and imminent realization, thereby increasing our confidence in the ultimate consummation of God's purposes. In its own unique way Revelation underscores the salvation accomplished by God through the slain Lamb. The kingdom represented by the vision of the new heavens and the new earth cannot be fully realized until evil is destroyed. And the promise of the end of evil is meant to lift the spirits of the church living between the times.

Like other NT books, the Apocalypse preserves the tension between realized and future eschatology. But here the fulfillment of salvation in Christ is pushed to the logical conclusion that the consummation not only is assured but also, precisely because of that fact, must be imminent. John does not shrink from that theologically correct conclusion. What he will speak of "must soon [*en tachei*] take place" (1:1; 21:6). "The time is near" (1:3). And the Lord promises him and the church, "Behold, I am coming soon" (22:7, 12); "Surely I am coming soon" (22:20). This theme has rightly given comfort and encouragement to generation after generation of Christians. For to each generation the end is potentially imminent.

We must not allow abuse of the book of Revelation to rob us of its beauty and power. It stands at the end of the NT like a great doxology or series of doxologies, with its magnificent outbursts of praise, as a worthy conclusion to the whole story of the Bible. God and the Lamb have set right what went wrong at the beginning. And therefore we will not wait futilely or long for the joyful experience of God's reign in the perfect age to come.

Bibliography

See also the bibliography in chapter 41, "The Apocalypse."

Books and Articles

Bauckham, Richard J. *The Theology of the Book of Revelation*. NTT. Cambridge: Cambridge University Press, 1993.

Bauckham Richard, and Trevor A. Hart. *Hope against Hope: Christian Eschatology at the Turn of the Millennium*. Grand Rapids: Eerdmans, 1999.

Bietenhard, Hans. "The Millennial Hope in the Early Church." *SJT* 6 (1953): 12–30.

Blaising, Craig A., Kenneth L. Gentry, and Robert B. Strimple. *Three Views on the Millennium and Beyond*. Edited by Darrell L. Bock. Grand Rapids: Zondervan, 1999.

Blomberg, Craig L., and Sung Wook Chung. *A Case for Historic Premillennialism: An Alternative to the "Left Behind" Eschatology*. Grand Rapids: Baker Academic, 2009.

Boxall, Ian. *Revelation: Vision and Insight; An Introduction to the Apocalypse*. London: SPCK, 2002.

Brown, Raymond E. *An Introduction to the New Testament*. New York: Doubleday, 1997.

Charles, R. H. *A Critical and Exegetical Commentary on the Revelation of St. John: With Introduction, Notes, and Indices; Also the Greek Text and Translation*. ICC. 2 vols. Edinburgh: T&T Clark, 1920.

———. *Studies in the Apocalypse*. 2nd ed. Edinburgh: T&T Clark, 1915.

Childs, Brevard S. *The New Testament as Canon: An Introduction*. Philadelphia: Fortress, 1985.

Collins, Adela Yarbro. *Crisis and Catharsis: The Power of the Apocalypse*. Philadelphia: Westminster, 1984.

Collins, John J. *The Apocalyptic Imagination: An Introduction to Jewish Apocalyptic Literature.* 2nd ed. Grand Rapids: Eerdmans, 1998.

———. "Introduction: Early Christian Apocalypticism." *Semeia* 36 (1986): 1–11.

Cook, Stephen L. *The Apocalyptic Literature.* IBT. Nashville: Abingdon, 2003.

———. *Prophecy and Apocalypticism: The Postexilic Social Setting.* Minneapolis: Fortress, 1995.

deSilva, David A. *Seeing Things John's Way: The Rhetoric of the Book of Revelation.* Louisville: Westminster John Knox, 2009.

Erickson, Millard J. *A Basic Guide to Eschatology: Making Sense of the Millennium.* Grand Rapids: Baker Academic, 1998.

Faley, Roland J. *Apocalypse Then and Now: A Companion to the Book of Revelation.* Mahwah, NJ: Paulist Press, 1999.

Festinger, Leon, Henry W. Riecken, and Stanley Schachter. *When Prophecy Fails: A Social and Psychological Study of a Modern Group that Predicted the Destruction of the World.* New York: Harper & Row, 1964.

Fuller, Robert C. *Naming the Antichrist: The History of an American Obsession.* New York: Oxford University Press, 1995.

Gorman, Michael J. *Reading Revelation Responsibly: Uncivil Worship and Witness; Following the Lamb into the New Creation.* Eugene, OR: Wipf & Stock, 2010.

Gourgues, Michel. "The Thousand-Year Reign (Rev. 20:1–6): Terrestrial or Celestial?" *CBQ* 47 (1985): 676–81.

Gundry, Robert H. *The Church and the Tribulation: A Biblical Examination of Posttribulationism.* Grand Rapids: Zondervan, 1973.

Hanson, Paul D. *The Dawn of Apocalyptic: The Historical and Sociological Roots of Jewish Apocalyptic Eschatology.* Rev. ed. Philadelphia: Fortress, 1979.

Harrington, Wilfrid J. *Understanding the Apocalypse.* Washington, DC: Corpus, 1969.

Harrison, J. F. C. *The Second Coming: Popular Millenarianism, 1780–1850.* New Brunswick, NJ: Rutgers University Press, 1979.

Hellholm, David W. "The Problem of Apocalyptic Genre and the Apocalypse of John." *Semeia* 36 (1986): 13–64.

Hendricksen, William. *More than Conquerors: An Interpretation of the Book of Revelation.* Reprint, Grand Rapids: Baker Academic, 1978.

Hill, Craig C. *In God's Time: The Bible and the Future.* Grand Rapids: Eerdmans, 2002.

Holman, Charles L. *Till Jesus Comes: Origins of Christian Apocalyptic Expectation.* Peabody, MA: Hendrickson, 1996.

Howard-Brook, Wes, and Anthony Gwyther. *Unveiling Empire: Reading Revelation Then and Now.* Maryknoll, NY: Orbis, 1999.

Jewett, Robert. *Jesus against the Rapture: Seven Unexpected Prophecies.* Philadelphia: Westminster, 1979.

Kallas, James. "The Apocalypse—An Apocalyptic Book?" *JBL* 86 (1967): 69–80.

Kik, J. Marcellus. *The Eschatology of Victory.* Phillipsburg, NJ: Presbyterian & Reformed, 1971.

Koch, Klaus. *The Rediscovery of Apocalyptic: A Polemical Work on a Neglected Area on Biblical Studies and Its Damaging Effects on Theology and Philosophy.* Translated by Margaret Kohl. SBT. Naperville, IL: Allenson, 1972.

Koester, Craig R. "On the Verge of the Millennium: A History of the Interpretation of Revelation." *WW* 15 (1995): 128–36.

Kümmel, Werner Georg. *Introduction to the New Testament.* Translated by A. J. Mattill Jr. 14th ed. Nashville: Abingdon, 1966.

Ladd, George Eldon. *The Blessed Hope.* Grand Rapids: Eerdmans, 1956.

———. *Crucial Questions about the Kingdom of God: The Sixth Annual Mid-Year Lectures of 1952, Delivered at Western Conservative Baptist Theological Seminary of Portland, Oregon.* Grand Rapids: Eerdmans, 1952.

Mazzaferri, Frederick David. *The Genre of the Book of Revelation from a Source-Critical Perspective*. BZNW 54. Berlin: de Gruyter, 1989.

Mealy, J. Webb. *After the Thousand Years: Resurrection and Judgment in Revelation 20*. JSNTSup 70. Sheffield: JSOT Press, 1992.

Metzger, Bruce M. *Breaking the Code: Understanding the Book of Revelation*. Nashville, Abingdon, 1993.

Metzger, Bruce M., and Bart D. Ehrman. *The Text of the New Testament: Its Transmission, Corruption, and Restoration*. 4th ed. New York: Oxford University Press, 2005.

Michaels, J. Ramsey. *Interpreting the Book of Revelation*. GNTE. Grand Rapids: Baker Academic, 1992.

Minear, Paul S. *I Saw a New Earth: An Introduction to the Visions of the Apocalypse*. Washington, DC: Corpus, 1968.

———. *New Testament Apocalyptic*. IBT. Nashville: Abingdon, 1981.

Morris, Leon. *Apocalyptic*. Grand Rapids: Eerdmans, 1983.

Newport, Kenneth G. C. *Apocalypse and Millennium: Studies in Biblical Eisegesis*. Cambridge: Cambridge University Press, 2000.

O'Leary, Stephen D. *Arguing the Apocalypse: A Theory of Millennial Rhetoric*. New York: Oxford University Press, 1994.

Pate, C. Marvin, ed. *Four Views on the Book of Revelation*. Grand Rapids: Zondervan, 1998.

———. *What Does the Future Hold? Exploring Various Views on the End Times*. Grand Rapids: Baker Academic, 2010.

Pate, C. Marvin, and Douglas W. Kennard. *Deliverance Now and Not Yet: The New Testament and the Great Tribulation*. SBL 54. New York: Peter Lang, 2003.

Pentecost, J. Dwight. *Prophecy for Today: God's Purpose and Plan for Our Future*. Grand Rapids: Discovery House, 1989.

———. *Things to Come: A Study in Biblical Eschatology*. Findlay, OH: Dunham, 1958.

Poythress, Vern S. "Genre and Hermeneutics in Rev 20:1–6." *JETS* 36 (1993): 41–54.

———. *The Returning King: A Guide to the Book of Revelation*. Phillipsburg, NJ: Presbyterian & Reformed, 2000.

Prévost, Jean-Pierre. *How to Read the Apocalypse*. Translated by John Bowden and Margaret Lydamore. New York: Crossroad, 1993.

Rossing, Barbara R. *The Rapture Exposed: The Message of Hope in the Book of Revelation*. Boulder, CO: Westview, 2004.

Rowland, Christopher. *The Open Heaven: A Study of Apocalyptic in Judaism and Early Christianity*. New York: Crossroad, 1982.

Rowley, H. H. *The Relevance of Apocalyptic: A Study of Jewish and Christian Apocalypses from Daniel to the Revelation*. 3rd ed. London: Lutterworth, 1963.

Russell, D. S. *The Method and Message of Jewish Apocalyptic, 200 BC–AD 100*. Philadelphia: Westminster, 1964.

Sandeen, Ernest R. *The Roots of Fundamentalism: British and American Millenarianism, 1800–1930*. Chicago: University of Chicago Press, 1970.

Scholer, David M. "Breaking the Code: Interpretive Reflections on Revelation." *EvRT* 25 (2001): 304–17.

Stevens, Gerald L., ed. *Essays on Revelation: Appropriating Yesterday's Apocalypse in Today's World*. Eugene, OR: Wipf & Stock, 2010.

Stone, Jon R., ed. *Expecting Armageddon: Essential Readings in Failed Prophecy*. New York: Routledge, 2000.

Tenney, Merrill C. *Interpreting Revelation*. Grand Rapids: Eerdmans, 1957.

Wainwright, Arthur W. *Mysterious Apocalypse: Interpreting the Book of Revelation*. Nashville: Abingdon, 1993.

Walhout, Edwin. *Revelation Down to Earth: Making Sense of the Apocalypse of John*. Grand Rapids: Eerdmans, 2000.

Walvoord, John F. *The Millennial Kingdom*. Findlay, OH: Dunham, 1959.

———. *The Rapture Question*. Grand Rapids: Zondervan, 1979.

———. *The Revelation of Jesus Christ*. Chicago: Moody, 1966.

Weber, Timothy P. *Living in the Shadow of the Second Coming: American Premillennialism, 1875–1982*. Grand Rapids: Zondervan, 1983.

———. *On the Road to Armageddon: How Evangelicals Became Israel's Best Friend*. Grand Rapids: Baker Academic, 2004.

Commentaries

See the bibliography for chapter 41, "The Apocalypse."

41

The Apocalypse

The single book of the NT that represents the apocalyptic genre opens with the three words *Apokalypsis Iēsou Christou*, "the revelation of Jesus Christ"— that is, the revelation *from* Jesus Christ. This revelation is further described as given by God to Jesus, and then given through an intermediary angel to "his servant John." Although we know of other early apocalypses from the Second Temple literature, this book apparently is the first to bear as its title "Apocalypse." The apocalypse that bears John's name does so because John was the person responsible for writing it down.[1]

"Apocalypse" is not merely the title of the book; it also is descriptive of a literary genre. The now-classic definition of this genre is the following: "a genre of revelatory literature with a narrative framework, in which a revelation is mediated by an otherworldly being to a human recipient, disclosing a transcendent reality which is both temporal insofar as it envisages eschatological salvation and spatial insofar as it involves another, supernatural world."[2] As will be immediately evident, this description fits the book of Revelation well. But while it reflects the fact that other apocalyptic books resemble Revelation, it does not indicate the unique aspects of the Christian Apocalypse.

---

1. Arguably, the book should be called "The Apocalypse of Jesus Christ," in agreement with the opening words. But in the early centuries the book took on the title "The Apocalypse of John," focusing attention on the actual author of the book rather than the source of the revelation. The manuscripts of the Textus Receptus have the title *apokalypsis iōannou tou theologou*, the "revelation of John the theologian," which gives rise to the archaic title of the KJV, "The Revelation of St. John the Divine" (the expression "the divine" means "the theologian").

2. From volume 14 of the journal *Semeia* (1979), which is devoted to the subject of apocalyptic. Quoted in J. J. Collins, *The Apocalyptic Imagination*, 5.

> **Author**: Almost certainly not by the Apostle John. Possibly by John "the Elder," but more probably by another John, otherwise unknown to us, who may have been a member of the Johannine circle.
>
> **Date**: Probably during the reign of the Roman emperor Domitian or shortly after, thus sometime in the 90s.
>
> **Addressees**: The seven churches of Asia Minor addressed in chapters 2–3.
>
> **Purpose**: To strengthen and encourage Christians undergoing persecution.
>
> **Message/Argument**: The sovereignty of God over present and future contradicts present appearances and discloses the truth that the future is secure in God's purpose and will. Evil will be finally destroyed, and God's people will enjoy the blessings of the new heaven and new earth.
>
> **Significance**: Provides a stunning conclusion to the macronarrative of the entire Bible, describing not merely fulfillment but the consummation of salvation history.

The Distinctiveness of John's Apocalypse

The Apocalypse of John is both similar to and different from apocalypses of its time. The characteristics of other apocalypses usually include things such as tours (i.e., glimpses) of heaven and hell, heavy use of mythological imagery and a variety of symbols—pictorial, especially of animals, and numerological—to point to future events, the promise of usually imminent judgment of the wicked and the reward of the righteous, as well as a deterministic view of history. The most important examples of contemporary parallel apocalypses are *1 Enoch*, *2 Baruch*, and *4 Ezra* (= 2 Esdras).

Material from the OT often serves as the inspiration and partial source of Second Temple apocalypses (especially important is the fountainhead of Dan. 7–12; also significant are Ezek. 38–39; 40–48; Zech. 4–6; 9–14; Isa. 24–27; 40–66). This is also true of John's Apocalypse. John clearly was immersed in the OT Scriptures, and although he does not directly cite the OT, his language is thoroughly scriptural.[3] Even though he never uses a fulfillment formula, the continual use of scriptural allusions (estimated to be more than two hundred)[4] itself points to the reality of fulfillment of the apocalyptic expectation that the book describes.[5]

---

3. For a full study of the subject, see Beale, *John's Use of the Old Testament in Revelation*. See also idem, *The Use of Daniel in Jewish Apocalyptic Literature and in the Revelation of St. John*; Moyise, *The Old Testament in the Book of Revelation*.

4. Thus Moyise, *The Old Testament in the Book of Revelation*, 137.

5. Richard Bauckham concludes that Revelation "is a book designed to be read in constant intertextual relationship with the Old Testament. John was writing what he understood to be a work of prophetic scripture, the climax of prophetic revelation, which gathered up the prophetic meaning of the Old Testament scriptures and disclosed the way in which it was being and was to be fulfilled in the last days" (*The Climax of Prophecy*, xi).

While Revelation is similar to other apocalypses, its Christian orientation makes it distinctive and marks it out from others. In effect, Revelation is a Christianizing of the apocalyptic genre. "The apocalyptic view of history has received a new substructure through the historical appearance of Jesus. On this the entire weight of the structure rests."[6] The frequent hymnic/liturgical passages that constitute the essence of Revelation celebrate the victory already won by the Lamb. They transform the apocalyptic tone of the book from negative to uniquely positive. John's Apocalypse is a book of worship and seems to have been intended to be read liturgically in the churches of Asia Minor (1:3).

Another distinctive about John's Apocalypse is its mixed genre, combining the form of an apocalypse with the form of a letter. Although the opening words begin like an apocalypse, after the first three verses we encounter the standard formula for the beginning of a letter: "John to the seven churches that are in Asia," followed by the Pauline-sounding blessing of "grace to you and peace" (1:4), and a full doxology (1:5b–6). Revelation also ends like a letter, with a benediction, albeit a general one: "The grace of the Lord Jesus be with all" (22:21).

Letters to the Seven Churches

A further unique formal feature of Revelation are the seven short letters to the churches of Asia Minor (2:1–3:22). Here alone in the book do we find specific connections with the particular intended readers that we expect to find in a letter.

The churches are, in order, Ephesus, Smyrna, Pergamum, Thyatira, Sardis, Philadelphia, and Laodicea. Of these, only Ephesus, Thyatira, and Laodicea are mentioned elsewhere in the NT. In exile on the island of Patmos (southwest of Ephesus), John was "in the Spirit" (1:10) on a Sunday when he received a vision of "one like a son of man" (1:13 [cf. Dan. 7:13]) telling him to "write what you see in a book and send it to the seven churches" (1:11). The book referred to is the whole book of Revelation, including the specific letters to the seven churches. These letters contain specifics pertaining to each local church, but they also are to be read by all seven congregations, while at the same time the entire book is meant for the church universal, as the seven churches, representing the number of perfection, already suggests.[7]

The seven letters form a unit wherein each letter consists of the same elements:

- the introductory formula "To the angel of the church in . . . write:"
- identification of the speaker by "the words of"

6. Kümmel, *Introduction to the New Testament*, 461.
7. The number "seven" is of very great importance in Revelation, occurring some fifty-four times.

> "him who holds the seven stars in his right hand, who walks among the seven golden lampstands" (to Ephesus)
>
> "the first and the last, who died and came to life" (to Smyrna)
>
> "him who has the sharp two-edged sword" (to Pergamum)
>
> "the Son of God, who has eyes like a flame of fire, and whose feet are like burnished bronze" (to Thyatira)
>
> "him who has the seven spirits of God and the seven stars" (to Sardis)
>
> "the holy one, the true one, who has the key of David, who opens and no one shall shut, who shuts and no one opens" (to Philadelphia)
>
> "the Amen, the faithful and true witness, the beginning of God's creation" (to Laodicea)

- description and criticism of the church, introduced by the formula "I know your works" (but to Smyrna, "I know your tribulation and your poverty"; and to Pergamum, "I know where you dwell, where Satan's throne is")
- the promise to the one "who conquers"
- exhortation to hear (sometimes occurring before the promise to the one who conquers): "He who has an ear, let him hear what the Spirit says to the churches"

It appears that Revelation may have been intended to be a circular letter to the churches of eastern Asia Minor, including not only an apocalyptic treatise relevant to all of them but also a more specific message for each of the seven churches. Each letter has the ring of a prophetic oracle: "Thus says the Lord." The descriptions and criticisms of the individual churches indicate that John probably was very familiar with these congregations.[8] What is unusual is that the specific material is restricted to these seven short, initial letters and makes no further appearance in the book.

Authorship

Apocalypses of the Second Temple period usually were written under a pseudonym, using the name of a famous person of the distant past, such as Enoch, Baruch, or Ezra. So unless the name "John" in Revelation is a pseudonym, which seems highly unlikely, the book was written by a contemporaneous person of that name. Ironically, this is the only book in the "Johannine corpus" (Gospel, Epistles, Apocalypse) that provides the author's name, yet the identity of this John is much disputed. His name occurs four times in the book (1:1, 4, 9; 22:8), but he is never identified as an Apostle. John possibly

8. The most helpful volume on the letters is Hemer, *The Letters to the Seven Churches of Asia in Their Local Setting.*

had some leadership role in the area, although it is interesting that he does not appeal to any personal authority, but instead refers to himself simply as a "servant" (1:1) of Jesus Christ and as "your brother" (1:9). He is basically one "who bore witness" (1:2). Probably we are to classify John as a "seer" or "prophet." His book is repeatedly referred to as a "prophecy" (1:3; 22:7, 10, 18–19). When John falls down at the feet of the revealing angel at the end of the book, the angel states, "I am a fellow servant with you and your brethren the prophets" (22:9). The identity of this John remains a mystery. If, as we will see, it is improbable that he is to be identified as the John the Apostle, he may be the Elder of 2 John and 3 John. More probably, however, he is yet another John altogether, about whom we know virtually nothing.

In the middle of the second century Justin Martyr shows that he knew Revelation (he refers to the millennium and the resurrection [20:4–5]) and says that it was written by "a certain man with us, whose name is John, one of the apostles of Christ" (*Dial.* 81.4, trans. *ANF* 1:240), making him the first to state that Revelation was written by the Apostle. Other early church fathers joining Justin in this view are Irenaeus, Clement of Alexandria, Tertullian, and Origen. Although from the late second century Revelation was accepted as the work of John the Apostle, it was not long before this conclusion was challenged. Eusebius did not think much of the book and is happy to quote at length the third-century bishop Dionysius, who argued against the conclusion that had begun to establish itself, that John the Apostle was the author:

> That, then, he was certainly named John and that this book is by one John, I will not gainsay; for I fully allow that it is the work of some holy and inspired person. But I should not readily agree that he was the apostle, the son of Zebedee, the brother of James, whose are the Gospel entitled According to John and the Catholic Epistle. For I form my judgement from the character of each and from the nature of the language and from what is known as the general construction of the book, that [the John therein mentioned] is not the same. For the evangelist nowhere adds his name, nor yet proclaims himself, throughout either the Gospel or the Epistle. (Eusebius, *Hist. eccl.* 7.25.7–8, trans. Oulton)

Eusebius quotes Dionysius further:

> That the writer of these words, therefore, was John, one must believe, since he says it. But what John, is not clear. (*Hist. eccl.* 7.25.12, trans. Oulton)

> The Apocalypse is utterly different from, and foreign to, these [Johannine] writings; it has no connexion, no affinity, in any way with them; it scarcely, so to speak, has even a syllable in common with them. Nay more, neither does the Epistle (not to speak of the Gospel) contain any mention or thought of the Apocalypse, nor the Apocalypse of the Epistle. (*Hist. eccl.* 7.25.22, trans. Oulton)

And further, by means of the style one can estimate the difference between the Gospel and Epistle and the Apocalypse. (*Hist. eccl.* 7.25.25, trans. Oulton)

I will not deny that the other writer had seen revelations and received knowledge and prophecy; nevertheless I observe his style and that his use of the Greek language is not accurate, but that he employs barbarous idioms, in some places committing downright solecisms. (*Hist. eccl.* 7.25.26, trans. Oulton)[9]

The uniqueness of Revelation had already been noted by others before Dionysius, and he records the opinion of some "that the author of this book was not only not one of the apostles, nor even one of the saints or those belonging to the Church, but Cerinthus, the same who created the sect called 'Cerinthian' after him, since he desired to affix to his own forgery a name worthy of credit" (according to Eusebius, *Hist. eccl.* 7.25.2, trans. Oulton).[10]

A key issue in deciding the question of the author of Revelation is whether it was written by the same person who wrote the Fourth Gospel and the Johannine Epistles. There is some evidence in favor of this conclusion. To begin with, we have the strong, if not unanimous, tradition of the early church that attributed the whole of the Johannine corpus to the Apostle. There is also some internal evidence that seems to point in the same direction.

Beyond the fact that the author identifies himself as John, there are some concepts and themes distinctive to the Gospel and Epistles that are also found in the Apocalypse. Thus we find a linking of the *logos* and Jesus (of the rider on the white horse it is said in 19:13, "the name by which he is called is The Word of God" [cf. 1:2, 9; 6:9; 20:4]), reference to Jesus as the "Lamb" (*arnion*, nearly 30x [cf. John 1:29, 36, although here *amnos* is used]),[11] and several "I am" sayings (e.g., 1:8, 17–18; 21:6; 22:13, 16). Among common themes are life and death, hunger and thirst, witness and victory.

But there are significant differences between the Apocalypse and the other Johannine writings. Very important here is the different quality of the Greek. As we already noted in Dionysius's comment, Revelation often exhibits a certain roughness in its Greek. It is true that some of the grammatical abnormalities may be deliberate.[12] But even apart from these, there is considerable difference in style. Some of this is perhaps explainable by the

---

9. This viewpoint is anything but naive or uncritical. On the contrary, Dionysius (and others in the early church, such as Origen) had a keen sense of critical judgment and drew informed conclusions.

10. This attribution of Revelation to the second-century Gnostic Cerinthus apparently was made by the contemporaneous group known as the Alogoi (who did not accept the *logos* doctrine of the Gospel and opposed the Montanists), a group known to us from Epiphanius (*Pan.* 51).

11. In Revelation the Lamb is not only a slain sacrificial lamb (e.g., 5:6) but also a victorious, apocalyptic lamb (e.g., 6:16; 17:14; 22:3). The Lamb is "the Lion of the tribe of Judah" (5:5–6).

12. As in *apo* followed by designations of God in the nominative case, where John chooses not to inflect the divine name (1:4), and in the strange construction *ho ēn* (1:4; 4:8). See also

apocalyptic genre and the liturgical portions of the text, but the problem remains. Some have maintained that although the author writes in Greek, he thinks in Hebrew/Aramaic.[13] So distinctive is the Greek of the Apocalypse that R. H. Charles compiled a special grammar for the book as a part of the introduction to his monumental and still important commentary.[14] Charles concluded, "John the Seer used a unique style, the true character of which no Grammar of the New Testament has as yet recognized. . . . The language which he adopted in his old age formed for him no rigid medium of expression. Hence he remodelled its syntax freely, and created a Greek that is absolutely his own."[15]

A great difference in content between the Apocalypse and the other writings of the Johannine corpus is to be expected simply because of the difference in genre between the writings. But it remains the case that if the same author did write the Apocalypse, one might expect more similarity than exists. The similarities already observed could well be explained by the author being associated with the Johannine school in Ephesus.

Some reputable scholars (e.g., C. K. Barrett, Raymond Brown, George Beasley-Murray) think that the content of the Apocalypse fits the profile of the Apostle better than the content of the Fourth Gospel and thus it is more likely that the Apostle was the author of the former than of the latter. But if the John who authored the Apocalypse was the Apostle, why would he be so shy about giving his name in the Gospel or Epistles when in the Apocalypse he offers it so freely? And why, when he gives it, does he not identify himself as the Apostle, or as the Beloved Disciple, or as the brother of James?

With Dionysius and others after him, in the end all we are able to say is that the book very probably was authored by someone named "John," who possibly was the Elder, but improbably the Apostle. This John appears to have been an Aramaic-speaking Palestinian Jew who may have been a refugee to Asia Minor, and who belonged to a group of Christian prophets, possibly associated with the Johannine school.[16]

---

the discussion of OT influence on the grammar of Revelation in Beale, *John's Use of the Old Testament in Revelation*, 318–55.

13. R. H. Charles concluded, "Frequently it is not the Greek but the Hebrew in the mind of the writer that has to be translated" (*A Critical and Exegetical Commentary on the Revelation of St. John*, 1:clxxxvii).

14. Ibid., 1:cxvii–clix. David Aune, in an equally monumental commentary, remarks, "The Greek of Revelation is the most peculiar Greek in the NT" (*Revelation*, 1:clxii), and he follows suit with his own syntax of the Apocalypse (ibid., 1:clx–ccvii).

15. Charles, *A Critical and Exegetical Commentary on the Revelation of St. John*, 1:x–xi. How Charles knows that the author was of an advanced age is unclear.

16. See further discussion in chapters 14 and 39 above. The association of the Apocalypse with the Johannine school has recently been challenged by Elisabeth Schüssler Fiorenza, *The Book of Revelation*, 85–113. In my opinion, her reasons for doing so are insufficient.

The Structure of Revelation

A number of the specific structural elements of Revelation are clear, but the relation of the separate elements is not clear and continues to challenge interpreters. Many find two major divisions of the book after the letters to the seven churches, the first beginning with 4:1 (the open door in heaven) and the second with 12:1 (the open temple in heaven [11:19]). The statement in 1:19 often is taken as programmatic: "Now write what you see, what is and what is to take place hereafter." This points to the book's concern with both present and future, and many take the reference to the future as beginning already from the start of chapter 4. However, it is not always easy to differentiate future eschatology from what might be taken as presently realized eschatology. What was future for John is not necessarily future for us, and what John describes as being future may already have been something that occurred in the past (prophecy *ex eventu*).

The opening chapter, setting the tone for the whole book, contains the vision of "one like a son of man" (a deliberate allusion to Dan. 7) in which John is commissioned to write the revelation (1:9–20). This is followed by the letters to the seven churches (chaps. 2–3). Then in turn, following the vision of the heavenly throne room (chaps. 4–5), is the heart of the book: the three cycles of judgment—the seven seals (6:1–8:1), seven trumpets (8:2–11:19), and seven bowls "full of the wrath of God" (chaps. 15–16). Between the trumpets and the pouring out of the bowls/plagues, however, several intervening accounts occur (chaps. 12–14):

1. war in heaven, wherein Michael defeats the dragon (Satan, who opposes the woman and her child, Jesus), while the dragon is cast down to the earth;
2. the rise of the blasphemous beast from the sea, who makes war on the saints, which account is described as "a call for the endurance and faith of the saints" (13:10 [cf. 14:12]);
3. the rise of a second beast, this one from the earth, with great power, who forces the worship of the first beast, and whose number is 666, probably pointing to the persecuting emperor Nero;
4. the Lamb and the 144,000 saints (again symbolic: 12 x 12,000, pointing to the church as eschatological Israel);
5. warning angels, some of whom have sickles in hand, pointing to the imminence of the harvest (judgment).

After the pouring out of the bowls comes a lengthy section (chaps. 17–18) on the judgment of "Babylon" (code for Rome and the Roman Empire), followed by a liturgical section of worship with a threefold "Hallelujah" (19:1–10). The climax of the book appears to be reached beginning in 19:11–16 with the return of Christ and a further account of judgment in which the beast and the false prophet (the second beast) are cast into the lake of fire (19:17–21). There follows, however, the millennium (20:1–6), at the end of which, somewhat surprisingly, is the release of Satan and his gathering of Gog and Magog for yet one more battle. They are destroyed, and Satan is sent to be with the beast and the false prophet, a kind of evil trinity (20:7–10). At last, the final judgment occurs with the destruction of Death and Hades (20:11–15). Apart from the epilogue (22:6–21), the book essentially ends with the vision of the heavenly Jerusalem, with the reference to God's worshiping servants, who "shall reign for ever and ever" (21:1–22:5). Appropriately, this ending points to the fulfillment of God's promises, with much allusion to the OT and the final realization of the kingdom of God in all its perfection, with the redeemed saints reigning for eternity.

The Three Cycles of Judgment: Seals, Trumpets, Bowls

The foregoing survey, though brief, is sufficient to indicate the complexity of the book and to give an idea of the challenges facing the interpreter. Chief among these is to determine whether the book is to be understood as presenting a sustained, chronologically sequential account of last things. Although there are some who take this linear view, the more convincing view, in the opinion of many, is that the various sections are recapitulations—that is, chronological flashbacks: retellings of essentially the same sequence of judgments coming upon the earth during the interim period between the first and second comings of Christ, and especially prior to the end of the age. Thus, the seals, trumpets, and bowls need not necessarily be taken as successive or serial. Rather, the trumpets and bowls are a retelling and perhaps an extending further of the judgments revealed in the opening of the seals. Each sequence of seven can be understood as covering approximately the same period of time, bringing us to the day of the Lord, the judgment at the end of the age. Thus the words of the sixth seal seem to portray the final judgment itself (6:12–17).[17] The contents of the seventh seal are not specified; when the seal is opened, it is said only that there was an ominous "silence in heaven for about half an hour" (8:1). Perhaps it is meant that the trumpets and bowls are the content of the seventh seal. So too the seventh trumpet concludes with words that can easily be taken as bringing us to the end (11:15–19).[18] The section that interrupts the vision of the three sevens, chapters 12–14, also describes what sounds like the end. With

---

17. The reference to "the great tribulation" (7:14) may well indicate the Neronian persecution in the 60s.

18. The repeated references in Revelation to the period of tribulation lasting three and a half years—"forty-two months" (11:2 [cf. "one thousand two hundred and sixty days" in 11:3]); "a time, and times, and half a time" (12:14)—reflect Daniel 7:25 and allude to the persecution of

the pouring out of the seventh bowl, a voice from the heavenly throne says, "It is done!" (16:17), which likewise seems to convey a note of finality. Then again, the section that includes the return of Christ and the establishment of the millennium (19:11–20:6) sounds like it could be the end.

The recapitulation in these sections means that the book actually could end with practically any one of them, for they all point to the final judgment of evil and the victory of the redeemed. What this unusual structure of the book does, however, is heighten the dramatic effect. The narrative of the Apocalypse builds to a great climax as it uses the various images of John's visions for the portrayal of the grand conclusion of salvation history.

Unity of the Book

The unusual, asymmetrical structure of the book has raised the question of its unity. Especially the unexpected interruptions of the flow of the narrative can give the impression that they might be later interpolations. David Aune observes, "The most striking literary characteristic in Revelation is the presence of approximately twelve relatively independent textual units that have little to do with their immediate contexts or indeed with the macronarrative of Revelation."[19] In light of this, Aune thus prefers to speak of the "author-editor" of the Apocalypse. He speculates that there were two major editions of the Apocalypse (ca. 70 and in the 90s) that come into existence in three stages, beginning with the twelve discrete units just mentioned, and that were then redacted and embedded in the series of sevens (seals, trumpets, bowls). The second edition, formed in stage three, is marked by an escalated christology.[20] Clearly, a proposal such as this is highly conjectural, as Aune readily admits. It is, however, an interesting way to account for the structural peculiarities of the book. However, it is much simpler to assume that the author appropriated some preexisting textual units when he composed the book and used them as he deemed appropriate. Given the genre of apocalypse, the bewildering order of the text hardly needs to be explained as pointing to the disunity of the text.

The Millennium and Eschatological Expectation

The millennium, already discussed briefly in the preceding chapter, seems as it stands in Revelation to be an unnecessary oddity. The notion of a literal

---

Israel under Antiochus Epiphanes (168–165 BC), so that the formula becomes a prototype of eschatological persecution.

19. Aune, *Revelation*, 1:cxix. These units are 7:1–17; 10:1–11; 11:1–13; 12:1–18; 13:1–18; 14:1–20; 17:1–18; 18:1–24; 19:11–16; 20:1–10; 20:11–15; 21:9–22:5.

20. Ibid., 1:cxx–cxxxiv.

thousand-year period of earthly quasi-fulfillment, however, did not originate with John. Other apocalyptic writers also thought it necessary to have a kind of literal earthly fulfillment of the promises, with the Messiah reigning, prior to the end of the age and the coming of the new heavens and earth. The so-called Apocalypse of Weeks, contained in *1 Enoch*, divides all of history into ten weeks, each of which has seven parts (*1 En.* 93:1–10; 91:12–17). The earthly kingdom is established in the eighth week, with the ninth week bringing the judgment of the wicked, leading in the tenth week to the eternal age.[21] A similar interim earthly period lasting a thousand years is found in *Jubilees* 23:26–31. Underlying some conceptions is the idea that all of history is to be contained in a seven-thousand-year period, analogous to the six days of creation, with the last thousand years analogous to God's resting on the seventh day, and the eighth day beginning eternity. We find this view in *2 Enoch* 25–33 (cf. 65:6–8) and also in Barnabas, among the Apostolic Fathers: the six days of creation mean that "in six thousand years the Lord will complete all things, for a day with him is as a thousand years. . . . Hence in six thousand years shall all be completed"; God's resting on the seventh day means that when the Messiah comes, he will do his work of judgment and re-creation "and will truly rest on the seventh day"; then the eighth day "is the beginning of another cosmos" (*Barn.* 15:4–5, 8 [cf. Irenaeus, *Haer.* 5.28.3]).[22] Interim periods of messianic rule are found also in *Apocalypse of Baruch* 39–40 and in *4 Ezra* 7:26–30, where the period lasts four hundred years. In both books, as in Revelation, the dawn of the messianic age is connected with the fall of Rome.[23] The length of the expected interim messianic age can vary greatly. If we include views of the later rabbinic writings (see *b. Sanh.* 99a), the time can range from as short as 40 years to as long as 365,000 years.[24]

There are significant difficulties with taking John's depiction of the millennium literally, especially if we try to relate it chronologically to the immediately preceding material in chapter 19. At the end of that chapter all the enemies of

---

21. Because of the uncertainty and ambiguity of the texts of *Jubilees* and *2 Enoch*, Larry Kreitzer concludes, "The *Apocalypse of Weeks* is the *sole* unambiguous evidence for belief in a temporary, earthly Kingdom in Jewish pseudepigraphical literature of the second to first centuries BCE" (*Jesus and God in Paul's Eschatology*, 87). But Kreitzer notes that in the Apocalypse of Weeks the kingdom is not related to the coming of the Messiah.

22. On a view such as this, one can see how those who accept a creation date of about 4000 BC would have their expectations of the imminence of the end whipped up as the calendar turned to AD 2000.

23. Larry Kreitzer notes a shift in the first-century *4 Ezra* and *2 Baruch*, which "quite clearly maintain a distinction between the temporary, earthly Kingdom and the eternal Age to Come," but is now clearly associated with the Messiah (*Jesus and God in Paul's Eschatology*, 87). See also Bailey, "The Temporary Messianic Reign in the Literature of Early Judaism." It is interesting that after the fall of Rome and the subsequent non-return of Christ, the popularity of Revelation declined.

24. For a helpful survey of the subject, see Beale, *The Book of Revelation*, 1017–21.

God are destroyed, and in the millennium in chapter 20 it is the resurrected martyrs who reign with Christ. What nations are there to deceive (20:3, 8) and to start another battle against God (20:8–9)? It is not necessary, however, to take John's account of the millennium literally. The earthly promises to Israel can also be understood as pictorial anticipations of something greater. The prevalent symbolism of the Apocalypse should also encourage us to take the millennium as a symbolic representation. Two attractive options offer themselves here.

The first is what traditionally has been known as amillennialism, although, as G. K. Beale rightly suggests, the term "inaugurated millennialism" is more accurate. Here John's millennium refers essentially to the church age, beginning with the death and resurrection of Christ, and hence already exists. "Christ's death and resurrection have inaugurated both the binding of Satan and the era of the saints' reign with Christ. If the reign in 20:4–6 has been influenced by the general Jewish idea of an intermediate reign on earth, then the intermediate period is now the church age and the reign takes place in heaven, though 1:6 and 5:10 show that it also takes place on earth among those who are regenerate."[25] Here the millennium in a sense represents the whole story of fulfillment in a microcosm. It is a picture of what God is presently doing in and through the church. The redeemed already reign with Christ (cf. Col. 3:1; Eph. 2:6). A second option is that the millennium represents a proleptic picture of the coming new earth at the end of the present age.[26]

We get little help elsewhere in the NT concerning how the end of the age will come. When it comes to future eschatology, what interests the NT writers is the *that*, not the *how* or *when*. Although some would dispute this statement, there is no other clear reference in the NT to the millennium of Revelation 20 (1 Cor. 15:25–28 is a possible exception, although it can bear different interpretations). Eschatological passages in the NT, such as Matthew 24, 2 Thessalonians 2, and 2 Peter 3, share with Revelation the basic perspective, perhaps drawn initially from Daniel, concerning a time of escalating trouble prior to the coming of the Son of Man and the dawning of the new age. These are referred to as the birth pangs of the end time, the so-called messianic woes, the persecution of the saints—that is, the time of tribulation preceding the end, together with the appearance of the antichrist, who attempts to thwart the purpose and plan of God. There is no suggestion of an interim period such as the millennium in any of these passages. The Lord Jesus will destroy the antichrist "by his appearing and his coming" (2 Thess. 2:8). The old heaven and earth are also to be destroyed and replaced by "new heavens and a new earth in which righteousness dwells" (2 Pet. 3:10–13).

---

25. Ibid., 1021.
26. See Marshall, "The Christian Millennium."

Text

The Greek text of Revelation is poorly attested in comparison with other NT books. There are, for example, only three majuscule manuscripts that contain the whole of the book (Sinaiticus, Alexandrinus, and the tenth-century 046; C contains most of the book). The earliest papyrus fragment of Revelation is $\mathfrak{P}^{98}$, from the late second century, containing 1:13–20; the other four extant papyrus fragments are no earlier than the late third century. This sparsity of early textual evidence probably is the result of the debate in the early church about the canonical status of the book.[27] The book is lacking even in most later minuscule manuscripts,[28] and even when it is present, often there are signs that it was added later.[29] When Erasmus produced the first printed edition of the Greek NT in 1516, he had access to but one late, twelfth-century manuscript of the Apocalypse. Because it lacked the last six verses of the book, Erasmus translated them back into Greek from the Latin Vulgate translation of the NT. He had to do that also for other passages in the book that were not clear from the Greek manuscript that he had.[30]

A number of the textual variants in Revelation were created by copyists intent on improving the strange and sometimes questionable grammatical constructions in the book. David Aune notes that when John's Apocalypse is found in nonecclesiastical (i.e., nonbiblical) collections of writings, the number of harmonizing and theologically motivated variants is smaller.[31]

Date

The main clue to the date of the Apocalypse is the evidence of the persecution presently being experienced by the readers or imminently expected (2:3, 10, 13, 19; 3:2, 8). Much attention is given to the reality of martyrdom (6:9, 11) and the vindication of the martyrs (12:11; 20:4, 6). The source of the

27. However, there are at least thirty-five instances where copies of Revelation are included in codices containing nonbiblical documents. See Metzger and Ehrman, *The Text of the New Testament*, 51n80. See also chapter 42 below.

28. Robert Hull notes that "there are fifty-nine Greek manuscripts containing the entire New Testament, but there are 150 manuscripts that contain the whole New Testament *except for* Revelation" (*The Story of the New Testament Text*, 189n36).

29. Oddly enough, even though Revelation probably was written to be used liturgically, it apparently was not used this way in the early church, and thus it is lacking altogether in the lectionary manuscripts.

30. Metzger and Ehrman point out that these passages, like the final six verses, accordingly contain readings not found in a single Greek manuscript known to us, but that nonetheless are perpetuated in modern printings of the Greek Textus Receptus (*The Text of the New Testament*, 145 [italics in original]).

31. Aune, *Revelation*, 1:cxxxvi. For a full study of the text of Revelation, see Parker, *An Introduction to the New Testament Manuscripts and Their Texts*, 227–45. See also chapter 42 below.

persecution is Rome (17:4–6 [note the seven hills in 17:9–10]); repeated references to "Babylon" point to Rome (14:8; 16:19; 17:5; 18:2, 10, 21).[32] But under which emperor did the persecution take place? From what can be determined, the most likely possibilities are Nero (54–68) and Domitian (81–96),[33] most probably the latter. Although the number 666 (13:18) may well point to Nero,[34] the beast had received a mortal wound (13:12; cf. 17:8), meaning that probably Nero was dead. The reference to his being healed of the mortal wound could thus point to a later emperor, a kind of antitype to Nero. The antichrist was to be another Nero. Two key problems with identifying Nero as the emperor during whose time, or shortly thereafter, the book was written are that he did not promote the imperial cult of emperor worship and that he did not engage in persecution of Christians outside of Rome. Domitian, on the contrary, is known to have proclaimed himself as *dominus ac deus noster* ("our Lord and God"), and the imperial cult was especially strong in Asia Minor in the time of Domitian (though some doubt this). Christians who refused to participate in the worship of the emperor (= worship of the beast) were severely persecuted.

It was furthermore the opinion of Irenaeus, Clement of Alexandria, Origen, and Eusebius (*Hist. eccl.* 3.18–20; 5.8.6) that the Apocalypse was written during the reign of Domitian. The current consensus of NT scholarship is that Revelation was written toward the end of Domitian's reign, in the mid-90s of the first century. But the possibility of an earlier date cannot entirely be excluded.

The attempt to discern the sources and prehistory of the document that we presently possess is fraught with difficulty. David Aune, who, as we have seen, detects early units of tradition in Revelation, finds truth in both an early and a later date for the book and has proposed a three-stage process in its production:

1. the creation of textual units in the 60s or earlier,
2. the production of a first edition of the book at about 70, and
3. a revision and expansion of this into a second edition sometime in the 90s.[35]

This hypothesis enables Aune to account for all the data, whether pointing to an earlier or later date for the book. But this suggested prehistory of the book necessarily remains speculative.

32. Both Babylon and Rome had destroyed Jerusalem. A similar equation is made in *2 Baruch* and *4 Ezra*.

33. Suggestions have ranged, however, from very early, before 70, to very late, in the time of Trajan (98–117).

34. It is impossible to identify with any certainty the "kings" mentioned in 17:10.

35. Aune, *Revelation*, 1:lviii.

Admission into the Canon

The Apocalypse had its difficulties in gaining admission into the canon. From the start, the unusual content of the book together with its passage concerning the millennium raised the question of whether it belonged at all in the collection of the writings of the new covenant. Although many accepted it as apostolic as early as the late second century, it did not find a secure place in the Western canon until the late fourth century, while in the Eastern church it was not generally accepted until the fourteenth century—a thousand years later!

Revelation was rejected by Marcion and by the Alogoi (Epiphanius, *Pan.* 51.3). The late second-century Muratorian Canon lists two apocalypses, one of John and the other of Peter, noting, however, that "some of us are not willing that the latter be read in church." Early in the third century Gaius, perhaps because of his distaste for its millennialism, rejected Revelation as part of the Johannine corpus, denying its apostolic authorship. So too, as we noted above, Dionysius of Alexandria rejected apostolic authorship because of the book's thought and style, arguing that therefore it was by another John.

Eusebius exhibits his own ambivalence in his tabulation of NT books. Thus he first lists Revelation among the recognized books: "After these must be put, if it really seems right, the Apocalypse of John, concerning which we shall give the different opinions at the proper time" (*Hist. eccl.* 3.25.2, trans. Lake). In the next paragraph, however, he lists Revelation among the spurious books (along with the NT apocryphal books *Acts of Paul* and *Apocalypse of Peter*, and the Apostolic Fathers *Shepherd of Hermas*, *Barnabas*, and the *Didache*): "And, in addition, as I said, the Apocalypse of John, if it seems right. This last, as I said, is rejected by some, but others count it among the recognized books" (*Hist. eccl.* 3.25.3–4, trans. Lake).

In the Eastern church uncertainty continued about the canonicity of Revelation. It is not found in the Syriac (known as the Peshitta) translation of the NT. In the West there was far less uncertainty about the Apocalypse; Athanasius accepted it and so too the Synod of Carthage in 397. But in the Reformation period there was again hesitation about Revelation. Erasmus expressed doubt about its authorship. Zwingli was said not to have liked it, and it is the only book of the NT for which Calvin did not write a commentary. Although like the other Reformers, Luther was willing to use the book against the papacy, he was notoriously critical of Revelation. He regarded it as "neither apostolic or prophetic" and objected to its extensive visions and figures in place of "clear, plain words" such as used by Peter, Paul, and Christ. Above all, he says, "There is one sufficient reason for me not to think highly of it—Christ is not taught or known in it." Of course, by this he means that his beloved doctrine of justification by faith is not taught in the book. But certainly he is wrong to conclude that Christ "is not taught or known in it." On the contrary, Revelation is continuously about Christ. Indeed, Christ is fundamental in the Apocalypse, and if one were to remove Christ from the book, it would fall apart.

The Apocalypse has a key role to fulfill in the NT. As we have seen, it beautifully rounds out the whole story of salvation. It builds on the reality of the saving work of Christ, not only lifting the veil—as a worthy apocalypse should—for us to see the presently realized dimensions of eschatological reality in the midst of this world's evil but also providing glimpses of the future reality guaranteed to the children of God, with the final removal of evil and the effects of human rebellion against God, concluding with the experience of a perfection that can be expressed only by means of remarkable images and metaphors. The NT needs the Apocalypse as the capstone of its narrative, just as the Apocalypse needs the NT to be intelligible and to make its message clear.

Bibliography

See also the bibliography for chapter 40, "The Message of the Apocalypse."

Books and Articles

Adams, Edward. *The Stars Will Fall from Heaven: Cosmic Catastrophe in the New Testament and Its World*. LNTS 347. London: T&T Clark, 2007.

Aune, David E. "The Apocalypse of John and Palestinian Jewish Apocalyptic." *Neot* 40 (2006): 1–33.

———. "The Apocalypse of John and the Problem of Genre." *Semeia* 36 (1986): 65–96.

———. "The Form and Function of the Proclamations to the Seven Churches (Revelation 2–3)." *NTS* 36 (1990): 182–204.

———. "The Prophetic Circle of John of Patmos and the Exegesis of Revelation 22:16." *JSNT* 37 (1989): 103–16.

———. "The Social Matrix of the Apocalypse of John." *BR* 26 (1981): 16–32.

Bailey, John W. "The Temporary Messianic Reign in the Literature of Early Judaism." *JBL* 53 (1934): 170–87.

Bandstra, Andrew J. "A Kingship and Priests: Inaugurated Eschatology in the Apocalypse." *CTJ* 27 (1992): 10–25.

Barker, Margaret. *The Revelation of Jesus Christ: Which God Gave Him to Show His Servants What Must Soon Take Place (Revelation 1:1)*. Edinburgh: T&T Clark, 2000.

Barr, David L. "The Apocalypse as a Symbolic Transformation of the World: A Literary Analysis." *Int* 38 (1984): 39–50.

———, ed. *Reading the Book of Revelation: A Resource for Students*. RBS 44. Atlanta: Society of Biblical Literature, 2003.

Bauckham, Richard. *The Climax of Prophecy: Studies on the Book of Revelation*. Edinburgh: T&T Clark, 1993.

———. *The Theology of the Book of Revelation*. NTT. Cambridge: Cambridge University Press, 1993.

Beagley, Alan James. *The "Sitz im Leben" of the Apocalypse, with Particular Reference to the Role of the Church's Enemies*. BZNW 50. Berlin: de Gruyter, 1987.

Beale, G. K. *John's Use of the Old Testament in Revelation*. JSNTSup 166. Sheffield: Sheffield Academic Press, 1998.

————. *The Use of Daniel in Jewish Apocalyptic Literature and in the Revelation of St. John.* Lanham, MD: University Press of America, 1984.

Beasley-Murray, George R. "The Relation of the Fourth Gospel to the Apocalypse." *EvQ* 18 (1946): 173–86.

Bell, Albert A., Jr. "The Date of John's Apocalypse: The Evidence of Some Roman Historians Reconsidered." *NTS* 25 (1978–79): 93–102.

Blevins, James L. *Revelation.* KPG. Atlanta: John Knox, 1984.

Blount, Brian K. *Can I Get a Witness? Reading Revelation through African American Culture.* Louisville: Westminster John Knox, 2005.

Boesak, Allan A. *Comfort and Protest: Reflections on the Apocalypse of John of Patmos.* Philadelphia: Westminster, 1987.

Boring, M. Eugene. "The Voice of Jesus in the Apocalypse of John." *NovT* 34 (1992): 334–59.

Boxall, Ian. *Revelation; Vision and Insight; An Introduction to the Apocalypse.* London: SPCK, 2002.

Bruce, F. F. "The Spirit in the Apocalypse." In *Christ and Spirit in the New Testament: Studies in Honour of Charles Francis Digby Moule,* edited by Barnabas Lindars and Stephen S. Smalley, 333–44. Cambridge: Cambridge University Press, 1973.

Carrell, Peter R. *Jesus and the Angels: Angelology and Christology in the Apocalypse of John.* SNTSMS 95. Cambridge: Cambridge University Press, 1997.

Collins, Adela Yarbro. *The Combat Myth in the Book of Revelation.* HDR 9. Missoula, MT: Scholars Press, 1976.

Collins, John J. *The Apocalyptic Imagination: An Introduction to Jewish Apocalyptic Literature.* 2nd ed. Grand Rapids: Eerdmans, 1998.

————. "Pseudonymity, Historical Reviews, and the Genre of the Revelation of John." *CBQ* 39 (1977): 329–43.

Cook, Stephen L. *Prophecy and Apocalypticism: The Postexilic Social Setting.* Minneapolis: Fortress, 1995.

Court, John M. *Myth and History in the Book of Revelation.* Atlanta: John Knox, 1979.

————. *Revelation.* NTG. Sheffield: JSOT Press, 1994.

Duff, Paul B. *Who Rides the Beast? Prophetic Rivalry and the Rhetoric of Crisis in the Churches of the Apocalypse.* New York: Oxford University Press, 2001.

Dumbrell, William J. *The End of the Beginning: Revelation 21–22 and the Old Testament.* Exeter: Paternoster, 1985.

Ellul, Jacques. *Apocalypse: The Book of Revelation.* Translated by George W. Schreiner. New York: Seabury, 1977.

Ewing, Ward. *The Power of the Lamb: Revelation's Theology of Liberation for You.* Cambridge, MA: Cowley Publications, 1994.

Faley, Roland J. *Apocalypse Then and Now: A Companion to the Book of Revelation.* Mahwah, NJ: Paulist Press, 1999.

Farrer, Austin. *A Rebirth of Images: The Making of St. John's Apocalypse.* Westminster, UK: Dacre, 1949.

Fekkes, Jan, III. *Isaiah and Prophetic Traditions in the Book of Revelation: Visionary Antecedents and Their Development.* JSNTSup 93. Sheffield: JSOT Press, 1994.

Fiorenza, Elisabeth Schüssler. *The Book of Revelation: Justice and Judgment.* 2nd ed. Minneapolis: Fortress, 1998.

Friesen, Steven J. *Imperial Cults and the Apocalypse of John: Reading Revelation in the Ruins.* New York: Oxford University Press, 2001.

Frilingos, Christopher A. *Spectacles of Empire: Monsters, Martyrs, and the Book of Revelation.* Philadelphia: University of Pennsylvania Press, 2004.

Giblin, Charles H. "Structure and Thematic Correlations in the Theology of Revelation 16–22." *Bib* 55 (1974): 487–504.

Gunther, John J. "The Elder John, Author of Revelation." *JSNT* 11 (1981): 3–20.

Hanson, A. T. *The Wrath of the Lamb*. London: SPCK, 1957.

Hellholm, David, ed. *Apocalypticism in the Mediterranean World and the Near East: Proceedings of the International Colloquium on Apocalypticism, Uppsala, August 12–17, 1979*. Tübingen: Mohr Siebeck, 1983.

Hemer, Colin J. *The Letters to the Seven Churches of Asia in Their Local Setting*. JSNTSup 11. Sheffield: JSOT Press, 1986.

Herms, Ronald. *An Apocalypse for the Church and for the World: The Narrative Function of Universal Language in the Book of Revelation*. BZNW 143. Berlin: de Gruyter, 2006.

Hill, David. "Prophecy and Prophets in the Revelation of St. John." *NTS* 18 (1971–1972): 401–18.

Hoffmann, Matthias Reinhard. *The Destroyer and the Lamb: The Relationship between Angelomorphic and Lamb Christology in the Book of Revelation*. WUNT 203. Tübingen: Mohr Siebeck, 2005.

Howard-Brook, Wes, and Anthony Gwyther. *Unveiling Empire: Reading Revelation Then and Now*. Maryknoll, NY: Orbis, 1999.

Hull, Robert F., Jr. *The Story of the New Testament Text: Movers, Materials, Motives, Methods, and Models*. SBLRBS 58. Atlanta: Society of Biblical Literature, 2010.

Jauhiainen, Marko. *The Use of Zechariah in Revelation*. WUNT 2/199. Tübingen: Mohr Siebeck, 2005.

Johns, Loren L. *The Lamb Christology of the Apocalypse of John: An Investigation into Its Origins and Rhetorical Force*. WUNT 167. Tübingen: Mohr Siebeck, 1998.

King, Karen L. *The Secret Revelation of John*. Cambridge, MA: Harvard University Press, 2006.

Kirby, John T. "The Rhetorical Situations of Revelation 1–3." *NTS* 34 (1988): 197–207.

Koester, Craig R. *Revelation and the End of All Things*. Grand Rapids: Eerdmans, 2001.

Kraybill, J. Nelson. *Imperial Cult and Commerce in John's Apocalypse*. JSNTSup 132. Sheffield: Sheffield Academic Press, 1996.

Kreitzer, Larry J. *Jesus and God in Paul's Eschatology*. JSNTSup 19. Sheffield: JSOT Press, 1987.

Kümmel, Werner Georg. *Introduction to the New Testament*. Translated by A. J. Mattill Jr. 14th ed. Nashville: Abingdon, 1966.

Lambrecht, Jan. "A Structuration of Revelation 4:1–22:5." In *L'Apocalypse johannique et l'apocalyptique dans le Nouveau Testament*, 77–104. BETL 53. Gembloux: Duculot; Leuven: Leuven University Press, 1980.

Laws, Sophie. *In the Light of the Lamb: Imagery, Parody, and Theology in the Apocalypse of John*. GNS 31. Wilmington, DE: Michael Glazier, 1988.

Lee, Dal. *The Narrative Asides in the Book of Revelation*. Lanham, MD: University Press of America, 2002.

Maier, Harry O. *Apocalypse Recalled: The Book of Revelation after Christendom*. Minneapolis: Fortress, 2000.

Malina, Bruce J. *On the Genre and Message of Revelation: Star Visions and Sky Journeys*. Peabody, MA: Hendrickson, 1995.

Marshall, I. Howard. "The Christian Millennium" *EvQ* 72 (2000): 217–35.

Marshall, John W. *Parables of War: Reading John's Jewish Apocalypse*. Waterloo, ON: Wilfrid Laurier University Press, 2001.

McKelvey, R. J. *The Millennium and the Book of Revelation*. Cambridge: Lutterworth, 1999.

Metzger, Bruce M., and Bart D. Ehrman. *The Text of the New Testament: Its Transmission, Corruption, and Restoration*. 4th ed. New York: Oxford University Press, 2005.

Minear, Paul S. *I Saw a New Earth: An Introduction to the Visions of the Apocalypse*. Washington, DC: Corpus, 1968.

Mojtabai, A. G. *Blessed Assurance: At Home with a Bomb in Amarillo, Texas*. Boston: Houghton Mifflin, 1987.

Moyise, Steve. *The Old Testament in the Book of Revelation.* JSNTSup 115. Sheffield: Sheffield Academic Press, 1995.

Mussies, Gerard. *The Morphology of Koine Greek, as Used in the Apocalypse of St. John: A Study in Bilingualism.* NovTSup 27. Leiden: Brill, 1971.

Nwachukwu, Oliver O. *Beyond Vengeance and Protest: A Reflection on the Macarisms in Revelation.* SBL 71. New York: Peter Lang, 2005.

O'Leary, Stephen D. *Arguing the Apocalypse: A Theory of Millennial Rhetoric.* New York: Oxford University Press, 1994.

Parker, D. C. *An Introduction to the New Testament Manuscripts and Their Texts.* Cambridge: Cambridge University Press, 2008.

Pattemore, Stephen. *The People of God in the Apocalypse: Discourse, Structure, and Exegesis.* SNTSMS 128. New York: Cambridge University Press, 2005.

Paulien, Jon. "Recent Developments in the Study of the Book of Revelation." *AUSS* 26 (1988): 159–70.

Peerbolte, L. J. Lietaert. *The Antecedents of Antichrist: A Traditio-Historical Study of the Earliest Christian View on Eschatological Opponents.* JSJSup 49. Leiden: Brill, 1996.

Pilch, John J. *What Are They Saying about the Book of Revelation?* Mahwah, NJ: Paulist Press, 1978.

Pippin, Tina. *Apocalyptic Bodies: The Biblical End of the World in Text and Image.* London: Routledge, 1999.

———. *Death and Desire: The Rhetoric of Gender in the Apocalypse of John.* LCBI. Louisville: Westminster John Knox, 1992.

Porter, Stanley E. "The Language of the Apocalypse in Recent Discussion." *NTS* 35 (1989): 582–603.

Ramsay, W. M. *The Letters to the Seven Churches of Asia and Their Place in the Plan of the Apocalypse.* New York: Armstrong, 1909.

Rissi, Mathias. *The Future of the World: An Exegetical Study of Revelation 19:11–22:15.* SBT 2/23. Naperville, IL: Allenson, 972.

———. "The Kerygma of the Revelation to John." *Int* 22 (1968): 3–17.

———. *Time and History: A Study of the Revelation.* Richmond: John Knox, 1966.

Rossing, Barbara R. *The Choice between Two Cities: Whore, Bride, and Empire in the Apocalypse.* HTS 48. Harrisburg, PA: Trinity Press International, 1999.

Royalty, Robert M., Jr. *The Streets of Heaven: The Ideology of Wealth in the Apocalypse of John.* Macon, GA: Mercer University Press, 1998.

Shepherd, Massey Hamilton. *The Paschal Liturgy and the Apocalypse.* ESW 6. Richmond: John Knox, 1960.

Siew, Antoninus King Wai. *The War between the Two Beasts and the Two Witnesses: A Chiastic Reading of Revelation 11:1–14:5.* LNTS 283. New York: T&T Clark, 2005.

Smalley, Stephen S. *Thunder and Love: John's Revelation and John's Community.* Dallas: Word, 1993.

Smith, Christopher R. "The Structure of the Book of Revelation in Light of Apocalyptic Literary Conventions." *NovT* 36 (1994): 373–93.

Stonehouse, N. B. *The Apocalypse in the Ancient Church: A Study in the History of the New Testament Canon.* Goes: Oosterbann & Le Cointre, 1929.

Stuckenbruck, Loren T. *Angel Veneration and Christology: A Study in Early Judaism and in the Christology of the Apocalypse of John.* WUNT 2/70. Tübingen: Mohr Siebeck, 1995.

Thompson, Damian. *The End of Time: Faith and Fear in the Shadow of the Millennium.* London: Minerva, 1997.

Thompson, Leonard L. *The Book of Revelation: Apocalypse and Empire.* Oxford: Oxford University Press, 1990.

Thompson, Stephen. *The Apocalypse and Semitic Syntax.* SNTSMS 52. Cambridge: Cambridge University Press, 1985.

Tonstad, Sigve K. *Saving God's Reputation: The Theological Function of* Pistis Iesou *in the Cosmic Narratives of Revelation.* LNTS 337. London: T&T Clark, 2006.

Ulfgard, Håkan. *Feast and Future: Revelation 7:9–17 and the Feast of Tabernacles.* ConBNT 22. Stockholm: Almqvist & Wiksell, 1989.

Wenig, Laurin J. *The Challenge of the Apocalypse: Embracing the Book of Revelation with Hope and Faith.* Mahwah, NJ: Paulist Press, 2002.

Wilson, J. Christian. "The Problem of the Domitianic Date of Revelation." *NTS* 39 (1995): 587–605.

Wilson, Mark. *Charts on the Book of Revelation: Literary, Historical, and Theological Perspectives.* Grand Rapids: Kregel, 2007.

Worth, Roland H., Jr. *The Seven Cities of the Apocalypse and Greco-Asian Culture.* Mahwah, NJ: Paulist Press, 1999.

———. *The Seven Cities of the Apocalypse and Roman Culture.* Mahwah, NJ: Paulist Press, 1999.

Commentaries

Aune, David E. *Revelation.* 3 vols. WBC 52. Nashville: Thomas Nelson, 1997–98.

Beale, G. K. *The Book of Revelation: A Commentary on the Greek Text.* NIGTC. Grand Rapids: Eerdmans, 1999.

Beasley-Murray, George R. *The Book of Revelation.* NCB. Rev. ed. Greenwood, SC: Attic Press, 1978.

Blount, Brian K. *Revelation.* NTL. Louisville: John Knox, 1989.

Boring, M. Eugene. *Revelation.* IBC. Louisville: John Knox, 1989.

Boxall, Ian. *The Revelation of St. John.* BNTC. Peabody, MA: Hendrickson, 2006.

Brighton, Louis A. *Revelation.* ConC. St. Louis: Concordia, 2000.

Caird, G. B. *A Commentary on the Revelation of St. John the Divine.* 2nd ed. BNTC. London: Black, 1984.

Charles, R. H. *A Critical and Exegetical Commentary on the Revelation of St. John: With Introduction, Notes, and Indices; Also the Greek Text and Translation.* ICC. 2 vols. Edinburgh: T&T Clark, 1920.

Collins, Adela Yarbro. *The Apocalypse.* NTM. Wilmington, DE: Michael Glazier, 1979.

Farmer, Ronald L. *Revelation.* CCT. St. Louis: Chalice, 2005.

Farrer, Austin. *The Revelation of St. John the Divine.* Oxford: Oxford University Press, 1964.

Fee, Gordon D. *Revelation.* NCC. Eugene, OR: Cascade, 2010.

Fiorenza, Elisabeth Schüssler. *Invitation to the Book of Revelation: A Commentary on the Apocalypse with Complete Text from the Jerusalem Bible.* Garden City, NY: Image Books, 1981.

———. *Revelation: Vision of a Just World.* PC. Minneapolis: Fortress, 1991.

Ford, J. Massyngberde. *Revelation: Introduction, Translation, and Commentary.* AB 38. Garden City, NY: Doubleday, 1975.

Garrow, A. J. P. *Revelation.* NTR. London: Routledge, 1997.

Giblin, Charles H. *The Book of Revelation: The Open Book of Prophecy.* GNS 34. Collegeville, MN: Liturgical Press, 1991.

Glasson, T. F. *The Revelation of John.* CBC. Cambridge: Cambridge University Press, 1965.

Harrington, Wilfrid J. *Revelation.* SP 16. Collegeville, MN: Liturgical Press, 1993.

Hort, F. J. A. *The Apocalypse of St. John I–III: The Greek Text with Introduction, Commentary, and Additional Notes.* London: Macmillan, 1908.

Hughes, Philip E. *The Book of the Revelation: A Commentary.* Leicester, UK: Inter-Varsity; Grand Rapids: Eerdmans, 1990.

Johnson, Alan F. "Revelation." In *The Expositor's Bible Commentary*, edited by Tremper Longman III and David E. Garland, 13:571–789. Rev. ed. Grand Rapids: Zondervan, 2005.

Johnson, Dennis E. *Triumph of the Lamb: A Commentary on Revelation*. Phillipsburg, NJ: Presbyterian & Reformed, 2001.

Keener, Craig S. *Revelation*. NIVAC. Grand Rapids: Zondervan, 2000.

Kistemaker, Simon J. *Exposition of the Book of Revelation*. NTComm. Grand Rapids: Baker Academic, 2001.

Kovacs, Judith, and Christopher Rowland, with Rebekah Callow. *Revelation: The Apocalypse of Jesus Christ*. BBC. Oxford: Blackwell, 2004.

Krodel, Gerhard A. *Revelation*. ACNT. Minneapolis: Augsburg, 1989.

Ladd, George Eldon. *A Commentary on the Revelation of John*. Grand Rapids: Eerdmans, 1972.

Lupieri, Edmondo F. *A Commentary on the Apocalypse of John*. Translated by Maria Poggi Johnson and Adam Kamesar. Grand Rapids: Eerdmans, 2006.

Malina, Bruce J., and John J. Pilch. *Social-Science Commentary on the Book of Revelation*. Minneapolis: Fortress, 2000.

Michaels, J. Ramsey. *Revelation*. IVPNTC. Downers Grove, IL: InterVarsity, 1997

Morris, Leon. *The Book of Revelation: An Introduction and Commentary*. TNTC. Grand Rapids: Eerdmans, 1987.

Mounce, Robert H. *The Book of Revelation*. Rev. ed. NICNT. Grand Rapids: Eerdmans, 1997.

Murphy, Frederick J. *Fallen Is Babylon: The Revelation to John*. NTC. Harrisburg, PA: Trinity Press International, 1998.

Osborne, Grant R. *Revelation*. BECNT. Grand Rapids: Baker Academic, 2002.

Reddish, Mitchell G. *Revelation*. SHBC. Macon, GA: Smyth & Helwys, 2001.

Resseguie, James L. *The Revelation of John: A Narrative Commentary*. Grand Rapids: Baker Academic, 2009.

Roloff, Jürgen. *The Revelation of John*. Translated by John E. Alsup. CC. Minneapolis: Fortress, 1993.

Rowland, Christopher C. "The Book of Revelation." *NIB* 12:501–743.

Smalley, Stephen S. *The Revelation to John: A Commentary on the Greek Text of the Apocalypse*. Downers Grove, IL: InterVarsity, 2005.

Sweet, J. P. M. *Revelation*. WestPC. Philadelphia: Westminster; London: SCM, 1979.

Swete, H. B. *The Apocalypse of St. John: The Greek Text with Introduction, Notes and Indices*. 3rd ed. London: Macmillan, 1917.

Talbert, Charles H. *The Apocalypse: A Reading of the Revelation of John*. Louisville: Westminster John Knox, 1994.

Thompson, Leonard L. *Revelation*. ANTC. Nashville: Abingdon, 1998.

Trafton, Joseph L. *Reading Revelation: A Literary and Theological Commentary*. RNT. Macon, GA: Smyth & Helwys, 2005.

Witherington, Ben, III. *Revelation*. NCamBC. Cambridge: Cambridge University Press, 2003.

THE TEXT AND CANON OF THE NEW TESTAMENT

42

The Transmission of the Text

Today we are so used to copy machines, electronic copying, and the mass production of printed books that it is difficult to put ourselves back into the era before the late fifteenth century, when texts had to be copied by hand. Anyone who has copied something out in longhand, or even copied something by typing it into a word processor, knows that errors easily creep into the copy. The eye skips over something or sees something not there, the imagination creates something new, unconscious correction takes place—it is hard, for example, to copy a spelling or grammatical error. Exact copying by hand is very difficult. Add to this a poorly written or unclear original manuscript, bad lighting, cold chambers, uncomfortable conditions, and fatigue, and one may expect mistakes as a common occurrence in the copying of manuscripts.

Given that the NT was copied by hand for more than fourteen centuries, one might expect the manuscripts that came down to the modern era to be full of errors and the text of our NT to be extremely unreliable. However, we have far better evidence for the text of the NT than for any other ancient writing, and, as we will see, we have every reason to believe in the basic reliability of the text that we now have.

We do not possess any original manuscripts—autographs—of the NT writings. What we do have is a large number of copies of copies, usually themselves copies of copies. It is the task of textual criticism to evaluate the textual witnesses available to us and thus to reconstruct the original text as far as is possible.

The Resources for Textual Criticism

Textual criticism of the NT works with three types of evidence:

1. direct evidence of the Greek manuscripts themselves, including Greek lectionaries
2. indirect evidence of the ancient versions (i.e., translations) of the Greek NT
3. patristic quotations of the Greek NT

Greek Manuscripts

We currently possess nearly six thousand Greek manuscripts, and the number continues to grow as more are discovered. These divide into three basic categories, from earliest to later texts: papyri, majuscule manuscripts, and minuscule manuscripts.[1] Most of these are partial manuscripts, and some consist of only fragments. An extra group of Greek witnesses to the text, but considered separately because of their indirect character, are the Greek lectionaries, which are worship books containing Scripture passages for reading in church services.

The following list shows the breakdown in the number of manuscripts in these categories as of 2003:[2]

Papyri	116
Majuscule Manuscripts	310
Minuscule Manuscripts	2877
Lectionary Manuscripts	2432
Total	5735

The majority of these manuscripts are fragmentary. Of the above total, only about sixty manuscripts contain the entire NT, and of those, only one, Codex Sinaiticus, is a majuscule.[3]

---

1. These categories are a little confusing because they involve different criteria, and thus there is some overlapping. "Papyrus," of course, concerns the material used in writing, whereas "majuscule" and "minuscule" refer to the type of writing: capitals or lower case, which connected letters (cursive). Papyri can be written in either style of writing. All writing is in one of the two forms. Lectionaries bring yet another dimension in play: the location of a text within another text.

2. Thus Metzger and Ehrman, *The Text of the New Testament*, 50. These numbers have increased since then. For the current count, visit the website of the Münster Institute for New Testament Textual Research and access the Kurzgefaßte Liste. Their numbered manuscripts now total as follows: papyri, 127; majuscules, 322; minuscules, 2911; and lectionaries, 2453. It is important to note that, for a variety of reasons, this should not be understood to be the exact number of manuscripts, but only an approximation. Images of many of these manuscripts can be seen on the Münster website.

3. Ibid., 51.

Papyri

The earliest manuscripts were written on papyrus, a writing surface made of dried, flattened strips of the stem of the papyrus plant pasted horizontally over vertical strips. A single papyrus sheet was adequate for a relatively short letter, such as 2 John or 3 John. Sheets could be joined to form papyrus rolls (scrolls) up to some thirty feet in length, used for lengthier works such as the Gospels or the book of Acts. Perhaps already as early as the late first century the codex came into use, and soon it was favored over the roll. The codex, the forerunner of the modern book, consisted of sheets of folded papyrus sewn in the middle. The codex enabled a reader to move about in different sections of the text far more conveniently than did the scroll. It had the further advantage of making it possible to write on both sides of the papyrus. The codex also made it possible to combine related writings in a single physical manuscript, something not so easily done with rolls. Papyrus manuscripts survived only in the driest climates and therefore have been preserved only in places such as Egypt and the Judean desert.

Since they represent the earliest manuscripts that we have, the papyri are held in the highest esteem. Among the most important are the Beatty papyri codices: $\mathfrak{P}^{45}$ (early third century), containing parts of the Gospels and Acts; $\mathfrak{P}^{46}$ (ca. 200), containing nine letters of Paul and Hebrews; and $\mathfrak{P}^{47}$ (mid-to-late third century), containing approximately a third of Revelation. Also important are the Bodmer papyri, among which the following are noteworthy: $\mathfrak{P}^{66}$ (ca. 200), containing large portions of the Gospel of John; $\mathfrak{P}^{72}$ (third century), containing Jude and 1–2 Peter among other, noncanonical writings; $\mathfrak{P}^{75}$ (ca. 200), containing Luke and John, but only two-thirds of the leaves survive.

Majuscule Manuscripts

After the papyri, the most important manuscripts are the earliest written on vellum, a parchment made of animal skin and prepared as a writing surface. This far more durable material replaced papyri near the beginning of the fourth century, although papyrus stayed in use for several more centuries. Parchment continued as the preferred material until the introduction of paper in the mid-fourteenth century. Like the papyri, the early vellum manuscripts were written in a book hand—that is, majuscules,[4] carefully formed discrete letters of the same height, usually capitals, and without spaces between the words. But the papyri are never called "majuscules." The name is reserved for vellum manuscripts even though papyri are also written in majuscules. These early majuscule manuscripts written on durable vellum, and therefore surviving in relatively complete form, are among the major witnesses to the text of the NT. The three most important are as follows.

---

4. These are sometimes referred to as "uncials," but Metzger and Ehrman regard this as technically incorrect. See ibid., 17.

1. Sinaiticus (designated with the Hebrew letter **א**) is from the fourth century and is the only complete extant majuscule manuscript of the NT. It also contains the OT (LXX), not all of which has survived. The manuscript was discovered under unusual circumstances at the St. Catherine monastery at the foot of the traditional Mount Sinai, hence its name. Constantin von Tischendorf, a young scholar from Leipzig, visited the monastery in 1844 and discovered that the monks were using sheets of a manuscript to light the fires for their oven. These turned out to be pages from a larger OT manuscript. It was some fifteen years later before Tischendorf was able to see the remainder of the manuscript, containing the complete NT as well as *Epistle of Barnabas* (until then known only in a Latin translation) and most of *Shepherd of Hermas*, the first evidence of a document known only by title (two writings classified now as Apostolic Fathers), and was allowed to copy it by hand. Eventually at Tischendorf's suggestion the manuscript was sold for pragmatic reasons to the czar of Russia, Alexander II, then protector of the Orthodox Church, and published in Leipzig in a special four-folio edition (1862) on the occasion of the celebrations of the millennium of the Russian Empire.[5] The British Museum was able to buy the manuscript from the Soviets in 1933 for the equivalent of half a million dollars, half of which was paid by public subscriptions. As late as 1975, in a sealed chamber at St. Catherine's, a cache of manuscripts was discovered, among which were a further twelve missing leaves and some fragments from the Sinaiticus manuscript.[6]

2. Alexandrinus (designated with the letter A) dates from the fifth century and contains the whole of the OT and most of the NT, except for the majority of Matthew (which begins at 25:7),[7] John 6:50–8:52, and 2 Corinthians 4:13–12:6. It was presented to the English king Charles I by the patriarch of Constantinople in 1627, and today it remains with Sinaiticus in the British Library. A photographic edition was made in the late nineteenth century, and a reduced facsimile edition was produced by F. G. Kenyon in 1909.

3. Vaticanus (designated with the letter B) dates from the mid-fourth century and contained the OT, NT, and Apocrypha (except for the books of Maccabees). In its present form it lacks most of Genesis (up to chap. 46), and some thirty psalms are missing, as well as the following NT books: Hebrews from 9:14, the Pastoral Epistles, Philemon, and Revelation. This manuscript, located in the Vatican, was first published in photographic facsimile in 1889–90.

Only two further majuscule manuscripts need be mentioned here. Ephraemi Rescriptus (designated with the letter C) dates from the fifth century and is a palimpsest, a vellum biblical manuscript that was erased and written over,

---

5. The definitive facsimile edition of the NT was published by Oxford University Press in 1911 from photographs taken by Kirsopp Lake.

6. See Skeat, "The Last Chapter in the History of Codex Sinaiticus."

7. While much of the NT manuscript represents the highly respected Alexandrian text, the Gospels reflect the later Byzantine text.

in this case in the twelfth century with a text consisting of various writings and sermons of Ephraem, a well-known fourth-century Syrian saint. With the help of chemicals, Tischendorf was able to read the original text of this manuscript. A mere 64 leaves of the OT remain and 145 leaves of NT writings (five-eighths of what the original required).[8] In the leaves that remain every NT book is represented except 2 Thessalonians and 2 John. The text is not regarded highly, despite its early date.

Undoubtedly one of the most unusual and interesting witnesses to the text of the NT is the codex Bezae (designated with the letter D), sometimes known as Cantabrigiensis, because the French reformer Beza presented it to the Cambridge University library in 1581. It dates from the fifth century and contains almost all of the four Gospels (in the order Matthew, John, Luke, Mark) and Acts, together with a brief fragment of 3 John, all in both Greek and Latin.[9] A critical edition of the manuscript was published in 1864 by F. H. Scrivener, and then it was published in a facsimile edition by Cambridge University Press in 1899.[10]

Codex Bezae is remarkable for its inclusive readings; it contains a large variety of additions: words, phrases, and sentences that are lacking in other Greek manuscripts. Famous for its additions to the book of Acts, Bezae here is usually reckoned as nearly one-tenth longer than the text of other manuscripts. This form of the text is known as the Western Text (some readings of which are also found in a few other witnesses). Given the persistent tendency of Bezae to add material, the instances where it *omits* material are bound to attract attention. B. F. Westcott and F. J. A. Hort (see "The History of the New Testament Text" below) gave these readings the attractive name "Western non-interpolations"—that is, readings omitted by a text that wants to include everything available in the tradition.

Minuscule Manuscripts

Written in smaller letters, in cursive script (i.e., connected letters rather than separate capitals), minuscule manuscripts could be produced more quickly and economically. This style of writing became popular in the ninth century. A clever system of abbreviation of case endings that came into use also reduced the size of these manuscripts. As can be seen from the statistics provided above, the overwhelming majority of manuscripts of the Greek NT fall into this category, and they are relatively late. Of these numerous manuscripts, identified by Arabic numerals, the following are noteworthy.

8. Thus Metzger and Ehrman, *The Text of the New Testament*, 70.

9. A second manuscript assigned the letter D, with superscript "p" or subscript "2," is the sixth-century Claromontanus, which contains the Pauline Epistles and Hebrews in both Greek and Latin, and also exhibits the traits of the Western Text. This manuscript was published by Tischendorf in 1852.

10. For thorough treatments, see Read-Heimerdinger, *The Bezan Text of Acts*; Parker, *Codex Bezae*.

33 ("The Queen of the Cursives"). This ninth-century codex contains the entire NT except for Revelation (and a few short passages in Mark and Luke). It was given the designation "queen of the cursives" because of the superiority of its text, which usually agrees with the Alexandrian witnesses.

Family 1. As we will see in the section below on text types, manuscripts often display family resemblances; that is, they reveal similar patterns of variants that enable them to be grouped together. There are certain resemblances among the minuscule manuscripts that have caused scholars to group them into families. Family 1 consists of manuscripts 1, 118, 131, and 209, which derive from the twelfth to fourteenth centuries. The text of Mark in these manuscripts agrees with Codex Θ and reflects the text that was current in Caesarea in the third and fourth centuries.

Family 13. This family, also known as the Ferrar group, from the scholar who identified the family resemblances, consists of a dozen or so manuscripts (e.g., 13, 69, 124, 346) dating from the eleventh century to the fifteenth century. The manuscript that underlies this family seems to have come from Italy. Bruce Metzger and Bart Ehrman point out that these manuscripts contain the pericope of the woman caught in adultery (John 7:53–8:11 [but lacking in the early manuscripts]), placing it in Luke's Gospel after 21:38.[11]

LECTIONARIES

Greek passages of the NT found in lectionaries are, of course, witnesses to some form of the NT text, albeit in a secondary way. Although they are relatively late, mainly from the period of the minuscule manuscripts, because of the conservatism of liturgies, lectionaries often may reflect a much older form of the text than the actual date of the lectionary.

Lectionaries are organized in two different ways: by contents (Gospel and Apostolos [i.e., Acts, Catholic Epistles, and Paul]) or by calendar sequence. There are two forms of the latter, the *synaxarion*, which is the church year, beginning at Easter rather than Advent, and the *menologion*, which is the civil year of the Byzantine Empire, starting September 1. The latter form also contains many nonbiblical readings.[12]

Ancient Versions

As early as the second century the NT began to be translated into other languages. These early translations, of course, become witnesses to the Greek text used by the translators. The task of discerning the underlying text is often a challenge, however, not only because of the different ability of the translators, but also because of the freedom exercised by some of them. Some ancient translations themselves may depend on other translations of the Greek. Another

---

11. Metzger and Ehrman, *The Text of the New Testament,* 87.
12. On the lectionaries, see Osburn, "The Greek Lectionaries of the New Testament."

problem is that because of the proliferation of manuscripts, it is necessary to engage in text-critical restoration of the version's original manuscript itself. Beyond this, there are also limitations of the languages themselves, such as the lack of the definite article in Latin, the lack of the passive voice in Coptic, and the inability of Syriac to differentiate the aorist and perfect tenses of Greek.

The Old Latin (Itala)

The Bible probably was first translated into Latin in North Africa sometime in the last quarter of the second century, if not earlier. Apparently, several further translations were made into Latin, thus accounting for the great divergence that exists between the manuscripts. Oddly, no single codex containing the entire Old Latin Bible exists today. The earliest manuscripts of the Gospels, of Acts, and of the Pauline Epistles date from the fourth century, but some are as late as the thirteenth century.

The Vulgate

Because of the greatly differing Latin translations, in 382 Pope Damasus asked Jerome to revise the Old Latin translation, bringing it into closer accord with the Greek text. Jerome stayed as close as he could to the Latin translation with which he started; his Greek manuscripts seem to have been Alexandrian in type. He soon presented the Gospels to the pope, but it is apparently less than clear whether he himself revised the remainder of the NT, producing the Vulgate version accepted still today as the official translation of the Roman Catholic Church.[13]

The Old Syriac

With a text from the end of the second century or beginning of the third, two partial manuscripts from the fourth (Sinaitic, a palimpsest, discovered at St. Catherine's monastery) and fifth centuries (Curetonian) represent the Old Syriac. Influence from Tatian's *Diatessaron* (see above, p. 149) on the Gospel texts in these manuscripts is possible.

Other Syrian versions to be noted are the Peshitta (Syrian Vulgate) from the beginning of the fifth century, which became the official translation of the Syrian church. The books of 2 Peter, 2–3 John, Jude, and Revelation were not in this translation. These books finally appeared in Syriac translation in the Philoxenian and Harclean versions (sixth and seventh centuries), but some argue that these two were really a single version with variant readings. Finally, there is a Palestinian Syriac (i.e., Aramaic) version dating perhaps from the fifth century, known primarily from an eleventh- or twelfth-century Gospel lectionary and which is independent from the other Syriac versions.

---

13. Jerome's revision soon became corrupted by "correctors," and thus this situation virtually returned to that existing in the pre-Jerome era. Bruce Metzger and Bart Ehrman conclude that "the more than 8,000 Vulgate manuscripts that are extant today exhibit the greatest amount of cross-contamination of textual types" (*The Text of the New Testament*, 106).

THE COPTIC

Translation of the NT into the Egyptian language (written in Greek letters plus a few supplementary letters) took place in the beginning of the third century. The first Coptic translations were into the Sahidic dialect of Upper Egypt. A little later, translations were made into Bohairic, the dialect of the delta region of Lower Egypt. Translations into other Egyptian dialects are also known.

Other, less important versions may also be listed here: Gothic, Armenian, Georgian, Ethiopic, Arabic, and Old Slavonic.[14]

Patristic Quotations

When the fathers of the church who wrote in Greek quote the NT, this too becomes an important witness to the Greek NT of their time and locale. (Of course, those who wrote in other languages also witness to their NT texts, but these may have already been available in their own respective languages.) So extensive is this quotation that Metzger and Ehrman say that practically the entire Greek NT could be restored from the quotations of the fathers alone.[15] A key problem with using the quotations for information about their NT texts is that it is not always possible to be certain about whether the fathers intend to quote accurately, or whether they may be consciously paraphrasing, or whether they are looking at a manuscript or perhaps relying on memory (and if so, how successfully?) in their citations. There is furthermore the problem that copyists of these writings were constantly tempted to conform the quotations to agree more exactly with the biblical text.

There are dozens of patristic writers whose manuscripts are yet to be thoroughly studied for their use of NT writings and what light this might throw on the history of the NT text.[16]

Text Types

We have already noted that manuscripts often can exhibit similar patterns of variants showing a kind of familial relationship (e.g., Family 1 and Family 13). This is also true of larger groupings of manuscripts into what are called "text types." That some manuscripts are similar to one another in contrast to others is the result of their genealogy. If all our manuscripts came from the same, single original manuscript, these families would not emerge, at least not until

14. For details, see Metzger, *The Early Versions of the New Testament.*
15. Metzger and Ehrman, *The Text of the New Testament,* 126.
16. Bruce Metzger and Bart Ehrman call attention to the series of monographs with just this purpose that have begun to appear (see ibid., 129). The series, titled "The New Testament in the Greek Fathers: Texts and Analyses," is published by the Society of Biblical Literature.

there was further copying of copies. But what we have is manuscripts that are copied from different manuscripts, themselves perhaps copied from others. Descendants of manuscript A will resemble one another in a way that will not be true of manuscripts that are descendants of manuscript B; each group will have its own familial similarities.

For this reason, the large text types probably emerged in specific geographic areas, and indeed their designations are geographical, since we may assume that manuscripts coming from a particular area will have a similar genealogy. Nevertheless, manuscripts containing a particular text type are not always from the geographical locale one might expect, nor is it clear where a particular text type originated.[17] It is the consequence of genealogical relationships that one cannot decide on a variant by merely counting manuscripts. As J. A. Bengel, the first to isolate text types ("African" and "Asiatic"), said already in the eighteenth century, "Manuscripts must be weighed, rather than counted." Everything depends on the genealogy. One corrupt manuscript copied by others that are again further copied can produce a large number of manuscripts that are inferior.[18] This is also the reason why earlier manuscripts are likely to be superior to later ones. These considerations, together with a pattern of internal probabilities concerning variants themselves, have led scholars to the following main three text types. It should be noted that the text type of a manuscript is not always consistent throughout. Texts can vary in different parts and sometimes can reflect a mixed text type within the same corpus of writings. The key figures in the determining of text types were B. F. Westcott and F. J. A. Hort (see below).

Alexandrian

The earliest Greek manuscripts, the papryri, and the early majuscule manuscripts (a handful of manuscripts) were preserved in the desert climate of Egypt, and a number of these texts clearly resemble one another and are members of the same family or text type. This text type is accordingly given the name "Alexandrian." The vast majority of textual critics regard this family as representing the most reliable text of the NT. This, of course, does not mean that its readings are always and automatically correct. The Alexandrian text tends to be shorter and less polished than other text types. Westcott and Hort called this text type the "Neutral" text.[19]

Manuscripts that contain the Alexandrian text type are the Bodmer papyri $\mathfrak{P}^{66}$ and $\mathfrak{P}^{72}$ (mentioned above); the Beatty papyri $\mathfrak{P}^{45}$ and $\mathfrak{P}^{46}$; so too the majority, but not all, of the other papyri; and the majuscules Sinaiticus and

---

17. See Parker, *An Introduction to the New Testament Manuscripts and Their Texts*, 171.

18. This single fact undermines the argument of the defenders of the Majority Text (i.e., the Textus Receptus).

19. See Westcott and Hort, *The New Testament in the Original Greek*, 126–30; 169–72.

Vaticanus. Among the versions it is found in the Coptic translations (both Sahidic and Bohairic); it is also found in quotations of Clement of Alexandria and Origen (in part), both of course associated with Alexandria. Bruce Metzger lists as secondary witnesses to the Alexandrian text, 33 (the "queen"; among other cursives, 81, 104, and 326), Alexandrinus for Acts, the Pauline Epistles, the Catholic Epistles, and Revelation. The majuscule Ephraemi (C) is mentioned for the entire NT but is noted as a mixed text. And there are $\mathfrak{P}^{50}$ for Acts, and $\mathfrak{P}^{20}$ and $\mathfrak{P}^{23}$ for the Catholic Epistles.

Western

This name comes from the fact that this text type was used in the Western church, though it is also found elsewhere. Kurt Aland and Barbara Aland say that the origin of this text "lies anywhere but in the direction its name suggests."[20] As already indicated, the Western Text is known for its expansiveness, containing almost always the fullest text. D. C. Parker, commenting on the freedom represented by the changes and additions, concludes, "We have in Codex Bezae a text that takes up a remarkable attitude, not only in its reproduction of the text, but in its recording of the sayings of Jesus and of the apostles."[21]

According to Metzger, this text type, like the Alexandrian, can be traced back to the second century. Some papyri manuscripts ($\mathfrak{P}^{69}$ in the Gospels; $\mathfrak{P}^{29}$, $\mathfrak{P}^{38}$, and $\mathfrak{P}^{48}$ in Acts) reflect the Western Text. So too Sinaiticus in the Gospels. The prime majuscule manuscript here is Codex Bezae (D). Also representing the Western text are the Old Latin for the Gospels and Epistles, and the Latin fathers in general.[22]

Byzantine (or Antiochan, Syrian [thus Westcott and Hort], Koine)

The vast majority of Greek manuscripts (80 percent of all minuscules and practically all the lectionaries) contain this text type. This text is "characterized by stylistic clarity and completeness."[23] It is lucid and polished, and it harmonizes conflicting readings and has a tendency to conflate variant readings. It may derive from Syrian Antioch and then have been taken to Constantinople and distributed throughout the Byzantine Empire. It became the overwhelmingly dominant text type from the sixth or seventh century until the mid-fifteenth century. The great proliferation of copies soon made it the authoritative, accepted text, and thus it became known as the *textus receptus* ("received text").

20. Aland and Aland, *The Text of the New Testament*, 67.
21. Parker, *Codex Bezae*, 286.
22. Bruce Metzger notes that there are no Western Text manuscripts for Revelation (*A Textual Commentary on the Greek New Testament*, 15*).
23. Omanson, *A Textual Guide to the Greek New Testament*, 23*.

Although outside the Gospels the majuscule manuscript Alexandrinus witnesses to the Alexandrian text, in the Gospels its text is Byzantine. Virtually all majuscule manuscripts from the sixth century on contain the Byzantine text.[24]

A fourth text type(s) has been proposed by some text-critical scholars: the Caesarean, now called (the) Eastern. It lacks the definition of the other text types because it is has a very few exemplars.[25] Roger Omanson refers to it as "a mixture of Western and Alexandrian readings."[26] Bruce Metzger mentions only the ninth-century majuscule Θ, minuscules 565 and 700, and the Armenian and Georgian versions.[27]

The Future of Text Types

Determining text types and their relationships is extremely difficult at best. Kurt Aland and Barbara Aland use the analogy of pebbles making ripples in a pool. Each manuscript is like a pebble making its own ripples. The ripples intersect and influence one another, "producing a textual mixture and starting a new pattern of ripples—a process that would be repeated continually," making it impossible to trace sources and mutual relationships.[28]

We should note that the cutting edge of NT textual criticism seems to be moving away from the usefulness of text types altogether. The discipline is in a time of ferment. D. C. Parker, for example, is ready to abandon traditional text types in favor of new, revolutionary tools and methods.[29]

The Practice of Textual Criticism

Having surveyed the available resources, we turn now to the actual practice of textual criticism: the reconstruction of the original text of the NT. The text-critical scholar works with a combination of two basic kinds of evidence: external and internal, with the careful and sensitive weighing of both, freshly considered

24. For a full tabulation of witnesses to the major text types, see Metzger, *A Textual Commentary on the Greek New Testament*, 15–16*.

25. Kurt Aland and Barbara Aland regard this text type as "purely hypothetical" and resting on "dubious foundations" (*The Text of the New Testament*, 66).

26. Omanson, *A Textual Guide to the Greek New Testament*, 23*.

27. Metzger, *A Textual Commentary on the Greek New Testament*, 6*. Roger Omanson mentions another Eastern text, associated with Antioch, found in some Old Syriac witnesses and in the fourth-century Syrian fathers Aphraates and Ephraem (*A Textual Guide to the Greek New Testament*, 23*).

28. Aland and Aland, *The Text of the New Testament*, 70.

29. D. C. Parker writes, "I venture to predict that the Coherence-Based Genealogical Method and the use of phylogenetic software will prove to be equal to any past advance in their significance" (*An Introduction to the New Testament Manuscripts and Their Texts*, 178). These new, computer-based approaches (see ibid., 169) open new possibilities because they enable the scholar to work with exhaustive databases. See too Wachtel and Holmes, *The Textual History of the New Testament*.

for each variant. Although certain principles are involved, as we will see shortly, there is nothing automatic about their application or the conclusions to be drawn.

External Evidence

This concerns the manuscripts themselves.[30] First and foremost are their date and character. The earlier the date of the manuscript, or rather the text contained in the manuscript, the more likely it is to be the preferred text. Second, the geographical distribution of the manuscripts can be important. That is, all else being equal, variants that are represented by manuscripts from different locales would be favored over variants known only from one locale. Third, the genealogical relationship of texts and families of witnesses must be considered as over against simply counting manuscripts. A single variant that happens to have been copied in twenty different manuscripts should be given no more value than a variant found in only one manuscript. This leads to the fundamental principle, stated by J. A. Bengel in the eighteenth century, that witnesses are to be weighed rather than counted. Thus manuscripts that are generally regarded as trustworthy, such as those containing the Alexandrian text, are to be preferred where the evidence is otherwise ambiguous.

Internal Evidence

Two kinds of consideration are in view here: (1) transcriptional probabilities having to do with the habits of scribes and paleographical aspects of the manuscripts; and (2) intrinsic probabilities based on what seems most likely to have been written by the author (not the copyist).

As far as the activity of scribes is concerned, the following must be noted.

1. *The more difficult reading is generally to be preferred*, since scribes are likely to be tempted to emend the text to remove the difficulty.
2. *The shorter reading is generally to be preferred*, since scribes are more likely to add than to omit text. There are important exceptions to this rule: obvious inadvertent errors of the eye, such as homoeoarcton (skipping from the beginning of a line or word to a different line or word that begins the same way) or homoeoteleuton (skipping from the end of a line or word to a different line or word that ends the same way), and deliberate omission of material regarded by the scribe as superfluous, harsh, or contrary to pious belief or the practice of the church.
3. *The reading that differs from parallel passages, such as a quotation from the OT or a parallel in a different Gospel, is generally to be preferred*, since scribes are tempted to harmonize the differences.

---

30. The following paragraphs on the practice of textual criticism depend heavily on Metzger, *A Textual Commentary on the Greek New Testament*, 11*–14*.

    4. Scribes have a tendency to replace an unfamiliar word with a more famil-
       iar synonym; to improve texts grammatically and lexically; and to add
       pronouns, conjunctions, and expletives to smooth the flow of the text.

A host of other inadvertent errors must also be considered, common mistakes
not only of the eye but also of the ear, since it was not unusual for several
copyists to work at the same time by listening to someone read the text aloud.[31]
    As far as the activity of the *author* is concerned, the following should be
considered in making decisions about variants: the style and vocabulary of the
author in the same book and in other writings, if available; and, of course,
the immediate context. Variant readings in the Gospels require attention to
the Aramaic background of the teaching of Jesus, the priority of Mark, and the
influence of the community on the formulation and transmission of the passage.
    The practice of textual criticism is an art that can be truly learned only by
doing it. There is nothing mechanical about it, and no decisions can be automatic. The challenge is "to know when it is appropriate to give greater consideration to one kind of evidence and less to another."[32] Just for this reason, Bruce
Metzger's *Textual Commentary on the Greek New Testament* is very valuable.
It provides, in effect, a record of deliberations of the blue-ribbon committee
that produced the text of the United Bible Societies' *Greek New Testament*.
Reading a few pages of it, with the principles that we have just reviewed in mind,
will give the student a good idea of how informed textual criticism proceeds.

The History of the New Testament Text

The rapid growth of the church in the early centuries meant that the demand
for copies of the Gospels and the Epistles must have increased dramatically. No
doubt the demand outran the possibility of producing highly reliable copies.
Copies often were made by church members rather than professional scribes.
Errors in the manuscripts began to multiply and were perpetuated in copies
of the copies. The large majority of significant variant readings originated in
the first three centuries, and by the fourth century the variant readings were
causing problems. In an apparent effort to bring more uniformity to the NT
text, in 331 the emperor Constantine asked Eusebius, bishop of Caesarea, to
arrange for the production of fifty new copies of the NT for use in the churches

31. In this event we encounter not only mishearing a text but also the phenomenon known
as itacism: in Koine Greek the vowels *ē* and *i* and *u*, together with dipthongs *ei* and *oi* and *ui*,
were pronounced the same, with a long *e* sound. See Caragounis, *The Development of Greek
and the New Testament*, 339–96.

32. Metzger, *A Textual Commentary on the Greek New Testament*, 14*. Metzger mentions
the examples of where the more difficult reading is found only in later witnesses or the longer
reading is found only in earlier witnesses.

of Constantinople, "to be written on prepared parchment in a legible manner, and in a convenient, portable form, by professional transcribers thoroughly practiced in their art" (Eusebius, *Vit. Const.* 4.36, *NPNF*[2] 1:549). The text used for this is thought to have been the recension of Lucian of Antioch (250?–312), a forerunner to the Majority or Byzantine text.

The first Bible to be produced from a printing press was the famous Gutenberg Bible published in the 1450s, containing the text of Jerome's Latin translation, the translation favored by the church. The first Greek NT in printed form, in 1514, was produced under the sponsorship of the Spanish cardinal Francisco Ximenes de Cisneros. It was part of a larger project, a printed polyglot Bible in Hebrew, Aramaic, Greek, and Latin, which was delayed in being published until 1522. Because of the delay, the Greek NT edited by the famous Erasmus and published in 1516 became the first to be published in printed form. It also contained the Latin Vulgate in columns parallel to the Greek. For this edition Erasmus relied on several twelfth-century Greek manuscripts that were available to him in Basel. None of these had the final verses of Revelation, so he translated them back from the Latin into Greek, and in like manner he interpolated here and there where necessary from the Vulgate (e.g., 1 John 5:7–8 [see chap. 39 above]). Erasmus's Greek NT went through five editions. It reflected the Majority or Byzantine text that had long since become the dominant text. This *textus receptus* ("received text") retained its favored position until its collapse in the nineteenth century.

The next printed Greek NT that should be noted is that of the Parisian Robert Estienne (= Stephanus), who in the first half of the sixteenth century produced four editions. The third of these is the first Greek NT with an apparatus that makes reference to variant readings. It was in his fourth edition (1551) that Stephanus added verse numberings to the text that, despite their occasional oddness, endure to this day. (Our chapter numbers had already been added in 1205 by Stephen Langton, archbishop of Canterbury.) In the latter half of the sixteenth century Theodore Beza, a colleague of John Calvin, published nine editions of the Greek NT, used by the translators of the King James Bible in 1611, thereby ensuring the extensive and lasting influence of the *textus receptus*—"the text now received by all," as the 1633 edition of the Elzevir brothers in Leiden described it. Bruce Metzger and Bart Ehrman comment: "So superstitious has been the reverence accorded the Textus Receptus that in some cases attempts to criticize it or emend it have been regarded as akin to sacrilege. Yet, its textual basis is essentially a handful of late and haphazardly collected minuscule manuscripts, and in a dozen passages its rendering is supported by no known Greek witness."[33]

But as British scholars such as Brian Walton, John Fell, John Mill, and Richard Bentley began to gather manuscripts, the awareness of variant readings

---

33. Metzger and Ehrman, *The Text of the New Testament*, 152.

increased. It was, however, the work of the Lutheran Pietist Johann Albrecht Bengel that would spell the beginning of the end for *textus receptus*. In 1725 he outlined fundamental principles for the scientific practice of textual criticism that remain in place today. He organized manuscripts into families (two: "Asiatic" and "African"), and he posited the rules that manuscripts are to be weighed rather than counted in making decisions between variants, and that the more difficult reading is to be preferred to the easier reading. In his 1734 edition of the Greek NT he ranked variants in five categories, ranging from the original reading to readings that should be rejected.

In the last decades of the eighteenth century Johann Jakob Griesbach, whom we encountered in chapter 9 as the advocate for Mark as the latest of the Synoptic Gospels, laid out fifteen detailed canons of textual criticism. Finally, Karl Lachmann, known also as a pioneer arguing for the priority of Mark, was the first to make a complete break with *textus receptus* in his 1831 edition of the Greek NT, listing passages where his text differed. In the nineteenth century Constantin von Tischendorf, mentioned earlier in this chapter as the discoverer of Codex Sinaiticus, produced celebrated editions of the Greek NT, his ninth edition having an exceptionally rich apparatus, listing variants from the three major categories of manuscripts, versions, and patristic citations.

It was, however, B. F. Westcott and F. J. A. Hort in 1881 who put textual criticism on a firm foundation.[34] The practice of textual criticism outlined above is essentially the method of Westcott and Hort as presented in the second volume of their Greek NT. So too their identification of text types remains fundamentally important. The latest and poorest type they identified as "Syrian" (i.e., Byzantine); the text represented by D (Bezae) and the Old Latin, with its inflated readings, they designated "Western"; the name "Alexandrian" they gave to C (Ephraemi) and 33, Coptic versions, and the Alexandrian fathers; their respect for the main majuscule manuscripts Vaticanus and Sinaiticus is indicated in their naming this text as "Neutral," closest to the originals, and generally to be preferred, except in the case of "Western non-interpolations" (i.e., readings not contained in the Western Text, which usually has the fullest readings).[35] Westcott and Hort mark the end of *textus receptus* by having demonstrated its weaknesses. Metzger and Ehrman observe, "When the Syrian readings are compared with the rival readings, their claim to be regarded as original is found gradually to diminish and at last to disappear."[36]

One important result of the work of Westcott and Hort was that it also meant the end of the hegemony of the King James Version. In the same year as their Greek NT (1881), a new English translation of the Bible, the Revised Version, was published (in 1901, the equivalent American Standard Version

34. Westcott and Hort, *The New Testament in the Original Greek*.
35. Bruce Metzger and Bart Ehrman note that Westcott and Hort probably could not tolerate the idea of "Neutral interpolations" (*The Text of the New Testament*, 179).
36. Ibid., 181.

was published). The Revised Version itself was revised in the Revised Standard Version, the NT of which first appeared in 1946, and virtually all major
English translations have followed suit in depending on the best text-critical
research available in their day.

The two standard critical editions of the Greek NT in use today are the
Nestle-Aland and that of the United Bible Societies. As of the twenty-sixth
edition of the former (1979),[37] the two texts agree exactly, reflecting the nuanced application of the principles of Westcott and Hort and making use of
the latest manuscript discoveries. The former has many more variant readings
listed than the latter together with an excellent collection of cross-references
in the margins, while the latter has much fuller documentation for the readings that it lists (selected for their importance to Bible translators) and also
a useful apparatus that compares the punctuation of various translations.
The United Bible Societies text (the first edition appeared in 1966) also rates
the variants in terms of confidence (from A to D), and in the fourth edition
(1993) the level of confidence has increased.[38] The fullest and most up-to-date
resource for textual critical evidence is, or will be (the projected completion
date is 2030), the huge, ongoing project of the Münster Institute for New
Testament Textual Research: *Novum Testamentum graecum: Editio critica
maior*. The fourth volume of this project is now in print (in four parts):
Catholic Letters (edited by Barbara Aland et al., published by Deutsche Bibelgesellschaft, 1998–2005).

The Reliability of the Text of the Greek New Testament

There are, of course, many thousands of variant readings in the manuscripts
of the Greek NT. Statistically, this could give the impression that the text
of the NT is poorly attested and highly unreliable. What must be stressed,
however, is that the vast majority of these variants involve small details that
are of little or no consequence. Westcott and Hort summed up the situation
in these words: "Setting aside differences of orthography, the words in our
opinion still subject to doubt only make up about one sixtieth of the whole
New Testament." They continue by noting that substantial variation "can
hardly form more than a thousandth part of the entire text."[39] If such a large
percentage of the variants is insubstantial and inconsequential (e.g., spelling
variations, difference in word order, use or nonuse of definite article), only
a relatively few are even potentially disconcerting. But, to quote Westcott

37. The first edition, produced by Eberhard Nestle, was printed in 1898; the latest, the
twenty-seventh edition, appeared in 1993.
38. See Clarke, *Textual Optimism*, 184. Clarke suggests that these more confident ratings
may create "a false sense of optimism."
39. Westcott and Hort, *The New Testament in the Original Greek*, 2:2.

and Hort once again, "Even among the numerous unquestionably spurious readings of the New Testament there are no signs of deliberate falsification of the text for dogmatic purposes."[40] And further, as Frederic Kenyon remarked, "No fundamental doctrine of the Christian faith rests upon a disputed reading."[41]

The situation regarding the Greek text of the NT is so positive, and the textual critics have done such exemplary work, that confidence in the overall reliability of the text is justified. We are in a far better position with the Greek NT than with any other writing from antiquity, with an embarrassment of riches by comparison. And our Greek text is probably more reliable now than it has been since the earliest centuries of the church. This is something to be grateful for. But this by no means suggests that all has been settled. Textual criticism remains an ongoing challenge: we must beware of allowing today's critical text, as good as it is, to become a new unquestioned, and unquestionable, *textus receptus*.[42] There remains an important future for textual criticism.

Bibliography

Aland, Kurt, and Barbara Aland. *The Text of the New Testament: An Introduction to the Critical Editions and to the Theory and Practice of Modern Textual Criticism*. Translated by Erroll F. Rhodes. 2nd ed. Grand Rapids: Eerdmans; Leiden: Brill, 1989.

Amphoux, Christian-B., and J. K. Elliott. *The New Testament Text in Early Christianity: Proceedings of the Lille Colloquium, July 2000*. HTB 6. Lausanne: Éditions du Zèbre, 2003.

Bentley, James. *Secrets of Mount Sinai: The Story of the World's Oldest Bible—Codex Sinaiticus*. Garden City, NY: Doubleday, 1986.

Birdsall, J. Neville. "The New Testament Text." In *From the Beginning to Jerome*. Vol. 1 of *The Cambridge History of the Bible*, edited by P. R. Ackroyd and C. F. Evans, 308–77. Cambridge: Cambridge University Press, 1970.

———. "The Recent History of New Testament Textual Criticism (from Westcott and Hort, 1881, to Present)." *ANRW* II.26.1 (1992): 99–197.

Black, David Alan. *New Testament Textual Criticism: A Concise Guide*. Grand Rapids: Baker Academic, 1994.

40. Ibid., 2:282. The opposite is claimed now by Ehrman, *The Orthodox Corruption of Scripture*; idem, *Misquoting Jesus*. If scribes were as active in altering the text for theological reasons as Ehrman maintains, one might expect much more evidence of it in the NT than he is able to muster. For critique of Ehrman's views, see Köstenberger and Kruger, *The Heresy of Orthodoxy*, 179–231.

41. Kenyon, *Our Bible and the Ancient Manuscripts*, 55. Even, for example, the hardest textual questions that Ehrman can raise (see *Whose Word Is It?* 207–8) present nothing that overturns any Christian doctrine.

42. Textual criticism will take new directions in the future, becoming more complex, especially in the use of computers, and more interdisciplinary in its agenda. See Parker, *An Introduction to the New Testament Manuscripts and Their Texts*; Hull, *The Story of the New Testament Text*, chapters 8–9; Wachtel and Holmes, *The Textual History of the Greek New Testament*.

————, ed. *Rethinking New Testament Textual Criticism*. Grand Rapids: Baker Academic, 2002.

Caragounis, Chrys C. *The Development of Greek and the New Testament*. Grand Rapids: Baker Academic, 2006.

Childers, J. W., and D. C. Parker, eds. *Transmission and Reception: New Testament Text-Critical and Exegetical Studies*. TSt 3/4. Piscataway, NJ: Gorgias, 2006.

Clarke, Kent D. *Textual Optimism: A Critique of the United Bible Societies' Greek New Testament*. JSNTSup 138. Sheffield: Sheffield Academic Press, 1997.

Colwell, Ernest C. *Studies in Methodology in Textual Criticism of the New Testament*. NTTS 9. Leiden: Brill, 1969.

Comfort, Philip W. *Early Manuscripts and Modern Translations of the New Testament*. Grand Rapids: Baker Academic, 1996.

————. *Encountering the Manuscripts: An Introduction to New Testament Paleography and Textual Criticism*. Nashville: Broadman & Holman, 2005.

————. *New Testament Text and Translation Commentary: Commentary on the Variant Readings of the Ancient New Testament Manuscripts and How They Relate to the Major English Translations*. Carol Stream, IL: Tyndale House, 2008.

————. *The Quest for the Original Text of the New Testament*. Grand Rapids: Baker Academic, 1992.

Comfort, Philip W., and David P. Barrett. *The Complete Text of the Earliest New Testament Manuscripts*. Grand Rapids: Baker Academic, 1999.

Ehrman, Bart D. *Misquoting Jesus: The Story behind Who Changed the Bible and Why*. New York: Oxford University Press, 2005.

————. *The Orthodox Corruption of Scripture: The Effects of Early Christological Controversies on the Text of the New Testament*. New York: Oxford University Press, 1993.

————. *Studies in the Textual Criticism of the New Testament*. NTTS 33. Leiden: Brill, 2006.

————. *Whose Word Is It? The Story behind Who Changed the New Testament and Why*. New York: Continuum, 2006.

Ehrman, Bart D., and Michael W. Holmes, eds. *The Text of the New Testament in Contemporary Research: Essays on the Status Quaestionis*. SD 46. Grand Rapids: Eerdmans, 1995.

Elliott, J. K. *A Bibliography of Greek New Testament Manuscripts*. SNTSMS 109. Cambridge: Cambridge University Press, 1989.

————. "The Case for Thoroughgoing Eclecticism." In *Rethinking New Testament Textual Criticism*, edited by David Alan Black, 101–24. Grand Rapids: Baker Academic, 2002.

————. *A Survey of Manuscripts Used in Editions of the Greek New Testament*. NovTSup 57. Leiden: Brill, 1987.

Elliott, J. K., and Ian Moir. *Manuscripts and the Text of the New Testament: An Introduction for English Readers*. Edinburgh: T&T Clark, 1995.

————. *The Theological Tendency of Codex Bezae Cantabrigiensis in Acts*. SNTSMS 3. Cambridge: Cambridge University Press, 1966.

Epp, Eldon Jay. *Perspectives on New Testament Textual Criticism: Collected Essays, 1962–2004*. NovTSup 116. Leiden: Brill, 2005.

Epp, Eldon Jay, and Gordon D. Fee, eds. *New Testament Textual Criticism: Its Significance for Exegesis; Essays in Honour of Bruce M. Metzger*. Oxford: Clarendon, 1981.

————. *Studies in the Theory and Method of New Testament Textual Criticism*. SD 45. Grand Rapids: Eerdmans, 1993.

Fee, Gordon D. "The Use of Greek Patristic Citations in New Testament Textual Criticism: The State of the Question." *ANRW* II.26.1 (1992): 246–65.

Finegan, Jack. *Encountering New Testament Manuscripts: A Working Introduction to Textual Criticism*. Grand Rapids: Eerdmans, 1974.

Gamble, Harry Y. *Books and Readers in the Early Church: A History of Early Christian Texts*. New Haven: Yale University Press, 1995.

Greenlee, J. Harold. *Introduction to New Testament Textual Criticism*. Rev. ed. Peabody, MA: Hendrickson, 1995.

———. *The Text of the New Testament: From Manuscript to Modern Edition*. Peabody, MA: Hendrickson, 2008.

Head, Peter M. "Some Recently Published NT Papyri from Oxyrhynchus: An Overview and Preliminary Assessment." *TynBul* 51 (2000): 1–16.

Hodges, Zane C., and Arthur L. Farstad, eds. *The Greek New Testament Text according to the Majority Text*. 2nd ed. Nashville: Thomas Nelson, 1985.

Holmes, Michael W. "The Case for Reasoned Eclecticism." In *Rethinking New Testament Textual Criticism*, edited by David Alan Black, 77–100. Grand Rapids: Baker Academic, 2002.

Hull, Robert F., Jr. *The Story of the New Testament Text: Movers, Materials, Motives, Methods, and Models*. SBLRBS 58. Atlanta: Society of Biblical Literature, 2010.

Kenyon, Frederic G. *Our Bible and the Ancient Manuscripts*. Revised by A. W. Adams. London: Eyre & Spottiswoode, 1958.

Kilpatrick, G. D. *The Principles and Practice of New Testament Textual Criticism: Collected Essays of G. D. Kilpatrick*. Edited by J. K. Elliott. BETL 96. Leuven: Leuven University Press, 1990.

Köstenberger, Andreas J., and Michael J. Kruger. *The Heresy of Orthodoxy: How Contemporary Culture's Fascination with Diversity Has Reshaped Our Understanding of Early Christianity*. Wheaton, IL: Crossway, 2010.

McKendrick, Scot, and Orlaith A. O'Sullivan, eds. *The Bible as Book: The Transmission of the Greek Text*. New Castle, DE: Oak Knoll, 2003.

Metzger, Bruce M. *Chapters in the History of New Testament Textual Criticism*. NTTS 4. Leiden: Brill, 1963.

———. *The Early Versions of the New Testament*. Oxford: Clarendon, 1977.

———. *Manuscripts of the Greek Bible: An Introduction to Paleography*. New York: Oxford University Press, 1981.

———. *A Textual Commentary on the Greek New Testament*. 2nd ed. Stuttgart: Deutsche Bibelgesellschaft, 1994.

Metzger, Bruce M., and Bart D. Ehrman. *The Text of the New Testament: Its Transmission, Corruption, and Restoration*. 4th ed. New York: Oxford University Press, 2005.

Millard, Alan R. *Reading and Writing in the Time of Jesus*. New York: New York University Press, 2000.

Omanson, Roger L. *A Textual Guide to the Greek New Testament: An Adaptation of Bruce M. Metzger's Textual Commentary for the Needs of Translators*. Stuttgart: German Bible Society, 2006.

Osburn, Carroll D. "The Greek Lectionaries of the New Testament." In *The Text of the New Testament in Contemporary Research: Essays on the Status Quaestionis*, edited by Bart D. Ehrman and Michael W. Holmes, 61–74. SD 46. Grand Rapids: Eerdmans, 1995.

Parker, D. C. *Codex Bezae: An Early Christian Manuscript and Its Text*. Cambridge: Cambridge University Press, 1992.

———. *An Introduction to the New Testament Manuscripts and Their Texts*. Cambridge: Cambridge University Press, 2008.

———. *The Living Text of the Gospels*. Cambridge: Cambridge University Press, 1997.

Read-Heimerdinger, Jenny. *The Bezan Text of Acts: A Contribution of Discourse Analysis to Textual Criticism*. JSNTSup 236. London: Sheffield Academic Press, 2002.

Rius-Camps, Josep, and Jenny Read-Heimerdinger. *The Message of Acts in Codex Bezae: A Comparison with the Alexandrian Tradition*. 2 vols. JSNTSup 257. New York: T&T Clark International, 2004.

Roberts, Colin H., and T. C. Skeat. *The Birth of the Codex*. London: Oxford University Press, 1983.

Robinson, Maurice A., and William G. Pierpont, eds. *The New Testament in the Original Greek according to the Byzantine/Majority Textform*. Atlanta: Original Word, 1991.

Royse, James R. *Scribal Habits in Early Greek New Testament Papyri*. NTTS 36. Leiden: Brill, 1998.

Skeat, T. C. "The Last Chapter in the History of Codex Sinaiticus." *NovT* 42 (2000): 313–15.

Stewart, R. B., ed. *The Reliability of the New Testament: Bart Ehrman and Daniel Wallace in Dialogue*. Minneapolis: Fortress, 2011.

Sturz, Harry A. *The Byzantine Text-Type and New Testament Textual Criticism*. Nashville: Thomas Nelson, 1984.

Swanson, Reuben J., ed. *New Testament Greek Manuscripts: Variant Readings Arranged in Horizontal Lines against Codex Vaticanus*. 7 vols. Wheaton, IL: Tyndale House; Pasadena, CA: William Carey International University Press, 1995–2001.

Wachtel, Klaus, and Michael W. Holmes, eds. *The Textual History of the Greek New Testament: Changing Views in Contemporary Research*. Atlanta: SBL, 2011.

Westcott, B. F., and F. J. A. Hort. *Introduction to the New Testament in the Original Greek: With Notes on Selected Readings*. Reprint, Peabody, MA: Hendrickson, 1988.

———. *The New Testament in the Original Greek*. 2 vols. London: Macmillan, 1881–96.

Williams, C. S. C. *Alterations to the Text of the Synoptic Gospels and Acts*. Oxford: Blackwell, 1951.

Yoder, James D., ed. *Concordance to the Distinctive Greek Text of Codex Bezae*. NTTS 2. Leiden: Brill, 1961.

Zuntz, Günther. *The Text of the Epistles: A Disquisition upon the Corpus Paulinum*. London: Oxford University Press, 1953.

43

The Formation of the Canon

The books that compose the NT form an authoritative collection of writings, gradually selected over a considerable period of time, from a much larger body of near-contemporary writings that were available. God revealed no authoritative list, nor did the church first decide on such a list at a specific point in time. On the contrary, the formation of the canon was a process that proceeded over several centuries and was the result of decisions made by fallible human beings based on the best evidence available to them. When later church councils did declare decisions about canon, in effect they put their stamp of approval only on books that already enjoyed that status. This is not to imply that they made mistakes, but only to stress that the formation of the canon was a process determined by human reasoning.

The word "canon" simply means "rule" or "standard" by which things are measured. The Greek word *kanōn* initially referred to a "reed" that was used in making measurements. The word is used in the NT to refer to rule of conduct (2 Cor. 10:13 [where it means "limit" and is combined with *metron*, lit. "measure"], 15–16; Gal. 6:16, "rule" [where it refers to standard of conduct]). Already in the second century the phrase *kanōn tēs pisteōs*, "rule of faith" (*regula fidei*), is used to refer to the orthodox belief of the church (cf. Rom. 6:17; *1 Clem.* 7:2). Canonical books are those that set the standard of truth. Canonization refers to the placing of a limited number of books in a special category. By its nature, then, "canon" refers to something more or less closed. But canon need not be fully fixed; there may always be books on the fringe of the canon that remain of debatable status.

The interesting question is why we have *these* books in the Bible and not *those*. How and where were the decisions made and by what criteria? We begin with a brief look at these questions for the OT canon as background to the same questions for the NT canon.

The Formation of the Old Testament Canon

The Three Divisions of the Hebrew Canon

Sacred tradition exists before canon exists. This certainly is true both for Israel and the church. For Israel, it begins with Moses. Although the five books of our Bible under his name were written long after his day, they probably do enshrine traditions that go back to Moses. This material plays an important role in the history of Israel, and these five books (hence the name "Pentateuch" for them) soon come to constitute the first and foundational collection of the three divisions of the Hebrew Bible, the Law (Torah). This is officially recognized in the postexilic era (Ezra 7:10, 14, 26: Neh. 8:1–2), and from that time on the Pentateuch held an unquestioned primacy among the Scriptures of Israel. Probably within the next century or so, the books that comprise the second division, the Prophets (Nebiim), began to gain acceptance as a group. It included historical books, the Former Prophets (= the "Deuteronomistic" history books of Joshua, Judges, Samuel, and Kings, giving a prophetic view of history) and the Latter Prophets (= Isaiah, Jeremiah, Ezekiel, and the Book of the Twelve).[1] The expression "the law and the prophets" refers to the core of the canon (cf. Matt. 5:17; Luke 24:27). Meanwhile, some writings that eventually would compose the third division, known as the Writings (Ketubim), were also highly valued. An early, established fixture of this division is the book of Psalms, which was placed at its head.

A key piece of datable historical evidence comes from the prologue to the book of Sirach (the full name is "The Wisdom of Jesus [Gk. for "Joshua"] the Son of Sirach [Gk. for "Sira"]," given the name "Ecclesiasticus" by the church), a book now found in the OT Apocrypha. The book itself was written in about 180 BC in Hebrew, but the prologue, written by the author's grandson, who translated the book into Greek, dates to 132 BC. In this prologue we find the following: "Many great teachings have been given to us through the law and the prophets and the others that followed them. . . . My grandfather Jesus, after devoting himself especially to the reading of the law and the prophets and the other books of our fathers, . . . was himself also led to write something pertaining to instruction and wisdom." This is perhaps the

---

1. Josephus (*Ag. Ap.* 1.38–41), however, has an additional five books in the "Prophets" (making a total of thirteen). These are possibly Job, Esther, Daniel, Chronicles, and Ezra-Nehemiah—all in the third division, the Writings, in the Hebrew Bible. This puts in Josephus's third division Psalms, Proverbs, Ecclesiastes, and Song of Songs.

earliest reference to the threefold division of the Hebrew Bible. The manner of reference suggests that the Law and Prophets are settled categories, while the third is referred to more vaguely as simply "other" books, suggesting that it was not yet a defined group.[2]

A further very important piece of evidence for the three divisions of the Hebrew canon comes from Luke's Gospel, where the risen Jesus is reported as saying, "Everything written about me in the law of Moses and the prophets and the psalms must be fulfilled" (Luke 24:44).[3] A threefold division is also witnessed to by Philo, who refers to "laws and the oracles delivered through the mouth of prophets, and psalms" (*Contempl.* 25, trans. Colson).[4]

By the time of the NT, the Law and the Prophets are well established as having canonical authority (although the Sadducees and the Samaritans accepted only the Torah). There are signs, however, that the third division of the canon, the Writings, was not yet fully established in the first century.[5] A few books, such as Ecclesiastes, Song of Songs, and Esther, were subject to ongoing debate. Their content was controversial, as none of the three contains the name "YHWH," and Esther does not even contain a reference to God. In the rabbinic deliberations in the 90s at Yavneh (Jamnia), discussion of Qohelet (i.e., Ecclesiastes) and Song of Songs took place.[6] There is evidence of discussion in the rabbinic period concerning which books "defile the hands"—that is, which books are holy and therefore require washing of hands before and after touching the scrolls. A famous passage in the Mishnah (*m. Yad.* 3.5) records a discussion of what books "defile the hands," with the specific books of Song of Songs and Qohelet in view. A statement in the Tosefta suggests that Qohelet and Sirach (and books later than Sirach) do not defile the hands. Yet Sirach is quoted three times, twice with introductory formula, as Scripture in the rabbinic writings.[7]

2. Other evidence suggests the threefold division. At Qumran we find this: "To you we have written that you must understand the book of Moses and the words of the prophets and of David and the annals of each generation" ([4QMMT [4Q397], fragments 14–21, lines 10–11. Trans. Martínez). The reference to David probably indicates Psalms, and "the annals" may refer to Chronicles. Second Maccabees 2:13 also refers to the "prophets and writing of David," possibly the second and third divisions of the canon.

3. A further possible indication in Luke of the third division of the Hebrew canon is found in Luke 11:50–51: "the blood of all the prophets . . . from the blood of Abel to the blood of Zechariah" (cf. Matt. 24:35). Zechariah is the last martyr mentioned in the Hebrew Bible (2 Chron. 24:20–22), which ends with 2 Chronicles, the last book of the Writings.

4. See also Josephus, *Against Apion* 1.39.

5. Roger Beckwith goes rather too far in concluding that the OT had "reached its final form in the time of Judas Maccabeus, about 164 BC, and did so for all schools of thought alike" (*The Old Testament Canon of the New Testament Church*, 406).

6. Often too much has been claimed for the rabbis at Yavneh, such as the contention that they formally established the Hebrew canon. But they issued no list of canonical books and by no means brought the discussion to an end. See Lewis, "Jamnia Revisited."

7. For references, see ibid., 158n105.

The Number of Books in the Hebrew Bible

The number of books in the Hebrew Bible is usually counted as twenty-four: five in the Torah, eight in the Prophets, eleven in the Writings. This number corresponds to the thirty-nine books of the OT of the English Bible. The difference in reckoning is due to the Hebrew canon's combining of books: the books of Samuel, Kings, Ezra-Nehemiah, and Chronicles are counted as four books, and the twelve Minor Prophets as one book. It became popular, however, to refer to twenty-two books in order to agree with the number of letters of the Hebrew alphabet (this number could be reached by joining Ruth to Ezra-Nehemiah, and Lamentations to Jeremiah). Thus already in *Jubilees* (ca. 160–140 BC) we read, "There were twenty-two chief men from Adam until Jacob, and twenty-two kinds of works were made before the seventh day" (2:23).[8] So too Josephus: "We have . . . twenty-two books, which contain the records of all the past times; which are justly believed to be [*pepisteumena*] divine" (*Ag. Ap.* 1.38, trans. Whiston). The church fathers Origen and Jerome follow the Jewish authorities in also referring to the twenty-two books.

But despite the numerical symbolism, the exact number of the books that came to be in the canon was not fully fixed until rather later. The first Jewish text that identifies the books of the Hebrew Bible, and assigns them in the three divisions, is in the Babylonian Talmud, *Baba Batra* 14b, a *baraita*—a Tanaaitic saying probably from the second half of the second century but not contained in the Mishnah.

Meanwhile, there is abundant evidence, beginning with the NT itself, but also in the Apostolic Fathers and later fathers, that the Christians were making use of a much larger number of writings than those of the Jewish canon, sometimes indeed citing them with introductory formulae in the same way the Scriptures of the OT were cited.

Books Excluded from the Hebrew Canon

There were many other writings known in the first century that could be thought of as vying for inclusion in the still-open third division of the Jewish canon, writings that we now place in the categories of Apocrypha and Pseudepigrapha.

An acknowledgment of these writings is found in the first-century document known as *4 Ezra* (= 2 Esdras in our Apocrypha). There, in an account of the restoration of the Scriptures to Ezra, dictated during a period of forty days, we read: "So during the forty days ninety-four books were written. And when the forty days were ended, the Most High spoke to me, saying, 'Make public the

---

8. Epiphanius, fourth-century bishop of Salamis, refers to twenty-two letters in the Hebrew alphabet and twenty-two sacred books (*Weights and Measures* 22).

twenty-four books that you wrote first and let the worthy and the unworthy read them; but keep the seventy that were written last, in order to give them to the wise among your people. For in them is the spring of understanding the fountain of wisdom, and the river of knowledge'" (14:44–47). Epiphanius, in the fourth century, similarly refers to twenty-two canonical and seventy-two apocryphal books (*Weights and Measures* 10).

The LXX used by the Alexandrian Christians contained a number of books from the category that we designate as the Apocrypha, traditionally some fourteen in number, but with a few extra books, such as an additional psalm (Ps. 151) and two extra books of Maccabees (3–4 Maccabees). Some deduced from this that among the Jews of Alexandria a larger OT canon was accepted. This is widely regarded as an unwarranted conclusion, however. What it apparently does represent is the Christian use of a larger number of writings than were eventually accepted into the Hebrew Bible.[9] Philo of Alexandria never cites the Apocrypha. The Apocrypha are distinguished from the Pseudepigrapha because of their association with the LXX. They have maintained their special, deuterocanonical status in large parts of the Christian church.

Among the Qumran scrolls, all books of the Hebrew Bible have been discovered, even if only in fragments, except for Esther (possibly just a coincidence, but an interesting one because we know that the book was under debate). But at Qumran a considerable number of noncanonical books are represented. These include not only the various writings that stem from the community itself but also books such as *Enoch* and *Jubilees*, and books of the Apocrypha such as Sirach, Tobit, Letter of Jeremiah, and Psalm 151.

The pattern of quotation of Jewish Scriptures in the NT is revealing. The overwhelming majority of quotations are from the books that eventually would be incorporated into the Hebrew canon. There are, to be sure, abundant allusions to other books, from both the Apocrypha and the Pseudepigrapha, but only a very few citations from those writings (e.g., most famously *1 En.* 1:9, quoted in Jude 14–15).[10]

By What Criteria Were Books Excluded?

We are not in a good position to articulate the criteria used in Jewish decisions to include or exclude books from the OT canon. When finally canonical lists began to be drawn up, no underlying rationale was stated. It seemed more a matter of what for the most part was regarded as self-evident, at least for the majority of books. These were simply writings that were regarded with high esteem, writings that had been in use for some considerable time. It was the recognition of a de facto canon already in use.

9. See Sundberg, *The Old Testament of the Early Church*.
10. For a full listing, see Evans, *Ancient Texts for New Testament Studies*, 342–409. A list also is found in McDonald, *The Biblical Canon*, 452–64.

Some statements give the impression of a belief that prophecy had ceased in the postexilic period.[11] Several passages in 1 Maccabees point in this direction. First Maccabees 4:46 refers to stones of the defiled temple altar that were stored on the temple hill "until a prophet should come to tell what to do with them." According to 1 Maccabees 14:41, Simon was to remain leader "until a trustworthy prophet should arise." Even more striking is 1 Maccabees 9:27: "So there was great distress in Israel, such as had not been since the time that the prophets ceased to appear among them" (cf. Ps. 74:9: "there is no longer any prophet"). Josephus mentions history books "from Artaxerxes to our own time" not comparable with earlier works "because of the failure of the exact succession of the prophets" (*Ag. Ap.* 1.41, trans. Thackeray). And in the Babylonian Talmud it is said, "Our rabbis taught: Since the death of the last prophets, Haggai, Zechariah, and Malachi, the Holy Spirit [of prophetic inspiration] departed from Israel" (*b. Sanh.* 11a).

But at the same time, there is evidence at Qumran and in Philo and Josephus that contradicts this viewpoint. Much points to the ongoing activity of the Holy Spirit in the Second Temple period. If it was not the belief that the Holy Spirit had ceased working in Israel, it seems to have been the conviction specifically that prophecy and prophetic inspiration had come to an end. As Jack Lightstone points out, "Moses and Ezra are portrayed as the architects of the world defined in rabbinic teaching."[12] The time of the prophets was from Moses to Ezra, and therefore no books after Ezra could ultimately qualify for the canon, no matter how appealing. According to Josephus, "The prophets alone learned the highest and oldest matters by the inspiration of God," and prophets were responsible for the thirteen books after Moses (*Ag. Ap.* 1.37, 40, trans. Mason). Josephus and Philo (*Contempl.* 25) regarded all writers of the OT as prophets. Prophecy, in the sense of special individuals speaking on behalf of God, was ultimately the deciding factor in the stabilizing of the Hebrew canon.

Summary

It is simplistic and misleading to say that there was no Hebrew canon in the first century. The books of Moses surely were canonical even if no list of them is provided. Very probably the same may be said about the second division of the canon, the Prophets. So too with some writings of the third division, at least the psalms, but probably others too. From the available evidence, it appears that already in the first century there was a de facto Jewish canon that corresponded rather closely to our present OT. Certain books were already regarded as authoritative, sacred, and inspired, and were treated differently from other writings. The fact that some questionable

---

11. On this subject, see Meyer, "προφήτης."
12. Lightstone, "The Rabbis' Bible," 184.

books were lingering on the fringe of the canon does not mean that other books did not have essentially canonical status and function canonically. Thus, before the stabilizing of the Hebrew canon in its fixed form there was an intermediate stage of an informal, functional canon, not quite closed, but nearly so.

In the early church, by contrast, a much wider collection of Second Temple writings was being cited and thereby given informal canonical status. Thus, for example, in *1 Clement* we find not only quotations from all three divisions of the Hebrew canon, as might be expected, but also from Wisdom of Solomon and, with introductory formulae, from lesser-known writings such as perhaps *Eldad and Modad*, *Assumption of Moses*, and *Apocryphon of Ezekiel*.[13] This use of a larger canon than what would be finalized as the Jewish canon was typical of the early church,[14] which tended to function by the principle articulated by Tertullian in reference to *1 Enoch*: "Nothing at all must be rejected by us which pertains to us" (*Cult. fem.* 1.3, trans. *ANF* 4:16). Since by the hermeneutic of the early church it was not difficult to see a text as pointing to Christ, many books could be regarded as useful and acceptable, perhaps even inspired.

The church, however, eventually narrowed its de facto OT canon to agree with the Hebrew canon, perhaps more for utilitarian than theological reasons, since they made no headway in their disputations with the Jews by appealing to books that the Jews simply dismissed as noncanonical. Nevertheless, the Apocrypha and other books too continued to be used by the Christians, even if regarded now as in a deuterocanonical status.

The Formation of the New Testament Canon

The process of canonization begins with the collection of selected writings. And in a way similar to the history of the formation of the OT, the formation of the NT begins with the gradual collection of three groups of writings, beginning with the Pauline Epistles, followed by the Gospels, and then the Catholic Epistles. These collections undoubtedly were facilitated by the invention of the codex, the new format coming into use toward the end of the first century, which enabled separate writings to be combined in a single physical entity.

---

13. See Hagner, *The Use of the Old and New Testament in Clement of Rome*, 111–20.

14. "When Origen and the Greek fathers who follow him fix the number of the books at twenty-two or twenty-four, they follow, not the earlier tradition of the Church, but the corrected estimate of Christian scholars who had learned it from Jewish teachers. An earlier tradition is represented by the line of Christian writers beginning with Clement of Rome, who quoted the 'Apocryphal' books apparently without suspecting that they were not part of the Canon" (Swete, *An Introduction to the Old Testament in Greek*, 224).

The Collection of New Testament Writings

The Pauline Epistles

The first writings to be collected were the letters of Paul. Although Paul never dreamed that his writings some day would be regarded as Holy Scripture, he did think of them as authoritative and important for the churches to which he wrote, and others too. Thus he urged the churches to exchange his letters: "And when this letter has been read among you, have it read also in the church of the Laodiceans; and see that you read also the letter from Laodicea" (Col. 4:16). We noted earlier that Ephesians and Romans may well have originally been encyclicals. Undoubtedly, the churches valued these letters from the Apostle and, as well as treasuring any letter written to them, would have made copies of letters to other churches for their own archives.

We can get an idea of these church collections by looking at the Apostolic Fathers, writers spanning the time from Clement of Rome (96) to the middle of the second century. Clement shows a knowledge of a number of the Pauline Epistles. Although there is room for disagreement, Clement knows at least Romans and 1 Corinthians, but also probably Galatians, Ephesians, and Philippians, and possibly 2 Corinthians, Colossians, and the Pastoral Epistles.[15] Clement also, and unquestionably, knows Hebrews, which could be included as evidence of a Pauline collection were it not for the fact that in the Western church the Pauline authorship of Hebrews, as we have noted earlier, was accepted only very late. If Clement knows so many Pauline Letters, perhaps as many as do the later Apostolic Fathers,[16] the likelihood increases that they were available to him already in a collection, partial at the least if not the full collection, probably in codex form.[17]

Within the NT itself there is possible evidence of a collection of the Pauline Letters in 2 Peter 3:15–16: "So also our beloved brother Paul wrote to you according to the wisdom given him, speaking of this as he does in all his letters. There are some things in them hard to understand, which the ignorant

15. For details, see Hagner, *The Use of the Old and New Testaments in Clement of Rome*, 179–237. My conclusions have been criticized, not without some justification, for being maximalist. I worked with the following premise: "When a known source is readily available, it is difficult to argue probable dependence in another direction without the strongest of evidence" (ibid., 15).

16. The other two Apostolic Fathers who show considerable knowledge of Paul's writings are Ignatius and Polycarp. Ignatius gives evidence of knowing 1 Corinthians, Ephesians, 1–2 Timothy; Polycarp probably of knowing 1 Corinthians, Ephesians (referring to it as "scripture"), 1–2 Timothy; and perhaps more. These are the conclusions of Paul Foster and Michael Holmes, respectively, in Gregory and Tuckett, *The Reception of the New Testament in the Apostolic Fathers*, a volume that marks the centenary of the Oxford Society of Historical Theology's *New Testament in the Apostolic Fathers*, published in 1905.

17. In view of the clear citations of 1 Corinthians and Romans in *1 Clement*, Kurt Aland and Barbara Aland conclude, "This must reflect the existence in Rome at this time of a collection of Paul's letters, although its extent cannot be determined precisely because the quotations and allusions to other letters of Paul cannot be identified conclusively" (*The Text of the New Testament*, 49); the beginnings of the Pauline corpus, they conclude, reach "back into the first century" (ibid., 67).

and unstable twist to their own destruction, as they do the other scriptures [*graphas*]." Besides the indication concerning a collection of Paul's Letters, the author seems to put the letters in the category of "scriptures"—that is, alongside the writings of the OT. The authorship and date of 2 Peter are, as we have seen, uncertain, but the letter probably dates from late in the first century, perhaps not far from the time of Clement.

In the middle of the second century the first actual list of NT books that we have comes from Marcion (144), who lists one Gospel (Luke) and ten letters of Paul, but not the Pastoral Epistles. At the end of the century the earliest manuscript of the Pauline Letters, $\mathfrak{P}^{46}$ (ca. 200), has the Pauline corpus in codex form, again minus the Pastorals.

A recent explanation of the origin of the Pauline letter collection speculates that, in keeping with the custom of ancient authors to keep copies of their letters, Paul himself had collected copies of his letters in a private codex.[18]

The Four Gospels

In Clement of Rome and writers of the early second century the Gospels are seldom quoted. There is a strong preference to cite the words of Jesus from the oral tradition, as we had occasion to note above in chapter 7.[19]

There is a general consensus that the Gospels were collected in the mid-second century. At that time, Marcion had published a canon of one Gospel (a severely edited Luke) and the ten letters of Paul. It probably was in response to Marcion's attenuated canon that the church's canon consciousness was raised. The church was aware of four important Gospels. At about the same time, Justin Martyr refers to "the memoirs [*apomnēmoneumata*] of Peter," probably with the Gospel of Mark in mind (*Dial.* 106.3). Earlier in the *Dialogue with Trypho* he speaks of "the memoirs of the apostles" (*Dial.* 100.4), probably meaning the Gospels. In the *First Apology*, Justin also refers to "the memoirs of the Apostles" (i.e., Gospels) being read in church along with "the compositions of the prophets" (*1 Apol.* 66.3; 67.3).

Tatian's *Diatessaron* (lit. "through the four"), usually dated to about 165, was a harmony of the four Gospels into one comprehensive narrative, omitting doublets. It clearly indicates that the four Gospels were already separated out as a distinct collection.

Before the end of the second century Irenaeus, in a well-known passage, defends the reasonableness of four Gospels: "Since there are four zones of the world in which we live, and four principal winds, . . . and the 'pillar and ground' of the Church is the Gospel . . . it is fitting that she should have four

18. See Trobisch, *Paul's Letter Collection*; Richards, "The Codex and the Early Collection of Paul's Letters."

19. For discussion, see Hagner, "The Sayings of Jesus in the Apostolic Fathers and Justin Martyr."

pillars"; therefore God "has given us the Gospel under four aspects, but bound together by one Spirit" (*Haer.* 3.11.8, *ANF* 1:428).[20]

THE CATHOLIC EPISTLES

The latest collection (fourth century?) to be gathered was the seven Catholic Epistles. These letters, representing the "pillar Apostles," stand together as kind of "literary witness to the Jerusalem mission to the Jews," and function not only as anti-Marcionite polemic, but canonically as a "theological counterweight to the Pauline collection."[21] Of this group, only two individual letters had much of a strong candidacy in the early church: 1 Peter and 1 John. Several reasons can be mentioned for the difficulties of the Catholic Epistles and their slowness in coming into the canon. First, none of these letters was written to a specific, named church, and therefore there were no particular churches that could vouch for their authenticity, and the authorship of the letters thus remained uncertain. Second, a couple of the letters, 2 John and 3 John, are extremely brief. Third, questions could be raised about the content of a few of them—for example, whether James was contradictory of Paul, and the unusual content of Jude and its overlap with 2 Peter. The idea of a seven-epistle corpus, on the model of the seven churches (not counting second letters to two of them) to which Paul wrote and the letters to the seven churches in Revelation 2–3, undoubtedly made possible the inclusion of the shorter letters. It is thus as a collection of seven that they find their way into the canon.

Eventually, toward the end of the process, the seven letters became a familiar component of the canon, often being bound together with Acts, which they follow in many codices of the NT (e.g., all three of the main majuscules: Sinaiticus, Alexandrinus, and Vaticanus).

Canonical Lists and Virtual Canonical Lists

Basic to the idea of canon is a list of writings that are designated as special, as uniquely inspired and authoritative. A formal canon, in contrast to an informal or functional canon, is a closed canon, specifying which books are accepted and, by silence, which are rejected.[22] A few canonical lists begin to appear in the second century. It is also possible to consider the list that some

20. See Stanton, "The Fourfold Gospel."

21. Nienhuis, *Not By Paul Alone*, 88, 90. Nienhuis's interesting proposal that James was written in the middle of the second century to consolidate the Catholic Epistles as a corpus must, unfortunately, remain speculation.

22. The consensus is that we do not reach a closed canon until the fourth century. David Trobisch (*The First Edition of the New Testament*), appealing to early manuscripts of the NT, has argued that the entire NT canon was published as a single book as early as the mid-second century. But this highly improbable conclusion is difficult to reconcile with the church's discussion of canon in the second, third, and fourth centuries.

writers could have produced, given their quotations of, and allusions to, NT writings, but did not—in other words, a virtual or implied list.[23]

MARCION (144)

We have already noted that as far as we know, Marcion was the first to produce an actual canonical list, consisting of one Gospel and ten letters of Paul. This hardly means, however, that Marcion was the first to think about canonical issues. The structure of the canon into Gospel and Apostle (i.e., Epistles) was not an innovation of Marcion. As François Bovon notes: "A New Testament containing Gospels and Epistles is the logical outgrowth and materialization of a revelation that articulates an event and the proclamation that follows, i.e., Jesus and his disciples. Thus the need for a New Testament and its two-part configuration is inscribed in the very nature of the Christian faith from the beginnings of Christianity."[24] There can be little doubt, however, that the church had to counteract the influence of Marcion.

VALENTINUS (140–150, ROME)

The Coptic *Gospel of Truth*, found in the gnostic library of Nag Hammadi in Egypt, is a meditation on the gospel, rather than an actual Gospel. It witnesses to a virtual canon consisting of Matthew, Luke (and possibly Acts), John, and 1 John, together with the letters of Paul (excluding the Pastoral Epistles), and Hebrews and Revelation.

MURATORIAN CANON

This canonical list is one of the most important pieces of evidence for the history of the NT canon. It takes its name from the Italian librarian and archivist Ludovico Antonio Muratori (1672–1750), who discovered it in the Ambrosian Library in Milan and published it in 1740. It has been commonly dated late in the second century, in about 180, but although this remains the majority view, it has been challenged by some scholars who now date it late in the fourth century.[25] The manuscript is not in good condition and is missing its beginning and ending.

---

23. The following depends heavily on Bruce, *The Canon of Scripture*, 134–207. See also Metzger, *The Canon of the New Testament*, 75–164; Westcott, *A General Survey of the History of the Canon of the New Testament*.

24. Bovon, "The Canonical Structure of Gospel and Apostle," 516.

25. Thus Sundberg, "Canon Muratori"; followed by Gamble, "Canon, New Testament"; Hahneman, *The Muratorian Fragment and the Development of the Canon*; McDonald, *The Biblical Canon*, all of whom put it about two centuries later. Against this view, see Ferguson, "Canon Muratori"; Horbury, "The Wisdom of Solomon in the Muratorian Fragment"; Metzger, *The Canon of the New Testament*, 193–94; Stanton, "The Fourfold Gospel," 322–25; Hill, "The Debate over the Muratorian Fragment and the Development of the Canon." Jozef Verheyden writes at the end of his long study on the subject, "I am afraid I have to conclude that the suggestion of a fourth-century, eastern origin for the Fragment should be put to rest not for a thousand years, but for eternity" ("The Canon Muratori," 556).

It lists the four Gospels and Acts, as well as thirteen epistles of Paul—nine written to "seven churches," but also four written to individuals, thus including the Pastoral Epistles. The document calls attention to the existence of a letter to the Laodiceans and one to the Alexandrians, "forged under Paul's name to further the heresy of Marcion, and several others which cannot be received into the catholic Church—for it is not fitting that gall be mixed with honey."[26]

Also listed are Revelation, Jude, and two letters of John. Wisdom of Solomon also seems to be accepted, pointing to the larger canon of the early church, although it may represent the first of four disputed books, being followed by the Apocalypse of John, *Apocalypse of Peter*, and *Shepherd of Hermas*.[27] Some refused to have *Apocalypse of Peter* read in the church; so too the Muratorian Canon says that *Shepherd of Hermas* is not to be read in the church to the people, since it belongs neither to "the Prophets" nor to "the Apostles," indicating the two basic categories of Holy Scripture. Not mentioned in the list are Hebrews, 1–2 Peter, James, and one letter of John's three.

Irenaeus (ca. 130–ca. 200)

Writing close to the end of the second century, Irenaeus nowhere provides a list. But Eusebius (*Hist. eccl.* 5.8.1–8) give us an account of Irenaeus's use of NT writings, mentioning the four Gospels, 1 John, 1 Peter, and also *Shepherd of Hermas* and Wisdom of Solomon. Although Eusebius does not mention it, Irenaeus also accepted thirteen letters of Paul (though he makes no use of Philemon) and Hebrews (though denying Pauline authorship). Of the remainder, Irenaeus knows 1 Peter, 2 John, James, and the Apocalypse.

Tertullian (Active 196–212)

Tertullian seems to be the first person to use "New Testament [*novum testamentum*]" for the second part of the Christian Bible. From his writings it appears that he knew the four Gospels and Acts, the thirteen letters of Paul, Hebrews (by Barnabas, he guesses), 1 Peter, 1 John, Jude, and Revelation.

Clement of Alexandria (ca. 200)

Clement also speaks of Old Testament and New Testament, the latter consisting of the four Gospels, Acts, the fourteen Pauline Epistles (i.e., including Hebrews), James (possibly), 1 Peter, the three Johannine Epistles, and the Apocalypse. Clement also made free use of many other writings that were not accepted into the canon.

Origen (ca. 185–ca. 254)

In his commentary on Matthew, Origen writes, "I accept the traditional view of the four gospels which alone are undeniably authentic in the church of

---

26. Metzger's translation, in *The Canon of the New Testament*, Appendix IV.
27. Thus Horbury, "The Wisdom of Solomon in the Muratorian Fragment."

God on earth" (according to Eusebius, *Hist. eccl.* 6.25.3–14, trans. Oulton).
He also accepted as undisputed Acts, the thirteen Pauline Epistles, 1 Peter,
1 John, and the Apocalypse. Among the disputed documents he put 2 Peter,
2–3 John, James, Jude, and Hebrews. As far as we know, Origen is the first
writer to mention 2 Peter at all.

Eusebius (ca. 325)

Eusebius provides a report on the state of the canon in his day (*Hist. eccl.*
3.25.1–7, trans. Lake), using three categories:

1. Universally acknowledged (*homologoumena*). The books indicated
   here are "the holy tetrad of the gospels," Acts, the Pauline Epistles
   (fourteen, including Hebrews), 1 John, 1 Peter, and, "if it seem right,"
   the Apocalypse of John.
2. Disputed (*antilegomena*). This category contains writings doubted by
   some, "but recognized by the majority," all books from the Catholic
   Epistles: James, Jude, 2 Peter, 2–3 John.
3. Spurious (*nōtha*). Books rejected as not genuine are *Acts of Paul*, *Shepherd of Hermas*, *Apocalypse of Peter*, *Barnabas*, the *Didache*, and,
   surprisingly appearing a second time in the lists, the Apocalypse of John,
   "should it seem right." Eusebius adds these explanatory words: "For,
   as I said, some reject it, while others count it among the acknowledged
   books."

Some other books, which do not deserve being classified with the spurious
writings, are the *Gospel according to the Hebrews* and books "put forward
by heretics under the name of the apostles containing gospels such as those of
Peter, and Thomas, and Matthias, and some others besides, or Acts such as
those of Andrew and John and the other apostles" (*Hist. eccl.* 3.25.6, trans.
Lake). Eusebius goes on to give reasons for the rejection of these books, and
in so doing he articulates his criteria for canonicity. "To none of these has
any who belonged to the succession of the orthodox ever thought it right to
refer in his writings. Moreover, the type of phraseology differs from apostolic
style, and the opinion and tendency of their contents is widely dissonant from
true orthodoxy and clearly shows that they are the forgeries of heretics. They
ought, therefore, to be reckoned not even among spurious books but shunned
as altogether wicked and impious" (*Hist. eccl.* 3.25.6–7, trans. Lake). As we
have already had occasion to note, the emperor Constantine, who looked to
Eusebius for counsel concerning the church, asked him in 331 to produce fifty
parchment copies of the Scriptures, done by professional scribes. The contents
of the NT in these manuscripts probably included both the recognized and
the disputed books mentioned by Eusebius, and Revelation too, despite his
dislike of it.

ATHANASIUS (367)

In his Easter Letter of 367, his Thirty-Ninth Festal Letter, Athanasius, bishop of Alexandria, gives us the earliest known list of NT books that agrees exactly with our NT. All of them are accepted without distinction. These are, he says, the "springs of salvation . . . let no one add to them or take away aught of them." Athanasius mentions "other books" and suggests that they are worth reading: Wisdom of Solomon, Sirach, Esther, Judith, Tobit, the *Didache*, and *Shepherd of Hermas*. The Council of Hippo (393) was the first ecumenical church council to affirm a list (agreeing with Athanasius's), and subsequently this was confirmed by the Council of Carthage in 397.

Conclusions

In the early years of the church the rule of faith was more important than canonical lists. But an implicit canon began to function already toward the end of the first century and on into the second century. John Barton correctly notes, "In the first stage, which was complete astonishingly early, the great central core of the present New Testament was already being treated as the main authoritative source for Christians. There is little to suggest that there were any serious controversies about the Synoptics, John, or the major Pauline epistles."[28] With the appearance of a number of Gnostic writings outside the ambit of the church proper, there was a raising of canon consciousness in the second half of the first century. The church had to begin to emphasize the writings that it accepted as authoritative: the writings of the apostolic period.

The decisive period for the development of the NT canon was the first and second centuries, not the fourth and fifth centuries. To be sure, the lists reflecting a closed canon come late. But very early a de facto canon begins to evolve, an informal canon that, though beginning to take concrete shape, was open at the fringes. A handful of books remain debated, while at the same time the church continues to make use of a much larger number of writings.

In a helpful essay, Harry Gamble notes that despite differences among students of the development of the canon, all recognize the following: (1) by the end of the second century the four Gospels, the Pauline Epistles, 1 Peter, and 1 John had acquired very broad use and high authority in almost all regions of early Christianity; (2) the status and use of other writings continued to be variable through the third century and well into the fourth; and (3) lists that strictly delimit the scope of authoritative writings clearly belong mainly, perhaps exclusively, to the fourth and fifth centuries.[29]

28. Barton, *Holy Writings, Sacred Text*, 18.
29. Gamble, "The New Testament Canon," 271.

Criteria for Canonicity

What criteria were used to determine which books were admitted into the canon and which were excluded? Although no ancient author lists the criteria for us, we can, from what is said in various places, put together the following list, beginning with the most important. A writing had to meet all the criteria to a sufficient degree. Often the criteria were used "to justify *a posteriori* the high respect in which a writing had already been held for some time past, or the disapproval it had already incurred."[30]

Apostolic Authority or Apostolic Association

For the early church, authority is located in Jesus and the Apostles. The authority of the Apostles depends on their having been chosen by Jesus, and this stands in direct parallel to the paradigm of God and the prophets in the OT. The Scriptures of the OT stem from prophets; those of the NT stem from Apostles. Inspiration—the divine origination of Scripture—is not entirely intrinsic to the documents, but more a matter of the identity of the author. The writings that comprise the canon of Scripture are inspired because of their source. Inspiration is thus a corollary of apostolicity.

The trouble with this argument is that of the five or six (if we take John the Elder [2–3 John] and John the seer [Revelation] as different authors) named NT authors, only one or two (Peter and possibly one of the Johns) actually were members of the Twelve. Paul, of course, stands unique as an Apostle extraordinaire. Even if we accept the traditional designation of Matthew and John as authors of those Gospels, and count Paul as an exceptional case, together with Peter, we have a total of only four Apostles.

The early church was well aware of this problem. Thus we have noted the association of Mark with Peter, and Luke with Paul. It is clear that direct apostolic authority was extended to apostolic association (as was the case with the disciples of the prophets in the OT). This is the principle that alleviates the problem of pseudonymity, as we have seen. As F. F. Bruce remarks, "Even at an earlier period, apostolic authorship in the direct sense was not insisted on, if some form of apostolic authority could be established."[31]

We can postulate, then, that all the books of the NT were written either by Apostles or members of the apostolic circle—that is, associates of, or co-workers with, the Apostles. And, by extension of the principle, we can assume that the anonymous Hebrews was written either by an Apostle or an associate of an Apostle.

---

30. De Jonge, "The New Testament Canon," 313.

31. Bruce, *The Canon of Scripture*, 258. Bruce adds, with James and Jude in mind, "Membership of the holy family apparently carried with it near-apostolic status . . . good enough reason for accepting [their writings] among the apostolic writings" (ibid.).

Books lacking this supreme credential, though in other respects worthy, apparently were not finally accepted—for example, *1 Clement* and the letters of Ignatius and Polycarp, among the Apostolic Fathers (who are designated "apostolic," not because of apostolic association or apostolic succession, but because they perpetuate the sound doctrine of the Apostles).

An entailment of this criterion is the antiquity of canonical writings. That is, if a document was not within reach of the lifetime of an Apostle's disciple or associate, it was automatically disqualified. This meant, of course, that writings determined as stemming from the mid-second century or later had no chance of becoming part of the NT canon.

Orthodoxy

The importance of orthodoxy is very great; it stands alongside apostolic derivation as one of the two main criteria for canonicity. Orthodoxy is, of course, inextricably linked with apostolicity, the one implying the other. Orthodoxy was measured by agreement with the rule of faith (*regula fidei*), the central doctrinal convictions of the churches established by the Apostles and their co-workers.[32] H. J. de Jonge concludes that "the test whether the contents of a writing agreed with the traditional teaching of the Church played a more important part than our sources suggest at first sight," and that "in the final analysis it was mostly the criterion of orthodoxy that decided a writing's fate."[33] Very probably in cases where there was uncertainty about other criteria, orthodoxy became determinative.

Ecclesiastical Acknowledgment

Writings that became canonical were writings that were used in the churches; they were read in public worship and known to be useful for study, doctrine, and edification. And this recognition of the worthiness of a writing had to be in more than just one locality. Thus catholicity is also an aspect of canonicity.[34]

The Canon Today

Today the canon has come under strong criticism. One reason for this is the discovery and publication of noncanonical writings (especially the much-touted "lost gospels") of the early church era,[35] and particularly the idea that the canon

---

32. In the second century the succession of bishops in churches became an important factor. See especially the letters of Ignatius.

33. De Jonge, "The New Testament Canon," 318.

34. F. F. Bruce quotes the "Vincentian canon": "what has been believed everywhere, always, by all" (*The Canon of Scripture*, 262).

35. See, for example, Ehrman, *Lost Christianities*; King, *The Gospel of Mary of Magdala*; Krosney, *The Lost Gospel*.

represents but one strand of Christianity that was powered into "orthodoxy" over other equally worthy strands of Christianity. The result, it is argued, was the suppression of writings that demand equal respect and attention.

These other writings are indeed important historical documents and worth our attention. Whether they represent a parallel and equally valid expression of early Christianity that should cancel out the notion of orthodoxy is another question.[36] Even the early, orthodox church, as we have seen, valued and made use of apocryphal books that were not a part of the emerging canon.

Some question the propriety of the canon we have. They wonder whether the church was right in finally limiting its OT canon to that of the Hebrew Bible. What if the church was wrong in some of its judgments about canon? What if it were discovered beyond any question that a book of the NT was a late forgery? Or what if a manuscript of an undoubtedly original letter of an Apostle were discovered? In other words, what if some books that are in the canon should not be, and some that should be are not? There are some, for example, especially members of the Jesus Seminar, who would very much like to ditch the book of Revelation. Should the canon be regarded as fully and finally closed?

At this point in history, the canon stands as a given under the sovereign providence of God. It stands as it is, a gift of the church to all later generations. The most that one might do for books in the canon, if pressed, is to subordinate some books to others. This is what Martin Luther infamously did by relegating Hebrews, James, Jude, and Revelation to an appendix of his newly translated NT, but not by rejecting them altogether. Most Christians, like Luther, consciously or unconsciously work with a canon within the canon. For Luther, the principle was "what preaches Christ." For many Christians, including myself, it is Paul's Letters, especially Romans and Galatians, where we have the clearest exposition of salvation and the meaning of the death of Christ. Even those who champion being people of the "whole Bible" often unconsciously function with a canon within the canon. The reason for this is the presence of tensions within the canon that are difficult to hold in balance. However, while all the books of the NT deserve to be heard, some are more valuable than others and therefore take priority. Similarly, if a book not in the canon was newly discovered, and its authenticity was impeccable, the most that could be done is to add it to the canon as an appendix. The canon of the church remains fixed. Even so, however, there still remain some relatively minor differences between a few Christian churches on the contents of the OT canon.

A significant recent trend will serve as a protection against the inherent dangers of affirming a canon within the canon: canon criticism.[37] This approach

---

36. For useful responses, see Jenkins, *Hidden Gospels*; Bock, *The Missing Gospels*; Wright, *Judas and the Gospel of Judas*.

37. See Childs, *The New Testament as Canon*; Wall and Lemcio, *The New Testament as Canon*.

attempts to affirm the canon as a totality and its components as constituent parts of that totality. Canon criticism focuses on the positive dimensions of the diverse canon that we have, working with it as a datum—given by God for the church.

Bibliography

Aland, Kurt, and Barbara Aland. *The Text of the New Testament: An Introduction to the Critical Editions and to the Theory and Practice of Modern Textual Criticism*. Translated by Erroll F. Rhodes. 2nd ed. Grand Rapids: Eerdmans; Leiden: Brill, 1989.

Allert, Craig D. *Revelation, Truth, Canon, and Interpretation: Studies in Justin Martyr's Dialogue with Trypho*. VCSup 64. Leiden: Brill, 2002.

———. "The State of the New Testament Canon in the Second Century: Putting Tatian's *Diatessaron* in Perspective." *BBR* 9 (1999): 1–18.

Auwers, J.-M., and H. J. de Jonge, eds. *The Biblical Canons*. BETL 163. Leuven: Leuven University Press, 2003.

Balla, Peter. "Evidence for an Early Christian Canon (Second and Third Century)." In *The Canon Debate*, edited by Lee Martin McDonald and James A. Sanders, 372–85. Peabody, MA: Hendrickson, 2002.

Barr, James. *Holy Scripture: Canon, Authority, Criticism*. Philadelphia: Westminster, 1983.

Barrera, Julio C. Trebolle. *The Jewish Bible and the Christian Bible: An Introduction to the History of the Bible*. Translated by Wilfred G. E. Watson. Grand Rapids: Eerdmans; Leiden: Brill, 1998.

Barton, John. *Holy Writings, Sacred Text: The Canon in Early Christianity*. Louisville: Westminster John Knox, 1997.

Beckwith, Roger. *The Old Testament Canon of the New Testament Church*. Grand Rapids: Eerdmans, 1985.

Berding, Kenneth. *Polycarp and Paul: An Analysis of Their Literary and Theological Relationship in Light of Polycarp's Use of Biblical and Extra-Biblical Literature*. VCSup 62. Leiden: Brill, 2002.

Bock, Darrell L. *The Missing Gospels: Unearthing the Truth behind Alternative Christianities*. Nashville: Thomas Nelson, 2006.

Bovon, François. "The Canonical Structure of Gospel and Apostle." In *The Canon Debate*, edited by Lee Martin McDonald and James A. Sanders, 516–27. Peabody, MA: Hendrickson, 2002.

Bruce, F. F. *The Canon of Scripture*. Downers Grove, IL: InterVarsity, 1988.

———. "Some Thoughts on the Beginning of the New Testament Canon." *BJRL* 65 (1982): 37–60.

Campenhausen, Hans von. *The Formation of the Christian Bible*. Translated by John Austin Baker. London: Black, 1972.

Childs, Brevard S. *The Church's Guide for Reading Paul: The Canonical Shaping of the Pauline Corpus*. Grand Rapids: Eerdmans, 2008.

———. *The New Testament as Canon: An Introduction*. Philadelphia: Fortress, 1985.

Christensen, Duane L. *Explosion of the Canon: The Greek New Testament in Early Church History*. North Richland Hills, TX: Bibal Press, 2004.

Cullmann, Oscar. "Pluralism and Unity in the New Testament." In *Faith and History: Essays in Honor of Paul W. Meyer*, edited by John T. Carroll, Charles H. Cosgrove, and E. Elizabeth Johnson, 352–59. Atlanta: Scholars Press, 1990.

Davies, Philip R. *Scribes and Schools: The Canonization of the Hebrew Scriptures*. LAI. Louisville: Westminster John Knox, 1988.

de Jonge, H. J. "The New Testament Canon." In *The Biblical Canons*, edited by J.-M. Auwers and H. J. de Jonge, 309–19. BETL 163. Leuven: Leuven University Press, 2003.

Dungan, David L. *Constantine's Bible: Politics and the Making of the New Testament*. Minneapolis: Fortress, 2007.

Ehrman, Bart D. *Lost Christianities: The Battles for Scripture and the Faiths We Never Knew*. New York: Oxford University Press, 2002.

Ellis, E. Earle. *The Making of the New Testament Documents*. BIS 39. Leiden: Brill, 1999.

———. *The Old Testament in Early Christianity: Canon and Interpretation in Light of Modern Research*. Grand Rapids: Baker Academic, 1992.

Evans, Craig A. *Ancient Texts for New Testament Studies: A Guide to the Background Literature*. Peabody, MA: Hendrickson, 2005.

Farkasfalvy, Denis M. "The Ecclesial Setting and Pseudepigraphy in 2 Peter and Its Role in the Formation of the Canon." *SecCent* 5 (1985–86): 3–29.

Farmer, William R., and Denis M. Farkasfalvy. *The Formation of the New Testament Canon: An Ecumenical Approach*. New York: Paulist Press, 1983.

Ferguson, Everett, ed. *The Bible in the Early Church*. Vol. 3 of *Studies in Early Christianity: A Collection of Scholarly Essays*. New York: Garland, 1993.

———. "Canon Muratori: Date and Provenance." *StPatr* 17.2 (1982): 677–83.

Gamble, Harry Y. *Books and Readers in the Early Church: A History of Early Christian Texts*. New Haven: Yale University Press, 1995.

———. "Canon, New Testament." *ABD* 1:852–61.

———. *The New Testament Canon: Its Making and Meaning*. GBS. Philadelphia: Fortress, 1985.

———. "The New Testament Canon: Recent Research and the *Status Quaestionis*." In *The Canon Debate*, edited by Lee Martin McDonald and James A. Sanders, 267–94. Peabody, MA: Hendrickson, 2002.

———. "The Redaction of the Pauline Letters and the Formation of the Pauline Corpus." *JBL* 94 (1975): 403–18.

Goodspeed, Edgar J. *The Formation of the New Testament*. Chicago: University of Chicago Press, 1926.

Grant, Robert M. *The Formation of the New Testament*. New York: Harper & Row, 1965.

———. *Second-Century Christianity: A Collection of Fragments*. London: SPCK, 1946.

Gregory, Andrew F., and Christopher M. Tuckett, eds. *The Reception of the New Testament in the Apostolic Fathers*. NTAF 1. New York: Oxford University Press, 2005.

———, eds. *Trajectories through the New Testament and the Apostolic Fathers*. NTAF 2. New York: Oxford University Press, 2005.

Gregory, Caspar René. *Canon and Text of the New Testament*. ITL. Edinburgh: T&T Clark, 1907.

Grosheide, F. W., ed. *Some Early Lists of the Books of the New Testament*. TM 1. Leiden: Brill, 1948.

Hagner, Donald A. "The Sayings of Jesus in the Apostolic Fathers and Justin Martyr." In *The Jesus Tradition outside the Gospels*, edited by David Wenham, 233–68. GP 5. Sheffield: JSOT Press, 1985.

———. *The Use of the Old and New Testaments in Clement of Rome*. NovTSup 34. Leiden: Brill, 1973.

Hahneman, Geoffrey Mark. *The Muratorian Fragment and the Development of the Canon*. OTM. Oxford: Clarendon, 1992.

Hartog, Paul. *Polycarp and the New Testament: The Occasion, Rhetoric, Theme, and Unity of the Epistle to the Philippians and Its Allusions to New Testament Literature*. WUNT 2/134. Tübingen: Mohr Siebeck, 2002.

Helmer, Christine, and Christof Landmesser, eds. *One Scripture or Many? Canon from Biblical, Theological, and Philosophical Perspectives*. Oxford: Oxford University Press, 2004.

Hill, Charles E. "The Debate over the Muratorian Fragment and the Development of the Canon." *WTJ* 57 (1995): 437–52.

Horbury, William. "The Wisdom of Solomon in the Muratorian Fragment." *JTS* 45 (1994): 149–59.

Jenkins, Philip. *Hidden Gospels: How the Search for Jesus Lost Its Way.* New York: Oxford University Press, 2001.

Kalin, Everett R. "The New Testament Canon of Eusebius." In *The Canon Debate,* edited by Lee Martin McDonald and James A. Sanders, 386–404. Peabody, MA: Hendrickson, 2002.

King, Karen L. *The Gospel of Mary of Magdala: Jesus and the First Woman Apostle.* Santa Rosa, CA: Polebridge, 2003.

Knox, John. *Marcion and the New Testament: An Essay in the Early History of the Canon.* Chicago: University of Chicago Press, 1942.

Köstenberger, Andreas J., and Michael J. Kruger. *The Heresy of Orthodoxy: How Contemporary Culture's Fascination with Diversity Has Reshaped Our Understanding of Early Christianity.* Wheaton, IL: Crossway, 2010.

Krosney, Herbert. *The Lost Gospel: The Quest for the Gospel of Judas Iscariot.* Washington, DC: National Geographic, 2006.

Levison, John R. "Did the Spirit Withdraw from Israel? An Evaluation of the Earliest Jewish Data." *NTS* 43 (1997): 35–57.

———. *The Spirit in First-Century Judaism.* Leiden: Brill, 1997.

Lewis, Jack P. "Jamnia Revisited." In *The Canon Debate,* edited by Lee Martin McDonald and James A. Sanders, 146–62. Peabody, MA: Hendrickson, 2002.

Lightstone, Jack N. "The Rabbis' Bible: The Canon of the Hebrew Bible and the Early Rabbinic Guild." In *The Canon Debate,* edited by Lee Martin McDonald and James A. Sanders, 163–84. Peabody, MA: Hendrickson, 2002.

McDonald, Lee Martin. *The Biblical Canon: Its Origin, Transmission, and Authority.* Peabody, MA: Hendrickson, 2007.

———. *Forgotten Scriptures: The Selection and Rejection of Early Religious Writings.* Louisville: Westminster John Knox, 2009.

———. "The Integrity of the Biblical Canon in Light of Its Historical Development." *BBR* 6 (1996): 95–132.

McDonald, Lee Martin, and James A. Sanders, eds. *The Canon Debate.* Peabody, MA: Hendrickson, 2002.

Meade, David G. *Pseudonymity and Canon: An Investigation into the Relationship of Authorship and Authority in Jewish and Earliest Christian Tradition.* Grand Rapids: Eerdmans, 1986.

Metzger, Bruce M. *The Canon of the New Testament: Its Origin, Development, and Significance.* Oxford: Clarendon, 1987.

Meyer, Rudolf. "προφήτης." *TDNT* 6:812–19.

Miller, John W. *How the Bible Came to Be: Exploring the Narrative and the Message.* New York: Paulist Press, 2004.

———. *The Origins of the Bible: Rethinking Canon History.* New York: Paulist Press, 1994.

Mitton, C. Leslie. *The Formation of the Pauline Corpus of Letters.* London: Epworth, 1955.

Moore, George F. "The Definition of the Jewish Canon and the Repudiation of Christian Scriptures." In *The Canon and Masorah of the Hebrew Bible: An Introductory Reader,* edited by Sid Z. Leiman, 99–125. New York: Ktav, 1974.

Nienhuis, David R. *Not by Paul Alone: The Formation of the Catholic Epistle Collection and the Christian Canon.* Waco: Baylor University Press, 2007.

Oliver, William G. "Origen and the New Testament Canon." *ResQ* 31 (1989): 13–26.

Patzia, Arthur G. *The Making of the New Testament: Origin, Collection, Text and Canon.* Downers Grove, IL: InterVarsity, 1995.

Petersen, William L. *Tatian's Diatessaron: Its Creation, Dissemination, Significance and History in Scholarship.* VCSup 25. Leiden: Brill, 1994.

Porter, Stanley E., ed. *The Pauline Canon.* PS 1. Leiden: Brill, 2004.

———. "When and How Was the Pauline Canon Completed? An Assessment of Theories." In *The Pauline Canon*, edited by Stanley E. Porter, 95–127. PS 1. Leiden: Brill, 2004.

Richards, E. Randolph. "The Codex and the Early Collection of Paul's Letters." *BBR* 8 (1998): 151–66.

Schniedewind, William M. *How the Bible Became a Book: The Textualization of Ancient Israel.* Cambridge: Cambridge University Press, 2004.

Skeat, T. C. "Irenaeus and the Four-Gospel Canon." *NovT* 34 (1992): 194–99.

———. "The Origins of the Christian Codex." *ZPE* 102 (1994): 263–68.

Smith, D. Moody. "When Did the Gospels Become Scripture?" *JBL* 119 (2000): 3–20.

Souter, Alexander. *The Text and Canon of the New Testament.* Revised by C. S. C. Williams. London: Duckworth, 1954.

Stanton, Graham N. "The Fourfold Gospel." *NTS* 43 (1997): 317–46.

———. "Jesus Traditions and Gospels in Justin Martyr and Irenaeus." In *The Biblical Canons*, edited by J.-M. Auwers and H. J. de Jonge, 353–70. BETL 163. Leuven: Leuven University Press, 2003.

Sundberg, Albert C., Jr. "Canon Muratori: A Fourth-Century List." *HTR* 66 (1973): 1–11.

———. *The Old Testament of the Early Church.* HTS 20. Cambridge, MA: Harvard University Press, 1964.

———. "Towards a Revised History of the New Testament Canon." *SE* 4 [= TU 102] (1968): 452–61.

Swete, H. B. *An Introduction to the Old Testament in Greek.* Cambridge: Cambridge University Press, 1902.

Thomassen, Einar, ed. *Canon and Canonicity: The Formation and Use of Scripture.* Copenhagen: Museum Tusculanum, 2010.

Trobisch, David. *The First Edition of the New Testament.* New York: Oxford, 2000.

———. *Paul's Letter Collection: Tracing the Origins.* Minneapolis: Fortress, 1994.

Verheyden, Jozef. "The Canon Muratori: A Matter of Dispute." In *The Biblical Canons*, edited by J.-M. Auwers and H. J. de Jonge, 487–556. BETL 163. Leuven: Leuven University Press, 2003.

Wall, Robert W., and Eugene E. Lemcio. *The New Testament as Canon: A Reader in Canonical Criticism.* JSNTSup 76. Sheffield: JSOT Press, 1992.

Westcott, B. F. *The Bible in the Church: A Popular Account of the Collection and Reception of the Holy Scriptures in the Christian Churches.* London: Macmillan, 1882.

———. *A General Survey of the History of the Canon of the New Testament.* 6th ed. London: Macmillan, 1889.

Wright, N. T. *Judas and the Gospel of Judas: Have We Missed the Truth about Christianity?* Grand Rapids: Baker Books, 2006.

A Final Word

Few books in history have been revered as much as the Bible. Because of its content, its special place in the church, and its acceptance as the word of God, it has been easy for some to fall prey to an unabashed bibliolatry and to think of the Bible as practically dictated by God, coming directly from heaven untouched by human hands. Held in such high esteem, the Bible takes on an almost magical quality that often prevents it from being studied and interpreted responsibly. A supernatural book is thought by many to be beyond critical interpretation and this attitude opens the door to the abuse of the Bible.

A key insight, however, gained from a study of the writings of the NT such as we have undertaken here is the full humanity of these writings, their fully human historical context, and their human mediation. It does indeed involve mystery to assert that Scripture is the word of God in the words of humans. But just as it is basic to the biblical narrative that God acts through human agency, so it is a fundamental truth of the biblical writings that God speaks to us in and through normal human language.

The only responsible approach to interpreting the NT involves the recognition of, and allowance for, its full humanity. As God has come to us supremely in the human incarnation of his Son, so too in the revelation of his word in the NT documents he speaks to us in human language fully rooted in human contexts. This is indeed the essence and the glory of our faith: revelation in history.

Given its historical origins, it should be no surprise that the NT canon contains diversity. This diversity is directly related to the different authors and to the diverse problems that they had to address in various churches. At the same time, however, it should be stressed that the diversity of the NT has its limits and that there is an underlying unity in these writings. The NT constitutes a unity in and with its diversity. Together with the OT, the NT in its three kinds of writings—historical, epistolary, and apocalyptic—presents the fulfillment of one great story of salvation. If we seek a unifying principle, a common theological center of the NT, it will be in the kerygmatic utterances—the short confessions of faith about human salvation and its basis in the work of Christ. In most books of the NT this kerygma is quite explicit, but, in a few instances, it is assumed and implied rather than articulated. Here is the heart of the NT, its very essence.

Oscar Cullmann, the great Swiss NT scholar, captures the essence of the NT exceptionally well in these words:

> What especially unifies all of New Testament theology is the authors' conviction, shared with the Jews, that they belong to a *salvation history* that runs from the suprahistorical events of creation, through events unfolding on a straight line within secular history, toward the history of Israel and from there toward the Kingdom of God, and finally to the new creation. . . . This vision of the great stages in the second part of salvation history explains at once both the plurality of the New Testament as the result of the unfolding of time (gospels, Acts, letters, the Apocalypse) and the unity of the New Testament as the result of the plan of God that binds the different stages together.[1]

The NT above all else records the announcement of something new. It provides the story of the arrival of this new reality, encapsulated in the gospel. It argues that this gospel constitutes a major turning point in the whole of human history and is the fulfillment of a long history of promise and preparation. As the Gospels show us, central to the coming of the kingdom—indeed, its very foundation—is the cross of Christ, for it is his atoning death that brings the new reality into existence. The gospel of the kingdom and the cross are thus inseparable.

The new reality of the kingdom is experienced in the church through the power of the Holy Spirit. Its significance in terms of both doctrine and ethics is explored in the NT Epistles. Life in the kingdom may be described as eschatological existence in the present fallen age, for in the church the fulfillment of the promises has begun. In that sense, the kingdom is already here as well as being something that will reach its consummation in the future. The Apocalypse brings us full circle, back to the glory and perfection of God's unspoiled creation, but now with the stunning, unparalleled story of redemption as its history and basis.

The writings of the NT soon will be two thousand years old. They are ancient writings. Can documents this old offer anything to the world of the twenty-first century? Are they not passé, outdated, of interest only to antiquarians? Are they of any more than sentimental value to modern people?

---

1. O. Cullmann, "Pluralism and Unity in the New Testament," in *Faith and History: Essays in Honor of Paul W. Meyer.* J. T. Carroll, C. H. Cosgrove and E. E. Johnson, eds. (Atlanta: Scholars Press, 1990), 358–59.

The continued relevance and significance of the NT to the present world rest on two facts. First, the fundamental need of humanity remains. All the changes brought to human existence in the modern world affect only life's external trappings. The basic and deepest needs of humanity are universal, and they remain essentially the same as they were in the first century, indeed, through all of human history, for human beings remain basically unchanged. The veil that lies over our existence as the result of our fallenness remains in place: alienation from one another, enmity, suffering, sickness, and death. Second, the solution to the human predicament remains the same as in the first century. The God of grace and redemption remains unchanged, as does his provision of a Savior and his loving offer of salvation to unworthy sinners. For these reasons the NT, rooted in a specific time in the distant past, will remain a timeless book that is pertinent to every age. For those willing to hear what it says, it will continue to meet the universal need of humankind.

But in our modern religiously pluralistic environment, can we continue to believe in and affirm the truthfulness of these documents? The gospel of Christianity cannot be proved to be true. The evidence that we have, however, is sufficient to warrant acceptance of its truth, beginning with the resurrection of Jesus and the growth of the church. The inadequacy of all alternate explanations of the origin of Christianity itself points to the truth of the NT. It is the further step of faith, however, together with the inner testimony of the Holy Spirit, that brings final assurance to the believer. For those who believe, the narratives and teachings of the NT become and remain the source of life, enabling the transformation of present existence and offering the hope of future life. Thanks be to God!

Author Index

Ancient Writings Index

Old Testament

Genesis

1:26–27 400n11
2:9 749
3:1–6 636n57
3:11 445
3:15 14n4, 15
3:17–18 464n20
6:1–3 709
6:1–4 698
9:4 337n29
12:1–3 14, 15
12:3 14n5, 445
12:7 14, 15
13:14–17 14, 15
14 659
15:5–6 14, 15
15:6 384, 445, 451,
    529, 680
17 529
17:1–8 14, 15
17:5 529
18:18 14n5
22:15–18 14, 15
22:18 14n5, 446
26:3–4 14
26:4 14n5
26:24 14
28:3–4 14
28:13–15 14
32:9–12 14
35:9–12 14
46 786
48:3–4 14
48:16 14
48:19 14
50:24 14

Exodus

3:14 172n23, 202, 285
12:10 286n104
12:14 40
12:46 286n104
16 279
19:3–6 15, 16
19:5–6 695
20:1–17 16, 367
23:7 384n6, 529
23:16 41
23:17 40
25:9 661
25:17–22 383
25:40 661
26:30 661
26:34 383
27:8 661

Leviticus

16 41
16:13–15 528
16:13–16 383
18:5 445
23:26–32 41
23:42–43 41

Numbers

6:1–21 370
9:12 286n104
16:41–50 505n8
24:17 719

Deuteronomy

1:8 16
1:10–11 16
3:18 16
4:1 16
4:8 17
4:13–14 16
4:31 16
4:39 17
4:40 16
5:3 17
5:6–21 367
6:4 17, 41
6:5 5
6:7 41
6:10 16
6:18 16
6:23 16
7:6 16
7:6–9 15
7:7–8 367
7:8 16
7:9 16
7:12–13 16
7:14 16
16:16 40
18:15 71n7
21:23 446
27:6 445
28:58 367
30:14 534
30:15–20 367

Judges

1:8 213

2 Samuel

7 72
7:4–17 17
7:8–16 15
7:13 17, 754
7:16 754

2 Kings

17 30
24:10–17 30

1 Chronicles

28:5 69
28:19 661
29:11 69

2 Chronicles

13:8 69
24:20–22 805n3

Ezra

1:2–4 30
3:12–13 30
5:12 367
7:10 367, 804
7:14 804
7:26 804
9:10–15 30, 367

3:12 570
3:13 572
3:14 570
3:16 360, 567
3:17 571
3:18 570
3:18–4:1 565, 570,
   609
3:22–25 570
3:22–4:1 576
3:24 572
4:2 570
4:3 565, 571, 573
4:4 427
4:7 610, 618
4:7–8 586, 588
4:7–9 562, 573,
   623n23
4:9 600
4:10 164, 165, 183,
   562, 573
4:10–17 246n58
4:11 313
4:12 562, 570
4:12–13 562
4:13 562
4:14 228, 245, 246,
   308, 562, 600
4:16 411, 479n11,
   589, 810
4:17 562
4:18 427, 566, 573

1 Thessalonians

1:1 412, 458
1:2–10 458
1:3 360, 458, 461
1:5 470
1:6 459, 467, 470
1:7–8 459
1:8 470
1:9–10 360, 459,
   459n3, 470n33
1:10 468, 470
2–3 467
2:1–12 459, 459n6
2:2 313, 381, 467,
   470, 548
2:4 460, 470
2:6 460
2:7 460

2:8 460, 470
2:8–9 381
2:9 470
2:10 460
2:11 460
2:12 403n22
2:13 108, 459, 460,
   462, 464, 470, 610
2:14 466
2:14–16 460, 462
2:17 460
2:17–18 413
2:1–3:13 460
2:18 460
2:19 460, 468
3:1–2 458
3:1–10 422
3:2 381, 467, 470
3:3–4 467
3:5 459
3:6 458, 460
3:6–10 459
3:7 467
3:10 460
3:11–13 461, 462, 464
3:13 462, 468, 469
4–5 358, 461n10
4:1 459, 462, 467
4:1–12 461
4:1–5:22 461
4:6 396
4:9 466
4:11 466, 468
4:11–12 609n4
4:13–18 79n18, 469,
   699n28
4:13–5:11 461
4:14 461
4:15 404
4:15–17 357, 609
4:16 461, 469
4:17 461, 469
4:18 461
5:1 466, 467
5:1–7 357
5:1–11 461, 462
5:2 468
5:3 357n7
5:5 461
5:8 360, 461
5:11 461
5:12 618

5:12–13 611
5:12–22 462
5:14 466, 468
5:23 468
5:23–24 462
5:25 462
5:26 411
5:26–28 462
5:28 396

2 Thessalonians

1:1 412
1:2 463
1:3–4 463
1:3–12 463
1:4–5 466, 468
1:5 313
1:7–8 463
1:8 465
1:11–12 463
2:1–2 427
2:1–12 463, 466, 468,
   469
2:2 404, 463, 464,
   465, 467, 468
2:3 463, 469
2:4 463, 465, 470
2:5 463, 467
2:5–6 470
2:6 463, 470
2:7 470
2:8 463, 619, 771
2:9 460, 469
2:10 463, 465
2:12 463, 465
2:13 463, 464, 465
2:14 465, 470
2:15 112, 463, 465,
   467, 610
2:16 464
2:16–17 463
3:1 470
3:1–2 463
3:3–4 463
3:5 463
3:6 108, 112, 465
3:6–13 468
3:6–15 463, 466
3:7 464
3:11 466
3:12 464

3:17 427, 465, 466
3:17–18 464

1 Timothy

1:2 628
1:3 548, 620, 626, 631
1:4 619, 626, 634
1:5 626, 631
1:8–11 619
1:10 626, 629
1:11 381, 628, 629
1:11–12 620
1:15 630
1:18 628, 631
1:19 626, 628
2:1–15 571, 629
2:3–6 635
2:4 628
2:5 631
2:5–6 360
2:6 362
2:7 620, 628, 629
2:11–12 635
2:11–15 635
2:13–15 630n40
3:1 630
3:2 112
3:2–7 632, 633
3:5 634
3:8–13 632, 633
3:9 626, 628
3:11 634
3:13 628
3:14–15 624
3:15 626, 629, 634,
   638
3:16 325n1, 628, 631
4:1 628
4:3 619, 629
4:6 112, 626, 628, 629
4:8 630, 630n41
4:9 630
4:11–16 112
4:13 624, 629
4:14 618, 632
4:16 112, 626, 629
5:1–2 571
5:1–16 629
5:17 112
5:17–22 632, 633
5:21 627, 631

Apocrypha and Septuagint

Old Testament Pseudepigrapha

Subject Index